UNIVERSITY CASEBOOK SERIES

REGULATION

WHY AND HOW THE STATE REGULATES

by

BARAK ORBACH

Professor of Law
The University of Arizona College of Law

FOUNDATION PRESS
2013

1 New York Plaza, 34th Floor

New York, NY 10004

Phone Toll Free 1–877–888–1330

Fax 646–424–5201

foundation–press.com

Printed in the United States of America

ISBN 978–1–59941–925–1

Mat #41102564

To Sivan and Eli

PREFACE

Lawyers are "messengers of regulation." They negotiate regulatory reforms, draft regulations, enforce regulations, assist their clients in complying with regulations, lobby for and against regulations, and often challenge the validity of regulations. The need for a course on regulation in law school cannot be overstated. It is only an oddity that many law schools have neglected this expertise.

I began working on this book during (and inspired by) the housing bubble of the 2000s that led to the Great Recession. Financial bubbles are a social phenomenon of irrational exuberance. Unrealistic optimism drives individuals and institutions to increase financial risk through the accumulation of debt in an unsustainable fashion. At the core of every bubble, naiveté and excessive confidence inflate prices and dismiss doubts regarding the real value of assets. Ultimately, however, every bubble bursts, exposing individuals and institutions to monetary losses and consequential damages. In many ways, the implosion of financial bubbles illuminates the costs individuals and society pay for human imperfections. Similar human shortcomings have been shaping approaches to regulation.

Three years after the official end of the Great Recession, in June 2012, the Supreme Court handed down its historic health-care decision, *National Federation of Independent Business v. Sebelius* ("*NFIB*"). *NFIB* is a milestone in regulation. The decision and the political controversy over the Patient Protection and Affordable Care Act of 2010 provide another powerful example for the strong positions people tend to take about regulatory issues.

"*Regulation*" is one of the most misunderstood concepts in modern legal thinking. The word is frequently used to evoke images of unproductive and wasteful government bureaucracy, and a source of concern regarding a large government that seeks to expand its power. The *NFIB* Court, for example, was divided over the meaning of the term "to regulate," and consequently also over the potential relationship between mandating health insurance and "ordering everyone to buy vegetables." Our law requires regulations to be reasonably related to the public welfare, but not all regulations achieve this goal or are even designed to do so. All institutions suffer from some degree of inefficiency, among other reasons, because their agents act with other people's money. The government and courts are no exception. Regulation is a byproduct of our imperfect reality and human limitations.

Many people firmly believe that the state (or the "government") should not intervene in the private domain, or to do so only in very limited circumstances. Alas, unregulated free markets fail; they are not viable in theory or in practice. Moreover, unregulated freedom means freedom to harm. A Society that protects the right of some "to be let alone" sacrifices the rights of others. Society, therefore, has at its disposal imperfect regulatory tools and must choose among imperfect realities, which may be ugly and costly. The choices are far from obvious.

While the scope of federal and state regulations and the design of particular regulatory policies raise many legitimate debates, the concept of "regulation" itself is benign. Yet, even *laissez faire* advocates tend to demand regulations that promote their own perceptions of morality, property rights, contractual rights, and other entitlements. This inconsistency is particularly apparent in certain regulatory issues, such as abortion restrictions, firearms and tobacco control, healthcare reforms, financial regulation, environmental policies, national security, welfare entitlements, civil rights, same-sex marriage, and freedom of speech.

This book is designed for a first-year or an upper-level course on regulation. The objective of this course is to teach students how to analyze and design substantive legal rules and public policies. The course serves as a foundation for other courses that focus on particular regulatory areas, including administrative law, antitrust, bankruptcy, corporate law, employment law, environmental law, health law, insurance law, intellectual property, and securities regulation. It equips students with critical analytical tools needed in today's legal practice and complex business environment.

The book's approach is practical: Human beings are imperfect and must make decisions under uncertainty with transaction costs. Legal rules are products of an imperfect reality. The understanding of regulatory systems and specific legal rules, therefore, demands a nuanced appreciation of the impediments to a frictionless world—transaction costs, inadequate information, bounded rationality, and diverse preferences. The state regulates—wisely or unwisely—because of these sources of market inefficiencies. The book helps students understand why legal rules exist, why they are imperfect, and why and how they may be misused in practice.

The book consists of three parts. Part I focuses on the concept of "regulation" and its controversial nature. This part includes two chapters that introduce the distinction between rules and standards, indirect regulation (third-party liability), cost-benefit analysis, the "invisible hand" theory and the pursuit of self-interest, the concepts of unintended consequences and government failures, and public choice. Part I begins with a concise discussion of the Great Recession and concludes with the Supreme Court's 2012 health-care decision. The interrelated controversies over the Great Recession and the 2010 health-care reform frame many of the themes discussed in the book. Part II explores the motivations for regulation—why the state may regulate, or more precisely why people rightly or wrongly believe that the state should regulate. This part includes five chapters, each examines a different category of motivations: (a) externalities, (b) risk, (c) inadequate information, (d) unfair prices and contractual terms, and (e) legal paternalism (morality and bounded rationality). Part III introduces general regulatory methods—how the state typically regulates. This part includes four chapters that analyze key regulatory methods: (a) bans, mandates, and permits (b) standard setting and price regulation, (c) information regulation, and (d) preference shaping.

I have been using drafts of this book in the classroom since the spring of 2006. Its design and approach have evolved through teaching and student feedback. The encouragement and input I have received from my students over the years convinced me of the practical value of this course. Many students have enormously helped me to develop the book. I cannot list them all. Frances Sjoberg, Alexis Danneman, Grace Campbell Rebling, Darcy Elgin, Meredith Marder, Erin Norris, Andrew Floyd, Corey Mantei, Anne Nelson, Blake Rebling, and Julie Wilson made substantial contributions to the book and my thinking. I also greatly benefitted from comments and suggestions of many friends and colleagues. Bob Mundheim, Jean Braucher, Jack Chin, Carol Rose, and Danny Sokol particularly influenced my work throughout the years and I owe them a great deal for their invaluable advice and support. Throughout the writing of this book, Maureen Garmon helped me with numerous research challenges. I was fortunate to have her assistance. During the writing and publication process, the individuals who make Foundation Press what it is have become friends and helped me to finish the manuscript. I am particularly grateful to John Bloomquist, Tessa Boury, Laura Holle, and Greg Olson of Foundation Press for their help, support, and friendship. Finally, this book is about imperfections and limitations. Its writing was possible because of the individuals who help me the most with my own imperfections and flaws, my family—Sivan and Eli.

The book's website, *www.regulationonline.net*, contains over 1,000 documents and images related to materials discussed in the book. Students can conveniently download relevant primary sources from this website. Many materials are available only through short hyperlinks that the book provides in the footnotes. My contact information for questions, comments, and feedback is available on the website. I hope you will enjoy the book.

BARAK ORBACH

October 2012

SUMMARY OF CONTENTS

Preface v
Table of Cases xxiii

PART I. INTRODUCTORY CONCEPTS 1

CHAPTER 1. What Is Regulation? 2

Sec.
1.1 Paying for Misunderstanding Regulation 2
1.2 Shaping Conduct With Legal Norms 22
1.3 Rules vs. Standards 74
1.4 Direct and Indirect Regulation 81
1.5 Unintended Consequences 107
1.6 Cost–Benefit Analysis 113

CHAPTER 2. Inescapable Controversy and Critique 137

Sec.
2.1 (Mis)Perceptions of Reality 137
2.2 The Invisible Hand's Fingerprints 144
2.3 Private Interest and Change 160
2.4 Institutional Weaknesses 165
2.5 Government Failures 225
2.6 National Controversy 231

PART II. MOTIVATIONS FOR REGULATION 267

CHAPTER 3. Externalities 274

Sec.
3.0 Affecting Others 274
3.1 Social Regulation 275
3.2 Sic Utere Tuo Ut Alienum Non Lædas 288
3.3 Entitlements and Effects on Others 297
3.4 Coordination breakdowns 328
3.5 Network Effects 348

CHAPTER 4. Risk 355

Sec.
4.1 Safety First, Wisdom Later 355
4.2 Misuse of Risk 363
4.3 Risk, Chance, and Hope 370
4.4 Willingness and Ability to Pay the Costs 375
4.5 Conflicting Values and Disbelief 382
4.6 Systemic Risk, Too Big to Fail, and Government Relief 400

CHAPTER 5. Inadequate Information 404

Sec.
5.1 What Is Inadequate Information? 404
5.2 Insufficient Information 409
5.3 Misleading Information 424
5.4 Confusing Information 445

CHAPTER 6. Unfair Prices and Other Contractual Terms 457

Sec.
6.1 Concentration of Ownership 457
6.2 Rent, Price, and Motivations for Regulation 463
6.3 The Rhetoric of Bargaining 471
6.4 Natural Monopoly 488

CHAPTER 7. Legal Paternalism 527

Sec.
7.1 What Is Paternalism? 527
7.2 Morality 530
7.3 Inalienability and Commodification 558
7.4 Bounded Rationality 599

PART III. REGULATORY METHODS 631

CHAPTER 8. Bans, Mandates, and Permits 632

Sec.
8.1 Commands and Controls 632
8.2 Bans and Prohibitions 634
8.3 Mandates 661
8.4 Permits and Entry Regulation 665

CHAPTER 9. Standard Setting and Price Regulation 691

Sec.
9.1 Standard Setting 691
9.2 Price Regulation 695
9.3 Quality and Other Standards 740

CHAPTER 10. Information Regulation 757

Sec.
10.1 Information and Beliefs 757
10.2 Centralized Information Regulation 763
10.3 Decentralized Information Regulation 778

CHAPTER 11. Preference Shaping 799

Sec.

11.1 Do We Have Defined Preferences? 799
11.2 Why Regulate Preferences? 802
11.3 Traditional Preference Shaping 806
11.4 Censorship 807
11.5 Compulsory Expressions 810
11.6 Voluntary Expressions 838
11.7 Curbing Immediate Gratification Options 844

INDEX 847

TABLE OF CONTENTS

PREFACE v
TABLE OF CASES xxiii

PART I. INTRODUCTORY CONCEPTS 1

CHAPTER 1. What Is Regulation? 2

Sec.

1.1 Paying for Misunderstanding Regulation 2
1.1.1 Background of the Great Recession 3
1.1.2 Some Costs of the Great Recession 11
1.1.3 The Causes of the Great Recession 15
1.1.3a Irrational Exuberance 15
1.1.3b The Financial Crisis Inquiry Commission ("FCIC") 16
1.1.3c The Senate Permanent Subcommittee on Investigation 19
Questions 21
1.2 Shaping Conduct With Legal Norms 22
1.2.1 The Meaning of the Word 22
Questions 25
Lochner and the Bakeshop Act 25
Lochner v. New York 27
Notes on Lochner 33
Questions 34
1.2.2 The Regulator: Who Has the Authority to Regulate? 40
Cipollone v. Liggett Group, Inc. 44
Altria Group, Inc. v. Good 50
Questions 60
Food and Drug Administration v. Brown & Williamson Tobacco Corp. 61
Questions 69
1.2.3 The Regulatee: Whose Conduct Is Targeted? 70
Hogs in New York City 70
Questions 71
Rogers v. Higgins 72
Questions 74
1.3 Rules vs. Standards 74
Montana's Basic Rule 76
Questions 81
1.4 Direct and Indirect Regulation 81
The Tennessee Movie Rating Law 84
Questions 85
File Sharing 86
In re: Aimster Copyright Litigation 86
The Bono Rule 93
Fox Television Stations, Inc. v. Federal Communications Commission 94
Federal Communications Commission v. Fox Television Stations, Inc. 103
Questions 106

Sec.
1.5 Unintended Consequences 107
Plastic Bags and Legal Definitions 109
Questions 110
Smoking in Atlantic City 110
Questions 113
1.6 Cost–Benefit Analysis 113
1.6.1 The Underlying Intuition 114
1.6.2 Executive Order 12866 115
1.6.3 (Why) Is Cost–Benefit Analysis Controversial? 116
The Delaney Clause 118
Les v. Reilly 119
Questions 122
Entergy Corp. v. Riverkeeper, Inc. 123
Questions 128
Center for Biological Diversity v. National Highway Traffic Safety Administration 128
Questions 136

CHAPTER 2. Inescapable Controversy and Critique 137

Sec.
2.1 (Mis)Perceptions of Reality 137
Coalition for Responsible Regulation, Inc. v. Environmental Protection Agency 139
2.2 The Invisible Hand's Fingerprints 144
2.2.1 What's in the Hand? 144
Questions 149
2.2.2 The Pursuit of Self–Interest 150
2.2.2a The Butcher 150
2.2.2b The Brewer 154
2.2.2c The Baker 155
Questions 155
Seattle's Green Fee 157
Questions 159
2.3 Private Interest and Change 160
2.3.1 Regulating Conflicting Private Interests 160
2.3.2 Pareto Efficiency 161
2.3.3 Kaldor–Hicks Efficiency 162
Questions 164
2.4 Institutional Weaknesses 165
2.4.1 The Benevolent Public Decisionmaker 166
Oregon Trollers Association v. Gutierrez 166
Questions 169
2.4.2 The Self–Interested Public Decisionmaker 169
2.4.2a Self–Serving Regulations 171
Tennessee's T–Bo Act 171
Questions 173
Defamation of Public Officials 173
Anti–Cartoon Laws 175
Questions 185
Randall v. Evening News Association 188
Questions 191
2.4.2b Bribery and Cinch Bills 191
Questions 195

Sec.
2.4 Institutional Weaknesses—Continued
2.4.3 The Public Decisionmaker and Interest Groups ... 197
Question ... 200
2.4.3a Earmarks ... 200
Questions ... 202
2.4.3b Pressure Groups in Action Crush Videos ... 202
United States v. Stevens ... 205
Notes ... 210
Questions ... 211
2.4.3c Agreements With Interest Groups ... 211
Sanders v. Brown ... 211
Questions ... 217
2.4.3d The Judiciary and Interest Groups ... 218
Caperton v. A.T. Massey Coal Co., Inc. ... 220
2.5 Government Failures ... 225
Smallpox in America ... 227
Questions ... 230
2.6 National Controversy ... 231
National Federation of Independent Business v. Sebelius ... 231
Questions ... 264

PART II. MOTIVATIONS FOR REGULATION ... 267

Questions ... 273

CHAPTER 3. Externalities ... 274

Sec.
3.0 Affecting Others ... 274
3.1 Social Regulation ... 275
3.1.1 Uncompensated Effects on Others' Well–Being ... 277
3.1.1a Pigou: Private and Social Interests ... 277
3.1.1b Externalities Defined ... 278
3.1.2 The Coase Theorem ... 279
3.1.2a Critique of the Pigonvian Tradition ... 279
3.1.2b Coasean Bargaining and Sparks From Railway Engines ... 281
3.1.2c Public Goods ... 282
3.1.3 Fables and Myths: Do Externalities Justify Regulation? ... 286
3.2 Sic Utere Tuo Ut Alienum Non Lædas ... 288
Questions ... 291
"Smoke From Factory Chimneys" ... 293
Boomer v. Atlantic Cement Co. ... 293
Questions ... 297
3.3 Entitlements and Effects on Others ... 297
Ladies' Hats ... 298
Oldknow v. City of Atlanta ... 298
Questions ... 300
Cellphones at the Theater ... 301
Questions ... 302
Urban Nuisances ... 303
Questions ... 306
Tobacco and Odors ... 307
In re Jacobs ... 308

Sec.
3.3 Entitlements and Effects on Others—Continued
Questions 313
Smallpox Vaccination 313
Jacobson v. Massachusetts 315
Questions 320
Regulation of Social Diseases 323
Harry A. Rider, Regulation of Social Diseases 324
Questions 327
3.4 Coordination breakdowns 328
Game and Fish 330
Minnesota v. Rodman 333
Questions 334
The Fragmented American Indian Land 334
Hodel v. Irving 334
Babbitt v. Youpee 343
Questions 348
3.5 Network Effects 348
Decoding and Circumvention 350
Chartwell Communications Group v. Westbrook 351
The Digital Millennium Copyright Act 352
Questions 354

CHAPTER 4. Risk 355

Sec.
4.1 Safety First, Wisdom Later 355
4.1.1 Shaky Intuitions 355
4.1.2 Flawed Decisionmaking 357
4.1.3 Risk Misperceptions and Regulation 360
4.2 Misuse of Risk 363
Anti–Spitting Laws 363
Questions 369
4.3 Risk, Chance, and Hope 370
United States v. Rutherford 370
Questions 374
4.4 Willingness and Ability to Pay the Costs 375
Mine Safety 375
Commonwealth v. Bonnell 379
Questions 381
4.5 Conflicting Values and Disbelief 382
Auto Safety Regulation 382
American Motorcycle Association v. Davids 385
Adrian v. Poucher 388
Illinois v. Kohrig 390
Picou v. Gillum 396
Questions 399
4.6 Systemic Risk, Too Big to Fail, and Government Relief 400
4.6.1 What Is Systemic Risk? 400
4.6.2 Too Big to Fail (TBTF) 401
4.6.3 Government Regulation and Relief 401

CHAPTER 5. Inadequate Information 404

Sec.
5.1 What Is Inadequate Information? 404
Questions 406

Sec.
5.2 Insufficient Information 409
5.2.1 Decisionmaking Under Ignorance 409
5.2.1a Risk, Uncertainty, and Ignorance 409
5.2.1b Information About Others' Choices 411
The T.J. Hooper 413
Questions 415
5.2.2 Information Asymmetry 416
5.2.2a Caveat Emptor 417
Laidlaw v. Organ 418
Questions 418
5.2.2b Implied Warranties 419
Ingalls v. Hobbs 419
Horton v. Marston 420
Questions 421
Bedbugs 421
Questions 424
5.3 Misleading Information 424
The Tobacco Industry 425
United States v. Philip Morris USA Inc. 425
Questions 436
The Stolen Valor Act 437
United States v. Alvarez 437
Questions 445
5.4 Confusing Information 445
Eastman Kodak Co. v. Image Technical Services 447
Questions 456

CHAPTER 6. Unfair Prices and Other Contractual Terms 457

Sec.
6.1 Concentration of Ownership 457
Hawaii Housing Authority v. Midkiff 457
Questions 461
6.2 Rent, Price, and Motivations for Regulation 463
Dodge v. Ford Motor Co. 467
Questions 471
6.3 The Rhetoric of Bargaining 471
Adkins v. Children's Hospital of the District of Columbia 474
West Coast Hotel Co. v. Parrish 482
Questions 488
6.4 Natural Monopoly 488
6.4.1 Market Concentration and Competitiveness 488
6.4.2 The Monopolist 489
Laboratories of Ice 490
New State Ice Co. v. Liebmann 490
Questions 501
The Evolution of Monopolists 501
United States v. Terminal Railroad Association of St. Louis 504
Questions 510
News Networks 512
International News Service v. Associated Press 512
Questions 521
Telephone Networks 521
National Rural Telecom Association v. Federal Communications Commission 521
Questions 526

CHAPTER 7. Legal Paternalism 527

Sec.
7.1 What Is Paternalism? 527
7.2 Morality 530
The Kentucky Model 532
Commonwealth v. Campbell 532
Commonwealth v. Wasson 535
Questions 544
Public Moral Code and Private Intimate Conduct 545
Reliable Consultants, Inc. v. Earle 546
Questions 552
Regulating What We Eat 554
Illinois Restaurant Association v. Chicago 555
Notes 558
Questions 558
7.3 Inalienability and Commodification 558
7.3.1 "Some Things That Money Cannot Buy" 560
In the Matter of Baby M 564
Questions 576
7.3.2 Suppression of Information 578
44 Liquormart, Inc. v. Rhode Island 578
Coyote Publishing, Inc. v. Miller 591
Questions 599
7.4 Bounded Rationality 599
7.4.1 Predictable Failures of the Pursuit of Self–Interest 599
7.4.2 Bounded Rationality in Action 603
Defunding Law 604
Palmer v. Thompson 604
Graphic Warnings 613
R.J. Reynolds Tobacco Co. v. United States Food and Drug Administration 614
Informed Consent 620
Texas Medical Providers Performing Abortion Services v. Lakey 620
Texas Medical Providers Performing Abortion Services v. Lakey 626
Questions 630

PART III. REGULATORY METHODS 631

CHAPTER 8. Bans, Mandates, and Permits 632

Sec.
8.1 Commands and Controls 632
8.2 Bans and Prohibitions 634
Pollution Regulation 636
Pugh v. Des Moines 636
Questions 639
Banning Smoking in Public 639
Roark & Hardee LP v. Austin 641
Questions 645

Sec.
8.2 Bans and Prohibitions—Continued
Regulating What We Eat 646
Questions 649
Restrictions on Relationships 650
Toledo v. Tellings 650
Notes 653
Questions 655
The Incandescent Light Bulb 656
Questions 660
8.3 Mandates 661
Wickard v. Filburn 662
Questions 664
8.4 Permits and Entry Regulation 665
8.4.1 Participation and Exclusion Through Permits 665
8.4.2 Occupational Licensure 667
Dent v. West Virginia 669
Questions 670
S.S. Kresge Co. v. Couzens 671
Questions 674
Dyrek v. Garvey 675
Questions 678
8.4.3 Regulation through Permits 678
Dog Permits 678
McGlone v. Womack 679
Questions 682
Movie Censorship 682
Block v. Chicago 683
Questions 684
Tabooing Tattooing 685
Anderson v. Hermosa Beach 685
Questions 690

CHAPTER 9. Standard Setting and Price Regulation 691

Sec.
9.1 Standard Setting 691
9.2 Price Regulation 695
Munn v. Illinois (1876) 696
9.2.1 Regulation of Prices 698
9.2.1a Ratemaking 699
Fire Insurance 699
German Alliance Insurance Co. v. Lewis 700
Questions 707
9.2.1b Price Floors and Ceilings 708
In re Kazas 708
State Board of Dry Cleaners v. Thrift–D–Lux Cleaners 712
Questions 717
Price Gouging 717
Questions 721
The Durbin Amendment 722
Questions 725
9.2.2 Regulation Through Prices and Taxes 726
9.2.2a Sin Taxes 727
Child Labor 728
Bailey v. Drexel Furniture Co. Child Labor Tax Case 729

Sec.
9.2 Price Regulation—Continued
9.2.2b Rent Seeking 731
Butter and Margarine 731
A. Magnano Co. v. Hamilton 733
9.2.2c Internalization 735
Pay as You Throw 736
Questions 739
9.3 Quality and Other Standards 740
Bread Standardization 740
Schmidinger v. Chicago 741
Questions 744
Water Fluoridation 745
Paduano v. City of New York 746
Coshow v. Escondido 751
Questions 756

CHAPTER 10. Information Regulation 757

Sec.
10.1 Information and Beliefs 757
Personal Hygiene 760
Questions 762
10.2 Centralized Information Regulation 763
Advertising 764
Questions 765
Education and the State 765
Edwards v. Aguillard 766
Questions 776
10.3 Decentralized Information Regulation 778
10.3.1 Warnings 779
Skyhook Corp. v. Jasper 779
Klopp v. Wackenhut Corp. 783
Question 784
10.3.2 Disclosures 784
Grade Cards and Restaurant Hygiene 784
Calorie Labeling in Food Establishments 785
New York State Restaurant Association v. New York City Board of Health 789
Questions 796

CHAPTER 11. Preference Shaping 799

Sec.
11.1 Do We Have Defined Preferences? 799
11.2 Why Regulate Preferences? 802
11.2.1 Addressing Conflicting Preferences 802
11.2.2 Debiasing Bounded Rationality 804
11.3 Traditional Preference Shaping 806
11.4 Censorship 807
Maryland v. West 807
Questions 809
11.5 Compulsory Expressions 810
The Pledge of Allegiance 810
Minersville School District v. Gobitis 811
West Virginia State Board of Education v. Barnette 816
Questions 823

Sec.
11.5 Compulsory Expressions—Continued
Live Free or Die ... 824
Wooley v. Maynard ... 825
Questions ... 829
Cigarettes in Pharmacies ... 830
Walgreen Co. v. San Francisco ... 831
Questions ... 838
11.6 Voluntary Expressions ... 838
The Pledge of Allegiance ... 839
Freedom From Religion Foundation v. Hanover School District ... 839
Questions ... 844
11.7 Curbing Immediate Gratification Options ... 844
Small Stake Gambling ... 844
Questions ... 845

INDEX ... 847

TABLE OF CASES

The principal cases are in bold type. Cases cited or discussed in the text are in roman type. References are to pages. Cases cited in principal cases and within other quoted materials are not included.

Adkins v. Children's Hospital of the District of Columbia, 261 U.S. 525, 43 S.Ct. 394, 67 L.Ed. 785 (1923), 22, 34, **474,** 559, 636, 696

Adrian v. Poucher, 67 Mich.App. 133, 240 N.W.2d 298 (Mich.App.1976), **388**

Agurs, United States v., 427 U.S. 97, 96 S.Ct. 2392, 49 L.Ed.2d 342 (1976), 417

Aimster Copyright Litigation, In re, 334 F.3d 643 (7th Cir.2003), 82, **86**

Alcorn v. Mitchell, 63 Ill. 553 (Ill.1872), 369

Altria Group, Inc. v. Good, 555 U.S. 70, 129 S.Ct. 538, 172 L.Ed.2d 398 (2008), 43, **50**

Alvarez, United States v., ___ U.S. ___, 132 S.Ct. 2537, 183 L.Ed.2d 574 (2012), 24, **437,** 801

Alvarez, United States v., 638 F.3d 666 (9th Cir.2011), 425

Amadeo v. Principal Mut. Life Ins. Co., 290 F.3d 1152 (9th Cir.2002), 269

A. Magnano Co. v. Hamilton, 292 U.S. 40, 54 S.Ct. 599, 78 L.Ed. 1109 (1934), 163, 464, **733**

Ambach v. Norwick, 441 U.S. 68, 99 S.Ct. 1589, 60 L.Ed.2d 49 (1979), 269

American Booksellers Ass'n, Inc. v. Hudnut, 771 F.2d 323 (7th Cir.1985), 760, 806

American Motorcycle Ass'n v. Davids, 11 Mich.App. 351, 158 N.W.2d 72 (Mich.App. 1968), **385**

American Tradition Partnership, Inc. v. Bullock, ___ U.S. ___, 132 S.Ct. 2490, 183 L.Ed.2d 448 (2012), 198

A&M Records, Inc. v. Napster, Inc., 239 F.3d 1004 (9th Cir.2001), 86

Anderson v. City of Hermosa Beach, 621 F.3d 1051 (9th Cir.2010), **685**

Application of (see name of party)

Ashcroft v. Free Speech Coalition, 535 U.S. 234, 122 S.Ct. 1389, 152 L.Ed.2d 403 (2002), 545

Babbitt v. Youpee, 519 U.S. 234, 117 S.Ct. 727, 136 L.Ed.2d 696 (1997), 334, **343,** 463

Baby M, Matter of, 109 N.J. 396, 537 A.2d 1227 (N.J.1988), **564**

Bagley, United States v., 473 U.S. 667, 105 S.Ct. 3375, 87 L.Ed.2d 481 (1985), 417

Bailey v. Drexel Furniture Co. (United States Reports Title: Child Labor Tax Case), 259 U.S. 20, 42 S.Ct. 449, 66 L.Ed. 817 (1922), **729**

Barnes v. New Hampshire Karting Ass'n, Inc., 128 N.H. 102, 509 A.2d 151 (N.H. 1986), 269

Barthet v. City of New Orleans, 24 F. 563 (C.C.E.D.La.1885), 153

Bates v. State Bar of Arizona, 433 U.S. 350, 97 S.Ct. 2691, 53 L.Ed.2d 810 (1977), 692, 764

Belden, State ex rel. v. Fagan, 1870 WL 92 (La.1870), 152

Bell v. Burson, 402 U.S. 535, 91 S.Ct. 1586, 29 L.Ed.2d 90 (1971), 682

Berman v. Parker, 348 U.S. 26, 75 S.Ct. 98, 99 L.Ed. 27 (1954), 40, 273

Block v. City of Chicago, 239 Ill. 251, 87 N.E. 1011 (Ill.1909), **683,** 758

Blodgett, People ex rel. Twitchell v., 13 Mich. 127 (Mich.1865), 107, 108

Board of Trade of City of Chicago v. United States, 246 U.S. 231, 38 S.Ct. 242, 62 L.Ed. 683 (1918), 76

Bonnell, Commonwealth v., 1872 WL 11223 (Pa.Com.Pl.1872), **379**

Boomer v. Atlantic Cement Co., 26 N.Y.2d 219, 309 N.Y.S.2d 312, 257 N.E.2d 870 (N.Y.1970), **293**

Boston, C. & M.R.R. v. Gilmore, 37 N.H. 410 (N.H.1858), 291

Bowers v. Hardwick, 478 U.S. 186, 106 S.Ct. 2841, 92 L.Ed.2d 140 (1986), 531, 553

Brady v. Maryland, 373 U.S. 83, 83 S.Ct. 1194, 10 L.Ed.2d 215 (1963), 417

Brakeman v. Potomac Ins. Co., 472 Pa. 66, 371 A.2d 193 (Pa.1977), 472, 473

Brendale v. Confederated Tribes and Bands of Yakima Indian Nation, 492 U.S. 408, 109 S.Ct. 2994, 106 L.Ed.2d 343 (1989), 290

Brigance v. Velvet Dove Restaurant, Inc., 725 P.2d 300 (Okla.1986), 82

Brown v. Board of Ed. of Topeka, Shawnee County, Kansas, 347 U.S. 483, 74 S.Ct. 686, 98 L.Ed. 873 (1954), 275

Brown v. New Haven Taxicab Co., 93 Conn. 251, 105 A. 706 (Conn.1919), 77
Bruesewitz v. Wyeth LLC, ___ U.S. ___, 131 S.Ct. 1068, 179 L.Ed.2d 1 (2011), 321, 408, 777
Buck v. Bell, 274 U.S. 200, 47 S.Ct. 584, 71 L.Ed. 1000 (1927), 655, 762
Bunting v. State of Oregon, 243 U.S. 426, 37 S.Ct. 435, 61 L.Ed. 830 (1917), 34, 473
Burnham v. Beverly Airways, 311 Mass. 628, 42 N.E.2d 575 (Mass.1942), 279
Burstyn, Inc. v. Wilson, 343 U.S. 495, 72 S.Ct. 777, 96 L.Ed. 1098 (1952), 84
Butchers' Union Slaughter–House & Live–Stock Landing Co. v. Crescent City Live–Stock Landing & Slaughter–House Co., 111 U.S. 746, 4 S.Ct. 652, 28 L.Ed. 585 (1884), 153, 418, 667, 671

Camden County Board of Chosen Freeholders v. Beretta, USA Corp., 273 F.3d 536 (3rd Cir.2001), 83
Campbell, Commonwealth v., 133 Ky. 50, 117 S.W. 383 (Ky.1909), **532**
Caperton v. A.T. Massey Coal Co., Inc., 556 U.S. 868, 129 S.Ct. 2252, 173 L.Ed.2d 1208 (2009), **220**
Caremark International Inc. Derivative Litigation, In re, 698 A.2d 959 (Del.Ch.1996), 75
Carroll Towing Co., United States v., 159 F.2d 169 (2nd Cir.1947), 113
CBS Corp. v. F.C.C., 535 F.3d 167 (3rd Cir. 2008), 94
Cedillo v. Secretary of Health and Human Services, 617 F.3d 1328 (Fed.Cir.2010), 321, 408, 777
Center for Biological Diversity v. National Highway Traffic Safety Admin., 538 F.3d 1172 (9th Cir.2008), **128,** 659, 693
Chamber of Commerce of United States v. Whiting, ___ U.S. ___, 131 S.Ct. 1968, 179 L.Ed.2d 1031 (2011), 82
Charles Wolff Packing Co. v. Court of Industrial Relations of State of Kansas, 262 U.S. 522, 43 S.Ct. 630, 67 L.Ed. 1103 (1923), 268
Charles River Bridge v. Warren Bridge, 36 U.S. 420, 11 Pet. 420, 9 L.Ed. 773 (1837), 289, 464
Chartwell Communications Group v. Westbrook, 637 F.2d 459 (6th Cir.1980), **351**
Chevron, USA., Inc. v. Natural Resources Defense Council, Inc., 467 U.S. 837, 104 S.Ct. 2778, 81 L.Ed.2d 694 (1984), 43
Chicago, City of v. Schmidinger, 243 Ill. 167, 90 N.E. 369 (Ill.1909), 741
Chicago, City of v. Stratton, 162 Ill. 494, 44 N.E. 853 (Ill.1896), 305
Cipollone v. Liggett Group, Inc., 505 U.S. 504, 112 S.Ct. 2608, 120 L.Ed.2d 407 (1992), 43, **44**
Citizens United v. Federal Election Com'n, 558 U.S. 310, 130 S.Ct. 876, 175 L.Ed.2d 753 (2010), 108, 198
City of (see name of city)
Clippinger v. Hepbaugh, 1843 WL 5037 (Pa. 1843), 191
Coalition for Responsible Regulation, Inc. v. E.P.A., 684 F.3d 102 (D.C.Cir. 2012), **139**
Cohens v. State of Virginia, 19 U.S. 264, 5 L.Ed. 257 (1821), 290
Colusa County v. Welch, 122 Cal. 428, 55 P. 243 (Cal.1898), 193
Commonwealth v. ______ (see opposing party)
Combs v. Texas Entertainment Ass'n, Inc., 347 S.W.3d 277 (Tex.2011), 728
Commonwealth v. ______ (see opposing party)
Compas, Montana v., 290 Mont. 11, 964 P.2d 703 (Mont.1998), 279
Coshow v. City of Escondido, 34 Cal. Rptr.3d 19 (Cal.App. 4 Dist.2005), **751**
Coyote Pub., Inc. v. Miller, 598 F.3d 592 (9th Cir.2010), **591,** 758, 764
Craigmiles v. Giles, 312 F.3d 220 (6th Cir. 2002), 163

Darcantel v. People's Slaughterhouse & Refrigerating Co., 11 So. 239 (La.1892), 153
Delaware & Raritan Canal Co. v. Camden & Atlantic Railroad Co., 1863 WL 63 (N.J.Ch.1863), 291
Delta Air Corp. v. Kersey, 193 Ga. 862, 20 S.E.2d 245 (Ga.1942), 279
Dent v. State of West Virginia, 129 U.S. 114, 9 S.Ct. 231, 32 L.Ed. 623 (1889), **669**
District of Columbia v. Heller, 554 U.S. 570, 128 S.Ct. 2783, 171 L.Ed.2d 637 (2008), 76, 219
Dodge v. Ford Motor Co., 204 Mich. 459, 170 N.W. 668 (Mich.1919), **467**
Dun & Bradstreet, Inc. v. Greenmoss Builders, Inc., 472 U.S. 749, 105 S.Ct. 2939, 86 L.Ed.2d 593 (1985), 269
Duquesne Light Co. v. Barasch, 488 U.S. 299, 109 S.Ct. 609, 102 L.Ed.2d 646 (1989), 466
Dyrek v. Garvey, 334 F.3d 590 (7th Cir. 2003), **675**

Eastman Kodak Co. v. Image Technical Services, Inc., 504 U.S. 451, 112 S.Ct. 2072, 119 L.Ed.2d 265 (1992), **447**
East Saginaw Mfg. Co. v. City of East Saginaw, 19 Mich. 259 (Mich.1869), 291
eBay Inc. v. MercExchange, L.L.C., 547 U.S. 388, 126 S.Ct. 1837, 164 L.Ed.2d 641 (2006), 307
Edwards v. Aguillard, 482 U.S. 578, 107 S.Ct. 2573, 96 L.Ed.2d 510 (1987), **766**
Entergy Corp. v. Riverkeeper, Inc., 556 U.S. 208, 129 S.Ct. 1498, 173 L.Ed.2d 369 (2009), **123**
Euclid, Ohio, Village of v. Ambler Realty Co., 272 U.S. 365, 47 S.Ct. 114, 71 L.Ed. 303 (1926), 290

Fagan, State ex rel. Belden v., 1870 WL 92 (La.1870), 152

FCC v. AT & T Inc., ___ U.S. ___, 131 S.Ct. 1177, 179 L.Ed.2d 132 (2011), 108

F.C.C. v. Fox Television Stations, Inc., ___ U.S. ___, 132 S.Ct. 2307, 183 L.Ed.2d 234 (2012), **103**

F.C.C. v. Fox Television Stations, Inc., 556 U.S. 502, 129 S.Ct. 1800, 173 L.Ed.2d 738 (2009), 42

F.C.C. v. Pacifica Foundation, 438 U.S. 726, 98 S.Ct. 3026, 57 L.Ed.2d 1073 (1978), 42, 107

Federal Power Commission v. Hope Natural Gas Co., 320 U.S. 591, 64 S.Ct. 281, 88 L.Ed. 333 (1944), 466, 698

Florida Lime & Avocado Growers, Inc. v. Paul, 373 U.S. 132, 83 S.Ct. 1210, 10 L.Ed.2d 248 (1963), 41

Flynn v. Holder, 684 F.3d 852 (9th Cir.2012), 562

Foley v. Interactive Data Corp., 254 Cal.Rptr. 211, 765 P.2d 373 (Cal.1988), 269

Fonovisa, Inc. v. Cherry Auction, Inc., 76 F.3d 259 (9th Cir.1996), 82

FDA v. Brown & Williamson Tobacco Corp., 529 U.S. 120, 120 S.Ct. 1291, 146 L.Ed.2d 121 (2000), **61,** 197, 374

44 Liquormart, Inc. v. Rhode Island, 517 U.S. 484, 116 S.Ct. 1495, 134 L.Ed.2d 711 (1996), **578,** 758

Fox Television Stations, Inc. v. F.C.C., 613 F.3d 317 (2nd Cir.2010), **94,** 161, 197, 758

Freedman v. State of Md., 380 U.S. 51, 85 S.Ct. 734, 13 L.Ed.2d 649 (1965), 84

Freedom From Religion Foundation v. Hanover School Dist., 626 F.3d 1 (1st Cir.2010), **839**

Freedom Holdings, Inc. v. Spitzer, 357 F.3d 205 (2nd Cir.2004), 218

Freeman, People v., 250 Cal.Rptr. 598, 758 P.2d 1128 (Cal.1988), 38

Fruit v. Schreiner, 502 P.2d 133 (Alaska 1972), 82

Gagliardi v. TriFoods Intern., Inc., 683 A.2d 1049 (Del.Ch.1996), 75

Gempp v. Bassham, 60 Ill.App. 84 (Ill.App. 3 Dist.1895), 304

Gentile v. Altermatt, 169 Conn. 267, 363 A.2d 1 (Conn.1975), 682

German Alliance Ins. Co. v. Lewis, 233 U.S. 389, 34 S.Ct. 612, 58 L.Ed. 1011 (1914), **700**

Gibbons v. Ogden, 22 U.S. 1, 6 L.Ed. 23 (1824), 464

Ginsberg v. State of N. Y., 390 U.S. 629, 88 S.Ct. 1274, 20 L.Ed.2d 195 (1968), 84

Goedert v. City of Ferndale, 596 F.Supp.2d 1027 (E.D.Mich.2008), 279

Goldblatt v. Town of Hempstead, New York, 369 U.S. 590, 82 S.Ct. 987, 8 L.Ed.2d 130 (1962), 41

Goldfarb v. Virginia State Bar, 421 U.S. 773, 95 S.Ct. 2004, 44 L.Ed.2d 572 (1975), 692

Goldstein v. Chestnut Ridge Volunteer Fire Co., 218 F.3d 337 (4th Cir.2000), 269

Gonzales v. Raich, 545 U.S. 1, 125 S.Ct. 2195, 162 L.Ed.2d 1 (2005), 43, 561

Grace v. Howlett, 51 Ill.2d 478, 283 N.E.2d 474 (Ill.1972), 682

Graham v. Allis–Chalmers Manufacturing Co., 41 Del.Ch. 78, 188 A.2d 125 (Del. Supr.1963), 75

Granholm v. Heald, 544 U.S. 460, 125 S.Ct. 1885, 161 L.Ed.2d 796 (2005), 164

Graves v. Secretary of Dept. of Health and Human Services, 2011 WL 3010753 (Fed. Cl.2011), 321, 408, 777

Gunter v. Dale County, 44 Ala. 639 (Ala. 1870), 291

Hammer v. Dagenhart, 247 U.S. 251, 38 S.Ct. 529, 62 L.Ed. 1101 (1918), 728

Hardy v. Georgia, 25 Ga.App. 287, 103 S.E. 267 (Ga.App.1920), 77

Hawaii Housing Authority v. Midkiff, 467 U.S. 229, 104 S.Ct. 2321, 81 L.Ed.2d 186 (1984), **457,** 489

Hay v. Cohoes Co., 2 N.Y. 159, 2 Comst. 159 (N.Y.1849), 288

Helsley, United States v., 615 F.2d 784 (9th Cir.1979), 72

Hershberg v. City of Barbourville, 142 Ky. 60, 133 S.W. 985 (Ky.1911), 544

Hines v. Davidowitz, 312 U.S. 52, 61 S.Ct. 399, 85 L.Ed. 581 (1941), 41

Hinman v. Pacific Air Lines Transport Corp., 84 F.2d 755 (9th Cir.1936), 279

Hodel v. Irving, 481 U.S. 704, 107 S.Ct. 2076, 95 L.Ed.2d 668 (1987), 334, **334,** 463

Holden v. Hardy, 169 U.S. 366, 18 S.Ct. 383, 42 L.Ed. 780 (1898), 28, 381, 473

Horton v. Marston, 352 Mass. 322, 225 N.E.2d 311 (Mass.1967), **420**

Ileto v. Glock Inc., 349 F.3d 1191 (9th Cir. 2003), 83

Illinois v. Kohrig, 113 Ill.2d 384, 101 Ill. Dec. 650, 498 N.E.2d 1158 (Ill.1986), **390**

Illinois v. Kuchta, 296 Ill. 180, 129 N.E. 528 (Ill.1920), 77

Illinois Restaurant Ass'n v. City of Chicago, 492 F.Supp.2d 891 (N.D.Ill.2007), **555**

Ingalls v. Hobbs, 156 Mass. 348, 31 N.E. 286 (Mass.1892), **419**

In re (see name of party)

International News Service v. Associated Press, 248 U.S. 215, 39 S.Ct. 68, 63 L.Ed. 211 (1918), **512,** 764

Interstate Circuit, Inc. v. City of Dallas, 390 U.S. 676, 88 S.Ct. 1298, 20 L.Ed.2d 225 (1968), 84

Jackson v. Metropolitan Edison Co., 419 U.S. 345, 95 S.Ct. 449, 42 L.Ed.2d 477 (1974), 269

Jacobs, In re, 98 N.Y. 98 (N.Y.1885), **308**

Jacobson v. Commonwealth of Massachusetts, 197 U.S. 11, 25 S.Ct. 358, 49 L.Ed. 643 (1905), 227, **315,** 632, 661, 762
Jardine v. Upper Darby Lodge No. 1973, Inc., 413 Pa. 626, 198 A.2d 550 (Pa.1964), 82
J.W. Hampton, Jr., & Co. v. United States, 276 U.S. 394, 48 S.Ct. 348, 72 L.Ed. 624 (1928), 42

Kalem Co. v. Harper Bros., 222 U.S. 55, 32 S.Ct. 20, 56 L.Ed. 92 (1911), 81
Kamin v. American Express Co., 54 A.D.2d 654, 387 N.Y.S.2d 993 (N.Y.A.D. 1 Dept. 1976), 75
Kansas v. Bailey, 107 Kan. 637, 193 P. 354 (Kan.1920), 77
Kazas, In re, 22 Cal.App.2d 161, 70 P.2d 962 (Cal.App. 4 Dist.1937), **708,** 731
Kelo v. City of New London, 268 Conn. 1, 843 A.2d 500 (Conn.2004), 163
Kelo v. City of New London, Connecticut, 545 U.S. 469, 125 S.Ct. 2655, 162 L.Ed.2d 439 (2005), 162
Kendall v. Visa USA, Inc., 518 F.3d 1042 (9th Cir.2008), 724
Klopp v. Wackenhut Corp., 113 N.M. 153, 824 P.2d 293 (N.M.1992), **783**

Laidlaw v. Organ, 15 U.S. 178, 4 L.Ed. 214 (1817), **418**
Lanphear v. Commonwealth, 2001 WL 36244749 (Mass.Super.2001), 690
Lasky v. State Farm Ins. Co., 296 So.2d 9 (Fla.1974), 682
Lawrence v. Texas, 539 U.S. 558, 123 S.Ct. 2472, 156 L.Ed.2d 508 (2003), 531
Ledbetter v. Goodyear Tire & Rubber Co., Inc., 550 U.S. 618, 127 S.Ct. 2162, 167 L.Ed.2d 982 (2007), 160
Leis v. Cleveland R. Co., 101 Ohio St. 162, 128 N.E. 73 (Ohio 1920), 78
Les v. Reilly, 968 F.2d 985 (9th Cir.1992), **119**
Lewis v. Gollner, 129 N.Y. 227, 29 N.E. 81 (N.Y.1891), 305
Lochner v. New York, 198 U.S. 45, 25 S.Ct. 539, 49 L.Ed. 937 (1905), **27,** 34, 40, 360, 559
Lopez, United States v., 514 U.S. 549, 115 S.Ct. 1624, 131 L.Ed.2d 626 (1995), 40, 43
Loving v. Virginia, 388 U.S. 1, 87 S.Ct. 1817, 18 L.Ed.2d 1010 (1967), 530
Lowell v. Boston & L.R. Corp., 40 Mass. 24 (Mass.1839), 290
Lucas v. South Carolina Coastal Council, 505 U.S. 1003, 112 S.Ct. 2886, 120 L.Ed.2d 798 (1992), 291

Manzanares v. Bell, 214 Kan. 589, 522 P.2d 1291 (Kan.1974), 682
Marks v. Mobil Oil Corp., 562 F.Supp. 759 (E.D.Pa.1983), 79
Maryland v. West, 9 Md.App. 270, 263 A.2d 602 (Md.App.1970), **807**
Mary M. v. City of Los Angeles, 285 Cal.Rptr. 99, 814 P.2d 1341 (Cal.1991), 82
Massachusetts v. Alger, 61 Mass. 53 (Mass. 1851), 40
Matter of (see name of party)
McCardle v. Indianapolis Water Co., 272 U.S. 400, 47 S.Ct. 144, 71 L.Ed. 316 (1926), 466, 698
McCarty v. Pheasant Run, Inc., 826 F.2d 1554 (7th Cir.1987), 114
McDonald v. City of Chicago, Illinois, ___ U.S. ___, 130 S.Ct. 3020, 177 L.Ed.2d 894 (2010), 76, 219
McGlone v. Womack, 129 Ky. 274, 111 S.W. 688 (Ky.1908), **679,** 696, 727
McGowan v. State of Maryland, 366 U.S. 420, 81 S.Ct. 1101, 6 L.Ed.2d 393 (1961), 37, 693
McLaughlin v. State of Florida, 379 U.S. 184, 85 S.Ct. 283, 13 L.Ed.2d 222 (1964), 530
M'Culloch v. Maryland, 17 U.S. 316, 4 L.Ed. 579 (1819), 41
Meaney v. Dever, 326 F.3d 283 (1st Cir.2003), 279
Mellen, People v., 172 N.Y.S. 165 (N.Y.Co.Ct. 1918), 78
MGM Studios Inc. v. Grokster, Ltd., 545 U.S. 913, 125 S.Ct. 2764, 162 L.Ed.2d 781 (2005), 82, 86
Metropolitan Board of Health v. Heister, 37 N.Y. 661 (N.Y.1868), 151, 156
Microsoft Corp., United States v., 253 F.3d 34, 346 U.S.App.D.C. 330 (D.C.Cir.2001), 510
Millbank v. Jones, 127 N.Y. 370, 38 N.Y.St. Rep. 910, 28 N.E. 31 (N.Y.1891), 191
Miller v. California, 413 U.S. 15, 93 S.Ct. 2607, 37 L.Ed.2d 419 (1973), 693
Miller, United States v., 307 U.S. 174, 59 S.Ct. 816, 83 L.Ed. 1206 (1939), 76
Mills v. Mills, 40 N.Y. 543 (N.Y.1869), 191
Minersville School Dist. v. Gobitis, 310 U.S. 586, 60 S.Ct. 1010, 84 L.Ed. 1375 (1940), **811**
Minnesota v. Rodman, 58 Minn. 393, 59 N.W. 1098 (Minn.1894), **333**
Mitchell v. Williams, 27 Ind. 62 (Ind.1866), 291
Montana v. Stanko, 292 Mont. 192, 974 P.2d 1132 (Mont.1998), 80
Morrison, United States v., 529 U.S. 598, 120 S.Ct. 1740, 146 L.Ed.2d 658 (2000), 40, 43
Mulgrew v. Board of Educ. of City School Dist. of City of New York, 87 A.D.3d 506, 928 N.Y.S.2d 701 (N.Y.A.D. 1 Dept.2011), 796
Muller v. State of Oregon, 208 U.S. 412, 28 S.Ct. 324, 52 L.Ed. 551 (1908), 34, 477
Munn v. Illinois, 94 U.S. 113, 4 Otto 113, 24 L.Ed. 77 (1876), 267, 291, 466, 696
Mutual Film Corp. v. Industrial Commission of Ohio, 236 U.S. 230, 35 S.Ct. 387, 59 L.Ed. 552 (1915), 84

Nash v. Port Authority of New York and New Jersey, 51 A.D.3d 337, 856 N.Y.S.2d 583 (N.Y.A.D. 1 Dept.2008), 84

National Ass'n of Regulatory Utility Com'rs v. F.C.C., 525 F.2d 630, 173 U.S.App.D.C. 413 (D.C.Cir.1976), 269
National Basketball Ass'n v. Motorola, Inc., 105 F.3d 841 (2nd Cir.1997), 521
National Federation of Independent Business v. Sebelius, ___ U.S. ___, 132 S.Ct. 2566, 183 L.Ed.2d 450 (2012), 20, 22, 34, 40, **231,** 320, 356, 382, 399, 527, 633, 803
National Rural Telecom Ass'n v. F.C.C., 988 F.2d 174, 300 U.S.App.D.C. 226 (D.C.Cir.1993), **521,** 696, 708
National Soc. of Professional Engineers v. United States, 435 U.S. 679, 98 S.Ct. 1355, 55 L.Ed.2d 637 (1978), 692
Nebbia v. New York, 291 U.S. 502, 54 S.Ct. 505, 78 L.Ed. 940 (1934), 268, 299, 714
New State Ice Co. v. Liebmann, 285 U.S. 262, 52 S.Ct. 371, 76 L.Ed. 747 (1932), 40, 60, **490,** 527, 666, 717
New York, City of v. Beretta USA Corp., 315 F.Supp.2d 256 (E.D.N.Y.2004), 83
New York State Restaurant Ass'n v. New York City Bd. of Health, 556 F.3d 114 (2nd Cir.2009), **789**
New York State Restaurant Ass'n v. New York City Bd. of Health, 509 F.Supp.2d 351 (S.D.N.Y.2007), 786
New York Times Co. v. Sullivan, 376 U.S. 254, 84 S.Ct. 710, 11 L.Ed.2d 686 (1964), 174
New York Times Co. v. Sullivan, 273 Ala. 656, 144 So.2d 25 (Ala.1962), 174
Nollan v. California Coastal Com'n, 483 U.S. 825, 107 S.Ct. 3141, 97 L.Ed.2d 677 (1987), 40
Nye & Nissen v. United States, 336 U.S. 613, 69 S.Ct. 766, 93 L.Ed. 919 (1949), 82

Office of Communication of United Church of Christ v. F.C.C., 359 F.2d 994, 123 U.S.App.D.C. 328 (D.C.Cir.1966), 275
Oldknow v. City of Atlanta, 9 Ga.App. 594, 71 S.E. 1015 (Ga.App.1911), **298**
Olmstead v. United States, 277 U.S. 438, 48 S.Ct. 564, 72 L.Ed. 944 (1928), 2, 21, 161, 411, 745
Onan, United States v., 190 F.2d 1 (8th Cir. 1951), 269
Opinion of the Justices, 113 N.H. 205, 304 A.2d 881 (N.H.1973), 682
Oregon Trollers Ass'n v. Gutierrez, 452 F.3d 1104 (9th Cir.2006), **166**
Oyama v. California, 332 U.S. 633, 68 S.Ct. 269, 92 L.Ed. 249 (1948), 269

Pace v. Alabama, 106 U.S. 583, 16 Otto 583, 1 S.Ct. 637, 27 L.Ed. 207 (1883), 530
Pacific Gas and Elec. Co. v. State Energy Resources Conservation & Development Com'n, 461 U.S. 190, 103 S.Ct. 1713, 75 L.Ed.2d 752 (1983), 41
Paduano v. City of New York, 257 N.Y.S.2d 531 (N.Y.Sup.1965), **746**
Palmer v. Thompson, 403 U.S. 217, 91 S.Ct. 1940, 29 L.Ed.2d 438 (1971), **604**
Paris Adult Theatre I v. Slaton, 413 U.S. 49, 93 S.Ct. 2628, 37 L.Ed.2d 446 (1973), 530
Peoni, United States v., 100 F.2d 401 (2nd Cir.1938), 82
People v. ______ (see opposing party)
People v. Two Wheel Corp., 71 N.Y.2d 693, 530 N.Y.S.2d 46, 525 N.E.2d 692 (N.Y. 1988), 720
People ex rel. v. ______ (see opposing party and relator)
Perry v. Brown, 671 F.3d 1052 (9th Cir. 2012), 530
Philip Morris USA Inc., United States v., 566 F.3d 1095, 386 U.S.App.D.C. 49 (D.C.Cir.2009), 59, **425**
Picou v. Gillum, 874 F.2d 1519 (11th Cir. 1989), **396,** 403
Pinkerton v. United States, 328 U.S. 640, 66 S.Ct. 1180, 90 L.Ed. 1489 (1946), 82
Pinnick v. Cleary, 360 Mass. 1, 271 N.E.2d 592 (Mass.1971), 682
Planned Parenthood of Southeastern Pennsylvania v. Casey, 505 U.S. 833, 112 S.Ct. 2791, 120 L.Ed.2d 674 (1992), 416
Plumley v. Commonwealth of Massachusetts, 155 U.S. 461, 15 S.Ct. 154, 39 L.Ed. 223 (1894), 163
Poe v. Ullman, 367 U.S. 497, 81 S.Ct. 1752, 6 L.Ed.2d 989 (1961), 40
Powell v. Commonwealth of Pennsylvania, 127 U.S. 678, 8 S.Ct. 992, 32 L.Ed. 253 (1888), 163
Powers v. Harris, 379 F.3d 1208 (10th Cir. 2004), 163
Pugh v. City of Des Moines, 176 Iowa 593, 156 N.W. 892 (Iowa 1916), **636**

Randall v. Evening News Ass'n, 97 Mich. 136, 56 N.W. 361 (Mich.1893), 191
Randall v. Evening News Ass'n, 79 Mich. 266, 44 N.W. 783 (Mich.1890), **188**
Reader v. Ottis, 147 Minn. 335, 180 N.W. 117 (Minn.1920), 78
Reliable Consultants, Inc. v. Earle, 517 F.3d 738 (5th Cir.2008), 83, **546**
Rice v. Santa Fe Elevator Corp., 331 U.S. 218, 67 S.Ct. 1146, 91 L.Ed. 1447 (1947), 42
Richmond, F. & P.R. Co. v. Louisa R. Co., 54 U.S. 71, 13 How. 71, 14 L.Ed. 55 (1851), 289
Riviello v. Waldron, 47 N.Y.2d 297, 418 N.Y.S.2d 300, 391 N.E.2d 1278 (N.Y. 1979), 82
R.J. Reynolds Tobacco Co. v. United States Food and Drug Admin., 845 F.Supp.2d 266 (D.D.C.2012), **614,** 645, 805
Roark & Hardee LP v. City of Austin, 522 F.3d 533 (5th Cir.2008), **641**
Roe v. Wade, 410 U.S. 113, 93 S.Ct. 705, 35 L.Ed.2d 147 (1973), 108, 198
Rogers v. Higgins, 48 Ill. 211 (Ill.1868), **72**
Ronwin, In re, 113 Ariz. 357, 555 P.2d 315 (Ariz.1976), 408

Ronwin v. Shapiro, 657 F.2d 1071 (9th Cir. 1981), 408
Rush–Presbyterian–St. Luke's Medical Center v. Hellenic Republic, 877 F.2d 574 (7th Cir.1989), 269
Rutherford, United States v., 442 U.S. 544, 99 S.Ct. 2470, 61 L.Ed.2d 68 (1979), **370**

Sanders v. Brown, 504 F.3d 903 (9th Cir. 2007), **211**
Schmidinger v. City of Chicago, 226 U.S. 578, 33 S.Ct. 182, 57 L.Ed. 364 (1913), **741**
Schmitt v. Nord, 71 S.D. 575, 27 N.W.2d 910 (S.D.1947), 163
Schollenberger v. Commonwealth of Pennsylvania, 171 U.S. 1, 18 S.Ct. 757, 43 L.Ed. 49 (1898), 163
Scopes v. State, 154 Tenn. 105, 289 S.W. 363 (Tenn.1927), 766
Semler v. Oregon State Bd. of Dental Examiners, 294 U.S. 608, 55 S.Ct. 570, 79 L.Ed. 1086 (1935), 764
Shavers v. Kelley, 402 Mich. 554, 267 N.W.2d 72 (Mich.1978), 291
Sheldon v. Weeks, 51 Ill.App. 314 (Ill.App. 1 Dist.1893), 305
Singer v. Sheppard, 464 Pa. 387, 346 A.2d 897 (Pa.1975), 682
Skinner, Nevada, State of v., 884 F.2d 445 (9th Cir.1989), 79
Skyhook Corp. v. Jasper, 90 N.M. 143, 560 P.2d 934 (N.M.1977), **779**
Slaughter–House Cases, 83 U.S. 36, 21 L.Ed. 394 (1872), 152, 418, 636, 667, 668
Smith v. New England Aircraft Co., 270 Mass. 511, 170 N.E. 385 (Mass.1930), 279
Smith v. Van Gorkom, 488 A.2d 858 (Del. Supr.1985), 75
Smyth v. Ames, 169 U.S. 466, 18 S.Ct. 418, 42 L.Ed. 819 (1898), 466, 698
Sony Corp. of America v. Universal City Studios, Inc., 464 U.S. 417, 104 S.Ct. 774, 78 L.Ed.2d 574 (1984), 82, 86
Hing v. Crowley, 113 U.S. 703, 5 S.Ct. 730, 28 L.Ed. 1145 (1885), 36, 693
Souza v. Estate of Bishop, 821 F.2d 1332 (9th Cir.1987), 462
S.S. Kresge Co. v. Couzens, 290 Mich. 185, 287 N.W. 427 (Mich.1939), **671**
Standard Oil Co. of New Jersey v. United States, 221 U.S. 1, 31 S.Ct. 502, 55 L.Ed. 619 (1911), 76, 466
State v. ______ (see opposing party)
State Bd. of Dry Cleaners v. Thrift–D–Lux Cleaners, 40 Cal.2d 436, 254 P.2d 29 (Cal.1953), 269, **712**
State ex rel. v. ______ (see opposing party and relator)
State of (see name of state)
Stevens, United States v., ___ U.S. ___, 130 S.Ct. 1577, 176 L.Ed.2d 435 (2010), **205,** 219
Stevens, United States v., 533 F.3d 218 (3rd Cir.2008), 205

TCF Nat. Bank v. Bernanke, 643 F.3d 1158 (8th Cir.2011), 727
TDM, Inc. v. Tax Com'n, 103 P.3d 190 (Utah App.2004), 728
Terminal R. R. Ass'n of St. Louis, United States v., 224 U.S. 383, 32 S.Ct. 507, 56 L.Ed. 810 (1912), **504,** 666
Texas Medical Providers Performing Abortion Services v. Lakey, 2012 WL 373132 (W.D.Tex.2012), **626,** 779
Texas Medical Providers Performing Abortion Services v. Lakey, 667 F.3d 570 (5th Cir.2012), 416, **620,** 779, 805
The T.J. Hooper v. Northern Barge Corp., 60 F.2d 737 (2nd Cir.1932), 25, **413**
Thorpe v. Rutland & B.R. Co., 27 Vt. 140 (Vt.1854), 289
Thrasher v. City of Atlanta, 178 Ga. 514, 173 S.E. 817 (Ga.1934), 279
Toledo v. Tellings, 114 Ohio St.3d 278, 871 N.E.2d 1152 (Ohio 2007), **650**
Twitchell, People ex rel. v. Blodgett, 13 Mich. 127 (Mich.1865), 107, 108
Tyson & Bro.–United Theatre Ticket Offices v. Banton, 273 U.S. 418, 47 S.Ct. 426, 71 L.Ed. 718 (1927), 268, 299

United States v. ______ (see opposing party)
Universe Life Ins. Co. v. Giles, 950 S.W.2d 48 (Tex.1997), 269

Varnum v. Brien, 763 N.W.2d 862 (Iowa 2009), 530
Village of (see name of village)

Wagner, People v., 86 Mich. 594, 49 N.W. 609 (Mich.1891), 740
Walgreen Co. v. City and County of San Francisco, 110 Cal.Rptr.3d 498 (Cal.App. 1 Dist.2010), **831**
Walt Disney Co. Derivative Litigation, In re, 907 A.2d 693 (Del.Ch.2005), 75, 553
Walz v. Tax Commission of City of New York, 397 U.S. 664, 90 S.Ct. 1409, 25 L.Ed.2d 697 (1970), 464
Washington v. Randall, 107 Wash. 695, 182 P. 575 (Wash.1919), 78
Washington v. Immelt, 173 Wash.2d 1, 267 P.3d 305 (Wash.2011), 139, 279
Wasson, Commonwealth v., 842 S.W.2d 487 (Ky.1992), 532, **535**
Weil v. McClough, 618 F.Supp. 1294 (S.D.N.Y.1985), 139, 279
West Coast Hotel Co. v. Parrish, 300 U.S. 379, 57 S.Ct. 578, 81 L.Ed. 703 (1937), 34, **482,** 559, 696
West Virginia State Board of Education v. Barnette, 319 U.S. 624, 63 S.Ct. 1178, 87 L.Ed. 1628 (1943), **816**
Weygandt v. Bartle, 88 Or. 310, 171 P. 587 (Or.1918), 78
White v. R.M. Packer Co., Inc., 635 F.3d 571 (1st Cir.2011), 721

Wickard v. Filburn, 317 U.S. 111, 63 S.Ct. 82, 87 L.Ed. 122 (1942), **662**
Wiggins Ferry Co. v. City of East St. Louis, 107 U.S. 365, 17 Otto 365, 2 S.Ct. 257, 27 L.Ed. 419 (1883), 502
Wildey v. Collier, 7 Md. 273 (Md.1854), 191
William Deering & Co. v. Cunningham, 63 Kan. 174, 65 P. 263 (Kan.1901), 191
Williams v. Attorney General of Alabama, 378 F.3d 1232 (11th Cir.2004), 83
Williams v. Morgan, 478 F.3d 1316 (11th Cir.2007), 83
Williams v. Pryor, 240 F.3d 944 (11th Cir. 2001), 83
Williams, United States v., 553 U.S. 285, 128 S.Ct. 1830, 170 L.Ed.2d 650 (2008), 545
Williams v. Walker–Thomas Furniture Co., 350 F.2d 445, 121 U.S.App.D.C. 315 (D.C.Cir.1965), 471, 472
Williams v. Walker–Thomas Furniture Co., 198 A.2d 914 (D.C.App.1964), 471
Williamson v. Lee Optical of Oklahoma Inc., 348 U.S. 483, 75 S.Ct. 461, 99 L.Ed. 563 (1955), 267, 764
Williamson v. Mazda Motor of America, Inc., ___ U.S. ___, 131 S.Ct. 1131, 179 L.Ed.2d 75 (2011), 60
Wilson v. Handley, 119 Cal.Rptr.2d 263 (Cal. App. 3 Dist.2002), 279
Wisconsin v. Yoder, 406 U.S. 205, 92 S.Ct. 1526, 32 L.Ed.2d 15 (1972), 765
Womack v. Von Rardon, 133 Wash.App. 254, 135 P.3d 542 (Wash.App. Div. 3 2006), 172
Wooley v. Maynard, 430 U.S. 705, 97 S.Ct. 1428, 51 L.Ed.2d 752 (1977), **825**
World Trade Center Bombing Litigation, In re, 17 N.Y.3d 428, 933 N.Y.S.2d 164, 957 N.E.2d 733 (N.Y.2011), 84
Wright v. State, 88 Md. 436, 41 A. 795 (Md. 1898), 163

REGULATION

WHY AND HOW THE STATE REGULATES

PART I

Introductory Concepts

CHAPTER 1

WHAT IS REGULATION?

Regulation is state intervention in the private domain, which is a byproduct of our imperfect reality and human limitations. We live in a complex world of finite resources, in which the pursuit of self-interest often fails the individual and causes harm to others. These imperfections and limitations motivate society to adopt regulations—to promote economic efficiency, environmental sustainability, morality, and the general welfare of the public. The same imperfections and limitations, however, also guarantee the imperfect nature of regulation. Our human flaws allow, for example, the promulgation of excessive and redundant regulations, and enable the adoption of regulations that serve private interest groups. Society's challenge, therefore, is to acknowledge that imperfections and limitations impair decisionmaking, communication, and trade, and to utilize legal institutions to address them. In other words, we should accept the fact that regulation is here to stay, and work to maximize its benefits and minimize its costs.*

§ 1.1 PAYING FOR MISUNDERSTANDING REGULATION

"Ignorance more frequently begets confidence than does knowledge."

—Charles Darwin[1]

"The greatest dangers to liberty lurk in insidious encroachment by men of zeal, well-meaning but without understanding."

—Louis Brandeis[2]

Lawyers are key participants in the regulatory process. They negotiate regulatory reforms, draft regulations, enforce regulations, assist their clients in complying with regulations, lobby for and against regulations, and often challenge the validity of regulations. Our goal this semester is to acquire basic legal tools lawyers need in the modern regulatory state.

We will see how people tend to agree that misunderstandings of regulation may entail significant costs to society, and seem to believe that they understand complex regulatory issues, while identify flaws in the

* See Barak Orbach, *What Is Regulation?*, 30 YALE JOURNAL ON REGULATION ONLINE 1 (2012).

1. CHARLES DARWIN, DESCENT OF MAN AND SELECTION IN RELATION TO SEX 4 (1871).

2. Olmstead v. United States, 277 U.S. 438, 478 (1928) (Brandeis, J., dissenting). Friedrich Hayek endorsed the quotation in F.A. HAYEK, THE CONSTITUTION OF LIBERTY 253 (1960). Milton and Rose Friedman used the quotation to open their book MILTON & ROSE FRIEDMAN, FREE TO CHOOSE: A PERSONAL STATEMENT (1980). Friedman's and Hayek's regulatory philosophies were remarkably inconsistent with Brandeis' philosophy.

views of others. Political, academic, and everyday debates often create the impression that each one of us knows how to design optimal regulatory regimes for complex issues, such as the healthcare system, the financial system, the environment, transportation, abortion, firearms, and innovation. The problem appears to be with "other people" who misunderstand these issues and many others. This Section describes the potential costs of such misunderstandings.

§ 1.1.1 Background of the Great Recession

The Great Depression and the Great Recession are two economic crises that deeply scarred the American economy and threatened the viability of our financial system.[3] Congress responded to both crises with massive regulatory reforms. These actions incited fierce debates over the costs and benefits of regulation. Economists and historians have extensively studied the Great Depression, but no single account of its causes or consequences has gained national consensus. Similarly, the public continues to be divided over accounts of the Great Recession. These enduring controversies frame our introduction and highlight the ongoing disagreement over the role of the state in the private domain.

The American colonies and later the new American states issued their own money to collect revenues.[4] This so-called currency-finance system ended when, under the Constitution, states relinquished money their power to coin to the federal government. Losing a significant source of income, states substituted "bank finance" for "currency finance"—they turned to banks and used regulatory powers to draw revenues from them.[5] Because they relied on local banks for revenues, states suppressed competition among banks to enhance their profitability. By prohibiting out-of-state banks from their jurisdictions and imposing branch banking restrictions, which reduced competition among local banks, states created local monopolies in towns and counties.[6] Within a few decades, states developed additional regulatory schemes, the most controversial of which was "free banking."

Between 1837 and 1865, states allowed individuals with capital to establish banks wherever they chose and to issue notes. These bank notes were used for everyday transactions and could be redeemed for gold or silver at the issuing banks. Because of the lack of regulatory constraints, free banking encouraged "wildcat banking:" The practice of opening banks in inaccessible locations to hamper attempts to redeem their notes. Although the free banking system had many problems, studies show that its

---

3. Another significant crisis is the Panic of 1893. *See, e.g.*, CHARLES HOFFMANN, THE DEPRESSION OF THE NINETIES (1956); DOUGLAS STEEPLES & DAVID O. WHITTEN, DEMOCRACY IN DESPERATION: THE DEPRESSION OF 1893 (1998).

4. *See generally* E. James Ferguson, *Currency Finance: An Interpretation of Colonial Monetary Practices*, 10 WILLIAM & MARY QUARTERLY 153 (1953).

5. See Richard Sylla et al., Bank and State Public Finance in the New Republic: *The United States, 1790–1860*, 47 JOURNAL OF ECONOMIC HISTORY 391 (1987).

6. *See* REY BERT WESTERFIELD, HISTORICAL SURVEY OF BRANCH BANKING IN THE UNITED STATES (1939). *See also* Daniel C. Giedeman, *Branch Banking Restrictions and Finance Constraints in Early–Twentieth–Century America*, 65 JOURNAL OF ECONOMIC HISTORY 129 (2005).

competitiveness made it superior to the prior restrictive regime.[7] The growth of wildcat banking and increase in the number of bank failures, however, led to the enactment of the National Banking Act of 1863 and federal regulation of the banking system. Thus, by the Stock Market Crash of 1929, the United States had experience with state and federal regulation of the banking industry.[8]

In the four years that followed the Stock Market Crash of 1929, over 9,500 commercial banks in the United States failed. In June 1933, Congress enacted the Banking Act of 1933[9] that reformed the banking system, separated commercial and investment banking, and established the Federal Deposit Insurance Corporation ("FDIC"). The Act became known as the Glass–Steagall Act for its two primary sponsors, Senator Carter Glass and Congressman Henry B. Steagall. It required separation between commercial and investment banking. Only a few days after President Franklin Roosevelt signed the Glass–Steagall Act into law, *Time* magazine focused public attention on the transformation of the financial sector: "[T]he Banking Act of 1933 ... requires private bankers to give up either their banking or their securities business."[10]

In 1956, Congress expanded the restrictions of the Glass–Steagall Act by passing the Bank Holding Company Act.[11] The new Act limited the activities of commercial banks to those activities most closely related to banking. Together, the two statutes greatly restricted the ability of banks to conduct activities associated with securities firms, insurance companies, merchant banks, and other financial companies. The statutes prevented commercial banks and bank holding companies from entering these markets either directly or through their subsidiaries.

In 1980, Congress began deregulating the financial sector by stripping restrictions from the Glass–Steagall Act and the Bank Holding Company Act.[12] The deregulation of the financial sector was spurred by the belief that increased competition is beneficial, serving businesses, consumers, and

---

7. *See* Gerald P. Dwyer, Jr., *Wildcat Banking, Banking Panics, and Free Banking in the United States*, 81 ECONOMIC REVIEW 1 (1996); Andrew Economopoulous & Heather O'Neill, Bank Entry during the Antebellum Period, 27 JOURNAL OF MONEY, CREDIT & BANKING 1071 (1995); Hugh Rockoff, *The Free Banking Era: A Reexamination*, 6 JOURNAL OF MONEY, CREDIT & BANKING 141 (1974).

8. *See* Randall S. Kroszner & Philip E. Strahan, *Regulation and Deregulation of the U.S. Banking Industry: Causes, Consequences and Implications for the Future* in ECONOMIC REGULATION AND ITS REFORM: WHAT HAVE WE LEARNED? (Nancy L. Rose ed., 2012).

9. Pub. L. No. 73–66, 48 Stat. 162 (June 16, 1933).

10. Pub. L. No. 84–511, 70 Stat. 133 (May 9, 1956).

11. Pub. L. No. 84–511, 70 Stat. 133 (May 9, 1956).

12. *See generally* James R. Barth, *The Repeal of Glass–Steagall and the Advent of Broad Banking*, 14 JOURNAL OF ECONOMIC PERSPECTIVES 191 (2000); CHARLES W. CALOMIRIS, U.S. BANK DEREGULATION IN HISTORICAL PERSPECTIVE (2000); Yongil Jeon & Stephen M. Miller, *Deregulation and Structural Change in the U.S. Commercial Banking Industry*, 29 EASTERN ECONOMIC JOURNAL 391 (2003); Randall S. Kroszner & Philip E. Strahan, *What Drives Deregulation? Economics and Politics of the Relaxation of Bank Branching Restrictions*, 114 QUARTERLY JOURNAL OF ECONOMICS 1437 (1999); Patricia McCoy et al., *Systemic Risk Through Securitization: The Result of Deregulation and Regulatory Failure*, 41 CONNECTICUT LAW REVIEW 493, 499–509 (2009).

the economy as a whole. Financial deregulation contributed to efficiency and innovation in the financial sector. Among other things, economists believed that financial innovation flattened business cycles. From the mid–1980s until the start of the Great Recession, business cycle fluctuations were small relative to those experienced in previous decades. This phenomenon of reduced volatility was dubbed the "*Great Moderation*."[13] In 2003, delivering the Presidential Address at the annual meeting of the American Economic Association, Nobel Laureate Robert Lucas explained the significance of the Great Moderation: "Macroeconomics was born as a distinct field in the 1940s, as a part of the intellectual response to the Great Depression. The term then referred to the body of knowledge and expertise that we hoped would prevent the recurrence of that economic disaster.... [M]acroeconomics in this original sense has succeeded: *Its central problem of depression prevention has been solved*."[14]

The scope of financial deregulation, however, has also entailed social costs. In the financial sector, firms often compete in risk. Being a competitive financial institution means offering a product that carries more risk than comparable products competitors are willing to offer. With limited regulatory constraints, an individual or firm that cannot receive a loan from one institution will receive it from another; a firm whose risk is too great for one insurer will insure its risk with another insurer; and so forth. That is, absent regulatory restrictions, financial institutions tend to increase the risk of their products to remain competitive. The financial deregulation that began in 1980 corresponded to massive changes in risk practices among financial institutions.[15] Global markets were becoming more competitive and technological progress allowed for the development and utilization of risky financial instruments. Financial markets are about trade in risk (risky investments, insurance products, and so forth). Financial innovation and efficiency allowed trade in riskier products. However, within existing limitations, an enduring increase in risk is unsustainable and inevitably concludes with "accidents."[16] Financial deregulation was followed by two big waves of bank failures—a first wave in the 1980s,

13. James H. Stock & Mark W. Watson, *Has the Business Cycle Changed and Why?*, in NBER MACROECONOMICS ANNUAL 2002 159 (Mark Gertler & Kenneth Rogoff eds. 2002); Governor Ben S. Bernanke, *What Have We Learned Since October 1979?*, Remarks at the Conference on Reflections on Monetary Policy 25 Years after October 1979 (Federal Reserve Bank of St. Louis, St. Louis, Missouri, October 8, 2004)

14. Robert E. Lucas, Jr., *Macroeconomic Priorities*, 93 AMERICAN ECONOMIC REVIEW 1 (2003) (emphasis added).

15. *See* Michael C. Keeley, *Deposit Insurance, Risk and Market Power in Banking*, 80 AMERICAN ECONOMIC REVIEW 1183 (1990).

16. *See* Franklin Allen & Douglas Gale, *Competition and Financial Stability*, 36 JOURNAL OF MONEY, CREDIT, AND BANKING 453 (2004). Section 619 of the 2010 Dodd–Frank Wall Street Reform and Consumer Protection Act, commonly known as *the Volcker Rule*, 12 U.S.C. 1851, prohibits proprietary trading by banking institutions. The Volcker Rule reintroduced the Glass–Steagall Act's conceptual divide between banks and securities firms. It intends to ban engagement in risky activities unrelated to essential bank services on financial institutions that benefit from public support by access to the Federal Reserve and FDIC insurance. *See generally* Charles K. Whitehead, *The Volcker Rule and Evolving Financial Markets*, 1 HARVARD BUSINESS LAW REVIEW 39 (2011).

before the Great Moderation, and a second one was part of the Great Recession and marked the end of the Great Moderation (see *Figure 1.4*).[17]

With the deregulation wave of the 1980s, income inequality began to rise (*see Figures 1.3–1.4*). From 1979 to 2007, the average inflation-adjusted household income, measured after government transfers and federal taxes, grew by 62%.[18] During the same period, the top 1% of earners had their average real household after tax income grow by more than 275%. For the remaining top 20% of the earners, average real household income after tax grew by 65%. For the 60% of earners in the middle, average real household after tax income grew by 40%. For the 20% of earners with the lowest income, average real household after tax income grew by 18%. Thus, although income inequality in the United States was visible in 1979, before financial deregulation began. By 2007, the eve of the Great Recession, income disparity had grown significantly.

Table 1.1

Income Group	*Growth in Income After Federal Taxes and Transfers, 1979-2007*	*Share of Household Income After Federal Taxes and Transfers*		
		1979	*2007*	*Change*
Top 1%	277.5%	7.7%	17.1%	122.1%
Fifth Quintile Without Top 1% (81st–99th Percentiles)	65%	35.1%	35.6%	1.4%
Fourth Quintile (61st–80th Percentiles)	43.3%	22%	19.9%	-9.6%
Middle Quintile (41st–60th Percentiles)	35.2%	16.2%	14%	-13.6%
Second Quintile (21st–40th Percentiles)	27.5%	12.2%	9.2%	-24.6%
Lowest Quintile (0–20th Percentiles)	18.3%	7.1%	5.1%	-28.1%

Using the Gini Index, the standard measure of income inequality, we can see the trend in income distribution in the United States between 1979 and 2007 (see *Figure 1.1*). During that period, income inequality went up by 33%.[19]

---

17. *See* David A. Moss, *Reversing the Null: Regulation, Deregulation, and the Power of Ideas*, in CHALLENGES TO BUSINESS IN THE TWENTY-FIRST CENTURY 35 (Gerald Rosenfeld et al. eds. 2011).

18. CONGRESSIONAL BUDGET OFFICE, TRENDS IN THE DISTRIBUTION OF HOUSEHOLD INCOME BETWEEN 1997 AND 2007 (Oct. 2011).

19. *The Gini Index* is a standard, simple summary measure of income inequality that is based on the relationship between shares of income and shares of the population. It ranges in value from zero to one, with zero indicating complete equality (for example, if each fifth of the population, ranked by income, received one-fifth of total income) and one indicating complete inequality (for example, if one household received all the income). A Gini Index that increases over time indicates rising income inequality.

Figure 1.1

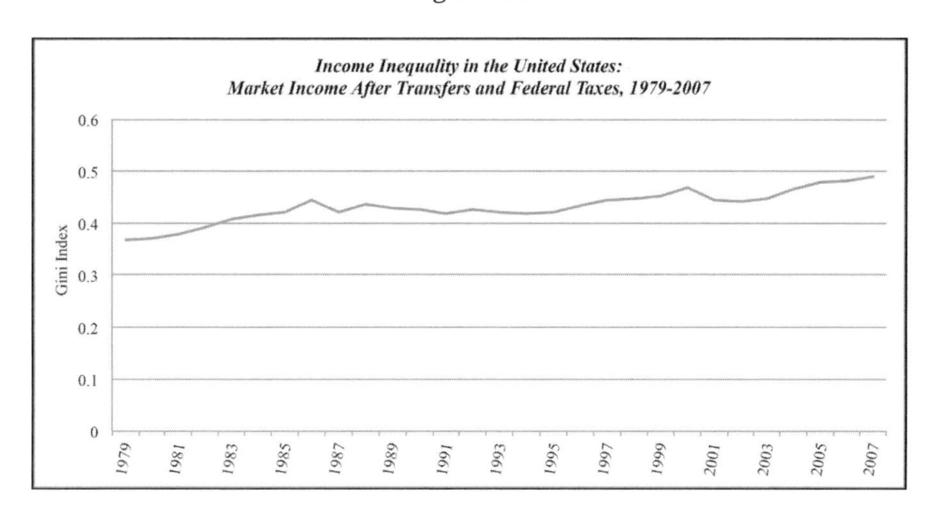

Prior to the Great Depression, before the era of significant financial regulation, levels of income inequality were also relatively high. The decline in income inequality in the 1930s and 1940s (*see Figures 1.2–1.4*) also took place in other countries following the Great Depression and two World Wars. During that era, massive social and economic changes occurred in many countries that account for the decline in income inequality, including large tax increases enacted to finance the wars.[20] By contrast, the rise in income inequality in recent decades in the United States was much less pronounced in other countries.[21] Beginning in the 1980s, top earners in the United States have increased their share of income much more than top earners in other developed countries.

20. *See generally* Thomas Piketty & Emmanuel Saez, *Income Inequality in the United States, 1913–1998*, 118 QUARTERLY JOURNAL OF ECONOMICS 1 (2003); Thomas Piketty & Emmanuel Saez, *The Evolution of Top Incomes: A Historical and International Perspective*, 96 AMERICAN ECONOMIC REVIEW 200 (2006).

21. Piketty & Saez, *The Evolution of Top Incomes*, *id.*

Figure 1.2

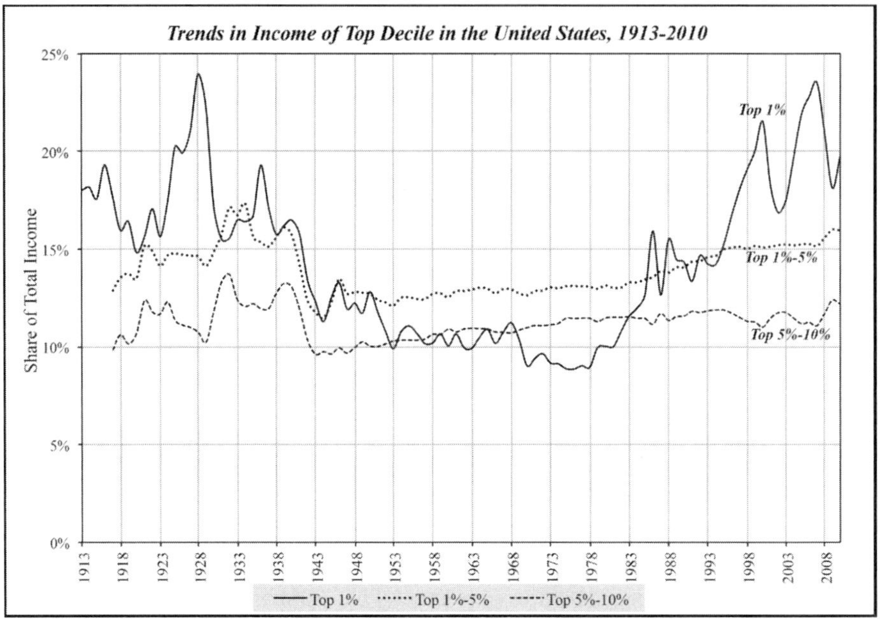

Trends in Income of Top Decile in the United States, 1913-2010

Source: Thomas Piketty & Emmanuel Saez, Income Inequality in the United States, Tables and Figures (March 2012).

One central question in the study of income inequality is how much the recent trend reflects the ability of top earners to extract rents at the expense of other groups in society and how much of it represents compensation for innovation and increased productivity.[22] *Both* forces contributed to changes in the distribution of income in the United States. Entrepreneurship and creativity paid off for many individuals. However, in some sectors of the economy, including the financial industry, many individuals benefitted from engaging in business activities that increased market risks, while shifting the cost of those increased risks onto the public.[23] The Great Recession elevated concerns that the American regulatory system allows (or allowed) individuals to increase the market risks in the pursuit of the own private gains.

---

22. *See* Janet Currie, *Inequality at Birth: Some Causes and Consequences*, 101 AMERICAN ECONOMIC REVIEW 1 (2011); Louis Kaplow, *Why Measure Inequality?* 3 JOURNAL OF ECONOMIC INEQUALITY 65 (2005).

23. *See, e.g.*, LUCIAN BEBCHUK & JESSE FRIED, PAY WITHOUT PERFORMANCE: THE UNFULFILLED PROMISE OF EXECUTIVE COMPENSATION (2006); Lucian A. Bebchuk & Holger Spamann, *Regulating Bankers' Pay*, 98 GEORGETOWN LAW JOURNAL 247 (2010). *See also* Lucian A. Bebchuk, *The Pursuit of a Bigger Pie: Can Everyone Expect a Bigger Slice?* 8 HOFSTRA LAW REVIEW 671 (1980).

Figure 1.3

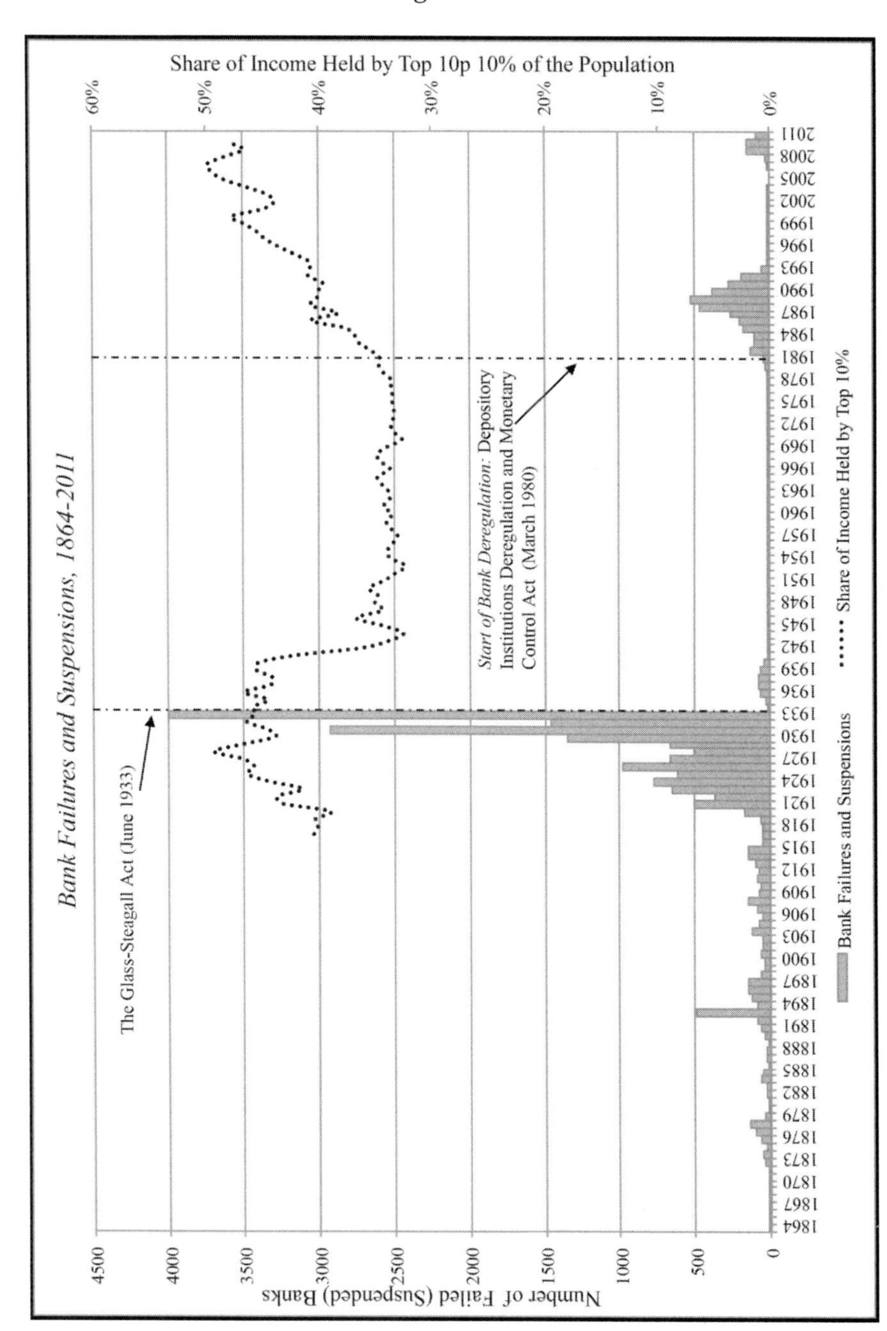

Source: David Moss, Harvard Business School.

Figure 1.4

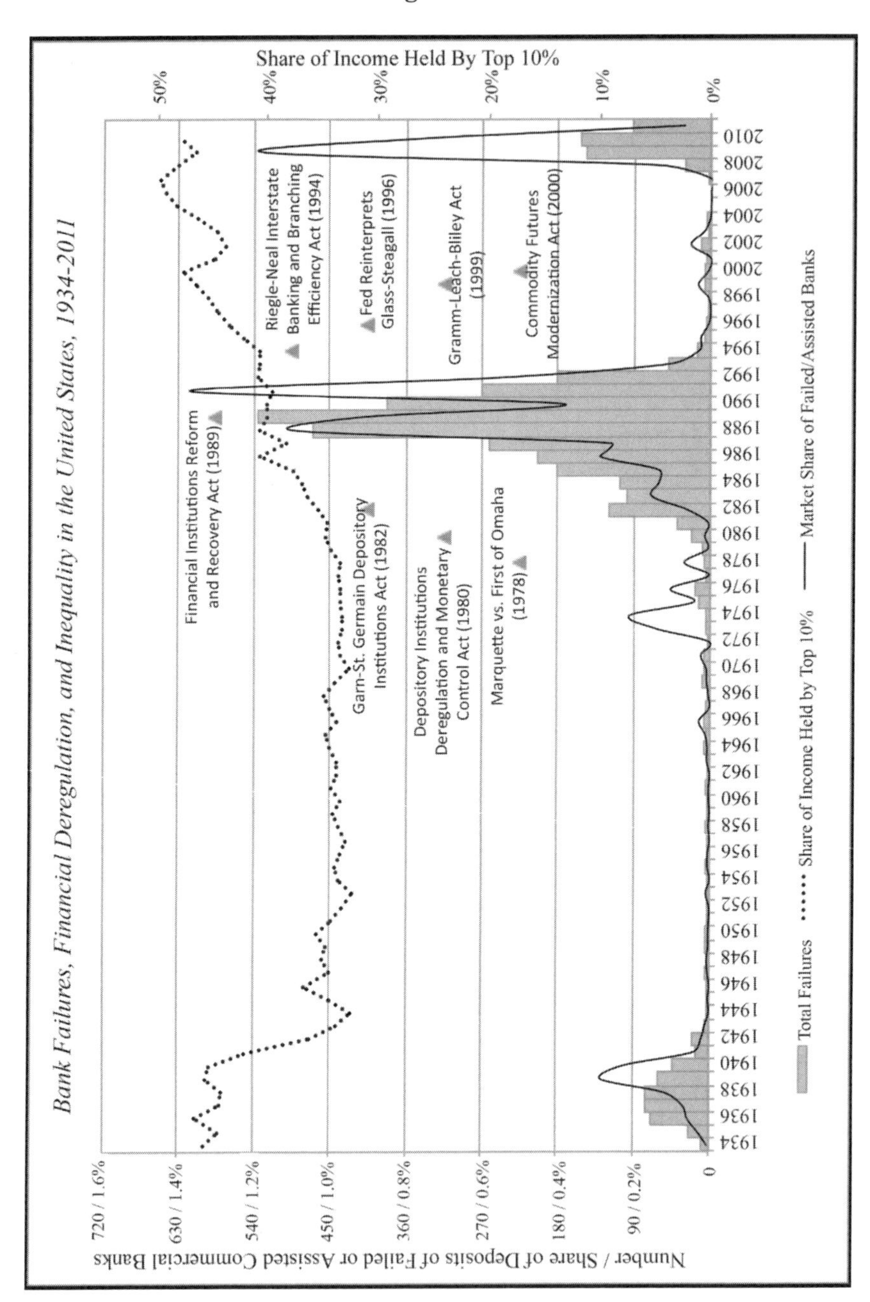

Source: David Moss, Harvard Business School.

§ 1.1.2 *Some Costs of the Great Recession*

The Great Recession, the worst economic crisis since the Great Depression, began in December 2007 and ended in June 2009.[24] From December 2007 to March 2009, the Dow Jones Industrial Average Index, S & P 500 Index, and Nasdaq Composite Index saw their value decline by 50%. The GDP, a measure of how much is produced in the economy declined in 2008 and 2009. By July 2009, the stock market showed significant signs of recovery—the Dow Jones Industrial Average, S & P 500, Nasdaq Composite indices gained 30% to 45% from their lowest point in March 2009.

In economics, the end of a recession merely means the beginning of an economic expansion. Despite the economic expansion, in July 2009, the American economy was operating at a lower capacity than it was in November 2007, housing prices continued to fall, and unemployment remained high. Many households continued feeling the consequences of the crisis and will continue to do so for years to come.

The burden of the Great Recession spread across the economy, affecting employment, production, sales, and other vital economic activities.[25] The two most conspicuous hardships of the recession have been unemployment and the collapse of real estate markets. In 2007, the *annual* average unemployment rate was 4.6%. It climbed to 5.8% in 2008, soared to 9.3% in 2009, and rose to 9.6% in 2010. The unemployment rate reached 10.1% in October 2009 and then slowly declined to the level of 9% at which it fluctuated for some time. Unemployment remained above 9% until October 2011. To simplify the figures: during the Great Recession, unemployment in the United States more than doubled itself, and began declining slowly in 2011. Correspondingly, the percentage of people in the United States living in poverty continued to grow.[26]

---

24. *See* National Bureau of Economic Research, Determination of the December 2007 Peak in Economic Activity (Nov. 28, 2008); National Bureau of Economic Research, Announcement of June 2009 Business Cycle Trough/End of Last Recession (September 20, 2010).

25. *See* Robert E. Hall, *Why Does the Economy Fall to Pieces after a Financial Crisis?*, 24 JOURNAL OF ECONOMIC PERSPECTIVES 3 (2010); Robert E. Hall, *The Long Slump*, 101 AMERICAN ECONOMIC REVIEW 431 (2011).

26. The U.S. Census Bureau measures poverty since 1959. In September 2011, the Bureau announced that the poverty rate in 2010 was the highest since 1993. According the Bureau's statistics, the percentage of U.S. population in poverty was approximately 12.5% in 2007 and started increasing in 2008. In 2010 it was 15.1%. The official poverty measure for the years of the Great Recession was deficient because it did not factor taxes and transfers. An adjusted measure for 2010, using available data shows that the percentage of people in poverty for that year was 16%. *See* Kathleen Short, *The Research Supplemental Poverty Measure: 2010* (U.S. Census Bureau, Nov. 2011).

Figure 1.5

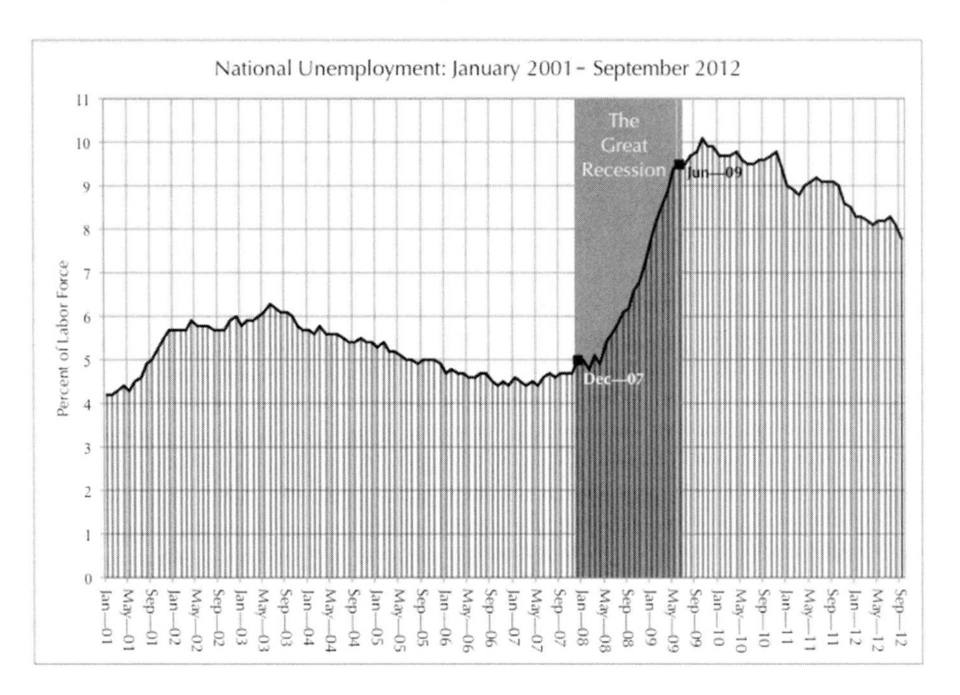

Source: Bureau of Labor Statistics.

Prior to the financial crisis, the U.S. housing market witnessed an excessive accumulation of debt, unsustainable volumes of trade, and a continuing increase in home prices—three basic properties of a financial bubble. Like all other financial bubbles, the U.S. housing bubble was fed by the irrational belief that the upward trend would last forever.[27] The collapse of the housing bubble shook the financial system and depressed real estate markets.[28] Real estate investments lost value, while corresponding liabilities (mortgages) have generally remained intact. During the bubble years, the use of risky loans and the insurance products that backed them steadily grew: inexpensive loans were available to almost all, and the household debt-to-income ratio soared. The bubble generated continuing appreciation in housing prices and motivated many households to use the available mortgage credit either to purchase homes or to borrow against

27. *See* CARMEN M. REINHART & KENNETH ROGOFF, THIS TIME IS DIFFERENT: EIGHT CENTURIES OF FINANCIAL FOLLY (2009).

28. *See* Markus K. Brunnermeier, *Deciphering the Liquidity and Credit Crunch 2007–2008*, 23 Journal of Economic Perspectives 77 (2009); Gary Gorton, *Information, Liquidity, and the (Ongoing) Panic of 2007*, 99 AMERICAN ECONOMIC REVIEW 567 (2009); Christopher Mayer et al., *The Rise in Mortgage Defaults*, 23 JOURNAL OF ECONOMIC PERSPECTIVES 27 (2009); Robert J. Shiller, *Understanding Recent Trends in House Prices Homeownership*, in Housing, Housing Finance and Monetary Policy 85 (Jackson Hole Conference Series, Federal Reserve Bank of Kansas City, 2008).

their home equity ("equity-based borrowers").[29] The bubble burst when the untenable high debt-to-income ratios began to unravel and the number of delinquent mortgages soared. Home prices fell to levels that, for many homes, were below the remaining mortgage balance. Many homeowners could no longer sell their homes and pay off their debts. Rising unemployment rates and a decline in real income levels only exacerbated these problems.

One of the financial products that fueled the housing bubble was subprime mortgages—high interest loans extended to high-risk borrowers (non-prime borrowers).[30] To increase the supply of these risky products, financial institutions developed and traded in related products in securities and insurance, thereby enhancing market risks. When the bubble began imploding, the risk carried by subprime loans triggered a chain reaction that affected the entire financial system.

As the recession progressed, the rates of mortgage delinquencies and home foreclosures multiplied. Homeowners' financial hardship accounted for the vast majority of delinquencies and foreclosures. However, changing norms in the crumbling mortgage market greatly contributed to the number of "strategic defaulters"—underwater borrowers who were not financially distressed.[31] During the Great Recession, foreclosure rates soared and they remained high after the end of the recession in June 2009 (see *Figure 1.6*).

Figure 1.6

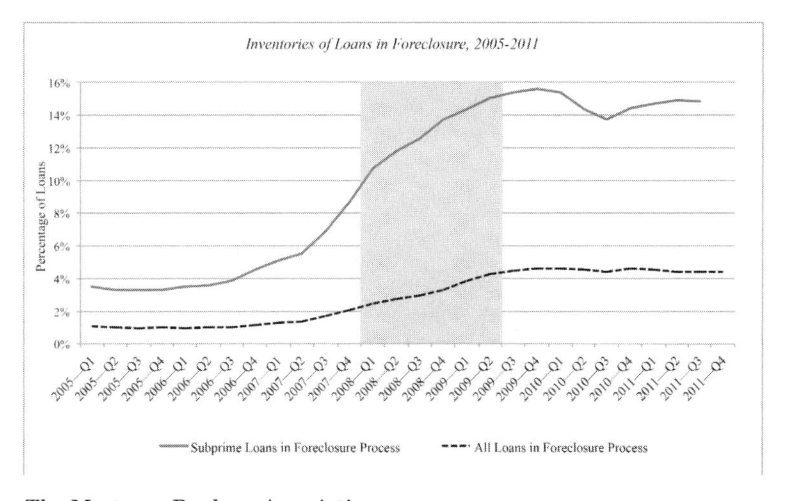

Source: The Mortgage Bankers Association.

---

29. *See* Atif Mian & Amir Sufi, House *Prices, Home Equity-Based Borrowing, and the US Household Leverage Crisis*, 101 AMERICAN ECONOMIC REVIEW 2132 (2011).

30. In January 2008, the American Dialect Society voted "*subprime*" as the 2007 word of the year, defining it as "an adjective used to describe a risky or less than ideal loan, mortgage, or investment."

31. *See* Neil Bhutta et al. *Consumer Ruthlessness and Strategic Default During the 2007–2009 Housing Bust*, Federal Reserve Working Paper (March 2011); Nasser Daneshvary & Terrence M. Clauretie, *Toxic Neighbors: Foreclosures and Short-Sales Spillover Effects from the Current Housing-Market Crash*, 50 ECONOMIC INQUIRY 217 (2012); Ryan M. Goodstein et al., *Are Foreclosures Contagious?*, FDIC Working Paper No. 2011–4 (2011).

House prices in the United States reached their peak in 2006 and began sliding before the bursting of the housing bubble in December 2007. During the bubble years, real estate properties were traded at prices divorced from realistic values. The collapse was inevitable and it brought about a foreclosure tide. Home foreclosures reduced the value of neighboring homes and further adversely affected the well-being of households that had initially been unaffected by foreclosure processes.[32]

In the course of the recession, Congress adopted several comprehensive programs to reinvigorate the economy.[33] The programs provided cash and government guarantees to unfreeze credit markets and rescue firms in several industries. Government aid to the private sector sparked bitter debates over their design and necessity. Proponents of the recovery programs argued that, although the programs were not perfect, the cost of financial catastrophe would have been much greater than the costs paid by taxpayers.[34] Critics argued that the programs increased the debt burden on the public in a time of recession, burdened future taxpayers, and established an unhealthy precedent of government bailouts for failing organizations.[35] Regardless of one's views of the value of the recovery programs, their costs are among the consequences of the recession for the American taxpayer.

The Great Recession heavily taxed the economy and touched every American household. Its impact, however, varied across socioeconomic groups and geographic regions. Four states experienced the most severe effects of the housing downturn—Arizona, California, Florida, and Nevada.[36] Homeowners who purchased their first homes during the housing bubble were more affected by its collapse, because their first real estate investment was made when prices were high. Unemployment and decreased income burdened the population at the bottom of the income scale much more than top earners. Some financial institutions that had fed the housing bubble and encouraged subprime lending benefitted from transfers at the expense of taxpayers.[37] In contrast, families that lost their homes in the crisis incurred additional costs, such as failing health.[38] These distribu-

---

32. *See* John Y. Campbell et al., *Forced Sales and House Prices*, 101 AMERICAN ECONOMIC REVIEW 2108 (2011).

33. The key measures include the Economic Stimulus Act of 2008, Pub. L. No. 110–185, 122 Stat. 613 (Feb. 13, 2008); the Housing and Economic Recovery Act of 2008, Pub. L. No. 110–289, 122 Stat. 2654 (July 30, 2008); the Emergency Economic Stabilization Act of 2008, Pub. L. No. 110–343, 122 Stat. 3765 (Oct. 3, 2008); the American Recovery and Reinvestment Act of 2009, Pub. L. No. 111–5, 123 Stat. 115 (Feb. 17, 2009); the Helping Families Save Their Homes Act of 2009, Pub. L. No. 111–22, 123 Stat. 1632 (May 20, 2009).

34. *See* Alan S. Blinder & Mark Zandi, *How the Great Recession Was Brought to an End* (July 27, 2010).

35. *See, e.g.*, Kenneth Ayotte & David A. Skeel, *Bankruptcy or Bailouts*, 35 JOURNAL OF CORPORATION LAW 469 (2010); Mark J. Roe & David Skeel, *Assessing the Chrysler Bankruptcy*, 108 MICHIGAN LAW REVIEW 727 (2010); Jeffrey A. Miron, *Bailout or Bankruptcy*, 29 CATO JOURNAL 1 (2009); Pietro Veronesi & Luigi Zingales, *Paulson's Gift*, 97 JOURNAL OF FINANCIAL ECONOMICS 339 (2010).

36. *See, e.g.*, Shayna M. Olesiuk & Kathy R. Kalser, *The Sand States: Anatomy of a Perfect Housing–Market Storm*, 3 FDIC QUARTERLY 30 (2009).

37. *See* Veronesi & Zingales, *Paulson's Gift*, *supra* note 35.

38. See Craig Evan Pollack et al., A Case–Control Study of Home Foreclosure, Health Conditions, and Health Care Utilization, 88 JOURNAL OF URBAN HEALTH 469 (2011).

tional effects and increased socioeconomic disparities are yet another cost of the recession.

Every crisis raises the question whether it could have been avoided. The Great Recession was no exception. Even if the recession itself was not avoidable, then its scope and depth could possibly be mitigated. After all, the sequence of events and their consequences were ordinary for financial bubbles.

§ 1.1.3 The Causes of the Great Recession

§ 1.1.3a Irrational Exuberance

In December 1996, the Chairman of the Federal Reserve Board, Alan Greenspan delivered a speech about the role of central banking in a democratic society.[39] At some point, Greenspan posed a rhetorical question: "But how do we know when *irrational exuberance* has unduly escalated asset values, which then become subject to unexpected and prolonged contractions * * *?" He replied: "We as central bankers need not be concerned if a collapsing financial asset bubble does not threaten to impair the real economy, its production, jobs and price stability."

The economist Robert Shiller borrowed Greenspan's phrase "irrational exuberance" to describe the "psychological basis of a speculative bubble."[40] Shiller defined a "speculative bubble" as:

> a situation in which news of price increases spurs investor enthusiasm, which spreads by psychological contagion from person to person, in the process amplifying stories that might justify the price increases and bringing in a larger and larger class of investors, who, despite doubts about the real value of an investment, are drawn to it partly through envy of others' successes and partly through a gambler's excitement.[41]

Ultimately every bubble bursts and is followed by a crisis.[42] The housing bubble in the United States was indeed no exception. Irrational exuberance explains speculative bubbles and spurs borrowers to invest in assets despite their growing prices and irrespective of their real values. Such price increases are unsustainable, and the loans that fund them become riskier over time. The collapse of this house of cards is inevitable—bubbles burst and then the prices of the assets that spur the borrowing fall sharply. When prices drop, many borrowers find themselves with assets whose value is lower than the debt incurred to finance their purchase.

In retrospect, most speculative bubbles raise two key questions: (1) whether any party intentionally enhanced the irrational exuberance that fed the bubble, and (2) whether any party had the power to temper the escalating irrational exuberance.

---

39. Chairman Alan Greenspan, *The Challenge of Central Banking in a Democratic Society*, Remarks at the Annual Dinner and Francis Boyer Lecture of the American Enterprise Institute (Dec. 5, 1996).

40. Robert J. Shiller, Irrational Exuberance 2 (2d ed., 2005).

41. *Id.*

42. Shiller, *id.*; Franking Allen & Douglas Gale, *Bubbles and Crises*, 110 Economic Journal 236 (2000).

Two official reports examine the causes of the Great Recession: the report of the National Commission on the Causes of the Financial and Economic Crisis in the United States[43] and the report of the U.S. Senate Permanent Subcommittee on Investigation.[44] Both criticize the financial sector and specific firms for feeding the housing bubble and conclude that regulatory failures account for the financial crisis.

§ 1.1.3b The Financial Crisis Inquiry Commission ("FCIC")

The Fraud Enforcement and Recovery Act ("FERA") established the Financial Crisis Inquiry Commission ("FCIC") and empowered it "to examine the causes of the current financial and economic crisis in the United States, specifically the role of— * * * fraud and abuse in the financial sector, * * * Federal and State financial regulators, * * * the concept that certain institutions are 'too-big-to-fail' and its impact on market expectations, * * * legal and regulatory structure of the United States housing market, [and] the legal and regulatory structure governing investor and mortgagor protection."[45]

FCIC consisted of ten members, six of whom were appointed by the Democratic leadership of Congress and four by the Republican leadership. This bipartisan initiative to examine the causes of the Great Recession resulted in a majority's report of the six members appointed by the Democratic leadership and two dissenting statements from the FCIC members appointed by the Republican leadership.

The majority's report concludes that the "financial crisis was avoidable" and was "the result of human action and inaction." It finds that the "captains of finance and the public stewards of our financial system ignored warnings and failed to question, understand, and manage evolving risks within a system essential to the well-being of the American public." The report lists several categories of deficiencies and failures of the financial sector and regulatory agencies that brought about the economic catastrophe. First and foremost, it identifies widespread failures in financial regulation. The majority charged that regulators had the power to protect the financial system and chose not to do so. More specifically, the majority wrote:

> More than 30 years of deregulation and reliance on self-regulation by financial institutions, championed by former Federal Reserve Chairman Alan Greenspan and others, supported by successive administrations and Congresses, and actively pushed by the powerful financial industry at every turn, had stripped away key safeguards, which could have helped avoid catastrophe. * * * In addition, the government permitted financial firms to pick their preferred regulators in what became a race to the weakest supervisor.

---

43. NATIONAL COMMISSION ON THE CAUSES OF THE FINANCIAL AND ECONOMIC CRISIS IN THE UNITED STATES, THE FINANCIAL CRISIS: INQUIRY REPORT (final report, Jan. 2011) available at *regti.me/FCIC-Report* (case sensitive).

44. U.S. SENATE PERMANENT SUBCOMMITTEE ON INVESTIGATION, COMMITTEE ON HOMELAND SECURITY AND GOVERNMENTAL AFFAIRS, WALL STREET AND THE FINANCIAL CRISIS: ANATOMY OF A FINANCIAL COLLAPSE (Apr. 13, 2011), available at *regti.me/WS-report* (case sensitive).

45. Pub L. No. 111–21, 123 Stat. 1617 § 5 (2009).

The majority's conclusions regarding the role of deregulation and lax regulation are largely consistent with observations made by Alan Greenspan. In February 1997, after almost ten years in office as the Chairman of the Board of Governors of the Federal Reserve, Greenspan summarized his view of regulation:

> [I]t is critically important to recognize that no market is ever truly unregulated. The self-interest of market participants generates private market regulation. Thus, the real question is not whether a market should be regulated. Rather, the real question is whether government intervention strengthens or weakens private regulation. If incentives for private market regulation are weak or if market participants lack the capabilities to pursue their interests effectively, then the introduction of government regulation may improve regulation. But if private market regulation is effective, then government regulation is at best unnecessary. At worst, the introduction of government regulation may actually weaken the effectiveness of regulation if government regulation is itself ineffective or undermines incentives for private market regulation.[46]

In October 2008, testifying before the House Oversight and Government Reform Committee on the Financial Crisis, Greenspan stated: "[T]hose of us who have looked to the self-interest of lending institutions to protect shareholders' equity (myself included) are in a state of shocked disbelief * * * The whole intellectual edifice * * * collapsed in the summer of last year."[47]

The majority's criticism of regulatory policies was not limited to the events that brought about the crisis. It also concluded that the government was ill-prepared for the crisis and its response added to the panic in the financial markets and the overall costs of the recession. The majority, therefore, assigned responsibility to most sectors in society and the economy:

> We conclude there was a systemic breakdown in accountability and ethics. * * * Unfortunately—as has been the case in past speculative booms and busts—we witnessed an erosion of standards of responsibility and ethics that exacerbated the financial crisis. This was not universal, but these breaches stretched from the ground level to the corporate suites. They resulted not only in significant financial consequences but also in damage to the trust of investors, businesses, and the public in the financial system. * * *
>
> These conclusions must be viewed in the context of human nature and individual and societal responsibility. First, to pin this crisis on mortal flaws like greed and societal responsibility. First, to pin this crisis on mortal flaws like greed and hubris would be simplistic. It was the failure to account for human weakness that is relevant to this crisis. * * *

---

46. Alan Greenspan, *Government Regulation and Derivative Contracts*, Speech at the Financial Markets Conference of the Federal Reserve Bank of Atlanta, Coral Gables, Florida, Feb. 21, 1997.

47. *The Financial Crisis and the Role of Federal Regulators: Hearing Before the H. Comm. on Gov't Oversight and Reform*, 110th Cong. 17 (Oct. 23, 2008) (testimony of Alan Greenspan, Former Chairman of the Federal Reserve).

> Second, we clearly believe the crisis was a result of human mistakes, misjudgments, and misdeeds that resulted in systemic failures for which our nation has paid dearly. [S]pecific firms and individuals acted irresponsibly. Yet a crisis of this magnitude cannot be the work of a few bad actors, and such was not the case here. * * *
>
> We do place special responsibility with the public leaders charged with protecting our financial system, those entrusted to run our regulatory agencies, and the chief executives of companies whose failures drove us to crisis. These individuals sought and accepted positions of significant responsibility and obligation. Tone at the top does matter and, in this instance, we were let down. * * *
>
> But as a nation, we must also accept responsibility for what we permitted to occur. Collectively, but certainly not unanimously, we acquiesced to or embraced a system, a set of policies and actions, that gave rise to our present predicament.

The two dissenting statements maintain that "poorly designed government housing policies" were one of the driving forces behind the housing bubble. Unlike the majority, the four dissenting members stressed poor government policies as opposed to lack of action. They believed that policies that encouraged homeownership, rather than lax supervision of financial institutions, were some of the most significant causes of the crisis.

The four dissenting members were not convinced that the crisis was avoidable. Their statements list several global factors in credit and housing markets that, they argued, suggest that the causes of the crisis might not be local. Furthermore, the dissenting statements criticize the recovery programs for further increase in the costs of the recession.

One of the dissenting members who wrote an independent statement, stressed that "[e]xplanations that rely on lack of regulation or deregulation as a cause of the financial crisis are * * * deficient." This member did not consider the financial deregulation a relevant event and stated that "no significant deregulation of financial institutions occurred in the last 30 years." A few months before the conclusion of the FCIC's work and the publication of its report, this member published an essay, expressing the view that "[t]he connection between the current recession and the government housing policy is clear." In the essay, he also warned against the "focus on the lack of or insufficiency of regulation."[48]

In sum, the dissenting statements in the FCIC report reject the conclusion that failures to regulate financial institutions contributed to the crisis, and attribute significant weight to "poor housing policies." Thus, the disagreements in the FCIC report are over which regulatory policies were the major causes of the bubble, rather than whether regulatory failures were among the key causes of the recession.

---

48. Peter J. Wallison, *Government Housing Policy and the Financial Crisis*, 30 CATO JOURNAL 397, 402 (2010).

§ 1.1.3c The Senate Permanent Subcommittee on Investigation

The Senate Permanent Subcommittee on Investigation prepared another report on the causes of the recession and also concluded that regulatory failures were among the key causes of the Great Recession. It summarized the conclusions of its 600–page report in one short paragraph:

> Lenders introduced new levels of risk into the U.S. financial system by selling and securitizing complex home loans with high risk features and poor underwriting. The credit rating agencies labeled the resulting securities as safe investments, facilitating their purchase by institutional investors around the world. Federal banking regulators failed to ensure safe and sound lending practices and risk management, and stood on the sidelines as large financial institutions active in U.S. financial markets purchased billions of dollars in mortgage related securities containing high risk, poor quality mortgages. Investment banks magnified the risk to the system by engineering and promoting risky mortgage related structured finance products, and enabling investors to use naked credit default swaps and synthetic instruments to bet on the failure rather than the success of U.S. financial instruments. Some investment banks also ignored the conflicts of interest created by their products, placed their financial interests before those of their clients, and even bet against the very securities they were recommending and marketing to their clients.

The Senate Subcommittee identified specific regulatory failures, correction of which it concluded may prevent future crises and mitigate risks to the economy. It recommended new regulations for practices and products of financial institutions that would be sensitive to various factors of risk.

In September 2010, the National Bureau of Economic Research announced that the Great Recession had ended in June 2009.[49] The macroeconomic indicators used to establish this determination confused the public. In September 2010, the national unemployment rate was still above 9.5% and real estate prices were still declining.[50] The recession continued to affect most American households.

The two national reports of the causes of the Great Recession conclude that regulatory failures were behind the housing bubble that brought about the crisis. The FCIC dissenting members shared this view, although they had reservations about which regulatory failures explain the crisis. The broad agreement that regulatory failures caused the Great Recession illuminates that we may still not understand fundamental concepts in regulation. In June 2012, three years after the official end of the Great Recession, the Supreme Court handed down a milestone decision in regulation: *National Federation of Independent Business*, also known as the health-care

---

49. A copy of the announcement is available at *regti.me/NBER2010* (case sensitive).

50. *See, e.g.*, *A Tale of Two Recoveries*, WALL STREET JOURNAL, Sept. 21, 2010, at A20; Sara Murray, *Slump Over, Pain Persists*, WALL STREET JOURNAL, Sept. 21, 2010, at A1.

decision.[51] The decision and the controversy over the 2010 health-care reform stressed the common use of outdated concepts and misguided perceptions of regulation.

This book takes a small step toward a better future, providing a framework for lawyers and policymakers to learn the concepts and principles of regulation.

Figure 1.7

Source: *Puck*, November 27, 1907.

---

51. National Federation of Independent Business v. Sebelius, 132 S.Ct. 2566 (2012).

Questions

1. What is "irrational exuberance"? In his famous dissent in *Olmstead v. United States*,[52] Justice Louis Brandeis described the "right to be let alone" as "the most comprehensive of rights and the right most valued by civilized men." If so, should "civilized" men and women expect any government agency to have the power and duty to temper and possibly prevent irrational exuberance in order to eliminate the social costs of speculative bubbles and subsequent crises?

2. "Trends" and "fashions" are common social phenomena. People tend to follow others. What are the similarities and differences between financial bubbles and other trends (say, fashionable colors, popular music, or cool gadgets)? If government regulation is needed to protect the public from fads that create financial bubbles, is it also needed to protect the public from other fads?

3. In late 2010, a few months before the FCIC released its report, Nobel Laureate Joseph Stiglitz published his book *Freefall* in which he wrote: "Bankers are (for the most part) not born any greedier than other people. It is just that they may have more opportunity and the strongest incentives to do mischief at others' expense."[53] Criticizing financial institutions, the FCIC majority wrote: "Like Icarus, they never feared flying ever closer to the sun." The majority, however, stressed that "it was the failure to account for human weakness that is relevant to this crisis." Policymakers and regulators have all human flaws, including greed and hubris. Can we realistically expect policymakers and regulators to account for human weaknesses?

4. Governments, organizations, and individuals usually reconsider their approaches toward regulation during recessions. Immediate economic pressures tend to influence in three common directions: (a) a willingness to cut the budget of programs that used to be regarded as important;[54] (b) a willingness to relax restrictions on activities that are (or used to be) regarded as harmful in order to raise revenues;[55] and (c) a willingness to raise taxes.[56] Such regulatory measures intend to accomplish temporary

---

52. Olmstead v. United States, 277 U.S. 438, 478 (1928).

53. JOSEPH E. STIGLITZ, FREEFALL: AMERICA, FREE MARKETS, AND THE SINKING OF THE WORLD ECONOMY 151 (2010).

54. For examples of such budget cuts *see* Michael Cooper, *Budget Ax Falls, and Schools and Streetlights Go Dark*, NEW YORK TIMES, Aug. 7, 2010, at A1; Sam Dillon, *Tight Budgets Mean Squeeze in Classrooms*, NEW YORK TIMES, Mar. 7, 2011, at A1; Robin Pogrebin, *Arts Outposts Stung By Cuts in State Aid*, NEW YORK TIMES, Aug. 2, 2011, at C1; Lizette Alvarez, *Looking to Save Money, More Places Decide to Stop Fluoridating the Water*, NEW YORK TIMES, October 14, 2011, at A20.

55. For examples of relaxation of restrictions on alcohol, gambling, insurance, and anti-smoking policies *see* § 2.4; Shaila Dewan, *States Look at Tobacco to Balance the Budget*, NEW YORK TIMES, Mar. 21, 2009, at A9; Peter Applebome, *States Hooked on Gambling for Revenues*, NEW YORK TIMES, July 26, 2010, at A18; Matt Richtel, *Starved Budget Inspire New Look at Web Gambling*, NEW YORK TIMES, Aug. 14, 2011, at A1; Kevin Severson, *States Putting Hopes in 'Bottoms Up' to Help the Bottom Line*, NEW YORK TIMES, Sept. 30, 2011, at A1; Mary Williams Walsh & Louise Story, *Seeking Business, States Loosen Insurance Rules*, NEW YORK TIMES, May 9, 2011, at A1.

56. For examples of tax increases in attempt to relief budget problems *see* Nicholas Confessore, *Cigarette Tax Is Increased to Keep New York Running*, NEW YORK TIMES, June 22,

reliefs through compromises and reconsideration of choices and preferences. What are the pros and cons of a reevaluation of social choices and preferences during recessions?

§ 1.2 SHAPING CONDUCT WITH LEGAL NORMS

"But pretty much all law consists in forbidding men to do some things that they want to do."

—Oliver Wendell Holmes[57]

*§ 1.2.1 The Meaning of the Word***

National Federation of Independent Business is a milestone decision in regulation jurisprudence.[58] Yet, the Court was fractured over the meaning of the term "to regulate." The unsettled meaning of the term contributed to a debate among the Justices over the question whether a federal requirement to purchase health insurance is equivalent to "address[ing] the diet problem by ordering everyone to buy vegetables,"[59] or even to mandatory purchases of "cars and broccoli."[60]

Despite the perpetual controversy over regulation, the meaning of the term "regulation" (or "to regulate") is vague, elusive, and perplexing.[61] The firm beliefs and opinions people hold regarding simple and complex regulatory issues, and regulation in general, are therefore perplexing as well. In essence, people argue about a concept whose meaning they do not really understand.

The legal concept of "*regulation*" refers to government intervention in the private domain or a legal rule that implements such intervention.[62] The implementing rule is defined as *a binding legal norm created by a state*

2010, at A20; Kevin Sack, *States Look to Tobacco Tax to Fill Their Budget Holes*, NEW YORK TIMES, Apr. 21, 2008, at A14; Michael Cooper, *Squeezed Cities Ask Nonprofits for More Money*, NEW YORK TIMES, May 12, 2011, at A1.

57. Adkins v. Children's Hospital of the District of Columbia, 261 U.S. 525, 568 (1923) (Holmes, J., dissenting).

** Based on Barak Orbach, *What Is Regulation?*, 30 YALE JOURNAL ON REGULATION ONLINE 1 (2012).

58. National Federation of Independent Business v. Sebelius, 132 S.Ct. 2566 (2012).

59. *Id.* at 2588 (Roberts, C.J.)

60. *Id.* at 2591 (Roberts, C.J.). *See also Id.* at 2619–20, 2624–25 (Ginsburg, J.) (discussing the proposition), 2650 (Scalia, Kennedy, Thomas, and Alito, dissenting) (same).

61. *See, e.g.*, STEPHEN BREYER, REGULATION AND ITS REFORM 7 (1982) (stressing that the book makes "no serious effort * * * to define 'regulation' " and this choice is a limitation of the book.); BARRY M. MITNICK, THE POLITICAL ECONOMY OF REGULATION 1 (1980) ("[t]he concept of regulation is not often defined; * * * it is not often discussed as a concept. It has no accepted definition."); William J. Novak, *Common Regulation: Legal Origins of State Power in America*, 45 HASTINGS LAW JOURNAL 1061, 1071 (1994) ("[d]espite a vast academic literature and constant public usage, [the concept of] 'regulation' defies close circumscription."); ANTHONY I. OGUS, REGULATION: LEGAL FORM AND ECONOMIC THEORY 1 (1994) ("The expression 'regulation' * * * is not a term of art, and unfortunately it has acquired a bewildering variety of meanings").

62. *See, e.g.*, JOHN STUART MILL, 2 PRINCIPLES OF POLITICAL ECONOMY 525–571 (1848) (referring to "governmental intervention in the affairs of society" and applicable laws).

organ that intends to shape the conduct of individuals and firms.[63] The state organ, the *regulator*, may be any legislative, executive, administrative, or judicial body that has the legal power to create a binding legal norm.

In 1976, the Congressional Budget Office (CBO) tried to define the term "regulation" in response to a Congressional inquiry regarding the number of federal employees who engaged in regulatory activities:

> There is no single accepted definition of what constitutes regulation by the federal government. * * * A "traditional" definition would include those activities which impact major aspects of private enterprise operations, such as market entry and exit; rate, price, and profit structures; and competitive environment. This definition would—at a minimum—cover the oldest and some of the best known independent regulatory agencies; e.g., the Interstate Commerce Commission, Federal Trade Commission, Federal Communications Commission, Federal Power Commission, and the Securities and Exchange Commission. Many activities of the federal government in the areas of health, safety, environmental and consumer protection, and employment standards have significant regulatory impact on private enterprise operations. The broadest definition of federal regulation would include all governmental activities which somehow affect the operations of private industry or the lives of private citizens. Such a definition would result in the identification of most federal activities as regulatory.[64]

The CBO took the approach that not all "federal activities" were regulatory and excluded activities related to national defense, foreign policy, law enforcement, revenue collection, and internal management of the federal government and economic policy. A few years later, in February 1981, shortly after taking office, President Ronald Reagan issued Executive Order 12291, which intended "to reduce the burdens of existing and future regulations, increase agency accountability for regulatory actions, provide for presidential oversight of the regulatory process, minimize duplication and conflict of regulations, and insure well-reasoned regulations." Executive Order 12291 defined the word "regulation" as "an agency statement of general applicability and future effect designed to implement, interpret, or prescribe law or policy or describing the procedure or practice requirements of an agency."[65] This narrow, bureaucratic meaning is rather prevalent among lawyers.

Some define the term "regulation" as an approach to *control* market failures that "relies on relatively specific rules developed and enforced by administrative agencies."[66] This perspective of control often understates

---

63. David P. Baron, *Design of Regulatory Mechanisms and Institutions*, in 2 HANDBOOK OF INDUSTRIAL ORGANIZATION 1349, 1349 (Richard Schmalensee & Robert D. Willig eds., 1989) ("Regulation involves government intervention in markets in response to some combination of normative objectives and private interests reflected through politics").

64. Staff Paper, Congressional Budget Office, *The Number of Federal Employees Engaged in Regulatory Activities*, Prepared for the Subcommittee on Oversight and Investigation (Aug. 1976).

65. In 1993, President Bill Clinton issued Executive Order 12866 that replaced Executive Order 12291. Executive Order 12866 maintained the definition of the term "regulation." Executive Order 12866 of September 30, 1993, as amended by E.O. 13258 of February 26, 2002 and E.O. 13422 of January 18, 2007 § 3.

66. Daniel P. Kessler, *Introduction*, in REGULATION VS. LITIGATION 1, 1 (2011).

the significance of social and moral control. Regulation is often used to control human conduct in an effort to impose religious and other values.[67] Government control is indeed one common understanding of the word "regulation." For example, the definitive legal dictionary, *Black's Law Dictionary*, defines "regulation" as "the act or process of controlling by rule or restriction."[68]

Until the late 1970s, "regulation" and "government control" were often used interchangeably. Regulations were understood as "command-and-control" measures that require or proscribes conduct, such as bans, mandates, and permit requirements.[69] Regulations, however, often do not intend to require or proscribe conduct; rather, many regulatory measures aim to influence choices among options by altering incentives. Many simple regulatory schemes utilize legal sanctions and rewards to influence conduct by modifying the consequences of choices.[70] *Command-and-control measures* supposedly only eliminate or add practically feasible courses of action, while *incentive regulations* use taxes, subsidies, and other means to change consequences of actions. Familiar examples of incentive regulations include subsidies, entitlements, exemptions, sin taxes, public education, pay-as-you-throw programs, and regulation of information. Since the late 1970s, the trend has been toward the use of incentives in regulation.[71]

---

67. *See generally* Chapter 7. *See also* United States v. Alvarez, 132 S.Ct. 2537 (2012).

68. Black's Law Dictionary (9th ed. 2009). *The Oxford English Dictionary* defines "regulation" as an act of controlling and governing and indicates that the word has been in use since the seventeenth century.

69. *See, e.g.*, Harry V. Ball & Lawrence M. Friedman, *The Use of Criminal Sanctions in the Enforcement of Economic Legislation: A Sociological View*, 17 STANFORD LAW REVIEW 197 (1965); LUDWIG VON MISES, INTERVENTIONISM: AN ECONOMIC ANALYSIS 10 (Bettina Bien Greaves ed. 1998) (1940) ("The intervention is an isolated order by the authority in command of the social power apparatus; it forces the entrepreneur and the owner of the means of production to use these means in a way different from what they would do under the pressure of the market. The order may be by command or interdiction."); Robert L. Rabin, *Federal Regulation in Historical Perspective*, 38 STANFORD LAW REVIEW 1189, 1318 (1986) (noting that Congress embraced deregulation when "traditional administrative rulemaking—so-called command and control rulemaking—came under general attack for its economic inefficiency in failing to discriminate between low-cost and high-cost compliance activity").

70. *See generally* James M. Buchanan & Gordon Tullock, *Polluters' Profits and Political Response: Direct Controls versus Taxes*, 65 AMERICAN ECONOMIC REVIEW 139 (1975); MILL, 2 PRINCIPLES OF POLITICAL ECONOMY, *supra* note 5, 526–527 (distinguishing between regulations in the form of "command" and regulations in the form of "advice" and "information"); OGUS, REGULATION, *supra* note 4, at 79–89. *See also* Brian Galle, *The Tragedy of the Carrots: Economics and Politics in the Choice of Price Instruments*, 64 STANFORD LAW REVIEW 797 (2012); Sonzinsky v. United States, 300 U.S. 506, 513 (1937) ("Every tax is in some measure regulatory. To some extent it interposes an economic impediment to the activity taxed as compared with others not taxed.")

71. *See, e.g.*, FREDRICK R. ANDERSON ET AL., ENVIRONMENTAL IMPROVEMENT THROUGH ECONOMIC INCENTIVES (1977); Robert E. Goodin, *Selling Environmental Indulgences*, 47 KYKLOS 573, 574 (1994) ("The standard 'legalistic' approach operates by manipulating rights and duties. It is essentially a command-and-control strategy, specifying what people may or must or must not do and attaching penalties to violation of those commands. The newer 'economistic' approach works by manipulating incentives."); JODY FREEMAN & CHARLES D. KOLSTAD EDS., MOVING TO MARKETS IN ENVIRONMENTAL REGULATION (2007); Richard B. Stewart, *Regulation, Innovation, and Administrative Law: A Conceptual Framework*, 69 CALIFORNIA LAW REVIEW 1256, 1264 (1981) ("The present system of administrative remedies relies almost exclusively on 'command-and-

Incentive regulation may be criticized for many reasons, but is profoundly different from command-and-control measures. For example, many forms of incentive regulations focus on decisionmaking, addressing problems of inadequate information and situations in which one's conduct harms others. Their goal is to increase the likelihood that decisions of individuals and firms are informed and factor costs to others. Put differently, the perception that regulation is a legal instrument of control is inconsistent with the common use of regulations. Control is a rudimentary form of regulation that may be useful for some purposes but is ineffective for many others.[72]

To summarize, although regulation is a common legal instrument, it is one of the most misunderstood concepts in modern legal thinking. The meaning of the word "regulation" is often convoluted and obscured. As a concept, "regulation" means government intervention in the private domain. As a legal instrument "regulation" means a binding legal norm created by a state organ that intends to shape the conduct of individuals and firms. As stated at the outset, regulation is a byproduct of our imperfect reality and human limitations. We have regulations for the imperfections in our world.

Questions

1. Many drivers frequently exceed the speed limit and violate other traffic rules. Are traffic rules regulations? Does the frequency of traffic violations suggest that they are ineffective?

2. In *The T.J. Hooper*,[73] Judge Learned Hand held that a tugboat not carrying a properly working radio receiver was liable for an accident that could have been avoided with weather information, although at the time many tugboats did not have any.[74] Subsequently, all tugboats were equipped with radio receivers. *The T.J. Hooper* ruling had a regulatory effect—it established a new negligence standard that motivated tugboats to modify their operations. Many judicial decisions have regulatory effects, although the overwhelming majority of decisions have none. What types of cases may have regulatory effects? What are their general characteristics?

Lochner and the Bakeshop Act

The Industrial Revolution brought about many changes, including greater concentration of employment—industrialized businesses became large employers. Technology and competition also brought about an in-

---

control' measures that require or proscribe specific conduct."); Ingo Vogelsang, *Incentive Regulation and Competition in Public Utility Markets: A 20-Year Perspective*, 22 JOURNAL OF REGULATORY ECONOMICS 5 (2002).

72. In practice, even controls are frequently used as incentive regulations. *See* § 8.1.

73. The T.J. Hooper v. Northern Barge Corp., 60 F.2d 737 (1932).

74. *See generally* Richard A. Epstein, *The Path to the T.J. Hooper: The Theory and History of Custom in the Law of Tort*, 21 JOURNAL OF LEGAL STUDIES 1 (1992).

crease in work hours. Most industrialized countries witnessed a rise of social movements lobbying for a cap on working hours.[75] In the United States, during the last decade of the nineteenth century, the American labor movement began focusing on working hours. Unions organized mass strikes, participated in electoral campaigns, and commenced legislative initiatives to further their goals.[76] In New York, the Journeymen Bakers' Union lobbied to secure favorable legislation for bakers; primarily to cap the number of hours a baker could work per day and week.[77] Bakers were typically paid by the day, but believed they were not fully compensated for the length of their days or the health risks associated with their constant exposure to flour dust, gas fumes, dampness, and extreme heat and cold. The bakers' campaign was successful and in May 1895, the New York Governor signed into law the "*Bakeshop Act*:"[78]

An Act to Regulate the Manufacture of Flour and Meal Food Product

SECTION 1. *Hours of labor in bakeries and confectionery establishments.*—No employee shall be required, permitted or suffered to work in a biscuit, bread or cake bakery or confectionery establishment more than sixty hours in any one week, or more than ten hours in any one day of the week, nor more hours in any one week than will make an average of ten hours per day for the whole number of days in which such person shall so work during such week.

SECTION 2. *Drainage and plumbing of buildings and rooms occupied by bakeries.*—All buildings occupied as a biscuit, bread or cake bakeries shall be drained and plumbed in a manner to conduce to the proper and healthful sanitary condition thereof, as the factory, inspector or any of his deputies shall direct.

* * *

SECTION 4. *Products how kept.*—The manufactured flour or meal food products shall be kept in perfectly dry and airy rooms, so arranged that the floors, shelves and all other facilities for storing the same can be easily and perfectly cleaned.

SECTION 5. *Washrooms and water-closets.*—Every such bakery shall be provided with a proper washroom and water-closet or

75. *See, e.g.*, Peter Scott & Anna Spadavecchia, *Did the 48–Hour Week Damage Britain's Industrial Competitiveness*, 64 ECONOMIC HISTORY REVIEW 1266 (2011) (finding that, in Britain, reduced working hours were compensated for by higher hourly productivity).

76. *See* EDWARD & ELEANOR MARX AVELING, WORKING-CLASS MOVEMENT IN AMERICA 67–76 (1888); MARION C. CAHILL, SHORTER HOURS: A STUDY OF THE MOVEMENT SINCE THE CIVIL WAR (1932).

77. *See* David E. Bernstein, *The Story of Lochner v. New York: Impediment to the Growth of the Regulatory State*, in CONSTITUTIONAL LAW STORIES 299 (Michael C. Dorf ed., 2d ed. 2009); *Matthew S. Bewig, Lochner v. The Journeymen Bakers of New York: The Journeymen Bakers, Their Hours of Labor, and The Constitution: A Case Study in the Social History of Legal Thought*, 38 AMERICAN JOURNAL OF LEGAL HISTORY 413 (1994); PAUL KENS, LOCHNER V. NEW YORK: ECONOMIC REGULATION ON TRIAL (1998).

78. A copy of the 1895 Bakeshop Act is available at *regti.me/NY-bakeshop* (case sensitive).

closets, apart from the bakeroom or rooms where the manufacturing of such food products is conducted; and no water closet, earth-closet, privy or ash-pit shall be within or communicate directly with the bakeroom of any bakery, hotel or public restaurant.

SECTION 6. *Sleeping places.*—The sleeping places for the person employed in a baker shall be separate from the room or rooms where flour or meal food products are manufactured or stored.

SECTION 7. *Violation of act, etc.*—Any person who violates any of the previsions of this act * * * shall be guilty of a misdemeanor, and on conviction shall be punished by a fine of not less than twenty or more than fifty dollars for a first offense, and not less than fifty nor more than one hundred dollars for a second offense, or imprisonment for not more than ten days, and for a third offense by a fine of not less than two hundred and fifty dollars and not more than thirty days imprisonment.

In April 1902, Joseph Lochner, a New York bakery owner, was arrested for violation of Section 1 of the Bakeshop Act. Lochner challenged the constitutionality of the Bakeshop Act and reached the Supreme Court.

Lochner v. New York

198 U.S. 45 (1905)

■ MR. JUSTICE PECKHAM delivered the opinion of the court.

The indictment, it will be seen, charges that the plaintiff in error violated [Section 1 of the Bakeshop Act*] in that he wrongfully and unlawfully required and permitted an employee working for him to work more than sixty hours in one week. * * * The mandate of the statute, that 'no employee shall be required or permitted to work,' is the substantial equivalent of an enactment that 'no employee shall contract or agree to work,' more than ten hours per day. * * * The employee may desire to earn the extra money which would arise from his working more than the prescribed time, but this statute forbids the employer from permitting the employee to earn it.

The statute necessarily interferes with the right of contract between the employer and employees, concerning the number of hours in which the latter may labor in the bakery of the employer. The general right to make a contract in relation to his business is part of the liberty of the individual protected by the Fourteenth Amendment of the Federal Constitution. * * * Under that provision no state can deprive any person of life, liberty, or property without due process of law. The right to purchase or to sell labor is part of the liberty protected by this amendment, unless there are circumstances which exclude the right. There are, however, certain powers, existing in the sovereignty of each state in the Union, somewhat vaguely termed police powers, the exact description and limitation of which have

* [Section 1 of the Bakeshop Act was codified as Section 110, Article 8, Chapter 415 the labor law of the state of New York (1897). By the time the case reached the Supreme Court, New York slightly amended the Bakeshop Act].

not been attempted by the courts. Those powers, broadly stated, and without, at present, any attempt at a more specific limitation, relate to the safety, health, morals, and general welfare of the public. Both property and liberty are held on such reasonable conditions as may be imposed by the governing power of the state in the exercise of those powers, and with such conditions the Fourteenth Amendment was not designed to interfere. * * *

The state, therefore, has power to prevent the individual from making certain kinds of contracts, and in regard to them the Federal Constitution offers no protection. If the contract be one which the state, in the legitimate exercise of its police power, has the right to prohibit, it is not prevented from prohibiting it by the Fourteenth Amendment. * * *

This Court has recognized the existence and upheld the exercise of the police powers of the states in many cases. * * * [For example, in *Holden v. Hardy*, 169 U. S. 366 (1898),] the legislature of Utah * * * limit[ed] the employment of workmen in all underground mines or workings, to eight hours per day, 'except in cases of emergency, where life or property is in imminent danger.' It also limited the hours of labor in smelting and other institutions for the reduction or refining of ores or metals to eight hours per day, except in like cases of emergency. The act was held to be a valid exercise of the police powers of the state. * * *

It will be observed that * * * the statute * * * now before this Court has no emergency clause in it, and, if the statute is valid, there are no circumstances and no emergencies under which the slightest violation of the provisions of the act would be innocent. * * *

In every case that comes before this Court * * * where legislation of this character is concerned, and where the protection of the Federal Constitution is sought, the question necessarily arises: Is this a fair, reasonable, and appropriate exercise of the police power of the state, or is it an unreasonable, unnecessary, and arbitrary interference with the right of the individual to his personal liberty, or to enter into those contracts in relation to labor which may seem to him appropriate or necessary for the support of himself and his family? Of course the liberty of contract relating to labor includes both parties to it. The one has as much right to purchase as the other to sell labor.

This is not a question of substituting the judgment of the Court for that of the legislature. If the act be within the power of the state it is valid, although the judgment of the Court might be totally opposed to the enactment of such a law. But the question would still remain: Is it within the police power of the state? and that question must be answered by the Court.

The question whether this act is valid as a labor law, pure and simple, may be dismissed in a few words. There is no reasonable ground for interfering with the liberty of person or the right of free contract, by determining the hours of labor, in the occupation of a baker. There is no contention that bakers as a class are not equal in intelligence and capacity to men in other trades or manual occupations, or that they are not able to assert their rights and care for themselves without the protecting arm of the state, interfering with their independence of judgment and of action.

They are in no sense wards of the state. Viewed in the light of a purely labor law, with no reference whatever to the question of health, we think that a law like the one before us involves neither the safety, the morals, nor the welfare, of the public, and that the interest of the public is not in the slightest degree affected by such an act. The law must be upheld, if at all, as a law pertaining to the health of the individual engaged in the occupation of a baker. It does not affect any other portion of the public than those who are engaged in that occupation. Clean and wholesome bread does not depend upon whether the baker works but ten hours per day or only sixty hours a week. The limitation of the hours of labor does not come within the police power on that ground.

* * *

We think the limit of the police power has been reached and passed in this case. There is, in our judgment, no reasonable foundation for holding this to be necessary or appropriate as a health law to safeguard the public health, or the health of the individuals who are following the trade of a baker. * * *

We think that there can be no fair doubt that the trade of a baker, in and of itself, is not an unhealthy one to that degree which would authorize the legislature to interfere with the right to labor, and with the right of free contract on the part of the individual, either as employer or employee In looking through statistics regarding all trades and occupations, it may be true that the trade of a baker does not appear to be as healthy as some other trades, and is also vastly more healthy than still others. To the common understanding the trade of a baker has never been regarded as an unhealthy one. Very likely physicians would not recommend the exercise of that or of any other trade as a remedy for ill health. Some occupations are more healthy than others, but we think there are none which might not come under the power of the legislature to supervise and control the hours of working therein, if the mere fact that the occupation is not absolutely and perfectly healthy is to confer that right upon the legislative department of the government. It might be safely affirmed that almost all occupations more or less affect the health. There must be more than the mere fact of the possible existence of some small amount of unhealthiness to warrant legislative interference with liberty. It is unfortunately true that labor, even in any department, may possibly carry with it the seeds of unhealthiness. But are we all, on that account, at the mercy of legislative majorities? A printer, a tinsmith, a locksmith, a carpenter, a cabinetmaker, a dry goods clerk, a bank's, a lawyer's, or a physician's clerk, or a clerk in almost any kind of business, would all come under the power of the legislature, on this assumption. No trade, no occupation, no mode of earning one's living, could escape this all-pervading power, and the acts of the legislature in limiting the hours of labor in all employments would be valid, although such limitation might seriously cripple the ability of the laborer to support himself and his family. In our large cities there are many buildings into which the sun penetrates for but a short time in each day, and these buildings are occupied by people carrying on the business of bankers, brokers, lawyers, real estate, and many other kinds of business, aided by many clerks, messengers, and other employees. Upon the assumption of the validity of this act under review, it is not possible to say that an act, prohibiting lawyers' or bank clerks, or others, from contracting to labor for their employers more than eight hours a day would be invalid. It might be said that it is unhealthy to work more than that number of hours in an apartment lighted by artificial light during the working hours of the day; that the occupation of the bank clerk, the lawyer's clerk, the real estate clerk, or the broker's clerk, in such offices is therefore unhealthy, and the legislature, in its paternal wisdom, must, therefore, have the right to legislate on the subject of, and to limit, the hours for such labor; and, if it exercises that power, and its validity be questioned, it is sufficient to say, it has reference to the public health; it has reference to the health of the employees condemned to labor day after day in buildings where the sun never shines; it is a health law, and therefore it is valid, and cannot be questioned by the courts.

It is also urged, pursuing the same line of argument, that it is to the interest of the state that its population should be strong and robust, and therefore any legislation which may be said to tend to make people healthy must be valid as health laws, enacted under the police power. If this be a valid argument and a justification for this kind of legislation, it follows that the protection of the Federal Constitution from undue interference with liberty of person and freedom of contract is visionary, wherever the law is sought to be justified as a valid exercise of the police power. Scarcely any law but might find shelter under such assumptions, and conduct, properly so called, as well as contract, would come under the restrictive sway of the legislature. Not only the hours of employees, but the hours of employers, could be regulated, and doctors, lawyers, scientists, all professional men, as well as athletes and artisans, could be forbidden to fatigue their brains and bodies by prolonged hours of exercise, lest the fighting strength of the state be impaired. We mention these extreme cases because the contention is extreme. We do not believe in the soundness of the views which uphold this law. On the contrary, we think that such a law as this, although passed in the assumed exercise of the police power, and as relating to the public health, or the health of the employees named, is not within that power, and is invalid. The act is not, within any fair meaning of the term, a health law, but is an illegal interference with the rights of individuals, both employers and employees, to make contracts regarding labor upon such terms as they may think best, or which they may agree upon with the other parties to such contracts. Statutes of the nature of that under review, limiting the hours in which grown and intelligent men may labor to earn their living, are mere meddlesome interferences with the rights of the individual, and they are not saved from condemnation by the claim that they are passed in the exercise of the police power and upon the subject of the health of the individual whose rights are interfered with, unless there be some fair ground, reasonable in and of itself, to say that there is material danger to the public health, or to the health of the employees, if the hours of labor are not curtailed. If this be not clearly the case, the individuals whose rights are thus made the subject of legislative interference are under the protection of the Federal Constitution regarding their liberty of contract as well as of person; and the legislature of the state has no power to limit their right as proposed in this statute. All that it could properly do has been done by it with regard to the conduct of bakeries, as provided for in the other sections of the act, above set forth. These several sections provide for the inspection of the premises where the bakery is carried on, with regard to furnishing proper wash rooms and waterclosets, apart from the bake room, also with regard to providing proper drainage, plumbing, and painting; the sections, in addition, provide for the height of the ceiling, the cementing or tiling of floors, where necessary in the opinion of the factory inspector, and for other things of that nature; alterations are also provided for, and are to be made where necessary in the opinion of the inspector, in order to comply with the provisions of the statute. These various sections may be wise and valid regulations, and they certainly go to the full extent of providing for the cleanliness and the healthiness, so far as possible, of the quarters in which bakeries are to be conducted. Adding to all these requirements a prohibition to enter into any contract of labor in a bakery for more than a certain number of hours a week is, in our judgment, so wholly beside the matter of a proper, reasonable, and fair provision as to run counter to that liberty of person and of free contract provided for in the Federal Constitution.

It was further urged on the argument that restricting the hours of labor in the case of bakers was valid because it tended to cleanliness on the part of the workers, as a man was more apt to be cleanly when not overworked, and if cleanly then his 'output' was also more likely to be so. What has already been said applies with equal force to this contention. We do not admit the reasoning to be sufficient to justify the claimed right of such interference. The state in that case would assume the position of a supervisor * * * over every act of the individual, and its right of governmental interference with his hours of labor, his hours of exercise, the character thereof, and the extent to which it shall be carried would be recognized and upheld. In our judgment it is not possible in fact to discover the connection between the number of hours a baker may work in the bakery and the healthful quality of the bread made by the workman. The connection, if any exist, is too shadowy and thin to build any argument for the interference of the legislature. If the man works ten hours a day it is all right, but if ten and a half or eleven his health is in danger and his bread may be unhealthy, and, therefore, he shall not be permitted to do it. This, we think, is unreasonable and entirely arbitrary. * * *

This interference on the part of the legislatures of the several states with the ordinary trades and occupations of the people seems to be on the increase. * * * It is impossible for us to shut our eyes to the fact that many of the laws of this character, while passed under what is claimed to be the police power for the purpose of protecting the public health or welfare, are, in reality, passed from other motives. * * *

The judgment * * * must be reversed and the case remanded * * * for further proceedings not inconsistent with this opinion.

Reversed.

■ Mr. Justice Holmes dissenting:

I regret sincerely that I am unable to agree with the judgment in this case, and that I think it my duty to express my dissent.

This case is decided upon an economic theory which a large part of the country does not entertain. * * * It is settled by various decisions of this court that state constitutions and state laws may regulate life in many ways which we as legislators might think as injudicious, or if you like as tyrannical, as this, and which, equally with this, interfere with the liberty to contract. Sunday laws and usury laws are ancient examples. A more modern one is the prohibition of lotteries. * * * [The] Constitution is not intended to embody a particular economic theory, whether of paternalism and the organic relation of the citizen to the state or of *laissez faire*. It is made for people of fundamentally differing views. * * *

I think that the proposition just stated, if it is accepted, will carry us far toward the end. Every opinion tends to become a law. I think that the word 'liberty,' in the Fourteenth Amendment, is perverted when it is held to prevent the natural outcome of a dominant opinion, unless it can be said that a rational and fair man necessarily would admit that the statute proposed would infringe fundamental principles as they have been understood by the traditions of our people and our law. It does not need research to show that no such sweeping condemnation can be passed upon the statute before us. A reasonable man might think it a proper measure on the score of health. Men whom I certainly could not pronounce unreasonable would uphold it as a first installment of a general regulation of the hours of work. Whether in the latter aspect it would be open to the charge of inequality I think it unnecessary to discuss.

■ MR. JUSTICE HARLAN (with whom MR. JUSTICE WHITE and MR. JUSTICE DAY concurred) dissenting:

While this court has not attempted to mark the precise boundaries of what is called the police power of the state, the existence of the power has been uniformly recognized, equally by the Federal and State courts.

All the cases agree that this power extends at least to the protection of the lives, the health, and the safety of the public against the injurious exercise by any citizen of his own rights.

* * *

I take it to be firmly established that what is called the liberty of contract may, within certain limits, be subjected to regulations designed and calculated to promote the general welfare, or to guard the public health, the public morals, or the public safety. * * * If there be doubt as to the validity of the statute, that doubt must therefore be resolved in favor of its validity, and the courts must keep their hands off, leaving the legislature to meet the responsibility for unwise legislation. * * *

It is plain that [the statute in question] was enacted in order to protect the physical well-being of those who work in bakery and confectionery establishments. It may be that the statute had its origin, in part, in the belief that employers and employees in such establishments were not upon an equal footing, and that the necessities of the latter often compelled them to submit to such exactions as unduly taxed their strength. Be this as it may, the statute must be taken as expressing the belief of the people of New York that, as a general rule, and in the case of the average man, labor in excess of sixty hours during a week in such establishments may endanger the health of those who thus labor. Whether or not this be wise legislation it is not the province of the court to inquire. Under our systems of government the courts are not concerned with the wisdom or policy of legislation. * * *

We judicially know that the question of the number of hours during which a workman should continuously labor has been, for a long period, and is yet, a subject of serious consideration among civilized peoples, and by those having special knowledge of the laws of health. Suppose the statute prohibited labor in bakery and confectionery establishments in excess of eighteen hours each day. No one, I take it, could dispute the power of the state to enact such a statute. But the statute before us does not embrace extreme or exceptional cases. It may be said to occupy a middle ground in respect of the hours of labor. What is the true ground for the state to take between legitimate protection, by legislation, of the public health and liberty of contract is not a question easily solved, nor one in respect of which there is or can be absolute certainty. There are very few, if any, questions in political economy about which entire certainty may be predicated. * * *

I do not stop to consider whether any particular view of this economic question presents the sounder theory. What the precise facts are it may be difficult to say. It is enough for the determination of this case, and it is enough for this court to know, that the question is one about which there is room for debate and for an honest difference of opinion. There are many reasons of a weighty, substantial character, based upon the experience of mankind, in support of the theory that, all things considered, more than ten hours' steady work each day, from week to week, in a bakery or confectionery establishment, may endanger the health and shorten the lives of the workmen, thereby diminishing their physical and mental capacity to serve the state and to provide for those dependent upon them.

If such reasons exist that ought to be the end of this case, for the state is not amenable to the judiciary, in respect of its legislative enactments, unless such enactments are plainly, palpably, beyond all question, inconsistent with the Constitution of the United States. We are not to presume that the state of New York has acted in bad faith. Nor can we assume that its legislature acted without due deliberation, or that it did not determine this question upon the fullest attainable information and for the common good. We cannot say that the state has acted without reason, nor ought we to proceed upon the theory that its action is a mere sham. Our duty, I submit, is to sustain the statute as not being in conflict with the Federal Constitution. * * *

The judgment, in my opinion, should be affirmed.

Notes on Lochner

Lochner v. New York is one of the most controversial decisions in the history of the U.S. Supreme Court. The so-called *Lochner* era of laissez-faire jurisprudence defines a period of limited economic regulation that lasted until 1937. During these years, the judiciary closely scrutinized many forms of regulations that intervened in the freedom of contract, trying to assure that the intervention served a valid purpose of protecting the public health, safety, or morals. Applying these principles, the Supreme Court upheld many federal and state social and economic regulations, but declared many others as unconstitutional. The decisions that followed *Lochner* cannot be reconciled. For example, in 1908, three years after *Lochner*, the Court upheld an Oregon law that set a ten-hour day for women in laundries. In that case, *Muller v. Oregon*,[79] Louis Brandeis wrote a 113–page brief that convinced the Court that women were physically weaker than men and deserved to be protected from overwork. Nine years later, in *Bunting v. Oregon*,[80] the Court upheld a ten-hour work day for men and women. But then in *Adkins v. Children's Hospital of the District of Columbia*,[81] the Court held that federal minimum wage legislation for women was an unconstitutional intervention in the freedom of contract.

In 1937, the Supreme Court handed down a decision that signaled the end of its laissez-faire jurisprudence. In *West Coast Hotel Co. v. Parrish*,[82] the Court upheld a Washington State statute that fixed the minimum wage for women and minors, reversing its decision in *Adkins*. The controversy over *Lochner*, however, has never faded.[83]

In *National Federation of Independent Business*,[84] Justice Ruth Bader Ginsburg referred to the Lochner era and its controversy, writing: "In the early 20th century, this Court regularly struck down economic regulation enacted by the peoples' representatives in both the States and the Federal Government. See, *e.g.*, * * * *Lochner v. New York*, 198 U.S. 45 (1905). The Chief Justice's Commerce Clause opinion, and even more so the joint dissenters' reasoning, bear a disquieting resemblance to those long-overruled decisions."

Questions

1. Toward the end of his opinion, Justice Peckham stressed that

> [The] interference on the part of the legislatures of several states with the ordinary trades and occupations of the people seems to be on the increase. * * * It is impossible for us to shut our eyes to the fact that many of the laws of this character, while passed under what is claimed to be * * * protecting the public health or welfare, are, in reality, passed from other motives.

---

79. 208 U.S. 412 (1908).

80. 243 U.S. 426 (1917).

81. 261 U.S. 525 (1923).

82. 300 U.S. 379 (1937).

83. *See, e.g.*, DAVID E. BERNSTEIN, REHABILITATING LOCHNER (2011); Richard A. Epstein, *The Mistakes of 1937*, 11 GEORGE MASON UNIVERSITY LAW REVIEW 5 (1988); Cass Sunstein, *Lochner's Legacy*, 87 COLUM. L. REV. 873 (1987).

84. National Federation of Independent Business v. Sebelius, 132 S.Ct. 2566 (2012).

Did the New York Bakeshop Act intend to protect the public health or welfare? What were the "other motives" behind the New York Bakeshop Act? Did Justices Peckham, Holmes, and Harlan agree on the nature of these "other motives"?

2. One of the arguments *in favor* of the New York Bakeshop Act was that at least some bakers assumed excessive risks that threatened their health. The counter-argument is that all occupations are risky and some are have serious occupational hazards (*e.g.*, firefighters, police officers, miners, and deep-water divers). Society, however, needs most existing occupations and pays a risk premium that varies with the job and its characteristics.[85] Under this theory, bakers at the turn of the twentieth century were compensated for risks associated with their jobs. In *Lochner*, Justice Peckham made a similar point:

> The mandate of the statute, that 'no employee shall be required or permitted to work,' is the substantial equivalent of an enactment that 'no employee shall contract or agree to work,' more than ten hours per day. * * * The employee may desire to earn the extra money which would arise from his working more than the prescribed time, but this statute forbids the employer from permitting the employee to earn it.

Is the risk-compensation theory persuasive? How should we evaluate this theory? To the extent that the risk-compensation theory is valid, on what grounds could the state intervene in choices of employers and employees?

3. In June 1883 the San Francisco Board of Supervisors passed Order No. 1719: *Regulating the Establishment and Maintenance of Public Laundries and Public Wash–Houses Within Certain Limits in the City and County of San Francisco*. The preamble of the Order provided that "the indiscriminate establishment of public laundries and public washhouses, where clothes and other articles are cleansed for hire, is injurious and dangerous to public health and public safety, and prejudicial to the well-being and comfort of the community, and depreciates the value of property in those neighborhoods where such public laundries and such public washhouses are situate." The Order created a regulatory regime for public laundries and washhouses. Interested businesses were required to obtain appropriate certificates from the City Health Officer and the City Board of Fire Wardens. The Order also provided:

> SEC. 4. No person or persons owning or employed in the public laundries or public wash-houses * * * shall wash or iron clothes between the hours of 10 o'clock p. m. and 6 o'clock a. m., nor upon any portion of that day known as Sunday.
>
> SEC. 5. No Person or person engaged in the laundry business * * * shall permit any person suffering from any infectious or contagious disease to lodge, sleep, or remain within or upon the premises used by him, her, or them for the purposes or a public laundry.

---

85. *See, e.g.*, W. KIP VISCUSI, RISK BY CHOICE: REGULATING HEALTH AND SAFETY IN THE WORKPLACE (1983).

> SEC. 6. Any person or persons establishing, maintaining, or carrying on the business of a public laundry or a public wash-house, * * * who shall violate the provisions of section 4 or 5 of this Order shall be guilty of a misdemeanor, and upon conviction thereof shall be punished by a fine of not less than five dollars nor more than fifty dollars, or by imprisonment not more than one month, or by both such fine and imprisonment.

On Monday, February 25, 1884, 11 p.m., Soon Hing, an employee of a Chinese public laundry in San Francisco, was arrested and imprisoned for ironing clothing in a public laundry in violation of Ordinance 1719. Hing's habeas corpus petition reached the Supreme Court. His petition argued:

> [In San Francisco had existed] great antipathy and hatred on the part of the residents * * * against the subjects of the Emperor of China residing and doing business in said city and county of San Francisco.
>
> That such antipathy and hatred has manifested itself in various ways and under various forms for the purpose and with the intent of expelling and compelling the subjects of said Emperor of China to quit and abandon doing business. * * *
>
> That owing to the aforesaid feeling of antipathy and hatred prevailing against the * * * subjects of the Emperor of China, and not otherwise, and not for any sanitary, police, or other legitimate purpose, but for the purpose and with the intent of forcing said subjects of the Emperor of China engaged in carrying on the business of a laundry in * * * San Francisco to abandon the exercise of their lawful vocation and their only means of earning a livelihood, the * * * Board of Supervisors did enact and pass [Ordinance 1719].
>
> * * *
>
> That said ordinance was enacted, framed, and adopted, not from any legitimate police regulation or sanitary purpose, but for the purpose and with the intent of oppressing the Chinese engaged in the laundry business.
>
> That petitioner has been and is earning his living exclusively by working at washing and ironing for hire in a laundry, and in order to gain a livelihood is obliged to work late in the night, and has no other lawful vocation or pursuit to earn his living except such business.
>
> * * * Section Four of said Order No. 1719 * * * is null and void, and in * * * contravention of the provisions of article 14 of the amendments to the Constitution of the United States.

The Supreme Court upheld the Ordinance, reasoning that "regulations in this matter are not subject to any interference by the federal tribunals unless they are made the occasion for invading the substantial rights of persons, and no such invasion is caused by the regulation in question."[86]

---

86. Hing v. Crowley, 113 U.S. 703 (1885).

The Court further noted that "occupations in which continuous fires are necessary should cease at certain hours of the night would seem to be under such circumstances a reasonable regulation as a measure of precaution."

(a) Could the San Francisco Ordinance survive a challenge after *Lochner*?

(b) Writing for the *Hing* Court, Justice Stephen Johnson Field summarized several legal principles related to state interference with the freedom of contract:

> The objection that [Section Four] is void on the ground that it deprives a man of the right to work at all times is * * * without force. However broad the right of every one to follow such calling and employ his time as he may judge most conducive to his interests, it must be exercised subject to such general rules as are adopted by society for the common welfare. All sorts of restrictions are imposed upon the actions of men, notwithstanding the liberty which is guarantied to each. It is liberty regulated by just and impartial laws. Parties, for example, are free to make any contracts they choose for a lawful purpose, but society says what contracts shall be in writing and what may be verbally made, and on what days they may be executed, and how long they may be enforced if their terms are not complied with. So, too, with the hours of labor. On few subjects has there been more regulation. How many hours shall constitute a day's work in the absence of contract, at what time shops in our cities shall close at night, are constant subjects of legislation. Laws setting aside Sunday as a day of rest are upheld, not from any right of the government to legislate for the promotion of religious observances, but from its right to protect all persons from the physical and moral debasement which comes from uninterrupted labor. Such laws have always been deemed beneficent and merciful laws, especially to the poor and dependent, to the laborers in our factories and workshops, and in the heated rooms of our cities; and their validity has been sustained by the highest courts of the states.

Twenty years later, the Supreme Court handed down *Lochner*. Did *Lochner* necessarily depart from Justice Field's statement in *Hing v. Crowley* (1885)?

(c) In *Lochner*, Justice Holmes dissented arguing that the "Constitution is not intended to embody a particular economic theory, whether of paternalism and the organic relation of the citizen to the state or of *laissez faire*." Holmes reminded the Court that "[it] is settled * * * that state constitutions and state laws may regulate life in many ways which we as * * * might think as injudicious, or * * * tyrannical, * * * which, * * * interfere with the liberty to contract. Sunday laws * * * are ancient examples." In *Hing*, Justice Field chose to stress the established constitutionality of Sunday laws, although the case focused on the regulation of businesses at night.[87] In *McGowan v. Maryland* (1961),[88] the Supreme Court upheld

---

87. *See* Andrew J. King, *Sunday Law in the Nineteenth Century*, 64 ALBANY LAW REVIEW 675 (2000).

88. McGowan v. Maryland, 366 U.S. 420 (1961).

again the constitutionality of Sunday laws, also known as Sunday Closing Laws:

> Throughout this century and longer, both the federal and state governments have oriented their activities very largely toward improvement of the health, safety, recreation and general well-being of our citizens. Numerous laws affecting public health, safety factors in industry, laws affecting hours and conditions of labor of women and children, week-end diversion at parks and beaches, and cultural activities of various kinds, now point the way toward the good life for all. Sunday Closing Laws * * * have become part and parcel of this great governmental concern wholly apart from their original purposes or connotations. The present purpose and effect of most of them is to provide a uniform day of rest for all citizens; the fact that this day is Sunday, a day of particular significance for the dominant Christian sects, does not bar the State from achieving its secular goals. To say that the States cannot prescribe Sunday as a day of rest for these purposes solely because centuries ago such laws had their genesis in religion would give a constitutional interpretation of hostility to the public welfare rather than one of mere separation of church and State.

Are Sunday laws consistent with *Lochner*? Did *McGowan* introduce a new justification for interference with employment contracts? Is a uniform day of rest likely to contribute to public health and safety? Do Sunday laws intend to command conduct or manipulate incentives?

4. In *People v. Freeman* (1988),[89] the California Supreme Court held that the production of adult films is not pandering or prostitution, and thus falls within the protection of the First Amendment. The state was prohibited from intervening in the freedom of contract of producers and performers in the adult movie industry. A 1998 HIV outbreak in the industry inspired the establishment of voluntary institutions to enhance occupational safety among performers in adult movies. Performers in the adult film industry, however, have remained exposed to a relatively high risk of acquiring and transmitting sexually transmitted diseases, including HIV infections. This risk sparked a debate on regulation of the industry. Many industry insiders defended their freedom of choice, and argued that industry practices are superior to state regulation. In contrast, health professionals, HIV activists, and others posited that the state should regulate the industry and require various protective measures, such as mandatory condoms, routine screening of performers, mandatory vaccinations when those are available, and mandatory education on health and safety hazards.[90] In January 2012, the Los Angeles City Council passed the City of Los Angeles Safer Sex in the Adult Film Industry Act that requires the use condoms in adult films

---

89. People v. Freeman, 46 Cal.3d 419 (1988).

90. *See generally* Corita R. Grudzen et al., *Pathways to Health Risk Exposure in Adult Film Performers*, 86 JOURNAL OF URBAN HEALTH 67 (2008); Melanie M. Taylor et al., *Epidemiologic Investigation of a Cluster of Workplace HIV Infections in the Adult Film Industry: Los Angeles, California, 2004*, 44 CLINICAL INFECTIOUS DISEASES 301 (2007). *See also* Assemb. B. 2798, 2003–04 Leg., Reg. Sess. (Cal. 2004).

produced in the City.[91] Sections 2 and 3 of the Ordinance provide the rationale to the interference with the employment agreements used in the adult film industry:

> **SEC. 2. Findings and Declaration.**
>
> The people of the City of Los Angeles hereby find and declare all of the following:
>
> (a) The HIV/AIDS crisis, and the ongoing epidemic of sexually transmitted infections as a result of the making of adult films, has caused a negative impact on public health and the quality of life of citizens living in Los Angeles.
>
> (b) Safer sex practices are a prime method of preventing and reducing the spread of HIV/AIDS and other sexually transmitted infections.
>
> (c) The Los Angeles County Department of Public Health has documented widespread transmission of sexually transmitted infections associated with the activities of the adult film industry within the City of Los Angeles.
>
> (d) The Los Angeles County Department of Public Health has opined that the use of condoms is the best and most effective way to stem the spread of sexually transmitted infections within the adult film industry.
>
> (e) Multiple organizations committed to protecting the public health have called for mandatory use of condoms in the production of adult films, including the American Medical Association, the American Public Health Association, the California Conference of Local AIDS Directors, the California STD Controllers Association, the National Coalition of STD Directors, the National Association of City and County Health Officials, AIDS Healthcare Foundation and the California Medical Association.
>
> * * *
>
> **SEC. 3. Purpose and Intent.**
>
> The people of the City of Los Angeles hereby declare their purpose and intent in enacting this ordinance to be to minimize the spread of sexually transmitted infections resulting from the production of adult films in the City of Los Angeles, which have caused a negative impact on public health and the quality of life of citizens living in Los Angeles.

Individuals employed in the adult film industry and in the bread and pastry industry assume risks when they perform services for compensation. In *Lochner*, Justice Peckham observed that "[i]t is unfortunately true that labor, even in any department, may possibly carry with it the seeds of unhealthiness."

(a) Do the occupational risks in the adult film industry justify interference with employment agreements? (b) Does the Los Angeles Safer Sex Ordi-

---

91. A copy of the Los Angeles Safer Sex in the Adult Film Industry Act is available at *regti.me/LA-sex* (case sensitive).

nance meet the *Lochner*'s standard of legitimate interference with ordinary trades and occupations? (c) Should Los Angeles distinguish between the adult film industry and the bread and pastry industry? (d) Should Los Angeles craft unique regulatory standards for the adult film industry? (e) Does the Los Angeles Safer Sex Ordinance intend to command conduct or manipulate incentives?

---

§ 1.2.2 The Regulator: Who Has the Authority to Regulate?

In many ways, the 2012 health-care decision, *National Federation of Independent Business*, symbolizes the controversy over the scope of government regulation.[92] Writing for the Court, Chief Justice Roberts summarized the distinction between federal and state regulatory authorities. The federal government possesses only limited powers: the enumerated powers granted by the Constitution. All other regulatory powers are reserved to the states. Chief Justice Roberts noted that the Court has traditionally used the term "police power" to refer to the "general power of governing, possessed by the States but not by the Federal Government."[93]

Since the nineteenth century, courts have been struggling with the concept of the "police power." The Supreme Court conceded that any "attempt to define its reach or trace its outer limits is fruitless."[94] Within this ambiguity, it is settled that states invoke the police power only in aid of the safety, health, morals, and general welfare of the public.[95] Thus, courts examine whether a regulation is within the scope of the state's police power in two steps. First, the court examines whether any constitutional restriction or federal preemption bars the regulation in question. Second, the court determines whether the regulation is *reasonably* related to the safety, health, morals, and general welfare of the public.[96]

---

92. 132 S.Ct. 2566 (2012).

93. National Federation of Independent Business v. Sebelius, 132 S.Ct. 2566 (2012). *See also* United States v. Lopez, 514 U.S. 549, 566 (1995) (Rehnquist, C.J.) ("The Constitution * * * withhold[s] from Congress a plenary police power"); United States v. Morrison, 529 U.S. 598, 599 (2000) (Rehnquist, C.J.) ("[W]e can think of no better example of the police power, which the Founders denied the National Government and reposed in the States."); Walter Wheeler Cook, *What Is the Police Power*, 7 COLUMBIA LAW REVIEW 322 (1907).

94. Berman v. Parker, 348 U.S. 26, 32 (1954). *See also* Massachusetts v. Alger, 61 Mass. 53, 85 (1851) ("It is much easier to perceive and realize the existence and sources of this power, than to mark its boundaries, or prescribe limits to its exercise").

95. *See, e.g.*, Lochner v. New York, 198 U.S. 45, 53 (1905) (Peckham, J.) ("There are, however, certain powers, existing in the sovereignty of each state in the Union, somewhat vaguely termed police powers, the exact description and limitation of which have not been attempted by the courts. Those powers, broadly stated * * * relate to the safety, health, morals, and general welfare of the public."); New State Ice Co. v. Liebmann, 285 U.S. 262, 304 (1932) (Brandeis, J., dissenting) ("It is settled that the police power commonly invoked in aid of health, safety, and morals extends equally to the promotion of the public welfare."); Poe v. Ullman, 367 U.S. 497, 539 (1961) ("the State's police powers [refer to] provision for the health, safety, morals or welfare of its people.")

96. *See, e.g.*, Nollan v. California Coastal Commission, 483 U.S. 825, (1987) ("The term 'police power' connotes the time-tested conceptional limit of public encroachment upon private interests. Except for the substitution of the familiar standard of 'reasonableness,' this Court

The distinction Chief Justice Roberts drew in *National Federation of Independent Business* between the enumerated powers and the police power is in practice one of the thorniest issues in the controversy over regulation. Already in 1819, Chief Justice Marshall observed that "the question respecting the extent of the powers actually granted" to the Federal Government "is perpetually arising, and will probably continue to arise, as long as our system shall exist."[97] *NFIB* illustrates that disputes over the allocation of powers between the federal and state governments are frequently a pretext for objections to regulation.

In this Section, we discuss several key principles that govern the allocation of powers between the federal and state governments.

Since the rise of the modern regulatory state, the federal government's primary source of regulatory authority has been the Commerce Clause, which empowers Congress "[t]o regulate Commerce with foreign Nations, and among the several States, and with the Indian Tribes."[98] The federal government's increasing reliance on the Commerce Clause to assert its regulatory power has shaped most struggles between federal and state governments over the use of police power.[99]

Once Congress acts in a certain area, the question is whether it preempts state laws in that area. The *preemption doctrine*, arguably "the most frequently used doctrine of constitutional law in practice,"[100] intends to resolve such questions.[101] The doctrine articulates conditions under which a federal law preempts state laws. Under the doctrine, within constitutional limits, Congress may expressly preempt state regulatory authority.[102] Absent explicit preemptive language, courts may infer implied preemption. There are three categories of implied preemption—conflict preemption, obstacle preemption, and field preemption. Conflict preemption may exist when it is impossible to comply with both the federal law and a state law.[103] Obstacle preemption may be triggered in situations in which compliance with the state law "stands as an obstacle to the accomplishment and execution of the full purposes and objectives of Congress."[104] Field preemption may be inferred when "[t]he scheme of federal regulation [is] so pervasive as to make reasonable the inference that Congress left no

---

has generally refrained from announcing any specific criteria.") (quoting Goldblatt v. Hempstead, 369 U.S. 590, 594–595 (1962)).

97. M'Culloch v. Maryland, 17 U.S. 316, 405 (1819).

98. U.S. Const. art. I, § 8, cl. 3

99. *See generally* Jack M. Balkin, *Commerce*, 109 MICHIGAN LAW REVIEW 1 (2010); Barak Orbach et al., *Arming States' Rights: Federalism, Private Lawmakers, and the Battering Ram Strategy*, 52 ARIZONA LAW REVIEW 1161 (2010).

100. Stephen A. Gardbaum, *The Nature of Preemption*, 79 CORNELL LAW REVIEW 767, 768 (1994).

101. *See* Gardbaum, *id*; Caleb Nelson, *Preemption*, 86 VIRGINIA LAW REVIEW 225 (2000).

102. Pacific Gas and Elec. Co. v. State Energy Resources Conservation & Development Commission, 461 U.S. 190, 203 (1983).

103. M'Culloch v. Maryland, 17 U.S. 316, 427 (1819); Florida Lime & Avocado Growers, Inc. v. Paul, 373 U.S. 132, 142–43 (1963).

104. Hines v. Davidowitz, 312 U.S. 52, 67 (1941).

room for the States to supplement it."[105] Applying this classification has proved to be a challenging task, and thus uncertainties related to the allocation of powers between the federal and state governments are often litigated.

We saw that one meaning of the term "regulation" is "agency statement of general applicability and future effect, which the agency intends to have the force and effect of law, that is designed to implement, interpret, or prescribe law or policy or to describe the procedure or practice requirements of an agency."[106] Administrative agencies acquire regulatory powers when legislatures delegate such powers to them. This delegation is necessary for practical reasons to address the growing complexity of the economy and new technologies. However, the increasing costs of the regulatory system, including in terms of accountability to the public and effectiveness, have been another source of controversy. At the federal level, the *delegation doctrine* defines the authorities Congress cannot delegate to administrative agencies.[107] Although Article I of the Constitution declares that "[a]ll legislative Powers herein granted shall be vested in a Congress,"[108] applying the delegation doctrine, the Supreme Court has consistently upheld statutes that contained an "intelligible principle" to guide the administrative agency and constrain the delegation.[109]

The so-called intelligible principle still leaves uncertainty with respect to the allocation of regulatory authorities. When administrative agencies, such as the EPA, FDA, or FCC, promulgate rules or act in other ways, their regulatory activities must be within the ambit of their specific statutory authority. However, statutory construction is often needed to identify these boundaries. For example, the Federal Communications Commission Act (the "FCC Act") authorizes the FCC to license and regulate radio and television broadcast stations and vests in the FCC the responsibility for enforcing the its rules and applicable statutory provisions concerning the operation of those stations. The FCC Act provides that "[w]hoever utters any obscene, indecent, or profane language by means of radio communication shall be fined under this title or imprisoned not more than two years, or both."[110] The meanings of "obscene," "indecent" or "profane" language are products of statutory interpretation.[111] Congress, the FCC, and the judiciary are plausible candidates to provide such interpretations. This interpretive authority encompasses significant regulatory implications and thus it is meaningful.

---

105. Rice v. Santa Fe Elevator Corp., 331 U.S. 218, 230 (1947).

106. Executive Order 12866 of September 30, 1993, as amended by E.O. 13258 of February 26, 2002 and E.O. 13422 of January 18, 2007 § 3.

107. *See generally* Peter H. Aranson et al., *A Theory of Legislative Delegation*, 66 CORNELL LAW REVIEW (1982); Cass R. Sunstein, *Nondelegation Canons*, 67 UNIVERSITY OF CHICAGO LAW REVIEW 315 (2000).

108. U.S. Const. art. I, § 1.

109. J.W. Hampton, Jr., & Co. v. United States, 276 U.S. 394 (1928).

110. 18 U.S.C. § 1464.

111. *See, e.g.*, F.C.C. v. Pacifica Foundation, 438 U.S. 726 (1978); F.C.C. v. Fox Television Stations, Inc., 556 U.S. 502 (2009).

In *Chevron USA Inc. v. Natural Resources Defense Council, Inc.* (1984),[112] the Supreme Court reshaped the division of statutory interpretation authorities between courts and agencies, effectively changing the scope of powers Congress can delegate to agencies.[113] In *Chevron*, the Court laid down a two-step framework for reviewing the statutory interpretation of agencies. At step one, courts using "traditional tools of statutory construction," examine whether Congress had a "specific intention" and "has directly spoken to the precise question at issue." "If the intent of Congress is clear, that is the end of the matter." If no clear congressional intent can be discerned, then at step two, "the question for the court is whether the agency's [interpretation was] a permissible construction of the statute." The "court does not * * * impose its own construction on the statute," and "[it] need not conclude that the agency construction was the only one it permissibly could have adopted to uphold the construction, or even the reading the court would have reached if the question initially had arisen in a judicial proceeding." Prior to *Chevron*, courts often assessed agency interpretations against multiple contextual factors and, thus, agencies had a narrower scope of powers. The *Chevron* Court justified a deference to agencies' constructions by noting that "[t]he responsibilities for assessing the wisdom of * * * policy choices and resolving the struggle between competing views of the public interest are not judicial ones."[114] The *Chevron* Court further clarified that it is within the power of Congress to delegate implicitly or explicitly the authority to interpret statutes to the agencies that administer them.[115] When agencies fill gaps Congress leaves explicitly or implicitly in statutes (such as definitions of terms), their rules "are given controlling weight unless they are arbitrary, capricious, or manifestly contrary to the statute."[116] By deferring to statutory construction of agencies, *Chevron* allows Congress to delegate to agencies somewhat less detailed statutes and rely on their work.

The following pair of decisions—*Cipollone v. Liggett Group, Inc.*, 505 U.S. 504 (1992) and *Altria Group, Inc. v. Good*, 555 U.S. 70 (2008)—illustrates one dimension of the controversy over allocation of regulatory authorities between the federal government and states. In *Cipollone* and *Altria*, Justice John Paul Stevens led the Court to adopt an interpretation that gives weight to state laws, although in other cases Justice Stevens adopted interpretations that sided with the federal government.[117]

112. Chevron USA Inc. v. Natural Resources Defense Council, Inc., 467 U.S. 837 (1984).

113. *See generally* Thomas W. Merrill, *The Story of* Chevron USA v. Natural Resources Defense Council, Inc.: *Sometimes Great Cases Are Made Not Born*, in STATUTORY INTERPRETATION STORIES 164 (William Eskridge, Jr. et al. eds. 2011).

114. *Id.* at 866.

115. *Id.* at 844–45.

116. *Id.* at 844.

117. *See, e.g.*, United States v. Lopez, 514 U.S. 549 (1995) (dissenting); United States v. Morrison, 529 U.S. 598 (2000) (dissenting); Gonzales v. Raich, 545 U.S. 1 (2005).

Cipollone v. Liggett Group, Inc.

505 U.S. 504 (1992)

■ JUSTICE STEVENS delivered the opinion of the Court, except as to Parts V and VI.

"WARNING: THE SURGEON GENERAL HAS DETERMINED THAT CIGARETTE SMOKING IS DANGEROUS TO YOUR HEALTH." A federal statute enacted in 1969 requires that warning (or a variation thereof) to appear in a conspicuous place on every package of cigarettes sold in the United States. The questions presented to us by this case are whether that statute * * * pre-empted petitioner's common-law claims against respondent cigarette manufacturers.

Petitioner is the son of Rose Cipollone, who began smoking in 1942 and who died of lung cancer in 1984. He claims that respondents are responsible for Rose Cipollone's death because they breached express warranties contained in their advertising, because they failed to warn consumers about the hazards of smoking, because they fraudulently misrepresented those hazards to consumers, and because they conspired to deprive the public of medical and scientific information about smoking. The Court of Appeals held that petitioner's state-law claims were pre-empted by federal statutes * * * and other courts have agreed with that analysis. The highest court of the State of New Jersey, however, has held that the federal statutes did not pre-empt similar common-law claims. Because of the manifest importance of the issue, we granted certiorari to resolve the conflict. * * * We now reverse in part and affirm in part.

I

[Petitioner's] complaint alleged that Rose Cipollone developed lung cancer because she smoked cigarettes manufactured and sold by the three respondents. * * *

As one of their defenses, respondents contended that the Federal Cigarette Labeling and Advertising Act, enacted in 1965, and its successor, the Public Health Cigarette Smoking Act of 1969, protected them from any liability based on their conduct after 1965. * * *

II

Although physicians had suspected a link between smoking and illness for centuries, the first medical studies of that connection did not appear until the 1920's. [By] the time the Surgeon General convened an advisory committee to examine the issue in 1962, there were more than 7,000 publications examining the relationship between smoking and health. * * *

In 1964, the advisory committee issued its report, which stated as its central conclusion: "Cigarette smoking is a health hazard of sufficient importance in the United States to warrant appropriate remedial action." * * * In July 1965, Congress enacted the Federal Cigarette Labeling and Advertising Act (1965 Act or Act). The 1965 * * * mandated warnings on cigarette packages (§ 5(a)), but barred the requirement of such warnings in cigarette advertising (§ 5(b)).

Section 2 of the Act declares the statute's two purposes: (1) adequately informing the public that cigarette smoking may be hazardous to health, and (2) protecting the national economy from the burden imposed by diverse, nonuniform, and confusing cigarette labeling and advertising regulations. In furtherance of the first purpose, § 4 of the Act made it unlawful to sell or distribute any cigarettes in the United States unless the package bore a conspicuous label stating: "CAUTION: CIGARETTE SMOKING MAY BE HAZARDOUS TO YOUR HEALTH." In furtherance of the second purpose, § 5, captioned "Preemption," provided in part:

> "(a) No statement relating to smoking and health, other than the statement required by section 4 of this Act, shall be required on any cigarette package.
>
> "(b) No statement relating to smoking and health shall be required in the advertising of any cigarettes the packages of which are labeled in conformity with the provisions of this Act."

[T]he Public Health Cigarette Smoking Act of 1969 (1969 Act or Act) * * * amended the 1965 Act in several ways. First, the 1969 Act strengthened the warning label, in part by requiring a statement that cigarette smoking "is dangerous" rather than that it "may be hazardous." Second, the 1969 Act banned cigarette advertising in "any medium of electronic communication subject to [FCC] jurisdiction." Third, and related, the 1969 Act modified the pre-emption provision by replacing the original § 5(b) with a provision that reads:

> "(b) No requirement or prohibition based on smoking and health shall be imposed under State law with respect to the advertising or promotion of any cigarettes the packages of which are labeled in conformity with the provisions of this Act."

* * *

III

Article VI of the Constitution provides that the laws of the United States "shall be the supreme Law of the Land; * * * any Thing in the Constitution or Laws of any state to the Contrary notwithstanding." Art. VI, cl. 2. * * * Consideration of issues arising under the Supremacy Clause "start[s] with the assumption that the historic police powers of the States [are] not to be superseded by * * * Federal Act unless that [is] the clear and manifest purpose of Congress." Rice v. Santa Fe Elevator Corp., 331 U.S. 218, 230 (1947). * * *

* * * In the absence of an express congressional command, state law is pre-empted if that law actually conflicts with federal law, * * *or if federal law so thoroughly occupies a legislative field " 'as to make reasonable the inference that Congress left no room for the States to supplement it.' " * * *

In our opinion, the pre-emptive scope of the 1965 Act and the 1969 Act is governed entirely by the express language in § 5 of each Act. When Congress has considered the issue of pre-emption and has included in the enacted legislation a provision explicitly addressing that issue. * * * Congress' enactment of a provision defining the pre-emptive reach of a statute implies that matters beyond that reach are not pre-empted. In this case, the other provisions of the 1965 and 1969 Acts offer no cause to look beyond § 5 of each Act. Therefore, we need only identify the domain expressly pre-empted by each of those sections. As the 1965 and 1969 provisions differ substantially, we consider each in turn.

IV

In the 1965 pre-emption provision regarding advertising (§ 5(b)), Congress spoke precisely and narrowly: "No *statement* relating to smoking and health shall be required *in the advertising* of [properly labeled] cigarettes." Section 5(a) used the same phrase ("No *statement* relating to smoking and health") with regard to cigarette labeling. As § 5(a) made clear, that phrase referred to the sort of warning provided for in § 4, which set forth verbatim the warning Congress determined to be appropriate. Thus, on their face, these provisions merely prohibited state and federal rulemaking bodies from mandating particular cautionary statements on cigarette labels (§ 5(a)) or in cigarette advertisements (§ 5(b)).

Beyond the precise words of these provisions, this reading is appropriate for several reasons. First, as discussed above, we must construe these provisions in light of the presumption against the pre-emption of state police power regulations. This presumption reinforces the appropriateness of a narrow reading of § 5. Second, the warning required in § 4 does not by its own effect foreclose additional obligations imposed under state law. That Congress requires a particular warning label does not automatically pre-empt a regulatory field. * * * Third, there is no general, inherent conflict between federal pre-emption of state warning requirements and the continued vitality of state common-law damages actions. * * * All of these considerations indicate that § 5 is best read as having superseded only positive enactments by legislatures or administrative agencies that mandate particular warning labels.

This reading comports with the 1965 Act's statement of purpose, which expressed an intent to avoid "diverse, nonuniform, and confusing cigarette labeling and advertising *regulations* with respect to any relationship between smoking and health." Read against the backdrop of regulatory activity undertaken by state legislatures and federal agencies in response to the Surgeon General's report, the term "regulation" most naturally refers to positive enactments by those bodies, not to common-law damages actions.

V

Compared to its predecessor in the 1965 Act, the plain language of the pre-emption provision in the 1969 Act is much broader. First, the later Act bars not simply "statement[s]" but rather "requirement[s] or prohibition[s] * * * imposed under State law." Second, the later Act reaches beyond statements "in the advertising" to obligations "with respect to the advertising or promotion" of cigarettes.

Notwithstanding these substantial differences in language, both petitioner and respondents contend that the 1969 Act did not materially alter the pre-emptive scope of federal law. Their primary support for this contention is a sentence in a Committee Report which states that the 1969 amendment "clarified" the 1965 version of § 5(b). * * * We reject the parties' reading as incompatible with the language and origins of the amendments. * * * The 1969 Act worked substantial changes in the law: rewriting the label warning, banning broadcast advertising, and allowing the FTC to regulate print advertising. In the context of such revisions and in light of the substantial changes in wording, we cannot accept the parties' claim that the 1969 Act did not alter the reach of § 5(b).

Petitioner next contends that § 5(b), however broadened by the 1969 Act, does not pre-empt *common-law* actions. He offers two theories for limiting the reach of the amended § 5(b). First, he argues that common-law damages actions do not impose "requirement[s] or prohibition[s]" and that Congress intended only to trump "state statute[s], injunction[s], or executive pronouncement[s]." We disagree; such an analysis is at odds both with the plain words of the 1969 Act and with the general understanding of common-law damages actions. The phrase "[n]o requirement or prohibition" sweeps broadly and suggests no distinction between positive enactments and common law; to the contrary, those words easily encompass obligations that take the form of common-law rules. * * *

Petitioner's second argument for excluding common-law rules from the reach of § 5(b) hinges on the phrase "imposed under State law." This argument fails as well. At least since Erie R. Co. v. Tompkins, 304 U.S. 64, (1938), we have recognized the phrase "state law" to include common law as well as statutes and regulations. * * *

That the pre-emptive scope of § 5(b) cannot be limited to positive enactments does not mean that that section pre-empts all common-law claims. * * *

VI

[T]he 1969 Act does not pre-empt petitioner's claims based on express warranty, intentional fraud and misrepresentation, or conspiracy.

The judgment of the Court of Appeals is accordingly reversed in part and affirmed in part, and the case is remanded for further proceedings consistent with this opinion.

It is so ordered.

■ JUSTICE BLACKMUN, with whom JUSTICE KENNEDY and JUSTICE SOUTER join, concurring in part, concurring in the judgment in part, and dissenting in part.

I

The Court today would craft a compromise position concerning the extent to which federal law pre-empts persons injured by cigarette manufacturers' unlawful conduct from bringing state common-law damages claims against those manufacturers. I, however, find the Court's divided holding with respect to the original and amended versions of the federal statute entirely unsatisfactory. Our precedents do not allow us to infer a scope of pre-emption beyond that which clearly is mandated by Congress' language. In my view, *neither* version of the federal legislation at issue here provides the kind of unambiguous evidence of congressional intent necessary to displace state common-law damages claims. I therefore join Parts I, II, III, and IV of the Court's opinion, but dissent from Parts V and VI. * * *

II

* * * Given the Court's proper analytical focus on the scope of the express pre-emption provisions at issue here and its acknowledgment that the 1965 Act does not pre-empt state common-law damages claims, I find the plurality's conclusion that the 1969 Act pre-empts at least some common-law damages claims little short of baffling. In my view, the modified language of § 5(b) * * * no more "clearly" or "manifestly" exhibits an intent to pre-empt state common-law damages actions than did the language of its predecessor in the 1965 Act. Nonetheless, the plurality reaches a different conclusion, and its reasoning warrants scrutiny.

A

The plurality premises its pre-emption ruling on what it terms the "substantial changes" wrought by Congress in § 5(b), notably, the rewording of the provision to pre-empt any "requirement or prohibition" (as opposed merely to any "statement") "imposed under State law." As an initial matter, I do not disagree with the plurality that the phrase "State law," in an appropriate case, can encompass the common law as well as positive enactments such as statutes and regulations. I do disagree, however, with the plurality's conclusion that "State law" as used in § 5(b) represents such an all-inclusive reference. Congress' intention in selecting that phrase cannot be understood without considering the narrow range of actions—any "requirement or prohibition"—that Congress specifically described in § 5(b) as "imposed under" state law. * * *

Although the plurality flatly states that the phrase "no requirement or prohibition" "sweeps broadly" and "easily encompass[es] obligations that take the form of common-law rules," those words are in reality far from unambiguous and cannot be said clearly to evidence a congressional mandate to pre-empt state common-law damages actions. * * *

More important, the question whether common-law damages actions exert a regulatory effect on manufacturers analogous to that of positive enactments—an assumption crucial to the plurality's conclusion that the phrase "requirement or prohibition" encompasses common-law actions—is significantly more complicated than the plurality[] * * * suggest[s].

The effect of tort law on a manufacturer's behavior is necessarily indirect. Although an award of damages by its very nature attaches additional consequences to the manufacturer's continued unlawful conduct, no particular course of action (*e.g.*, the adoption of a new warning label) is required. * * * The level of choice that a defendant retains in shaping its own behavior distinguishes the indirect regulatory effect of the common law from positive enactments such as statutes and administrative regulations. * * *

In light of the recognized distinction in this Court's jurisprudence between direct state regulation and the indirect regulatory effects of common-law damages actions, it cannot be said that damages claims are clearly or unambiguously "requirements" or "prohibitions" imposed under state law. The plain language of the 1969 Act's modified pre-emption provision simply cannot bear the broad interpretation the plurality would impart to it.

B

Not only does the text of the revised § 5(b) fail clearly or manifestly to require pre-emption of state common-law damages actions, but there is no suggestion in the legislative history that Congress intended to expand the scope of the pre-emption provision when it amended the statute in 1969. * * *

Viewing the revisions to § 5(b) as generally nonsubstantive in nature makes sense. By replacing the word "statement" with the slightly broader term, "requirement," and adding the word "prohibition" to ensure that a State could not do through negative mandate (*e.g.*, banning all cigarette advertising) that which it already was forbidden to do through positive mandate (*e.g.*, mandating particular cautionary statements), Congress sought to "clarif[y]" the existing precautions against confusing and non-uniform state laws and regulations. * * *

Finally, there is absolutely no suggestion in the legislative history that Congress intended to leave plaintiffs who were injured as a result of cigarette manufacturers' unlawful conduct without any alternative remedies; yet that is the regrettable effect of the ruling today that many state common-law damages claims are pre-empted. The Court in the past has hesitated to find pre-emption where federal law provides no comparable remedy. * * *

■ JUSTICE SCALIA, with whom JUSTICE THOMAS joins, concurring in the judgment in part and dissenting in part.

Today's decision announces what, on its face, is an extraordinary and unprecedented principle of federal statutory construction: that express pre-emption provisions must be construed narrowly, "in light of the presumption against the pre-emption of state police power regulations." * * * In my view, there is no merit to this newly crafted doctrine of narrow construction. Under the Supremacy Clause, * * * our job is to interpret Congress's decrees of pre-emption neither narrowly nor broadly, but in accordance with their apparent meaning. If we did that job in the present case, we would find, under the 1965 Act, pre-emption of petitioner's failure-to-warn claims; and under the 1969 Act, we would find pre-emption of petitioner's claims complete.

* * * The Court goes beyond the[] traditional [pre-emption] principles * * * to announce two new ones. First, it says that express pre-emption provisions must be given the narrowest possible construction. This is in its view the consequence of our oft-repeated assumption that, absent convincing evidence of statutory intent to pre-empt, " 'the historic police powers of the States [are] not to be superseded.' " But it seems to me that assump-

tion dissolves once there is conclusive evidence of intent to pre-empt in the express words of the statute itself, and the only remaining question is what the *scope* of that pre-emption is meant to be. Thereupon, I think, our responsibility is to apply to the text ordinary principles of statutory construction.

* * *

In light of our willingness to find pre-emption in the absence of *any* explicit statement of pre-emptive intent, the notion that such explicit statements, where they exist, are subject to a "plain-statement" rule is more than somewhat odd. * * *

The results seem odder still when one takes into account the second new rule that the Court announces: "When Congress has considered the issue of pre-emption and has included in the enacted legislation a provision explicitly addressing that issue, * * * we need only identify the domain expressly pre-empted by [that provision]." * * * To my knowledge, we have never expressed such a rule before, and our prior cases are inconsistent with it. When this second novelty is combined with the first, the result is extraordinary: The statute that says *anything* about pre-emption must say *everything;* and it must do so with great exactitude, as any ambiguity concerning its scope will be read in favor of preserving state power. If this is to be the law, surely only the most sporting of Congresses will dare to say anything about pre-emption.

* * *

Altria Group, Inc. v. Good

555 U.S. 70 (2008)

■ JUSTICE STEVENS delivered the opinion of the Court.

Respondents, who have for over 15 years smoked "light" cigarettes manufactured by petitioners, Philip Morris USA, Inc., and its parent company, Altria Group, Inc., claim that petitioners violated the Maine Unfair Trade Practices Act (MUTPA). Specifically, they allege that petitioners' advertising fraudulently conveyed the message that their "light" cigarettes deliver less tar and nicotine to consumers than regular brands despite petitioners' knowledge that the message was untrue. Petitioners deny the charge, asserting that their advertisements were factually accurate. The * * * District Court entered summary judgment in favor of petitioners on the ground that respondents' state-law claim is pre-empted by the Federal Cigarette Labeling and Advertising Act, as amended (Labeling Act or Act). The Court of Appeals reversed that judgment, and we granted certiorari to review its holding that the Labeling Act neither expressly nor impliedly pre-empts respondents' fraud claim. We affirm.

I

Respondents are Maine residents and longtime smokers of Marlboro Lights and Cambridge Lights cigarettes, which are manufactured by petitioners. [R]espondents filed a complaint alleging that petitioners deliberately deceived them about the true and harmful nature of "light" cigarettes in violation of the MUTPA. * * * Respondents claim that petitioners fraudulently marketed their cigarettes as being "light" and containing " '[l]owered [t]ar and [n]icotine' " to convey to consumers that they deliver less tar and nicotine and are therefore less harmful than regular cigarettes. * * *

Respondents acknowledge that testing pursuant to the Cambridge Filter Method [that weighs and measures the tar and nicotine collected by a smoking machine] indicates that tar and nicotine yields of Marlboro Lights and Cambridge Lights are lower than those of regular cigarettes. * * * Respondents allege, however, that petitioners have known at all relevant times that human smokers unconsciously engage in compensatory behaviors not registered by Cambridge Filter Method testing that negate the effect of the tar- and nicotine-reducing features of "light" cigarettes. * * * By covering filter ventilation holes with their lips or fingers, taking larger or more frequent puffs, and holding the smoke in their lungs for a longer period of time, smokers of "light" cigarettes unknowingly inhale as much tar and nicotine as do smokers of regular cigarettes. "Light" cigarettes are in fact more harmful because the increased ventilation that results from their unique design features produces smoke that is more mutagenic per milligram of tar than the smoke of regular cigarettes. * * * Respondents claim that petitioners violated the MUTPA by fraudulently concealing that information and by affirmatively representing, through the use of "light" and "lowered tar and nicotine" descriptors, that their cigarettes would pose fewer health risks. * * *

Petitioners moved for summary judgment on the ground that the Labeling Act * * * expressly pre-empts respondents' state-law cause of action. Relying on our decisions in *Cipollone v. Liggett Group, Inc.*, 505 U.S. 504 (1992), and *Lorillard Tobacco Co. v. Reilly*, 533 U.S. 525 (2001), the District Court concluded that respondents' MUTPA claim is pre-empted. The court recast respondents' claim as a failure-to-warn or warning neutralization claim of the kind pre-empted in *Cipollone*. * * *

Respondents appealed, and the Court of Appeals reversed. The Court of Appeals first rejected the District Court's characterization of respondents' claim as a warning neutralization claim akin to the pre-empted claim in *Cipollone*. Instead, the court concluded that respondents' claim is in substance a fraud claim that alleges that petitioners falsely represented their cigarettes as "light" or having "lowered tar and nicotine" even though they deliver to smokers the same quantities of those components as do regular cigarettes. "The fact that these alleged misrepresentations were unaccompanied by additional statements in the nature of a warning does not transform the claimed fraud into failure to warn" or warning neutralization. * * *

II

Article VI, cl. 2, of the Constitution provides that the laws of the United States "shall be the supreme Law of the Land; . . . any Thing in the Constitution or Laws of any state to the Contrary notwithstanding."

Consistent with that command, we have long recognized that state laws that conflict with federal law are "without effect." * * *

* * * If a federal law contains an express pre-emption clause, it does not immediately end the inquiry because the question of the substance and scope of Congress' displacement of state law still remains. Pre-emptive intent may also be inferred if the scope of the statute indicates that Congress intended federal law to occupy the legislative field, or if there is an actual conflict between state and federal law. * * *

When addressing questions of express or implied pre-emption, we begin our analysis "with the assumption that the historic police powers of the States [are] not to be superseded by the Federal Act unless that was the clear and manifest purpose of Congress." *Rice v. Santa Fe Elevator Corp.*, 331 U.S. 218, 230 (1947). That assumption applies with particular force when Congress has legislated in a field traditionally occupied by the States. * * *

Congress enacted the Labeling Act in 1965 in response to the Surgeon General's determination that cigarette smoking is harmful to health. The Act required that every package of cigarettes sold in the United States contain a conspicuous warning, and it pre-empted state-law positive enactments that added to the federally prescribed warning. * * * Congress amended the Labeling Act a few years later by enacting the Public Health Cigarette Smoking Act of 1969. The amendments strengthened the language of the prescribed warning * * * and prohibited cigarette advertising in "any medium of electronic communication subject to [Federal Communications Commission] jurisdiction," * * * They also broadened the Labeling Act's pre-emption provision. * * * The Labeling Act has since been amended further to require cigarette manufacturers to include four more explicit warnings in their packaging and advertisements on a rotating basis.

The stated purpose of the Labeling Act is

> "to establish a comprehensive Federal program to deal with cigarette labeling and advertising with respect to any relationship between smoking and health, whereby—
>
> "(1) the public may be adequately informed that cigarette smoking may be hazardous to health by inclusion of a warning to that effect on each package of cigarettes; and
>
> "(2) commerce and the national economy may be (A) protected to the maximum extent consistent with this declared policy and (B) not impeded by diverse, nonuniform, and confusing cigarette labeling and advertising regulations with respect to any relationship between smoking and health." 79 Stat. 282, 15 U.S.C. § 1331.

The requirement that cigarette manufacturers include in their packaging and advertising the precise warnings mandated by Congress furthers the Act's first purpose. And the Act's pre-emption provisions promote its second purpose.

As amended, the Labeling Act contains two express pre-emption provisions. Section 5(a) protects cigarette manufacturers from inconsistent state labeling laws by prohibiting the requirement of additional statements relating to smoking and health on cigarette packages. 15 U.S.C. § 1334(a). Section 5(b), which is at issue in this case, provides that "[n]o requirement or prohibition based on smoking and health shall be imposed under State law with respect to the advertising or promotion of any cigarettes the packages of which are labeled in conformity with the provisions of this chapter." § 1334(b).

Together, the labeling requirement and pre-emption provisions express Congress' determination that the prescribed federal warnings are both necessary and sufficient to achieve its purpose of informing the public of the health consequences of smoking. Because Congress has decided that no additional warning statement is needed to attain that goal, States may not impede commerce in cigarettes by enforcing rules that are based on an assumption that the federal warnings are inadequate. Although both of the Act's purposes are furthered by prohibiting States from supplementing the federally prescribed warning, neither would be served by limiting the States' authority to prohibit deceptive statements in cigarette advertising. Petitioners acknowledge that "Congress had no intention of insulating tobacco companies from liability for inaccurate statements about the relationship between smoking and health." * * * But they maintain that Congress could not have intended to permit the enforcement of *state* fraud rules because doing so would defeat the Labeling Act's purpose of preventing nonuniform state warning requirements. * * * As we observed in *Cipollone*, however, fraud claims "rely only on a single, uniform standard: falsity." * * * (plurality opinion).

Although it is clear that fidelity to the Act's purposes does not demand the pre-emption of state fraud rules, the principal question that we must decide is whether the text of § 1334(b) nevertheless requires that result.

III

We have construed the operative phrases of § 1334(b) [and] recognized that the phrase "based on smoking and health" modifies the state-law rule at issue rather than a particular application of that rule. * * *

In *Cipollone*, the plurality * * * read the pre-emption provision in the 1969 amendments to the Labeling Act to pre-empt common-law rules as well as positive enactments. [T]he plurality concluded that the provision does not preclude all common-law claims that have some relationship to smoking and health. * * * To determine whether a particular common-law claim is pre-empted, the plurality inquired "whether the legal duty that is the predicate of the common-law damages action constitutes a 'requirement or prohibition based on smoking and health ... with respect to ... advertising or promotion,' giving that clause a fair but narrow reading." * * *

* * * The duty [not to deceive] codified in [MUPTA], like the duty imposed by the state common-law rule at issue in *Cipollone,* has nothing to do with smoking and health.

* * * Petitioners nonetheless contend that respondents' claim is like the pre-empted warning neutralization claim because it is based on statements that "might create a false impression" rather than statements that

are "inherently false." * * * But the extent of the falsehood alleged does not alter the nature of the claim. Nothing in the Labeling Act's text or purpose or in the plurality opinion in *Cipollone* suggests that whether a claim is pre-empted turns in any way on the distinction between misleading and inherently false statements. * * * Certainly, the extent of the falsehood alleged may bear on whether a plaintiff can prove her fraud claim, but the merits of respondents' claim are not before us.

Once that erroneous distinction is set aside, it is clear that our holding in *Cipollone* that the common-law fraud claim was not pre-empted is directly applicable to the statutory claim at issue in this case. [R]espondents' claim that the deceptive statements "light" and "lowered tar and nicotine" induced them to purchase petitioners' product alleges a breach of the duty not to deceive. * * *

IV

As an alternative to their express pre-emption argument, petitioners contend that respondents' claim is impliedly pre-empted because, if allowed to proceed, it would present an obstacle to a longstanding policy of the FTC. According to petitioners, the FTC has for decades promoted the development and consumption of low tar cigarettes and has encouraged consumers to rely on representations of tar and nicotine content based on Cambridge Filter Method testing in choosing among cigarette brands. Even if such a regulatory policy could provide a basis for obstacle pre-emption, petitioners' description of the FTC's actions in this regard are inaccurate. The Government itself disavows any policy authorizing the use of "light" and "low tar" descriptors. * * *

V

We conclude, as we did in *Cipollone*, that the Labeling Act does not pre-empt state-law claims like respondents' that are predicated on the duty not to deceive. We also hold that the FTC's various decisions with respect to statements of tar and nicotine content do not impliedly pre-empt respondents' claim. Respondents still must prove that petitioners' use of "light" and "lowered tar" descriptors in fact violated the state deceptive practices statute, but neither the Labeling Act's pre-emption provision nor the FTC's actions in this field prevent a jury from considering that claim. Accordingly, the judgment of the Court of Appeals is affirmed, and the case is remanded for further proceedings consistent with this opinion.

It is so ordered.

■ JUSTICE THOMAS, with whom CHIEF JUSTICE ROBERTS, JUSTICE SCALIA, and JUSTICE ALITO join, dissenting.

This appeal requires the Court to revisit its decision in *Cipollone v. Liggett Group, Inc.*, 505 U.S. 504 (1992). As in that case, the question before us is whether state-law claims alleging that cigarette manufacturers misled the public about the health effects of cigarettes are pre-empted by the Federal Cigarette Labeling and Advertising Act, as amended in 1969 (Labeling Act or Act). The Labeling Act requires that specific health warnings be placed on all cigarette packaging and advertising, 15 U.S.C. § 1333, in order to eliminate "diverse, nonuniform, and confusing cigarette labeling and advertising regulations with respect to any relationship between smoking and health," § 1331. To that end, § 5(b) of the Labeling Act pre-empts any "requirement or prohibition based on smoking and health ... imposed under State law with respect to the advertising or promotion of any cigarettes." § 1334(b).

Whether § 5(b) pre-empts state common-law claims divided the Court in *Cipollone*. The plurality opinion found some claims expressly pre-empted and others not, depending on whether "the legal duty that is the predicate of the common-law damages action constitutes a requirement or prohibition based on smoking and health ... imposed under State law with respect to ... advertising or promotion." * * * A majority of the Court disagreed with the plurality's predicate-duty approach. * * * (Blackmun, J., concurring in part, concurring in judgment in part, and dissenting in part); * * * (Scalia, J., concurring in judgment in part and dissenting in part). In particular, Justice Scalia recognized that the plurality's interpretation of § 5(b) created an unworkable test for pre-emption with little or no relationship to the text of the statute. * * * The intervening years have vindicated Justice Scalia's critical assessment; the lower courts have consistently expressed frustration at the difficulty in applying the *Cipollone* plurality's test. Moreover, this Court's recent pre-emption decisions have undermined, and in some cases overruled, central aspects of the plurality's atextual approach to express pre-emption generally.

The majority today ignores these problems and adopts the methodology of the *Cipollone* plurality as governing law. As a consequence, the majority concludes that state-law liability for deceiving purchasers about the health effects of smoking light cigarettes is not a "requirement or prohibition based on smoking and health" under the Labeling Act. The Court's fidelity to *Cipollone* is unwise and unnecessary. The Court should instead provide the lower courts with a clear test that advances Congress' stated goals by interpreting § 5(b) to expressly pre-empt any claim that "imposes an obligation ... because of the effect of smoking upon health." *Cipollone*, at 554 (opinion of Scalia, J.).

Respondents' lawsuit under [MUPTA] is expressly pre-empted under § 5(b) of the Labeling Act. The civil action is premised on the allegation that the cigarette manufacturers misled respondents into believing that smoking light cigarettes would be healthier for them than smoking regular cigarettes. A judgment in respondents' favor will thus result in a "requirement" that petitioners represent the effects of smoking on health in a particular way in their advertising and promotion of light cigarettes. Because liability in this case is thereby premised on the effect of smoking on health, I would hold that respondents' state-law claims are expressly pre-empted by § 5(b) of the Labeling Act. I respectfully dissent.

I

In *Cipollone*, a smoker and her spouse brought state common-law claims for fraud, breach of warranty, and failure to warn against cigarette manufacturers for their alleged failure to adequately disclose the health risks of smoking. * * * As here, the cigarette manufacturer asserted that the claims were pre-empted by § 5(b) of the Labeling Act.

In deciding the case, the Court could not agree on the meaning of the Labeling Act's express pre-emption provision. It produced three separate opinions, none of which reflected the views of a majority of Justices. Relying heavily on a "presumption against the pre-emption of state police power regulations," * * * a plurality opinion by Justice Stevens settled on a "narrow reading" of the Labeling Act that tested § 5(b)'s pre-emptive effect under a claim-by-claim approach. * * * This approach considered each state-law claim and asked whether it is predicated "on a duty 'based on smoking and health.' " * * * If so, the claim is pre-empted. * * * If, however, the claim is predicated on a "more general obligation" under state law, it may proceed. * * *

Applying a test that it conceded lacked "theoretical elegance," * * * the plurality held that the failure-to-warn claims were pre-empted "to the extent that those claims rel[ied] on omissions or inclusions in ... advertising or promotions" of cigarettes. * * * The same was true for one of the fraud claims, which alleged that the cigarette manufacturers had used their advertising to neutralize the federally required warning labels. * * * The plurality determined that these claims were "predicated on a state-law prohibition against statements ... that tend to minimize the health hazards associated with smoking." * * * Thus, according to the plurality, these state-law claims sought recovery under the theory that the cigarette manufacturer breached a duty based on smoking or health. But the plurality found that the other fraud claim, which alleged misrepresentation or concealment of a material fact, was not pre-empted because it was based on a more general state-law obligation: "the duty not to deceive." * * *

Justice Blackmun, writing for three Justices, departed from the plurality on the antecedent question whether the Labeling Act pre-empted state common-law damages claims at all. * * * He concluded that the phrase " 'State law' " in § 5(b) referred only to "positive enactments such as statutes and regulations." * * * But Justice Blackmun specifically noted that even if state common-law claims were within the scope of the Labeling Act, he could not join the plurality's claim-by-claim approach because he "perceive[d] no principled basis for many of the plurality's asserted distinctions among the common-law claims." * * * Justice Blackmun wrote that Congress could not have "intended to create such a hodgepodge of allowed and disallowed claims when it amended the pre-emption provision in 1970," and lamented the "difficulty lower courts w[ould] encounter in attempting to implement" the plurality's test. * * *

Justice Scalia, writing for two Justices, also faulted the plurality for its claim-by-claim approach. * * * Although he agreed with the plurality that the phrase " 'State law' " in § 5(b) encompassed state common-law claims as well as state statutes and regulations, * * * Justice Scalia objected to the plurality's invocation of a presumption against pre-emption to narrowly interpret § 5(b). * * *Because Congress had expressed its intent to pre-empt state law by enacting § 5(b), the Court's "responsibility [was] to apply to the text ordinary principles of statutory construction." * * * By employing its "newly crafted doctrine of narrow construction," Justice Scalia wrote, the plurality arrived at a cramped and unnatural construction of § 5(b) that failed to give effect to the statutory text. * * *

Applying "ordinary principles" of statutory construction, * * * Justice Scalia determined that the proper test for pre-emption of state-law claims under § 5(b) was far less complicated than the plurality's claim-by-claim approach. As he explained, "[o]nce one is forced to select a consistent methodology for evaluating whether a given legal duty is 'based on smoking and health,' it becomes obvious that the methodology must focus not upon the ultimate source of the duty * * * but upon its proximate application." * * * This "proximate application" test, therefore, focuses not on the state-law duty invoked by the plaintiff, but on the effect of the suit on the cigarette manufacturer's conduct—i.e., the "requirement" or "prohibition" that would be imposed under state law. Put simply, if, "whatever the source of the duty, [the claim] imposes an obligation * * * because of the effect of smoking upon health," it is pre-empted * * * ("The test for pre-emption in this setting should be one of practical compulsion, i.e., whether the law practically compels the manufacturers to engage in behavior that Congress has barred the States from prescribing directly"). Justice Scalia also seconded Justice Blackmun's concern that the lower courts would find the plurality's distinctions between materially identical state-law claims to be incapable of application: "A disposition that raises more questions than it answers does not serve the country well." * * *

II

Sixteen years later, we must confront *Cipollone* to resolve the question presented in this case: whether respondents' class-action claims for fraudulent marketing under the MUTPA are pre-empted by § 5(b) of the Labeling Act. The majority adheres to *Cipollone* because it "remain[s] persuaded" that the plurality's construction of § 5(b) was " 'fair.' " * * * I disagree. The Court should discard the *Cipollone* plurality's ill-conceived predicate-duty approach and replace it with Justice Scalia's far more workable and textually sound "proximate application" test.

The majority does not assert that the *Cipollone* plurality opinion is binding precedent, and rightly so. Because the "plurality opinion ... did not represent the views of a majority of the Court, we are not bound by its reasoning." * * * At most, *Cipollone* is a "point of reference for further discussion." * * * But even if the plurality opinion had some force beyond its mere persuasive value, it nevertheless should be abandoned. It is unworkable; it has been overtaken by more recent decisions of this Court; and it cannot be reconciled with a commonsense reading of the text of § 5(b).

A

As predicted by a majority of the Justices in *Cipollone,* the plurality opinion's claim-by-claim approach has proved unworkable in the lower federal courts and state courts. The District Court in this case properly observed that "courts remain divided about what the decision means and how to apply it" and that "*Cipollone*'s distinctions, though clear in theory, defy clear application." * * * Other courts have expressed similar frustration with the *Cipollone* framework. * * *

* * * We owe far more to the lower courts, which depend on this Court's guidance, and to litigants, who must conform their actions to the Court's interpretation of federal law. The *Cipollone* plurality's test for pre-emption under § 5(b) should be abandoned for this reason alone.

B

Furthermore, in the years since *Cipollone* was decided, this Court has altered its doctrinal approach to express pre-emption. The *Cipollone* plurality justified what it described as the "theoretical [in] elegance" of its construction of § 5(b) by relying on the presumption against pre-emption, which, it argued, required a narrow, but "fair," construction of the statute. * * * Of course, as Justice Scalia explained, there was nothing "fair" about imposing an artificially narrow construction on the Labeling Act's pre-emption provision. * * *

Since *Cipollone*, the Court's reliance on the presumption against pre-emption has waned in the express pre-emption context. * * * Most * * * decisions since *Cipollone* also * * * refrained from invoking the presumption in the context of express pre-emption. * * * The Court has invoked the presumption sporadically during this timeframe.

* * *

D

Finally, * * * Congress chose a uniform federal standard. Under the Labeling Act, Congress "establish[ed] a comprehensive Federal Program to deal with cigarette labeling and advertising," 15 U.S.C. § 1331, so that "commerce and the national economy may . . . not [be] impeded by diverse, nonuniform, and confusing cigarette labeling and advertising regulations with respect to any relationship between smoking and health," § 1331(2)(B)4 The majority's distorted interpretation of § 5(b) defeats this express congressional purpose, opening the door to an untold number of deceptive-practices lawsuits across the country. The question whether marketing a light cigarette is " 'misrepresentative' " in light of compensatory behavior "would almost certainly be answered differently from State to State." *Cipollone*, 505 U.S. at 553 (Scalia, J., concurring in judgment in part and dissenting in part). This will inevitably result in the nonuniform imposition of liability for the marketing of light and/or low-tar cigarettes—the precise problem that Congress intended § 5(b) to remedy.

In light of these serious flaws in the majority's approach, even if the *Cipollone* plurality opinion were binding precedent, the Court "should not hesitate to allow our precedent to yield to the true meaning of an Act of Congress when our statutory precedent is 'unworkable' or 'badly reasoned.' " * * * Where, as here, there is "confusion following a splintered decision," that "is itself a reason for reexamining that decision." * * *

III

* * * Respondents, longtime smokers of Marlboro Lights, claim that they have suffered an injury as a result of petitioners' decision to advertise these cigarettes as "light" and/or "low-tar and low-nicotine products." * * * They claim that petitioners marketed their cigarettes as "light"

and/or "low-tar and low-nicotine products" despite knowledge that light-cigarette smokers would engage in compensatory behavior causing them to inhale at least as much tar and nicotine as smokers of regular cigarettes. * * * Respondents thus allege that they were misled into thinking that they were gaining a health advantage by smoking the light cigarettes, and, as a result, petitioners' conduct was an "unfair or deceptive act or practice" under the MUTPA.

Respondents' claims seek to impose liability on petitioners because of the effect that smoking light cigarettes had on their health. The alleged misrepresentation here—that "light" and "low-tar" cigarettes are not as healthy as advertised—is actionable *only* because of the effect that smoking light and low-tar cigarettes had on respondents' health. Otherwise, any alleged misrepresentation about the effect of the cigarettes on health would be immaterial for purposes of the MUTPA and would not be the source of the injuries that provided the impetus for the class-action lawsuit. * * * Therefore, with this suit, respondents seek to *require* the cigarette manufacturers to provide additional warnings about compensatory behavior, or to *prohibit* them from selling these products with the "light" or "low-tar" descriptors. This is exactly the type of lawsuit that is pre-empted by the Labeling Act. * * *

IV

The Court today elects to convert the *Cipollone* plurality opinion into binding law, notwithstanding its weakened doctrinal foundation, its atextual construction of the statute, and the lower courts' inability to apply its methodology. The resulting confusion about the nature of a claim's "predicate duty" and inevitable disagreement in the lower courts as to what type of representations are "material" and "misleading" will have the perverse effect of increasing the nonuniformity of state regulation of cigarette advertising, the exact problem that Congress intended § 5(b) to remedy. It may even force us to yet again revisit the Court's interpretation of the Labeling Act. Because I believe that respondents' claims are pre-empted under § 5(b) of the Labeling Act, I respectfully dissent.

A few months after the Supreme Court handed down its decision in *Altria*, the D.C. Circuit delivered a victory to the Department of Justice in an action against the tobacco industry, ending an eleven-year litigation battle. In *United States v. Philip Morris USA, Inc.*,[118] the court held that cigarette manufacturers and tobacco-related trade organizations deceived the American public about health effects of smoking and environmental tobacco smoke, addictiveness of nicotine, and health benefits from low tar "light" cigarettes. The court specifically found that cigarette manufacturers' use of terms "light" and "low tar" to describe their low tar and nicotine cigarettes was misleading, that cigarette manufacturers fraudulently denied adverse health effects of secondhand smoke and intentionally

118. United States v. Philip Morris USA, Inc., 566 F.3d 1095 (D.C. Cir. 2009).

made representations disputing addictiveness of cigarettes to mislead the public. Moreover, the court upheld the district court's decision that cigarette manufacturers violated the Racketeer Influenced and Corrupt Organizations Act ("RICO") by conspiring to engage in some of these actions. Pursuant to the D.C. Circuit's decision, cigarette manufacturers rebranded their product lines, stopped using banned words like "light" or "mild," and instead started using visual codes to suggest that the newly packaged cigarettes are better in some way from "regular cigarettes" and look like "light cigarettes."[119]

Questions

1. What are the characteristics of federal laws that are likely to make them favorable to defendants like the tobacco companies, or at least more favorable than state laws? What are the characteristics of state laws that may make them more favorable to plaintiffs than to defendants like the tobacco companies?

2. The National Traffic and Motor Vehicle Safety Act of 1966 (the "Safety Act") provides that "[c]ompliance with a motor vehicle safety standard prescribed under this chapter does not exempt a person from liability at common law."[120] In *Williamson v. Mazda Motor of America, Inc.*,[121] motor vehicle accident victims brought suit against a minivan manufacturer arguing that although the manufacturer installed seatbelts in compliance with the federal safety standards, under state law it was liable for not installing safer seatbelts. The Supreme Court ruled for the plaintiffs, holding that the federal safety standards did not preempt their state tort claims. In a concurring opinion, Justice Thomas stressed his view that the plain text of the relevant statute, rather than the majority's more complex analysis, should resolve the case: The Safety Act's saving clause speaks directly to the question and bans preemption.

(a) Is liability under state law for design choices equivalent to liability under state law for advertising and misrepresentations? (b) When, if ever, is it desirable to have both federal and state regulations of manufacturers?

3. In his famous dissent in *New State Ice Co. v. Liebmann*, Justice Brandeis summarized his views of state regulation: "To stay experimentation in things social and economic is a grave responsibility. Denial of the right to experiment may be fraught with serious consequences to the nation. It is one of the happy incidents of the federal system that a single courageous state may, if its citizens choose, serve as a laboratory; and try novel social and economic experiments without risk to the rest of the country."[122] Under what circumstances is state regulation "without risk to the rest of the country"? Should federal regulations preempt all state

---

119. *See, e.g.*, Duff Wilson, *Coded to Obey Law, Lights Become Marlboro Gold*, NEW YORK TIMES, Feb. 19, 2010, at B1.

120. 49 U.S.C. § 30103(e).

121. 131 S.Ct. 1131 (2011).

122. New State Ice Co. v. Liebmann, 285 U.S. 262 (1932).

regulations that create or increase risks to other states or to the country as a whole?

On June 22, 2009, President Barack Obama signed into law the Family Smoking Prevention and Tobacco Control Act (the "Tobacco Control Act").[123] Earlier that month, an overwhelming majority at both houses of Congress voted for the Act. The Tobacco Control Act, which grants the Food and Drug Administration (FDA) the power to regulate tobacco products, reshapes the mandatory cigarette label and advertising warnings, and requires tobacco companies to disclose to the FDA all delivery methods of nicotine, all ingredients of their products and changes thereof, and any research into the health, toxicological, behavioral, or physiologic effects of tobacco products. The Tobacco Control Act reformed tobacco regulation in the United States and its most significant innovation was the express delegation of the power to regulate tobacco to the FDA. In *FDA v. Brown & Williamson Tobacco Corp.*, 529 U.S. 120 (2000), the Supreme Court ruled that under prior law the FDA had no jurisdiction to regulate tobacco.

Food and Drug Administration v. Brown & Williamson Tobacco Corp.

529 U.S. 120 (2000)

■ JUSTICE O'CONNOR delivered the opinion of the Court.

This case involves one of the most troubling public health problems facing our Nation today: the thousands of premature deaths that occur each year because of tobacco use. In 1996, the Food and Drug Administration (FDA), after having expressly disavowed any such authority since its inception, asserted jurisdiction to regulate tobacco products. *See* 61 Fed. Reg. 44619–45318. The FDA concluded that nicotine is a "drug" within the meaning of the Food, Drug, and Cosmetic Act (FDCA or Act), 52 Stat. 1040, as amended, 21 U.S.C. § 301 et seq., and that cigarettes and smokeless tobacco are "combination products" that deliver nicotine to the body. 61 Fed.Reg. 44397 (1996). Pursuant to this authority, it promulgated regulations intended to reduce tobacco consumption among children and adolescents. * * * The agency believed that, because most tobacco consumers begin their use before reaching the age of 18, curbing tobacco use by minors could substantially reduce the prevalence of addiction in future generations and thus the incidence of tobacco-related death and disease. * * *

Regardless of how serious the problem an administrative agency seeks to address, however, it may not exercise its authority "in a manner that is inconsistent with the administrative structure that Congress enacted into law." * * * And although agencies are generally entitled to deference in the interpretation of statutes that they administer, a reviewing "court, as well as the agency, must give effect to the unambiguously expressed intent of

---

123. Pub. L. No. 111–31, 123 Stat. 1845 (2009).

Congress." *Chevron U.S.A. Inc. v. Natural Resources Defense Council, Inc.*, 467 U.S. 837, 842–843 (1984). In this case, we believe that Congress has clearly precluded the FDA from asserting jurisdiction to regulate tobacco products. * * *

I

The FDCA grants the FDA, as the designee of the Secretary of Health and Human Services (HHS), the authority to regulate, among other items, "drugs" and "devices." *See* 21 U.S.C. §§ 321(g)–(h), 393 * * * The Act defines "drug" to include "articles (other than food) intended to affect the structure or any function of the body." 21 U.S.C. § 321(g)(1)(C). It defines "device," in part, as "an instrument, apparatus, implement, machine, contrivance, * * * or other similar or related article, including any component, part, or accessory, which is * * * intended to affect the structure or any function of the body." § 321(h). The Act also grants the FDA the authority to regulate so-called "combination products," which "constitute a combination of a drug, device, or biological product." § 353(g)(1). The FDA has construed this provision as giving it the discretion to regulate combination products as drugs, as devices, or as both. *See* 61 Fed.Reg. 44400 (1996). * * *

On August 28, 1996, the FDA issued a final rule entitled "Regulations Restricting the Sale and Distribution of Cigarettes and Smokeless Tobacco to Protect Children and Adolescents." * * * The FDA determined that nicotine is a "drug" and that cigarettes and smokeless tobacco are "drug delivery devices," and therefore it had jurisdiction under the FDCA to regulate tobacco products as customarily marketed—that is, without manufacturer claims of therapeutic benefit. * * * First, the FDA found that tobacco products " 'affect the structure or any function of the body' " because nicotine "has significant pharmacological effects." * * * Specifically, nicotine "exerts psychoactive, or mood-altering, effects on the brain" that cause and sustain addiction, have both tranquilizing and stimulating effects, and control weight. * * * Second, the FDA determined that these effects were "intended" under the FDCA because they "are so widely known and foreseeable that [they] may be deemed to have been intended by the manufacturers," * * *; consumers use tobacco products "predominantly or nearly exclusively" to obtain these effects, * * *; and the statements, research, and actions of manufacturers revealed that they "have 'designed' cigarettes to provide pharmacologically active doses of nicotine to consumers," * * *. Finally, the agency concluded that cigarettes and smokeless tobacco are "combination products" because, in addition to containing nicotine, they include device components that deliver a controlled amount of nicotine to the body. * * *

Having resolved the jurisdictional question, the FDA next explained the policy justifications for its regulations, detailing the deleterious health effects associated with tobacco use. It found that tobacco consumption was "the single leading cause of preventable death in the United States." * * * According to the FDA, "[m]ore than 400,000 people die each year from tobacco-related illnesses, such as cancer, respiratory illnesses, and heart disease." *Ibid*. The agency also determined that the only way to reduce the amount of tobacco-related illness and mortality was to reduce the level of addiction, a goal that could be accomplished only by preventing children and adolescents from starting to use tobacco. * * * The FDA found that 82% of adult smokers had their first cigarette before the age of 18, and more than half had already become regular smokers by that age. * * *

Based on these findings, the FDA promulgated regulations concerning tobacco products' promotion, labeling, and accessibility to children and adolescents. * * *

The FDA promulgated these regulations pursuant to its authority to regulate "restricted devices." *See* 21 U.S.C. § 360j(e). The FDA construed § 353(g)(1) as giving it the discretion to regulate "combination products" using the Act's drug authorities, device authorities, or both, depending on "how the public health goals of the act can be best accomplished." 61 Fed.Reg. 44403 (1996). * * * The FDA reasoned that its regulations fell within the authority granted by § 360j(e) because they related to the sale or distribution of tobacco products and were necessary for providing a reasonable assurance of safety. 61 Fed.Reg. 44405–44407 (1996).

Respondents, a group of tobacco manufacturers, retailers, and advertisers [are] challenging the regulations. * * * We granted the federal parties' petition for certiorari * * * to determine whether the FDA has authority under the FDCA to regulate tobacco products as customarily marketed.

II

The FDA's assertion of jurisdiction to regulate tobacco products is founded on its conclusions that nicotine is a "drug" and that cigarettes and smokeless tobacco are "drug delivery devices." Again, the FDA found that tobacco products are "intended" to deliver the pharmacological effects of satisfying addiction, stimulation and tranquilization, and weight control because those effects are foreseeable to any reasonable manufacturer, consumers use tobacco products to obtain those effects, and tobacco manufacturers have designed their products to produce those effects. 61 Fed.Reg. 44632–44633 (1996). As an initial matter, respondents take issue with the FDA's reading of "intended," arguing that it is a term of art that refers exclusively to claims made by the manufacturer or vendor about the product. * * * That is, a product is not a drug or device under the FDCA unless the manufacturer or vendor makes some express claim concerning the product's therapeutic benefits. * * * We need not resolve this question, however, because assuming, arguendo, that a product can be "intended to affect the structure or any function of the body" absent claims of therapeutic or medical benefit, the FDA's claim to jurisdiction contravenes the clear intent of Congress.

A threshold issue is the appropriate framework for analyzing the FDA's assertion of authority to regulate tobacco products. Because this case involves an administrative agency's construction of a statute that it administers, our analysis is governed by *Chevron U.S.A. Inc. v. Natural Resources Defense Council, Inc.*, 467 U.S. 837 (1984). Under *Chevron*, a reviewing court must first ask "whether Congress has directly spoken to the precise question at issue." * * * If Congress has done so, the inquiry is at an end; the court "must give effect to the unambiguously expressed intent of Congress." * * * But if Congress has not specifically addressed the question, a reviewing court must respect the agency's construction of the statute so long as it is permissible. * * * Such deference is justified because "[t]he responsibilities for assessing the wisdom of such policy choices and resolving the struggle between competing views of the public interest are not judicial ones," *Chevron*, at 866, and because of the agency's greater familiarity with the ever-changing facts and circumstances surrounding the subjects regulated, *see Rust v. Sullivan*, 500 U.S. 173, 187 (1991).

In determining whether Congress has specifically addressed the question at issue, a reviewing court should not confine itself to examining a particular statutory provision in isolation. The meaning—or ambiguity—of certain words or phrases may only become evident when placed in context. * * *

With these principles in mind, we find that Congress has directly spoken to the issue here and precluded the FDA's jurisdiction to regulate tobacco products.

A

Viewing the FDCA as a whole, it is evident that one of the Act's core objectives is to ensure that any product regulated by the FDA is "safe" and "effective" for its intended use. *See* 21 U.S.C. § 393(b)(2) * * * (defining the FDA's mission). * * * This essential purpose pervades the FDCA. For instance, 21 U.S.C. § 393(b)(2) * * * defines the FDA's "[m]ission" to include "protect[ing] the public health by ensuring that * * * drugs are safe and effective" and that "there is reasonable assurance of the safety and effectiveness of devices intended for human use." * * * Thus, the Act generally requires the FDA to prevent the marketing of any drug or device where the "potential for inflicting death or physical injury is not offset by the possibility of therapeutic benefit." *United States v. Rutherford*, 442 U.S. 544, 556 (1979).

In its rulemaking proceeding, the FDA quite exhaustively documented that "tobacco products are unsafe," "dangerous," and "cause great pain and suffering from illness." 61 Fed.Reg. 44412 (1996). It found that the consumption of tobacco products presents "extraordinary health risks," and that "tobacco use is the single leading cause of preventable death in the United States." * * * These findings logically imply that, if tobacco products were "devices" under the FDCA, the FDA would be required to remove them from the market. * * *

In fact, * * * the FDA itself has previously taken the position that if tobacco products were within its jurisdiction, "they would have to be removed from the market because it would be impossible to prove they were safe for their intended us[e]." * * *

Congress, however, has foreclosed the removal of tobacco products from the market. A provision of the United States Code currently in force states that "[t]he marketing of tobacco constitutes one of the greatest basic industries of the United States with ramifying activities which directly affect interstate and foreign commerce at every point, and stable conditions therein are necessary to the general welfare." 7 U.S.C. § 1311(a).* More

---

* [The Fair and Equitable Tobacco Reform Act ("FETRA") of 2004 that was part of the American Job Creation Act of 2004, Pub L. No. 108–357, 118 Stat. 1418 (Oct. 22, 2004)

importantly, Congress has directly addressed the problem of tobacco and health through legislation on six occasions since 1965. *See* Federal Cigarette Labeling and Advertising Act (FCLAA), Pub. L. No. 89–92, 79 Stat. 282 (1965); Public Health Cigarette Smoking Act of 1969, Pub. L. No. 91–222, 84 Stat. 87 (1969); Alcohol and Drug Abuse Amendments of 1983, Pub. L. No. 98–24, 97 Stat. 175 (1983); Comprehensive Smoking Education Act, Pub. L. No. 98–474, 98 Stat. 2200 (1984); Comprehensive Smokeless Tobacco Health Education Act of 1986, Pub. L No. 99–252, 100 Stat. 30 (1986); Alcohol, Drug Abuse, and Mental Health Administration Reorganization Act, Pub. L. No. 102–321, § 202, 106 Stat. 394 (1988). When Congress enacted these statutes, the adverse health consequences of tobacco use were well known, as were nicotine's pharmacological effects. * * * Nonetheless, Congress stopped well short of ordering a ban. Instead, it has generally regulated the labeling and advertisement of tobacco products, expressly providing that it is the policy of Congress that "commerce and the national economy may be * * * protected to the maximum extent consistent with" consumers "be[ing] adequately informed about any adverse health effects." 15 U.S.C. § 1331. Congress' decisions to regulate labeling and advertising and to adopt the express policy of protecting "commerce and the national economy * * * to the maximum extent" reveal its intent that tobacco products remain on the market. * * *

The FDA apparently recognized this dilemma and concluded, somewhat ironically, that tobacco products are actually "safe" within the meaning of the FDCA. In promulgating its regulations, the agency conceded that "tobacco products are unsafe, as that term is conventionally understood." 61 Fed.Reg. 44412 (1996). Nonetheless, the FDA reasoned that, in determining whether a device is safe under the Act, it must consider "not only the risks presented by a product but also any of the countervailing effects of use of that product, including the consequences of not permitting the product to be marketed." *Id.*, at 44412–44413. Applying this standard, the FDA found that, because of the high level of addiction among tobacco users, a ban would likely be "dangerous." *Id.*, at 44413. In particular, current tobacco users could suffer from extreme withdrawal, the health care system and available pharmaceuticals might not be able to meet the treatment demands of those suffering from withdrawal, and a black market offering cigarettes even more dangerous than those currently sold legally would likely develop. *Ibid.* The FDA therefore concluded that, "while taking cigarettes and smokeless tobacco off the market could prevent some people from becoming addicted and reduce death and disease for others, the record does not establish that such a ban is the appropriate public health response under the act." *Id.*, at 44398.

It may well be, as the FDA asserts, that "these factors must be considered when developing a regulatory scheme that achieves the best public health result for these products." *Id.*, at 44413. But the FDA's judgment that leaving tobacco products on the market "is more effective in achieving public health goals than a ban," *ibid.*, is no substitute for the specific safety determinations required by the FDCA's various operative

---

repealed this statutory language. FETRA terminated the federal tobacco quota and price support programs that this finding justified. 118 Stat. 1522.].

provisions. Several provisions in the Act require the FDA to determine that the product itself is safe as used by consumers. That is, the product's probable therapeutic benefits must outweigh its risk of harm. * * * In contrast, the FDA's conception of safety would allow the agency, with respect to each provision of the FDCA that requires the agency to determine a product's "safety" or "dangerousness," to compare the aggregate health effects of alternative administrative actions. This is a qualitatively different inquiry. Thus, although the FDA has concluded that a ban would be "dangerous," it has not concluded that tobacco products are "safe" as that term is used throughout the Act.

* * * To accommodate the FDA's conception of safety, * * * one must read "any probable benefit to health" to include the benefit to public health stemming from adult consumers' continued use of tobacco products. * * * In other words, the FDA is forced to contend that the very evil it seeks to combat is a "benefit to health." This is implausible.

* * *

Considering the FDCA as a whole, it is clear that Congress intended to exclude tobacco products from the FDA's jurisdiction. * * *

B

In determining whether Congress has spoken directly to the FDA's authority to regulate tobacco, we must also consider in greater detail the tobacco-specific legislation that Congress has enacted over the past 35 years. At the time a statute is enacted, it may have a range of plausible meanings. Over time, however, subsequent acts can shape or focus those meanings. * * *

Congress has enacted six separate pieces of legislation since 1965 addressing the problem of tobacco use and human health. * * * Those statutes, among other things, require that health warnings appear on all packaging and in all print and outdoor advertisements* * *; prohibit the advertisement of tobacco products through "any medium of electronic communication" subject to regulation by the Federal Communications Commission (FCC), * * *; require the Secretary of HHS to report every three years to Congress on research findings concerning "the addictive property of tobacco," * * *; and make States' receipt of certain federal block grants contingent on their making it unlawful "for any manufacturer, retailer, or distributor of tobacco products to sell or distribute any such product to any individual under the age of 18."

In adopting each statute, Congress has acted against the backdrop of the FDA's consistent and repeated statements that it lacked authority under the FDCA to regulate tobacco absent claims of therapeutic benefit by the manufacturer. In fact, on several occasions over this period, * * * Congress considered and rejected bills that would have granted the FDA such jurisdiction. Under these circumstances, it is evident that Congress' tobacco-specific statutes have effectively ratified the FDA's long-held position that it lacks jurisdiction under the FDCA to regulate tobacco products. Congress has created a distinct regulatory scheme to address the problem of tobacco and health, and that scheme, as presently constructed, precludes any role for the FDA.

* * *

C

* * * Deference under *Chevron* to an agency's construction * * * is premised on the theory that a statute's ambiguity constitutes an implicit delegation from Congress to the agency to fill in the statutory gaps. * * * In extraordinary cases, however, there may be reason to hesitate before concluding that Congress has intended such an implicit delegation. * * *

This is hardly an ordinary case. Contrary to its representations to Congress since 1914, the FDA has now asserted jurisdiction to regulate an industry constituting a significant portion of the American economy. * * * Owing to its unique place in American history and society, tobacco has its own unique political history. Congress, for better or for worse, has created a distinct regulatory scheme for tobacco products, squarely rejected proposals to give the FDA jurisdiction over tobacco, and repeatedly acted to preclude any agency from exercising significant policymaking authority in the area. Given this history and the breadth of the authority that the FDA has asserted, we are obliged to defer not to the agency's expansive construction of the statute, but to Congress' consistent judgment to deny the FDA this power.

* * *

* * *

By no means do we question the seriousness of the problem that the FDA has sought to address. * * * Nonetheless, no matter how "important, conspicuous, and controversial" the issue, and regardless of how likely the public is to hold the Executive Branch politically accountable, * * * an administrative agency's power to regulate in the public interest must always be grounded in a valid grant of authority from Congress. * * *

It is so ordered.

■ JUSTICE BREYER, with whom JUSTICE STEVENS, JUSTICE SOUTER, and JUSTICE GINSBURG join, dissenting.

The Food and Drug Administration (FDA) has the authority to regulate "articles (other than food) intended to affect the structure or any function of the body." Federal Food, Drug, and Cosmetic Act (FDCA), 21 U.S.C. § 321(g)(1)(C). Unlike the majority, I believe that tobacco products fit within this statutory language.

In its own interpretation, the majority nowhere denies the following two salient points. First, tobacco products (including cigarettes) fall within the scope of this statutory definition, read literally. Cigarettes achieve their mood-stabilizing effects through the interaction of the chemical nicotine and the cells of the central nervous system. Both cigarette manufacturers and smokers alike know of, and desire, that chemically induced result. Hence, cigarettes are "intended to affect" the body's "structure" and "function," in the literal sense of these words.

Second, the statute's basic purpose—the protection of public health—supports the inclusion of cigarettes within its scope. * * * Unregulated tobacco use causes "[m]ore than 400,000 people [to] die each year from tobacco-related illnesses, such as cancer, respiratory illnesses, and heart disease." 61 Fed.Reg. 44398 (1996). Indeed, tobacco products kill more people in this country every year "than * * * AIDS * * * car accidents, alcohol, homicides, illegal drugs, suicides, and fires, *combined*." *Ibid.* (emphasis added).

Despite the FDCA's literal language and general purpose (both of which support the FDA's finding that cigarettes come within its statutory authority), the majority nonetheless reads the statute as excluding tobacco products for two basic reasons:

(1) the FDCA does not "fit" the case of tobacco because the statute requires the FDA to prohibit dangerous drugs or devices (like cigarettes) outright, and the agency concedes that simply banning the sale of cigarettes is not a proper remedy; and

(2) Congress has enacted other statutes, which, when viewed in light of the FDA's long history of denying tobacco-related jurisdiction and considered together with Congress' failure explicitly to grant the agency tobacco-specific authority, demonstrate that Congress did not intend for the FDA to exercise jurisdiction over tobacco.

In my view, neither of these propositions is valid. Rather, the FDCA does not significantly limit the FDA's remedial alternatives. * * * And the later statutes do not tell the FDA it cannot exercise jurisdiction, but simply leave FDA jurisdictional law where Congress found it. * * *

The majority nonetheless reaches the "inescapable conclusion" that the language and structure of the FDCA as a whole "simply do not fit" the kind of public health problem that tobacco creates. That is because, in the majority's view, the FDCA requires the FDA to ban outright "dangerous" drugs or devices (such as cigarettes); yet, the FDA concedes that an immediate and total cigarette-sale ban is inappropriate.

This argument is curious because it leads with similarly "inescapable" force to precisely the opposite conclusion, namely, that the FDA *does* have jurisdiction but that it must ban cigarettes. More importantly, the argument fails to take into account the fact that a statute interpreted as requiring the FDA to pick a more dangerous over a less dangerous remedy would be a perverse statute, *causing,* rather than preventing, unnecessary harm whenever a total ban is likely the more dangerous response. And one can at least imagine such circumstances.

* * *

I concede that, as a matter of logic, one could consider the FDA's "safety" evaluation to be different from its choice of remedies. But to read the statute to forbid the agency from taking account of the realities of consumer behavior either in assessing safety or in choosing a remedy could increase the risks of harm. * * *

In my view, where linguistically permissible, we should interpret the FDCA in light of Congress' overall desire to protect health. That purpose requires a flexible interpretation that both permits the FDA to take into account the realities of human behavior and allows it, in appropriate cases, to choose from its arsenal of statutory remedies. * * *

In the majority's view, laws enacted since 1965 require us to deny jurisdiction, whatever the FDCA might mean in their absence. * * * [These] later statutes do not support the majority's conclusion. That is because, whatever individual Members of Congress after 1964 may have assumed about the FDA's jurisdiction, the laws they enacted did not embody any such "no jurisdiction" assumption. * * *

I now turn to the final historical fact that the majority views as a factor in its interpretation of the subsequent legislative history: the FDA's former denials of its tobacco-related authority.

Until the early 1990's, the FDA expressly maintained that the 1938 statute did not give it the power that it now seeks to assert. It then changed its mind. The majority agrees with me that the FDA's change of positions does not make a significant legal difference. See * * * also *Chevron*, 467 U.S., at 863 ("An initial agency interpretation is not instantly carved in stone"). * * * Nevertheless, it labels those denials "important context" for drawing an inference about Congress' intent. In my view, the FDA's change of policy, like the subsequent statutes themselves, does nothing to advance the majority's position.

* * *

Consequently, I dissent.

Questions

1. In *Brown & Williamson Tobacco Corp.*, the Court applied the *Chevron* doctrine to examine the FDA's interpretation of the FDCA. Justices O'Connor and Breyer presented different approaches to permitted interpretations of risk regulation under FDCA. What are the differences between these approaches?

2. The 2009 Tobacco Control Act gave the FDA authority to regulate tobacco products. Section 907 of the Act, however, provides that "a cigarette or any of its component parts (including the tobacco, filter, or paper) shall not contain, as a constituent (including a smoke constituent) or additive, an artificial or natural flavor (*other than tobacco or menthol*) or an herb or spice, including strawberry, grape, orange, clove, cinnamon, pineapple, vanilla, coconut, licorice, cocoa, chocolate, cherry, or coffee, that is a characterizing flavor of the tobacco product or tobacco smoke. Nothing in this subparagraph shall be construed to limit the [Secretary of Health & Human Services'] authority to take action under this section or other sections of this chapter applicable to menthol or any artificial or natural flavor, herb, or spice not specified in this subparagraph."[124] Empirical evidence shows that menthol is one of the most effective flavors to promote addiction to cigarettes, especially among African Americans, Hispanics, and

124. 21 U.S.C. § 387g (emphasis added).

other racial and ethnic minorities.[125] Why would Congress expressly exempt menthol? Could the FDA still regulate menthol in cigarettes?

---

§ 1.2.3 The Regulatee: Whose Conduct Is Targeted?

Decision-making capacity is a required element for legal liability. Although definitions of "capacity" vary, the general principle is that only a person with decision-making capacity can be liable for his actions. Voluminous bodies of literature have attempted to address the many layers and nuances of this principle. One reflection of the principle in regulatory design is that regulations can be directed only at legal persons with a decision-making capacity to assure that the regulated party (the "regulatee") is responsive to incentives.

* * *

Hogs in New York City

In the eighteenth century and early nineteenth century, pigs were an ordinary feature in the streets of New York and other cities.[126] They provided a necessary public service: Pigs cleaned the streets and other common areas by eating waste and garbage. At the time, local governments operated on a very low budget and could not provide many services. Deploying workers to clean public areas and collect waste and garbage on a regular basis was not a possibility that localities could afford. Pigs therefore served a useful function in the city. In some respects, pigs were a substitute for regulation. Rather than collecting taxes and increasing the size of the government to provide services, nineteenth-century communities relied on private pigs.

On October 19, 1809, the Aldermen in the Common Council of New York City passed the following ordinance:[127]

A Law Respecting Swine

> Whereas, the great number of Swine, which, at present, run at large, in the City of New York, are extremely destructive to the pavements, and in other respects injurious; for remedy whereof

---

125. *See, e.g.*, Neal L. Benowitz & Jonathan M. Samet, *The Threat of Menthol Cigarettes to U.S. Public Health*, 364 NEW ENGLAND JOURNAL OF MEDICINE 2179 (2011); Phillip S. Gardiner, *The African Americanization of Menthol Cigarette Use in the United States*, 6 NICOTINE & TOBACCO RESEARCH S55 (2004); Youn Ok Lee & Stanton A. Glantz, *Menthol: Putting the Pieces Together*, 20 TOBACCO CONTROL ii1 (2011); William J. McCarthy et al., *Menthol vs. Nonmenthol Cigarettes: Effects on Smoking Behavior*, 85 AMERICAN JOURNAL OF PUBLIC HEALTH 67 (1995).

126. *See generally* Henrik Hertog, *Pigs and Positivism*, 1985 WISCONSIN LAW REVIEW 899 (1985). *See also* John Duffy, Hogs, Dogs, and Dirt: Public Health in Early Pittsburgh, 87 PENNSYLVANIA MAGAZINE OF HISTORY AND BIOGRAPHY 294 (1963); David J. Grettler, *Environmental Change and Conflict over Hogs in Early Nineteenth–Century Delaware*, 19 JOURNAL OF THE EARLY REPUBLIC 197 (1999).

127. A copy of the Ordinance is available at *regti.me/NYC-hogs* (case sensitive).

> Be it Ordained by the Mayor, Aldermen and Commonalty of the City of New York in Common Council convened, this nineteenth day of October one thousand eight hundred and nine That from and after the first day of November next no Hog Shoat, pig, or Swine shall be permitted to run at large in any road, street, lane, or alley of the said City unless such hog shoat pig or swine shall have a ring or rings in its nose; so as to prevent it from rooting up any ground or pavement, under the penalty of Three Dollars to be recovered against the owner of any such animal, in any Court having cognizance thereof with costs of suit.
>
> * * *
>
> And be it further Ordained, That the Attorney of the Board [of Health] shall be authorized, after the recovery and receipt of any penalty under & by virtue of this Ordinance, to pay to the person who shall give the said Attorney such information of any offence against this ordinance as shall enable the said Attorney to prosecute the offender to judgment such part thereof, not exceeding one half of the said penalty so recovered and received as in his judgment he shall deem just and proper.

Questions

1. Was the 1809 New York Ordinance a regulation? If so, whose conduct did the Ordinance intend to shape?

2. What was the effect of the Ordinance on cleaning services provided by pigs? If pigs provided an important public service to the City in the early nineteenth century, why did the Aldermen adopt an ordinance that had such an effect?

3. Under the Ordinance, the Attorney of the City's Board of Health was authorized to compensate individuals who informed the authorities about pigs with no nose rings that were running at large in the City. What was the purpose of this provision? What would be the contemporary equivalent of such an award?

4. In November 1969, NBC broadcasted the documentary *The Wolf Men*, depicting the hunting of wolves from aircrafts. The film generated significant public pressure to ban the slaughter of wolves and other wildlife shot from aircrafts.[128] Congress responded to the pressures and passed the Airborne Hunting Act of 1971.[129] The Act prohibits the use of aircraft for harassing, capturing, or killing wildlife. In *United States v. Helsley*, the Ninth Circuit upheld the constitutionality of the Act, holding that the enactment of Airborne Hunting Act of 1971 was within Congressional

---

128. *See Hunting From Aircraft*, Report No. 91–1632, 91st Cong., 2d Sess. (Nov. 25, 1970); *Shooting Animals from Aircraft*, Report No. 92–202, 92nd Cong., 1st Sess. (May 13, 1971); *Shooting Animals from Aircraft*, Report No. 92–202, 92nd Cong., 1st Sess. (Nov. 2, 1971). *See also Alaska Assailed Over Wolf Policy*, New York Times, Dec. 28, 1969.

129. Pub.L.No.92–159, 85 Stat. 480 (1971), available at *regti.me/AHA1971* (case sensitive).

power to regulate interstate commerce.[130] In 2011, forty years after the enactment of the Airborne Hunting Act, the Texas Legislature learned that "feral hogs in Texas are responsible for approximately $400 million in direct damages to Texas every year. There are an estimated two million feral hogs in Texas and feral hogs are found in nearly every county of the state. It is also estimated that for every dollar spent on feral hog control, more than $7.50 in agricultural products is saved. In addition, it is estimated that predation by coyotes causes millions of dollars in economic losses to agricultural producers in the state." And that "[a]ccording to the Department of Agriculture, more than 75 percent of the state has suitable terrain and vegetative cover for hunting feral hogs from helicopters, and such hunting is a cost-effective method."[131] The State Legislature therefore passed the so-called the Pork Copper Bill that allows landowners to contract licensed hunters to shoot feral hogs from helicopters.[132] In June 2011, Governor Rick Perry signed the bill into law.

Whose conduct do the 1971 federal Airborne Hunting Act and the 2011 Texas Pork Chopper law intend to shape?

Rogers v. Higgins

48 Ill. 211 (1868)

■ MR. JUSTICE WALKER delivered the opinion of the Court.

Ann Wright, a married woman, purchased the property in question, in June, 1842, * * * and received a deed of conveyance in May, 1845. Mrs. Wright, and her husband * * * sold the premises in controversy to Mrs. Elizabeth Rogers, the mother of complainant, for the sum of four hundred dollars, and executed to her a conveyance for the property on the 31st day of October, 1845. * * * Mrs. Rogers took possession of the premises soon after the purchase. * * *

Mrs. Wright remained married until early in the year 1860, at which time her husband died, leaving her surviving him as his widow. [O]n or about the 22d day of December, 1863, Mrs. Wright conveyed the premises to Milton O. Higgins, by a quit claim deed; and that Higgins purchased with full notice of the sale to Mrs. Rogers, [who] had paid in full for the lot. [A]fter his purchase, Higgins had commenced a suit * * * against * * * the tenant of complainant, to recover the property. The court below, on a hearing, dismissed the bill at the costs of complainant.

It is not disputed, nor can it be, that at the time this deed was executed and delivered, there was no statute of this State which authorized a married woman, holding real estate in Illinois, to execute a deed for its conveyance. There is no principle of the common law more firmly estab-

130. United States v. Helsley, 615 F.2d 784 (9th Cir. 1979).

131. Committee Report for H.B. 716, 82nd Leg. (Tex. 2011), May 3, 2011.

132. H.B. 716, 82nd Leg. (Tex. 2011), available at *regti.me/TX-Pork* (case sensitive). *See also* Becca Aaronson, *Hogs Can't Fly, but a Texas Bill Allows Their Hunters To*, TEXAS TRIBUNE, May 13, 2011, at A23A.

lished, or uniformly recognized, than, a married woman is incapable of conveying her property by any of the usual deeds executed for the assurance of title to land. Nor can she make any binding contract, unless authorized by legislative enactment. Without such authority, a deed executed by her for the conveyance of her land, or any other contract, is void, and not merely voidable. These are rules familiar to all, * * * but appellant insists that there are equities in this case that entitle him to the relief which he asks. That there is hardship, no one will or can deny. He and his mother, for many years after having paid for it, have occupied the lot, and supposed it to be theirs, never suspecting their title to be defective. * * *

From the earliest antiquity that we can trace the common law, we find that its policy has been to disarm the wife of all power to make any contract valid or binding. It acted upon the principle, that to secure harmony and domestic quiet in the family, there must be a head, and, as far as possible, to avoid the introduction of separate and conflicting interests into its peaceful and quiet domain. And it was supposed that the well-being of society could be best promoted, and the general good advanced, by not permitting the wife to sell or dispose of her separate property, whether real or personal.

As commerce advanced, art and science contributed their mighty influence to the march of progress; the fetters that clogged alienations have from time to time been removed, to answer the wants of the people; and by legislative enactment married women were enabled, with the concurrence of, and by joining with their husbands in a deed, to convey their real estate, and divest themselves of their title. This is as far as our legislature has ever gone in this direction. * * *

As a general rule, all persons deal with individuals laboring under disability, at their peril. The law has not favored such transactions, and it is not its policy to afford relief, or remove the disability for the benefit of those who have so dealt. * * * To enforce and give effect to such agreements in courts of equity, instead of following the law, would be to disregard and violate its provisions, and this is never done. A party dealing with a married woman, must be presumed to know the fact, and to contemplate the legal effect of the act, as he must be presumed to know the law. If this were not so, there could be no protection to idiots, minors or married women, so far as relates to their property. If equity would decree a specific performance of their agreements, * * * it would be simply to permit persons to acquire property in a mode prohibited by the law, and to transfer property which the parties themselves were unable to do, and the law has said they could not, and that such efforts would not be aided or enforced.

A party attempting to purchase from a person under legal disability, does that which he knows the law will not sanction * * * To grant relief in such a case, would violate the policy of the law; would render all the safeguards thrown around the weak and incompetent ineffectual; would invite a violation of the law; would be contrary to the rules of equity, and although it might, in a few cases, promote justice, its general operation would be productive of great wrong and injustice. Parties knowing that the law confers no rights by such agreements, must be left to the consequences of their own rash or inconsiderate acts.

* * * In this case, Mrs. Rogers could not but have known that Mrs. Wright was a married woman, and attempting to sell her real estate, without authority of law. She is presumed to have known the law, and with this presumption, when she received the deed from which she learned, if not before, that Mrs. Wright was a married woman. * * * She should have refused to receive the deed. * * *

We do not propose to consider whether the changes in society require a change of the law placing married women under disability. We find that the common law, as it has descended to us, has, from the remotest period of its history to the present, recognized such disabilities, and our legislature has declared it to be the rule of decision until altered or repealed. If a further change is required, further disabilities removed, it must be left to the general assembly, where it belongs, to afford the relief. It is our province to administer the law as we find it, and not to repeal or modify well settled principles. However forcible and able the arguments presented, to show that the policy of the law should be changed, they should be urged upon the legislative department, and not the judicial, for the change desired.

We perceive no error in this record, and the decree must therefore be affirmed.

Decree affirmed.

Questions

1. In *Higgins*, the court invalidated a sale of property by a married couple because the wife was an active participant in that transaction. What were the stated reasons for the ruling?

2. The *Higgins* court stated two legal rules: (1) married women have no power to make any valid or binding contract, and (2) the legal system does not enforce agreements made with individuals with legal disabilities, such as idiots, minors, and married women. Whose conduct did these rules aim to shape? Was decisionmaking capacity relevant to these rules?

§ 1.3 RULES VS. STANDARDS

When lawmakers design legal norms, they consider (or should consider) whether to craft them as rules or standards.[133] "Rules" state a binding

133. *See generally* Isaac Ehrlich & Richard A. Posner, *An Economic Analysis of Legal Rulemaking*, 3 JOURNAL OF LEGAL STUDIES 257 (1974); Daniel J. Gifford, *Communication of Legal Standards, Policy Development, and Effective Conduct Regulation*, 56 CORNELL LAW REVIEW 409 (1971); Louis Kaplow, *Rules versus Standards: An Economic Analysis*, 42 DUKE LAW JOURNAL 557 (1992); Finn E. Kydland & Edward C. Prescott, *Rules Rather than Discretion: The Inconsistency of Optimal Plans*, 85 JOURNAL OF POLITICAL ECONOMY 473 (1977); Pierre J. Schlag, *Rules and Standards*, 33 UCLA LAW REVIEW 379 (1985); Cass R. Sunstein, *Problems with Rules*, 83 CALIFORNIA LAW REVIEW 953 (1995).

legal outcome that follows from particular facts. Speed limits provide an intuitive illustration of rules. If a person drives faster than the specified speed limit (say, 65 miles per hour), she has violated the law. If she drives at the specified speed limit or below, she has not violated the speed-limit law. "Statutory rape" is another example of rules—a prohibited sexual intercourse with a person under a specified age, where the victim's age precludes the ability to consent to the proscribed activity.[134] Rules confine the discretion that regulatees and law enforcement authorities may exercise. They restrict judgment to facts and negate the need for using discretion and legal analysis. For example, speed limit laws reduce all inquiries into two primaries questions: (1) what is the legal speed limit? and (2) what is the driver's speed?

"Standards" incorporate discretion into the legal norm and assume that the regulatee's judgment can be trusted. For example, the "reasonable person" standard that applies in most areas of law assumes that the regulatee has the time and capacity to determine what a reasonable person of ordinary prudence would have done under the same or similar circumstances. Because standards require discretion, there is uncertainty regarding their application: In hindsight, the regulatee's choices may appear unreasonable to the relevant agency, judge, or jury.[135]

In practice, rules and standards lie on one spectrum: Sometimes vagueness is introduced into legal norms that are worded like rules and precision emerges in legal norms that are framed like standards. For example, the duty of care that applies to directors and officers of businesses—corporations, partnerships, and alike—is the duty to perform their tasks in good faith, with such care, including inquiry, as an ordinarily prudent person in a like position would act under similar circumstances.[136] This norm is framed like a standard. Courts, however, interpret it almost like a rule: in the absence of facts showing self-dealing or improper motives, officers or directors are not legally responsible for losses resulting from decisions they made in good faith.[137] In contrast, the First Amendment is worded like a rule: "Congress shall make no law * * * abridging the freedom of speech." Congress and the Supreme Court, however, have always treated the First Amendment like a standard. Similarly, one dimension of the debate over the Second Amendment is that it is framed like a

---

134. *See, e.g.*, Tenn. Code Ann. § 39–13–506 ("Statutory rape is sexual penetration of a victim by the defendant or of the defendant by the victim when: (1) The victim is at least thirteen (13) but less than fifteen (15) years of age and the defendant is at least four (4) years but less than ten (10) years older than the victim; or (2) The victim is at least fifteen (15) but less than eighteen (18) years of age and the defendant is more than five (5) but less than ten (10) years older than the victim.")

135. *See generally* Kim A. Kamin & Jeffrey J. Rachlinski, *Ex Post ≠ Ex Ante: Determining Liability in Hindsight*, 19 LAW & HUMAN BEHAVIOR 89 (1995); Erin M. Harley, *Hindsight Bias in Legal Decision Making*, 25 SOCIAL COGNITION 48 (2007).

136. *See, e.g.*, Graham v. Allis–Chalmers Manufacturing Co., 188 A.2d 125 (Del. 1963); In re Caremark International Inc. Derivative Litigation, 698 A.2d 959 (Del. Ch. 1996); Smith v. Van Gorkom, 488 A.2d 858 (Del. 1985); In re Walt Disney Co. Derivative Litigation, 907 A.2d 693 (Del. Ch. 2005).

137. *See, e.g.*, Gagliardi v. Trifoods International, Inc., 683 A.2d 1049 (Del. Ch. 1996); Kamin v. American Express Co., 54 A.D.2d 654 (N.Y. 1976); In re Walt Disney Co. Derivative Litigation, 907 A.2d 693 (Del. Ch. 2005).

rule—"the right of the people to keep and bear Arms, shall not be infringed"—but state legislatures, Congress, and courts have always treated this norm like a standard. Some restrictions on the right to bear arms will always exist.[138]

Another example is Section 1 of the Sherman Act. The Act provides: "[e]very contract * * * in restraint of trade * * * is declared to be illegal." Shortly after Congress enacted the Act in 1890, courts discovered that contracts in restraint of trade may be reasonable. For instance, exclusivity agreements between manufacturers and distributors are reasonable when they serve consumers.[139] Thus, in 1911, the Supreme Court determined that the "standard of reason" should guide the interpretation of the phrase "restraint of trade" in Section 1.[140] Since then, Section 1 of the Sherman Act has been governed by rules (per se prohibitions) and standards (the rule of reason).[141]

Many considerations explain the choice of norm.[142] We, however, stress two key considerations. Complexity of activities and uncertainty around their outcome make standards superior to rules. For example, the reasonable person standard is used in law because of the difficulties in defining all contingencies in reality and framing them as rules. Imposing liability on physicians or lawyers through rules is unlikely to be an effective way to accomplish any goal. In contrast, when the targeted activities are simple and can be defined precisely, rules tend to be superior to standards.[143] For example, the speed of driving, the number of hours an employee works a day, and sales of certain products to minors can be defined precisely and using rules to regulate such activities is likely to save resources to all parties.

Montana's Basic Rule

In September 1908, Henry Ford released his revolutionary Ford Model T, the first car that was affordable for middle-class Americans.[144] The Model T was equipped with a 2.9 liter four-cylinder engine that produced

---

138. *See, e.g.*, United States v. Miller, 307 U.S. 174 (1939); District of Columbia v. Heller, 554 U.S. 570 (2008); McDonald v. Chicago, 130 S.Ct. 3020 (2010).

139. *See generally* Howard P. Marvel, *Exclusive Dealing*, 25 JOURNAL OF LAW & ECONOMICS 1 (1982).

140. Standard Oil Co. of New Jersey v. United States, 221 U.S. 1, 60 (1911).

141. Board of Trade of the City of Chicago v. United States, 246 U.S. 231, 238 (1918). *See generally* Daniel A. Crane, *Rules versus Standards in Antitrust Adjudication*, 64 WASHINGTON & LEE LAW REVIEW 49 (2007).

142. *See, e.g.*, Kydland & Prescott, *supra* note 124; Howard Kunreuther & Mark Pauly, *Rules Rather Than Discretion: Lessons from Hurricane Katrina*, 33 JOURNAL OF RISK & UNCERTAINTY 101 (2006).

143. For a related discussion *see* Steven Shavell, *Liability for Harm versus Regulation for Safety*, 13 JOURNAL OF LEGAL STUDIES 357 (1984); Donald Wittman, *Prior Regulation versus Post Liability: The Choice between Input and Output Monitoring*, 6 JOURNAL OF LEGAL STUDIES 193 (1977).

144. *See* ROBERT H. CASEY, THE MODEL T: A CENTENNIAL HISTORY (2008).

20 horsepower and could propel the car at a speed of up to 45 miles per hour. The commercial introduction of the Ford Model T made its mark on American roads: cars appeared everywhere and brought with them new risks and costly accidents. States and localities responded by adjusting their laws to address the risks presented by the new powerful machines.[145]

In March 1915, Montana revised its rudimentary traffic laws, *Montana's Laws of the Road*. The 1915 Act defined the new technology of "motor vehicles" as "all vehicles propelled by any power other than muscular power, excepting rail road and railway cars and motor vehicles running only upon rails or tracks." The Act also introduced some new traffic rules for motor vehicles, such as restrictions against employing drunk drivers[146] and basic driving measures to mitigate the risks of accidents.[147] Most importantly, the 1915 Act introduced the first standardized speed limit for motor vehicles in Montana. The 1915 Act provided:

> No automobile or other motor vehicle shall be run on any public highway outside of the limits of any city, fire district, or thickly settled or business part of a town, at a speed exceeding thirty miles an hour; and no such vehicle shall be run on any public way within the limits of a city, fire district, or of any thickly settled or business part of a town at a speed exceeding eight miles an hour.[148]

Two years later, in March 1917, Montana replaced the speed-limit rule with a standard:

> *Speed Regulations.*—Every person operating or driving a vehicle of any character on a public highway of this state shall drive the same in a careful and prudent manner and at a rate of speed no greater than is reasonable and proper under the conditions existing at the point of operation, taking into account amount and character of traffic, condition of brakes, weight of vehicle, grade and width of highway, condition of surface, and freedom of obstruction to view ahead, and so as not to unduly or unreasonably endanger the life, limb, property or other rights of any person entitled to the use of the street or highway. Provided, however, that cities and towns may by ordinance, regulate speed and traffic upon the streets, within the incorporated limits.[149]

The Montana's "reasonable and proper" speed-limit standard was not innovative in any way. Montana followed the footsteps of many other states that had already adopted this standard.[150] Montana, however, adhered to a

---

145. *See generally* STEPHEN B. GODDARD, GETTING THERE: THE EPIC STRUGGLE BETWEEN ROAD AND RAIL IN THE AMERICAN CENTURY (1994).

146. Section 2 of the 1915 Act (codified as § 1406 of Montana Political Code of 1915) provided: "No person must employ to drive any vehicle for the conveyance of passengers upon any public highway or road, a person addicted to drunkenness, under penalty of five dollars ($5) for every day such person in his employ."

147. Section 1 of the 1915 Act (codified as § 1405 of Montana Political Code of 1915) provided: "When vehicles meet, the driver of each must turn reasonable to the right of the center of the highway of road, so as to pass without interference * * *."

148. Section 2 of the 1915 Act (codified as § 1414 of Montana Political Code of 1915).

149. Section 7 of the 1917 Act, Mt. Rev. Codes § 1742 (1917).

150. *See, e.g.*, Brown v. New Haven Taxicab Co., 93 Conn. 251 (1919); Hardy v. Georgia, 25 Ga.App. 287 (1920); Illinois v. Kuchta, 296 Ill. 180 (1920); Kansas v. Bailey, 107 Kan. 637

speed-limit standard, many years after other states switched to speed-limit rules. In 1955, Montana revised again its speed-limit law and introduced its "*Basic Rule*":

ARTICLE I
WORDS AND PHRASES DEFINED

* * *

Section 2. (a) *Vehicle.* Every device, in upon, or by which any person or property is or may be transported or drawn upon a highway, except devices moved by human power or used exclusively upon stationary rails or tracks.

(b) *Motor Vehicle.* Every vehicle which is self-propelled and every vehicle which is propelled by electric power obtained from overhead trolley wired, but not operated upon train rails.

* * *

ARTICLE V
SPEED RESTRICTIONS

Section 41. (a) *Basic Rule.* Every person operating or driving a vehicle of any character on a public highway of this state shall drive the same in a careful and prudent manner, at a rate of speed no greater than is reasonable and proper under the conditions existing at the point of operation, taking into account amount and character of traffic, condition of brakes, weight of vehicle, grade and width of highway, condition of surface, and freedom of obstruction to view ahead, and so as not to unduly or unreasonably endanger the life, limb, property, or other rights of any person entitled to the use of the street or highway.

(b) *Maximums Otherwise.* Where no special hazard exist that requires lower speed for compliance with paragraph (a) of this section the speed of any vehicle not in excess of the limits specified in this section or established as hereinafter authorized, shall be lawful, but any speed in excess of the limits specified in this section or established as hereinafter authorized shall be unlawful:

1. Twenty-five (25) miles per hour in any urban district;

2. Thirty-five (35) miles per hour on any highways under construction or repairs;

3. Fifty-five (55) miles per hour in such other locations during the night time;

"Daytime" Defined. Daytime means from a half (½) hour before sunrise to a half (½) hour after sunset. Nighttime means at any other hour.[151]

(1920); Leis v. Cleveland R. Co., 101 Ohio St. 162 (1920); People v. Mellen, 172 N.Y.S. 165 (Co.Ct. 1918); Reader v. Ottis, 147 Minn. 335 (1920); Washington v. Randall, 107 Wash. 695 (1919); Weygandt v. Bartle, 88 Or. 310 (1918).

151. Mont. Code Ann. § 61–8–303 (1973).

This law governed the Montana's roads until 1974. In the wake of the Arab oil embargo in 1974, Congress enacted the Federal Aid Highways Amendments of 1974[152] that imposed national maximum speed limit of 55 miles per hour.[153] Although the triggering event for a national standard of speed limit was increasing energy costs, Congress also linked speed to risk and emphasized that the new standard could save lives.[154] Congress did not order states to adjust their speed limits to the new national standard, but attached a painful sanction for noncompliance: denial of all future federal highway grants.[155] Montana immediately adopted the national standard and amended its speed restrictions as follows:

> 61–8–303. *Speed restrictions—Basic Rule.* (1) A person operating or driving a vehicle * * * shall drive it in a careful and prudent manner, and at a rate of speed no greater than is reasonable and proper under the conditions * * *
>
> (2) Where no special hazard exists that requires lower speed for compliance with subsection (1) of this section, * * * but a speed in excess of those limits is unlawful:
>
> (a) 25 miles per hour in an urban district;
>
> (b) 35 miles per hour on a highway under construction or repair;
>
> (c) 55 miles per hour in other locations during the nighttime, except that the nighttime speed limit on completed sections of interstate highways is 65 miles per hour.
>
> (3) "Daytime" means from one-half hour before sunrise to one-half hour after sunset. "Nighttime" means at any other hour.
>
> * * *
>
> 61–8–304. *Declaration of Speed Limits—Exception to the Basic Rule.* The attorney general shall declare by proclamation filed with the secretary of state a speed limit for all motor vehicles on all public streets and highways in the state whenever the establishment of such a speed limit by the state is required by federal law as a condition to the state's continuing eligibility to receive funds authorized by the Federal Aid Highway Act of 1973 [sic] and all acts amendatory thereto or any other federal statute. Such speed limit may not be less than that required by federal law, and the attorney general shall by further proclamation change the speed limit adopted pursuant to this section to comply with federal law. * * * A speed limit imposed pursuant to this section is an exception to the basic rule requirements of 61–8–303 and a speed in

---

152. Pub. L. 93–239, 87 Stat. 1046 (1974).

153. § 2 of the Federal Aid Highways Amendments of 1974.

154. *See* H.R. Rep. No. 93–1567 (Dec. 11, 1974); Marks v. Mobil Oil Corp., 562 F.Supp. 759, 771–72 (E.D. Pa. 1983). *See also* Lilliard E. Richardson Jr. & David J. Houston, *Federalism and Safety on America's Highways*, 39 JOURNAL OF FEDERALISM 117, 122–124 (2008).

155. *See* Nevada v. Skinner, 884 F.2d 445 (9th Cir.1989), *cert. denied*, 493 U.S. 1070 (1990).

excess of the speed limit established pursuant to this section is unlawful notwithstanding any provision of 61–8–303.

In November 1995, Congress passed the National Highway System Designation Act[156] that repealed the national maximum speed limit.[157] The repeal of the national speed limit revived Montana's Basic Rule. A few months later, in March 1996, a Montanan, Rudy Stanko, received a speeding ticket for driving his car at a speed of 85 miles per hour at a location where the police officer concluded it was unsafe to do so. Stanko was subsequently convicted for violating Montana's Basic Rule.[158] He appealed and challenged the constitutionality of the Basic Rule, arguing that it was "unconstitutionally vague." The Montana Supreme Court held that

> It is evident * * * that the average motorist in Montana would have no idea of the speed at which he or she could operate his or her motor vehicle on this State's highways without violating Montana's "basic rule" based simply on the speed at which he or she is traveling. Furthermore, the basic rule not only permits, but requires the kind of arbitrary and discriminatory enforcement that the Due Process clause in general, and the void-for-vagueness doctrine in particular, are designed to prevent.[159]

The Court reversed Stanko's conviction and held that "Montanans cannot be charged, prosecuted, and punished for speed alone without notifying them of the speed at which their conduct violates the law."[160] Following the *Stanko* decision, the Montana Legislature amended the state speed limits to be as follows:

> 61–8–303. *Speed Restrictions*
>
> (1) * * * the speed limit for vehicles traveling:
>
> (a) on a federal-aid interstate highway outside an urbanized area of 50,000 population or more is 75 miles an hour at all times and the speed limit for vehicles traveling on federal-aid interstate highways within an urbanized area of 50,000 population or more is 65 miles an hour at all times;
>
> (b) on any other public highway of this state is 70 miles an hour during the daytime and 65 miles an hour during the nighttime;
>
> (c) in an urban district is 25 miles an hour.
>
> (2) A vehicle subject to the speed limits imposed in subsection (1) traveling on a two-lane road may exceed the speed limits imposed in subsection (1) by 10 miles an hour in order to

---

156. Pub. L. 104–59, 109 Stat. 568 (1995).

157. President Clinton signed the bill into law, noting that he is "deeply disturbed by the repeal of * * * the national maximum speed limit law." Statement on Signing the National Highway System Designation Act of 1995, 1995 U.S.C.C.A.N. 618–1 (Nov. 28, 1995).

158. Montana v. Stanko, 292 Mont. 192 (1998).

159. *Id.* at 197.

160. *Id.*

overtake and pass a vehicle and return safely to the right-hand lane.

(3) Subject to the maximum speed limits set forth in subsection (1), a person shall operate a vehicle in a careful and prudent manner and at a reduced rate of speed no greater than is reasonable and prudent under the conditions existing at the point of operation, taking into account the amount and character of traffic, visibility, weather, and roadway conditions.

* * *

Questions

1. The "reasonable and proper" speed-limit standard governed in many states after commercial cars were introduced, and then vanished. Why did the standard vanish? What would that standard mean today?

2. A person who drives a motor vehicle in Montana must travel at a speed that is "no greater than is *reasonable and prudent* under the conditions existing at the point of operation, taking into account the amount and character of traffic, visibility, weather, and roadway conditions." Does Montana have a rule or a standard of speed limit? In what ways the legal norm has changed after *Stanko*?

3. Many drivers consciously exceed well-defined speed limits. The national standard of 55 miles per hours was poorly enforced in Montana and many Montanans ignored that standard between 1974 and 1995 when it was in effect.[161] Do frequent violations of speed limits affect the design of speeding laws?

4. What could explain the evolution of the Montana's speed limits? What could explain the relative longevity of the Montana's Basic Rule?

§ 1.4 DIRECT AND INDIRECT REGULATION

In the early nineteenth century, New York City chose to address the problem of potentially harmful pigs by banning pigs without nose rings from running at large in the City. The City imposed liability on pig owners whose pigs ran free without nose rings and offered monetary awards to individuals who provided the City Attorney with information about violations of the law. This regulatory measure included a direct measure that targeted pig owners and an indirect measure that sought to motivate individuals who possessed information about disobedient pig owners. The use of indirect measures—regulating one party in order to shape the conduct of another party—is popular and "recognized in every part of the law."[162]

---

161. *See* Robert E. King & Cass R. Sunstein, *Doing Without Speed Limits*, 79 BOSTON UNIVERSITY LAW REVIEW 155 (1999).

162. Kalem Co. v. Harper Bros., 222 U.S. 55 (1911) (Justice Holmes discussing the use of contributory liability in copyright law and other areas of law).

Indirect regulation intends to shape the conduct of individuals and firms by motivating third parties to disrupt misconduct or encourage desirable conduct. Indirect regulatory techniques may impose liability on third parties for the misconduct of others or award third parties for preventing misconduct or for providing information about the misconduct of others. The state employs indirect regulation when direct regulation is ineffective or too costly. The New York City hog Ordinance that offered awards to informants intended to reduce the City's enforcement costs.

Indirect regulation is a common regulatory technique that typically intends to supplement direct regulation and deter third parties from inducing or assisting misconduct. Indirect regulation is used when the third party is in a superior position to disrupt misconduct and available public resources cannot afford effective direct regulation. Indirect regulation as a means to deter third parties from inducing or assisting misconduct focuses on the role of the third party in the misconduct and is extracted from common law doctrines that impose liability on parties that knowingly participate or further misconduct (*e.g.*, a tortious act or crime) with the prime offender.

Many familiar and less familiar legal norms utilize this technique. For example, an employer may be vicariously liable for injuries caused by her employee in the scope of his employment.[163] A dram-shop owner who serves alcoholic beverages to intoxicated patrons may be liable to parties injured by his intoxicated patrons.[164] In copyright law, flea-market operators may be liable for sales of counterfeit by vendors and operators of file-sharing technologies may be liable for infringement by users.[165] In criminal law, one may be liable for crimes committed by another as a principal, aider, abettor, or accomplice.[166] In *Chamber of Commerce v. Whiting*,[167] the

---

163. See, e.g., Riviello v. Waldron, 47 N.Y.2d 297 (1979) (holding a bar owner liable for an accident in which his cook struck a patron in the eye); Fruit v. Schreiner, 502 P.2d 133 (AK 1972) (holding an employer liable for car accident injuries caused by his salesman); Mary M. v. City of Los Angeles, 54 Cal.3d 202 (CA 1991) (holding the City liable for a rape committed by a police officer on duty). See generally Reinier H. Kraakman, Gatekeepers: The Anatomy of a Third–Party Enforcement Strategy, 2 JOURNAL OF LAW, ECONOMICS, AND ORGANIZATION 53 (1986); Alan O. Sykes, The Economics of Vicarious Liability, 93 YALE LAW JOURNAL 1231 (1984).

164. See, e.g., Jardine v. Upper Darby Lodge No. 1973, Inc., 413 Pa. 626 (PA 1964); Brigance v. Velvet Dove Restaurant, Inc., 725 P.2d 300 (OK 1986). See also FRANK A. SLOAN ET AL., DRINKERS, DRIVERS AND BARTENDERS: BALANCING PRIVATE CHOICES AND PUBLIC ACCOUNTABILITY (2000).

165. *See, e.g.*, Fonovisa, Inc. v. Cherry Auction, Inc., 76 F.3d 259 (9th Cir. 1996) (holding a flea-market operator liable for trade in counterfeit by vendors); MGM Studios v. Grokster, 545 U.S. 913 (2005) (holding owners of file-sharing technologies liable for copyright infringements by users); *In re* Aimster Copyright Litig., 334 F.3d 643 (7th Cir. 2003) (same). *Cf.* Sony Corp. of Am. v. Universal City Studios, 464 U.S. 417 (1984) (absolving VCR a manufacturer of liability for infringing activities of VCR users). *See generally* Barak Y. Orbach, *Indirect Free Riding on the Wheels of Commerce: Dual–Use Technologies and Copyright Liability*, 58 EMORY LAW JOURNAL 409 (2008).

166. For accomplice liability, *see* Nye & Nissen v. United States, 336 U.S. 613 (1949); United States v. Peoni 100 F.2d 401 (2d. Cir. 1938); For the Pinkerton liability, *see* Pinkerton v. United States, 328 U.S. 640 (1946) (holding that one may be liable for crimes committed by another in furtherance of a conspiracy in which both are involved). *See also* Francis Bowes Sayre, *Criminal Responsibility for the Acts of Another*, 43 HARVARD LAW REVIEW 689 (1930).

167. 131 S.Ct. 1968 (2011).

Supreme Court upheld a state law that suspended and revoked business licenses for employing unauthorized aliens and required every employer to verify the employment eligibility of hired employees through a specific Internet-based system.

Indirect regulation is also used to eliminate markets by imposing liability on market facilitators, rather than consumers. For example, to protect the "public health and morals," Alabama seeks to reduce the use of "any device designed or marketed as useful primarily for the stimulation of human genital organs," by prohibiting commercial distribution of such devices.[168] The Combat Methamphetamine Epidemic Act of 2005 imposes a wide range of restrictions on the sale of products that could be used for the production of "meth."[169] The universe of indirect regulations is rich and diverse and indeed reaches every area of law.

Furthermore, because indirect regulation claims are common in litigation (third-party liability),[170] Congress and state legislatures have expressly exempted certain parties from liability that indirect regulation theories might have created or could create. For example, the Digital Millennium Copyright Act of 1998 creates safe harbors for Internet service providers (ISPs) that meet certain conditions against suits for copyright infringements conducted by the ISPs users.[171] The 2005 federal Protection of Lawful Commerce in Arms Act limits the types of civil actions that can be brought against firearms manufacturers and dealers from liability for crimes committed with their products. Congress passed this Act in response to actions brought against manufacturers and dealers of firearms for crimes conducted with firearms and ammunition they distributed and sold.[172] Similarly, several states enacted anti-dram shop statutes that exempt dram-shop owners and social hosts from liability for injuries caused by intoxicated patrons and guests.[173]

As the examples illustrate, legislatures, agencies, and courts utilize indirect regulation. The origins of indirect regulation are in common law, and courts have always developed liability rules in the form of indirect regulation. Despite its popularity, indirect regulation is a controversial legal instrument—it imposes liability on one party for the misconduct of another party. This form of liability sometimes appears unfair, unjust, or unwarranted.

---

168. Ala.Code § 13A–12–200.2(a)(1). *See* Williams v. Pryor, 240 F.3d 944 (11th Cir. 2001) (upholding the constitutionality of the ban); Williams v. Attorney General of Alabama, 378 F.3d 1232 (11th Cir. 2004) (same); Williams v. Morgan, 478 F.3d 1316 (11th Cir. 2007) (same). *Cf.* Reliable Consultants, Inc. v. Earle, 517 F.3d 738 (5th Cir. 2008) (holding that a similar Texas ban was unconstitutional).

169. The Combat Methamphetamine Epidemic Act of 2005, Pub L. No. 109–177, 120 Stat. 256 (2006).

170. *See generally* William M. Landes & Richard A. Posner, *The Private Enforcement of Law*, 4 JOURNAL OF LEGAL STUDIES 1 (1975).

171. 17 U.S.C. § 512.

172. *See*, e.g., City of New York v. Beretta U.S.A Corp., 315 F.Supp.2d 256 (E.D.N.Y. 2004); Camden County Bd. of Chosen Freeholders v. Beretta U.S.A. Corp., 273 F.3d 536 (3d Cir. 2001); Ileto v. Glock, Inc., 349 F.3d 1191 (9th Cir. 2003).

173. *See, e.g.*, Cal. Bus. & Prof.Code § 25602(b); La. Rev. Stat. Ann. § 9:2800.1; Miss. Code Ann. § 67–3–73.

To illustrate the pervasiveness and potential perceived oddities of indirect regulation, consider the World Trade Center Bombing Litigation that was about the question of whether the Port Authority of New York and New Jersey (the Port Authority) could be held liable for the 1993 terrorist truck bombing at the World Trade Center.[174] In October 2005, a New York jury was asked to determine the availability of tort recovery to victims of the terror attack. The jury assigned fault to the terrorists who had deliberately planted and ignited a bomb in the building's underground parking garage and to the World Trade Center's owner and operator, the Port Authority, for its failure to adopt the more rigorous security measures recommended by its experts. The jury apportioned 68% of the fault to Port Authority and 32% to the terrorists. The New York state courts affirmed the jury's finding of liability and apportionment of fault. An application of indirect regulation in torts (third-party liability) persuaded a jury and at least the New York state courts that the owner and operator of the World Trade Center should have significant liability for the consequences of a terror attack.

The Tennessee Movie Rating Law

Movie censorship in the United States was born in 1897.[175] Until 1952, movie censorship did not encounter any significant legal challenges because movies were outside the scope of the First Amendment.[176] The motion picture industry therefore developed self-censorship institutions in an effort to reduce pressures from state legislatures. These early self-censorship institutions had limited levels of effectiveness: the industry did not control producers and censorship laws gradually became tighter. In 1934, the industry introduced the so-called the Production Code that served as an effective censorship device and eliminated pressures from the industry. Despite its effectiveness, in 1968, the industry abandoned the Production Code, after the Supreme Court handed down three cases that substantially narrowed the scope of permitted censorship and suggested that institutional censorship was unconstitutional.[177] The industry replaced its censorship code with the rating system that we have today. In 1993, Dallas, the last locality in the country to have active censorship laws, retired its Motion Picture Classification Board. Government censorship of films vanished. Film exhibitors were no longer required to receive permits from a censor for every film they considered showing and producers were relieved from the strict morality standards of local censorship boards.

---

174. *See* Nash v. Port Authority of New York and New Jersey, 856 N.Y.S.2d 583 (A.D. 2008); In re World Trade Center Bombing Litigation, 17 N.Y.3d 428 (2011). *See also* Ellen M. Bublick, *Upside Down? Terrorists, proprietors, and Civil Responsibility for Crime Prevention in the Post-9/11 Tort-Reform World*, 41 LOYOLA OF LOS ANGELES LAW REVIEW 1483 (2008).

175. *See* Barak Orbach, *Prizefighting and the Birth of Movie Censorship*, 21 YALE JOURNAL OF LAW & THE HUMANITIES 251 (2009).

176. *See* Mutual Film Corp. v. Industrial Commission of Ohio, 236 U.S. 230 (1915); Burstyn v. Wilson, 343 U.S. 495 (1952).

177. Freedman v. Maryland, 380 U.S. 51 (1965); Ginsberg v. New York, 390 U.S. 629 (1968); Interstate Circuit, Inc. v. Dallas, 390 U.S. 676 (1968).

In 1989, Tennessee incorporated the industry's movie rating system into its law.

Tennessee Code Annotated

§ 39–17–901. Definitions

* * *

(14) "Sexual conduct" means:

(A) Patently offensive representations or descriptions of ultimate sexual acts, normal or perverted, actual or simulated. A sexual act is simulated when it depicts explicit sexual activity that gives the appearance of ultimate sexual acts, anal, oral or genital. "Ultimate sexual acts" means sexual intercourse, anal or otherwise, fellatio, cunnilingus or sodomy; or

(B) Patently offensive representations or descriptions of masturbation, excretory functions, and lewd exhibition of the genitals;

* * *

§ 39–17–907. Theaters; regulation of showings

(a) It is unlawful for any person to exhibit for public consumption, whether or not the exhibition is for compensation, any motion picture, film, movie, or videotape that depicts sexual conduct as defined in § 39–17–901, unless the exhibition is within a theater auditorium or other enclosed area that effectively removes the exhibition from the view of members of the public who are not voluntarily engaged in viewing the motion picture, film, movie, or videotape.

(b) Each theater at which two (2) or more motion pictures are shown in the same building shall maintain adequate supervision of the customers to prevent minors from purchasing a ticket or admission pass to a motion picture designated by the rating board of the Motion Picture Association of America by the letter "G" for general audiences or "PG" for all ages, parental guidance advised, and then viewing a motion picture designated "R" for restricted audiences, persons under eighteen (18) years of age not admitted unless accompanied by parent or adult guardian, or "X," persons under eighteen (18) years of age not admitted.

(c) A violation of this section is a Class A misdemeanor.

Questions

1. What was the possible rationale behind the incorporation of movie ratings into law? Is the reliance on indirect regulation necessary? If so, should the law focus on exhibitors?

2. What is film the rating "X"? What could it mean in Tennessee? Why did the Tennessee Legislature choose to include this rating in the statute? Could it make better choices?

3. Assuming you are unfamiliar with patterns of movie-going in Tennessee, how effective do you think this statute is? To the extent that you are

familiar with patterns of movie going in Tennessee: Can you explain the level of effectiveness?

File Sharing

In the mid–1970s, Sony introduced an expensive video recording technology that had the capacity of taping up to 60 minutes: The Betamax. Fearing that the Betamax would threaten its viability, the motion picture industry sued Sony for alleged copyright infringements by Betamax users and sought to ban the technology. In 1984, after lengthy litigation, the Supreme Court absolved Sony of liability for the potentially infringing activities of Betamax users, holding that a manufacturer is not liable for the copyright infringements conducted by users of its products when the products are capable of "substantial-noninfringing-use."[178]

In the late 1990s, when the Internet became popular in many households, new technologies emerged that facilitated file sharing among users. File-sharing technologies had various models, but all built on the concept of allowing users to choose which files to exchange while the operator monetized or planned to monetize the volume of users for profit.[179] Users of file-sharing technologies exchanged mostly files of copyrighted songs and, despite the differences among the file-sharing technologies, courts found their operators liable for users' copyright infringements. Napster, Grokster, StreamCast, Aimster, and others rose and fell.[180] The file-sharing technologies transformed music distribution from bundled tangible media (albums) to unbundled online media (downloaded songs and tracks). Their business models, however, skipped copyright holders, as their users paid no royalties for the downloaded music. On April 23, 2003, Apple launched its iTunes Store, a virtual store where people could buy and download digital music on-demand. Within the first eighteen hours, Apple sold approximately 275,000 songs. iTunes sold over one million tracks in its first week of operation and over 70 million tracks in its first year. A new model of music distribution emerged that protected the interests of copyright holders.

In re: Aimster Copyright Litigation

334 F.3d 643 (7th Cir. 2003)

■ POSNER, CIRCUIT JUDGE.

Owners of copyrighted popular music filed a number of closely related suits * * * against John Deep and corporations that are controlled by him.

---

178. *See* Sony Corp. of Am. v. Universal City Studios, 464 U.S. 417 (1984). For the story of the litigation *see* JAMES LARDNER, FAST FORWARD: A MACHINE AND THE COMMOTION IT CAUSED (rev. ed. 1987)

179. *See generally* Orbach, *Indirect Free Riding on the Wheels of Commerce*, *supra* note 157.

180. *See* A & M Records, Inc. v. Napster, Inc., 239 F.3d 1004 (9th Cir. 2001); *In re* Aimster Copyright Litig., 334 F.3d 643 (7th Cir. 2003); MGM Studios v. Grokster, 545 U.S. 913 (2005).

* * * The numerous plaintiffs, who among them appear to own most subsisting copyrights on American popular music, claim that Deep's "Aimster" Internet service (recently renamed "Madster") is a contributory and vicarious infringer of these copyrights. The district judge entered a broad preliminary injunction, which had the effect of shutting down the Aimster service until the merits of the suit are finally resolved, from which Deep appeals. Aimster is one of a number of enterprises (the former Napster is the best known) that have been sued for facilitating the swapping of digital copies of popular music, most of it copyrighted, over the Internet. * * * To simplify exposition, we refer to the appellant as "Aimster" and to the appellees (the plaintiffs) as the recording industry.

Teenagers and young adults who have access to the Internet like to swap computer files containing popular music. If the music is copyrighted, such swapping, which involves making and transmitting a digital copy of the music, infringes copyright. The swappers, who are ignorant or more commonly disdainful of copyright and in any event discount the likelihood of being sued or prosecuted for copyright infringement, are the direct infringers. But firms that facilitate their infringement, even if they are not themselves infringers because they are not making copies of the music that is shared, may be liable to the copyright owners as contributory infringers. Recognizing the impracticability or futility of a copyright owner's suing a multitude of individual infringers, the law allows a copyright holder to sue a contributor to the infringement instead, in effect as an aider and abettor. Another analogy is to the tort of intentional interference with contract, that is, inducing a breach of contract. * * * If a breach of contract (and a copyright license is just a type of contract) can be prevented most effectively by actions taken by a third party, it makes sense to have a legal mechanism for placing liability for the consequences of the breach on him as well as on the party that broke the contract.

* * *

The Aimster system has the following essential components: proprietary software that can be downloaded free of charge from Aimster's Web site; Aimster's server * * *, which hosts the Web site and collects and organizes information obtained from the users but does not make copies of the swapped files themselves and that also provides the matching service described below; computerized tutorials instructing users of the software on how to use it for swapping computer files; and "Club Aimster," a related Internet service owned by Deep that users of Aimster's software can join for a fee and use to download the "top 40" popular-music files more easily than by using the basic, free service. The "AIM" in "Aimster" stands for AOL instant-messaging service. Aimster is available only to users of such services (of which AOL's is the most popular) because Aimster users can swap files only when both are online and connected in a chat room enabled by an instant-messaging service.

* * *

In principle, [because of Aimster's services] the purchase of a single CD could be levered into the distribution within days or even hours of millions of identical, near-perfect (depending on the compression format used) copies of the music recorded on the CD-hence the recording industry's anxiety about file-sharing services oriented toward consumers of popular music. But because copies of the songs reside on the computers of the users and not on Aimster's own server, Aimster is not a direct infringer of the copyrights on those songs. Its function is similar to that of a stock exchange, which is a facility for matching offers rather than a repository of the things being exchanged (shares of stock). But unlike transactions on a stock exchange, the consummated "transaction" in music files does not take place in the facility, that is, in Aimster's server.

What we have described so far is a type of Internet file-sharing system that might be created for innocuous purposes such as the expeditious exchange of confidential business data among employees of a business firm. * * * The fact that copyrighted materials might sometimes be shared between users of such a system without the authorization of the copyright owner or a fair-use privilege would not make the firm a contributory infringer. Otherwise AOL's instant-messaging system, which Aimster piggybacks on, might be deemed a contributory infringer. For there is no doubt that some of the attachments that AOL's multitudinous subscribers transfer are copyrighted, and such distribution is an infringement unless authorized by the owner of the copyright. The Supreme Court made clear in the *Sony* decision that the producer of a product that has substantial noninfringing uses is not a contributory infringer merely because some of the uses actually made of the product (in that case a machine, the predecessor of today's videocassette recorders, for recording television programs on tape) are infringing. *Sony Corp. of America, Inc. v. Universal City Studios, Inc.*, 464 U.S. 417, 104 (1984). * * *

Sony's Betamax video recorder was used for three principal purposes, as Sony was well aware (a fourth, playing home movies, involved no copying). The first, which the majority opinion emphasized, was time shifting, that is, recording a television program that was being shown at a time inconvenient for the owner of the Betamax for later watching at a convenient time. The second was "library building," that is, making copies of programs to retain permanently. The third was skipping commercials by taping a program before watching it and then, while watching the tape, using the fast-forward button on the recorder to skip over the commercials. The first use the Court held was a fair use (and hence not infringing) because it enlarged the audience for the program. The copying involved in the second and third uses was unquestionably infringing to the extent that the programs copied were under copyright and the taping of them was not authorized by the copyright owners-but not all fell in either category. Subject to this qualification, building a library of taped programs was infringing because it was the equivalent of borrowing a copyrighted book from a public library, making a copy of it for one's personal library, then returning the original to the public library. The third use, commercial-skipping, amounted to creating an unauthorized derivative work, * * * namely a commercial-free copy that would reduce the copyright owner's income from his original program, since "free" television programs are financed by the purchase of commercials by advertisers.

Thus the video recorder was being used for a mixture of infringing and noninfringing uses and the Court thought that Sony could not demix them because once Sony sold the recorder it lost all control over its use. * * *

In our case the recording industry * * * points out that the provider of a service, unlike the seller of a product, has a continuing relation with its customers and therefore should be able to prevent, or at least limit, their infringing copyright by monitoring their use of the service and terminating them when it is discovered that they are infringing. * * *

* * * If a service facilitates both infringing and noninfringing uses, as in the case of AOL's instant-messaging service, and the detection and prevention of the infringing uses would be highly burdensome, the rule for which the recording industry is contending could result in the shutting down of the service or its annexation by the copyright owners (contrary to the clear import of the *Sony* decision), because the provider might find it impossible to estimate its potential damages liability to the copyright holders and would anyway face the risk of being enjoined. The fact that the recording industry's argument if accepted might endanger AOL's instant-messaging service * * * is not only alarming; it is paradoxical, since subsidiaries of AOL's parent company (AOL Time Warner), such as Warner Brothers Records and Atlantic Recording Corporation, are among the plaintiffs in this case and music chat rooms are among the facilities offered by AOL's instant-messaging service.

* * *

The recording industry's hostility to the *Sony* decision is both understandable, given the amount of Internet-enabled infringement of music copyrights, * * * [b]ut it is being articulated in the wrong forum.

* * *

[W]hen a supplier is offering a product or service that has noninfringing as well as infringing uses, some estimate of the respective magnitudes of these uses is necessary for a finding of contributory infringement. The Court's action in striking the cost-benefit tradeoff in favor of Sony came to seem prescient when it later turned out that the principal use of video recorders was to allow people to watch at home movies that they bought or rented rather than to tape television programs. (In 1984, when *Sony* was decided, the industry was unsure how great the demand would be for prerecorded tapes compared to time shifting. The original Betamax played one-hour tapes, long enough for most television broadcasts but too short for a feature film. Sony's competitors used the VHS format, which came to market later but with a longer playing time; this contributed to VHS's eventual displacement of Betamax.) An enormous new market thus opened for the movie industry-which by the way gives point to the Court's emphasis on potential as well as actual noninfringing uses. But the balancing of costs and benefits is necessary only in a case in which substantial noninfringing uses, present or prospective, are demonstrated.

We * * * reject Aimster's argument that because the Court said in *Sony* that mere "constructive knowledge" of infringing uses is not enough for contributory infringement and the encryption feature of Aimster's service prevented Deep from knowing what songs were being copied by the users of his system, he lacked the knowledge of infringing uses that liability for contributory infringement requires. Willful blindness is knowledge, in copyright law (where indeed it may be enough that the defendant *should* have known of the direct infringement, * * * as it is in the law generally. * * * One who, knowing or strongly suspecting that he is involved in shady dealings, takes steps to make sure that he does not acquire full or exact knowledge of the nature and extent of those dealings is held to have a criminal intent, * * * because a deliberate effort to avoid guilty knowledge is all that the law requires to establish a guilty state of mind. * * * In *United States v. Diaz*, 864 F.2d 544, 550 (7th Cir.1988), the defendant, a drug trafficker, sought "to insulate himself from the actual drug transaction so that he could deny knowledge of it," which he did sometimes by absenting himself from the scene of the actual delivery and sometimes by pretending to be fussing under the hood of his car. He did not escape liability by this maneuver; no more can Deep by using encryption software to prevent himself from learning what surely he strongly suspects to be the case: that the users of his service-maybe *all* the users of his service-are copyright infringers.

This is not to say that the provider of an encrypted instant-messaging service or encryption software is ipso factor a contributory infringer should his buyers use the service to infringe copyright, merely because encryption, like secrecy generally, facilitates unlawful transactions. ("Encryption" comes from the Greek word for concealment.) Encryption fosters privacy, and privacy is a social benefit though also a source of social costs. * * * Our point is only that a service provider that would otherwise be a contributory infringer does not obtain immunity by using encryption to shield itself from actual knowledge of the unlawful purposes for which the service is being used.

* * *

There are analogies in the law of aiding and abetting, the criminal counterpart to contributory infringement. A retailer of slinky dresses is not guilty of aiding and abetting prostitution even if he knows that some of his customers are prostitutes-he may even know which ones are. * * * The extent to which his activities and those of similar sellers actually promote prostitution is likely to be slight relative to the social costs of imposing a risk of prosecution on him. But the owner of a massage parlor who employs women who are capable of giving massages, but in fact as he knows sell only sex and never massages to their customers, is an aider and abettor of prostitution (as well as being guilty of pimping or operating a brothel). * * * The slinky-dress case corresponds to *Sony,* and, like *Sony,* is not inconsistent with imposing liability on the seller of a product or service that, as in the massage-parlor case, is capable of noninfringing uses but in fact is used only to infringe. To the recording industry, a single known infringing use brands the facilitator as a contributory infringer. To the Aimsters of this world, a single noninfringing use provides complete immunity from liability. Neither is correct.

To situate Aimster's service between these unacceptable poles, we need to say just a bit more about it. In explaining how to use the Aimster software, the tutorial gives as its *only* examples of file sharing the sharing of copyrighted music, including copyrighted music that the recording industry had notified Aimster was being infringed by Aimster's users. The tutorial is the invitation to infringement that the Supreme Court found was missing in *Sony*. In addition, membership in Club Aimster enables the member for a fee of $4.95 a month to download with a single click the music most often shared by Aimster users, which turns out to be music copyrighted by the plaintiffs. Because Aimster's software is made available free of charge and Aimster does not sell paid advertising on its Web site, Club Aimster's monthly fee is the only means by which Aimster is financed and so the club cannot be separated from the provision of the free software. When a member of the club clicks on "play" next to the name of a song on the club's Web site, Aimster's server searches through the computers of the Aimster users who are online until it finds one who has listed the song as available for sharing, and it then effects the transmission of the file to the computer of the club member who selected it. Club Aimster lists only the 40 songs that are currently most popular among its members; invariably these are under copyright.

The evidence that we have summarized does not exclude the *possibility* of substantial noninfringing uses of the Aimster system, but the evidence is sufficient, especially in a preliminary-injunction proceeding, which is summary in character, to shift the burden of production to Aimster to demonstrate that its service has substantial noninfringing uses. * * *

Aimster has failed to produce any evidence that its service has ever been used for a noninfringing use, let alone evidence concerning the frequency of such uses. * * * We have to assume for purposes of deciding this appeal that no such evidence exists. * * *

Even when there are noninfringing uses of an Internet file-sharing service, moreover, if the infringing uses are substantial then to avoid liability as a contributory infringer the provider of the service must show that it would have been disproportionately costly for him to eliminate or at least reduce substantially the infringing uses. Aimster failed to make that showing too, by failing to present evidence that the provision of an encryption capability *effective against the service provider itself* added important value to the service or saved significant cost. Aimster blinded itself in the hope that by doing so it might come within the rule of the *Sony* decision.

* * *

[W]e are less confident * * * that the recording industry would also be likely to prevail on the issue of vicarious infringement should the case be tried, though we shall not have to resolve our doubts in order to decide the appeal. "Vicarious liability" generally refers to the liability of a principal, such as an employer, for the torts committed by his agent, an employee for example, in the course of the agent's employment. The teenagers and young adults who use Aimster's system to infringe copyright are of course not Aimster's agents. But one of the principal rationales of vicarious liability, namely the difficulty of obtaining effective relief against an agent, who is likely to be impecunious, * * * has been extended in the copyright area to cases in which the only effective relief is obtainable from someone who bears a relation to the direct infringers that is analogous to the relation of a principal to an agent. * * * The canonical illustration is the owner of a dance hall who hires dance bands that sometimes play copyrighted music without authorization. The bands are not the dance hall's agents, but it may be impossible as a practical matter for the copyright holders to identify and obtain a legal remedy against the infringing bands yet quite feasible for the dance hall to prevent or at least limit infringing performances. And so the dance hall that fails to make reasonable efforts to do this is liable as a vicarious infringer. * * * The dance hall could perhaps be described as a contributory infringer. But one thinks of a contributory infringer as someone who benefits directly from the infringement that he encourages, and that does not seem an apt description of the dance hall, though it does benefit to the extent that competition will force the dance band to charge the dance hall a smaller fee for performing if the band doesn't pay copyright royalties and so has lower costs than it would otherwise have.

How far the doctrine of vicarious liability extends is uncertain. It could conceivably have been applied in the *Sony* case itself, on the theory that while it was infeasible for the producers of copyrighted television fare to sue the viewers who used the fast-forward button on Sony's video recorder to delete the commercials and thus reduce the copyright holders' income, Sony could have reduced the likelihood of infringement, as we noted earlier, by a design change. But the Court, treating vicarious and contributory infringement interchangeably, held that Sony was not a vicarious infringer either. By eliminating the encryption feature and monitoring the use being made of its system, Aimster could like Sony have limited the amount of infringement. Whether failure to do so made it a vicarious infringer notwithstanding the outcome in *Sony* is academic, however; its ostrich-like refusal to discover the extent to which its system was being used to infringe copyright is merely another piece of evidence that it was a contributory infringer.

We turn now to Aimster's defenses under the Online Copyright Infringement Liability Limitation Act, Title II of the Digital Millennium Copyright Act (DMCA), 17 U.S.C. § 512. The DMCA is an attempt to deal with special problems created by the so-called digital revolution. One of these is the vulnerability of Internet service providers such as AOL to liability for copyright infringement as a result of file swapping among their subscribers. Although the Act was not passed with Napster-type services in mind, the definition of Internet service provider is broad ("a provider of online services or network access, or the operator of facilities therefor," 17 U.S.C. § 512(k)(1)(B)), and, * * * Aimster fits it. The Act provides a series of safe harbors for Internet service providers and related entities, but none in which Aimster can moor. The Act does not abolish contributory infringement. The common element of its safe harbors is that the service provider must do what it can reasonably be asked to do to prevent the use of its service by "repeat infringers." 17 U.S.C. § 512(i)(1)(A). Far from doing anything to discourage repeat infringers of the plaintiffs' copyrights, Aimster invited them to do so, showed them how they could do so with ease using its system, and by teaching its users how to encrypt their unlawful distribution of copyrighted materials disabled itself from doing anything to prevent infringement.

This completes our discussion of the merits of Aimster's appeal. But the fact that the recording industry is likely to win this case if it is ever tried is not by itself a sufficient basis for the issuance of a preliminary injunction. A court asked to issue such an injunction must also consider which party will suffer the greater harm as a result of a ruling for or against issuance. Aimster points out that the preliminary injunction has put it out of business. * * * On this record, therefore, the harm to Aimster from the grant of the injunction must be reckoned comparable to the harm that the recording industry would suffer from denial of the preliminary injunction.

The only harm that is relevant to the decision to grant a preliminary injunction is irreparable harm, since if it is reparable by an award of damages at the end of trial there is no need for preliminary relief. The recording industry's harm should the preliminary injunction be dissolved would undoubtedly be irreparable. The industry's damages from Aimster's contributory infringement cannot be reliably estimated and Aimster would in any event be unlikely ever to have the resources to pay them. Aimster's irreparable harm from the grant of the injunction is, if anything, less, because of the injunction bond of $500,000 that the industry was required to post and that Aimster does not contend is inadequate. * * * Even if the irreparable harms are deemed the same, since the plaintiffs have a stronger case on the merits than Aimster does the judge was right to grant the injunction.

* * *

AFFIRMED.

The Bono Rule

The Super Bowl XXXVIII was held on February 1, 2004 and it was broadcasted by CBS and its affiliates. MTV organized the halftime show that was performed by Janet Jackson, Justin Timberlake, and others. During Timberlake's song, *Rock Your Body*, in which he promises his dance partner to "have you naked by the end of this song," Timberlake ripped off the right side of Jackson's bustier. The event was broadcasted live to nearly 90 million people. CBS had implemented a five-second audio delay to guard against the possibility of indecent language being transmitted on air, but it did not employ such a precautionary technology for video images. As a result, Jackson's bare right breast was exposed on camera for nine-sixteenths of one second. Shortly after the performance, MTV released a statement: "The tearing of Janet Jackson's costume was unrehearsed, unplanned, completely unintentional and was inconsistent with assurances we had about the content of the performance. MTV regrets this incident occurred, and we apologize to anyone who was offended by it." Timberlake released a statement, too: "I am sorry if anyone was offended by the wardrobe malfunction during the halftime performance of the Super Bowl. It was not intentional and is regrettable."[181] The incident was immediately dubbed the "wardrobe malfunction."

---

181. *See* Daniel Henninger, *Right and Left Have a Problem With Janet's Breast*, WALL STREET JOURNAL, Feb. 6, 2004, at A16; Kelefa Sanneh, *During Halftime Show, a Display Tailored for Video Review*, NEW YORK TIMES, Feb. 2, 2004, at D1.

Because the wardrobe malfunction was broadcasted, the Federal Communications Commission ("FCC") imposed on the broadcaster, CBS, a monetary forfeiture of $550,000.[182] The FCC found that the Halftime Show broadcast was indecent and that the brevity of the image was outweighed by the nature of the indecency. The FCC further determined that CBS's actions in broadcasting the indecent image were "willful" and therefore sanctionable by a monetary forfeiture under the Federal Communications Commission Act, because CBS "consciously and deliberately failed to take reasonable precautions to ensure that no actionably indecent material was broadcast." Moreover, applying a respondeat superior theory, the FCC found CBS vicariously liable for the willful actions of its agents, Jackson and Timberlake. CBS filed a petition for review and the Third Circuit vacated the FCC's ruling,[183] holding that the FCC departed from its existing policy to sanction CBS, without proper notice and reasoned explanation. The court also dismissed the FCC's vicarious liability theory.

Immediately after the wardrobe malfunction, the FCC increased enforcement efforts and Congress increased the maximum fines the FCC could imposed on broadcasters by factor 10—from $32,500 to $325,000.

In January 2003, more than a year *before* the wardrobe malfunction took place, at the 2003 Golden Globe Awards, Bono had his own incident that was broadcasted live. The Parents Television Council, a non-profit organization whose "primary mission is to promote and restore responsibility and decency to the entertainment industry," filed a complaint with the FCC, and so did numerous individuals affiliated with the Council. On October 3, 2003, three months *before* the wardrobe malfunction, the FCC's Chief, Enforcement Bureau issued a Memorandum Opinion and Order, denying the complaints and holding that Bono's act was not indecent or obscenity and that the broadcasters did not violate the Federal Communications Commission Act. The Council appealed. On March 3, 2004, a month *after* the wardrobe malfunction, the FCC reversed the October 2003 order, creating a new rule of indecency that acquired the informal name "the Bono Rule."

Fox Television Stations, Inc. v. Federal Communications Commission

613 F.3d 317 (2d Cir. 2010)

■ POOLER, CIRCUIT JUDGE.

This petition for review comes before us on remand from the Supreme Court. Previously we held, with Judge Leval dissenting, that the indecency policy of the Federal Communications Commission ("FCC" or "Commission") was arbitrary and capricious under the Administrative Procedure Act ("APA"), 5 U.S.C. § 706(2)(A). See *Fox Television Stations, Inc. v.*

182. *See* In re Complaints Against Various Television Licensees Concerning Their February 1, 2004 Broadcast of the Super Bowl XXXVIII Halftime Show, 21 F.C.C.R. 2760 (2006); In re Complaints Against Various Television Licensees Concerning Their February 1, 2004 Broadcast of the Super Bowl XXXVIII Halftime Show, 21 F.C.C.R. 6653 (2006).

183. CBS Corp. v. FCC, 535 F.3d 167 (3d Cir. 2008).

FCC, 489 F.3d 444, 462 (2d Cir.2007). The Supreme Court reversed, upholding the policy under the APA and remanding for consideration of petitioners' constitutional arguments. *See FCC v. Fox Television Stations, Inc.*, 556 U.S. 502 (2009) (Scalia, J.). We now hold that the FCC's policy violates the First Amendment because it is unconstitutionally vague, creating a chilling effect that goes far beyond the fleeting expletives at issue here. Thus, we grant the petition for review and vacate the FCC's order and the indecency policy underlying it.

BACKGROUND

Section 1464 of Title 18 of United States Code provides that "[w]hoever utters any obscene, indecent, or profane language by means of radio communication shall be fined under this title or imprisoned not more than two years, or both." In 1960, Congress authorized the FCC to impose civil forfeitures for violations of Section 1464. *See* 47 U.S.C. § 503(b)(1)(D). It was not until 1975, however, that the FCC first exercised its authority to regulate speech it deemed indecent but not obscene. The speech at issue was comedian George Carlin's "Filthy Words" monologue, a 12–minute string of expletives broadcast on the radio at 2:00 in the afternoon.

The FCC brought forfeiture proceedings against the Pacifica Foundation, the broadcaster that had aired the Carlin monologue. *Citizen's Complaint Against Pacifica Found. Station WBAI (FM), N.Y, N.Y.*, 56 F.C.C.2d 94 (1975). In finding that *Pacifica* had violated Section 1464, the Commission defined "indecent" speech as "language that describes, in terms patently offensive as measured by contemporary community standards for the broadcast medium, sexual or excretory activities and organs, at times of the day when there is a reasonable risk that children may be in the audience." *Id.* at ¶ 11. *Pacifica* petitioned for review to the D.C. Circuit, which declared the FCC's indecency regime invalid. *See Pacifica Found. v. FCC*, 556 F.2d 9 (D.C.Cir.1977). In finding the FCC's order both vague and overbroad, the court pointed out that the Commission's definition of indecent speech would prohibit "the uncensored broadcast of many of the great works of literature including Shakespearian plays and contemporary plays which have won critical acclaim, the works of renowned classical and contemporary poets and writers, and passages from the *Bible*." Id. at 14. Such a result, the court concluded, amounted to unconstitutional censorship. *Id.* at 18.

In a plurality opinion authored by Justice Stevens, the Supreme Court reversed. *See FCC v. Pacifica Found.*, 438 U.S. 726 (1978). The Court limited its review to the question of whether the FCC could impose a civil forfeiture for the Carlin monologue and declined to address Pacifica's argument that the regulation was overbroad and would chill protected speech. * * *

The Court then went on to hold that the FCC could, at least in the situation before it, restrict indecent speech in the broadcast context that did not meet the legal definition of obscenity. * * * Resting on a nuisance rationale, the Court first noted that "of all forms of communication, it is broadcasting that has received the most limited First Amendment protection" because of its "uniquely pervasive presence in the lives of all

Americans." *Id.* at 748. Moreover, the nature of broadcast television—as opposed to printed materials—made it "uniquely accessible to children, even those too young to read." *Id.* at 749. The Court, however, "emphasize[d] the narrowness of [its] holding." *Id.* at 750. "[N]uisance may be merely a right thing in the wrong place,—like a pig in the parlor instead of the barnyard. We simply hold that when the Commission finds that a pig has entered the parlor, the exercise of its regulatory power does not depend on proof that the pig is obscene." *Id.* at 750–51 (internal quotation marks omitted).

Justices Powell and Blackmun, who concurred in a separate opinion, also made clear that the FCC's regulatory authority was limited, stating that the Court's holding did not give the FCC "an unrestricted license to decide what speech, protected in other media, may be banned from the airwaves in order to protect unwilling adults from momentary exposure to it in their homes." *Id.* at 759–60 (Powell, J., concurring). Nor, they explained, did the holding "speak to cases involving the isolated use of a potentially offensive word in the course of a radio broadcast, as distinguished from the verbal shock treatment administered by respondent here." *Id.* at 760–61. * * *

In the years after *Pacifica,* the FCC did indeed pursue a restrained enforcement policy, taking the position that its enforcement powers were limited to the seven specific words in the Carlin monologue. *See Infinity Broadcasting Corp., et al.*, 3 F.C.C.R. 930, at ¶ 5 (1987) ("Infinity Order"). No enforcement actions were brought between 1978 and 1987. * * * Then, in 1987, the FCC abandoned its focus on specific words [and] adopt[ed] a contextual approach to indecent speech.

Despite its move to a more flexible standard, the FCC continued to exercise restraint. In particular, it consistently held that a single, non-literal use of an expletive was not actionably indecent. * * *

In 2001, in an attempt to "provide guidance to the broadcast industry regarding * * * [its] enforcement policies with respect to broadcast indecency," the FCC issued a policy statement in which it set forth its indecency standard in more detail. *Industry Guidance on the Commission's Case Law Interpreting 18 U.S.C. § 1464*, 16 F.C.C.R. 7999, at ¶ 1 (2001) ("*Industry Guidance*"). In *Industry Guidance*, the FCC explained that an indecency finding involved the following two determinations: (1) whether the material "describe[s] or depict[s] sexual or excretory organs or activities"; and (2) whether the broadcast is "patently offensive as measured by contemporary community standards for the broadcast medium." *Id.* at ¶¶ 7–8 (emphasis omitted). The FCC further explained that it considered the following three factors in determining whether a broadcast is patently offensive: (1) "the explicitness or graphic nature of the description or depiction"; (2) "whether the material dwells on or repeats at length" the description or depiction; and (3) "whether the material appears to pander or is used to titillate, or whether the materials appears to have been presented for its shock value." *Id.* at ¶ 10 (emphasis omitted). The *Industry Guidance* reiterated that under the second prong of the patently offensive test, "fleeting and isolated" expletives were not actionably indecent. *Id.* at ¶ 18.

In 2004, however, the FCC's policy on indecency changed. During the 2003 Golden Globe Awards, U2 band member Bono exclaimed, upon receiving an award, "this is really, really, fucking brilliant. Really, really, great." *In re Complaints Against Various Broadcast Licenses Regarding the Airing of the "Golden Globe Awards" Program*, 19 F.C.C.R. 4975, at ¶ 3 n. 4 (2004) ("*Golden Globes Order*"). In response to complaints filed after the incident, the FCC declared, for the first time, that a single, nonliteral use of an expletive (a so-called "fleeting expletive") could be actionably indecent.[2] Finding that "the 'F-Word' is one of the most vulgar, graphic, and explicit descriptions of sexual activity in the English language," *id.* at ¶ 9, and therefore "inherently has a sexual connotation," *id.* at ¶ 8, the FCC concluded that the fleeting and isolated use of the word was irrelevant and overruled all prior decisions in which fleeting use of an expletive was held *per se* not indecent, *id.* at ¶¶ 8–12. The FCC also found that the broadcast was "profane" within the meaning of Section 1464, abandoning its previous interpretation of the term to mean blasphemy. *Id.* at ¶¶ 13–14.

At the same time that the FCC expanded its enforcement efforts to include even fleeting expletives, the FCC also began issuing record fines for indecency violations.[3] While the Commission had previously interpreted the maximum fines in the statute as applying on a per-program basis, it began treating *each* licensee's broadcast of the same program as a separate violation, thereby multiplying the maximum fine the FCC could order for each instance of indecent speech. In addition, Congress amended Section 503(b)(2)(c)(ii) to increase the maximum fine permitted by a factor of 10—from $32,500 to $325,000—meaning that the fine for a single expletive uttered during a broadcast could easily run into the tens of millions of dollars. * * *

NBC Universal, Inc. ("NBC"), along with numerous other parties, filed petitions for reconsideration of the *Golden Globes Order* before the FCC, raising statutory and constitutional challenges to the new policy. While the petitions for reconsideration were pending, the FCC applied the *Golden Globes Order* policy in *In re Complaints Regarding Various Television Broadcasts Between February 2, 2002 and March 8, 2005*, 21 F.C.C. Rcd. 2664 (2006) ("*Omnibus Order*"), which the Commission stated was intended to "provide substantial guidance to broadcasters and the public" about what was considered indecent under the new policy. *Id.* at ¶ 2. In the Omnibus Order (which dealt with many more programs than are at issue in the present case), the Commission found four programs—the 2002 Billboard Music Awards, the 2003 Billboard Music Awards, various episodes of ABC's NYPD Blue, and CBS's The Early Show—indecent and profane under the *Golden Globes* standard.

2. The FCC's increased enforcement efforts—as well as Congress's decision to increase the maximum fines—were in large part caused by the broadcast of the 2004 Super Bowl, during which Justin Timberlake exposed Janet Jackson's breast for a fraction of a second during their halftime show, an event that came to be known as "Nipplegate." * * * The FCC imposed a $550,000 fine, which was overturned by the Third Circuit. *See CBS Corp. v. FCC*, 535 F.3d 167, 209 (3d Cir.2008).

3. In 2003, the FCC imposed $440,000 in fines. In 2004, it imposed a record $8 million in fines* * *.

All four programs involved what could be characterized as fleeting expletives. For instance, during the 2002 Billboard Music Awards, Cher, in an unscripted moment from her acceptance speech, stated: "People have been telling me I'm on the way out every year, right? So fuck 'em." *Id.* at ¶ 101. Similarly, during the 2003 Billboard Music Awards, Nicole Ritchie—on stage to present an award with Paris Hilton—made the following unscripted remark: "Have you ever tried to get cow shit out of a Prada purse? It's not so fucking simple." *Id.* at ¶ 112 n. 164. Episodes of NYPD Blue were found indecent based on several instances of the word "bullshit," *id.* at ¶ 125, while the CBS's The Early Show was found indecent on the basis of a guest's use of the word "bullshitter" to describe a fellow contestant on the reality TV show, Survivor: Vanuatu, *id.* at ¶ 137.

In finding these programs indecent and profane, the FCC reaffirmed its decision in the *Golden Globes Order* that any use of the word "fuck" was presumptively indecent and profane, *id.* at ¶¶ 102, 107, further concluding that any use of the word "shit" was also presumptively indecent and profane, *id.* at ¶¶ 138, 143. It also held that the four broadcasts in question were "patently offensive" because the material was explicit, shocking, and gratuitous, notwithstanding the fact that the expletives were fleeting and isolated. *Id.* ¶¶ 106, 120, 131, 141.

Fox Television Stations, Inc. ("Fox"), CBS Broadcasting Inc. ("CBS"), and ABC Inc. ("ABC"), as well as several network affiliates, filed petitions for review of the *Omnibus Order*. The FCC moved for a voluntary remand, which we granted. * * * After soliciting public comments, the FCC issued a second order on November 6, 2006. See *In re Complaints Regarding Various Television Broadcasts Between February 2, 2002 and March 8, 2005*, 21 F.C.C.R. 13299 (2006) ("*Remand Order*"). In the *Remand Order*, the FCC reaffirmed its finding that the 2002 and 2003 Billboard Music Awards were indecent and profane. However, the FCC reversed its finding with respect to The Early Show and dismissed the complaint against NYPD Blue on procedural grounds.[5]

In the *Remand Order*, the FCC rejected the petitioners' argument that non-literal uses of expletives were not indecent, reasoning that "any strict dichotomy between expletives and descriptions or depictions of sexual or excretory functions is artificial and does not make sense in light of the fact that an expletive's power to offend derives from its sexual or excretory meaning." *Id.* at ¶ 23 (internal quotation marks omitted). However, the Commission did "not take the position that any occurrence of an expletive is indecent or profane under its rules," allowing that expletives that were "integral" to an artistic work or occurring during a "*bona fide* news interview" might not run afoul of the indecency standard. *Id.* at ¶ 70 (emphasis added). As such, it reversed its previous decision concerning the CBS's The Early Show because the utterance of the word "bullshitter" took place during a *bona fide* news interview. The Commission made clear, however, that "there is no outright news exemption from our indecency rules."

---

5. The Commission dismissed the complaints against NYPD Blue because the only person who complained of the material resided in the Eastern time zone, where NYPD Blue aired during the "safe harbor" period after 10pm.

Petitioners and intervenors, which collectively represented all the major broadcast networks as well as local affiliates affected by the FCC's indecency policy (hereinafter, the "Networks"), returned to this Court for review of the Remand Order, making a variety of administrative, statutory, and constitutional arguments. In a 2–1 decision (with Judge Leval in dissent), we held that the FCC's indecency policy was arbitrary and capricious under the APA. We reached this decision because we believed that the FCC had failed to adequately explain why it had changed its nearly–30–year policy on fleeting expletives. Moreover, we noted that the FCC's justification for the policy—that children could be harmed by hearing even one fleeting expletive (the so-called "first blow" theory)—bore "no rational connection to the Commission's actual policy," because the FCC had not instituted a blanket ban on expletives.

Because we struck down the indecency policy on APA grounds, we declined to reach the constitutional issues in the case. We noted, however, that we were "skeptical that the Commission [could] provide a reasoned explanation for its 'fleeting expletive' regime that would pass constitutional muster." We expressed sympathy for "the Networks' contention that the FCC's indecency test [wa]s undefined, indiscernible, inconsistent, and consequently, unconstitutionally vague." We were also troubled that the FCC's policy appeared to permit it to "sanction speech based on its subjective view of the merit of that speech." However, because it was unnecessary for us to reach them, we left those issues for another day. The FCC subsequently filed a writ of certiorari, which the Supreme Court granted.

In a 5–4 decision, the Supreme Court reversed our APA ruling, holding that the FCC's "fleeting expletive" policy was not arbitrary and capricious because "[t]he Commission could reasonably conclude that the pervasiveness of foul language, and the coarsening of public entertainment in other media such as cable, justify more stringent regulation of broadcast programs so as to give conscientious parents a relatively safe haven for their children." * * * However, the Court declined to address the Networks' constitutional arguments, "see[ing] no reason to abandon our usual procedures in a rush to judgment without a lower court opinion," and remanded for us to consider them in the first instance. Thus, * * * we now turn to the question that we deferred in our previous decision—whether the FCC's indecency policy violates the First Amendment.

DISCUSSION

I

It is well-established that indecent speech is fully protected by the First Amendment. * * * Broadcast radio and television, however, have always occupied a unique position when it comes to First Amendment protection. The categorization of broadcasting as different from all other forms of communication pre-dates *Pacifica*. * * * And the Supreme Court has continuously reaffirmed the distinction between broadcasting and other forms of media since *Pacifica*. * * * However, it was in *Pacifica* that the Supreme Court gave its fullest explanation for why restrictions on broadcast speech were subject to a lower level of scrutiny, relying on the twin pillars of pervasiveness and accessibility to children. * * *

* * * The past thirty years has seen an explosion of media sources, and broadcast television has become only one voice in the chorus. Cable television is almost as pervasive as broadcast—almost 87 percent of households subscribe to a cable or satellite service—and most viewers can alternate between broadcast and non-broadcast channels with a click of their remote control. * * *

Moreover, technological changes have given parents the ability to decide which programs they will permit their children to watch. Every television, 13 inches or larger, sold in the United States since January 2000 contains a V-chip, which allows parents to block programs based on a standardized rating system. 47 U.S.C. § 303(x). Moreover, since June 11, 2009, when the United States made the transition to digital television, anyone using a digital converter box also has access to a V-chip. *CSVA Report,* 24 F.C.C. Rcd. 11413, at ¶ 11. In short, there now exists a way to block programs that contain indecent speech in a way that was not possible in 1978. * * *

[W]e are bound by Supreme Court precedent, regardless of whether it reflects today's realities. The Supreme Court may decide in due course to overrule *Pacifica* and subject speech restrictions in the broadcast context to strict scrutiny. * * *

II

It is a basic principle that a law or regulation " 'is void for vagueness if its prohibitions are not clearly defined.' " *Piscottano v. Murphy*, 511 F.3d 247, 280 (2d Cir.2007) * * * A law or regulation is impermissibly vague if it does not "give the person of ordinary intelligence a reasonable opportunity to know what is prohibited." *Farrell v. Burke*, 449 F.3d 470, 485 (2d Cir.2006) * * * The First Amendment places a special burden on the government to ensure that restrictions on speech are not impermissibly vague. * * *

* * * The FCC set forth its indecency policy in its 2001 *Industry Guidance*, in which the FCC explained that an indecency finding involved the following two determinations: (1) whether the material "describe[s] or depict [s] sexual or excretory organs or activities"; and (2) whether the broadcast is "patently offensive as measured by contemporary community standards for the broadcast medium." Under the policy, whether a broadcast is patently offensive depends on the following three factors: (1) "the explicitness or graphic nature of the description or depiction"; (2) "whether the material dwells on or repeats at length" the description or depiction; and (3) "whether the material appears to pander or is used to titillate, or whether the materials appears to have been presented for its shock value." Since 2001, the FCC has interpreted its indecency policy in a number of decisions, including *Golden Globes Order* and the orders on review here.

The FCC argues that the indecency policy in its *Industry Guidance*, together with its subsequent decisions, give the broadcasters sufficient notice as to what will be considered indecent. The Networks argue that the policy is impermissibly vague and that the FCC's decisions interpreting the policy only add to the confusion of what will be considered indecent.

We agree with the Networks that the indecency policy is impermissibly vague. The first problem arises in the FCC's determination as to which words or expressions are patently offensive. For instance, while the FCC concluded that "bullshit" in a "NYPD Blue" episode was patently offensive, it concluded that "dick" and "dickhead" were not. Other expletives such as "pissed off," "up yours," "kiss my ass," and "wiping his ass" were also not found to be patently offensive. The Commission argues that its three-factor "patently offensive" test gives broadcasters fair notice of what it will find indecent. However, in each of these cases, the Commission's reasoning consisted of repetition of one or more of the factors without any discussion of how it applied them. Thus, the word "bullshit" is indecent because it is "vulgar, graphic and explicit" while the words "dickhead" was not indecent because it was "not sufficiently vulgar, explicit, or graphic." This hardly gives broadcasters notice of how the Commission will apply the factors in the future.

The English language is rife with creative ways of depicting sexual or excretory organs or activities, and even if the FCC were able to provide a complete list of all such expressions, new offensive and indecent words are invented every day. * * *

The FCC's current indecency policy undoubtedly gives the FCC more flexibility, but this flexibility comes at a price. The "artistic necessity" and "*bona fide* news" exceptions allow the FCC to decide, in each case, whether the First Amendment is implicated. The policy may maximize the amount of speech that the FCC can prohibit, but it results in a standard that even the FCC cannot articulate or apply consistently. Thus, it found the use of the word "bullshitter" on CBS's The Early Show to be "shocking and gratuitous" because it occurred "during a morning television interview," before reversing itself because the broadcast was a "bona fide news interview." In other words, the FCC reached diametrically opposite conclusions at different stages of the proceedings for precisely the same reason—that the word "bullshitter" was uttered during a news program. And when Judge Leval asked during oral argument if a program about the dangers of pre-marital sex designed for teenagers would be permitted, the most that the FCC's lawyer could say was "I suspect it would." With millions of dollars and core First Amendment values at stake, "I suspect" is simply not good enough.

With the FCC's indiscernible standards come the risk that such standards will be enforced in a discriminatory manner. The vagueness doctrine is intended, in part, to avoid that risk. If government officials are permitted to make decisions on an "ad hoc" basis, there is a risk that those decisions will reflect the officials' subjective biases. * * *

We have no reason to suspect that the FCC is using its indecency policy as a means of suppressing particular points of view. But even the risk of such subjective, content-based decision-making raises grave concerns under the First Amendment. Take, for example, the disparate treatment of "Saving Private Ryan" and the documentary, "The Blues." The FCC decided that the words "fuck" and "shit" were integral to the "realism and immediacy of the film experience for viewers" in "Saving Private Ryan," but not in "The Blues." We query how fleeting expletives could be more essential to the "realism" of a fictional movie than to the "realism" of interviews with real people about real life events, and it is hard not to speculate that the FCC was simply more comfortable with the themes in "Saving Private Ryan," a mainstream movie with a familiar cultural milieu, than it was with "The Blues," which largely profiled an outsider genre of musical experience. But even if there were a perfectly benign way of explaining these particular outcomes, nothing would prevent the FCC from applying its indecency policy in a discriminatory manner in the future. * * *

III

Under the current policy, broadcasters must choose between not airing or censoring controversial programs and risking massive fines or possibly even loss of their licenses, and it is not surprising which option they choose. Indeed, there is ample evidence in the record that the FCC's indecency policy has chilled protected speech.

For instance, several CBS affiliates declined to air the Peabody Award-winning "9/11" documentary, which contains real audio footage—including occasional expletives—of firefighters in the World Trade Center on September 11th. Although the documentary had previously aired twice without complaint, following the *Golden Globes Order* affiliates could no longer be sure whether the expletives contained in the documentary could be found indecent. * * *

The FCC's application of its policy to live broadcasts creates an even more profound chilling effect. In the case of the 2003 Billboard Music Awards broadcasts, Fox had an audio delay system in place to bleep fleeting expletives. It also pre-cleared the scripts of the presenters. Ritchie, however, departed from her script and used three expletives in rapid sequence. While the person employed to monitor and bleep expletives was bleeping the first, the following two slipped through. Even elaborate precautions will not protect a broadcaster against such occurrences. The FCC argues that Fox should simply implement a more effective screening system, but, short of giving up live broadcasting altogether, no system will ever be one hundred percent effective. Instead, Fox may decide not to ask individuals with a history of using profanity to present at its awards shows. But, of course, this will not prevent someone who wins an award—such as Cher or Bono—from using fleeting expletives. In fact, the only way that Fox can be sure that it won't be sanctioned by the FCC is by refusing to air the broadcast live.

This chilling effect extends to news and public affairs programming as well. Broadcasters may well decide not to invite controversial guests on to their programs for fear that an unexpected fleeting expletive will result in fines. The FCC points to its "*bona fide* news" exception to show that such fears would be unfounded. But the FCC has made clear that it considers the decision to apply this exception a matter within its discretion. * * * If the FCC's policy is allowed to remain in place, there will undoubtedly be countless other situations where broadcasters will exercise their editorial judgment and decline to pursue contentious people or subjects, or will eschew live programming altogether, in order to avoid the FCC's fines. This chill reaches speech at the heart of the First Amendment.

The chill of protected speech has even extended to programs that contain no expletives, but which contain reference to or discussion of sex, sexual organs, or excretion. For instance, Fox decided not to re-broadcast an episode of "That 70s Show" that dealt with masturbation, even though it neither depicted the act or discussed it in specific terms. The episode subsequently won an award from the Kaiser Family Foundation for its honest and accurate depiction of a sexual health issue. Similarly, an episode of "House" was re-written after concerns that one of the character's struggles with psychiatric issues related to his sexuality would be considered indecent by the FCC.

As these examples illustrate, the absence of reliable guidance in the FCC's standards chills a vast amount of protected speech dealing with some of the most important and universal themes in art and literature. Sex and the magnetic power of sexual attraction are surely among the most predominant themes in the study of humanity since the Trojan War. The digestive system and excretion are also important areas of human attention. By prohibiting all "patently offensive" references to sex, sexual organs, and excretion without giving adequate guidance as to what "patently offensive" means, the FCC effectively chills speech, because broadcasters have no way of knowing what the FCC will find offensive. To place any discussion of these vast topics at the broadcaster's peril has the effect of promoting wide self-censorship of valuable material which should be completely protected under the First Amendment.

IV

For the foregoing reasons, we strike down the FCC's indecency policy. We do not suggest that the FCC could not create a constitutional policy. We hold only that the FCC's current policy fails constitutional scrutiny. The petition for review is hereby GRANTED.

Federal Communications Commission v. Fox Television Stations, Inc.

132 S.Ct. 2307 (2012)

■ Justice Kennedy delivered the opinion of the Court.

In *FCC v. Fox Television Stations, Inc.*, 556 U.S. 502 (2009) (*Fox I*), the Court held that the Federal Communication Commission's decision to modify its indecency enforcement regime to regulate so-called fleeting expletives was neither arbitrary nor capricious. The Court then declined to address the constitutionality of the policy, however, because the United States Court of Appeals for the Second Circuit had yet to do so. On remand, the Court of Appeals found the policy was vague and, as a result, unconstitutional. The case now returns to this Court for decision upon the constitutional question.

I

* * * This Court first reviewed the Commission's indecency policy in *FCC v. Pacifica Foundation*, 438 U.S. 726 (1978). In *Pacifica*, the Commission determined that George Carlin's "Filthy Words" monologue was indecent. * * * This Court upheld the Commission's ruling. * * * Finding no First Amendment violation, the decision explained the constitutional standard under which regulations of broadcasters are assessed. It observed that "broadcast media have established a uniquely pervasive presence in the lives of all Americans," * * * and that "broadcasting is uniquely accessible to children, even those too young to read." In light of these considerations, "broadcasting ... has received the most limited First Amendment protection." * * *

In 2001, the Commission issued a policy statement. * * * In that document the Commission restated that for material to be indecent it must depict sexual or excretory organs or activities and be patently offensive as measured by contemporary community standards for the broadcast medium. Describing the framework of what it considered patently offensive, the Commission explained that three factors had proved significant:

> (1) [T]he explicitness or graphic nature of the description or depiction of sexual or excretory organs or activities; (2) whether the material dwells on or repeats at length descriptions of sexual or excretory organs or activities; (3) whether the material appears to pander or is used to titillate, or whether the material appears to have been presented for its shock value.

* * * It was against this regulatory background that the three incidents of alleged indecency at issue here took place. First, in the 2002 Billboard Music Awards, broadcast by respondent Fox Television Stations, Inc., the singer Cher exclaimed during an unscripted acceptance speech: "I've also had my critics for the last 40 years saying that I was on my way out every year. Right. So f * * * 'em." Second, Fox broadcast the Billboard Music Awards again in 2003. There, a person named Nicole Richie made the following unscripted remark while presenting an award: "Have you ever tried to get cow s* * * out of a Prada purse? It's not so f * * *ing simple." The third incident involved an episode of NYPD Blue, a regular television show broadcast by respondent ABC Television Network. The episode broadcast on February 25, 2003, showed the nude buttocks of an adult female character for approximately seven seconds and for a moment the side of her breast. During the scene, in which the character was preparing to take a shower, a child portraying her boyfriend's son entered the bathroom. A moment of awkwardness followed. The Commission received indecency complaints about all three broadcasts.

After these incidents, but before the Commission issued Notices of Apparent Liability to Fox and ABC, the Commission issued a decision sanctioning NBC for a comment made by the singer Bono during the 2003 Golden Globe Awards. Upon winning the award for Best Original Song, Bono exclaimed: " 'This is really, really, f* * *ing brilliant. Really, really great.' " *In re Complaints Against Various Broadcast Licensees Regarding Their Airing of the "Golden Globe Awards" Program*, 19 FCC Rcd. 4975, 4976, n. 4 (2004) (Golden Globes Order). Reversing a decision by its enforcement bureau, the Commission found the use of the F-word actionably indecent. The Commission held that the word was "one of the most vulgar, graphic and explicit descriptions of sexual activity in the English language," and thus found "any use of that word or a variation, in any context, inherently has a sexual connotation." Turning to the isolated nature of the expletive, the Commission reversed prior rulings that had found fleeting expletives not indecent. The Commission held "the mere fact that specific words or phrases are not sustained or repeated does not mandate a finding that material that is otherwise patently offensive to the broadcast medium is not indecent." * * *

Even though the incidents at issue in these cases took place before the Golden Globes Order, the Commission applied its new policy regarding fleeting expletives and fleeting nudity. It found the broadcasts by respondents Fox and ABC to be in violation of this standard. * * **

II

A fundamental principle in our legal system is that laws which regulate persons or entities must give fair notice of conduct that is forbidden or required. * * * This requirement of clarity in regulation is essential to the protections provided by the Due Process Clause of the Fifth Amendment. * * * It requires the invalidation of laws that are impermissibly vague. A conviction or punishment fails to comply with due process if the statute or regulation under which it is obtained "fails to provide a person of ordinary intelligence fair notice of what is prohibited, or is so standardless that it authorizes or encourages seriously discriminatory enforcement." As this Court has explained, a regulation is not vague because it may at times be difficult to prove an incriminating fact but rather because it is unclear as to what fact must be proved.

Even when speech is not at issue, the void for vagueness doctrine addresses at least two connected but discrete due process concerns: first, that regulated parties should know what is required of them so they may act accordingly; second, precision and guidance are necessary so that those enforcing the law do not act in an arbitrary or discriminatory way. * * * When speech is involved, rigorous adherence to those requirements is necessary to ensure that ambiguity does not chill protected speech.

These concerns are implicated here because, at the outset, the broadcasters claim they did not have, and do not have, sufficient notice of what is proscribed. And leaving aside any concerns about facial invalidity, they contend that the lengthy procedural history set forth above shows that the broadcasters did not have fair notice of what was forbidden. Under the 2001 Guidelines in force when the broadcasts occurred, a key consideration was " 'whether the material dwell[ed] on or repeat[ed] at length' " the offending description or depiction. In the 2004 Golden Globes Order, issued after the broadcasts, the Commission changed course and held that fleeting expletives could be a statutory violation. In the challenged orders now under review the Commission applied the new principle promulgated in the Golden Globes Order and determined fleeting expletives and a brief moment of indecency were actionably indecent. This regulatory history, however, makes it apparent that the Commission policy in place at the time of the broadcasts gave no notice to Fox or ABC that a fleeting expletive or a brief shot of nudity could be actionably indecent; yet Fox and ABC were found to be in violation. The Commission's lack of notice to Fox and ABC that its interpretation had changed so the fleeting moments of indecency contained in their broadcasts were a violation of § 1464 as interpreted and enforced by the agency "fail[ed] to provide a person of ordinary intelligence fair notice of what is prohibited." This would be true with respect to a regulatory change this abrupt on any subject, but it is surely the case when applied to the regulations in question, regulations that touch upon "sensitive areas of basic First Amendment freedoms." * * *

III

It is necessary to make three observations about the scope of this decision. First, because the Court resolves these cases on fair notice grounds under the Due Process Clause, it need not address the First Amendment implications of the Commission's indecency policy. It is argued that this Court's ruling in *Pacifica* (and the less rigorous standard of scrutiny it provided for the regulation of broadcasters, should be overruled because the rationale of that case has been overtaken by technological change and the wide availability of multiple other choices for listeners and viewers. * * * In light of the Court's holding that the Commission's policy failed to provide fair notice it is unnecessary to reconsider *Pacifica* at this time.

This leads to a second observation. Here, the Court rules that Fox and ABC lacked notice at the time of their broadcasts that the material they were broadcasting could be found actionably indecent under then-existing policies. Given this disposition, it is unnecessary for the Court to address the constitutionality of the current indecency policy as expressed in the Golden *Globes Order* and subsequent adjudications. The Court adheres to its normal practice of declining to decide cases not before it. * * *

Third, this opinion leaves the Commission free to modify its current indecency policy in light of its determination of the public interest and applicable legal requirements. And it leaves the courts free to review the current policy or any modified policy in light of its content and application.

The judgments of the United States Court of Appeals for the Second Circuit are vacated, and the cases are remanded for further proceedings consistent with the principles set forth in this opinion.

It is so ordered.

■ JUSTICE GINSBURG, concurring in the judgment.

In my view, the Court's decision in *FCC v. Pacifica Foundation*, 438 U.S. 726 (1978), was wrong when it issued. Time, technological advances, and the Commission's untenable rulings in the cases now before the Court show why Pacifica bears reconsideration. * * *

Questions

1. What were the justifications the courts in *Aimster* and *Fox* provided for indirect liability?

2. Court decisions that found operators of file-sharing technologies liable for users' copyright infringements were highly controversial. Similarly, the FCC's indecency ruling was controversial. Under what circumstances is indirect liability likely to be popular?

3. Copyright law imposes on certain technology operators a duty to prevent copyright infringements. The Federal Communications Commission Act and FCC's policies impose a duty on broadcasters to prevent indecency. What are the similarities and differences between the standards?

4. In *Pacifica*, the Supreme Court endorsed the FCC's regulation of the broadcast media in part because broadcasted indecent material enters into the privacy of the home uninvited and without warning.[184] The Court rejected the argument that the audience could simply tune-out: "To say that one may avoid further offense by turning off the radio when he hears indecent language is like saying that the remedy for an assault is to run away after the *first blow*."[185] In *Fox*, the Second Circuit mentioned the "first blow" theory that the FCC had adopted for its indecency policy. Does the 'first blow' theory provide a good motivation for indirect regulation of indecency?

5. In *Fox*, the broadcasters persuaded the Supreme Court that they did not have sufficient notice of what was proscribed. Was this claim plausible? Were the broadcasters unaware of the FCC's approach to nudity during primetime and the use of the F-word? Why did the Court accept the claim of insufficient notice?

§ 1.5 UNINTENDED CONSEQUENCES

> *"Restrictions have, it is true, been found more likely than grants to be unsuited to unforeseen circumstances."*
>
> —*Twitchell v. Blodgett* (1865)[186]

Regulations are designed to influence conduct in certain ways, but often interference in the private domain has some *unintended consequences—desirable* and *undesirable* effects that arise from state intervention in a complex reality.[187]

Examples of unintended consequences span a diverse range of regulations. Economists have shown that the Americans with Disabilities Act (ADA), which requires employers to accommodate disabled workers and outlaws discrimination in hiring, firing, and wage decisions against this class of workers, has led to a decrease in the employment of disabled workers since its enactment.[188] To avoid land-use regulations imposed by

184. FCC v. Pacifica Found., 438 U.S. 726, 748 (1978).

185. *Id.* at 748–49 (emphasis added).

186. Twitchell v. Blodgett, 13 Mich. 127, 139 (1865).

187. *See generally* Robert K. Merton, *The Unanticipated Consequences of Purposive Social Action*, 1 AMERICAN SOCIOLOGICAL REVIEW 894 (1936).

188. Daron Acemoglu & Joshua D. Angrist, *Consequences of Employment Protection? The Case of the Americans with Disabilities Act*, 109 JOURNAL OF POLITICAL ECONOMY 915 (2001).

the Endangered Species Act, some landowners destroyed habitat that could be used by endangered species.[189] Researchers established an empirical a link between the legalization of abortions in *Roe v. Wade*[190] and the substantial drop in crime rates during the 1990s.[191] When scientists examined the consequences of "selective fishing" regulatory policies, which were intended to protect the overexploitation of specific fish species, they found that these policies alter biodiversity; this effect, in turn changes ecosystem functioning and may affect the fisheries production, hindering rather than helping achieve the goals of ecosystem-based management.[192] Mandatory disclosure rules in civil litigation were adopted to curtail litigation costs, but in many circumstances have actually had the opposite effect.[193]

Unintended consequences sometimes create business opportunities. Such opportunities, *regulatory arbitrage*, exploit the gap between the economic substance of some matter (*e.g.*, a transaction, litigation, or product) and its regulatory treatment, taking advantage of the legal system's limited ability to capture the richness of reality with sufficient precision.[194] For example, the word "person" is frequently used in legal contexts to refer to any legal entity. However, in other contexts the word "person" simply refers to a human being. When a regulation affects a person but does not expressly define the term, firms try to take advantage of the ambiguity to argue they are eligible to "personal privacy,"[195] to invest in political campaigns,[196] and other things.

Unintended consequences, therefore, are a byproduct of regulations. However, lack of regulation may also have unintended consequences. Climate change, financial meltdowns, endangered species, epidemic breakouts, and other social harms are unintended consequences that happen in the absence of regulation, and may be avoided or mitigated with regulation. Thus, the belief that "[r]estrictions [are] more likely than grants to be unsuited to unforeseen circumstances"[197] is generally misguided.

---

189. *See, e.g.*, Dean Lueck & Jeffrey Michael, *Preemptive Habitat Destruction Under the Endangered Species Act*, 46 JOURNAL OF LAW & ECONOMICS 27 (2003).

190. 410 U.S. 113 (1973).

191. John J. Donohue III & Steven D. Levitt, *The Impact of Legalized Abortion on Crime*, 116 QUARTERLY JOURNAL OF ECONOMICS 379 (2001).

192. Shijie Zhoua et al., *Ecosystem–Based Fisheries Management Requires a Change to the Selective Fishing Philosophy*, 107 PROCEEDINGS OF THE NATIONAL ACADEMY OF SCIENCES 9485 (2010).

193. *See* Samuel Issacharoff & George Loewenstein, *Unintended Consequences of Mandatory Disclosure*, 73 TEXAS LAW REVIEW 753 (1995).

194. *See* Victor Fleicher, *Regulatory Arbitrage*, 89 TEXAS LAW REVIEW 227, 230 (2010); Frank Partnoy, *Financial Derivatives and the Costs of Regulatory Arbitrage*, 22 JOURNAL OF CORPORATE LAW 211, 227 (1997) ("Regulatory arbitrage consists of those financial transactions designed specifically to reduce costs or capture profit opportunities created by differential regulations or laws").

195. *See, e.g.*, F.C.C. v. AT & T Inc., 131 S.Ct. 1177 (2011).

196. *See, e.g.*, Citizens United v. Federal Election Commission, 130 S.Ct. 876 (2010).

197. Twitchell v. Blodgett, 13 Mich. 127, 139 (1865).

Plastic Bags and Legal Definitions

In April 2007, the San Francisco Board of Supervisors adopted the Plastic Bag Reduction Ordinance,[198] making the City the first jurisdiction in the United States to restrict the use of plastic bags. The ordinance required all stores to provide customers with three types of "checkout bags": recyclable paper bags, compostable plastic bags, or reusable plastic bags.[199] To avoid confusion, the ordinance listed several clear definitions:

- "Compostable Plastic Bag" means a plastic bag that (1) conforms to California labeling law * * *; (2) is certified and labeled as meeting the ASTM–Standard* * *; (3) conforms to requirements to ensure that the renewable based product content is maximized over time as set forth in Department of the Environment regulations; (4) conforms to requirements to ensure that products derived from genetically modified feedstocks are phased out over time as set forth in Department of the Environment regulations; and (5) displays the phrase "Green Cart Compostable" and the word "Reusable" in a highly visible manner on the outside of the bag.
- "Checkout bag" means a carryout bag that is provided by a store to a customer at the point of sale.
- "Recyclable" means material that can be sorted, cleansed, and reconstituted using San Francisco's available recycling collection programs for the purpose of using the altered form in the manufacture of a new product. Recycling does not include burning, incinerating, converting, or otherwise thermally destroying solid waste.
- "Recyclable Paper Bag" means a paper bag that meets all of the following requirements: (1) contains no old growth fiber, (2) is 100% recyclable overall and contains a minimum of 40% post-consumer recycled content, and (3) displays the words "Reusable" and "Recyclable" in a highly visible manner on the outside of the bag.
- "Reusable Bag" means a bag with handles that is specifically designed and manufactured for multiple reuse and is either (1) made of cloth or other machine washable fabric, and/or (2) made of durable plastic that is at least 2.25 mils thick.

In April 2010, just three years later, the Board of Supervisors adopted a resolution calling for an amendment to the 2007 regulation:[200]

> WHEREAS, Checkout bags use increasingly scarce resources including energy, and create pollution from production through disposal; and,
>
> WHEREAS, The City and County of San Francisco adopted the Plastic Bag Reduction Ordinance * * * in 2007; and
>
> WHEREAS, The intention of the Ordinance was to reduce the use of single-use plastic bags by banning them at supermarkets and drugstores; and,

---

198. San Francisco Plastic Bag Reduction Ordinance 81–07 (Apr. 20, 2007), available at *regti.me/SF-pb2007* (case sensitive).

199. *Id.* § 1703.

200. A copy of the resolution is available at *regti.me/SF-pb2010* (case sensitive).

WHEREAS, The Plastic Bag Reduction Ordinance allows stores to give away reusable bags, which are defined as including any plastic bag at least 2.5 mil thick; and

WHEREAS, This definition has resulted in the unintended consequence of some stores distributing 2.5 mil thick polyethylene plastic bags, which may not be suitably durable, to customers for free; and,

WHEREAS, Plastic bags provided for free at checkout are usually perceived as disposable products who consumers then continue to treat as single-use plastic bags being used on average for just a few minutes, thus creating an impediment to increasing bag reuse; and,

* * *

WHEREAS. The Plastic Bag Reduction Ordinance allows the Director of the Department of the Environment, after a public hearing, to adopt or amend guideline rules and regulation in order to implement the Ordinance; now, therefore, be it

RESOLVED. That the Board of Supervisors requests the Director of the Department of the Environment to promulgate new. or amend existing, regulations to ensure that reusable bags are suitably durable, and do not contribute to the landfill waste stream.

Questions

1. What were the unintended consequences of the San Francisco's 2007 Ordinance? Could have they been avoided?

2. Did the 2007 Ordinance create any opportunities for regulatory arbitrage? If so, what were these opportunities?

3. San Francisco was the first jurisdiction in the United States to restrict the use of plastic bags. In 2010, the City sought to address the unintended consequences created by its plastic bag regulation. What were the lessons other localities could have drawn from the identified unintended consequences?

Smoking in Atlantic City

In January 2006, the New Jersey legislature passed the Smoke–Free Air Act.[201] In the statute, the legislature described the history and motivation underlying the regulation:

26:3D–56. Legislative findings and declarations; smoking in enclosed indoor places of public access and workplaces

The Legislature finds and declares that: tobacco is the leading cause of preventable disease and death in the State and the nation, and tobacco smoke constitutes a substantial health hazard to the nonsmoking majority of the public; the separation of smoking and

201. N.J.S.A. §§ 26:3D–55 et seq.

> nonsmoking areas in indoor public places and workplaces does not eliminate the hazard to nonsmokers if these areas share a common ventilation system; and, therefore, subject to certain specified exceptions, it is clearly in the public interest to prohibit smoking in all enclosed indoor places of public access and workplaces.

The Smoke–Free Air Act prohibits smoking "in an indoor public place or workplace, except as otherwise provided in this act,"[202] but it exempts indoors smoking in casinos. The exemption Section provides:

> (1) any casino * * * approved by the Casino Control Commission that contains at least 150 stand-alone slot machines, 10 table games, or some combination thereof approved by the commission, which machines and games are available to the public for wagering; and
>
> (2) any casino simulcasting facility approved by the Casino Control Commission * * * that contains a simulcast counter and dedicated seating for at least 50 simulcast patrons or a simulcast operation and at least 10 table games, which simulcast facilities and games are available to the public for wagering.[203]

In November 2006, a few months after the enactment of the Smoke–Free Air Act, the City Council of Atlantic City adopted a smoking ordinance that imposed restrictions on indoor smoking in casinos:[204]

> **Section 221–6—Where Smoking Not Regulated**
>
> Notwithstanding any other provision of this Article to the contrary, the following areas shall be exempt from the [prohibition of smoking]:
>
> * * *
>
> F. Gaming Floors within licensed casino hotel facilities; provided, however, that not more than twenty-five percent (25%) of such Gaming Floor * * * may be so designated; and further provided * * * that the exempt areas so designated shall be (a) enclosed by solid walls or windows, a ceiling and a solid door; and (b) equipped with a ventilation system separately exhausted from the nonsmoking areas of the casino hotel facility so that air from the exempt areas is not recirculated to and smoke is not back streamed into such nonsmoking areas.

Shortly after the adoption of the Ordinance, casino employees and other interest groups began lobbying the City Council to expand its scope. They argued that "the reduction of smoking areas from 100% of the casino floor down to a concentrated area of 25% places a greater burden on the employees who are forced to work in the smoking areas." The employees further argued that the casinos did not comply with the requirement to

---

202. N.J.S.A § 26:3D–58(a).

203. N.J.S.A § 26:3D–59(e).

204. City of Atlantic City, N.J., Ordinance 86 (November 15, 2006, as amended on January 24, 2007).

build barriers to separate the smoking areas from the non-smoking areas, as the Ordinance mandated.[205]

In light of these complaints, in March 2008, the City Council voted unanimously for a complete ban on smoking in casinos and issued another ordinance that eliminated the casino exemption of the 2006 Ordinance.[206] In the summer of 2008, when the magnitude of the economic downturn became apparent, and casinos revenues began declining sharply, the City adopted yet another Ordinance.

Ordinance

Ordinance No. 95	OF THE CITY OF ATLANTIC CITY, N.J.	Date: 10–08–08 Date to Mayor 10–27–08

AN ORDINANCE TO AMEND CHAPTER 221–SMOKING–AMENDING THE RESTRICTIONS ON SMOKING AREAS UPON A CASINO FLOOR AND REQUIRING THE RECONSIDERATION OF THIS AMENDMENT IN ONE YEAR

WHEREAS, in January 2006, the New Jersey legislature adopted the Smoke Free Air Act (the "Act") (N.J.S.A. 26:3D–55 et. seq.) which, in addition to prohibiting smoking in most indoor workplaces throughout the state, limited smoking within casino properties to gaming floors and certain guest rooms; and
WHEREAS, on February 2007, the Atlantic City Council ("Council") adopted Ordinance 86, which prohibited smoking on all but twenty five (25%) percent of the area of the casino gaming floor; and
WHEREAS, on April 2008, the Council adopted Ordinance 27, which will effectively restrict smoking on the casino floor to non-gaming areas beginning on October 15, 2008; and
WHEREAS, since the adoption of Ordinance 27, however, the regional and national economic conditions have significantly deteriorated and that deterioration has had a destabilizing effect on the local economy and the welfare of many Atlantic City residents;
WHEREAS, Atlantic City casino industry performance has also declined over that period causing a loss of current and future local employment opportunities, a reduction in funding for senior programs, and a delay in the construction of commercial development needed to reduce the property tax liability of Atlantic City residents; and
WHEREAS, based on the consequences of similar restrictions placed on casino patrons' smoking in other jurisdictions around the country, the implementation at this time of the additional Ordinance 27 restrictions would likely cause a significant, immediate and further decline in the Atlantic City casino industry; and
WHEREAS, in light of the current situation as described above, the implementation of the further smoking restrictions of Ordinance 27 at this time would be imprudent and should be delayed to permit the economic recovery of the region and the national financial markets, and the provisions of Ordinance 86 of 2007 reinstated to restrict smoking to twenty five (25%) percent of a casino gaming floor;
NOW, THEREFORE, BE IT ORDAINED that Chapter 221 of the Code of Atlantic City–SMOKING be amended as follows:

SECTION ONE
Chapter 221–6 "Exemptions from smoking regulations" shall be amended to provide:
Add: Chapter 221–6(A)(6). Gaming Floors within licensed casino hotel facilities; provided, however, that not more than twenty-five (25%) percent of such Gaming

205. City of Atlantic City, N.J., Ordinance 27 (March 26, 2008).

206. *Id.*

Floor, as particularly determined by the casino licensee operator of the casino hotel facility within which the Gaming Floor is located, may be so designated. Replace: Chapter 221–6(B). On the one year anniversary of the adoption of the ordinance amending this section, Council, through its Revenue and Finance Committee, shall review this Chapter and determine whether the factors then impacting the general welfare of Atlantic City residents and the Atlantic City casino industry and the employment, development, competitive and other economic conditions which affect them warrant a continuation of the provisions of Subsection 6(a)(6) or the restrictions of Ordinance 27 should be re-implemented.

SECTION TWO
Any Ordinance or parts of any Ordinance inconsistent with the provisions of this Ordinance are hereby repealed to the extent of any such inconsistency.

SECTION THREE
This Ordinance shall take effect immediately as provided by law.

Questions

1. Whose interests can a ban on smoking in Atlantic City casinos serve? Is such a prohibition likely to promote the interests of the City?

2. What were the unintended consequences of the 2006 Ordinance? Did the March 2008 Ordinance also have unintended consequences?

3. Did the smoking restrictions in Atlantic City create any opportunities for regulatory arbitrage? If so, what were these opportunities?

§ 1.6 COST-BENEFIT ANALYSIS

In *United States v. Carroll Towing Co.*,[207] Judge Learned Hand famously penned the modern negligence standard:

> [The defendant's] duty, as in other similar situations, to provide against resulting injuries is a function of three variables: (1) The probability that [accident would occur]; (2) the gravity of the resulting injury* * *; (3) the burden of adequate precautions. Possibly it serves to bring this notion into relief to state it in algebraic terms: if the probability be called P; the injury, L; and the burden, B; liability depends upon whether B is less than L multiplied by P: i.e., whether B < PL.[208]

Known as the "Learned Hand formula," courts use this standard to compare the costs and benefits of particular precautions the defendant did not take.[209]

The Learned Hand formula is canonized in law and economics literature as the first use of cost-benefit analysis for determining negligence and assigning liability.[210] Courts, however, do not always follow it,[211] and in

---

207. 159 F.2d 169 (2d Cir. 1947).

208. *Id.* at 173.

209. *See* Mark Grady, *Untaken Precautions*, 18 JOURNAL OF LEGAL STUDIES 139 (1989). *See also* Allan M. Feldman & Jeonghyun Kim, *The Hand Rule and* United States v. Carroll Towing *Reconsidered*, 7 AMERICAN LAW & ECONOMICS REVIEW 523 (2005).

210. For an earlier cost-benefit formulation of the concept of negligence in torts *see* Harry T. Terry, *Negligence*, 29 HARVARD LAW REVIEW 40 (1915); Restatement of Torts § 291 (1934).

211. *See, e.g.*, McCarty v. Pheasant Run, Inc., 826 F.2d 1554 (7th Cir. 1987).

many instances it is inconsistent with adequate cost-benefit analysis because it focuses on the analysis of *particular untaken precautions*. The formula does not factor take the victim's ability to mitigate harm or even avoid the accident. It also does not identify the best precaution for the circumstances, namely the most cost-effective precaution. The formula merely evaluates if a specific untaken precaution could be cost-effective. Nonetheless, despite its limitations, the Learned Hand formula has offered guidance in analyzing negligence.[212] More broadly, the Learned Hand formula has integrated cost-benefit analysis in the American legal tradition.

§ 1.6.1 The Underlying Intuition

Regulatory policies involve governmental choices to act or not to act to influence the conduct of firms and individuals. These policies intend to benefit the public or at least certain sectors therein, but any policy—whether to act or not to act—also entails social costs that can be rather significant. The Great Recession offers an extreme example of such costs. An informed regulatory choice takes into account (1) the social costs of not acting, (2) the regulatory budget—the amount of resources society is willing to commit to the address the issue in question, and (3) the costs and benefits of the regulatory options available within the regulatory budget.

To illustrate, assume that without any regulatory inspection, there is a 1% chance that tainted eggs will create a social harm of $100,000 (say, due to a salmonella outbreak[213]). At a cost of $2,000 the risk can be eliminated and at a cost of $500 the likelihood of the risk can be reduced to 0.1%. Which regulatory option is socially desirable? (a) No government action, (b) Eliminating the risk at a cost of $2,000, or (c) Reducing the risk at a cost of $500.

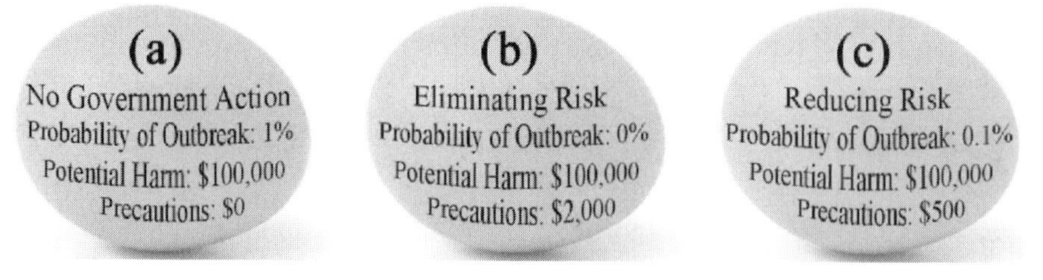

(a)
No Government Action
Probability of Outbreak: 1%
Potential Harm: $100,000
Precautions: $0

(b)
Eliminating Risk
Probability of Outbreak: 0%
Potential Harm: $100,000
Precautions: $2,000

(c)
Reducing Risk
Probability of Outbreak: 0.1%
Potential Harm: $100,000
Precautions: $500

The expected social cost of option (a), government inaction, is $1,000 (0.01*$100,000). For $2,000 the government can eliminate an expected social cost of $1,000 to 0. Thus, the expected social cost of option (b) is also $1,000. For $500, the government can reduce an expected social cost of

212. *See generally* GUIDO CALABRESI, THE COST OF ACCIDENTS: A LEGAL AND ECONOMIC ANALYSIS (1970).

213. In August 2010, more than half a billion eggs were recalled because of a salmonella outbreak originated on two egg farms in Iowa. *See* Lindsey Layton, *Unsafe Eggs Linked to U.S. Failure to Act*, WASHINGTON POST, Dec. 11, 2010, at A1; William Neuman, *Fried, Scrambled, Infected*, NEW YORK TIMES, Sept. 26, 2010, at WK5. A timeline of the events is available at *regti.me/2010SE* (case sensitive).

$1,000 to $100 (0.001*$100,000). Thus, the expected social cost of option (c) is $600 ($100+$500). We see then that decisions to regulate or not to regulate may entail social costs of a similar magnitude, although the costs tend spread in different ways.

§ 1.6.2 Executive Order 12866

In September 1993, President Bill Clinton issued Executive Order 12866 (E.O. 12866), which outlines the general regulatory principles of the federal government. E.O. 12866 declares:

> The American people deserve a regulatory system that works for them, not against them: a regulatory system that protects and improves their health, safety, environment, and well-being and improves the performance of the economy without imposing unacceptable or unreasonable costs on society; regulatory policies that recognize that the private sector and private markets are the best engine for economic growth; regulatory approaches that respect the role of State, local, and tribal governments; and regulations that are effective, consistent, sensible, and understandable. * * * We do not have such a regulatory system today.[214]

At the core of E.O. 12866 is a "Statement of Regulatory Philosophy and Principles" that intends to guide federal agencies and provides a general criterion for assessing their performance: "In deciding whether and how to regulate, [federal] agencies should assess all costs and benefits of available regulatory alternatives, including the alternative of not regulating." Put simply, cost-benefit analysis should guide federal agencies when they consider and develop regulatory policies. Using our egg inspection hypothetical, E.O. 12866 instructs the relevant regulatory agency to consider the costs and benefits of all available regulatory alternatives, including the alternative of not regulating.

Furthermore, E.O. 12866 emphasizes that the agencies should be inclusive in considering costs and benefits:

> Costs and benefits shall be understood to include both quantifiable measures (to the fullest extent that these can be usefully estimated) and qualitative measures of costs and benefits that are difficult to quantify, but nevertheless essential to consider. Further, in choosing among alternative regulatory approaches, agencies should select those approaches that maximize net benefits (including potential economic, environmental, public health and safety, and other advantages; distributive impacts; and equity), unless a statute requires another regulatory approach.

E.O. 12866 has greatly improved regulatory efficiency by forcing federal agencies to conduct cost-benefit analysis. As we shall see, the (present) critique of the regulatory system consists of objections to regulation,

---

214. A copy of E.O. 12866 is available at *regti.me/EO12866* (case sensitive). E.O. 12866 replaced Executive Order 12291, which President Ronald Reagan issued in February 1981. Executive Order 12291 adopted a rudimentary cost-benefit analysis framework. It determined that the "[r]egulatory objectives shall be chosen to maximize the net benefits to society." § 2(c).

objections to changes and improvements, demands for more regulation, and evaluations of specific regulatory policies.

§ 1.6.3 (Why) Is Cost–Benefit Analysis Controversial?

In 1967, a year before becoming the youngest tenured professor in the history of Harvard University, Stephen Marglin, published a book entitled *Public Investment Criteria: Benefit–Cost Analysis for Planned Economic Growth*. Summarizing his critique of federal agencies' use of cost-benefit analysis, he wrote:

> Benefit-cost analysis was introduced as a means of project 'justification' alone * * *, not as a tool for project planning; in American practice (as distinct from theory) it often has served as window dressing for projects whose plans have already been formulated with little if any reference to economic criteria.[215]

Cost-benefit analysis (CBA) is indeed a controversial concept. But this "concept" is not a black box whose content is unknown or whose nature does not change. Rather, CBA methodologies have been constantly evolving.[216] Correspondingly, the debate over CBA has been changing as well. Although old arguments are still occasionally raised, they do not necessarily refer to modern CBA or its contemporary practices.[217]

CBA is unlikely to be universally embraced for many reasons. We discuss here five major dimensions of critique:

(1) Conflicts with preexisting views and beliefs.

(2) Confusions caused by campaigns of interest groups.

(3) Critique of the CBA methodology.

(4) Objections to the pricing of certain values.

(5) Irreversibility of certain harms.

1. *Conflicts with Preexisting Views and Beliefs*. Although CBA methodology appears intuitive, many of its applications are often counterintuitive and controversial.[218] CBA is rationally appealing because it claims to promote regulations whose benefits outweigh their costs, and it can provide the tools to design, implement, and assess such regulations.[219] Those who endorse CBA because of its rational appeal, often abandon such reasoning

---

215. Stephen Marglin, Public Investment Criteria: Benefit-Cost Analysis for Planned Economic Growth 18 (1967).

216. See, *e.g.*, Cass R. Sunstein, The Cost-Benefit State (2002).

217. *See, e.g., See also* Joseph Persky, *Cost-Benefit Analysis and the Classical Creed*, 15 Journal of Economic Perspectives 199 (2001). *See also* Matthew D. Adler & Eric A. Posner, *Rethinking Cost–Benefit Analysis*, 109 Yale Law Journal 165 (1999); Shi–Ling Hsu & John Loomis, *A Defense of Cost–Benefit Analysis for Natural Resource Policy*, 32 Environmental Law Reporter 10239 (2002).

218. *See, e.g.*, Robert H. Frank, *Why Is Cost–Benefit Analysis So Controversial*, 29 Journal of Legal Studies 913 (2000); Robert Kuttner, Everything for Sale: The Virtues and Limits of Markets (1997); Amartya Sen, *The Discipline of Cost–Benefit Analysis*, 29 Journal of Legal Studies 931 (2000).

219. *See generally* Sunstein, *supra* note 209; Cass R. Sunstein, *Cognition and Cost–Benefit Analysis*, 29 Journal of Legal Studies 1059 (2000).

when it advises actions that contradict their beliefs or expectations. This logical flaw is not unique to CBA. Rather, it is an innate human tendency to reject inconvenient information.[220]

2. *Confusions Caused By Interest Groups.* Interest groups promote their agendas, not the public interest. To this end, they frequently employ persuasion techniques to obscure scientific data, undermining public confidence in the scientific community.[221] Interest groups often work to erode the validity of CBA. In some instances, such as smoking[222] and baby food,[223] the debates focus on costs *or* benefits and do not systematically compare them. In other areas, however, such as climate change and vaccinations,[224] the public discourse relies on a *partial* comparison of costs and benefits.

3. *Critique of the CBA Methodology.* Some CBA critics argue that the CBA philosophy is flawed and cannot serve society well.[225] To illustrate these arguments, consider our egg inspection hypothetical. What are the legitimate methods to estimate the social benefits of eggs, the social costs of tainted eggs, and the costs of inspecting eggs? Some argue that the methods used for CBA are not legitimate. For example, CBA analysis requires accounting for future values, since some costs and benefits accrue over time. Some argue that such adjustments are illegitimate for one reason or another. This critique is more about the implementation of CBA, although it is often framed as a criticism of CBA.

4. *Objections to the Pricing of Certain Values.* Most CBA critiques focus on two values—human lives and the environment. Some CBA critics have expressed discomfort with or raised ethical concerns about the pricing and discounting of these values.[226] CBA methodologies require "pricing" everything to estimate how much society is willing to invest in saving one human life, a particular environmental resource, or something else.[227] This

---

220. *See* § 2.1.

221. *See, e.g.*, THOMAS O. MCGARITY, BENDING SCIENCE, HOW SPECIAL INTERESTS GROUP CORRUPT PUBLIC HEALTH RESEARCH (2010); DAVID MICHAELS, DOUBT IN THEIR PRODUCT: HOW INDUSTRY'S ASSAULT ON SCIENCE THREATENS YOUR HEALTH (2008); NAOMI ORESKES & ERIK M. M. CONWAY, MERCHANTS OF DOUBT: HOW A HANDFUL OF SCIENTISTS OBSCURED THE TRUTH ON ISSUES FROM TOBACCO SMOKE TO GLOBAL WARMING (2011).

222. *See generally* ALLAN BRANDT, THE CIGARETTE CENTURY: THE RISE, FALL, AND DEADLY PERSISTENCE OF THE PRODUCT THAT DEFINED AMERICA (2009).

223. *See* Toby Milgrom Levin, *The Infant Formula Act of 1980: A Case Study of Congressional Delegation to the Food and Drug Administration*, 42 FOOD DRUG COSMETIC LAW JOURNAL 101 (1987).

224. For vaccinations *see* §§ 2.5, 3.3.3. For climate change *see, e.g.*, SPENCER R. WEART, THE DISCOVERY OF GLOBAL WARMING (rev. ed. 2008); Mary–Elena Carr et al., *Climate Change: Addressing the Major Skeptic Arguments*, Deutche Bank Climate Change Advisors (Sept. 2010).

225. *See, e.g.*, FRANK ACKERMAN & LISA HEINZERLING, PRICELESS: ON KNOWING THE PRICE OF EVERYTHING AND THE VALUE OF NOTHING (2004); ROBERT KUTTNER, EVERYTHING FOR SALE, *supra* note 211; DOUGLAS A. KYSAR, REGULATING FROM NOWHERE: ENVIRONMENTAL LAW AND THE SEARCH FOR OBJECTIVITY (2010). *See also* Frank, *Why Is Cost–Benefit Analysis So Controversial*, *supra* note 211.

226. *See, e.g.*, ACKERMAN & HEINZERLING, PRICELESS, *supra* note 218; ROBERT KUTTNER, EVERYTHING FOR SALE, *supra* note 211; KYSAR, REGULATING FROM NOWHERE, *id.*

227. *See generally* Orley Ashenfelter, *Measuring the Value of Statistical Life: Problems and Prospects*, 116 ECONOMIC JOURNAL C10 (2006); Dasgupta, *Discounting Climate Change*,

line of critique has been losing ground, since for practical purposes society must consider costs.[228]

5. *Irreversibility of Certain Harms*. Some critics point out that certain activities pose such a great threat to the environment, endangered species, or human lives that they should be avoided altogether. This *Precautionary Principle* (PP) follows the intuitive rules of thumb "first, do no harm" and "better safe than sorry."[229] People often rely on these simple rules. For example, "better safe than sorry" is the recommended approach to driving and fire safety. Intuitive rules of thumb, however, do not have the details needed for legal rules and are not necessarily good for public policy.[230] Framed as a legal rule, PP bans a risky activity, until its safety is proved. For example, in 2003, San Francisco adopted PP "as a general City policy,"[231] dictating "that where threats of serious or irreversible damage to people or natural systems exist, lack of full scientific certainty relating to cause and effect shall not be viewed as sufficient reason to postpone measures to prevent the degradation of the environment or protect human health." The City therefore integrated "a precautionary principle approach into the * * * existing process for the purchase of commodities" and into several others areas. PP critics argue that its application requires active regulation of activities, even when the risk is unknown.[232] To illustrate, consider San Francisco's PP regulation. The City's process of commodity purchases is burdened with inquiries and constraints, regardless of whether risks exist. PP proponents believe that this burden is justified—although it means greater public spending or reduction in scope of activities. For them, potential risks to human health and the environment should supersede CBA.

The Delaney Clause

Rising rates of death associated with cancer in the 1930s and 1940s motivated Congress to consider how to reduce potential cancer risks. In

---

supra note 217; John D. Graham, *Saving Lives Through Administrative Law and Economics*, 157 UNIVERSITY OF PENNSYLVANIA LAW REVIEW 395 (2008); Hsu & Loomis, *A Defense of Cost–Benefit Analysis for Natural Resource Policy*, *supra* note 210; W. Kip Viscusi, *The Devaluation of Life*, 3 REGULATION & GOVERNANCE 103 (2009).

228. *See* Goodin, *Selling Environmental Indulgences*, *supra* note 57.

229. *See generally* Kenneth J. Arrow & Anthony C. Fisher, Environmental Preservation, Uncertainty, and Irreversibility, 88 QUARTERLY JOURNAL OF ECONOMICS 312 (1974); Christian Gollier & Nicholas Treich, *Decision–Making Under Scientific Uncertainty: The Economics of the Precautionary Principle*, 27 JOURNAL OF RISK & UNCERTAINTY 77 (2003); KYSAR, REGULATING FROM NOWHERE, *supra* note 218; Robert S. Pindyck, *Irreversibilities and the Timing of Environmental Policy*, 22 RESOURCES AND ENERGY ECONOMICS 233 (2000).

230. *See generally* §§ 4.1.2, 7.4. *See also* Cass R. Sunstein, *Moral Heuristics and Risk*, in EMOTIONS AND RISKY TECHNOLOGIES 3 (Sabine Roeser ed., 2010).

231. City and County of San Francisco, Resolution No. 129–03 (Mar. 13, 2003); San Francisco Environment Code and Precautionary Principle Policy, Ordinance No. 171–03 (July 3, 2003), available at *regti.me/SF-PP* (case sensitive).

232. *See generally* CASS R. SUNSTEIN, LAWS OF FEAR: BEYOND THE PRECAUTIONARY PRINCIPLE (2005); Cass Sunstein, *Irreversibility*, 9 LAW PROBABILITY & RISK 227 (2010).

1950, the House of Representatives established a House Select Committee to Investigate the Use of Chemicals in Food Products, chaired by Representative James Delaney of New York. After several hearings, Delaney became convinced that too many chemicals, including pesticide chemicals, were used in foods. In 1957, Congress began debating the Federal Food Drug and Cosmetic Act (FFDCA). One of the amendments to the original bill introduced by Delaney dealt with food additives and contained anticancer language. Congress passed the FFDCA with a so-called Delaney Clause, which applies to food additives, precludes approvals of food additives that could induce cancer risk of any kind and level and bans consideration of any possible benefits of such food additives. In 1996, Congress passed the Food Quality Protection Act, excluding pesticide residues from the scope of the Delaney Clause.

Les v. Reilly

968 F.2d 985 (9th Cir. 1992)

■ SCHROEDER, CIRCUIT JUDGE:

Petitioners seek review of a final order of the Environmental Protection Agency permitting the use of four pesticides as food additives although they have been found to induce cancer. Petitioners challenge the final order on the ground that it violates the provisions of the Delaney clause, 21 U.S.C. § 348(c)(3), which prohibits the use of any food additive that is found to induce cancer.

* * * Notwithstanding the Delaney clause, the EPA [argued that] although the chemicals posed a measurable risk of causing cancer, that risk was "de minimis."

We set aside the EPA's order because we agree with the petitioners that the language of the Delaney clause, its history and purpose all reflect that Congress intended the EPA to prohibit all additives that are carcinogens, regardless of the degree of risk involved.

Background

The Federal Food, Drug, and Cosmetic Act (FFDCA) * * * is designed to ensure the safety of the food we eat by prohibiting the sale of food that is "adulterated." 21 U.S.C. § 331(a). Adulterated food is in turn defined as food containing any unsafe food "additive." 21 U.S.C. § 342(a)(2)(C). A food "additive" is defined broadly as "any substance the intended use of which results or may reasonably be expected to result * * * in its becoming a component * * * of any food." 21 U.S.C. § 321(s). A food additive is considered unsafe unless there is a specific exemption for the substance or a regulation prescribing the conditions under which it may be used safely. 21 U.S.C. § 348(a).

Before 1988, the four pesticide chemicals with which we are here concerned—benomyl, mancozeb, phosmet and trifluralin—were all the subject of regulations issued by the EPA permitting their use. In October 1988, however, the EPA published a list of substances, including the pesticides at issue here, that had been found to induce cancer. Regulation of Pesticides in Food: Addressing the Delaney Paradox Policy Statement, 53 Fed.Reg. 41,104, 41,119 (Oct. 19, 1988). As known carcinogens, the four pesticides ran afoul of a special provision of the FFDCA known as the Delaney clause, which prescribes that additives found to induce cancer can never be deemed "safe" for purposes of the FFDCA. The Delaney clause is found in FFDCA section 409. That section limits the conditions under which the Secretary may issue regulations allowing a substance to be used as a food additive:

> No such regulation shall issue if a fair evaluation * * * (A) fails to establish that the proposed use of the food additive, under the conditions of use to be specified in the regulation, will be safe: *Provided,* That no additive shall be deemed to be safe if it is found to induce cancer when ingested by man or animal, or if it is found, after tests which are appropriate for the evaluation of the safety of food additives, to induce cancer in man or animal. * * *
>
> 21 U.S.C. § 348(c)(3).

* * * It is undisputed that the EPA regulations at issue in this case allow for the concentration of cancer-causing pesticides during processing to levels in excess of those permitted in the raw foods.

The proceedings in this case had their genesis in October 1988 when the EPA published a list of substances, including these pesticides, that were found to induce cancer. * * * Simultaneously, the EPA announced a new interpretation of the Delaney clause: the EPA proposed to permit concentrations of cancer-causing pesticide residues greater than that tolerated for raw foods so long as the particular substances posed only a "de minimis" risk of actually causing cancer. 53 Fed.Reg. at 41,110. Finding that benomyl, mancozeb, phosmet and trifluralin (among others) posed only such a de minimis risk, the Agency announced that it would not immediately revoke its previous regulations authorizing use of these substances as food additives. * * *

Petitioners filed an administrative petition in May 1989 requesting the EPA to revoke those food additive regulations. * * *

Discussion

The issue before us is whether the EPA has violated section 409 of the FFDCA, the Delaney clause, by permitting the use of carcinogenic food additives which it finds to present only a de minimis or negligible risk of causing cancer. The Agency acknowledges that its interpretation of the law is a new and changed one. From the initial enactment of the Delaney clause in 1958 to the time of the rulings here in issue, the statute had been strictly and literally enforced. 56 Fed.Reg. at 7751–52. The EPA also acknowledges that the language of the statute itself appears, at first glance, to be clear on its face. *Id.* at 7751 ("[S]ection 409 mandates a zero risk standard for carcinogenic pesticides in processed foods in those instances where the pesticide concentrates during processing or is applied during or after processing.").

The language is clear and mandatory. The Delaney clause provides that no additive shall be deemed safe if it induces cancer. * * * The EPA states in its final order that appropriate tests have established that the pesticides at issue here induce cancer in humans or animals. 56 Fed.Reg. at 7774–75. The statute provides that once the finding of carcinogenicity is made, the EPA has no discretion. As a leading work on food and drug regulation notes:

> [T]he Delaney Clause leaves the FDA room for scientific judgment in deciding whether its conditions are met by a food additive. * * * A food additive that has been found in an appropriate test to induce cancer in laboratory animals may not be approved for use in food for any purpose, at any level, regardless of any "benefits" that it might provide.
>
> RICHARD A. MERRILL AND PETER B. HUTT, FOOD AND DRUG LAW 78 (1980).

* * *

The legislative history * * * reflects that Congress intended the very rigidity that the language it chose commands. The food additive Delaney clause was enacted in response to increasing public concern about cancer. It was initially part of a bill, introduced in the House of Representatives in 1958 by Congressman Delaney, to amend the FFDCA. H.R. 7798, 85th Cong., 1st Sess. (1957), *reprinted in* XIV *A Legislative History of the Federal Food, Drug, and Cosmetic Act and its Amendments* 91 (1979) (hereinafter, *"Legislative History"*). The bill, intended to ensure that no carcinogens, no matter how small the amount, would be introduced into food, was at least in part a response to a decision by the FDA to allow a known carcinogen, the pesticide Aramite, as an approved food additive. *Food Additives: Hearings Before a Subcommittee of the House Committee on Interstate and Foreign Commerce,* 85th Cong., 1st and 2d Sess. 171 (1958), *reprinted in* XIV *Legislative History* 163, 336. Of the FDA's approval for sale of foods containing small quantities of Aramite, Congressman Delaney stated:

> The part that chemical additives play in the cancer picture may not yet be completely understood, but enough is known to put us on our guard. * * * The precedent established by the Aramite decision has opened the door, even if only a little, to the use of carcinogens in our foods. That door should be slammed shut and locked. That is the purpose of my anticarcinogen provision.

Id. at 498, *reprinted in* XIV *Legislative History* at 660. The scientific witnesses who testified before Congress stressed that because current scientific techniques could not determine a safe level for carcinogens, all carcinogens should be prohibited. While Congressman Delaney's bill was not ultimately passed, the crucial anticancer language from the bill was incorporated into the Food Additives Amendment of 1958 which enacted section 409 of the FFDCA into law. * * * Thus, the legislative history supports the conclusion that Congress intended to ban all carcinogenic food additives, regardless of amount or significance of risk, as the only safe alternative.

Throughout its 30–year history, the Delaney clause has been interpreted as an absolute bar to all carcinogenic food additives. * * * Further, Congress has repeatedly ratified a strict interpretation of the Delaney clause by reenacting all three FFDCA provisions which contain Delaney clauses without changing the Agency's interpretation. *See* 21 U.S.C. § 348 (amended 1960, 1962, 1984); 21 U.S.C. § 360b (amended 1988, 1991); 21 U.S.C. § 376 (amended 1960, 1962, 1970, 1976). "When the statute giving rise to the longstanding interpretation has been reenacted without pertinent change, the congressional failure to revise or repeal the agency's interpretation is persuasive evidence that the interpretation is the one intended by Congress." *Federal Deposit Ins. Corp. v. Philadelphia Gear Corp.*, 476 U.S. 426, 437 (1986) (quotation omitted).

* * *

Finally, the EPA argues that a de minimis exception to the Delaney clause is necessary in order to bring about a more sensible application of the regulatory scheme. It relies particularly on a recent study suggesting that the criterion of concentration level in processed foods may bear little or no relation to actual risk of cancer. * * * *See* National Academy of Sciences, *Regulating Pesticides in Food: The Delaney Paradox* (1987). The EPA in effect asks us to approve what it deems to be a more enlightened system than that which Congress established. The EPA is not alone in criticizing the scheme established by the Delaney clause. * * * Revising the existing statutory scheme, however, is neither our function nor the function of the EPA. There are currently bills pending before the House and the Senate which would amend the food additive provision to allow * * * tolerance levels for carcinogens, including pesticide residues in processed foods, which impose a negligible risk. * * * If there is to be a change, it is for Congress to direct.

The EPA's refusal to revoke regulations permitting the use of benomyl, mancozeb, phosmet and trifluralin as food additives on the ground the cancer risk they pose is de minimis is contrary to the provisions of the Delaney clause prohibiting food additives that induce cancer. The EPA's final order is set aside.

Questions

1. In *Reilly*, the court pointed out that "[during the debates over the Delaney Clause, the] scientific witnesses who testified before Congress stressed that because * * * scientific techniques could not determine a safe level for carcinogens, all carcinogens should be prohibited." Today, scientific techniques still cannot determine a safe level for greenhouse gas emissions. Should we ban all activities that emit greenhouse gases? Do we necessarily need to know a safe level of activity for regulatory purposes?

2. The Delaney Clause takes a zero-risk approach to cancer in food additives. Tobacco smoking is unsafe and induces cancer. The ordinary consumption of some of the food additives that the Delaney Clause bans does not create any risk to health, while this is not true for smoking. Should Congress ban smoking?

3. The human papillomavirus (HPV) is a common sexually transmitted infection and the major cause of cervical cancer. Since 2006, safe HPV vaccines are commercially available. The age at which the vaccine produces

the best immune response in the body is 11 or 12 for females and males. Should Congress (or states) require HPV vaccines to reduce certain risks of cancer?

Entergy Corp. v. Riverkeeper, Inc.

556 U.S. 208 (2009)

■ JUSTICE SCALIA delivered the opinion of the Court.

These cases concern a set of regulations adopted by the Environmental Protection Agency (EPA or agency) under § 316(b) of the Clean Water Act, 33 U.S.C. § 1326(b). 69 Fed.Reg. 41576 (2004). Respondents—environmental groups and various States—challenged those regulations, and the Second Circuit set them aside. * * * The issue for our decision is whether, as the Second Circuit held, the EPA is not permitted to use cost-benefit analysis in determining the content of regulations promulgated under § 1326(b).

I

Petitioners operate—or represent those who operate—large powerplants. In the course of generating power, those plants also generate large amounts of heat. To cool their facilities, petitioners employ "cooling water intake structures" that extract water from nearby water sources. These structures pose various threats to the environment, chief among them the squashing against intake screens (elegantly called "impingement") or suction into the cooling system ("entrainment") of aquatic organisms that live in the affected water sources. Accordingly, the facilities are subject to regulation under the Clean Water Act, 33 U.S.C. § 1251 *et seq.*, which mandates:

> "Any standard established pursuant to section 1311 of this title or section 1316 of this title and applicable to a point source shall require that the location, design, construction, and capacity of cooling water intake structures reflect *the best technology available* for minimizing adverse environmental impact." § 1326(b) [(emphasis added)].

The § 1326(b) regulations at issue here were promulgated by the EPA after nearly three decades in which the determination of the "best technology available for minimizing [cooling water intake structures] adverse environmental impact" was made by permit-issuing authorities on a case-by-case basis, without benefit of a governing regulation. * * *

[After extensive litigation, in 1995,] the EPA * * * set a multiphase timetable * * * to promulgate regulations under § 1326(b). * * * In the first phase the EPA adopted regulations governing certain new, large cooling water intake structures. 66 Fed.Reg. 65256 (2001) (Phase I rules) [that were upheld by the Second Circuit and are irrelevant to the cases before us].

The EPA then adopted the so-called "Phase II" rules at issue here. 69 Fed.Reg. 41576. They apply to existing facilities that are point sources, whose primary activity is the generation and transmission (or sale for transmission) of electricity, and whose water-intake flow is more than 50 million gallons of water per day, at least 25 percent of which is used for cooling purposes. *Ibid.* Over 500 facilities, accounting for approximately 53 percent of the Nation's electric-power generating capacity, fall within Phase II's ambit. * * * Those facilities remove on average more than 214 billion gallons of water per day, causing impingement and entrainment of over 3.4 billion aquatic organisms per year. 69 Fed.Reg. 41586.

To address those environmental impacts, the EPA set "national performance standards," requiring Phase II facilities (with some exceptions) to reduce "impingement mortality for all life stages of fish and shellfish by 80 to 95 percent from the calculation baseline"; a subset of facilities must also reduce entrainment of such aquatic organisms by "60 to 90 percent from the calculation baseline." 40 CFR § 125.94(b)(1), (2); *see* § 125.93 (defining "calculation baseline"). Those targets are based on the environmental improvements achievable through deployment of a mix of remedial technologies, * * * which the EPA determined were "commercially available and economically practicable," *id.*, at 41602.

In its Phase II rules, however, the EPA expressly declined to mandate adoption of closed-cycle cooling systems or equivalent reductions in impingement and entrainment, as it had done for new facilities subject to the Phase I rules. It refused to take that step in part because of the "generally high costs" of converting existing facilities to closed-cycle operation, and because "other technologies approach the performance of this option." *Id.*, at 41605. Thus, while closed-cycle cooling systems could reduce impingement and entrainment mortality by up to 98 percent, *id.*, at 41601, (compared to the Phase II targets of 80 to 95 percent impingement reduction), the cost of rendering all Phase II facilities closed-cycle-compliant would be approximately $3.5 billion per year, nine times the estimated cost of compliance with the Phase II performance standards. Moreover, Phase II facilities compelled to convert to closed-cycle cooling systems "would produce 2.4 percent to 4.0 percent less electricity even while burning the same amount of coal," possibly requiring the construction of "20 additional 400–MW plants * * * to replace the generating capacity lost." *Id.*, at 41605. The EPA thus concluded that "[a]lthough not identical, the ranges of impingement and entrainment reduction are similar under both options * * * [Benefits of compliance with the Phase II rules] can approach those of closed-cycle recirculating at less cost with fewer implementation problems." *Id.*, at 41606.

* * *

Respondents challenged the EPA's Phase II regulations, and the Second Circuit granted their petition for review and remanded the regulations to the EPA. The Second Circuit identified two ways in which the EPA could permissibly consider costs under 33 U.S.C. § 1326(b): (1) in determining whether the costs of remediation "can be 'reasonably borne' by the industry," and (2) in determining which remedial technologies are the most cost-effective, that is, the technologies that reach a specified level of benefit at the lowest cost. * * * It concluded, however, that cost-benefit analysis, which "compares the costs and benefits of various ends, and chooses the end with the best net benefits," is impermissible under § 1326(b).

* * *

II

In setting * * * Phase II * * * the EPA relied on its view that § 1326(b)'s "best technology available" standard permits consideration of the technology's costs, and of the relationship between those costs and the environmental benefits produced. That view governs if it is a reasonable interpretation of the statute—not necessarily the only possible interpretation, nor even the interpretation deemed most reasonable by the courts. *Chevron U.S.A. Inc. v. Natural Resources Defense Council, Inc.*, 467 U.S. 837, 843–844 (1984).

As we have described, § 1326(b) instructs the EPA to set standards for cooling water intake structures that reflect "the best technology available for minimizing adverse environmental impact." The Second Circuit took that language to mean the technology that achieves the greatest reduction in adverse environmental impacts at a cost that can reasonably be borne by the industry. * * * That is certainly a plausible interpretation of the statute. The "best" technology—that which is "most advantageous," Webster's New International Dictionary 258 (2d ed.1953)—may well be the one that produces the most of some good, here a reduction in adverse environmental impact. But "best technology" may also describe the technology that *most efficiently* produces some good. In common parlance one could certainly use the phrase "best technology" to refer to that which produces a good at the lowest per-unit cost, even if it produces a lesser quantity of that good than other available technologies.

Respondents contend that this latter reading is precluded by the statute's use of the phrase "for minimizing adverse environmental impact." Minimizing, they argue, means reducing to the smallest amount possible, and the "best technology available for minimizing adverse environmental impacts," must be the economically feasible technology that achieves the greatest possible reduction in environmental harm. * * * But "minimize" is a term that admits of degree and is not necessarily used to refer exclusively to the "greatest possible reduction." For example, elsewhere in the Clean Water Act, Congress declared that the procedures implementing the Act "shall encourage the drastic minimization of paperwork and interagency decision procedures." 33 U.S.C. § 1251(f). If respondents' definition of the term "minimize" is correct, the statute's use of the modifier "drastic" is superfluous.

Other provisions in the Clean Water Act also suggest the agency's interpretation. When Congress wished to mandate the greatest feasible reduction in water pollution, it did so in plain language: The provision governing the discharge of toxic pollutants into the Nation's waters requires the EPA to set "effluent limitations [which] shall require the *elimination* of discharges of all pollutants if the Administrator finds * * * that such elimination is technologically and economically achievable," § 1311(b)(2)(A) (emphasis added). See also § 1316(a)(1) (mandating "where practicable, a standard [for new point sources] permitting *no discharge* of pollutants" (emphasis added)). Section 1326(b)'s use of the less ambitious goal of "minimizing adverse environmental impact" suggests, we think, that the agency retains some discretion to determine the extent of reduction that is warranted under the circumstances. That determination could plausibly involve a consideration of the benefits derived from reductions and the costs of achieving them. * * * It seems to us, therefore, that the phrase "best technology available," even with the added specification "for minimizing adverse environmental impact," does not unambiguously preclude cost-benefit analysis.

* * *

* * *

We conclude that the EPA permissibly relied on cost-benefit analysis in setting the national performance standards and in providing for cost-benefit variances from those standards as part of the Phase II regulations.

* * *

It is so ordered.

* * *

■ JUSTICE BREYER, concurring in part and dissenting in part.

I agree with the Court that the relevant statutory language authorizes the Environmental Protection Agency (EPA) to compare costs and benefits. Nonetheless the drafting history and legislative history of related provisions make clear that those who sponsored the legislation intended the law's text to be read as restricting, though not forbidding, the use of cost-benefit comparisons. And I would apply that text accordingly.

I

Section 301 provides that, not later than 1977, effluent limitations for point sources shall require the application of "*best practicable* control technology," § 301(b)(1)(A), 86 Stat. 845 (emphasis added); and that, not later than 1983 (later extended to 1989), effluent limitations for categories and classes of point sources shall require application of the "*best available* technology economically achievable," § 301(b)(2)(A), *ibid.* (emphasis added). Section 304(b), in turn, identifies the factors that the Agency shall take into account in determining (1) "*best practicable* control technology" and (2) "*best available* technology." 86 Stat. 851 (emphasis added).

With respect to the first, the statute provides that the factors taken into account by the Agency "shall include consideration of the total cost of application of technology in relation to the effluent reduction benefits to be achieved from such application * * * and such other factors as the Administrator deems appropriate." § 304(b)(1)(B), *ibid.* With respect to the second, the statute says that the Agency "shall take into account * * * the cost of achieving such effluent reduction" and "such other factors as the Administrator deems appropriate." § 304(b)(2)(B), *ibid.*

The drafting history makes clear that the statute reflects a compromise. In the House version of the legislation, the Agency was to consider "the cost and the economic, social, and environmental impact of achieving such effluent reduction" when determining both "*best practicable*" and "*best available*" technology. * * * The House Report explained that the "*best available* technology" standard was needed—as opposed to mandating the elimination of discharge of pollutants—because "the difference in the cost of 100 percent elimination of pollutants as compared to the cost of removal of 97–99 percent of the pollutants in an effluent can far exceed any reasonable benefit to be achieved. In most cases, the cost of removal of the last few percentage points increases expo[n]entially." H.R.Rep. No. 92–911, p. 103 (1972).

In the Senate version, the Agency was to consider "the cost of achieving such effluent reduction" when determining both "*best practicable*" and "*best available*" technology. S. 2770, 92d Cong., 1st Sess., §§ 304(b)(1)(B), (b)(2)(B) (1971) (as reported from committee). The Senate Report explains that "the technology must be available at a cost * * * which the Administrator determines to be reasonable." S.Rep. No. 92–414, p. 52 (1971), U.S.Code Cong. & Admin.News 1972, pp. 3668, 3718 (hereinafter S. Rep.). But it said nothing about comparing costs and benefits.

The final statute reflects a modification of the House's language with respect to "*best practicable,*" and an adoption of the Senate's language with respect to "*best available.*" * * * The final statute does not *require* the Agency to compare costs to benefits when determining "*best available* technology," but neither does it expressly *forbid* such a comparison.

* * *

Most of what the majority says is consistent with this view, and to that extent I agree with its opinion.

II

The cases before us, however, present an additional problem. We here consider a rule that permits variances from national standards if a facility demonstrates that its costs would be "significantly greater than the benefits of complying." * * * The EPA must adequately explain why it has changed its standard* * *

I am not convinced the EPA has successfully explained the basis for the change. * * *

Consequently, like the majority, I would remand these cases to the Court of Appeals. But unlike the majority I would permit that court to remand the cases to the EPA so that the EPA can either apply its traditional "wholly disproportionate" standard or provide an adequately reasoned explanation for the change.

■ JUSTICE STEVENS, with whom JUSTICE SOUTER and JUSTICE GINSBURG join, dissenting.

Section 316(b) of the Clean Water Act (CWA), which governs industrial powerplant water intake structures, provides that the Environmental Protection Agency (EPA or Agency) "shall require" that such structures "reflect the best technology available for minimizing adverse environmental impact." The EPA has interpreted that mandate to authorize the use of cost-benefit analysis in promulgating regulations under § 316(b). For instance, under the Agency's interpretation, technology that would otherwise qualify as the best available need not be used if its costs are "significantly greater than the benefits" of compliance. 40 CFR § 125.94(a)(5)(ii) (2008).

* * * I am convinced that the EPA has misinterpreted the plain text of § 316(b). Unless costs are so high that the best technology is not "available," Congress has decided that they are outweighed by the benefits of minimizing adverse environmental impact. Section 316(b) neither expressly nor implicitly authorizes the EPA to use cost-benefit analysis when setting regulatory standards; fairly read, it prohibits such use.

* * *

Questions

1. In *Reilly* and *Riverkeeper*, EPA deviated from the plain meaning of a statutory language to conduct cost-benefit analysis. How did the *Reilly* and *Riverkeeper* courts address this choice? What can explain the differences between the courts?

2. The *Riverkeeper* Court accepted the EPA's interpretation that term "the best available technology" in the Clean Water Act accommodates CBA. Technologies are not static, rather they develop and evolve. What could a CBA that relies on "the best available technology" mean for businesses and industries? Is this a real problem?

Center for Biological Diversity v. National Highway Traffic Safety Administration

538 F.3d 1172 (9th Cir. 2008)

■ BETTY B. FLETCHER, CIRCUIT JUDGE:

Eleven states, the District of Columbia, the City of New York, and four public interest organizations petition for review of a rule issued by the National Highway Traffic Safety Administration (NHTSA) entitled "Average Fuel Economy Standards for Light Trucks, Model Years 20082011," 71 Fed.Reg. 17,566 (Apr. 6, 2006) ("Final Rule") (codified at C.F.R. pt. 533). Pursuant to the Energy Policy and Conservation Act of 1975 (EPCA), 49 U.S.C. §§ 32901–32919 (2007), the Final Rule sets corporate average fuel economy (CAFE) standards for light trucks, defined by NHTSA to include many Sport Utility Vehicles (SUVs), minivans, and pickup trucks, for Model Years (MYs) 2008–2011. For MYs 2008–2010, the Final Rule sets new CAFE standards using its traditional method, fleet-wide average (Unreformed CAFE). For MY 2011 and beyond, the Final Rule creates a new CAFE structure that sets varying fuel economy targets depending on vehicle size and requires manufacturers to meet different fuel economy levels depending on their vehicle fleet mix (Reformed CAFE).

* * * We hold that the Final Rule is arbitrary and capricious, contrary to the EPCA in its failure to monetize the value of carbon emissions, failure

to set a backstop,* failure to close the SUV loophole, and failure to set fuel economy standards for all vehicles in the 8,500 to 10,000 gross vehicle weight rating ("GVWR") class. * * * Therefore, we remand to NHTSA to promulgate new standards as expeditiously as possible. * * *

I. FACTUAL AND PROCEDURAL BACKGROUND

A. *CAFE Regulation Under the Energy Policy and Conservation Act*

In the aftermath of the energy crisis created by the 1973 Mideast oil embargo, Congress enacted the Energy Policy and Conservation Act of 1975. Congress observed that "[t]he fundamental reality is that this nation has entered a new era in which energy resources previously abundant, will remain in short supply, retarding our economic growth and necessitating an alteration in our life's habits and expectations." The goals of the EPCA are to "decrease dependence on foreign imports, enhance national security, achieve the efficient utilization of scarce resources, and guarantee the availability of domestic energy supplies at prices consumers can afford." These goals are more pressing today than they were thirty years ago: since 1975, American consumption of oil has risen from 16.3 million barrels per day to over 20 million barrels per day, and the percentage of U.S. oil that is imported has risen from 35.8 to 56 percent. * * *

In furtherance of the goal of energy conservation, * * * the EPCA establishes automobile fuel economy standards. An "average fuel economy standard" (often referred to as a CAFE standard) is "a performance standard specifying a minimum level of average fuel economy applicable to a manufacturer in a model year." 49 U.S.C. § 32901(a)(6). Only "automobiles" are subject to fuel economy regulation, and passenger automobiles must meet a statutory standard of 27.5 mpg, 49 U.S.C. § 32902(b), whereas non-passenger automobiles must meet standards set by the Secretary of Transportation. Congress directs the Secretary to set fuel economy standards at "the maximum feasible average fuel economy level that the Secretary decides the manufacturers can achieve in that model year." [T]he Secretary is authorized to "prescribe separate standards for different classes of automobiles." [EPCA] also provides that "[w]hen deciding maximum feasible average fuel economy * * *, the Secretary of Transportation shall consider technological feasibility, economic practicability, the effect of other motor vehicle standards of the Government on fuel economy, and the need of the United States to conserve energy." *Id.* § 32902(f).

Under the EPCA's definitional scheme, vehicles not manufactured primarily for highway use and vehicles rated at 10,000 lbs. gross vehicle weight or more are excluded from fuel economy regulation altogether because they are not "automobiles."[6] An "automobile" is defined as:

> a 4-wheeled vehicle that is propelled by fuel, or by alternative fuel, manufactured primarily for use on public streets, roads, and highways * * *, and rated at—

* ["Backstop" is a required fuel economy level applicable to a manufacturer.—ed.]

6. For example, the Hummer H1 is more than 10,000 lbs. GVWR [the value specified by the manufacturer as the loaded weight of a single vehicle-BYO] and thus not subject to CAFE regulation.

(A) not more than 6,000 pounds gross vehicle weight; or

(B) more than 6,000, but less than 10,000, pounds gross vehicle weight, if the Secretary decides by regulation that—

(i) an average fuel economy standard under this chapter for the vehicle is feasible; and

(ii) an average fuel economy standard under this chapter for the vehicle will result in significant energy conservation or the vehicle is substantially used for the same purposes as a vehicle rated at not more than 6,000 pounds gross vehicle weight.

* * *

For MYs 1996 to 2004, Congress froze the light truck CAFE standard at 20.7 mpg. After the legislative restrictions were lifted, NHTSA set new light truck CAFE standards in April 2003: 21.0 mpg for MY 2005, 21.6 mpg for MY 2006, and 22.2 mpg for MY 2007.

In response to a request from Congress, the National Academy of Sciences (NAS) published in 2002 a report entitled "Effectiveness and Impact of Corporate Average Fuel Economy (CAFE) Standards." The NAS committee made several findings and recommendations. It found that from 1970 to 1982, CAFE standards helped contribute to a 50 percent increase in fuel economy for new light trucks. In the subsequent decades, however, light trucks became more popular since domestic manufacturers faced less competition in the light truck category and could generate greater profits. The "less stringent CAFE standards for trucks . . . provide[d] incentives for manufacturers to invest in minivans and SUVs and to promote them to consumers in place of large cars and station wagons." When the CAFE regulations were originally promulgated in the 1970s, "light truck sales accounted for about 20 percent of the new vehicle market," but now they account for about half. This shift has had a "pronounced" effect on overall fuel economy. As the market share of light trucks has increased, the overall average fuel economy of the new light duty vehicle fleet (light trucks and passenger automobiles) has declined "from a peak of 25.9 MPG in 1987 to 24.0 MPG in 2000." Vehicle miles traveled (VMT) by light trucks has also been growing more rapidly than passenger automobile travel.

The NAS committee found that the CAFE program has increased fuel economy, but that certain aspects of the program "have not functioned as intended," including "[t]he distinction between a car for personal use and a truck for work use/cargo transport," which "has been stretched well beyond the original purpose." The committee also found that technologies exist to "significantly reduce fuel consumption," for cars and light trucks and that raising CAFE standards would reduce fuel consumption. Significantly, the committee found that of the many reasons for improving fuel economy, "[t]he most important * * * is concern about the accumulation in the atmosphere of so-called greenhouse gases, principally carbon dioxide. Continued increases in carbon dioxide emissions are likely to further global warming." In addition, the committee found "externalities of about $0.30/gal of gasoline associated with the combined impacts of fuel consumption on greenhouse gas emissions and on world oil market conditions" that "are not necessarily taken into account when consumers purchase new vehicles."

* * *

D. The Final Rule: CAFE Standards for Light Trucks MYs 2008–2011

NHTSA issued the Final Rule on April 6, 2006. * * * NHTSA set the CAFE standards for MY 2008–2010 (Unreformed CAFE). * * * NHTSA has reformed the structure of the CAFE program for light trucks, effective MY 2011 (Reformed CAFE).

During MYs 2008–2010, manufacturers may choose to comply with Unreformed CAFE or Reformed CAFE.

NHTSA used the manufacturers' preexisting product plans as the baseline for its analyses of technical and economic feasibility under both Unreformed and Reformed CAFE. * * * NHTSA did not monetize the benefit of reducing carbon dioxide emissions, which it recognized was the "the main greenhouse gas emitted as a result of refining, distribution, and use of transportation fuels." * * * NHTSA acknowledged the estimates suggested in the scientific literature, * * * but concluded:

> [T]he value of reducing emissions of CO2 and other greenhouse gases [is] too uncertain to support their explicit valuation and inclusion among the savings in environmental externalities from reducing gasoline production and use. There is extremely wide variation in published estimates of damage costs from greenhouse gas emissions, costs for controlling or avoiding their emissions, and costs of sequestering emissions that do occur, the three major sources for developing estimates of economic benefits from reducing emissions of greenhouse gases.

71 Fed.Reg. at 17,638. * * *

* * *

NHTSA rejected the idea of a "backstop" under Reformed CAFE. * * * NHTSA argued that "EPCA permits the agency to consider consumer demand and the resulting market shifts in setting fuel economy standards," and that a backstop "would essentially limit the ability of manufacturers to respond to market shifts arising from changes in consumer demand. If consumer demand shifted towards larger vehicles, a manufacturer potentially could be faced with a situation in which it must choose between limiting its production of the demanded vehicles, and failing to comply with the CAFE light truck standard."

Finally, NHTSA declined to change the regulatory definition of cars and light trucks to close the SUV loophole and refused to regulate vehicles between 8,500 and 10,000 lbs. * * *

II. STANDARD OF REVIEW

The Administrative Procedure Act (APA) provides that agency action must be set aside by the reviewing court if it is " 'arbitrary, capricious, an abuse of discretion, or otherwise not in accordance with law.' " *Competitive Enter. Inst. v. NHTSA (CEI III)*, 45 F.3d 481, 484 (D.C.Cir.1995) (quoting 5

U.S.C. § 706(2)(A)) (applying the APA to review a rulemaking under the EPCA). * * *

III. DISCUSSION

* * *

1. *NHTSA's use of marginal cost-benefit analysis to determine "maximum feasible average fuel economy level"*

With respect to non-passenger automobiles (i.e., light trucks), the fuel economy standard "shall be the maximum feasible average fuel economy level that the Secretary decides the manufacturers can achieve in that model year." 49 U.S.C. § 32902(a). "Maximum feasible" is not defined in the EPCA. However, the EPCA provides that "[w]hen deciding maximum feasible average fuel economy under this section, the Secretary of Transportation shall consider technological feasibility, economic practicability, the effect of other motor vehicle standards of the Government on fuel economy, and the need of the United States to conserve energy." *Id.* § 32902(f).

Petitioners argue that the meaning of "maximum feasible" is plain, and that NHTSA's decision to maximize economic benefits is contrary to the plain language of the EPCA because "feasible" means "capable of being done," not economically optimal. But even if "feasible" means "capable of being done," technological feasibility, economic practicability, the effect of other motor vehicle standards, and the need of the nation to conserve energy must be considered in determining the "maximum feasible" standard. * * * Here, "maximum feasible" standards are to be determined in light of technological feasibility, economic practicability, the effect of other motor vehicle standards, and the need of the nation to conserve energy.

The EPCA clearly requires the agency to consider these four factors, but it gives NHTSA discretion to decide how to balance the statutory factors-as long as NHTSA's balancing does not undermine the fundamental purpose of the EPCA: energy conservation.

* * *

In this rulemaking, NHTSA does not set forth its interpretation of the four factors in 49 U.S.C. § 32902(f). It simply states that in determining the "maximum feasible" fuel economy level, NHTSA "assesses what is technologically feasible for manufacturers to achieve without leading to adverse economic consequences, such as a significant loss of jobs or the unreasonable elimination of consumer choice." * * *

2. *Failure to monetize benefits of greenhouse gas emissions reduction*

Even if NHTSA may use a cost-benefit analysis to determine the "maximum feasible" fuel economy standard, it cannot put a thumb on the scale by undervaluing the benefits and overvaluing the costs of more stringent standards. NHTSA fails to include in its analysis the benefit of carbon emissions reduction in either quantitative or qualitative form. It did, however, include an analysis of the employment and sales impacts of more stringent standards on manufacturers.

To determine the "maximum feasible" CAFE standards, NHTSA began with the fuel economy baselines for each of the seven largest manufacturers [and adjusted it to maximize net benefits in the industry]. Maximization occurs when the incremental change in industry-wide compliance costs from adjusting it further would be exactly offset by the resulting incremental change in benefits." NHTSA claims that this "cost-benefit analysis carefully considers and weighs all of the benefits of improved fuel savings," and that "there is no compelling evidence that the unmonetized benefits would alter our assessment of the level of the standard for MY 2011."

Under this methodology, the values that NHTSA assigns to benefits are critical. Yet, NHTSA assigned no value to the most significant benefit of more stringent CAFE standards: reduction in carbon emissions. * * * NHTSA acknowledged that "[c]onserving energy, especially reducing the nation's dependence on petroleum, benefits the U.S. in several ways. [It] has benefits for economic growth and the environment, as well as other benefits, such as reducing pollution and improving security of energy supply." 71 Fed.Reg. at 17,644. NHTSA also acknowledged the comments it received that recommended values for the benefit of carbon emissions reduction; however, the agency refused to place a value on this benefit. *See id.* at 17,638. NHTSA stated:

> The agency continues to view the value of reducing emissions of CO2 and other greenhouse gases as too uncertain to support their explicit valuation and inclusion among the savings in environmental externalities from reducing gasoline production and use. * * *
>
> *Id.*

NHTSA's reasoning is arbitrary and capricious for several reasons. First, while the record shows that there is a range of values, the value of carbon emissions reduction is certainly not zero. NHTSA conceded as much during oral argument when, in response to questioning, counsel for NHTSA admitted that the range of values begins at $3 per ton carbon. NHTSA insisted at argument that it placed no value on carbon emissions reduction rather than zero value. We fail to see the difference. The value of carbon emissions reduction is nowhere accounted for in the agency's analysis, whether quantitatively or qualitatively. * * *

Second, NHTSA gave no reasons why it believed the range of values presented to it was "extremely wide"; in fact, several commenters and the NAS committee recommended the *same* value: $50 per ton carbon. The NAS committee selected the value of $50 per ton carbon although it acknowledged the wide range of values in the literature and the potential controversy in selecting a particular value. * * *

Third, NHTSA's reasoning is arbitrary and capricious because it has monetized other uncertain benefits, such as the reduction of criteria pollutants, crash, noise, and congestion costs, and "the value of increased energy security." * * *

Fourth, NHTSA's conclusion that commenters did not "reliably demonstrate" that monetizing the value of carbon reduction would have affected the stringency of the CAFE standard runs counter to the evidence. * * *

Thus, NHTSA's decision not to monetize the benefit of carbon emissions reduction was arbitrary and capricious, and we remand to NHTSA for it to include a monetized value for this benefit in its analysis of the proper CAFE standards.

* * *

4. Backstop for Reformed CAFE

Under Reformed CAFE, a manufacturer's required CAFE level would depend on its fleet mix. Reformed CAFE (setting individual fuel economy targets for vehicles of every footprint size) plus a backstop (overall fleet-wide average) would prevent manufacturers from upsizing their vehicles or producing too many large footprint vehicles, if the backstop were set high enough. Under Unreformed CAFE, manufacturers had to meet only a fleet-wide average, which means that they could increase the number of small vehicles (with higher fuel economy) they produced in order to balance out the larger vehicles (with lower fuel economy) and achieve the required CAFE standard.

* * *

NHTSA argues that a backstop would unduly limit consumer choice. * * * Neither the EPCA's language nor structure explicitly *requires* NHTSA to adopt a backstop. The issue is whether it was arbitrary or capricious in not adopting a backstop. Under Reformed CAFE, manufacturers would still be required to meet a minimum average fuel economy level-there would simply be no *corporate* minimum average fuel economy level. That is, each vehicle of a particular footprint would be required to meet a minimum average fuel economy level, but there would be no fleet-wide minimum. The corporate or fleet-wide minimum would depend entirely on the number of vehicles of each footprint that the manufacturer decided to produce.

* * *

We do agree with NHTSA that the continuous function of Reformed CAFE will likely reduce the incentive to upsize. * * * But, Petitioners raise well-founded concerns (given the historical trend) that a floating fleet-mix-based standard would continue to permit upsizing—which is not just a function of consumer demand, but also a function of manufacturers' own design and marketing decisions. We remand to NHTSA for it to reconsider under the proper standard whether to adopt a backstop based on the factors in 49 U.S.C. § 32902(f).

* * *

6. Changing the definition of passenger and non-passenger automobiles in order to close the SUV loophole

Petitioners challenge NHTSA's decision not to reform the SUV loophole. They argue that this decision is arbitrary and capricious because it runs counter to the evidence showing that the majority of SUVs, minivans, and pickup trucks function solely or primarily as passenger vehicles, and because NHTSA has not provided a reasoned explanation for why the transition to Reformed CAFE could not be accomplished at the same time as a revision in the definitions.

* * *

We conclude that NHTSA's decision not to otherwise revise the passenger automobile/light truck definitions is arbitrary and capricious. First, NHTSA has not provided a reasoned explanation of why an orderly transition to Reformed CAFE could not be accomplished at the same time that the passenger automobile/light truck definitions are revised.

Second, NHTSA asserts that it reasonably decided to look to the purpose for which a vehicle is manufactured instead of consumers' use of a vehicle because it is a more objective way of differentiating between passenger and non-passenger automobiles. But this overlooks the fact that many light trucks today *are* manufactured primarily for transporting passengers. * * *

Third, NHTSA's decision runs counter to the evidence showing that SUVs, vans, and pickup trucks are manufactured primarily for the purpose of transporting passengers and are generally not used for off-highway operation.

* * * We agree with Petitioners that NHTSA's decision not to do the same was arbitrary and capricious, especially in light of EPCA's overarching goal of energy conservation. Thus, we remand to NHTSA to revise its regulatory definitions of passenger automobile and light truck or provide a valid reason for not doing so.

7. Exclusion of 8,500–10,000 lb. pickup trucks from CAFE regulation

Petitioners argue that NHTSA's decision not to regulate the fuel economy of vehicles between 8,500 and 10,000 lbs. * * * is arbitrary and capricious because fuel economy standards for these vehicles are feasible and will result in significant energy conservation. * * * We agree.

* * *

IV. CONCLUSION

NHTSA's failure to monetize the value of carbon emissions in its determination of the MY 2008–2011 light truck CAFE standards, failure to set a backstop, failure to revise the passenger automobile/light truck classifications, and failure to set fuel economy standards for all vehicles in the 8,500 to 10,000 lb. * * * was arbitrary and capricious and contrary to the EPCA. We therefore remand to NHTSA to promulgate new standards consistent with this opinion as expeditiously as possible and for the earliest model year practicable.

* * *

REVERSED AND REMANDED.

■ SILER, CIRCUIT JUDGE, concurring in part and dissenting in part:

I concur in the conclusions by the majority on all points, with the exception of its conclusion [related to NHTSA's failure] to adopt a backstop for a minimum level of average fuel economy. The majority admits that the EPCA does not require NHTSA to adopt a backstop. We must realize that the arbitrary or capricious standard is one that grants an agency a significant amount of deference. Its failure to adopt this backstop was not an act which ignored factors that Congress required to be taken into account. Under those circumstances, when the EPCA did not require the adoption of a backstop, I would not find that NHTSA acted arbitrarily or capriciously by failing to do so.

Questions

1. NHTSA did not include in its cost-benefit analysis potential effects of greenhouse gas emissions because of the "extremely wide variation in published estimates of damage costs from greenhouse gas emissions." In *Reilly*, the court noted that Congress adopted the Delaney Clause because at the time "scientific techniques could not determine a safe level for carcinogens." How should regulators address uncertainty?

2. "Backstop" is a required fuel economy level applicable to a manufacturer. Under backstop rules, the fleet sold by a manufacturer must meet certain average fuel economy standards. Backstop standards intend to prevent manufacturer from producing more large footprint vehicles and fewer small footprint ones. NHTSA chose not to include backstop standards in its rulemaking, arguing that they would unduly limit consumer choice. The Energy Policy and Conservation Act (EPCA) does not explicitly requires NHTSA to adopt a backstop. The Ninth Circuit held that the failure to set a backstop was arbitrary and capricious. Do backstop standards affect consumer choices? If so, should we be concerned about such interference with choices?

CHAPTER 2

INESCAPABLE CONTROVERSY AND CRITIQUE

§ 2.1 (MIS)PERCEPTIONS OF REALITY

> *I had * * * followed a golden rule * * * that whenever a published fact, a new observation or thought came across me, which was opposed to my general results, to make a memorandum of it without fail and at once; for I had found by experience that such facts and thoughts were far more apt to escape from the memory than favorable ones.*
>
> —Charles Darwin[1]

In 1848, John Stuart Mill observed that "[n]o subject has been more keenly contested in the present age" than "the limits of the province of government." Mill posited that the source of controversy was largely an ideological divide between two groups in society—"the supporters of interference [who believe the government should act] wherever its intervention would be useful" and the "*laissez-faire* school [that believes] the province of government [should be] restricted * * * to the protection of person and property against force and fraud."[2] Mill's account of the controversy over regulation and its sources appears timeless.[3]

In every era, "supporters of interference" and members of the "*laissez-faire* school" consist of ideologues and other individuals whose views of regulations are predictable. These individuals tend to be dismissive of any analysis of factual inquiry that is inconsistent with their own beliefs and perceptions of reality. They are convinced that their own views, if implemented, will enhance the public interest. Their over-confidence is a common human trait. Mill explained and criticized this tendency:

> But on every subject on which difference of opinion is possible, the truth depends on a balance to be struck between two sets of conflicting reasons. * * * [W]e do not [always] understand the grounds of our opinion. But when we turn to * * * to morals, religion, politics, social relations, and the business of life, three-fourths of the arguments for every disputed opinion consist in dispelling the appearances which favour some opinion different

1. Charles Darwin, *Autobiography*, *in* THE LIFE AND LETTERS OF CHARLES DARWIN 71 (Francis Darwin ed., 1896).

2. JOHN STUART MILL, II PRINCIPLES OF POLITICAL ECONOMY 525 (1848).

3. *See, e.g.*, James M. Buchanan, *Afraid to Be Free: Dependency As Desideratum*, 124 PUBLIC CHOICE 19 (2005).

> from it. * * * He who knows only his own side of the case, knows little of that. * * * The rational position for him would be suspension of judgment, and unless he contents himself with that, he is either led by authority, or adopts, like the generality of the world, the side to which he feels most inclination. * * * That is not the way to do justice to the arguments, or bring them into real contact with his own mind.[4]

Francis Bacon also addressed the this phenomenon: "The human understanding when it has once adopted an opinion * * * draws all things else to support and agree with it. And though there be a greater number and weight of instances to be found on the other side, yet these it either neglects and despises, or else by some distinction sets aside and rejects; in order that by this great and pernicious predetermination the authority of its former conclusions may remain inviolate."[5]

Indeed, studies in psychology consistently find that people tend to seek or interpret evidence in ways that are partial to their existing beliefs and expectations.[6] Considerable evidence demonstrates that people are more likely to arrive at conclusions they want to find, and use reasoning skills and ability to construct justifications to do so; that is, to reach the conclusions they have in mind in the first place.[7] This tendency is further exacerbated by another common tendency—the inclination of people to hold overly favorable views of their own skills and abilities.[8] The long-term effect of the common pattern of drawing opposite conclusions from the same evidence is polarization in society.[9]

---

4. JOHN STUART MILL, ON LIBERTY 66–67 (1859).

5. Francis Bacon, *Novum Organum*, in THE WORKS OF FRANCIS BACON 59, 74 (James Spedding et al. eds., 1869) (originally published in 1620).

6. *See generally* § 7.4; Albert H. Hastorf & Hadley Cantril, *They Saw a Game: A Case Study*, 49 JOURNAL OF ABNORMAL & SOCIAL PSYCHOLOGY 129 (1954); Peter Lamont, *The Making of Extraordinary Psychological Phenomena*, 48 JOURNAL OF THE HISTORY OF BEHAVIORAL SCIENCES 1 (2012); Raymond S. Nickerson, *Confirmation Bias: A Ubiquitous Phenomenon in Many Guises*, 2 REVIEW OF GENERAL PSYCHOLOGY 175 (1998).

7. *See generally* Ziva Kunda, *The Case for Motivated Reasoning*, 108 PSYCHOLOGICAL BULLETIN 480 (1990); Hugo Mercier & Dan Sperber, *Why Do Humans Reason? Arguments for an Argumentative Theory*, 34 BEHAVIORAL & BRAIN SCIENCES 57 (2011).

8. *See* Dan Lovallo & Daniel Kahneman, *Delusions of Success: How Optimism Undermines Executives Decisions*, 81(7) HARVARD BUSINESS REVIEW 56 (Jul. 2003); Frank P. McKenna, *It Won't Happen to Me: Unrealistic Optimism or Illusion of Control?* 84 BRITISH JOURNAL OF PSYCHOLOGY 39 (1993); Ola Svenson, *Are We All Less Risky and More Skillful Than Our Fellow Drivers?* 47 ACTA PSYCHOLOGICA 143 (1981); Shelly E. Taylor & J. D. Brown, *Illusion and Well–Being: A Social Psychological Perspective on Mental Health*, 103 PSYCHOLOGICAL BULLETIN, 193 (1988); Neil D. Weinstein, *Unrealistic Optimism About Future Life Events*, 39 JOURNAL OF PERSONALITY & SOCIAL PSYCHOLOGY 806 (1980); Neil D. Weinstein, *Unrealistic Optimism About Susceptibility to Health Problems*, 5 JOURNAL OF BEHAVIORAL MEDICINE 441 (1982). *See also* Tali Sharot et al., *Neural Mechanism Mediating Optimism Bias*, 450 NATURE 102 (2007).

9. *See generally* James Andreoni & Tymofiy Mylovanov, *Diverging Opinions*, 4(1) AMERICAN ECONOMIC JOURNAL: MICROECONOMICS 209 (2012); Avinash K. Dixit & Jörgen W. Weibull, Political Polarization, 104 PROCEEDINGS OF THE NATIONAL ACADEMY OF SCIENCES 7351 (2007); Barak Orbach, *On Hubris, Civility, and Incivility*, 54 ARIZONA LAW REVIEW 443 (2012); Rajiv Sethi & Muhamet Yildiz, *Public Disagreement*, 4(3) AMERICAN ECONOMIC JOURNAL: MICROECONOMICS 57 (2012).

Regulation as a concept of interference inevitably offends individuals' personal beliefs and sparks controversy. When a person cannot engage in an activity of choice, her personal beliefs involving the value of that activity or the right to engage in this activity may motivate her to contest the regulatory restrictions.[10] Similarly, a person who believes that the *laissez faire* principle is a desirable state practice may object to many regulatory policies without actually considering their value to society.[11] In the same spirit, an individual who believes that the state should take some regulatory action may be reluctant to consider its cost-effectiveness. Such tensions between personal beliefs and regulatory policies frequently lead to extended debates and disputes over regulation.[12] In such disagreements, people often have predetermined positions before any analysis is even conducted.[13]

This Chapter examines some of the characteristics of the controversy over regulation. Specifically, we will explore some implications of reality imperfections for regulation. We shall see that, in the real world, the unrestricted pursuit of self-interest can compromise public interests and result in harm. We will also see that government regulation is likely to be imperfect and controversial. In such imperfect world, it appears somewhat arbitrary and capricious to have a predetermined view about any regulatory issue, and specifically factually complex ones. Yet, people tend to have very strong views about many issues in regulation: speed limits, tax rates, immigration policies, abortion restrictions, gun control, financial regulation, health care laws, environmental policies, and others. The confidence people have in their own views is often inconsistent with the knowledge and understanding they can have. This discrepancy is the primary source of controversy over regulation.

Coalition for Responsible Regulation, Inc. v. Environmental Protection Agency

684 F.3d 102 (D.C. Cir. 2012)

■ PER CURIAM:

Following the Supreme Court's decision in *Massachusetts v. EPA*, 549 U.S. 497 (2007)—which clarified that greenhouse gases are an "air pollutant" subject to regulation under the Clean Air Act (CAA)—the Environmental Protection Agency promulgated a series of greenhouse gas-related rules. * * *

---

10. *See, e.g.*, Washington v. Immelt, 173 Wash.2d 1 (2011) (holding that noise ordinance, which prohibited honking of a vehicle horn, was unconstitutional); Weil v. McClough, 618 F.Supp. 1294 (S.D.NY. 1985) (upholding the constitutionality of an anti-honking noise ordinance).

11. *See generally* 2.6; Mark Francis, *Herbert Spencer and the Myth of Laissez-Faire*, 39 JOURNAL OF THE HISTORY OF IDEAS 317 (1978); Jacob Viner, *The Intellectual History of Laissez Faire*, 3 JOURNAL OF LAW & ECONOMICS 45 (1960).

12. *See generally* Barak Orbach & Frances Sjoberg, *Excessive Speech, Civility Norms, and the Clucking Theorem*, 44 CONNECTICUT LAW REVIEW 1 (2011).

13. *See* Orbach, *On Hubris, Civility, and Incivility*, *supra* note 9.

Petitioners, various states and industry groups, challenge all these rules, arguing that they are based on improper constructions of the CAA and are otherwise arbitrary and capricious. * * *

I.

We begin with a brief primer on greenhouse gases. As their name suggests, when released into the atmosphere, these gases act "like the ceiling of a greenhouse, trapping solar energy and retarding the escape of reflected heat." *Massachusetts v. EPA*, 549 U.S. at 505. A wide variety of modern human activities result in greenhouse gas emissions; cars, power plants, and industrial sites all release significant amounts of these heat-trapping gases. In recent decades "[a] well-documented rise in global temperatures has coincided with a significant increase in the concentration of [greenhouse gases] in the atmosphere." *Id.* at 504–05. Many scientists believe that mankind's greenhouse gas emissions are driving this climate change. These scientists predict that global climate change will cause a host of deleterious consequences, including drought, increasingly severe weather events, and rising sea levels.

The genesis of this litigation came in 2007, when the Supreme Court held in *Massachusetts v. EPA* that greenhouse gases "unambiguous[ly]" may be regulated as an "air pollutant" under the Clean Air Act ("CAA"). Squarely rejecting the contention—then advanced by EPA—that "greenhouse gases cannot be 'air pollutants' within the meaning of the Act," the Court held that the CAA's definition of "air pollutant" "embraces all airborne compounds of whatever stripe." Moreover, because the CAA requires EPA to establish motor-vehicle emission standards for "any air pollutant ... which may reasonably be anticipated to endanger public health or welfare," 42 U.S.C. § 7521(a)(1) (emphasis added), the Court held that EPA had a "statutory obligation" to regulate harmful greenhouse gases. "Under the clear terms of the Clean Air Act," the Court concluded, "EPA can avoid taking further action only if it determines that greenhouse gases do not contribute to climate change or if it provides some reasonable explanation as to why it cannot or will not exercise its discretion to determine whether they do." The Court thus directed EPA to determine "whether sufficient information exists to make an endangerment finding" for greenhouse gases.

Massachusetts v. EPA spurred a cascading series of greenhouse gas-related rules and regulations. [In] direct response to the Supreme Court's directive, EPA issued an Endangerment Finding for greenhouse gases. * * * After compiling and considering a considerable body of scientific evidence, EPA concluded that motor-vehicle emissions of * * * gases "contribute to the total greenhouse gas air pollution, and thus to the climate change problem, which is reasonably anticipated to endanger public health and welfare."* * * *

A number of groups—including states and regulated industries-filed petitions for review of EPA's greenhouse gas regulations, contending that

* [The decision addressed challenges to two other regulations.—BYO]

the agency misconstrued the CAA and otherwise acted arbitrarily and capriciously. * * *

II.

State and Industry [Petitioners challenged] the Endangerment Finding, the first of the series of rules EPA issued after the Supreme Court remanded *Massachusetts v. EPA*. In the decision ordering the remand, the Supreme Court held that EPA had failed in its statutory obligations when it "offered no reasoned explanation for its refusal to decide whether greenhouse gases cause or contribute to climate change." *Massachusetts v. EPA*, 549 U.S. at 534. On remand, EPA compiled a substantial scientific record, which is before us in the present review, and determined that "greenhouse gases in the atmosphere may reasonably be anticipated both to endanger public health and to endanger public welfare." Endangerment Finding, 74 Fed. Reg. at 66,497. EPA went on to find that motor-vehicle emissions of greenhouse gases "contribute to the total greenhouse gas air pollution, and thus to the climate change problem, which is reasonably anticipated to endanger public health and welfare."

State and Industry Petitioners challenge several aspects of EPA's decision, including (1) EPA's interpretation of CAA § 202(a)(1), which sets out the endangerment-finding standard; (2) the adequacy of the scientific record supporting the Endangerment Finding; (3) EPA's decision not to "quantify" the risk of endangerment to public health or welfare created by climate change; (4) EPA's choice to define the "air pollutant" at issue as an aggregate of six greenhouse gases; (5) EPA's failure to consult its Science Advisory Board before issuing the Endangerment Finding; and (6) EPA's denial of all petitions for reconsideration of the Endangerment Finding. We ultimately conclude that the Endangerment Finding is consistent with *Massachusetts v. EPA* and the text and structure of the CAA, and is adequately supported by the administrative record.

A.

Industry Petitioners contend that EPA improperly interpreted CAA § 202(a)(1) as restricting the Endangerment Finding to a science-based judgment devoid of considerations of policy concerns and regulatory consequences. * * *

In *Massachusetts v. EPA*, the Supreme Court rebuffed an attempt by EPA itself to inject considerations of policy into its decision. At the time, EPA had "offered a laundry list of reasons not to regulate" greenhouse gases, including

> that a number of voluntary Executive Branch programs already provide an effective response to the threat of global warming, that regulating greenhouse gases might impair the President's ability to negotiate with "key developing nations" to reduce emissions, and that curtailing motor-vehicle emissions would reflect "an inefficient, piecemeal approach to address the climate change issue."

The Court noted that "these policy judgments . . . have nothing to do with whether greenhouse gas emissions contribute to climate change. Still less do they amount to a reasoned justification for declining to form a scientific judgment." In the Court's view, EPA's policy-based explanations contained "no reasoned explanation for [EPA's] refusal to decide" the key part of the endangerment inquiry: "whether greenhouse gases cause or contribute to climate change."

As in *Massachusetts v. EPA*, a "laundry list of reasons not to regulate" simply has "nothing to do with whether greenhouse gas emissions contribute to climate change." The additional exercises State and Industry Petitioners would have EPA undertake * * * do not inform the "scientific judgment" that § 202(a)(1) requires of EPA. Instead of focusing on the question whether greenhouse gas emissions may reasonably be anticipated to endanger public health or welfare, the factors State and Industry Petitioners put forth only address what might happen were EPA to answer that question in the affirmative. As EPA stated in the Endangerment Finding, such inquiries "muddle the rather straightforward scientific judgment about whether there may be endangerment by throwing the potential impact of responding to the danger into the initial question." 74 Fed. Reg. at 66, 515. * * *

B.

State and Industry Petitioners next challenge the adequacy of the scientific record underlying the Endangerment Finding, objecting to both the type of evidence upon which EPA relied and EPA's decision to make an Endangerment Finding in light of what Industry Petitioners view as significant scientific uncertainty. Neither objection has merit.

1.

As an initial matter, State and Industry Petitioners question EPA's reliance on "major assessments" addressing greenhouse gases and climate change issued by the Intergovernmental Panel on Climate Change (IPCC), the U.S. Global Climate Research Program (USGCRP), and the National Research Council (NRC). These peer-reviewed assessments synthesized thousands of individual studies on various aspects of greenhouse gases and climate change and drew "overarching conclusions" about the state of the science in this field. The assessments provide data and information on, *inter alia*, "the amount of greenhouse gases being emitted by human activities"; their continued accumulation in the atmosphere; the resulting observed changes to Earth's energy balance, temperature and climate at global and regional levels, and other "climate-sensitive sectors and systems of the human and natural environment"; the extent to which these changes "can be attributed to human-induced buildup of atmospheric greenhouse gases"; "future projected climate change"; and "projected risks and impacts to human health, society and the environment."

State and Industry Petitioners assert that EPA improperly "delegated" its judgment to the IPCC, USGCRP, and NRC by relying on these assessments of climate-change science. This argument is little more than a semantic trick. EPA did not delegate, explicitly or otherwise, any decision-making to any of those entities. EPA simply did here what it and other decision-makers often must do to make a science-based judgment: it sought out and reviewed existing scientific evidence to determine whether a particular finding was warranted. It makes no difference that much of the scientific evidence in large part consisted of "syntheses" of individual studies and research. Even individual studies and research papers often synthesize past work in an area and then build upon it. This is how science works. EPA is not required to re-prove the existence of the atom every time it approaches a scientific question.

Moreover, it appears from the record that EPA used the assessment reports not as substitutes for its own judgment but as evidence upon which it relied to make that judgment. * * *

2.

Industry Petitioners also assert that the scientific evidence does not adequately support the Endangerment Finding. As we have stated before in reviewing the science-based decisions of agencies such as EPA, * * * "we give an extreme degree of deference to the agency when it is evaluating scientific data within its technical expertise."

The body of scientific evidence marshaled by EPA in support of the Endangerment Finding is substantial. EPA's scientific evidence of record included support for the proposition that greenhouse gases trap heat on earth that would otherwise dissipate into space; that this "greenhouse effect" warms the climate; that human activity is contributing to increased atmospheric levels of greenhouse gases; and that the climate system is warming. * * *

EPA had before it substantial record evidence that anthropogenic emissions of greenhouse gases "very likely" caused warming of the climate over the last several decades. EPA further had evidence of current and future effects of this warming on public health and welfare. Relying again upon substantial scientific evidence, EPA determined that anthropogenically induced climate change threatens both public health and public welfare. It found that extreme weather events, changes in air quality, increases in food-and water-borne pathogens, and increases in temperatures are likely to have adverse health effects. The record also supports EPA's conclusion that climate change endangers human welfare by creating risk to food production and agriculture, forestry, energy, infrastructure, ecosystems, and wildlife. Substantial evidence further supported EPA's conclusion that the warming resulting from the greenhouse gas emissions could be expected to create risks to water resources and in general to coastal areas as a result of expected increase in sea level. Finally, EPA determined from substantial evidence that motor-vehicle emissions of greenhouse gases contribute to climate change and thus to the endangerment of public health and welfare.

Industry Petitioners do not find fault with much of the substantial record EPA amassed in support of the Endangerment Finding. Rather, they contend that the record evidences too much uncertainty to support that judgment. But the existence of some uncertainty does not, without more, warrant invalidation of an endangerment finding. If a statute is "precautionary in nature" and "designed to protect the public health," and the relevant evidence is "difficult to come by, uncertain, or conflicting because it is on the frontiers of scientific knowledge," EPA need not provide "rigorous step-by-step proof of cause and effect" to support an endangerment finding. *Ethyl Corp. v. EPA*, 541 F.2d 1, 28 (D.C.Cir.1976). As we have stated before, "Awaiting certainty will often allow for only reactive, not preventive, regulation." *Id.* at 25. * * *

In the end, Petitioners are asking us to re-weigh the scientific evidence before EPA and reach our own conclusion. This is not our role. * * * When EPA evaluates scientific evidence in its bailiwick, we ask only that it take the scientific record into account "in a rational manner." * * * Industry Petitioners have not shown that EPA failed to do so here.

C.

State Petitioners, here led by Texas, contend that the Endangerment Finding is arbitrary and capricious because EPA did not "define," "measure," or "quantify" either the atmospheric concentration at which greenhouse gases endanger public health or welfare, the rate or type of climate change that it anticipates will endanger public health or welfare, or the risks or impacts of climate change. According to Texas, without defining these thresholds and distinguishing "safe" climate change from climate change that endangers, EPA's Endangerment Finding is just a "subjective conviction."

It is true that EPA did not provide a quantitative threshold at which greenhouse gases or climate change will endanger or cause certain impacts to public health or welfare. The text of CAA § 202(a)(1) does not require that EPA set a precise numerical value as part of an endangerment finding. Quite the opposite; the § 202(a)(1) inquiry necessarily entails a case-by-case, sliding-scale approach to endangerment. * * *

In its essence, Texas's call for quantification of the endangerment is no more than a specialized version of Industry Petitioners' claim that the scientific record contains too much uncertainty to find endangerment. * * *

For the foregoing reasons, we dismiss all petitions for review * * * and deny the remainder of the petitions.

So ordered.

§ 2.2 THE INVISIBLE HAND'S FINGERPRINTS

§ 2.2.1 What's in the Hand?

Adam Smith's *invisible hand* metaphor is a common currency in the controversy over regulation: Legal and political arguments routinely refer to the invisible hand metaphor to enhance or criticize reliance on private enterprise, protection of individual liberties, and government interference with private domains.[14] The metaphor refers the belief that unrestricted market forces serve society as a whole. It is unclear whether any person

14. *See generally* Adrian Vermeule, *The Invisible Hand in Legal and Political Theory*, 96 VIRGINIA LAW REVIEW 1416 (2010).

seriously believes that market forces are so effective that regulation is always redundant. Some use the metaphor to argue that specific regulations are redundant or that the general burden of regulations is too heavy. In contrast, others use it to argue that the reliance on market forces is excessive and is more likely to be a source of many problems. Adam Smith believed that "the most persistent, the most universal, and therefore the most reliable of man's motives was the pursuit of his own interests."[15]

The housing bubble that led to the Great Recession, we saw, was framed by related beliefs. In 1997, the Chairman of the Federal Reserve Board, Alan Greenspan, described the U.S. philosophy for financial regulation, declared that "self-interest of market participants generates private market regulation."[16] In October 2008, reflecting on the causes of the Great Recession, Chairman Greenspan stated that "those of us who have looked to the self-interest of lending institutions to protect shareholders' equity (myself included) are in a state of shocked disbelief. * * * The whole intellectual edifice * * * collapsed in the summer of last year."[17] Studies of the recession charged Greenspan with excessive reliance on the pursuit of self-interest.[18]

In his famous 1776 book, *The Wealth of Nations*, Adam Smith wrote:

> [E]very individual * * * neither intends to promote the public interest, nor knows how much he is promoting it. * * * [H]e intends [to promote] only his own gain, and he is * * * led by an *invisible hand* to promote an end which was no part of his intention. * * * By pursuing his own interest he frequently promotes that of the society more effectually than when he really intends to promote it. I have never known much good done by those affected to trade for the public good.[19]

As stated in *The Wealth of Nations*, the invisible hand metaphor *supposedly* posits that the pursuit of self-interest is a reliable way to promote public interests. For example, in *Free to Choose*, a book advocating against government regulation, economists Milton and Rose Friedman explained their reading of the metaphor:

> [Adam Smith] analyzed the way in which a market system could combine the freedom of individuals to pursue their own objectives

---

15. George J. Stigler, *Preface*, in AN INQUIRY INTO THE NATURE AND CAUSES OF THE WEALTH OF NATIONS xii (1976).

16. Alan Greenspan, *Government Regulation and Derivative Contracts*, Speech at the Financial Markets Conference of the Federal Reserve Bank of Atlanta, Coral Gables, Florida, Feb. 21, 1997.

17. *The Financial Crisis and the Role of Federal Regulators: Hearing Before the H. Comm. on Gov't Oversight and Reform*, 110th Cong. 17 (Oct. 23, 2008) (testimony of Alan Greenspan, Former Chairman of the Federal Reserve).

18. *See, e.g.*, NATIONAL COMMISSION ON THE CAUSES OF THE FINANCIAL AND ECONOMIC CRISIS IN THE UNITED STATES, THE FINANCIAL CRISIS: INQUIRY REPORT (final report, Jan. 2011) available at *regti.me/FCIC–Report* (case sensitive), § 1.1.3; Gary B. Gorton, SLAPPED BY THE INVISIBLE HAND: THE PANIC OF 2007 (2010).

19. ADAM SMITH, AN INQUIRY INTO THE NATURE AND CAUSES OF THE WEALTH OF NATIONS 477–478 (1976).

> with the extensive cooperation and collaboration needed in the economic field to produce our food, our clothing, our housing. Adam Smith's key insight was that both parties to an exchange can benefit and that, *so long as cooperation is strictly voluntary*, no exchange will take place unless both parties do benefit. No external force, no coercion, no violation of freedom is necessary to produce cooperation among individuals all of whom can benefit. That is why, as Adam Smith put it, an individual who "intends only his own gain" is "led by an invisible hand to promote an end which was no part of his intention. * * * I have never known much good done by those who affected to trade for the public good."[20]

Furthermore, Milton and Rose Friedman stressed, "[i]n the government sphere, as in the market, there seems to be an invisible hand, but it operates precisely the opposite direction from Adam Smith's: an individual who intends to serve the public interest by fostering government intervention is 'led by an invisible hand to promote' private interests, 'which was no part of his intention.' * * * Adam Smith's invisible hand has been powerful enough to overcome the deadening effects of the invisible hand that operates in the political sphere."[21]

Adam Smith did not coin the phrase "invisible hand," nor did he popularize it. It was a common phrase during his time.[22] For example, in the early seventeenth century, William Shakespeare had already used the phrase in *Macbeth*. Historians of economic thought concluded that that the metaphor's meaning was theological and related to God's work; however, they could not determine with certainty the exact meaning Smith had attributed to the phrase.[23] Whatever meaning Smith had for the invisible hand metaphor, he did not refer to the market forces. Ultimately, the modern meaning of the phrase "invisible hand" is somewhat related to Smith's criticism of government regulation, but it is unrelated to the meaning Smith attributed to the phrase.

The modern meaning of the invisible hand metaphor is also inconsistent with economic principles. Economists have rejected the proposition that the pursuit of self-interest is a reliable way to promote public interests.[24] The Great Recession is an unfortunate reminder that the metaphor

---

20. MILTON & ROSE FRIEDMAN, FREE TO CHOOSE: A PERSONAL STATEMENT 1–2 (1980).

21. *Id.* at 5–6.

22. *See generally* Peter Harrison, *Adam Smith and the History of the Invisible Hand*, 72 JOURNAL OF THE HISTORY OF IDEAS 29 (2011); Alec Mafie, *The Invisible Hand of Jupiter*, 32 JOURNAL OF THE HISTORY OF IDEAS 595 (1971).

23. *See, e.g.*, Anthony Brewer, *On the Other (Invisible) Hand . . .*, 41 HISTORY OF POLITICAL ECONOMY 519 (2009); Andy Denis, *The Invisible Hand of God in Adam Smith*, 23 RESEARCH IN THE HISTORY OF ECONOMIC THOUGHT & METHODOLOGY 1 (2005); William D. Grampp, *What Did Smith Mean by the Invisible Hand*, 108 JOURNAL OF POLITICAL ECONOMY 441 (2000); Harrison, *Adam Smith and the History of the Invisible Hand*, *id.*; Mafie, *The Invisible Hand of Jupiter*, *id*; Joseph Persky, *Adam Smith's Invisible Hands*, 3 JOURNAL OF ECONOMIC PERSPECTIVES 195 (1989); Emma Rothschild, *Adam Smith and the Invisible Hand*, 84 AMERICAN ECONOMIC REVIEW 319 (1994).

24. *See, e.g.*, Frank Hahn, *Reflections on the Invisible Hand*, 144 LLOYD BANK REVIEW 1 (1982); Paul A. Samuelson, *A Modern Theorist's Vindication of Adam Smith*, 67 AMERICAN

is not and has never been a principle in economics.[25] Contrary to the argument of Milton and Rose Friedman, voluntary exchanges do not necessarily promote public interests. Voluntary exchanges may adversely affect third parties.[26] For example, when a person opens a bar in a residential neighborhood, all transactions between the bar owner and patrons are voluntary. However, noise and traffic will burden the local residents. Similarly, the assumption that voluntary exchanges necessarily serve the pursuit of self-interest is misguided. Financial bubbles are the outcome of voluntary exchanges.[27] They do not serve the interests of those who enter into voluntary exchanges and surely do not serve the public. Along the same lines, society bans and restricts voluntary exchanges in drugs, sex, firearms, alcohol, tobacco, and bodily organs. The rationale behind these restrictions is that voluntary exchanges do not always promote self-interest.[28]

In practice, society relies on many institutions to assure that the pursuit of self-interest will not harm public interests.[29] Regulations ban or at least to attempt to curb the negative consequences resulting from the pursuit of self-interest and may actually stimulate the pursuit of self-interest. However, state intervention in society is costly, not necessarily effective, and in certain instances unnecessarily burdens pursuits of self-interest that could benefit the public.

In sum, many people have strong views about the effectiveness of the "invisible hand" and often use invisible hand arguments. These views are diverse and often in conflict. The concept that sparks the beliefs and controversies has no actual theoretical foundation and has never been implemented in practice. This concept, however, influenced approaches regulation.

Sidebar 2–1

Inalienable Rights

The Declaration of Independence provides: "We hold these truths to be self-evident, that all men are created equal, that they are endowed by their Creator with certain unalienable rights, that among these are life, liberty and the pursuit of happiness."

An *inalienable right* is one that its possessor cannot waive or transfer.[30] By extension, "if there are any rights properly called 'inalienable,' assertions of these rights cannot, for any reason and under any circumstances, be denied. It is a

ECONOMIC REVIEW 42 (1977); George A. Selgin & Lawrence H. White, *How Would the Invisible Hand Handle Money?*, 32 JOURNAL OF ECONOMIC LITERATURE 1178 (1994); Oliver E. Williamson, *Visible and Invisible Governance,* 84 AMERICAN ECONOMIC REVIEW 323 (1994).

25. *See, e.g.*, Gary B. Gorton, SLAPPED BY THE INVISIBLE HAND: THE PANIC OF 2007 (2010).

26. *See* Chapter 3.

27. *See* § 1.1.

28. *See* Chapter 7.

29. ARTHUR CECIL PIGOU, THE ECONOMICS OF WELFARE 128–129 (4th ed. 1932); Williamson, *Visible and Invisible Governance, supra* note 16.

30. *See generally infra* § 7.3; Stuart M. Brown, Jr., *Inalienable Rights*, 64 PHILOSOPHICAL REVIEW 192 (1955); Terrance McConnell, *The Nature and Basis of Inalienable Rights*, 3 LAW & PHILOSOPHY 25 (1984); Margaret Jane Radin, *Market-Inalienability*, 100 HARVARD LAW REVIEW 1849 (1987).

moral impossibility, because the refusal to honor an asserted inalienable right is the most intolerable and inexcusable injustice against a man."[31] It follows that the state should protect inalienable rights from interference and not intrude upon such rights.[32]

Like many other concepts in regulation, people attribute opposite meanings to "inalienable rights." Some use the phrase to argue against state interference with choices. Others posit that the state should protect these inalienable rights with regulations.[33] Certain issues, such as voluntary euthanasia and abortion may blur individual positions about inalienable rights. Some of those who perceive the concept of inalienable rights as a limit on government regulation may believe that regulation is needed to avoid voluntary euthanasia and abortion. In contrast, some of those who believe that the state should regulate to protect inalienable rights may prefer that the state refrain from banning such choices.[34]

The absolute nature of inalienable rights is another topic of controversy.[35] All rights are waived, traded, and transferred in one way or another. People waive their right to life when they engage in risky activities such as smoking, excessive drinking, driving under the influence of alcohol, or riding a motorcycle.[36] Similarly, the right to liberty is compromised when we take on commitments, or when financial constraints prevent us from actually carrying out our choices. In this system of risks and commitments, people, at least indirectly transfer rights to life and liberty.

Inalienable rights symbolize core debates in regulation. People with opposite views use the same rights to support their positions. These rights do not exist or at best are rather controversial.

Sidebar 2–2

The Pursuit of Happiness

As we shall see, the right to the pursuit of happiness—which is one of the Declaration of Independence's "unalienable rights"—is occasionally treated as a right to pursue self-interest. Henry Campbell Black, the creator of Black's Law Dictionary, wrote the one of the most famous analyses of the pursuit of happiness.[37]

In 1895, Black published the first edition of his *Handbook of American Constitutional Law*. In describing the handbook, Black wrote that it was "intended primarily for the use of students at law and instructors in the law schools and

31. Brown, *Inalienable Rights*, *id.*, at 192.

32. *See generally* Amartya Sen, *The Impossibility of a Paretian Liberal*, 78 JOURNAL OF POLITICAL ECONOMY 152 (1970); Amartya Sen, *Freedom of Choice: Concept and Content*, 32 EUROPEAN ECONOMIC REVIEW 269 (1988).

33. *See*, *e.g.*, Radin, *Market–Inalienability*, *supra* note 21.

34. *See*, *e.g.*, Joel Feinberg, *Voluntary Euthanasia and the Inalienable Right to Life*, 7 PHILOSOPHY & PUBLIC AFFAIRS 93 (1978).

35. *See*, *e.g.*, Brown, *Inalienable Rights*, *id.*; H.L.A. Hart, *Are There Any Natural Rights?* 64 PHILOSOPHICAL REVIEW 175, 175 (1955); McConnell, *The Nature and Basis of Inalienable Rights*, *supra* note 21; Marvin Schiller, *Are There Any Inalienable Rights*, 79 ETHICS 309 (1969); Lance K. Stell, *Dueling and the Right to Life*, 90 ETHICS 7 (1979).

36. For risks associated with motorcycle riding *see* Sidebar 11–1.

37. *See* David Jayne Hill, *In Memoriam: Doctor Henry Campbell Black*, 11 CONSTITUTIONAL REVIEW 67 (1927); Sarah Yates, *Black's Law Dictionary: The Making of an American Standard*, 103 LAW LIBRARY JOURNAL 175 (2011).

universities."[38] Critics disagreed and noted that Black understated the value of his "admirable" work.[39] One of the handbook's chapters was dedicated to "civil rights and their protection by the constitutions." In that chapter, Black defined "rights" as "powers of free action" and discussed the pursuit of happiness.

THE PURSUIT OF HAPPINESS

145. All men are invested with a natural, inherent, and inalienable right to the pursuit of happiness.

This principle is formally declared in the constitutions of many of the states. And moreover the framers of the Declaration of Independence announced that they "held these truths to be self-evident, that all men are created equal; that they are endowed by their Creator with certain inalienable rights; that among these are life, liberty, and the pursuit of happiness." This latter expression is one of a general nature, and the right thus secured is not capable of specific definition or limitation, but is really the aggregate of many particular rights, some of which are enumerated in the constitutions, and others included in the general guaranty of "liberty." The happiness of men may consist in many things or depend on many circumstances. But in so far as it is likely to be acted upon by the operations of government, it is clear that it must comprise personal freedom, exemption from oppression or invidious discrimination, the right to follow one's individual preference in the choice of an occupation and the application of his energies, liberty of conscience, and the right to enjoy the domestic relations and the privileges of the family and the home. The search for happiness is the mainspring of human activity. And a guaranteed constitutional right to pursue happiness can mean no less than the right to devote the mental and physical powers to the attainment of this end, without restriction or obstruction, in respect to any of the particulars just mentioned, except in so far as may be necessary to secure the equal rights of others. Thus it appears that this guaranty, though one of the most indefinite, is also one of the most comprehensive to be found in the constitutions.[40]

Questions

1. *Stealing*, taking property illegally with the intent to keep it unlawfully, is a certain type of a pursuit of self-interest. *Opportunism*, "self-interest seeking with guile,"[41] is "behavior that is undesirable but that cannot be cost-effectively captured—defined, detected, and deterred—by explicit ex ante rulemaking."[42] What is the primary difference between stealing and opportunism? Is stealing or opportunism necessarily inconsistent with the idea that the pursuit of self-interest is a reliable way to promote public interests? Is stealing or opportunism inconsistent with Milton and Rose Friedman's reading of the invisible hand metaphor?

2. The "*agency problem*" refers to situations in which a person (agent) has some control over assets of another person (principal), and their

38. HENRY CAMPBELL BLACK, HANDBOOK OF AMERICAN CONSTITUTIONAL LAW iii (1895).

39. *See, e.g.*, A.B. Weimer, *Handbook of American Constitutional Law. By Henry Campbell Black*, 43 AMERICAN LAW REGISTER & REVIEW 274 (1895); *Handbook of American Constitutional Law. By Henry Campbell Black*, 7 GREEN BAG 208 (1895).

40. HENRY CAMPBELL BLACK, HANDBOOK OF AMERICAN CONSTITUTIONAL LAW 404 (1895).

41. OLIVER E. WILLIAMSON, MARKET AND HIERARCHIES 26 (1975).

42. Henry E. Smith, *An Economic Analysis of Law Versus Equity* (unpublished manuscript, 2010).

interests are not perfectly aligned.[43] In such situations, the agent may use her control to pursue her private interests, including having more leisure time, rather than diligently managing the principal's assets. Examples of agency problems include the relationships between a management (agent) and shareholders (principals), and between employees (agents) and employers (principals). Adam Smith considered the agency problem in *The Wealth of Nations*:

> The directors of * * * companies, * * * being the managers rather of other people's money than of their own, it cannot well be expected, that they should watch over it with the same anxious vigilance with which the partners in a private copartnery frequently watch over their own. * * * Negligence and profusion * * * must always prevail, more or less, in the management of the affairs of * * * a company.[44]

Do agency problems necessarily undermine the idea that the pursuit of self-interest is a reliable way to promote public interests?

§ 2.2.2 The Pursuit of Self–Interest

In *The Wealth of Nations*, Adam Smith explored the persistence of the pursuit of self-interest. In a famous passage he wrote: "It is not from the benevolence of *the butcher, the brewer, or the baker*, that we expect our dinner, but from their regard to their own interest. We address ourselves, not to their humanity but to their self-love, and never talk to them of our own necessities but of their advantages."[45]

Modern interpretations of the invisible hand metaphor treat this passage as an illustration of the "invisible hand principle," although such a principle never existed in Smith's thinking. We will examine the question of whether the pursuit of self-interest of butchers, brewers, and bakers is a reliable way to promote public interests.

§ 2.2.2a The Butcher

In April 1866, New York enacted the Metropolitan Health Act, which established a Board of Health for New York City with broad regulatory powers "to prevent the spread of disease[s]."[46] At the time, New York was one of the few large cities that failed to reduce death rates.[47] Studies

---

43. *See generally* Eugene F. Fama & Michael C. Jensen, *Agency Problems and Residual Claims*, 26 JOURNAL OF LAW & ECONOMICS 327 (1983); Eugene F. Fama & Michael C. Jensen, *Separation of Ownership and Control*, 26 JOURNAL OF LAW & ECONOMICS 301 (1983); Michael C. Jensen & William H. Meckling, Theory of the Firm: Managerial Behavior, Agency Costs and Ownership Structure, 3 JOURNAL OF FINANCE ECONOMICS 305 (1976); Sanford J. Grossman & Oliver D. Hart, *An Analysis of the Principal–Agent Problem*, 51 ECONOMETRICA 7 (1983).

44. At 741.

45. SMITH, *supra* note 11, at 741.

46. *See generally* Gert H. Brieger, *Sanitary Reform in New York City: Stephen Smith and the Passage of the Metropolitan Health Bill*, 40 BULLETIN OF THE HISTORY OF MEDICINE 407 (1966).

47. METROPOLITAN BOARD OF HEALTH, 1866 ANNUAL REPORT TO THE GOVERNOR OF THE STATE OF NEW YORK 8–9 (1867).

unequivocally showed that the cause of the City's high death rate resulted from poor sanitary conditions, which arose primarily from local slaughterhouses. The slaughterhouses operated in crowded residential areas, and they were often constructed in such a way that their cesspools flowed into gutters or even the streets. Large amounts of animal remains and waste were discharged onto the streets and into the sewer system. The City's air became noxious and poisonous.[48] No invisible hand cleared the air or streets. In the process of promoting their private interests, the butchers created a costly public nuisance.

To combat the pollution resulting from this commercial activity, the Board of Health's adopted a Code of Health Ordinances that imposed restrictions on the construction and operation of slaughterhouses.[49] Butchers challenged the constitutionality of the Metropolitan Health Act and the Code of Health Ordinances, arguing that these regulations deprived them of liberty and property without proper due process. The Court of Appeals of New York sided with the City and upheld the law.[50]

Butchers caused similar problems in New Orleans, where nineteenth century slaughterhouses operations turned the city into a decaying health hazard. Like many cities during the era, New Orleans had no sewer system and could not afford to collect public waste or provide cleaning services for public areas. Local butchers slaughtered animals and dumped the waste into the Mississippi River and streets. The dumped waste did not mix well with the local humidity and created a sanitation nightmare in the City's swampy environment.[51] The pursuit of self-interest of butchers in New Orleans resulted in frequent epidemics of cholera and yellow fever and a rising death rate.

In 1869, the Louisiana legislature responded by endorsing an initiative proposed by a group of entrepreneurs and passed *An Act for the Protection of the Health of the City of New Orleans*.[52] The Act gave a charter to Crescent City Live Stock Landing and Slaughter House Company to build a slaughterhouse on the east bank of the Mississippi River south of the City; it also granted the Company an exclusive right to conduct all butchering for the City, and regulated its rules and prices to allow access to all the City's butchers. This regulatory framework cleaned the City from slaughterhouses by concentrating butchering in one regulated facility. Prior to the reform, New Orleans' butchers did not internalize the full costs of their operation, as the *public* bore the nuisance cost. Under the reform, *butchers* paid for the cost of safe operations. The New Orleans model was not an innovative regulatory concept. It was extremely successful in improving the City's health conditions and boosting the beef industry.[53]

---

48. *Id.* at 33–37.

49. *Id.*

50. Metropolitan Bd. of Health v. Heister, 37 N.Y. 661 (1868).

51. Ronald M. Labbé & Jonathan Lurie, The Slaughterhouse Cases 6, 17–65 (2003).

52. Act No. 118, Louisiana (1869).

53. Herbert Hovenkamp, Enterprise and American Law 1839–1937 116–124 (1991); Labbé & Lurie, *supra* note 41, at 82–102.

The 1869 slaughterhouse reform, however, sparked a heated controversy, carried by almost 300 lawsuits. Some of the cases reached the Supreme Court, and in a famous decision known as *The Slaughter–House Cases*, it upheld the law by a five-to-four decision.[54] *The Slaughter–House Cases* was one of the most misunderstood Supreme Court decisions in regulation.[55] Mainly, the majority's reasoning is widely denounced for its narrow interpretation of the Fourteenth Amendment.[56] Moreover, throughout much of the twentieth century, the decision symbolized corrupt regulation.

During the Reconstruction Era, corruption was pervasive in Louisiana and eroded the public confidence in the state government. Henry Clay Warmoth, the "Prince of the Carpetbaggers," was the Louisiana Governor who signed the Slaughterhouse Bill into law allegedly in exchange for a bribe. He was impeached at the end of his gubernatorial term after being accused of corruption throughout his term.[57] In assessing the legality of the Bill, one of the trial courts ruled against the state by holding that "deception, fraud, bribery, [and] corruption" motivated state politicians to create a monopoly and deprive butchers of livelihood. On appeal, the district court, and subsequently the Louisiana Supreme Court, held that the allegations "were too vague and indefinite to admit of proof."[58] The press, however, never acquitted the government that was believed to be corrupt.

A 1918 study, which relied on publicly available historical reports, concluded that bribery and corruption led to the enactment of the 1869 Act.[59] In his 1922 influential text, *The Supreme Court in United States History*, Charles Warren relied on this study to critique the 1869 reform: "The 'carpet-bag' Legislature of Louisiana, undoubtedly under influence of corruption and bribery, had passed a statute which granted a monopoly of the slaughterhouse business within certain parishes of New Orleans in favor of one corporation, and which deprive over one thousand persons of the right to engage in that business."[60] Warren's influential book established the corruption claims as a fact in American legal literature.

Until the twenty-first century, no evidence was found for payments to politicians beyond "sandwiches, whiskey, brandy, * * * wine, * * * and

54. The Slaughter–House Cases, 83 U.S. 36 (1873).

55. *See* Herbert Hovenkamp, *Technology, Politics, and Regulated Monopoly: An American Historical Perspective*, 62 TEXAS LAW REVIEW 1263, 1295–1308 (1984); HERBERT HOVENKAMP, ENTERPRISE AND AMERICAN LAW, 1839–1937 116–124 (1991); LABBÉ & LURIE, *supra* note 41, at 82–102. *See also* Mitchell Franklin, *The Foundations and Meaning of the Slaughterhouse Cases*, 18 TULANE LAW REVIEW 1 (1943).

56. *See, e.g.*, CHARLES BLACK JR., A NEW BIRTH OF FREEDOM: HUMAN RIGHTS, NAMED AND UNNAMED 55–59 (1999) ("[T]he Slaughterhouse Cases * * * is probably the worst holding, in its effect on human rights, ever uttered by the Supreme Court").

57. *See generally* Charles L. Dufour, *The Age of Warmoth*, 6 LOUISIANA HISTORY 335 (1965); JOE G. TAYLOR, LOUISIANA RECONSTRUCTED, 1863–1877 209–252 (1974).

58. Belden v. Fagan, La.Ann. 545, 547 (1870).

59. ELLA LONN, RECONSTRUCTION IN LOUISIANA AFTER 1868 42–44 (1918).

60. CHARLES WARREN, THE SUPREME COURT IN UNITED STATES HISTORY, vol. 3, at 258 (1922). Warren won the 1923 Pulitzer Prize for History for this book.

that kind of thing."[61] Herbert Hovenkamp, who uncovered how the 1869 Act became associated with corruption, argued that the alleged corruption was nothing more than "skillful lobbying."[62] Analyzing the economics of the reform and its effects, Hovenkamp determined that the regulated slaughterhouse monopoly was "a work of great genius," while the allegations regarding driving butchers out of business were "nonsense." In 2003, 130 years after the Supreme Court delivered *The Slaughter–House Cases*, two researchers published a comprehensive study, documenting possible evidence of significant payments to state politicians who supported the 1869 Act.[63] Yet, the study concludes that "[h]owever controversial, the act represented an effective means of addressing a persistent public problem in a manner consistent with the * * * emphasis on minimal government."[64]

Shortly after the events of *The Slaughter–House Cases*, New Orleans learned again that the pursuit of self-interest of unregulated butchers could harm public interests. In 1879, Louisiana adopted a new constitution that vested in localities the authority to regulate slaughterhouses, as long as "no monopoly or exclusive privilege [is granted to] any individual or corporation."[65] The new constitution abolished all "monopoly features in the charter of any corporation."[66] Instead, the 1879 constitution authorized localities to regulate slaughterhouses through licenses and inspection.[67] Once the Crescent City Company lost its exclusive rights and butchers returned to New Orleans,[68] the health conditions quickly deteriorated. The City therefore responded by adopting a new regulatory framework similar to the 1869 reform. Louisiana courts approved this reinstated monopolistic framework.[69]

The reforms of urban butchers in New York and New Orleans were part of a broad sanitary revolution that transformed urban planning in the United States between 1840 and 1890.[70] Massive urbanization trends in industrialized countries were strongly correlated with increased death rates. Improved scientific understanding of infectious disease in the mid-nineteenth century showed that sanitary conditions contributed to the deteriorated health conditions in cities. The unrestricted pursuit of self-interest of urban butchers was found to be one of the leading preventable causes of death and illness. Sanitary regulation indeed greatly contributed to decline in death rates.

---

61. Franklin, *supra* note 45, at 24.

62. HOVENKAMP, *supra* note 45, at 117, 124.

63. LABBÉ & LURIE, *supra* note 41, at 82–102.

64. *Id.* at 101–102.

65. Louisiana Constitution of 1879, art. 248.

66. *Id.* art. 258.

67. *Id.* art. 248.

68. *See* Butchers' Union Slaughter–House & Live–Stock Landing Co. v. Crescent City Live Stock Landing & Slaughter House Co., 111 U.S. 746 (1884).

69. *See, e.g.*, Barthet v. New Orleans, 24 Fed. 563 (1885); Darcantel v. People's Slaughterhouse & Refrigerating Co., 44 La.Ann. 632 (1892).

70. *See generally* Jon A. Peterson, *The Impact of Sanitary Reform Upon American Urban Planning, 1840–1890*, 13 JOURNAL OF SOCIAL HISTORY 83 (1979).

§ 2.2.2b The Brewer

Brewers are members of the alcohol industry. Brewers' gains increase when society consumes more alcohol, but the consumption of alcohol products is related to illness and accidents. Empirical evidence shows that drivers with alcohol in their blood are seven times more likely to cause a fatal crash and legally drunk drivers pose a risk 13 times greater than sober drivers.[71] Thus, when the brewer succeeds in the pursuit of self-interest, society as a whole may lose.[72]

Although the interests of the alcohol industry and society have never aligned, alcohol regulation has always been a source of endless debate and dispute. Conflating perceptions of risk and morality, early twentieth century alcohol regulation took an ineffective, highly controversial form of zero-tolerance regulation—prohibition.[73] The 18th Amendment regime reduced the level of alcohol consumption only by 30% to 40%, failed to stigmatize alcohol, inflated and distorted enforcement resources, and is believed to increase the level of violent crimes.[74] By many accounts, the Prohibition was a failure.

The 18th Amendment regime, however, has very limited resemblance to modern alcohol control policies. Contemporary alcohol regulations include blue laws,[75] DUI laws,[76] age limits,[77] dram-shop liability laws,[78]

---

71. *See* Steven D. Levitt & Jack Porter, *How Dangerous Are Drinking Drivers?*, 109 JOURNAL OF POLITICAL ECONOMY 1198 (2001).

72. *See* Christopher S. Carpenter, *Heavy Alcohol Use and the Commission of Nuisance Crime: Evidence from Underage Drunk Driving Laws*, 95 AMERICAN ECONOMIC REVIEW 267 (2005).

73. *See generally* RICHARD H. HAMM, SHAPING THE EIGHTEENTH AMENDMENT (1995); DANIEL OKRENT, LAST CALL: THE RISE AND FALL OF PROHIBITION (2010). *See also* ROBERT H. HOHNER, PROHIBITION AND POLITICS: THE LIFE OF BISHOP JAMES CANNON, JR. (1999).

74. *See, e.g.*, Jeffrey A. Miron, *Violence and the U.S. Prohibitions of Drugs and Alcohol*, 1 AMERICAN LAW & ECONOMICS REVIEW 78 (1999); Jeffrey A. Miron & Jeffrey Zwiebel, *Alcohol Consumption During Prohibition*, 81 AMERICAN ECONOMIC REVIEW 242 (1991); Jeffrey A. Miron & Jeffrey Zwiebel, *The Economic Case Against Drug Prohibition*, 9 JOURNAL OF ECONOMIC PERSPECTIVES 175 (1995). *Cf.* Emily Greene Owens, *Are Underground Market Really More Violent? Evidence from Early 20th Century America*, 13 AMERICAN LAW & ECONOMICS REVIEW 1 (2011).

75. *See generally* DAVID N. LABAND & DEBORAH HENDRY HEINBUCH, BLUE LAWS: THE HISTORY, ECONOMICS, AND POLITICS OF SUNDAY CLOSING LAWS (1987); Michael F. Lovenheim & Daniel P. Steefel, *Do Blue Laws Save Lives? The Effect of Sunday Alcohol Sales Bans on Fatal Vehicle Accidents*, 30 JOURNAL OF POLICY ANALYSIS & MANAGEMENT 798 (2011).

76. *See generally* Thomas S. Dee, *Does Setting Limits Save Lives? The Case of 0.08 BAC Laws*, 20 JOURNAL OF POLICY ANALYSIS & MANAGEMENT 111 (2001); Daniel Eisenberg, *Evaluating the Effectiveness of Policies Related to Drunk Driving*, 22 JOURNAL OF POLICY ANALYSIS & MANAGEMENT 249 (2003); David S. Kenkel, *Do Drunk Drivers Pay Their Way? A Note on Optimal Penalties for Drunk Driving*, 12 JOURNAL OF HEALTH ECONOMICS 137 (1993).

77. *See generally* Christopher Carpenter & Carlos Dobkin, *The Minimum Legal Drinking Age and Public Health*, 25 Journal of Economic Perspectives 133 (2011).

78. *See, e.g.*, FRANK A. SLOAN ET AL., DRINKERS, DRIVERS AND BARTENDERS: BALANCING PRIVATE CHOICES AND PUBLIC ACCOUNTABILITY (2000); Angela K. Dills, *Social Host Liability for Minors and Underage Drunk Driving Accidents*, 29 JOURNAL OF HEALTH ECONOMICS 241 (2010).

alcohol taxes,[79] and others. Although these regulations still conflate risk analysis and morality, they have helped reduce the number of fatalities associated with alcohol consumption.[80] Alcohol control laws have several goals, but the primary one is reducing the potential harm to society when the alcohol industry seeks to maximize profit, as it should.

§ 2.2.2c The Baker

Lochner v. New York involved state interference with employment agreements to protect one of the parties. Some firmly believe that New York unjustifiably infringed on liberty of contract. Others believe that the state protected parties who had no liberty to negotiate employment agreements and its interference was within the scope of the police power.

Lochner dealt with Section 1 of the New York Bakeshop Act that regulated the work hours of bakers and prohibited bakeries and bakers from contracting around its restrictions. The New York Bakeshop Act did not exclusively regulate the work hours of bakers. It also included provisions intended to protect the public from the hidden risks that bakeries created. The Act prohibited bakers from sleeping in "rooms where flour or meal food products [were] manufactured or stored."[81] It also required every bakery to have "a proper washroom and water-closet or closets, apart from the bakeroom or rooms where the manufacturing of such food products [was] conducted."[82] Further, it demanded that all bakeries "be drained and plumbed in a manner to conduce to the proper and healthful sanitary condition,"[83] and imposed other requirements designed to remedy unsanitary bakery conditions that would have horrified the average bread-buyer.

In *Lochner*, the Court concluded that"[c]lean and wholesome bread does not depend upon whether the baker works but ten hours per day or only sixty hours a week." However, sanitary conditions of bakeries undeniably affect the supply of "clean and wholesome bread." Thus, *Lochner* and the New York Bakeshop Act illuminate that the pursuit of self-interest of bakers may risk public interests. The controversy over state interference with the freedom of contract is somewhat irrelevant to this point.

Questions

1. The discussion of butchers, brewers and bakers presents three different ways in which the pursuit of self-interest may not serve society. What are the differences among the potential adverse effects on society in these three instances similar?

2. The Code of Health Ordinances that New York City Board of Health adopted pursuant to the 1866 Metropolitan Health Act included many restrictions on slaughterhouses. One of these restrictions was Section 45 of the Ordinances, which regulated the delivery of cattle to slaughterhouses:

---

79. Susan Farrell et al., *Alcohol Dependence and the Price of Alcoholic Beverages*, 22 JOURNAL OF HEALTH ECONOMICS 117 (2003); Christopher J. Ruhm, *Alcohol Policies and Highway Vehicle Fatalities*, 15 JOURNAL OF HEALTH ECONOMICS 435 (1996).

80. *See generally* Douglas J. Young & Thomas W. Likens, *Alcohol Regulation and Auto Fatalities*, 20 INTERNATIONAL REVIEW OF LAW & ECONOMICS 107 (2000).

81. The New York 1895 Bakeshop Act § 6.

82. *Id.* § 5.

83. *Id.* § 2.

> [N]o cattle shall be driven in the generally built up portion of either of the cities of New–York or Brooklyn, except between the hours of nine of the evening and one hour after Sunrise of the next morning; nor shall more than twenty cattle, or more than one hundred hogs, or more than one hundred sheep be driven together; and they shall be driven in streets and avenues (leading towards their destination) where they will least endanger the lives of human beings.

The Board firmly enforced its Code and imposed penalties on individuals who violated its provisions. In *Metropolitan Board of Health v. Heister*, the Court of Appeals of New York examined the question of whether the Metropolitan Health Law and the Code of Health Ordinances unconstitutionally "deprived of life, liberty or property [of people in New York], without due process of law."[84] Specifically, the court examined the constitutionality of Section 45 and held that "[t]hese regulations take away no man's property. If [a person] owns cattle, his ownership is not interfered with. He may sell, exchange and traffic in the same manner as any other person owning cattle may do * * *. Simply the health regulations of the district operate upon his cattle * * * in the same manner that they do upon live property owned by all others, and the use of the streets for dangerous purposes of the prosecution of a business dangerous to the public health is regulated by the Ordinances in question."

What was the rationale for Section 45? Was it similar to the general rationale for slaughterhouse regulation? Was it similar to the rationale for the enactment of Section 1 of the New York Bakeshop Act? Was the *Lochner* Court likely to upheld Section 45?

---

84. Metropolitan Board of Health v. Heister, 37 N.Y. 661 (1868).

Figure 2.1

JOURNEY TO THE SLAUGHTER-HOUSE.

Journey to the Slaughter-House, Harper's Weekly, February 4, 1860.

The pursuit of self-interest takes many forms. Consider the role of the pursuit of self-interest in the following events, and specifically whether the pursuit of self-interest is a reliable way to promote public interests.

Seattle's Green Fee

Unusual political storms troubled Seattle during the summer of 2009: A battle occurred over the "Green Fee," the City's proposed tax for disposable shopping bags. In July 2008, the City Council passed an ordinance imposing a 20¢ tax on disposable shopping bags.[85] Many cities and states across the country had already acted to reduce or even ban the use of disposable shopping bags because of the bags' environmental costs. The Seattle City Council and Mayor were similarly determined to reduce the

85. On July 28, 2008, the City Council passed the Seattle Public Utilities Green Fee Ordinance (Ordinance No. 122752) that Mayor Gregory Nickels signed on July 30, 2008.

use of plastic bags in their town. In a statement to the City Council, Mayor Gregory Nickels, highlighted some of the advantages of the Green Fee:

> The Green Fee, which will be collected by all grocery, drug, and convenience stores, is expected to substantially reduce Seattle's consumption of 360 million disposable shopping bags and help subsidize solid waste utility rates. It is also expected to reduce greenhouse gas emissions by more than 4,000 tons per year, the equivalent of taking 665 cars off the road.[86]

A sufficient number of voters signed a petition to refer the ordinance to a public vote. The plastic industry launched a massive campaign against the Green Fee, investing approximately $1.4 million to outspend environmental groups and other proponents of the ordinance 15 to 1.[87] Referendum No. 1, on which Seattleites voted in August 2009, provided:

> The Seattle City Council passed Ordinance No. 122752 concerning imposing a 20–cent fee on disposable shopping bags. A sufficient number of voters signed a petition to refer the ordinance to a public vote.
>
> This ordinance would require grocery, drug and convenience stores to collect the fee for every disposable shopping bag provided to customers. Stores with annual gross sales of under $1,000,000 could keep all of the fees they collected, to cover their costs. Other stores could keep 25% of the fees they collected, and would send the remainder to the City to support garbage reduction and recycling programs. The stores would get a business-tax deduction for the fees they collected.

The Referendum further included statements for and against the ordinance:

Statement For	***Statement Against***
SEND A MESSAGE TO BIG OIL: HANDS OFF SEATTLE! The American Chemical Council, funded by Exxon/Mobil and other major polluters spent more than $250,000 on paid signatures to force this referendum. Now they are spending even more on a misleading campaign to protect industry profits at the expense of Puget Sound wildlife and Seattle's right to make our own laws. Let's send the message that our elections and environment are not for sale: APPROVE Referendum 1 * * * Every year, the average Seattle resident uses more than 500 single-use bags—more than 360 million citywide.	We are asking you to **Vote No on Referendum 1** because we are tired of seeing the City of Seattle make the same mistakes over-and-over again. By voting **NO on Referendum 1**, Seattle residents will send a message to Mayor Greg Nickels and the City Council that we don't want any more failed programs run by unresponsive city bureaucrats. And that means saying NO to the so-called advance recovery fee-commonly called the "bag tax." Seattleites have been taking care of the environment for decades. It comes naturally to us. So why do we need a taxpayer funded program when most us already reuse and recycle our bags right now? And without a tax!

86. A letter from Mayor Gregory Nickels to President of Seattle City Council, Richard Conlin, dated June 17, 2008.

87. The proponents spent approximately $93,000 on campaign related activities. Phuong Le, *Seattle Votes Down Fee on Plastic, Paper Bags,* ASSOCIATED PRESS, August 19, 2009; William Yardley, *Seattle Votes Down Fee on Bags*, NEW YORK TIMES, August 19, 2009, at 19.

These bags are costly to recycle, and many end up clogging landfills, choking waterways, and threatening the health of marine life in the Sound. In the Pacific Ocean a floating soup of plastic pollution the size of Connecticut is integrating into the marine food chain—including fish we consume.

The law underlying Referendum 1 will curb the use of disposable bags—no wonder the industry is willing to mislead voters to protect their profits.

* * *

Curbing plastic bag use is a simple step toward reducing our dependence on foreign petroleum. Production and transport of paper bags also contributes to climate change.

Referendum 1 is an easy, convenient way to reduce climate emissions and make progress on other critical issues.

Seattle's leadership has inspired several other cities like Edmonds, Washington, D.C., New York, and Philadelphia to consider or institute similar actions.

* * *

You only pay the fee if you choose not to bring your own bags.

Every day we use reusable bags for work, school, and sports. Tens of thousands in Seattle have already started using convenient reusable bags for shopping as well.

Some cities have chosen to ban plastic bags outright. Referendum 1 strikes a middle ground: preserve consumer choice but reflect the real cost of these bags through an optional fee.

APPROVE Referendum 1.

Well, we don't. And here's why:

- The 2,300 word City Ordinance (now Referendum 1) is filled with loopholes. For example, there are nine different kinds of paper and plastic bags that are exempt. And, somehow, big box stores like Target and Fred Meyer are given special treatment—if you buy groceries at one of these stores the tax does not apply!
- The ordinance indicates that Our Mayor and City Council will need to hire at least two permanent city employees to "carry out the purpose of the ordinance."
- The fiscal note to the ordinance indicates that Our Mayor and City Council will need to spend over $1.4 million in the first two years of the program. $1 million just to "purchase and distribute" reusable shopping bags to Seattle residents.
- Similar to the hundreds-of-thousands spent for the SDOT consultant, the Mayor and the City Council will spend 150,000 for "public education activities" to tell us how to keep our cloth bags "clean." [Page 5, Fiscal Note for Non–Capital Projects.]
- This ordinance will make hard lives even harder. The poor, seniors, disabled, those living on fixed incomes, and even food banks will be forced to use discretionary income for necessities.

Vote No on Referendum 1. Seattle deserves so much better.

At the polls, the Seattleites rejected the proposed Green Fee by a large margin, 58% to 42%.

In Seattle, the public decisionmakers (the City Council and the Mayor) sought to promote an environmental interest, believing that it would serve the public. Many Seattleites opposed this initiative and, together with a trade association representing national and international businesses with no known interest in the welfare Seattle's residents, effectively campaigned to defeat the proposal. The 2009 events in Seattle parallel regulatory struggles at federal, state, and municipal levels.

Questions

1. The plastic bag industry, supported by big oil companies, had no stated or otherwise known interest in the prosperity of Seattle or the welfare of its

citizens. Nevertheless, it funded a successful campaign against the Green Fee. Is the industry's lack of interest in the prosperity of the City or the welfare of its citizens relevant to the legitimacy of its campaign funding?

2. Seattle was neither the first nor the last municipality to introduce a regulatory measure that imposes tax on plastic bags. The plastic bag industry obviously cannot afford to invest $1.4 million each time a municipality considers such a measure. Why did the industry invest so much money in this specific campaign?

3. Public decisionmakers—either elected or appointed officials—often engage in campaigns. They spend considerable time and other resources explaining their agendas to media representatives. Should public decisionmakers be allowed to engage in such activities?

4. Seattle considered a 20¢ tax on disposable shopping bags. The vast majority of cities have adopted similar measures impose a tax of 5¢ tax per disposable shopping bag. For example, the District of Columbia Anacostia River Clean Up and Protection Act of 2009 established a 5¢ tax on disposable carryout bags and created a fund to clean up the Anacostia River, using these tax revenues.[88] What are the possible differences between the 5¢ tax and the 20¢ tax?

5. Cities including San Francisco (California), Westport (Connecticut), and Edmonds (Washington), chose to address the environmental problems caused by disposable shopping bags by banning them altogether. What are the similarities and differences between bans and taxes on disposable shopping bags?

§ 2.3 PRIVATE INTEREST AND CHANGE

§ 2.3.1 Regulating Conflicting Private Interests

Regulations may serve certain private interests at no cost to others. Often, however, regulations that intend to protect or promote the interest of one person adversely affect the interests of another. Consider, for example, *Ledbetter v. Goodyear Tire & Rubber Co.*[89] In a five-to-four decision, the Supreme Court held that an employee must assert a Title VII pay discrimination claim within 180 days of employer's *first* discriminatory pay decision. That is, serving as a court-created statute of limitations, the ruling shielded employers paying discriminatory wages from Title VII claims when their employees failed to sue them within this 180–day period. Responding to this decision, Congress passed the Lilly Ledbetter Fair Pay Act of 2009.[90] The Act overruled the *Ledbetter* decision by specifying that the 180–day statute of limitations starts with the *last* discriminatory act. The Lilly Ledbetter Fair Pay Act therefore protects the interests of employ-

88. A copy of the Anacostia River Clean Up and Protection Act of 2009 is available at *regti.me/Anacostia* (case sensitive).

89. Ledbetter v. Goodyear Tire & Rubber Co., 550 U.S. 618 (2007).

90. Pub. L. No. 111–2, 123 Stat. 5 (2009).

ees experiencing wage discrimination, but increases the costs to discriminatory employers.

Many people consider workplace discrimination to be categorically objectionable conduct; therefore, the adverse effects of the Lilly Ledbetter Fair Pay Act on discriminatory employers may actually be appropriate and, perhaps, even insufficient. The normative merit of the statute, however, does not change the fact that this regulation adversely affects the interests of discriminatory employers.

Regulatory policies frequently make choices among groups in society, even when the normative choice is controversial. For example, the FCC's indecency policy affects the interests of several groups in society—prudent parents, children, advertisers, broadcasters, and entertainers, among others. Decency and indecency are a matter of perspective. *Fox Television Stations* dealt with a change in indecency policy in favor of some groups at the expense of others.[91] California effectively "censors" beggars. Panhandling is illegal in the state.[92] Panhandlers and beggars cause some inconvenience to residents, and because of these adverse effects, the California legislature considered clean, unobstructed streets and sidewalks paramount to the interest of this trade. Panhandling is not categorically socially condemned, yet anti-panhandling laws burden beggars in favor of other groups.

The comparison between regulations that benefit some and do not affect others and regulations that benefit some and burden others somewhat parallels to the distinction between two economic concepts: *Pareto efficiency* and *Kaldor–Hicks efficiency*.

§ 2.3.2 Pareto Efficiency

Pareto efficiency exists when no change in the present allocation of resources in society could make any person better off without making any other person worse off. Correspondingly, a *Pareto improvement* is a change in the allocation of resources that makes at least one person better off but no other person is worse off. Pareto improvements therefore seem uncontroversial. The Pareto principle establishes some kind of an inalienable right that protects every person from involuntary state interference. Justice Brandeis described the "right to be let alone" as "the most comprehensive of rights and the right most valued by civilized men."[93] The Pareto principle guards the right to be let alone.

In practice, however, the "right to be let alone" means, among other things, "freedom to harm others," and sometimes also an expectation that

91. Fox Television Stations, Inc. v. Federal Communications Commission, 613 F.3d 317 (2d Cir. 2010).

92. *See, e.g.*, California Penal Code § 647(c) ("Who accosts other persons in any public place or in any place open to the public for the purpose of begging or soliciting alms."). *Cf.* Indiana Code ch. 17 (prohibiting panhandling at night, at bus stops, in public transportation, in the sidewalk of restaurant dining areas, and within twenty feet of an ATM or bank entrance); District of Columbia Code ch. 23 (prohibiting panhandling in an 'aggressive manner').

93. Olmstead v. United States, 277 U.S. 438, 478 (1928) (Brandeis, J., dissenting).

the state will interfere with the liberty of others. Because private interests often interact and conflict, an attempt to guard one's interests often requires sacrificing the interests of others. To illustrate this point, consider Alexis, who likes the color black—for her outfit, home, bicycle, car, and everything else. Alexis expresses her individualism and style with color. Alas, everyone else in society finds the color black terribly depressing.[94] Should society intervene in the freedom of Alexis (and individuals with similar preferences) to serve the majority's preferences? Or should we follow the Pareto principle and leave Alexis alone because any intervention would harm her interests? The Pareto principle protects individual liberty and restricts government regulation. It will protect Alexis' liberty (*i.e.*, her personal style) by preventing the majority from using the state power to interfere with individual choices.

If the hypothetical appears impractical, replace the phrase "likes the color black" with phrases such as "discriminates against females and minorities," "makes sexist and racist remarks in the workplace," "bullies classmates in school," or "smokes in public." Assume that the majority's preferences are always opposite to those of Alexis. The right to be let alone turns into a freedom to harm others, and the Pareto principle into a justification for such freedom.[95]

§ 2.3.3 Kaldor–Hicks Efficiency

Kaldor–Hicks efficiency exists when no change in the present allocation of resources in society could increase the total social welfare. A *Kaldor–Hicks improvement* is a change in the allocation of resources that increases the total social welfare, although it may have distributive effects. Robin Hood "lived" by a Kaldor–Hicks principle, robbing from the rich to give to the poor, believing that a dollar in the pocket of the poor was worth more than a dollar in the pocket of the rich. In essence, the cost-benefit analysis methodology is an advanced version of the Kaldor–Hicks principle.

Because Kaldor–Hicks improvements entail losses to some people, they tend to invoke controversies and provoke aggrieved parties to lobby against them and challenge their validity. Thus, for the purpose of public policy, the choice to implement a Kaldor–Hicks improvement must take into account potential costs of controversies and challenges.[96]

Kelo v. City of New London[97] illustrates some of the inescapable problems related to policies that attempt to implement Kaldor–Hicks improvements. In *Kelo*, New London launched a development plan in response to an announcement of the pharmaceutical giant, Pfizer, Inc., that it

---

94. The example builds on Amartya Sen's Liberal Paradox. *See* Amartya Sen, *The Impossibility of a Paretian Liberal*, 78 JOURNAL OF POLITICAL ECONOMY 152 (1970). *See also* Barak Orbach, *On Hubris, Civility, and Incivility*, 54 ARIZONA. LAW REVIEW 443 (2012).

95. *See generally* Amartya Sen, *Liberty, Unanimity and Rights*, 43 ECONOMICA 217 (1976). *See also* Louis Kaplow & Steven Shavell, *The Conflict Between Notions of Fairness and the Pareto Principle*, 1 AMERICAN LAW & ECONOMICS REVIEW 63 (1999).

96. *See generally* Barak Orbach & Frances R. Sjoberg, *Excessive Speech, Civility Norms and the Clucking Theorem*, 44 CONNECTICUT LAW REVIEW 1 (2011).

97. Kelo v. City of New London, 545 U.S. 469 (2005).

planned to build a $300 million global research facility in the City. The City's plan assumed that Pfizer would "create jobs, increase tax and other revenues, encourage public access to and use of the city's waterfront, and eventually 'build momentum' for the revitalization of the rest of the city."[98] Based on this assumption, the City decided to exercise its eminent domain power to acquire properties that were necessary to execute its development plan. Property owners' refusal to sell their properties triggered a controversial exercise of the City's powers. The owners challenged the City's decision by arguing that the "public use" restriction in the Fifth Amendment prohibited the City from exercising its eminent domain power for the purpose of economic development. In a five-to-four decision, the Supreme Court upheld the City's taking policy. Ultimately, however, the reallocation of resources did not yield the desired economic benefits. The City's decision to endorse a Kaldor–Hicks improvement not only affected the interests of property owners, but also generated heavy lobbying and litigation costs, and did not result in the promised economic outcome. *Kelo*, therefore, illustrates that a decision to implement a Kaldor–Hicks improvement may be both controversial and costly.

Moreover, regulatory policies that make choices among groups in society are not always consistent with Kaldor–Hicks principles. When public decisionmakers act to protect or promote private interests, they do not always consider the public interest. To illustrate this point, consider state "butter laws."[99] To protect the interests of local dairy industries, many state legislatures enacted laws that restrict the distribution and availability of butter substitutes. These laws prohibit sales of butter substitutes,[100] outlaw the serving of substitutes to "students, patients or inmates of any state institutions,"[101] imposing tax on substitutes,[102] and restricting the permitted scope of advertising.[103] Rather than preventing the fraudulent sale of butter substitutes (margarine) as butter, state butter laws penalize affordable, and possibly healthier, butter substitutes to protect the interests of butter producers. States have taken similar regulatory approaches to caskets and alcohol by forcing consumers to purchase caskets directly from the funeral home,[104] and prohibiting direct distribution of out-

---

98. Kelo v. City of New London, 268 Conn. 1, 7–8 (2004).

99. *See generally* W.T. Mickle, *Margarine Legislation*, 23 JOURNAL OF FARM ECONOMICS 567 (1941); Geoffrey Miller, *Public Choice at the Dawn of the Special Interest State: The Story of Butter and Margarine*, 77 CALIFORNIA LAW REVIEW 83 (1989); William H. Nicholls, *Some Economic Aspects of the Margarine Industry*, 54 JOURNAL OF POLITICAL ECONOMY 221 (1946).

100. *See, e.g.*, Wright v. State, 88 Md. 436 (1898) (upholding the constitutionality of a state prohibition); Powell v. Pennsylvania, 127 U.S. 678 (1888) (upholding a stat prohibition); Schollenberger v. Pennsylvania, 171 U.S. 1 (1898) (holding that a prohibition against the manufacture or sale of butter substitutes is "void as an interference with interstate commerce"); Plumley v. Massachusetts, 155 U.S. 461 (1894) (same).

101. *See, e.g.*, Wisc. Stat. Ann. § 97.18(5) (Wisconsin).

102. *See, e.g.*, A. Magnano Co. v. Hamilton, 292 U.S. 40 (1934); *Margarine Legislation Hearings in Washington*, 8 JOURNAL OF THE AMERICAN OIL CHEMISTS' SOCIETY 65, 77 (1931); Schmitt v. Nord, 71 S.D. 575, 27 N.W.2d 910 (1947).

103. *See, e.g.*, AZ. Rev. Stat. § 3–629 (Arizona); Ala. Code § 2–13–19 (Alabama); Miss. Stat. § 196.725 (Missouri); N.H. Rev. Stat. § 184.53 (New Hampshire).

104. *See* Craigmiles v. Giles, 312 F.3d 220 (6th Cir. 2002) (holding that a state casket law is unconstitutional); Powers v. Harris, 379 F.3d 1208 (10th Cir. 2004) (upholding a state

of-state wines.[105] By serving the interests of certain industries, rather than applying Kaldor–Hicks principles, states raise the cost of living and the cost of death.

Questions

1. Commitments to Pareto or Kaldor–Hicks principles may burden certain groups in society, but in different ways. What are the differences?

2. In his 1895 treatise, *Handbook of American Constitutional Law*, Henry Campbell Black, addressed the constitutionality of Sunday laws:

> Laws requiring the observance of the first day of the week as a holiday, at least to the extent of forbidding all ordinary labor, trade, and traffic on that day, enforcing quiet upon the public streets, and directing the cessation of public amusements, such as theatrical exhibitions and the closing of saloons and grog-shops, are universally in force in the states, and their constitutional validity is sustained by the decisions of the courts * * *. [T]he requirement of the observance of Sunday, if it is distinctly as a matter of religious principle, violates the religious liberty of the Jews and perhaps others. The fact is that the great majority of the American people are Christians, and the laws are made with reference to this fact. And although others may be put to inconvenience by laws of this kind, it is but an application of the principle that the wishes and preferences of the majority must govern.[106]

Did the enactment of Sunday laws constitute a Pareto or Kaldor–Hicks improvement? Can society make any improvements once Sunday laws are adopted?

3. The Precautionary Principle (PP) has several forms. Its main axiom is "first, do no harm."[107] Regulations that adopt PP may ban activities that pose risk to human lives or the environment until safety is established. PP imposes the burden of proving safety on the party that wishes to engage in risky activities. For example, San Francisco adopted a resolution that interprets PP to dictate "where threats of serious or irreversible damage to people or natural systems exist, lack of full scientific certainty relating to cause and effect shall not be viewed as sufficient reason to postpone

---

casket law). *See generally* Asheesh Agarwal, *Protectionism as a Rational Basis? The Impact on E-Commerce in the Funeral Industry*, 3 JOURNAL OF LAW, ECONOMICS & POLICY 189 (2007); Daniel Sutter, *Casket Sales Restrictions and the Funeral Market*, 3 JOURNAL OF LAW, ECONOMICS & POLICY 219 (2007)

105. In Granholm v. Heald, 544 U.S. 460 (2005), the Supreme Court struck down the restrictions on direct distribution of alcohol. 544 U.S. 460 (2005). *See generally* Maureen K. Ohlhausen & Gregory P. Luib, *Moving Sideways: Post–Granholm Developments in Wine Direct Shipping and Their Implications for Competition*, 75 ANTITRUST LAW JOURNAL 505 (2008); James Alexander Tanford, *E–Commerce in Wine*, 3 JOURNAL OF LAW, ECONOMICS & POLICY 275 (2007).

106. HENRY CAMPBELL BLACK, HANDBOOK OF AMERICAN CONSTITUTIONAL LAW 392–393 (1895).

107. *See* § 1.5.3.

measures to prevent the degradation of the environment or protect human health."[108]

Is PP consistent with Pareto or Kaldor–Hicks principles?

§ 2.4 INSTITUTIONAL WEAKNESSES

> RED TAPE is everywhere and everywhere it is abhorred. * * * Lexicographers seem to agree that the term red tape derives from the ribbon once used to tie up legal documents in England. Because the common law gives great weight to precedent, every judicial decision must have been preceded by a thorough search of the records for guidance and authority. * * * [L]egions of clerks and lawyers spent a good deal of their time tying and untying the ribbon-bound folders.
>
> Meanwhile citizens and administrative officers trying to get action must have fretted and fumed while they waited. * * * And they must have exploded in outrage when, after all that, action was blocked grounds of some obscure ancient decision or, still worse, because no unequivocal precedent could be found.
>
> * * * The ribbon has long since disappeared, but the hated conditions and practices it represents continue, keeping the symbol alive.[109]

Regulation requires "government action." Thus, if we believe that the government is an inefficient bureaucratic institution, we should be concerned about the cost of the bureaucracy and the effects of invaluable regulations on welfare. Failure and success, however, are relative concepts. The notion that the government always fails and cannot perform any task adequately is extreme and implausible. It is inconsistent with the great pride so many people have in the military, which is a government organization. It is also inconsistent with trust in the legal system that relies on government agencies. When parties seek to avoid government interference with their agreements, they still rely on state institutions to settle disputes between them and enforce the agreements. In the same spirit, firms and individuals expect the government to maintain security and conditions for economic activity. The government engages in a wide range of activities at some level of success.

State institutions, however, also fail and underperform. In this Section, we will discuss institutional aspects that contribute to controversies and debates over regulations.

---

108. City and County of San Francisco, Resolution No. 129–03 (Mar. 13, 2003). *See also* San Francisco Environment Code and Precautionary Principle Policy, Ordinance No. 171–03 (July 3, 2003).

109. HERBERT KAUFMAN, RED TAPE: ITS ORIGINS, USES, AND ABUSES 1–2 (1977). *See also* BARRY BOZEMAN, BUREAUCRACY AND RED TAPE (2000).

§ 2.4.1 *The Benevolent Public Decisionmaker*

Because private interests may conflict or not be aligned in other respects, serving the public is a delicate task. A public decisionmaker can never please all members of society. In theory, the ideal public official is a benevolent public decisionmaker who works tirelessly to serve the public and only the public. A benevolent public decisionmaker never protects or promotes private interests at the public expense. However, by being "ideal," the benevolent public decisionmaker must sacrifice the interests of some individuals and firms to protect others or to promote the well-being of society as a whole. Therefore, controversy over regulation is likely to arise even when the public decisionmaker is benevolent.

In the case of *Seattle's Green Fee*, the Mayor and the City Council supposedly acted like benevolent public decisionmakers. They sought to promote a public interest with a regulatory measure but failed to garner the public vote for it. Their failure offers three related lessons about benevolent public decisionmakers. First, regulatory policies of benevolent public decisionmakers may be controversial and possibly detrimental to society. Second, controversies and debates over regulatory policies benevolent public decisionmakers introduce may not be motivated by the public interest. Rather, the pursuit of self-interest in guise may be the driving force. Third, regulatory policies of benevolent public decisionmakers are vulnerable to the influence of private interests.

Oregon Trollers Association v. Gutierrez

452 F.3d 1104 (9th Cir. 2006)

■ WILLIAM A. FLETCHER, CIRCUIT JUDGE:

The 250–mile Klamath River originates in eastern Oregon and empties into the Pacific Ocean at Crescent City, California. The Klamath River fall chinook, an anadromous salmon species, begin life in the river's upper reaches and tributaries, either in hatcheries or in the wild. As juveniles the Klamath chinook migrate to sea and spend much of their lives in the Klamath Management Zone, an area off the coasts of California and Oregon. At age 3, 4, or 5, they return, usually to their natal tributaries or hatcheries, to spawn and die.

In early 2005, the National Marine Fisheries Service ("NMFS") projected that a critically low number of Klamath chinook would escape that season's harvest to survive and to spawn in the wild. To increase the projected number of wild-spawning Klamath chinook, the NMFS adopted fishery management measures that substantially limited commercial and, to a lesser extent, recreational fishing in the Klamath Management Zone for 2005.

Plaintiffs, who include fishermen, fishing-related businesses, and fishing organizations, filed this action against the NMFS and other governmental entities to challenge the 2005 management measures. Plaintiffs allege that the measures conflict with a number of substantive and procedural requirements set forth in the Magnuson–Stevens Fishery Conservation and Management Act ("Magnuson Act"). The district court granted summary judgment to defendants, and we affirm.

I. Introduction

* * *

A. *Regulatory Background*

* * *

Congress passed the Magnuson Act in 1976 in order "to take immediate action to conserve and manage the fishery resources found off the coasts of the United States. * * * " 16 U.S.C. § 1801(b)(1). The statute established eight Regional Fishery Management Councils, including the Pacific Fishery Management Council ("PFMC" or "the Council"). *Id.* § 1852(a)(1)(F). The councils, composed of federal and state officials as well as private experts appointed by the NMFS, draft "fishery management plans" ("FMPs"), *id.* § 1852(h)(1), that are designed to "achieve and maintain, on a continuing basis, the optimum yield from each fishery[.]" *Id.* § 1801(b)(4). * * *

B. *Klamath Chinook and 2005 Management Measures*

Klamath River salmon have suffered dramatically in recent years. In the spring of 2002, thousands of juvenile salmon died in the river before reaching the ocean. That fall, 34,000 mature chinook, coho, and steelhead died in the river's lower 20 miles as they tried to swim upstream. The proliferation of a salmon parasite, exacerbated by low water levels caused by drought and irrigation use, may have caused this mass fish kill. * * * Problems continued in 2004 and 2005.

[In April 2005, the Council formally proposed a natural spawner escapement goal of 35,000 for Klamath Chinook salmon.]

There is little doubt that the restricted salmon fishing season under the 2005 management measures imposed significant hardship on Pacific fishing communities. One estimate pegged the loss caused to commercial fishermen and related businesses at $40 million, * * * Several of the individual plaintiffs in this suit attested to the threats the 2005 management measures posed to their livelihoods.

* * *

[II]. Merits

* * *

Plaintiffs claim (1) that the management measures are inconsistent with the "national standard" under 16 U.S.C. § 1851(a)(8) requiring that the "importance of fishery resources to fishing communities" be taken into account; [and] (2) that they are inconsistent with the "national standard" under 16 U.S.C. § 1851(a)(10) requiring the NMFS "to the extent practicable" to "promote the safety of human life at sea." * * * We take these three claims in turn.

1. "Importance of Fishery Resources to Fishing Communities"

By its explicit terms, § 1851(a) requires only that FMPs and their implementing regulations be consistent with the "national standards." * * * Plaintiffs claim that the Council inadequately analyzed the economic impact of its 2005 management measures, and that the NMFS inadequately reviewed the measures for consistency with National Standard No. 8.

The regulation implementing National Standard No. 8 provides that an economic analysis must "identify affected fishing communities and then assess their differing levels of dependence and engagement in the fishery being regulated * * *. The analysis should discuss each alternative's likely effect on the sustained participation of these fishing communities in the fishery." 50 C.F.R. § 600.345(c)(3). In addition, "[t]he analysis should assess the likely positive and negative social and economic impacts of the alternative management measures, over both the short and the long term, on fishing communities[,]" *id.* § 600.345(c)(4), as well as "identify those alternatives that would minimize adverse impacts on those fishing communities within the constraints of conservation and management goals of the FMP." *Id.* § 600.345(c)(5).

In 2004, the Council and the NMFS considered the socio-economic impact of that year's proposed management measures and issued a lengthy report titled an "Environmental Assessment." That assessment discussed various alternatives to measures satisfying the 35,000 natural spawner escapement floor, addressing their short- and long-term impacts on fishing communities. In April 2005, the NMFS concluded that, "[f]or the fisheries to be conducted under the proposed 2005 ocean salmon regulations[,] the analysis from the 2004 [Environmental Assessment] is sufficient to understand the range of options developed and the impacts projected . . . for the 2005 season." The NMFS's "Supplemental Finding of No Significant Impact" updated the Environmental Assessment's conclusions for the 2005 management measures and concluded as follows:

> The overall 2005 community income impact of the commercial fishery is projected to be $33.7 million, down 28% from the 2004 value of $46.8 million, and 74% below the 1976–1990 average. The overall community income impact of the recreational fishery is projected to be $394 million, down 16% from the 2004 value of $471 million, and 44% below the 1976–1990 average. Community income impacts projected for both the commercial and recreational fisheries off Washington, Oregon, and California, are well above the disaster levels of the 1994 season.

So long as the agency appropriately updates its analysis under National Standard No. 8, there is no reason why it must start from scratch every year * * *. We conclude the that NMFS did not abuse its discretion when it relied on a 2004 analysis, updated for 2005, to review the 2005 management measures for consistency with National Standard No. 8.

2. "Safety of Human Life at Sea"

National Standard No. 10 provides that "[c]onservation and management measures shall, to the extent practicable, promote the safety of human life at sea." 16 U.S.C. § 1851(a)(10). Plaintiffs contend that, by shortening the fishing season, the 2005 management measures unnecessarily obliged fishermen to go to sea regardless of the weather or other dangers. Thus, according to plaintiffs, the management measures did not, "to the extent practicable," "promote" human safety.

The NMFS addressed safety concerns in an April 2005 memorandum commenting on the Council's recommendations:

> The proposed action is expected to be neutral with respect to health and safety. The proposed regulations are within the range of annual regulations implemented since adoption of the salmon framework plan in 1984 and meet the considerations for weather-related safety and harvest opportunity . . .

* * * The fact that the measures are "neutral," and do not affirmatively promote safety, does not mean that they do not promote safety "to the extent practicable." We conclude that the NMFS did not act arbitrarily and capriciously when it assessed the management measures for compliance with National Standard No. 10.

* * *

Affirmed.

Questions

1. Whose interests did the National Marine Fisheries Service (NMFS) try to protect? What were the motivations behind the plaintiffs' objections to the regulation?

2. Judge Fletcher describes the factors contributing to the decline in numbers of Klamath Chinook and points out that "the proliferation of a salmon parasite, exacerbated by low water levels caused by drought and irrigation use, may have caused this mass fish kill." According to *The Washington Post*, much of the irrigation use was attributable to a 2001 political decision by then Vice President Dick Cheney, who decided to support the interests of Oregon farmers after "declaring that there was no threat to the fish"[100] from use of the river water for irrigation. Nevertheless, "what followed was the largest fish kill the West had ever seen, with tens of thousands of salmon rotting on the banks of the Klamath River."[101] Assume that some of the decline in numbers the Klamath Chinook was related to water use in Oregon and, possibly, in other locations.

Was the disputed regulation the optimal regulatory mechanism to protect the Klamath Chinook?

§ 2.4.2 The Self–Interested Public Decisionmaker

In April 2006, George Ryan, the 39th Governor of Illinois, was convicted of racketeering, bribery, extortion, money laundering, and tax fraud for

---

100. Jo Becker & Barton Gellman, *Leaving No Tracks*, WASHINGTON POST, June 27, 2007, at A1.

101. *Id. See generally* HOLLY D. DOREMUS & A. DAN TARLOCK, WATER WAR IN THE KLAMATH BASIN: MACHO LAW, COMBAT BIOLOGY, AND DIRTY POLITICS (2008).

conduct while he was governor and secretary of state. On the day of his conviction, Ryan's successor, Rod Blagojevich, announced: "*Today's verdict proves that no one is above the law. And just as important, it proves that government is supposed to exist for the good of the people, not the other way around, and certainly not for the personal enrichment of those who hold public office.*"[112] True to his own words, Governor Blagojevich was arrested in December 2008. He was later charged with 20 felony counts, including racketeering conspiracy, wire fraud, extortion conspiracy, attempted extortion, and making false statements to federal agents. In June 2011, a federal jury found the by-then impeached governor guilty on 17 counts of corruption. These counts ranged from using official appointments, business, legislation and pension fund investments to obtain financial benefits, campaign contributions, and lucrative employment for himself and others, to an attempt to sell the U.S. Senate seat vacated by President Barack Obama.[113] Blagojevich was sentenced to 14 years in prison. Ryan and Blagojevich were self-interested public decisionmakers. They used state power to promote their interests at the expense of the public. This Section addresses several potential effects of self-interested public decisionmakers on the regulatory process.

Although arguments against self-interested public decisionmakers are popular, they are quite difficult to establish. The unresolved question of whether Louisiana politicians were bribed to pass the 1869 slaughterhouse reform in New Orleans provides a useful example of this point.[114] In *The Slaughter–House Cases*, even if corruption motivated state politicians to pass the law, the law still served the public. Ordinarily, however, when self-interest influences the regulatory process, the outcome is unlikely to serve the public. These circumstances still introduce evidentiary challenges. One characteristic of self-interest is that it is not always observable, let alone verifiable. When a public decisionmaker acts to promote his private interests, the public may not be able to observe his actions or verify his motives. Information about motives is relevant because, with the exception of blatant corruption, such as bribery, actions of public decisionmakers in the pursuit of self-interest often also benefit other parties. Under such circumstances, the action can be framed as advocacy for a constituency or promotion of an important social need.

To illustrate some of these points, consider Senator Patrick ("Pat") McCarran of Nevada and his legislative work for ranchers.[115] Senator McCarran's family owned a large ranch in Nevada. When Senator McCarran acted to promote the interests of ranchers in Nevada, supposedly he

---

112. *Politicians Speak Out on Ryan's Racketeering Conviction*, CHICAGO DEFENDER, April 19, 2006, at 3.

113. *See* Douglas Belkin & Stephanie Banchero, *Blagojevich Convicted On Corruption Charges*, WALL STREET JOURNAL, June 28, 2011, at A3; Monica Davey & Emma G. Fitzsimmons, *Ex–Governor Found Guilty of Corruption*, NEW YORK TIMES, June 28, 2011, at A1; Bob Secter & Jeff Coen, *Gulity*, CHICAGO TRIBUNE, June 28, 2011, at 1.

114. *See* § 2.2.2b.

115. *See, e.g.*, George Cameron Coggins & Margaret Lindberg–Johnson, *The Law of Public Rangeland Management II: The Commons and the Taylor Act*, 13 ENVIRONMENTAL LAW 1 (1982).

served his constituency, not only his family.[116] Senator McCarran was generally hostile toward immigration and opposed to any concessions on immigration issues. Nevertheless, he drafted a special quota visa bill that allowed 250 skilled sheepherders to immigrate into the United States in 1950.[117] At the time Congress considered his bill, Senator McCarran felt that "[t]here [was] no more important bill on the calendar than this one."[118] McCarran's actions do not reveal whether the family business motivated him to create an exemption to his hard-lined immigration policies, or whether constituents' interests softened his heart.

§ 2.4.2a Self–Serving Regulations

Tennessee's T–Bo Act

In August 1999, a 12–year–old Shih Tzu named T–Bo lost his life in his owner's backyard. A neighbor's dog, which roamed unsupervised in the neighborhood, entered the yard and viciously attacked T–Bo. T–Bo's owner, Tennessee State Senator Steve Cohen, spent the three days that followed the brutal attack taking his little furry friend on frantic trips to veterinarian clinics. These trips generated bills, but did not save T–Bo.

After his personal tragedy, Cohen realized that "the law didn't deal with loss of affection and companionship. The civil suit against the owners of the attacking dog resulted in $3,436 damages that covered the bills. Dogs, cats, pets were treated as any inanimate, personal property—like losing a shirt or damaging a lamp. The law provided for replacement value."[119] Cohen felt that replacement and repair costs (vet bills) were utterly inadequate, especially because under the formula, "if the dog is a mutt somebody adopted from the pound, there's no value." Cohen therefore felt that "if the dog is killed through an unlawful, negligent act, there should be damages."[120] He took action and introduced his T–Bo Bill, stating: "We want this to be a deterrent to people who let their dogs loose, without fences or leashes * * *. I think it's an important bill because it recognizes pets as living things and not merely as property, which is how they are treated by the law today."[121]

Senator Cohen convinced his peers in the state legislature that companion animals have some intrinsic value and the law should reflect this principle. In May 2000, Tennessee passed the T–Bo Act:

---

116. For a comprehensive biography of Senator McCarran, see MICHAEL J. YBARRA, WASHINGTON GONE CRAZY: SENATOR PAT MCCARRAN AND THE GREAT AMERICAN COMMUNIST HUNT (2004).

117. An Act to Provide Relief for Sheep–Raising Industry by Making Special Quota Immigration Visas Available to Certain Alien Sheepherders, 64 Stat. 306 (1950).

118. YABARRA, *supra* note 104, at 465 (quoting Senator McCarran).

119. *Canine Loss Spurs New Law*, STATE LEGISLATURES, October 2000, at 6.

120. *Id.*

121. Richard Locker, *T–Bo Act 'Recognizes Pets As Living Things, Not Merely Property,'* COMMERCIAL APPEAL, February 10, 2000, at B1.

AN ACT To amend Tennessee Code Annotated, Title 44, Chapter 17, relative to damages for injured or killed pets.

BE IT ENACTED BY THE GENERAL ASSEMBLY OF THE STATE OF TENNESSEE:

SECTION 1. Tennessee Code Annotated, Title 44, Chapter 17, Part 4, is amended by adding the following as a new, appropriately designated section:

Section 44–17–4___. (a) If a person's pet is killed or sustains injuries which result in death caused by the unlawful and intentional, or negligent, act of another or the animal of another, the trier of fact may find the individual causing the death or the owner of the animal causing the death liable for up to five thousand dollars ($5,000) in non-economic damages; provided that if such death is caused by the negligent act of another, the death or fatal injury must occur on the property of the deceased pet's owner or care-taker, or while under the control and supervision of the deceased pet's owner or care-taker.

(b) As used in this section, "pet" means any domesticated dog or cat normally maintained in or near the household of its owner;

(c) Limits for non-economic damages set out in subsection (a) shall not apply to causes of action for intentional infliction of emotional distress or any other civil action other than the direct and sole loss of a pet.

(d) Non-economic damages awarded pursuant to this section shall be limited to compensation for the loss of the reasonably expected society, companionship, love and affection of the pet.

(e) This section shall not apply to any not-for-profit entity or governmental agency, or their employees, negligently causing the death of a pet while acting on the behalf of public health or animal welfare; to any killing of a dog that has been or was killing or worrying livestock as in § 44–17–203; nor shall this section be construed to authorize any award of non-economic damages in an action for professional negligence against a licensed veterinarian.

SECTION 2. This act shall be known and may be cited as the "T–Bo Act."

* * *

SECTION 4. This act shall take effect upon becoming a law, the public welfare requiring it, and shall apply to any fatal injury sustained on or after the effective date of this act.

Tennessee's T–Bo Act inspired several other states to adopt similar laws,[122] acknowledging the non-economic losses of pet owners losing their pets in intentional and negligent incidents.

---

122. *See* Womack v. Von Rardon, 133 Wash.App. 254 (2006); Margit Livingston, *The Calculus of Animal Valuation: Crafting a Viable Remedy*, 82 NEBRASKA LAW REVIEW 783 (2004).

Questions

1. Senator Cohen championed the enactment of a statute that was named after his four-legged friend because of his personal interest in the issue. Did the T–Bo Act benefit Cohen? Did Cohen sponsored the T–Bo Act in the pursuit of self-interest? Was the T–Bo Act necessarily socially undesirable because its sponsor's personal interest?

2. Assume that a state legislator is found liable in court for the non-economic losses caused by his dog's attack on a neighbor's dog. Subsequently, this legislator leads legislative efforts to restrict the compensation that courts are permitted to award against dog owners. His legislative initiative specifically prohibits damages for non-economic losses. Is such action necessarily socially undesirable? Is this legislative initiative substantially different from the T–Bo Act?

Defamation of Public Officials

On February 17, 1960, Martin Luther King was apprehended, after a grand jury in Montgomery, Alabama issued a warrant for his arrest. This arrest was based on two felony counts for perjury, which allegedly resulted from King's signing of fraudulent tax returns in 1956 and 1958.[123] On March 29, 1960, *The New York Times* published a full-page advertisement, entitled *Heed Their Rising Voices*. The advertisement responded to King's arrest, and it began by noting: "*As the whole world knows by now, thousands of Southern Negro students are engaged in widespread non-violent demonstrations in positive affirmation of the right to live in human dignity as guaranteed by the U.S. Constitution and the Bill of Rights.*"

---

123. *See* Claude Sitton, *Dr. King Is Seized In Tax Indictment*, NEW YORK TIMES, February 18, 1960, at 14.

Figure 2.2

The New York Times.

NEW YORK, TUESDAY, MARCH 29, 1960.

"*The growing movement of peaceful mass demonstrations by Negroes is something new in the South, something understandable. . . . Let Congress heed their rising voices, for they will be heard.*"

—*New York Times editorial Saturday, March 19, 1960*

Heed Their Rising Voices

As the whole world knows by now, thousands of Southern Negro students are engaged in widespread non-violent demonstrations in positive affirmation of the right to live in human dignity as guaranteed by the U. S. Constitution and the Bill of Rights. In their efforts to uphold these guarantees, they are being met by an unprecedented wave of terror by those who

protagonists of democracy. Their courage and amazing restraint have inspired millions and given a new dignity to the cause of freedom.

Small wonder that the Southern violators of the Constitution fear this new, non-violent brand of freedom fighter . . . even as they fear the upswelling right-to-vote movement. Small wonder that they

of others—look for guidance and support, and thereby to intimidate *all* leaders who may rise in the South. Their strategy is to behead this affirmative movement, and thus to demoralize Negro Americans and weaken their will to struggle. The defense of Martin Luther King, spiritual leader of the student sit-in movement, clearly, therefore, is an integral part of the total

The advertisement continued with allegations of "an unprecedented wave of terror by those who would deny and negate that document which the whole world looks upon as setting the pattern for modern freedom." L. B. Sullivan supervised the Montgomery Police Department as the town's elected Commissioner of Public Affairs. Sullivan brought a libel action against the publisher of *The New York Times*. Although the advertisement did not mention Sullivan by name, he contended that it referred to Montgomery Police Department and, therefore, to him. A jury in the Circuit Court of Montgomery County awarded Sullivan damages of $500,000 and the Supreme Court of Alabama upheld this judgment. The case subsequently reached the U.S. Supreme Court.[124]

When Sullivan brought his case against the New York Times Company, Alabama had an established "libel per se" doctrine. Applying this doctrine, Alabama courts found libel per se whenever published words could injure a person "in his reputation, profession, trade or business, or charge him with an indictable offense, or * * * bring the individual into public contempt."[125] Once libel per se was established, the defendant was left to persuade the jury that all statements were true. If the defense was unsuccessful, general damages were presumed without proof of injury. In *Sullivan*, the trial judge instructed the jury that the statements in the New York advertisement were "libelous per se." The Alabama Supreme Court upheld this ruling.

124. New York Times Co. v. Sullivan, 376 U.S. 254 (1964).

125. New York Times Co. v. Sullivan, 273 Ala. 656 (1962).

The Supreme Court, however, held that "the rule of law applied by the Alabama courts [was] constitutionally deficient for failure to provide the safeguards for freedom of speech and of the press that are required by the First and Fourteenth Amendments in a libel action brought by a public official against critics of his official conduct." Therefore, the Court ruled that public officials cannot recover damages for alleged defamatory publications, even false ones, unless they can prove that a statement was made with "actual malice;" that is, with knowledge or reckless disregard that the statement was false. Specifically, the *Sullivan* Court emphasized that the law must reflect "a profound national commitment to the principle that debate on public issues should be uninhibited, robust, and wide-open, and that it may well include vehement, caustic, and sometimes unpleasantly sharp attacks on government and public officials."

New York Times Co. v. Sullivan (1964) and its progeny impose limits on the state's power to award damages for libel in actions brought by public officials against critics of their official conduct. Since *Sullivan*, public officials cannot legally suppress criticism in the press by using the state police powers or liability rules.

Anti–Cartoon Laws

In the 1860s, as printing technologies developed, cartoonists became effective participants in political debates, shaping public views and mobilizing social forces against corrupt politicians.[126] In New York City, Thomas Nast discredited "Boss Tweed" with cartoons he published in the *Harper's Magazine*, which ultimately led to public outrage and forced reforms in the city. Boss William Tweed headed Tammany Hall—the Democratic Party political machine—from 1858 to 1871 and his "Ring" controlled the government of New York City and looted its treasury.[127] Tweed's Ring reached and influenced every dimension of life and law in New York City. Although for the most part the law and public criticism did not restrain Boss Tweed, he felt threatened by Thomas Nast's cartoons. On one occasion he said: "Let's stop the damned pictures. I don't care so much what the papers write about me—my constituents can't read; but damn it, they can see pictures."[128] Nast's cartoons increased the pressures. Tweed was arrested in 1871 and tried.[129] In November 1873, a jury convicted Tweed on 204

---

126. *See generally* WILLIAM MURRELL, A HISTORY OF AMERICAN GRAPHIC HUMOR, 1865–1938 (1938). Images and materials related to this section are available at *regti.me/anti-cartoon* (case sensitive).

127. For the crusade of Thomas Nast against Boss Tweed *see* JOHN ADLER, DOOMED BY CARTOON: HOW CARTOONIST THOMAS NAST AND THE NEW YORK TIMES BROUGHT DOWN BOSS TWEED AND HIS RING OF THIEVES (2008). *See also The Tweed Ring: Its Beginnings and Its Methods,* NEW YORK TIMES, September 18, 1901, Jubilee Supplement at 12. Tweed inspired a good number of biographies, most notably, DENIS TILDEN LYNCH, "BOSS" TWEED: THE STORY OF A GRIM GENERATION (1927); KENNETH D. ACKERMAN, BOSS TWEED: THE RISE AND FALL OF THE CORRUPT POL WHO CONCEIVED THE SOUL OF MODERN NEW YORK (2005).

128. Albert Bigelow Paine, *'Harper's Weekly' and Thomas Nast*, HARPER'S WEEKLY, January 5, 1907, at 14, 17.

129. *Tweed Under Arrest: How the Great Criminal Was Captured in His Den*, NEW YORK TIMES, October 28, 1871, at 3.

counts of criminal offenses related to the embezzlement of public funds.[130] A month later, the trial judge sentenced him to 12 years in prison. After sentencing, Tweed fled to Spain, but was apprehended and extradited back to New York. He spent the last years of his life in prison, dying in 1878. Tweed's death ended the most corrupt era in New York history, but did it not end the role of cartoons in the fight against corruption.[131]

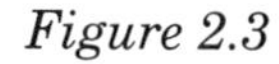

Figure 2.3

"STONE WALLS DO NOT A PRISON MAKE."—*Old Song.*
"NO PRISON IS BIG ENOUGH TO HOLD THE BOSS." IN ON ONE SIDE, AND OUT AT THE OTHER.

---

130. *Justice at Last: W. M. Tweed Convicted*, NEW YORK TIMES, NOVEMBER 20, 1873, at 1.

131. *See* MURRELL, *supra* note 114.

Figure 2.4

In the post-Boss Tweed era, one of most powerful political leaders in New York was Thomas C. Platt. Known commonly as "Boss Platt," he was the leader of the Republican Party in New York State. Boss Platt was not shy about political influence, but was dismissive of the "popular idea" that "a successful political leader, or a boss * * * possesses ability to pull strings while puppets dance."[132] His prescription for a boss was to "[c]onduct a political organization as a general commands an army, or the heads of a great business concern conducts its affairs."[133] Platt considered himself the "political godfather" of four consecutive Republican New York Governors: Levi Morton (1895–1896), Frank Black (1897–1898), Theodore Roosevelt (1899–1900), and Benjamin Odell (1901–1904).[134]

Leveraging the power of his position, Platt was actively involved in state and Presidential elections. The 1896 state and Presidential elections that followed an economic depression were particularly intense. The Republican candidate for the White House, William McKinley, won the national election, and in New York, Platt's protégée, Frank Black, was elected as a State Governor.[135] After the 1896 elections, Platt felt that he was "subjected to almost daily cuts and thrusts from enemies of the Republican Party and the New York Organization" and that "those who preferred to misunderstand [him] and [his] friends, saw fit to misconstrue every word and

---

132. THOMAS COLLIER PLATT, THE AUTOBIOGRAPHY OF THOMAS COLLIER PLATT xii (1910).

133. *Id.*

134. *Id.* at xx.

135. McKinley managed an effective campaign remaining at his home in Canton, Ohio, delivering speeches from his front porch. His rival, William Jennings Bryan, conducted a vigorous railroad campaign that was not nearly as effective as McKinley's campaign. *See* PAUL W. GLAD, MCKINLEY, BRYAN, AND THE PEOPLE (1964); STANLEY JONES, THE PRESIDENTIAL ELECTION OF 1896 (1964). PLATT, *supra* note 120, at 334–348.

act." The "attacks upon his private and public character" compelled him to run for the state vacated seat in the Senate.[136] In January 1897, he was elected by the State Legislature to serve as a Senator for the state.

Figure 2.5

Thomas C. Platt
NEW YORK TRIBUNE, January 21, 1897

136. PLATT, *supra* note 132, at 334.

On January 21, 1897, the *New York Tribune* announced his election to the U.S. Senate and printed his photo on the front page.[137] Boss Platt's portrait in the *New York Tribune* is a landmark in photojournalism. It revolutionized the press, being the first printed image in a newspaper with a new halftone technology that allowed mass printing of photos.

By January 1897, Platt, however, became sensitive to printed portraits, especially cartoons. He believed that the criticism against him amounted to "unreasonable prejudice" and thought that at best the Party would "have hard time electing a Republican Governor [in New York] in 1898." Platt was particularly troubled by the political cartoons.

In February 1897, one of Platt's "field-marshals" at the New York State Senate, Senator Timothy Ellsworth,[138] introduced an anti-cartoon bill:

> *An Act to restrain the unauthorized printing and publishing of portraits or alleged portraits of individuals.*
>
> **SECTION 1.** No person * * * shall print or publish in any newspaper, periodical, magazine, pamphlet, or book, any portrait or alleged portrait of any person * * * living in this State without first having obtained his or her written consent to such printing or publication.
>
> **SEC. 2.** The printing or publishing of the portrait or alleged portrait of such person * * * without such consent in writing shall be a misdemeanor, and shall be punishable by a fine not less than $1,000 and by imprisonment for not less than one year.
>
> **SEC. 3.** This act shall take effect immediately.

The bill drew substantial public attention. A month later, the State Senate Committee on Codes favorably reported on the bill with a few amendments. The Committee amended the proposed Section 1 to provide: "No person * * * shall print or publish in any newspaper, periodical, magazine, pamphlet, or book, any portrait or alleged portrait of any person * * * living in this State, *except fugitives from justice*, without first having obtained his or her written consent to such printing, publication, *or circulation*." The amended Section 2 provided: "The printing, publishing *or circulation* of the portrait or alleged portrait of such person * * * without such consent in writing shall be a misdemeanor, and shall be punishable by a fine not less than $1,000 and by imprisonment for not less than one year, *upon the complaint of the person whose portrait, or alleged portrait, has been so printed, published or circulated, without such consent*."

---

137. *Platt Elected Senator*, NEW YORK TRIBUNE, January 21, 1897, at 1.

138. Concluding his 1910 autobiography, Platt praised the "field-marshals who were faithful, [and] in victory or defeat, exhibited fighting qualities and a devotion." Among these "field-marshals," Platt listed Ellsworth and praised his "unswerving fealty." PLATT, *supra* note 122, at 513–14.

Figure 2.6

Misfit, Homer Development (1897)
Boss Platt "encouraging" his marshals to gag the press. Boss Tweed is in the Background.

In the legislative debates over the bill, Senator Ellsworth argued that its purpose was "to insure the right of privacy." He dismissed his colleagues' criticism that "[n]o public man of integrity has ever been harmed by a caricature" and that "[if] such a law had existed when Tweed was stealing millions in New York City it was doubtful if the illustrated newspapers would have dared to make such damaging attacks on him as they did." Although the New York anti-cartoon bill was known as the "Ellsworth Bill," it was publicly known that Platt stood behind it, and that "above all, Platt wanted the Anti–Cartoon bill placed upon the statute book." The *New York Tribune* reported that Governor Black was "considerably annoyed at the persistence with which Thomas C. Platt pushe[d] along the bill to abridge the liberty of the press."[139] According to the *Tribune*, the governor expected Mr. Platt to try to "jam" the bill through the Senate, the Assembly, and the Executive Chamber.[140]

---

139. *Platt the Prime Mover*, NEW YORK TRIBUNE, April 18, 1897, at 1.

140. "Jamming a bill through" refers to a self-interested voting of "legislators [who] do not listen to argument or appeal, do not deliberate, do not consult the opinions and wishes of constituents. The caucus upon measures coming before them, not as to their effect upon the general welfare but as to whether or not they will * * * promote the personal fortunes of the legislators themselves—and upon the decision of that question determine whether to drop them or 'jam them through.'" *Jamming*, NEW YORK DAILY TRIBUNE, April 16, 1897, at 6.

Ultimately, the New York Senate voted down the bill. In January 1898, Senator Ellsworth introduced a new anti-cartoon bill that provided:

> **SECTION 1.** A person who, either as principal or agent, conducts or engages in the business of editing, publishing, printing, distributing, or circulating any licentious, indecent, corrupt, depraved, or libelous paper, or a paper which corrupts, depraves, degrade, or injure the mind or morals of the public, or of its readers, or of the people among whom it circulates, is guilty of a misdemeanor, and upon conviction of such offence shall be punished by a fine of not more than $1,000 or by imprisonment for not more than one year, or by both such fine and imprisonment, for the first offence; and upon conviction of any subsequent offence shall be punished by imprisonment for not less than one year or more than five years; and in addition thereto the defendant and his agents and employees shall be prohibited from thereafter publishing, printing, selling, distributing, or circulating such paper, or any paper of the same name. * * *
>
> **SEC. 2.** Every paper published, sold, distributed or circulated in this State shall contain a printed statement setting forth the names of every owner, proprietor and publisher and editor. * * * Any person who edits, publishes, prints, sells, distributes or circulates any paper which fails to contain the statement above required is guilty of a misdemeanor, and upon conviction of any such offence shall be punished by a fine of not more than $1,000 or by imprisonment of not more than one year, or by both such fine and imprisonment. Upon the trial of any indictment for an offence under the first section of this act, a statement in any paper that the defendant is an owner, proprietor, publisher or editor thereof is presumptive evidence of the fact so stated.
>
> **SEC. 3.** An indictment for any violation of a provision of the first section of this act may be substantially in the words of the statute and need not specify or set forth any particular document, issue or number of any such paper nor any particular matter contained therein, but shall state the name by which such paper is commonly known or shall otherwise describe or identify it, and shall state the period of time within which the defendant is charged with having carried on the prohibited business. * * * The jury may find whether the offence has been committed from such evidence without proof that any particular person or persons have been, corrupted, depraved, degraded or injured. * * *
>
> **SEC. 4.** The District Attorney of any county in which any prosecution or trial for a violation of the provisions of this act shall take place shall appoint the counsel designated by the person making complaint against the defendant to assist him in such prosecution or trial, provided that the expense of such employment shall be paid by such complainant, and shall not be a public charge. * * *

SEC. 7. Whenever a judgment has been entered for a violation of the first section of this act as a second offence, or whenever a paper is deemed to be a licentious paper, as herein before defined, it shall be the duty of the Attorney General to bring an action or actions against the owner and the proprietor thereof. * * *

SEC. 8. The word person, as used in this act, includes any person, partnership, corporation, association, and any officer of any corporation or association engaged in the business herein prohibited. The word paper as used in this act includes any newspaper, journal, serial, magazine, periodical, and any publication of and kind.

SEC. 9. This act shall take effect immediately.

Like its 1897 predecessor, the 1898 Ellsworth Bill failed in the New York Senate and never became law.

Figure 2.7

No Honest Man Need Fear Cartoons.

In other states, politicians actually succeeded in passing anti-cartoon laws. For example, in 1899, California adopted an anti-cartoon law. The local press attributed the law to the "revulsion of feeling on part of the Legislature, left by an unfeeling, brutal caricature attack by the *San Francisco Call*." The California law provided:

SECTION 258. It shall be unlawful to publish in any newspaper, handbill, poster, book or serial publication, or supplement thereto,

> the portrait of any living person a resident of California, other than that of a person holding a public office in this state, without the written consent of such person first had and obtained; *provided*, that it shall be lawful to publish the portrait of a person convicted of a crime. It shall likewise be unlawful to publish in any newspaper, handbill, poster, book or serial publication or supplement thereto, any caricature of any person residing in this state, which caricature will in any manner reflect upon the honor, integrity, manhood, virtue, reputation, or business or political motives of the person so caricatured, or which tends to expose the individual so caricatured to public hatred, ridicule, or contempt. A violation of this section shall be a misdemeanor, and shall be punished by a fine of not less than one hundred dollars, nor more than five hundred dollars, or by imprisonment in the county jail for not less than one month nor more than six months, or by both such fine and imprisonment * * *.

Pennsylvania joined the states that banned cartoons in 1903. Governor Samuel Pennypacker secured an anti-cartoon legislation after a cartoonist ridiculed him in a series of cartoons that depicted him as a parrot.[141] Section 2 of the Pennsylvania anti-cartoon statute provided:

> In all civil actions * * * against the proprietor, owner, publisher or managing editor of any newspaper published in this Commonwealth, * * * if it shall be shown that the publication complained of resulted from negligence on the part of such owner, proprietor, manager or editor, to the ascertainment of the facts or in the publication thereof, compensatory damages may be recovered for injuries to business and reputation resulting from such publication, as well as damages for the physical and mental suffering endured by the injured party or parties; and whenever in any such action it shall be shown that the matter complained of is libelous, and that such libelous matter has been given special prominence by the use of pictures, cartoons, head-lines, displayed type, or any other matter calculated to specially attract attention, the jury shall have the right to award punitive damages against the defendant or defendants.

---

141. *See* Steven Piott, *The Right of the Cartoonist: Samuel Pennypacker and Freedom of the Press*, 55 PENNSYLVANIA HISTORY 78 (1988). Images and materials related to Samuel Pennypacker and his fight against cartoons are available at *regti.me/PA-gag* (case sensitive).

Figure 2.8

"Polly Got a Cracker." — Charles Nelan. Philadelphia North American, May 16, 1903 (commenting on Governor Pennypacker's anti-cartoon bill that was introduced in response to Charles Nelan's cartoon that caricatured him as a parrot).

When signing the anti-cartoon bill, Governor Pennypacker released a lengthy official statement explaining why he believed the law was needed:

> The questions raised by Senate bill No. 690 are of very grave importance. They affect large business interests, the freedom of speech and the press, the right of the citizen to be informed concerning current affairs and the conduct of government, as well as his right to protect his reputation and home from the injuries that result from careless or negligent, as well as malicious false report.
>
> * * *
>
> The bill in its application is not confined to officials, but affects as well the citizen or business man, whose conduct constitutes no part of the right of the public to information. The corporation officer who has been falsely charged with crimes, the manufacturer who has been falsely accused of being a drunken brawler; * * * the quiet citizen whose peace of mind has been destroyed by the publication of evil gossip; the merchant whose credit has been affected by groundless rumors; the sufferers from reckless but not necessarily malicious publications are given the right, not to prohibit publication, but to recover the damages which they have sustained, provided they prove negligence or lack of care on the part of the publishing newspaper. All of these are instances of what has in fact recently occurred.
>
> * * *

A [recent] cartoon in a daily journal * * * defines the question with entire precision. An ugly little dwarf representing the Governor of the Commonwealth stands on a crude stool. The stool is subordinate to and placed alongside of a huge printing press with wheels as large as those of an ox team and all are so arranged as to give the idea that when the press starts the stool and its occupant will be thrown to the ground.

Put into words, the cartoon asserts to the world that the press is above the law and greater in strength than the government. No self-respecting people will permit such an attitude to be long maintained. * * *

If such abuse of the privileges allowed to the press is to go unpunished, if such tales are permitted to be poured into the ears of men and to be profitable, it is idle to contend that reputable newspapers can maintain their purity. Evil communications corrupt good manners. One rotten apple will ere long spoil all in the barrel. The flaring headlines, the meretricious art, the sensational devices and the disregard of truth in time will creep over them all. * * *

The motive which leads to the degradation of the press is very plain and by no means unusual. It is the same motive which causes men to put deleterious chemicals into food, weak iron into the boilers of engines and wood into the flues of houses, the desire to produce cheaply in order that there may be a profitable sale. * * *

The bill offers as a remedy for these ills, or some of them, the application of the principles of the law of negligence to the publication of newspapers. All that this means is that they shall exercise "reasonable care" in the ascertainment of facts, and the announcement of comment which may injuriously affect the reputation or business of other people.

It is a law of almost universal application in the affairs of men. When we walk the streets or drive a horse, or light a fire, or make a shoe or build a house, we must take care that we do not cause harm to others. * * * It applies to the lawyer, the doctor and the dentist in the exercise of his profession. Why should it not apply to the editor? * * *

Questions

1. What was the significance of the amendments to the 1897 Ellsworth Bill? What were the major differences between the 1898 Ellsworth Bill and the amended 1897 Ellsworth Bill?

2. What are the differences among the New York anti-cartoon bill, the California anti-cartoon statute, and the Pennsylvania anti-cartoon statute?

3. One of the key arguments Senator Timothy Ellsworth made in support of his anti-cartoon bill in New York was that its purpose was "to insure the

right of privacy."[142] *The New York Times* described the proposed criminalization of publication of any portrait or alleged portrait of a person without obtaining his or her written consent as a "hasty and ill-directed shot at an undoubted evil."[143] Yet, *The Times* criticized the "outrageous invasion of private rights which has become so common in publishing portraits of persons who have no relations to the public."[144]

In 1890, a few years prior to the events in New York, a Boston paper manufacturer became annoyed by the unflattering press coverage his wife received. The paper manufacturer, Samuel D. Warren was a classmate of Louis Brandeis at Harvard Law School, and upon graduation the two founded a successful law firm.[145] Warren left the practice for a short time to run a family business. Responding to the invasion to Mrs. Warren's privacy, Warren and Brandeis published an article in *Harvard Law Review* that quickly became a classic in the law of privacy.[146] Warren and Brandeis' article addresses the "right to be let alone." They argued that "inventions and business methods" allowed newspapers to invade the "scared precincts of private and domestic life." Their analysis led them to conclude that "[t]he right of one who has remained a private individual, to prevent his public portraiture, presents the simplest case for such extension; the right to protect one's self from pen portraiture, from a discussion by the press of one's private affairs, would be a more important and far-reaching one." Warren and Brandeis further explored the limits of the rule and stressed that the "right to privacy does not prohibit any publication of matter which is of public or general interest. * * * In general, * * * the matters of which the publication should be repressed may be described as those which concern the private life, habits, acts, and relations of an individual, and have no legitimate connection with his fitness for a public office * * *, and have no legitimate relation to or bearing upon any act done by him in a public or quasi public capacity."

What are the similarities and differences between the Warren–Brandeis' right of privacy and the anti-cartoon bills and laws in New York, California, and Pennsylvania?

---

142. *Even the Cartoon Barred*, NEW YORK TRIBUNE, April 2, 1897, at 2.

143. *The Protection of Privacy*, NEW YORK TIMES, March 14, 1897, at 16.

144. *Id. See also Portraiture and Privacy*, NEW YORK TIMES, June 3, 1897, at 6.

145. *See* MELVIN I. UROFSKY, LOUIS D. BRANDEIS: A LIFE 40–74 (2009).

146. Samuel D. Warren & Louis D. Brandeis, *The Right to Privacy*, 4 HARVARD LAW REVIEW 193 (1890).

In the mid–1870s, Detroit began constructing Grand Boulevard to improve the traffic across the City. The first person to build a house on the new boulevard was James Andrus Randall, a native of Detroit who began practicing law in 1869.[147] In the 1880s, Randall was defeated in several attempts to obtain an appointment on a state court and thus diverted his attention to real estate. The development of Grand Boulevard was slow, and investors like James Randall regularly participated in City committees to secure budget appropriations and other supporting actions from the City. Randall's zeal earned him the nickname "Boulevard Randall." In 1888, Randall was elected to the Michigan House of Representatives; his public agenda was all about promoting the interests of the boulevard. As a state legislator, he sponsored legislation that authorized a $500,000 loan to Detroit for the purpose of paving a road in Grand Boulevard.[148] Within 20 years, Detroit's Grand Boulevard project became one of the City's major attractions.[149]

On May 8, 1889, the date Michigan Governor signed into law the legislation Randall sponsored, Detroit's leading evening news paper, *The Evening News*, published an article criticizing Randall's legislation and expressing the view that the loan would "help the land speculators" and "totally ignore[]" "the wishes of the people of Detroit."[150] Along with the article, *The Evening News* published a cartoon of Randall. Randall sued the publisher, the Evening News Association, for libel.

---

147. Images of Grand Boulevard and the Randall house are available at *regti.me/B–Randall* (case sensitive).

148. *An Act to Empower the Common Council of the City of Detroit to Borrow Money for the Purpose of Improving the Boulevard*, MI Act. No. 389 (May 8, 1889).

149. CLARENCE M. BURTON ET AL., THE CITY OF DETROIT MICHIGAN, 1701–1922, 430–34 (1922); GILBERT R. OSMUN, OFFICIAL DIRECTORY AND LEGISLATIVE MANUAL OF THE STATE OF MICHIGAN FOR THE YEARS 1889–90 654 (1889).

150. *Boulevard Bonds*, EVENING NEWS, May 8, 1889, at 1.

Figure 2.9

THE BOULEVARD NAPOLEON.

[in the course of his remarks in the legislature, yesterday, Mr. Randall stated that within five years the grateful citizens of Detroit would erect a monument in his honor. THE NEWS submit the following design.]

'Rah! for Randall.
'Rah! 'Rah! 'Rah!
Here's his statue
Looking at you;
Bless the boy, he's like his pa!

'Rah! for Randall; 'Rah! for gall!
What's Cadillac?
A saddle back;
Such old fans don't count all all.

'Rah! for Randall; shake old pard!
All the land 'll
Roar for Randall;
Napoleon of the boulevard!

THE EVENING NEWS, May 8, 1889.

Randall v. Evening News Association

Supreme Court of Michigan
79 Mich. 266 (1890)

■ Judge Morse

The plaintiff commenced a suit in a plea of trespass on the case for libel against the defendants. * * * His declaration averred that he was and is a good, true, honest, just and faithful citizen of this state, and as such had always behaved and conducted himself; that at the time of the printing and publication of the articles of which he complains he was a member of the legislature of the state of Michigan, from the city of Detroit, being such member from the 2d day of January, 1889, up to the present time; that as such member he has at all times conducted himself as a good, honest, and faithful official, and has executed and performed his duties as such representative in an honest and conscientious manner, and for the best interests of the state, and of the constituency represented by him. * * *

[T]he said plaintiff, as a member of the said house of representatives, * * * introduce[d] a bill * * * entitled "*A bill to empower the common council of the city of Detroit to borrow money for the purpose of improving the boulevard*," and which said bill was duly passed * * * on the 7th day of May, 1889. * * *

[T]he said defendants * * * contriving, and wickedly and maliciously intending, to injure the said plaintiff in his good name, fame, and credit, and to bring him into public scandal, disrepute, ridicule, and disgrace with and among his neighbors, and other good and worthy citizens * * * published, in a certain newspaper, known and styled *The Evening News*, and of which numerous copies, to-wit, of the number of 40,000, are circulated * * * the words following, to-wit, and the picture hereinafter delineated, to-wit:

> *A GREAT VICTORY—WHAT NEXT?* Rep. Randall is receiving congratulations on every hand over his success in inducing the Michigan legislature to pass a bill designed to enrich a few speculators at the general expense of the city of Detroit. The next move of the speculators will be to corrupt the caucuses of both parties, and bribe and bulldoze a sufficient number of the common council and board of estimates to vote to issue the bonds. * * * And all to enrich a few men who have grabbed a street and are determined that other people's money shall make them wealthy. However, the *NEWS* can stand it a great deal better than the majority of citizens, who must foot the bills. We therefore join the others who are congratulating Mr. Randall on his victory over the solid opposition of his fellow-citizens. There probably never was so signal a victory against such great odds in the history of Michigan legislation. Here was a measure proposed avowedly in the personal interests of its introducer and his partners. He made no secret of it. * * * He went there for this bill, and this bill alone; and he represented himself and his copartners in the deal, who, like himself, had pecuniary interests in the measure. The bill was denounced by * * * the common council, denounced by the board of estimates, denounced by 5,000 petitioners; and Mr. Randall candidly acknowledged before the senate committee that if it were submitted to the popular vote of Detroit it would be overwhelmed by an adverse majority. Furthermore, the majority of Detroit's representatives at Lansing opposed it. * * * When the legislature was carefully sized up, it was found to be the smallest, cheapest, rottenest body that ever assembled in Lansing. The premonitory symptoms of a desire to steal something manifested themselves from the beginning. Scarcely a day passed that some measure was not introduced

> containing promises of boodle, or that the legislature did not resolve upon some expedition or junket, for which the members voted themselves extra pay or allowance. Nothing was too small for them to despise, nothing too large for them to grasp at. * * *

The picture cannot well be reproduced here, but it was a caricature of Mr. Randall standing upon a platform, supported at each corner, and resting upon bottles, one of which was marked "Rye." Upon the platform was a cask marked "Gin," with faucet all ready for opening. Mr. Randall's right foot rested upon this cask. His left hand was pressed against his heart, and his right arm was extended, and clasped in his right hand was a bag marked "$." Above the picture was the following heading: "*THE BOULEVARD NAPOLEON*. (In the course of his remarks in the legislature yesterday Mr. Randall stated that within five years the grateful citizens of Detroit would erect a monument in his honor. The News submits the following design.)"

* * *

The plaintiff claims * * * that these articles and the picture impute to him, among other things, these three things: *First*, that he had, for bad and corrupt motives, induced the legislature to pass a bill designed to enrich a certain number of persons at the expense of the city of Detroit; *second*, that he, as a member of the legislature, had accepted and received bribes, and was corrupted thereby in his official action in respect to the bills pending in or passed by the said house of representatives; and, *third*, that he had, by the giving of a bribe, or by other corrupt means, influenced or controlled the giving of votes by members of said legislature.

The second imputation does not follow from the articles, or any language contained within them, or from the picture, and was so admitted upon the argument in this court by plaintiff's counsel. But we think that the first and last imputations are found within the articles. The plain meaning of the articles are—*First*, that Mr. Randall did not go to Lansing as a member of the legislature to serve the public, and so publicly expressed himself, but that he went there alone for the purpose of passing this boulevard bill, to enrich himself and his copartners in the boulevard scheme at the expense of the people of the city of Detroit; and, *secondly*, that the legislature was of such a character that they were grasping for boodle, (meaning money,) and that the members were susceptible of bribery, in the shape of liquor and money, from those interested in the passage of bills, and that Mr. Randall, taking advantage of this characteristic of said members, used both liquor and money to accomplish the passage of this bill, which was to put money in his own pocket at the tax-payers' expense.

The picture itself is capable of but one meaning, and that is that Randall's monument should show that liquor and money was the source of his Napoleon-like success in passing the bill. This is libelous, if not true. It is gravely argued that men are elected to the legislature and to the congress of the United States at every election, avowedly in the interest of private schemes of plunder, and not in the interest of the public, to represent corporations and other bodies or associations of men for their financial advancement and profit, without reference to the interests of the people at large, or even the constituency of the member so elected; that there is nothing illegal in this, because there is no law or statute providing that a member shall lose his seat by so doing; that it is at least perfectly legal for a member of the legislature to devote his whole time and energies as such member to enrich himself, or the class or corporation he represents, at the expense of the public. If there is now no law against such action by a member of the legislature, it is high time that statutes be enacted looking towards not only the unseating of a member guilty of prostituting his high place to personal and corrupt greed, but providing, also, a punishment for such misconduct.

Be that as it may, however, we are satisfied that public sentiment is not yet such as to look with either favor or complacency upon a member of the legislature whose whole avowed aim and effort is to enrich himself, or those who hire him, at the expense of the tax-payers. And we are satisfied that if the charge made against Mr. Randall in this respect be true, he deserves the scorn and contempt of every good citizen, and would receive it. Consequently, if untrue, it is libelous, and has damaged him in the estimation of good men and honest citizens, and whom we believe to be yet largely in the majority in every community in our state. It is equally libelous, if untrue, to state that Mr. Randall accomplished the passage of this boulevard bill by keeping open house, with liquors, (which is the true and plain meaning of these publications,) or that he did it by the use of boodle.

* * *

The judgment of the court below is therefore reversed, and the demurrer of the defendant overruled. The record will be remanded, and the usual time will be allowed the defendants in which to plead to the declaration if they so desire. * * *

[On remand, Randall recovered verdict and judgment for $11,000.[151]]

Questions

1. In *Randall v. Evening News Association*, the Michigan Supreme Court held that a cartoon is capable of having a libelous meaning. James Randall therefore contributed to the establishment of a liability rule against cartoons. What are the similarities and differences between the Randall liability rule and anti-cartoon laws?

2. One meaning of *Randall v. Evening News Association* is that, in the 1890s, public officials could successfully sue publishers for defamation by cartoons. Nevertheless, in several states, public officials preferred anti-cartoon laws over libel laws. What could explain this preference?

§ 2.4.2b Bribery and Cinch Bills

Under common law, the offering, acceptance or solicitation of bribery for influencing the regulatory process is illegal.[152] More broadly, all activi-

---

151. Randall v. Evening News Association, 97 Mich. 136 (1893).

152. *See, e.g.*, Clippinger v. Hepbaugh, 40 Am.Dec. 519 (Pa. 1843); William Deering & Co. v. Cunningham, 63 Kan. 174 (1901); Millbank v. Jones, 127 N.Y. 370 (1891); Mills v. Mills, 40 N.Y. 543 (1869); Wildey v. Collier, 7 Md. 273 (1854).

ties in which a benefit is offered, promised, solicited, or accepted in exchange for influence over the discretion of a lawmaker, regulator, or judge are illegal. Acknowledging the importance of this common law ban, all states have opted to incorporate it into their statutes to reduce enforcement costs. Most states have relied on the Model Penal Code version of the ban, which provides:

> *Model Penal Code § 240.1: Bribery in Official and Political Matters*
>
> A person is guilty of bribery, a felony of the third degree, if he offers, confers or agrees to confer upon another, or solicits, accepts or agrees to accept from another:
>
> (1) any pecuniary benefit as consideration for the recipient's decision, opinion, recommendation, vote or other exercise of discretion as a public servant, party official or voter; or
>
> (2) any benefit as consideration for the recipient's decision, vote, recommendation or other exercise of official discretion in a judicial or administrative proceeding; or
>
> (3) any benefit as consideration for a violation of a known legal duty as public servant or party official.
>
> It is no defense to prosecution under this section that a person whom the actor sought to influence was not qualified to act in the desired way whether because he had not yet assumed office, or lacked jurisdiction, or for any other reason.

Many states, however, have incorporated alternative versions of the ban. For example, the California 1879 Constitution included a provision that addressed improper influence on lawmakers:

> Any person who seeks to influence the vote of the legislature by bribery, promise of reward, intimidation, or any other dishonest means, shall be guilty of lobbying, which is hereby declared a felony, and it shall be the duty of the Legislature to provide, by law, for the punishment of this crime. Any member of the Legislature who shall be influenced in his vote or action upon any matter pending before the Legislature by any reward, or promise of future reward, shall be deemed guilty of a felony, and upon conviction thereof, in addition to such punishment as may provided by law, shall be disfranchised and forever disqualified from holding any office or public trust. * * *[153]

In 1966, California chose to rely on statutory bans and repealed the constitutional provision. Current California law includes three provisions that are parallel to the Model Penal Code and the statutory bans of other states.

> *Cal. Gov. Code § 9054*
>
> Every person who obtains, or seeks to obtain, money or other thing of value from another person upon a pretense, claim, or representation that he can or will improperly influence in any

---

153. Cal. Const., Art. IV, § 35 (repealed).

manner the action of any member of a legislative body in regard to any vote or legislative matter, is guilty of a felony. * * *

Cal. Penal Code § 85

Every person who gives or offers to give a bribe to any Member of the Legislature, any member of the legislative body of a city, county, city and county, school district, or other special district, or to another person for the member, or attempts by menace, deceit, suppression of truth, or any corrupt means, to influence a member in giving or withholding his or her vote, or in not attending the house or any committee of which he or she is a member, is punishable by imprisonment in the state prison for two, three or four years.

Cal. Penal Code § 86

Every Member of either house of the Legislature, or any member of the legislative body of a city, county, city and county, school district, or other special district, who asks, receives, or agrees to receive, any bribe, upon any understanding that his or her official vote, opinion, judgment, or action shall be influenced thereby, * * * or she may be required to act in his or her official capacity, or gives, or offers or promises to give, any official vote in consideration that another Member of the Legislature, or another member of the legislative body of a city, county, city and county, school district, or other special district shall give this vote either upon the same or another question, is punishable by imprisonment in the state prison for two, three, or four years and, in cases in which no bribe has been actually received, by a restitution fine of not less than two thousand dollars ($2,000) or not more than ten thousand dollars ($10,000) or, in cases in which a bribe was actually received, by a restitution fine of at least the actual amount of the bribe received or two thousand dollars ($2,000), whichever is greater, or any larger amount of not more than double the amount of any bribe received or ten thousand dollars ($10,000), whichever is greater.

In imposing a fine under this section, the court shall consider the defendant's ability to pay the fine.

In addition to these three statutory provisions, in 1949, California adopted a unique statutory ban against "cinch bills." *Cinch bills*, in the Californian political jargon of the nineteenth and twentieth century,[154] are measures introduced for the purpose of obtaining benefits to kill or pigeonhole them. A legislator introduces a cinch bill to induce affected parties to bribe her to either eliminate the bill or reduce its effect. In the words of a Californian politician: "[A] 'cinch' bill [is] a measure farmed for the purpose of blackmail; one that its author [has] no idea of passing, but

154. *See, e.g.*, Colusa County v. Welch, 122 Cal. 428 (1898) (holding that that an agreement "to secure by means of personal solicitation, and by means of private interview with members of the legislature of California, and by means of lobbying, the defeat of said senate bill" was invalid).

simply introduce[s] it to give weight to his demand that his silence be purchased with gold."[155] The California ban on cinch bills provides:

Cal. Gov. Code § 9056

Any person who shall secure through his influence, knowingly exerted for that purpose, the introduction of any bill, resolution or amendment into the State Legislature and shall thereafter solicit or accept from any person other than a person upon whose request he secured such introduction, any pay or other valuable consideration for preventing or attempting to prevent, the enactment or adoption of such measure, while it retains its original purpose, shall be guilty of a crime and upon conviction thereof shall be punishable by a fine of not exceeding ten thousand dollars ($10,-000) or by imprisonment in the county jail for not more than one year or in the state prison, or by both such fine and imprisonment.

GENESIS OF "CINCH" BILLS.

February 23, 1899 at 6.

Cinch bills may properly be designated as the invention of legislative devils. They are introduced, not for the purpose of being enacted into laws, but to alarm the corporations against which they are directed and to make business for a corrupt and reckless lobby. Every Legislature is afflicted with large numbers of them. Some "cinch" bills are popular, having for their object the reformation of acknowledged evils or the correction of acknowledged abuses. A "cinch" bill is effective in producing blood just in proportion as it is reasonable and fair. When the lobby directs its attention to something that needs reformation it is very apt to strike a popular chord and obtain for itself the assistance of large numbers of well-meaning people. It is only when things go along smoothly and there is no cause for popular outcry that "cinch" bills become poor and poverty-stricken.

But there is never any intention to pass "cinch" bills. * * * There being no intention on the part of the legislative devils to do anything more than frighten individuals and corporations into providing money with which to defeat the "cinch" bills, it is dangerous for any sensible person to pay the slightest attention to them. In ninety-nine cases out of a hundred, if "cinch" bills are let run, they will die of their own corruption. Sometimes the newspapers help the "cinchers" by applauding their bills as reform measures, but this is always done without a proper knowledge of the purposes of those who introduce and advocate them.

---

155. *Irish Now Knows What A "Cinch" Is*, SAN FRANCISCO CALL, Feb. 8, 1905, at 3.

The files of [every] Legislature are loaded down with "cinch" bills. Where the corporations affected have not become alarmed the legislative devils have appointed committees to investigate and report information which is intended to work upon the fears of the stockholders and officers. But where a bill is a bald "cinch" neither the newspapers nor the victims should encourage it. To do so is merely to make money for a corrupt and debased lobby.

It is difficult, however, to expose the men who concoct "cinch" bills and further their enactment up to a certain point. They cover their tracks pretty effectually, and at every stage of their progress loudly proclaim their virtue and righteousness. But if no one put up to defend "cinch" bills, we are sure in time they would cease to be a source of profit to the lobby or a cause for fear among their victims.

Questions

1. What are the differences between the California statutory bans on bribery of public officials and the Model Penal Code ban? Are there any substantial differences between the California statutory bans and the 1879 constitutional ban?

2. At the turn of the nineteenth century, the term "cinch bill" was occasionally misused and referred to measures "authorizing the destruction of property or favoring a certain section against the whole people."[156] Most frequently, when misused, the term referred to bills "purchased" by firms and wealthy individuals. The Southern Pacific Railroad Company, the largest railroad in western United States, for example, was known to buy bills in California.

Cinch bills and more "traditional bribery schemes" in which a public official accepts or solicits a benefit to promote private interest, share at least one characteristic in common: a public official is inappropriately using the legislative process for her own private benefit. What are the similarities and differences between cinch bills and the "traditional bribery schemes"? Which scheme is likely to impose higher costs on the public?

---

156. *Irish Now Knows What A "Cinch" Is*, SAN FRANCISCO CALL, Feb. 8, 1905, at 3.

Figure 2.10

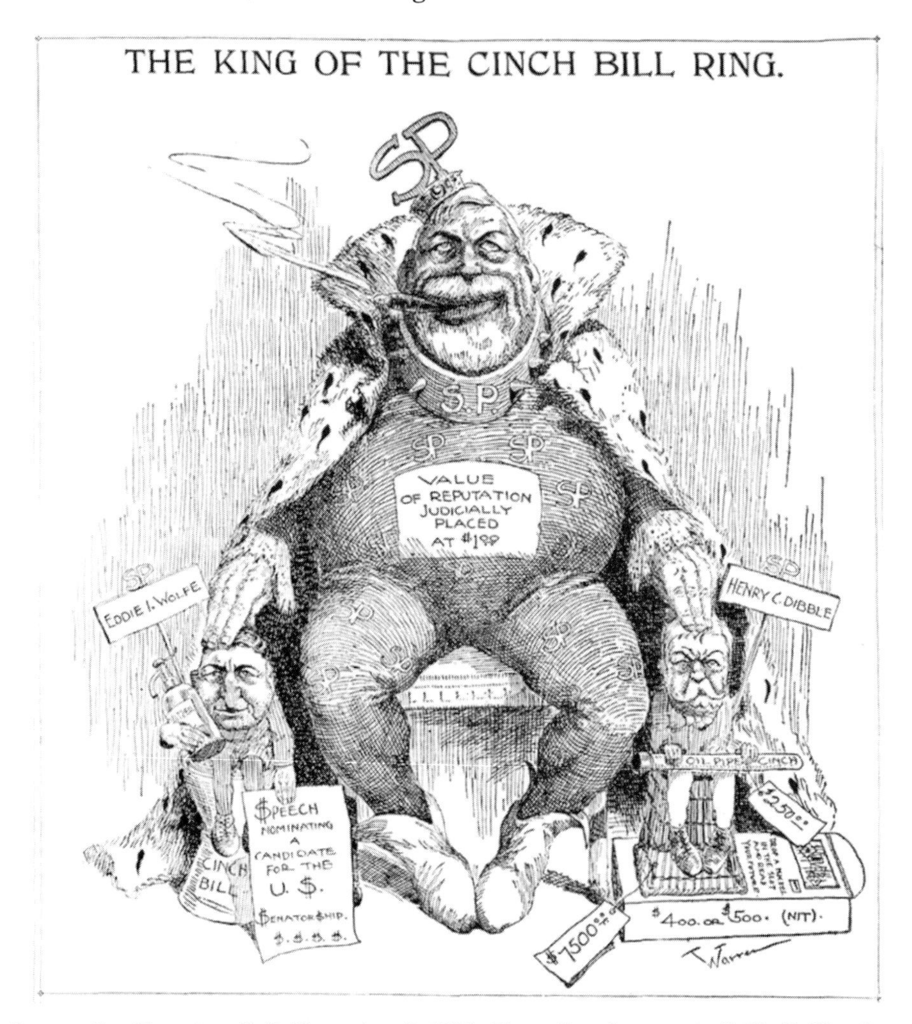

Source: San Francisco Call, November 5, 1900. The railroad magnate Collis P. Huntington served as the President of Southern Pacific (SP) from 1890 to 1900, and was nationally known for his aggressive lobbying strategies.[157] Wolfe and Dibble were state politicians who were allegedly paid for their legislative services.

3. Cinch bills were popular mostly in California. "Legislative threats" are prevalent in all states and in Congress. Under this practice, "[a] legislator * * * exercise[s] his legislative mandate and enact adverse legislation in order to regulate * * *, unless the threat recipients alter their behavior to bring it in line with the legislator's demands. Implicit in the threat is the inverse promise that the legislator will forgo the threatened legislation if,

---

157. *See* C.W. EVANS, COLLIS POTTER HUNTINGTON (1954); DAVID SIEVERT LEVENDER, THE GREAT PERSUADER (1970).

and only if, the threat recipients duly meet such expectations. Under certain conditions, legislative threats induce entities to modify their conduct and abandon targeted practices, averting the risk and consequences of the threatened legislation."[158] Regulatory threats are similar but performed by administrative agencies, rather than lawmakers. What are the similarities and differences between cinch bills and legislative (or regulatory) threats? Do legislative and regulatory threats raise any concerns?

4. What may explain the popularity of cinch bills in California and not in other states? Why did powerful political leaders, such as the New York "Bosses," not frequently use cinch bills or similar influence instruments?

§ 2.4.3 The Public Decisionmaker and Interest Groups

Interest groups form to promote the causes of their members by exerting pressure on public decisionmakers and influencing public views. Manifested in various forms, interest groups influence the regulatory process in significant ways.

Consider the following examples. The Interstate Commerce Commission ("ICC"), the first independent federal regulatory agency, was tasked with regulating the railroad and trucking industries. In many respects, ICC primarily served the interests of regulated industries.[159] In the battle over Seattle's Green Fee, a trade association that represented national and international businesses effectively lobbied against the City. Senator Timothy Ellsworth introduced his anti-cartoon bill in New York to protect the interests of a specific interest group—powerful New York politicians, who were displeased with criticism of the press. The Parents Television Council, a non-profit organization whose "primary mission is to promote and restore responsibility and decency to the entertainment industry," successfully persuaded the FCC to revise its indecency policy.[160] In 2000, the tobacco industry convinced five Supreme Court Justices that the FDA erred in asserting authority to regulate tobacco products.[161] The motion picture industry has persuaded Congress to enact many statutes that directly benefit the industry. Walt Disney Company, which lobbied for the Sonny Bono Copyright Term Extension Act ("CTEA") of 1998, saddled the statute with a particularly unflattering nickname: the Mickey Mouse Protection Act.[162] Philip Morris, the largest tobacco company in the United States, strategically participated in the legislative process for the Family Smoking Prevention and Tobacco Control Act of 2009.[163] The statute protects the

---

158. Guy Halfteck, *Legislative Threats*, 61 STANFORD LAW REVIEW 629, 633 (2008).

159. *See, e.g.*, MARVER H. BERNSTEIN, REGULATING BUSINESS BY INDEPENDENT COMMISSION (1955).

160. *See* Fox Television Stations, Inc. v. Federal Communications Commission, 613 F.3d 317 (2d Cir. 2010).

161. *See* Food and Drug Administration v. Brown & Williamson Tobacco Corp., 529 U.S. 120 (2000).

162. Pub. L. No. 105–298, 112 Stat. 2827 (1998). *See* Lawrence Lessig, *Copyright's First Amendment*, 48 UCLA LAW REVIEW 1057, 1065 (2001).

163. Pub. L. No. 111–31, 123 Stat. 1845 (2009). *See* P.A. McDanieal & R.E. Malone, *Understanding Philip Morris's Pursuit of US Government Regulation of Tobacco*, 14 TOBACCO CONTROL 193 (2005).

competitive advantage of Philip Morris over its rivals. For that, some call the statute "the Marlboro Man Act."[164] Interest groups influence, manipulate, and sometimes even control the regulatory process.[165]

Interest groups are not always motivated by financial motives. The National Rifle Association was created in 1871 to promote and encourage rifle shooting on a scientific basis and became America's foremost defender of Second Amendment rights. The Humane Society of the United States is the nation's largest animal rights organization, and it strives to reduce the suffering of animals and to create meaningful social change for them. The Planned Parenthood Federation of America is one of the leading organizations defending a woman's right to make informed and independent decisions about health, sex, and family planning. The National Right to Life Committee is the largest pro-life organization in the United States. It was established after the Supreme Court decision in *Roe v. Wade*.[166] Such organizations regularly participate in regulatory processes by attempting to influence public decisionmakers; specifically, they hope to promote their causes and encourage the public to support these perspectives.

To be sure, interest groups are important participants in the public discourse, frequently contributing knowledge and expertise. However, they may also circumvent the democratic process to influence laws and regulations.[167] In *Citizens United*, in a 5–4 decision, the Supreme Court dismantled legal restrictions imposed on interest groups, holding that the First Amendment prohibits the government from restricting political spending by corporations and unions, reasoning that such "prohibitions are classic examples of censorship."[168] In *American Tradition Partnership*, again in a 5–4 decision, the Court reaffirmed its decision in *Citizens United*.[169] Effectively, the Supreme Court empowered interest groups.

---

164. The person who coined the name is Steve Watson, a former Vice–President of External Affairs of Lorillard one of the largest four tobacco companies. An email from Lorillard's External Affairs, June 17, 2009. The statute is advantageous to Philip Morris in several ways, including Section 907 that exempts menthol additives from FDA regulation. Philip Morris is the leading tobacco producer in the lucrative segment of menthol-flavored cigarettes. *See* Samuel Loewenberg, *Smoke Screen*, SLATE, July 25, 2002; Duff Wilson, *Philip Morris's Support Shadow Over a Bill to Limit Tobacco*, NEW YORK TIMES, April 1, 2009, at B3; *Washington's Marlboro Men*, WALL STREET JOURNAL, June 13, 2009, at A12.

165. *See, e.g.* MARVER H. BERNSTEIN, REGULATING BUSINESS BY INDEPENDENT COMMISSION (1955); KENNETH G. CRAWFORD, THE PRESSURE BOYS: THE INSIDE STORY OF LOBBYING IN AMERICA (1939); Cass R. Sunstein, *Interest Groups in American Public Law*, 38 STANFORD LAW REVIEW 29 (1985); HARMON ZEIGLER, INTEREST GROUPS IN AMERICAN SOCIETY (1964). *See also* Gary S. Becker, *A Theory of Competition among Pressure Groups for Political Influence*, 98 QUARTERLY JOURNAL OF ECONOMICS 371 (1983); Gary S. Becker, *Public Policies, Pressure Groups, and Dead Weight Costs*, 28 JOURNAL OF PUBLIC ECONOMICS 329 (1985); Jean–Jacques Laffont et al., *Cartelization by Regulation*, 5 JOURNAL OF REGULATORY ECONOMICS 111 (1993).

166. 410 U.S. 113 (1973).

167. *See generally* Barak Orbach, *Invisible Lawmaking*, 79 UNIVERSITY OF CHICAGO LAW REVIEW ONLINE (2012); Barak Orbach, et al., 52 *Arming States' Rights: Federalism, Private Lawmakers, and the Battering Ram Strategy*, 52 ARIZONA LAW REVIEW 1161 (2010).

168. Citizens United v. Federal Election Commission, 130 S. Ct. 876, 896 (2010).

169. American Tradition Partnership, Inc. v. Bullock, 132 S. Ct. 2490 (2012).

The term "*rent seeking*" is often used to describe the pursuit of private interest through regulation.[170] Rent-seeking activities are all actions that interest groups may take to promote their goals, and their costs are added to the burden interest groups impose on society. Another term frequently used is "*regulatory capture*." It describes a regulator that is "captured" by the regulatee.[171] A popular critique of regulation maintains that regulators are captured by the regulatees; that is, they serve those they intend to regulate rather than the public. Nobel Laureate George Stigler popularized this criticism: "[A]s a rule, regulation is acquired by the industry and is designed and operated primarily for its benefit."[172] Studies of regulation find some support for this view. However, reality tends to be more complex than the Stiglerian explanation.

Industries and firms sometimes strategically support regulation, among other reasons because they realize that restrictive regulation will be adopted. The support may enable the industry (or industry members) to influence the design for its (or their) benefit. Such support, however, is not equivalent to "acquisition" of the regulation and the influence does not amount to control over the design and operation. Railroad companies supported, rather than opposed, federal regulation and the establishment of ICC. Railroads also captured and influenced ICC throughout the history of the agency.[173] This undisputed history does *not* suggest that the railroads controlled the federal regulation. ICC served the public interest in the sense that imperfect, flawed regulation was still much better than no regulation.[174] Similarly, although Philip Morris strategically participated in the legislative process of the Prevention and Tobacco Control Act of 2009, the act still serves the public.

Many factors explain actions taken by lawmakers, agencies, and judges.[175] Capture is only one of them.[176] The challenge facing interest groups is to capture a critical mass of individuals in strategic positions with

---

170. Anne Krueger coined the term "rent seeking," although she wrote about the concept a few years after Gordon Tullock who presented an old idea in modern neoclassic economic framework. Anne Krueger, *The Political Economy of the Rent-seeking Society*, 64 AMERICAN ECONOMIC REVIEW 291 (1974); Gordon Tullock, *The Welfare Costs of Tariffs, Monopolies, and Theft*, 5 WESTERN ECONOMIC JOURNAL 224 (1967).

171. *See generally* Ernesto Dal Bó, *Regulatory Capture: A Review*, 22 OXFORD REVIEW OF ECONOMIC POLICY 203 (2006); Paul Sabatier, *Social Movements and Regulatory Agencies: Toward a More Adequate: And Less Pessimistic: Theory of "Clientele Capture,"* 6 POLICY SCIENCES 301 (1975). *See also* DANIEL CARPENTER & DAVID MOSS EDS., PREVENTING CAPTURE: SPECIAL INTEREST INFLUENCE IN REGULATION AND HOW TO LIMIT IT (2012).

172. Stigler, *The Theory of Economic Regulation*, 2 BELL JOURNAL OF ECONOMIC & MANAGEMENT SCIENCE 3, 5 (1971). *See also* Sam Pelzman, *Toward a More General Theory of Regulation*, 19 JOURNAL OF LAW & ECONOMICS 211 (1976).

173. *See, e.g.*, BERNSTEIN, REGULATING BUSINESS BY INDEPENDENT COMMISSION, *supra* note 151; GABRIEL KOLKO, THE TRIUMPH OF CONSERVATISM, A REINTERPRETATION OF AMERICAN HISTORY, 1900–1916 3 (1963) (Studying the establishment of ICC and its early years and concluding that "regulation itself was invariably controlled by leaders of the regulated industry, and directed toward ends they deemed acceptable or desirable.")

174. *See* Robert W. Harbeson, *Railroads and Regulation, 1877–1916: Conspiracy or Public Interest?*, 27 JOURNAL OF ECONOMIC HISTORY 230 (1967).

175. *See, e.g.*, STEVEN P. CROLEY, REGULATION AND PUBLIC INTERESTS: THE POSSIBILITY OF GOOD REGULATORY GOVERNMENT (2007); RICHARD A. POSNER, HOW JUDGES THINK (2008); Michael P. Vandenbergh, *The Private Life of Public Law*, 105 COLUMBIA LAW REVIEW 2029 (2005); Barry R. Weingast, *Regulation, Reregulation, and Deregulation: The Political Foundations of Agency*

a limited budget available for rent-seeking activities.[177] For this reason, regulatory independence from political control may reduce capture costs for interest groups. Independence curtails the ability of new governments to radically change policies, which creates a stabilization effect that in turn could make capture more effective.[178]

Question

In his book, *The Great Crash 1929*, John Kenneth Galbraith wrote:

> To the economist embezzlement is the most interesting of crimes. Alone among the various forms of larceny it has a time parameter. Weeks, months, or years, may elapse between the commission of the crime and its discovery. * * * At any given time there exists an inventory of undiscovered embezzlement in—or more precisely not in—the country's businesses and banks. This inventory—it should be perhaps be called bezzle—amounts at any moment to many millions of dollars. It also varies with the size of the business cycle. In good times people are relaxed, trusting, and money is plentiful. But even though money is plentiful, there are always many people who need more. Under these circumstances the rate of embezzlement grows, the rate of discovery falls off, and the bezzle increases rapidly. In depression all this is reversed. Money is watched with a narrow, suspicious eye. The man who handles it is assumed to be dishonest until he proves himself otherwise. Audits are penetrating and meticulous. Commercial morality is enormously improved. The bezzle shrinks.[179]

What possible effects do the fluctuations of bezzle inventory have on the influence of interest groups?

§ 2.4.3a Earmarks

Earmarks: "Funds provided by Congress for projects, programs, or grants where the purported congressional direction (whether in

---

Clientele Relationships, 44 LAW & CONTEMPORARY PROBLEMS 147 (1981); Barry R. Weingast & William J. Marshall, *The Industrial Organization of Congress; or, Why Legislatures, Like Firms, Are Not Organized as Markets*, 96 JOURNAL OF POLITICAL ECONOMY 132 (1996).

176. *See* Barry R. Weingast & Mark J. Moran, *Bureaucratic Discretion or Congressional Control? Regulatory Policymaking by the Federal Trade Commission*, 91 JOURNAL OF POLITICAL ECONOMY 765 (1983).

177. *See generally* Joseph P. Kalt & Mark A. Zupan, *Capture and Ideology in the Economic Theory of Politics*, 74 AMERICAN ECONOMIC REVIEW 279 (1984).

178. *See generally* Antoine Faure-Grimaud and David Martimort, *Regulatory Inertia*, 34 RAND JOURNAL OF ECONOMICS 413 (2003). The ICC, the first independent federal regulatory agency is the archetype of captured regulators. *See* MARVER H. BERNSTEIN, REGULATING BUSINESS BY INDEPENDENT COMMISSION (1955); Samuel P. Huntington, *The Marasmus of the ICC: The Commission, The Railroads, and the Public Interest*, 61 YALE LAW JOURNAL 467, 508 (1952) ("When such a commission loses its objectivity and impartiality by becoming dependent upon the support of a single narrow interest group, obviously the rationale for maintaining its independence has ceased to exist.") In practice, Congress maintains some control or at least influence over federal agencies. *See* Weingast & Moran, *Bureaucratic Discretion or Congressional Control*, *supra* note 159.

179. JOHN KENNETH GALBRAITH, THE GREAT CRASH 1929, at 137–138 (1954).

statutory text, report language, or other communication) circumvents otherwise applicable merit-based or competitive allocation processes, or specifies the location or recipient, or otherwise curtails the ability of the executive branch to manage its statutory and constitutional responsibilities pertaining to the funds allocation process."

—Office of Management and Budget
Executive Office of the President[180]

On October 3, 2008, in the wake of the worst financial crisis since the Great Depression, President George W. Bush signed into law the Emergency Economic Stabilization Act of 2008.[181] The statute clearly defined its goals:

(1) to immediately provide authority and facilities that the Secretary of the Treasury can use to restore liquidity and stability to the financial system of the United States; and

(2) to ensure that such authority and such facilities are used in a manner that—

(A) protects home values, college funds, retirement accounts, and life savings;

(B) preserves homeownership and promotes jobs and economic growth;

(C) maximizes overall returns to the taxpayers of the United States; and

(D) provides public accountability for the exercise of such authority.[182]

The Emergency Economic Stabilization Act was comprehensive, complex legislation intended to unfreeze paralyzed credit markets and save the economy. The statute had a critical mission but it also included several earmarks. One of them was Section 503 that provided an "exemption from excise tax for certain wooden arrows designed for use by children."[183] In medieval England, Robin Hood allegedly used wooden arrows during his efforts to help the poor, but in 2008 no one believed that toy wooden arrows could really energize the troubled American economy. Oregon Senators Gordon Smith (Republican) and Ron Wyden (Democrat), however, drafted Section 503 to benefit several wooden arrow manufacturers in their state.

Earmarks, the practice by which individual legislators insert pet projects of their choosing into a bill, constitute one technique to promote private interests. Most earmarks serve certain sectors of society; some of them may be worthy, but others are vehicles for waste, fraud, and abuse.

180. Memorandum for the Heads of Departments and Agencies from Rob Portman, Director of Office of Management and Budget (January 25, 2007).

181. The Emergency Economic Stabilization Act of 2008, Pub. L. No. 110–343, 122 Stat. 3765 (2008).

182. Section 2, codified as 12 U.S.C. § 5201.

183. Codified as 26 U.S.C. § 4161.

They are the fingerprints interest leave when they squeeze benefits through the legislative process. Section 503 illustrates how a small, supposedly powerless interest group—manufacturers of toy wooden arrows—can influence the regulatory process.

Very often interest groups with a small number of members are much more effective than large interest groups in securing favorable regulations. This happens because groups always face some form of *collective action problems*—the marginal value of each member encourages commitment in small groups and free riding in large groups. As a result, small groups are often more cohesive and effective than large groups with many members.[184]

Questions

1. Why do earmarks, rather than stand-alone legislative measures, serve as common vehicles for the promotion of interest group agendas?

2. Because earmarks are associated with interest groups, they also symbolize one of the illnesses the regulatory process, although elected legislators, not regulators, enact earmarks. Legislators often insert earmarks into bills even after they pledge to eliminate them.[185] Could lawmakers effectively ban earmarks? If so, how?

§ 2.4.3b Pressure Groups in Action Crush Videos[186]

In 1998, the Humane Society of the United States contacted Ventura County District Attorney's Office in California to complain about a relatively unknown film genre—"crush videos." The films featured women, barefoot or in spiked heels, slowly crushing small animals to death. The subsequent investigation revealed a national market with over 2,000 available titles for which consumers were paying $30 to $300 per video.

The underlying acts of animal cruelty were illegal in every state, but law enforcement officers struggled to detect and convict wrongdoers. Although the government had the videos as evidence, it was difficult to identify the participants in the films that featured mostly women's legs. It

---

184. *See generally* Gary S. Becker, *A Theory of Competition among Pressure Groups for Political Influence*, 98 QUARTERLY JOURNAL OF ECONOMICS 371 (1983); Gary S. Becker, *Public Policies, Pressure Groups, and Dead Weight Costs*, 28 JOURNAL OF PUBLIC ECONOMICS 329 (1985); MANCUR OLSON, THE LOGIC OF COLLECTIVE ACTION: PUBLIC GOODS AND THE THEORY OF GROUPS (1965); Sam Pelzman, *Toward a More General Theory of Regulation*, 19 JOURNAL OF LAW & ECONOMICS 211 (1976); Richard A. Posner, *Theories of Economic Regulation*, 5 BELL JOURNAL OF ECONOMICS & MANAGEMENT SCIENCE 335 (1974); Stigler, *The Theory of Economic Regulation*, *supra* note 153; George J. Stigler, *Free Riders and Collective Action: An Appendix to Theory of Economic Regulation*, 5 BELL JOURNAL OF ECONOMIC & MANAGEMENT SCIENCE 359 (1974).

185. In November 2010, Congress adopted a two-year earmark moratorium. However, supporters of the pledge started circumventing it within a few weeks. *See, e.g.*, *The Empty Earmark Pledge*, NEW YORK TIMES, November 17, 2010, at 31; Dana Milbank, *Pork Is Back On the Menu*, WASHINGTON POST, December 15, 2010, at 21; Philip Rucker & Paul Kane, *Senators Load Spending Bill With Earmarks*, WASHINGTON POST, December 15, 2010; Philip Rucker & Paul Kane, *A Vow to Vote Down Their Own Earmarks*, WASHINGTON POST, December 16, 2010, at A1.

186. This section relies on Barak Orbach & Allison S. Woolston, *Censoring Crimes*, 29 CARDOZO ARTS & ENTERTAINMENT LAW JOURNAL 251 (2011).

was also challenging to determine where and when the films were produced for jurisdictional and statute of limitation considerations. At the time, state and federal laws did not prohibit the production, sale, or possession of crush films or any films that depicted animal cruelty. Moreover, censorship laws did not expressly address animal cruelty. Crush videos were commonly available through the Internet and almost exclusively distributed for sale through interstate or foreign commerce; therefore, they appeared as an appropriate subject for federal regulation.

As his district was struggling to prosecute these cases, California Representative Elton Gallegly brought the issue of crush videos Congress. With the help of "[s]ome of the leading constitutional lawyers in the nation," he drafted a bill "very narrowly" to target "the profits made from promoting illegal cruel acts toward animals." In May 1999, Gallegly introduced the bill, H.R. 1887, in the House with a strong statement:

> Sick criminals are taking advantage of the loopholes in the local law and the lack of federal law on animal cruelty videos. This is a serious problem. Thousands of these videos are being sold. Thousands of dollars are being made. By not closing these loopholes and allowing this sick behavior, we are encouraging people to profit from violating the state animal cruelty laws. This must be stopped!
>
> H.R. 1887 will put a stop to this offensive behavior. This legislation is narrowly tailored to prohibit the creation, sale or possession of a depiction of animal cruelty in interstate commerce for commercial gain. H.R. 1887 does not preempt state laws on animal cruelty. Rather, it incorporates the animal cruelty law of the state where the offense occurs.
>
> I urge all of my colleagues to join me in pursuing this legislation which will put an end to profiting from these disgusting criminal acts.

H.R. 1887 banned the creation, sale, or possession of a "depiction of animal cruelty" when the person who engages in such activity has knowledge of it and does so "with the intention of placing that depiction in interstate or foreign commerce for commercial gain."[187] The bill defined "depiction of animal cruelty" as:

> [A]ny visual or auditory depiction, including any photograph, motion-picture film, video recording, electronic image, or sound recording of conduct in which a living animal is intentionally maimed, mutilated, tortured, wounded, or killed, if such conduct is illegal under Federal law or the law of the State in which the creation, sale, or possession takes place, regardless of whether the maiming, mutilation, torture, wounding, or killing took place in the State.[188]

Despite Gallegly's expressed commitment to protect freedom of speech by drafting the bill very narrowly, the original bill was clearly broad. H.R. 1887 banned the use of films for educational purposes and, by relying on

187. H.R. 1887, 106th Cong. § 1 (1999).

188. *Id.* § (1)(b)(1).

state law, it expanded the scope of illegal conduct. In September 1999, four months after introducing H.R. 1887, Representative Gallegly acknowledged that it contained some "unforeseen problems;" he soon introduced an amendment to his original bill. The amendment defined an exception to the term "animal cruelty" to exclude "any depiction that has serious political, scientific, educational, historical, or artistic value."

In September 1999, the Subcommittee on Crime of the Committee on the Judiciary held a one-day hearing on H.R. 1887. The witnesses appearing before the Subcommittee included Representative Gallegly, two members of the Ventura County District Attorney Office who had investigated the crush films, and an animal rights activist. The Subcommittee did not invite any First Amendment experts or other interested parties.

The House Committee Report that accompanied H.R. 1887 was titled "Punishing Depictions of Animal Cruelty," and indeed it focused on the federal government's "interest in regulating the treatment of animals." The Report emphasized the values of preventing animal cruelty and the importance of "[o]rganizations which work to improve the treatment of animals in our society [and] are active participants in political dialog."

The House Committee Report included the dissenting view of two Congressmen who questioned the legislation's constitutionality. They argued that, while all states have laws that prohibit the underlying animal cruelty inherent in crush videos, the "films of animals being crushed are communications about the acts depicted, not the doing of the acts. Shooting, possessing or selling such films are distinct from the act [of] crushing an animal."

In October 1999, the House passed H.R. 1887 by a vote of 372 to 42. A month later, the Senate passed the bill unanimously. On December 9, 1999, President Clinton signed the bill into law, expressing support for the legislation's objectives that he believed "should assist in reducing or eliminating some of these deplorable and indefensible practices." President Clinton, however, warned that "[i]t is important to avoid constitutional challenge to this legislation and to ensure that the Act does not chill protected speech." To protect the law, President Clinton declared that:

> I will broadly construe the Act's exception and will interpret it to require a determination of the value of the depiction as part of a work or communication, taken as a whole. So construed, the Act would prohibit the types of depictions, described in the statute's legislative history, of wanton cruelty to animals designed to appeal to a prurient interest in sex. I will direct the Department of Justice to enforce the Act accordingly.[189]

H.R. 1887 became law and was codified as 18 U.S.C. § 48, *Depiction of Animal Cruelty*.

Robert Stevens was a Virginian entrepreneur who owned a business selling certain specialized videos and merchandise. He occasionally advertised his products in *Sporting Dog Journal*, an underground publication

---

189. Presidential Statement on Signing Legislation to Establish Federal Criminal Penalties for Commerce in Depiction of Animal Cruelty, 2 PUB. PAPERS 2245 (Dec. 9, 1999).

featuring articles on illegal dogfighting. In 2003, law enforcement officers purchased from Stevens three videotapes that contained graphic images of dogfighting. Two of these tapes showed old films that were produced in the United States during the 1960s and 1970s. The third one was a gruesome film imported from Japan that showed a pit bull attacking a domesticated pig. Stevens supplemented the three videos with introductions, narration and commentary. He also provided buyers with complementary literature that he had written himself.

In March 2004, a federal grand jury returned a three-count indictment against Stevens. "All three counts charged Stevens with knowingly selling depictions of animal cruelty with the intention of placing those depictions in interstate commerce for commercial gain, in violation of 18 U.S.C. § 48." In November of 2004, "the District Court denied Stevens' motion to dismiss the indictment based on his assertion that § 48 abridged his First Amendment right to freedom of speech," holding that the statute was not substantially overbroad because the exceptions clause sufficiently narrowed the statute to only constitutional applications. The case proceeded to trial, which was the very first time a prosecution under § 48 was tried in court. In January 2005, a jury returned a guilty verdict on each of the three counts. The trial judge sentenced Stevens to thirty-seven months of imprisonment, in addition to three years of supervised release.

Stevens appealed his conviction to the Third Circuit Court of Appeals. The en banc court declared § 48 facially unconstitutional and vacated Stevens' conviction, holding that § 48 could not survive strict scrutiny as a content-based regulation of protected speech and declining to recognize a new category of unprotected speech for animal cruelty. The Third Circuit stressed that "[t]he *acts* of animal cruelty * * * are reprehensible, and indeed warrant strong legal sanctions," but distinguished the criminalization of animal cruelty from its depiction.[190]

The federal government appealed this decision to the United States Supreme Court.

United States v. Stevens

130 S.Ct. 1577 (2010)

■ CHIEF JUSTICE ROBERTS delivered the opinion of the Court.

Congress enacted 18 U.S.C. § 48 to criminalize the commercial creation, sale, or possession of certain depictions of animal cruelty. The statute does not address underlying acts harmful to animals, but only portrayals of such conduct. The question presented is whether the prohibition in the statute is consistent with the freedom of speech guaranteed by the First Amendment.

Section 48 establishes a criminal penalty of up to five years in prison for anyone who knowingly "creates, sells, or possesses a depiction of animal cruelty," if done "for commercial gain" in interstate or foreign commerce. § 48(a). A depiction of "animal cruelty" is defined as one "in which a living animal is intentionally maimed, mutilated, tortured, wounded, or killed," if

---

190. United States v. Stevens, 533 F.3d 218, 220–21 (3d Cir. 2008) (en banc).

that conduct violates federal or state law where "the creation, sale, or possession takes place." § 48(c)(1). In what is referred to as the "exceptions clause," the law exempts from prohibition any depiction "that has serious religious, political, scientific, educational, journalistic, historical, or artistic value." § 48(b).

The legislative background of § 48 focused primarily on the interstate market for "crush videos." According to the House Committee Report on the bill, such videos feature the intentional torture and killing of helpless animals, including cats, dogs, monkeys, mice, and hamsters * * *. Crush videos often depict women slowly crushing animals to death "with their bare feet or while wearing high heeled shoes," sometimes while "talking to the animals in a kind of dominatrix patter" over "[t]he cries and squeals of the animals, obviously in great pain." * * * Apparently these depictions "appeal to persons with a very specific sexual fetish who find them sexually arousing or otherwise exciting." * * * The acts depicted in crush videos are typically prohibited by the animal cruelty laws enacted by all 50 States and the District of Columbia * * *. But crush videos rarely disclose the participants' identities, inhibiting prosecution of the underlying conduct. * * *

This case, however, involves an application of § 48 to depictions of animal fighting. Dogfighting, for example, is unlawful in all 50 States and the District of Columbia * * * and has been restricted by federal law since 1976. * * *

We read § 48 to create a criminal prohibition of alarming breadth. To begin with, the text of the statute's ban on a "depiction of animal cruelty" nowhere requires that the depicted conduct be cruel. That text applies to "any * * * depiction" in which "a living animal is intentionally maimed, mutilated, tortured, wounded, or killed." § 48(c)(1). "[M]aimed, mutilated, [and] tortured" convey cruelty, but "wounded" or "killed" do not suggest any such limitation.

The Government contends that the terms in the definition should be read to require the additional element of "accompanying acts of cruelty." * * * But the phrase "wounded * * * or killed" at issue here contains little ambiguity. The Government's opening brief properly applies the ordinary meaning of these words, stating for example that to " 'kill' is 'to deprive of life.' " * * * We agree that "wounded" and "killed" should be read according to their ordinary meaning. * * * Nothing about that meaning requires cruelty.

While not requiring cruelty, § 48 does require that the depicted conduct be "illegal." But this requirement does not limit § 48 along the lines the Government suggests. There are myriad federal and state laws concerning the proper treatment of animals, but many of them are not designed to guard against animal cruelty. Protections of endangered species, for example, restrict even the humane "wound[ing] or kill[ing]" of "living animal[s]." § 48(c)(1). Livestock regulations are often designed to protect the health of human beings, and hunting and fishing rules (seasons, licensure, bag limits, weight requirements) can be designed to raise revenue, preserve animal populations, or prevent accidents. The text of § 48(c) draws no distinction based on the reason the intentional killing of an animal is made illegal, and includes, for example, the humane slaughter of a stolen cow.

What is more, the application of § 48 to depictions of illegal conduct extends to conduct that is illegal in only a single jurisdiction. Under subsection (c)(1), the depicted conduct need only be illegal in "the State in which the creation, sale, or possession takes place, regardless of whether the ... wounding ... or killing took place in [that] State." A depiction of entirely lawful conduct runs afoul of the ban if that depiction later finds its way into another State where the same conduct is unlawful. This provision greatly expands the scope of § 48, because although there may be "a broad societal consensus" against cruelty to animals, ... there is substantial disagreement on what types of conduct are properly regarded as cruel. Both views about cruelty to animals and regulations having no connection to cruelty vary widely from place to place.

In the District of Columbia, for example, all hunting is unlawful. * * * Other jurisdictions permit or encourage hunting, and there is an enormous national market for hunting-related depictions in which a living animal is intentionally killed. Hunting periodicals have circulations in the hundreds of thousands or millions * * * and hunting television programs, videos, and Web sites are equally popular * * *. The demand for hunting depictions exceeds the estimated demand for crush videos or animal fighting depictions by several orders of magnitude. Compare * * * Brief for National Rifle Association of America, Inc., as Amicus Curiae 12 (hereinafter NRA Brief) (estimating that hunting magazines alone account for $135 million in annual retail sales) with Brief for United States 43–44, 46 (suggesting $1 million in crush video sales per year, and noting that Stevens earned $57,000 from his videos). Nonetheless, because the statute allows each jurisdiction to export its laws to the rest of the country, § 48(a) extends to *any* magazine or video depicting lawful hunting, so long as that depiction is sold within the Nation's Capital.

Those seeking to comply with the law thus face a bewildering maze of regulations from at least 56 separate jurisdictions. Some States permit hunting with crossbows, * * * while others forbid it * * *, or restrict it only to the disabled. * * * Missouri allows the "canned" hunting of ungulates held in captivity, * * * but Montana restricts such hunting to certain bird species. * * * The sharp-tailed grouse may be hunted in Idaho, but not in Washington. * * *

The disagreements among the States * * * extend well beyond hunting. State agricultural regulations permit different methods of livestock slaughter in different places or as applied to different animals. * * * Even cockfighting, long considered immoral in much of America * * * is legal in Puerto Rico * * * and was legal in Louisiana until 2008. * * * An otherwise-lawful image of any of these practices, if sold or possessed for commercial gain within a State that happens to forbid the practice, falls within the prohibition of § 48(a).

The only thing standing between defendants who sell such depictions and five years in federal prison-other than the mercy of a prosecutor-is the statute's exceptions clause. Subsection (b) exempts from prohibition "any depiction that has serious religious, political, scientific, educational, journalistic, historical, or artistic value." The Government argues that this clause substantially narrows the statute's reach: News reports about animal cruelty have "journalistic" value; pictures of bullfights in Spain have "historical" value; and instructional hunting videos have "educational" value. * * * Thus, the Government argues, § 48 reaches only crush videos, depictions of animal fighting (other than Spanish bullfighting * * * and perhaps other depictions of "extreme acts of animal cruelty."

The Government's attempt to narrow the statutory ban, however, requires an unrealistically broad reading of the exceptions clause. * * * But the text says "serious" value, and "serious" should be taken seriously. We decline the Government's invitation-advanced for the first time in this Court-to regard as "serious" anything that is not "scant." * * *

Quite apart from the requirement of "serious" value in § 48(b), the excepted speech must also fall within one of the enumerated categories. Much speech does not. Most hunting videos, for example, are not obviously instructional in nature, except in the sense that all life is a lesson. According to Safari Club International and the Congressional Sportsmen's Foundation, many popular videos "have primarily entertainment value" and are designed to "entertai[n] the viewer, marke[t] hunting equipment, or increas[e] the hunting community." Brief for Safari Club International *et al.* as Amici Curiae 12. The National Rifle Association agrees that "much of the content of hunting media * * * is merely recreational in nature." NRA Brief 28. The Government offers no principled explanation why these depictions of hunting or depictions of Spanish bullfights would be inherently valuable while those of Japanese dogfights are not. The dissent contends that hunting depictions must have serious value because hunting has serious value, in a way that dogfights presumably do not. * * * But § 48(b) addresses the value of the depictions, not of the underlying activity. There is simply no adequate reading of the exceptions clause that results in the statute's banning only the depictions the Government would like to ban. * * *

Not to worry, the Government says: The Executive Branch construes § 48 to reach only "extreme" cruelty * * * and it "neither has brought nor will bring a prosecution for anything less." * * * The Government hits this theme hard, invoking its prosecutorial discretion several times * * *. But the First Amendment protects against the Government; it does not leave us at the mercy of noblesse oblige. We would not uphold an unconstitutional statute merely because the Government promised to use it responsibly. * * *

This prosecution is itself evidence of the danger in putting faith in government representations of prosecutorial restraint. When this legislation was enacted, the Executive Branch announced that it would interpret § 48 as covering only depictions "of wanton cruelty to animals designed to appeal to a prurient interest in sex." See Statement by President William J. Clinton upon Signing H.R. 1887, 34 Weekly Comp. Pres. Doc. 2557 (Dec. 9, 1999). No one suggests that the videos in this case fit that description. The Government's assurance that it will apply § 48 far more restrictively than its language provides is pertinent only as an implicit acknowledgment of the potential constitutional problems with a more natural reading.

* * *

Our construction of § 48 decides the constitutional question; the Government makes no effort to defend the constitutionality of § 48 as applied beyond crush videos and depictions of animal fighting. It argues that those particular depictions are intrinsically related to criminal conduct or are analogous to obscenity (if not themselves obscene), and that the ban on such speech is narrowly tailored to reinforce restrictions on the underlying conduct, prevent additional crime arising from the depictions, or safeguard public mores. But the Government nowhere attempts to extend these arguments to depictions of any other activities—depictions that are presumptively protected by the First Amendment but that remain subject to the criminal sanctions of § 48. * * * However "growing" and "lucrative" the markets for crush videos and dogfighting depictions might be * * * they are dwarfed by the market for other depictions, such as hunting magazines and videos, that we have determined to be within the scope of § 48. * * * We therefore need not and do not decide whether a statute limited to crush videos or other depictions of extreme animal cruelty would be constitutional. We hold only that § 48 is not so limited but is instead substantially overbroad, and therefore invalid under the First Amendment.

The judgment of the United States Court of Appeals for the Third Circuit is affirmed.

It is so ordered.

■ JUSTICE ALITO, dissenting.

The Court strikes down in its entirety a valuable statute, 18 U.S.C. § 48, that was enacted not to suppress speech, but to prevent horrific acts of animal cruelty—in particular, the creation and commercial exploitation of "crush videos," a form of depraved entertainment that has no social value. The Court's approach, which has the practical effect of legalizing the sale of such videos and is thus likely to spur a resumption of their production, is unwarranted. Respondent was convicted under § 48 for selling videos depicting dogfights. On appeal, he argued, among other things, that § 48 is unconstitutional as applied to the facts of this case, and he highlighted features of those videos that might distinguish them from other dogfight videos brought to our attention * * *. Today's decision * * * strikes down § 48 using what has been aptly termed the "strong medicine" of the overbreadth doctrine. * * *

I do not have the slightest doubt that Congress, in enacting § 48, had no intention of restricting the creation, sale, or possession of depictions of hunting. Proponents of the law made this point clearly. See H.R. Rep. No. 106–397, p. 8 (1999) (hereinafter H.R. Rep.) ("[D]epictions of ordinary hunting and fishing activities do not fall within the scope of the statute"); 145 Cong. Rec. 25894 (Oct. 19, 1999) (Rep. McCollum) ("[T]he sale of depictions of legal activities, such as hunting and fishing, would not be illegal under this bill"); *id.*, at 25895 (Rep. Smith) ("[L]et us be clear as to what this legislation will not do. It will in no way prohibit hunting, fishing, or wildlife videos"). Indeed, even opponents acknowledged that § 48 was not intended to reach ordinary hunting depictions. See ibid. (Rep. Scott); *id.*, at 25897 (Rep. Paul).

For these reasons, I am convinced that § 48 has no application to depictions of hunting. * * *

§ 48 may validly be applied to at least two broad real-world categories of expression covered by the statute: crush videos and dogfighting videos. Thus, the statute has a substantial core of constitutionally permissible applications. * * * I would reject respondent's claim that § 48 is facially unconstitutional under the overbreadth doctrine.

For these reasons, I respectfully dissent.

Notes

A day after the Supreme Court delivered its decision in *Stevens*, Representative Elton Gallegly rushed to fill the void with a bill amending § 48 to ban "animal crush videos,"[191] rather than "depictions of animal cruelty."[192] First amendment experts advised Congress that bill was still too broad.

On September 27, 2010, Senator Kyl introduced S. 3841, The Animal Crush Video Prohibition Act of 2010. Senator Kyl's introductory statement underscored the obscene nature of crush videos, stressing that his bill "would ban animal crush videos that fit squarely within the obscenity doctrine, a well-established exception to the First Amendment." Senator Kyl also referred to the "long-history of prohibiting speech that is essential to criminal conduct," stating that "[i]n the case of animal crush videos, the videos themselves drive the criminal conduct depicted in them."[193]

The final form of H.R. 5566 captured the language of Senator Kyl's bill and focused on the obscene nature of crush videos as a specific criterion for their prohibition.[194] The bill defined "animal crush video" as

> [A]ny photograph, motion-picture film, video or digital recording, or electronic image that—
>
> (1) depicts actual conduct in which 1 or more living non-human mammals, birds, reptiles, or amphibians is intentionally crushed, burned, drowned, suffocated, impaled, or otherwise subjected to serious bodily injury * * *; and
>
> (2) is obscene.[195]

---

191. H.R. 5092, 111th Cong. (2010). The bill defined "animal crush video" as:

[A]ny visual depiction, including any photograph, motion-picture film, video recording, or electronic image, which depicts animals being intentionally crushed, burned, drowned, or impaled, that

(A) depicts actual conduct in which a living animal is tortured, maimed, or mutilated that violates any criminal prohibition on intentional cruelty under Federal law or the law of the State in which the depiction is sold; and

(B) taken as a whole, does not have religious, political, scientific, educational, journalistic, historical, or artistic value.

192. H.R. 5092, 111th Cong. (2010).

193. 156 CONG. REC. S7509 (daily ed. Sept. 27, 2010) (statement of Sen. Kyl).

194. H.R. 5566, 111th Cong. (2010) (as referred in Senate, July 22, 2010).

195. *Id.* § 3(a).

H.R. 5566 specifically exempted visual depictions of "customary and normal veterinary or agricultural husbandry practices," "the slaughter of animals for food," and "hunting, trapping, or fishing." The bill also exempted good-faith distribution to law enforcement officers and to third parties to determine whether a referral to a law enforcement agency is appropriate.

On December 9, 2010, President Obama signed into law H.R. 5566, the "Animal Crush Video Prohibition Act of 2010."

Questions

1. Senator Gallegly's 1999 bill received the overwhelming support of the House of Representatives. Only 42 members voted against it. In the Senate, the bill gained a unanimous vote. In *United States v. Stevens*, the Court referred several times to the NRA amicus brief, endorsing several of the organization's arguments regarding the unconstitutionality of the 1999 Act. The NRA has always found many representatives and senators committed to protect Second Amendment rights. Why would these members of Congress support the 1999 Act?

2. The Humane Society invested political and other capital in crush video legislation. What were gains and losses of the organization in the process?

§ 2.4.3c Agreements With Interest Groups

Sanders v. Brown

504 F.3d 903 (9th Cir. 2007)

■ CLIFTON, CIRCUIT JUDGE:

This case involves an indirect legal challenge to the massive settlement agreement between the nation's largest tobacco companies and the attorneys general of 46 states and several territories. The 1998 settlement known as the Master Settlement Agreement, or "MSA," resolved all of these states' and territories' claims against those tobacco companies, which the states had sued for billions of dollars in damages related to the harmful effects of smoking.

Plaintiff Steve Sanders, a smoker, alleges that cigarette prices have skyrocketed in the nine years since the MSA, and that the price increases are the result of an illegal price-fixing scheme that the MSA enabled. On behalf of a putative class of cigarette smokers, Sanders sued the Attorney General of the State of California and the four largest tobacco companies: Philip Morris USA Inc., R.J. Reynolds Tobacco Co., Brown & Williamson Tobacco Corp., and Lorillard Tobacco Co. Sanders does not allege that the MSA itself is illegal, but rather alleges that the MSA, the post-MSA price increases, and the state statutes implementing the MSA's terms (the "implementing statutes") are evidence of a cigarette price-fixing cartel that violates the Sherman Act, 15 U.S.C. § 1 *et seq.*; the Cartwright Act, Cal. Bus. & Prof.Code §§ 16720 *et seq.*; other California unfair competition statutes, Cal. Bus. & Prof.Code §§ 17200 *et seq.*; and California's common law of unfair competition. Sanders also alleges that the Sherman Act preempts the implementing statutes.

The defendants moved to dismiss. * * * The district court granted the motions. * * * We affirm.

I. Background

The United States cigarette market is dominated by four companies: Philip Morris USA Inc., R.J. Reynolds Tobacco Co., Brown & Williamson Tobacco Corp., and Lorillard Tobacco Co. Their combined sales have accounted for more than 90 percent of cigarette sales for at least the last decade.

These four companies in the 1990s faced coordinated lawsuits by the attorneys general of most states and U.S. territories, who sought money and other relief to help their governments cope with the harmful effects of smoking and the costs imposed by those effects. In late 1998, the tobacco companies and the attorneys general signed the MSA. State courts, including the California Superior Court, then approved the MSA in consent decrees and dismissed the lawsuits against the tobacco companies.

The MSA requires the four major tobacco companies—who, as the initial signatories of the MSA, are known as the "Original Participating Manufacturers"—to pay the states billions of dollars each year. The total annual payments are based on a formula that considers inflation and the total number of individual cigarettes sold in the fifty United States, the District of Columbia and Puerto Rico. Each Original Participating Manufacturer (or "OPM") must annually contribute a portion of the total payment that is equal to the OPM's share of that year's cigarette sales (the OPM's "market share"). For example, if an OPM's market share is 25 percent, that OPM must contribute 25 percent of that year's settlement payment.

The OPMs expected to raise cigarette prices to help pay for the settlement and feared that smaller manufacturers, which were not part of the negotiations, would seize the chance to compete with cheaper cigarettes, possibly cutting into the OPMs' market share. The settling parties addressed this problem in three ways. First, the MSA offered a carrot to non-OPM tobacco companies to join the settlement agreement. These "Subsequent Participating Manufacturers" ("SPMs") could join the settlement within 90 days of the enactment of the MSA. They would not have to make any part of the payments due to the states so long as their market share remained at or below their 1998 market share (or 125 percent of their 1997 market share, whichever was greater). If an SPM's market share increased, however, the SPM would have to contribute to the settlement payment, with the contribution based on the sales in excess of the SPM's 1998 sales (or 125 percent of 1997 sales, if applicable). For example, if an SPM sold 250,000 cigarettes in 1998, and then one year later sold a larger share of the market-say, 300,000 cigarettes-the SPM would have to contribute to the settlement payment. If the extra 50,000 cigarettes equaled 1 percent of the market share, the SPM would have to pay 1 percent of the settlement payment. As of August 15, 2007, forty-four smaller tobacco companies are participating in the MSA as SPMs.

Second, the OPMs would pay less money under the MSA if their total sales dropped below a certain amount. If the reason for this drop is competition by tobacco companies that did not participate in the MSA, the settlement payment would be reduced even further.

Third, most states have enacted two sets of statutes that allegedly make it harder for non-signatory tobacco companies (and any future market entrants) to undercut the OPMs' and SPMs' market shares. Sanders alleges that the states were motivated to pass these statutes out of fear that the OPMs' higher prices would cause their market share to fall, thereby reducing the amount of the settlement payments to the states. These "implementing statutes" are known in most states as the "Qualifying Act" and the "Contraband Amendment."

Under the "Qualifying Act," non-signatory tobacco companies (also known as "Non–Participating Manufacturers," or "NPMs") have to pay a portion of their revenues into an escrow account. The money in the escrow account acts as a liability reserve. If the NPMs are successfully sued for cigarette-related harms, the money in the escrow accounts will pay the damage awards. Each NPM's payment is based on market share, and is roughly the same per-cigarette cost as the amount that OPMs must pay to abide by the MSA. The payments can only be used to pay a judgment or settlement on a claim against the NPM, up to the amount that the NPM would otherwise pay under the MSA. Any remaining funds in the escrow account revert back to the NPM after twenty-five years.

This law allegedly prevents the NPMs from undercutting the prices of OPMs' cigarettes by taking away the extra profitability that an NPM would enjoy. For example, say that OPMs' sales are such that for a given year, they must pay 25 cents per cigarette to the states under the MSA. This would seem to give NPMs a cost advantage of 25 cents per cigarette. But under the Qualifying Act, if an NPM also sold cigarettes that year, the NPM would have to pay roughly 25 cents per cigarette into an escrow account, which the NPM could not touch for 25 years. In other words, the NPM's cost advantage over the OPMs is erased.

The "Contraband Amendment," for its part, penalizes NPMs who refuse to make escrow payments under the Qualifying Act. The Contraband Amendment allows a state to "de-list" NPMs from a list of approved tobacco manufacturers. De-listing effectively prevents the offending NPM from selling cigarettes in that state.

The California legislature has enacted a Qualifying Act and a Contraband Amendment. Cal. Health & Safety Code §§ 104556, 104557 (Qualifying Act); Cal. Bus. & Prof.Code § 22979(a), (b), and Cal. Rev. & Tax Code § 30165.1(d), (e) (Contraband Amendment).

As expected, the OPMs' cigarette prices rose when the MSA took effect. Sanders alleges, however, that the price increases have far exceeded the tobacco companies' costs of complying with the MSA. The OPMs allegedly raised their prices by $12.20 per carton between late 1998 and early 2002—more than twice the amount necessary to meet the OPMs' obligations under the MSA. Also, the price increases have been "parallel." Whenever one OPM has raised its cigarette prices, the others have generally matched the increase. Despite these increases, the OPMs' cigarette sales still account for more than 90 percent of the market.

The price increases and other factors have prompted several legal challenges against the MSA, most alleging antitrust and constitutional violations. The challenges have been largely unsuccessful. * * *

II. The Present Case

Sanders alleges that the MSA has spawned a "cartel" because it lets the participating tobacco companies "raise prices without fear of losing sales or market share." Sanders does not allege that the tobacco companies have agreed amongst themselves to fix prices. Instead, he alleges that the MSA penalizes tobacco companies for competing on price, because they have to pay more money under the MSA as their market shares increase. As a result, tobacco companies allegedly will be reluctant to increase market share. Thus, when one tobacco company raises its prices, all other tobacco companies allegedly can raise prices in lockstep without fearing that their rivals will try to undercut them. "[I]n effect," the complaint alleges, "the OPMs have agreed to compensate each other [f]or any market share increase * * * by imposing a proportionate increase in the settlement payment for such market share gain."[4]

Sanders also alleges that the MSA encouraged other tobacco companies to join the cartel. Any company that has joined the MSA as an SPM will be reluctant to increase its market share beyond 1998 levels, because by doing so it would be forced to pay some money to the states.[5] As a result, the SPMs followed the OPMs when they increase their prices.

Sanders further alleges that the MSA encouraged the states to pass anti-competitive laws protecting the alleged cartel from price competition. This is because the OPMs' payments to the states drop if their total sales drop below a threshold level, or if non-signatory NPMs take away OPMs' market share. The states, Sanders alleges, therefore passed the Qualifying Acts and Contraband Amendments to keep NPMs from entering the market.

The sum of these parts, Sanders alleges, is an illegal "horizontal output-restriction cartel" in which the OPMs, backed by state authority (or, at least, state acquiescence), have raised cigarette prices to artificially high (or "supracompetitive") levels without fear of price competition. This scheme is preempted by the Sherman Act, Sanders argues, because it so obviously conflicts with federal antitrust law. Furthermore, Sanders argues that even if the scheme consisting of the MSA and its implementing statutes is not facially preempted, the tobacco defendants have still committed illegal price-fixing, as evidenced by the parallel price increases. Finally, Sanders

4. It is not clear that a proportionate price increase, which would not affect the per-cigarette cost of doing business, would dissuade a tobacco company from attempting to increase its market share. We need not, however, address the merits of this claim, as the following discussion will show.

5. It is not clear whether this extra payment would really dissuade the SPM from seeking extra market share. If an SPM would pay to the states less money than it would make by selling extra cigarettes, an SPM still might turn a higher profit by increasing its market share. Again, we need not address the merits of this claim.

argues that the State of California failed to adequately supervise the tobacco companies' pricing actions.[6]

* * *

III. Analysis

* * *

A. Preemption

Sanders argues that California's Qualifying Act and Contraband Amendment are preempted by Section 1 of the Sherman Act, which states that "[e]very contract, combination in the form of trust or otherwise, or conspiracy, in restraint of trade or commerce * * * is declared to be illegal." 15 U.S.C. § 1. To be preempted by this Act, a state statute must be in "irreconcilable" conflict with the federal antitrust regulatory scheme. * * * The only way such a conflict can exist, according to the Supreme Court, is if the state statute "mandates or authorizes conduct that necessarily constitutes a violation of the antitrust laws in all cases, or if it places irresistible pressure on a private party" to violate those laws. *Fisher v. City of Berkeley*, 475 U.S. 260, 265 (1986). * * *

The statutes do place some pressure on some new entrant tobacco companies to charge higher prices if they decide to enter the market. The Qualifying Act forces NPMs to place into escrow a per-cigarette payment roughly equal to the per-cigarette payment that participating manufacturers pay under the MSA. The Contraband Amendment prevents NPMs who fail to make the escrow payments from distributing their cigarettes. If NPMs wish to remain profitable, they must factor the escrow payments into the prices they charge per cigarette. The statutes thus may cause higher prices and dissuade some potential market entrants. Nothing, however, forces the NPMs to either peg their prices to those of participating manufacturers, or to refrain altogether from entering the market. If the OPMs really are charging artificially high prices, and thus making artificially high profits, an NPM conceivably could compete on price by charging a "normal" price and still make a "normal" profit, even taking the escrow payment into account.

Sanders therefore has failed to adequately allege that the implementing statutes mandate or authorize conduct that "in all cases" violates federal antitrust law. * * * The implementing statutes are thus not preempted by the Sherman Act. * * *

---

6. The relief Sanders seeks includes:

(1) A declaratory judgment that California's Qualifying Act and Contraband Amendment are both "facially void as a per se restraint of trade," and therefore preempted by the Sherman Act.

(2) An injunction against the state to keep it from enforcing the MSA and the implementing statutes, and against the tobacco defendants to make them "cease their anticompetitive activity taken in furtherance of the MSA."

(3) Money damages against the tobacco defendants for operating an illegal price-fixing cartel.

Sanders's complaint also seeks to enjoin implementation of the "anticompetitive provisions" of the MSA. His appeal, however, does not address whether the MSA itself is illegal. Sanders instead argues that the MSA is one part of a larger illegal scheme. We therefore need not address whether the MSA itself would be legal in the absence of the alleged larger scheme.

B. Immunity

Sanders next argues that even if the Sherman Act does not preempt the implementing statutes, the tobacco companies have nonetheless violated the Act by using the MSA and implementing statutes to create a price-fixing cartel. * * *

The defendants argue * * * that even if Sanders has adequately pleaded Sherman Act violations, they are nonetheless immune from prosecution under the *Noerr–Pennington* immunity doctrine, the state action doctrine, or both.

1. Noerr–Pennington immunity

The *Noerr–Pennington* doctrine arises from two Supreme Court cases, *E. R.R. Presidents Conf. v. Noerr Motor Freight, Inc.*, 365 U.S. 127, 135–145 (1961), and *United Mine Workers of America v. Pennington*, 381 U.S. 657, 669–70 (1965). The Court, citing First Amendment and federalism concerns, held that private actors are immune from antitrust liability for petitioning the government, even when the private actors' motives are anticompetitive. *Noerr–Pennington* immunity protects petitions to all departments of the government. * * *

The Supreme Court has interpreted "petitioning" to encompass activities other than legislative lobbying. For example, *Noerr–Pennington* immunity protects private actors when they file court documents and enter contracts with the government. * * *

Neither the Supreme Court nor the Ninth Circuit have specifically held that a settlement agreement like the MSA qualifies as "petitioning" that may be protected by *Noerr–Pennington* immunity. The Seventh Circuit, however, has explicitly held that *Noerr–Pennington* immunity protects private parties from liability for negotiating and entering into settlements or other agreements with the government. *See Campbell v. City of Chicago*, 823 F.2d 1182, 1186–87 (7th Cir.1987). We now join that circuit in so holding.

* * *

The act of negotiating a settlement with a state undoubtedly is a form of speech directed at a government entity. Given the Court's desire to protect free speech from Sherman Act attack, it is clear why *Noerr–Pennington* immunity should protect a private party from liability for such an act. If a person undertaking to negotiate a way out of his legal troubles were to fear that the very act of negotiating would expose him to further liability, he might be afraid to attempt a settlement in the first place. The result would be fewer settlements, even when the parties would otherwise be willing to reach a principled compromise, and more cases dragging on for years to the detriment of all parties, not to mention the court system.

Furthermore, holding that a private party's settlements with the government are exposed to antitrust liability would surely, as the Supreme Court in *Noerr* warned, "substantially impair the power of [state] government to take actions through its legislature and executive that operate to restrain trade." * * * If a state can restrain trade through its "legislature and executive," that means the attorney general, an executive officer, can negotiate trade restraints in the context of litigation, so long as those restraints are not preempted by the Sherman Act.

We therefore hold that *Noerr–Pennington* immunity protects a private party from liability for the act of negotiating a settlement with a state entity. Immunity thus protects the tobacco defendants from liability for the act of negotiating the MSA with the State of California. * * *

2. State action immunity

The State of California, for its part, argues that state action immunity, or "*Parker* immunity," protects it from liability both for entering into the MSA and for enacting the implementing statutes. We agree.

The *Parker* immunity doctrine protects most state laws and actions from antitrust liability. The doctrine originated in *Parker v. Brown*, 317 U.S. 341, 350–52 (1943). In *Parker*, the Court dismissed a Sherman Act challenge to a California law that restricted competition among raisin manufacturers. The Court held that nothing in the Sherman Act suggests its purpose is "to restrain a state or its officers or agents from activities directed by its legislature." * * * Thus, even a state law that would violate the Sherman Act is immune from attack on antitrust grounds * * *. The only exception to this rule is a state law that attempts to "give immunity to those who violate the Sherman Act by authorizing them to violate it, or by declaring that their action is lawful." * * *

Since the California attorney general's act of entering into the MSA is a sovereign act, as are the legislature's actions in enacting the Qualifying Act and Contraband Amendment, the state is immune from antitrust liability for these actions, unless the MSA scheme is an attempt to "give immunity to those who violate the Sherman Act by authorizing them to violate it, or by declaring that their action is lawful." *Parker*, 317 U.S. at 351. The MSA and the implementing statutes authorize no illegal activity, as we discussed above. * * * We therefore hold that *Parker* immunity protects the state from antitrust liability for entering into the MSA and for passing the implementing statutes.

* * *

D. Conclusion

Sanders has failed to show that the MSA implementing statutes are *per se* illegal under the Sherman Act. Sanders also has failed to show that any of the defendants are liable under either the Sherman Act or under California antitrust law. Sanders therefore has failed to state a claim entitling him to relief, and the district court properly dismissed his lawsuit.

Affirmed.

Questions

1. In *Sanders v. Brown*, the plaintiff challenged an agreement between the tobacco industry and 46 states, arguing it improperly served industry

members.[196] The Ninth Circuit affirmed the district's court's grant of summary judgment in favor of the defendants. Three years earlier, in *Freedom Holdings Inc v. Spitzer*,[197] the Second Circuit ruled on a similar challenge against the MSA. In finding a Sherman Act violation, the court held that:

> The alleged arrangement, even without the protection of the Contraband Statutes as enforced by wholesalers, would be a *per se* violation because it is a naked restraint on competition. * * * With the Contraband Statutes in force, the scheme as alleged threatens to become a permanent, nationwide cartel. * * * Had the executives of the major tobacco companies entered into such an arrangement without the involvement of the States and their attorneys general, those executives would long ago have had depressing conversations with their attorneys about the United States Sentencing Guidelines. * * * We therefore hold that appellants have sufficiently alleged a *per se* violation of the Sherman Act.[198]

Under the MSA, the tobacco industry agreed to pay the states $206 billion over 25 years and to certain advertising restrictions. Can such a costly agreement serve collusion?

2. Consumer welfare is the stated goal of U.S. antitrust laws.[199] Assume that the MSA does serve the interests of participating industry members. Does the agreement between the states and the industry necessarily sacrifice public interests or consumer welfare? What injury did the plaintiff, Steve Sanders, experience?

3. *Sanders v. Brown* applies *Noerr–Pennington* immunity, which shields private parties from antitrust liability for lobbying or otherwise influencing public decisionmakers. This immunity applies even though a party's motives may be to promote private interests such as suppression of competition. What may be the justifications for such immunity? What are the differences between *Noerr–Pennington* immunity and state action immunity?

§ 2.4.3d The Judiciary and Interest Groups

The Coase Theorem provides that, in the absence of sources of market inefficiency such as transaction costs, markets are efficient and hence government regulation is unnecessary.[200]

One corollary of the Coase Theorem is that regulation may be needed when parties cannot efficiently reach private agreements or settle disputes. In practice, interest groups use legal disputes to shape legal rules. Private

---

196. Several commentators shared this view. *See, e.g.*, ANDREW P. MORRISS ET AL., REGULATION BY LITIGATION 126–159 (2008).

197. 357 F.3d 205 (2d Cir. 2004).

198. *Id.* at 226.

199. *See generally* Barak Orbach, *The Antitrust Consumer Welfare Paradox*, 7 JOURNAL OF COMPETITION LAW & ECONOMICS 133 (2010).

200. Despite its tautological nature, the Theorem offers many insights. *See* § 3.1.2.

and public parties often use lawsuits to influence legal rules that govern industries, or obtain concessions, and squeeze rents from industries.[201] The 1998 MSA between 46 states and the four largest U.S. tobacco companies is an example of a party using litigation to impose regulatory constraints on an industry.[202] Firearms litigation also demonstrates how interest groups may use lawsuits against regulation.[203] In *United States v. Stevens*,[204] one interest group was involved in the legislative process and others became active when Mr. Stevens challenged the constitutionality of the regulation in court. Many, if not most, of the concerns regarding the influence of interest groups on the regulatory process can be extended to the influence of interest groups on the judicial process.[205]

First and foremost, unlike other public decisionmakers, judges do not select their cases. When they have the opportunity to analyze a regulatory issue, the case brought by the litigating parties addresses certain narrow issues related to very specific circumstances.[206] Sophisticated interest groups actively select cases that are more likely to serve their interests than to promote "good law."[207]

Second, litigation is often advantageous to well-funded interest groups. Wealthy parties can hire better lawyers and experts than their adversaries, and they can strategically bankrupt opponents with transaction costs, thereby discouraging future litigation and claims against them.

Third, 39 states elect their judges, and in these states judicial candidates seek campaign contributions that at least theoretically make them vulnerable to interest groups.

A 2006 study of *The New York Times* shows that, in the states that elect their judges by popular election, many of these candidates raised $2

---

201. *See, e.g.*, ANDREW P. MORRISS ET AL., REGULATION BY LITIGATION (2009); W. KIP VISCUSI ED., REGULATION THROUGH LITIGATION (2002).

202. *See* W. Kip Viscusi & Joni Hersch, *Tobacco Regulation Through Litigation: The Master Settlement Agreement*, in REGULATION VS. LITIGATION 71 (2011).

203. *See* District of Columbia v. Heller, 554 U.S. 570 (2008). McDonald v. Chicago, 130 S.Ct. 3020 (2010). *See also* Philip J. Cook et al., *Gun Control After* Heller: *Litigating Against Regulation*, in REGULATION VS. LITIGATION 103 (2011).

204. 130 S.Ct. 1577 (2010). *See* § 2.5.2.

205. *See generally* Einer R. Elhauge, *Does Interest Group Theory Justify More Intrusive Judicial Review?*, 101 YALE LAW JOURNAL 31 (1991); Frederick Schauer, *Do Cases Make Bad Law?* 73 UNIVERSITY OF CHICAGO LAW REVIEW 883 (2006). *See also* Thomas W. Merrill, *Capture Theory and the Courts: 1967–1983*, 72 CHICAGO-KENT LAW REVIEW 1039 (1997) (documenting a trend among many federal judges who were convinced that agencies were prone to capture and related defects and felt they were in a position to do something about it); John Shepard Wiley Jr., *A Capture Theory of Antitrust Federalism*, 99 HARVARD LAW REVIEW 713 (1986) (same).

206. *See generally* Richard A. Posner, *Regulation (Agencies) versus Litigation (Courts): An Analytical Framework*, in REGULATION VS. LITIGATION: PERSPECTIVES FROM ECONOMICS AND LAW (Daniel P. Kessler ed. 2011); Steven Shavell, *Liability for Harm versus Regulation for Safety*, 13 JOURNAL OF LEGAL STUDIES 357 (1984); Donald Wittman, *Prior Regulation versus Post Liability: The Choice Between Input and Output Monitoring*, 6 JOURNAL OF LEGAL STUDIES 193 (1977).

207. *See* Lynn M. LoPucki & Walter O. Weyrauch, *A Theory of Legal Strategy*, 49 DUKE LAW JOURNAL 1405 (2000).

million or more for their election campaigns.[208] The study also found that, in Ohio, "justices routinely sat on cases after receiving campaign contributions from the parties involved or from groups that filed supporting briefs. On average, judges voted in favor of their contributors 70 percent of the time. Justice [Terrence] O'Donnell voted for his contributors 91 percent of the time, the highest rate of any justice on the court." The study also finds that a significant portion of the corporate contributions came after the court agreed to hear the case but before a decision was actually reached.

In a letter responding to the findings of *The New York Times*, Justice O'Donnell wrote:[209]

> The Ohio Constitution provides for the popular election of all judges in Ohio and in 1987, the voters overwhelmingly rejected efforts to change that process. Thus, all judges in Ohio are compelled to run in contested judicial races and they are permitted * * * to raise funds for advertising. Judges, however, are not permitted to personally solicit or accept campaign contributions. * * *
>
> Any effort to link judicial campaign contributions * * * to case outcomes is misleading and erodes public confidence in the judiciary. Everyone knows that correlation is not equivalent to causation.

Caperton v. A.T. Massey Coal Co., Inc.

556 U.S. 868 (2009)

■ JUSTICE KENNEDY delivered the opinion of the Court.

In this case the Supreme Court of Appeals of West Virginia reversed a trial court judgment, which had entered a jury verdict of $50 million. Five justices heard the case, and the vote to reverse was 3 to 2. The question presented is whether the Due Process Clause of the Fourteenth Amendment was violated when one of the justices in the majority denied a recusal motion. The basis for the motion was that the justice had received campaign contributions in an extraordinary amount from, and through the efforts of, the board chairman and principal officer of the corporation found liable for the damages.

Under our precedents there are objective standards that require recusal when "the probability of actual bias on the part of the judge or decisionmaker is too high to be constitutionally tolerable." * * * Applying those precedents, we find that, in all the circumstances of this case, due process requires recusal.

In August 2002 a West Virginia jury returned a verdict that found respondents A.T. Massey Coal Co. and its affiliates (hereinafter Massey) liable for fraudulent misrepresentation, concealment, and tortious interference with existing contractual relations. The jury awarded petitioners

---

208. Adam Liptak and Janet Roberts, *Campaign Cash Mirrors a High Court's Rulings*, NEW YORK TIMES, October 1, 2006, at A1.

209. Undated letter to *The New York Times*.

Hugh Caperton, Harman Development Corp., Harman Mining Corp., and Sovereign Coal Sales (hereinafter Caperton) the sum of $50 million in compensatory and punitive damages.

In June 2004 the state trial court denied Massey's post-trial motions challenging the verdict and the damages award, finding that Massey "intentionally acted in utter disregard of [Caperton's] rights and ultimately destroyed [Caperton's] businesses because, after conducting cost-benefit analyses, [Massey] concluded it was in its financial interest to do so." * * * In March 2005 the trial court denied Massey's motion for judgment as a matter of law.

Don Blankenship is Massey's chairman, chief executive officer, and president. After the verdict but before the appeal, West Virginia held its 2004 judicial elections. Knowing the Supreme Court of Appeals of West Virginia would consider the appeal in the case, Blankenship decided to support an attorney who sought to replace Justice McGraw. Justice McGraw was a candidate for reelection to that court. The attorney who sought to replace him was Brent Benjamin.

In addition to contributing the $1,000 statutory maximum to Benjamin's campaign committee, Blankenship donated almost $2.5 million to "And For The Sake Of The Kids," a political organization [that] opposed McGraw and supported Benjamin. * * * Blankenship's donations accounted for more than two-thirds of the total funds it raised. * * * This was not all. Blankenship spent, in addition, just over $500,000 on independent expenditures-for direct mailings and letters soliciting donations as well as television and newspaper advertisements—"to support * * * Brent Benjamin." * * *

To provide some perspective, Blankenship's $3 million in contributions were more than the total amount spent by all other Benjamin supporters and three times the amount spent by Benjamin's own committee. * * * Caperton contends that Blankenship spent $1 million more than the total amount spent by the campaign committees of both candidates combined. * * * Benjamin won. He received 382,036 votes (53.3%), and McGraw received 334,301 votes (46.7%). * * *

In October 2005, before Massey filed its petition for appeal in West Virginia's highest court, Caperton moved to disqualify now-Justice Benjamin under the Due Process Clause and the West Virginia Code of Judicial Conduct, based on the conflict caused by Blankenship's campaign involvement. Justice Benjamin denied the motion in April 2006. He indicated that he "carefully considered the bases and accompanying exhibits proffered by the movants." But he found "no objective information * * * to show that this Justice has a bias for or against any litigant, that this Justice has prejudged the matters which comprise this litigation, or that this Justice will be anything but fair and impartial." * * * In December 2006 Massey filed its petition for appeal to challenge the adverse jury verdict. The West Virginia Supreme Court of Appeals granted review.

In November 2007 that court reversed the $50 million verdict against Massey. The majority opinion, authored by then-Chief Justice Davis and joined by Justices Benjamin and Maynard, found that "Massey's conduct warranted the type of judgment rendered in this case." * * * Justice Starcher dissented, stating that the "majority's opinion is morally and legally wrong." * * * Justice Albright also dissented, accusing the majority of "misapplying the law and introducing sweeping 'new law' into our jurisprudence that may well come back to haunt us." * * *

Caperton sought rehearing, and the parties moved for disqualification of three of the five justices who decided the appeal. Photos had surfaced of Justice Maynard vacationing with Blankenship in the French Riviera while the case was pending. * * * Justice Maynard granted Caperton's recusal motion. On the other side Justice Starcher granted Massey's recusal motion, apparently based on his public criticism of Blankenship's role in the 2004 elections. In his recusal memorandum Justice Starcher urged Justice Benjamin to recuse himself as well. He noted that "Blankenship's bestowal of his personal wealth, political tactics, and 'friendship' have created a cancer in the affairs of this Court." * * * Justice Benjamin declined Justice Starcher's suggestion and denied Caperton's recusal motion.

The court granted rehearing. Justice Benjamin, now in the capacity of acting chief justice, selected Judges Cookman and Fox to replace the recused justices. Caperton moved a third time for disqualification, arguing that Justice Benjamin had failed to apply the correct standard under West Virginia law—*i.e.,* whether "a reasonable and prudent person, knowing these objective facts, would harbor doubts about Justice Benjamin's ability to be fair and impartial." * * * Justice Benjamin again refused to withdraw, noting that the "push poll" was "neither credible nor sufficiently reliable to serve as the basis for an elected judge's disqualification." * * *

In April 2008 a divided court again reversed the jury verdict, and again it was a 3–to–2 decision. Justice Davis filed a modified version of his prior opinion, repeating the two earlier holdings. She was joined by Justice Benjamin and Judge Fox. Justice Albright, joined by Judge Cookman, dissented: "Not only is the majority opinion unsupported by the facts and existing case law, but it is also fundamentally unfair. Sadly, justice was neither honored nor served by the majority." * * * The dissent also noted "genuine due process implications arising under federal law" with respect to Justice Benjamin's failure to recuse himself. * * *

Caperton contends that Blankenship's pivotal role in getting Justice Benjamin elected created a constitutionally intolerable probability of actual bias. Though not a bribe or criminal influence, Justice Benjamin would nevertheless feel a debt of gratitude to Blankenship for his extraordinary efforts to get him elected. That temptation, Caperton claims, is as strong and inherent in human nature. * * *

Justice Benjamin was careful to address the recusal motions and explain his reasons why, on his view of the controlling standard, disqualification was not in order. In four separate opinions issued during the course of the appeal, he explained why no actual bias had been established. He found no basis for recusal because Caperton failed to provide "objective evidence" or "objective information," but merely "subjective belief" of bias * * *. In other words, based on the facts presented by Caperton, Justice Benjamin conducted a probing search into his actual motives and inclinations; and he found none to be improper. We do not question his subjective findings of impartiality and propriety. Nor do we determine whether there was actual bias.

* * * Blankenship's campaign efforts had a significant and disproportionate influence in placing Justice Benjamin on the case. Blankenship contributed some $3 million to unseat the incumbent and replace him with Benjamin. His contributions eclipsed the total amount spent by all other Benjamin supporters and exceeded by 300% the amount spent by Benjamin's campaign committee * * *. Caperton claims Blankenship spent $1 million more than the total amount spent by the campaign committees of both candidates combined. * * *

Massey responds that Blankenship's support, while significant, did not cause Benjamin's victory. In the end the people of West Virginia elected him, and they did so based on many reasons other than Blankenship's efforts. Massey points out that every major state newspaper, but one, endorsed Benjamin. * * * It also contends that then-Justice McGraw cost himself the election by giving a speech during the campaign, a speech the opposition seized upon for its own advantage. * * *

Justice Benjamin raised similar arguments. He asserted that "the outcome of the 2004 election was due primarily to [his own] campaign's message," as well as McGraw's "devastat[ing]" speech in which he "made a number of controversial claims which became a matter of statewide discussion in the media, on the internet, and elsewhere." * * *

Justice Benjamin did undertake an extensive search for actual bias. But, as we have indicated, that is just one step in the judicial process; objective standards may also require recusal whether or not actual bias exists or can be proved. Due process "may sometimes bar trial by judges who have no actual bias and who would do their very best to weigh the scales of justice equally between contending parties." * * * We find that Blankenship's significant and disproportionate influence—coupled with the temporal relationship between the election and the pending case—"offer a possible temptation to the average * * * judge to . . . lead him not to hold the balance nice, clear and true." * * * On these extreme facts the probability of actual bias rises to an unconstitutional level.

* * *

The judgment of the Supreme Court of Appeals of West Virginia is reversed, and the case is remanded for further proceedings not inconsistent with this opinion.

It is so ordered.

■ CHIEF JUSTICE ROBERTS, with whom JUSTICE SCALIA, JUSTICE THOMAS, and JUSTICE ALITO join, dissenting.

I, of course, share the majority's sincere concerns about the need to maintain a fair, independent, and impartial judiciary—and one that appears to be such. But I fear that the Court's decision will undermine rather than promote these values.

* * *

Today, * * * the Court enlists the Due Process Clause to overturn a judge's failure to recuse because of a "probability of bias." Unlike the established grounds for disqualification, a "probability of bias" cannot be defined in any limited way. The Court's new "rule" provides no guidance to judges and litigants about when recusal will be constitutionally required. This will inevitably lead to an increase in allegations that judges are biased, however groundless those charges may be. The end result will do far more to erode public confidence in judicial impartiality than an isolated failure to recuse in a particular case.

* * * With little help from the majority, courts will now have to determine:

1. How much money is too much money? What level of contribution or expenditure gives rise to a "probability of bias"?

2. How do we determine whether a given expenditure is "disproportionate"? Disproportionate *to what*?

3. Are independent, non-coordinated expenditures treated the same as direct contributions to a candidate's campaign? What about contributions to independent outside groups supporting a candidate?

4. Does it matter whether the litigant has contributed to other candidates or made large expenditures in connection with other elections?

5. Does the amount at issue in the case matter? What if this case were an employment dispute with only $10,000 at stake? What if the plaintiffs only sought non-monetary relief such as an injunction or declaratory judgment?

6. Does the analysis change depending on whether the judge whose disqualification is sought sits on a trial court, appeals court, or state supreme court?

7. How long does the probability of bias last? Does the probability of bias diminish over time as the election recedes? Does it matter whether the judge plans to run for reelection?

8. What if the "disproportionately" large expenditure is made by an industry association, trade union, physicians' group, or the plaintiffs' bar? Must the judge recuse in all cases that affect the association's interests? Must the judge recuse in all cases in which a party or lawyer is a member of that group? Does it matter how much the litigant contributed to the association?

9. What if the case involves a social or ideological issue rather than a financial one? Must a judge recuse from cases involving, say, abortion rights if he has received "disproportionate" support from individuals who feel strongly about either side of that issue? If the supporter wants to help elect judges who are "tough on crime," must the judge recuse in all criminal cases?

10. What if the candidate draws "disproportionate" support from a particular racial, religious, ethnic, or other group, and the case involves an issue of particular importance to that group?

11. What if the supporter is not a party to the pending or imminent case, but his interests will be affected by the decision? Does the Court's analysis apply if the supporter "chooses the judge" not in *his* case, but in someone else's?

12. What if the case implicates a regulatory issue that is of great importance to the party making the expenditures, even though he has no direct financial interest in the outcome (*e.g.*, a facial challenge to an agency rulemaking or a suit seeking to limit an agency's jurisdiction)?

13. Must the judge's vote be outcome determinative in order for his non-recusal to constitute a due process violation?

* * *

[14]. What if the judge voted against the supporter in many other cases?

* * *

[15]. Should we assume that elected judges feel a "debt of hostility" towards major *opponents* of their candidacies? Must the judge recuse in cases involving individuals or groups who spent large amounts of money trying unsuccessfully to defeat him?

* * *

[16]. Does a debt of gratitude for endorsements by newspapers, interest groups, politicians, or celebrities also give rise to a constitutionally unacceptable probability of bias? How would we measure whether such support is disproportionate?

[17]. Does close personal friendship between a judge and a party or lawyer now give rise to a probability of bias?

* * *

These are only a few uncertainties that quickly come to mind. * * *

It is an old cliché, but sometimes the cure is worse than the disease. I am sure there are cases where a "probability of bias" should lead the prudent judge to step aside, but the judge fails to do so. Maybe this is one of them. But I believe that opening the door to recusal claims under the Due Process Clause, for an amorphous "probability of bias," will itself bring our judicial system into undeserved disrepute, and diminish the confidence of the American people in the fairness and integrity of their courts. I hope I am wrong.

I respectfully dissent.

§ 2.5 GOVERNMENT FAILURES

Our discussion thus far has addressed several ways in which private interest intertwined with criticism of regulation. We now turn to the core of this critique and discuss the characteristics of "*government failure*." The intuitive meaning of the term refers to costly and dysfunctional regulatory systems and unreasonable restrictions on society. In practice, the meaning of the term "government failure" is rather vague. The phrase emerged with the modern critique of regulation in the mid–1960s as a governmental counterpart to "market failure," which at the time economists considered the only legitimate justification for government regulation.[210] As such, the term mostly connotes too much government intervention or poor regulatory policies.[211] Government failures, however, may have other meanings as well. They may include government inaction or inadequate action with respect to social problems. Examples of such government failures include unregulated activities of urban slaughterhouses and unsustainable risk activities of financial institutions.

Figure 2.11

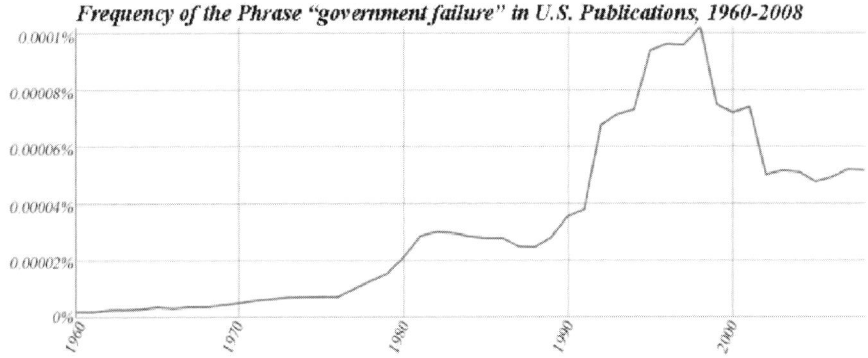

Frequency of the Phrase "government failure" in U.S. Publications, 1960-2008

Source: Google Ngram Viewr.

We define *government failure* as a regulatory policy that does not satisfy cost-benefit analysis. This definition includes under-regulation, over-regulation, and poor regulation. We should expect the government to fail, because any deviation from perfection means a "failure"—too lenient regulatory policies, excessively strict policies, ineffective policies, overenforcement, and underenforcement.[212] One way to interpret the term "government failure" is simply a measure of government performance, used to

---

210. *See, e.g.*, Ronald N. McKean, The Unseen Hand in Government, 55 AMERICAN ECONOMIC REVIEW 496 (1965); Charles Wolf Jr., *A Theory of Nonmarket Failure: Framework for Implementation Analysis*, 22 JOURNAL OF LAW & ECONOMICS 107 (1979).

211. *See, e.g.*, CLIFFORD WINSTON, GOVERNMENT FAILURE VERSUS MARKET FAILURE 2–3 (2006) ("Government failure * * * arises when government has created inefficiencies because it should not have intervened [in the market] in the first place or when it could have solved a given problem or set of problems more efficiently, that is, by generating greater net benefits.")

212. *See, e.g.*, EUGENE BARDACH & ROBERT A. KAGAN, GOING BY THE BOOK: THE PROBLEM OF REGULATORY UNREASONABLENESS (1982); Sara Sun Beale, *The Many Faces of Overcriminalization: From Morals and Mattress Tags to Overfederalization*, 54 AMERICAN UNIVERSITY LAW REVIEW 747 (2005); Richard A. Bierschbach & Alex Stein, *Overenforcement*, 93 GEORGETOWN LAW JOURNAL 1743 (2005); Stuart P. Green, *Why It's A Crime to Tear the Tag Off a Mattress: Overcriminalization and the Moral Content of Regulatory Offenses*, 46 EMORY LAW JOURNAL 1533 (1997); Erik Luna, *The Overcriminalization Phenomenon*, 54 AMERICAN UNIVERSITY LAW REVIEW 703 (2005); Alexandra Natapoff, *Underenforcement*, 75 FORDHAM LAW REVIEW 1715 (2006).

assess deviations from perfection. Public attention is drawn to major government failures, and instances of poor performance.

Smallpox in America

Smallpox was one of the deadliest diseases in human history; it killed millions and disfigured most survivors. In the last decade of the eighteenth century, a British scientist, Edward Jenner, introduced an effective smallpox vaccination to policymakers and the medical community.[213] Despite its effectiveness, Jenner's vaccine was controversial in many countries, including England and the United States. An anti-vaccine movement emerged with branches in every major city. The anti-vaccinationists warned the public about the risks associated with the vaccine, argued that it interfered with God's will and opposed any laws required citizens to be vaccinated.[214]

In the early nineteenth century, the United States launched a rudimentary national program to vaccinate the population. However, it abandoned this program in 1822. Subsequently, states and municipalities tried to vaccinate local communities but were saddled with opposition from the anti-vaccination movement.[215] The question of whether states could lawfully institute compulsory vaccination programs remained unsettled until the Supreme Court's 1905 decision in *Jacobson v. Massachusetts*.[216] In this case, the Court upheld a Massachusetts law that gave municipal health boards the authority to require the vaccination of adults against smallpox; specifically, the Court determined that such programs had "a real and substantial relation to the protection of the public health and safety."[217] The decision had a dramatic impact on health policies in the United States. States and localities began mandating vaccinations that they believed protected the public.[218] The last known outbreak of smallpox in the United States occurred in 1949 in Texas; eight confirmed cases were reported and one death from this outbreak.[219]

After several successful experiments in England, the smallpox vaccine reached the United States. President Thomas Jefferson was a key support-

213. *See generally* HERVÉ BAZIN, THE ERADICATION OF SMALLPOX, EDWARD JENNER AND THE FIRST AND ONLY ERADICATION OF HUMAN INFECTIOUS DISEASE (2000).

214. *See generally* Martin Kaufman, *The American Anti-Vaccinationists and Their Arguments*, 41 BULLETIN OF THE HISTORY OF MEDICINE 463 (1967); MICHAEL WILLRICH, POX: AN AMERICAN HISTORY (2011). *See also* Illana Ritov & Jonathan Baron, *Reluctance to Vaccinate: Omission Bias and Ambiguity*, 3 JOURNAL OF BEHAVIORAL DECISION MAKING 263 (1990).

215. *See generally* Martin Kaufman, *The American Anti-Vaccinationists and Their Arguments*, 41 BULLETIN OF THE HISTORY OF MEDICINE 463 (1967).

216. Jacobson v. Massachusetts, 197 U.S. 11 (1905).

217. *Id.* at 31.

218. *See generally* JAMES COLGROVE, STATE OF IMMUNITY (2006).

219. David T. Karzon, *Smallpox Vaccination in the United States: The End of an Era*, 81 JOURNAL OF PEDIATRICS 600 (1972).

er of the smallpox vaccine and he vaccinated many citizens himself.[220] In February 1813, Congress passed the Vaccine Act. President James Madison immediately signed the Act into law.[221]

An Act to Encourage Vaccination

> [SECTION 1.] *Be it enacted by the Senate and House of Representatives of the United States of America in Congress assembled*, That the President of the United States * * * is hereby authorized to appoint an agent to preserve the genuine vaccine matter, and to furnish the same to any citizen of the United States, whenever it may be applied for, through the medium of the post-office; and such agent shall, previous to his entering upon the execution of the duties assigned to him by this act, and before he shall be entitled to the privilege of franking any letter or package as herein allowed. * * *
>
> SEC. 2. *And be it further enacted*, That all letters or packages not exceeding half an ounce in weight, containing vaccine matter, or relating to the subject of vaccination, and that alone, shall be carried by the United States' mail free of any postage, either to or from the agent who may be appointed to carry the provisions of this act into effect. * * * [I]f said agent shall frank any letter or package, in which shall be contained any thing relative to any subject other than vaccination, he shall, on conviction of every such offence, forfeit and pay a fine of fifty dollars, to be recovered in the same manner as other fines or violations of law establishing the post-office: *Provided* * * *, that the discharge of any agent, and the appointment of another in his stead, be at the discretion of the President of the United States.

The pioneering Vaccine Act established a regulatory authority for vaccinations. It authorized the President to appoint a national vaccine agent who would assure the supply of genuine vaccinations to all citizens. When Congress passed the Vaccine Act, it considered the death toll of smallpox, the discovery of an effective smallpox vaccine, problems in the existing market for vaccines, including deceit and fraud, and the failure of the market to address the national vaccine needs.

President Madison appointed Dr. James Smith as the National Vaccine Agent. Smith was the most experienced vaccinator in the country and had proven administrative skills. Upon his appointment, Smith established the National Vaccine Institution to facilitate the supply and administration of vaccines across the country.[222] For eight years, Smith and the Institution successfully promoted the well-being of the American public.

---

220. *See* Henry Austin Martin, *Jefferson as a Vaccinator*, 7 NORTH CAROLINA MEDICAL 1 (1881). An illustration of the procedure is available at *regti.me/small-pox* (case sensitive).

221. 2 Stat. 806 (1813).

222. Petition for National Vaccine Institution, No. 477, 16th Cong. (Jan. 1, 1820); Act of Incorporation of a National Vaccine Institution for the United States of America (Jan. 1, 182) (appended to the petition). See also Joseph Smith, *National Vaccine Institution*, 5 VACCINE INQUIRER 822 (1822).

In November 1821, Dr. Smith inadvertently mailed live smallpox scabs, rather than the vaccine, to a local physician in Tarborough, North Carolina.[223] Trusting the package received from Dr. Smith, the physician used its contents to "vaccinate" residents in Tarborough.[224] A local epidemic broke out. Sixty individuals became sick with the smallpox virus and ten of them died. Smith's mistake, or "regulatory failure," eroded the public confidence in his competency and in the enterprise itself.[225]

The failure of the national vaccine regulator shook the nation. In early 1822, Congress held hearings and received reports about the success of European vaccination programs.[226] In April 1822, the Congressional Committee that examined the "North Carolina Accident" submitted a report, together with a bill to repeal the 1813 Act.[227] The report provided:

> The recent unfortunate occurrences in the s[t]ate of North Carolina, having involved considerations of the utmost importance to society, and intimately connected with the dearest interests of humanity. [The] committee feel[s] it to be due to the occasion to commence their remarks by a distinct and unequivocal declaration of their entire and unshaken confidence in the efficacy of the vaccine disease, as a preventive of small pox. * * *
>
> The inquiry, therefore appears to be very properly limited to the mere expediency of the existing law, which authorizes the appointment of an agent, from, and to whom, letters be transmitted free of postage. While the committee would on no account offer a suggestion, which would be construed to imply a doubt of the efficacy of vaccination, [it questions] whether the general government can beneficially interpose for the furtherance of an object, which seems in a peculiar manner to appertain to the municipal authorities in the several states. * * * All our regulations for the preservation of the public health are questions of police, wisely committed to those who are immediately interested, and therefore, most likely to adopt efficient measures for their own safety; and it is doubted whether Congress can, in any instance devise a system which will not be more liable to abuses in its operations, and less subject to a prompt and salutary control, than such as may be adopted by the local authorities. * * *
>
> An establishment of this kind, under the authority of the general government, naturally commands attention of all portion of the country [and] must reduce any single agent to the necessity of

223. *Small Pox*, 1 VACCINE INQUIRER 45 (1822).

224. *Id.*

225. *See, e.g.*, ABRIDGEMENT OF THE DEBATES OF CONGRESS, FROM 1789 TO 1859, vol. III, 243–44, 256–57 (1858); Henry W. Ducachet, *Strictures on the Late Circular Addressed to the Citizens of the United States by James Smith*, 1 MEDICAL & PHYSICAL JOURNAL 42 (1822); James Smith, A Letter Addressed to the Citizens of the United States, 3 VACCINE INQUIRER 125 (1822).

226. *See, e.g.*, House Report No. 517 (Feb. 22, 1822); *On Vaccination*, 6 VACCINE INQUIRER 255 (1822).

227. *Report of the Committee Appointed to Inquire into the Propriety of Repealing the Act of 1813* (Apr. 18, 1822). *See also Letter of the Vaccine Agent to the Speaker of the House of Representative* (Feb. 7, 1822); *The North Carolina Accident*, 3 VACCINE INQUIRER 109 (1822).

> either relinquishing the proffered fee, or of transmitting matter of doubtful character. Sub-agents must necessarily be employed to furnish a supply equal to the demand. Careless or incompetent assistants, guided more by cupidity than intelligence, may thus be instrumental in producing mischief, by the distribution of inert matter, or by the more fatal error of disseminating pestilence instead of prophylactic. That such unhappy mistakes may occur, is but too-well attested by the recent events in North Carolina. The committee are therefore inclined to the belief, that any single agency, for the whole Union, must always be liable to similar objections; and from which they apprehend no institution, clothed with the character of a lucrative monopoly or privilege, can be entirely exempted. If, however, it should be deemed advisable for Congress to continue to aid in facilitating the distribution of vaccine matter, by the mode now in operation, the committee are of opinion, that some of the evils to which they have adverted might be obviated by the appointment of two or more agents, judiciously located in our large cities, in different quarters of the Union. But after mature deliberation, [we] have come to the conclusion, that it would be still better to commit the subject altogether to the local authorities, who with the aid of professional men, will be more competent to the successful management of it, and to whom [we] believe it properly belongs.[228]

In May 1822, Congress repealed the 1813 Vaccine Act, and President James Monroe immediately signed this repealing bill into law.[229] Ten years later, Congress passed the Indian Vaccination Act of 1832,[230] which established a new federal program dedicated to promoting of immunization among Indian tribes. Congress granted the Secretary of War absolute authority over the program, and it was implemented selectively to protect Indian nations viewed as friendly or economically important to the United States.[231] Smallpox continued to infect individuals in the United States for more than a century. In 1921, almost a century after Congress repealed the 1813 Vaccine Act, more than 100,000 cases of smallpox were reported.

Questions

1. What government failures affected smallpox rates in the United States?

2. The Congressional Committee that examined the North Carolina accident expressed its confidence in "the efficacy of vaccination," but concluded that "any single agency" was likely to fail. How did the Committee

228. *Report of the Committee Appointed to Inquire into the Propriety of Repealing the Act of 1813* (Apr. 18, 1822).

229. An Act to repeal the Act to encourage vaccination, 3 Stat. 677 (1922).

230. An Act to provide the means of extending the benefits of vaccination, as preventive of the small-pox, to the Indian tribes, and thereby, as far as possible, to save from the destructive ravages of that disease, 4 Stat. 514 (1832).

231. *See generally* J. Diane Pearson, *Lewis Cass and the Politics of Disease: The Indian Vaccination Act of 1832*, 18 WICAZO SA REVIEW 9 (2003).

justify this conclusion? What alternative model did the Committee propose? What were the strengths and weaknesses of the proposed model?

§ 2.6 NATIONAL CONTROVERSY

We conclude this chapter stressing our initial observation: people tend to have strong views about regulatory issues, but exhibit less interest in the facts and the meaning of the terms they use. This Chapter used several dimensions of reality imperfections to illustrate four practical points. First, unrestricted freedom, or unrestricted pursuit of self-interest, is unlikely to serve society. Second, regulation is needed to protect the general well being of the public and prevent harm. Third, regulation is likely to be imperfect and controversial. Fourth, regulations do not necessarily serve the public. In the real world, a great degree of oversimplification is needed to believe that one approach toward regulation can serve society.

National Federation of Independent Business v. Sebelius closed one chapter in a bitter national controversy over regulation and over a specific health care reform. The challenged health care reform was rather complex. Nine Supreme Court Justices analyzed two provisions in one statute and issued three opinions. They saw different things when they analyzed one regulatory framework.

National Federation of Independent Business v. Sebelius

132 S.Ct. 2566 (2012)

■ CHIEF JUSTICE ROBERTS announced the judgment of the Court and delivered the opinion of the Court with respect to Parts I, II, and III–C, an opinion with respect to Part IV, in which JUSTICE BREYER and JUSTICE KAGAN join, and an opinion with respect to Parts III–A, III–B, and III–D.

Today we resolve constitutional challenges to two provisions of the Patient Protection and Affordable Care Act of 2010: the individual mandate, which requires individuals to purchase a health insurance policy providing a minimum level of coverage; and the Medicaid expansion, which gives funds to the States on the condition that they provide specified health care to all citizens whose income falls below a certain threshold. We do not consider whether the Act embodies sound policies. That judgment is entrusted to the Nation's elected leaders. We ask only whether Congress has the power under the Constitution to enact the challenged provisions. * * *

I

In 2010, Congress enacted the Patient Protection and Affordable Care Act, 124 Stat. 119. The Act aims to increase the number of Americans covered by health insurance and decrease the cost of health care. * * *

The individual mandate [provision] requires most Americans to maintain "minimum essential" health insurance coverage. 26 U.S.C. § 5000A. The mandate does not apply to some individuals, such as prisoners and undocumented aliens. Many individuals will receive the required coverage through their employer, or from a government program such as Medicaid or Medicare. But for individuals who are not exempt and do not receive health insurance through a third party, the means of satisfying the requirement is to purchase insurance from a private company.

Beginning in 2014, those who do not comply with the mandate must make a "[s]hared responsibility payment" to the Federal Government. § 5000A(b)(1). That payment, which the Act describes as a "penalty," is calculated as a percentage of household income, subject to a floor based on a specified dollar amount and a ceiling based on the average annual premium the individual would have to pay for qualifying private health insurance. In 2016, for example, the penalty will be 2.5 percent of an individual's household income, but no less than $695 and no more than the average yearly premium for insurance that covers 60 percent of the cost of 10 specified services (e.g., prescription drugs and hospitalization). The Act provides that the penalty will be paid to the Internal Revenue Service with an individual's taxes, and "shall be assessed and collected in the same manner" as tax penalties, such as the penalty for claiming too large an income tax refund. The Act, however, bars the IRS from using several of its normal enforcement tools, such as criminal prosecutions and levies. § 5000A(g)(2). And some individuals who are subject to the mandate are nonetheless exempt from the penalty—for example, those with income below a certain threshold and members of Indian tribes. § 5000A(e).

On the day the President signed the Act into law, Florida and 12 other States filed a complaint in the Federal District Court for the Northern District of Florida. Those plaintiffs * * * were subsequently joined by 13 more States, several individuals, and the National Federation of Independent Business. The plaintiffs alleged, among other things, that the individual mandate provisions of the Act exceeded Congress's powers under Article I of the Constitution. * * *

The second provision of the Affordable Care Act directly challenged here is the Medicaid expansion. Enacted in 1965, Medicaid offers federal funding to States to assist pregnant women, children, needy families, the blind, the elderly, and the disabled in obtaining medical care. See 42 U.S.C. § 1396a(a)(10). In order to receive that funding, States must comply with federal criteria governing matters such as who receives care and what services are provided at what cost. By 1982 every State had chosen to participate in Medicaid. Federal funds received through the Medicaid program have become a substantial part of state budgets, now constituting over 10 percent of most States' total revenue.

The Affordable Care Act expands the scope of the Medicaid program and increases the number of individuals the States must cover. For example, the Act requires state programs to provide Medicaid coverage to adults with incomes up to 133 percent of the federal poverty level, whereas many States now cover adults with children only if their income is considerably lower, and do not cover childless adults at all. The Act increases federal funding to cover the States' costs in expanding Medicaid coverage, although States will bear a portion of the costs on their own. If a State does not comply with the Act's new coverage requirements, it may lose not only the federal funding for those requirements, but all of its federal Medicaid funds. * * *

III

The Government advances two theories for the proposition that Congress had constitutional authority to enact the individual mandate. First, the Government argues that Congress had the power to enact the mandate under the Commerce Clause. Under that theory, Congress may order individuals to buy health insurance because the failure to do so affects interstate commerce, and could undercut the Affordable Care Act's other reforms. Second, the Government argues that if the commerce power does not support the mandate, we should nonetheless uphold it as an exercise of Congress's power to tax. According to the Government, even if Congress lacks the power to direct individuals to buy insurance, the only effect of the individual mandate is to raise taxes on those who do not do so, and thus the law may be upheld as a tax.

A

The Government's first argument is that the individual mandate is a valid exercise of Congress's power under the Commerce Clause and the Necessary and Proper Clause. According to the Government, the health care market is characterized by a significant cost-shifting problem. Everyone will eventually need health care at a time and to an extent they cannot predict, but if they do not have insurance, they often will not be able to pay for it. Because state and federal laws nonetheless require hospitals to provide a certain degree of care to individuals without regard to their ability to pay, * * * hospitals end up receiving compensation for only a portion of the services they provide. To recoup the losses, hospitals pass on the cost to insurers through higher rates, and insurers, in turn, pass on the cost to policy holders in the form of higher premiums. Congress estimated that the cost of uncompensated care raises family health insurance premiums, on average, by over $1,000 per year.

In the Affordable Care Act, Congress addressed the problem of those who cannot obtain insurance coverage because of preexisting conditions or other health issues. It did so through the Act's "guaranteed-issue" and "community-rating" provisions. These provisions together prohibit insurance companies from denying coverage to those with such conditions or charging unhealthy individuals higher premiums than healthy individuals.

The guaranteed-issue and community-rating reforms do not, however, address the issue of healthy individuals who choose not to purchase insurance to cover potential health care needs. In fact, the reforms sharply exacerbate that problem, by providing an incentive for individuals to delay purchasing health insurance until they become sick, relying on the promise of guaranteed and affordable coverage. The reforms also threaten to impose massive new costs on insurers, who are required to accept unhealthy individuals but prohibited from charging them rates necessary to pay for their coverage. This will lead insurers to significantly increase premiums on everyone. * * *

The individual mandate was Congress's solution to these problems. By requiring that individuals purchase health insurance, the mandate prevents cost-shifting by those who would otherwise go without it. In addition, the mandate forces into the insurance risk pool more healthy individuals, whose premiums on average will be higher than their health care expenses. This allows insurers to subsidize the costs of covering the unhealthy individuals the reforms require them to accept. The Government claims that Congress has power under the Commerce and Necessary and Proper Clauses to enact this solution.

1

The Government contends that the individual mandate is within Congress's power because the failure to purchase insurance "has a substantial and deleterious effect on interstate commerce" by creating the cost-shifting problem. * * * Given its expansive scope, it is no surprise that Congress has employed the commerce power in a wide variety of ways to address the pressing needs of the time. But Congress has never attempted to rely on that power to compel individuals not engaged in commerce to purchase an unwanted product. * * *

The Constitution grants Congress the power to "*regulate* Commerce." Art. I, § 8, cl. 3 (emphasis added). The power to *regulate* commerce presupposes the existence of commercial activity to be regulated. * * * there is already something to be regulated. * * * The language of the Constitution reflects the natural understanding that the power to regulate assumes there is already something to be regulated. * * *

The individual mandate, however, does not regulate existing commercial activity. It instead compels individuals to *become* active in commerce by purchasing a product, on the ground that their failure to do so affects interstate commerce. Construing the Commerce Clause to permit Congress to regulate individuals precisely *because* they are doing nothing would open a new and potentially vast domain to congressional authority. Every day individuals do not do an infinite number of things. In some cases they decide not to do something; in others they simply fail to do it. Allowing Congress to justify federal regulation by pointing to the effect of inaction on commerce would bring countless decisions an individual could *potentially* make within the scope of federal regulation, and—under the Government's theory—empower Congress to make those decisions for him.

Applying the Government's logic to the familiar case of *Wickard v. Filburn*, 317 U.S. 111 (1942), shows how far that logic would carry us from the notion of a government of limited powers. In *Wickard*, the Court famously upheld a federal penalty imposed on a farmer for growing wheat for consumption on his own farm. That amount of wheat caused the farmer to exceed his quota under a program designed to support the price of wheat by limiting supply. The Court rejected the farmer's argument that growing wheat for home consumption was beyond the reach of the commerce power. It did so on the ground that the farmer's decision to grow wheat for his own use allowed him to avoid purchasing wheat in the market. That decision, when considered in the aggregate along with similar decisions of others, would have had a substantial effect on the interstate market for wheat.

Wickard has long been regarded as "perhaps the most far reaching example of Commerce Clause authority over intrastate activity," *United States v. Lopez*, 514 U.S. 549, 560 (1995), but the Government's theory in this case would go much further. Under *Wickard* it is within Congress's power to regulate the market for wheat by supporting its price. But price can be supported by increasing demand as well as by decreasing supply. The aggregated decisions of some consumers not to purchase wheat have a substantial effect on the price of wheat, just as decisions not to purchase health insurance have on the price of insurance. Congress can therefore command that those not buying wheat do so, just as it argues here that it may command that those not buying health insurance do so. The farmer in *Wickard* was at least actively engaged in the production of wheat, and the Government could regulate that activity because of its effect on commerce. The Government's theory here would effectively override that limitation, by establishing that individuals may be regulated under the Commerce Clause whenever enough of them are not doing something the Government would have them do.

Indeed, the Government's logic would justify a mandatory purchase to solve almost any problem. * * * To consider a different example in the health care market, many Americans do not eat a balanced diet. That group makes up a larger percentage of the total population than those without health insurance. The failure of that group to have a healthy diet increases health care costs, to a greater extent than the failure of the uninsured to purchase insurance. * * * Those increased costs are borne in part by other Americans who must pay more, just as the uninsured shift costs to the insured. * * * Congress addressed the insurance problem by ordering everyone to buy insurance. Under the Government's theory, Congress could address the diet problem by ordering everyone to buy vegetables. * * *

People, for reasons of their own, often fail to do things that would be good for them or good for society. Those failures—joined with the similar failures of others—can readily have a substantial effect on interstate commerce. Under the Government's logic, that authorizes Congress to use its commerce power to compel citizens to act as the Government would have them act.

That is not the country the Framers of our Constitution envisioned. * * * While Congress's authority under the Commerce Clause has of course expanded with the growth of the national economy, our cases have "always recognized that the power to regulate commerce, though broad indeed, has limits." *Maryland v. Wirtz*, 392 U.S. 183, 196 (1968). The Government's theory would erode those limits, permitting Congress to reach beyond the natural extent of its authority. * * * Congress already enjoys vast power to regulate much of what we do. Accepting the Government's theory would give Congress the same license to regulate what we do not do, fundamentally changing the relation between the citizen and the Federal Government.

To an economist, perhaps, there is no difference between activity and inactivity; both have measurable economic effects on commerce. But the distinction between doing something and doing nothing would not have been lost on the Framers, who were "practical statesmen," not metaphysical philosophers. As we have explained, "the framers of the Constitution were not mere visionaries, toying with speculations or theories, but practical men, dealing with the facts of political life as they understood them, putting into form the government they were creating, and prescribing in language clear and intelligible the powers that government was to take." *South Carolina v. United States*, 199 U.S. 437, 449 (1905). The Framers gave Congress the power to regulate commerce, not to compel it, and for over 200 years both our decisions and Congress's actions have reflected this understanding. There is no reason to depart from that understanding now.

The Government sees things differently. It argues that because sickness and injury are unpredictable but unavoidable, "the uninsured as a class are active in the market for health care, which they regularly seek and obtain." The individual mandate "merely regulates how individuals finance and pay for that active participation—requiring that they do so through insurance, rather than through attempted self-insurance with the back-stop of shifting costs to others."

The Government repeats the phrase "active in the market for health care" throughout its brief, but that concept has no constitutional significance. An individual who bought a car two years ago and may buy another in the future is not "active in the car market" in any pertinent sense. The phrase "active in the market" cannot obscure the fact that most of those regulated by the individual mandate are not currently engaged in any commercial activity involving health care, and that fact is fatal to the Government's effort to "regulate the uninsured as a class." * * *

The proposition that Congress may dictate the conduct of an individual today because of prophesied future activity finds no support in our precedent. * * *

Everyone will likely participate in the markets for food, clothing, transportation, shelter, or energy; that does not authorize Congress to direct them to purchase particular products in those or other markets today. The Commerce Clause is not a general license to regulate an individual from cradle to grave, simply because he will predictably engage in particular transactions. Any police power to regulate individuals as such, as opposed to their activities, remains vested in the States.

The Government argues that the individual mandate can be sustained as a sort of exception to this rule, because health insurance is a unique product. According to the Government, upholding the individual mandate would not justify mandatory purchases of items such as cars or broccoli because, as the Government puts it, "[h]ealth insurance is not purchased for its own sake like a car or broccoli; it is a means of financing health-care consumption and covering universal risks." But cars and broccoli are no more purchased for their "own sake" than health insurance. They are purchased to cover the need for transportation and food.

* * *

B

That is not the end of the matter. Because the Commerce Clause does not support the individual mandate, it is necessary to turn to the Government's second argument: that the mandate may be upheld as within Congress's enumerated power to "lay and collect Taxes." Art. I, § 8, cl. 1.

The Government's tax power argument asks us to view the statute differently than we did in considering its commerce power theory. In making its Commerce Clause argument, the Government defended the mandate as a regulation requiring individuals to purchase health insurance. The Government does not claim that the taxing power allows Congress to issue such a command. Instead, the Government asks us to read the mandate not as ordering individuals to buy insurance, but rather as imposing a tax on those who do not buy that product.

The text of a statute can sometimes have more than one possible meaning. To take a familiar example, a law that reads "no vehicles in the park" might, or might not, ban bicycles in the park. And it is well established that if a statute has two possible meanings, one of which violates the Constitution, courts should adopt the meaning that does not do so. Justice Story said that 180 years ago: "No court ought, unless the terms of an act rendered it unavoidable, to give a construction to it which should involve a violation, however unintentional, of the constitution." *Parsons v. Bedford, Breedlove & Robeson*, 28 U.S. 433, 448–449 (1830). Justice Holmes made the same point a century later: "[T]he rule is settled that as between two possible interpretations of a statute, by one of which it would be unconstitutional and by the other valid, our plain duty is to adopt that which will save the Act." *Blodgett v. Holden*, 275 U.S. 142, 148 (1927) (concurring opinion).

The most straightforward reading of the mandate is that it commands individuals to purchase insurance. * * * Under our precedent, it is therefore necessary to ask whether the Government's alternative reading of the statute—that it only imposes a tax on those without insurance—is a reasonable one.

Under the mandate, if an individual does not maintain health insurance, the only consequence is that he must make an additional payment to the IRS when he pays his taxes. That, according to the Government, means the mandate can be regarded as establishing a condition—not owning health insurance—that triggers a tax—the required payment to the IRS. Under that theory, the mandate is not a legal command to buy insurance. Rather, it makes going without insurance just another thing the Government taxes, like buying gasoline or earning income. And if the mandate is in effect just a tax hike on certain taxpayers who do not have health insurance, it may be within Congress's constitutional power to tax.

The question is not whether that is the most natural interpretation of the mandate, but only whether it is a "fairly possible" one. * * * The Government asks us to interpret the mandate as imposing a tax, if it would otherwise violate the Constitution. * * *

C

The exaction the Affordable Care Act imposes on those without health insurance looks like a tax in many respects. The "[s]hared responsibility payment," as the statute entitles it, is paid into the Treasury by "taxpayer[s]" when they file their tax returns. * * * For taxpayers who do owe the payment, its amount is determined by such familiar factors as taxable income, number of dependents, and joint filing status. The requirement to pay is found in the Internal Revenue Code and enforced by the IRS, which—as we previously explained—must assess and collect it "in the same manner as taxes." This process yields the essential feature of any tax: it produces at least some revenue for the Government. * * *

It is of course true that the Act describes the payment as a "penalty," not a "tax." But [the] label * * * does not determine whether the payment may be viewed as an exercise of Congress's taxing power. * * *

Our cases confirm this functional approach. For example, in *Bailey v. Drexel Furniture Co.*, 259 U.S. 20 (1922), we focused on three practical characteristics of the so-called tax on employing child laborers that convinced us the "tax" was actually a penalty. First, the tax imposed an exceedingly heavy burden—10 percent of a company's net income—on those who employed children, no matter how small their infraction. Second, it imposed that exaction only on those who knowingly employed underage laborers. Such scienter requirements are typical of punitive statutes, because Congress often wishes to punish only those who intentionally break the law. Third, this "tax" was enforced in part by the Department of Labor, an agency responsible for punishing violations of labor laws, not collecting revenue. * * *

The same analysis here suggests that the shared responsibility payment may for constitutional purposes be considered a tax, not a penalty: First, for most Americans the amount due will be far less than the price of insurance, and, by statute, it can never be more.[8] It may often be a reasonable financial decision to make the payment rather than purchase insurance, unlike the "prohibitory" financial punishment in *Drexel Furniture*. Second, the individual mandate contains no scienter requirement. Third, the payment is collected solely by the IRS through the normal means of taxation—except that the Service is *not* allowed to use those means most suggestive of a punitive sanction, such as criminal prosecution. The reasons the Court in *Drexel Furniture* held that what was called a "tax" there was a penalty support the conclusion that what is called a "penalty" here may be viewed as a tax.

None of this is to say that the payment is not intended to affect individual conduct. Although the payment will raise considerable revenue, it is plainly designed to expand health insurance coverage. But taxes that seek to influence conduct are nothing new. Some of our earliest federal taxes sought to deter the purchase of imported manufactured goods in order to foster the growth of domestic industry. * * * Today, federal and state taxes can compose more than half the retail price of cigarettes, not just to raise more money, but to encourage people to quit smoking. And we have upheld such obviously regulatory measures as taxes on selling mari-

---

8. In 2016, for example, individuals making $35,000 a year are expected to owe the IRS about $60 for any month in which they do not have health insurance. Someone with an annual income of $100,000 a year would likely owe about $200. The price of a qualifying insurance policy is projected to be around $400 per month. See D. Newman, CRS Report for Congress, Individual Mandate and Related Information Requirements Under PPACA 7, and n. 25 (2011).

juana and sawed-off shotguns. See *United States v. Sanchez*, 340 U.S. 42, 44–45 (1950); *Sonzinsky v. United States*, 300 U.S. 506, 513 (1937). Indeed, "[e]very tax is in some measure regulatory. To some extent it interposes an economic impediment to the activity taxed as compared with others not taxed." *Sonzinsky, supra*, at 513. That § 5000A seeks to shape decisions about whether to buy health insurance does not mean that it cannot be a valid exercise of the taxing power.

* * * While the individual mandate clearly aims to induce the purchase of health insurance, it need not be read to declare that failing to do so is unlawful. Neither the Act nor any other law attaches negative legal consequences to not buying health insurance, beyond requiring a payment to the IRS. The Government agrees with that reading, confirming that if someone chooses to pay rather than obtain health insurance, they have fully complied with the law.

Indeed, it is estimated that four million people each year will choose to pay the IRS rather than buy insurance. We would expect Congress to be troubled by that prospect if such conduct were unlawful. That Congress apparently regards such extensive failure to comply with the mandate as tolerable suggests that Congress did not think it was creating four million outlaws. It suggests instead that the shared responsibility payment merely imposes a tax citizens may lawfully choose to pay in lieu of buying health insurance.

* * *

The Affordable Care Act's requirement that certain individuals pay a financial penalty for not obtaining health insurance may reasonably be characterized as a tax. Because the Constitution permits such a tax, it is not our role to forbid it, or to pass upon its wisdom or fairness.

* * *

IV

A

The States also contend that the Medicaid expansion exceeds Congress's authority under the Spending Clause. They claim that Congress is coercing the States to adopt the changes it wants by threatening to withhold all of a State's Medicaid grants, unless the State accepts the new expanded funding and complies with the conditions that come with it. This, they argue, violates the basic principle that the "Federal Government may not compel the States to enact or administer a federal regulatory program." *New York v. United States*, 505 U.S. 144, 188 (1992).

There is no doubt that the Act dramatically increases state obligations under Medicaid. The current Medicaid program requires States to cover only certain discrete categories of needy individuals—pregnant women, children, needy families, the blind, the elderly, and the disabled. 42 U.S.C. § 1396a(a)(10). There is no mandatory coverage for most childless adults, and the States typically do not offer any such coverage. The States also enjoy considerable flexibility with respect to the coverage levels for parents of needy families. On average States cover only those unemployed parents who make less than 37 percent of the federal poverty level, and only those employed parents who make less than 63 percent of the poverty line.

The Medicaid provisions of the Affordable Care Act, in contrast, require States to expand their Medicaid programs by 2014 to cover *all* individuals under the age of 65 with incomes below 133 percent of the federal poverty line. The Act also establishes a new "[e]ssential health benefits" package, which States must provide to all new Medicaid recipients—a level sufficient to satisfy a recipient's obligations under the individual mandate. The Affordable Care Act provides that the Federal Government will pay 100 percent of the costs of covering these newly eligible individuals through 2016. In the following years, the federal payment level gradually decreases, to a minimum of 90 percent. In light of the expansion in coverage mandated by the Act, the Federal Government estimates that its Medicaid spending will increase by approximately $100 billion per year, nearly 40 percent above current levels. * * *

The Spending Clause grants Congress the power "to pay the Debts and provide for the . . . general Welfare of the United States." U.S. Const., Art. I, § 8, cl. 1. We have long recognized that Congress may use this power to grant federal funds to the States, and may condition such a grant upon the States' "taking certain actions that Congress could not require them to take." * * *

At the same time, our cases have recognized limits on Congress's power under the Spending Clause to secure state compliance with federal objectives. "We have repeatedly characterized . . . Spending Clause legislation as 'much in the nature of a *contract*.' " *Barnes v. Gorman*, 536 U.S. 181, 186 (2002) (quoting *Pennhurst State School and Hospital v. Halderman*, 451 U.S. 1, 17 (1981)). The legitimacy of Congress's exercise of the spending power "thus rests on whether the State voluntarily and knowingly accepts the terms of the 'contract.' " *Pennhurst, supra*, at 17. Respecting this limitation is critical to ensuring that Spending Clause legislation does not undermine the status of the States as independent sovereigns in our federal system. * * * For this reason, "the Constitution has never been understood to confer upon Congress the ability to require the States to govern according to Congress' instructions." *New York, supra*, at 162. Otherwise the two-government system established by the Framers would give way to a system that vests power in one central government, and individual liberty would suffer.

* * * Permitting the Federal Government to force the States to implement a federal program would threaten the political accountability key to our federal system. "[W]here the Federal Government directs the States to regulate, it may be state officials who will bear the brunt of public disapproval, while the federal officials who devised the regulatory program may remain insulated from the electoral ramifications of their decision." *Id.*, at 169. Spending Clause programs do not pose this danger when a State has a legitimate choice whether to accept the federal conditions in exchange for federal funds. In such a situation, state officials can fairly be held politically accountable for choosing to accept or refuse the federal offer. But when the State has no choice, the Federal Government can achieve its objectives without accountability. * * * Indeed, this danger is heightened

when Congress acts under the Spending Clause, because Congress can use that power to implement federal policy it could not impose directly under its enumerated powers.

* * *

The States * * * argue * * * that Congress has "crossed the line distinguishing encouragement from coercion," * * * in the way it has structured the funding: Instead of simply refusing to grant the new funds to States that will not accept the new conditions, Congress has also threatened to withhold those States' existing Medicaid funds. The States claim that this threat serves no purpose other than to force unwilling States to sign up for the dramatic expansion in health care coverage effected by the Act.

Given the nature of the threat and the programs at issue here, we must agree. * * *

* * *

The Affordable Care Act is constitutional in part and unconstitutional in part. The individual mandate cannot be upheld as an exercise of Congress's power under the Commerce Clause. That Clause authorizes Congress to regulate interstate commerce, not to order individuals to engage in it. In this case, however, it is reasonable to construe what Congress has done as increasing taxes on those who have a certain amount of income, but choose to go without health insurance. Such legislation is within Congress's power to tax.

As for the Medicaid expansion, that portion of the Affordable Care Act violates the Constitution by threatening existing Medicaid funding. Congress has no authority to order the States to regulate according to its instructions. Congress may offer the States grants and require the States to comply with accompanying conditions, but the States must have a genuine choice whether to accept the offer. * * * The remedy for that constitutional violation is to preclude the Federal Government from imposing such a sanction. That remedy does not require striking down other portions of the Affordable Care Act.

The Framers created a Federal Government of limited powers, and assigned to this Court the duty of enforcing those limits. The Court does so today. But the Court does not express any opinion on the wisdom of the Affordable Care Act. Under the Constitution, that judgment is reserved to the people.

The judgment of the Court of Appeals for the Eleventh Circuit is affirmed in part and reversed in part.

It is so ordered.

■ JUSTICE GINSBURG, with whom JUSTICE SOTOMAYOR joins, and with whom JUSTICE BREYER and JUSTICE KAGAN join as to Parts I, II, III, and IV, concurring in part, concurring in the judgment in part, and dissenting in part.

I agree with THE CHIEF JUSTICE that * * * the minimum coverage provision is a proper exercise of Congress' taxing power. * * * Unlike THE

CHIEF JUSTICE, however, I would hold, alternatively, that the Commerce Clause authorizes Congress to enact the minimum coverage provision. I would also hold that the Spending Clause permits the Medicaid expansion exactly as Congress enacted it.

I

* * * Since 1937, our precedent has recognized Congress' large authority to set the Nation's course in the economic and social welfare realm. See *United States v. Darby*, 312 U.S. 100, 115 (1941) (overruling *Hammer v. Dagenhart*, 247 U.S. 251 (1918), and recognizing that "regulations of commerce which do not infringe some constitutional prohibition are within the plenary power conferred on Congress by the Commerce Clause"). * * * THE CHIEF JUSTICE's crabbed reading of the Commerce Clause harks back to the era in which the Court routinely thwarted Congress' efforts to regulate the national economy in the interest of those who labor to sustain it. * * * It is a reading that should not have staying power.

A

In enacting the Patient Protection and Affordable Care Act (ACA), Congress comprehensively reformed the national market for health-care products and services. By any measure, that market is immense. Collectively, Americans spent $2.5 trillion on health care in 2009, accounting for 17.6% of our Nation's economy. Within the next decade, it is anticipated, spending on health care will nearly double.

The health-care market's size is not its only distinctive feature. Unlike the market for almost any other product or service, the market for medical care is one in which all individuals inevitably participate. Virtually every person residing in the United States, sooner or later, will visit a doctor or other health-care professional. * * *

When individuals make those visits, they face another reality of the current market for medical care: its high cost. In 2010, on average, an individual in the United States incurred over $7,000 in health-care expenses. * * * Over a lifetime, costs mount to hundreds of thousands of dollars. * * * When a person requires nonroutine care, the cost will generally exceed what he or she can afford to pay. A single hospital stay, for instance, typically costs upwards of $10,000. * * * Treatments for many serious, though not uncommon, conditions similarly cost a substantial sum. * * *

Although every U.S. domiciliary will incur significant medical expenses during his or her lifetime, the time when care will be needed is often unpredictable. An accident, a heart attack, or a cancer diagnosis commonly occurs without warning. Inescapably, we are all at peril of needing medical care without a moment's notice. * * *

To manage the risks associated with medical care—its high cost, its unpredictability, and its inevitability—most people in the United States obtain health insurance. Many (approximately 170 million in 2009) are insured by private insurance companies. Others, including those over 65 and certain poor and disabled persons, rely on government-funded insurance programs, notably Medicare and Medicaid. Combined, private health insurers and State and Federal Governments finance almost 85% of the medical care administered to U.S. residents. * * *

Not all U.S. residents, however, have health insurance. In 2009, approximately 50 million people were uninsured, either by choice or, more likely, because they could not afford private insurance and did not qualify for government aid. * * * As a group, uninsured individuals annually consume more than $100 billion in healthcare services, nearly 5% of the Nation's total. * * * Over 60% of those without insurance visit a doctor's office or emergency room in a given year. * * *

B

The large number of individuals without health insurance, Congress found, heavily burdens the national health-care market. * * * As just noted, the cost of emergency care or treatment for a serious illness generally exceeds what an individual can afford to pay on her own. Unlike markets for most products, however, the inability to pay for care does not mean that an uninsured individual will receive no care. Federal and state law, as well as professional obligations and embedded social norms, require hospitals and physicians to provide care when it is most needed, regardless of the patient's ability to pay. * * *

As a consequence, medical-care providers deliver significant amounts of care to the uninsured for which the providers receive no payment. In 2008, for example, hospitals, physicians, and other health-care professionals received no compensation for $43 billion worth of the $116 billion in care they administered to those without insurance.

Health-care providers do not absorb these bad debts. Instead, they raise their prices, passing along the cost of uncompensated care to those who do pay reliably: the government and private insurance companies. In response, private insurers increase their premiums, shifting the cost of the elevated bills from providers onto those who carry insurance. The net result: Those with health insurance subsidize the medical care of those without it. As economists would describe what happens, the uninsured "free ride" on those who pay for health insurance.

The size of this subsidy is considerable. Congress found that the cost-shifting just described "increases family [insurance] premiums by on average over $1,000 a year." *Ibid.* Higher premiums, in turn, render health insurance less affordable, forcing more people to go without insurance and leading to further cost-shifting.

And it is hardly just the currently sick or injured among the uninsured who prompt elevation of the price of health care and health insurance. Insurance companies and health-care providers know that some percentage of healthy, uninsured people will suffer sickness or injury each year and will receive medical care despite their inability to pay. In anticipation of this uncompensated care, health-care companies raise their prices, and insurers their premiums. In other words, because any uninsured person may need medical care at any moment and because health-care companies must account for that risk, every uninsured person impacts the market price of medical care and medical insurance.

The failure of individuals to acquire insurance has other deleterious effects on the health-care market. * * *

C

States cannot resolve the problem of the uninsured on their own. Like Social Security benefits, a universal health-care system, if adopted by an individual State, would be "bait to the needy and dependent elsewhere, encouraging them to migrate and seek a haven of repose." *Helvering v. Davis*, 301 U.S. 619, 6447 (1937). * * * An influx of unhealthy individuals into a State with universal health care would result in increased spending on medical services. To cover the increased costs, a State would have to raise taxes, and private health-insurance companies would have to increase premiums. Higher taxes and increased insurance costs would, in turn, encourage businesses and healthy individuals to leave the State.

States that undertake health-care reforms on their own thus risk "placing themselves in a position of economic disadvantage as compared with neighbors or competitors." *Davis*, 301 U.S., at 644. * * * Facing that risk, individual States are unlikely to take the initiative in addressing the problem of the uninsured, even though solving that problem is in all States' best interests. Congress' intervention was needed to overcome this collective action impasse.

D

Aware that a national solution was required, Congress could have taken over the health-insurance market by establishing a tax-and-spend federal program like Social Security. Such a program, commonly referred to as a single-payer system (where the sole payer is the Federal Government), would have left little, if any, room for private enterprise or the States. Instead of going this route, Congress enacted the ACA, a solution that retains a robust role for private insurers and state governments. To make its chosen approach work, however, Congress had to use some new tools, including a requirement that most individuals obtain private health insurance coverage. * * *

A central aim of the ACA is to reduce the number of uninsured U.S. residents. * * * The minimum coverage provision advances this objective by giving potential recipients of health care a financial incentive to acquire insurance. Per the minimum coverage provision, an individual must either obtain insurance or pay a toll constructed as a tax penalty.

The minimum coverage provision serves a further purpose vital to Congress' plan to reduce the number of uninsured. Congress knew that encouraging individuals to purchase insurance would not suffice to solve the problem, because most of the uninsured are not uninsured by choice. Of particular concern to Congress were people who, though desperately in need of insurance, often cannot acquire it: persons who suffer from preexisting medical conditions.

Before the ACA's enactment, private insurance companies took an applicant's medical history into account when setting insurance rates or deciding whether to insure an individual. Because individuals with preexisting medical conditions cost insurance companies significantly more than those without such conditions, insurers routinely refused to insure these individuals, charged them substantially higher premiums, or offered only limited coverage that did not include the preexisting illness. * * *

To ensure that individuals with medical histories have access to affordable insurance, Congress devised a three-part solution. First, Congress imposed a "guaranteed issue" requirement, which bars insurers from denying coverage to any person on account of that person's medical condition or history. Second, Congress required insurers to use "community rating" to price their insurance policies. Community rating, in effect, bars insurance companies from charging higher premiums to those with preexisting conditions.

But these two provisions, Congress comprehended, could not work effectively unless individuals were given a powerful incentive to obtain insurance. * * * In the 1990's, several States—including New York, New Jersey, Washington, Kentucky, Maine, New Hampshire, and Vermont—enacted guaranteed-issue and community-rating laws without requiring universal acquisition of insurance coverage. The results were disastrous. "All seven states suffered from skyrocketing insurance premium costs, reductions in individuals with coverage, and reductions in insurance products and providers." * * *

Congress comprehended that guaranteed-issue and community-rating laws alone will not work. When insurance companies are required to insure the sick at affordable prices, individuals can wait until they become ill to buy insurance. Pretty soon, those in need of immediate medical care—*i.e.*, those who cost insurers the most—become the insurance companies' main customers. This "adverse selection" problem leaves insurers with two choices: They can either raise premiums dramatically to cover their ever-increasing costs or they can exit the market. In the seven States that tried guaranteed-issue and community-rating requirements without a minimum coverage provision, that is precisely what insurance companies did. * * *

* * *

In sum, Congress passed the minimum coverage provision as a key component of the ACA to address an economic and social problem that has plagued the Nation for decades: the large number of U.S. residents who are unable or unwilling to obtain health insurance. Whatever one thinks of the policy decision Congress made, it was Congress' prerogative to make it. Reviewed with appropriate deference, the minimum coverage provision, allied to the guaranteed-issue and community-rating prescriptions, should survive measurement under the Commerce and Necessary and Proper Clauses.

II

A

The Commerce Clause, it is widely acknowledged, "was the Framers' response to the central problem that gave rise to the Constitution itself." *EEOC v. Wyoming*, 460 U.S. 226, 244, 245, n. 1 (1983) (Stevens, J., concurring) (citing sources). Under the Articles of Confederation, the Constitution's precursor, the regulation of commerce was left to the States.

This scheme proved unworkable, because the individual States, understandably focused on their own economic interests, often failed to take actions critical to the success of the Nation as a whole. * * *

The Framers' solution was the Commerce Clause, which, as they perceived it, granted Congress the authority to enact economic legislation "in all Cases for the general Interests of the Union, and also in those Cases to which the States are separately incompetent." * * *

The Framers understood that the "general Interests of the Union" would change over time, in ways they could not anticipate. Accordingly, they recognized that the Constitution was of necessity a "great outlin[e]," not a detailed blueprint, see *McCulloch v. Maryland*, 17 U.S. 316 (1819). * * *

B

Consistent with the Framers' intent, we have repeatedly emphasized that Congress' authority under the Commerce Clause is dependent upon "practical" considerations, including "actual experience." * * * To deal with it effectively, Congress must be able to act in terms of economic and financial realities." * * * We afford Congress the leeway "to undertake to solve national problems directly and realistically." *American Power & Light Co. v. SEC*, 329 U.S. 90, 103 (1946).

Until today, this Court's pragmatic approach to judging whether Congress validly exercised its commerce power was guided by two familiar principles. First, Congress has the power to regulate economic activities "that substantially affect interstate commerce." *Gonzales v. Raich*, 545 U.S. 1, 17 (2005). This capacious power extends even to local activities that, viewed in the aggregate, have a substantial impact on interstate commerce. * * *

Second, we owe a large measure of respect to Congress when it frames and enacts economic and social legislation. * * * In answering these questions, we presume the statute under review is constitutional and may strike it down only on a "plain showing" that Congress acted irrationally. *United States v. Morrison*, 529 U.S. 598, 607 (2000).

C

Straightforward application of these principles would require the Court to hold that the minimum coverage provision is proper Commerce Clause legislation. * * *

D

Rather than evaluating the constitutionality of the minimum coverage provision in the manner established by our precedents, THE CHIEF JUSTICE relies on a newly minted constitutional doctrine. The commerce power does not, THE CHIEF JUSTICE announces, permit Congress to "compe[l] individuals to become active in commerce by purchasing a product."

1

a

THE CHIEF JUSTICE's novel constraint on Congress' commerce power gains no force from our precedent and for that reason alone warrants disapprobation. But even assuming, for the moment, that Congress lacks authority under the Commerce Clause to "compel individuals not engaged in commerce to purchase an unwanted product," such a limitation would be inapplicable here. Everyone will, at some point, consume health-care products and services. Thus, if THE CHIEF JUSTICE is correct that an insurance-purchase requirement can be applied only to those who "actively" consume health care, the minimum coverage provision fits the bill.

THE CHIEF JUSTICE does not dispute that all U.S. residents participate in the market for health services over the course of their lives. [In his opinion, THE CHIEF JUSTICE writes:] "Everyone will eventually need health care at a time and to an extent they cannot predict." But, THE CHIEF JUSTICE insists, the uninsured cannot be considered active in the market for health care, because "[t]he proximity and degree of connection between the [uninsured today] and [their] subsequent commercial activity is too lacking."

This argument has multiple flaws. First, more than 60% of those without insurance visit a hospital or doctor's office each year. Nearly 90% will within five years. An uninsured's consumption of health care is thus quite proximate: It is virtually certain to occur in the next five years and more likely than not to occur this year.

* * *

Second, it is Congress' role, not the Court's, to delineate the boundaries of the market the Legislature seeks to regulate. THE CHIEF JUSTICE defines the health-care market as including only those transactions that will occur either in the next instant or within some (unspecified) proximity to the next instant. But Congress could reasonably have viewed the market from a long-term perspective, encompassing all transactions virtually certain to occur over the next decade, not just those occurring here and now.

Third, contrary to THE CHIEF JUSTICE'S contention, our precedent does indeed support "[t]he proposition that Congress may dictate the conduct of an individual today because of prophesied future activity." In *Wickard*, the Court upheld a penalty the Federal Government imposed on a farmer who grew more wheat than he was permitted to grow under the Agricultural Adjustment Act of 1938 ("AAA"). He could not be penalized, the farmer argued, as he was growing the wheat for home consumption, not for sale on the open market. The Court rejected this argument. Wheat intended for home consumption, the Court noted, "overhangs the market, and if induced by rising prices, tends to flow into the market and check price increases [intended by the AAA]."

* * * Our decisions thus acknowledge Congress' authority, under the Commerce Clause, to direct the conduct of an individual today (the farmer in *Wickard*, stopped from growing excess wheat * * *) because of a prophesied future transaction (the eventual sale of that wheat or marijuana in the interstate market). Congress' actions are even more rational in this case, where the future activity (the consumption of medical care) is certain to occur, the sole uncertainty being the time the activity will take place.

Maintaining that the uninsured are not active in the health-care market, THE CHIEF JUSTICE draws an analogy to the car market. An individual "is not 'active in the car market,'" THE CHIEF JUSTICE observes, simply because he or she may someday buy a car. The analogy is inapt. The inevitable yet unpredictable need for medical care and the guarantee that emergency care will be provided when required are conditions nonexistent in other markets. That is so of the market for cars, and of the market for broccoli as well. Although an individual *might* buy a car or a crown of broccoli one day, there is no certainty she will ever do so. And if she eventually wants a car or has a craving for broccoli, she will be obliged to pay at the counter before receiving the vehicle or nourishment. She will get no free ride or food, at the expense of another consumer forced to pay an inflated price. * * *

Nor is it accurate to say that the minimum coverage provision "compel[s] individuals ... to purchase an unwanted product." If unwanted today, medical service secured by insurance may be desperately needed tomorrow. Virtually everyone, I reiterate, consumes health care at some point in his or her life. Health insurance is a means of paying for this care, nothing more. In requiring individuals to obtain insurance, Congress is therefore not mandating the purchase of a discrete, unwanted product. Rather, Congress is merely defining the terms on which individuals pay for an interstate good they consume: Persons subject to the mandate must now pay for medical care in advance (instead of at the point of service) and through insurance (instead of out of pocket). Establishing payment terms for goods in or affecting interstate commerce is quintessential economic regulation well within Congress' domain. * * *

THE CHIEF JUSTICE also calls the minimum coverage provision an illegitimate effort to make young, healthy individuals subsidize insurance premiums paid by the less hale and hardy. This complaint, too, is spurious. Under the current health-care system, healthy persons who lack insurance receive a benefit for which they do not pay: They are assured that, if they need it, emergency medical care will be available, although they cannot afford it. Those who have insurance bear the cost of this guarantee. By requiring the healthy uninsured to obtain insurance or pay a penalty structured as a tax, the minimum coverage provision ends the free ride these individuals currently enjoy.

In the fullness of time, moreover, today's young and healthy will become society's old and infirm. Viewed over a lifespan, the costs and benefits even out: The young who pay more than their fair share currently will pay less than their fair share when they become senior citizens. And even if, as undoubtedly will be the case, some individuals, over their lifespans, will pay more for health insurance than they receive in health services, they have little to complain about, for that is how insurance works. Every insured person receives protection against a catastrophic loss, even though only a subset of the covered class will ultimately need that protection.

b

In any event, THE CHIEF JUSTICE's limitation of the commerce power to the regulation of those actively engaged in commerce finds no home in the text of the Constitution or our decisions. Article I, § 8, of the Constitution grants Congress the power "[t]o regulate Commerce ... among the several

States." Nothing in this language implies that Congress' commerce power is limited to regulating those actively engaged in commercial transactions. Indeed, as the D.C. Circuit observed, "[a]t the time the Constitution was [framed], to 'regulate' meant," among other things, "to require action." See *Seven–Sky v. Holder*, 661 F.3d 1, 16 (2011).

Arguing to the contrary, THE CHIEF JUSTICE * * * asserts, "[t]he language of the Constitution reflects the natural understanding that the power to regulate assumes there is already something to be regulated."

This argument is difficult to fathom. Requiring individuals to obtain insurance unquestionably regulates the interstate health-insurance and health-care markets, both of them in existence well before the enactment of the ACA. * * *

Nor does our case law toe the activity versus inactivity line. In *Wickard*, for example, we upheld the penalty imposed on a farmer who grew too much wheat, even though the regulation had the effect of compelling farmers to purchase wheat in the open market. * * * In another context, this Court similarly upheld Congress' authority under the commerce power to compel an "inactive" landholder to submit to an unwanted sale. See *Monongahela Nav. Co. v. United States*, 148 U.S. 312, 335–337 (1893) ("[U]pon *the [great] power to regulate commerce* [,]" Congress has the authority to mandate the sale of real property to the Government, where the sale is essential to the improvement of a navigable waterway (emphasis added)). * * *

In concluding that the Commerce Clause does not permit Congress to regulate commercial "inactivity," and therefore does not allow Congress to adopt the practical solution it devised for the health-care problem, THE CHIEF JUSTICE views the Clause as a "technical legal conception," precisely what our case law tells us not to do. * * *

These line-drawing exercises were untenable, and the Court long ago abandoned them. * * * Failing to learn from this history, THE CHIEF JUSTICE plows ahead with his formalistic distinction between those who are "active in commerce" and those who are not.

It is not hard to show the difficulty courts (and Congress) would encounter in distinguishing statutes that regulate "activity" from those that regulate "inactivity." As Judge Easterbrook noted, "it is possible to restate most actions as corresponding inactions with the same effect." *Archie v. Racine*, 847 F.2d 1211, 1213 (7th Cir. 1988) (en banc). * * *

2

Underlying THE CHIEF JUSTICE'S view that the Commerce Clause must be confined to the regulation of active participants in a commercial market is a fear that the commerce power would otherwise know no limits. * * * The joint dissenters express a similar apprehension. * * * This concern is unfounded.

First, THE CHIEF JUSTICE could certainly uphold the individual mandate without giving Congress *carte blanche* to enact any and all purchase mandates. As several times noted, the unique attributes of the health-care market render everyone active in that market and give rise to a significant free-riding problem that does not occur in other markets.

* * *

Consider the chain of inferences the Court would have to accept to conclude that a vegetable-purchase mandate was likely to have a substantial effect on the health-care costs borne by lithe Americans. The Court would have to believe that individuals forced to buy vegetables would then eat them (instead of throwing or giving them away), would prepare the vegetables in a healthy way (steamed or raw, not deep-fried), would cut back on unhealthy foods, and would not allow other factors (such as lack of exercise or little sleep) to trump the improved diet.[9] * * *

Other provisions of the Constitution also check congressional overreaching. A mandate to purchase a particular product would be unconstitutional if, for example, the edict impermissibly abridged the freedom of speech, interfered with the free exercise of religion, or infringed on a liberty interest protected by the Due Process Clause.

* * * As the controversy surrounding the passage of the Affordable Care Act attests, purchase mandates are likely to engender political resistance. This prospect is borne out by the behavior of state legislators. Despite their possession of unquestioned authority to impose mandates, state governments have rarely done so. See Mark A. Hall, *Commerce Clause Challenges to Health Care Reform*, 159 U. Pa. L. Rev. 1825 (2011).

When contemplated in its extreme, almost any power looks dangerous. The commerce power, hypothetically, would enable Congress to prohibit the purchase and home production of all meat, fish, and dairy goods, effectively compelling Americans to eat only vegetables. Yet no one would offer the "hypothetical and unreal possibilit[y]," of a vegetarian state as a credible reason to deny Congress the authority ever to ban the possession and sale of goods. THE CHIEF JUSTICE accepts just such specious logic when he cites the broccoli horrible as a reason to deny Congress the power to pass the individual mandate. * * *

3

To bolster his argument that the minimum coverage provision is not valid Commerce Clause legislation, THE CHIEF JUSTICE emphasizes the provision's novelty. * * * While an insurance-purchase mandate may be novel, THE CHIEF JUSTICE'S argument certainly is not. "[I]n almost every instance of the exercise of the [commerce] power differences are asserted from previous exercises of it and made a ground of attack." *Hoke v. United States*, 227 U.S. 308, 320 (1913). * * * For decades, the Court has declined to override legislation because of its novelty, and for good reason. As our national economy grows and changes, we have recognized, Congress must adapt to

---

9. The failure to purchase vegetables in, THE CHIEF JUSTICE'S hypothetical, then, is not what leads to higher health-care costs for others; rather, it is the failure of individuals to maintain a healthy diet, and the resulting obesity, that creates the cost-shifting problem. Requiring individuals to purchase vegetables is thus several steps removed from solving the problem. The failure to obtain health insurance, by contrast, is the immediate cause of the cost-shifting Congress sought to address through the ACA. Requiring individuals to obtain insurance attacks the source of the problem directly, in a single step.

the changing "economic and financial realities." Hindering Congress' ability to do so is shortsighted; if history is any guide, today's constriction of the Commerce Clause will not endure.

* * *

IV

In the early 20th century, this Court regularly struck down economic regulation enacted by the peoples' representatives in both the States and the Federal Government. See, *e.g., Carter v. Carter Coal Co.*, 298 U.S. 238 (1936); *Hammer v. Dagenhart*, 247 U.S. 251 (1918); *Lochner v. New York*, 198 U.S. 45 (1905). THE CHIEF JUSTICE'S Commerce Clause opinion, and even more so the joint dissenters' reasoning, bear a disquieting resemblance to those long-overruled decisions.

Ultimately, the Court upholds the individual mandate as a proper exercise of Congress' power to tax and spend "for the ... general Welfare of the United States." Art. I, § 8, cl. 1. I concur in that determination, which makes THE CHIEF JUSTICE'S Commerce Clause essay all the more puzzling. Why should THE CHIEF JUSTICE strive so mightily to hem in Congress' capacity to meet the new problems arising constantly in our ever-developing modern economy? I find no satisfying response to that question in his opinion.

V

Through Medicaid, Congress has offered the States an opportunity to furnish health care to the poor with the aid of federal financing. To receive federal Medicaid funds, States must provide health benefits to specified categories of needy persons, including pregnant women, children, parents, and adults with disabilities. Guaranteed eligibility varies by category: for some it is tied to the federal poverty level (incomes up to 100% or 133%); for others it depends on criteria such as eligibility for designated state or federal assistance programs. The ACA enlarges the population of needy people States must cover to include adults under age 65 with incomes up to 133% of the federal poverty level. The spending power conferred by the Constitution, the Court has never doubted, permits Congress to define the contours of programs financed with federal funds. * * * And to expand coverage, Congress could have recalled the existing legislation, and replaced it with a new law making Medicaid as embracive of the poor as Congress chose.

* * * Medicaid is a prototypical example of federal-state cooperation in serving the Nation's general welfare. Rather than authorizing a federal agency to administer a uniform national health-care system for the poor, Congress offered States the opportunity to tailor Medicaid grants to their particular needs, so long as they remain within bounds set by federal law. In shaping Medicaid, Congress did not endeavor to fix permanently the terms participating states must meet; instead, Congress reserved the "right to alter, amend, or repeal" any provision of the Medicaid Act. 42 U.S.C. § 1304. States, for their part, agreed to amend their own Medicaid plans consistent with changes from time to time made in the federal law. And

from 1965 to the present, States have regularly conformed to Congress' alterations of the Medicaid Act.

THE CHIEF JUSTICE acknowledges that Congress may "condition the receipt of [federal] funds on the States' complying with restrictions on the use of those funds," but nevertheless concludes that the 2010 expansion is unduly coercive. His conclusion rests on three premises, each of them essential to his theory. First, the Medicaid expansion is, in THE CHIEF JUSTICE'S view, a new grant program, not an addition to the Medicaid program existing before the ACA's enactment. Congress, THE CHIEF JUSTICE maintains, has threatened States with the loss of funds from an old program in an effort to get them to adopt a new one. Second, the expansion was unforeseeable by the States when they first signed on to Medicaid. Third, the threatened loss of funding is so large that the States have no real choice but to participate in the Medicaid expansion. THE CHIEF JUSTICE therefore—*for the first time ever*—finds an exercise of Congress' spending power unconstitutionally coercive.

Medicaid, as amended by the ACA, however, is not two spending programs; it is a single program with a constant aim—to enable poor persons to receive basic health care when they need it. Given past expansions, plus express statutory warning that Congress may change the requirements participating States must meet, there can be no tenable claim that the ACA fails for lack of notice. Moreover, States have no entitlement to receive any Medicaid funds; they enjoy only the opportunity to accept funds on Congress' terms. Future Congresses are not bound by their predecessors' dispositions; they have authority to spend federal revenue as they see fit. The Federal Government, therefore, is not, as THE CHIEF JUSTICE charges, threatening States with the loss of "existing" funds from one spending program in order to induce them to opt into another program. Congress is simply requiring States to do what States have long been required to do to receive Medicaid funding: comply with the conditions Congress prescribes for participation.

A majority of the Court, however, buys the argument that prospective withholding of funds formerly available exceeds Congress' spending power. Given that holding, I entirely agree with THE CHIEF JUSTICE as to the appropriate remedy. It is to bar the withholding found impermissible—not, as the joint dissenters would have it, to scrap the expansion altogether. The dissenters' view that the ACA must fall in its entirety is a radical departure from the Court's normal course. When a constitutional infirmity mars a statute, the Court ordinarily removes the infirmity. It undertakes a salvage operation; it does not demolish the legislation. * * * That course is plainly in order where, as in this case, Congress has expressly instructed courts to leave untouched every provision not found invalid. See 42 U.S.C. § 1303. Because THE CHIEF JUSTICE finds the withholding—not the granting—of federal funds incompatible with the Spending Clause, Congress' extension of Medicaid remains available to any State that affirms its willingness to participate.

A

Expansion has been characteristic of the Medicaid program. Akin to the ACA in 2010, the Medicaid Act as passed in 1965 augmented existing federal grant programs jointly administered with the States. States were not required to participate in Medicaid. But if they did, the Federal Government paid at least half the costs. * * *

Since 1965, Congress has amended the Medicaid program on more than 50 occasions, sometimes quite sizably. Most relevant here, between 1988 and 1990, Congress required participating States to include among their beneficiaries pregnant women with family incomes up to 133% of the federal poverty level, children up to age 6 at the same income levels, and children ages 6 to 18 with family incomes up to 100% of the poverty level. * * *

Between 1966 and 1990, annual federal Medicaid spending grew from $631.6 million to $42.6 billion; state spending rose to $31 billion over the same period. See Dept. of Health and Human Services, National Health Expenditures by Type of Service and Source of Funds: Calendar Years 1960 to 2010. And between 1990 and 2010, federal spending increased to $269.5 billion. Enlargement of the population and services covered by Medicaid, in short, has been the trend.

Compared to past alterations, the ACA is notable for the extent to which the Federal Government will pick up the tab. Medicaid's 2010 expansion is financed largely by federal outlays. In 2014, federal funds will cover 100% of the costs for newly eligible beneficiaries; that rate will gradually decrease before settling at 90% in 2020. By comparison, federal contributions toward the care of beneficiaries eligible pre-ACA range from 50% to 83%, and averaged 57% between 2005 and 2008. * * *

Nor will the expansion exorbitantly increase state Medicaid spending. The Congressional Budget Office (CBO) projects that States will spend 0.8% more than they would have, absent the ACA. * * * Whatever the increase in state obligations after the ACA, it will pale in comparison to the increase in federal funding.[15]

Finally, any fair appraisal of Medicaid would require acknowledgment of the considerable autonomy States enjoy under the Act. * * * States, as first-line administrators, will continue to guide the distribution of substantial resources among their needy populations.

The alternative to conditional federal spending, it bears emphasis, is not state autonomy but state marginalization. In 1965, Congress elected to nationalize health coverage for seniors through Medicare. It could similarly have established Medicaid as an exclusively federal program. Instead, Congress gave the States the opportunity to partner in the program's administration and development. Absent from the nationalized model, of course, is the state-level policy discretion and experimentation that is Medicaid's hallmark; undoubtedly the interests of federalism are better

---

15. Even the study on which the plaintiffs rely, * * * concludes that "[w]hile most states will experience some increase in spending, this is quite small relative to the federal matching payments and low relative to the costs of uncompensated care that [the states] would bear if the[re] were no health reform." * * * Thus there can be no objection to the ACA's expansion of Medicaid as an "unfunded mandate." Quite the contrary, the program is impressively well funded.

served when States retain a meaningful role in the implementation of a program of such importance. * * *

B

The Spending Clause authorizes Congress "to pay the Debts and provide for the . . . general Welfare of the United States." Art. I, § 8, cl. 1. To ensure that federal funds granted to the States are spent "to 'provide for the . . . general Welfare' in the manner Congress intended," Congress must of course have authority to impose limitations on the States' use of the federal dollars. This Court, time and again, has respected Congress' prescription of spending conditions, and has required States to abide by them. * * * In particular, we have recognized Congress' prerogative to condition a State's receipt of Medicaid funding on compliance with the terms Congress set for participation in the program. * * *

Yes, there are federalism-based limits on the use of Congress' conditional spending power. In the leading decision in this area, *South Dakota v. Dole*, 483 U.S. 203 (1987), the Court identified four criteria. The conditions placed on federal grants to States must (a) promote the "general welfare," (b) "unambiguously" inform States what is demanded of them, (c) be germane "to the federal interest in particular national projects or programs," and (d) not "induce the States to engage in activities that would themselves be unconstitutional."

The Court in *Dole* mentioned, but did not adopt, a further limitation, one hypothetically raised a half-century earlier: In "some circumstances," Congress might be prohibited from offering a "financial inducement . . . so coercive as to pass the point at which 'pressure turns into compulsion.' " (quoting *Steward Machine Co. v. Davis*, 301 U.S. 548, 590 (1937)). Prior to today's decision, however, the Court has never ruled that the terms of any grant crossed the indistinct line between temptation and coercion.

Dole involved the National Minimum Drinking Age Act, 23 U.S.C. § 158, enacted in 1984. That Act directed the Secretary of Transportation to withhold 5% of the federal highway funds otherwise payable to a State if the State permitted purchase of alcoholic beverages by persons less than 21 years old. Drinking age was not within the authority of Congress to regulate, South Dakota argued, because the Twenty–First Amendment gave the States exclusive power to control the manufacture, transportation, and consumption of alcoholic beverages. The small percentage of highway-construction funds South Dakota stood to lose by adhering to 19 as the age of eligibility to purchase 3.2% beer, however, was not enough to qualify as coercion, the Court concluded.

This case does not present the concerns that led the Court in *Dole* even to consider the prospect of coercion. In *Dole*, the condition—set 21 as the minimum drinking age—did not tell the States how to use funds Congress provided for highway construction. Further, in view of the Twenty–First Amendment, it was an open question whether Congress could directly impose a national minimum drinking age.

The ACA, in contrast, relates solely to the federally funded Medicaid program; if States choose not to comply, Congress has not threatened to withhold funds earmarked for any other program. Nor does the ACA use Medicaid funding to induce States to take action Congress itself could not undertake. The Federal Government undoubtedly could operate its own health-care program for poor persons, just as it operates Medicare for seniors' health care.

That is what makes this such a simple case, and the Court's decision so unsettling. Congress, aiming to assist the needy, has appropriated federal money to subsidize state health-insurance programs that meet federal standards. The principal standard the ACA sets is that the state program cover adults earning no more than 133% of the federal poverty line. Enforcing that prescription ensures that federal funds will be spent on health care for the poor in furtherance of Congress' present perception of the general welfare.

C

THE CHIEF JUSTICE asserts that the Medicaid expansion creates a "new health care program." Moreover, States could "hardly anticipate" that Congress would "transform [the program] so dramatically." Therefore, THE CHIEF JUSTICE maintains, Congress' threat to withhold "old" Medicaid funds based on a State's refusal to participate in the "new" program is a "threa[t] to terminate [an]other . . . independent gran[t]." And because the threat to withhold a large amount of funds from one program "leaves the States with no real option but to acquiesce [in a newly created program]," THE CHIEF JUSTICE concludes, the Medicaid expansion is unconstitutionally coercive.

1

The starting premise on which THE CHIEF JUSTICE'S coercion analysis rests is that the ACA did not really "extend" Medicaid; instead, Congress created an entirely new program to co-exist with the old. THE CHIEF JUSTICE calls the ACA new, but in truth, it simply reaches more of America's poor than Congress originally covered.

Medicaid was created to enable States to provide medical assistance to "needy persons." * * * By bringing health care within the reach of a larger population of Americans unable to afford it, the Medicaid expansion is an extension of that basic aim.

* * *

Endeavoring to show that Congress created a new program, THE CHIEF JUSTICE cites three aspects of the expansion. First, he asserts that, in covering those earning no more than 133% of the federal poverty line, the Medicaid expansion, unlike pre-ACA Medicaid, does not "care for the neediest among us." What makes that so? Single adults earning no more than $14,856 per year—133% of the current federal poverty level—surely rank among the Nation's poor.

Second, according to THE CHIEF JUSTICE, "Congress mandated that newly eligible persons receive a level of coverage that is less comprehensive than the traditional Medicaid benefit package." That less comprehensive benefit package, however, is not an innovation introduced by the ACA; since 2006,

States have been free to use it for many of their Medicaid beneficiaries. The level of benefits offered therefore does not set apart post-ACA Medicaid recipients from all those entitled to benefits pre-ACA.

Third, THE CHIEF JUSTICE correctly notes that the reimbursement rate for participating States is different regarding individuals who became Medicaid-eligible through the ACA. But the rate differs only in its generosity to participating States. Under pre-ACA Medicaid, the Federal Government pays up to 83% of the costs of coverage for current enrollees; under the ACA, the federal contribution starts at 100% and will eventually settle at 90%. Even if one agreed that a change of as little as 7 percentage points carries constitutional significance, is it not passing strange to suggest that the purported incursion on state sovereignty might have been averted, or at least mitigated, had Congress offered States *less* money to carry out the same obligations?

* * * Thereafter, Congress could have enacted Medicaid II, a new program combining the pre–2010 coverage with the expanded coverage required by the ACA. By what right does a court stop Congress from building up without first tearing down?

2

THE CHIEF JUSTICE finds the Medicaid expansion vulnerable because it took participating States by surprise. * * * When amendment of an existing grant program has no [substantial] retroactive effect, however, we have upheld Congress' instruction. * * * [This is not the case here, since] from the start, the Medicaid Act put States on notice that the program could be changed: "The right to alter, amend, or repeal any provision of [Medicaid]," the statute has read since 1965, "is hereby reserved to the Congress." 42 U.S.C. § 1304. * * *

3

THE CHIEF JUSTICE ultimately asks whether "the financial inducement offered by Congress . . . pass[ed] the point at which pressure turns into compulsion." The financial inducement Congress employed here, he concludes, crosses that threshold: The threatened withholding of "existing Medicaid funds" is "a gun to the head" that forces States to acquiesce. * * *

When future Spending Clause challenges arrive, as they likely will in the wake of today's decision, how will litigants and judges assess whether "a State has a legitimate choice whether to accept the federal conditions in exchange for federal funds"? Are courts to measure the number of dollars the Federal Government might withhold for noncompliance? The portion of the State's budget at stake? And which State's—or States'—budget is determinative: the lead plaintiff, all challenging States (26 in this case, many with quite different fiscal situations), or some national median? * * * Or that the coercion state officials in fact fear is punishment at the ballot box for turning down a politically popular federal grant?

The coercion inquiry, therefore, appears to involve political judgments that defy judicial calculation. * * * At bottom, my colleagues' position is that the States' reliance on federal funds limits Congress' authority to alter its spending programs. This gets things backwards: Congress, not the States, is tasked with spending federal money in service of the general welfare. And each successive Congress is empowered to appropriate funds as it sees fit. * * * There is only money States *anticipate* receiving from future Congresses.

* * *

For the reasons stated, I agree with THE CHIEF JUSTICE that, as to the validity of the minimum coverage provision, the judgment of the Court of Appeals for the Eleventh Circuit should be reversed. In my view, the provision encounters no constitutional obstruction. Further, I would uphold the Eleventh Circuit's decision that the Medicaid expansion is within Congress' spending power.

■ JUSTICE SCALIA, JUSTICE KENNEDY, JUSTICE THOMAS, and JUSTICE ALITO, dissenting.

Congress has set out to remedy the problem that the best health care is beyond the reach of many Americans who cannot afford it. It can assuredly do that, by exercising the powers accorded to it under the Constitution. The question in this case, however, is whether the complex structures and provisions of the Patient Protection and Affordable Care Act (Affordable Care Act or ACA) go beyond those powers. We conclude that they do.

This case is in one respect difficult: it presents two questions of first impression. The first of those is whether failure to engage in economic activity (the purchase of health insurance) is subject to regulation under the Commerce Clause. Failure to act does result in an effect on commerce, and hence might be said to come under this Court's "affecting commerce" criterion of Commerce Clause jurisprudence. But in none of its decisions has this Court extended the Clause that far. The second question is whether the congressional power to tax and spend, U.S. Const., Art. I, § 8, cl. 1, permits the conditioning of a State's continued receipt of all funds under a massive state-administered federal welfare program upon its acceptance of an expansion to that program. Several of our opinions have suggested that the power to tax and spend cannot be used to coerce state administration of a federal program, but we have never found a law enacted under the spending power to be coercive. Those questions are difficult.

The case is easy and straightforward, however, in another respect. What is absolutely clear, affirmed by the text of the 1789 Constitution, by the Tenth Amendment ratified in 1791, and by innumerable cases of ours in the 220 years since, is that there are structural limits upon federal power—upon what it can prescribe with respect to private conduct, and upon what it can impose upon the sovereign States. Whatever may be the conceptual limits upon the Commerce Clause and upon the power to tax and spend, they cannot be such as will enable the Federal Government to regulate all private conduct and to compel the States to function as administrators of federal programs.

That clear principle carries the day here. The striking case of *Wickard v. Filburn*, 317 U.S. 111 (1942), which held that the economic activity of growing wheat, even for one's own consumption, affected commerce sufficiently that it could be regulated, always has been regarded as the *ne plus ultra* of expansive Commerce Clause jurisprudence. To go beyond that, and to say the *failure* to grow wheat (which is *not* an economic activity, or any activity at all) nonetheless affects commerce and therefore can be federally regulated, is to make mere breathing in and out the basis for federal prescription and to extend federal power to virtually all human activity.

As for the constitutional power to tax and spend for the general welfare: The Court has long since expanded that beyond (what Madison thought it meant) taxing and spending for those aspects of the general welfare that were within the Federal Government's enumerated powers. * * * Thus, we now have sizable federal Departments devoted to subjects not mentioned among Congress' enumerated powers, and only marginally related to commerce: the Department of Education, the Department of Health and Human Services, the Department of Housing and Urban Development. The principal practical obstacle that prevents Congress from using the tax-and-spend power to assume all the general-welfare responsibilities traditionally exercised by the States is the sheer impossibility of managing a Federal Government large enough to administer such a system. That obstacle can be overcome by granting funds to the States, allowing them to administer the program. That is fair and constitutional enough when the States freely agree to have their powers employed and their employees enlisted in the federal scheme. But it is a blatant violation of the constitutional structure when the States have no choice.

The Act before us here exceeds federal power both in mandating the purchase of health insurance and in denying nonconsenting States all Medicaid funding. These parts of the Act are central to its design and operation, and all the Act's other provisions would not have been enacted without them. In our view it must follow that the entire statute is inoperative.

I

The Individual Mandate

Article I, § 8, of the Constitution gives Congress the power to "regulate Commerce . . . among the several States." The Individual Mandate in the Act commands that every "applicable individual shall for each month beginning after 2013 ensure that the individual, and any dependent of the individual who is an applicable individual, is covered under minimum essential coverage." 26 U.S.C. § 5000A(a). If this provision "regulates" anything, it is the *failure* to maintain minimum essential coverage. One might argue that it regulates that failure by requiring it to be accompanied by payment of a penalty. But that failure—that abstention from commerce—is not "Commerce." To be sure, *purchasing* insurance *is* "Commerce"; but one does not regulate commerce that does not exist by compelling its existence.

In *Gibbons v. Ogden*, 22 U.S. 1 (1824), Chief Justice Marshall wrote that the power to regulate commerce is the power "to prescribe the rule by which commerce is to be governed." That understanding is consistent with the original meaning of "regulate" at the time of the Constitution's ratification, when "to regulate" meant "[t]o adjust by rule, method or established mode," 2 N. Webster, An American Dictionary of the English Language (1828); "[t]o adjust by rule or method," 2 S. Johnson, A Dictionary of the English Language (7th ed. 1785); "[t]o adjust, to direct according to rule," 2 J. Ash, New and Complete Dictionary of the English Language (1775); "to put in order, set to rights, govern or keep in order," T. Dyche & W. Pardon, A New General English Dictionary (16th ed. 1777).[1] It can mean to direct the manner of something but not to direct that something come into being. There is no instance in which this Court or Congress (or anyone else, to our knowledge) has used "regulate" in that peculiar fashion. If the word bore that meaning, Congress' authority "[t]o make Rules for the Government and Regulation of the land and naval Forces," U.S. Const., Art. I, § 8, cl. 14, would have made superfluous the later provision for authority "[t]o raise and support Armies," id., § 8, cl. 12, and "[t]o provide and maintain a Navy," id., § 8, cl. 13.

We do not doubt that the buying and selling of health insurance contracts is commerce generally subject to federal regulation. But when Congress provides that (nearly) all citizens must buy an insurance contract, it goes beyond "adjust[ing] by rule or method," * * * or "direct[ing] according to rule;" * * * it directs the creation of commerce.

In response, the Government offers two theories as to why the Individual Mandate is nevertheless constitutional. Neither theory suffices to sustain its validity.

A

First, the Government submits that § 5000A is "integral to the Affordable Care Act's insurance reforms" and "necessary to make effective the Act's core reforms." * * * [T]he Act contains numerous health insurance reforms, but most notable for present purposes are the "guaranteed issue" and "community rating" provisions, §§ 300gg to 300gg–4. * * *

Under ordinary circumstances, of course, insurers would respond by charging high premiums to individuals with pre-existing conditions. The Act seeks to prevent this through the community-rating provision. * * * Aside from the rough proxies of age and tobacco use * * *, the Act does not allow an insurer to factor the individual's health characteristics into the price of his insurance premium. This creates a new incentive for young and healthy individuals without pre-existing conditions. The insurance premiums for those in this group will not reflect their own low actuarial risks but will subsidize insurance for others in the pool. Many of them may decide that purchasing health insurance is not an economically sound decision—especially since the guaranteed-issue provision will enable them to purchase it at the same cost in later years and even if they have developed a pre-existing condition. But without the contribution of above-risk premiums from the young and healthy, the community-rating provision will not

1. The most authoritative legal dictionaries of the founding era lack any definition for "regulate" or "regulation," suggesting that the term bears its ordinary meaning (rather than some specialized legal meaning) in the constitutional text. See R. Burn, A New Law Dictionary 281 (1792); G. Jacob, A New Law Dictionary (10th ed. 1782); 2 T. Cunningham, A New and Complete Law Dictionary (2d ed. 1771).

enable insurers to take on high-risk individuals without a massive increase in premiums.

The Government presents the Individual Mandate as a unique feature of a complicated regulatory scheme governing many parties with countervailing incentives that must be carefully balanced. * * * This is not a dilemma unique to regulation of the health-insurance industry. Government regulation typically imposes costs on the regulated industry—especially regulation that prohibits economic behavior in which most market participants are already engaging. * * * And many industries so regulated face the reality that, without an artificial increase in demand, they cannot continue on. * * * Congress might protect the imperiled industry by prohibiting low-cost competition, or by according it preferential tax treatment, or even by granting it a direct subsidy.

Here, however, Congress has impressed into service third parties, healthy individuals who could be but are not customers of the relevant industry, to offset the undesirable consequences of the regulation. Congress' desire to force these individuals to purchase insurance is motivated by the fact that they are further removed from the market than unhealthy individuals with pre-existing conditions, because they are less likely to need extensive care in the near future. If Congress can reach out and command even those furthest removed from an interstate market to participate in the market, then the Commerce Clause becomes a font of unlimited power. * * *

At the outer edge of the commerce power, this Court has insisted on careful scrutiny of regulations that do not act directly on an interstate market or its participants. * * * [The] Commerce Clause, even when supplemented by the Necessary and Proper Clause, is not *carte blanche* for doing whatever will help achieve the ends Congress seeks by the regulation of commerce. * * *

[T]here are many ways other than this unprecedented Individual Mandate by which the regulatory scheme's goals of reducing insurance premiums and ensuring the profitability of insurers could be achieved. For instance, those who did not purchase insurance could be subjected to a surcharge when they do enter the health insurance system. Or they could be denied a full income tax credit given to those who do purchase the insurance. * * *

B

The Government's second theory in support of the Individual Mandate is that § 5000A is valid because it is actually a "regulat[ion of] activities having a substantial relation to interstate commerce. * * *

The primary problem with this argument is that § 5000A does not apply only to persons who purchase all, or most, or even any, of the health care services or goods that the mandated insurance covers. * * * [T]he health care "market" that is the object of the Individual Mandate not only includes but principally consists of goods and services that the young people primarily affected by the Mandate *do not purchase*. They are quite simply not participants in that market, and cannot be made so (and thereby subjected to regulation) by the simple device of defining participants to include all those who will, later in their lifetime, probably purchase the goods or services covered by the mandated insurance. Such a definition of market participants is unprecedented, and were it to be a premise for the exercise of national power, it would have no principled limits.

* * * All of us consume food, and when we do so the Federal Government can prescribe what its quality must be and even how much we must pay. But the mere fact that we all consume food and are thus, sooner or later, participants in the "market" for food, does not empower the Government to say when and what we will buy. That is essentially what this Act seeks to do with respect to the purchase of health care. It exceeds federal power.

C

A few respectful responses to JUSTICE GINSBURG'S dissent on the issue of the Mandate are in order. * * * The dissent dismisses the conclusion that the power to compel entry into the health-insurance market would include the power to compel entry into the new-car or broccoli markets. The latter purchasers, it says, "will be obliged to pay at the counter before receiving the vehicle or nourishment," whereas those refusing to purchase health-insurance will ultimately get treated anyway, at others' expense. "[T]he unique attributes of the health-care market ... give rise to a significant free-riding problem that does not occur in other markets." And "a vegetable-purchase mandate" (or a car-purchase mandate) is not "likely to have a substantial effect on the health-care costs" borne by other Americans. Those differences make a very good argument by the dissent's own lights, since they show that the failure to purchase health insurance, unlike the failure to purchase cars or broccoli, creates a national, social-welfare problem that is (in the dissent's view) included among the unenumerated "problems" that the Constitution authorizes the Federal Government to solve. But those differences do not show that the failure to enter the health-insurance market, unlike the failure to buy cars and broccoli, is an activity that Congress can "regulate." (Of course one day the failure of some of the public to purchase American cars may endanger the existence of domestic automobile manufacturers; or the failure of some to eat broccoli may be found to deprive them of a newly discovered cancerfighting chemical which only that food contains, producing health-care costs that are a burden on the rest of us—in which case, under the theory of JUSTICE GINSBURG'S dissent, moving against those inactivities will also come within the Federal Government's unenumerated problem-solving powers.)

II

The Taxing Power

As far as § 5000A is concerned, we would stop there. Congress has attempted to regulate beyond the scope of its Commerce Clause authority, and § 5000A is therefore invalid. The Government contends, however, as expressed in the caption to Part II of its brief, that "THE MINIMUM COVERAGE PROVISION IS INDEPENDENTLY AUTHORIZED BY CONGRESS'S TAXING POWER." * * * The issue is not whether Congress had the *power* to frame the minimum-coverage provision as a tax, but whether it *did* so.

* * * Our cases establish a clear line between a tax and a penalty: " '[A] tax is an enforced contribution to provide for the support of government; a penalty . . . is an exaction imposed by statute as punishment for an unlawful act.' " *United States v. Reorganized CF & I Fabricators of Utah, Inc.*, 518 U.S. 213, 224 (1996) (quoting *United States v. La Franca*, 282 U.S. 568, 572 (1931)). In a few cases, this Court has held that a "tax" imposed upon private conduct was so onerous as to be in effect a penalty. But we have never held—*never*—that a penalty imposed for violation of the law was so trivial as to be in effect a tax. We have never held that *any* exaction imposed for violation of the law is an exercise of Congress' taxing power—even when the statute *calls* it a tax, much less when (as here) the statute repeatedly calls it a penalty. When an act "adopt[s] the criteria of wrongdoing" and then imposes a monetary penalty as the "principal consequence on those who transgress its standard," it creates a regulatory penalty, not a tax. *Child Labor Tax Case*, 259 U.S. 20, 38 (1922).

So the question is, quite simply, whether the exaction here is imposed for violation of the law. It unquestionably is. * * *

IV

The Medicaid Expansion

We now consider respondents' second challenge to the constitutionality of the ACA, namely, that the Act's dramatic expansion of the Medicaid program exceeds Congress' power to attach conditions to federal grants to the States.

The ACA does not legally compel the States to participate in the expanded Medicaid program, but the Act authorizes a severe sanction for any State that refuses to go along: termination of all the State's Medicaid funding. For the average State, the annual federal Medicaid subsidy is equal to more than one-fifth of the State's expenditures. A State forced out of the program would not only lose this huge sum but would almost certainly find it necessary to increase its own health-care expenditures substantially, requiring either a drastic reduction in funding for other programs or a large increase in state taxes. And these new taxes would come on top of the federal taxes already paid by the State's citizens to fund the Medicaid program in other States.

* * *

Seven Members of the Court agree that the Medicaid Expansion, as enacted by Congress, is unconstitutional. * * *

V

Severability

The Affordable Care Act seeks to achieve "near-universal" health insurance coverage. The two pillars of the Act are the Individual Mandate and the expansion of coverage under Medicaid. In our view, both these central provisions of the Act—the Individual Mandate and Medicaid Expansion—are invalid. It follows, as some of the parties urge, that all other provisions of the Act must fall as well. * * * This Court must not impose risks unintended by Congress or produce legislation Congress may have lacked the support to enact. For those reasons, the unconstitutionality of both the Individual Mandate and the Medicaid Expansion requires the invalidation of the Affordable Care Act's other provisions.

* * *

The Court today decides to save a statute Congress did not write. It rules that what the statute declares to be a requirement with a penalty is instead an option subject to a tax. And it changes the intentionally coercive sanction of a total cut-off of Medicaid funds to a supposedly noncoercive cut-off of only the incremental funds that the Act makes available.

* * * The values that should have determined our course today are caution, minimalism, and the understanding that the Federal Government is one of limited powers. But the Court's ruling undermines those values at every turn. In the name of restraint, it overreaches. In the name of constitutional avoidance, it creates new constitutional questions. In the name of cooperative federalism, it undermines state sovereignty.

The Constitution, though it dates from the founding of the Republic, has powerful meaning and vital relevance to our own times. The constitutional protections that this case involves are protections of structure. Structural protections—notably, the restraints imposed by federalism and separation of powers—are less romantic and have less obvious a connection to personal freedom than the provisions of the Bill of Rights or the Civil War Amendments. Hence they tend to be undervalued or even forgotten by our citizens. It should be the responsibility of the Court to teach otherwise, to remind our people that the Framers considered structural protections of freedom the most important ones, for which reason they alone were embodied in the original Constitution and not left to later amendment. The fragmentation of power produced by the structure of our Government is central to liberty, and when we destroy it, we place liberty at peril. Today's decision should have vindicated, should have taught, this truth; instead, our judgment today has disregarded it.

For the reasons here stated, we would find the Act invalid in its entirety. We respectfully dissent.

■ JUSTICE THOMAS, dissenting.

I dissent for the reasons stated in our joint opinion, but I write separately to say a word about the Commerce Clause. The joint dissent and THE CHIEF JUSTICE correctly apply our precedents to conclude that the Individual Mandate is beyond the power granted to Congress under the Commerce Clause and the Necessary and Proper Clause. Under those precedents, Congress may regulate "economic activity [that] substantially affects interstate commerce." *United States v. Lopez*, 514 U.S. 549, 560 (1995). I adhere to my view that "the very notion of a 'substantial effects' test under the Commerce Clause is inconsistent with the original understanding of Congress' powers and with this Court's early Commerce Clause cases." *United States v. Morrison*, 529 U.S. 598, 627 (2000) (THOMAS, J., concurring); see also *Lopez, supra*, at 584–602 (THOMAS, J., concurring);

Gonzales v. Raich, 545 U.S. 1, 67–69 (2005) (THOMAS, J., dissenting). As I have explained, the Court's continued use of that test "has encouraged the Federal Government to persist in its view that the Commerce Clause has virtually no limits." *Morrison, supra*, at 627. The Government's unprecedented claim in this suit that it may regulate not only economic activity but also *inactivity* that substantially affects interstate commerce is a case in point.

Questions

1. Who are the individuals the Patient Protection and Affordable Care Act compels to purchase health insurance? Did the plaintiffs in *NFIB* represent the interests of the compelled individuals? Whose interests did the plaintiffs represent?

2. One of the government's justifications for requiring minimum essential health insurance coverage was the so-called "cost-shifting problem." What is the cost-shifting problem? How did the Court analyze the problem? What are the functions of the "guaranteed-issue" and "community-rating" provisions of the Patient Protection and Affordable Care Act? How do the "guaranteed-issue" and "community-rating" provisions address the cost-shifting problem?

3. In *Lochner v. New York*, defending the liberty of contract, the majority rejected the argument that bakers were coerced to accept unfavorable contractual terms. In the context of the Medicaid expansion provision, the *NFIB* Court held that Congress exceeded its constitutional authority by "forc[ing] the States to implement a federal program * * * threaten[ing] the political accountability [that is] key to our federal system." What are the characteristics of coercion that the *NFIB* Court identified? Should courts apply this test to ordinary commercial relationships in the marketplace? Explain.

4. Are "mandatory purchases of items such as cars or broccoli" equivalent to a "requirement to maintain minimum essential [health insurance] coverage"? What are the similarities and differences between a "requirement to maintain minimum essential [health insurance] coverage" and "address[ing] the diet problem by ordering everyone to buy vegetables"?

5. Urban fire was a common risk until the 1920s. Urban fires destroyed many cities across the United States. A very partial list of "great fires" includes the Great Fire of New York City (1776), the Second Great Fire of New York City (1835), the Great Chicago Fire of 1871, the Great Boston Fire of 1872, the Great Seattle Fire of 1889, the Great Baltimore Fire of 1904, and the Great Atlanta Fire of 1917. The 1906 San Francisco Earthquake was followed by fire that destroyed most buildings. The prevalence and magnitude of urban fires established fire insurance as a critically important financial instrument at the turn of the nineteenth century. Would the government's justifications for individual health insurance mandates also apply to fire insurance?

6. With the brief exception of the National Vaccine Act, the United States had no federal smallpox vaccination program. The localization of the vaccination programs substantially delayed the eradication of the deadly disease. The overwhelming majority of smallpox cases and deaths in the United States occurred during the period in which a safe vaccination was available. (a) Under the 2012 health-care ruling, could Congress create a regulatory framework requiring smallpox vaccination for all U.S. residents? (b) Assume we are back in 1900, forty-nine years before the eradication of smallpox in the United States and before several exceptionally deadly smallpox epidemics broke out. The anti-vaccination movement has a significant number of members who refuse to be vaccinated and to vaccinate their children. Should Congress use any regulatory powers to establish a mandate smallpox vaccination across the United States?

7. A government failure is any regulatory policy that does not satisfy cost-benefit analysis and, as such, may include a governmental failure to regulate. Society ordinarily evaluates the government by its actions and inactions—too many regulations that burden businesses, inadequate border security, poor responses to economic problems and national disasters, and so forth. How did the *NFIB* Court address the distinction between action and inaction? Was the Court's approach consistent with public perceptions of government failures?

PART II

MOTIVATIONS FOR REGULATION

"It is enough that there is an evil at hand for correction, and that it might be thought that the particular legislative measure was a rational way to correct it."

—Justice William O. Douglas[1]

Justifications vs. Motivations

What justifies regulation? In the late 1670s, Sir Matthew Hale, then Lord Chief Justice of the King's Bench of England, wrote an essay on the ports of the sea that he filed among his private papers. The essay analyzes the laws applied to harbors and their facilities, noting that wharves are "affected with a publick interest." In 1787, his retired essay was published in an influential legal treatise,[2] which Chief Justice Morrison Waite invoked eighty-nine years later, in *Munn v. Illinois* (1876), to justify a new doctrine of state regulation of private businesses:

> This brings us to inquire as to the principles upon which this power of regulation rests. * * * Looking, then, to the common law, from whence came the right which the Constitution protects, we find that when private property is 'affected with a public interest, it ceases to be *juris privati only*.' This was said by Lord Chief Justice Hale more than two hundred years ago, in his treatise *De Portibus Maris*, 1 Harg. Law Tracts, 78, and has been accepted without objection as an essential element in the law of property ever since.[3]

---

1. Williamson v. Lee Optical of Oklahoma, 348 U.S. 483, 488 (1955).

2. FRANCIS HALGRAVE, A COLLECTION OF TRACTS RELATIVE TO THE LAW OF ENGLAND 77–78 (1787).

3. Munn v. Illinois, 94 U.S. 113, 125–126 (1876). *See generally* Walton H. Hamilton, *Affection with Public Interest*, 39 YALE LAW JOURNAL 1089 (1930); Breck P. McAllister, *Lord Hale and Business Affected with a Public Interest*, 43 HARVARD LAW REVIEW 759 (1930). *See also* Robert L. Rabin, *Federal Regulation in Historical Perspective*, 38 STANFORD LAW REVIEW 1189,

Dissenting, Justice Stephen Johnson Field stressed the ambiguity of the distinction between businesses that are affected and those that are not affected with a public interest and warned that the distinction "gives unrestrained license to legislative will."[4] *Munn*, however, established a new doctrine in regulation: "Businesses * * * clothed with a public interest justif[y] some public regulation."[5]

For fifty years after *Munn*, courts developed the "affected with a public interest" doctrine as a justification for regulation. In *Tyson v. Banton* (1927), a New York ticket broker challenged the constitutionality of an anti-scalping statute that regulated the markup of ticket brokers. Striking down the statute in a five-to-four decision, the Supreme Court refused to apply the "affected with a public interest" doctrine "in the absence of some controlling emergency" and held that the police power did not reach "amusements and entertainments."[6] Moreover, the Court stressed that a business was not affected with a public interest merely because it was large. In a famous dissent, Justice Oliver Wendell Holmes expressed his view of the "affected with a public interest" doctrine and regulatory powers: "We fear to grant power and are unwilling to recognize it when it exists. * * * [W]hen Legislatures are held to be authorized to do anything considerably affecting public welfare it is covered by apologetic phrases like the police power, or the statement that the business concerned has been dedicated to a public use. * * * I do not believe in such apologies. I think the proper course is to recognize that a state Legislature can do whatever it sees fit to do unless it is restrained by some express prohibition in the Constitution of the United States or of the State. * * * *[T]he notion that a business is clothed with a public interest and has been devoted to the public use is little more than a fiction intended to beautify what is disagreeable agreeable to the sufferers.*"[7]

Seven years later, the Supreme Court again examined the "affected with a public interest" doctrine. In *Nebbia v. New York* (1934), the Court declared that "[i]t is clear that there is no closed class or category of businesses affected with a public interest." The Court, therefore, concluded that " 'affected with a public interest' is the equivalent of 'subject to the exercise of the police power'; and it is plain that nothing more was intended by the expression."[8] That is, the "phrase 'affected with a public interest' can * * * mean no more than that an industry, for adequate reason, is subject to control for the public good."[9] The Court did not explain the meaning of the "adequate reason" nor did it offer appropriate justifications for regulation.

1208 (1986) ("*Munn v. Illinois* is often regarded as the cornerstone of Supreme Court regulatory jurisprudence, and in a sense it seems appropriate that the case should be granted this pivotal position.")

4. *Munn*, 94 U.S. at 148. *See also* Charles W. McCurdy, *Justice Field and the Jurisprudence of Government–Business Relations: Some Parameters of Laissez–Faire Constitutionalism, 1863–1897*, 62 JOURNAL OF AMERICAN HISTORY 970 (1975).

5. Charles Wolff Packing Co. v. Court of Industrial Relations of State of Kansas, 262 U.S. 522, 535 (1923). *See generally* FORD P. HALL, THE CONCEPT OF BUSINESS AFFECTED WITH A PUBLIC INTEREST (1940).

6. Tyson v. Banton, 273 U.S. 418, 440 (1927).

7. *Id.* at 445–446 (Holmes, J., dissenting) (emphasis added).

8. Nebbia v. New York, 291 U.S. 502, 533 (1934).

9. *Id.* at 536.

Figure II.1 depicts the frequency of the use of the phrase "affected with a public interest" in U.S. publications between 1860 and 2008. This frequency roughly parallels the use of the "affected with a public interest" doctrine by courts and reflects the doctrine's rise after its adoption in *Munn v. Illinois* until its decline in 1938, four years after *Nebbia*.[10] Since then, the use of the doctrine has continued to decline. Federal and state courts still occasionally use the "affected with a public interest" doctrine, although the *Nebbia* Court repudiated its logic.[11] The "public interest" standard may be an intuitive justification for regulation, but it offers no guidance for why or when the state should intervene in the private domain. As a justification for regulation, the "affected with a public interest" doctrine is too vague and can also be used as a justification against regulation.[12] The survival of the doctrine in courts, despite its 1934 rejection by the Supreme Court illuminates the power of shaky intuitions in regulation.

We saw that states can invoke the police power only in aid of the safety, health, morals, and general welfare of the public.[13] The "affected with a public interest" doctrine attempted to provide a justification for the use of the police power in order to regulate private property. The doctrine, however, mostly satisfied legal reasoning and indeed did not add much to the understanding of the police power. We describe the doctrine here for two reasons. First, many important cases and other texts refer to the

---

10. The Supreme Court delivered *Nebbia* on March 5, 1934. Between March 5, 1934 and December 31, 1938, 209 reported court decisions referred to the doctrine. *See also* ALFRED E. KAHN, THE ECONOMICS OF REGULATION, vol. 1, 3 (1971) (noting that "roughly in the period 1877–1934," "the Supreme Court treated certain industries as affected with a public interest").

11. *See, e.g.*, State Bd. of Dry Cleaners v. Thrift–D–Lux Cleaners, 40 Cal.2d 436 (1953), § 9.1. *See also* Amadeo v. Principal Mutual Life Insurance Co., 290 F.3d 1152, 1161 (9th Cir. 2002) (noting that "the insurance business is affected with a public interest and offers services of a quasi-public nature"); Ambach v. Norwick, 441 U.S. 68, 73 (1979) (noting that, Oyama v. California, 332 U.S. 633 (1948), the Supreme Court appeared to be willing to "question the constitutionality of discrimination against aliens even in areas affected with a 'public interest'."); Barnes v. New Hampshire Karting Association, Inc., 128 N.H. 102 (1986) (holding that racing facilities were not "affected with a public interest" because they were "not a service of great importance to the public, nor is racing a matter of practical necessity."); Foley v. Interactive Data Corp., 47 Cal.3d 654, 685 (1988) ("Suppliers of services affected with a public interest must take the public's interest seriously, where necessary placing it before their interest in maximizing gains"); Goldstein v. Chestnut Ridge Volunteer Fire Co., 218 F.3d 337, 347 (4th Cir. 2000) (noting that volunteer fire companies "become so affected with a public interest that the corporation thus becomes quasi-public."); Jackson v. Metropolitan Edison Co., 419 U.S. 345 (1974) (examining the status of services "affected with a public interest"); National Association of Regulatory Utility Commissioners v. F.C.C., 525 F.2d 630, 640–41 (D.C. Cir. 1976) (suggesting that the justification for common carriers may be the affected with a public interest doctrine); Rush–Presbyterian–St. Luke's Med. Ctr. v. Hellenic Republic, 877 F.2d 574, 578 (7th Cir. 1989) (noting that "natural resources, to the extent they are 'affected with a public interest,' are goods in which only the sovereign may deal."); United States v. Onan, 190 F.2d 1, 6 (8th Cir. 1951) ("The practice of law is affected with a public interest and an attorney at law as distinguished from a layman, has both public and private obligations, being sworn to act with all good fidelity toward both his client and the court."); Universe Life Ins. Co. v. Giles, 950 S.W.2d 48, 53 (Tex. 1997) ("[W]e have long-recognized that the insurance industry is peculiarly affected with a public interest.")

12. *See, e.g.*, Dun & Bradstreet, Inc. v. Greenmoss Builders, Inc., 472 U.S. 749, 788 (1985) (Brennan, J., dissenting) (explaining that the First Amendment protection of advertising relies on the "[recognition] that even pure advertising may well be affected with a public interest, [and] that 'the free flow of commercial information is indispensable'.")

13. *See* § 1.2.2.

Figure II.1
Frequency of the Phrase "affected with a public interest" in U.S. Publications, 1860–2008

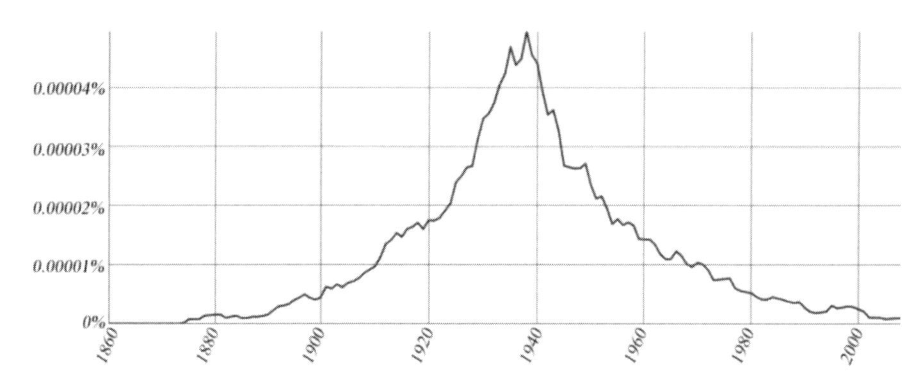

Source: Google Ngram Viewer.

doctrine. Second, the doctrine is a powerful example of a hollow legal justification for regulation. Its framing, "affected with a public interest," had an intuitive appeal; it suggested that societal interests were at stake. The story of the doctrine, therefore, stresses that intuitive motivations for regulation and traditional justifications do not necessarily warrant state interference with the private domain.

Theory and practice provide justifications for regulation in three general categories of situations: (1) failures in market performance, (2) uncompensated effects on others' well being, and (3) self-inflicted harm. Both in theory and practice, however, it is often challenging to classify circumstances and determine whether they warrant regulation.

The chapters in this Part of the book review common *motivations* for regulation; reasons individuals, firms, and organizations believe or use to justify state interference with the private domain. We will examine the nature of these motivations and the circumstances under which they may align with societal interests. Ultimately, a regulation is justified only when it benefits society; however, cost-benefit analysis is not always consistent with fairness perceptions, and it may contradict preexisting beliefs. Such conflicts, as we saw, contribute to disagreements over regulation and regulatory policies.

The starting point of the discussion of motivations for regulation is that *"problems" do not justify government regulation.*[14] This point is intuitive but may run against human sentiments. It is only natural to have incentives to address problems, since they are bothering. However, it is not always worth doing so. Does a problem that bothers a few people but benefits society justify regulation? Do "small problems" justify regulation, or only "large problems"? Does a problem justify regulation regardless of the cost to the taxpayer? Should society allocate resources to address all

---

14. *See, e.g.*, CHARLES L. SCHULTZE, THE PUBLIC USE OF PRIVATE INTEREST 46 (1977); HENRY SIDGWICK, PRINCIPLES OF POLITICAL ECONOMY 414 (1887) ("It does not follow that whenever *laissez faire* falls short government interference is expedient; since the inevitable drawbacks of the latter, may in any particular case, be worse than the shortcomings of the private enterprise.")

problems? "Problems" may have powerful influence on decisionmaking processes, but as we shall see perceptions of problems may be misleading.

In 1969, the Congressional Joint Economic Committee held a hearing on public expenditures and the appropriate function of the government. One of the witnesses testifying before the Committee was the economist Kenneth Arrow, who wrote for the Committee a short essay about justifications for economic regulation:[15]

> Before beginning a discussion of the role of economic analysis in Government expenditure policy one must determine that set of activities in which the public sector should properly be engaged. While the price system of the private sector is an efficient resource allocating mechanism under many conditions, it fails to function appropriately when certain conditions prevail. [T]his paper * * * presents the conditions under which the private competitive market system will lead to an efficient allocation of resources and deals with those conditions in which nonmarket allocating mechanisms appear superior to the price system. * * *
>
> [T]he analysis * * * lead to criteria for non-market allocation. We are tempted to set forth these criteria in terms analogous to the profit-and-loss statements of private business; in this form, we are led to benefit-cost analysis. There are, moreover, two possible aims for benefit-cost analysis; one, more ambitious but theoretically simpler, * * * which will restore Pareto efficiency; the second involves the recognition that the instruments available to the Government or other non-market forces are scarce resources for one reason or another, so that all that can be achieved is a "second-best."
>
> * * *
>
> [M]arket failure is not absolute; it is better to consider a broader category that of transaction costs, which in general impede and in particular cases completely block the formation of markets. It is usually though not always emphasized that transaction costs are costs of running the economic system. * * * The identification of transaction costs * * * should be a major item on the research agenda. * * *
>
> Given the existence of Pareto inefficiency in a free market equilibrium, there is a pressure in the market to overcome it by some sort of departure from the free market; *i.e.*, some form of collective action. This need not be undertaken by the Government.
>
> * * *
>
> *Collective Action: The Political Process*
>
> The State may frequently have a special role to play in resource allocation because, by its nature, it has a monopoly of coercive power, and coercive power can be used to economize on transaction costs. The most important use of coercion in the economic context is the collection of taxes; others are regulatory legislation and eminent domain proceedings.
>
> * * *

---

15. Kenneth Arrow, *The Organization of Economic Activity: Issues Pertinent to the Choice of Market Versus Nonmarket Allocation*, in 1 The Analysis and Evaluation of Public Expenditures: The PPB System, 91st Cong., 1st Sess. 47 (May 28, 1969).

> Political policy is not made by voters, not even in the sense that they choose the vector of political actions which best suits them. It is in fact made by representatives in one form or another. Political representation is an outstanding example of the principal-agent relation. This means that the link between individual utility functions and social action is tenuous, though by no means completely absent.
>
> * * *
>
> *Collective Action: Social Norms*
>
> It is a mistake to limit collective action to State action; many other departures from the anonymous atomism of the price system are observed regularly. Indeed, firms of any complexity are illustrations of collective action, the internal allocation of their resources being directed by authoritative and hierarchical controls.
>
> I want, however, to conclude by calling attention to a less visible form of social action: norms of social behavior, including ethical and moral codes. I suggest as one possible interpretation that they are reactions of society to compensate for market failures. It is useful for individuals to have some trust in each other's word. In the absence of trust it would become very costly to arrange for alternative sanctions and guarantees, and many opportunities for mutually beneficial cooperation would have to be, foregone.
>
> It is difficult to conceive of buying trust in any direct way. * * * As an alternative, society may proceed by internalization of these norms to the achievement of the desired agreement on an unconscious level.
>
> There is a whole set of customs and norms which might be similarly interpreted as agreements to improve the efficiency of the economic system * * * by providing commodities to which the price system is inapplicable.

Arrow, therefore, argued that market failures alone do not offer a justification for government regulation. Rather, market failures constitute an economic *problem*: a situation where free market forces cannot overcome impediments to efficient allocation of resources, and, possibly, contribute to such impediments. According to Arrow, government regulation may be justified when cost-benefit analysis indicates that such intervention may benefit the public and reduce the burden of the market failure. He cautioned, however, that even when government regulation is justified, the most it can accomplish is a "second-best" solution.[16] Under this realistic perspective, "for one reason or another," government intervention could never yield the optimal outcome.[17] From Arrow's analysis, we can posit that justifications for regulation should be developed through a cost-benefit analysis that compares regulatory alternatives, including the alternative of not regulating.[18]

---

16. *See generally* R.G. Lipsey & Kelvin Lancaster, *The General Theory of Second Best*, 24 REVIEW OF ECONOMIC STUDIES 11 (1956).

17. *See also* Paul L. Joskow & Roger C. Noll, *Regulation in Theory and Practice: An Overview*, in STUDIES IN PUBLIC REGULATION 1, 1 (Gary Fromm ed. 1981) ("[E]conomists have had to come to grips with important contradictions between theoretical prescriptions to remedy market imperfections so as to increase economic welfare and the actual behavior and performance of regulatory agencies.")

18. *See also* Stephen Breyer, *Analyzing Regulatory Failure: Mismatches, Less Restrictive Alternatives, and Reform*, 92 HARVARD LAW REVIEW 549, 553 (1979) (arguing that "regulation is

In sum, for the most part, the common reference to "justification for regulation" means willingness to allocate resources to address a perceived problem. People use the word "justification" but mean "*motivation*"—the willingness to pay for a regulatory measure to address a perceived problem is not necessarily justified; it merely exists. In other words, a regulatory measure is not necessarily cost-effective ("justified") because it was adopted.

Questions

In *Tyson*, the Supreme Court struck down an attempt of the New York legislature to outlaw the ticket brokerage industry. One of the key provisions in this 1922 legislation provided:

> **Restriction as to Price**. No licensee shall resell * * * ticket or other evidence of the right of entry to any theater, place of amusement or entertainment, or other place where public exhibitions, games, contests, or performances are given at a price in excess of fifty cents in advance of the price printed on the face of such ticket or other evidence of the right to entry. * * *

Justice Holmes' dissent in *Tyson* reflected his position that the Court should refrain from scrutinizing the economic policies of legislatures: "I think the proper course is to recognize that a state Legislature can do whatever it sees fit to do unless it is restrained by some express prohibition in the Constitution of the United States or of the State." Justice Louis Brandeis joined this dissent.

One of the debates among the other seven Justices was whether the "virtual monopoly [over] the best seats" that enabled ticket brokers to charge "extortionate prices" justified the regulation of the resale prices of theater tickets. Writing for the majority, Justice Sutherland argued that the ban would fix prices and facilitate "collusive alliances between the proprietors of theaters and ticket brokers or scalpers." Justices Stone and Sanford in separate dissents concluded that ticket brokers deprived the public of access to the theaters and thus the ban was justified. From the economic perspective, both arguments are wrong. Anti-scalping laws are befuddling because they prevent a matching of demand and supply,[19] but they do not establish collusions on the market.

(1) Consider the possibility that judges may be wrong in determining whether a policy would serve the public. Is Justice Holmes' judicial approach to justifying regulation socially desirable?

(2) In *Berman v. Parker* (1954), Justice William Douglas declared: "When the legislature has spoken, the public interest has been declared in terms well-nigh conclusive."[20] Is this position similar to Justice Holmes' approach?

---

justified only if it achieves without too great a corresponding cost policy objectives that a consensus of reasonable observers would consider to be in the public interest.")

19. *See, e.g.*, Stephen K. Happel & Marianne M. Jennings, *Assessing the Economic Rationale and Legal Remedies for Ticket Scalping*, 16 JOURNAL OF LEGISLATION 1 (1989); Andrew T. Williams, *Do Anti–Ticket Scalping Laws Make a Difference?* 15 MANAGERIAL & DECISION ECONOMICS 503 (1994).

20. Berman v. Parker, 348 U.S. 26, 32 (1954).

CHAPTER 3

EXTERNALITIES

§ 3.0 AFFECTING OTHERS

Should the state protect our aesthetic and other sensitivities? In *Berman v. Parker*, Justice William Douglas examined the scope of the state's police power and wrote: "The concept of the public welfare is broad and inclusive. The values it represents are spiritual as well as physical, aesthetic as well as monetary. It is within the power of the legislature to determine that the community should be beautiful as well as healthy, spacious as well as clean, well-balanced as well as carefully patrolled."[1] Our discussion of Pareto efficiency demonstrated that such interpretation of regulatory powers may result in harm.[2] We used the following hypothetical:

> Consider Alexis, who likes the color black—for her outfit, home, bicycle, car, and everything else. Alexis expresses her individualism and style with color. Alas, everyone else in society finds the color black terribly depressing. Should society intervene in the freedom of Alexis (and individuals with similar preferences) to serve the majority's preferences? Or should we follow the Pareto principle and leave Alexis alone because any intervention would harm her interests?

This hypothetical builds on Amartya Sen's Liberal Paradox.[3] We can consider Alexis' preference for black as one of her traits. The majority's dislike of particular traits may be broad and related to ethnicity, sexual orientation, intellectual deficiencies, illnesses, height, or just appearance. Some traits have historically offended the public, or significant portions of the public. The state can devise and has devised regulatory techniques to address such social discomfort and preferences. For example, many states engaged in eugenics to serve particular social preferences. Between 1929 and 1974, North Carolina sterilized about 7,600 people "for the best interest of the[ir] mental, moral or physical improvement."[4] Similarly, localities addressed the unpleasantness "ugliness" can inflict on the public. For example, in 1867, San Francisco issued an ordinance to "restrain

---

1. Berman v. Parker, 348 U.S. 26, 33 (1954).

2. *See* § 2.3.2.

3. *See* Amartya Sen, *The Impossibility of a Paretian Liberal*, 78 JOURNAL OF POLITICAL ECONOMY 152 (1970). *See also* Amartya Sen, *Freedom of Choice: Concept and Content*, 32 EUROPEAN ECONOMIC REVIEW 269 (1988); Barak Orbach, *On Hubris, Civility, and Incivility*, 54 ARIZONA. LAW REVIEW 443 (2012).

4. Copies of North Carolina sterilization laws are available at *regti.me/NC-sterilization* (case sensitive). In 2010, Governor Bev Perdue established the N.C. Justice for Sterilization Victims Foundation to provide justice and compensation for victims who were sterilized by the state. The state estimated that 2,944 victims were alive in 2010.

certain persons from appearing in streets and public places."[5] The ordinance banned the "practice of begging," "whether by look, word, sign or deed" and prohibited people who are "diseased, maimed, mutilated or in any way deformed so as to be an unsightly or disgusting object" from exposing themselves to public view. In 1881, Chicago revised its municipal code and used the opportunity to borrow San Francisco's "ugly law:"

> Any person who is diseased, maimed, mutilated or in any way deformed so as to be an unsightly or disgusting object, or an improper person to be allowed in or on the streets, highways, thoroughfares or public places in this city shall not therein or thereon expose himself or herself to public view under penalty of one dollar for each offense. On the conviction of any person for a violation of this section, if it shall seem proper and just, the fine provided for may be suspended, and such person detained at the police station, where he shall be well cared for, until he can be committed to the county poor house.

The City Council repealed this regulation in October 1973.[6] "Ugly laws" used to be rather prevalent.[7] The issues raised by both the unpleasantness that "ugly people" allegedly inflict on others and the possibility of addressing such ugliness through regulation are, of course, parallel to many discussions of freedom, harm, and regulation. Not all forms of alleged "ugliness" impose harm on others, nor do all forms of "beauty" produce any benefit to society. This Chapter presents a broad framework for analyzing harm and benefit to others. As we shall see, harm and benefit may be reciprocal concepts. Social definitions of "ugliness" and "beauty" may define entitlements, although such definitions may not necessarily promote prosperity. The history of civil rights—minorities', women's, and gays' rights—illuminates this point.

§ 3.1 SOCIAL REGULATION

In the 1970s, scholars started drawing a distinction between regulations that "cope with various kinds of market-failure problems" and regulations that address "environmental, health, occupational-safety, and product-quality" issues.[8] The latter group of regulations was regarded as "[t]he most vigorous recent extensions of government intervention * * * intended to improve the quality of the environment, of consumer products, and of workplaces."[9] This regulatory trend was much more "vigorous" than traditionally described, since it also includes some civil right regulations that followed *Brown v. Board of Education*.[10] Public policy toward

5. A copy of the ordinance is available at *regti.me/SF-ugly* (case sensitive).

6. *See* Adrienne Phelps Coco, *Diseased, Maimed Mutilated: Categorization of Disability and an Ugly Law in Late Nineteenth Century Chicago*, 44 JOURNAL OF SOCIAL HISTORY 23 (2010).

7. *See generally* SUSAN M. SCHWEIK, UGLY LAWS: DISABILITY IN PUBLIC (2009).

8. Paul L. Joskow & Roger C. Noll, *Regulation in Theory and Practice: An Overview*, in STUDIES IN PUBLIC REGULATION 1, 3 (Gary Fromm ed. 1981).

9. *Id.* at 21.

10. Brown v. Board of Education, 347 U.S. 483 (1954). *See, e.g.*, Office of Communication of United Church of Christ v. F.C.C., 359 F.2d 994 (D.C. Cir. 1966):

these two groups of regulations moved in opposite directions. *Economic regulations*, which intend to address market failures with command-and-control measures, were slashed. In the 1970s, critiques of and disappointment with regulatory policies gave rise to deregulation and changes in approaches toward government regulation. By contrast, new regulations, called social regulations, that addressed certain social problems were on the rise.[11] These legislative and regulatory reforms paralleled the pro-plaintiff revolution in products liability that began in the early 1960s and expended into other "social" areas.[12]

Social regulation may be the oldest form of regulation. It addresses *externalities*—involuntary effects on well-being one person imposes on others;[13] that is, the *uncompensated effects of one's actions on others' well-being*.[14] Pollution, discrimination, unknown risks in products, and other "social problems" are examples of externalities. The regulation of actions that affect others' well-being is indeed an ancient concept in law and order that rationalizes criminal and tort laws.[15] For example, in the mid-nineteenth century, John Stuart Mill argued that "[t]he only purpose for which [the state] power can be rightfully exercised over any member of a civilized

---

> The theory that the Commission can always effectively represent the listener interests in a renewal proceeding without the aid and participation of legitimate listener representatives fulfilling the role of private attorney general is one of those assumptions we collectively try to work with so long as they are reasonably adequate. When it becomes clear, as it does to us now, that it is no longer a valid assumption which stands up under the realities of actual experience, neither we nor the Commission can continue to rely on it.

See also Robert L. Rabin, *Federal Regulation in Historical Perspective*, 38 STANFORD LAW REVIEW 1189, 1296–1298 (1986).

11. *See generally* Rabin, *Federal Regulation in Historical Perspective*, *supra* note 3, at 1278–1315. *See also* EUGENE BARDACH & ROBERT A. KAGAN EDS., SOCIAL REGULATION: STRATEGIES FOR REFORM (1982); E. Donald Elliott et al., *Toward a Theory of Statutory Evolution: The Federalization of Environmental Law*, 1 JOURNAL OF LAW, ECONOMICS & ORGANIZATION 313 (1985); LESTER B. LAVE, THE STRATEGY OF SOCIAL REGULATION: DECISION FRAMEWORKS FOR POLICY (1981); JERRY L. MASHAW & DAVID L. HARFST, THE STRUGGLE FOR AUTO SAFETY (1990).

12. *See generally* James A. Henderson, Jr. & Theodore Eisenberg, *The Quiet Revolution in Products Liability: An Empirical Study of Legal Change*, 37 UCLA LAW REVIEW 479 (1990).

13. For the meaning of the term "well-being" *see* Matthew D. Adler, *Risk, Death and Harm: The Normative Foundations of Risk Regulation*, 87 MINNESOTA LAW REVIEW 1293, 1303–1310 (2003); LOUIS KAPLOW & STEVEN SHAVELL, FAIRNESS VERSUS WELFARE 18–28, 409–449 (2002).

14. *See, e.g.*, Richard B. Stewart, *Regulation, Innovation, and Administrative Law: A Conceptual Framework*, 69 CALIFORNIA LAW REVIEW 1256, 1263 (1981) ("The basic justification for environmental, health, and safety regulation is preventing or reducing harmful spillovers or externalities such as pollution generated by producers and consumers in a market economy.") Some scholars have maintained the abstract definition of "social regulation" that uses the areas of regulation, implicitly equating social regulation with "risk regulation." *See, e.g.*, W. KIP VISCUSI, FATAL TRADEOFFS: PUBLIC AND PRIVATE RESPONSIBILITIES FOR RISK 13 (1995) ("The ultimate objective of social regulation policies is to influence health, safety, and environmental outcomes."); WESLEY A. MAGAT & W. KIP VISCUSI, INFORMATIONAL APPROACHES TO REGULATION viii (1992) ("[S]ocial regulation * * * focuses on workplace safety, environmental preservation, consumer protection, and related goals.")

15. *See generally* JOEL FINBERG, OFFENSE TO OTHERS (1985). *See also* Elizabeth C. Tandy, *The Regulation of Nuisances in the American Colonies*, 13 AMERICAN JOURNAL OF PUBLIC HEALTH 810 (1923).

community, against his will, is to prevent harm to others."[16] Mill also believed that state regulation might be needed to guarantee that positive externalities—uncompensated goods and services—are produced and benefit the public:

> [I]t is a proper office of government to build and maintain lighthouses, establish buoys, etc., for the security of navigation: for since it is impossible that the ships at sea which are benefited by a lighthouse, should be made to pay a toll on the occasion of its use, no one would build lighthouses from motives of personal interest, unless indemnified and rewarded from a compulsory levy made by the state.[17]

The trend that began in the 1970s, the so-called the Public Interest era of regulation,[18] refers to the increasing scope of social regulation at the federal level, not to new motivations for regulation.

§ 3.1.1 Uncompensated Effects on Others' Well–Being

§ 3.1.1a Pigou: Private and Social Interests

The first scholar to articulate the meaning of uncompensated effects on others' well-being was the British economist Arthur Cecil Pigou. In his 1912 book, *Wealth and Welfare*, Pigou explored potential societal consequences of the pursuit of self-interest.[19] As we have seen, Adam Smith's invisible hand theory *supposedly* predicts that the pursuit of self-interest tends to serve society as a whole, even though this end is not the express intent of the individual or the firm.[20] Pigou posited that the pursuit of self-interest to maximize private gains ("private net product") could compromise societal interests and diminish social wealth ("social net product.") Thus, he argued that there are common situations of "divergences between social and private net product," when a person promotes his private gains, but does not increase the social gain by the same amount. Rather, there may be spillovers—other parties may capture some gains or incur some losses because of his private actions. These spillovers, effects on others' well-being, are "*externalities*."

Pigou's analysis therefore was a direct challenge to the "validity of the classical doctrine that self-interest, if not interfered with, tends to" promote societal interests—Adam Smith's invisible hand theory.

In 1920, Pigou published a revised and enlarged version of his book that he retitled: *The Economics of Welfare*. This book popularized his theory of externalities and influenced the development of many public policies.[21] In his 1920 book, Pigou surveyed several classic examples of

---

16. JOHN STUART MILL, ON LIBERTY 22 (1859).

17. JOHN STUART MILL, PRINCIPLES OF POLITICAL ECONOMY, vol. 2, 567 (1848).

18. *See* Rabin, *Federal Regulation in Historical Perspective*, *supra* note 3, at 1278–1315. *See also* STEPHEN P. CROLEY, REGULATION AND PUBLIC INTERESTS: THE POSSIBILITY OF GOOD REGULATORY GOVERNMENT (2007).

19. ARTHUR CECIL PIGOU, WEALTH AND WELFARE 148–171 (1912).

20. *Supra* § 2.1.1.

21. In *The Economics of Welfare*, Pigou defined "divergences between social and private net product," as situations in which "person A, in the course of rendering some service, for

externalities. He began by stressing that the effects on others' well-being may be positive, not only negative. For this point, he borrowed a famous nineteenth-century analysis of lighthouses: "[I]t may easily happen that the benefits of a well-placed lighthouse must be largely enjoyed by ships on which no toll could be conveniently imposed."[22] Pigou contributed another example of positive effects: "uncompensated services are rendered when resources are invested in private parks in cities; for these, even though the public is not admitted to them, improve the air of the neighbourhood." Pigou also discussed negative effects on others' well-being, providing a famous example of "smoke from factory chimneys * * * in large towns [that] inflicts a heavy uncharged loss on the community, [such as] injury to buildings and vegetables, expenses for washing clothes and cleaning rooms, [and] expenses for the provision of extra artificial light." Another famous example of negative effects Pigou identified was "uncompensated damage done to surrounding woods by sparks from railway engines."[23] Pigou posited that such uncompensated effects may warrant government regulation:

> It is plain that divergences between private and social net product * * * cannot * * * be mitigated by a modification of the contractual relation between any two contracting parties, because the divergence arises out of a service or disservice rendered to persons other than the contracting parties. It is, however, possible for the State * * * to remove the divergence * * * by "extraordinary encouragements" or "extraordinary restraints."[24]

§ 3.1.1b Externalities Defined

Pigou himself did not use the term "*externalities*." The term was coined in the 1950s to simplify the Pigonvian phrase "divergences between social and private net product," which stands for uncompensated effects of one's actions on others' well-being.[25] A more technical definition of the term externality that modern economists sometimes use is: a transfer of value from one economic agent to another in the absence of any related

---

which payment is made, to * * * person B, incidentally also renders services or disservices to other persons * * * of such a sort that payment cannot be exacted from the benefitted parties or compensation enforced on behalf of the injured parties." ARTHUR CECIL PIGOU, THE ECONOMICS OF WELFARE 159–171 (1920).

22. HENRY SIDGWICK, PRINCIPLES OF POLITICAL ECONOMY 407 (1887).

23. PIGOU, THE ECONOMICS OF WELFARE, *supra* note 21, at 115.

24. *Id.* at 168. A similar passage appeared *Wealth and Welfare*. PIGOU, WEALTH AND WELFARE, *supra* note 19, at 164.

25. Economists started using the term "external economies" in the early 1950s. *See, e.g.*, J. E. Meade, *External Economies and Diseconomies in a Competitive Situation*, 62 ECONOMIC JOURNAL 54, 56 (1952); Paul A. Samuelson, *The Pure Theory of Public Expenditure*, 36 REVIEW ECONOMICS & STATISTICS 387, 389 (1954); Tibor Scitovsky, *Two Concepts of External Economies*, 62 JOURNAL OF POLITICAL ECONOMICS 143, 143–45 (1954). It is unknown who coined the term "externality," but by 1958 it was part of the economic jargon. *See, e.g.*, Francis M. Bator, *The Anatomy of Market Failure*, 72 QUARTERLY JOURNAL OF ECONOMICS 351, 363–71 (1958); Paul A. Samuelson, *Aspects of Public Expenditure Theories*, 40 REVIEW OF ECONOMICS & STATISTICS 332, 336 (1958).

economic transactions between the agents.[26] In plain English, externalities exist whenever a person does not internalize the full costs and benefits of her actions and these actions affect others' well-being. Under such circumstances, the pursuit of self-interest may not serve society. For example, a butcher operating in a residential neighborhood does not take into account the effects of his business on the health of residents and their quality of life. A railway may disregard the relationship between the number of trains it operates and the damage to surrounding trees done by sparks. Similarly, when a person does not capture the full benefits associated with her activities, she may not engage in desirable activities or she may choose a suboptimal level of activity because she does not take into account the benefits to others. For these reasons, there may also be too few lighthouses and they may operate irregularly.

The concept of *externalities* does not provide any meaningful threshold to justify regulation. Externalities are social problems in which society may or may not be willing to invest resources. Does horn-honking justify regulation?[27] Does airplane noise justify regulation?[28] Does potential sky trespassing justify regulation?[29] Does a mountain view blocked by neighbors' evergreen trees justify regulation?[30] Does a junk fax justify regulation?[31] Pigou noted that we benefit from "resources invested in lamps erected at the doors of private houses [that] throw light also on the streets."[32] Is government regulation needed to pay homeowners for these uncompensated positive effects? Externalities often provide motivations for social regulation, and should be tolerated if feasible regulatory alternatives cannot address them cost-effectively.

§ 3.1.2 The Coase Theorem

§ 3.1.2a Critique of the Pigonvian Tradition

Ronald Coase's article *The Problem of Social Cost* is one of the most influential works in law *and* economics.[33] He wrote this article in response to the theories of a person he considered an intellectual nemesis: Arthur

---

26. *See* DANIEL F. SPULBER, REGULATION AND MARKETS 46 (1989).

27. *See, e.g.*, Goedert v. City of Ferndale, 596 F. Supp.2d 1027 (E.D. Mich. 2008); Meaney v. Dever, 326 F.3d 283, 287–88 (1st Cir. 2003); Montana v. Compas, 290 Mont. 11 (1998); Washington v. Immelt, 173 Wash.2d 1 (2011); Weil v. McClough, 618 F.Supp. 1294 (S.D.N.Y. 1985).

28. *See, e.g.*, Burnham v. Beverly Airways, 311 Mass. 628 (1942); Delta Air Corp. v. Kersey, 193 Ga. 862 (1942); Smith v. New England Aircraft Co., 270 Mass. 511 (1930); Thrasher v. Atlanta, 178 Ga. 514 (1934). *See also* William B. Harvey, *Landowners' Rights in the Air Age: The Airport Dilemma*, 56 MICHIGAN LAW REVIEW 1313 (1958); Steven A. Morrison et al., *Fundamental Flaws of Social Regulation: The Case of Airplane Noise*, 42 JOURNAL OF LAW & ECONOMICS 723 (1999).

29. *See, e.g.*, Hinman v. Pacific Air Transport, 84 F.2d 755 (9th Cir. 1936). *See also* Howard H. Hackley, *Trespassers in the Sky*, 21 MINNESOTA LAW REVIEW 773 (1937).

30. *See, e.g.*, Wilson v. Handley, 97 Cal.App.4th 1301 (2002).

31. *See* the Junk Fax Act of 2005, Pub. L. No. 109–21, 119 Stat. 359 (2005).

32. PIGOU, THE ECONOMICS OF WELFARE, *supra* note 21, at 160.

33. Ronald H. Coase, *The Problem of Social Cost*, 3 JOURNAL OF LAW & ECONOMICS 1 (1960).

Cecil Pigou.[34] Pigou died at age 81 in 1959, a year before the publication of *The Problem of Social Cost*. Coase, however, remained preoccupied, criticizing Pigou's intellectual legacy throughout his career.[35] In 1972, Coase even published an article criticizing Pigou's 1908 appointment as a successor to Alfred Marshall at Cambridge University.[36]

The Problem of Social Cost opens by crediting Pigou for persuading "most economists" that "it would be desirable to make the owner of the factory liable for the damage caused to those injured by the smoke, or alternatively, to place a tax on the factory owner varying with the amount of smoke produced and equivalent in money terms to the damage it would cause, or * * * to exclude the factory from residential districts."[37] Coase argued that "the suggested courses of action are inappropriate, in that they lead to results which are not necessarily, or even usually, desirable." He considered Pigou a radical interventionist whose influence on economic analysis was mostly harmful.[38] Coase firmly believed that regulation is socially costly and proposed to minimize state intervention in markets. He was convinced that the gains that could be attained from government regulation smaller than the costs.

The Problem of Social Cost criticizes the traditional framing of externalities as "A inflicts harm on B" and examines the question "how should we restrain A?" Coase stressed that "[w]e are dealing with a problem of a reciprocal nature. To avoid the harm to B would inflict harm on A. The real question to be decided is: should A be allowed to harm B, or should B be allowed to harm A?" Coase had a clear answer to the question: "What has to be decided is whether the gain from preventing the harm is greater than the loss which would be suffered elsewhere as a result of stopping the action which produces the harm." That is, Coase believed that society should conduct cost-benefit analysis, evaluate activities according to their social value, and ignore distributional effects.

At the core of Coase's thesis is the analysis of the impediments to market transactions:

> In order to carry out a market transaction it is necessary to discover who it is that one wishes to deal with, to inform people that one wishes to deal and on what terms, to conduct negotiations

---

34. *See generally* Barak Orbach & Frances R. Sjoberg, *Excessive Speech, Civility Norms and the Clucking Theorem*, 44 CONNECTICUT LAW REVIEW 1, 3–18 (2011).

35. In 1988, Coase published a short collection of his own works. The book included a thirty-page introduction, of which ten pages were dedicated to criticism of Pigou's support of government regulation. R.H. COASE, THE FIRM, THE MARKET, AND THE LAW 20–30 (1988). In 1991, Ronald Coase was awarded the Nobel Prize in Economics. For a critique of Coase's criticism of Pigou's work, see generally Herbert Hovenkamp, *The Coase Theorem and Arthur Cecil Pigou*, 51 ARIZONA LAW REVIEW 633 (2009); A.W. Brian Simpson, Coase v. Pigou *Reexamined*, 25 JOURNAL OF LEGAL STUDIES 53 (1996). Coase responded to Simpson's critique in his own article. Ronald H. Coase, *Law and Economics and A.W. Brian Simpson*, 25 JOURNAL OF LEGAL STUDIES 103 (1996). For additional commentary, *see* Harold Demsetz, *The Problem of Social Cost: What Problem?*, 7 REVIEW OF LAW & ECONOMICS 1 (2011).

36. Ronald H. Coase, *The Appointment of Pigou as Marshall's Successor*, 15 JOURNAL OF LAW & ECONOMICS 473 (1972).

37. For Pigonvian taxes *see* § 9.2.2c.

38. COASE, *supra* note 33, at 20–30.

> leading up to a bargain, to draw up the contract, to undertake the inspection needed to make sure that the terms of the contract are being observed, and so on. These operations are often extremely costly—sufficiently costly at any rate to prevent many transactions that would be carried out in a world in which the pricing system worked without cost.

The genius of this thesis, *the Coase Theorem*,[39] is its focus on *transaction costs*, information, and the (in)efficacy of government regulation. The Coase Theorem states that when transaction costs are zero then private and social costs are equal, no externalities exist, and prices are perfectly competitive.[40] Thus, reduction of transaction costs (*e.g.*, by cutting the bureaucracy and supporting the enforcement of private contracts) may be far more cost-effective than regulation of externalities and other market failures.[41] The flip side of this corollary is that regulation whose principal purpose is control may generate transaction and information costs.[42]

§ 3.1.2b Coasean Bargaining and Sparks From Railway Engines

For Ronald Coase, the term "externalities" was associated with the interventionist approach of the Pigonvian tradition. *The Problem of Social Cost* uses the phrase "harmful effects" rather than the word "externalities." Coase laid out his thesis by examining several disputes related to the types of externalities Pigou described in his book. A central example in this analysis is the case of "damage done to surrounding woods by sparks from railway engines."

Coase explained that, when a person does not internalize the full costs of her actions, the actions may be socially undesirable:

> Suppose a railway is considering whether to run an additional train or to increase the speed of an existing train or to install spark-preventing devices on its engines. If the railway were not liable for fire damage, then, when making these decisions, it would

---

39. George Stigler coined the phrase the "Coase Theorem" and formulated it. *See* RONALD H. COASE, *Notes on the Problem of Social Cost*, THE FIRM, THE MARKET, AND THE LAW 157 (1988). In his autobiography, *Memoirs of an Unregulated Economist*, Stigler writes:

> When, in 1960, Ronald Coase criticized Pigou's theory rather casually, * * * Chicago economists could not understand how so fine an economist as Coase could make so obvious a mistake. Since he persisted, we invited Coase * * * to come and give a talk on it. * * * I christened [Coase's] proposition the "Coase Theorem" and that is how it is known today.

GEORGE J. STIGLER, MEMOIRS OF AN UNREGULATED ECONOMIST 76–77 (1988).

40. *See generally* George J. Stigler, *The Law and Economics of Public Policy: A Plea to the Scholars*, 1 JOURNAL OF LEGAL STUDIES 1 (1972); Richard O. Zerbe Jr. & Howard E. McCurdy, *The Failure of Market Failure*, 18 JOURNAL OF POLICY ANALYSIS & MANAGEMENT 558 (1999).

41. *See generally* Kenneth Arrow, *The Organization of Economic Activity: Issues Pertinent to the Choice of Market Versus Nonmarket Allocation*, in 1 The Analysis and Evaluation of Public Expenditures: The PPB System, 91st Cong., 1st Sess. 47, 59–60 (May 28, 1969); Joseph Farrell, *Information and the Coase Theorem*, 1 JOURNAL OF ECONOMIC PERSPECTIVES 113 (1987). Carl J. Dahlman, *The Problem of Externality*, 22 JOURNAL OF LAW & ECONOMICS 141 (1979); Harold Demsetz, *The Cost of Transacting*, 82 QUARTERLY JOURNAL OF ECONOMICS 33 (1968).

42. *See, e.g.*, John S. Applegate, *The Perils of Unreasonable Risk: Information, Regulatory Policy, and Toxic Substances Control*, 91 COLUMBIA LAW REVIEW 261 (1991).

not take into account as a cost the increase in damage resulting from the additional train or the faster train or the failure to install spark-preventing devices. This is the source of the divergence between private and social net products.

He illustrated this point with a simple "arithmetical example" that is summarized in the table below.

	Annual Revenues	*Annual Cost*	*Destruction of Crops*
One Train	$150	$50	$60
Two Trains	$250	$100	$120

The "social net product" associated with the railway operations ("social welfare" in modern economics jargon) is the annual revenues minus the annual costs minus the cost to farmers (destruction of crops)—namely, $40 when one train is running, and $30 when two trains are running. Under such circumstances, the choice to operate two trains rather than one is socially undesirable. When the railway *is* liable for damages, it internalizes the costs of its operations and will run one train to maximize profit. However, when the railway is *not* liable for damages, the second train would allow the railway to increase profit by $50. *Cost internalization* is therefore the technique to assure that the pursuit of self-interest does not result in social costs.

Coase disagreed with the "Pigonvian position" that to reach the socially desirable level of activity society should impose liability on the railway. He pointed out that "if the railway could make a bargain with everyone having property adjoining the railway line and there were no costs involved in making such bargains, it would not matter whether the railway was liable for damage caused by fires or not." Thus, "[t]he problem is whether it would be desirable to make the railway liable in conditions in which it is too expensive for such bargains to be made." More broadly, Coase clarified that "[t]he question at issue is not whether it is desirable to run an additional train or a faster train or to install smoke-preventing devices; the question * * * is whether it is desirable to have a system in which the railway has to compensate those who suffer damage from the fires which it causes or one in which the railway does not have to compensate them."

§ 3.1.2c Public Goods

Lighthouse. *n.* A tall building on the seashore in which the government maintains a lamp and the friend of a politician.

—The Devil's Dictionary (1911)[43]

The Problem of Social Cost analyzed "harmful effects"—namely, only negative externalities. In the mid–1970s, when social regulation was expanding, Coase returned to externalities to address positive ones. He chose to write about the "lighthouse in economics" that Pigou and other econo-

---

43. AMBROSE BIERCE, THE DEVIL'S DICTIONARY 198 (1911).

mists used "because of the light it [was] supposed to throw on the question of the economic functions of government."[44]

Lighthouses belong to a class of goods and services that have two properties: non-exclusivity and non-rivalry. *Non-exclusivity* means that a supplier of a good or service cannot control its consumption nor exclude consumers and users.[45] A lighthouse owner cannot exclude ships in the sea from benefiting from the light and cannot charge them for her services. Similarly, television broadcasters and radio stations cannot exclude viewers and listeners and cannot charge them for using receivers. Absent a solution to the non-excludability problems, market participants have no incentives to offer non-excludable goods and services. In the case of broadcasting, television networks and radio stations overcome the problem by drawing revenues from advertisers. *Non-rivalry* means that "each individual's consumption of such a good leads to no subtraction from any other individual's consumption of that good."[46] That is, the consumption (or use) of a good by one person does not diminish the benefits to other people. Light and publicly available information are examples of non-rivalrous goods (also known as "collective consumption goods"). Private firms have limited incentives to offer non-rivalrous goods because "each individual, in seeking as a competitive buyer to [cut costs], would be led as if by an Invisible Hand to the grand solution" of avoiding paying for collective consumption goods, hoping to free ride on the purchases of others.[47] The combination of non-exclusivity and non-rivalry turns goods into *public goods* (or *public services*).

The supposed failure of markets to provide public goods and services convinced many economists that the government should finance the provision of such goods and services. To rebut this interventionist position, Coase studied the British lighthouse system.[48] He concluded that it utilized a relatively efficient privately financed framework:

> The lighthouses were built, operated, financed and owned by private individuals, who could sell the lighthouse or dispose of it by bequest. The role of the government was limited to the establishment and enforcement of property rights in the lighthouse. The charges were collected at the ports by agents for the lighthouses. The problem of enforcement was no different for them than for other suppliers of goods and services to the shipowner.

Coase therefore argued that "economists should not use the lighthouse as an example of a service which could only be provided by the government. * * * [E]conomists wishing to point to a service which is best provided by the government should use an example which has more solid backing." Yet,

---

44. Ronald H. Coase, *The Lighthouse in Economics*, 17 JOURNAL OF LAW & ECONOMICS 357 (1974).

45. *See generally* Garret Hardin, *The Competitive Exclusion Principle*, 131 SCIENCE 1292 (1960).

46. Samuelson, *The Pure Theory of Public Expenditure*, *supra* note 25.

47. *Id.*

48. Coase, *The Lighthouse in Economics*, *supra* note 44, at 376.

a more detailed examination of the lighthouse system Coase studied shows that that the government played a substantial role in that system.[49]

The concept of "public goods" is somewhat theoretical. Private and public institutions have many creative solutions to the non-*exclusivity* problem. Toll roads, for example, utilize a wide range of solutions to establish exclusivity. Pure non-rivalry rarely exists, because normally the use of a resource gives a person an advantage over people who do not use that resource, and the simultaneous use of most resources tends to lead congestion. When many ships in the sea simultaneously benefit from a single lighthouse, they are crowded and should consider the possibility of collusion. Similarly, highway congestion means that the use of a highway by one person may diminish the benefits to other people. Thus, it is unclear whether any good or service meets the textbook definition of "public good" under all conditions.

The practical way to think about public goods is that the efficient production of certain necessary goods and services is by one entity (centralized production), but for one reason or another free markets are unlikely to produce such goods and services in a sufficiently reliable manner.[50] Under such circumstances, there may be reasons for state participation in the central function of production. Social and private institutions provide many so-called "public goods."[51] But the private provision of such goods and services depends on local circumstances. Circumstances change over time and vary geographically. *Lighthouse A* may successfully devise and utilize a system to charge ships for its services, but *Lighthouse B* may fail to do so. Over time, changes in economic conditions may prevent *Lighthouse A* from charging ships for services and enable *Lighthouse B* to do so.[52] Moreover, public provision of a particular good or service may be needed in one place, but not in another; and such local needs may change over time. Thus, the government and private entities may concurrently provide lighthouses, firefighting services,[53] turnpikes,[54] and other so-called "public goods." In many instances, the state and private institutions collaborate in the production and provision of goods that are regarded as "public goods."

In sum, the term "public good" is frequently used as a motivation and even as a justification for regulation. As a term, "public good" is a useful shortcut for a concept. However, a decision to invest public resources

---

49. David E. van Zandt, *The Lessons of the Lighthouse: "Government" or "Private" Provision of Goods*, 22 JOURNAL OF LEGAL STUDIES 47 (1993).

50. For centralized production *see* § 6.4 (natural monopoly).

51. *See generally* James Anderoni, *Privately Provided Public Goods in a Large Economy: The Limits of Altruism*, 35 JOURNAL OF PUBLIC ECONOMICS 57 (1988); Theodore C. Bergstrom et al., *On the Private Provision of Public Goods*, 29 JOURNAL OF PUBLIC ECONOMICS 25 (1986); B. Douglas Bernheim, *On Voluntary and Involuntary Provision of Public Goods*, 76 AMERICAN ECONOMIC REVIEW 789 (1986).

52. *See also* John Morgan, *Financing Public Goods by Means of Lotteries*, 67 REVIEW OF ECONOMIC STUDIES 761 (2000).

53. *See* Fred S. McChesney, *Government Prohibitions on Volunteer Fire Fighting in Nineteenth-Century America: A Property Rights Perspective*, 15 JOURNAL OF LEGAL STUDIES 69 (1986).

54. Daniel B. Klein, *The Voluntary Provision of Public Goods? The Turnpike Companies of Early America*, 28 ECONOMIC INQUIRY 788 (1990).

should rely on the analysis of the relevant facts, not on textbook definitions. In certain instances, public provision of certain goods and services may be warranted.[55]

To illuminate the advantages of the refined definition of the term "public good," consider protection from low-probability, high-impact events, such as natural disasters, terrorism, financial crises, and deadly pandemics ("catastrophes").[56] Although uncontrolled factors, such as nature or terror groups, are the sources of most catastrophes, the human factor influences the risks associated with every type of catastrophe[57] and our financial capacity to recover from them (insurance).[58] Choices related to levees, floodplains and wetlands, trees and plants, construction standards and roads, health programs and evacuation plans, complex financial instruments, and other matters increase or decrease the potential costs of catastrophes.[59] Decentralized market mechanisms are unlikely to yield the coordination necessary to invest in required projects and to avoid risk-increasing activities.[60] Thus, the state provides such coordination, as a "public good" to reduce the costs of catastrophes. This public service may rely on market institutions, such as private investments in certain projects and private insurance, but the state operates as a risk manager.[61]

In August 2005, Hurricane Katrina, the costliest and one of the deadliest natural disasters in the history of United States, struck the Golf

---

55. *See also* Charles M. Tiebout, *A Pure Theory of Local Expenditures*, 64 JOURNAL OF POLITICAL ECONOMY 416 (1956).

56. *See generally* RONALD J. DANIELS ET AL. EDS., ON RISK AND DISASTER: LESSONS FROM HURRICANE KATRINA (2006).

57. *See generally* Richard Zeckhauser, *The Economics of Catastrophes*, 12 JOURNAL OF RISK AND UNCERTAINTY 113 (1996). *See also* STEPHEN J. PYNE, FIRE IN AMERICA: A CULTURAL HISTORY OF WILDLAND AND RURAL FIRE (1982).

58. *See, e.g.*, HOWARD KUNREUTHER ET AL., DISASTER INSURANCE PROTECTION: PUBLIC POLICY LESSONS (1978); *Howard Kunreuther & Mark Pauly, Neglecting Disaster: Why Don't People Insure Against Large Losses?* 28 JOURNAL OF RISK & UNCERTAINTY 5 (2004); James Stone, *A Theory of Capacity and the Insurance of Catastrophe Risks*, 40 JOURNAL OF RISK & INSURANCE 231–243 (Part I), 339–355 (Part II) (1973); Richard Zeckhauser, *Insurance and Catastrophes*, 20 GENEVA PAPERS ON RISK AND INSURANCE THEORY 157 (1995).

59. *See generally* Matthew E. Kahn, *The Death Toll from Natural Disasters: The Role of Income, Geography, and Institutions*, 87 REVIEW OF ECONOMICS AND STATISTICS 271 (2005); ROGER G. KENNEDY, WILDFIRE AND AMERICANS: HOW TO SAVE LIVES, PROPERTY, AND YOUR TAX DOLLARS (2006); Ruthenford H. Platt et al., *Rebuilding the North Carolina Coast after Hurricane Fran: Did Public Regulation Matter?* 30 COASTAL MANAGEMENT 249 (2002); Stephen Pyne, TENDING FIRE: COPING WITH AMERICA'S WILDLAND FIRES (2004); Robin Spence, *Risk and Regulation: Can Improved Government Action Reduce the Impacts of Natural Disasters*, 32 BUILDING RESEARCH & INFORMATION 391 (2004).

60. *See* DANIELS ET AL., ON RISK AND DISASTER, *supra* note 49. *See also* James Chivers & Nicholas E. Flores, *Market Failure in Information: The National Flood Insurance Program*, 78 LAND ECONOMICS 515 (2002); James M. Holway & Raymond J. Burby, *The Effects of Floodplain Development Controls on Residential Land Values*, 66 LAND ECONOMICS 259 (1990); John V. Krutilla, *An Economic Approach to Coping with Flood Damage*, 2 WATER RESOURCES RESEARCH 183 (1966).

61. *See, e.g.*, Carolyn Kousky, *Private Investment and Government Protection*, 33 JOURNAL OF RISK & UNCERTAINTY 73 (2006); Michael J. Trebilcock & Ronald J. Daniels, *Rationales and Instruments for Government Intervention in Natural Disasters*, in ON RISK AND DISASTER: LESSONS FROM HURRICANE KATRINA 89 (Ronald J. Daniels et al. eds. 2006). *See also* DAVID A. MOSS, WHEN ALL ELSE FAILS: GOVERNMENT AS THE ULTIMATE RISK MANAGER (2002).

Coast causing 1,833 deaths and damages estimated at $108 billion.[62] The national commission that studied the federal government's response to Katrina concluded that "there is no question that the Nation's current incident management plans and procedures fell short of what was needed and that improved operational plans could have better mitigated the Hurricane's tragic effects."[63] The long chain of government failures related to Hurricane Katrina stresses two points relevant to the general debate over private and public provision of public goods. First, the government may fail, including in adequately preparing for or responding to catastrophes. Second, the alternative to government action *may* still be worse. Public perceptions and preferences are inconsistent and tend to change after catastrophes.[64] *Ex ante* unwillingness to pay for a protection plan may evaporate in the face of a catastrophe, such as a terror attack, major earthquake, or a hurricane. The public tends to expect the government to respond to catastrophes. For this preference inconsistency, protection plans *may* be desirable.[65] Generalizing this observation, *ex ante* public provision of public goods should be considered when public expenditure is expected *ex post*.[66]

§ 3.1.3 *Fables and Myths: Do Externalities Justify Regulation?*

The proposition that externalities may justify state regulation has energized a body of empirical literature that examines many examples of externalities. Coase's study of the lighthouse in economics is part of this literature. Another famous study is *The Fable of the Bees*,[67] which examined an important 1950s study of externalities. This study illustrated the meaning of cost internalization by employing the example of the relationships between the apple orchard owners and beekeepers:

> Suppose that in a given region there is a certain amount of apple-growing and a certain amount of bee-keeping and that the bees feed on the apple-blossom. If the apple-farmers apply 10% more labour, land and capital to apple-farming they will increase the output of apples by 10%; but they will also provide more food for the bees. On the other hand, the beekeepers will not increase the output of honey by 10% by increasing the amount of land, labour and capital applied to bee-keeping by 10% unless at the same time

---

62. Richard D. Knabb et al., *Tropical Cyclone Report: Hurricane Katrina*, National Hurricane Center (Sept. 14, 2011).

63. HURRICANE KATRINA LESSONS LEARNED STAFF, THE FEDERAL RESPONSE TO HURRICANE KATRINA: LESSONS LEARNED (Feb. 2006).

64. *See* §§ 4.1, 4.6.3.

65. *See generally* Scott E. Harrington, *Rethinking Disaster Policy*, 23 REGULATION 40 (2000); Howard Kunreuther & Mark Pauly, *Rules Rather Than Discretion: Lessons from Hurricane Katrina*, 33 JOURNAL OF RISK & UNCERTAINTY 101 (2006); W. Kip Viscusi, *Valuing Risks of Death from Terrorism and Natural Disasters*, 38 JOURNAL OF RISK & UNCERTAINTY 191 (2009).

66. *See generally* Amihai Glazer, *Politics and the Choice of Durability*, 79 AMERICAN ECONOMIC REVIEW 1207 (1989); Dani Rodrik & Richard Zeckhauser, *The Dilemma of Government Responsiveness*, 7 JOURNAL OF POLICY ANALYSIS & MANAGEMENT 601 (1988).

67. Steven N.S. Cheung, *The Fable of the Bees: An Economic Investigation*, 16 JOURNAL OF LAW & ECONOMICS 11 (1973).

the apple-farmers also increase their output and so the food of the bees by 10%.[68]

The "apple and bees" became a textbook example of externalities, suggesting that apple farmers cannot capture the full benefits that apple blossoms confer upon beekeepers because markets for feeding bees in which beekeepers pay farmers do not exist. The "bee and the apple" example was therefore understood as a form of market failure in which "apple producers are unable to protect their equity in apple-nectar and markets do not impute to apple blossoms their correct shadow value."[69] The original example was also applied to a reciprocal situation: "While the apples may provide the food of the bees, the bees may fertilize the apples." This application highlighted the fact that beekeepers also confer some benefits on the apple farmers.

Sidebar 3–1
The Fable of the Bees

"All Trades and Places knew some Cheat,
No Calling was without Deceit."

In 1705, Bernard Mandeville (1670–1733), a Dutch–Anglo philosopher, published a satire: *The Fable of the Bees: Or Private Vices, Publick Benefits*, originally titled *The Grumbling Hive, or Knaves Turn'd Honest.*[70]

Mandeville's satire includes several layers of moral philosophy that influenced, among others, classic economists. A central message of the satire is that vicious greed motivates individuals, but their aggregate acts promote societal interests. Or, as Mandeville's subtitle frames the idea, private vices promote public benefits. Adam Smith's 1776 invisible hand theory utilizes the same concept, using self-interest rather than vicious greed. Mandeville's work is credited for being "the first systematic presentation of the *laissez faire* philosophy."[71]

The Fable of the Bees (1973) studied the beekeeping industry and concluded that bees provide invaluable pollination services for apple trees and, therefore, apple farmers hire the services of beekeepers. They pay for the services of the bees. The correct analysis of the relationships between apple farmers and beekeepers is that a hive is producing two products: honey and pollination services. The beekeeper is paid for placing the hive on a farm with honey and money. As far as government policy goes, for several decades, American beekeepers have successfully secured subsidies

68. J. E. Meade, *External Economies and Diseconomies in a Competitive Situation*, 62 ECONOMIC JOURNAL 54 (1952).

69. Bator, *The Anatomy of Market Failure*, *supra* note 25, at 364.

70. A copy of Mandeville's *The Fable of the Bees* is available at *regti.me/f-bees* (case sensitive).

71. Alfred F. Chalk, *Natural Law and the Rise of Economic Individualism in England*, 59 JOURNAL OF POLITICAL ECONOMY 332 (1951). *See also* Alfred F. Chalk, *Mandeville's Fable of the Bees: A Reappraisal*, 33 SOUTHERN ECONOMIC JOURNAL 1 (1966); Sterling P. Lamprecht, *The Fable of the Bees*, 23 JOURNAL OF PHILOSOPHY 561 (1926); Nathan Rosenberg, *Mandeville and Laissez Faire*, 24 JOURNAL OF THE HISTORY OF IDEAS 183 (1963).

for honey production and some protection from imports.[72] Since farmers pay for beekeeping services and the public pays for honey, it is hard to justify these programs for which the taxpayer pays.

The *Lighthouse in Economics* and the *Fable of the Bees* offer many lessons about desirable modesty in public policy and political discourse. Regulation is a costly state action that involves deployment and reallocation of societal resources. Theoretical models that explain the existence of positive and negative externalities may provide theoretical *motivations* for regulation, but do not necessarily *justify* government intervention in markets and society. The use of examples to illustrate theoretical points does not provide any grounds for government regulation, unless those examples are supported empirically. Nonetheless, undermining the validity of theoretical examples, such as the "apples and the bees" illustration, does not suggest that a theoretical concept, such as regulation of externalities, is wrong.

§ 3.2 SIC UTERE TUO UT ALIENUM NON LÆDAS

We now turn to the regulation of externalities and begin with the common law maxim *sic utere tuo ut alienum non lædas* ("use your own in such manner as not to injure that of another"). The maxim "is an elementary principle in reference to private rights, that every individual is entitled to the undisturbed possession and lawful enjoyment of his own property. The mode of enjoyment is necessarily limited by the rights of others—otherwise it might be made destructive of their rights altogether."[73] The maxim underscores one of the key differences between the approaches of Pigou and Coase. It treats harm as an outcome of a unilateral conduct, and prohibits actions that may impose harm on others. The maxim does not seem to consider the reciprocal nature of harm.

In November 1849, the Vermont General Assembly passed *An Act in relation to Railroad Corporations* that established a regulatory framework for railroads in Vermont.[74] Three key sections in the new statute addressed accidents with cattle:

> **SEC. 44**. Each railroad corporation shall erect and maintain fences on the sides of their road, (so far as the same shall be necessary,) of the height and strength of a division fence as required by law, and farm crossings of the road for the use of the proprietors of lands adjoining such railroad, and also construct and maintain cattle guards at all farm and road crossings, suitable and sufficient to prevent cattle and animals from getting on to the railroad. Until such fences and cattle guards shall be duly made, the corporation and its agents shall be liable for all damages which shall be done by their agents or engines to cattle, horses, or other animals. * * *

72. Mary K. Muth, *The Fable of the Bees Revisited: Cases and Consequences of the U.S. Honey Program*, 46 JOURNAL OF LAW AND ECONOMICS 479 (2003). *See also* Dan Eggen, *U.S. Honey Industry Asks FDA for National Purity Standard*, WASHINGTON POST, July 1, 2010, at A13.

73. Hay v. Cohoes Co., 2 N.Y. 159, 161 (1849).

74. A copy of the statute is available at *regti.me/VT1849* (case sensitive).

> [I]f occasioned by want of such fences and cattle guards, and after such fences and guards shall be duly made, the corporation shall not be liable for any such damages, unless negligently or willfully [*sic*] done; and if any person shall ride, lead, or drive any horse or other animal, upon such road, and within such fences and guards, other than at road and farm crossings, without the consent of the corporation, he shall for every such offence forfeit a sum not exceeding ten dollars, to be recovered by such corporation in an action on the case, and shall also pay all damages which shall be sustained thereby to the party aggrieved.
>
> **SEC. 45**. The provision in the preceding section, requiring such corporations to erect and maintain fences shall not apply to any case where the corporation shall have settled with and paid the land owner for building and maintaining such fence.—And if any person, having been thus settled with and paid for keeping any such fence in repair, shall neglect so to do, such railroad corporation may make such repairs and recover the necessary expense thereof of such person or his grantee.
>
> * * *
>
> **SEC. 47**. If any horse or other beast shall be found going at large, within the limits of any railroad, * * * the person, through whose fault or negligence such horse or other beast shall be so found, shall, for every such offence, forfeit a sum not exceeding twenty dollars, for every horse or other beast so found going at large, and shall also be liable for any damages thereby sustained by any person, to be recovered in an action on the case, by the person sustaining such damages.

In *Thorpe v. Rutland*,[75] the Rutland & Burlington Railroad Company challenged Section 44, arguing it increased its obligations beyond those stated in its charter from the state. More broadly, the railroad contended that the state acted outside the reach of its police powers by requiring the company to pay damages for cattle killed or injured by its trains, unless the company met new requirements intended to protect property of others (cattle). The case reached the Supreme Court of Vermont. Writing for the Court, Chief Justice Isaac Redfield dismissed the argument regarding the scope of the corporate charter, relying on the well-established rule that "public grants are to be construed strictly, that any ambiguity in the terms of the grant must operate against the corporation and in favor of the public."[76] Chief Justice Redfield then articulated a rationale for the police power:

> Th[e] police power of the state extends to the protection of the lives, limbs, health, comfort, and quiet of all persons, and the protection of all property within the state. According to the maxim, *Sic utere tuo ut alienum non lædas*, which being of universal application, it must of course, be within the range of legislative

75. Thorpe v. Rutland, 27 Vt. 140 (1855).

76. *See, e.g.*, Charles River Bridge v. Warren Bridge, 36 U.S. 420, 544 (1837); Richmond v. Louisa, 54 U.S. 71, 81 (1851).

action to define the mode and manner in which every one may so use his own as not to injure others. * * *

Applying this rule to the case in front of him, Chief Justice Redfield held:

[A] statute requiring land owners to build all their fences of a given quality or height, would no doubt be invalid, as an unwarrantable interference with matters of exclusively private concern. But [imposing] farm-crossings upon a railway are by no means of this character. They are division fences between adjoining occupants, to all intents. In addition to this, they are the safeguards which one person, in the exercise of a dangerous business, is required to maintain in order to prevent the liability to injure his neighbor. This is a control by legislative action coming within the obligation of the maxim, *Sic utere tuo [ut alienum non lædas]*, and which has always been exercised in this manner in all free states, in regard to those whose business is dangerous and destructive to other persons, property or business. Slaughter-houses, powder-mills, or houses for keeping powder, unhealthy manufactories, the keeping of wild animals, and even domestic animals, dangerous to persons or property, have always been regarded as under the control of the legislature. It seems incredible how any doubt should have arisen upon the point now before the court.

Thorpe v. Rutland is a classic application of the common law maxim *sic utere tuo ut alienum non lædas*, use your own in such a manner as not to injure another.[77] Courts have used the maxim as a justification for the exercise of the state's police power to regulate harm.[78] One form of such regulation is *ex-post* liability for harm. For example, criminal law and torts comply with this model.[79] Another form includes *ex-ante* regulatory schemes that intend to prevent harm or reduce the risk of harm. For example, states and localities find authority in nuisance law to establish zoning plans.[80] A third form of regulations involves *ex-ante* requirements that do not directly affect risk but assure that potential injurers could

77. *See generally* Elmer E. Smead, *Sic Utere Tuo Ut Alienum Non Laedas: A Basis of the State Police Power*, 21 CORNELL LAW QUARTERLY 276 (1935).

78. *Sees* THOMAS M. COOLEY, GENERAL PRINCIPLES OF CONSTITUTIONAL LAW 227 (1880) (defining the police power as "rules of good conduct and good neighborhood which are calculated to prevent a conflict of rights and to insure to each the uninterrupted enjoyment of his own, so far as is reasonably consistent with a corresponding enjoyment of others.")

79. *See, e.g.*, Cohens v. Virginia, 19 U.S. 264, 374 (1821) ("Nobody objects to a State enforcing its own penal laws: all that is claimed is, that in executing them, it should not violate the laws of the Union, which are paramount: *Sic utere tuo ut alienum non laedas*."); Lowell v. Boston & Lowell Rail Road Corp., 40 Mass. 24, 30 (1839) ("Corporations as well as individuals, by the principles of the common law, are bound so to exercise their rights as not to injure others. The principle, *sic utere tuo ut alienum non lædas*, is of universal application.")

80. *See, e.g.*, Euclid v. Ambler Realty Co., 272 U.S. 365, 387 (1926) ("In solving doubts, the maxim 'sic *utere tuo ut alienum non laedas*,' which lies at the foundation of so much of the common low of nuisances, ordinarily will furnish a fairly helpful clew."). *See also* Brendale v. Confederated Tribes and Bands of Yakima Indian Nation, 492 U.S. 408, 434 (1989).

compensate victims. Statutory insurance requirements illustrate this form of regulation.[81]

In *Lucas v. South Carolina Coastal Council*,[82] the Supreme Court held that the maxim in and of itself does not absolve the state from paying "just compensation" when it exercises its eminent domain power. The *Lucas* Court examined the question of whether a South Carolina statute that restricted the use of property to protect the state's eroding beaches and had a "dramatic effect on the economic value" of certain lots was a taking of private property under the Fifth and Fourteenth Amendments. Writing for the Court, Justice Scalia ruled: "We emphasize that to win [such a] case [the state] must do more than proffer the legislature's declaration that the uses [a property owner] desires are inconsistent with the public interest, or the conclusory assertion that they violate a common-law maxim such as *sic utere tuo ut alienum non lædas*." Dissenting, Justice Blackmun opened his opinion by announcing: "Today the Court launches a missile to kill a mouse." Justice Blackmun disagreed with the majority's dismissive view of the maxim: "Once one abandons the level of generality of *sic utere tuo ut alienum non lædas,* * * * one searches in vain * * * for anything resembling a principle in the common law of nuisance."

Questions

1. How did Sections 44, 45, and 47 of the 1849 Vermont railroad corporations act allocate rights and liabilities between railroads and property owners? What was the function of Section 45? Did the Vermont legislature adopt a Pigonvian or Coasean approach?

2. The Precautionary Principle's basic axiom is "first, do no harm."[83] Regulations that adopt the Precautionary Principle may ban activities that pose risk to human lives or the environment until safety is established and impose the burden of proving safety on the party that wishes to engage in risky activities. Is the Precautionary Principle consistent with the maxim *sic utere tuo ut alienum non lædas*?

3. The Vermont Supreme Court handed down *Thorpe* in 1855. The decision has been cited by many courts, including the U.S. Supreme Courts.[84] In *Thorpe*, Vermont Chief Justice Isaac Redfield noted: "Slaughter-houses, * * * unhealthy manufactories, the keeping of wild animals,

---

81. *See, e.g.*, Shavers v. Kelley, 402 Mich. 554, 596–97 (1978) ("The No-Fault Act's self-insurance concept is embraced within the traditional scope of the police power as stated in the maxim '*sic utere tuo ut alienum non laedas*.' "). *See also* Michael Spence, *Consumer Misperceptions, Product Failure and Producer Liability*, 44 REVIEW OF ECONOMIC STUDIES 561 (1977).

82. Lucas v. South Carolina Coastal Council, 505 U.S. 1003 (1992). *See generally* Vicki Breen, *Lucas v. The Green Machine: Using the Taking Clause to Promote More Efficient Regulation?* in PROPERTY STORIES 299 (Gerald Korngold & Andrew P. Morriss eds., 2d ed., 2009).

83. *See supra* § 1.5.3.

84. The Supreme Court first cited *Thorpe* in *Munn v. Illinois*, 94 U.S. 113 (1876), which is a landmark in regulation we will discuss in Chapter 9. For prior decisions in lower courts *see, e.g.*, Boston, Concord & Montreal Railroad v. Gilmore, 37 N.H. 410, 418 (1858); Delaware & Raritan Canal Co. v. Camden & Atlantic Railroad Co., 16 N.J. Eq. 321, 350 (Ch. 1863); Mitchell v. Williams, 27 Ind. 62, 63 (1866); East Saginaw Mfg. Co. v. East Saginaw, 19 Mich. 259, 281 (1869); Gunter v. Dale County, 44 Ala. 639, 645 (1870).

and even domestic animals, dangerous to persons or property, have always been regarded as under the control of the legislature. It seems incredible how any doubt should have arisen upon the point now before the court." We saw, however, that, in the second half of the nineteenth century, regulation of slaughterhouses was highly controversial.[85] Could courts apply the *sic utere tuo ut alienum non lædas* maxim to resolve disputes over slaughterhouse regulation? If the maxim was so established, why did slaughterhouse regulation encounter so many challenges?

4. Railroad transportation began to develop in the United States in the 1830s. Railroads introduced a new set of risks, some of which we have already discussed. The intersections of railroads with roads, grade crossings, were one of the primary sources of risks (*see Figures 3.1, 3.2*). Reliable data about such accidents was is available only from 1920 (*see Figure 3.2*). Do accidents at grade crossings involve any externalities? How would Pigou and Coase address such accidents? What may be the explanation for the changes in the number of fatalities in accidents at grade crossings between 1920 and 2004?

Figure 3.1
The Railroad Monster

Source: New York Herald, July 26, 1911.

85. *See* § 2.2.2a.

Figure 3.2

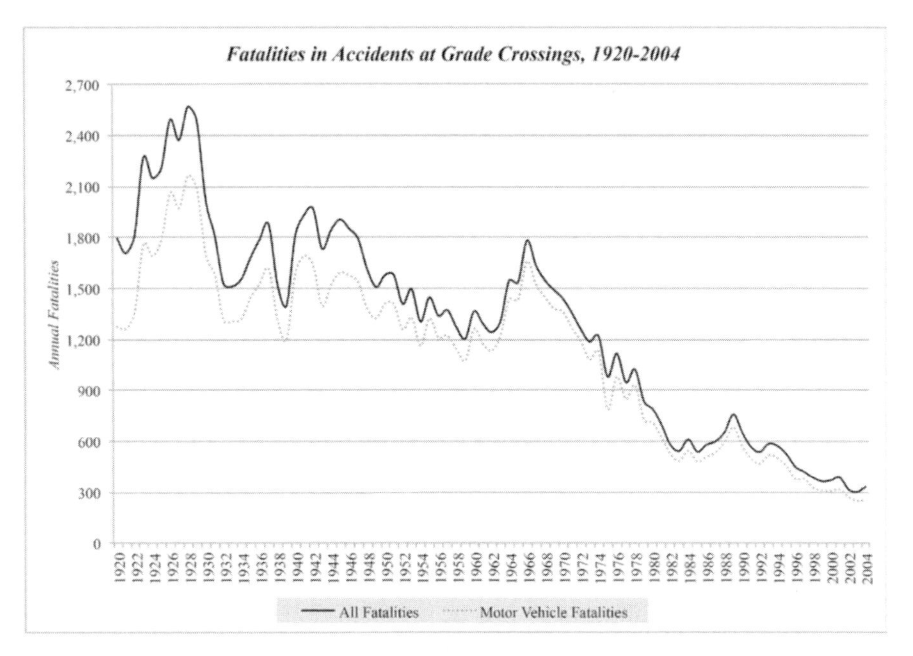

Source: U.S. Department of Transportation, Federal Highway Administration.

"Smoke From Factory Chimneys"

Boomer v. Atlantic Cement Co.

Court of Appeals of New York
26 N.Y.2d 219 (1970)

■ BERGAN, JUDGE.

Defendant operates a large cement plant near Albany. These are actions for injunction and damages by neighboring land owners alleging injury to property from dirt, smoke and vibration emanating from the plant. A nuisance has been found after trial, temporary damages have been allowed; but an injunction has been denied.

The public concern with air pollution arising from many sources in industry and in transportation is currently accorded ever wider recognition accompanied by a growing sense of responsibility in State and Federal Governments to control it. Cement plants are obvious sources of air pollution in the neighborhoods where they operate.

But there is now before the court private litigation in which individual property owners have sought specific relief from a single plant operation. The threshold question raised by the division of view on this appeal is whether the court should resolve the litigation between the parties now before it as equitably as seems possible; or whether, seeking promotion of the general public welfare, it should channel private litigation into broad public objectives.

A court performs its essential function when it decides the rights of parties before it. Its decision of private controversies may sometimes greatly affect public issues. Large questions of law are often resolved by the manner in which private litigation is decided. But this is normally an incident to the court's main function to settle controversy. It is a rare exercise of judicial power to use a decision in private litigation as a purposeful mechanism to achieve direct public objectives greatly beyond the rights and interests before the court.

Effective control of air pollution is a problem presently far from solution even with the full public and financial powers of government. In large measure adequate technical procedures are yet to be developed and some that appear possible may be economically impracticable.

It seems apparent that the amelioration of air pollution will depend on technical research in great depth; on a carefully balanced consideration of the economic impact of close regulation; and of the actual effect on public health. It is likely to require massive public expenditure and to demand more than any local community can accomplish and to depend on regional and interstate controls.

A court should not try to do this on its own as a by-product of private litigation and it seems manifest that the judicial establishment is neither equipped in the limited nature of any judgment it can pronounce nor prepared to lay down and implement an effective policy for the elimination of air pollution. This is an area beyond the circumference of one private lawsuit. It is a direct responsibility for government and should not thus be undertaken as an incident to solving a dispute between property owners and a single cement plant—one of many—in the Hudson River valley.

The cement making operations of defendant have been found by the court at Special Term to have damaged the nearby properties of plaintiffs in these two actions. That court, * * * accordingly found defendant maintained a nuisance. * * * The total damage to plaintiffs' properties is, however, relatively small in comparison with the value of defendant's operation and with the consequences of the injunction which plaintiffs seek.

The ground for the denial of injunction, notwithstanding the finding both that there is a nuisance and that plaintiffs have been damaged substantially, is the large disparity in economic consequences of the nuisance and of the injunction. This theory cannot, however, be sustained without overruling a doctrine which has been consistently reaffirmed in several leading cases in this court and which has never been disavowed here, namely that where a nuisance has been found and where there has been any substantial damage shown by the party complaining an injunction will be granted.

The rule in New York has been that such a nuisance will be enjoined although marked disparity be shown in economic consequence between the effect of the injunction and the effect of the nuisance.

The problem of disparity in economic consequence was sharply in focus in *Whalen v. Union Bag & Paper Co.*, 208 N.Y. 1 (1913). A pulp mill entailing an investment of more than a million dollars polluted a stream in which plaintiff, who owned a farm, was "a lower riparian owner". The economic loss to plaintiff from this pollution was small. This court, reversing the Appellate Division, reinstated the injunction granted by the Special Term against the argument of the mill owner that in view of "the slight advantage to plaintiff and the great loss that will be inflicted on defendant" an injunction should not be granted. "Such a balancing of injuries cannot be justified by the circumstances of this case," Judge Werner noted. He continued: "Although the damage to the plaintiff may be slight as compared with the defendant's expense of abating the condition, that is not a good reason for refusing an injunction."

Thus the unconditional injunction granted at Special Term was reinstated. The rule laid down in that case, then, is that whenever the damage resulting from a nuisance is found not "unsubstantial", *viz.*, $100 a year, injunction would follow. This states a rule that had been followed in this court with marked consistency. * * *

Although the court at Special Term and the Appellate Division held that injunction should be denied, it was found that plaintiffs had been damaged in various specific amounts up to the time of the trial and damages to the respective plaintiffs were awarded for those amounts. * * * The court at Special Term also found the * * * total of permanent damages to all plaintiffs * * * were $185,000. * * *

This result at Special Term and at the Appellate Division is a departure from a rule that has become settled; but to follow the rule literally in these cases would be to close down the plant at once. This court is fully agreed to avoid that immediately drastic remedy; the difference in view is how best to avoid it.*

One alternative is to grant the injunction but postpone its effect to a specified future date to give opportunity for technical advances to permit defendant to eliminate the nuisance; another is to grant the injunction conditioned on the payment of permanent damages to plaintiffs which would compensate them for the total economic loss to their property present and future caused by defendant's operations. For reasons which will be developed the court chooses the latter alternative.

If the injunction were to be granted unless within a short period—*e.g.*, 18 months—the nuisance be abated by improved methods, there would be no assurance that any significant technical improvement would occur.

The parties could settle this private litigation at any time if defendant paid enough money and the imminent threat of closing the plant would build up the pressure on defendant. If there were no improved techniques found, there would inevitably be applications to the court at Special Term for extensions of time to perform on showing of good faith efforts to find such techniques.

* Respondent's investment in the plant is in excess of $45,000,000. There are over 300 people employed there.

Moreover, techniques to eliminate dust and other annoying by-products of cement making are unlikely to be developed by any research the defendant can undertake within any short period, but will depend on the total resources of the cement industry Nationwide and throughout the world. The problem is universal wherever cement is made.

For obvious reasons the rate of the research is beyond control of defendant. If at the end of 18 months the whole industry has not found a technical solution a court would be hard put to close down this one cement plant if due regard be given to equitable principles.

On the other hand, to grant the injunction unless defendant pays plaintiffs such permanent damages as may be fixed by the court seems to do justice between the contending parties. All of the attributions of economic loss to the properties on which plaintiffs' complaints are based will have been redressed.

The nuisance complained of by these plaintiffs may have other public or private consequences, but these particular parties are the only ones who have sought remedies and the judgment proposed will fully redress them. The limitation of relief granted is a limitation only within the four corners of these actions and does not foreclose public health or other public agencies from seeking proper relief in a proper court.

It seems reasonable to think that the risk of being required to pay permanent damages to injured property owners by cement plant owners would itself be a reasonable effective spur to research for improved techniques to minimize nuisance.

The power of the court to condition on equitable grounds the continuance of an injunction on the payment of permanent damages seems undoubted. * * * This should be placed beyond debate by a provision of the judgment that the payment by defendant and the acceptance by plaintiffs of permanent damages found by the court shall be in compensation for a servitude on the land.

Although the Trial Term has found permanent damages as a possible basis of settlement of the litigation, on remission the court should be entirely free to re-examine this subject. It may again find the permanent damage already found; or make new findings.

The orders should be reversed, without costs. * * *

■ JASEN, JUDGE (dissenting).

I agree with the majority that a reversal is required here, but I do not subscribe to the newly enunciated doctrine of assessment of permanent damages, in lieu of an injunction, where substantial property rights have been impaired by the creation of a nuisance. * * *

The specific problem faced here is known as particulate contamination because of the fine dust particles emanating from defendant's cement plant. The particular type of nuisance is not new, having appeared in many cases for at least the past 60 years. * * * It is interesting to note that cement production has recently been identified as a significant source of particulate contamination in the Hudson Valley. This type of pollution, wherein very small particles escape and stay in the atmosphere, has been denominated as the type of air pollution which produces the greatest hazard to human health. We have thus a nuisance which not only is damaging to the plaintiffs, but also is decidedly harmful to the general public.

I see grave dangers in overruling our long-established rule of granting an injunction where a nuisance results in substantial continuing damage. * * *

Questions

1. *Boomer v. Atlantic Cement Co.* applies the Coasean framing of externalities as a reciprocal problem.[86] What are the possible effects of *Boomer* on polluters' choices of investments and technology?

2. In *Boomer*, owners of eight properties sought an injunctive relief against the dust and noise produced by a neighboring cement plant. The trial court found the total damages to all plaintiffs were $185,000. By the time the trial judge on remand awarded damages, all cases but one were settled. The judge found that, for the property of that plaintiff, the decline in market value was $140,000 and awarded the plaintiff $175,000.[87] The courts assumed that the stakes of the cement plant were much higher than those of homeowners. The *Boomer* court noted that "[r]espondent's investment in the plant is in excess of $45,000,000 and [there] are over 300 people employed there."

(a) What are the figures the court should have compared?

(b) Assume that the aggregate damages of the plaintiffs were very small compared to the potential loss from closing the cement plant. Litigation costs tend to be very high. Why did the *Boomer* litigation take place? Could all parties save costs by settling before the litigation began?

3. Did the *Boomer* court implicitly reject the maxim *sic utere tuo ut alienum non lædas*?

§ 3.3 ENTITLEMENTS AND EFFECTS ON OTHERS

Our discussion of "ugly laws" illuminated that normative values may determine the direction and magnitude of "effects on others."[88] Normative values and other considerations may change the meaning of externalities because, in a world of scarce resources, friction and conflict among market participants are inevitable: Most actions of any person entail effects on others, but society regulates only some actions and ignores others. Regula-

---

86. *See* Louise A. Halper, *Nuisance, Courts and Markets in the New York Court of Appeal, 1850–1915*, 54 ALBANY LAW REVIEW 301 (1990) (documenting earlier decisions that adopted a similar approach).

87. Daniel A. Farber, *The Story of Boomer: Pollution and the Common Law*, 25 ECOLOGY LAW QUARTERLY 113 (2005).

88. *See* § 3.0.

tion of externalities, therefore, may establish entitlements—private rights that can be enforced through the legal system.[89] This Section utilizes several settings to stress the reciprocal nature of externalities and the use of externalities-related entitlements.

Ladies' Hats

In August 1897, the City Council of Atlanta, Georgia amended its charter and added two new provisions:

> SEC. **1980.** It shall be the duty of the proprietor, lessee, or other person in charge of each and every opera house or theatre in the City of Atlanta to require ladies who attend performances in such theatre or opera house to remove their hats before the performance begins, and to keep them off during the performance.
>
> SEC. **1981.** Any such proprietor, lessee or other person in charge of an opera house or theatre, who shall violate the preceding section of this ordinance, upon conviction shall be fined in the Recorder's Court not exceeding one hundred dollars or imprisoned not exceeding thirty days.

Oldknow v. City of Atlanta

Court of Appeals of Georgia
9 Ga.App. 594 (1911)

■ JUDGE RUSSELL:

William Oldknow was convicted in the recorder's court of the city of Atlanta for a violation of a city ordinance which makes it "the duty of the proprietor, lessee, or other person in charge of every opera house, or theater, or moving picture show, or vaudeville performance, or similar exhibition in the city of Atlanta to require ladies who attend performances in such theater or opera house to remove their hats before the performance begins and to keep them off during the performance." * * *

He challenges the legality of the ordinance in question on various grounds, such as that no authority in law existed for the enactment of such ordinance, that it was discriminatory and class legislation * * *, and that the ordinance, if otherwise valid, was wholly unreasonable, because it imposed a penalty for an offense over which the defendant had no control and was powerless to prevent. * * *

It will hardly be questioned that the city has the power to regulate all classes of exhibitions * * * and that the police power of the city is properly exercised over places of public resort, although owned and operated by private citizens. * * *

---

89. *See generally* Guido Calabresi & A. Douglas Melamed, *Property Rules, Liability Rules, and Inalienability: One View of the Cathedral*, 85 HARVARD LAW REVIEW 1089 (1972).

Generally speaking, it is well settled that the Legislature has the same authority over the theatrical business as over any other lawful private business.* Besides the requirement of a license, it is authorized to regulate the conduct of places of public amusement, where the public health, safety, morality, comfort, and tranquility are concerned and the general welfare requires. This is the exercise of police power, which has always been declared by the courts as that inherent and plenary power in the state which enables it to prohibit all things hurtful to the comfort, safety, and welfare of society. The "general welfare clause" contained in the charter of the city of Atlanta confers upon the municipality authority to pass ordinances "for the prevention of disorderly conduct and conduct liable to disturb the peace and tranquility of any citizen," and such as "may seem to [it] proper for the security of the peace, health, order, and good government of said city." City Code, § 33. Under this welfare clause we think the state conferred upon the city the authority to adopt the ordinance in question. * * *

The [defendant] was proprietor of what is known as a "moving picture show" in the City of Atlanta. This character of amusement has become one of the most popular methods of recreation and pleasure, and is resorted to almost universally by all classes of citizens. The business is clearly lawful, as well as entertaining, and sometimes instructive, and the public has the right to resort to these places, and, while there, to be protected in the full enjoyment furnished by this class of entertainment. It is a matter of common knowledge that the style of modern hats worn by ladies, if permitted to be worn by them while the performance is in progress, will prevent those who may be so unfortunate as to sit in the rear of ladies from seeing the stage or from enjoying the spectacular entertainment there presented, which is a most important part of the performance. Nothing more greatly mars the pleasure of an entertainment, or disturbs the comfort of those who may be so unfortunate as to be located behind these obstructions, or more irritably disturbs or interferes with the comfort of the audience attending the theaters or moving picture shows, than these large hats worn by ladies, which in many cases completely obstruct the view of the performance. The spectacular is the principal part of moving picture shows. The evil aimed at by this ordinance, the mischief it was intended to prevent, and the nuisance it was passed to abate, all clearly show that the ordinance in question is within the police power of the city and is authorized by the "general welfare clause" of its charter.

Nor do we think that the ordinance is an unwarranted interference with the right of the citizen to conduct his private business in such manner as he may see proper. * * * This is not an interference with the right of the proprietor to operate his private business, but is simply a requirement that he shall operate it in such manner as not to disturb the public tranquility, peace, and comfort of those who may be assembled there. The proprietors,

* [In Tyson v. Banton, 273 U.S. 418 (1927), the Supreme Court held that, despite any past practices, the police power did not reach "amusements and entertainments." Seven years later, the Court eliminated this distinction between the entertainment industry and other industry, holding that the "affected with a public interest" doctrine was meaningless. Nebbia v. New York, 291 U.S. 502 (1934). *See* pp. 267–270].

or those who operate such establishments, have themselves the right to make any reasonable rules and regulations for the orderly conduct of such places, and, where they cannot effectually do so, it becomes the duty of the municipality to interfere and make such regulations as will secure the orderly conduct of such places and the peaceful and full enjoyment of those who have a right to assemble at such places. Neither is the ordinance unreasonable because it imposes upon the proprietor a burdensome duty which he cannot enforce. If the ordinance is lawful, he can enforce it by simply calling to his aid the police of the city to arrest any lady who refuses to obey the regulation and remove her hat. Besides, it is a matter of common knowledge that the ladies of our country are always amenable to reasonable requests conducing to the comfort of others.

The ordinance is not discriminatory because it does not include men within its operation. Men do not need any regulation on this subject. Public opinion, which demands that the man shall take off his hat in the presence of ladies, is sufficient, and does not need the aid of any police regulation. If it were the fashion for men to wear hats of such description as those worn by ladies in this day and to keep them on in public places, could it be doubted that there would be a loud and vociferous demand on the part of the ladies for the abatement of such a nuisance? But we will not extend the discussion. We hold that the ordinance in question, reasonably construed, is clearly within the police power of the city of Atlanta, that it does not discriminate, that it does not impose on the proprietor of such places any unnecessary or unusual hardship, and that it is in the interest of public order and comfort. * * *

Judgment affirmed.

Questions

1. What was the rationale behind requiring all women to remove their hats in amusement houses?

2. Mr. Oldknow, the defendant, argued that the Atlanta Ordinance was discriminatory because it applied only to women. The court dismissed this argument, holding that "[m]en do not need any regulation on this subject. Public opinion, which demands that the man shall take off his hat in the presence of ladies, is sufficient, and does not need the aid of any police regulation." (a) Why did public opinion not demand women to take off their hats at amusement houses? Assume public opinion did not establish any requirement for women to remove their hats at amusement houses. (b) Did the ordinance serve the public? (c) Did the court adopt some sort of an "invisible hand" theory that worked well with men but not with women?

3. Mr. Oldknow also asserted that the Atlanta Ordinance was "wholly unreasonable, because it imposed a penalty for an offense over which the defendant had no control and was powerless to prevent." What was the court's justification for the imposition of liability on proprietors and operators of amusement houses, rather than on inconsiderate women? Was the

imposition of liability on proprietors and operators of amusement houses unreasonable?

4. How would Pigou and Coase address the problem of ladies hats in amusement houses in the early twentieth century?

Cellphones at the Theater

In August 2002, a large group of New York Council members introduced a bill that addressed the use of mobile telephones in places of public performance. The bill was referred to the Committee on Consumer Affairs that summarized the background for its inquiry. The Committee wrote:

> New York City has long been one of the major cultural centers of the world. Long-time citizens and tourists alike attend our city's theatres, cinemas, and cultural institutions to enjoy high-caliber performances, films, and lectures at every price level. In the last several years, however, the growing presence of mobile or cellular phones in theatres and performance spaces has made enjoyment of the arts more difficult. Increasingly, theatre and movie patrons are failing to turn off their mobile phones during performances. Disregarding the rest of the audience members, these individuals may answer phone calls and engage in prolonged, audible conversations in the middle of stage performances, films, dance recitals, and lectures. A number of stage actors have even found themselves in the unenviable position of hushing audience members who have interrupted pivotal scenes by taking phone calls. * * *[90]

The Committee held several hearings and received testimonies from representatives from the Mayor's Office, a good number of trade associations, and several patrons of the arts. In February 2003, over the Mayor's veto, the City Council passed the bill, adding to the City Code the following sections.

> ***§ 24–218.1 Use of mobile telephones restricted in a place of public performance.***
>
> *a.* *Definitions*. For purposes of this section:
>
> (1) The term "mobile telephone" shall mean a cellular, analog, wireless, digital or other similar telephone or communications device, which can be used to access two-way real time voice telecommunications service that is interconnected to a public switched telephone network and is provided by a commercial mobile radio service, as such term is defined by 47 CFR § 20.3.
>
> (2) The term "use" shall mean to receive a mobile telephone call signaled by an audible sound, dial a mobile telephone, or talk or listen on a mobile telephone.

---

90. New York City Committee on Consumer Affairs Report, Int. No. 257 (Sept. 24, 2002).

(3) The term "place of public performance" shall mean the area, room, or chamber of any indoor theatre, library, museum, gallery, motion picture theatre, concert hall, or building in which theatrical, musical, dance, motion picture, lecture, or other similar performances are exhibited. This term shall not include any area or venue in which professional or amateur sporting events are taking place.

b. No person shall use a mobile telephone in a place of public performance while a theatrical, musical, dance, motion picture, lecture or other similar performance is taking place.

c. *Exception*. The provisions of this section shall not apply to an individual who uses a mobile telephone to contact an emergency response operator, hospital, physician's office or health clinic, ambulance company, fire company, first aid squad or police department in an emergency situation or in any other circumstance which may be deemed an emergency.

d. *Notice to patrons*.

(1) The owner, operator, manager or other person having control of any place of public performance shall, at every theatrical, musical, dance, motion picture, lecture or other similar performance, provide prominent and conspicuous notice to patrons by means of announcement, signage, printed material, or other similar means indicating that mobile telephone use is prohibited. * * *

(2) In addition, the owner, operator, manager or other person having control of any motion picture theatre in which motion pictures are exhibited to the public shall, prior to the showing of each feature motion picture, show upon the movie screen information indicating that mobile telephone use is prohibited. * * *

§ 24–257 Penalties

Violations related to section and subdivision	First Violation		Second Violation		Third and Subsequent Violations	
	Max.	Min.	Max.	Minimum	Maximum	Minimum
24–218.1(b)	$50	$50	$50	$50	$50	$50

Questions

1. What are the differences between cellphone and hat externalities?

2. What are the key differences between the 2003 New York regulation of cellphone in amusement houses and the 1897 Atlanta regulation of ladies' hats in amusement houses?

3. Is the 2003 New York regulation of cellphones in amusement houses likely to be more effective than the 1897 Atlanta regulation of ladies' hats in amusement houses? Could Pigou or Coase offer insight into the relative effectiveness of these ordinances?

Urban Nuisances

In 1866, Chicago adopted a comprehensive ordinance that addressed nuisances in the City. Among other things the ordinance provided:

> 1. CATTLE AND SWINE KEPT IN CITY—LIMIT TO NUMBER—OFFENCE—PENALTY. Any person or persons who shall own, keep or use any yard, pen, place or premises within the City of Chicago, in or upon which more than ten cattle or swine shall be confined or kept at any one time, and any person or persons who shall own, keep or use any yard, pen, place or premises, in or upon which a less number of cattle or swine than ten shall be so kept as to be offensive to those residing in the vicinity, or an annoyance to the public, shall be deemed the author of a nuisance, and, on conviction, shall be subject to a fine of not less than twenty-five dollars and not exceeding one hundred dollars in every case, and to a like fine for every day he or they shall neglect or refuse to abate such nuisance, when notified by the mayor or board of health to abate the same.
>
> * * *
>
> 8. OFFENSIVE PREMISES—PENALTY. Any owner or occupant of any tallow chandler's shop, soap factory, tannery, distillery, livery stable, cattle yard or shed, barn, packing house, slaughter house, or rendering establishment, who shall suffer the same to become nauseous, foul or offensive, shall be fined in a sum not less than twenty-five dollars and not exceeding one-hundred dollars in every case.
>
> 9. OFFENSIVE GROUNDS—PENALTY. If any person shall own, occupy, or keep any grounds or other premises in such condition as to be offensive and a nuisance to the neighborhood, he shall be subject to a fine of not less than twenty-five dollars, and not exceeding one hundred dollars, and to a like fine for every day such nuisance shall continue after the first conviction.
>
> * * *
>
> 12. HOGS, ETC., AT LARGE—PENALTY. If any person, being the owner of any hog, shoat or pig, shall suffer the same to run, or be, at large, or to be found at large, he shall be subject to a penalty of two dollars in every case.
>
> * * *
>
> 17. INFORMER—MOIETY OF FINE, ETC. Any person or persons, other than members of the police force, who may hereafter give information that shall lead to the conviction of any person or persons guilty of a violation of this chapter, shall be entitled to one-half the fine imposed for such violation, to be paid when the same shall be collected, upon the certificate of the clerk of the police court, stating the person who gave such information, and the time when it was given.

By adopting the 1866 ordinance, Chicago took a firm approach toward externalities that created a nuisance in the City.[91] Its used of informers emphasized the significance the City attributed to the problem. Nevertheless, the City struggled with the status of its livery stables—a building where horses or vehicles were kept or let for hire.[92] Prior to the commercialization of motor vehicles, urban livery stables were needed, but they were also a source of nuisance for nearby houses. Property owners, of course, preferred to have livery stables in other neighborhoods, rather than in their own. "It [was] well known that the owners of nice residence propert[ies] object[ed] to the intrusion of a livery stable. It [was] not thought to be a desirable neighbor. It [brought] stable smells, extra flies, and horsy manners, and [was] not a good lounging place for children. Property-owners occasionally [were] blackmailed by a man who would buy a lot in a good residence neighborhood, and then threaten unless bought off at a high price to start a livery stable next their to front doors."[93]

Illinois courts were not generous with property owners injured by livery stables. They awarded damages only for physical discomfort and deprivation of the use and comforts of the premises. Consider *Gempp v. Bassham*.[94] The defendant built a livery stable on a lot "adjoining, and not more than two feet distant from the dwelling house of the [plaintiff], in which he and his family resided. * * * [U]nwholesome and noxious stenches from the [defendant's] stable permeated [plaintiff's] dwelling and loud and offensive noises caused by the stamping, kicking * * * of the horses * * * deprived in a large degree of the comfortable and wholesome enjoyment of [the plaintiff's] home." At trial, the plaintiff was awarded damages that measured the difference between the premises' rental value with and without the stable. The court of appeals accepted the defendant's argument that "[w]here the injury is to physical comfort and results in deprivation of the comfortable enjoyments of a home, the measure of damages is not the depreciation in the rental value of the premises occupied by the plaintiff, but compensation for such physical discomfort, and deprivation of the use and comforts of the home."

In 1883, the Chicago realtors formed a trade association, the Chicago Real Estate Board (CREB), which aggressively promoted the interests of the industry, including preserving the value of real estate in Chicago.[95] In June 1890, CREB concluded a successful campaign by securing from the City Council a new ordinance that provided:

> *An Ordinance Regulating the Location of Livery, Boarding and Sale Stables.*
>
> Passed June 16, 1890

---

91. For the general regulatory trend *see* Jon A. Peterson, *The Impact of Sanitary Reform Upon American Urban Planning, 1840–1890*, 13 JOURNAL OF SOCIAL HISTORY 83 (1979).

92. For livery stables *see* Clark C. Spence, *The Livery Stable in the American West*, 36 MONTANA: MAGAZINE OF WESTERN HISTORY 36 (1986).

93. *Saloons and Livery Stables*, CHICAGO DAILY TRIBUNE, June 29, 1890, at 12.

94. Gempp v. Bassham, 60 Ill. App. 84 (1895).

95. *See generally* EVERRETT C. HUGHES, THE GROWTH OF AN INSTITUTION: THE CHICAGO REAL ESTATE BOARD (1931).

> **Consent to location required, when—permit—violation, penalty**. *Be it ordained by the city council of the City of Chicago:* That it shall not be lawful for any person to locate, build, construct or keep a livery, boarding and sale stable in any block in which a majority of the buildings are devoted to exclusive residence purposes, within two hundred feet of such residences, on either side of the street, unless the owners of a majority of the lots in such block fronting or abutting on the street, consent in writing to the location or construction of such livery stable therein; *provided*, that this ordinance shall not apply to livery, boarding and sale stables now constructed and in operation, or now in process of construction. That such written consent of the property owners shall be filed with the department of public works before a permit be granted for the construction or keeping of such livery stable. Any person who violates this ordinance shall be fined not less than fifty ($50) dollars and not exceeding one hundred ($100) dollars, and a further penalty of twenty-five ($25) dollars for each day the person persists in such violation, after a conviction for the first offense.

Initially, courts were reluctant to enjoin construction of livery stables, because it could "not be known in advance that [a] stable [would] be a nuisance."[96] However, in 1896, the Supreme Court of Illinois upheld constitutionality and enforceability of the 1890 ordinance.[97]

The practice of blackmailing neighborhoods was not invented nor exclusively used in Chicago. Consider, for example, *Lewis v. Gollner* (1891).[98] In the early 1890s, the houses on President and Union Streets between Seventh and Eighth Avenues in Brooklyn had unique qualities that property owners wanted to maintain:

> President Street * * * and Union Street, which runs parallel with it one block away, [were] occupied by private residences constructed by citizens of some wealth and social standing whose homes are more or less creditable to their taste, and in which, as giving character to their neighborhood, they [felt] a pardonable pride. That part of the city had never been invaded by flats or tenement-houses, which brought together a changing and floating population under one roof, having no ownership of their own, and caring little for anything beyond their personal comfort and immediate needs. * * * Into this locality came the defendant Gollner, a builder of tenement-houses and flats. He bought a lot fronting on Union Street * * * and at once announced his intention of erecting there a seven-story flat [building]. Such a building in such a locality was regarded as offensive and injurious by the residents of the vicinity, and * * * its construction in that locality would cause injury and damage to the neighboring premises. Gollner was not without experience, and apparently knew what he was about when he took

96. *See* Sheldon v. Weeks, 51 Ill. App. 314, 315 (1893).

97. Chicago v. Stratton, 162 Ill. 494 (1896).

98. Lewis v. Gollner, 129 N.Y. 227 (1891).

some pains to let his plans be generally understood. The neighbors at first remonstrated, but found Gollner immovable and standing upon his rights. They then sought to buy him out for the sole and declared purpose of saving the neighborhood from flats. Gollner had no title but simply a contract. The price he had agreed to pay was eighteen thousand dollars, which was the full and fair value of the property, and upon that he had paid only the sum of five hundred dollars. He began the negotiations with a very large price, but finally agreed to sell out for twenty-four thousand and five hundred dollars, or a net profit of six thousand dollars, and upon the further contract that 'he would not construct or erect any flats in plaintiff's immediate neighborhood or trouble him any more.' It is evident * * * that the six thousand dollars was the consideration for the restrictive agreement of Gollner, and was the price paid for his covenant not to build flats in the neighborhood or trouble its residents with similar injurious and disagreeable enterprises. Neither party at all misunderstood that this was the material point of the contract. * * * Gollner himself, * * * accurately understood and clearly stated the pith of the agreement when he said, that after making it, if he should build flats in the vicinity, he 'should be considered a blackmailer;' and when other lots were suggested * * *, Gollner said, 'What, go for more blood money after I had taken blood money out of those people; I would not do it.' And yet he did attempt to do it. At the moment when his contract with plaintiff was closed and the down payment was made, he began negotiations for the purchase of a lot on Union street diagonally opposite his first purchase and, obtaining title, at once commenced the erection of a seven-story flat. When reminded of his agreement and remonstrated with he seems, according to one witness, to have regarded it as a good joke upon his vendees, and added that 'he guessed he could fight them with their own money, that he had $6,000 of it in his clothes—patting his pocket—and he would see that go as far as it would last in that direction.

Questions

1. Did livery stables in Chicago and apartment buildings in the Brooklyn neighborhood create externalities?

2. Section 17 of the 1866 Chicago ordinance established a revenue sharing scheme between the City and informers. Did this provision encourage people to obey nuisance laws? Did it motivate blackmailing?

3. In the late 1990s, Peter Detkin, the assistant general counsel for Intel, coined the term "*patent troll*" to describe "somebody who tries to make a lot of money off a patent that they are not practicing and have no intention of practicing and in most cases never practiced."[99] Patent trolls collect

99. Brenda Sandburg, *You May Not Have a Choice: Trolling for Dollars*, RECORDER–SAN FRANCISCO, Jul. 30, 2001. *See generally* John R. Allison et al., *Extreme Value or Trolls on Top? The Characteristics of the Most-Litigated Patents*, 158 University of Pennsylvania Law Review

patents, but never commercialize them. They use injunctions or the threat of injunctions to inflate the licensing fees they can collect. In *eBay Inc. v. MercExchange L.L.C.*,[100] the Supreme Court narrowed the availability of injunctions to patent trolls, holding that the decision whether to grant injunctive relief rests within the equitable discretion of the courts, so that the remedy would not disserve the public. In a concurring opinion, Justice Kennedy expressed concerns regarding the practice of "[using] patents not as a basis for producing and selling goods but, instead, primarily for obtaining licensing fees."

(a) Patent trolls and urban "entrepreneurs" who threaten property owners with nuisances make profits through blackmail.[101] What is needed for a successful blackmail?

(b) Injunctions allow property to enforce their rights.[102] How are injunctions related to the *sic utere tuo ut alienum non lædas* maxim? When can injunctions promote societal interests? When injunctions can impede societal interests? Would Pigou and Coase endorse injunctions as regulatory measures? If so, how would they use injunctions?

Tobacco and Odors

In March 1883, the New York Legislature passed *An Act to Improve the Public Health in the City of New York by Prohibiting the Manufacture of Cigars and Preparation of Tobacco in Any Form in the Tenement–Houses of Said City*. In 1884, the Legislature decided to expand the regulation to other cities, and replaced the 1883 Act with a new statute:

> *An Act to Improve the Public Health by Prohibiting the Manufacture of Cigars and Preparation of Tobacco in Any Form in Tenement–Houses in Certain Cases, and Regulating the Use of Tenement–Houses in Certain Cases.*

---

1 (2009); James Bessen et al., *The Private and Social Costs of Patent Trolls*, 34 REGULATION 26 (2011); John M. Golden, *"Patent Trolls" and Patent Remedies*, 85 TEXAS LAW REVIEW 2111 (2007).

100. eBay Inc. v. MercExchange L.L.C., 547 U.S. 388 (2006).

101. *See generally* Oren Bar–Gill & Omri Ben–Shahar, Credible Coercion, TEXAS LAW REVIEW 717 (2005); Ronald H. Coase, *Blackmail*, 74 VIRGINIA LAW REVIEW 655 (1988); Richard A. Epstein, *Blackmail, Inc.*, 50 UNIVERSITY OF CHICAGO LAW REVIEW 553 (1983); George P. Fletcher, *Blackmail: The Paradigmatic Crime*, 141 UNIVERSITY OF PENNSYLVANIA LAW REVIEW 1617 (1993); Douglas H. Ginsburg & Paul Shechtman, *Blackmail: An Economic Analysis of the Law*, 141 UNIVERSITY OF PENNSYLVANIA LAW REVIEW 1849 (1993); Leo Katz, *Blackmail and Other Forms of Arm–Twisting*, 141 UNIVERSITY OF PENNSYLVANIA LAW REVIEW 1567 (1993); James Lindgren, *Unraveling the Paradox of Blackmail*, 84 COLUMBIA LAW REVIEW 670 (1984); James Lindgren, *The Theory, History, and Practice of the Bribery–Extortion Distinction*, 141 UNIVERSITY OF PENNSYLVANIA LAW REVIEW 1695 (1993); Richard H. McAdams, *Group Norms, Gossip, and Blackmail*, 144 UNIVERSITY OF PENNSYLVANIA LAW REVIEW 2237 (1996); *Richard A. Posner, Blackmail, Privacy, and Freedom of Contract*, 141 UNIVERSITY OF PENNSYLVANIA LAW REVIEW 1817 (1993); Henry E. Smith, *The Harm in Blackmail*, 92 NORTHWESTERN UNIVERSITY LAW REVIEW 861 (1998).

102. *See generally* Guido Calabresi & A. Douglas Melamed, *Property Rules, Liability Rules, and Inalienability: One View of the Cathedral*, 85 HARVARD LAW REVIEW 1089 (1972).

Passed May 12, 1884.

The People of the State of New York, represented in Senate and Assembly, do enact as follows.

Manufacture of cigars and tobacco prohibited in tenant houses.

Section 1. The manufacture of cigars or preparation of tobacco in any form on any floor, or in any part of any floor in any tenement-house is hereby prohibited if such floor or any part of such floor is by any person occupied as a home or residence for the purpose of living, sleeping, cooking or doing any household work therein.

What is a tenant house.

§ 2. Any house, building or portion thereof occupied as home or residence of more than three families, living independently of one another, and doing their cooking upon the premises, is a tenement-house within the meaning of this act.

First floor exempted.

§ 3. The first floor of said tenement-house on which there is a store for the sale of cigars and tobacco shall be exempt from the prohibition provided in section one of this act.

Sanitary inspector to report violations.

§ 4. It shall be the duty of every sanitary inspector of any city to which this act is applicable, to report any violation of this act coming to his knowledge forthwith to a police magistrate, and to procure the punishment of the person or persons having committed such violation; but this provision shall not be construed to preclude any other citizen from performing the duty herein assigned to said sanitary inspector.

Penalty.

§ 5. Every person who shall be found guilty of a violation of this act, or of having caused another to commit such violation, shall be deemed guilty of misdemeanor and shall be punished for every offense by a fine of not less than ten dollars and not more than one hundred dollars, or by imprisonment for not less than ten days and not more than six months, or both such fine and imprisonment.

Application of act.

§ 6. This act shall apply only to cities having over five hundred thousand inhabitants.

§ 7. All acts or parts of act inconsistent with this act are hereby repealed.

§ 8. This act shall take effect immediately.

In re Jacobs

Court of Appeals of New York
98 N.Y. 98 (1885)

■ Robert Earl, Judge

The relator Jacobs was arrested on the 14th day of May, 1884, on a warrant issued by a police justice in the city of New York under the act * * * entitled *'An act to improve the public health by prohibiting the manufacture of cigars and preparation of tobacco in any form in tenement-houses in certain cases, and regulating the use of tenement-houses in certain cases.'* * * * [U]pon his petition, a justice of the Supreme Court granted a writ of *habeas corpus,* * * * and upon the hearing thereon the justice made an order dismissing the writ and remanding him to prison. From that order he appealed to the General Term of the Supreme Court, which reversed the order and discharged him from prison, on the ground that the act under which he was arrested was unconstitutional and therefore void. The district attorney on behalf of the people then appealed to this court, and the sole question for our determination is, whether the act of 1884 creating the offense for which the relator was arrested was a constitutional exercise of legislative power.

The facts as they appeared before the police justice were as follows: The relator at the time of his arrest lived with his wife and two children in a tenement-house in the city of New York in which three other families also lived. There were four floors in the house, and seven rooms on each floor, and each floor was occupied by one family living independently of the others, and doing their cooking in one of the rooms so occupied. The relator at the time of his arrest was engaged in one of his rooms in preparing tobacco and making cigars, but there was no smell of tobacco in any part of the house except the room where he was thus engaged.

* * *

What does this act attempt to do? In form, it makes it a crime for a cigarmaker in New York and Brooklyn, the only cities in the State having a population exceeding 500,000, to carry on a perfectly lawful trade in his own home. Whether he owns the tenement-house or has hired a room therein for the purpose of prosecuting his trade, he cannot manufacture therein his own tobacco into cigars for his own use or for sale, and he will become a criminal for doing that which is perfectly lawful outside of the two cities named—everywhere else, so far as we are able to learn, in the whole world. He must either abandon the trade by which he earns a livelihood for himself and family, or, if able, procure a room elsewhere, or hire himself out to one who has a room upon such terms as, under the fierce competition of trade and the inexorable laws of supply and demand, he may be able to obtain from his employer. * * * In the unceasing struggle for success and existence which pervades all societies of men, he may be deprived of that which will enable him to maintain his hold, and to survive. * * * It is, therefore, plain that this law interferes with the profitable and free use of his property by the owner or lessee of a tenement-house who is a cigarmaker, and trammels him in the application of his industry and the disposition of his labor, and thus, in a strictly legitimate sense, it arbitrarily deprives him of his property and of some portion of his personal liberty.

The constitutional guaranty that no person shall be deprived of his property without due process of law may be violated without the physical taking of property for public or private use. Property may be destroyed, or its value may be annihilated; it is owned and kept for some useful purpose and it has no value unless it can be used. Its capability for enjoyment and adaptability to some use are essential characteristics and attributes without which property cannot be conceived; and hence any law which destroys it or its value, or takes away any of its essential attributes, deprives the owner of his property.

The constitutional guaranty would be of little worth, if the legislature could, without compensation, destroy property or its value, deprive the owner of its use, deny him the right to live in his own house, or to work at any lawful trade therein. If the legislature has the power under the Constitution to prohibit the prosecution of one lawful trade in a tenement-house, then it may prevent the prosecution of all trades therein. * * *

All laws * * * which impair or trammel these rights, which limit one in his choice of a trade or profession, or confine him to work or live in a specified locality, or exclude him from his own house, or restrain his otherwise lawful movements (except as such laws may be passed in the exercise by the legislature of the police power, which will be noticed later), are infringements upon his fundamental rights of liberty, which are under constitutional protection. In *Butchers' Union Company v. Crescent City Co.*, 111 U.S. 746 (1884), Justice [Stephen Johnson] Field says that among the inalienable rights as proclaimed in the Declaration of Independence "is the right of men to pursue any lawful business or vocation in any manner not inconsistent with the equal rights of others, which may increase their property or develop their faculties, so as to give them their highest enjoyment. The common business and callings of life, the ordinary trades and pursuits which are innocent in themselves, and have been followed in all communities from time immemorial, must, therefore, be free in this country to all alike upon the same terms. The right to pursue them without let or hindrance, except that which is applied to all persons of the same age, sex and condition, is a distinguishing privilege of citizens of the United States, and an essential element of that freedom which they claim as their birthright." In the same case Justice [Joseph] Bradley says: "I hold that the liberty of pursuit, the right to follow any of the ordinary callings of life, is one of the privileges of a citizen of the United States," of which he cannot be deprived without invading his right to liberty within the meaning of the Constitution. In *Live-Stock Dealers' & Butchers' Ass'n v. Crescent City Live-Stock Landing & Slaughter-House Co.*, 15 F. Cas. 649 (C.C.D. La. 1870), the learned presiding justice* says: "There is no more sacred right of citizenship than the right to pursue unmolested a lawful employment in a lawful manner. It is nothing more nor less than the sacred right of labor." * * *

But the claim is made that the legislature could pass this act in the exercise of the police power which every sovereign State possesses. That power is very broad and comprehensive, and is exercised to promote the health, comfort, safety and welfare of society. * * * It is used to regulate the use of property by enforcing the maxim *sic utere tuo, ut alienum non lædas*. Under it the conduct of an individual and the use of property may be regulated so as to interfere, to some extent, with the freedom of the one and the enjoyment of the other; and in cases of great emergency engendering overruling necessity, property may be taken or destroyed without compensation, and without what is commonly called due process of law. The limit of the power cannot be accurately defined, and the courts have not been able or willing definitely to circumscribe it. But the power, however broad and extensive, is not above the Constitution. * * *

---

* [Joseph Bradley.—BYO.]

Generally it is for the legislature to determine what laws and regulations are needed to protect the public health and secure the public comfort and safety, and while its measures are calculated, intended, convenient and appropriate to accomplish these ends, the exercise of its discretion is not subject to review by the courts. But they must have some relation to these ends. Under the mere guise of police regulations, personal rights and private property cannot be arbitrarily invaded, and the determination of the legislature is not final or conclusive. If it passes an act ostensibly for the public health, and thereby destroys or takes away the property of a citizen, or interferes with his personal liberty, then it is for the courts to scrutinize the act and see whether it really relates to and is convenient and appropriate to promote the public health. It matters not that the legislature may in the title to the act, or in its body, declare that it is intended for the improvement of the public health. * * *

We will now once more recur to the law under consideration. It does not deal with tenement-houses as such; it does not regulate the number of persons who may live in any one of them, or be crowded into one room, nor does it deal with the mode of their construction for the purpose of securing the health and safety of their occupants or of the public generally. It deals mainly with the preparation of tobacco and the manufacture of cigars, and its purpose obviously was to regulate them. We must take judicial notice of the nature and qualities of tobacco. It has been in general use among civilized men for more than two centuries. It is used in some form by a majority of the men in this State, by the good and bad, learned and unlearned, the rich and the poor. Its manufacture into cigars is permitted without any hindrance, except for revenue purposes, in all civilized lands. It has never been said, so far as we can learn, and it was not affirmed even on the argument before us, that its preparation and manufacture into cigars were dangerous to the public health. We are not aware, and are not able to learn, that tobacco is even injurious to the health of those who deal in it, or are engaged in its production or manufacture. We certainly know enough about it to be sure that its manipulation in one room can produce no harm to the health of the occupants of other rooms in the same house. It was proved in this case that the odor of the tobacco did not extend to any of the other rooms of the tenement, house. Mr. Secretary McCulloch in his late annual report to congress, in which he recommends the removal of the internal tax from tobacco that it might thus be placed upon a footing with other agricultural products, says: "An article which is so generally used and which adds so much to the comfort of the large numbers of our population who earn their living by manual labor, cannot properly be considered a luxury." To justify this law it would not be sufficient that the use of tobacco may be injurious to some persons, or that its manipulation may be injurious to those who are engaged in its preparation and manufacture; but it would have to be injurious to the public health. This law was not intended to protect the health of those engaged in cigarmaking, as they are allowed to manufacture cigars everywhere except in the forbidden tenement-houses. It cannot be perceived how the cigarmaker is to be improved in his health or his morals by forcing him from his home and its hallowed associations and beneficent influences, to ply his trade elsewhere. It was not intended to protect the health of that portion of the public not residing in the forbidden tenement-houses, as cigars are allowed to be manufactured in private houses, in large factories and shops in the two crowded cities, and in all other parts of the State. What possible relation can cigarmaking in any building have to the health of the general public? Nor was it intended to improve or protect the health of the occupants of tenement-houses. If there are but three families in the tenement-house, however numerous and gregarious their members may be, the manufacture is not forbidden; and it matters not how large the number of the occupants may be if they are not divided into more than three families living and cooking independently. If a store is kept for the sale of cigars on the first floor of one of these houses, and thus more tobacco is kept there than otherwise would be, and the baneful influence of tobacco, if any, is thus increased, that floor, however numerous its occupants, or the occupants of the house, is exempt from the operation of the act. What possible relation to the health of the occupants of a large tenement-house could cigarmaking in one of its remote rooms have? If the legislature had in mind the protection of the occupants of tenement-houses, why was the act confined in its operation to the two cities only? It is plain that this is not a health law, and that it has no relation whatever to the public health. Under the guise of promoting the public health the legislature might as well have banished cigarmaking from all the cities of the State, or confined it to a single city or town, or have placed under a similar ban the trade of a baker, of a tailor, of a shoemaker, of a woodcarver, or of any other of the innocuous trades carried on by artisans in their own homes. The power would have been the same, and its exercise, so far as it concerns fundamental, constitutional rights, could have been justified by the same arguments. Such legislation may invade one class of rights to-day and another to-morrow, and if it can be sanctioned under the Constitution, while far removed in time we will not be far away in practical statesmanship from those ages when governmental prefects supervised the building of houses, the rearing of cattle, the sowing of seed and the reaping of grain, and governmental ordinances regulated the movements and labor of artisans, the rate of wages, the price of food, the diet and clothing of the people, and a large range of other affairs long since in all civilized lands regarded as outside of governmental functions. Such governmental interferences disturb the normal adjustments of the social fabric, and usually derange the delicate and complicated machinery of industry and cause a score of ills while attempting the removal of one.

When a health law is challenged in the courts as unconstitutional on the ground that it arbitrarily interferes with personal liberty and private property without due process of law, the courts must be able to see that it has at least in fact some relation to the public health, that the public health is the end actually aimed at, and that it is appropriate and adapted to that end. This we have not been able to see in this law, and we must, therefore, pronounce it unconstitutional and void. * * *

Order affirmed.

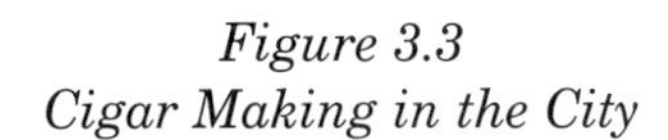

Figure 3.3
Cigar Making in the City

CIGAR MAKING.

Source: Scientific American, November 30, 1872.

Questions

1. What was the stated motivation for anti-tobacco regulation? What was the actual motivation?

2. In *Jacobs*, Judge Earl stressed that cigars were "used in some form by a majority of the men," and no knowledge existed that "preparation and manufacture [of] cigars were dangerous to the public health [or that] tobacco [was] injurious to the health of those who deal in it, or are engaged in its production or manufacture." Were any of these statements relevant to the decision?

Smallpox Vaccination

In May 1901, smallpox broke out in Boston. During the two years in which the epidemic affected the city, there were 1596 cases of smallpox with 270 deaths. In 1901, Boston's population was approximately 560,900. The disease attacked 0.3% of the population and 17% of the infected individuals died.[103] At the time of the outbreak, the deadly disease has been a preventable for more than a century. Dr. Benjamin Waterhouse, Harvard's first Professor of the Theory and Practice of Physic, was the first physician to administer smallpox vaccinations in the United States.[104] Boston was the first City in the country to acquire successful experience with the vaccine already in 1799. Despite this legacy, smallpox frequently attacked the state. Boston was one of the most vocal centers of anti-vaccinationists in the United States. By 1902, Massachusetts law included several provisions regarding "vaccination." Three of the key provisions provided:

> **SECTION 136.** A parent or guardian who neglects to cause his child or ward to be vaccinated before the child or ward attains the age two years, except as provided in Section 137, shall forfeit five dollars for every year during which such neglect continues.
>
> **SECTION 137.** The board of health of a city or town if, in its opinion it is necessary for the public health or safety, shall require and enforce the vaccination and re-vaccination of all inhabitants thereof and shall provide them with the means of free vaccination. Whoever refuses or neglects to comply with such requirement shall forfeit five dollars.
>
> * * *
>
> **SECTION 139.** Any person over twenty-one years of age who * * * is under guardianship shall not be subject to the provisions of Section 137; and any child * * * [about whom] a registered physician * * * is of the opinion that the physical condition of the child is such that his health will be endangered by vaccination shall not, while such condition continues, be subject to the provisions of * * * this chapter; and the parent or guardian of such child shall not be liable to the penalties imposed by section 136 of this chapter.

Under the authority of Section 137, on February 27, 1902, the Cambridge Board of Health passed the following Order:

> *Whereas*, smallpox has been prevalent to some extent in the city of Cambridge, and still continues to increase; and
>
> *Whereas*, it is necessary for the speedy extermination of the disease that all persons not protected by vaccination should be vaccinated; and
>
> *Whereas*, in the opinion of the board, the public health and safety require the vaccination or revaccination of all the inhabitants of Cambridge;
>
> *Therefore,* be it ordered, that all the inhabitants habitants of the city who have not been successfully vaccinated since March 1st, 1897, be vaccinated or revaccinated forthwith.

---

103. Michael R. Albert et al., *The Last Smallpox Epidemic in Boston and the Vaccination Controversy, 1901–1903*, 344 NEW ENGLAND JOURNAL OF MEDICINE 375 (2001).

104. PHILIP CASH, DR. BENJAMIN WATERHOUSE: A LIFE IN MEDICINE AND PUBLIC SERVICE (2006).

On March 15, 1902, Reverend Henning Jacobson refused to be vaccinated. He was convicted and fined $5. His conviction was upheld by the state courts and he appealed to the Supreme Court. In his briefs, Jacobson made the following arguments:

> 1. That vaccination, as usually performed, is an operation that quite often causes or results in a serious and permanent injury to the health of the person vaccinated.
>
> 2. Also, that it is an operation which occasionally causes and results in the death of the vaccinated person.
>
> 3. That among the diseases that are caused, or often result from vaccination, are eczema, salt rheum, erysipelas, syphilis, some forms of scrofula, paralysis, consumptions, tetanus, and various forms of blood poisoning, including septicæmia and pyæmia, and some forms of insanity—all loathsome and dangerous diseases, to be dreaded and feared.
>
> 4. That it is impossible to tell in any particular case, what the results of vaccination will be, whether or not it will cause serious injury to the health, or result in the death of the vaccinated person.
>
> 5. That, as a rule, vaccination of a person results ill a sickness more or less prolonged and serious, which renders the person vaccinated incapable of performing his usual duties and labors, whether physical or mental, for a longer or shorter time sometimes incapacitating him for a period of several weeks, or even months—and this in cases where the is an ultimate complete recovery from the effects of the vaccination itself.
>
> 6. That it is a fact that quite often a person blood is in such a condition of impurity, that it is not prudent or safe to vaccinate him while in that condition, and that it cannot be done at such It time without a risk or danger to his health or life.
>
> * * *
>
> 8. That the so-called virus, or vaccine matter, or points, that is used for the purpose of vaccination, as manufactured and sold for use, quite often is impure and in a condition unfit and dangerous to be so used, and that there is no known practical test that can be resorted to by the ordinarily skillful und experienced practising physician, to determine whether or not the vaccine matter that is to be used is pure and suitable to be used, or is by reason of its impurity, necessarily a source of danger if used at all.* * *[105]

Jacobson v. Massachusetts

197 U.S. 11 (1905)

■ MR. JUSTICE HARLAN delivered the opinion of the court.

This case involves the validity, under the Constitution of the United States, of certain provisions in the statutes of Massachusetts relating to

105. Jacobson v. Massachusetts, Transcript of the Record, Docket No. 70–175 (June 29, 1903).

vaccination. [After the Cambridge Board of Health adopted the smallpox order in February 1902,] the Board adopted an additional regulation empowering a named physician to enforce the vaccination of persons. * * *

The [original] complaint charged that [Jacobson], being over twenty-one years of age and not under guardianship, refused and neglected to comply [with the Order's] requirement.

* * *

[P]ursuant to the verdict of the jury, [Jacobson] was sentenced by the court to pay a fine of $5. And the court ordered that he stand committed until the fine was paid.

* * *

The supreme judicial court of Massachusetts said in the present case [some of Jacobson's propositions were nothing more than] his personal opinion, which could not be taken as correct, or given effect, merely because he made it a ground of refusal to comply with the requirement. Moreover, his views could not affect the validity of the statute, nor entitle him to be excepted from its provisions. The other * * * propositions all relate to alleged injurious or dangerous effects of vaccination. * * * The only 'competent evidence' that could be presented to the court to prove these propositions was the testimony of experts, giving their opinions. It would not have been competent to introduce the medical history of individual cases. * * * [However,] for nearly a century most of the members of the medical profession have regarded vaccination * * * as a preventive of smallpox; that, while they have recognized the possibility of injury to an individual from carelessness in the performance of it, or even in a conceivable case without carelessness, they generally have considered the risk of such an injury too small to be seriously weighed as against the benefits coming from the discreet and proper use of the preventive. * * *

The authority of the state to enact this statute is to be referred to what is commonly called the police power. * * * Although this court has refrained from any attempt to define the limits of that power, yet it has distinctly recognized the authority of a state to enact quarantine laws and 'health laws of every description.' * * * It is equally true that the state may invest local bodies called into existence for purposes of local administration with authority in some appropriate way to safeguard the public health and the public safety. * * *

We come, then, to inquire whether any right given or secured by the Constitution is invaded by the statute as interpreted by the state court. The defendant insists that his liberty is invaded when the state subjects him to fine or imprisonment for neglecting or refusing to submit to vaccination; that a compulsory vaccination law is unreasonable, arbitrary, and oppressive, and, therefore, hostile to the inherent right of every freeman to care for his own body and health in such way as to him seems best; and that the execution of such a law against one who objects to vaccination, no matter for what reason, is nothing short of an assault upon his person. But the liberty secured by the Constitution of the United States to every person within its jurisdiction does not import an absolute right in each person to be, at all times and in all circumstances, wholly freed from restraint. There are manifold restraints to which every person is necessarily subject for the common good. On any other basis organized society could not exist with safety to its members. Society based on the rule that each one is a law unto himself would soon be confronted with disorder and anarchy. Real liberty for all could not exist under the operation of a principle which recognizes the right of each individual person to use his own, whether in respect of his person or his property, regardless of the injury that may be done to others. * * *

Applying these principles to the present case, it is to be observed that the legislature of Massachusetts required the inhabitants of a city or town to be vaccinated only when, in the opinion of the board of health, that was necessary for the public health or the public safety. The authority to determine for all what ought to be done in such an emergency must have been lodged somewhere or in some body; and surely it was appropriate for the legislature to refer that question, in the first instance, to a board of health composed of persons residing in the locality affected, and appointed, presumably, because of their fitness to determine such questions. To invest such a body with authority over such matters was not an unusual, nor an unreasonable or arbitrary, requirement. Upon the principle of self-defense, of paramount necessity, a community has the right to protect itself against an epidemic of disease which threatens the safety of its members. It is to be observed that when the regulation in question was adopted smallpox * * * was prevalent to some extent in the city of Cambridge, and the disease was increasing. If such was the situation, * * * the court would usurp the functions of another branch of government if it adjudged, as matter of law, that the mode adopted under the sanction of the state, to protect the people at large was arbitrary, and not justified by the necessities of the case. * * * If the mode adopted by the Commonwealth of Massachusetts for the protection of its local communities against smallpox proved to be distressing, inconvenient, or objectionable to some—if nothing more could be reasonably affirmed of the statute in question—the answer is that it was the duty of the constituted authorities primarily to keep in view the welfare, comfort, and safety of the many, and not permit the interests of the many to be subordinated to the wishes or convenience of the few. There is, of course, a sphere within which the individual may assert the supremacy of his own will, and rightfully dispute the authority of any human government—especially of any free government existing under a written constitution, to interfere with the exercise of that will. But it is equally true that in every well-ordered society charged with the duty of conserving the safety of its members the rights of the individual in respect of his liberty may at times, under the pressure of great dangers, be subjected to such restraint, to be enforced by reasonable regulations, as the safety of the general public may demand. An American citizen arriving at an American port on a vessel in which, during the voyage, there had been cases of yellow fever or Asiatic cholera, he, although apparently free from disease himself, may yet, in some circumstances, be held in quarantine against his will on board of such vessel or in a quarantine station, until it be ascertained by inspection, conducted with due diligence, that the danger of the spread of the disease among the community at large has disappeared. The liberty secured by the 14th Amendment, this court has said, consists, in part, in the right of a person 'to live and work where he will' *Allgeyer v. Louisiana*, 165 U. S. 578 (1897); and yet he may be compelled, by force if need be, against his will and without regard to his personal wishes or his pecuniary interests, or even his religious or political convictions, to take his place in the ranks of the army of his country, and risk the chance of being shot down in its defense. It is not, therefore, true that the power of the public to guard itself against imminent danger depends in every case involving the control of one's body upon his willingness to submit to reasonable regulations established by the constituted authorities, under the sanction of the state, for the purpose of protecting the public collectively against such danger.

* * *

Looking at the propositions embodied in the defendant's rejected offers of proof, it is clear that they are more formidable by their number than by their inherent value. Those offers in the main seem to have had no purpose except to state the general theory of those of the medical profession who attach little or no value to vaccination as a means of preventing the spread of smallpox, or who think that vaccination causes other diseases of the body. * * * Whatever may be thought of the expediency of this statute, it cannot be affirmed to be, beyond question, in palpable conflict with the Constitution. Nor, in view of the methods employed to stamp out the disease of smallpox, can anyone confidently assert that the means prescribed by the state to that end has no real or substantial relation to the protection of the public health and the public safety. Such an assertion would not be consistent with the experience of this and other countries whose authorities have dealt with the disease of smallpox. And the principle of vaccination as a means to prevent the spread of smallpox has been enforced in many states by statutes making the vaccination of children a condition of their right to enter or remain in public schools. * * *

Did the offers of proof made by the defendant present a case which entitled him, while remaining in Cambridge, to claim exemption from the operation of the statute and of the regulation adopted by the board of health? We have already said that his rejected offers, in the main, only set forth the theory of those who had no faith in vaccination as a means of preventing the spread of smallpox, or who thought that vaccination, without benefiting the public, put in peril the health of the person vaccinated. But there were some offers which it is contended embodied distinct facts that might properly have been considered. Let us see how this is.

The defendant offered to prove that vaccination 'quite often' caused serious and permanent injury to the health of the person vaccinated; that the operation 'occasionally' resulted in death; that it was 'impossible' to tell 'in any particular case' what the results of vaccination would be, or whether it would injure the health or result in death; that 'quite often' one's blood is in a certain condition of impurity when it is not prudent or safe to vaccinate him; that there is no practical test by which to determine 'with any degree of certainty' whether one's blood is in such condition of impurity as to render vaccination necessarily unsafe or dangerous; that vaccine matter is 'quite often' impure and dangerous to be used, but whether impure or not cannot be ascertained by any known practical test; that the defendant refused to submit to vaccination for the reason that he had, 'when a child,' been caused great and extreme suffering for a long period by a disease produced by vaccination; and that he had witnessed a similar result of vaccination, not only in the case of his son, but in the cases of others.

These offers, in effect, invited the court and jury to go over the whole ground gone over by the legislature when it enacted the statute in question. The legislature assumed that some children, by reason of their condition at the time, might not be fit subjects of vaccination; and it is suggested-and we will not say without reason-that such is the case with some adults. But the defendant did not offer to prove that, by reason of his then condition, he was in fact not a fit subject of vaccination at the time he was informed of the requirement of the regulation adopted by the board of health. It is entirely consistent with his offer of proof that, after reaching full age, he had become, so far as medical skill could discover, and when informed of the regulation of the board of health was, a fit subject of vaccination, and that the vaccine matter to be used in his case was such as any medical practitioner of good standing would regard as proper to be used. The matured opinions of medical men everywhere, and the experience of mankind, as all must know, negative the suggestion that it is not possible in any case to determine whether vaccination is safe. Was defendant exempted from the operation of the statute simply because of his dread of the same evil results experienced by him when a child, and which he had observed in the cases of his son and other children? Could he reasonably claim such an exemption because 'quite often,' or 'occasionally,' injury had resulted from vaccination, or because it was impossible, in the opinion of some, by any practical test, to determine with absolute certainty whether a particular person could be safely vaccinated?

It seems to the court that an affirmative answer to these questions would practically strip the legislative department of its function to care for the public health and the public safety when endangered by epidemics of disease. Such an answer would mean that compulsory vaccination could not, in any conceivable case, be legally enforced in a community, even at the command of the legislature, however widespread the epidemic of smallpox, and however deep and universal was the belief of the community and of its medical advisers that a system of general vaccination was vital to the safety of all.

We are not prepared to hold that a minority, residing or remaining in any city or town where smallpox is prevalent, and enjoying the general protection afforded by an organized local government, may thus defy the will of its constituted authorities, acting in good faith for all, under the legislative sanction of the state. If such be the privilege of a minority, then a like privilege would belong to each individual of the community, and the spectacle would be presented of the welfare and safety of an entire population being subordinated to the notions of a single individual who chooses to remain a part of that population. * * *

The judgment of the court below must be affirmed.

It is so ordered.

Questions

1. What were the regulatory measures available to localities in Massachusetts to address smallpox in 1902?

2. Who was vaccinated and who was not vaccinated under Massachusetts law in 1902? What was the function of the Cambridge Order of February 1902? What were Jacobson's arguments against the Cambridge Order? What was the reasoning of the *Jacobson* Court?

3. Was smallpox an externality? Assume smallpox is an externality. Should smallpox vaccines be mandated? If so, should state governments or the federal government mandate smallpox vaccines?[106]

4. Smallpox was the deadliest disease in human history until was eradicated. Aggressive influenza strains are highly contagious and can be also deadly. Every year, flu imposes high cost on society due, in part, to decreased productivity of employees and healthcare costs.[107] It is estimated that in an average flu season at least 5% of Americans are infected, of whom 30,000 to 50,000 die. In the course of history, aggressive influenza threads have caused global pandemics and great panics. The Influenza Pandemic of 1918 killed more than 50,000,000 people around the world—a larger number than the victims of WWI.[108] In 2009, a new strain of the flu virus that originated in swine created a life-threatening flu outbreak. The ensuing public panic diverted substantial private and public resources toward flu prevention and control. During the swine flu pandemic in the United States, 642 cases of human infections were confirmed, 42 of which resulted in death.[109] Flu vaccines have eliminated major outbreaks. However, they are not legally mandatory.[110] Private firms produce and supply the vaccines. Employers provide them to employees, and many who do not receive them at the workplace purchase them on the private market. In some years, there is a shortage of flu vaccines at the beginning of the season. The Centers for Disease Control and Prevention (CDC), a federal agency under the Department of Health and Human Services, actively studies influenza strains in collaboration with other countries, research institutions, and private organizations. CDC recommends "[r]outine annual influenza vaccination * * * for all persons aged ≥6 months" and disseminates information about seasonal flu.

---

106. *See* National Federation of Independent Business v. Sebelius, 132 S.Ct. 2566 (2012).

107. *See, e.g.*, William Porter, *Epidemic Influenza*, 14 JOURNAL OF THE AMERICAN MEDICAL ASSOCIATION 113 (1890).

108. *See* K. David Patterson & Gerald F. Pyle, *The Geography and Mortality of the 1918 Influenza Pandemic*, 65 BULLETIN OF THE HISTORY OF MEDICINE 4 (1991).

109. The Novel Swine–Origin Influenza A (H1N1) Investigation Team, *Emergence of a Novel Swine–Origin Influenza A (H1N1) Virus in Humans*, 360 NEW ENGLAND JOURNAL OF MEDICINE 2605 (2009).

110. Karl G. Nicholson, *Influenza*, 362 LANCET 1733 (2003).

(a) Is state regulation needed to address seasonal flu? Are the CDC's informational services needed?

(b) Section 137 of the Massachusetts smallpox law authorized local health boards to adopt mandatory smallpox vaccination plans when "it is necessary for the public health or safety." Should states adopt similar laws for flu vaccines? Would such measures be desirable for other diseases?

5. Vaccines have made many diseases preventable. In 1954, two prominent members from the Department of Epidemiology at Harvard School of Public Health noted that "measles is as inevitable as death and taxes."[111] Developed in the late 1960s, the measles, mumps, and rubella (MMR) vaccination changed that and quickly became a standard childhood vaccine. In February 1998, a group of researchers, led by Dr. Andrew J. Wakefield, published in the prestigious medical journal *The Lancet* an article that linked the MMR vaccination to autism.[112] Although the article's methodology was questionable, it spurred a public scare. In the years that followed, epidemiological studies consistently found no evidence of a link between the MMR vaccine and autism. In January 2010, a Fitness to Practise Panel of the UK General Medical Council issued a judgment determining that the researchers had no evidence to support their claims. A few days later *The Lancet* retracted the 1998 article, stating: "Following the judgment of the UK General Medical Council's Fitness to Practise Panel, * * * it has become clear that several elements of the 1998 paper by Wakefield et al. are incorrect. * * * In particular, the claims in the original paper * * * have been proven to be false. Therefore we fully retract this paper from the published record."[113] Subsequently, the General Medical Council revoked Wakefield's medical license after a lengthy hearing, citing numerous ethical violations that tainted his work, such as failing to disclose financial interests.[114] The MMR vaccine scare created uncertainty regarding the safety of the MMR vaccine and vaccines in general, resulting in increased litigation, public campaigns, and some reduced use of vaccination.[115]

(a) Does misleading information regarding vaccines constitute an externality? (b) Are there any unique reasons for state regulation of vaccines administered to infants?

6. In 2012, when this book was printed, the most common sexually transmitted infection in the United States and the major cause of cervical

---

111. Frank L. Babbot, Jr. & John E. Gordon, *Modern Measles*, 268 AMERICAN JOURNAL OF THE MEDICAL SCIENCES 361 (1954).

112. A. J. Wakefield et al., *Ileal–Lymphoid–Nodular Hyperplasia, Non–Specific Colitis, and Pervasive Developmental Disorder in Children*, 351 LANCET 637 (1998).

113. *Retraction*, 375 LANCET 445 (Feb. 6, 2010).

114. *See* Brian Deer, *How the Case Against the MMR Vaccine Was Fixed*, 342 BRITISH MEDICAL JOURNAL 77 (Jan. 8, 2011); *generally* Susan Dominus, *The Denunciation of Dr. Wakefield*, NEW YORK TIMES MAGAZINE, April 24, 2011, at 36.

115. *See generally* INSTITUTE OF MEDICINE, IMMUNIZATION, SAFETY REVIEW: VACCINES AND AUTISM (2004); KATHLEEN STRATTON, ADVERSE EFFECTS OF VACCINES: EVIDENCE AND CAUSALITY (2011). *See also* Cedillo v. Secretary of Health and Human Services, 617 F.3d 1328 (Fed. Cir. 2010); Bruesewitz v. Wyeth LLC, 131 S.Ct. 1068 (2011); Graves v. Secretary of Dept. of Health and Human Services, 2011 WL 3010753 (2011). *See also* Illana Ritov & Jonathan Baron, *Reluctance to Vaccinate: Omission Bias and Ambiguity*, 3 JOURNAL OF BEHAVIORAL DECISION MAKING 263 (1990).

cancer was the human papillomavirus (HPV).[116] In June 2006, the FDA approved the use of a commercial HPV vaccine for females aged 9 to 26 years to prevent four common threads of HPV. Later that month, the Advisory Committee on Immunization Practices (ACIP) recommended routine vaccination of females aged 11 to 12 years.[117] In October 2011, ACIP recommended routine vaccination of males aged 11 to 12.[118] Shortly after the approval of the HPV vaccine, many states considered and some adopted laws that added the HPV vaccine to the list of school vaccination requirements.[119] The HPV vaccine—and much more so initiatives to mandate it—sparked a bitter public debate that echoed many of the arguments raised in *Jacobson*, including skepticism about the efficacy of the vaccine, concerns regarding side effects, and resentment toward mandatory vaccinations. Some argued that because cervical cancer is not contagious, the traditional rationale for required vaccinations does not apply to HPV. The American Academy of Pediatrics, the Centers for Disease Control and Prevention (CDC), and the American Academy of Family Physicians "recommend that girls receive HPV vaccine around age 11 or 12 because this is the age at which the vaccine produces the best immune response in the body, and because it's important to protect girls well before the onset of sexual activity."[120]

(a) Are the motivations for HPV vaccinations substantially different from smallpox vaccines?

(b) Are there any unique considerations that should be taken into account in the case of the HPV vaccines?

---

116. *See generally* Anil K. Chaturvedi et al., *Human Papillomavirus and Rising Oropharyngeal Cancer Incidence in the United States*, 29 JOURNAL OF CLINICAL ONCOLOGY 4294 (2011).

117. *See generally* James Colgrove et al., *HPV Vaccination Mandates—Lawmaking Amid Political and Scientific Controversy*, 638 NEW ENGLAND JOURNAL OF MEDICINE 785 (2010); Barbara A. Slade et al., Postlicensure Safety Surveillance for Quadrivalent Human Papillomavirus Recombinant Vaccine, 302 JAMA 750 (2009); Win Techakehakij & Roger D. Feldman, *Cost–Effectiveness of HPV Vaccination Compared With Pap Smear Screening on a National Scale: A Literature Review*, 26 VACCINE 6258 (2008).

118. *See Recommendations on the Use of Quadrivalent Human Papillomavirus Vaccine in Males—Advisory Committee on Immunization Practices (ACIP), 2011*, 60 MORBIDITY AND MORTALITY WEEKLY REPORT 1705 (Dec. 23, 2011).

119. *See generally* James G. Hodge, Jr. et al., *School Vaccination Requirements: Historical, Social, and Legal Perspectives*, 90 KENTUCKY LAW JOURNAL 831 (2001–2002).

120. *See American Academy of Pediatrics Statement on HPF Vaccine* (Sept. 13, 2011). *See also* Colgrove et al., *HPV Vaccination Mandates*, *supra* note 106.

Regulation of Social Diseases

American Journal of Public Health
Official Monthly Publication of the American Public Health Association
126 Massachusetts Ave., Boston, Mass.
Vol. VIII FEBRUARY, 1918 No. 2

VENEREAL DISEASES AND THE WAR.

SURGEON GENERAL W. C. GORGAS, U. S. A.,
Washington, D. C.

Address before the General Sessions, American Public Health Association, October 19, 1917, at Washington, D.C.

THERE is probably no occasion for pointing out to this association the enormous importance to the military establishment which lays in a proper control of the venereal diseases as far as the army is concerned; It is the greatest cause of disability in the army. The army loses more days of service from its men due to venereal diseases than from any other cause. If the medical department of the army had a choice presented to it, say if some man came with a wand and it were demonstrated that with this wand every wounded man could be gotten back into the line at the end of the second day, with his wound cured; and another course were presented by which all venereal diseases could be eradicated from the army, and our choice were given, permitting us to leave out all sentimental reasons, such as the moral effect upon the community, and allowing us merely to consider the good of the army, and our ability to keep in the line the largest and most efficient fighting force, I think there would be very little hesitation on the part of our department in choosing the eradication of venereal disease. We, in the course of the year, would be able to keep more men in the trenches and have a more efficient force by having eradicated venereal diseases than by eradicating wounds. It does not take long to see how important and how true this is. A man with a flesh wound through the thigh is back in the trenches within ten days or two weeks, frequently in less time. If he contracts a venereal disease, his average disability is very much longer. In other words, to the commanding general, the loss is greater for a man who contracts gonorrhea than for a man who is shot through the thigh, and if the commanding general could lay aside all question of morality, he would probably choose the eradication of venereal disease rather than the prevention of wounds. I merely point that out to show the great importance of the control of venereal diseases as a practical measure to the military sanitarian. * * *

Harry A. Rider, Regulation of Social Diseases

14 The American Political Science Review 298 (1920)

The effect of the war on public opinion and on the mores of the American people is most clearly reflected in the legislation on the subject of venereal diseases. Not many years ago, this subject was ignored by all classes of people, except in vulgar jest, not only by polite and conventional society but by most clear-thinking and well-intentioned minds. It was a subject to be spoken under a bated breath, and written about only in scientific treatises in foreign languages. Even in the medical profession, professional ethics made such diseases the sacred secrets of the physician's 'confessional,' and professional policy usually prevented the disclosure to the patient as well as to the public. Parental prudity and time-honored custom kept adolescents in the dark concerning the devastating nature of these diseases, and, contrary to the rule, the unknown was not feared. Although the contagious nature of these diseases became known to medical science after the establishment of their germ origin, they were not placed in the category of contagious and infectious diseases like small-pox and diphtheria. A few safeguards—the abolition of the public drinking cup and the roller towel—were imposed in many states, but there prevention rested, while practical police methods in dealing with prostitution actually encouraged the spread of venereal diseases.

The power of the national government, under war time conditions, dispelled the former views as to the necessity of "the most ancient of professions," and demonstrated that an army of millions of men might be raised without subjecting the young men of the country to exposure to a terrible epidemic. The success of the war department undoubtedly encouraged the new legislation checking the ravages of venereal disease, and our state authorities display every indication of thoroughgoing cooperation with the United States public health service in clinics and propaganda.

Sixteen states * * * have passed similar laws covering the situation rather completely, providing for examination, reporting, and treatment of syphilis, chancroid, and gonorrhea. The Iowa law provides that physicians and hospital superintendents shall report, on forms supplied by the state board of health, every case of venereal disease which they discover in their practice, with a penalty attached for failure to do so and with a further penalty for the patient who gives false information concerning his previous history. The local board of health is given all powers, in relation to venereal diseases, already given to prevent the spread of other contagious, infectious, or communicable diseases. General publicity is alone excepted, and records are open to inspection only by the infected person, physicians, and public officers in performance of their official duties, and are to be destroyed at the end of one year after the disease has been pronounced cured. * * *

Missouri's law simply declares these diseases to be contagious and places them under the regulations of the state board of health, creating a separate division thereof, named "preventable diseases," including tuberculosis, child hygiene, and venereal diseases, with full powers for enforcing measures of prevention. New York has gone into more detail as to prevention measures, and vests their enforcement in the state board of health, creating therefor a bureau of venereal diseases.

Colorado authorizes the erection of a state detention home for women, for the confinement and free treatment of women suffering with venereal diseases. * * *

Another group of states * * * have * * * laws, providing for the examination of persons convicted on charges of prostitution, and for reporting cases of venereal disease by physicians. Massachusetts and South Dakota make compulsory the examination of inmates of all prisons, state, county, or city, and the treatment of cases found therein.

* * * Michigan prohibits the employment of persons affected with infectious or venereal disease in bakeries, restaurants and other places manufacturing, preparing, or serving food or drink, and requiring the examination of employees of such establishments at the order of any local health officer. The same regulation governs cigar factories. New Jersey has the same prohibitions on handling milk or manufacturing milk products, and on persons engaged in nursing or the care of children or the sick.

Massachusetts takes the further step of attacking the rule of medical ethics relating to secrecy in respect to venereal diseases, by authorizing physicians and surgeons to disclose information pertaining thereto to parents or guardians of any minor from whom the infected person has received a promise of marriage. This disclosure is optional and not mandatory, but, if given in good faith, cannot constitute a slander or libel. Maine and Oklahoma go still further, and prohibit the marriage of infected persons, making it unlawful for such infected persons to fail to report to a physician for examination and punishing physicians for issuing false certificates of freedom from disease. Alabama makes compulsory the examination of males before marriage and prohibits infected men from marrying.

One instance of the difficulties encountered by the national authorities in their campaign for public knowledge concerning these diseases is to be found in the suppression of such knowledge by state laws against literature and pictures on "obscene subjects." Pennsylvania, for instance, forbids the advertisement of treatment with no exception. * * *

Many of these states and some others have already evinced their willingness to enter into cooperation with the national government in enlightening the people and suppressing venereal disease. Arkansas, California, Indiana, Iowa, Montana, Nebraska, New Hampshire and New York have made appropriations for this purpose to their state boards of health, ranging in amount from $5000 to $50,000.

Figure 3.4
Venereal Disease Rules

VENEREAL DISEASE RULES

ILLINOIS HEALTH NEWS

"THE GREATEST WEALTH OF THE COMMONWEALTH IS HEALTH"

STATE DEPARTMENT OF PUBLIC HEALTH
OFFICIAL MONTHLY BULLETIN

[Printed by authority of the State of Illinois.]

Vol. IV. No. 4 APRIL, 1918 New Series

BRINGING·IT·INTO·THE·OPEN.

"IT·CAN·BE·OVERCOME—IF·BROUGHT·OUT·OF·ITS·AMBUSH."

Questions

1. What were the motivations for venereal diseases control mentioned by Surgeon General Gorgas and Harry Rider?[121] What were the differences between them?

2. Unlike smallpox, flu, and many other contagious diseases, in the case of sexually transmitted diseases (STDs), people can substantially reduce their own risk of infection. Should this difference affect the analysis of diseases? Could mandatory vaccinations against STDs be justified?

3. Some of the laws mentioned in Rider's article rely on third parties—physicians, members of boards of health, publishers, bakeries, food establishments, and others. What may be the rationale for such reliance in the context of STDs?

4. Rider's article notes that "[a] few safeguards—the abolition of the public drinking cup and the roller towel—were imposed in many states, but there prevention rested, while practical police methods in dealing with prostitution actually encouraged the spread of venereal diseases." At the end of the first decade of the twentieth century, the movement against the use of the common drinking cup gained power when scientists argued that a drinking glass can transmit tuberculosis, typhoid, and syphilis.[122] "Common drinking cups" were durable cups available in public places for the use of any person who wanted to use a local faucet, fountain, river, or other source of drink. Common drinking cups were used also for communion services. In 1911 and 1912, many states and localities adopted laws and ordinances that banned the common drinking cup, increasing the demand for paper cups that were under the monopoly of the Individual Drinking Cup Company. The Individual Drinking Cup Company was organized in Maine in December 1910 for the purpose of taking over all assets related to the inventions and patents of Lawrence W. Luellen and his associates related to paper drinking cups.[123] The bans on common drinking cups boosted the prices of paper drinking cups. In August 1911, *Domestic Engineering* reviewed other aspects of the problem:

> We are a sanitary people. It must be true, because we ourselves admit it. We are a fighting sanitary people. We fight drinking-cups, roller-towels, kissing, public and private, and any other fightable thing that the medical practitioner may conjure into our notice. At the same time, we are often unbalanced in our fighting. We commit ourselves to a policy the aftereffects of which are often disregarded. The public drinking-cup, for instance, has been demonstrated to be a menace to public health. Immediately every one commenced to fight the drinking-cup evil. This was good, and *Domestic Engineering* took its share in the fighting. Our lack of balance was shown in the inadequate form of the laws enforcing the individual drinking cup. No provision, whatever, was made for

---

121. *See also* Walter Clarke, *The Promotion of Social Hygiene in War Time*, 79 ANNALS OF THE AMERICAN ACADEMY OF POLITICAL AND SOCIAL SCIENCE 178 (1918).

122. *See generally* Howard S. Andres, *The Progress of the Individual Cup Movement, Especially Among Churches*, 29 JOURNAL OF THE AMERICAN MEDICAL ASSOCIATION 789 (1897); L. DUNCAN BULKLEY, SYPHILIS AND THE INNOCENT (1894); W. A. Matheny, *The Common Drinking Cup*, 18 PEDAGOGICAL SEMINARY 205 (1911).

123. Luellen realized the commercial future of individual drinking cups in 1907, when he began developing his technologies and raising capital.

> the relief of public thirst, as should have been done. The railway companies removed the public drinking-cup, according to the law, and left the travelers to fend for themselves in assuaging their thirst. They were at the mercy of the train-peddler, who conscientiously charged 25 cents for a drinking-cup which could be secured for 15 cents anywhere else.[124]

The bans on public drinking cups contributed to reducing the rates of several diseases. They were less effective in addressing STDs. Were there any externalities associated with public drinking cups? Was government intervention needed? Were bans the only available regulatory measure?

§ 3.4 COORDINATION BREAKDOWNS

Coordination breakdowns refer to situations in which the pursuit of self-interest result in inefficient outcomes because market participants undermine each other or fail to reach mutually beneficial agreements. In essence, whenever two or more parties operate in one environment, a coordination breakdown may arise because of one reason or another. The pursuit of self-interest is not a guarantee for successful coordination.[125] Specifically, transaction costs, inadequate information, bounded rationality, peculiar preferences, and fallibility may fail coordination.[126] Here we use two examples of coordination breakdowns the *tragedy of commons* and *tragedy of anticommons*.

The *tragedy of commons* describes a situation where multiple parties overexploit a resource to which they have access. Garrett Hardin coined the term and framed it as a "rebuttal to the invisible hand" theory:

> Picture a pasture open to all. It is to be expected that each herdsman will try to keep as many cattle as possible on the commons. Such an arrangement may work reasonably satisfactorily for centuries because tribal wars, poaching, and disease keep the numbers of both man and beast well below the carrying capacity of the land. Finally, however, comes the day of reckoning, that is, the day when the long-desired goal of social stability becomes a reality. At this point, the inherent logic of the commons remorselessly generates tragedy. As a rational being, each herdsman seeks to maximize his gain. Explicitly or implicitly, more or less consciously, he asks, "What is the utility to me of adding one more animal

---

124. *Wanted—A National Sanitary University and a National Board of Health*, 56 DOMESTIC ENGINEERING 203 (Aug. 26, 1911). A copy of an advertisement of a disposable cup, Tulip Cup, is available at *regti.me/paper-cup* (case sensitive).

125. *See* Joseph Farrel, *Information and the Coase Theorem*, 1 JOURNAL OF ECONOMIC PERSPECTIVES 113, 114 (1987) ("The Coase theorem dispenses with the heavy assumptions of perfect competition, but replaces them with the strong assumption that no mutually beneficial agreement is missed. So while it economizes on formal institutions, it demands a lot of coordination and negotiation.")

126. For the combination of these factors *see* § 6.2. For inadequate information *see* Chapter 5. For bounded rationality and fallibility *see* § 7.4.

> to my herd?" This utility has one negative and one positive component.
>
> 1) The positive component is a function of the increment of one animal. Since the herdsman receives all the proceeds from the sale of the additional animal, the positive utility is nearly *+1*.
>
> 2) The negative component is a function of the additional overgrazing created by one more animal. Since, however, the effects of overgrazing are shared by all the herdsmen, the negative utility for any particular decisionmaking herdsman is only a fraction of *−1*.
>
> Adding together the component partial utilities, the rational herdsman concludes that the only sensible course for him to pursue is to add another animal to his herd. And another; and another * * * But this is the conclusion reached by each and every rational herdsman sharing a commons. Therein is the tragedy. Each man is locked into a system that compels him to increase his herd. * * * Ruin is the destination toward which all men rush, each pursuing his own best interest in a society that believes in the freedom of the commons. Freedom in a commons brings ruin to all.[127]

The overexploitation of common goods arises from the fact that every user internalizes only a fraction of the costs of her actions and imposes costs on others (externalities). This happens whenever several parties share a common resource or when no party owns the resource and any person can use it. The tragedy of commons applies to all natural resources, such as fisheries, hunting areas, oil fields, water sources, and clean air.[128] As Nobel Laureate Elinor Ostrom observed: "Much of the world is dependent on resources that are subject to the possibility of a tragedy of the commons."[129]

The tragedy of anticommons describes a different coordination breakdown, which arises when multiple legal rights frustrate each other and the promotion of societal interests: a gridlock of legal rights.[130] Michael Heller, who coined the term, was inspired by a post-Soviet symptom of bureaucratic decay: many storefronts in Moscow were empty, but street kiosks in front were full of goods. Bureaucratic corruption and inefficiency established a regime in which related economic rights were held by different owners. "In a typical Moscow storefront, one owner [was] endowed initially with the right to sell, another to receive sale revenue, and still others to lease, receive lease revenue, occupy, and determine use. Each owner [could] block the others from using the space as a storefront. No one can set up

---

127. Garrett Hardin, *The Tragedy of Commons*, 162 SCIENCE 1243, 1244 (1968).

128. *See, e.g.*, Ian W.H. Parry et al. *Automobile Externalities and Policies*, 45 JOURNAL OF ECONOMIC LITERATURE 373 (2007) (discussing the nature and magnitude of externalities associated with automobile use, including local and global pollution, oil dependence, traffic congestion and traffic accidents.) *See also* Nicholas Z. Muller & Robert Mendelsohn, *Efficient Pollution Regulation: Getting the Prices Right*, 99 AMERICAN ECONOMIC REVIEW 1714 (2009).

129. ELINOR OSTROM, GOVERNING THE COMMONS: THE EVOLUTION OF INSTITUTIONS FOR COLLECTIVE ACTION 3 (1990).

130. *See generally* MICHAEL HELLER, THE GRIDLOCK ECONOMY: HOW TOO MUCH OWNERSHIP WRECKS MARKETS, STOPS INNOVATION, AND COSTS LIVES (2010).

shop without collecting the consent of all of the other owners."[131] The problem gridlock of rights was well understood before Heller framed the issue. For example, in *The Wealth of Nations*, Adam Smith noted that "[t]he navigation of the Danube is of very little use to the different states of Bavaria, Austria, and Hungary, in comparison of what it would be if any of them possessed the whole of its course till it falls into the Black Sea." Similarly, the history of innovation shows that blocking patents may delay technological progress.[132] Heller's major contribution is clarifying that "too many" rights may result in inefficiencies. This insight may apply to every locality, state, or federal agency.

The tragedies of commons and anticommons are are related to the characteristics of excludability and rivalry.[133] Both tragedies involve rivalries. In the case of the tragedy of commons, the overexploitation is a symptom of non-excludability. In the case of the tragedy of anticommons, the frustration of utilization is a symptom of unproductive excludability.

Game and Fish

In 1891, Minnesota established a state agency to protect and preserve the game and fish of the state.

An Act for the Preservation, Propagation and Protection of the Game and Fish of the State.

Approved April 20, 1891

Be it enacted by the State Legislature of the State of Minnesota:

Board of game and fish commissioners.

SECTION 1. There is hereby created a board to be known by the name of The Board of Game and Fish Commissioners of the State of Minnesota, which board shall be composed of five (5) members, who shall be appointed by the governor, for the term of six (6) years each, * * * and who shall serve without compensation, either direct or indirect. * * *

To propagate and distribute food fishes.

SEC. 3. It shall be the duty of the said board of game and fish commissioners to propagate and distribute food fishes and to keep up the supply thereof in the various waters of the state, and to secure through and by their agents and subordinates the enforcement of all the laws of this state for the preservation, propagation and protection of the game and fish of the state. * * *

---

131. Michael A. Heller, *The Tragedy of the Anticommons: Property in the Transition from Marx to Markets*, 111 HARVARD LAW REVIEW 621, 623 (1998).

132. *See generally* Michael A. Heller & Rebecca S. Eisenberg, *Can Patents Deter Innovation? The Anticommons in Biomedical Research*, 280 SCIENCE 698 (1998); Carl Shapiro, *Navigating the Patent Thicket: Cross Licenses, Patent Pools and Standard–Setting*, *in* 1 INNOVATION POLICY AND THE ECONOMY 119–26 (Adam B. Jaffe, Josh Lerner & Scott Stern eds. 2001). *See also* Adam Mossof, *The Rise and Fall of the First American Patent Thicket: The Sewing Machine War of the 1850s*, 53 ARIZONA LAW REVIEW 165 (2011).

133. *See* § 3.1.2c.

Duties of board, and annual report to governor.

SEC. 4. It shall be the duty of said board to collect, classify and preserve all such statistics, data and information as they may think will tend to promote the objects of act, to conduct all the necessary correspondence, to take charge of and keep all reports, books, papers, documents or specimens which they may collect in the discharge of their duties under this act, and to prepare an annual report to the governor. * * *

Fish-breeding establishment to be located.

SEC. 5. It shall be the further duty of said board to select suitable locations within the state whereon to establish and maintain fish-breeding establishments for the propagation and cultivation of such kinds of food fishes as they may direct, for the purpose of stocking with such fish such of the inland and bordering waters of the state as they may know or have reason to believe are suitable for the kinds of fish so selected by them, and replenishing the supply of the same.

No property in game or fish taken out of season.

SEC. 6. No person shall at any time acquire any property in any game or fish within the state of Minnesota, or subject any of the same to his own dominion or control, save only by killing the same within the periods and by the means permitted by the laws of' the state, and except as permitted by such laws, the game and fish within the state be and remain the property of the state.

Closed season.

SEC. 7. No person shall kill, or pursue with intent to kill, any of the animals or birds hereinafter mentioned. within the period hereinafter limited:

Woodcock.

Woodcock, between the thirty-first (31st) day of October and the fourth (4th) day of July following.

Prairie Chickens.

Prairie chickens, or white-breasted or sharp-tailed grouse, between the first (1st) day of November and the first (1st) day of September following.

Quail, partridge, grouse, or pheasant.

Quail, partridge, ruffled grouse, or pheasant, between the first (1st) day of November and the first (1st) day of September following.

Wild duck, goose or brant.

Wild duck of any variety, or wild goose or brant of any variety, or snipe of any variety, or any aquatic fowl whatever, between the twenty-fifth (25th) day of April and the twentieth (20th) day of August following.

Provided, The possession of anyone of such birds or animals (except alive), by any person during the time the killing thereof is prohibited shall be *prima facie* evidence of the fact that such person killed the same contrary to the provisions of this section.

Penalty for violation of close season.

Whoever shall offend against any of the provisions of this section shall be guilty misdemeanor, and shall, on conviction thereof, be punished by a fine of not less than ten (10) dollars nor more than twenty-five (25) dollars for each and every bird or animal so killed and the costs of prosecution, and, in default of the payment of anyone such fine, shall be imprisoned in the county jail not less than ten (10) days nor more than thirty (30) days, for each and every bird or animal killed.

Moose, caribou, or reindeer.

Provided, That no moose, caribou or reindeer shall be killed or sold or offered for sale in this state for five (5) years next after the passage of this act.

Any person offending under this provision shall be guilty of a misdemeanor.* * *

Elk, moose, deer, antelope, buck, doe or fawn.

SEC. 9. No persons shall hunt with hounds or dogs any elk, moose, deer, antelope, buck, doe or fawn at any time; and no person shall by any means, contrivance or device whatever kill or take by any means, or pursue with intent to kill, or take or worry any elk, moose, deer, antelope, buck, doe or fawn, at any time between the thirtieth (30th) day of November and the first (1st) day of November following.

Penalty for offenses in this section.

Whoever shall offend against any of the provisions of this section shall be guilty of a misdemeanor, and shall, upon conviction thereof, be punished by a fine of not less than fifty (50) dollar nor more than one hundred (100) dollars and costs of prosecution for each animal so destroyed or pursued, and, in default of the payment of each such fine, shall be imprisoned in the county jail for a period of not less than thirty (30) days nor more than sixty (60) days.

Possession of carcass *prima facie* evidence.

The possession by anyone of the carcass, or any part thereof, of any such animal between the fifteenth (15th) day of December any year and the first (1st) day of November following shall be *prima facie* evidence of the fact that such person killed the same contrary to the provisions of this section.

Manner of taking or killing, prohibition of traps or snares.

SEC. 10. No person shall at any time catch or kill any of the animals aforesaid in any other manner than by shooting them with a gun held to the shoulder by the person discharging the same. And no person shall at any time set, lay or prepare any trap, snare or other contrivance or device whatever, with the intent to kill or catch any of the animals aforesaid.

Penalty on conviction of violation.

And whoever shall offend against any of the provisions of this section, whether any such animal is taken or killed or not, shall be deemed guilty of a misdemeanor and shall, upon conviction thereof, be punished by a fine of not less than fifty (50) dollars nor more than one hundred (100) dollars and costs of prosecution, or, in default of the payment of any such fine, be imprisoned in the county jail not less than thirty (30) days nor more than sixty (60) days.* * *

Minnesota v. Rodman

Supreme Court of Minnesota
58 Minn. 393 (1894)

■ THOMAS COLLINS, JUDGE

These defendants were separately indicted for having in possession, more than five days after the end of the open season, parts of the flesh and meat of deer, contrary to the provisions of General Laws [of Minnesota]. * * * [I]t was admitted by the prosecution that the deer referred to had been killed in the open season. * * *

The contention of defendants is that the act should be construed as prohibiting only the having in possession, during the closed season, game unlawfully caught, taken, or killed. On this we need but to say that the language of the act is so clear, plain, and unambiguous as to leave no room for any such construction. It is perfectly obvious that it makes it an offense to have in possession, during the closed season, any game caught or killed in the state, the time when it was caught or killed being immaterial.

* * * Counsel for defendants contend strenuously that the state has no proprietary right in animals * * * and can acquire none by mere legislation. * * * We take it to be the correct doctrine in this country that the ownership of wild animals, so far as they are capable of ownership, is in the state, not as proprietor, but in its sovereign capacity, as the representative, and for the benefit, of all its people in common. The preservation of such animals as are adapted to consumption as food, or to any other useful purpose, is a matter of public interest; and it is within the police power of the state, as the representative of the people in their united sovereignty, to enact such laws as will best preserve such game, and secure its beneficial use in the future to the citizens, and to that end it may adopt any reasonable regulations, not only as to time and manner in which such game may be taken and killed, but also imposing limitations upon the right of property in such game after it has been reduced to possession. Such limitations deprive no person of his property, because he who takes or kills game had no previous right of property in it, and, when he acquires such right by reducing it to possession, he does so subject to such conditions and limitations as the legislature has seen fit to impose.

[T]he object to be attained is the preservation from extinction or undue depletion of game; and the legislature may pass any reasonable laws to affect that end, even to the extent of restricting the use of, or right of property in, the game after it is taken or killed. All so-called game laws proceed upon that principle, and their constitutionality has rarely, if ever, been successfully assailed. * * *

No court would be justified in declaring unreasonable the provision limiting the time to five days after the commencement of the closed season, during which a person may lawfully retain possession of game taken or killed during the open season. What this provision aims at is not the mere fact of possession of game lawfully obtained, but to prevent its being unlawfully taken or killed. If it were permitted to have possession during the closed season, without limitation, of game taken or killed during the open season, it would inevitably result in frequent violations of the law, without the least probability of a discovery. Game is usually found in secluded places, away from habitations of men, with no one to witness the killing but the hunter himself. The game would have no earmarks to show whether it was taken or killed in the open or the closed season, and hence conviction under this statute would ordinarily be impossible, and the law would become practically a dead letter. In these days of cold-storage warehouses, the mere lapse of time after the expiration of the open season would furnish little aid in an effort to prove that the game had been taken or killed out of season. The regulation is one which reasonably tends to prevent the taking or killing of game in the closed or forbidden season, and is therefore a legitimate exercise of the police power. * * *

Orders affirmed.

Questions

1. What were the goals of the 1891 Act? How did the Act define the term "closed season"? What was the open season?

2. What were the statutory restrictions on the hunting of elk, moose, deer, antelope, buck, doe, and fawn? What may explain these restrictions?

3. What was the explanation of the *Rodman* court regarding the Act's restrictions on possession of game? Do these restrictions promote the purpose of the Act? Are such restrictions likely to survive judicial scrutiny today?

The Fragmented American Indian Land

Seeking to address the problem of extreme fragmentation of American Indian land into tiny non-economic units, Congress passed the Indian Land Consolidation Act of 1983,[134] which provided for escheat (forfeit) to the tribe of units below a certain size and value at the death of the property holder. In *Hodel v. Irving*, 481 U.S. 704 (1987) and *Babbitt v. Youpee*, 519 U.S. 234 (1997) the Supreme Court held that that the right to pass on property at death, like the right to exclude, is a constitutionally protected property right and invalidated two versions of the escheat provision of the Act.[135]

Hodel v. Irving

481 U.S. 704 (1987)

■ Justice O'Connor delivered the opinion of the Court.

The question presented is whether the original version of the "escheat" provision of the Indian Land Consolidation Act of 1983 * * * effected a "taking" of appellees' decedents' property without just compensation.

I

Towards the end of the 19th century, Congress enacted a series of land Acts which divided the communal reservations of Indian tribes into individ-

134. Pub. L. No. 97–459, Tit. II, 96 Stat. 2515, 2519 (1983).

135. *See generally* Kristin T. Ruppel, Understanding Indian Land: Living with the Legacies of Allotment (2008).

ual allotments for Indians and unallotted lands for non-Indian settlement. This legislation seems to have been in part animated by a desire to force Indians to abandon their nomadic ways in order to "speed the Indians' assimilation into American society," * * * and in part a result of pressure to free new lands for further white settlement. Two years after the enactment of the General Allotment Act of 1887, Congress adopted a specific statute authorizing the division of the Great Reservation of the Sioux Nation into separate reservations and the allotment of specific tracts of reservation land to individual Indians, conditioned on the consent of three-fourths of the adult male Sioux. * * * Under the Act, each male Sioux head of household took 320 acres of land and most other individuals 160 acres. * * * In order to protect the allottees from the improvident disposition of their lands to white settlers, the Sioux allotment statute provided that the allotted lands were to be held in trust by the United States. * * * Until 1910, the lands of deceased allottees passed to their heirs "according to the laws of the State or Territory" where the land was located, and after 1910, allottees were permitted to dispose of their interests by will in accordance with regulations promulgated by the Secretary of the Interior. * * * Those regulations generally served to protect Indian ownership of the allotted lands.

The policy of allotment of Indian lands quickly proved disastrous for the Indians. Cash generated by land sales to whites was quickly dissipated, and the Indians, rather than farming the land themselves, evolved into petty landlords, leasing their allotted lands to white ranchers and farmers and living off the meager rentals. * * * The failure of the allotment program became even clearer as successive generations came to hold the allotted lands. Thus 40–, 80–, and 160–acre parcels became splintered into multiple undivided interests in land, with some parcels having hundreds, and many parcels having dozens, of owners. Because the land was held in trust and often could not be alienated or partitioned, the fractionation problem grew and grew over time.

A 1928 report commissioned by the Congress found the situation administratively unworkable and economically wasteful. * * * Good, potentially productive, land was allowed to lie fallow, amidst great poverty, because of the difficulties of managing property held in this manner. * * * In discussing the Indian Reorganization Act of 1934, Representative Howard said:

> "It is in the case of the inherited allotments, however, that the administrative costs become incredible.... On allotted reservations, numerous cases exist where the shares of each individual heir from lease money may be 1 cent a month. Or one heir may own minute fractional shares in 30 or 40 different allotments. The cost of leasing, bookkeeping, and distributing the proceeds in many cases far exceeds the total income. The Indians and the Indian Service personnel are thus trapped in a meaningless system of minute partition in which all thought of the possible use of land to satisfy human needs is lost in a mathematical haze of bookkeeping."

78 Cong. Rec. 11728 (1934).

In 1934, in response to arguments such as these, the Congress acknowledged the failure of its policy and ended further allotment of Indian lands. Indian Reorganization Act of 1934, 48 Stat. 984, 25 U.S.C. § 461 *et seq.*

But the end of future allotment by itself could not prevent the further compounding of the existing problem caused by the passage of time. Ownership continued to fragment as succeeding generations came to hold the property, since, in the order of things, each property owner was apt to have more than one heir. In 1960, both the House and the Senate undertook comprehensive studies of the problem. * * * These studies indicated that one-half of the approximately 12 million acres of allotted trust lands were held in fractionated ownership, with over 3 million acres held by more than six heirs to a parcel. * * * Further hearings were held in 1966, * * * but not until the Indian Land Consolidation Act of 1983 did the Congress take action to ameliorate the problem of fractionated ownership of Indian lands.

Section 207 of the Indian Land Consolidation Act—the escheat provision at issue in this case—provided:

> "No undivided fractional interest in any tract of trust or restricted land within a tribe's reservation or otherwise subjected to a tribe's jurisdiction shall descedent [*sic*] by intestacy or devise but shall escheat to that tribe if such interest represents 2 per centum or less of the total acreage in such tract and has earned to its owner less than $100 in the preceding year before it is due to escheat."
>
> 96 Stat. 2519.

Congress made no provision for the payment of compensation to the owners of the interests covered by § 207. The statute was signed into law on January 12, 1983, and became effective immediately.

The three appellees—Mary Irving, Patrick Pumpkin Seed, and Eileen Bissonette—are enrolled members of the Oglala Sioux Tribe. They are, or represent, heirs or devisees of members of the Tribe who died in March, April, and June 1983. Eileen Bissonette's decedent, Mary Poor Bear–Little Hoop Cross, purported to will all her property, including property subject to § 207, to her five minor children in whose name Bissonette claims the property. Chester Irving, Charles Leroy Pumpkin Seed, and Edgar Pumpkin Seed all died intestate. At the time of their deaths, the four decedents owned 41 fractional interests subject to the provisions of § 207. The Irving estate lost two interests whose value together was approximately $100; the Bureau of Indian Affairs placed total values of approximately $2,700 on the 26 escheatable interests in the Cross estate and $1,816 on the 13 escheatable interests in the Pumpkin Seed estates. But for § 207, this property would have passed, in the ordinary course, to appellees or those they represent.

Appellees filed suit in the United States District Court for the District of South Dakota, claiming that § 207 resulted in a taking of property without just compensation in violation of the Fifth Amendment. The District Court concluded that the statute was constitutional. It held that appellees had no vested interest in the property of the decedents prior to their deaths and that Congress had plenary authority to abolish the power of testamentary disposition of Indian property and to alter the rules of intestate succession. * * *

The Court of Appeals for the Eighth Circuit reversed. *Irving v. Clark*, 758 F.2d 1260 (1985). Although it agreed that appellees had no vested rights in the decedents' property, it concluded that their decedents had a right, derived from the original Sioux allotment statute, to control disposition of their property at death. The Court of Appeals held that appellees had standing to invoke that right and that the taking of that right without compensation to decedents' estates violated the Fifth Amendment.

* * *

III

The Congress, acting pursuant to its broad authority to regulate the descent and devise of Indian trust lands, *Jefferson v. Fink*, 247 U.S. 288, 294 (1918), enacted § 207 as a means of ameliorating, over time, the problem of extreme fractionation of certain Indian lands. By forbidding the passing on at death of small, undivided interests in Indian lands, Congress hoped that future generations of Indians would be able to make more productive use of the Indians' ancestral lands. We agree with the Government that encouraging the consolidation of Indian lands is a public purpose of high order. The fractionation problem on Indian reservations is extraordinary and may call for dramatic action to encourage consolidation. The Sisseton–Wahpeton Sioux Tribe, appearing as amicus curiae in support of the Secretary of the Interior, is a quintessential victim of fractionation. Forty-acre tracts on the Sisseton–Wahpeton Lake Traverse Reservation, leasing for about $1,000 annually, are commonly subdivided into hundreds of undivided interests, many of which generate only pennies a year in rent. The average tract has 196 owners and the average owner undivided interests in 14 tracts. The administrative headache this represents can be fathomed by examining Tract 1305, dubbed "one of the most fractionated parcels of land in the world." * * * Tract 1305 is 40 acres and produces $1,080 in income annually. It is valued at $8,000. It has 439 owners, one-third of whom receive less than $.05 in annual rent and two-thirds of whom receive less than $1. The largest interest holder receives $82.85 annually. The common denominator used to compute fractional interests in the property is 3,394,923,840,000. The smallest heir receives $.01 every 177 years. If the tract were sold (assuming the 439 owners could agree) for its estimated $8,000 value, he would be entitled to $.000418. The administrative costs of handling this tract are estimated by the Bureau of Indian Affairs at $17,560 annually * * * See also *Comment, Too Little Land, Too Many Heirs—The Indian Heirship Land Problem*, 46 WASHINGTON LAW REVIEW 709, 711–713 (1971).

This Court has held that the Government has considerable latitude in regulating property rights in ways that may adversely affect the owners. See *Keystone Bituminous Coal Assn. v. DeBenedictis*, 480 U.S. 470 (1987)*[1];

*1. [An action of coal companies challenging Pennsylvania Subsidence Act which requires that 50 percent of the coal beneath certain structures be kept in place to provide surface support.]

Penn Central Transportation Co. v. New York City, 438 U.S. 104, 125–127 (1978)*2. * * * The framework for examining the question whether a regulation of property amounts to a taking requiring just compensation is firmly established and has been regularly and recently reaffirmed. * * *

There is no question that the relative economic impact of § 207 upon the owners of these property rights can be substantial. Section 207 provides for the escheat of small undivided property interests that are unproductive during the year preceding the owner's death. Even if we accept the Government's assertion that the income generated by such parcels may be properly thought of as *de minimis,* their value may not be. While the Irving estate lost two interests whose value together was only approximately $100, the Bureau of Indian Affairs placed total values of approximately $2,700 and $1,816 on the escheatable interests in the Cross and Pumpkin Seed estates. * * * These are not trivial sums. There are suggestions in the legislative history regarding the 1984 amendments to § 207 that the failure to "look back" more than one year at the income generated by the property had caused the escheat of potentially valuable timber and mineral interests. * * * Of course, the whole of appellees' decedents' property interests were not taken by § 207. Appellees' decedents retained full beneficial use of the property during their lifetimes as well as the right to convey it *inter vivos.* There is no question, however, that the right to pass on valuable property to one's heirs is itself a valuable right. Depending on the age of the owner, much or most of the value of the parcel may inhere in this "remainder" interest. * * *

The extent to which any of appellees' decedents had "investment-backed expectations" in passing on the property is dubious. Though it is conceivable that some of these interests were purchased with the expectation that the owners might pass on the remainder to their heirs at death, the property has been held in trust for the Indians for 100 years and is overwhelmingly acquired by gift, descent, or devise. * * *

If we were to stop our analysis at this point, we might well find § 207 constitutional. But the character of the Government regulation here is extraordinary. In *Kaiser Aetna v. United States*, 444 U.S. 164, 176 (1979), we emphasized that the regulation destroyed "one of the most essential sticks in the bundle of rights that are commonly characterized as property—the right to exclude others." Similarly, the regulation here amounts to virtually the abrogation of the right to pass on a certain type of property—the small undivided interest—to one's heirs. In one form or another, the right to pass on property—to one's family in particular—has been part of the Anglo-American legal system since feudal times. * * * The fact that it may be possible for the owners of these interests to effectively control disposition upon death through complex *inter vivos* transactions such as revocable trusts is simply not an adequate substitute for the rights taken, given the nature of the property. Even the United States concedes that total abrogation of the right to pass property is unprecedented and likely unconstitutional. * * * Since the escheatable interests are not, as the United States argues, necessarily *de minimis,* nor, as it also argues, does

*2. [An action against New York City Landmarks Preservation Commission's refusal to approve plans for construction of 50-story office building over Grand Central Terminal.]

the availability of *inter vivos* transfer obviate the need for descent and devise, a *total* abrogation of these rights cannot be upheld. * * *

In holding that complete abolition of both the descent and devise of a particular class of property may be a taking, we reaffirm the continuing vitality of the long line of cases. * * * The difference in this case is the fact that both descent and devise are completely abolished; indeed they are abolished even in circumstances when the governmental purpose sought to be advanced, consolidation of ownership of Indian lands, does not conflict with the further descent of the property.

There is little doubt that the extreme fractionation of Indian lands is a serious public problem. It may well be appropriate for the United States to ameliorate fractionation by means of regulating the descent and devise of Indian lands. Surely it is permissible for the United States to prevent the owners of such interests from further subdividing them among future heirs on pain of escheat. * * *. It may be appropriate to minimize further compounding of the problem by abolishing the descent of such interests by rules of intestacy, thereby forcing the owners to formally designate an heir to prevent escheat to the Tribe. What is certainly not appropriate is to take the extraordinary step of abolishing both descent and devise of these property interests even when the passing of the property to the heir might result in consolidation of property. Accordingly, we find that this regulation, in the words of Justice Holmes, "goes too far." *Pennsylvania Coal Co. v. Mahon*, 260 U.S. 393, 415 (1922). The judgment of the Court of Appeals is

Affirmed.

* * *

■ JUSTICE STEVENS, with whom JUSTICE WHITE joins, concurring in the judgment.

The Government has a legitimate interest in eliminating Indians' fractional holdings of real property. Legislating in pursuit of this interest, the Government might constitutionally have consolidated the fractional land interests affected by § 207 of the Indian Land Consolidation Act of 1983, in three ways: It might have purchased them; it might have condemned them for a public purpose and paid just compensation to their owners; or it might have left them untouched while conditioning their descent by intestacy or devise upon their consolidation by voluntary conveyances within a reasonable period of time.

Since Congress plainly did not authorize either purchase or condemnation and the payment of just compensation, the statute is valid only if Congress, in § 207, authorized the third alternative. In my opinion, therefore, the principal question in this case is whether § 207 represents a lawful exercise of the sovereign's prerogative to condition the retention of fee simple or other ownership interests upon the performance of a modest statutory duty within a reasonable period of time.

I

The Court's opinion persuasively demonstrates that the Government has a strong interest in solving the problem of fractionated land holdings among Indians. It also indicates that the specific escheat provision at issue in this case was one of a long series of congressional efforts to address this problem. The Court's examination of the legislative history, however, is incomplete. An examination of the circumstances surrounding Congress' enactment of § 207 discloses the abruptness and lack of explanation with which Congress added the escheat section to the other provisions of the Indian Land Consolidation Act that it enacted in 1983. See *ante,* at 2079.

In 1982, the Senate passed a special bill for the purpose of authorizing the Devils Lake Sioux Tribe of North Dakota to adopt a land consolidation program with the approval of the Secretary of the Interior. That bill provided that the Tribe would compensate individual owners for any fractional interest that might be acquired; the bill did not contain any provision for escheat.[2]

When the Senate bill was considered by the House Committee on Indian Affairs, the Committee expanded the coverage of the legislation to authorize any Indian tribe to adopt a land consolidation program with the approval of the Secretary, and it also added § 207—the escheat provision at issue in this case—to the bill. * * * The Report on the House Amendments does not specifically discuss § 207. In its general explanation of how Indian trust or restricted lands pass out of Indian ownership, resulting in a need for statutory authorization to tribes to enact laws to prevent the erosion of Indian land ownership, the Report unqualifiedly stated that, "if an Indian allottee dies intestate, his heirs will inherit his property, whether they are Indian or non-Indian." * * *

The House returned the amended bill to the Senate, which accepted the House addition without hearings and without any floor discussion of § 207. * * * Section 207 provided:

> "No undivided fractional interest in any tract of trust or restricted land within a tribe's reservation or otherwise subjected to a tribe's jurisdiction shall [descend] by intestacy or devise but shall escheat to that tribe if such interest represents 2 per centum or less of the total acreage in such tract and has earned to its owner less than $100 in the preceding year before it is due to escheat."

In the text of the Act, Congress took pains to specify that fractional interests acquired by a tribe pursuant to an approved plan must be purchased at a fair price. See §§ 204, 205, and 206. There is no comparable provision in § 207. The text of the Act also does not explain why Congress omitted a grace period for consolidation of the fractional interests that were to escheat to the tribe pursuant to that section.

---

2. The Report of the Senate Select Committee on Indian Affairs described the purpose of the bill as follows:

> "The purpose of S. 503 is to authorize the purchase, sale, and exchange of lands by the Devils Lake Sioux Tribe of the Devils Lake Sioux Reservation, North Dakota. The bill is designed to allow the Tribe to consolidate land ownership with the reservation in order to maximize utilization of the reservation land base. The bill also would restrict inheritance of trust property to members of the Tribe provided that the Tribe paid fair market value to the Secretary of the Interior on behalf of the decedent's estate."

S.Rep. No. 97–507, p. 3 (1982).

The statute was signed into law on January 12, 1983, and became effective immediately. On March 2, the Bureau of Indian Affairs of the Department of the Interior issued a memorandum to all its area directors to advise them of the enactment of § 207 and to provide them with interim instructions pending the promulgation of formal regulations. The memorandum explained:

> Section 207 effects a major change in testate and intestate heirship succession for certain undivided fractional interests in trust and restricted Indian land. Under this section, certain interests in land, as explained below, will no longer be capable of descending by intestate succession or being devised by will. Such property interests will, upon the death of the current owner, escheat to the tribe. . . .

The three appellees—Mary Irving, Patrick Pumpkin Seed, and Eileen Bissonette—are enrolled members of the Oglala Sioux Tribe. They represent heirs or devisees of members of the Tribe who died in March, April, and June 1983. At the time of their deaths, the decedents owned 41 fractional interests subject to the provisions of § 207. * * * The size and value of those interests varied widely—the smallest was a 1/3645 interest in a 320–acre tract, having an estimated value of only $12.30, whereas the largest was the equivalent of 3½ acres valued at $284.44. If § 207 is valid, all of those interests escheated to the Tribe; if § 207 had not been enacted—or if it is invalid—the interests would have passed to appellees.

II

* * * The Court's grant of relief to appellees based on the rights of hypothetical decedents * * * necessarily rests on the implicit adoption of an overbreadth analysis that has heretofore been restricted to the First Amendment area. The Court uses the language of takings jurisprudence to express its conclusion that § 207 violates the Fifth Amendment, but the stated reason is that § 207 "goes too far," because it might interfere with testamentary dispositions, or inheritances, that result in the consolidation of property interests rather than their increased fractionation.[8] That reasoning may apply to some decedents, but it does not apply to these litigants' decedents. In one case, the property of Mary Poor Bear–Little Hoop Cross was divided among her five children. In two other cases, the fractional interests passed to the next generation.[9] I had thought it well settled by our precedents that "one to whom application of a statute is

8. The crux of the Court's holding is stated as follows:

> What is certainly not appropriate is to take the extraordinary step of abolishing both descent and devise of these property interests even when the passing of the property to the heir might result in consolidation of property. Accordingly, we find that this regulation, in the words of Justice Holmes, 'goes too far.'

9. Patrick Pumpkin Seed was a potential heir to four pieces of property in which both his father and his uncle had interests. However, because both his father and his uncle had other potential heirs, the net effect of the distribution of the uncle's and the father's estates would have been to increase the fractionalization of their property interests. Furthermore, even if the statute were considered invalid as applied to Patrick Pumpkin Seed, the Court does not explain why it would also be considered invalid as applied to Mary Irving and Eileen Bissonette.

constitutional will not be heard to attack the statute on the ground that impliedly it might also be taken as applying to other persons or other situations in which its application might be unconstitutional." *United States v. Raines*, 362 U.S. 17, 21 (1960) (citing cases). This rule rests on the wisdom that the "delicate power of pronouncing an Act of Congress unconstitutional is not to be exercised with reference to hypothetical cases thus imagined." *Id.*, at 22. In order to review the judgment of the Court of Appeals granting relief to these litigants, an analysis different from the Court's novel overbreadth approach is required.

III

The Secretary argues that special features of this legislation make it a reasonable exercise of Congress' power to regulate Indian property interests. The * * * Secretary contends that § 207 falls within the permissible boundaries of legislation that may operate to limit or extinguish property rights. The Secretary places great emphasis on the minimal value of the property interests affected by § 207, the legitimacy of the governmental purpose in consolidating such interests, and the fact that the tribe, rather than the United States, is the beneficiary of the so-called "escheat." * * *

The value of a property interest does not provide a yardstick for measuring "the scope of the dual constitutional guarantees that there be no taking of property without just compensation, and no deprivation of property without the due process of law." *Texaco, Inc. v. Short*, 454 U.S. 516, 540–541 (1982) (BRENNAN, J., dissenting). The sovereign has no license to take private property without paying for it and without providing its owner with any opportunity to avoid or mitigate the consequences of the deprivation simply because the property is relatively inexpensive. * * * The Fifth Amendment draws no distinction between grand larceny and petty larceny.

The legitimacy of the governmental purposes served by § 207 * * * do not excuse or mitigate whatever obligation to pay just compensation arises when an otherwise constitutional enactment effects a taking of property. Nor does it lessen the importance of giving a property owner fair notice of a major change in the rules governing the disposition of his property.

The fact that § 207 provides for an "escheat" to the tribe rather than to the United States does not change the unwarned impact of the statute on an individual Indian who wants to leave his property to his children. * * *

Assuredly Congress has ample power to require the owners of fractional interests in allotted lands to consolidate their holdings during their lifetimes or to face the risk that their interests will be deemed to have been abandoned. But no such abandonment may occur unless the owners have a fair opportunity to avoid that consequence. In this case, it is palpably clear that they were denied such an opportunity.

This statute became effective the day it was signed into law. It took almost two months for the Bureau of Indian Affairs to distribute an interim memorandum advising its area directors of the major change in Indian heirship succession effected by § 207. Although that memorandum identified three ways in which Indian landowners could avoid the consequences of § 207, it is not reasonable to assume that appellees' decedents—who died on March 18, March 23, April 2, and June 23, 1983—had anything approaching a reasonable opportunity to arrange for the consolidation of their respective fractional interests with those of other owners. With respect to these appellees' decedents, "the time allowed is manifestly so insufficient that the statute becomes a denial of justice." *Wilson v. Iseminger*, 185 U.S. 55, 63 (1902).

While citizens "are presumptively charged with knowledge of the law," *Atkins v. Parker*, 472 U.S. 115, 130 (1985), that presumption may not apply when "the statute does not allow a sufficient 'grace period' to provide the persons affected by a change in the law with an adequate opportunity to become familiar with their obligations under it." *Ibid.* Unlike the food-stamp recipients in *Parker*, who received a grace period of over 90 days and individual notice of the substance of the new law, 472 U.S., at 130–131, the Indians affected by § 207 did not receive a reasonable grace period. Nothing in the record suggests that appellees' decedents received an adequate opportunity to put their affairs in order.

* * * The Constitution vests Congress with plenary power "to deal with the special problems of Indians." *Morton v. Mancari*, 417 U.S. 535, 551 (1974). As the Secretary acknowledges, however, the Government's plenary power over the property of Indians "is subject to constitutional limitations." The Due Process Clause of the Fifth Amendment required Congress to afford reasonable notice and opportunity for compliance to Indians that § 207 would prevent fractional interests in land from descending by intestate or testate succession. In omitting any opportunity at all for owners of fractional interests to order their affairs in light of § 207, Congress has failed to afford the affected Indians the due process of law required by the Fifth Amendment.

Accordingly, I concur in the judgment.

Babbitt v. Youpee

519 U.S. 234 (1997)

■ JUSTICE GINSBURG delivered the opinion of the Court.

In this case, we consider for a second time the constitutionality of an escheat-to-tribe provision of the Indian Land Consolidation Act (ILCA). * * * Specifically, we address § 207 of the ILCA, as amended in 1984. Congress enacted the original provision in 1983 to ameliorate the extreme fractionation problem attending a century-old allotment policy that yielded multiple ownership of single parcels of Indian land. Amended § 207 provides that certain small interests in Indian lands will transfer—or "escheat"—to the tribe upon the death of the owner of the interest. In *Hodel v. Irving*, 481 U.S. 704 (1987), this Court held that the original version of § 207 of the ILCA effected a taking of private property without just compensation, in violation of the Fifth Amendment to the United States

Constitution. We now hold that amended § 207 does not cure the constitutional deficiency this Court identified in the original version of § 207.

I

In the late Nineteenth Century, Congress initiated an Indian land program that authorized the division of communal Indian property. Pursuant to this allotment policy, some Indian land was parceled out to individual tribal members. Lands not allotted to individual Indians were opened to non-Indians for settlement. * * * Allotted lands were held in trust by the United States or owned by the allottee subject to restrictions on alienation. On the death of the allottee, the land descended according to the laws of the State or Territory in which the land was located. Congress also provided that allottees could devise their interests in allotted land.

The allotment policy "quickly proved disastrous for the Indians." *Irving*, 481 U.S., at 707. The program produced a dramatic decline in the amount of land in Indian hands. * * * And as allottees passed their interests on to multiple heirs, ownership of allotments became increasingly fractionated, with some parcels held by dozens of owners. * * * A number of factors augmented the problem: Because Indians often died without wills, many interests passed to multiple heirs * * *; Congress' allotment Acts subjected trust lands to alienation restrictions that impeded holders of small interests from transferring those interests * * *; Indian lands were not subject to state real estate taxes, * * * which ordinarily serve as a strong disincentive to retaining small fractional interests in land. The fractionation problem proliferated with each succeeding generation as multiple heirs took undivided interests in allotments.

The administrative difficulties and economic inefficiencies associated with multiple undivided ownership in allotted lands gained official attention as early as 1928. * * * Governmental administration of these fractionated interests proved costly, and individual owners of small undivided interests could not make productive use of the land. Congress ended further allotment in 1934. See Indian Reorganization Act, 48 Stat. 984, 25 U.S.C. § 461 *et seq.* But that action left the legacy in place. As most owners had more than one heir, interests in lands already allotted continued to splinter with each generation. In the 1960's, congressional studies revealed that approximately half of all allotted trust lands were held in fractionated ownership; for over a quarter of allotted trust lands, individual allotments were held by more than six owners to a parcel. * * *

In 1983, Congress adopted the ILCA in part to reduce fractionated ownership of allotted lands. * * * Section 207 of the ILCA—the "escheat" provision—prohibited the descent or devise of small fractional interests in allotments.[1] Instead of passing to heirs, such fractional interests would escheat to the tribe, thereby consolidating the ownership of Indian lands.

1. As originally enacted, § 207 provided:

"No undivided fractional interest in any tract of trust or restricted land within a tribe's reservation or otherwise subjected to a tribe's jurisdiction shall descedent *[sic]* by intestacy or devise but shall escheat to that tribe if such interest represents 2 per centum or less of the total acreage in such tract and has earned to its owner less than $100 in the preceding year before it is due to escheat." 96 Stat. 2519.

Congress defined the targeted fractional interest as one that both constituted 2 percent or less of the total acreage in an allotted tract and had earned less than $100 in the preceding year. Section 207 made no provision for the payment of compensation to those who held such interests.

In *Hodel v. Irving,* this Court invalidated § 207 on the ground that it effected a taking of property without just compensation, in violation of the Fifth Amendment. The appellees in *Irving* were, or represented, heirs or devisees of members of the Oglala Sioux Tribe. But for § 207, the appellees would have received 41 fractional interests in allotments; under § 207, those interests would escheat to the Tribe. * * * This Court tested the legitimacy of § 207 by considering its economic impact, its effect on investment-backed expectations, and the essential character of the measure. * * * Turning first to the economic impact of § 207, the Court in Irving observed that the provision's income-generation test might fail to capture the actual economic value of the land. The Court next indicated that § 207 likely did not interfere with investment-backed expectations. Key to the decision in *Irving*, however, was the "extraordinary" character of the Government regulation. As this Court noted, § 207 amounted to the "virtua[l] abrogation of the right to pass on a certain type of property." Such a complete abrogation of the rights of descent and devise could not be upheld." * * *

II

In 1984, while *Irving* was still pending in the Court of Appeals for the Eighth Circuit, Congress amended § 207. Amended § 207 differs from the original escheat provision in three relevant respects. First, an interest is considered fractional if it both constitutes 2 percent or less of the total acreage of the parcel and "is incapable of earning $100 in any one of the five years [following the] decedent's death"—as opposed to one year before the decedent's death in the original § 207. 25 U.S.C. § 2206(a). If the interest earned less than $100 in any one of five years prior to the decedent's death, "there shall be a rebuttable presumption that such interest is incapable of earning $100 in any one of the five years following the death of the decedent." *Ibid*. Second, in lieu of a total ban on devise and descent of fractional interests, amended § 207 permits devise of an otherwise escheatable interest to "any other owner of an undivided fractional interest in such parcel or tract" of land. 25 U.S.C. § 2206(b). Finally, tribes are authorized to override the provisions of amended § 207 through the adoption of their own codes governing the disposition of fractional interests; these codes are subject to the approval of the Secretary of the Interior. 25 U.S.C. § 2206(c). * * *

Under amended § 207, the interests in this case would escheat to tribal governments. The initiating plaintiffs, respondents here, are the children and potential heirs of William Youpee. An enrolled member of the Sioux and Assiniboine Tribes of the Fort Peck Reservation in Montana, William Youpee died testate in October 1990. His will devised to respondents, all of them enrolled tribal members, his several undivided interests in allotted trust lands on various reservations in Montana and North Dakota. These interests, as the Ninth Circuit reported, were valued together at $1,239.

Youpee v. Babbitt, 67 F.3d 194, 199 (9th Cir. 1995). Each interest was devised to a single descendant. Youpee's will thus perpetuated existing fractionation, but it did not splinter ownership further by bequeathing any single fractional interest to multiple devisees.

In 1992, in a proceeding to determine the heirs to, and claims against, William Youpee's estate, an Administrative Law Judge (ALJ) in the Department of the Interior found that interests devised to each of the respondents fell within the compass of amended § 207 and should therefore escheat to the tribal governments of the Fort Peck, Standing Rock, and Devils Lake Sioux Reservations. * * * Respondents, asserting the unconstitutionality of amended § 207, appealed the ALJ's order to the Department of the Interior Board of Indian Appeals. * * *

III

In determining whether the 1984 amendments to § 207 render the provision constitutional, we are guided by *Irving*. * * * The Government maintains that the revisions moderate the economic impact of the provision and temper the character of the Government's regulation; the latter factor weighed most heavily against the constitutionality of the original version of § 207.

The narrow revisions Congress made to § 207, without benefit of our ruling in *Irving,* do not warrant a disposition different from the one this Court announced and explained in *Irving*. Amended § 207 permits a five-year window rather than a one-year window to assess the income-generating capacity of the interest. [A]rgument that this change substantially mitigates the economic impact of § 207 "misses the point." * * * Amended § 207 still trains on income generated from the land, not on the value of the parcel. The Court observed in *Irving* that "[e]ven if . . . the income generated by such parcels may be properly thought of as *de minimis*," the value of the land may not fit that description. * * * In short, the economic impact of amended § 207 might still be palpable.

Even if the economic impact of amended § 207 is not significantly less than the impact of the original provision, the United States correctly comprehends that *Irving* rested primarily on the "extraordinary" character of the governmental regulation. *Irving* stressed that the original § 207 "amount[ed] to virtually the abrogation of the right to pass on a certain type of property—the small undivided interest—to one's heirs." * * * ("both descent and devise are completely abolished"). The *Irving* Court further noted that the original § 207 "effectively abolish[ed] both descent and devise [of fractional interests] even when the passing of the property to the heir might result in consolidation of property." * * * As the United States construes *Irving,* Congress cured the fatal infirmity in § 207 when it revised the section to allow transmission of fractional interests to successors who already own an interest in the allotment.

Congress' creation of an ever-so-slight class of individuals equipped to receive fractional interests by devise does not suffice. * * * Amended § 207 severely restricts the right of an individual to direct the descent of his property. Allowing a decedent to leave an interest only to a current owner in the same parcel shrinks drastically the universe of possible successors. * * *

The United States also contends that amended § 207 satisfies the Constitution's demand because it does not diminish the owner's right to use or enjoy property during his lifetime, and does not affect the right to transfer property at death through nonprobate means. These arguments did not persuade us in *Irving* and they are no more persuasive today. * * *

The third alteration made in amended § 207 also fails to bring the provision outside the reach of this Court's holding in *Irving*. Amended § 207 permits tribes to establish their own codes to govern the disposition of fractional interests; if approved by the Secretary of the Interior, these codes would govern in lieu of amended § 207. * * * The United States does not rely on this new provision to defend the statute. Nor does it appear that the United States could do so at this time: Tribal codes governing disposition of escheatable interests have apparently not been developed. * * *

* * *

For the reasons stated, the judgment of the Court of Appeals for the Ninth Circuit is

Affirmed.

■ JUSTICE STEVENS, dissenting.

Section 207 of the Indian Land Consolidation Act did not, in my view, effect an unconstitutional taking of William Youpee's right to make a testamentary disposition of his property. As I explained in *Hodel v. Irving* * * * (opinion concurring in judgment), the Federal Government, like a State, has a valid interest in removing legal impediments to the productive development of real estate. For this reason, the Court has repeatedly "upheld the power of the State to condition the retention of a property right upon the performance of an act within a limited period of time." *Texaco, Inc. v. Short*, 454 U.S. 516, 529 (1982). I remain convinced that "Congress has ample power to require the owners of fractional interests in allotted lands to consolidate their holdings during their lifetimes or to face the risk that their interests will be deemed to be abandoned." *Hodel*, 481 U.S., at 732 (STEVENS, J., concurring in judgment). The federal interest in minimizing the fractionated ownership of Indian lands—and thereby paving the way to the productive development of their property—is strong enough to justify the legislative remedy created by § 207, provided, of course, that affected owners have adequate notice of the requirements of the law and an adequate opportunity to adjust their affairs to protect against loss. See *ibid.*

In my opinion, William Youpee did have such notice and opportunity. With regard to notice, the requirements of § 207 are set forth in the United States Code. "Generally, a legislature need do nothing more than enact and publish the law, and afford the citizenry a reasonable opportunity to familiarize itself with its terms and to comply* * * It is well established that persons owning property within a [jurisdiction] are charged with knowledge of relevant statutory provisions affecting the control or disposition of such property." *Texaco*, 454 U.S., at 531–532. Unlike the landowners in *Hodel,* Mr. Youpee also had adequate opportunity to comply. More than six years passed from the time § 207 was amended until Mr. Youpee died on October 19, 1990 (this period spans more than seven years if we count from the date § 207 was originally enacted). During this time, Mr. Youpee could have realized the value of his fractional interests (approximately $1,239) in a variety of ways, including selling the property, giving it to his children as a gift, or putting it in trust for them. I assume that he failed to do so because he was not aware of the requirements of § 207. This loss is unfortunate. But I believe Mr. Youpee's failure to pass on his property is the product of inadequate legal advice rather than an unconstitutional defect in the statute.

Accordingly, I respectfully dissent.

Questions

1. Does the Fragmentation of American Indian land create any externalities? What was the source of the fragmentation of American Indian land?

2. Under Section 207 of the Indian Land Consolidation Act, property owners remained entirely undisturbed in the use and enjoyment of their property throughout their lifetimes. The "right to pass on property" was restricted to units of some economic value. What was the significance of the holdings in *Hodel v. Irving* and *Babbitt v. Youpee*?

3. In *Hodel v. Irving*, Justice O'Connor conceded that the "extreme fractionation of Indian lands is a serious public problem" and that "encouraging the consolidation of Indian lands is a public purpose of high order." However, she concluded her opinion stating that "the extraordinary step of abolishing both descent and devise of these property interests even when the passing of the property to the heir might result in consolidation of property . . . 'goes too far'." What regulatory measures may encourage consolidation of Indian lands without going too far?

4. What was Justice Stevens' approach to the escheat provision?

§ 3.5 NETWORK EFFECTS

The last form of externalities we will discuss in this Chapter is those that stem from the use of the same standard—*network effects*.[136] When a person uses a standard, product, or service that person's well being may be affected by others' use of the same standard, product, or service. Such effects are called network effects or network externalities. For example, much of the value we derive from language is related to our ability to communicate with others. The value of our ability to communicate, which corresponds to the number of people who use the same language, is an

136. *See generally* Oz Shy, *A Short Survey of Network Economics*, 38 REVIEW OF INDUSTRIAL ORGANIZATION 119 (2011). Michael Katz and Carl Shapiro are credited for identifying "network externalities." *See* Michael L. Katz & Carl Shapiro, *Network Externalities, Competition, and Compatibility*, 75 AMERICAN ECONOMIC REVIEW 424 (1985); Michael L. Katz & Carl Shapiro, *System Competition and Network Effects*, 8 JOURNAL OF ECONOMIC PERSPECTIVES 93 (1994).

example of network effects. Similarly, the value of most communication methods is related to the number of people who use them. Consider, for instance, the telephone, facsimile, email, and text messages. The capacity to send and receive messages has very little value if it cannot be utilized.

Like all externalities, network effects may be negative or positive. Positive network externalities, often called *consumption network effects*, are created when value is added to a standard, product or service through an increase in the number of people (or firms) who use it. For example, many online vendors, such as eBay.com, Amazon.com, and online dating websites utilize consumption network effects because the size of the customer base increase value to each user and draws additional customers. The term *congestion network effects* is used as a mirror image to describe negative network externalities, which are defined as the decline in one's well-being when others use the same standard, product or service. Such effects arise in transportation and communication networks, where traffic may slow down as the number of users increases.[137] The more people who use the freeway, the less quickly each car travels; the more people using large amounts of bandwidth to stream videos, the less quickly each individual user is able to connect to the Internet. Increased usage of a product can also reduce the value of high-end fashion and other status goods, when popularity reduces the item's exclusivity.[138]

Sidebar 3–3
QWERTY
and the
Fable of the Keys

In 1985, Paul David published a paper that popularized the concept of "path dependence."[139] The paper argues that the standard keyboard arrangement (QWERTY) was developed to minimize the tendency of typebars to clash and jam when salesmen of early typewriters tried to impress customers by typing "TYPE WRITER," using only letters on the top row. It was believed that the Dvorak Simplified Keyboard (DSK) allowed users to type at least 20% faster than the QWERTY standard. The U.S. Navy held experiments that proved this efficiency, and Apple tried to launch computers with DSK keyboards. The QWERTY standard, however, survived.

In 1990, a new article, *The Fable of the Keys*, presented new evidence, showing that "the standard history of QWERTY versus Dvorak [was] flawed and incomplete[, since the] most dramatic claims are traceable to Dvorak himself."[140]

---

137. *See, e.g.*, Jonathan Leape, *The London Congestion Charge*, 20 JOURNAL OF ECONOMIC PERSPECTIVES 157 (2006).

138. *See generally* Harvey Leibenstein, *Bandwagon, Snob, and Veblen Effects in the Theory of Consumers' Demand*, 64 QUARTERLY JOURNAL OF ECONOMICS 183 (1950); Georg Simmel, *Fashion*, 10 INTERNATIONAL QUARTERLY 130 (1904); THORSTEIN VEBLEN, THE THEORY OF THE LEISURE CLASS: AN ECONOMIC STUDY IN THE EVOLUTION OF INSTITUTIONS (1899).

139. *See* Paul A. David, *Clio and the Economics of QWERTY*, 75 AMERICAN ECONOMICS REVIEW 332 (1985).

140. S. J. Liebowitz and Stephen E. Margolis, *The Fable of the Keys*, 33 JOURNAL OF LAW & ECONOMICS 1 (1990).

In the marketplace, users often stick to standards that are not the best available ones. In some circumstances, *switching costs*, the expenses associated with changing from one standard to another, bind users to a particular standard although they would prefer to use another. In other circumstances, a user does not switch to the better standard because it is not yet used by a critical mass of people (or people she cares about). *Lock-in* is the term that describes this situation.[141] Switching costs and lock-in may result in *path dependence*—the survival of an inefficient standard in the long run.

Any computer user who ever considered changing their operating system or word processing software has encountered this problem. In North America, the railway gauge is 4 feet and 8.5 inches, or 1,435 mm, because in the mid-nineteenth century many railroads adopted this standard. Railway engineers have never regarded the 4-foot-8.5-inch standard as efficient compared to other standards.[142] But the costs of retooling the railroad system have deterred conversion to a better standard. Analog television broadcasting and incandescent light bulbs are very inefficient compared to available technologies but survived in the market for many years, until Congress adopted regulatory frameworks to retire these standards.

From the legal perspective, network externalities raise several motivations for regulation. Consumption network effects create motivations to protect standards and networks. Congestion network effects may raise pressure to expand the capacity of such networks (*e.g.*, roads) or to limit their use. Switching costs, lock-in, and path dependence focus attention on *who* creates and owns standards and what can be done, if anything, when the governing standard is inefficient.[143]

Decoding and Circumvention

eBay.com, Amazon.com, iTunes, credit card companies, and many other private entities utilize network externalities. In their markets, consumers choose among competing services for various reasons, one of which is the price they have to pay the firm that operates the service. At any point of time, some "entrepreneurs" attempt to circumvent the billing system of the network to save the network fees.

---

141. *See generally* Joseph Farrell & Paul Klemperer, *Coordination and Lock-In: Competition with Switching Costs and Network Effects*, in HANDBOOK OF INDUSTRIAL ORGANIZATION, vol. 3, 1967 (Mark Armstrong & Robert H. Porter eds. 2007).

142. *See* Douglas J. Puffert, *The Standardization of Track Gauge on North American Railways, 1830–1890*, 60 JOURNAL OF ECONOMIC HISTORY 933 (2000); Douglas J. Puffert, *Path Dependence in Spatial Networks: The Standardization of Railway Track Gauge*, 39 EXPLORATION IN ECONOMIC HISTORY 282 (2002).

143. For "standards" *see* § 9.1.

Chartwell Communications Group v. Westbrook

637 F.2d 459 (6th Cir. 1980)

■ BAILEY BROWN, CIRCUIT JUDGE.

This case presents important questions concerning the nature of the over-the-air subscription television (STV) industry, and the extent to which it is protected by Section 605 of the Communications Act of 1934, 47 U.S.C. § 605. Appellants (Chartwell) operate a subscription television business in the Greater Metropolitan Detroit area. Chartwell's programming consists mainly of recently released movies, musical performances, and sporting events the typical fare of subscription and cable television services. Its services are marketed under the name "ON–TV."

Chartwell's programs are delivered to its subscribers by a television signal transmitted by WXON–TV, Channel 20, in Southfield, Michigan. WXON–TV has a subscription television license issued by the Federal Communications Commission (FCC), and Chartwell operates by virtue of a contract with WXON–TV. Subscribers are charged an installation fee of $49.50 and a monthly fee of $22.50, which covers programming and system rental and repairs. Chartwell's programs carry no advertising, and its sole source of operating income is from its subscription fees.

Chartwell's intent is that its programs be received only by paying subscribers. To ensure that its programming will only be received by its intended audience, Chartwell uses a Blonder–Tongue encoder-decoder system, installed at WXON–TV's transmitter, to encode the transmissions. The video and audio portions of the signal are encoded separately. The video portion of the signal transmitted over Channel 20's assigned frequency is "scrambled," so that a television set tuned to Channel 20 receives the signal but the image is unintelligible. The audio portion of the signal is transmitted via a separate sub-carrier frequency which cannot be received on a commercially available television or radio. Chartwell's subscribers are provided with decoders to enable them to receive the audio and unscramble the video. The decoders are leased to subscribers by Chartwell as part of the system rental. Chartwell is forbidden to sell decoders to subscribers by FCC regulations. * * * Without the use of a decoder, a television set tuned to Channel 20 during the hours of ON–TV's operation will receive no audio and unintelligible video.

Chartwell began operating in Michigan in June, 1979. In May, 1980 the appellees, Moser and Westbrook, began to make available to the public electronic decoders that would enable persons to receive Chartwell's programming without paying the subscription fees. On July 8, 1980, Chartwell filed this action seeking to enjoin appellees from selling equipment that would enable nonsubscribers to receive Chartwell's programs. * * *

Section 605 protects radio communications, (which include television communications * * *) from unauthorized reception, interception, divulgence, publication, etc. However, radio communications broadcast for the use of the general public are not protected. The relevant portion of Section 605 provides:

> No person not being authorized by the sender shall intercept any radio communication and divulge or publish the existence, contents, substance, purport, effect or meaning of such intercepted communication to any person. No person not being entitled thereto shall receive or assist in receiving any interstate or foreign communication (or any information therein contained) for his own benefit or for the benefit of another not entitled thereto ... This section shall not apply to the receiving, divulging, publishing, or utilizing the contents of any radio communication which is broadcast or transmitted by amateurs or others for the use of the general public, or which relates to ships in distress.

We think there is an important distinction between making a service available to the general public and intending a program for the use of the general public. The whole point of STV is to provide the service to as many members of the public as are interested. If the services could not be widely distributed there would be no business. However, the dual nature of STV is that while it may be available to the general public, it is intended for the exclusive use of paying subscribers. Availability and use are separate concepts. * * * We think STV is not broadcasting intended for use by the general public within the meaning of the proviso to Section 605. * * *

Having determined that Chartwell's communications are protected by Section 605, we now must determine whether the appellees' activity violates the statute. We think it clearly does. It is clear that by selling decoders or decoder schematics the appellees are assisting third parties in receiving communications to which they are not entitled.

* * *

The final question to be decided is whether the preliminary injunction should remain in effect until a trial can be had on the merits of Chartwell's claim. We think that it should. There is a substantial likelihood that Chartwell will prevail on the merits. A cause of action exists under Section 605, Chartwell's communications do not come within the proviso to the section and appellees' activity violates the section. Furthermore, Chartwell stands to suffer irreparable harm if appellees are allowed to sell decoders during the pendency of the trial. Once an individual buys a decoder he is lost to Chartwell forever as a potential subscriber. If the injunction does not remain in effect appellees may sell decoders and inflict significant harm on Chartwell's business. Therefore, the preliminary injunction is to remain in effect until final disposition.

* * *

The Digital Millennium Copyright Act

In 1998 Congress passed the Digital Millennium Copyright Act (DMCA). Section 1201 of the DMCA, the so-called anti-circumvention provision states as follows:[144]

---

144. 17 U.S.C. § 1201.

(a) Violations regarding circumvention of technological measures.

(1)(A) No person shall circumvent a technological measure that effectively controls access to a work protected under this title. * * *

(2) No person shall manufacture, import, offer to the public, provide, or otherwise traffic in any technology, product, service, device, component, or part thereof, that—

(A) is primarily designed or produced for the purpose of circumventing a technological measure that effectively controls access to a work protected under this title;

(B) has only limited commercially significant purpose or use other than to circumvent a technological measure that effectively controls access to a work protected under this title; or

(C) is marketed by that person or another acting in concert with that person with that person's knowledge for use in circumventing a technological measure that effectively controls access to a work protected under this title.

(3) As used in this subsection—

(A) to "circumvent a technological measure" means to descramble a scrambled work, to decrypt an encrypted work, or otherwise to avoid, bypass, remove, deactivate, or impair a technological measure, without the authority of the copyright owner; and

(B) a technological measure "effectively controls access to a work" if the measure, in the ordinary course of its operation, requires the application of information, or a process or a treatment, with the authority of the copyright owner, to gain access to the work.

(b) Additional violations.

(1) No person shall manufacture, import, offer to the public, provide, or otherwise traffic in any technology, product, service, device, component, or part thereof, that—

(A) is primarily designed or produced for the purpose of circumventing protection afforded by a technological measure that effectively protects a right of a copyright owner under this title in a work or a portion thereof;

(B) has only limited commercially significant purpose or use other than to circumvent protection afforded by a technological measure that effectively protects a right of a copyright owner under this title in a work or a portion thereof; or

(C) is marketed by that person or another acting in concert with that person with that person's knowledge for use in circumventing protection afforded by a technological measure that effectively protects a right of a copyright owner under this title in a work or a portion thereof.

(2) As used in this subsection—

(A) to "circumvent protection afforded by a technological measure" means avoiding, bypassing, removing, deactivating, or otherwise impairing a technological measure; and

(B) a technological measure "effectively protects a right of a copyright owner under this title" if the measure, in the ordinary course of its operation, prevents, restricts, or otherwise limits the exercise of a right of a copyright owner under this title.

* * *

(c) Other rights, etc., not affected.

* * *

(2) Nothing in this section shall enlarge or diminish vicarious or contributory liability for copyright infringement in connection with any technology, product, service, device, component, or part thereof.

Questions

1. What types of externalities do *Chartwell* and Section 1201 of the DMCA address?

2. Could the defendants in *Charwell* (Moser and Westbrook) blackmail Charwell? Could they use the model of urban "entrepreneurs" who threatened property owners with livery stables and apartment houses? What is the value of Section 1201 of the DMCA in negotiation with potential blackmailers?

3. Does Section 1201 of the DMCA address only network externalities?

CHAPTER 4

Risk

risk (risk), *n.* Exposure to the chance of injury or loss (as, a trip made at great *risk*; where there is *risk* there may be loss); hazard or danger; a hazard or dangerous chance (as, to run *risks*; "I promise to take care of myself * * * I won't take any *risks*," J. Conrad's "Lord Jim"); the hazard or chance (*of*: as, to persist at the *risk* of being fined or imprisoned; to run the *risk* of failure). * * *

safe (sāf), *a.* Free from hurt or injury (as, to arrive *safe* and sound); unharmed; also, free from danger or risk (as, "I greatly fear my money is not *safe*," Shakespeare's "Comedy of Errors"); secure from liability to harm, injury, etc.; also, affording freedom from danger or risk (as, a *safe* place; a *safe* distance); involving no risk of mishap, error, etc. (as a *safe* undertaking; a *safe* estimate); also, dependable or trustworthy (as, a *safe* guide or adviser); cautious in avoiding danger (as, in a *safe* player); also, sure or certain (colloq.: as, "an extremely clear-headed * * * young man, who was *safe* to rise in the world," Dickens's "Hard Times"); also in secure custody (as a criminal *safe* in jail); placed beyond the power of doing harm.

Safety (sāf'ty), *n.* The state of being safe; freedom from hurt or injury, or from danger or risk; the quality of insuring against hurt or injury, of affording freedom from danger or risk. * * *

—*The New Century Dictionary of the English Language* (1927)[1]

§ 4.1 Safety First, Wisdom Later

§ 4.1.1 Shaky Intuitions

No matter how people think about and perceive risk, many expect safety regulation to reduce and possibly eliminate danger because they equate safety with being free from risk.[2] Others feel "safe" because they ignore or deny risks, believing that no precautions or regulations are needed.[3] Risk is inherent to reality. We can neither regulate all risks nor

---

1. H.G. Emery & K.G. Brewster, The New Century Dictionary of the English Language (1927).

2. *See generally* Stephen G. Breyer, Breaking the Vicious Circle: Toward Effective Risk Regulation (Harvard University Press. 1993); W. Kip Viscusi, Risk by Choice: Regulating Health and Safety in the Workplace (1983). *See also* Paul Slovic, The Perception of Risk (2000).

3. *See generally* Frank P. McKenna, *It Won't Happen to Me: Unrealistic Optimism or Illusion of Control?* 84 British Journal of Psychology 39 (1993). *See also* Mary–Elena Carr et

eliminate regulated risks. For example, natural disasters, diseases, sharp objects, the use of energy, eating, and driving are mostly unavoidable, yet unsafe. Society has neither the capital nor will to reduce all miniscule risks. Whether we like it or not, we must embrace risk.

Individual risk management may entail social implications that are relevant to regulatory policies. For example, Congress enacted the Patient Protection and Affordable Care Act of 2010 "because every person is at risk of needing care at any moment, [and] all those who lack insurance, regardless of their current health status, adversely affect the price of health care and health insurance."[4] In the 2012 health care decision, *National Federation of Independent Business*, the Justices agreed that "[p]eople, for reasons of their own, often fail to do things that would be good for them or good for society. Those failures—joined with the similar failures of others—can readily have a substantial effect on interstate commerce [and society]."[5] They sharply disagreed, however, on whether the federal government had authority to mandate health insurance. In many ways, the legal-political battles over the 2010 health care reform reflect ordinary disagreements over risk management that stem from excessive confidence in risk analysis.

In his seminal book, *The Costs of Accidents*, Guido Calabresi stated: "I take it as axiomatic that the principal function of accident law is to reduce the sum of the costs of accidents and the costs of avoiding accidents."[6] Because tort law deals with materialization of risks (accidents), its function is to minimize the costs associated with risk—the costs of accidents and costs of precautions. "*Safety*," therefore, is not freedom from risk, but an assumption of reasonable risk.

In 1996, the National Research Council's Committee on Risk Characterization (CRC) published a comprehensive report entitled "*Understanding Risk*."[7] CRC pointed out that "[c]oping with risk situations can be complex and controversial. * * * One reason lies in inadequacies in the techniques available for analyzing risks. A second is the fundamental and continuing uncertainty in information about risks. Another, less well appreciated, reason for failure lies in a basic misconception of risk characterization."

This Chapter presents some perils of intuitive approaches to risk, stressing the human tendency to misunderstand risks. We begin with the obvious observation that a regulatory policy that ignores risks is unwise and can be costly.[8] Of course, risk regulation that aims at reducing hazards

---

al., *Climate Change: Addressing the Major Skeptic Arguments*, Deutche Bank Climate Change Advisors (Sept. 2010).

4. National Federation of Independent Business v. Sebelius, 132 S.Ct. 2566, 2617 (2012) (Ginsburg, J., dissenting).

5. *Id.* at 2588 (Roberts, C.J.).

6. GUIDO CALABRESI, THE COSTS OF ACCIDENTS 26 (1970).

7. NATIONAL RESEARCH COUNCIL, UNDERSTANDING RISK: INFORMING DECISION IN A DEMOCRATIC SOCIETY (1996).

8. *See* THOMAS O. MCGARITY, BENDING SCIENCE, HOW SPECIAL INTERESTS GROUP CORRUPT PUBLIC HEALTH RESEARCH (2010); DAVID MICHAELS, DOUBT IN THEIR PRODUCT: HOW INDUSTRY'S ASSAULT ON

with no cost-benefit analysis is also shortsighted and wasteful.[9] However, in politics, academic scholarship, business, everyday life, and legal disputes both approaches are very common.[10]

Having this starting point in mind, our focus is decisionmaking. CRC summarized its general conclusion as follows: "Risk characterization should be a *decision-driven activity*, directed toward informing choices and solving problems." As we shall see, human decisionmaking under uncertainty is often poor. One practical implication of this limitation is that there may be good reasons to regulate trade in risks. In the modern economy, many products involve some trade in risks—warranties, insurance policies, credit products, financial instruments, and others. Such reasons are about the ordinary decisionmaking capacity, not about risk itself.

People tend to casually use the words "risk," "uncertainty," "safety," "hazard" and related ones. For law and regulatory policies, the distinctions among these words are important. We use here CRC's definitions of *risk* and *hazard*. Later, we will discuss the concept of uncertainty.

> **Hazard**. An act or phenomenon that has the potential to produce harm or other undesirable consequences to humans or what they value. Hazards may come from physical phenomena (such as radioactivity, sound waves, magnetic fields, fire, floods, explosions), chemicals (ozone, mercury, dioxins, carbon dioxide, drugs, food additives), organisms (viruses, bacteria), commercial products (toys, tools, automobiles), or human behavior (drunk driving, firing guns). Hazards can also come from information (e.g., information that a person carries a gene that increases susceptibility to cancer may expose the person to job discrimination or increased insurance costs).
>
> **Risk**. A concept used to give meaning to things, forces, or circumstances that pose danger to people or to what they value. Descriptions of risk are typically stated in terms of the likelihood of harm or loss from a hazard and usually include: an identification of what is "at risk" and may be harmed or lost (e.g., health of human beings or an ecosystem, personal property, quality of life, ability to carry on an economic activity); the hazard that may occasion this loss; and a judgment about the likelihood that harm will occur.

§ 4.1.2 Flawed Decisionmaking

We possess imperfect information about future events. Benjamin Franklin wrote the immortal platitude: "In this world nothing can be said

SCIENCE THREATENS YOUR HEALTH (2008); NAOMI ORESKES & ERIK M. M. CONWAY, MERCHANTS OF DOUBT: HOW A HANDFUL OF SCIENTISTS OBSCURED THE TRUTH ON ISSUES FROM TOBACCO SMOKE TO GLOBAL WARMING (2011). *See also* Daniel A. Farber, *Uncertainty*, 99 GEORGETOWN LAW JOURNAL 901 (2011).

9. *See generally* Matthew D. Adler, *Risk, Death and Harm: The Normative Foundations of Risk Regulation*, 87 MINNESOTA LAW REVIEW 1293 (2003); Clayton P. Gillette & James E. Krier, *Risk Courts, and Agencies*, 138 UNIVERSITY OF PENNSYLVANIA LAW REVIEW 1027 (1990); Christopher H. Schroeder, *Rights Against Risks*, 86 COLUMBIA LAW REVIEW 495 (1986).

10. *See generally* Frank B. Cross, *The Public Role in Risk Control*, 24 ENVIRONMENTAL LAW 887 969 (1994).

to be certain, except death and taxes."[11] Even with respect to these two known future events, many people are overly optimistic or overly pessimistic. Our perceptions of future events tend to be flawed and, correspondingly, we frequently make poor decisions regarding future events.[12]

To acquaint ourselves with some of our human limitations, we begin with the distinction between "risk" and "uncertainty." The term "*risk*" refers to situations where the likelihood and other characteristics of future events are measurable. In contrast, the term "*uncertainty*" refers to situations where at least one significant characteristic of future events is immeasurable.[13] We make most of our personal decisions under uncertainty because we do not know something about future events—the possible events, their likelihood, magnitude, and so forth. Nevertheless, we can insure most risks. Insurance companies rely on *risk spreading*: they pool risks, price them with a markup, and distribute the costs of bad outcomes across a large pool of policyholders. The aggregation of risks allows insurance companies to calculate the statistical risk of insured individuals and firms.

FRANK H. KNIGHT, RISK, UNCERTAINTY AND PROFIT (1921):

> The ordinary decisions of life are made on the basis of "estimates" of a crude and superficial character. In general the future situation in relation to which we act depends upon the behavior of an indefinitely large number of [contingencies], and is influenced by so many factors that no real effort is made to take account of them all, much less estimate and summate their separate significances. It is only in very special and crucial cases that anything like a mathematical (exhaustive and quantitative) study can be made. * * *
>
> [Consider] the principle of insurance, as familiarly illustrated by the chance of fire loss. No one can say whether a particular building will burn, and most building owners do not operate on a sufficient scale to reduce the loss to constancy (though some do). But as is well known, the effect of insurance is to extend this base to cover the operations of a large number of persons and convert the contingency into a fixed cost. * * *
>
> [T]he fact that the [buildings] are not really homogeneous may be offset in part by the use of judgment, if not calculation. It is possible to tell with some accuracy whether the "real risk" in a particular case is higher or lower than that of a group as a whole, and by how much.

The state, like insurance companies, pools risks and calculates statistical risks to human lives, health, the environment, and other things for regulatory purposes. Much of the controversy over cost-benefit analysis is about the way the state calculates risks.

---

11. A letter from Benjamin Franklin to Jean-Baptiste Le Roy (Nov. 13, 1789), available at *regti.me/NOcertainty* (case sensitive).

12. *See generally* § 7.4 (bounded rationality).

13. *See generally* FRANK H. KNIGHT, RISK, UNCERTAINTY AND PROFIT 19–20, 197–232 (1921).

Many decisions people make are related to their assessments of future events, including investments in precautions and purchasing insurance. Empirical evidence, however, shows that people are unrealistically optimistic about future events, grossly underestimate ordinary risks, and are overconfident about their relative abilities. When assessing their position in a group on traits, like longevity, driving ability, and income prospects, the vast majority of individuals rate themselves as above average, although for such traits only half can be.[14] Studies also distinguish between two key cognitive biases that feed our overconfidence: an *optimism bias*, unfounded expectations for good outcomes, and an *illusion of control*, unfounded perceptions of ability to influence the future.[15] These biases affect the tendency to take excessive risks and explain some of the forces that fuel financial bubbles.[16] Moreover, under certain conditions, such as a vivid recollection of a dreadful event (*e.g.*, deadly natural disasters and horrible accidents), people tend to be unrealistically pessimistic about the future.[17] The quest for safety is often driven by highly publicized "bad events" that create pessimistic bias.[18] Thus, as a starting point, overconfidence about the nature of risks, which is based on personal perceptions as opposed to data and science, may be as accurate as a broken clock.

Patterns of decisionmaking under uncertainty reveal many other constraints. Bounded rationality curtails our cognitive skills. We rely on misguided intuitions—take shortcuts (use heuristics), and fail to optimize our decisions in other ways.[19] For example, the vividness of memories

14. *See* Ola Svenson, *Are We All Less Risky and More Skillful Than Our Fellow Drivers?* 47 ACTA PSYCHOLOGICA 143 (1981); Shelly E. Taylor & J. D. Brown, *Illusion and Well-Being: A Social Psychological Perspective on Mental Health*, 103 PSYCHOLOGICAL BULLETIN, 193 (1988); Neil D. Weinstein, *Unrealistic Optimism About Future Life Events*, 39 JOURNAL OF PERSONALITY & SOCIAL PSYCHOLOGY 806 (1980); Neil D. Weinstein, *Unrealistic Optimism About Susceptibility to Health Problems*, 5 JOURNAL OF BEHAVIORAL MEDICINE 441 (1982).

15. *See* McKenna, *It Won't Happen to Me*, *supra* note 3; Rachel Croson & James Sundali, *The Gambler's Fallacy and the Hot Hand: Empirical Data from Casinos*, 30 JOURNAL OF RISK & UNCERTAINTY 195 (2005); Ellen J. Langer, *The Illusion of Control*, 32 JOURNAL OF PERSONALITY & SOCIAL PSYCHOLOGY 311 (1975); DAN LOVALLO & DANIEL KAHNEMAN, *DELUSIONS OF SUCCESS: HOW OPTIMISM UNDERMINES EXECUTIVES DECISIONS*, 81(7) Harvard Business Review 56 (JUL. 2003).

16. *See* § 1.1.3a.

17. *See* Dariusz Doliski et al., *Unrealistic Pessimism*, 127 JOURNAL OF SOCIAL PSYCHOLOGY 511 (1987).

18. Deficiencies in a soy-based infant formula that was introduced into the market in 1978 were the cause of irreversible blood and growth disorders many children developed. In September 1980, Congress unanimously passed the Infant Formula Act, Pub. L. No. 96–359, 94 Stat. 1190 (1980), intending to make infant food perfectly safe. In implementing the statute, the FDA has always taken a more practical approach, taking into account that perfection in quality control would have adverse effects on the market for infant formula. *See* Toby Milgrom Levin, *The Infant Formula Act of 1980: A Case Study of Congressional Delegation to the Food and Drug Administration*, 42 FOOD DRUG COSMETIC LAW JOURNAL 101 (1987). *See also* Susan Chilton et al., *Public Perceptions of Risk and Preference–Based Values of Safety,* 25 JOURNAL OF RISK & UNCERTAINTY 211 (2002) (studying changes in public risk perceptions and safety preferences in response to a large-scale, highly publicized accident).

19. *See generally* Colin Camerer, *Individual Decision Making*, THE HANDBOOK OF EXPERIMENTAL ECONOMICS 587 (John H. Kagel & Alvin E. Roth eds. 1995); Geoffrey M. Hodgson, *The Ubiquity of Habits and Rules*, 21 CAMBRIDGE JOURNAL OF ECONOMICS 663 (1997); Robin Hogarth & Howard Kunreuther, *Decision Making Under Ignorance: Arguing with Yourself*, 10 JOURNAL OF RISK & UNCERTAINTY 15 (1995); DANIEL KAHNEMAN ET AL., JUDGMENT UNDER UNCERTAINTY: HEURISTICS

influences our perceptions of the likelihood and magnitude of events. We tend overreact to publicized stories about epidemics, terrorism, and natural disasters. In contrast, we tend to underestimate abstract risks, such as financial risks and health risks that are accrue over time. We tend to be overly concerned about low-probability, high-impact events,[20] such as natural disasters and terrorism, and terrible accidents.[21] But we do not prepare ourselves for ordinary health risks. These boundaries on our cognitive abilities tend to influence regulatory policies.[22] Regulators have ordinary human limitations and often respond to misplaced public concerns.[23]

§ 4.1.3 Risk Misperceptions and Regulation

We have already seen regulatory debates over risk that avoid risk analysis. For example, *Lochner* is about the regulation of occupational risks, although the word "risk" is not mentioned in the decision.[24] Justices Peckham and Harlan disagreed about which health risks justified government regulation. Writing for the Court, Justice Peckham maintained that "the trade of a baker, in and of itself, is not an unhealthy one to that degree which would authorize the legislature to interfere with the right to labor." He noted that "[i]t is unfortunately true that labor, even in any department, may possibly carry with it the seeds of unhealthiness." Justice Peckham felt that health risks were not a legitimate cause for regulation and expressed a concern that "[n]o trade, no occupation, no mode of earning one's living, could escape this all-pervading power."[25] Dissenting, Justice Harlan declared the New York Bakeshop Act was enacted "in order

---

AND BIASES (1982); DANIEL KAHNEMAN & AMOS TVERSKY, CHOICES, VALUES, AND FRAMES (2000); W. Kip Viscusi et al., *Measures of Mortality Risks*, 14 JOURNAL OF RISK & UNCERTAINTY 213 (1997).

20. *See generally* Colin Camerer & Howard Kunreuther, Decision Processes for Low Probability Events: Policy Implications, 8 JOURNAL OF POLICY ANALYSIS & MANAGEMENT 565 (1989); Howard Kunreuther et al., *Making Low Probabilities Useful*, 23 JOURNAL OF RISK & UNCERTAINTY 103 (2001); Peter P. Wakker et al., *Probabilistic Insurance*, 15 JOURNAL OF RISK & UNCERTAINTY 7 (1997).

21. *See, e.g.*, Susan Chilton et al., *Dread Risks*, 33 JOURNAL OF RISK & UNCERTAINTY 165 (2006); Cass Sunstein, *Bad Deaths,* 14 JOURNAL OF RISK & UNCERTAINTY 259 (1997); W. Kip Viscusi, *Valuing Risks of Death from Terrorism and Natural Disasters*, 38 JOURNAL OF RISK & UNCERTAINTY 191 (2009).

22. *See* Timur Kuran & Cass R. Sunstein, *Availability Cascades and Risk Regulation*, 51 STANFORD LAW REVIEW 683 (1999); Roger G. Noll & James E. Krier, *Some Implications of Cognitive Psychology for Risk Regulation*, 19 JOURNAL OF LEGAL STUDIES 747 (1990); Robert A. Pollak, *Imagined risks and cost-benefit analysis*, 88 AMERICAN ECONOMIC REVIEW 376 (1998); Paul R. Portney, *Trouble in Happyville*, 11 JOURNAL OF POLICY ANALYSIS AND MANAGEMENT 131 (1992); François Salanié & Nicolas Treich, *Regulation in Happyville*, 119 ECONOMIC JOURNAL 665 (2009); Nicolas Treich, *The Value of a Statistical Life Under Ambiguity Aversion*, 59 JOURNAL OF ENVIRONMENTAL ECONOMICS & MANAGEMENT 15 (2010).

23. *See* Baruch Fischhoff, *Debiasing*, in JUDGMENT UNDER UNCERTAINTY: HEURISTICS AND BIASES 422 (Daniel Kahneman et al. eds. 1982)

24. Lochner v. New York, 198 U.S. 45 (1905); *See supra* § 1.2.5.

25. Prior to his appointment to the Supreme Court, Justice Peckham served for nearly ten years as a judge in the New York Court of Appeals. During that time, he wrote more than 300 decisions, and "demonstrated skepticism about governmental regulation of the economy * * * and a disposition to define liberty as encompassing economic freedom." His opinion in *Lochner* was consistent with his record. *See* James W. Ely, Jr., *Rufus W. Peckham and the Pursuit of Economic Freedom*, 37 JOURNAL OF SUPREME COURT HISTORY 22, 23 (2012).

to protect the physical well-being of those who work in bakery and confectionery establishments." In contrast to Justice Peckham, he believed that such health risk was a legitimate justification for regulation. Moreover, Justice Harlan posited that the police power "extends at least to the protection of the lives, the health, and the safety of the public against the injurious exercise by any citizen of his own rights." Thus, one Justice believed that, because health risks were ordinary reality, the state should not have regulated them, while the other judge believed that health risks justified regulation. Both Justices expressed confidence about their understanding of health risks in bakeries and they strongly disagreed with each other. By definition, at least one Justice was overconfident.

Lochner is merely an example. Numerous studies document regulatory policies that employed myopic, inconsistent, blind, or generally unwise approaches to risk.[26] Lawmakers, agencies, and courts occasionally respond to high-profile events, establishing regulatory policies that are not sound, or consistent with cost-benefit analysis principles.[27] All financial crises share one known common theme—excessive debt; that is, unrealistically optimistic financial risks. Despite this understanding, "balancing the risk and opportunities of debt is * * * a challenge policy makers, investors, and ordinary citizens [often] forget."[28] Regulators often fail in their risk analysis or risk regulation.

The good news is that, although humans have always thought about risks, systemic efforts to regulate risk are a characteristic of modern times.[29] The improved understanding of risk analysis has substantially advanced regulatory approaches toward risk and has enabled us to identify biases and political influences.[30] As *Figure 4.1* illustrates, since the mid 1960s, the level of attention to the concept of risk has been skyrocketing.

---

26. *See, e.g.*, Matthew D. Adler, *Against "Individual Risk": A Sympathetic Critique of Risk Assessment*, 153 UNIVERSITY OF PENNSYLVANIA LAW REVIEW 1121(2005); BREYER, *supra* note 2; Maureen L. Cropper et al., *The Determinants of Pesticide Regulation: A Statistical Analysis of EPA Decision Making*, 100 JOURNAL OF POLITICAL ECONOMY 175 (1992); MADELEINE FERRIÈRES, SACRED COW, MAD COW: A HISTORY OF FOOD FEARS (2006); JOHN D. GRAHAM ET EL. EDS., RISK VS. RISK: TRADEOFFS IN PROTECTING HEALTH & THE ENVIRONMENT (1997); John F. Moral III, *A Review of the Record*, 10 REGULATION 25 (1985); CASS R. SUNSTEIN, LAWS OF FEAR (2005); Tammy O. Tengs et al., *Five-Hundred Life-Saving Interventions and Their Cost-Effectiveness*, 15 RISK ANALYSIS 369 (1995); Viscusi, *supra* note 2; W. Kip Viscusi, *Regulating the Regulators*, 63 UNIVERSITY OF CHICAGO LAW REVIEW 1423 (1996); W. Kip Viscusi, *Risk Equity*, 29 JOURNAL OF LEGAL STUDIES 843 (2000); W. Kip Viscusi & Jahn K. Hakes, *Synthetic Risks, Risk Potency, and Carcinogen Regulation*, 17 JOURNAL OF POLICY ANALYSIS & MANAGEMENT 52 (1998); W. Kip Viscusi & James T. Hamilton, *Are Risk Regulators Rational? Evidence from Hazardous Waste Cleanup Decisions*, 89 AMERICAN ECONOMIC REVIEW 1010 (1999).

27. *See, e.g.*, IAN AYRES & JOHN BRAITHWAITE, RESPONSIVE REGULATION: TRANSCENDING THE DEREGULATION DEBATE (1992); Anthony Downs, *Up and Downs with Ecology—the "Issue-Attention Cycle,"* 28 PUBLIC INTEREST 38 (1972).

28. CARMEN M. REINHART & KENNETH S. ROGOFF, THIS TIME IS DIFFERENT: EIGHT CENTURIES OF FINANCIAL FOLLY xxv (2009).

29. *See generally* PETER L. BERNSTEIN, AGAINST THE GODS: THE REMARKABLE STORY OF RISK (1996); DAVID A. MOSS, WHEN ALL ELSE FAILS: GOVERNMENT AS THE ULTIMATE RISK MANAGER (2002).

30. *See, e.g.*, Michael Spence, *Consumer Misperceptions, Product Failure and Producer Liability*, 44 REVIEW OF ECONOMIC STUDIES 561 (1977); Kenneth J. Arrow et al., *The Promise of Prediction Markets*, 320 SCIENCE 877 (2008); Partha Dasgupta, *Discounting Climate Change*, 37 JOURNAL OF RISK & UNCERTAINTY 141 (2008); Robert W. Hahn & Rohit Malik, *Is Regulation Good*

Figure 4.1
Frequency of the Words "risk" and "regulation" in U.S. Publications in English, 1800–2008

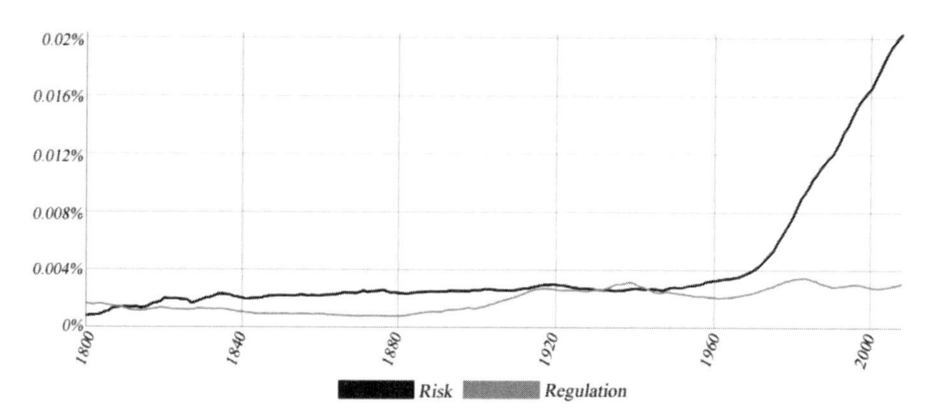

Source: Google Ngram Viewer.[31]

It is often said that people are *risk averse*. That is, people are willing to pay a premium to insurance companies to buy their risks.[32] However, people all do many things that are inconsistent with risk aversion—some gamble, some smoke, some do not buckle their seatbelts, some drive the under the influence of alcohol, some use firearms, some ski, some do not exercise enough, some do not maintain a healthy diet, and some do not floss their teeth daily. It is only human to exhibit inconsistency with our approach to risk.

---

for You?, 27 HARVARD JOURNAL OF LAW & PUBLIC POLICY 893 (2004); ROBERT W. HAHN ET AL. DO FEDERAL REGULATIONS REDUCE MORTALITY (2000); ROBERT W. HAHN & PAUL C. TETLOCK, INFORMATION MARKETS (2006); Winston Harrington et al., *On the Accuracy of Regulatory Cost Estimates*, 19 JOURNAL OF POLICY ANALYSIS & MANAGEMENT 297 (2000); Lawrence Summers & Richard Zeckhauser, *Policymaking for Prosperity*, 37 JOURNAL OF RISK & UNCERTAINTY 115 (2008); George Van Houtven & Maureen L. Cropper, *When Is a Life Too Costly to Save? The Evidence from U.S. Environmental Regulations*, 30 JOURNAL OF ENVIRONMENTAL ECONOMICS & MANAGEMENT 348 (1996); Richard J. Zeckhauser & W. Kip Viscusi, *Risk Within Reason*, 248 SCIENCE 559 (1990). *See also* Sam Peltzman, *The Effects of Automobile Safety Regulation*, 83 JOURNAL OF POLITICAL ECONOMY 677 (1975) (arguing that automobile safety regulation contributed to death rate); JOHN D. GRAHAM AND STEVEN GARBER, THE EFFECTS OF AUTOMOBILE SAFETY REGULATION, 3 Journal of Policy Analysis & Management 206 (1984) (showing that nuanced statistical analyses would conclude that automobile safety standards save lives).

31. For the methodology and its limitations *see* Jean–Baptiste Michel et al., *Quantitative Analysis of Culture Using Millions of Digitized Books*, 331 SCIENCE 176 (2011).

32. *See generally* KENNETH J. ARROW, ESSAYS IN THE THEORY OF RISK BEARING (1971); Peter A. Diamond & Joseph E. Stiglitz, *Increases in Risk and in Risk Aversion*, 8 JOURNAL OF ECONOMIC THEORY 337 (1974); Miles S. Kimball, *Standard Risk Aversion*, 61 ECONOMETRICA 589 (1993); David C. Nachman, *On the Theory of Risk Aversion of the Theory of Risk*, 21 JOURNAL OF ECONOMIC THEORY 317 (1979); Michael Rotschild & Joseph E. Stiglitz, *Increasing Risk I: A Definition*, 2 JOURNAL OF ECONOMIC THEORY 225 (1970); Michael Rotschild & Joseph E. Stiglitz, *Increasing Risk II: Its Economic Consequences*, 3 JOURNAL OF ECONOMIC THEORY 66 (1971); John W. Pratt, *Risk Aversion in the Small and in the Large*, 32 ECONOMETRICA 122 (1964); John W. Pratt & Richard Zeckhauser, *Proper Risk Aversion*, 55 ECONOMETRICA 143 (1987).

Moreover, denial of risk may be contagious and have broad social implications.[33] For example, studying the causes of the Great Recession, the National Commission concluded:

> There was a view that instincts for self-preservation inside major financial firms would shield them from fatal risk-taking without the need for a steady regulatory hand, which, the firms argued, would stifle innovation. Too many of these institutions acted recklessly, taking on too much risk, with too little capital, and with too much dependence on short-term funding. In many respects, this reflected a fundamental change in these institutions, particularly the large investment banks and bank holding companies, which focused their activities increasingly on risky trading activities that produced hefty profits. They took on enormous exposures in acquiring and supporting subprime lenders and creating, packaging, repackaging, and selling trillions of dollars in mortgage-related securities, including synthetic financial products. Like Icarus, they never feared flying ever closer to the sun.[34]

People think about and respond to risks in peculiar ways. *Risk is a common motivation for regulation, but in itself rarely provides good justifications for regulation*; rather, externalities, inadequate information, transaction costs, and bounded rationality *may* warrant risk regulation.

§ 4.2 MISUSE OF RISK

Should society deploy resources to eliminate risks of epidemics? Does a risk of epidemic provide good reasons to invest social resources in precautions?

Anti–Spitting Laws

In the 1880s, scientists concluded that human saliva could transmit contagious diseases, such as tuberculosis, pneumonia, and influenza. Health authorities and lawmakers began considering restrictions on practices they believed contributed to the spread of infectious diseases, such as spitting in public and the use of common drinking cups and spittoons. Despite the frequency of epidemics, many believed that restrictions on spitting in public were not feasible because "women can, but men can not, change their filthy spitting habits."[35] Others, however, thought that "most men had the natural instinct of cleanliness and could be educated in this

33. *See* § 1.1.3a (irrational exuberance).

34. NATIONAL COMMISSION ON THE CAUSES OF THE FINANCIAL AND ECONOMIC CRISIS IN THE UNITED STATES, THE FINANCIAL CRISIS: INQUIRY REPORT xviii-xix (final report, Jan. 2011) available at *regti.me/FCIC–Report* (case sensitive).

35. Elmer B. Borland, *Municipal Regulation of the Spitting Habit*, 35 JOURNAL OF THE AMERICAN MEDICAL ASSOCIATION 999 (1900).

respect up to the level with women; and further, that the ignorant, unteachable and vicious could be controlled by the absolute fiat."[36]

In November 1884, eleven New York middle-class women, "outraged at the continuance of the foul odors which polluted the atmosphere of th[eir] entire neighborhood, causing them to keep windows closed in the hottest weather, and depriving them of their inalienable right to pure air, that they resolved 'to investigate the cause of this nuisance," formed *The Ladies' Health Protective Association* (LHPA).[37] LHPA quickly became an effective interest group lobbying against nuisances in New York City.[38] One of the problems LHPA identified was "[t]he unsanitary condition of the surface and elevated [street] cars and the public buildings, in consequence of the vile habit of men and boys spitting over the floors."[39]

In September 1892, *The British Medical Journal* reported that "[n]either the sense of social decency nor the recent teachings of bacteriology have yet availed to restrain the average American citizen from exercising his privilege as a free man of voiding his sputum wherever he pleases. The ladies are now, we are pleased to observe, taking the matter in hand, and what the American woman sets her mind on doing she generally manages to effect."[40] "[In late 1895, LHPA] took the matter to the [New York City's] Health Board and urged the necessity for action."[41] Explaining the LHPA's position—the organization President Mary E. Trautmann stated: "The trouble was that spitting had become a habit, and so much so that persons intent on behaving well in public offended as much as those from whom one could not expect befitting conduct."[42] On January 18, 1896, two the pathologists presented a report "on the subject of expectoration in public buildings and conveyances" to the New York City Board of Health.[43] The report summarized a study New York City conducted, stating:

> [T]he expectoration of persons suffering from laryngeal or pulmonary tuberculosis, pneumonia, influenza or the grip, and from diphtheria, contains the specific germs of these different diseases, and is capable of inducing these diseases in others. There is, furthermore, much evidence that a similar condition exists in certain more readily communicable diseases, such as scarlet fever, measles and whooping cough. * * * It has long since been shown that the chief means for the transmission of consumption is the

---

36. *Id.*

37. Mrs. Ralph Trautmann (Mary E. Trautmann), *Twelve Years' Work of the Ladies Health Protective Association*, 24 NEW YORK MEDICAL TIMES 257 (Sept. 1896). *See also East Side Odors,* NEW YORK HERALD, Nov. 18, 1884, at 9.

38. *See generally* Felice Batlan, *Ladies' Health Protective Association: Lay Lawyers and Urban Cause Lawyering*, 41 AKRON LAW REVIEW 701 (2008).

39. Trautmann, *Twelve Years' Work of the Ladies Health Protective Association*, *supra* note 37.

40. *A Crusade Against Spitting*, 2 BRITISH MEDICAL JOURNAL 706 (Sept. 1892).

41. Trautmann, *Twelve Years' Work of the Ladies Health Protective Association*, *supra* note 37.

42. *Spitting in Conveyances*, NEW YORK TIMES, June 15, 1896, at 5.

43. *A More Aggressive Campaign Against Tuberculosis in New York*, 26 JOURNAL OF AMERICAN MEDICAL ASSOCIATION 240 (1896).

> dried and pulverized sputum of persons suffering from the disease. These germs are liable to be gathered on the feet and on the skirts of women, and taken into private houses, where the most perfect ventilation will not stay their evil effect. Expectorating in public places should be abated, as any other public nuisance which is brought to the attention of this department. That it is a habit and not a necessity, is clearly enough shown by the large number of men who are free from it, and the insignificant portion of women who practise it. There seems to be no good reason for the longer sufferance by the mass of people of the carelessness and the negligence of the few. We believe that this is a matter of great importance, and that on this ground alone it demands the interference of your Board. We believe that the time has now arrived when the people of the city of New York will heartily support the adoption of such sanitary measures as may seem necessary and expedient for the abatement of this widespread nuisance and source of danger.

The report recommended that "notices [would] be posted in all public places and in all surface and elevated cars in this city, signed by the Board of Health, warning passengers against expectoration upon the floor of those conveyances; and further that similar notices be posted in the stations of the elevated roads, warning people against expectoration upon the platforms and stairs, or on the floors of the stations."[44] Street car companies were willing to cooperate with the Board of Health and LHPA and posted notices in all their cars. However, the new policies were not enforced and individuals did not change their conduct. LHPA representatives communicated to the City authorities their concerns regarding the ineffectiveness of "education by moral suasion."[45] On May 12, 1896, New York City adopted the first anti-spitting law in the United States. The new ordinance, codified as § 222 of the New York City Sanitary Code, provided:

> SEC. **222**. Spitting upon the floors of public buildings and of railroad-cars and of ferry-boats is hereby forbidden, and officers in charge, or control of all such buildings, cars and boats shall keep posted permanently in each public building and in each railroad-car and in each ferry-boat a sufficient number of notices forbidding spitting upon the floors, and janitors of buildings, conductors of cars and employees upon ferry-boats shall call the attention of all violators of this ordinance to such notices.

The press favorably reported about the cultural effect of the ordinance. For example, four weeks after the City adopted the ordinance, *The New York Times* announced: "Spitting * * * in public places and conveyances may soon be accepted as evidence that the offender is callous to the sensibilities of his fellows and without regard for the comity of clean living which tends toward public comfort. Since the fulmination against a practice that is indecorous, a menace to health because of germ danger, and defiling, some strides have been made toward advancing the principles involved to

---

44. *Id.*

45. Trautmann, *Twelve Years' Work of the Ladies Health Protective Association*, *supra* note 37.

ethical importance."[46] Similarly, *The Harper's Weekly* noted: "The [Health] Board's mandate not yet effectual, but the public has begun to be familiar with it, and through it many citizens have for the first time had suggested them that miscellaneous spitting is not nice."[47] The powerful Police Commissioner, Theodore Roosevelt, expressed his support in LHPA's crusade, stating: "The only way to convince some kinds of human swine of their indecency is to punish some other human swine."[48]

Not all, however, fully endorsed the new anti-spitting ordinance. For example, in October 1896, *The Medical & Surgical Reporter* published an editorial criticizing the design of the new regulation.

THE

Medical and Surgical Reporter:

EDITORIAL.

SPITTING IN PUBLIC PLACES.

The American people have two ubiquitous manifestations of vulgarity. One is the irresistible desire to leave an autograph wherever the sublimity of nature or the ingenuity of man attracts a crowd; the other is indiscriminate spitting, regardless of the desecration of natural beauty, or of the contamination of places where human beings must live and congregate. We have used the word *spit*, rather than the supposedly more elegant one *expectorate*, because the ejected matter may consist of saliva, of mucus drawn backward from the nose or collected from the throat, of chyme eructated from the stomach, or matter raised from the lungs and thus strictly *expectorated*. * * *

THE REPORTER believes that the danger from ubiquitous spitting is practically limited to the possibility of the transmission of tubercle bacilli. The diplococcus of pneumonia is not likely to be present in the sputum of one able to appear in public. It is questionable if the bacteria found in the saliva of healthy persons and usually considered pneumonic, are truly so. * * * While it is desirable that highways, public buildings and conveyances of all kinds should be free from human filth, as well as from pathogenic bacteria, it is as yet impossible to enforce a rigid law against spitting. Reformers are always prone to forget that the refined, honest and conscientious members of society need no laws, and are affected by them only when their literal interpretation happens to be contrary to

46. *Spitting in Conveyances*, NEW YORK TIMES, Jun. 15, 1896, at 5.

47. *The Spitting Habit*, HARPER'S WEEKLY, Feb. 27, 1897, at 195.

48. *Roosevelt Says, Arrest Spitters*, NEW YORK LAW JOURNAL, Feb. 8, 1897, at 2.

the spirit which led to their enactment. Thus a law must always be framed, not with reference to stating an ideal condition, but with regard to its practical applicability to persons who are dishonest, vulgar and immoral. A law against spitting must not aim higher than the average sentiment of the policeman, the police court judge, the janitor, conductor or care-taker, upon whom its enforcement must depend. It must not too much curtail the highly-prized "personal liberty" of the two-legged swine, against whom it is directed; otherwise popular sympathy will immediately be aroused to prevent the enforcement of the law, to secure its repeal and to prevent an attempt to substitute a milder measure. * * * Some day we may hope for one simple prohibition applying to all bodily excretions, and protecting all public places from contamination, but the municipality cannot enforce nor consistently enact such an ordinance till it fulfills its own duty of furnishing freely, clean and convenient retiring places, at short distances, throughout its territory.

For the present, we believe that the best practical solution of the problem consists [of] an enactment against spitting in any inclosed place to which public access is possible. This would include not only public buildings, in the strict sense of the word, but railroad and streetcars, and other public conveyances, stores, offices, hotels, depots, theatres, churches and other congregating places. The act should not stop with providing a fine, but should make arrest easy and simple, preferably by granting police powers to all citizens. It should also compel, under suitable penalty, the owners or managers of the places named to enforce the law. Street cars, in most cities, have long contained conspicuous notices forbidding spitting, but no efficient method of enforcement has been reached, nor does the municipality usually lend its support to the feeble efforts of the street-car companies. * * * The man who has no more regard for his fellow-creatures than to force them to walk through slimy puddles of sputum, is capable of taking the meanest kind of vengeance on the officials to whom we must look for the enforcement of the law against spitting. * * * Any ordinance,* * * which deals with this crime against health and cleanliness, should give ample support to the complainant and should provide for the prompt and easy arrest of the offender and for efficient punishment. At the same time, the law should not destroy its own efficiency by forbidding spitting out-doors till a vast amount of work has been done in educating popular sentiment.[49]

The New York anti-spitting ordinance inspired many localities and states across the country. The 1901 treatise *Municipal Sanitation in the United States* reported:

The first anti-spitting law in the United States was adopted in* * * New York City. * * * It was adopted for the purpose of diminishing the spread of tuberculosis. * * * The danger was

49. *Spitting in Public Places*, MEDICAL & SURGICAL REPORTER, Oct. 31, 1896, at 563.

believed to be a very real one, and hence the ordinance. While the evidence in support of the view that this danger is great enough of itself to warrant such legislation is not entirely satisfactory, the legislation itself has met with very general approval. Spitting on the floor or sidewalk is a dirty nuisance, and is annoying to the majority of persons. It is probably because it prevents nuisance rather than because it prevents disease that the law meets with popular favor. It is, however, usually adopted by boards of health under authority to legislate for the prevention of disease.[50]

By the end of WWI, all states adopted anti-spitting laws. The vast majority of states repealed these laws by the end of the twentieth century. Some laws are still in effect.[51] The 1906 Massachusetts anti spitting law provides:

270: § 14 Spitting

Whoever expectorates or spits upon any public sidewalk, or upon any place used exclusively or principally by pedestrians, or, except in receptacles provided for the purpose, in or upon any part of any city or town hall, any court house or court room, any public library or museum, any church or theatre, any lecture or music hall, any mill or factory, any hall of any tenement building occupied by five or more families, any school building, any ferry boat or steamboat, any railroad car or elevated railroad car, except a smoking car, any street railway car, any railroad or railway station or waiting room, or on any track, platform or sidewalk connected therewith, and included within the limits thereof, shall be punished by a fine of not more than twenty dollars.

270 § 15: Arrest without warrant for spitting

Any person detected in the act of violating the preceding section may, if his name is unknown to the officer, be arrested without a warrant by any officer authorized to serve criminal process in the place where the offence is committed and kept in custody until he can be taken before a court having jurisdiction of such offence.

---

50. Charles Chaplin, Municipal Sanitation in the United States 158–159 (1901).

51. *See, e.g.*, Ga. Code Ann. § 16–12–120 (prohibiting spitting on public transportation); La. Rev. Stat. Ann. § 40:1121 (sanctioning spitting in certain public places); Mass. Gen. Laws Ann. ch. 270, § 14; N.H. Rev. Stat. Ann. § 147:18; Va. Code Ann. § 18.2–322.

Figure 4.2
A Nomination for the Hall of Shame: The Spitter

Source: Illinois Health News, vol. 8, January 1922.

Questions

1. What was the original motivation behind the ban on spitting in public places? What was the nature of the cost-benefit analysis? Who conducted the cost-benefit analysis? Was the regulator captured?

2. Spitting in public places was not a socially condemned activity in the United States at the turn of the nineteenth century. Today, spitting in public is not regarded as a polite (or civilized) activity. What has changed?

3. During the anti-spitting crusade at the turn of the nineteenth century, states and localities allocated resources to enforce public hygiene. Today, some states and localities still have anti-sitting laws on the book but no longer invest in their enforcement. Why have most states and localities repealed their anti-spitting laws? Why have some states and localities not repealed their laws?

4. In *Alcorn v. Mitchell*, 63 Ill. 553 (1872), the Supreme Court of Illinois upheld punitive damages of $1,000 against a person who spat in the face of another in the presence of a large number of people. Considering the availability of remedies in torts for harms caused by spitting, why did municipalities and states adopt anti-spitting laws?

5. Is or was spitting in public an externality? Why would the state ever intervene in habits of personal hygiene?

6. Today, the Metropolitan Transportation Authority operates the public transportation in New York City. About one third of all assaults on bus operators involve spitting and require drivers to be examined by a health-

care professional.[52] Should the City adopt any regulatory measures to address spitting on service providers?

§ 4.3 RISK, CHANCE, AND HOPE

People consider (or should consider) the risk of death, but healthy people are motivated to avoid illness while sick people focus on recovery. Their perspectives of risk of death are profoundly different.

In the nineteenth century, the American quack medicine industry capitalized on individuals' willingness to pay for hope, offering the public products of questionable curative and preventative power with water, alcohol, and cocaine as common ingredients.[53] Using deceit and fraud, the industry took advantage of trademark law, developing sophisticated branding and advertising strategies to persuade the public that its products can eliminate all health risks.[54] In 1906, Congress passed the Pure Food and Drug Act requiring manufacturers and sellers of drugs to disclose information believed to be relevant to health and risk. Nevertheless, by the Great Depression, quack medicines still accounted for half of all drug sales in the United States.[55] In 1938, Congress enacted the Food, Drug, and Cosmetic Act. Section 502 required every drug to bear "adequate directions for use" and warnings against unsafe uses on its label. Otherwise, it would be deemed misbranded and banned from sale. The FDA interpreted this provision to create a new category of drugs that could be sold only by prescription.[56] In 1951, Congress ratified this interpretation, creating a statutory category of nonnarcotic prescription drugs.

Studying the FDA's adoption of prescription drug requirements, Professor Peter Temin wrote: "The FDA had abandoned the assumption that people behaved rationally in their choice of medicines. * * * [P]olicy makers in the federal government lost faith in the ability of the market economy to protect individuals from a variety of economic and noneconomic ills."[57] This approach still governs today.

United States v. Rutherford

442 U.S. 544 (1979)

■ MR. JUSTICE MARSHALL delivered the opinion of the Court.

The question presented in this case is whether the Federal Food, Drug, and Cosmetic Act precludes terminally ill cancer patients from obtaining

---

52. *See* Jay Dwyer, *MTA's Budget Ills Are Worse Than Accounts of Spitting*, N.Y. TIMES, May 26, at A20.

53. *See, e.g.*, SAMUEL HOPKINS ADAMS, THE GREAT AMERICAN FRAUD (1906); STEWART H. HOLBROOK, THE GOLDEN AGE OF QUACKERY (1959); JAMES HARVEY YOUNG, THE TOADSTOOL MILLIONAIRES: A SOCIAL HISTORY OF PATENT MEDICINES IN AMERICA BEFORE FEDERAL REGULATION (1961); JAMES HARVEY YOUNG, THE MEDICAL MESSIAHS: A SOCIAL HISTORY OF HEALTH QUACKERY IN TWENTIETH-CENTURY AMERICA (1967); JAMES HARVEY YOUNG, PURE FOOD: SECURING THE FEDERAL FOOD AND DRUGS ACT OF 1906 (1989).

54. Materials about quack medicine are available at *regti.me/quack-m* (case sensitive).

55. Peter Temin, *The Origin of Compulsory Drug Prescriptions*, 22 JOURNAL OF LAW & ECONOMICS 91 (1979).

56. 3 Fed. Reg. 3168 (December 28, 1938).

57. Temin, *The Origin of Compulsory Drug Prescriptions*, *supra* note 55, at 105.

Laetrile, a drug not recognized as "safe and effective" within the meaning of § 201(p)(1) of the Act, 52 Stat. 1041, as amended, 21 U.S.C. § 321(p)(1).

I

Section 505 of the Federal Food, Drug, and Cosmetic Act * * * prohibits interstate distribution of any "new drug" unless the Secretary of Health, Education, and Welfare approves an application supported by substantial evidence of the drug's safety and effectiveness.[1] As defined in § 201(p)(1) of the Act, the term "new drug" includes

> "[a]ny drug* * * not generally recognized, among experts qualified by scientific training and experience to evaluate the safety and effectiveness of drugs, as safe and effective for use under the conditions prescribed, recommended, or suggested in the labeling. * * *"

Exemptions from premarketing approval procedures are available for drugs intended solely for investigative use and drugs qualifying under either of the Act's two grandfather provisions.

In 1975, terminally ill cancer patients and their spouses brought this action to enjoin the Government from interfering with the interstate shipment and sale of Laetrile, a drug not approved for distribution under the Act. [After completion of administrative hearings, the Commissioner of the FDA found that Laetrile constituted a "new drug" as defined in

---

1. Section 505, as set forth in 21 U.S.C. § 355, provides in part:

> "(a) ... No person shall introduce or deliver for introduction into interstate commerce any new drug, unless an approval of an application filed pursuant to subsection (b) of this section is effective with respect to such drug.
>
> "(b) ... Any person may file with the Secretary an application with respect to any drug subject to the provisions of subsection (a) of this section. Such person shall submit to the Secretary as a part of the application (1) full reports of investigations which have been made to show whether or not such drug is safe for use and whether such drug is effective in use....
>
> "(d) ... If the Secretary finds ... that (1) the investigations ... required to be submitted to the Secretary ... do not include adequate tests by all methods reasonably applicable to show whether or not such drug is safe for use under the conditions prescribed, recommended, or suggested in the proposed labeling thereof; (2) the results of such tests show that such drug is unsafe for use under such conditions or do not show that such drug is safe for use under such conditions; ... (4) ... he has insufficient information to determine whether such drug is safe for use under such conditions; or (5) ... there is a lack of substantial evidence that the drug will have the effect it purports or is represented to have under the conditions of use prescribed, recommended, or suggested in the proposed labeling thereof; or (6) based on a fair evaluation of all material facts, such labeling is false or misleading in any particular; he shall issue an order refusing to approve the application.... As used in this subsection ..., the term 'substantial evidence' means evidence consisting of adequate and well-controlled investigations, including clinical investigations, by experts qualified by scientific training and experience to evaluate the effectiveness of the drug involved, on the basis of which it could fairly and responsibly be concluded by such experts that the drug will have the effect it purports or is represented to have under the conditions of use prescribed, recommended, or suggested in the labeling or proposed labeling thereof.

§ 201(p)(1). The Commissioner determined first that no uniform definition of Laetrile exists. The Commissioner further found that Laetrile in its various forms constituted a "new drug" as defined in § 201(p)(1) of the Act because it was not generally recognized among experts as safe and effective for its prescribed use. The Commissioner concluded that there were no adequate well-controlled scientific studies of Laetrile's safety or effectiveness].

II

The Federal Food, Drug, and Cosmetic Act makes no special provision for drugs used to treat terminally ill patients. By its terms, § 505 of the Act requires premarketing approval for "any new drug" unless it is intended solely for investigative use. * * *

When construing a statute so explicit in scope, a court must act within certain well-defined constraints. If a legislative purpose is expressed in "plain and unambiguous language,* * * the* * * duty of the courts is to give it effect according to its terms." *United States v. Lexington Mill & Elevator Co.*, 232 U.S. 399, 409 (1914). * * * Exceptions to clearly delineated statutes will be implied only where essential to prevent "absurd results" or consequences obviously at variance with the policy of the enactment as a whole. *Helvering v. Hammel*, 311 U.S. 504, 510–511 (1941). * * * In the instant case, we are persuaded by the legislative history and consistent administrative interpretation of the Act that no implicit exemption for drugs used by the terminally ill is necessary to attain congressional objectives or to avert an unreasonable reading of the terms "safe" and "effective" in § 201(p)(1).

A

Nothing in the history of the 1938 Food, Drug, and Cosmetic Act, * * * suggests that Congress intended protection only for persons suffering from curable diseases. To the contrary, in deliberations preceding the 1938 Act, Congress expressed concern that individuals with fatal illnesses, such as cancer, should be shielded from fraudulent cures. * * * That same understanding is reflected in the Committee Reports on the 1962 Amendments. Both Reports note with approval the FDA's policy of considering effectiveness when passing on the safety of drugs prescribed for "life-threatening disease."[9]

---

9. The Senate Report states:

"The Food and Drug Administration now requires, in determining whether a 'new drug' is safe, a showing as to the drug's effectiveness where the drug is offered for use in the treatment of a life-threatening disease, or where it appears that the 'new drug' will occasionally produce serious toxic or even lethal effects so that only its usefulness would justify the risks involved in its use. In such cases, the determination of safety is, in the light of the purposes of the new drug provisions, considered by the Food and Drug Administration to be inseparable from consideration of the drug's effectiveness. The provisions of the bill are in no way intended to affect any existing authority of the Department of Health, Education, and Welfare to consider and evaluate the effectiveness of a new drug in the context of passing upon its safety." S.Rep.No.1744, 87th Cong., 2d Sess., pt. 1, p. 15 (1962), U.S.Code Cong. & Admin.News 1962, pp. 2884, 2891. . . .

In implementing the statutory scheme, the FDA has never made exception for drugs used by the terminally ill. As this Court has often recognized, the construction of a statute by those charged with its administration is entitled to substantial deference. * * * Such deference is particularly appropriate where, as here, an agency's interpretation involves issues of considerable public controversy, and Congress has not acted to correct any misperception of its statutory objectives. * * * Unless and until Congress does so, we are reluctant to disturb a longstanding administrative policy that comports with the plain language, history, and prophylactic purpose of the Act.

B

In the Court of Appeals' view, an implied exemption from the Act was justified because the safety and effectiveness standards set forth in § 201(p)(1) could have "no reasonable application" to terminally ill patients. * * * We disagree. Under our constitutional framework, federal courts do not sit as councils of revision, empowered to rewrite legislation in accord with their own conceptions of prudent public policy. * * * Only when a literal construction of a statute yields results so manifestly unreasonable that they could not fairly be attributed to congressional design will an exception to statutory language be judicially implied. * * * Here, however, we have no license to depart from the plain language of the Act, for Congress could reasonably have intended to shield terminal patients from ineffectual or unsafe drugs.

A drug is effective within the meaning of § 201(p)(1) if there is general recognition among experts, founded on substantial evidence, that the drug in fact produces the results claimed for it under prescribed conditions. * * * [E]ffectiveness does not necessarily denote capacity to cure. In the treatment of any illness, terminal or otherwise, a drug is effective if it fulfills, by objective indices, its sponsor's claims of prolonged life, improved physical condition, or reduced pain. * * *

For the terminally ill, as for anyone else, a drug is unsafe if its potential for inflicting death or physical injury is not offset by the possibility of therapeutic benefit. * * *

Moreover, there is a special sense in which the relationship between drug effectiveness and safety has meaning in the context of incurable illnesses. An otherwise harmless drug can be dangerous to any patient if it does not produce its purported therapeutic effect. * * * But if an individual suffering from a potentially fatal disease rejects conventional therapy in favor of a drug with no demonstrable curative properties, the consequences

---

The FDA's practice was further amplified by HEW Secretary Ribicoff in testimony on the bill that ultimately became the 1962 Amendments:

> "If the drug is offered for treatment of progressive or life-threatening diseases, such as cancer, . . . we now consider its effectiveness. In such cases the determination of safety is, in the light of the purpose of the new drug provisions, inseparable from consideration of the drug's effectiveness." Hearings on S. 1552 before the Subcommittee on Antitrust and Monopoly of the Senate Committee on the Judiciary, 87th Cong., 1st Sess., 2588 (1961).

can be irreversible. For this reason, * * * the FDA consider[s] effectiveness when reviewing the safety of drugs used to treat terminal illness. * * *

To accept the proposition that the safety and efficacy standards of the Act have no relevance for terminal patients is to deny the Commissioner's authority over all drugs, however toxic or ineffectual, for such individuals. If history is any guide, this new market would not be long overlooked. Since the turn of the century, resourceful entrepreneurs have advertised a wide variety of purportedly simple and painless cures for cancer, including liniments of turpentine, mustard, oil, eggs, and ammonia; peat moss; arrangements of colored floodlamps; pastes made from glycerin and limburger cheese; mineral tablets; and "Fountain of Youth" mixtures of spices, oil, and suet. In citing these examples, we do not, of course, intend to deprecate the sincerity of Laetrile's current proponents, or to imply any opinion on whether that drug may ultimately prove safe and effective for cancer treatment. But this historical experience does suggest why Congress could reasonably have determined to protect the terminally ill, no less than other patients, from the vast range of self-styled panaceas that inventive minds can devise.

We note finally that construing § 201(p)(1) to encompass treatments for terminal diseases does not foreclose all resort to experimental cancer drugs by patients for whom conventional therapy is unavailing. Section 505(i) of the Act, 21 U.S.C. § 355(i), exempts from premarketing approval drugs intended solely for investigative use if they satisfy certain preclinical testing and other criteria. An application for clinical testing of Laetrile by the National Cancer Institute is now pending before the Commissioner. * * * That the Act makes explicit provision for carefully regulated use of certain drugs not yet demonstrated safe and effective reinforces our conclusion that no exception for terminal patients may be judicially implied. Whether, as a policy matter, an exemption should be created is a question for legislative judgment, not judicial inference.

* * *

So ordered.

Questions

1. What is the risk in allowing terminally-ill cancer patients to purchase medications that are not FDA approved? Is this risk similar to the general risk associated with unapproved medications?

2. What was the Court's definition for effective drug? What does the word "safe" mean in the context of medications for terminally ill patients?

3. In *FDA v. Brown & Williamson Tobacco Corp.*, 529 U.S. 120 (2000), in a five-to-four decision, the Supreme Court overruled an attempt of the FDA to assert authority to regulate tobacco products. The core disagreement between the majority and dissent was over the Food, Drug, and Cosmetic Act's requirement that products the FDA approves would be safe as used by consumers. The majority held that no such interpretation could apply to tobacco products. Some medications do not intend to cure. Should the state impose restrictions on the marketing and distribution of such drugs?

§ 4.4 WILLINGNESS AND ABILITY TO PAY THE COSTS

Cost-benefit analysis may indicate that individuals should not take or produce particular risks. As we have seen, however, heuristics and biases may build reluctance to pay to mitigate risks. Moreover, liquidity constraints may impose an additional hurdle on the willingness to pay. Risks materialize in the future, but precaution costs must be paid at present. The need to pay such costs upfront may provide additional reasons to oppose risk regulation.

Mine Safety

On April 5, 2010, a powerful explosion tore through the Upper Big Branch mine in southern West Virginia. Twenty-nine miners died and one was seriously injured. On April 13, West Virginia Governor instructed his administration to conduct an independent investigation into the disaster. Thirteen months later, in May 2011, the Governor's Independent Investigation Panel submitted its report, entitled: *Upper Big Branch—The April 5, 10, Explosion: A Failure of a Basic Coal Mine Safety Practices*. The Panel concluded that the explosion could have been prevented and was the result of failures of basic systems designed to protect miners. Massey Energy, the mine owner, failed to meet a long line of federal and state safety standards. Concluding its report, the Panel wrote:

> Following all man-made disasters, such as coal mine explosions, government officials stand in front of the public and grieving family members and promise to take steps to ensure that such tragedies don't happen again. For a while people pay attention. Investigative bodies like this one are formed and spend months sifting through evidence to attempt to pinpoint the causes of the disaster and offer recommendations aimed at preventing another one.
>
> We have done so in this report, again with the genuine hope that reforms can be instituted and that the Upper Big Branch disaster is the last coal mining disaster ever in this country. However, we offer these recommendations with reservation. We have seen similar reports, written with the same good intent, gathering dust on the bookshelves of the national Mine Health and Safety Academy.
>
> We also have witnessed times when this country rolled up its sleeves and went to work with a steely determination to improve workplace conditions. Some of the most dramatic improvements for miners' health and safety in the United States came after some of the worst human tragedies—the disaster at Monongah in 1907 and the explosion at Farmington in 1968—when big, bold reforms were put in place by courageous lawmakers at both the state and federal level.

* * * The 1969 Coal Mine Health and Safety Act was the most comprehensive occupational safety and health law ever enacted in this nation and perhaps in the world. In the five years after its passage, the rate of coal mine fatalities declined 37 percent; the fatality rate again dropped 25 percent in the five years after passage of the Federal Mine and Health Act of 1977.

This tells us we can mine coal safely in this country. * * * However, laws and regulations are effective only if they are respected by companies and enforced with diligence by regulators. * * * Ultimately, the responsibility for the explosion at the Upper Big Branch mine lies with the management of Massey Energy. The company broke faith with its workers by frequently and knowingly violating the law and blatantly disregarding known safety practices while creating a public perception that its operations exceeded industry safety standards.

The story of Upper Big Branch is a cautionary tale of hubris. A company that was a towering presence in the Appalachian coalfields operated its mines in a profoundly reckless manner, and 29 coal miners paid with their lives for the corporate risk-taking. The April 5, 2010, explosion was not something that happened out of the blue, an event that could not have been anticipated or prevented. It was, to the contrary, a completely predictable result for a company that ignored basic safety standards and put too much faith in its own mythology.[58]

In March 1871, Pennsylvania Governor John W. Geary signed into law the Pennsylvania Coal Mine Law that provided:

Owners or agents to cause maps of workings of mines to be made.

SECTION 1. [T]he owner or agent of every anthracite coal mine or colliery shall make, or cause to be made, an accurate map or plan of the workings of such coal mine or colliery, on a scale of one hundred feet to the inch. * * *

* * *

Employment of persons in mines worked by shaft, etc., prohibited unless two outlets to each coal seam.

SECTION 3. [F]our months from and after the passage of this act, it shall not be lawful for the owner or agent of any anthracite coal mine or colliery, worked by or through a shaft or slope, to employ any person in working within such coal mine or colliery, or to permit any person to be in such coal mine or colliery, for the purpose of working therein, unless there are in communication with every seam or stratum of coal worked in such coal mine or colliery, for the time being at work, at least two

58. GOVERNOR'S INDEPENDENT INVESTIGATION PANEL, UPPER BIG BRANCH—THE APRIL 5, 10, EXPLOSION: A FAILURE OF A BASIC COAL MINE SAFETY PRACTICES 107–108 (May 2011), available at *regti.me/UB-report* (case sensitive).

shafts, or slopes, or outlets, separated by natural strata, of not less than one hundred and fifty feet in breadth, by which shafts, slopes or outlets distinct means of ingress and egress are always available to the persons employed in the coal mine or colliery; but it shall not be necessary for the two shafts, slopes or outlets to belong to the same coal mine or colliery, if the persons therein employed have ready and available means of ingress and egress by not less than two shafts, slopes or outlets, one or more of which may belong to another coal mine or colliery. * * *

* * *

Courts, upon application of inspectors, to prohibit workings of mines in contravention of act.

Section 5. Any of the courts of law or equity of this commonwealth, having jurisdiction where the coal mine or colliery proceeded against is situated, upon application of the inspector of coal mines and collieries of the proper district, acting in behalf of the commonwealth, shall prohibit by injunction or otherwise, the working of any mine in which any person is employed in working, or is permitted to be for the purpose of working in contravention of the provisions of this act, and may award such costs in the matter of the injunction or other proceeding as the court may think just; but this section shall be without prejudice to any other remedy permitted by law for enforcing the provisions of this act.

Building for use of men to be erected at mouth of mine.

Section 6. The owner, lessee, operator or agent of every coal mine or colliery, shall erect or provide, at or near the mouth or entrance to such mine, and maintain the same at all times when men are employed in such mine, a suitable building or buildings, supplied with soft water and properly lighted and warmed, for the use of the men employed in such mine, to wash and change their clothes when entering the mine and when returning therefrom.

Owners or agents to have mine properly ventilated.

Section 7. The owners or agent of every coal mine or colliery shall provide and establish, for every such coal mine or colliery, an adequate amount of ventilation of not less than fifty-five cubic feet per second of pure air, or thirty-three hundred feet per minute, for every fifty men at work in such mine, and as much more as circumstances may require, which shall be circulated through to the face of each and every working place throughout the entire mine, to dilute and render harmless and expel therefrom the noxious, poisonous gases, to such an extent, that the entire mine shall be in a fit state for men to work therein, and be free from danger to the health and lives of the men by reason of said noxious and poisonous gases, and all workings shall be kept clear of standing gas; the ventilation may be produced by using blowing engines, air-pumps, forcing or suction fans of sufficient capacity and power, or other suitable appliances, as to produce and insure constantly an abundant supply of fresh air throughout the entire mine; but in no case shall a furnace be used in the mine, where the coal breaker and schute buildings are built directly over and covering the top of the shaft, for the purpose of producing a hot upcast of air, and there shall be an intake air-way of not less than twenty square feet area, and the return air-way shall not be less than twenty-five square feet.

* * *

Safety-lamps.

Doors.

Mines containing explosive gases, how divided, etc.

SECTION 9. All and every of the safety-lamps used in coal mines or collieries shall be the property of the owner thereof, and shall be under the charge of a suitable person, under direction of the mining boss, who shall keep them clean and in good order; and the mining boss shall provide that all doors used in assisting, or in any way affecting ventilation of the mine, shall be so hung and adjusted as that they will close of their own accord, and cannot stand open; and the main air doors on the traveling roads shall be double, and an extra door shall be fixed, to be closed only in the event of an accident to one of the others, and the sides and top of such door shall be well built with stones and mortar, in mines in which the inspector shall deem it necessary and shall so order; and all main doors shall be provided with an attendant, whose constant duty shall be to guard them and prevent them being left open; and every mine having explosive gas, in each and every part of such mine or mines, shall be divided into two, four or more panels or districts, each ventilated by a separate spit or current of air, and fifty persons shall be the greatest number that shall work in any one panel or district at the same time; and bore holes shall be kept twenty feet in advance of the face of each and every place, and if necessary, on both sides, when the same is driven towards or approaching an abandoned mine, or part of a mine, suspected to contain inflammable gases, or which is inundated with water.

Boys under certain age not to work in mines.

Neglect to perform duties required by certain sections.

SECTION 10. * * * [N]o boy under twelve years of age shall work or enter any mine, and proof must be given of his age, by certificate or otherwise, before he shall be employed; and no father, or any other person, shall conceal or misrepresent the age of any boy; the neglect or refusal of any person or party to perform the duties provided for and required to be performed by Sections six, seven, eight, nine and ten of this Act, by the parties therein required to perform them, shall be taken and be deemed a misdemeanor by them, or either or any of them; and upon conviction thereof they, or any or either of them, shall be punished by imprisonment and fine of not exceeding five hundred dollars, or either, at the discretion of the court trying the same.

Commonwealth v. Bonnell

Court of Common Pleas of Supreme County
8 Phila. 534 (1871)

■ HARDING, JUDGE.

This proceeding had been instituted in this court under the provisions of the Act of the General Assembly of the Commonwealth of Pennsylvania, entitled, "An Act providing for the health and safety of persons employed in the coal mines," approved the third day of March, 1871.

The bill * * * charges that the mine or colliery is worked through a single shaft; and that the seams or strata of coal which are this being worked have no communication with any second opening or outlet, whereby another means of ingress and egress is available to the persons there employed in mining.

It charges that Samuel Bonnell, Jr., employs persons to work in the said mine or colliery for the purpose of mining coal for market, and that such persons, to the number of twenty persons and upwards, are there daily engaged in mining, raising and shipping coal in contravention of law.

It charges that Samuel Bonnell, Jr., has not provided and maintained a metal tube from the top to the bottom of said shaft, suitably calculated and adapted for the free passage of sound therein, and through which conversation may be had between persons at the bottom and at the top of the shaft; nor has he provided a sufficient cover over the carriage used for letting down and hoisting up the persons employed in the said mine; nor has he caused to be attached a suitable brake to the drum which is used by steam power for the purpose of letting down and hoisting up the persons employed in the said mine.

The bill concludes with a prayer, that an injunction may issue this court to restrain the [defendants and their agents] from working the said colliery, or permitting any persons to work therein, except such persons as may be adjudged sufficient by the relator in driving a second opening into the said mine, until full compliance with the provisions of the Act before referred to has been made by the said Samuel Bonnell, Jr.

[The defendants] press upon our consideration the manifest hardship and the great pecuniary loss to which they will be subjected in the use of their own property, if the provisions of the Act of Assembly in question be strictly enforced. Millions of capital, it is urged, invested here in good faith under former laws, must remain unproductive for months, and thousands of laborers must suffer in idleness, with hunger and want across their very hearthstones already, if the sole attention of operators must be given to strict compliance with the said Act.

We are not unmindful of some of the probable effects which may flow from the stringent enforcement of this law, nor are we insensible to the responsibility devolving upon us in connection with it; but we were placed here to take responsibilities incident to the position not to shirk them. We shall accordingly dispose of the questions raised under this law, alike novel in its features and destitute of analogies, yet vastly important in its general scope and effect, to the best of our ability. We can bring nothing to our aid, save an honest judgment grounded in ordinary common sense.

We recognize in this business the weakness of human nature. We are aware of the temptations, and even the difficulties which the owners or occupiers of such mines are obliged to encounter. In addition to the gains and savings to be derived from the continued and uninterrupted working of their property—often in themselves a sufficient inducement to warrant the risk of violating, or, at least, of chancing a violations of a statute, bristling all over with pains and penalties—come the pleadings and the beggings of the minors themselves, who have left hungry families at home, for the privilege of being allowed to go to work, promising to release the operators from all responsibility, and taking upon themselves all the risks and dangers attendant on the position they this voluntarily and anxiously seek.

We have seen that all mines or collieries of the character above described, were to be stopped on and after the expiration of four months as provided by the statute. We have seen also, that there was one condition, namely, if a second opening could be had through coal, on which their working could be continued.

Though we do not assume positively, that herein lies the explanation why so many mines or collieries in the region are yet without a second outlet, still such an explanation is not at all unreasonable, and must stand for what it is worth. At all events, such working, if indeed it is still carried on, had better case at once. It is without even the merit of shrewdness for its authors. On the contrary it can be regarded as little better than a stupid attempt at dodging the law; and the earlier, perhaps, a lesson in the pains and penalties of the Act is learned therefore, the better it will be for everybody.

We have sought for a construction [of the Act] which would harmonize the known, great interests of the operators in this behalf, with the safety of the miners and laborers in their employ; but, staring us in the face at every step of our investigation, were the plain, literal terms of the enactment itself, conforming in full rigor to its title—An Act providing for the health and safety of persons employed in coal mines—and we, therefore, have been obliged to adopt a construction, stringent though it be, alike in conformity therewith.

We say finally, and once for all, that, in the discharge of our duties arising under the provisions of this Act, and with no other motive than that springing from a sense of official obligation, we shall, whenever the occasion may arise, and as long as this law remains on the statute book, administer it strictly, and in accordance with its plain and unmistakable terms.

And now, to wit, July 3, 1871, after due consideration of the complainant's bill, and after hearing the arguments of counsel, the injunction heretofore granted in this case, is hereby continued until the further order of the court.

Questions

1. What risks did the 1871 Pennsylvania Act address?

2. Every workplace introduces some risks. As Justice Peckham observed in *Lochner*: "[i]t is unfortunately true that labor, even in any department, may possibly carry with it the seeds of unhealthiness." In *Lochner*, Justice Peckham distinguished between bakeries and "underground mines." What could motivate safety regulation of mines? Did the state have better information than miners about needed safety measures?

3. Did the defendants oppose the regulation? What were their arguments? Were the defendants' employees likely to support these arguments?

4. Writing for the *Lochner* Court, Justice Peckham mentioned the Court's decision in *Holden v. Hardy*, 169 U.S. 366 (1898). In that case, the defendant challenged the constitutionality of a Utah statute that provided:

> *An act regulating the hours of employment in underground mines and in smelters and ore reduction works.*
>
> **SECTION 1.** The period of employment of workingmen in all underground mines or workings shall be eight hours per day, except in cases of emergency where life or property is in imminent danger.
>
> **SECTION 2.** The period of employment of workingmen in smelters and all other institutions for the reduction or refining of ores or metals shall be eight hours per day, except in cases of emergency where life or property is in imminent danger.

The *Holden* Court held the Act a valid exercise of the state's police powers, providing on the following rationale:

> The conditions with respect to health of laborers in underground mines doubtless differ from those in which they labor in smelters and other reduction works on the surface. Unquestionably, the atmosphere and other conditions in mines and reduction works differ. Poisonous gases, dust, and impalpable substances arise and float in the air in stamp mills, smelters, and other works in which ores containing metals, combined with arsenic or other poisonous elements or agencies, are treated, reduced, and refined, and there can be no doubt that prolonged effort, day after day, subject to such conditions and agencies, will produce morbid, noxious, and often deadly effects in the human system. Some organisms and systems will resist and endure such conditions and effects longer than others. * * * The law in question is confined to the protection of [a] class of people engaged in labor in underground mines, and in smelters and other works wherein ores are reduced and refined. * * * Though reasonable doubts may exist as to the power of the legislature to pass a law, or as to whether the law is calculated or adapted to promote the health, safety, or comfort of the people, or to secure good order or promote the general welfare, we must resolve them in favor of the right of that department of government.

Do the described conditions justify regulation of work hours? Do they justify the restrictions in the 1871 Pennsylvania Act?

§ 4.5 CONFLICTING VALUES AND DISBELIEF

People tend to interpret information in ways that serve their existing beliefs and expectations. They use reasoning to serve their biases, rather than reexamine them. Debates and disputes over risks regulation (or any other topic in regulation) illuminate this tendency.

Risk misperceptions, especially overconfidence, tend to heat up controversy because they fail communication and compromise.[59] Again, the battles over the 2010 health-care reform illustrate this point.[60]

Auto Safety Regulation

Traffic Fatalities. Studies of risk perceptions consistently show that drivers tend to be overconfident about their driving skills and underestimate risks associated with their driving. Studies also show that not all drivers are alike: Men's risk bias is larger than women's.[61] The National Traffic and Motor Vehicle Safety Act of 1966 established the National Highway Traffic Safety Administration (NHTSA) and transformed the approached toward car accidents from focusing mostly on driver behavior toward a more comprehensive approach that takes into account other factors, including vehicle safety and road conditions.[62] Throughout its history, NHTSA has been criticized for its ineffectiveness. How should the agency be evaluated?

Figure 4.2 depicts the history of fatalities in motor vehicle accidents in the United States between 1900 and 2010. The graph shows that, over time, it has become safer to drive on US roads, as the risk of fatal accidents per mile has been consistently decreasing. In 1900, traffic fatalities were mostly caused by experimental vehicles. The spike in fatalities during 1907–1912 is attributed to the introduction of commercial motor vehicles. During the depicted period between 1900 and 2010, many other technological and legal changes have profoundly influenced the risk of traffic fatali-

59. *See generally* James Andreoni & Tymofiy Mylovanov, *Diverging Opinions*, 4(1) AMERICAN ECONOMIC JOURNAL: MICROECONOMICS 209 (2012); Roland Bénabou & Jean Tirole, *Self-Confidence and Personal Motivation*, 117 QUARTERLY JOURNAL OF ECONOMICS 871 (2002); Avinash K. Dixit & Jörgen W. Weibull, Political Polarization, 104 PROCEEDINGS OF THE NATIONAL ACADEMY OF SCIENCES 7351 (2007); Barak Orbach, *On Hubris, Civility, and Incivility*, 54 ARIZONA LAW REVIEW 443 (2012); Rajiv Sethi & Muhamet Yildiz, *Public Disagreement*, 4(3) AMERICAN ECONOMIC JOURNAL: MICROECONOMICS 57 (2012).

60. *See* National Federation of Independent Business v. Sebelius, 132 S.Ct. 2566 (2012).

61. *See, e.g.*, Henrik Andersson & Petter Lundborg, *Perception of Own Death Risk: An Analysis of Road–Traffic and Overall Mortality Risks*, 34 JOURNAL OF RISK & UNCERTAINTY 67 (2007); Svenson, *Are We All Less Risky and More Skillful Than Our Fellow Drivers*, *supra* note 14.

62. *See* JERRY L. MASHAW & DAVID L. HARFST, THE STRUGGLE FOR AUTO SAFETY (1990).

ties. Cars have become faster and lighter, but are equipped with additional safety devices, such as improved brakes, seatbelts, and airbags. Over time, the driver's space has filled with instruments such as an entertainment system, GPS, telephone, and other interactive communication devices. These additions to the driver's environment create value but also increase risk. Today's roads are longer, wider, better designed with computerized traffic light systems. The roads, however, have also become more congested. Thus, the performance analysis of NHTSA is rather complex and follows many interrelated developments.

Figure 4.2

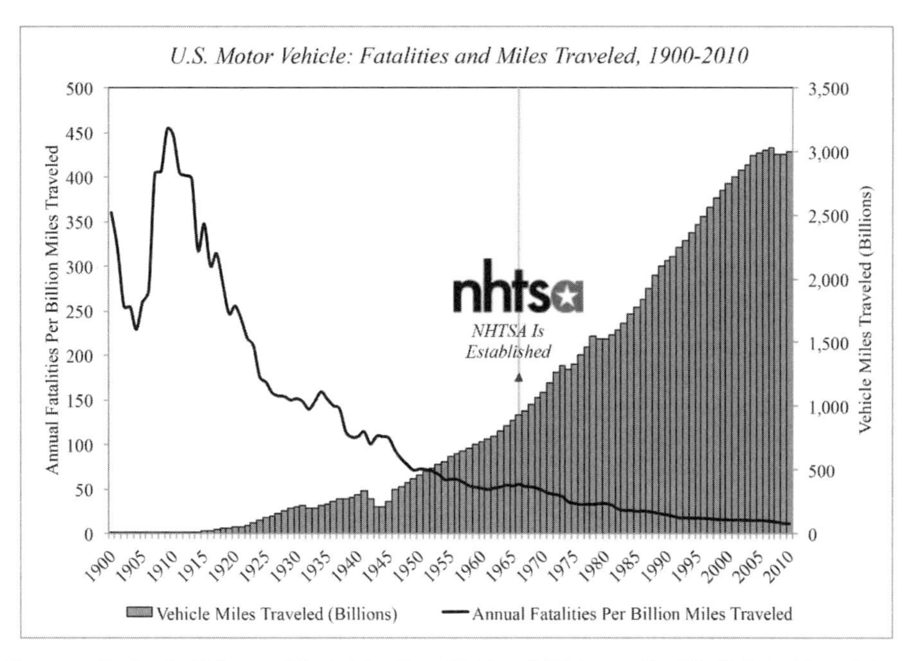

Sources: Federal Highway Administration, National Highway Traffic Safety Administration, U.S. Census Bureau.

Seatbelts. A few years after the establishment of the NHTSA, economists started publishing cost-benefit analyses of auto-safety features. For example, a 1970 study of mandatory safety devices noted that

> Government intervention is certainly one way to decrease the number of automobile accidents, but this accident reduction is not an economic justification for government intervention. Any sort of interference with the market has a cost which must be weighed against the possible benefits. The economic justification for government intervention is a substantial market failure. There is not sufficient evidence to conclude that various safety features ought to be mandatory.[63]

In 1975, economist Sam Peltzman published an article arguing that mandatory seatbelts had not contributed to any decrease in highway deaths, and more broadly that "safety regulation has had no effect on the

---

63. Lester B. Lave & Warren E. Webber, *A Benefit–Cost Analysis of Auto Safety Features*, 2 APPLIED ECONOMICS 265 (1970).

highway death toll."[64] His statistical analysis supported a compensating-behavior theory, proposing that "safety regulation has decreased the risk of death from an accident * * *, but drivers have offset this by taking greater accident risk." Peltzman's critique of NHTSA's costly safety regulation drew significant attention. Subsequent empirical studies, however, proved that seatbelts *and* mandatory seatbelt laws greatly decreased traffic fatalities. Moreover, these studies could not find empirical support for the compensating-behavior theory.[65] The critique of NHTSA, therefore, has not always been valid.[66] Moreover, the critique has not been exclusively academic. During the first two decades after the agency was established, many federal judges were convinced that regulatory agencies were prone to capture and other bureaucratic deficiencies and they felt they were in a position to do something about it.[67] Judicial hostility to regulations impaired the performance of NHTSA and contributed to a decrease in motor vehicle safety rulemaking.[68]

Motorcycle Helmets. Empirical studies uniformly show an inverse relationship between mandatory helmet laws and motorcyclist fatalities, or more accurately, the inverse relationship between helmet laws and helmet use and motorcycle fatalities.[69] Traffic experts endorse the requirement that all motorcyclists wear a helmet that complies with federal safety standards (universal helmet law) as the single most effective motorcycle safety strategy.

Section 402 of the National Traffic and Motor Vehicle Safety Act provides that "[e]ach State shall have a highway safety program approved by the Secretary, designed to reduce traffic accidents and deaths, injuries, and property damage resulting therefrom. Such programs shall be in accordance with uniform guidelines promulgated by the Secretary." Using his authority under this section, in June 1967 the Secretary released Highway Standard 4.4.3 (23 C.F.R. Part 204), entitled *Motorcycle Safety*. This required every state to mandate the wearing of an approved safety

---

64. Sam Peltzman, *The Effects of Automobile Safety Regulation*, 83 JOURNAL OF POLITICAL ECONOMY 677 (1975).

65. *See, e.g.*, Alma Cohen & Liran Einav, *The Effects of Mandatory Seat Belts Laws on Driving Behavior and Traffic Fatalities*, 85 REVIEW OF ECONOMICS & STATISTICS 828 (2003); William N. Evans & John D. Graham, *Risk Reduction or Risk Compensation? The Case for Mandatory Safety-Belt Use Laws*, 4 JOURNAL OF RISK & UNCERTAINTY 61 (1991).

66. *See also* Leon S. Robertson, *A Critical Analysis of Peltzman's "The Effects of Automobile's Safety Regulation,"* 11 JOURNAL OF ECONOMIC ISSUES 587 (1977).

67. *See generally* Thomas W. Merrill, *Capture Theory and the Courts: 1967–1983*, 72 CHICAGO-KENT LAW REVIEW 1039 (1997). *See also* John Shepard Wiley Jr., *A Capture Theory of Antitrust Federalism*, 99 HARVARD LAW REVIEW 713 (1986).

68. *See* MASHAW & HARFST, THE STRUGGLE FOR AUTO SAFETY, *supra* note 62.

69. *See* Sidebar 11-1. *See also* Rachel Dardis & Camille Lefkowitz, *Motorcycle Helmet Laws: A Case Study of Consumer Protection* 21 JOURNAL OF CONSUMER AFFAIRS 202 (1987); David J. Houston & Lilliard E. Richardson Jr., *Motorcycle Safety and the Repeal of Universal Helmet Laws*, 97 AMERICAN JOURNAL OF PUBLIC HEALTH 2063 (2007); Tim R. Sass & Paul R. Zimmerman, *Motorcycle Helmet Laws and Motorcyclist Fatalities*, 18 JOURNAL OF REGULATORY ECONOMICS 195 (2000); Daniel M. Sosin et al., *Head Injury—Associated Deaths From Motorcycle Crashes*, 264 JOURNAL OF AMERICAN MEDICAL ASSOCIATION 2395 (1990); Geoffrey S. Watson et al., *The Repeal of Helmet Use Laws and Increased Motorcyclist Mortality In the United States, 1975–1978*, 70 AMERICAN JOURNAL OF PUBLIC HEALTH 579 (1980).

helmet by every motorcycle operator and passenger wear an approved safety helmet. States enacted motorcycle helmet laws to receive federal highway construction funds, which were contingent on the enactment of such laws.[70] By the end of 1968, 38 states had universal helmet laws, and by 1975, 47 states and the District of Columbia had laws. In 1975, under pressure from the *American Motorcyclists Associations* (AMA) and *A Brotherhood Against Totality Enactment* (ABATE), Congress stopped requiring state helmet laws as a condition for the provision of federal highway construction funds.[71] By 1978, 26 states significantly modified or repealed existing state laws.[72] By the end of 2005, 46 states had helmet laws, but only 20 states required all motorcycle riders to wear helmets ("universal coverage statutes").[73] The effective lobbying of AMA and ABATE enhanced their members' freedom to choose.

American Motorcycle Association v. Davids

Court of Appeals of Michigan, Division No. 2
11 Mich.App. 351 (1968)

■ MILLER, JUDGE.

This is a review of a summary judgment granted in a proceeding requesting a declaration of rights as to the constitutionality of the amendment to the Motor Vehicle Code requiring motorcyclists and riders to wear crash helmets.

Plaintiffs challenge the act on the grounds that it violates the due process and reserved powers clauses of the Michigan Constitution3 and the due process, equal protection and right of privacy provisions of the Ninth and Fourteenth Amendments of the Constitution of the United States.

The statute in question reads as follows:

> 'A person operating or riding on a motorcycle or motor driven cycle shall wear a crash helmet approved by the department of state police. The department shall promulgate rules for the implementation of this section * * * '

Failure to wear the helmet by either the driver or rider of a motorcycle subjects such persons to criminal penalties provided for violation of the motor vehicle code.

It is contended by the plaintiffs that the legislative concern is solely related to the safety of the motorcyclist and passenger and can have no possible relationship to the safety and well-being of other persons, much

---

70. *See generally* Lilliard E. Richardson Jr. & David J. Houston, *Federalism and Safety on America's Highways*, 39 JOURNAL OF FEDERALISM 117 (2008). *See also supra* § 1.3 (discussing the standardization of the maximum speed limit of 55 miles per hour).

71. *See* Susan P. Baker, *On Lobbies, Liberties and the Public Good*, 70 AMERICAN JOURNAL OF PUBLIC HEALTH 573 (1980).

72. During this three-year period, 23 out of these 26 states witnessed an increased in the number of deaths associated with the repeal of the helmet laws. *See* Watson et al., *The Repeal of Helmet Use Laws*, *supra* note 69.

73. *See* Richardson & Houston, *Federalism and Safety on America's Highways*, *id.*, at 127–128.

less the public at large. Based on the premise that the individual in our society is still master of his fate and captain of his soul, plaintiffs cite the following maxim:

> The maxims are, first, that the individual is not accountable to society for his actions, insofar as these concern the interests of no person but himself.' John Stuart Mill, Utilitarianism, *Liberty and Representative Government*, E. P. Dutton & Co. Inc. (1950 ed., p. 201).

This is consistent with the time honored maxim: '*Sic utere tuo ut alienum non laedas.*' (So use your own that you do not injure that of another.)

The only case found in which the police power has been urged to require one to protect himself from himself is *Mugler v. Kansas* 123 U.S. 623 (1887). In that case the prohibition law of Kansas was attacked as a deprivation of property without due process of law. The broad implications of such regulations were argued as follows:

> 'It is, however, contended, that, although the state may prohibit the manufacture of intoxicating liquors for sale or barter within her limits, for general use as a beverage, 'no convention or legislature has the right, under our form of government, to prohibit any citizen from manufacturing for his own use, or for export, or storage, any article of food or drink not endangering or affecting the rights of others.' The argument made in support of the first branch of this proposition, briefly stated, is, that in the implied compact between the state and the citizen, certain rights are reserved by the latter, which are guaranteed by the constitutional provision protecting persons against being deprived of life, liberty, or property, without due process of law, and with which the State cannot interfere; that among those rights is that of manufacturing for one's use either food or drink; and that while, according to the doctrines of the commune, the state may control the tastes, appetites, habits, dress, food, and drink of the people, our system of government, based upon the individuality and intelligence of the citizen, does not claim to control him, except as to his conduct to others, leaving him the sole judge as to all that only affects himself.'

In this case the Court sustained the legislation because to permit individual manufacture 'would tend to cripple, if it did not defeat, the effort to guard the community' and ruled:

> 'No one may rightfully do that which the law-making power, upon reasonable grounds, declares to be prejudicial to the general welfare.'

No such enforcement problem can be urged to sustain the legislation here in question.

Does a direct relationship to the public, health, safety and welfare exist in the present case?

It is urged that the motorcycle is susceptible to loss of control because it has just two wheels and that other vehicles frequently pick up stones from the road or roadside and throw them at the head of the cyclist causing him to lose control and cross the centerline or otherwise injure others. This was the basis of two New York rulings. In *People v. Schmidt*, 283 N.Y.S.2d 290 (Co. Ct. 1967), the court said:

> 'The remaining question concerns the power of the state to regulate individual conduct. The court takes judicial notice of certain dangers inherent in the operation of motorcycles as compared to that of automobiles. The danger of flying stones or other objects from the wheels of moving vehicles is a real one. A blow on the head of a cyclist not only could endanger himself, but be the cause of injury or death to other users of the public highways. To prevent such possible occurrences is a valid objective for legislative action under the general police power of the state.'

And in *People v. Bielmeyer*, 282 N.Y.S.2d 797 (City Ct. 1967), the court reasoned:

> 'The old joke about the happy motorcyclist—'the one with the bugs on his teeth'—is not too funny when one hears or reads about instances where cyclists have been hit with hard-shelled beetles or bees and have lost control of their bikes, causing damage and injuries to others.'

The New York judge pointed out that motorcyclists normally ride near the edge of the road. In Michigan the law so requires. * * *

Nevertheless, such reasoning is obviously a strained effort to justify what is admittedly wholesome legislation.[9] If the purpose truly were to deflect flying objects, rather than to reduce cranial injuries, a windshield requirement imposed on the manufacturer would bear a reasonable relationship to the objective and not vary from the norm of safety legislation customarily imposed on the manufacturer for the protection of the public rather than upon the individual.

The Attorney General further contends that the State has an interest in the 'viability' of its citizens and can legislate to keep them healthy and self-supporting. This logic could lead to unlimited paternalism. A further contention pertains to the doctrine of *Parens patriae*, the special relationship of the State to youth, but this has little merit since the statute is not so limited.

* * *

This statute has a relationship to the protection of the individual motorcyclist from himself, but not to the public health, safety and welfare.

A discussion of the problem leads one to speculate on an analogy to suicide. This was a common law crime (4 Blackstone, *Homicide*, (Chap. 14 (Gavit's ed., 1940,), p. 830). * * * but it is not a statutory crime in

---

9. Michigan State Police datum 1962–66 (Exhibit A) show a mortality rate of 11.5 for 10,000 registrations of motorcycles, as compared with 5.2 per 10,000 for all vehicles in the same period.

Michigan. Our attorney general has opined that we did not adopt that part of the common law because of the abhorrent penalty. 1943 OAG 342.

Plaintiffs rely also upon the reserved powers under the Ninth Amendment to the United States Constitution and cites the recent decision[10] wherein Justice Goldberg, concurring, invoked this amendment to invalidate a Connecticut statute making the use of contraceptives a criminal offense. In holding that the use of contraceptives by the individual was a private right of the individual free from State coercion and control, he equated this right with the right 'to be let alone'. Justice Louis Brandeis stated this principle in his famous dissent in *Olmstead v. United States*, 277 U.S. 438, 478 (1928).

> 'The makers of our Constitution * * * sought to protect Americans in their beliefs, their thoughts, their emotions and their sensations. They conferred, as against the government, the right to be let alone-the most comprehensive of rights and the right most valued by civilized men. * * *
>
> 'Experience should teach us to be most on our guard to protect liberty when the government's purposes are beneficent. Men born to freedom are naturally alert to repel invasion of their liberty by evilminded rulers. The greatest dangers to liberty lurk in insidious encroachment by men of zeal, well-meaning but without understanding.'

The precedential consequences of 'stretching our imagination'[11] to find a relationship to the public health, safety and welfare, require the invalidation of this statute.

Reversed, but without costs, it being a public question.

Adrian v. Poucher

Court of Appeals of Michigan
67 Mich.App. 133 (1976)

■ PER CURIAM:

On June 14, 1974, defendant was cited by the Adrian City Police Department for not wearing a crash helmet while operating a motorcycle, a violation of a city ordinance. Defendant moved to quash the summons on the grounds that the ordinance is unconstitutional. The trial court held that ordinance unconstitutional basing its decision on our opinion in *American Motorcycle Association v. Department of State Police*, 11 Mich. App. 351 (1968).

* * *

---

10. *Griswold v. Connecticut*, 381 U.S. 479 (1965).

11. Judge Kaufman, *supra*, 'Here it just affects the individual, and while the individual is a member of the general public, his activity in doing what has been determined by the legislature to be a crime cannot in any way affect the general public unless one would stretch his imagination.'

The ordinance in question, § 6.23 of the Uniform Traffic Code, reads as follows:

> 'A person operating or riding on a motorcycle or motor driven cycle shall wear a crash helmet approved by the department of state police.'

The only issue raised on this appeal is whether the above ordinance is constitutional.

In *American Motorcycle Association v. Department of State Police*, *supra*, we held that a similar state statute was unconstitutional. This appeal challenges the validity of that decision. We held that the interest of the state in highway safety and in keeping its citizens healthy and self-supporting does not extend to requiring motorcyclists and their riders to wear crash helmets. The basis of that holding was that there is no real and substantial relationship between the statute and the protection of the public health, safety, morals or general welfare.

The controversy in this case centers around the proper exercise of the police power by the Legislature and the test of the legitimacy of an exercise of the police power. The city primarily argues that it is the Legislature's and not the court's function to determine what measures are proper subjects of the police power and that police regulations must be sustained unless so unreasonable and arbitrary as to invade fundamental constitutional rights. The city also asserts that the operation of a motor vehicle on the public highways is a privilege not a right, and that the Legislature's regulation of highway use is a proper exercise of the police power.

The defendant argues that it is not a proper function of the police power to protect the individual from his own acts; an individual is free to act according to his own notions of self-interest provided that what he does has no ill effect upon his fellow man. Defendant asserts that before the state can regulate individual conduct, it must demonstrate that such regulation is conducive to the public health, safety, morals or general welfare.

In reconsidering the issue raised by this appeal, we note that there is no paucity of authority on the subject. Courts in 29 states have held that legislation requiring the wearing of helmets by motorcyclists is constitutional. Several Federal courts have done the same, the United States Supreme Court affirming one such decision in *Simon v. Sargent*, 409 U.S. 1020 (1972). It appears that only one other state court has agreed with our holding in *American Motorcycle Association*, *supra*; *People v. Fries*, 42 Ill.2d 446 (1969).

In the instant case, the decisions of the courts below finding the ordinance in question unconstitutional were based solely upon the authority of *American Motorcycle Association*. Accordingly, we reexamine that decision to determine its validity.

The decision in *American Motorcycle Association*, *supra*, was based primarily upon a finding that the statute requiring motorcyclists to wear crash helmets was not a proper exercise of the police power. We failed to note, however, the proper test of legitimacy of the Legislature's exercise of the police power:

'The primary determination of public need and character of remedy in the exercise of the police power is in the legislature, and its statutes must be sustained unless the remedy is palpably unreasonable and arbitrary so as needlessly to invade property or personal rights as protected by the Constitution. *Carolene Products Co. v. Thomson*, 276 Mich. 172, (1936).

* * *

In neither *American Motorcycle Association*, *supra*, apparently, nor the instant case, was evidence presented by the parties challenging the validity of the legislation to overcome the presumption of validity. Nor is there any showing that the legislation affronted any of the party's constitutionally protected rights. * * *

We are not persuaded that the 'right to be let alone', at least in this case, or the fact that the legislation tends to protect particular individuals from their own folly warrants the conclusion that the measure is not a valid exercise of the police power. Nor can we say that a measure which seeks to protect a large number of individuals does not advance the health, safety or general welfare of the public in general. * * *

We are convinced that the reasoning of this Court in *American Motorcycle Association v. Department of State Police*, *supra*, was incorrect and decline to follow it.

The ordinance requiring motorcyclists to wear crash helmets is constitutionally valid. The judgment of the circuit court is reversed. No costs, a public question being involved.

Illinois v. Kohrig

Supreme Court of Illinois
113 Ill.2d 384 (1986)

■ PER CURIAM:

The defendants in these four consolidated cases were issued traffic citations for failure to wear seat safety belts while operating their motor vehicles on a street or highway in violation * * * of the Illinois Vehicle Code. * * * In each case, the trial court concluded that the section was unconstitutional and dismissed the charge. The State appealed each case * * * and the cases were consolidated for purposes of appeal. Only two of the four defendants * * * have filed briefs in this court; however, various parties have been permitted to file briefs as amicus curiae.

At issue is whether the section, which requires drivers of motor vehicles and their front-seat passengers to wear safety belts when driving on a public highway or street, violates the due process guarantees of the State and Federal constitutions. * * *

The section, which became effective on July 1, 1985, provides in part:

"(a) Each driver and front seat passenger of a motor vehicle operated on a street or highway in this State shall wear a properly adjusted and fastened seat safety belt; except that, a child less than 6 years of age shall be protected as required pursuant to the Child Passenger Protection Act. Each driver of a motor vehicle transporting a child 6 years of age or more, but less than 16 years of age, in the front seat of the motor vehicle shall secure the child in a properly adjusted and fastened seat safety belt." (Ill.Rev.Stat. 1985, ch. 95 ½, par. 12–603.1(a).)

The statute also provides that certain persons are exempt from complying with the seat-belt-use requirement, including persons with a written medical waiver from a physician or government agency; those persons frequently stopping and leaving the vehicle or delivering property from the vehicle if its speed between stops does not exceed 15 miles per hour; and drivers operating a vehicle in reverse. * * * Certain vehicles also are exempt from the statute's requirements, including motorcycles, motorized pedalcycles, and vehicles manufactured prior to 1965. * * * Violators of the section are guilty of a "petty offense and subject to a fine not to exceed $25." * * *

At the outset we note that, in reviewing the constitutionality of Illinois' mandatory-seat-belt law, this court does not join in the debate over whether the law is desirable or necessary. Our nation was founded in large part on the democratic principle that the powers of government are to be exercised by the people through their elected representatives in the legislature, subject only to certain constitutional limitations. Although this court has never hesitated to invalidate laws that it believes to be unconstitutional, we emphasize that our role is a limited one. The issue here in "not what the legislature should do but what the legislature can do." *Wichita v. White* 205 Kan. 408, 409 (1970).

[One defendant] contends that the section violates her fundamental right to privacy protected by the due process clause of the Fourteenth Amendment. * * * Additionally, both defendants argue that the section is beyond the police powers of the legislature and thus violates the due process clauses of the State and Federal constitutions. We first turn to the issue of whether the section violates defendants' fundamental right to privacy protected by the Fourteenth Amendment.

Regulations that limit a person's constitutional right to privacy may be justified only by a " 'compelling state interest,' " and the legislation "must be narrowly drawn to express only the legitimate state interests at stake." (*Roe v. Wade*, 410 U.S. 113, 115 (1973), * * *) However, " 'only personal rights that can be deemed "fundamental" or "implicit in the concept of ordered liberty" " (*Paris Adult Theatre I v. Slaton* 413 U.S. 49, 65 (1973), * * *) are included in the right of privacy guaranteed *by the Due Process Clause of the Fourteenth Amendment. The Supreme Court has selected only a few rights for such an esteemed status: the "privacy right encompasses and protects the personal intimacies of the home, the family, marriage, motherhood, procreation, and child rearing." *Paris Adult Theatre I v. Slaton* 413 U.S. 49, 65 (1973). * * *

[A]ttempts by litigants to expand the privacy right beyond matters relating to marriage, procreation, contraception, family relations, abortion, child rearing and education have largely been unsuccessful. See, *e.g.*, * * *

Kelley v. Johnson 425 U.S. 238, 244 (1976) (police officer does not have privacy right to choose hairstyle); * * * *Paris Adult Theatre I v. Slaton* 413 U.S. 49 (1973) (privacy right does not encompass right of adults to watch obscene movies in places of public accommodation).

In the present case it cannot be said that [the defendants'] claimed right to decide whether or not to wear a safety belt on a public highway resembles those liberties identified by the Supreme Court as being included in the right of privacy protected by the Fourteenth Amendment. Although the section in question implicates a person's interest in "liberty" in the sense that it restricts his freedom of choice, the law here does not regulate those intimate decisions relating to marriage, procreation, child rearing, education or family that have heretofore been recognized as deserving of heightened constitutional protection. * * * Nor do we think that the right to decide whether or not to wear a safety belt is "implicit in the concept of ordered liberty" such that "neither liberty nor justice would exist if [it] were sacrificed" * * *, or a liberty "deeply rooted in this Nation's history and tradition." * * * The States historically have been given a wide latitude to regulate the use of motor vehicles * * *, and the individual driver's autonomy on the road has, out of necessity for the public safety and welfare, been significantly curtailed by State regulation. * * * [W]e reject any notion that the right of privacy includes the right to "do one's thing" on an expressway:

> "There is no place where any such right to be let alone would be less assertable than on a modern highway with cars, trucks, busses and cycles whizzing by at sixty or seventy miles an hour. When one ventures onto such a highway, he must be expected and required to conform to public safety regulations and controls, including some that would neither have been necessary nor reasonable in the era of horse-drawn vehicles." *Bisenius v. Karns*, 42 Wis.2d 42, 55 (1969)

* * *

Defendants also argue that the section does not further the health, safety or welfare of the general public, asserting that the statute only protects the safety of the individual driver and passenger. They contend that since the section interferes with their right to decide whether or not to wear a safety belt, and has no corresponding public benefit, the statute exceeds the State's police power and violates the due process guarantees of the State and Federal constitutions.

It is well established that the legislatures, not the courts, have the primary role in our democratic society in deciding what the interests of the public require and in selecting the measures necessary to secure those interests. * * * Recognizing the legislature's broad power to provide for the public health, welfare and safety, the courts are hesitant to second-guess a legislative determination that a law is desirable or necessary. Only when the statute in question affects a fundamental constitutional right will the courts subject the legislation to strict or exacting scrutiny. * * *

In the present case we already have determined that the section here involved does not infringe upon the defendants' right of privacy protected by the Fourteenth Amendment, and defendants do not argue that the statute implicates any other fundamental constitutional right or liberty. * * * That is, the law will be upheld if it bears a rational relation to a legitimate legislative purpose and is neither arbitrary nor discriminatory. * * * Under the rational-basis test, a statute is presumed to be valid, and the party challenging the statute has the burden of proving that the statute is irrational. * * * As long as there is a conceivable basis for finding a rational relationship, the law will be upheld. * * *

In challenging the section as exceeding the scope of the State's police power, the defendants principally rely on the case of *People v. Fries*, 42 Ill.2d 446 (1969). In *Fries* the court held that a statute requiring the operator or passenger of a motorcycle to wear protective headgear was unconstitutional. The court reasoned that the purpose of the headgear requirement was to "safeguard the person wearing it" and was unrelated to the safety of the public at large. * * * It concluded that the statute constituted a "regulation of what is essentially a matter of personal safety" and exceeded the scope of the State's police power. * * * Here, too, defendants argue that the decision of whether or not to wear a safety belt is "essentially a matter of personal safety" and that any regulation restricting the individual's right to make such a decision exceeds the State's police power.

The State, on the other hand, maintains that *Fries* was wrongly decided, and it urges us to overrule that decision. It correctly notes that at present *Fries* stands alone in holding that a motorcycle helmet law is unconstitutional. The overwhelming weight of authority is that motorcycle-helmet laws are a valid exercise of the State's police power. * * * Alternatively, the State contends that the statute being challenged here promotes valid public interests and thus is distinguishable from the motorcycle helmet law found to be unconstitutional in *Fries*.

Defendants are correct in asserting that the primary goal of the section is to protect the individual driver and front-seat passenger from death or serious injury. As such, the statute interferes with the individual's choice concerning his or her personal safety. However, arriving at those conclusions does not ipso facto mean that the law is devoid of any public benefit and is unconstitutional. Regardless of a law's primary objective, it will be upheld if it bears a rational relation to a legitimate legislative purpose. * * * In that regard, the defendants have not persuaded us that the legislature could not have found that the law bears a rational relationship to a legitimate legislative purpose. The legislative debates clearly indicate that the legislators believed that safety-belt use would protect persons other than the belt wearers by helping drivers to maintain control of their vehicles, and that the law would promote that economic welfare of the State by reducing the public and private costs associated with serious injuries and deaths caused by automobile accidents. During debates in the House of Representatives, a principal sponsor of the safety-belt legislation remarked:

> "The Bill would not only protect drivers and passengers in the front seat, the Bill would also protect other people. It would protect other drivers. It would protect pedestrians on our high-

> ways and on our sidewalks. The reason for that, of course, is that even a minor * * * accident, can if * * * a car is driven by a person who doesn't have a seat belt, * * * result in that person losing control of the car and injuring other people on or about the car." (83d Ill.Gen.Assem., House Debates, May 16, 1984, at 212 (statement of Representative John Cullerton).)

Another legislator argues that if she were to drive an automobile without her safety belt fastened "and I lose control of my car, I am endangering others." * * * The Governor, in signing the seat-belt law, also agreed that the law would help drivers to maintain control of their vehicles and avoid accidents with other motorists and pedestrians:

> "Unbelted passengers in a motor vehicle literally become human projectiles in the event of a crash. Unbelted passengers can interfere with the ability of an operator to respond to the collision, and unbelted drivers may lose control of a vehicle and thus cause death and injury to others." Letter of Governor James R. Thompson to the General Assembly indicating his intent to sign House Bill 2800 (Jan. 8, 1985).

The State can enact laws aimed at reducing traffic accidents, since such laws are clearly related to the health, welfare and safety of the public. We also believe that the legislature could rationally conclude that unbelted drivers and passengers endanger the safety of others. In upholding a law similar to the one here under review, the court in *New York v. Weber*, 494 N.Y.S.2d 960 (1985) stated:

> "A driver who is injured or who is jolted away from his vehicle's controls during a skid or by an initial impact, may well be less able to prevent or minimize injuries caused by an accident. Also, an unrestrained occupant of a vehicle may injure others inside or out of the vehicle during an accident. The preventing or reduction of such an injury seems to the Court to be a valid State interest."

It also is conceivable that drivers who wear safety belts are less likely to fall asleep at the wheel, or to lose control of their vehicles in situations where the driver must apply the brakes suddenly, or in cases where a vehicle begins to skid or swerve. * * * Safety belts can also prevent passengers from being thrown against the driver. And, as the State observes, children and other occupants who are wearing safety belts are less likely to distract the driver. * * *

Defendants argue that there is no statistical evidence showing that seat-belt use helps the driver to maintain control of his vehicle and avoid accidents with other motorists or pedestrians. Even assuming this argument is correct, it is without merit. "The fact that a congressional directive reflects unprovable assumptions about what is good for the people is not a sufficient reason to find that statute unconstitutional" (*Paris Adult Theatre I v. Slaton* 413 U.S. 49, 62 (1973)), and a court "will not disturb a police regulation merely where there is room for a difference of opinion as to its wisdom, necessity and expediency." * * * Moreover, "the law need not be in every respect logically consistent with its aims to be constitutional. It is enough that there is an evil at hand for correction, and that it might be thought that the particular legislative measure was a rational way to correct it." (*Williamson v. Lee Optical of Oklahoma*, 348 U.S. 483, 488 (1955)). Here, we think that the legislature could rationally determine that the seat-belt-use law would serve the public safety and welfare by reducing the likelihood that a driver would lose control of his vehicle and jeopardize other motorists or pedestrians.

Another reason advanced by the State for the section is that the law promotes the economic welfare of the State by reducing the public costs associated with serious injuries and deaths caused by automobile accidents. The legislative history of the section indicates that legislators were concerned about the financial costs associated with highway accidents. Representative Cullerton remarked that the safety-belt legislation "would clearly save money," asserting that "it cost the State over 800,000 dollars for a 26 year old person who is made a paraplegic as a result of a car crash." * * * Another Representative stated: "The lives we save and the injuries that we avoid are the injuries and lives that we, the taxpayers, are very likely to be responsible for in the long run. We're not talking about somebody's own individual decision to end up in a car crash and find him or herself in a hospital for 20 years with that individual paying the bill. It's the taxpayers that are going to be paying those bills." * * * Senator James Philip, in urging passage of the seat-belt law, observed that "in 1982 in Illinois some seventy-five people were killed in automobiles [while] performing their job.... This costs Illinois employers some twelve million dollars." (83d Ill.Gen.Assem., Senate Debates, June 21, 1984, at 159 (statement of Senator James Philip).) * * * Governor Thompson, in explaining his reasons for signing the legislation, estimated that the seat belt law would "save more than 300 lives in Illinois in the first year, will avoid nearly 43,000 injuries and save more than $400 million in costs." Letter of Governor James R. Thompson to the General Assembly indicating his intent to sign House Bill 2800 (Jan. 8, 1985).

It cannot be seriously questioned that the police power may be used to promote the economic welfare of the State, its communities and its citizens. "[I]n the interest of general welfare, the police power may be exercised to protect citizens and their businesses in financial and economic matters, [and] it may be exercised to protect the government itself against potential financial loss." * * * A law whose aim is to reduce the private and public costs resulting from injuries and deaths caused by motor vehicle accidents is therefore within the police power of the State. In finding that a motorcycle helmet law was rationally related to the public welfare, the court in *Simon v. Sargent*, 346 F.Supp. 277, 279 (D.Mass.1972) stated:

> "From the moment of the injury, society picks the person up off the highway; delivers him to a municipal hospital and municipal doctors; provides him with unemployment compensation if, after recovery, he cannot replace his lost job, and, if the injury causes permanent disability, may assume the responsibility for his and his family's continued subsistence. We do not understand a state of mind that permits plaintiff to think that only he himself is concerned."

Because of the drain on private and public financial resources caused by highway accidents, society has a legitimate interest in minimizing injuries which result from such accidents. * * *

Defendants make several arguments concerning the effectiveness of safety belts in reducing injuries and arguments regarding the merits of alternative safety devices such as air bags. Defendants also contend that in some instances safety belts may cause injuries instead of preventing them. We need not consider these arguments, however, since they are proper subjects of discussion for the legislature, not the courts. * * * We believe that the General Assembly could reasonably assume that a law requiring drivers and front-seat passengers to wear safety belts will reduce traffic-related injuries and fatalities. * * * Therefore, we hold that section 12–603.1 does not violate the due process clauses of the State and Federal constitutions. To the extent that *People v. Fries*, 42 Ill.2d 446 (1969) is inconsistent with our opinion, it is overruled.

* * *

Picou v. Gillum

874 F.2d 1519 (11th Cir. 1989)

■ POWELL, ASSOCIATE JUSTICE.

The question presented is whether the federal Constitution prohibits Florida from requiring riders of motorcycles to wear protective headgear. We think Florida's statute a valid exercise of the State's police powers, and therefore affirm the district court.

I.

Appellant David L. Picou brought this suit against appellee Jim Gillum, Sheriff of Pasco County, Florida, and appellee James T. Russell, Florida State Attorney for Pasco County, seeking a declaratory judgment that Florida's mandatory motorcycle helmet law, Fla.Stat. § 316.211, is unconstitutional. The Florida statute provides in relevant part:

> (1) No person shall operate or ride upon a motorcycle unless he is properly wearing protective headgear securely fastened on his head which complies with standards established by the department.
>
> (2) No person shall operate a motorcycle unless he is wearing an eye-protective device over his eyes of a type approved by the department.

Appellant's complaint alleged that he uses a motorcycle as his primary means of transportation, that he wishes to ride without a helmet, and that appellees have enforced the statute by arresting and prosecuting violators in Pasco County and will continue to do so.

Appellant contended that the statute violated federal constitutional rights to Due Process, Equal Protection, and privacy. * * *

II.

This appeal presents us with the latest in a long line of challenges to the constitutionality of mandatory helmet laws. Helmet statutes have been the subject of numerous published opinions from state courts. Although a few courts in the late 1960's and early 1970's held motorcycle helmet laws unconstitutional,[1] each of these cases has been reversed or overruled. Courts in subsequent cases have uniformly upheld the provisions. Indeed, various constitutional challenges to Florida's statute have been rejected both by Florida courts, * * * and by a three-judge federal district court. * * *

A.

Appellant first relies on Supreme Court cases recognizing a right to privacy. The Due Process Clause of the Fourteenth Amendment embodies important protections against state intrusion on intimate and fundamental personal decisions. As in *Roe v. Wade*, 410 U.S. 113 (1973), and *Griswold v. Connecticut*, 381 U.S. 479 (1965), the right extends to reproductive decisions that are by their nature highly private. * * * But the rights involved in these cases do not resemble the right claimed here. There is little that could be termed private in the decision whether to wear safety equipment on the open road. Indeed, the Supreme Court has repeatedly declined to recognize a constitutional right that would cover appellant's case.

B.

Appellant concedes that his case is not covered by existing precedents defining the right to privacy. He contends, however, that those precedents stand for a broader proposition: that the Constitution protects the "right to be let alone." See *Bowers v. Hardwick*, 478 U.S. 186, 199 (1986) (BLACKMUN, J., dissenting); *Olmstead v. United States*, 277 U.S. 438, 478 (1928) (BRANDEIS, J., dissenting). He further casts his argument in terms of a right to be free from "paternalistic" legislation. In other words, appellant argues that the Constitution forbids enforcement of any statute aimed only at protecting a State's citizens from the consequences of their own foolish behavior and not at protecting others.

First, there is no broad legal or constitutional "right to be let alone" by government. In the complex society in which we live, the action and nonaction of citizens are subject to countless local, state, and federal laws and regulations. Bare invocation of a right to be let alone is an appealing rhetorical device, but it seldom advances legal inquiry, as the "right"—to the extent it exists—has no meaning outside its application to specific activities. The Constitution does protect citizens from government interference in many areas—speech, religion, the security of the home. But the unconstrained right asserted by appellant has no discernable bounds, and bears little resemblance to the important but limited privacy rights recog-

1. See *People v. Fries*, 42 Ill.2d 446 (1969), *overruled*, *People v. Kohrig*, 113 Ill.2d 384 (1986), 101 Ill.Dec. 650, 498 N.E.2d 1158 (1986); . . . *American Motorcycle Ass'n v. Davids*, 11 Mich. App. 351 (1968) *abrogated by Adrian v. Poucher*, 67 Mich. App. 133 (1976). These courts found that helmet laws were beyond the police power of the State because they were intended to safeguard only the cyclist, and did not benefit the public.

nized by our highest Court. As the Court has stated, "the protection of a person's *general* right to privacy—his right to be let alone by other people—is like the protection of his property and his very life, left largely to the law of the individual States." *Katz v. United States*, 389 U.S. 347, 350–51 (1967) (citations omitted).

Whatever merit may exist in appellant's further contention that paternalistic legislation is necessarily invalid, this argument is inapplicable to Fla.Stat. § 316.211. The helmet requirement does not implicate appellant alone. Motorcyclists normally ride on public streets and roads that are maintained and policed by public authorities. Traffic is often heavy, and on highways proceeds at high rates of speed. The required helmet and face-shield may prevent a rider from becoming disabled by flying objects on the road, which might cause him to lose control and involve other vehicles in a serious accident. * * *

It is true that a primary aim of the helmet law is prevention of unnecessary injury to the cyclist himself. But the costs of this injury may be borne by the public. A motorcyclist without a helmet is more likely to suffer serious head injury than one wearing the prescribed headgear. State and local governments provide police and ambulance services, and the injured cyclist may be hospitalized at public expense. If permanently disabled, the cyclist could require public assistance for many years. As Professor Tribe has expressed it, "[in] a society unwilling to abandon bleeding bodies on the highway, the motorcyclist or driver who endangers himself plainly imposes costs on others." L. Tribe, *American Constitutional Law* § 15–12, at 1372 (2d ed. 1988). * * * [W]e think Florida's helmet requirement a rational exercise of its police powers.

III.

There is a strong tradition in this country of respect for individual autonomy and mistrust of paternalistic legislation. Appellant, like many of his predecessors in helmet law cases, cites John Stuart Mill for the proposition that "the only purpose for which power can rightfully be exercised over any member of a civilised community, against his will, is to prevent harm to others. His own good, either physical or moral, is not a sufficient warrant." John Mill, *On Liberty* (1859). In fact, Thomas Jefferson presaged Mill by three quarters of century, writing in 1787 that "the legitimate powers of government extend to such acts only as are injurious to others." *Notes on the State of Virginia* in *Jefferson, Writings* 285 (Library of America ed. 1984) But the impressive pedigree of this political ideal does not readily translate into a constitutional right.

Legislatures and not courts have the primary responsibility for balancing conflicting interests in safety and individual autonomy. Indeed, the evidence suggests that arguments asserting the importance of individual autonomy may prevail in the political process. In the mid–1970's, opponents of helmet requirements successfully lobbied for amendment of a federal law that allowed withholding of federal highway funds from States without helmet statutes. See Dardis & Lefkowitz, *Motorcycle Helmet Laws: A Case Study of Consumer Protection,* 21 JOURNAL OF CONSUMER AFFAIRS 202 (1987). More recently, Massachusetts' mandatory seatbelt law was repealed by referendum after opponents attacked it as an infringement on personal liberties. See, e.g., Mandatory Seat Belt Foes Boycott Hearing, *The Boston Globe,* March, 9, 1989, at 16.

Subsequent studies suggest that repeal of these safety measures can have a substantial cost in lives and property. See, e.g., Dardis & Lefkowitz, *supra*; Prinzinger, *The Effect of the Repeal of Helmet Use Laws on Motorcycle Fatalities,* 10 ATLANTIC ECONOMIC JOURNAL 36 (1982). But it is no more our role to impose a helmet requirement on this ground than to invalidate Florida's helmet law on the grounds urged by appellant. Although a narrow range of privacy rights are shielded from the political process by the Constitution, the desirability of laws such as the Florida helmet requirement is a matter for citizens and their elected representatives to decide.

IV.

We think the district court was correct to conclude that appellant "has shown no reason in history, in policy, or in logic why a constitutional right should extend to his decision to forego a motorcycle helmet." The judgment of the district court is therefore

Affirmed.

Questions

1. Do people tend to oppose seatbelts and motorcycle helmets on similar grounds? Do similar motivations stand behind mandatory seatbelts and mandatory helmets?

2. In *National Federation of Independent Business,*[74] the federal government argued "that because sickness and injury are unpredictable but unavoidable," mandating minimum health insurance coverage 'merely regulates how individuals finance and pay for [health care services,] requiring that they do so through insurance, rather than through * * * shifting costs to others.' "[75] Some accidents, sickness, and injuries *are* avoidable. The costs of accidents, sickness, and injuries can be reduced. (a) Should society adopt regulations that prevent cost shifting through accidents? (b) Should society restrict or ban the use of motorcycles? (c) What are the similarities and differences between individual health care mandates and mandatory seatbelts (or helmets)?

3. *National Federation of Independent Business* was about the authority of the federal government to mandate health insurance. What are the pros and cons of state regulation of seatbelts and motorcycle helmets?

4. Should society replace the requirement for seatbelts and helmets with a tax that would measure the cost of an unbuckled driver (or passenger) and a motorcyclist without a helmet? Should society offer such a tax as an optional measure for car owners, passengers, and motorcyclists who would like to preserve their freedom of choice?

---

74. National Federation of Independent Business v. Sebelius, 132 S.Ct. 2566 (2012).

75. *Id.* at 2589–2590 (Roberts, C.J.).

§ 4.6 SYSTEMIC RISK, TOO BIG TO FAIL, AND GOVERNMENT RELIEF

§ 4.6.1 *What Is Systemic Risk?*

Systemic risk is a general risk resulting from interdependent actions of many parties. It is a "general risk" in the sense that it affects all parties in the relevant system—the community, economy, or society. The characteristics of the market participants (firms and individuals) and the nature of their actions determine their effect on the market risk. The London Millennium Bridge (LMB) illuminates one type of systemic risk. In 1996, *The Financial Times* newspaper and London's Southwark Borough Council launched a competition to design the first new footbridge across the Thames in more than a century. Construction of the new footbridge—the Millennium Bridge—began in April 1999. On its opening day, June 10, 2000, approximately 80,000 pedestrians used the new bridge. Although the bridge was designed to carry the weight of such traffic, it developed an unpleasant wobble. The bridge engineers insisted LMB would not collapse, but on June 12 the City closed it to traffic. Subsequent studies discovered that pedestrians' footsteps caused the bridge to sway and twist. Pedestrians responded to these oscillations by adjusting their gait, thereby increasing movement of the bridge.[76] Moreover, engineers realized that this phenomenon had many other examples in history.[77] In the case of swaying bridges, although the effect of every pedestrian on the vibrations is insignificant, these effects were not uniform. The pedestrian's weight and location on the bridge determine his contribution to the increasing oscillations.

Using our framework from Chapter 3, systemic risk is a network externality, in which risk is the externality.[78] One's use of a system—a bridge, the banking system, a communication network, or another—influences the general risk in the system that applies to all other users. Thus, because systemic risks are externalities, familiar motivations for state regulation apply. Furthermore, our discussion of externalities focused on Coasean bargaining as an alternative for state regulation of externalities. We saw that, under certain conditions, markets may address externalities efficiently. As the example of the London Millennium Bridge illustrates, however, informational problems and transaction costs *may* impede the possibility of market solutions to systemic risks. First and foremost, the relevant parties are often unaware of the risk and their contribution to the risk. Second, the complexity of the risk as an outcome of interdependent actions could forestall successful negotiations. Systemic risks exist in many

---

76. *See generally* Steven H. Strogatz et al., *Crowd Synchrony on the Millennium Bridge*, 483 NATURE 43 (2005); Ian Sample, *The Bridge of Sways*, NEW SCIENTIST, Mar. 31, 2001, at 38.

77. *See, e.g.*, John H.G. Macdonald, *Lateral Excitation of Bridges by Balancing Pedestrians*, 465 PROCEEDINGS OF THE ROYAL SOCIETY A 1055 (2008); STEVEN H. STROGATZ, SYNC: THE EMERGING SCIENCE OF SPONTANEOUS ORDER 153–178 (2003). *See also* LEON GLASS & MICHAEL C. MACKEY, FROM CLOCKS TO CHAOS (1988).

78. *See* § 3.5.

markets—health, energy, environment, and others—but are particularly salient in the financial system.

§ 4.6.2 *Too Big to Fail (TBTF)*

In the case of the London Millennium Bridge, the relative effects of pedestrians were not uniform, but no single pedestrian was particularly dominant. In other contexts, the effects of certain parties can be overwhelming. These market participants may be so large or strategically located that they have an extraordinary influence on systemic risks. For example, in the financial system, some institutions are very large or have a unique significance to the system. Because of the outsized influence such institutions have on systemic risk, they are defined as *systemically important financial institutions* (SIFIs).[79] The Great Recession and the bailouts that followed it sparked bitter controversies over a related term—"too big to fail" (TBTF). The TBTF concept suggests that the government will rescue a private entity whose collapse could threaten the viability of the financial market.[80] Many oppose such government reliefs. TBTF institutions are firms that because of their size are believed to be SIFIs (or systemically important in a non-financial market).

SIFIs (and TBTF institutions) raise concerns because our modern financial system relies on a high degree of interconnectedness among financial institutions. This interconnectedness reduces the costs of liquidity on the market: firms and individuals can do more with less cash, since financial institutions mobilize capital among themselves.[81] Interconnectedness, however, also enhances systemic risks. In a financial grid, liquidity or solvency problems of a systemically important institution can send shock waves throughout the entire system.[82] During the Great Recession, the collapse of Bear Stearns, Lehman Brothers, and AIG turned to threaten the viability of the entire financial system.

§ 4.6.3 *Government Regulation and Relief*

In October 2008, Congress passed the Emergency Economic Stabilization Act,[83] which rescued some of the key financial institutions that fed the housing bubble and several other private firms, such as the American car

---

79. Section 803(9) of the Dodd–Frank Wall Street Reform and Consumer Protection Act, Pub. L. No. 111–203, 129 Stat. 1377 (2009) defines the terms "systemically important" and "systemic importance" as:

> "[A] situation where the failure of or a disruption to the functioning of a financial market utility or the conduct of a payment, clearing, or settlement activity could create, or increase, the risk of significant liquidity or credit problems spreading among financial institutions or markets and thereby threaten the stability of the financial system of the United States."

80. *See generally* ANDREW ROSS SORKIN, TOO BIG TO FAIL (2009). *See also* GARY H. STERN & RON J. FELDMAN, TOO BIG TO FAIL: THE HAZARDS OF BANK BAILOUTS (2004).

81. *See generally* Jean Tirole, *Illiquidity and All Its Friends*, 49 JOURNAL OF ECONOMIC LITERATURE 287 (2011).

82. *See generally* Franklin Allen & Douglas Gale, *Financial Contagion*, 108 JOURNAL OF POLITICAL ECONOMY 1 (2000); Douglas M. Gale & Shachar Kariv, *Financial Networks*, 97 AMERICAN ECONOMIC REVIEW 99 (2007).

83. Pub. L. No. 110–343, 122 Stat. 3765 (Oct. 3, 2008).

manufacturers. This relief package, the so-called "bailout," caused public outrage. In January 2010, President Obama declared that "[n]ever again will the American taxpayer be held hostage by a bank that is 'too big to fail.' "[84] We conclude our discussion of risk with three observations regarding government commitments not to rescue TBTF institutions or not to respond to catastrophes.

First, these commitments are not credible. Government reliefs are controversial mostly because they create *moral hazard* problems: a person who knows that the government will bail her out if she fails is encouraged to take more and greater risks.[85] Objections to bailouts and reliefs rely on the idea that rescue of failing entities or relief to crisis victims undermines incentives to act responsibly. Putting aside the question whether individuals and firms are likely to prepare well to certain risks,[86] in many circumstances the objections are purely theoretical. Society cannot afford a financial catastrophe in order to punish a rogue financial institution or discipline careless individuals and institutions. Moreover, society is unlikely to be willing to take the risk of a financial catastrophe to engage in such disciplinary actions. The same point applies to other forms of government reliefs for catastrophes. Graphic images of catastrophes—terror attacks, earthquakes, wildfires, hurricanes, and deadly epidemics—generate public willingness to pay for reliefs. The decision to extend relief may be unwise and unjustified for many reasons, but public sentiments tend to require it. Commitments to ignore future cries for aid sentiments are just not realistic.[87]

Second, as we have seen,[88] *ex ante* investments in risk management are likely to reduce the costs of catastrophes. Using Calabresi's framing of the axiomatic principal function of accident law,[89] the question is only how society can reduce the sum of the costs of accidents and avoiding accidents. To the extent that *ex ante* regulation may reduce the cost of the catastrophe, than society should focus on such *ex ante* measures rather than *ex post* debates over why reliefs are provided. In *Picou v. Gillum*, the Eleventh Circuit cited Professor Laurence Tribe's treatise *American Constitutional Law*: "In a society unwilling to abandon bleeding bodies on the highway, the motorcyclist or driver who endangers himself plainly imposes costs on

---

84. Remarks by President Barack Obama on Financial Reform (January 21, 2010), available at *regti.me/Obama-bailout* (case sensitive).

85. *See generally* Louis Kaplow, *Incentives and Government Relief for Risk*, 4 JOURNAL OF RISK & UNCERTAINTY 167 (1991); *See also* Kenneth Ayotte & David A. Skeel, *Bankruptcy or Bailouts*, 35 JOURNAL OF CORPORATION LAW 469 (2010); Jeffrey A. Miron, *Bailout or Bankruptcy*, 29 CATO JOURNAL 1 (2009).

86. *See* §§ 4.1, 7.4.

87. *See generally* Amihai Glazer, *Politics and the Choice of Durability*, 79 AMERICAN ECONOMIC REVIEW 1207 (1989); Dani Rodrik & Richard Zeckhauser, *The Dilemma of Government Responsiveness*, 7 JOURNAL OF POLICY ANALYSIS & MANAGEMENT 601 (1988).

88. *See* § 3.1.2c.

89. *See* § 4.1.1.

others."[90] This rationale applies to all instances in which one party externalizes risks to others.

Third, after a decision to extend government relief is made, it is much more important to design a plan that serves society, rather than debating the wisdom of the decision that was made. Not all bailouts and government reliefs are alike. The government response to Hurricane Katrina in 2005 was a costly operational failure.[91] The bailout package of October 2008 rescued the economy; however, it also greatly benefitted the financial institutions that caused the crisis.[92] By way of comparison, in October 2011, while structuring a bailout for the Greek economy, the chancellor of Germany Angela Merkel forced the banking system to forego 50% of the Greek debt, reducing the costs of the bailout for taxpayers.[93] Put simply, the design of the government relief determines its costs to the taxpayer and its value to society.

In sum, when a systemic risk materializes, it tends to have the features of a "catastrophe" (a low probability, high-loss event). At that point, the state is very likely to extend some relief. From a practical perspective, it is foolish to pile objections to regulation of systemic risks and cry when reliefs are extended.

---

90. *See* Picou v. Gillum, 874 F.2d 1519 (11th Cir. 1989); § 4.5.

91. HURRICANE KATRINA LESSONS LEARNED STAFF, THE FEDERAL RESPONSE TO HURRICANE KATRINA: LESSONS LEARNED (Feb. 2006).

92. *See* Pietro Veronesi & Luigi Zingales, *Paulson's Gift*, 97 JOURNAL OF FINANCIAL ECONOMICS 339 (2010).

93. *See* Steven Erlanger & Stephen Castle, *Merkel Called Bankers' Bluff, Getting Europe a Financial Plan*, NEW YORK TIME, October 28, 2011, at A1.

CHAPTER 5

INADEQUATE INFORMATION

"Then you should say what you mean," the March Hare went on.

"I do," Alice hastily replied; "at least I mean what I say—that's the same thing you know."

"Not the same thing a bit!" said the Hatter. "Why you might just as well say that 'I see what I eat' is the same thing as 'I eat what I see'!"

"You might just as well say," added the March Hare "that 'I like what I get' is that the same thing as 'I get what I like'!"

—LEWIS CARROLL, ALICE'S ADVENTURES IN WONDERLAND

§ 5.1 WHAT IS INADEQUATE INFORMATION?

Question: *What inadequate information motivates regulation?* **Answer:** *Any inconvenient information or informational gap.* Our discussion of the Coase Theorem stressed that information is a critical ingredient in negotiations and transactions.[1] We saw that regulation, which improves information, may be superior to control-and-command measures because when individuals and firms have adequate information they can conclude private transactions that promote societal interests. With adequate information, market solutions for externalities may emerge and state regulation may be unnecessary. A corollary of this informational efficiency is that information adversarial parties possess influences the level of litigation, because when the parties have adequate information they have incentives to save legal fees and settle disputes.[2]

The traditional analysis of economic regulation indeed posits that markets can be competitive only when individuals and firms have adequate information to carry out transactions.[3] Therefore, insufficient, wrong, or misleading information may motivate government intervention.[4] By con-

1. *See supra* § 3.1.2a.

2. *See generally* Lucian Bebchuck, *Litigation and Settlement under Imperfect Information*, 15 RAND JOURNAL OF ECONOMICS 404 (1984); Andrew F. Daughety & Jennifer F. Reinganum, *Hush Money*, 30 RAND JOURNAL OF ECONOMICS 661 (1999).

3. *See, e.g.*, STEPHEN BREYER, REGULATION AND ITS REFORM 26–28 (1982); Friedrich A. Hayek, *The Use of Knowledge in Society*, 35 AMERICAN ECONOMIC REVIEW 519 (1945); Joseph E. Stiglitz, *Imperfect Information in the Product Market*, in HANDBOOK OF INDUSTRIAL ORGANIZATION, vol. I, 769 (Richard Schmalensee & Robert Willig eds. 1989).

4. *See, e.g.*, Phillip Nelson, *Information and Consumer Behavior*, 78 JOURNAL OF POLITICAL ECONOMY 311 (1970); Edward P. Lazear, *Bait and Switch*, 103 JOURNAL OF POLITICAL ECONOMY

trast, our discussion of the pursuit of self-interest highlighted inconvenient information that individuals and firms may prefer to keep private, such as unflattering reports and images.[5] We saw that privacy and defamation laws provide some protection against the dissemination of information that may be regarded as inadequate for public distribution.[6] By extension, paternalistic policies sometimes suppress information that is believed to disserve social order.[7] Invasion of privacy and defamation are certain forms of *informational externalities*, which are the ways in which information affects others' well-being.[8]

Negative informational externalities that motivate regulation include certain patterns of sexual harassment, racism, and bullying.[9] Frivolous demands for information offer another example for a negative informational externality.[10] Positive informational externalities that may motivate regulation include inventions, knowledge, creative works, and brands.[11] The ability of a person to obtain an unauthorized copy of a movie and the confidential customer list of his competitor or to produce a knockoff handbag reflects positive informational externalities. The person benefits

---

813 (1995); George J. Stigler, *The Economics of Information*, 69 JOURNAL OF POLITICAL ECONOMY 213 (1961)

5. *See supra* § 2.2.2a. *See also* Daughety & Reinganum, *Hush Money*, *supra* note 2; Owen M. Fiss, *Against Settlement*, 93 YALE LAW JOURNAL 1073 (1984); Alan E. Garfield, *Promises of Silence: Contract Law and Freedom of Speech*, 83 CORNELL LAW REVIEW 261 (1998).

6. *Id. See also* Melville B. Nimmer, *The Right of Publicity*, 19 LAW & CONTEMPORARY PROBLEMS 203 (1954).

7. *See* §§ 7.1, 7.2, 10.2.

8. For externalities *see* Chapter 3. For informational externalities *see generally* Kenneth J. Arrow, *Economic Welfare and the Allocation of Resources for Invention*, in THE RATE AND DIRECTION OF ECONOMIC ACTIVITY: ECONOMIC AND SOCIAL FACTORS 609 (1962); Jack Hirshleifer, *The Private and Social Value of Information and the Reward to Inventive Activity*, 61 AMERICAN ECONOMIC REVIEW 451 (1971); Sanford J. Grossman, *The Existence of Futures Markets, Noisy Rational Expectations and Informational Externalities*, 44 REVIEW OF ECONOMIC STUDIES 431 (1977); Jeremy C. Stein, *Informational Externalities and Welfare-Reducing Speculation*, 95 JOURNAL OF POLITICAL ECONOMY 1123 (1987); Eugene Volokh, *Crime-Facilitating Speech*, 57 STANFORD LAW REVIEW 1095 (2005).

9. *See, e.g.*, Jack M. Balkin, *Free Speech and Hostile Environments*, 99 COLUMBIA LAW REVIEW 2295 (1999); Kingsley R. Browne, *Title VII As Censorship: Hostile-Environment Harassment and the First Amendment*, 52 OHIO STATE LAW JOURNAL 481 (1991); JOHN B. GOULD, SPEAK NO EVIL: THE TRIUMPH OF HATE SPEECH REGULATION (2005); Eugene Volokh, *Freedom of Speech and Workplace Harassment*, 39 UCLA LAW REVIEW 1791 (1992); Eugene Volokh, *What Speech Does "Hostile Work Environment" Harassment Law Restrict?*, 85 GEORGETOWN LAW JOURNAL 627 (1997); JEREMY WALDRON, THE HARM IN HATE SPEECH (2012).

10. The noisy demands for the birth certificate of President Barack Obama exemplify this point. *See, e.g.*, Kirk Johnson, *Despite the Evidence, 'Birther' Bills Advance*, N.Y. TIMES, Apr. 22, 2011, at A11; Joel Achenbach, *Certificate Unlikely to Appease 'Birthers'*, WASHINGTON POST, Apr. 28, 2011, at A1; Michael D. Shear, *Citing 'Silliness,' Obama Shows Birth Certificate*, N.Y. TIMES, Apr. 28, 2011, at A1; Tamara Audi, *President's Birthplace Is Ballot Issue in Arizona*, WALL STREET JOURNAL, May 21, 2012, at A4; Tamara Audi, *Hawaii Verifies Obama Birth; Arizona Says Case Closed*, WALL STREET JOURNAL, May 24, 2012, at A5. President Obama's Remarks on the issue are available at *regti.me/O-birth* (case sensitive). In May 2012, Hawaii issued for Arizona Secretary of State a Verification of Birth that confirms the validity of President Obama's birth certificate. The document is available at *regti.me/AZ-O* (case sensitive).

11. *See* § 10.3 (discussing disclosures and health).

from the investments of others in creating inventions, knowledge, creative works, and brands. The primary function of intellectual property laws is to address informational externalities.[12]

Other informational externalities are associated with heuristics and cognitive biases. For example, *herd behavior* describes the tendency to follow others rather than following solid information.[13] Such a tendency helps individuals to save time when others take reasonable actions, but it can also fail people when others follow "irrational exuberance" during a bubble period.[14] We have also seen that misperceptions of risks are very prevalent.[15] Heuristics and cognitive biases influence our perceptions of reality and risk analysis, but adequate information may improve individual decisionmaking.

Finally, when we discussed network externalities we saw that standard ownership may give private entities control over information to which many people have access, and such control may raise concerns.[16]

In sum, inadequate information as a motivation for regulation may mean insufficient information, misleading information, or confusing information. In reality, demands for information regulation may be expressed in many ways.[17] Here, we discuss the key forms of motivations for information regulation. As we shall see, in many settings, there *are* good objective reasons to consider information regulation. However, the concept of "inadequate information" is somewhat analogous to beauty in the sense that both (or the perceptions of both) are in the eye of the beholder. The meaning of "inadequate information" may vary with the precision of the analysis and its assumptions, as well as the ideologies, beliefs, and situational factors of the person who conducts the analysis.

Questions

In September 1977, *Arizona Law Review* published an issue dedicated to "Arizona Appellate Decisions 1976–77."[18] The opening note of the issue stated:

> For the tenth consecutive year, the *Arizona Law Review* presents the "Arizona Note" issue, a review of recent Arizona appellate

---

12. *See, e.g.*, Beth Allen, *Information as an Economic Commodity*, 80 AMERICAN ECONOMIC REVIEW 268 (1990); Arrow, *Economic Welfare and the Allocation of Resources for Invention*, *supra* note 8; Hirshleifer, *The Private and Social Value of Information and the Reward to Inventive Activity*, *supra* note 8; Melville B. Nimmer, *The Law of Ideas*, 27 SOUTHERN CALIFORNIA LAW REVIEW 119 (1954).

13. *See generally* Sushil Bikhchandani et al., A Theory of Fads, Fashion, Custom, and Cultural Change as Informational Cascades, 100 JOURNAL OF POLITICAL ECONOMY 992 (1992).

14. *See* § 1.1.3.

15. *See* § 4.1.

16. *See* § 3.5. *See also* LAWRENCE LESSIG, CODE: AND OTHER LAWS OF CYBERSPACE, VERSION 2.0 (2006).

17. *See generally* Alan Schwartz & Louis L. Wilde, *Intervening in Markets on the Basis of Imperfect Information: A Legal and Economic Analysis*, 127 UNIVERSITY OF PENNSYLVANIA LAW REVIEW 630 (1979).

18. 19(3) ARIZONA LAW REVIEW (1977).

decisions and a Ninth Circuit case. The purpose of the "Arizona Note" issue is twofold: to develop the research, writing, and analytical skills of the first year candidates, and to provide the legal community with in-depth analyses of selected recent cases. The casenotes represent a joint effort on the part of the candidates and the editorial board, with candidates engaging in rigorous research and writing and the editors working closely with the candidates at every stage of the process. The result, we trust, is a quality overview of recent developments in Arizona law.

Figure 5.1

ARIZONA LAW REVIEW

VOLUME 19

1977

Published by
The College of Law of
The University of Arizona

COPYRIGHT © 1978

By the Arizona Board of Regents

The thirteenth note in the issue analyzed the "Arizona case of *In Ronwin* [that] exemplifie[d] the difficulties of balancing * * * the rights of the public and the rights of practicing attorneys and applicants to the [legal] profession to assure that fair and adequate standards are maintained."[19] In July 1976, the Arizona Supreme Court denied Edward Ronwin's motion seeking admission to the bar or, alternatively, permission to retake the bar exam, holding that Ronwin failed to demonstrate that he was mentally able to engage in the active and continuous practice of law."[20] Writing for the Court, Justice Frank Gordon noted "that there is significant expert testimony in the record to indicate that Ronwin has a 'paranoid personality' which is characterized by hypersensitivity, rigidity, unwarranted suspicion, excessive self-importance and a tendency to blame others and ascribe evil motives to them."[21] The casenote examined "the construction given to the Arizona Supreme Court rule requiring that an applicant be mentally * * * able to engage in [the] active and continuous practice of law," and diligently analyzed the "method of evaluation used [by the Court] to determine Ronwin's mental fitness."[22] Mr. Ronwin brought defamation action against the casenote author, the editor, and the Arizona Board of Regents as the copyright holders. Ronwin demanded that *Arizona Law Review* "print either a retraction or an article that [he] had prepared. Ronwin's proposed article contended that the Arizona Supreme Court's opinion was the result of fraud, perjured testimony and conspiracy."[23] The district court and the Ninth Circuit dismissed Ronwin claims.

1. Mr. Ronwin tried to use litigation to address an informational issue. What was the issue? What was the best remedy Mr. Ronwin could obtain? Could Ronwin's defamation action have any regulatory effects?

2. In 1998, a group of researchers, led by Dr. Andrew Wakefield, published an article in the prestigious medical journal *The Lancet* that linked the measles, mumps, and rubella (MMR) vaccination to autism.[24] In January 2010, a Fitness to Practise Panel of the UK General Medical Council issued a judgment determining that the researchers had no evidence to support their claims. A few days later *The Lancet* retracted the 1998 article, stating: "Following the judgment of the UK General Medical Council's Fitness to Practise Panel, * * * it has become clear that several elements of the 1998 paper by Wakefield et al. are incorrect. * * * In particular, the claims in the original paper * * * have been proven to be false. Therefore we fully retract this paper from the published record."[25] Dr. Wakefield's article and public engagements eroded the public trust in the MMR vaccine and vaccination in general.[26]

---

19. *Admission to the Bar: Mental Fitness, Requirements in Arizona—In re Ronwin*, 19 ARIZONA LAW REVIEW 672 (1977). The casenotes were published anonymously. Bruce Dickinson who wrote the note later became an Editor-in-Chief of the law review.

20. *In re Ronwin*, 113 Ariz. 357, 359 (1976).

21. *Id.*

22. *Admission to the Bar*, *supra* note 16, at 673.

23. Ronwin v. Shapiro, 657 F.2d 1071 (9th Cir. 1981).

24. A. J. Wakefield et al., *Ileal–Lymphoid–Nodular Hyperplasia, Non–Specific Colitis, and Pervasive Developmental Disorder in Children*, 351 LANCET 637 (1998).

25. *Retraction*, 375 LANCET 445 (Feb. 6, 2010). *See also See* Brian Deer, *How the Case Against the MMR Vaccine Was Fixed*, 342 BRITISH MEDICAL JOURNAL 77 (Jan. 8, 2011); *generally* Susan Dominus, *The Denunciation of Dr. Wakefield*, NEW YORK TIMES MAGAZINE, April 24, 2011, at 36.

26. *See generally* INSTITUTE OF MEDICINE, IMMUNIZATION, SAFETY REVIEW: VACCINES AND AUTISM (2004); KATHLEEN STRATTON, ADVERSE EFFECTS OF VACCINES: EVIDENCE AND CAUSALITY (2011). *See also* Cedillo v. Secretary of Health and Human Services, 617 F.3d 1328 (Fed. Cir. 2010); Bruesewitz v. Wyeth LLC, 131 S.Ct. 1068 (2011); Graves v. Secretary of Dept. of Health and Human Services, 2011 WL 3010753 (2011).

(a) What may be the value of retractions of publications? (b) What regulatory measures may be used to address misleading information that could harm the public? (c) Should the state intervene in instances of fraud or misleading information on the market?

3. Should concerns regarding reputational harms to market participants motivate regulation?

§ 5.2 INSUFFICIENT INFORMATION

Individuals and firms often do not have sufficient information to make good decisions. Should the state protect them from their own ignorance or lack of information? Insufficient information may motivate regulations, but it cannot serve as a good justification for regulation. Why would anyone ever invest in obtaining or creating valuable information if its disclosure is required by law? Valuable information is a commodity that market participants produce or purchase when it is not available for free.[27] It is an asset that is similar to many other goods we possess and own.[28]

Regulations that address insufficient information tend to distinguish between situations of asymmetric information in relationships and other circumstances of insufficient information. We follow this distinction. Our discussion begins with the general case of insufficient information as a motivation for state regulation.

§ 5.2.1 Decisionmaking Under Ignorance

§ 5.2.1a Risk, Uncertainty, and Ignorance

Risk is a property of meaningful decisions. Only decisions that have no effect on our well-being—namely, those whose outcomes we do not care about—are risk free. Such decisions have no significance for us. Our discussion of risk distinguished between *risk* and *uncertainty*.[29] We saw that the term "*risk*" refers to situations in which the likelihood and other characteristics of future events are quantifiable. In contrast, the term "*uncertainty*" refers to situations in which at least one significant characteristic of future events is unquantifiable. The purpose of that distinction was instrumental. Risk analysis may improve our decisions, but the problem is that individuals face uncertainty and have limited information about risks.[30]

Uncertainty, therefore, is some form of "ignorance"—imperfect information about the nature of future events. Human decisionmaking under

---

27. *See generally* Allen, *Information as an Economic Commodity*, *supra* note 10; Arrow, *Economic Welfare and the Allocation of Resources for Invention*, *supra* note 8; Hirshleifer, *The Private and Social Value of Information and the Reward to Inventive Activity*, *supra* note 8; Stigler, *The Economics of Information*, *supra* note 4.

28. *See generally* Anthony T. Kronman, *Mistakes, Disclosure, Information, and the Law of Contracts*, 7 JOURNAL OF LEGAL STUDIES 1 (1978).

29. *See* § 4.1.2.

30. *See generally* FRANK H. KNIGHT, RISK, UNCERTAINTY AND PROFIT 19–20, 197–232 (1921); Daniel A. Farber, *Uncertainty*, 99 GEORGETOWN LAW JOURNAL 901 (2011).

uncertainty is rarely optimal and tends to be influenced by cognitive biases and ordinary heuristics.[31] Information about risks can substantially improve the way people cope with uncertainty, although it cannot resolve the challenges. For example, many ordinary activities, such as driving, drinking alcohol, and smoking, involve risks to human lives. Information about the risks associated with activities changes how people approach them. Awareness of risks motivates people to modify their conduct. To be sure, situational factors, personal characteristics, among other things, create differences in responsiveness to information among individuals. It is unlikely that the entire population will respond to new information about a particular risk, and it is even less likely that the entire population will respond uniformly. Moreover, an individual's responsiveness to information tends to be inconsistent across types of risks. For example, a smoker may overinvest in safety accessories when she buys a new car. In other words, a person who does not respond to information about tobacco health risks may overreact to information about car accidents and safety.[32] Similarly, a nonsmoker who maintains her diet and physical fitness may not buckle her seatbelt. Information may improve decisionmaking under uncertainty, but it will never perfect it.

As individuals, we do not have time, resources, or expertise to collect information relevant to ordinary decisionmaking, such as how to minimize exposure to foodborne illnesses, when and what vaccines we should take, and how to avoid traffic jams. Without private or public institutions that produce information in a centralized fashion, we would have less information. Further, as individuals, we cannot even afford to research the question of *what information* we need to know in order to make decisions. We rely on private and public institutions to produce information for us. Consider, for example, the risks associated with outbreaks of new violent threads of influenza or foodborne diseases. People must know about their existence first in order to assess risks. A person cannot constantly investigate the question of whether such outbreaks do in fact occur. Put simply, sometimes a motivation for regulation of information is to provide information about options.

One of the reasons the state participates in the market for information is that many information goods have the characteristics of public goods. It is efficient to produce certain type of information in a centralized fashion and the market is unlikely to produce it in a reliable fashion.[33] To illustrate, consider the Centers for Disease Control and Prevention (CDC), a federal agency under the Department of Health and Human Services. CDC exercises discretion regarding what information to produce and relies on market institutions (*e.g.*, media and physicians) to disseminate this information to the public. CDC regularly produces alerts and periodical publications about health risks. Some people subscribe to the CDC's alerts

---

31. *See generally* Robin Hogarth & Howard Kunreuther, *Decision Making Under Ignorance: Arguing with Yourself*, 10 JOURNAL OF RISK & UNCERTAINTY 15 (1995).

32. Empirical evidence suggests that the risk-taking conduct U.S. smokers engage in is often consistent across risks (*e.g.*, driving, alcohol consumption, and smoking related risks). *See* Joni Hersch & W. Kip Viscusi, *Smoking and Other Risky Behaviors*, 28 JOURNAL OF DRUG ISSUES 645 (1998).

33. *See* § 3.1.2c.

and publications, but most people receive the information in a processed form from the media or their physician. The information CDC adds to the market about diseases, foodborne outbreaks, vaccines, and other health risk factors influences ordinary choices. However, people are not always aware of the source of information. Here, we do not evaluate the costs and benefits of information about health risks, nor do we assess CDC.

§ 5.2.1b Information About Others' Choices

Some resent the view that the state should assure that the public receive information for improved decisionmaking. They may even less fond of the state proving information about the *choices of others*.

Choices of market participants often externalize risks. Information about others' choices and their potential consequences is sometimes important to individual decisionmaking. As we have seen, most objections to regulation can be framed as concerns about privacy and freedom. But the "right to be let alone," which Justice Brandeis described as "the most comprehensive of rights and the right most valued by civilized men,"[34] is relative and has boundaries, especially when one's choices may harm others.

Consider information about the choice to smoke. Smoking is unhealthy. A smoker's decision to smoke, however, tends to affect others, including through secondhand smoking.[35] Smokers also increase fire risks in residential areas.[36] Cigarettes are the leading cause of death from fire and the second leading cause of fire-related injury.[37] Most people know that secondhand smoking creates risks, but it is doubtful that they properly estimate the risk. Further, it is unclear how many people are aware of, let alone properly estimate, risks associated with fire smoking-related incidents. Some apartment buildings ban smoking. Absent smoking restrictions, should people know about smokers in their building or neighborhood?

Consider now vaccine skeptics that we have discussed in several contexts. Vaccine skeptics tend to create informational problems. Although they debate with "others," this debate is not about information exchange. Both parties feel sufficiently informed. Vaccine skepticism may increase health risks. Do members of the community possess enough information about the increased risks unvaccinated individuals produce? Do they understand the actual costs to society the skeptics' approach entails? Such information is relevant to the decisions of those who trust vaccines. For example, during a flu season, an employee at a medical facility who is infected with flu can cause a chain reaction that begins with an outbreak of

---

34. Olmstead v. United States, 277 U.S. 438, 478 (1928) (Brandeis, J., dissenting).

35. *See, e.g.*, John Howard, *Smoking Is an Occupational Hazard*, 46 AMERICAN JOURNAL OF INDUSTRIAL MEDICINE 161 (2004). Sean Semple et al., *Secondhand Smoke Levels in Scottish Pubs: The Effect of Smoke-Free Legislation*, 16 TOBACCO CONTROL 127 (2007).

36. *See* Jane E. Ballard et al., *Association of Smoking and Alcohol Drinking with Residential Fire Injuries*, 135 AMERICAN JOURNAL OF EPIDEMIOLOGY 26 (1992); Carol W. Runyan et al., *Risk Factors for Fatal Residential Fires*, 327 NEW ENGLAND JOURNAL OF MEDICINE 859 (1992).

37. *See, e.g.*, Jeffrey J. Sacks & David E. Nelson, *Smoking and Injuries: An Overview*, 23 PREVENTIVE MEDICINE 515 (1994); Gerald McGwin, Jr. et al., *The Epidemiology of Fire-Related Deaths in Alabama, 1992–1997*, 21 JOURNAL OF BURN CARE & REHABILITATION 75 (2000).

flu among patients who cannot be vaccinated and continues with other medical complications and illnesses. Should people be aware of precise risks of this type? Should people know whether employees of medical facilities are vaccinated against contagious diseases, including seasonal flu?

In 2009, New York tried to address flu externalities of healthcare workers through a command-and-control measure: mandatory flu shots for healthcare workers. After a short battle with healthcare workers concerned about their freedom of choice, the state withdrew. Are regulatory measures that inform the public about the choices of healthcare workers desirable? To assess this question, consider some of the background facts. By 2009, abundant empirical literature conclusively showed that mandatory influenza vaccinations for health care workers could contribute to the decrease of flu and mortality among patients in medical facilities.[38] In August 2009, the State Health Commissioner issued a rule mandating influenza immunization for New York health care workers.[39] The Commissioner issued the regulation in response to problems that the 2009 swine flu (H1N1) pandemic presented.[40] The rule was not popular among many health workers. They launched an aggressive public campaign against it. Trying to rescue his initiative, in late September, the Commissioner released an open letter stressing the conflict of interests of health care workers. Among other things, the letter stated: "This is not the time for uninformed or self-interested parties to attempt to pump air into long-deflated arguments about vaccine safety in general or to use a single 33–year–old episode to deny decades of safety and saved lives achieved by influenza vaccines prepared in the same way as this year's formulations."[41] In October 2009, some of the organizations that opposed the required vaccination obtained a restraining order against the state, thereby protecting healthcare workers from being forcibly vaccinated.[42] A few days later the New York Governor announced the "suspension of [the] flu shot mandate for health care employees due to [a] shortage of [the] vaccine."[43]

---

38. *See, e.g.*, Carolyn Buxton Bridges, *Transmission of Influenza: Implications for Control in Health Care Settings*, 37 CLINICAL INFECTIOUS DISEASES 1094 (2003); Amanda Burls, *Vaccinating Healthcare Workers Against Influenza to Protect the Vulnerable: Is it A Good Use of Healthcare Resources?* 24 VACCINE 4212 (2006); William F. Carman, *Effects of Influenza Vaccination of Health–Care Workers on Mortality of Elderly People in Long–Term Care: A Randomised Controlled Trial*, 355 LANCET 93 (2000).

39. *See* Anemona Hartocollis, *State Requires Flu Vaccination for Caregivers*, NEW YORK TIMES, Aug. 19, 2009, at A20. A copy of the rule is available at *regti.me/NYS-flu-reg* (case sensitive).

40. *See, e.g.*, Donald G. McNeil Jr. & Karen Zraick, *New York Health Care Workers Resist Flu Vaccine Rule*, NEW YORK TIMES, Sept. 21, 2009, at A18.

41. Richard F. Daines, *Commissioner Tells Health Care Workers: Mandatory Flu Vaccine is in the Best Interest of Patients and Workers* (Sept. 24, 2009), available at *regti.me/NYS-flu* (case sensitive).

42. *See* Anemona Hartocollis & Sewell Chan, Albany Judge Blocks Vaccination Rule, NEW YORK TIMES, Oct. 17, 2009, at A17. A copy of the restraining order is available at *regti.me/NYS-flu-RO* (case sensitive).

43. *Governor David A. Paterson Announces Suspension of Flu Shot Mandate for Health Care Employees Due to Shortage of Vaccine*, Press Release (Oct. 22, 2009). The suspension was

The T.J. Hooper

60 F.2d 737 (2d Cir. 1932)

■ L. HAND, CIRCUIT JUDGE.

The barges No. 17 and No. 30, belonging to the Northern Barge Company, had lifted cargoes of coal at Norfolk, Virginia, for New York in March, 1928. They were towed by two tugs of the petitioner, the 'Montrose' and the 'Hooper,' and were lost off the Jersey Coast on March tenth, in an easterly gale. The cargo owners sued the barges under the contracts of carriage; the owner of the barges sued the tugs under the towing contract, both for its own loss and as bailee of the cargoes; the owner of the tug filed a petition to limit its liability. All the suits were joined and heard together, and the judge found that all the vessels were unseaworthy; the tugs, because they did not carry radio receiving sets by which they could have seasonably got warnings of a change in the weather which should have caused them to seek shelter in the Delaware Breakwater en route and barge jointly liable to each cargo owner, and each tug for half damages for the loss of its barge. The petitioner appealed, and the barge owner appealed and filed assignments of error.

* * *

The evidence of the condition of the barges was very extensive, the greater part being taken out of court. As to each, the fact remains that she foundered in weather that she was bound to withstand. A March gale is not unusual north of Hatteras; barges along the coast must be ready to meet one, and there is in the case at bar no adequate explanation for the result except that these were not well-found. The test of seaworthiness, being ability for the service undertaken, the case might perhaps be left with no more than this. As to the cargoes, the charters excused the barges if 'reasonable means' were taken to make them seaworthy; and the barge owners amended their answers during the trial to allege that they had used due diligence in that regard. [T]he barges were certainly not seaworthy in fact, and we do not think that the record shows affirmatively the exercise of due diligence to examine them. * * *

The weather bureau at Arlington broadcasts two predictions daily, at ten in the morning and ten in the evening. Apparently there are other reports floating about, which come at uncertain hours but which can also be picked up. The Arlington report of the morning read as follows: 'Moderate north, shifting to east and southeast winds, increasing Friday, fair weather to-night.' The substance of this, apparently from another souree, reached a tow bound north to New York about noon, and, coupled with a falling glass, decided the master to put in to the Delaware Breakwater in the afternoon. The glass had not indeed fallen much and perhaps the tug was over cautious; nevertheless, although the appearances were all fair, he thought discretion the better part of valor. Three other tows followed him, the masters of two of which testified. Their decision was in part determined by example; but they too had received the Arlington report or

---

not needed since the regulation provided that the "influenza vaccination(s) must be in accordance with the national recommendations in effect at the time of vaccination(s), unless the commissioner has determined that there is not an adequate supply of vaccine."

its equivalent, and though it is doubtful whether alone it would have turned the scale, it is plain that it left them in an indecision which needed little to be resolved on the side of prudence; they preferred to take no chances, and chances they believed there were. Courts have not often such evidence of the opinion of impartial experts, formed in the very circumstances and confirmed by their own conduct at the time.

Moreover, the 'Montrose' and the 'Hooper' would have had the benefit of the evening report from Arlington had they had proper receiving sets. This predicted worse weather; it read: 'Increasing east and southeast winds, becoming fresh to strong, Friday night and increasing cloudiness followed by rain Friday.' The bare 'increase' of the morning had become 'fresh to strong.' To be sure this scarcely foretold a gale of from forty to fifty miles for five hours or more, rising at one time to fifty-six; but if the four tows thought the first report enough, the second ought to have laid any doubts. The master of the 'Montrose' himself, when asked what he would have done had he received a substantially similar report, said that he would certainly have put in. The master of the 'Hooper' was also asked for his opinion, and said that he would have turned back also, but this admission is somewhat vitiated by the incorporation in the question of the statement that it was a 'storm warning,' which the witness seized upon in his answer. All this seems to us to support the conclusion of the judge that prudent masters, who had received the second warning, would have found the risk more than the exigency warranted; they would have been amply vindicated by what followed. * * * Taking the situation as a whole, it seems to us that these masters would have taken undue chances, had they got the broadcasts.

They did not, because their private radio receiving sets, which were on board, were not in working order. These belonged to them personally, and were partly a toy, partly a part of the equipment, but neither furnished by the owner, nor supervised by it. It is not fair to say that there was a general custom among coastwise carriers so to equip their tugs. One line alone did it; as for the rest, they relied upon their crews, so far as they can be said to have relied at all. An adequate receiving set suitable for a coastwise tug can now be got at small cost and is reasonably reliable if kept up; obviously it is a source of great protection to their tows. Twice every day they can receive these predictions, based upon the widest possible information, available to every vessel within two or three hundred miles and more. Such a set is the ears of the tug to catch the spoken word, just as the master's binoculars are her eyes to see a storm signal ashore. Whatever may be said as to other vessels, tugs towing heavy coal laden barges, strung out for half a mile, have little power to manoeuvre, and do not, as this case proves, expose themselves to weather which would not turn back stauncher craft. They can have at hand protection against dangers of which they can learn in no other way.

Is it then a final answer that the business had not yet generally adopted receiving sets? There are, no doubt, cases where courts seem to make the general practice of the calling the standard of proper diligence; we have indeed given some currency to the notion ourselves. * * * Indeed in most cases reasonable prudence is in fact common prudence; but strictly it is never its measure; a whole calling may have unduly lagged in the adoption of new and available devices. It never may set its own tests, however persuasive be its usages. Courts must in the end say what is required; there are precautions so imperative that even their universal disregard will not excuse their omission. * * * But here there was no custom at all as to receiving sets; some had them, some did not; the most that can be urged is that they had not yet become general. Certainly in such a case we need not pause; when some have thought a device necessary, at least we may say that they were right, and the others too slack. The [relevant] statute * * * does not bear on this situation at all. It prescribes not a receiving, but a transmitting set, and for a very different purpose; to call for help, not to get news. We hold the tugs therefore because had they been properly equipped, they would have got the Arlington reports. The injury was a direct consequence of this unseaworthiness.

Decree affirmed.

Questions

1. What was the informational problem Judge Learned Hand addressed in *The T.J. Hooper*? How does it differ from the problems discussed in this Section (§ 5.2.1)?

2. In *The T.J. Hooper*, Judge Learned Hand wrote:

> There are, no doubt, cases where courts seem to make the general practice of the calling the standard of proper diligence; we have indeed given some currency to the notion ourselves. * * * Indeed in most cases reasonable prudence is in fact common prudence; but strictly it is never its measure; a whole calling may have unduly lagged in the adoption of new and available devices.

What are the similarities and differences between radio receivers in the early twentieth century and influenza vaccines for health care workers in the early twenty-first century?

3. Judge Learned Hand effectively created a duty to be informed. Many states created a duty to be informed related to abortion.[44] These statutes, often called the Woman's Right to Know Act or Informed–Consent Act, ordinarily require the physician who is performing the abortion to inform the pregnant woman about potential health risks associated with abortions, the father's liability for assistance in the support of the child, and the availability of pregnancy prevention counseling. The statutes also require the physician to perform a sonogram on the pregnant woman, in a defined timeframe very close to the abortion, to display the images to the woman and to explain their meaning in plain English. For example, the Texas Woman's Right to Know Act requires the physician "to perform and display a sonogram of the fetus, make audible the heart auscultation of the fetus for the woman to hear, and explain to her the results of each procedure and to wait 24 hours, in most cases, between these disclosures and performing the abortion." A woman may "decline to view the images or hear the

44. *See generally* Robert Post *Informed Consent to Abortion: A First Amendment Analysis of Compelled Physician Speech*, 2007 UNIVERSITY OF ILLINOIS LAW REVIEW 939 (2007).

heartbeat, * * * but she may decline to receive an explanation of the sonogram images only on certification that her pregnancy falls into one of three statutory exceptions."[45] In *Texas Medical Providers Performing Abortion Services v. Lakey*, the Fifth Circuit upheld the constitutionality of the statute.[46] The opinion focused on the question of whether the statute abridged a physician's First Amendment rights by compelling the m to deliver information and vagueness. Concurring, Judge Patrick Higginbotham wrote:

> The doctor-patient relationship has long been conducted within the constraints of informed consent to the risks of medical procedures, as demanded by the common law, legislation, and professional norms. The doctrine itself rests on settled principles of personal autonomy, protected by a reticulated pattern of tort law, overlaid by both self- and state-imposed regulation. Speech incident to securing informed consent submits to the long history of this regulatory pattern.
>
> The Court's decision in *Casey** accented the state's interest in potential life, holding that its earlier decisions following *Roe* failed to give this interest force at all stages of a pregnancy and that in service of this interest the state may insist that a woman be made aware of the development of the fetus at her stage of pregnancy. Significantly, the Court held that the fact that such truthful, accurate information may cause a woman to choose not to abort her pregnancy only reinforces its relevance to an informed decision. Insisting that a doctor give this information in his traditional role of securing informed consent is permissible. Texas has done just this and affords three exceptions to its required delivery of information about the stage of fetal growth where in its judgment the information had less relevance, a legislative judgment that is at least rational.

(a) What are the similarities and differences between radio receivers in the early twentieth century and informed consent requirements for abortions in the early twenty-first century? (b) Judge Higginbotham appears to express a position about the functions of the regulatory state. What position does he take?

§ 5.2.2 Information Asymmetry

Information asymmetries exist in voluntary or involuntary relationships where one party is more informed than the other(s). In a transaction, a seller may know more about the product and its value and risks than the buyer. In litigation, the defendant often possesses information that may be valuable for the plaintiff. Under some circumstances, the informed party has a duty to share the information with the uninformed party (or parties).

---

45. A copy of the statute is available at *regti.me/TX-HB15* (case sensitive).

46. Texas Medical Providers Performing Abortion Services v. Lakey, 667 F.3d 570 (5th Cir. 2012); § 7.4.2.

* [Planned Parenthood of Southeastern Pennsylvania v. Casey, 505 U.S. 833 (1992)—BYO].

For example, packaged food of certain types must include nutrition information. Manufacturers have to provide warnings about certain risks in their products. Prosecutors have a constitutional duty to volunteer exculpatory evidence to the defense.[47] The Residential Lead–Based Paint Hazard Reduction Act of 1992 imposes an affirmative duty on sellers and landlords to address potential lead-based paint hazard in the sale and leasing of housing units. Information asymmetries often evoke perceptions of unfairness. The uninformed party feels that the informed party should have disclosed certain information because of the nature of the relationship or other fairness grounds.

Information asymmetry in and of itself, however, does not offer any viable justification for regulation. Individuals and firms will not bother to gather relevant information if they have to disclose it, or can receive it free. The nature of the informational gap could establish a justification for regulation.[48] The typical case is when the less-informed parties cannot obtain the relevant information or when obtaining it will cost them substantially more than the informed party.[49] Under such circumstances there may be disclosure duties. Such disclosure duties often expand market because they reduce information costs.[50]

§ 5.2.2a Caveat Emptor

Walton H. Hamilton, *The Ancient Maxim Caveat Emptor*, 40 Yale Law Journal 1133, 1186 (1930):

* * * The expression *caveat emptor* savors too much of the copybook and the almanac to have a clearcut history. A bit of wisdom may live long before it takes possession of a convenient verbal symbol; a collocation of words may be home to a succession of ideas. The notion that one had better look lest he rue his bargain is probably as old as trade; the phrase caveat emptor is a Latin proverb of late Anglican vintage. It hovered uncertainly on the fringes of respectability, but found no reputable place within the great authoritarian scheme by which Christian society was ordered. As a rule of law in the King's courts it was no more than shorthand for the want of an easy jurisdiction or the lack of a convenient writ. The common sense of individualism won for it judicial acceptance, fitted it out with legal trappings, and made it a vehicle of public policy. Its triumph was more complete in America than in England, in public than in private law. Not until the nineteenth century, did judges discover that caveat emptor

---

47. *See* Brady v. Maryland, 373 U.S. 83 (1963); United States v. Agurs, 427 U.S. 97 (1976); United States v. Bagley, 473 U.S. 667 (1985).

48. *See* Paul Milgrom, *What the Seller Won't Tell You: Persuasion and Disclosure in Markets*, 22 Journal of Economic Perspectives 115 (2008).

49. *See generally* Kronman, *Mistakes, Disclosure, Information*, *supra* note 28.

50. *See generally* George A. Akerlof, *The Market for "Lemons": Quality and the Market Mechanism*, 84 Quarterly Journal of Economics 488 (1970); Joseph E. Stiglitz, *Theory of "Screening," Education, and the Distribution of Income*, 65 American Economic Review 283 (1975); Charles Wilson, *The Nature of Equilibrium in Markets with Adverse Selection*, 11 Bell Journal of Economics 108 (1980).

sharpened wits, taught self-reliance, made a man—an economic man—out of the buyer, and served well its two masters, business and justice.

Laidlaw v. Organ

15 U.S. 178 (1817)

During the War of 1812, the British military set up an effective naval blockade against the southern ports of the United States to depress the American economy. In the absence of access to important trade distribution channels, the prices of many commodities, including tobacco, crashed. On the morning of February 19, 1815, Hector Organ, a New Orleans tobacco merchant, and Francis Girault, a partner in the New Orleans tobacco broker firm Laidlaw & Co., negotiated and closed a deal for the sale of 111 hogshead (111,000 pounds) of tobacco. Organ knew that earlier that day the United States and Britain signed a peace treaty and that the blockade that kept tobacco prices down was lifted. Girault was uninformed. Once the news of the peace treaty hit the market, tobacco prices went up by 30% to 50%.[51] Laidlaw & Co. refused to deliver the tobacco and Organ sued the firm. The case reached the Supreme Court. Chief Justice Marshall wrote a brief decision:

> The question in this case is, whether the intelligence of extrinsic circumstances, which might influence the price of the commodity, and which was exclusively within the knowledge of the vendee, ought to have been communicated by him to the vendor? The court is of opinion that he was not bound to communicate it. It would be difficult to circumscribe the contrary doctrine within proper limits, where the means of intelligence are equally accessible to both parties. But at the same time, each party must take care not to say or do any thing tending to impose upon the other.[52]

Questions

1. What does the *caveat emptor* maxim have to do with motivations for regulation?

2. In several decisions Justice Stephen Johnson Field wrote about the constitutional "inalienable right" of "the pursuit of happiness."[53] How may the pursuit of happiness be related to the *caveat emptor* maxim?

---

51. *See* M. H. Hoeflich, *Laidlaw v. Organ, Gulian C. Verplanck, and the Shaping of Early Nineteenth Century Contract Law: A Tale of A Case and A Commentary*, 1991 University of Illinois Law Review 55 (1991); Kronman, *Mistakes, Disclosure, Information, and the Law of Contracts*, *supra* note 28, at 9–11.

52. Laidlaw v. Organ, 15 U.S. 178 (1817).

53. *See, e.g.*, The Slaughter–House Cases, 83 U.S. 36 (1873); Butchers' Union Company v. Crescent City Co., 111 U.S. 746 (1884). *See also* Joseph R. Grodin, *Rediscovering the State Constitutional Right to Happiness and Safety*, 25 Hastings Constitutional Law Quarterly 1 (1997); Andrew R. Sheriff, *The Pursuit of Happiness*, 33 Commercial Law League Journal 709 (1928); sidebar 2-2.

3. Is the *caveat emptor* maxim consistent or inconsistent with the invisible hand theory? Does the maxim serve the invisible hand?

4. Externality is a particular outcome of involuntary relationships, or a nonconsensual dimension of a relationship. Arthur Pigou argued that the pursuit of self-interest is a source of externalities that may justify government regulation.[54] Responding to this proposition, Ronald Coase argued that market participants can address externalities better than the state.[55] What would Pigou and Coase likely to say about the *caveat emptor* maxim?

§ 5.2.2b Implied Warranties

Many standard transactions include expected warranties, such as: "This new toaster works." For practical reasons, parties do not specify all such warranties in every transaction. Instead, courts use *implied warranties* to guarantee certain qualities that a reasonable buyer would expect to have in the product.[56] These implied warranties are exceptions to the *caveat emptor* maxim and courts tend to interpret them narrowly. *The implied warranty of habitability or fitness for use of the premises* establishes that by making premises available for lease a landlord declares the premises are fit for human habitation. A tenant may recover damages for personal injuries caused by a breach of the warranty and may pursue other remedies. The standard of care owed by the landlord to the tenant under this cause of action is unsettled.

Ingalls v. Hobbs

Supreme Court of Massachusetts
156 Mass. 348 (1892)

■ KNOWLTON, JUSTICE.

This is an action to recover $500 for the use and occupation of a furnished dwelling house at Swampscott during the summer of 1890. [T]he defendant hired the premises of the plaintiffs for the season, as a furnished house, provided with beds, mattresses, matting, curtains, chairs, tables, kitchen utensils, and other articles which were apparently in good condition, and that when the defendant took possession it was found to be more or less infested with bugs, so that the defendant contended that it was unfit for habitation, and for that reason gave it up, and declined to occupy it. The agreed statement concludes as follows: "If, under the above circumstances, said house was not fit for occupation as a furnished house, and, being let as such, there was an implied agreement or warranty that the said house and furniture therein should be fit for use and occupation, judgment is to be for the defendant, with costs. If, however, under said circumstances, said house was fit for occupation as a furnished house, or there was no such implied

---

54. *See* § 3.1.1a.

55. *See* § 3.1.2.

56. *See, e.g.*, E. Allan, Farnsworth, *Implied Warranties of Quality in Non–Sales Cases*, 57 COLUMBIA LAW REVIEW 653 (1957).

agreement or warranty, judgment is to be for the plaintiffs in the sum of $500, with interest from the date of the writ, and costs." Judgment was ordered for the defendant, and the plaintiffs appealed to this court.

* * * The facts agreed warrant a finding that the house was unfit for habitation when it was hired, and we are therefore brought directly to the question whether there was an implied agreement on the part of the plaintiff that it was in a proper condition for immediate use as a dwelling house. It is well settled * * * that one who lets an unfurnished building to be occupied as a dwelling house does not impliedly agree that it is fit for habitation. * * * In the absence of fraud or a covenant, the purchaser of real estate, or the hirer of it for a term, however short, takes it as it is, and determines for himself whether it will serve the purpose for which he wants it. He may, and often does, contemplate making extensive repairs upon it to adapt it to his wants. But there are good reasons why a different rule should apply to one who hires a furnished room, or a furnished house, for a few days, or a few weeks or months. Its fitness for immediate use of a particular kind, as indicated by its appointments, is a far more important element entering into the contract than when there is a mere lease of real estate. One who lets for a short term a house provided with all furnishings and appointments for immediate residence may be supposed to contract in reference to a well-understood purpose of the hirer to use it as a habitation. An important part of what the hirer pays for is the opportunity to enjoy it without delay, and without the expense of preparing it for use. It is very difficult, and often impossible, for one to determine on inspection whether the house and its appointments are fit for the use for which they are immediately wanted, and the doctrine caveat emptor, which is ordinarily applicable to a lessee of real estate, would often work injustice if applied to cases of this kind. It would be unreasonable to hold, under such circumstances, that the landlord does not impliedly agree that what he is letting is a house suitable for occupation in its condition at the time. This distinction between furnished and unfurnished houses in reference to the construction of contracts for letting them, when there are no express agreements about their condition, has long been recognized in England, where it is held that there is an implied contract that a furnished house let for a short time is in proper condition for immediate occupation as a dwelling. * * * We are of opinion that in a lease of a completely furnished dwelling house for a single season at a summer watering place there is an implied agreement that the house is fit for habitation, without greater preparation than one hiring it for a short time might reasonably be expected to make in appropriating it to the use for which it was designed.

Judgment affirmed.

Horton v. Marston

Supreme Judicial Court of Massachusetts
352 Mass. 322 (1967)

■ WHITTEMORE, JUSTICE.

* * * On September 4, 1962, the plaintiff signed a written lease with Dana M. Marston for cottage No. 2 in Marston's development of rental

cottages. The lease was to run until the end of May, 1963. The cottage was rented with all furnishings except bed linen, including an apartment-sized gas stove. The plaintiff moved in on September 4, 1962, and used the stove from that date. It was at least ten years old. On May 8, 1963, when the plaintiff sought to light a burner on the top of the gas stove * * * an explosion occurred injuring the plaintiff. This was the first time the plaintiff had used all four top burners and the oven at the same time.

The trial judge found, with support in the evidence, including expert testimony, that "the oven * * * was insulated in a defective manner." As a result, either because much of the available oxygen had been used or because the air over the stove had become overheated, the flame of the * * * burner had been extinguished. The wall cabinets and side cabinets were "too close to the burner, closer than allowed by law." The combined effect of the defects was an accumulation of gas that exploded when the plaintiff struck a match.

* * *

Ingalls v. Hobbs, 156 Mass. 348 (1892) was an action by a landlord to recover for the rent of a furnished dwelling leased for the summer season. The tenant successfully defended on the ground of a breach of an implied warranty that the dwelling was fit for the intended use, the house having been infested with bugs. This court said, in respect of the renting of a dwelling for a short term ("a few days or a few weeks or months"): "Its fitness for immediate use of a particular kind, as indicated by its appointments, is a far more important element entering into the contract than when there is a mere lease of real estate. * * *"

* * *

We think that the length of the term in the case at bar was not such as to place the risk of concealed defects on the tenant. Here, as in the Ingalls case, an "important part of what the hirer * * * (paid for was) the opportunity to enjoy * * * (the dwelling) without delay, and without the expense of preparing it for use." * * *

So ordered.

Questions

1. At the time of closing the deal, were the landlords in *Ingalls* and *Horton* more informed than the prospective tenants?

2. What were the outcomes of in *Ingalls* and *Horton*? Are they equivalent to a duty to disclosure? If so, disclosure of what kind of information?

Bedbugs

In August 2010, CDC and the U.S. Environmental Protection Agency (EPA) released a joint statement "to highlight emerging public health issues associated with bed bugs (*Cimex lectularius*) in communities throughout the United States."[57]

Figure 5.2

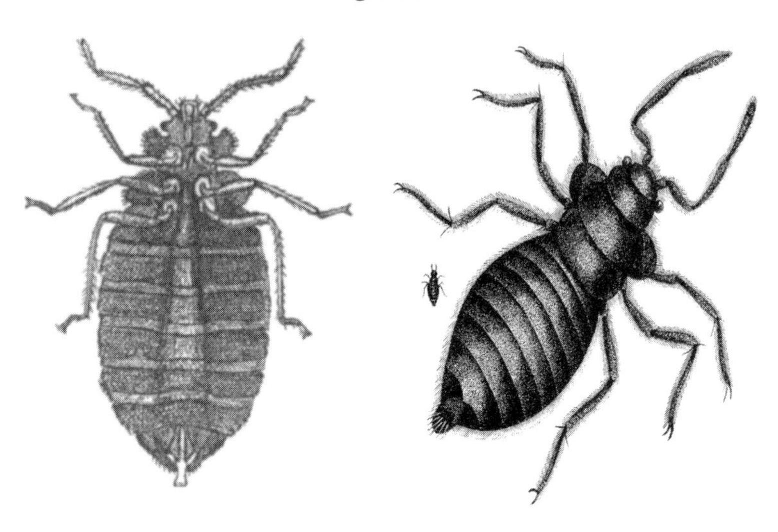

Source: Leland O. Howard, The Insect Book (1902). Source: *Unwelcome Guests,* Harper's New Monthly Magazine, December 1860.

Bedbugs are "are small, flat, parasitic insects that feed solely on the blood of people and animals while they sleep. Bed bugs are reddish-brown in color, wingless, range from 1mm to 7mm (roughly the size of Lincoln's head on a penny), and can live several months without a blood meal."[58] Bedbug bites are very unpleasant but they are not known to transmit diseases. However, some people develop allergic reactions to bedbug bites and coping with infestations ordinarily comes with significant challenges and distress. Bedbug infestations affect the mental health of many people. Bedbug victims also often cope with social consequences because many people and employers fear that the victims carry bedbugs in their clothes.[59]

Although bedbugs have been with us forever, very little is known about them. It is known, however, that bedbugs are resistant to most approved pesticides. Often the most effective strategy to treat bedbugs is to contain them and then to dismantle the bed and other infested furniture and vacuum the invaders.[60] The joint statement of the CDC and EPA pointed out that "in recent years, public health agencies across the country have been overwhelmed by complaints about bed bugs." In light of the bedbug outbreak in American cities, the statement summarized some concerns:

57. Joint Statement on Bed Bug Control in the United States from the U.S. Centers for Disease Control and Prevention (CDC) and the U.S. Environmental Agency (Aug. 2010), available at *regti.me/CDCbedbugs* (case sensitive).

58. http://www.cdc.gov/parasites/bedbugs/faqs.html.

59. *See, e.g.*, Emily B. Hager, *What Spreads Faster Than Bedbugs? Fear and Social Stigma*, NEW YORK TIMES, Aug. 2010, at A1.

60. Robert Lee Hotz, *Why Bedbugs Won't Die,* WALL STREET JOURNAL, Jan. 20, 2011, at A3; Donald G. McNeil Jr., *They Crawl, They Bite, They Baffle Scientists*, NEW YORK TIMES, Aug. 31, 2010, at D1; Donald G. McNeil Jr., *You Can Only Hope to Contain Them*, NEW YORK TIMES, Aug. 31, 2010, at D4.

> Research on the public health effects of bed bugs has been very limited over the past several decades, largely due to the * * * decline in bed bug populations in the latter half of the 20th century. Now that bed bug populations are rapidly increasing, additional research is needed to determine the reasons for the resurgence, the potential for bed bugs to transmit disease and their impact on public health.
>
> Economically, bed bug infestations are also a burden on society. Although the exact dollar amount is not known, the economic losses from health care, lost wages, lost revenue and reduced productivity can be substantial. The cost of effectively eliminating bed bugs may be significantly more than the cost of eliminating other pests because bed bug control usually requires multiple visits by a licensed pest control operator and diligence on the part of those who are experiencing the infestation. Control in multifamily homes is much more difficult than in single family homes because bed bugs frequently travel between units, either by direct transport by humans or through voids in the walls. There are additional costs and complexities associated with coordinating and encouraging participation from multiple residents.

In late 2009, a massive bedbug infestation began spreading in New York City.[61] The aggressive insects invaded to the Metropolitan Opera House, the Waldorf Astoria, and Google's New York Office. On August 30, 2010 the New York Governor signed into law a bill that amended the administrative code of New York and provided:

> **§ 27–2018.1 *Notice of bedbug infestation history*.** * * * For housing accommodations subject to this code, an owner shall furnish to each tenant signing a vacancy lease, a notice in a form promulgated or approved by the state division of housing and community renewal that sets forth the property's bedbug infestation history for the previous year regarding the premises rented by the tenant and the building in which the premises are located.

Pursuant to this legislation, on October 2010, the Housing Management Bureau of New York promulgated a tenant notice, officially titled: "Disclosure of Bedbug Infestation History." (*see Figure 5.3*).

---

61. Josh Brbanel, *Bedbug Disclosure Required*, NEW YORK TIMES, Sept. 15, 2010, at A25.

Figure 5.3

NOTICE TO TENANT
DISCLOSURE OF BEDBUG INFESTATION HISTORY

Pursuant to the NYC Housing Maintenance Code, an owner/managing agent of residential rental property shall furnish to each tenant signing a vacancy lease a notice that sets forth the property's bedbug infestation history.

Name of tenant(s):

Subject Premises:

Apt. #:

Date of vacancy lease:

BEDBUG INFESTATION HISTORY
(Only boxes checked apply)

[ ] There is no history of any bedbug infestation within the past year in the building or in any apartment.

[ ] During the past year the building had a bedbug infestation history that has been the subject of eradication measures. The location of the infestation was on the ______________ floor(s).

[ ] During the past year the building had a bedbug infestation history on the ____________ floor(s) and it has not been the subject of eradication measures.

[ ] During the past year the apartment had a bedbug infestation history and eradication measures were employed.

[ ] During the past year the apartment had a bedbug infestation history and eradication measures were not employed.

[ ] Other: ____.

Signature of Tenant(s): ______________________________ Dated: ______________

Signature of Owner/Agent: ______________________________ Dated: ______________

DBB-N (DHCR 10/10)

Questions

1. Does the New York Bedbug Disclosure Act add anything to the implied warranty of habitability?

2. Does the New York Bedbug Disclosure Act properly address information asymmetries?

§ 5.3 MISLEADING INFORMATION

Misleading information may cause a person to change her decision in a way that does not serve her. Many areas of law impose liability for the communication of misleading information.[62] Legal liability for misrepresentations and lies, however, is a nuanced matter.[63] The understanding of information tends to require interpretation. Interpretation and cultural references often inflect information with more than one meaning. As a result, regulation of misleading information is particularly challenging.

The Tobacco Industry

During the first half of the twentieth century scientists began exploring the possibility that tobacco smoking adversely affects health. In January 1964 Surgeon General Luther L. Terry issued a highly publicized report—*Smoking and Health*.[64] The report concluded that "[c]igarette smoking is associated with a 70 percent increase in the age specific death rates of males, and to a lesser extent with increased death rates of females."[65] It associated smoking with a wide range of health problems and diseases and determined that "the greater the number of cigarettes smoked daily, the higher the death rate."[66]

United States v. Philip Morris USA Inc.

566 F.3d 1095 (D.C. Cir. 2009)

■ PER CURIAM:

Defendants in this action, cigarette manufacturers and trade organizations, appeal from the district court's judgment finding them liable for conducting the affairs of their joint enterprise through a pattern of mail and wire fraud in a scheme to deceive American consumers. They also appeal from the district court's remedial order, which imposes numerous negative and affirmative duties on Defendants. * * * [W]e affirm in large part the finding of liability, remanding only for dismissal of the trade organizations. We also largely affirm the remedial order. * * *

I. Background

The United States initiated this civil action under the Racketeer Influenced and Corrupt Organizations Act ("RICO"), 18 U.S.C. §§ 1961–1968, in 1999. The government alleged that nine cigarette manufacturers

---

62. *See, e.g.*, David A. Anderson, *Libel and Press Self-Censorship*, 53 TEXAS LAW REVIEW 422 (1975); Howard Beales et al., *The Efficient Regulation of Consumer Information*, 24 JOURNAL OF LAW & ECONOMICS 491 (1981); W. Page Keeton, *Fraud–Concealment and Non-Disclosure*, 15 TEXAS LAW REVIEW 1 (1936); W. Page Keeton, *Defamation and Freedom of the Press*, 54 TEXAS LAW REVIEW 1221 (1976); Jonathan R. Macey, *Good Finance, Bad Economics: An Analysis of the Fraud-on-the-Market Theory*, 42 STANFORD LAW REVIEW 1059 (1990) Ellen S. Podgor, *Mail Fraud: Opening Letters*, 43 SOUTH CALIFORNIA LAW REVIEW 223 (1992).

63. *See, e.g.*, United States v. Alvarez, 638 F.3d 666 (9th Cir. 2011).

64. U.S. DEPARTMENT OF HEALTH, EDUCATION & WELFARE, SMOKING AND HEALTH (Jan. 1964). A copy of the report is available at *regti.me/1964report* (case sensitive).

65. *Id.* at 31.

66. *Id.* at 29.

and two tobacco-related trade organizations violated section 1962(c) and (d) of the Act. Those subsections make it unlawful for "any person employed by or associated with any enterprise engaged in, or the activities of which affect, interstate or foreign commerce, to conduct or participate, directly or indirectly, in the conduct of such enterprise's affairs through a pattern of racketeering activity" or to conspire to do so. * * * The eleven Defendants were Philip Morris, Inc., now Philip Morris USA, Inc. ("Philip Morris"); R.J. Reynolds Tobacco Company, now Reynolds American ("Reynolds"); Brown & Williamson Tobacco Company, now part of Reynolds ("Brown & Williamson"); Lorillard Tobacco Company ("Lorillard"); The Liggett Group, Inc. ("Liggett"); American Tobacco Company, which merged with Brown & Williamson and is now part of Reynolds ("American"); Philip Morris Companies, now Altria ("Altria"); British American Tobacco (Investments) Ltd. ("BATCo"); B.A.T. Industries p.l.c., now part of BATCo ("BAT Industries"); The Council for Tobacco Research–USA, Inc. ("CTR"); and The Tobacco Institute, Inc. ("TI"). The last two entities are trade organizations the cigarette manufacturers created; they do not manufacture or sell tobacco products. The district court dismissed BAT Industries from the case for lack of personal jurisdiction.

The government alleged that Defendants violated and continued to violate RICO by joining together in a decades-long conspiracy to deceive the American public about the health effects and addictiveness of smoking cigarettes. Specifically, the government alleged that Defendants fraudulently denied that smoking causes cancer and emphysema, that secondhand smoke causes lung cancer and endangers children's respiratory and auditory systems, that nicotine is an addictive drug and Defendants manipulated it to sustain addiction, that light and low tar cigarettes are not less harmful than full flavor cigarettes, and that Defendants intentionally marketed to youth. * * * In addition, the government alleged that Defendants concealed evidence and destroyed documents to hide the dangers of smoking and protect themselves in litigation. * * *

After years of pretrial proceedings and discovery, the case went to trial in September 2004. The bench trial lasted nine months and included live testimony from 84 witnesses, written testimony from 162 witnesses, and almost 14,000 exhibits in evidence. The government presented evidence that the presidents of Philip Morris, Reynolds, Brown & Williamson, Lorillard, and American assembled together in 1953 to strategize a response to growing public concern about the health risks of smoking and jointly retained a public relations firm to assist in the endeavor. From the beginning they agreed that no cigarette manufacturer would "seek a competitive advantage by inferring to its public that *its* product is less risky than others"; they would make no "claims that special filters or toasting, or expert selection of tobacco, or extra length in the butt, or anything else, makes a given brand less likely to cause you-know-what." * * * Acting on this agreement, the cigarette manufacturers jointly issued "*A Frank Statement to Cigarette Smokers*," published as a full-page advertisement in newspapers across the country on January 4, 1954. "The Frank Statement set forth the industry's 'open question' position that it would maintain for more than forty years—that cigarette smoking was not a proven cause of lung cancer; that cigarettes were not injurious to health; and that more research on smoking and health issues was needed." All of the Defendant manufacturers eventually joined this collective effort.

The government presented evidence from the 1950s and continuing through the following decades demonstrating that the Defendant manufacturers were aware—increasingly so as they conducted more research—that smoking causes disease, including lung cancer. Evidence at trial revealed that at the same time Defendants were disseminating advertisements, publications, and public statements denying any adverse health effects of smoking and promoting their "open question" strategy of sowing doubt, they internally acknowledged as fact that smoking causes disease and other health hazards. * * * Although the manufacturers conducted their own research and public relations regarding health and other issues, they also relied in part on a series of jointly-created entities. Among these entities were Defendants TI and CTR (formerly the Tobacco Industry Research Committee). The Defendant manufacturers created TI and CTR, composed their membership, staffed their boards of directors with executives from the manufacturers, and maintained frequent communication between high-level manufacturer and joint-entity officials. Evidence at trial showed that TI and CTR conducted the manufacturers' joint public relations through false and misleading press releases and publications, trained representatives from the manufacturers regarding their coordinated industry message, conducted some cigarette testing for the manufacturers, and funded "special projects" to produce favorable research results and witnesses specifically for use in litigation and for support of industry public statements.

In addition to the health hazards of smoking, the government presented evidence that Defendants intimately understood the addictiveness of nicotine and manipulated nicotine delivery in cigarettes to create and sustain addiction. Evidence showed that Defendants undertook extensive research into the physiological impact of nicotine, how it operates within the human body, and how the physical and chemical design parameters of cigarettes influence the delivery of nicotine to smokers. As a result of this research, they recognized and internally acknowledged that smoking and nicotine are addictive and they engineered their products around creating and sustaining this addiction. Evidence at trial suggested that despite this internal knowledge, for decades Defendants publicly denied and distorted the truth about the addictive nature of their products, suppressed research revealing the addictiveness of nicotine, and denied their efforts to control nicotine levels and delivery.

The government also presented evidence tending to show that Defendants marketed and promoted their low tar brands to smokers—who were concerned about the health hazards of smoking or considering quitting—as less harmful than full flavor cigarettes despite either lacking evidence to substantiate their claims or knowing them to be false. Internal industry documents introduced at trial revealed that by the late 1960s and early 1970s, Defendants were aware that lower tar cigarettes are unlikely to provide health benefits because they do not actually deliver the low levels of tar and nicotine advertised. Defendants researched and understood the phenomenon whereby smokers of low tar cigarettes, to satisfy their addiction, modify their smoking behavior to compensate for the reduced nicotine yields by "taking more frequent puffs, inhaling smoke more deeply, holding smoke in their lungs longer, covering cigarette ventilation holes with fingers or lips, and/or smoking more cigarettes." As a result of this nicotine-driven behavior, smokers of low tar cigarettes boost their intake of tar, so that lower tar cigarettes do not result in lower tar intake and therefore do not yield the touted health benefits or serve as a step toward quitting smoking. Evidence at trial suggested that Defendants understood this concept-for some time, better than the public health community or government regulators-while they promoted lower tar cigarettes as "health reassurance" brands.

Regarding secondhand smoke, the government presented evidence suggesting that Defendants became aware that secondhand smoke poses a health risk to nonsmokers but made misleading public statements and advertisements about secondhand smoke in an attempt to cause the public to doubt the evidence of its harmfulness. At trial, internal industry documents revealed that Defendants believed the public perception of secondhand smoke could determine the industry's survival and that secondhand smoke research by the cigarette manufacturers was a sensitive issue due to the absence of "objective science" supporting their position and the risk that their own research would lead to unfavorable results. As a result, the manufacturers jointly created the Center for Indoor Air Research ("CIAR") to coordinate and fund their secondhand smoke research with the appearance of independence. * * *

In addition to these topics, the government also presented evidence to the district court regarding Defendants' targeted marketing to youth under twenty-one years of age and their denials of such marketing, as well as evidence concerning Defendants' employees and attorneys destroying documents relevant to their public and litigation positions and suppressing or concealing scientific research.

* * *

We address Defendants' * * * general challenges to fraud liability in Part III, their challenges to specific aspects of the fraudulent scheme and the liability of specific Defendants in Part IV. * * *

III. General Challenges to Fraud Liability

A. Specific Intent

The predicate acts of racketeering in this case were all acts of mail or wire fraud, which require specific intent to defraud. * * * Defendants challenge the district court's conclusion that they acted with specific intent, arguing that the district court applied an impermissible "collective intent" standard and that the government did not present any evidence to support a finding of specific intent under the correct formulation.

Corporations may be held liable for specific intent offenses based on the "knowledge and intent" of their employees. *N.Y. Cent. & Hudson River R.R. Co. v. United States*, 212 U.S. 481, 495 (1909); see *United States v. A & P Trucking Co.*, 358 U.S. 121, 125 (1958). Because a corporation only acts and wills by virtue of its employees, the proscribed corporate intent depends on the wrongful intent of specific employees. * * * Thus, to determine whether a corporation made a false or misleading statement with specific intent to defraud, we look to the state of mind of the individual corporate officers and employees who made, ordered, or approved the statement. * * *

Here, the district court concluded that the chief executive officers and other highly placed officials in the Defendant corporations made or approved statements they knew to be false or misleading, evincing their specific intent to defraud consumers. In some instances, the court found by direct evidence that representatives of the Defendant companies "willfully stat[ed] something which they knew to be untrue." * * * For example, the court found that, in a televised interview in 1971, Philip Morris President Joseph Cullman III denied that cigarettes posed a health hazard to pregnant women or their infants, "contradict[ing] the information Helmut Wakeham, Philip Morris's Vice President for Corporate Research and Development, had given him two years earlier." In the main, however, the district court relied on indirect and circumstantial evidence indicating that the senior corporate officials knew that their public statements, and those that they approved for their corporations, were false or misleading.

In the majority of instances, the authors of the fraudulent statements alleged as Racketeering Acts were executives, including high level scientists—CEOs, Vice Presidents, Heads of Research & Development, not entry level employees—at each of the Defendant companies who would reasonably be expected to have knowledge of the company's internal research, public positions, and long term strategies.

The court reasoned:

> [I]t is absurd to believe that the highly-ranked representatives and agents of these corporations and entities had no knowledge that their public statements were false and fraudulent. The Findings of Fact are replete with examples of C.E.O.s, Vice–Presidents, and Directors of Research and Development, as well as the Defendants' lawyers, making statements which were inconsistent with the internal knowledge and practice of the corporation itself.

The district court did not commit legal error by imputing to Defendants' executives knowledge of the falsity of their statements based on inferences reasonably drawn from the facts shown, and sufficient evidence supported these inferences.

The government presented decades of evidence that scientists within the Defendant corporations and outside scientists hired by the corporations and their joint entities were continually conducting research and reviewing the research of other scientists regarding cigarettes and health, addiction, nicotine and tar manipulation, and secondhand smoke. The evidence at trial demonstrated that the results of this research-essential to the core of Defendants' operations, including strategic planning, product development, and advertising-were well known, acknowledged, and accepted throughout the corporations. These results established that cigarette smoking causes disease, that nicotine is addictive, that light cigarettes do not present lower health risks than regular cigarettes due to smoker compensation, and that secondhand smoke is hazardous to health. Dr. William Farone, a scientist who worked at Philip Morris for eighteen years and whom the district court found to be "impressive and credible as both a fact and expert witness," testified about the understanding within Philip Morris on the question of whether cigarette smoking is a cause of lung cancer and other diseases:

> There was widespread acceptance that smoking caused disease. I never talked with a scientist at Philip Morris who said that smoking doesn't cause disease. [This was based on the] compelling epidemiology such as that recounted in the Surgeon's [*sic*] General's reports, and our knowledge about the chemicals that were created by cigarettes and what was delivered to the smoker, hundreds of times per day on average.

* * * When asked whether, in his discussions with Philip Morris executives, any of them challenged the validity of the scientific evidence that smoking causes disease, Farone answered,

> No. Their comments generally focused on how the company could or should respond, not to whether the scientific evidence was valid. Remember, a main reason why they hired me in 1976 was to help develop a less hazardous cigarette. It seemed to me at the time I was hired, and certainly was the case during my entire time there, that hiring me for that job was itself implicit recognition that the cigarettes that were out there being sold were causing disease.

* * * Defendants' own documents also support the inference that Defendants' executives were aware that their public relations strategy of creating the impression of an "open question" about the link between smoking and disease did not square with their own knowledge about the established link between the two. For example, William Kloepfer, Vice President of Public Relations for the Tobacco Institute, wrote to Earle Clements, President of the Tobacco Institute, admitting that "[o]ur basic position in the cigarette controversy is subject to the charge, and may be subject to a finding, that we are making false or misleading statements to promote the sale of cigarettes." * * *

The government presented similar evidence regarding the other aspects of Defendants' scheme, such as addiction and nicotine. A few examples cannot adequately present the volumes of evidence underlying the district court's findings of fact, but the following provide a fair sample: A 1991 Reynolds Research and Development report acknowledged that "[w]e are basically in the nicotine business." Dr. Farone testified that during his time at Philip Morris there was "widespread acceptance internally throughout the company-among executives, scientists, and marketing people" that nicotine was primarily responsible for addiction to smoking. Indeed, the district court found that "internal documents and testimony from former company employees affirmed that within their corporate walls, Defendants openly recognized the addictiveness of cigarettes." Regarding light cigarettes, internal research reports and memoranda at the Defendant companies revealed that they understood the phenomenon of smoker compensation and studied how to manipulate it in order to make their light brands appealing to addicted smokers while continuing to be able to advertise the brands as low tar. For example, a 1978 BATCo memorandum about that company's internal research acknowledged that "a majority of habitual smokers compensate for changed delivery" and explained that if smokers "choose [a] lower delivery brand * * * than their usual brand" they "will in fact increase the amounts of tar and gas phase that they take in, in order to take in the same amount of nicotine." * * * Dr. Farone testified that Defendants' superior knowledge of compensation (compared to that of scientists outside the industry, including the government) was closely held within Philip Morris and the tobacco industry and there was an "effort on the part of [his] coworkers at Philip Morris, including [his] supervisors, to restrict any public acknowledgment on the part of Philip Morris of the phenomena of compensation."

As these examples and hundreds more findings in the district court's opinion demonstrate, the court had before it sufficient evidence from which to conclude that Defendants' executives, who directed the activities of the Defendant corporations and their joint entities, knew about the negative health consequences of smoking, the addictiveness and manipulation of nicotine, the harmfulness of secondhand smoke, and the concept of smoker compensation, which makes light cigarettes no less harmful than regular cigarettes and possibly more. * * *

Specific intent to defraud may be inferred where, as here, there is a pattern of corporate research revealing a particular proposition, for example, that smoking is addictive; an ensuing pattern of memoranda within the corporation acknowledging that smoking is addictive, even though the memoranda may or may not have gone directly to the executive who makes the contrary statement; and the corporate CEO or other official of high corporate status then makes a public statement stating that smoking is not addictive, contrary to the knowledge within the corporation. Based on this sort of evidence and the inferences reasonably drawn from it, a factfinder could permissibly infer that the speaker harbored specific intent to defraud at the time he or she made the false or misleading statement. Moreover, such pervasive knowledge throughout the organizations demonstrates that Defendants' executives at least acted with reckless disregard for the truth or falsity of their statements. As the district court correctly held, such reckless disregard suffices to demonstrate the requisite intent. * * * The law then imputes this specific intent to the corporation.

* * *

B. Materiality

In their next general challenge to fraud liability, Defendants argue that their false and misleading statements about the health effects of smoking cannot, as a legal matter, be fraudulent because their statements were not material. This argument is based on a flawed understanding of the materiality requirement.

In order for a false or misleading statement to qualify as mail or wire fraud, it "must concern a material or important fact or matter." *United States v. Winstead*, 74 F.3d 1313, 1320 (D.C.Cir.1996). This materiality requirement is met if the matter at issue is "of importance to a reasonable person in making a decision about a particular matter or transaction."

* * * [T]he test is only whether a reasonable person would consider the matter to be of importance regarding the transaction.

The false statements identified by the district court would be important to a reasonable person purchasing cigarettes. For example, statements about the adverse health effects of smoking * * * would be a matter of importance to a reasonable person deciding to purchase cigarettes. The fact that Defendants continually denied any link between smoking and cancer * * * suggests they themselves considered the matter material. So, too, regarding Defendants' false statements on other topics, including statements concerning: whether smoking is addictive, * * * whether Defendants manipulated their cigarettes to control nicotine delivery, * * * whether "light" cigarettes were less harmful than other cigarettes, * * * whether secondhand smoke is hazardous to non-smokers, * * * and whether Defendants concealed scientific research and destroyed documents.

Each of these topics is an important consideration for a reasonable person because each concerns direct and significant consequences of smoking. When deciding whether to smoke cigarettes, tobacco consumers must resolve initial reservations (or lingering qualms) about the potential for cancer, the risk of addiction, or the hazardous effects of secondhand smoke for friends, family, and others who may be exposed. Defendants' prevarications about each of these issues suggests full awareness of this obvious fact; reasonable purchasers of cigarettes would consider these statements important.

Defendants further argue that, because the scientific community had reached a consensus regarding the severely adverse health consequences of smoking, their statements to the contrary would not be believed. * * * The question, however, is not whether a reasonable person would have believed Defendants' false statements, but only whether a reasonable person would have considered the issue "of importance," and the issues considered by the district court clearly met the materiality threshold.

C. First Amendment

In their final general challenge to fraud liability, Defendants claim at least a portion of their statements qualify as protected activity under the First Amendment. Of course, it is well settled that the First Amendment does not protect fraud. * * * Recognizing this fact, Defendants argue their statements were not fraudulent, but those arguments are discussed and rejected elsewhere in this opinion. *See supra* Part III.A–B; *infra* Part IV.

Defendants next claim protection under the *Noerr–Pennington* doctrine—a doctrine, rooted in the Petition Clause of the First Amendment, that protects "an attempt to persuade the legislature or the executive to take particular action with respect to a law* * * " *E. R.R. Presidents Conference v. Noerr Motor Freight, Inc.*, 365 U.S. 127, 136 (1961). The protection does not "cover activity that was not genuinely intended to influence government action." *Allied Tube & Conduit Corp. v. Indian Head*, 486 U.S. 492, 508 n. 10, (1988).

Defendants' attempt to invoke *Noerr–Pennington* as protection fails because the doctrine does not protect deliberately false or misleading statements. "[N]either the Noerr–Pennington doctrine nor the First Amendment more generally protects petitions predicated on fraud or deliberate misrepresentation." *Edmondson & Gallagher v. Alban Towers Tenants Ass'n*, 48 F.3d 1260, 1267 (D.C. Cir. 1995) * * *

IV. Specific Challenges to Fraud Liability

A. "Light" Cigarettes

The first specific fraud finding Defendants challenge relates to their marketing of "light" cigarettes. The district court found: "As their internal documents reveal, Defendants engaged in massive, sustained, and highly sophisticated marketing and promotional campaigns to portray their light brands as less harmful than regular cigarettes." * * * The court concluded "Defendants have known for decades that filtered and low tar cigarettes do not offer a meaningful reduction of risk, and that their marketing which emphasized reductions in tar and nicotine was false and misleading."

Defendants contend they should be immune from liability because the Federal Trade Commission ("FTC") has blessed their use of labels such as "light" and "low tar." This argument is entirely foreclosed by the Supreme Court's recent decision in *Altria Group, Inc. v. Good*, 555 U.S. 70 (2008), concluding the FTC has never condoned the use of "light" or "low tar" descriptors. * * *

It is also worth noting that the district court in this case did not find liability solely based on the use of descriptors such as "light" and "low tar." The court found Defendants orchestrated "highly sophisticated marketing and promotional campaigns to portray their light brands as less harmful than regular cigarettes." * * * In addition to the misleading use of descriptors, the district court found "[Defendants'] public statements are blatantly false" in relation to the marketing of "light" cigarettes. * * * The district court went on to find that "[a]s part of the Enterprise's scheme to defraud smokers, Defendants withheld and suppressed their extensive knowledge and understanding of nicotine-driven smoker compensation." * * * These findings reveal that fraudulent activity surrounding "light" cigarettes was not merely limited to the use of misleading descriptors. In addition to the fact that the descriptors were not authorized by the FTC, the district court relied on other fraudulent activity by Defendants.

Independent of their FTC-authorization argument, Defendants also insist terms such as "light cigarettes" are not misleading to the public. They analogize "light" cigarettes to sodas which are "low caffeine" and cookies which are "low fat." According to Defendants, the public knows that drinking many "low caffeine" sodas can result in higher levels of caffeine consumption, and eating many "low fat" cookies can result in higher levels of fat consumption. Defendants thus analogize to "light" cigarettes, maintaining that it is obvious that smoking many "light" cigarettes can result in higher levels of nicotine and tar consumption. But the analogy to "light cigarettes" is inapt. Unlike drinking sodas and eating cookies, the factors behind compensation in "light" cigarettes are largely subconscious: "the smoker will subconsciously adjust his puff volume and frequency, and smoking frequency, so as to obtain and maintain his per hour and per day requirement for nicotine." *Philip Morris*, 449 F.Supp.2d at 467 (citing internal tobacco company documents). Not only is smoker compensation subconscious, but factors such as puff volume and frequency are not even tied to the number of "light" cigarettes smoked. The analogy to sodas and cookies fails; the subconscious nature of smoker compensation enabled Defendants to mislead the public about the health effects of "light" cigarettes.

Finally, Defendants argue their descriptors were simply verbal representations of numerical ratings authorized by the FTC, and thus were literally true. Even leaving aside the fact that literally true statements may nevertheless constitute fraud, this claim founders on the district court's finding that "there are lights of certain brands with higher tar levels than regulars of other brands from the same company, and there are also lights and regulars of the same brands that have the same FTC tar rating." * * * This finding, which Defendants do not attempt to show is clearly erroneous, reveals the descriptors were not simply representations of numerical ratings and thus were not "literally true."

B. Secondhand Smoke

We turn next to Defendants' claim that the district court erred in finding that they fraudulently denied the adverse health effects of secondhand smoke. Federal Rule of Civil Procedure 52 obliges us to uphold the district court's findings of fact unless they are "clearly erroneous." Fed. R. Civ. P. 52(a)(6). * * *

Defendants contend that their statements disputing the health hazards of secondhand smoke were merely good-faith expressions of opinion. But the district court found to the contrary—that Defendants' representations were fraudulent and not in good faith. Under Rule 52, then, the question for us is whether this finding was clearly erroneous.

The district court criticized Defendants' statements regarding secondhand smoke as contrary to the scientific consensus. Defendants object, emphasizing that the district court found no scientific consensus emerged until the issuance of the Surgeon General's 1986 report determining secondhand smoke to be hazardous. Moreover, they point to evidence of selected post–1986 scientific opinions casting doubt on the dangers of secondhand smoke, arguing that even then they possessed some basis for disputing the consensus.

Defendants' objections are beside the point. The district court based its finding of fraudulent intent not just on the existence of a consensus but also on evidence of Defendants' own knowledge. * * * Specifically, the district court found that dating back to the 1970s, Defendants' own research and analysis revealed the hazards of secondhand smoke. For example, the district court found that in 1980 a Philip Morris scientist reviewed a paper concluding that secondhand smoke caused "significant damage to airway function" in exposed nonsmokers, and found "little to criticize," deeming the paper "an excellent piece of work which could be very damaging" to the industry. * * * In 1982, a Philip Morris-sponsored research facility concluded that the "side stream" smoke composing the bulk of secondhand smoke is "more irritating and/or toxic" than the "main stream" smoke inhaled by smokers. * * * And several TI advertisements and press releases claimed that an independent 1981 study showing "a significant correlation between lung cancer and secondhand smoke" suffered from a statistical flaw yet the district court found that industry consultants told TI, Reynolds, and Brown & Williamson that TI knew at the time not only that the statistical error did not exist, but also that the study was in fact correct. * * *

In addition to these and other findings providing relatively direct evidence that Defendants were aware of the health risks of secondhand smoke, the district court found that Defendants concealed their role in making statements regarding secondhand smoke. * * * [T]he concealment of identity by Defendants over so long a period on a subject of such intense controversy is at the very least consistent with knowledge of the falsity of their statements.

Although Defendants insist they had no knowledge of the misleading character of their public statements, they nowhere challenge the accuracy of these or any of the district court's other findings suggestive of their knowledge. Instead, they argue that such findings reveal only facts that were known to the public and that had not, at the time, given rise to a scientific consensus. Again Defendants miss the point. The question is not whether *other* individuals knew that Defendants' claims were false or misleading; the question is whether *Defendants* did. Regardless of whether a scientific consensus existed at any point, Defendants may be liable for fraud if they made statements knowing they were false or misleading. Based on voluminous evidence, including that summarized above, the district court circumstantially inferred that Defendants did in fact possess such fraudulent intent. Given these unchallenged findings, we have no basis for saying that the district court clearly erred in drawing that conclusion.

C. Addiction

Defendants also claim that the district court clearly erred in finding their representations disputing the addictiveness of cigarettes to be intentionally misleading. We analyze the district court's factual finding as to the misleading character of Defendants' commercial statements for clear error. * * * We find none.

Defendants claim that their statements regarding addiction were not intentionally misleading because the term "addiction" is ambiguous. Pointing to the district court's findings that the meaning of the term "addiction" in the scientific community changed over time, Defendants insist that their statements merely clung to the earlier, narrower, definitions of the term, and claim that the district court erroneously converted a semantic dispute into a fraud case. But the district court did not find only that Defendants insisted on retaining an earlier definition of addiction. It found that they did so as part of a concerted effort to misrepresent the difficulty of quitting smoking. * * * Defendants fail to demonstrate that this finding was clearly erroneous.

To begin with, Defendants never challenge the district court's findings documenting the impact of nicotine on the body and, more importantly, Defendants' understanding of its effects. * * * As early as 1963, Brown &

Williamson's general counsel wrote a confidential memorandum stating: "We are, then, in the business of selling nicotine, an addictive drug effective in the release of stress mechanisms." (quotation marks omitted). Further, the district court found that Defendants were aware that cigarette dependence was stronger than mere habit formation. In 1974, a Philip Morris scientist told the company's president that it was "simply not an adequate explanation to say that smoking is a habit, or that it is social behavior." * * * In 1981, a Philip Morris executive wrote in an article: "Cigarettes are not just habit forming-the body builds up a requirement for them." Although several industry attorneys expressed dismay at the publication of the article, none disagreed with it. In 1985, Philip Morris's top management was informed that research showed that "the majority of smokers wished they did not smoke." * * * These and numerous other findings—all unchallenged—support the district court's conclusion that Defendants were aware that nicotine creates a chemical dependency far stronger than a mere habit.

The district court found that despite their knowledge Defendants made numerous statements trivializing and outright denying the dependence cigarettes cause. For example, in 1982 TI issued a press release summarizing testimony that smoking caused an "attachment" comparable to that produced by "tennis, jogging, candy, rock music, Coca-cola, members of the opposite sex and hamburgers." * * * In 1997, Philip Morris's CEO testified, "If [cigarettes] are behaviorally addictive or habit forming, they are much more like * * * Gummi Bears, and I eat Gummi Bears, and I don't like it when I don't eat my Gummi Bears, but I'm certainly not addicted to them." * * * In a 1994 television interview, a TI official claimed that there was "no chemical addiction" to nicotine and stated, "[S]ometimes we use the word 'addiction' in very broad terms. We talk about being, you know, news junkies. We talk about being chocoholics." * * * A 1988 TI press release declared that "it has been impossible to establish that the feelings persons have upon giving up smoking are *anything but* that which would be expected when one is frustrated by giving up *any desired habit.*" * * * Most directly, the district court found that Defendants had their representatives testify that nicotine "did not cause addiction *or dependence*," (emphasis added), rendering any supposed ambiguities in the word "addiction" beside the point.

The district court concluded that these and other findings reflected a campaign of statements intended to mislead the public into believing that giving up smoking is not markedly more difficult than giving up everyday habits. Although not every statement Defendants made was literally false, even partially true statements can be actionable fraud if intentionally misleading as to facts. * * *

Questions

1. At least since 1964, the public has known that smoking tobacco products is unhealthy and shortens life expectancy. The tobacco companies are in the business of selling unhealthy products, but they do not make

consumption decisions for individuals. How could they possibly mislead the public?

2. What were the legal standards the Court used to examine whether the tobacco industry communicated misleading information to the public?

3. Public officials and private individuals sometimes make statements that are "contrary to the scientific consensus" regarding public health, the environment, and other issues. Should they be held liable for disseminating misleading information? If so, under what circumstances?

The Stolen Valor Act

United States v. Alvarez

132 S.Ct. 2537 (2012)

■ JUSTICE KENNEDY announced the judgment of the Court and delivered an opinion, in which THE CHIEF JUSTICE, JUSTICE GINSBURG, and JUSTICE SOTOMAYOR join.

Lying was his habit. Xavier Alvarez, the respondent here, lied when he said that he played hockey for the Detroit Red Wings and that he once married a starlet from Mexico. But when he lied in announcing he held the Congressional Medal of Honor, respondent ventured onto new ground; for that lie violates a federal criminal statute, the Stolen Valor Act of 2005. 18 U.S.C. § 704.

In 2007, respondent attended his first public meeting as a board member of the Three Valley Water District Board. The board is a governmental entity with headquarters in Claremont, California. He introduced himself as follows: "I'm a retired marine of 25 years. I retired in the year 2001. Back in 1987, I was awarded the Congressional Medal of Honor. I got wounded many times by the same guy." None of this was true. For all the record shows, respondent's statements were but a pathetic attempt to gain respect that eluded him. The statements do not seem to have been made to secure employment or financial benefits or admission to privileges reserved for those who had earned the Medal.

Respondent was indicted under the Stolen Valor Act for lying about the Congressional Medal of Honor at the meeting. The United States District Court for the Central District of California rejected his claim that the statute is invalid under the First Amendment. Respondent pleaded guilty to one count, reserving the right to appeal on his First Amendment claim. The United States Court of Appeals for the Ninth Circuit, in a decision by a divided panel, found the Act invalid under the First Amendment and reversed the conviction. With further opinions on the issue, and over a dissent by seven judges, rehearing en banc was denied. This Court granted certiorari. * * *

After certiorari was granted, and in an unrelated case, the United States Court of Appeals for the Tenth Circuit, also in a decision by a divided panel, found the Act constitutional. *United States v. Strandlof*, 667 F.3d 1146 (10th Cir. 2012). So there is now a conflict in the Courts of Appeals on the question of the Act's validity. * * *

It is right and proper that Congress, over a century ago, established an award so the Nation can hold in its highest respect and esteem those who, in the course of carrying out the "supreme and noble duty of contributing to the defense of the rights and honor of the nation," *Selective Draft Law Cases*, 245 U.S. 366, 390 (1918), have acted with extraordinary honor. And it should be uncontested that this is a legitimate Government objective, indeed a most valued national aspiration and purpose. This does not end the inquiry, however. Fundamental constitutional principles require that laws enacted to honor the brave must be consistent with the precepts of the Constitution for which they fought.

The Government contends the criminal prohibition is a proper means to further its purpose in creating and awarding the Medal. When content-based speech regulation is in question, however, exacting scrutiny is required. Statutes suppressing or restricting speech must be judged by the sometimes inconvenient principles of the First Amendment. By this measure, the statutory provisions under which respondent was convicted must be held invalid, and his conviction must be set aside.

I

Respondent's claim to hold the Congressional Medal of Honor was false. There is no room to argue about interpretation or shades of meaning. On this premise, respondent violated § 704(b); and, because the lie concerned the Congressional Medal of Honor, he was subject to an enhanced penalty under subsection (c). Those statutory provisions are as follows:

> (b) FALSE CLAIMS ABOUT RECEIPT OF MILITARY DECORATIONS OR MEDALS.—Whoever falsely represents himself or herself, verbally or in writing, to have been awarded any decoration or medal authorized by Congress for the Armed Forces of the United States . . . shall be fined under this title, imprisoned not more than six months, or both.
>
> (c) ENHANCED PENALTY FOR OFFENSES INVOLVING CONGRESSIONAL MEDAL OF HONOR.—
>
> (1) IN GENERAL.—If a decoration or medal involved in an offense under subsection (a) or (b) is a Congressional Medal of Honor, in lieu of the punishment provided in that subsection, the offender shall be fined under this title, imprisoned not more than 1 year, or both.

Respondent challenges the statute as a content-based suppression of pure speech, speech not falling within any of the few categories of expression where content-based regulation is permissible. The Government defends the statute as necessary to preserve the integrity and purpose of the Medal, an integrity and purpose it contends are compromised and frustrated by the false statements the statute prohibits. It argues that false statements "have no First Amendment value in themselves," and thus "are protected only to the extent needed to avoid chilling fully protected speech." * * * The Government's arguments cannot suffice to save the statute.

II

* * * The Government * * * gives three examples of regulations on false speech that courts generally have found permissible: first, the crimi-

nal prohibition of a false statement made to a Government official, 18 U.S.C. § 1001; second, laws punishing perjury; and third, prohibitions on the false representation that one is speaking as a Government official or on behalf of the Government, see, *e.g.,* § 912; § 709. These restrictions, however, do not establish a principle that all proscriptions of false statements are exempt from exacting First Amendment scrutiny.

The federal statute prohibiting false statements to Government officials punishes "whoever, in any matter within the jurisdiction of the executive, legislative, or judicial branch of the Government ... makes any materially false, fictitious, or fraudulent statement or representation." § 1001. Section 1001's prohibition on false statements made to Government officials, in communications concerning official matters, does not lead to the broader proposition that false statements are unprotected when made to any person, at any time, in any context.

The same point can be made about what the Court has confirmed is the "unquestioned constitutionality of perjury statutes," both the federal statute, § 1623, and its state-law equivalents. * * * It is not simply because perjured statements are false that they lack First Amendment protection. Perjured testimony "is at war with justice" because it can cause a court to render a "judgment not resting on truth." Perjury undermines the function and province of the law and threatens the integrity of judgments that are the basis of the legal system. * * *

Statutes that prohibit falsely representing that one is speaking on behalf of the Government, or that prohibit impersonating a Government officer, also protect the integrity of Government processes, quite apart from merely restricting false speech. * * *

As our law and tradition show, then, there are instances in which the falsity of speech bears upon whether it is protected. * * * The Government has not demonstrated that false statements generally should constitute a new category of unprotected speech. * * *

III

The probable, and adverse, effect of the Act on freedom of expression illustrates, in a fundamental way, the reasons for the Law's distrust of content-based speech prohibitions.

The Act by its plain terms applies to a false statement made at any time, in any place, to any person. It can be assumed that it would not apply to, say, a theatrical performance. * * * Still, the sweeping, quite unprecedented reach of the statute puts it in conflict with the First Amendment. Here the lie was made in a public meeting, but the statute would apply with equal force to personal, whispered conversations within a home. The statute seeks to control and suppress all false statements on this one subject in almost limitless times and settings. And it does so entirely without regard to whether the lie was made for the purpose of material gain. * * *

Permitting the government to decree this speech to be a criminal offense, whether shouted from the rooftops or made in a barely audible whisper, would endorse government authority to compile a list of subjects about which false statements are punishable. That governmental power has no clear limiting principle. * * * Where false claims are made to effect a fraud or secure moneys or other valuable considerations, say offers of employment, it is well established that the Government may restrict speech without affronting the First Amendment. * * * But the Stolen Valor Act is not so limited in its reach. * * *

IV

* * * The Government is correct when it states military medals "serve the important public function of recognizing and expressing gratitude for acts of heroism and sacrifice in military service," and also " 'foste[r] morale, mission accomplishment and esprit de corps' among service members." General George Washington observed that an award for valor would "cherish a virtuous ambition in ... soldiers, as well as foster and encourage every species of military merit." * * * Time has not diminished this idea. In periods of war and peace alike public recognition of valor and noble sacrifice by men and women in uniform reinforces the pride and national resolve that the military relies upon to fulfill its mission.

These interests are related to the integrity of the military honors system in general, and the Congressional Medal of Honor in particular. Although millions have served with brave resolve, the Medal, which is the highest military award for valor against an enemy force, has been given just 3,476 times. Established in 1861, the Medal is reserved for those who have distinguished themselves "conspicuously by gallantry and intrepidity at the risk of his life above and beyond the call of duty." * * * The stories of those who earned the Medal inspire and fascinate, from Dakota Meyer who in 2009 drove five times into the midst of a Taliban ambush to save 36 lives, * * * to Desmond Doss who served as an army medic on Okinawa and on June 5, 1945, rescued 75 fellow soldiers, and who, after being wounded, gave up his own place on a stretcher so others could be taken to safety, * * * to William Carney who sustained multiple gunshot wounds to the head, chest, legs, and arm, and yet carried the flag to ensure it did not touch the ground during the Union army's assault on Fort Wagner in July 1863. The rare acts of courage the Medal celebrates led President Truman to say he would "rather have that medal round my neck than ... be president of the United States." * * * The Government's interest in protecting the integrity of the Medal of Honor is beyond question.

But to recite the Government's compelling interests is not to end the matter. The First Amendment requires that the Government's chosen restriction on the speech at issue be "actually necessary" to achieve its interest. * * * It must be acknowledged that when a pretender claims the Medal to be his own, the lie might harm the Government by demeaning the high purpose of the award, diminishing the honor it confirms, and creating the appearance that the Medal is awarded more often than is true. Furthermore, the lie may offend the true holders of the Medal. From one perspective it insults their bravery and high principles when falsehood puts them in the unworthy company of a pretender.

Yet these interests do not satisfy the Government's heavy burden when it seeks to regulate protected speech. * * * The Government points to no evidence to support its claim that the public's general perception of military awards is diluted by false claims such as those made by Alvarez. * * *

The Government [also] has not shown, and cannot show, why counter-speech would not suffice to achieve its interest. The facts of this case indicate that the dynamics of free speech, of counterspeech, of refutation, can overcome the lie. Respondent lied at a public meeting. Even before the FBI began investigating him for his false statements "Alvarez was perceived as a phony." Once the lie was made public, he was ridiculed online, his actions were reported in the press, and a fellow board member called for his resignation. There is good reason to believe that a similar fate would befall other false claimants. * * * Indeed, the outrage and contempt expressed for respondent's lies can serve to reawaken and reinforce the public's respect for the Medal, its recipients, and its high purpose. The acclaim that recipients of the Congressional Medal of Honor receive also casts doubt on the proposition that the public will be misled by the claims of charlatans or become cynical of those whose heroic deeds earned them the Medal by right. * * *

The remedy for speech that is false is speech that is true. This is the ordinary course in a free society. The response to the unreasoned is the rational; to the uninformed, the enlightened; to the straightout lie, the simple truth. See *Whitney v. California*, 274 U.S. 357, 377 (1927) (Brandeis, J., concurring) ("If there be time to expose through discussion the falsehood and fallacies, to avert the evil by the processes of education, the remedy to be applied is more speech, not enforced silence"). The theory of our Constitution is "that the best test of truth is the power of the thought to get itself accepted in the competition of the market," *Abrams v. United States*, 250 U.S. 616, 630 (1919) (Holmes, J., dissenting). The First Amendment itself ensures the right to respond to speech we do not like, and for good reason. Freedom of speech and thought flows not from the beneficence of the state but from the inalienable rights of the person. And suppression of speech by the government can make exposure of falsity more difficult, not less so. Society has the right and civic duty to engage in open, dynamic, rational discourse. These ends are not well served when the government seeks to orchestrate public discussion through content-based mandates.

* * * The American people do not need the assistance of a government prosecution to express their high regard for the special place that military heroes hold in our tradition. Only a weak society needs government protection or intervention before it pursues its resolve to preserve the truth. Truth needs neither handcuffs nor a badge for its vindication.

In addition, when the Government seeks to regulate protected speech, the restriction must be the "least restrictive means among available, effective alternatives." There is, however, at least one less speech-restrictive means by which the Government could likely protect the integrity of the military awards system. A Government-created database could list Congressional Medal of Honor winners. Were a database accessible through the Internet, it would be easy to verify and expose false claims. It appears some private individuals have already created databases similar to this, and at least one database of past winners is online and fully searchable. * * *

The Solicitor General responds that although Congress and the Department of Defense investigated the feasibility of establishing a database in 2008, the Government "concluded that such a database would be impracticable and insufficiently comprehensive." Without more explanation, it is difficult to assess the Government's claim, especially when at least one database of Congressional Medal of Honor winners already exists.

The Government may have responses to some of these criticisms, but there has been no clear showing of the necessity of the statute, the necessity required by exacting scrutiny.

* * *

The Nation well knows that one of the costs of the First Amendment is that it protects the speech we detest as well as the speech we embrace. Though few might find respondent's statements anything but contemptible, his right to make those statements is protected by the Constitution's guarantee of freedom of speech and expression. The Stolen Valor Act infringes upon speech protected by the First Amendment.

The judgment of the Court of Appeals is affirmed.

It is so ordered.

■ JUSTICE BREYER, with whom JUSTICE KAGAN joins, concurring in the judgment.

I agree with the plurality that the Stolen Valor Act of 2005 violates the First Amendment. But I do not rest my conclusion upon a strict categorical analysis. Rather, I base that conclusion upon the fact that the statute works First Amendment harm, while the Government can achieve its legitimate objectives in less restrictive ways.

I

* * * As the dissent points out, "there are broad areas in which any attempt by the state to penalize purportedly false speech would present a grave and unacceptable danger of suppressing truthful speech." Laws restricting false statements about philosophy, religion, history, the social sciences, the arts, and the like raise such concerns, and in many contexts have called for strict scrutiny. But this case does not involve such a law. The dangers of suppressing valuable ideas are lower where, as here, the regulations concern false statements about easily verifiable facts that do not concern such subject matter. Such false factual statements are less likely than are true factual statements to make a valuable contribution to the marketplace of ideas. And the government often has good reasons to prohibit such false speech. * * * But its regulation can nonetheless threaten speech-related harms. * * *

II

A

The Stolen Valor Act makes it a crime "falsely" to "represen[t]" oneself "to have been awarded any decoration or medal authorized by Congress for the Armed Forces of the United States." I would read the statute favorably to the Government as criminalizing only false factual statements made with knowledge of their falsity and with the intent that they be taken as true. * * * As so interpreted the statute covers only lies. But although this interpretation diminishes the extent to which the statute endangers First Amendment values, it does not eliminate the threat.

I must concede, as the Government points out, that this Court has frequently said or implied that false factual statements enjoy little First Amendment protection. See, e.g., *BE & K Constr. Co. v. NLRB*, 536 U.S. 516, 531 (2002) ("[F]alse statements may be unprotected for their own sake"); *Hustler Magazine, Inc. v. Falwell*, 485 U.S. 46, 52 (1988) ("False statements of fact are particularly valueless"); *Gertz v. Robert Welch, Inc.*, 418 U.S. 323, 340 (1974) ("[T]he erroneous statement of fact is not worthy of constitutional protection").

But these judicial statements cannot be read to mean "no protection at all." False factual statements can serve useful human objectives, for example: in social contexts, where they may prevent embarrassment, protect privacy, shield a person from prejudice, provide the sick with comfort, or preserve a child's innocence; in public contexts, where they may stop a panic or otherwise preserve calm in the face of danger; and even in technical, philosophical, and scientific contexts, where (as Socrates' methods suggest) examination of a false statement (even if made deliberately to mislead) can promote a form of thought that ultimately helps realize the truth. * * *

Moreover, as the Court has often said, the threat of criminal prosecution for making a false statement can inhibit the speaker from making true statements, thereby "chilling" a kind of speech that lies at the First Amendment's heart. * * *

I also must concede that many statutes and common-law doctrines make the utterance of certain kinds of false statements unlawful. Those prohibitions, however, tend to be narrower than the statute before us, in that they limit the scope of their application, sometimes by requiring proof of specific harm to identifiable victims; sometimes by specifying that the lies be made in contexts in which a tangible harm to others is especially likely to occur; and sometimes by limiting the prohibited lies to those that are particularly likely to produce harm.

Fraud statutes, for example, typically require proof of a misrepresentation that is material, upon which the victim relied, and which caused actual injury. * * * Torts involving the intentional infliction of emotional distress (like torts involving placing a victim in a false light) concern falsehoods that tend to cause harm to a specific victim of an emotional—dignitary—or privacy—related kind.

Perjury statutes prohibit a particular set of false statements—those made under oath—while requiring a showing of materiality. Statutes forbidding lying to a government official (not under oath) are typically limited to circumstances where a lie is likely to work particular and specific harm by interfering with the functioning of a government department, and those statutes also require a showing of materiality. * * *

Statutes prohibiting trademark infringement present, perhaps, the closest analogy to the present statute. Trademarks identify the source of a good; and infringement causes harm by causing confusion among potential customers (about the source) and thereby diluting the value of the mark to its owner, to consumers, and to the economy. Similarly, a false claim of possession of a medal or other honor creates confusion about who is entitled to wear it, thus diluting its value to those who have earned it, to their families, and to their country. But trademark statutes are focused upon commercial and promotional activities that are likely to dilute the value of a mark. Indeed, they typically require a showing of likely confusion, a showing that tends to assure that the feared harm will in fact take place. * * *

While this list is not exhaustive, it is sufficient to show that * * * virtually all these instances limitations of context, requirements of proof of injury, and the like, narrow the statute to a subset of lies where specific harm is more likely to occur. The limitations help to make certain that the statute does not allow its threat of liability or criminal punishment to roam at large, discouraging or forbidding the telling of the lie in contexts where harm is unlikely or the need for the prohibition is small.

The statute before us lacks any such limiting features. * * *

C

We must therefore ask whether it is possible substantially to achieve the Government's objective in less burdensome ways. In my view, the answer to this question is "yes." * * *

I recognize that in some contexts, particularly political contexts, such a narrowing will not always be easy to achieve. In the political arena a false statement is more likely to make a behavioral difference (say, by leading the listeners to vote for the speaker) but at the same time criminal prosecution is particularly dangerous (say, by radically changing a potential election result) and consequently can more easily result in censorship of speakers and their ideas. Thus, the statute may have to be significantly narrowed in its applications. * * *

The Government has provided no convincing explanation as to why a more finely tailored statute would not work. In my own view, such a statute could significantly reduce the threat of First Amendment harm while permitting the statute to achieve its important protective objective. That being so, I find the statute as presently drafted works disproportionate constitutional harm. It consequently fails intermediate scrutiny, and so violates the First Amendment.

For these reasons, I concur in the Court's judgment.

■ JUSTICE ALITO, with whom JUSTICE SCALIA and JUSTICE THOMAS join, dissenting.

Only the bravest of the brave are awarded the Congressional Medal of Honor, but the Court today holds that every American has a constitutional right to claim to have received this singular award. The Court strikes down the Stolen Valor Act of 2005, which was enacted to stem an epidemic of false claims about military decorations. These lies, Congress reasonably concluded, were undermining our country's system of military honors and inflicting real harm on actual medal recipients and their families.

Building on earlier efforts to protect the military awards system, Congress responded to this problem by crafting a narrow statute that presents no threat to the freedom of speech. The statute reaches only knowingly false statements about hard facts directly within a speaker's personal knowledge. These lies have no value in and of themselves, and proscribing them does not chill any valuable speech.

By holding that the First Amendment nevertheless shields these lies, the Court breaks sharply from a long line of cases recognizing that the right to free speech does not protect false factual statements that inflict real harm and serve no legitimate interest. I would adhere to that principle and would thus uphold the constitutionality of this valuable law. * * *

Questions

1. Does the criminalization of lying about "been awarded any decoration or medal authorized by Congress for the Armed Forces of the United States" *necessarily* serve the goals of the Stolen Valor Act? Could it disserve the goals of the Act?

2. In his dissent, Justice Alito wrote: "The Court strikes down the Stolen Valor Act of 2005, which was enacted to stem an epidemic of false claims about military decorations. These lies, Congress reasonably concluded, were undermining our country's system of military honors and inflicting real harm on actual medal recipients and their families." Is the Court's decision in *Alvarez* likely to lead to "an epidemic of false claims about military decorations"?

3. Lawmakers frequently introduce laws that accommodate denial of science and false claims about the evolution, climate change, and other scientific matters.[67] The *Alvarez* Court was divided about truth and lies. Does *Alvarez* offer any guidance regarding laws that accommodate lies about science, require teachers to lie about science, or penalize teachers who lie about science?

§ 5.4 CONFUSING INFORMATION

Bounded rationality constrains our ability to process information.[68] The human mind can cope with details, but the way details are framed and their volume may confuse us. *Framing*, the organization and presentation of details, influences outcomes of decisionmaking.[69] A simple example is the difference between our feeling toward "surcharges" and "discounts." People do not like surcharges but love discounts, although in effect they are

67. *See* § 10.2.

68. *See* § 7.4.

69. *See generally* Daniel Kahneman & Amos Tversky, *Choices, Values, and Frames*, 39 AMERICAN PSYCHOLOGIST 341 (1984); Daniel Kahneman & Amos Tversky, *Rational Choice and the Framing Decision*, 59 JOURNAL OF BUSINESS 5251 (1986). *See also* Eric J. Johnson et al., *Framing, Probability Distortions and Insurance Decisions*, 7 JOURNAL OF RISK & UNCERTAINTY 35 (1993); Richard H. Thaler, *Mental Accounting Matters*, 12 JOURNAL OF BEHAVIORAL DECISION MAKING 183 (1999).

often equivalent.[70] A business can set a price at $10 and give a $3 discount for certain people, or set the price at $7 and impose a surcharge of $3 on certain people. These pricing strategies are equivalent, but their framing affects their perception by the public. For a movie theater, it is better to give senior discounts of $3 on a ticket of $10, rather than charging a youth surcharge of $3 on a ticket of $7, although both pricing strategies are equivalent. The frame "surcharge" tends to deter buyers, whereas the frame "discount" tends to draw buyers.

Competitive market participants take advantage of decisionmaking patterns of other participants in order to make profit. This is one meaning of the pursuit of self-interest. Using Adam Smith's examples, we probably want the butcher, brewer, and baker to follow the patterns of demand.[71] The problem is with the patterns of decisionmaking.[72]

Consider, for example the cost of a vacation at a hotel. To boost revenues, hotels add "less-visible" fees that do not show up with the room rates in advertisements or on commercial websites. Example of such fees include mandatory "valet parking fees" for any customer who shows up with a car, required "resort fee" for a potential use of the pool or the exercise room, mandatory portage fees, housekeeping gratuities and bellman fees, in-room safe warranty surcharge, Internet services, and many others.[73] In the market for printers, the pricing structure is even more confusing. The printer price is relatively low, compared to the operational cost paid for toner, cartridges and other parts. Consumers often focus on the printer price, rather than the operational cost.

The described practices are known as the "add-on strategy."[74] To succeed, this strategy requires the availability of enough myopic consumers who fail to analyze, either fully or at all, the costs and benefits of the offered deal. Under some conditions, consumers may learn to factor simple pricing schemes, such as understanding the significance of airline luggage fees, asking about Internet services in hotels or calculating toner costs of printers. However, businesses that engage in the "add-on strategy" tend to keep many consumers in state of confusion by adding options and features.

Financial terms can be particularly confusing. Consider the Credit Card Accountability Responsibility and Disclosure Act of 2009 (the "Credit CARD Act").[75] The Act imposes restrictions on credit card companies, banning many practices that were customary until its enactment. Examples of the statute's innovations include: (1) a requirement of a 45–day advance

---

70. *See* Edmund W. Kitch, The *Framing Hypothesis: Is It Supported by Credit Card Issuer Opposition to a Surcharge on a Cash Price?* 6 JOURNAL OF LAW, ECONOMICS & ORGANIZATION 217 (1990).

71. *See* § 2.1.

72. *See* Xavier Gabaix & David Laibson, *Shrouded Attributes, Consumer Myopia, and Information Suppression in Competitive Markets*, 121 QUARTERLY JOURNAL OF ECONOMICS 505 (2006).

73. *See* Scott McCartney, *Paying for the Pool: Hotels Are Piling On Fees*, WALL STREET JOURNAL, Jun. 18, 2009, at D1.

74. *See* Gabaix & Laibson, *Shrouded Attributes, Consumer Myopia, and Information Suppression in Competitive Markets*, *supra* note 72.

75. Pub. L. No. 111–24, 123 Stat. 1734 (2009).

notice of increase in interest rate and other significant changes, (2) a prohibition on retroactive increases of interest rates and fees applicable to outstanding balances, (3) a ban on changing the terms governing the repayment of outstanding balances, (4) a ban on double-cycle billing,[76] and (5) subjecting penalty fees to standards of reasonableness and proportionality. Credit card holders were legally aware of all these practices and legally agreed to them prior to the enactment of the Credit CARD Act, since they received copies of the credit card agreements. The presentation of the information was too confusing for many people.[77]

Information often confuses people. We make mistakes all the time. Confusion, however, is not a motivation, let alone justification, for regulation. Something more than that is needed.

Eastman Kodak Co. v. Image Technical Services

504 U.S. 451 (1992)

■ JUSTICE BLACKMUN delivered the opinion of the Court.

Petitioner Eastman Kodak Company manufactures and sells photocopiers and micrographic equipment. Kodak also sells service and replacement parts for its equipment. Respondents are 18 independent service organizations (ISO's) that in the early 1980's began servicing Kodak copying and micrographic equipment. Kodak subsequently adopted policies to limit the availability of parts to ISO's and to make it more difficult for ISO's to compete with Kodak in servicing Kodak equipment.

I

A

Kodak manufactures and sells complex business machines—as relevant here, high-volume photocopiers and micrographic equipment. Kodak equipment is unique; micrographic software programs that operate on Kodak machines, for example, are not compatible with competitors' machines. Kodak parts are not compatible with other manufacturers' equipment, and vice versa. Kodak equipment, although expensive when new, has little resale value.

Kodak provides service and parts for its machines to its customers. It produces some of the parts itself; the rest are made to order for Kodak by independent original-equipment manufacturers (OEM's). Kodak does not sell a complete system of original equipment, lifetime service, and lifetime parts for a single price. Instead, Kodak provides service after the initial warranty period either through annual service contracts, which include all

---

76. Double-cycle billing occurs when a cardholder with no previous balance does not pay the entire balance of a new purchase by the payment due date, then—on the next periodic billing statement—the issuer computes interest on the original balance of the purchase. For example if the cardholder makes a $1000 purchase and pays off $950 in the first month, under double-cycle billing, she would be charged interest on the $1000 in the next month.

77. A sample of credit card agreements is available at *regti.me/CC-agreements* (case sensitive).

necessary parts, or on a per-call basis. It charges, through negotiations and bidding, different prices for equipment, service, and parts for different customers. Kodak provides 80% to 95% of the service for Kodak machines.

Beginning in the early 1980's, ISO's began repairing and servicing Kodak equipment. They also sold parts and reconditioned and sold used Kodak equipment. Their customers were federal, state, and local government agencies, banks, insurance companies, industrial enterprises, and providers of specialized copy and microfilming services. ISO's provide service at a price substantially lower than Kodak does. Some customers found that the ISO service was of higher quality.

Some ISO customers purchase their own parts and hire ISO's only for service. * * * Others choose ISO's to supply both service and parts. * * * ISO's keep an inventory of parts, purchased from Kodak or other sources, primarily the OEM's.

In 1985 and 1986, Kodak implemented a policy of selling replacement parts for micrographic and copying machines only to buyers of Kodak equipment who use Kodak service or repair their own machines.

As part of the same policy, Kodak sought to limit ISO access to other sources of Kodak parts. Kodak and the OEM's agreed that the OEM's would not sell parts that fit Kodak equipment to anyone other than Kodak. * * * Kodak also pressured Kodak equipment owners and independent parts distributors not to sell Kodak parts to ISO's. * * * In addition, Kodak took steps to restrict the availability of used machines. * * *

Kodak intended, through these policies, to make it more difficult for ISO's to sell service for Kodak machines. * * * Customers were forced to switch to Kodak service even though they preferred ISO service. * * *

B

In 1987, the ISO's filed the present action in the District Court, alleging, *inter alia,* that Kodak had unlawfully tied the sale of service for Kodak machines to the sale of parts, in violation of § 1 of the Sherman Act, and had unlawfully monopolized and attempted to monopolize the sale of service for Kodak machines, in violation of § 2 of that Act.

II

A tying arrangement is "an agreement by a party to sell one product but only on the condition that the buyer also purchases a different (or tied) product, or at least agrees that he will not purchase that product from any other supplier." * * * Such an arrangement violates § 1 of the Sherman Act if the seller has "appreciable economic power" in the tying product market and if the arrangement affects a substantial volume of commerce in the tied market.

Kodak did not dispute that its arrangement affects a substantial volume of interstate commerce. It, however, did challenge whether its activities constituted a "tying arrangement" and whether Kodak exercised "appreciable economic power" in the tying market. We consider these issues in turn.

A

For service and parts to be considered two distinct products, there must be sufficient consumer demand so that it is efficient for a firm to provide service separately from parts. * * * Evidence in the record indicates that service and parts have been sold separately in the past and still are sold separately to self-service equipment owners. Indeed, the development of the entire high-technology service industry is evidence of the efficiency of a separate market for service.

B

Having found sufficient evidence of a tying arrangement, we consider the other necessary feature of an illegal tying arrangement: appreciable economic power in the tying market. Market power is the power "to force a purchaser to do something that he would not do in a competitive market. " * * * It has been defined as 'the ability of a single seller to raise price and restrict output.' " * * * The existence of such power ordinarily is inferred from the seller's possession of a predominant share of the market. * * *

1

Respondents contend that Kodak has more than sufficient power in the parts market to force unwanted purchases of the tied market, service. Respondents provide evidence that certain parts are available exclusively through Kodak. Respondents also assert that Kodak has control over the availability of parts it does not manufacture. According to respondents' evidence, Kodak has prohibited independent manufacturers from selling Kodak parts to ISO's, pressured Kodak equipment owners and independent parts distributors to deny ISO's the purchase of Kodak parts, and taken steps to restrict the availability of used machines.

Respondents also allege that Kodak's control over the parts market has excluded service competition, boosted service prices, and forced unwilling consumption of Kodak service. Respondents offer evidence that consumers have switched to Kodak service even though they preferred ISO service, that Kodak service was of higher price and lower quality than the preferred ISO service, and that ISO's were driven out of business by Kodak's policies. Under our prior precedents, this evidence would be sufficient to entitle respondents to a trial on their claim of market power.

2

Kodak counters that even if it concedes monopoly *share* of the relevant parts market, it cannot actually exercise the necessary market *power* for a Sherman Act violation. This is so, according to Kodak, because competition exists in the equipment market. Kodak argues that it could not have the ability to raise prices of service and parts above the level that would be charged in a competitive market because any increase in profits from a higher price in the aftermarkets at least would be offset by a corresponding loss in profits from lower equipment sales as consumers began purchasing equipment with more attractive service costs.

Kodak does not present any actual data on the equipment, service, or parts markets. Instead, it urges the adoption of a substantive legal rule that "equipment competition precludes any finding of monopoly power in derivative aftermarkets." * * *

The extent to which one market prevents exploitation of another market depends on the extent to which consumers will change their consumption of one product in response to a price change in another, *i.e.*, the "cross-elasticity of demand." * * * Kodak's proposed rule rests on a factual assumption about the cross-elasticity of demand in the equipment and aftermarkets: "If Kodak raised its parts or service prices above competitive levels, potential customers would simply stop buying Kodak equipment. Perhaps Kodak would be able to increase short term profits through such a strategy, but at a devastating cost to its long term interests." * * *

Kodak's claim that charging more for service and parts would be "a short-run game" * * * is based on the false dichotomy that there are only two prices that can be charged—a competitive price or a ruinous one. But there could easily be a middle, optimum price at which the increased revenues from the higher priced sales of service and parts would more than compensate for the lower revenues from lost equipment sales. The fact that the equipment market imposes a restraint on prices in the aftermarkets by no means disproves the existence of power in those markets. * * *

We next consider the more narrowly drawn question: Does Kodak's theory describe actual market behavior so accurately that respondents' assertion of Kodak market power in the aftermarkets, if not impossible, is at least unreasonable?

To review Kodak's theory, it contends that higher service prices will lead to a disastrous drop in equipment sales. * * * According to the theory, one would have expected Kodak to take advantage of lower priced ISO service as an opportunity to expand equipment sales. Instead, * * * according to the record, * * * [s]ervice prices have risen for Kodak customers, but there is no evidence or assertion that Kodak equipment sales have dropped. * * * Kodak's theory does not explain the actual market behavior revealed in the record.

Respondents offer a forceful reason why Kodak's theory, although perhaps intuitively appealing, may not accurately explain the behavior of the primary and derivative markets for complex durable goods: the existence of significant information and switching costs. These costs could create a less responsive connection between service and parts prices and equipment sales.

For the service-market price to affect equipment demand, consumers must inform themselves of the total cost of the "package"—equipment, service, and parts—at the time of purchase; that is, consumers must engage in accurate lifecycle pricing. Lifecycle pricing of complex, durable equipment is difficult and costly. In order to arrive at an accurate price, a consumer must acquire a substantial amount of raw data and undertake sophisticated analysis. The necessary information would include data on price, quality, and availability of products needed to operate, upgrade, or enhance the initial equipment, as well as service and repair costs, including estimates of breakdown frequency, nature of repairs, price of service and parts, length of "downtime," and losses incurred from downtime.

Much of this information is difficult—some of it impossible—to acquire at the time of purchase. During the life of a product, companies may change the service and parts prices, and develop products with more advanced features, a decreased need for repair, or new warranties. In addition, the information is likely to be customer-specific; lifecycle costs will vary from customer to customer with the type of equipment, degrees of equipment use, and costs of down-time.

Kodak acknowledges the cost of information, but suggests, again without evidentiary support, that customer information needs will be satisfied by competitors in the equipment markets. * * * It is a question of fact, however, whether competitors would provide the necessary information. A competitor in the equipment market may not have reliable information about the lifecycle costs of complex equipment it does not service or the needs of customers it does not serve. Even if competitors had the relevant information, it is not clear that their interests would be advanced by providing such information to consumers. * * *

Moreover, even if consumers were capable of acquiring and processing the complex body of information, they may choose not to do so. Acquiring the information is expensive. If the costs of service are small relative to the equipment price, or if consumers are more concerned about equipment capabilities than service costs, they may not find it cost efficient to compile the information. Similarly, some consumers, such as the Federal Government, have purchasing systems that make it difficult to consider the complete cost of the "package" at the time of purchase. State and local governments often treat service as an operating expense and equipment as a capital expense, delegating each to a different department. These governmental entities do not lifecycle price, but rather choose the lowest price in each market. * * *

As Kodak notes, there likely will be some large-volume, sophisticated purchasers who will undertake the comparative studies and insist, in return for their patronage, that Kodak charge them competitive lifecycle prices. Kodak contends that these knowledgeable customers will hold down the package price for all other customers. * * * There are reasons, however, to doubt that sophisticated purchasers will ensure that competitive prices are charged to unsophisticated purchasers, too. As an initial matter, if the number of sophisticated customers is relatively small, the amount of profits to be gained by supracompetitive pricing in the service market could make it profitable to let the knowledgeable consumers take their business elsewhere. More importantly, if a company is able to price discriminate between sophisticated and unsophisticated consumers, the sophisticated will be unable to prevent the exploitation of the uninformed. A seller could easily price discriminate by varying the equipment/parts/service package, developing different warranties, or offering price discounts on different components.

Given the potentially high cost of information and the possibility that a seller may be able to price discriminate between knowledgeable and unsophisticated consumers, it makes little sense to assume, in the absence of any evidentiary support, that equipment-purchasing decisions are based on an accurate assessment of the total cost of equipment, service, and parts over the lifetime of the machine. * * *

A second factor undermining Kodak's claim that supracompetitive prices in the service market lead to ruinous losses in equipment sales is the cost to current owners of switching to a different product. * * * If the cost of switching is high, consumers who already have purchased the equipment, and are thus "locked in," will tolerate some level of service-price increases before changing equipment brands. Under this scenario, a seller profitably could maintain supracompetitive prices in the aftermarket if the switching costs were high relative to the increase in service prices, and the number of locked-in customers [was] high relative to the number of new purchasers.

Moreover, if the seller can price discriminate between its locked-in customers and potential new customers, this strategy is even more likely to prove profitable. The seller could simply charge new customers below-marginal cost on the equipment and recoup the charges in service, or offer packages with lifetime warranties or long-term service agreements that are not available to locked-in customers. * * *

In sum, there is a question of fact whether information costs and switching costs foil the simple assumption that the equipment and service markets act as pure complements to one another.

In the end, of course, Kodak's arguments may prove to be correct. It may be that its parts, service, and equipment are components of one unified market, or that the equipment market does discipline the aftermarkets so that all three are priced competitively overall, or that any anti-competitive effects of Kodak's behavior are outweighed by its competitive effects. But we cannot reach these conclusions as a matter of law on record this sparse. Accordingly, the judgment of the Court of Appeals denying summary judgment is affirmed.

It is so ordered.

■ JUSTICE SCALIA, with whom JUSTICE O'CONNOR and JUSTICE THOMAS join, dissenting.

This * * * case presents a very narrow—but extremely important—question of substantive antitrust law: whether, for purposes of applying our *per se* rule condemning "ties," and for purposes of applying our exacting rules governing the behavior of would-be monopolists, a manufacturer's conceded lack of power in the interbrand market for its equipment is somehow consistent with its possession of "market," or even "monopoly," power in wholly derivative aftermarkets for that equipment. In my view, the Court supplies an erroneous answer to this question, and I dissent.

I

Per se rules of antitrust illegality are reserved for those situations where logic and experience show that the risk of injury to competition from the defendant's behavior is so pronounced that it is needless and wasteful to conduct the usual judicial inquiry into the balance between the behavior's procompetitive benefits and its anticompetitive costs. * * *

The Court today finds in the typical manufacturer's inherent power over its own brand of equipment—over the sale of distinctive repair parts for that equipment, for example—the sort of "monopoly power" sufficient to bring the sledgehammer of § 2 [of the Sherman Act] into play. And, not surprisingly in light of that insight, it readily labels single-brand power over aftermarket products "market power" sufficient to permit an antitrust plaintiff to invoke the *per se* rule against tying. In my opinion, this makes no economic sense. The holding that market power can be found on the present record causes these venerable rules of selective proscription to extend well beyond the point where the reasoning that supports them leaves off. Moreover, because the sort of power condemned by the Court today is possessed by every manufacturer of durable goods with distinctive parts, the Court's opinion threatens to release a torrent of litigation and a flood of commercial intimidation that will do much more harm than good to enforcement of the antitrust laws and to genuine competition. I shall explain, in Parts II and III, respectively, how neither logic *nor* experience suggests, let alone compels, application of the *per se* tying prohibition and monopolization doctrine to a seller's behavior in its single-brand aftermarkets, when that seller is without power at the interbrand level.

II

* * *

A

We must assume, for purposes of deciding this case, that petitioner is without market, much less monopoly, power in the interbrand markets for its micrographic and photocopying equipment. * * *

Had Kodak—from the date of its entry into the micrographic and photocopying equipment markets—included a lifetime parts and service warranty with all original equipment, or required consumers to purchase a lifetime parts and service contract with each machine, that bundling of equipment, parts, and service would no doubt constitute a tie. * * * Nevertheless, it would be immune from *per se* scrutiny under the antitrust laws because the *tying* product would be *equipment,* a market in which (we assume) Kodak has no power to influence price or quantity. * * * The same result would obtain, I think, had Kodak—from the date of its market entry—consistently pursued an announced policy of limiting parts sales in the manner alleged in this case, so that customers bought with the knowledge that aftermarket support could be obtained only from Kodak. The foreclosure of respondents from the business of servicing Kodak's micrographic and photocopying machines in these illustrations would be undeniably complete—as complete as the foreclosure described in respondents' complaint. Nonetheless, we would inquire no further than to ask whether Kodak's *market power* in the equipment market effectively forced consumers to purchase Kodak micrographic or photocopying machines subject to the company's restrictive aftermarket practices. If not, that would end the case insofar as the *per se* rule was concerned. * * * The evils against which the tying prohibition is directed would simply not be presented. Interbrand competition would render Kodak powerless to gain economic power over an additional class of consumers, to price discriminate by charging each customer a "system" price equal to the system's economic value to that customer, or to raise barriers to entry in the interbrand equipment markets. * * *

It is quite simply anomalous that a manufacturer functioning in a competitive equipment market should be exempt from the *per se* rule when it bundles equipment with parts and service, but not when it bundles parts with service. This vast difference in the treatment of what will ordinarily be economically similar phenomena is alone enough to call today's decision into question.

B

[R]espondents sought to sidestep the impediment posed by interbrand competition to their invocation of the *per se* tying rule by zeroing in on the parts and service "aftermarkets" for Kodak equipment. By alleging a tie of *parts* to service, rather than of *equipment* to parts and service, they identified a tying product in which Kodak unquestionably held a near-monopoly share: the parts uniquely associated with Kodak's brand of machines. * * * The Court today holds that such a facial showing of market share in a single-brand aftermarket is sufficient to invoke the *per se* rule. The existence of even vibrant interbrand competition is no defense.

I find this a curious form of market power on which to premise the application of a *per se* proscription. It is enjoyed by virtually every manufacturer of durable goods requiring aftermarket support with unique, or relatively unique, goods. * * * Under the Court's analysis, the *per se* rule may now be applied to single-brand ties effected by the most insignificant players in fully competitive interbrand markets, as long as the arrangement forecloses aftermarket competitors from more than a *de minimis* amount of business. * * * This seems to me quite wrong. A tying arrangement "forced" through the exercise of such power no more implicates the leveraging and price discrimination concerns behind the *per se* tying prohibition than does a tie of the foremarket brand to its aftermarket derivatives, which—as I have explained—would not be subject to *per se* condemnation. As implemented, the Kodak arrangement challenged in this case may have implicated truth-in-advertising or other consumer protection concerns, but those concerns do not alone suggest an antitrust prohibition. * * *

In the absence of interbrand power, a seller's predominant or monopoly share of its single-brand derivative markets does not connote the power to raise derivative market prices *generally* by reducing quantity. As Kodak and its principal *amicus,* the United States, point out, a rational consumer considering the purchase of Kodak equipment will inevitably factor into his purchasing decision the expected cost of aftermarket support. "[B]oth the price of the equipment and the price of parts and service over the life of the equipment are expenditures that are necessary to obtain copying and micrographic services." Brief for United States as *Amicus Curiae* * * * If Kodak set generally supracompetitive prices for either spare parts or repair services without making an offsetting reduction in the price of its machines, rational consumers would simply turn to Kodak's competitors for photocopying and micrographic systems. * * * True, there are—as the Court notes, the occasional irrational consumers that consider only the hardware cost at the time of purchase (a category that regrettably includes the Federal Government, whose "purchasing system," we are told, assigns foremarket purchases and aftermarket purchases to different entities). But we have never before premised the application of antitrust doctrine on the lowest common denominator of consumer.

The Court attempts to counter this theoretical point with a theory of its own. It says that there are "information costs"—the costs and inconvenience to the consumer of acquiring and processing life-cycle pricing data for Kodak machines-that "could create a less responsive connection between service and parts prices and equipment sales." But this truism about the functioning of markets for sophisticated equipment cannot create "market power" of concern to the antitrust laws where otherwise there is none. "Information costs," or, more accurately, gaps in the availability and quality of consumer information, pervade real-world markets; and because consumers generally make do with "rough cut" judgments about price in such circumstances, in virtually any market there are zones within which otherwise competitive suppliers may overprice their products without losing appreciable market share. We have never suggested that the principal players in a market with such commonplace informational deficiencies (and, thus, bands of apparent consumer pricing indifference) exercise market power in any sense relevant to the antitrust laws. * * *

Respondents suggest that, even if the existence of interbrand competition prevents Kodak from raising prices *generally* in its single-brand aftermarkets, there remain certain consumers who are necessarily subject to abusive Kodak pricing behavior by reason of their being "locked in" to their investments in Kodak machines. The Court agrees; indeed, it goes further by suggesting that even a *general* policy of supracompetitive aftermarket prices might be profitable over the long run because of the "lock-in" phenomenon. "[A] seller profitably could maintain supracompetitive prices in the aftermarket," the Court explains, "if the switching costs were high relative to the increase in service prices, and the number of locked-in customers were high relative to the number of new purchasers." In speculating about this latter possibility, the Court is essentially repudiating the assumption on which we are bound to decide this case, viz., Kodak's lack of any power whatsoever in the interbrand market. If Kodak's *general* increase in aftermarket prices were to bring the total "system" price above competitive levels in the interbrand market, Kodak would be wholly unable to make further foremarket sales—and would find itself exploiting an ever-dwindling aftermarket, as those Kodak micrographic and photocopying machines already in circulation passed into disuse.

The Court's narrower point, however, is undeniably true. There will be consumers who, because of their capital investment in Kodak equipment, "will tolerate some level of service-price increases before changing equipment brands"; this is *necessarily* true for "every maker of unique parts for its own product." But this "circumstantial" leverage created by consumer investment regularly crops up in smoothly functioning, even perfectly competitive, markets, and in most—if not all—of its manifestations, it is of no concern to the antitrust laws. The leverage held by the manufacturer of a malfunctioning refrigerator (which is measured by the consumer's reluctance to walk away from his initial investment in that device) is no different in kind or degree from the leverage held by the swimming pool contractor when he discovers a 5–ton boulder in his customer's backyard and demands an additional sum of money to remove it; or the leverage held by an airplane manufacturer over an airline that has "standardized" its fleet around the manufacturer's models; or the leverage held by a drill press manufacturer whose customers have built their production lines around the manufacturer's particular style of drill press; or the leverage held by an insurance company over its independent sales force that has invested in company-specific paraphernalia; or the leverage held by a mobile home park owner over his tenants, who are unable to transfer their homes to a different park except at great expense. * * * Leverage, in the form of *circumstantial* power, plays a role in each of these relationships; but in none of them is the leverage attributable to the dominant party's *market* power in any relevant sense. Though that power can plainly work to the injury of certain consumers, it produces only "a brief perturbation in competitive conditions-not the sort of thing the antitrust laws do or should worry about." Parts & Elec. Motors, Inc. v. Sterling Elec., Inc., 866 F.2d 228, 236 (7th Cir. 1988) (Posner, J., dissenting).

* * *

III

* * * Because this case comes to us on the assumption that Kodak is without such interbrand power, I believe we are compelled to reverse the judgment of the Court of Appeals. I respectfully dissent.

Questions

1. What were the alleged informational problems in the market for copiers? Did the majority and dissent disagree about the nature of these problems? What were the major disagreements between the majority and dissent in *Kodak*?

2. Justice Scalia objected to the concept of identifying market power over a single brand and wrote: "I find this a curious form of market power. * * * It is enjoyed by virtually every manufacturer of durable goods requiring aftermarket support with unique, or relatively unique, goods." Gillette razors are rather durable, but its blades are in expensive.[78] The razors are incompatible with blades of rival firms. Are there any informational problems in the market for razors-and-blades? If so, are they similar to the problems in the markets for photocopiers?

---

78. *See* Randal C. Picker, *The Razors-and-Blades Myth(s)*, 78 UNIVERSITY OF CHICAGO LAW REVIEW 225 (2011).

CHAPTER 6

UNFAIR PRICES AND OTHER CONTRACTUAL TERMS

§ 6.1 CONCENTRATION OF OWNERSHIP

Imagine you own all the land in the Hawaiian Islands. Because your land is home to approximately 1.35 million people and is a popular vacation destination, you are able lease your land to businesses and individuals for a steady profit. Hawaii is a member of the United States and has an elected Governor, as well as an elected Senate and House of Representatives. You have never bothered to pursue any political position because your position as the islands' sole landlord has provided you with plenty of influence. Should your concentration of land ownership concern the Hawaiian government? If so, why and what should the Hawaiian government do about its concern? Is there any way for the Hawaiian government to address your matter without adopting measures that may be perceived as a "redistribution of wealth," which every politician knows is an unpopular idea?[1]

Hawaii Housing Authority v. Midkiff

467 U.S. 229 (1984)

■ JUSTICE O'CONNOR delivered the opinion of the Court.

The Fifth Amendment of the United States Constitution provides, in pertinent part, that "private property [shall not] be taken for public use, without just compensation." These cases present the question whether the Public Use Clause of that Amendment, made applicable to the States through the Fourteenth Amendment, prohibits the State of Hawaii from taking, with just compensation, title in real property from lessors and transferring it to lessees in order to reduce the concentration of ownership of fees simple in the State. We conclude that it does not.

I

A

The Hawaiian Islands were originally settled by Polynesian immigrants from the western Pacific. These settlers developed an economy around a feudal land tenure system in which one island high chief, the ali'i nui, controlled the land and assigned it for development to certain subchiefs.

---

1. *See, e.g.*, Arthur C. Brooks, *'Spreading the Wealth' Isn't Fair*, WALL STREET JOURNAL, Apr. 14, 2010, at A21; Michael Cooper, *'Spreading the Wealth' as Both Accusation and Prescription*, NEW YORK TIMES, Oct. 20, 2008, at A20. *See also* Steven A. Bank, *Origins of a Flat Tax*, 73 DENVER LAW REVIEW 329 (1996).

The subchiefs would then reassign the land to other lower ranking chiefs, who would administer the land and govern the farmers and other tenants working it. All land was held at the will of the ali'i nui and eventually had to be returned to his trust. There was no private ownership of land. * * *

Beginning in the early 1800's, Hawaiian leaders and American settlers repeatedly attempted to divide the lands of the kingdom among the crown, the chiefs, and the common people. These efforts proved largely unsuccessful, however, and the land remained in the hands of a few. In the mid–1960's, after extensive hearings, the Hawaii Legislature discovered that, while the State and Federal Governments owned almost 49% of the State's land, another 47% was in the hands of only 72 private landowners. * * * The legislature further found that 18 landholders, with tracts of 21,000 acres or more, owned more than 40% of this land and that on Oahu, the most urbanized of the islands, 22 landowners owned 72.5% of the fee simple titles. The legislature concluded that concentrated land ownership was responsible for skewing the State's residential fee simple market, inflating land prices, and injuring the public tranquility and welfare.

To redress these problems, the legislature decided to compel the large landowners to break up their estates. The legislature considered requiring large landowners to sell lands which they were leasing to homeowners. However, the landowners strongly resisted this scheme, pointing out the significant federal tax liabilities they would incur. Indeed, the landowners claimed that the federal tax laws were the primary reason they previously had chosen to lease, and not sell, their lands. Therefore, to accommodate the needs of both lessors and lessees, the Hawaii Legislature enacted the Land Reform Act of 1967 (Act), * * * which created a mechanism for condemning residential tracts and for transferring ownership of the condemned fees simple to existing lessees. By condemning the land in question, the Hawaii Legislature intended to make the land sales involuntary, thereby making the federal tax consequences less severe while still facilitating the redistribution of fees simple. * * *

Under the Act's condemnation scheme, tenants living on single-family residential lots within developmental tracts at least five acres in size are entitled to ask the Hawaii Housing Authority (HHA) to condemn the property on which they live. * * * When 25 eligible tenants,[1] or tenants on half the lots in the tract, whichever is less, file appropriate applications, the Act authorizes HHA to hold a public hearing to determine whether acquisition by the State of all or part of the tract will "effectuate the public purposes" of the Act. If HHA finds that these public purposes will be served, it is authorized to designate some or all of the lots in the tract for acquisition. It then acquires, at prices set either by condemnation trial or by negotiation between lessors and lessees, the former fee owners' full "right, title, and interest" in the land. § 516–25.

After compensation has been set, HHA may sell the land titles to tenants who have applied for fee simple ownership. HHA is authorized to

1. An eligible tenant is one who, among other things, owns a house on the lot, has a bona fide intent to live on the lot or be a resident of the State, shows proof of ability to pay for a fee interest in it, and does not own residential land elsewhere nearby. . . .

lend these tenants up to 90% of the purchase price, and it may condition final transfer on a right of first refusal for the first 10 years following sale. * * * If HHA does not sell the lot to the tenant residing there, it may lease the lot or sell it to someone else, provided that public notice has been given. * * * However, HHA may not sell to any one purchaser, or lease to any one tenant, more than one lot, and it may not operate for profit. * * * In practice, funds to satisfy the condemnation awards have been supplied entirely by lessees. * * * While the Act authorizes HHA to issue bonds and appropriate funds for acquisition, no bonds have issued and HHA has not supplied any funds for condemned lots. * * *

B

In April 1977, HHA held a public hearing concerning the proposed acquisition of some of appellees' lands. HHA made the statutorily required finding that acquisition of appellees' lands would effectuate the public purposes of the Act. Then, in October 1978, it directed appellees to negotiate with certain lessees concerning the sale of the designated properties. Those negotiations failed, and HHA subsequently ordered appellees to submit to compulsory arbitration.

Rather than comply with the compulsory arbitration order, appellees filed suit, in February 1979, in United States District Court, asking that the Act be declared unconstitutional and that its enforcement be enjoined. The District Court * * * declar[ed] the compulsory arbitration and compensation formulae provisions of the Act unconstitutional [and held] the remaining portion of the Act constitutional under the Public Use Clause. * * * The District Court found that the Act's goals were within the bounds of the State's police powers and that the means the legislature had chosen to serve those goals were not arbitrary, capricious, or selected in bad faith.

The Court of Appeals for the Ninth Circuit reversed. * * * The court concluded that the Act was simply "a naked attempt on the part of the state of Hawaii to take the private property of A and transfer it to B solely for B's private use and benefit." * * * We now reverse.

* * *

III

The majority of the Court of Appeals next determined that the Act violates the "public use" requirement of the Fifth and Fourteenth Amendments. * * *

The starting point for our analysis of the Act's constitutionality is the Court's decision in *Berman v. Parker*, 348 U.S. 26 (1954). In *Berman*, the Court held constitutional the District of Columbia Redevelopment Act of 1945. That Act provided both for the comprehensive use of the eminent domain power to redevelop slum areas and for the possible sale or lease of the condemned lands to private interests. In discussing whether the takings authorized by that Act were for a "public use," the Court stated:

> "We deal, in other words, with what traditionally has been known as the police power. An attempt to define its reach or trace its outer limits is fruitless, for each case must turn on its own facts.

> The definition is essentially the product of legislative determinations addressed to the purposes of government, purposes neither abstractly nor historically capable of complete definition. Subject to specific constitutional limitations, when the legislature has spoken, the public interest has been declared in terms well-nigh conclusive. In such cases the legislature, not the judiciary, is the main guardian of the public needs to be served by social legislation, whether it be Congress legislating concerning the District of Columbia * * * or the States legislating concerning local affairs. * * * This principle admits of no exception merely because the power of eminent domain is involved."

The Court explicitly recognized the breadth of the principle it was announcing, noting: "* * * Here one of the means chosen is the use of private enterprise for redevelopment of the area. Appellants argue that this makes the project a taking from one businessman for the benefit of another businessman. But the means of executing the project are for Congress and Congress alone to determine, once the public purpose has been established."

The "public use" requirement is thus coterminous with the scope of a sovereign's police powers.

There is, of course, a role for courts to play in reviewing a legislature's judgment of what constitutes a public use, even when the eminent domain power is equated with the police power. * * *

To be sure, the Court's cases have repeatedly stated that "one person's property may not be taken for the benefit of another private person without a justifying public purpose, even though compensation be paid." *Thompson v. Consolidated Gas Corp.*, 300 U.S. 55, 80 (1937). * * *

On this basis, we have no trouble concluding that the Hawaii Act is constitutional. The people of Hawaii have attempted, much as the settlers of the original 13 Colonies did,[5] to reduce the perceived social and economic evils of a land oligopoly traceable to their monarchs. The land oligopoly has, according to the Hawaii Legislature, created artificial deterrents to the normal functioning of the State's residential land market and forced thousands of individual homeowners to lease, rather than buy, the land underneath their homes. Regulating oligopoly and the evils associated with it is a classic exercise of a State's police powers. * * * We cannot disapprove of Hawaii's exercise of this power.

Nor can we condemn as irrational the Act's approach to correcting the land oligopoly problem. The Act presumes that when a sufficiently large number of persons declare that they are willing but unable to buy lots at fair prices the land market is malfunctioning. When such a malfunction is signaled, the Act authorizes HHA to condemn lots in the relevant tract.

---

5. After the American Revolution, the colonists in several States took steps to eradicate the feudal incidents with which large proprietors had encumbered land in the Colonies. *See, e.g.*, Act of May 1779, 10 Henning's Statutes At Large 64, ch. 13, § 6 (1822) (Virginia statute); Divesting Act of 1779, 1775–1781 Pa. Acts 258, ch. 139 (1782) (Pennsylvania statute). Courts have never doubted that such statutes served a public purpose. *See, e.g.*, Wilson v. Iseminger, 185 U.S. 55, 60–61 (1902); Stewart v. Gorter, 70 Md. 242, 244–245 (1889).

The Act limits the number of lots any one tenant can purchase and authorizes HHA to use public funds to ensure that the market dilution goals will be achieved. This is a comprehensive and rational approach to identifying and correcting market failure.

Of course, this Act, like any other, may not be successful in achieving its intended goals. But "whether in fact the provision will accomplish its objectives is not the question: the [constitutional requirement] is satisfied if * * * the * * * [state] Legislature rationally could have believed that the [Act] would promote its objective." *Western & Southern Life Ins. Co. v. State Bd. of Equalization*, 451 U.S. 648, 671–672, (1981). * * * When the legislature's purpose is legitimate and its means are not irrational, our cases make clear that empirical debates over the wisdom of takings—no less than debates over the wisdom of other kinds of socioeconomic legislation—are not to be carried out in the federal courts. Redistribution of fees simple to correct deficiencies in the market determined by the state legislature to be attributable to land oligopoly is a rational exercise of the eminent domain power. Therefore, the Hawaii statute must pass the scrutiny of the Public Use Clause.

* * *

IV

The State of Hawaii has never denied that the Constitution forbids even a compensated taking of property when executed for no reason other than to confer a private benefit on a particular private party. A purely private taking could not withstand the scrutiny of the public use requirement; it would serve no legitimate purpose of government and would thus be void. But no purely private taking is involved in these cases. The Hawaii Legislature enacted its Land Reform Act not to benefit a particular class of identifiable individuals but to attack certain perceived evils of concentrated property ownership in Hawaii—a legitimate public purpose. Use of the condemnation power to achieve this purpose is not irrational. * * *

* * *

It is so ordered.

Questions

1. In *Hawaii Housing Authority*, landowners were compensated for their condemned land. How should this compensation be characterized? Did the Hawaii Housing Authority (HHA) redistribute wealth or substitute assets?

2. Rather than reallocating land, the Hawaiian government could have regulated lease rates. Would rate regulation be preferable to land reallocation?

3. In a 1972 paper, Ronald Coase posed a hypothetical: "Assume that a supplier owns the total stock of a completely durable good. At what price will he sell it? To take a concrete example, assume that one person owns all the land in the United States, and to simplify the analysis, that all land is

of uniform quality."[2] Coase argued that the monopolistic landowner would have to sell land at a competitive price because if the landowner set any price higher than the competitive price, he could only sell land only to a limited number of consumers. After selling land to these consumers, he would still have unutilized hand, and would have to reduce the price to sell more. Anticipating a trajectory of price decreases, consumers would not buy land for any price higher than the competitive price. Coase also pointed out that the monopolist landowner could avoid this result and make profit by leasing the land for "relatively short period of time," rather than selling it.

In Hawaii, landowners that held a significant portion of the lands chose to implement a system of "lease-only policies" and did not sell their lands. Their choice to only lease their private lands kept rent levels in Hawaii very high. In *Souza v. Estate of Bishop*, 821 F.2d 1332 (9th Cir. 1987), the plaintiffs argued that the lease-only policy violated antitrust laws. The Ninth Circuit dismissed their suit. Should the state ban lease-only policies of property owners?

4. The Hawaii "legislature concluded that concentrated land ownership was responsible for * * * inflating land prices, and injuring the public tranquility and welfare." Therefore, "[t]he Hawaii Legislature enacted [the] Land Reform Act * * * to attack certain perceived evils of concentrated property ownership." The Supreme Court held that this was "a legitimate public purpose" for which the use of the condemnation power was not irrational. Put simply, the Court legitimized taking to address a problem of high prices.

In the pursuit of profit, businesses routinely take advantage of their market position to charge high prices. For example, movie theaters charge ridiculously high prices for popcorn and soda. Should Congress or state legislatures examine the "perceived evils" at movie theaters? When does state condemnation of property become an appropriate remedy for high prices?

5. In June 2012, Lawrence ("Larry") Ellison, Chief Executive of the software giant Oracle, acquired 98% of Lana'i, the smallest inhabited island in Hawaii. At the time of acquisition, Ellison was the third-richest person in the U.S., and seventh wealthiest person in the world.[3] The seller was Castle & Cooke, Inc. Responding to the transaction, Hawaii Governor Neil Abercrombie released the following statement:

> It is my understanding that Mr. Ellison has had a long-standing interest in Lana'i. His passion for nature, particularly the ocean is well known specifically in the realm of America's Cup sailing. He is also a businessman whose record of community involvement in medical research and education causes is equally notable.
>
> We look forward to welcoming Mr. Ellison in the near future.

---

2. Ronald H. Coase, *Durability and Monopoly*, 15 JOURNAL OF LAW & ECONOMICS 143 (1972). *See generally* Barak Orbach, *The Durapolist Puzzle: Monopoly Power in Durable-Goods Markets*, 21 YALE JOURNAL ON REGULATION 67 (2004).

3. *See* Don Clark & Ben Worthen, *Larry Ellison to Buy Island in Hawaii,* WALL STREET JOURNAL, June 21, 2012, at A7.

Was the unequivocal endorsement of the transaction consistent with the state's interests?

§ 6.2 RENT, PRICE, AND MOTIVATIONS FOR REGULATION

Rent is a payment for a use of a resource—land, labor, equipment, intellectual property, or another. Historically, the term "rent" was associated with a payment for the use of land. Eighteenth and nineteenth century economists debated what determined the level of rent—alternative land available to the tenant, improvements in the land made by the landowner, or the ability of the tenant to generate revenues from the land.[4] *Hawaii Housing Authority* illustrates that the relationships among these and other factors, such as the concentration of ownership and characteristics of demand, determine the level of rent. The concentration of ownership in Hawaii was believed to give landowners the power to charge high rent. In contrast, the extreme fragmentation of American Indian land, which we discussed in *Hodel v. Irving* and *Babbitt v. Youpee*,[5] forestalled the development of the land and limited the ability of landowners to charge any significant rent for it. In *Hawaii Housing Authority*, the regulatory solution for the high level of rent was deconcentration of ownership. In *Hodel v. Irving* and *Babbitt v. Youpee*, the regulatory solution for the inability to utilize the land was concentration of ownership.

What is the relationship between rent and price? Rent and price are related concepts in economics. *Rent* is a payment for the use of an asset, while *price* is a payment for the purchase of an asset or a service. In the past, economists also debated the distinction between rent and price,[6] but this distinction has been largely abandoned and forgotten. Today, people generally ask about the "price" of the right to use a certain asset for a particular period of time, even though the term for such us is technically "rent."

The term *rent seeking*, which we discussed earlier and defined as the pursuit of private interest through regulation,[7] alludes to the rent earned from a favorable regulation. Interest groups engage in "rent seeking" activities because favorable regulation is an asset that could generate a rent.[8] Examples of favorable regulations include an exclusive right to

---

4. *See, e.g.*, EDWARD HASTINGS CHAMBERLIN, THE THEORY OF MONOPOLISTIC COMPETITION 112–113, Appendix D (6th ed. 1948); Alfred Marshall, *On Rent*, 3 ECONOMIC JOURNAL 74 (1893); DAVID RICARDO, ON THE PRINCIPLES OF POLITICAL ECONOMY, AND TAXATION 49–81 (1817); ADAM SMITH, AN INQUIRY INTO THE NATURE AND CAUSES OF THE WEALTH OF NATIONS 161–162 (1976).

5. Hodel v. Irving, 481 U.S. 704 (1987); Babbitt v. Youpee, 519 U.S. 234 (1997).

6. *See generally* D.H. Buchanan, *The Historical Approach to Rent and Price Theory*, 26 ECONOMICA 123 (1929); Frank T. Carlton, *Price and Rent*, 26 QUARTERLY JOURNAL OF ECONOMICS 523 (1912).

7. *See* § 2.4.3.

8. *See generally* Richard A. Posner, *Theories of Economic Regulation*, 5 BELL JOURNAL OF ECONOMICS & MANAGEMENT SCIENCE 335 (1974); George Stigler, *The Theory of Economic Regulation*, 2 BELL JOURNAL OF ECONOMIC & MANAGEMENT SCIENCE 3, 5 (1971).

operate steamboats in the state or to build a bridge over a river;[9] subsidies;[10] exemptions from taxes;[11] and taxes that target competitors.[12] Regulation, therefore, is one way to secure and maintain a profitable rent. Regulation, however, is not the only device to advance profit. Market participants often use the power to influence prices to their benefit. Indeed, a common motivation for regulation is "unfair prices."[13] Unfair prices may refer to low salaries for employees, high levels of executive compensation, high consumer prices, and low rates for suppliers. They occasionally incite public outcry and demands for government regulation.

What are "unfair prices"? People tend to have strong feelings about prices, but concerns regarding prices can be misguided. Perceptions of prices are positional (*e.g.*, the differences between the views of buyers and sellers), related to available financial means, and shaped by alternatives.[14] To mitigate such subjective biases, the standard analysis of prices utilizes the competitive level as a benchmark.[15] Prices below the competitive level are unprofitable and are not sustainable in the long run. Prices above the competitive level result in misallocation of resources in the market.

Several economic characteristics of markets and market participants create conditions for prices that deviate from the competitive level.[16] These characteristics are the result of certain *sources of market inefficiencies*: transaction costs, inadequate information, preferences for differentiation, bounded rationality, and fallibility.[17] Such inefficiencies may vest some market participants with the power to influence prices, prevent some

9. *See, e.g.*, Charles River Bridge v. Warren Bridge, 36 U.S. 420 (1837); Gibbons v. Ogden, 22 U.S. 1 (1824).

10. *See, e.g.*, John M. Broder, *Oil Executives, Defending Tax Breaks, Say They'd Cede Them if Everyone Did*, N.Y. TIMES, May 13, 2011, at B4; *A Big Whine From Big Oil*, N.Y. TIMES, May 15, 2011, at WK7; *Big Oil's Bogus Campaign*, N.Y. TIMES, Mar. 31, 2012, at A18.

11. *See, e.g.*, Walz v. Tax Commission of City of New York, 397 U.S. 664 (1970).

12. *See, e.g.*, A. Magnano Co. v. Hamilton, 292 U.S. 40 (1934).

13. *See, e.g.*, Eliot Jones, *Is Competition in Industry Ruinous*, 34 QUARTERLY JOURNAL OF ECONOMICS 473 (1920).

14. *See, e.g.*, Daniel Kahneman et al., *Fairness as a Constraint on Profit Seeking: Entitlement in the Market*, 76 AMERICAN ECONOMIC REVIEW 728 (1986); SARAH MAXWELL, THE PRICE IS WRONG: UNDERSTANDING WHAT MAKES A PRICE SEEM FAIR AND THE TRUE COST OF UNFAIR PRICING (2008).

15. *See, e.g.*, Kenneth G. Elzinga & David E. Mills, *The Lerner Index of Monopoly Power: Origins and Uses*, 101 AMERICAN ECONOMIC REVIEW 558 (2011); Abba P. Lerner, *The Concept of Monopoly and the Measurement of Monopoly*, 1 REVIEW OF ECONOMIC STUDIES 157 (1934). *See also* Edward L. Glaeser & Erzo P. Luttmer, *The Misallocation of Housing under Rent Control*, 93 AMERICAN ECONOMIC REVIEW 1027 (2003).

16. In economics, the power to set prices profitably above the competitive level is called "market power." *See generally* Kenneth G. Elzinga & David E. Mills, *The Lerner Index of Monopoly Power: Origins and Uses*, 101 AMERICAN ECONOMIC REVIEW 558 (2011); William M. Landes & Richard A. Posner, *Market Power in Antitrust Cases*, 94 HARVARD LAW REVIEW 937 (1981).

17. Preferences for differentiation stimulate monopolistic competition, which is a competition among sellers of products that are not perfect substitutes (differentiated goods). *See generally* EDWARD H. CHAMBERLIN, THE THEORY OF MONOPOLISTIC COMPETITION: A RE-ORIENTATION OF THE THEORY OF VALUE (8th ed. 1965); JOAN ROBINSON, THE ECONOMICS OF IMPERFECT COMPETITION (1933).

participants from making good decisions, benefit arbitrageurs, and disrupt or crumble markets.

To see how the sources of market inefficiencies may disrupt the market system, consider urban slaughterhouses that dump animal waste into the streets.[18] Urban slaughterhouses underpriced their products by externalizing pollution costs to the public rather than internalizing their operation costs.[19] In such circumstances, as well as in any other externality case, transaction costs, inadequate information, and possibly other inefficiencies fail negotiation.

Now consider the concentration of land ownership in *Hawaii Housing Authority* and the extreme fragmentation of American Indian land. In these cases, opposite structures of land ownership corresponded to opposite levels of rent. In Hawaii, concentration of ownership in the hands of a limited number of landowners resulted in high rents. In the Indian land, extreme fragmentation of land in the hands of numerous landowners resulted in very low rents. These rent discrepancies were the result of a failure of the market system induced by transaction costs, inadequate information, preferences for differentiation, bounded rationality, and fallibility. Real estate transactions involve substantial transaction costs: relocation is very costly to tenants, preparing property for new tenants is costly for landowners, and lease agreements may generate costs to landowners and tenants. Real estate markets also suffer from inadequate information. Tenants and landowners invest resources in information to find each other, and often rely on middlemen (real estate agents). When a tenant and a landowner consider a lease, they are strangers to each other and often invest in acquiring some information about their respective credentials. Moreover, people have peculiar preferences for real estate and analyze real estate transactions in ways that are not necessarily consistent with the ways they analyze other market transactions, exhibiting vulnerability to bounded rationality and fallibility. For these reasons, concentration of ownership in land may influence the rent level. When the concentration is high, landowners may have the power to charge high rents. By contrast, when the ownership is highly fragmented landowners may not be able to fully utilize their assets and the rent will be low.[20] This analysis applies to most markets and parallel sources of market inefficiencies influence prices in other markets.

In sum, prices may reflect problems in the market, but they are not the source of any problem. Accordingly, price regulation is unlikely to effectively address most problems related to prices.[21] So long as transaction costs, inadequate information, preferences for differentiation, bounded rationality, and fallibility exist, the market system will not produce perfectly competitive prices. Some market participants will exploit market conditions

---

18. For a discussion of urban slaughterhouses *see* § 2.2.2a.

19. For externalities *see* Chapter 3.

20. This is the tragedy of anticommons. *See* § 3.3.

21. *See generally* Jeremy Bulow & Paul Klemperer, *Regulated Prices, Rent Seeking, and Consumer Surplus*, 120 JOURNAL OF POLITICAL ECONOMY 160 (2012).

to influence prices to advance their profits, and others will fail to protect their own well-being.[22]

The same factors, however, also impede the regulatory process. Regulations often exacerbate existing problems and create new problems in markets. In other words, the sources of market inefficiencies may also be the sources of regulatory failures. For example, in the cases of *Hawaii Housing Authority* and the fragmented American Indian land, past regulatory policies shaped he ownership structures that influenced rents. More recently, regulatory policies account for the housing bubble that brought about the Great Recession. These policies facilitated speculative price increases that resulted in the market crash.[23] Thus, uncompetitive prices, as unfair as they may be, may not always justify regulation.

Until the late 1970s, regulation was often associated with concerns regarding prices. Early federal regulatory frameworks, such as the Interstate Commerce Act of 1887 and the Sherman Act of 1890, intended to address problems in the market pricing system. The Interstate Commerce Act focused on railroad rates, prohibiting price discrimination and requiring rates to be "reasonable and just." The Sherman Act was enacted in response to the growth of big businesses in the United States ("trusts") and intended to protect competitive conditions in the markets.[24] Many landmark cases in regulation dealt with the state's authority to regulate prices and the appropriate formulas for price regulation.[25] Price control policies, however, have generally proved to be inefficient,[26] and indeed, over time, prices have become instruments of regulation rather than objects. Today, while the state still uses price regulation to obtain certain goals, such as reducing or encouraging consumption of certain goods and services; price regulation is much less prevalent than was before the 1980s.[27]

Dodge v. Ford Motor Company is one of the most famous cases in U.S. corporate law. It involves a minority shareholders' challenge to the authori-

22. For transaction costs *see* Chapter 3. For inadequate information *see* Chapter 5. For bounded rationality and fallibility *see* Chapter 7. Loopholes, unintended consequences, and regulatory arbitrage are often a consequence of these sources of inefficiencies in the regulatory process. For unintended consequences and regulatory arbitrage *see* § 1.4. For Loopholes *see* Leo Katz, *A Theory of Loopholes*, 39 JOURNAL OF LEGAL STUDIES 1 (2010).

23. *See* § 1.1.

24. *See* Standard Oil Co. v. United States, 221 U.S. 1, 58 (1911) (White, C.J.) (arguing that "the dread of enhancement of prices and of other wrongs which it was thought would flow from undue limitation[s] on competitive conditions" motivated the enactment of the Sherman Act.). *See also* Barak Orbach & Grace E. Campbell, *The Antitrust Curse of Bigness*, 85 SOUTHERN CALIFORNIA LAW REVIEW 605 (2012).

25. *See, e.g.*, Munn v. Illinois, 94 U.S. 113 (1876); Smyth v. Ames, 169 U.S. 466 (1898); McCardle v. Indianapolis Water Co., 272 U.S. 400 (1926); Federal Power Commission v. Hope Natural Gas Co., 320 U.S. 591 (1944); Duquesne Light Co. v. Barasch, 488 U.S. 299 (1989).

26. *See generally* Bulow & Paul Klemperer, *Regulated Prices, Rent Seeking, and Consumer Surplus*, *supra* note 21.

27. *See* Joseph D. Kearney & Thomas W. Merrill, *The Great Transformation of Regulated Industries Law*, 98 COLUMBIA LAW REVIEW 1323 (1998). For price regulation *see* Chapter 9.

ty of the board of directors to make business decisions that consciously compromise stock prices. The plaintiffs, John and Horace Dodge, were long time partners of Henry Ford, the founder of the defendant, Ford Motor Company, and a defendant himself. Founded in 1900, the Dodge Brothers Company supplied parts and assemblies to Ford beginning in 1903. In 1914, John and Horace introduced their own car.[28] By 1916, Henry Ford was already a very wealthy man. He identified himself with the successful development of his company, which he considered to be mass production of inexpensive goods and high wages for employees.[29] His company became a model of consumerism known as "Fordism."[30] The Dodge brothers were directly affected by Ford's decision to increase production capacity, cut prices, and raise salaries to employees. They challenged this decision.

Dodge v. Ford Motor Co.

Supreme Court of Michigan
204 Mich. 459 (1919)

Action by John F. Dodge and Horace E. Dodge against the Ford Motor Company and others. * * *

The following is admitted to be a substantially correct statement of the financial affairs of [Ford Motor Company] on July 31, 1916:

Assets		Liabilities	
Working—		**Working—**	
Cash on hand and in bank	$52,550,771.92	Accounts payable	$7,680,866.17
Michigan municipal bonds	1,259,029.01	Contract deposits	1,519,296.40
Accounts Receivable	8,292,778.41	Accrued pay rolls	847,953.68
Merchandise and supplies	31,895,434.69	Accrued salaries	338,268, 80
Investments—outside	9,200.00	Accrued expenses	1,175,070.72
Expense inventories	434,055.19	Contract rebates	2,199,988.00
Plant—		Buyers' P. S. rebate	48,099.00
Land	5,232,156.10	**Reserves—**	
Buildings and fixtures	17,293,293.40	For fire insurance	57,493.89
Machinery and power plant	8,896,342.31	For depreciation of plant	4,260,275.53
Factory Equipment	3,868,261.02	**Total liabilities**	**$18,127,312.05**
Tools	1,690,688.54		
Patterns	170,619.77	**Surplus**	**111,960,907.53**
Patents	64,339.85	**Capital stock**	**2,000,000.00**
Office Equipment	431,249 37		
Total assets	**$132,088,219.58**	**Total**	**$132,088,219.58**

* * *

The plaintiffs, who together own 2,000 shares, or one-tenth of the entire capital stock of the Ford Motor Company, * * * filed * * * their bill of complaint, * * * in which bill they charge that since 1914 they have not been represented on the board of directors of the Ford Motor Company, and that since that time the policy of the board of directors has been

---

28. *See* CHARLES K. HYDE, THE DODGE BROTHERS: THE MEN, THE MOTOR CARS, AND THE LEGACY (2005).

29. Copies of Ford Motors' advertisements of low prices are available at *regti.me/ford-prices* (case sensitive).

30. *See* DAVID A. HOUNSHELL, FROM THE AMERICAN SYSTEM TO MASS PRODUCTION, 1800–1932 (1984).

dominated and controlled absolutely by Henry Ford, the president of the company, who owns and for several years has owned 58% of the entire capital stock of the company. * * * [O]n the 31st of July, 1916, the end of its last fiscal year, * * * Henry Ford [released a statement about that the company would distribute a regular dividend of 5% and] declared it to be the settled policy of the company not to pay in the future any special dividends, but to put back into the business for the future all of the earnings of the company, other than the regular dividend of five per cent (5%). * * *

This declaration of the future policy, it is charged in the bill, was published in the public press in the city of Detroit and throughout the United States in substantially the following language:

> "My ambition,' declared Mr. Ford, 'is to employ still more men; to spread the benefits of this industrial system to the greatest possible number, to help them build up their lives and their homes. To do this, we are putting the greatest share of our profits back into the business."

* * *

When plaintiffs made their complaint and demand for further dividends, the Ford Motor Company had concluded its most prosperous year of business. The demand for its cars at the price of the preceding year continued. It could make and could market in the year beginning August 1, 1916, more than 500,000 cars. Sales of parts and repairs would necessarily increase. The cost of materials was likely to advance, and perhaps the price of labor; but it reasonably might have expected a profit for the year of upwards of $60,000,000. * * * It had been the practice, under similar circumstances, to declare larger dividends. Considering only these facts, a refusal to declare and pay further dividends appears to be not an exercise of discretion on the part of the directors, but an arbitrary refusal to do what the circumstances required to be done. These facts and others call upon the directors to justify their action, or failure or refusal to act. In justification, the defendants have offered testimony tending to prove, and which does prove, the following facts: It had been the policy of the corporation for a considerable time to annually reduce the selling price of cars, while keeping up, or improving, their quality. As early as in June, 1915, a general plan for the expansion of the productive capacity. * * * It is hoped, by Mr. Ford, that eventually 1,000,000 cars will be annually produced. The contemplated changes will permit the increased output.

The plan, as affecting the profits * * * calls for a reduction in the selling price of the cars. It is true that this price might be at any time increased, but the plan called for the reduction in price of $80 a car. The capacity of the plant, without the additions thereto voted to be made * * * would produce more than 600,000 cars annually. This number, and more, could have been sold for $440 instead of $360, a difference * * * of at least $48,000,000. In short, the plan does not call for and is not intended to produce immediately a more profitable business, but a less profitable one; not only less profitable than formerly, but less profitable than it is admitted it might be made. The apparent immediate effect will be to diminish the value of shares and the returns to shareholders.

It is the contention of plaintiffs that the apparent effect of the plan is intended to be the continued and continuing effect of it, and that it is deliberately proposed, not of record and not by official corporate declaration, but nevertheless proposed, to continue the corporation henceforth as a semi-eleemosynary institution and not as a business institution. In support of this contention, they point to the attitude and to the expressions of Mr. Henry Ford.

Mr. Henry Ford is the dominant force in the business of the Ford Motor Company. No plan of operations could be adopted unless he consented, and no board of directors can be elected whom he does not favor. * * *

'With regard to dividends, the company paid 60% on its capitalization of two million dollars, or $1,200,000, leaving $58,000,000 to reinvest for the growth of the company. This is Mr. Ford's policy at present, and it is understood that the other stockholders cheerfully accede to this plan.'

He had made up his mind in the summer of 1916 that no dividends other than the regular dividends should be paid, 'for the present.'

'**Q.** For how long? Had you fixed in your mind any time in the future, when you were going to pay?—**A.** No.

'**Q.** That was indefinite in the future?—**A.** That was indefinite; yes, sir.'

The record, and especially the testimony of Mr. Ford, convinces that he has to some extent the attitude towards shareholders of one who has dispensed and distributed to them large gains and that they should be content to take what he chooses to give. His testimony creates the impression, also, that he thinks the Ford Motor Company has made too much money, has had too large profits, and that, although large profits might be still earned, a sharing of them with the public, by reducing the price of the output of the company, ought to be undertaken. We have no doubt that certain sentiments, philanthropic and altruistic, creditable to Mr. Ford, had large influence in determining the policy to be pursued by the Ford Motor Company—the policy which has been herein referred to.

It is said by his counsel that—

> 'Although a manufacturing corporation cannot engage in humanitarian works as its principal business, the fact that it is organized for profit does not prevent the existence of implied powers to carry on with humanitarian motives such charitable works as are incidental to the main business of the corporation.'

And again:

> 'As the expenditures complained of are being made in an expansion of the business which the company is organized to carry on, and for purposes within the powers of the corporation as hereinbefore shown, the question is as to whether such expenditures are rendered illegal because influenced to some extent by humanitarian motives and purposes on the part of the members of the board of directors.'

* * * There should be no confusion (of which there is evidence) of the duties which Mr. Ford conceives that he and the stockholders owe to the general public and the duties which in law he and his codirectors owe to

protesting, minority stockholders. A business corporation is organized and carried on primarily for the profit of the stockholders. The powers of the directors are to be employed for that end. The discretion of directors is to be exercised in the choice of means to attain that end, and does not extend to a change in the end itself, to the reduction of profits, or to the nondistribution of profits among stockholders in order to devote them to other purposes.

There is committed to the discretion of directors, a discretion to be exercised in good faith, the infinite details of business, including the wages which shall be paid to employees, the number of hours they shall work, the conditions under which labor shall be carried on, and the price for which products shall be offered to the public.

It is said by [the defendants] that the motives of the board members are not material and will not be inquired into by the court so long as their acts are within their lawful powers. [However], it is not within the lawful powers of a board of directors to shape and conduct the affairs of a corporation for the merely incidental benefit of shareholders and for the primary purpose of benefiting others, and no one will contend that, if the avowed purpose of the defendant directors was to sacrifice the interests of shareholders, it would not be the duty of the courts to interfere.

We are not, however, persuaded that we should interfere with the proposed expansion of the business of the Ford Motor Company. In view of the fact that the selling price of products may be increased at any time, the ultimate results of the larger business cannot be certainly estimated. The judges are not business experts. It is recognized that plans must often be made for a long future, for expected competition, for a continuing as well as an immediately profitable venture. The experience of the Ford Motor Company is evidence of capable management of its affairs. * * *

Assuming the general plan and policy of expansion and the details of it to have been sufficiently, formally, approved at the * * * meetings of directors, and assuming further that the plan and policy and the details agreed upon were for the best ultimate interest of the company and therefore of its shareholders, what does it amount to in justification of a refusal to declare and pay a special dividend or dividends? The Ford Motor Company was able to estimate with nicety its income and profit. It could sell more cars than it could make. Having ascertained what it would cost to produce a car and to sell it, the profit upon each car depended upon the selling price. That being fixed, the yearly income and profit was determinable, and, within slight variations, was certain.

* * *

Defendants say, and it is true, that a considerable cash balance must be at all times carried by such a concern. But, as has been stated, there was a large daily, weekly, monthly, receipt of cash. * * * Moreover, the contemplated expenditures were not to be immediately made. The large sum appropriated for the smelter plant was payable over a considerable period of time. So that, without going further, it would appear that, accepting and approving the plan of the directors, it was their duty to distribute on or near the 1st of August, 1916, a very large sum of money to stockholders.

Questions

1. *Dodge v. Ford Motor Company* addresses several types of "prices." What are these "prices"? Which prices bothered the plaintiffs? Which prices did the plaintiffs ask the court to address? Was the court's decision likely to affect market prices?

2. Did any sources of market inefficiencies affect the market for cars? Were such factors relevant to car prices? If so, in what way?

3. The *Dodge* court noted that "judges are not business experts," yet it interfered with business decisions of a "capable management." What was the motivation for this intervention?

§ 6.3 THE RHETORIC OF BARGAINING

The phrase "unequal bargaining power" is often used to describe the ability of a party to a transaction to control its terms. For example, in *Williams v. Walker–Thomas Furniture Co.*, 350 F.2d 445 (D.C. Cir. 1965), a furniture company offered a financing plan to its customers that allowed customers to pay for the furniture in monthly installments. The contracts were "approximately six inches in length and each contained a long paragraph in extremely fine print."[31] One of the sentences in that paragraph provided:

> [T]he amount of each periodical installment payment to be made by [purchaser] to the Company under this present lease shall be inclusive of and not in addition to the amount of each installment payment to be made by [purchaser] under such prior leases, bills or accounts; and all payments now and hereafter made by [purchaser] shall be credited pro rata on all outstanding leases, bills and accounts due the Company by [purchaser] at the time each such payment is made.

In plain English, as long as there was a balance on purchased item, the company retained the title to all purchased items. Or, in the words of the D.C. Circuit: "The effect of this rather obscure provision was to keep a balance due on every item purchased until the balance due on all items, whenever purchased, was liquidated. As a result, the debt incurred at the time of purchase of each item was secured by the right to repossess all the items previously purchased by the same purchaser, and each new item purchased automatically became subject to a security interest arising out of the previous dealings." When buyers defaulted on their payments, the furniture company sought to repossess all the purchased items. Two purchasers contested these attempts and the company sued them. The trial court ruled in favor of the company. The case reached the Court of Appeals District of Columbia Circuit. Reversing the judgment against the purchasers, the court held:

> Ordinarily, one who signs an agreement without full knowledge of its terms might be held to assume the risk that he has entered a

31. Williams v. Walker–Thomas Furniture Co., 198 A.2d 914, 915 (D.C. 1964).

> one-sided bargain. But when a party of *little bargaining power*, and hence little real choice, signs a commercially unreasonable contract with little or no knowledge of its terms, it is hardly likely that his consent, or even an objective manifestation of his consent, was ever given to all the terms. In such a case the usual rule that the terms of the agreement are not to be questioned should be abandoned and the court should consider whether the terms of the contract are so unfair that enforcement should be withheld.[32]

In *Williams v. Walker–Thomas Furniture*, therefore, the court expressly used "unequal bargaining power" as the rationale to refuse to enforce one-sided contracts under the unconscionability doctrine.[33] But there was no bargaining between the Walker–Thomas Furniture Company and its customers. The company introduced the customers with a "take-it-or-leave-it" offer: an incomprehensible financing plan. Some customers possibly understood the one-page paragraph. Some customers could understand it if they took the time to analyze it. Other customers could never have understood it. Actual bargaining, however, never took place.

Insurance policies offer another example where the term "unequal bargaining power" is often used, no actual bargaining takes place. In *Brakeman v. Potomac Insurance Co.*, 472 Pa. 66 (1977), the Pennsylvania Supreme Court stressed this point. *Brakeman* involved a car insurance policy that required a notice of an accident "as soon as practicable." Specifically, the insurance policy provided:

> In the event of an accident, occurrence or loss, written notice containing particulars sufficient to identify the insured and also reasonably obtainable information with respect to the time, place and circumstances thereof, and the names and addresses of the injured and of available witnesses, Shall be given by or for the insured to the company or any of its authorized agents as soon as practicable.
>
> * * *
>
> No action shall lie against the company unless, As a condition precedent thereto, the insured shall have fully complied with all of the terms of this policy, nor until the amount of the insured's obligation to pay shall have been finally determined either By judgment against the insured after actual trial or by written agreement of the insured, the claimant and the company.

The court ruled that an insurer could deny claims that breach the notice provision only if it also proved that it suffered prejudice as a consequence of the breach. It explained that "insurance policies are [not] private contracts in the traditional sense * * * [because an] insurance contract is not a negotiated agreement; rather its conditions are by and large dictated by the insurance company to the insured. The only aspect of

---

32. Williams v. Walker–Thomas Furniture Co., 350 F.2d 445, 449–50 (D.C. Cir. 1965) (emphasis added).

33. *See generally* Eben Colby, *What Did the Doctrine of Unconscionability Do to the Walker–Thomas Furniture Company?*, 34 CONNECTICUT LAW REVIEW 625 (2002).

the contract over which the insured can 'bargain' is the monetary amount of coverage.''[34]

Standardized transactions that circumvent bargaining are indeed common in the marketplace. Bargaining involves transaction costs and thus happens only in particular circumstances. To save time and money, the vast majority of transactions do not involve any form of bargaining whatsoever. One party is in advantageous position to standardize certain transactions and economize transaction costs. That party inevitably determines the terms of the standardized transaction and, thus, is in a position to exploits every possible source of market inefficiencies. Even when competition appears to be intense, the opportunities to take advantage of particular market characteristics and human limitations are infinite.[35] The credit card market, in which issuers fiercely compete to seduce more people to take and use their cards, is one example.[36] The question we address is whether, and if so, when the state should intervene in standard form agreements.

Lochner was about the power of business owners to dictate employment terms to employees. Under certain theories of freedom of contract, sources of market inefficiencies do not exist or should be disregarded. The only question that matter is whether the parties entered into an agreement. *Lochner* applies such theories. The *Lochner* Court declared unconstitutional a state law that set maximum hours for bakers. Writing for the majority, Justice Peckham distinguished bakers from miners, for whom the Court upheld a maximum-hour law seven years prior to *Lochner*.[37] Three years after *Lochner*, in *Muller v. Oregon*, the Court upheld a maximum-hour law for women working in "in any mechanical establishment, or factory, or laundry." Louis Brandeis served as a counsel for the State of Oregon and wrote for the state an influential brief that pioneered the use of social science data. The so-called "Brandeis Brief" purported to document that women's reproductive health was related to the scope of non-domestic work. It persuaded the Court that the law protected the public safety, health, morals, or general welfare and as such was a legitimate exercise of the state police powers. In 1917, in *Bunting v. Oregon*, the Supreme Court upheld a maximum-hour law for men and women in manufacturing jobs.[38]

---

34. Brakeman v. Potomac Insurance Co., 472 Pa. 66, 72 (1977).

35. *See, e.g.*, Xavier Gabaix & David Laibson, *Shrouded Attributes, Consumer Myopia, and Information Suppression in Competitive Markets*, 121 QUARTERLY JOURNAL OF ECONOMICS 505 (2006).

36. *See* Oren Bar–Gill, *Seduction by Plastic*, 98 NORTHWESTERN UNIVERSITY LAW REVIEW 1373 (2004).

37. Holden v. Hardy, 169 U.S. 366 (1898).

38. Bunting v. Oregon, 243 U.S. 426 (1917).

Adkins v. Children's Hospital of the District of Columbia

261 U.S. 525 (1923)

■ MR. JUSTICE SUTHERLAND delivered the opinion of the Court.

The question presented for determination by these appeals is the constitutionality of the Act of September 19, 1918, providing for the fixing of minimum wages for women and children in the District of Columbia. * * *

The act provides for a board of three members to be constituted, as far as practicable, so as to be equally representative of employers, employees and the public. * * * By section 8 the board is authorized—

> (1) To investigate and ascertain the wages of women and minors in the different occupations in which they are employed in the District of Columbia;
>
> (2) to examine, through any member or authorized representative, any book, pay roll or other record of any employer of women or minors that in any way appertains to or has a bearing upon the question of wages of any such women or minors; and
>
> (3) to require from such employer full and true statements of the wages paid to all women and minors in his employment.

And by section 9—

> 'To ascertain and declare, in the manner hereinafter provided, the following things:
>
> (a) Standards of minimum wages for women in any occupation within the District of Columbia, and what wages are inadequate to supply the necessary cost of living to any such women workers to maintain them in good health and to protect their morals; and
>
> (b) standards of minimum wages for minors in any occupation within the District of Columbia, and what wages are unreasonably low for any such minor workers.'

The act then provides (section 10) that if the board, after investigation, is of opinion that any substantial number of women workers in any occupation are receiving wages inadequate to supply them with the necessary cost of living, maintain them in health and protect their morals, a conference may be called to consider and inquire into and report on the subject investigated, the conference to be equally representative of employers and employees in such occupation and of the public, and to include one or more members of the board.

The conference is required to make and transmit to the board a report including, among other things:

> 'Recommendations as to standards of minimum wages for women workers in the occupation under inquiry and as to what wages are inadequate to supply the necessary cost of living to women workers in such occupation and to maintain them in health and to protect their morals.'

The board is authorized (section 12) to consider and review these recommendations and to approve or disapprove any or all of them. * * * There is a provision (section 13) under which the board may issue a special license to a woman whose earning capacity 'has been impaired by age or otherwise,' authorizing her employment at less than the minimum wages fixed under the act.

All questions of fact (section 17) are to be determined by the board, from whose decision there is no appeal; but an appeal is allowed on questions of law.

Any violation of the act (section 18) by an employer or his agent or by corporate agents is declared to be a misdemeanor, punishable by fine and imprisonment.

Finally, after some further provisions not necessary to be stated, it is declared (section 23) that the purposes of the act are—

> 'To protect the women and minors of the District from conditions detrimental to their health and morals, resulting from wages which are inadequate to maintain decent standards of living; and the act in each of its provisions and in its entirety shall be interpreted to effectuate these purposes.'

The appellee in the first case is a corporation maintaining a hospital for children in the District. It employs a large number of women in various capacities, with whom it had agreed upon rates of wages and compensation satisfactory to such employees, but which in some instances were less than the minimum wage fixed by an order of the board made in pursuance of the act. The women with whom appellee had so contracted were all of full age and under no legal disability. * * *

In the second case the appellee, a woman 21 years of age, was employed by the Congress Hall Hotel Company as an elevator operator, at a salary of $35 per month and two meals a day. She alleges that the work was light and healthful, the hours short, with surroundings clean and moral, and that she was anxious to continue it for the compensation she was receiving, and that she did not earn more. Her services were satisfactory to the Hotel Company, and it would have been glad to retain her, but was obliged to dispense with her services by reason of the order of the board and on account of the penalties prescribed by the act. The wages received by this appellee were the best she was able to obtain for any work she was capable of performing, and the enforcement of the order, she alleges, deprived her of such employment and wages. She further averred that she could not secure any other position at which she could make a living, with as good physical and moral surroundings, and earn as good wages, and that she was desirous of continuing and would continue the employment, but for the order of the board. An injunction was prayed as in the other case.

* * * This court, by an unbroken line of decisions from Chief Justice Marshall to the present day, has steadily adhered to the rule that every possible presumption is in favor of the validity of an act of Congress until overcome beyond rational doubt. But, if by clear and indubitable demonstration a statute be opposed to the Constitution, we have no choice but to

say so. The Constitution, by its own terms, is the supreme law of the land, emanating from the people, the repository of ultimate sovereignty under our form of government. A congressional statute, on the other hand, is the act of an agency of this sovereign authority, and if it conflict with the Constitution must fall; for that which is not supreme must yield to that which is. * * *

The statute now under consideration is attacked upon the ground that it authorizes an unconstitutional interference with the freedom of contract included within the guaranties of the due process clause of the Fifth Amendment. That the right to contract about one's affairs is a part of the liberty of the individual protected by this clause is settled by the decisions of this court and is no longer open to question. * * * Within this liberty are contracts of employment of labor. In making such contracts, generally speaking, the parties have an equal right to obtain from each other the best terms they can as the result of private bargaining.

* * *

There is, of course, no such thing as absolute freedom of contract. It is subject to a great variety of restraints. But freedom of contract is, nevertheless, the general rule and restraint the exception, and the exercise of legislative authority to abridge it can be justified only by the existence of exceptional circumstances. Whether these circumstances exist in the present case constitutes the question to be answered. It will be helpful to this end to review some of the decisions where the interference has been upheld and consider the grounds upon which they rest:

(1) *Those dealing with statutes fixing rates and charges to be exacted by businesses impressed with a public interest*. There are many cases, but it is sufficient to cite *Munn v. Illinois*, 94 U.S. 113 (1876). The power here rests upon the ground that, where property is devoted to a public use, the owner thereby in effect grants to the public an interest in the use which may be controlled by the public for the common good to the extent of the interest thus created. It is upon this theory that these statutes have been upheld, and, it may be noted in passing, so upheld, even in respect of their incidental and injurious or destructive effect upon preexisting contracts. * * * In the case at bar the statute does not depend upon the existence of a public interest in any business to be affected, and this class of cases may be laid aside as inapplicable.

(2) *Statutes relating to contracts for the performance of public work. Atkin v. Kansas*, 191 U.S. 207 (1903). * * * These cases sustain such statutes as depending, not upon the right to condition private contracts, but upon the right of the government to prescribe the conditions upon which it will permit work of a public character to be done for it, or, in the case of a state, for its municipalities. We may therefore, in like manner, dismiss these decisions from consideration as inapplicable.

(3) *Statutes prescribing the character, methods, and time for payment of wages*. Under this head may be included *McLean v. Arkansas*, 211 U.S. 539 (1909), sustaining a state statute requiring coal to be measured for payment of miners' wages before screening; *Knoxville Iron Co. v. Harbison*, 183 U.S. 13 (1901), sustaining a Tennessee statute requiring the redemp-

tion in cash of store orders issued in payment of wages; *Erie Railway Co. v. Williams*, 233 U.S. 685 (1914), upholding a statute regulating the time within which wages shall be paid to employees in certain specified industries; and other cases sustaining statutes of like import and effect. In none of the statutes thus sustained was the liberty of employer or employee to fix the amount of wages the one was willing to pay and the other willing to receive interfered with. Their tendency and purpose was to prevent unfair, and perhaps fraudulent, methods in the payment of wages, and in no sense can they be said to be, or to furnish a precedent for, wage fixing statutes.

(4) *Statutes fixing hours of labor*. * * * In some instances the statute limited the hours of labor for men in certain occupations, and in others it was confined in its application to women. No statute has thus far been brought to the attention of this court which by its terms, applied to all occupations. In *Holden v. Hardy*, 169 U.S. 366 (1898), the court considered an act of the Utah Legislature, restricting the hours of labor in mines and smelters. This statute was sustained as a legitimate exercise of the police power, on the ground that the Legislature had determined that these particular employments, when too long pursued, were injurious to the health of the employees, and that, as there were reasonable grounds for supporting this determination on the part of the Legislature, its decision in that respect was beyond the reviewing power of the federal courts.

That this constituted the basis of the decision is emphasized by the subsequent decision in *Lochner v. New York*, 198 U.S. 45 (1905), reviewing a state statute which restricted the employment of all persons in bakeries to 10 hours in any one day. The court referred to *Holden v. Hardy* * * * and, declaring it to be inapplicable, held the statute unconstitutional as an unreasonable, unnecessary and arbitrary interference with the liberty of contract and therefore void under the Constitution. * * * Subsequent cases in this court have been distinguished from that decision, but the principles therein stated have never been disapproved.

In addition * * *, there are decisions of this court dealing with laws especially relating to hours of labor for women. * * *

In the Muller Case,* the validity of an Oregon statute, forbidding the employment of any female in certain industries more than 10 hours during any one day was upheld. The decision proceeded upon the theory that the difference between the sexes may justify a different rule respecting hours of labor in the case of women than in the case of men. It is pointed out that these consist in differences of physical structure, especially in respect of the maternal functions, and also in the fact that historically woman has always been dependent upon man, who has established his control by superior physical strength. * * * In view of the great-not to say revolutionary-changes which have taken place since that utterance, in the contractual, political, and civil status of women, culminating in the Nineteenth Amendment, it is not unreasonable to say that these differences have now come almost, if not quite, to the vanishing point. In this aspect of the matter, while the physical differences must be recognized in appropriate cases, and legislation fixing hours or conditions of work may properly take them into

* [Muller v. Oregon, 208 U.S. 412 (1908)—BYO].

account, we cannot accept the doctrine that women of mature age, *sui juris*, require or may be subjected to restrictions upon their liberty of contract which could not lawfully be imposed in the case of men under similar circumstances. To do so would be to ignore all the implications to be drawn from the present day trend of legislation, as well as that of common thought and usage, by which woman is accorded emancipation from the old doctrine that she must be given special protection or be subjected to special restraint in her contractual and civil relationships. In passing, it may be noted that the instant statute applies in the case of a woman employer contracting with a woman employee as it does when the former is a man.

The essential characteristics of the statute now under consideration, which differentiate it from the laws fixing hours of labor, will be made to appear as we proceed. * * * A law forbidding work to continue beyond a given number of hours leaves the parties free to contract about wages and thereby equalize whatever additional burdens may be imposed upon the employer as a result of the restrictions as to hours, by an adjustment in respect of the amount of wages. Enough has been said to show that the authority to fix hours of labor cannot be exercised except in respect of those occupations where work of long continued duration is detrimental to health. This court has been careful in every case where the question has been raised, to place its decision upon this limited authority of the Legislature to regulate hours of labor and to disclaim any purpose to uphold the legislation as fixing wages, thus recognizing an essential difference between the two. It seems plain that these decisions afford no real support for any form of law establishing minimum wages.

If now, in the light furnished by the foregoing exceptions to the general rule forbidding legislative interference with freedom of contract, we examine and analyze the statute in question, we shall see that it differs from them in every material respect. It is not a law dealing with any business charged with a public interest or with public work, or to meet and tide over a temporary emergency. It has nothing to do with the character, methods or periods of wage payments. It does not prescribe hours of labor or conditions under which labor is to be done. It is not for the protection of persons under legal disability or for the prevention of fraud. It is simply and exclusively a price-fixing law, confined to adult women (for we are not now considering the provisions relating to minors), who are legally as capable of contracting for themselves as men. It forbids two parties having lawful capacity—under penalties as to the employer—to freely contract with one another in respect of the price for which one shall render service to the other in a purely private employment where both are willing, perhaps anxious, to agree, even though the consequence may be to oblige one to surrender a desirable engagement and the other to dispense with the services of a desirable employee. The price fixed by the board need have no relation to the capacity or earning power of the employee, the number of hours which may happen to constitute the day's work, the character of the place where the work is to be done, or the circumstances or surroundings of the employment, and, while it has no other basis to support its validity than the assumed necessities of the employee, it takes no account of any independent resources she may have. It is based wholly on the opinions of the members of the board and their advisers—perhaps an average of their opinions, if they do not precisely agree—as to what will be necessary to provide a living for a woman, keep her in health and preserve her morals. It applies to any and every occupation in the District, without regard to its nature or the character of the work.

The standard furnished by the statute for the guidance of the board is so vague as to be impossible of practical application with any reasonable degree of accuracy. What is sufficient to supply the necessary cost of living for a woman worker and maintain her in good health and protect her morals is obviously not a precise or unvarying sum—not even approximately so. The amount will depend upon a variety of circumstances: The individual temperament, habits of thrift, care, ability to buy necessaries intelligently, and whether the woman live alone or with her family. To those who practice economy, a given sum will afford comfort, while to those or contrary habit the same sum will be wholly inadequate. The co-operative economies of the family group are not taken into account, though they constitute an important consideration in estimating the cost of living, for it is obvious that the individual expense will be less in the case of a member of a family than in the case of one living alone. The relation between earnings and morals is not capable of standardization. It cannot be shown that well-paid women safeguard their morals more carefully than those who are poorly paid. Morality rests upon other considerations than wages, and there is, certainly, no such prevalent connection between the two as to justify a broad attempt to adjust the latter with reference to the former. As a means of safeguarding morals the attempted classification, in our opinion, is without reasonable basis. No distinction can be made between women who work for others and those who do not; nor is there ground for distinction between women and men, for, certainly, if women require a minimum wage to preserve their morals men require it to preserve their honesty. For these reasons, and others which might be stated, the inquiry in respect of the necessary cost of living and of the income necessary to preserve health and morals presents an individual and not a composite question, and must be answered for each individual considered by herself and not by a general formula prescribed by a statutory bureau.

* * *

The law takes account of the necessities of only one party to the contract. It ignores the necessities of the employer by compelling him to pay not less than a certain sum, not only whether the employee is capable of earning it, but irrespective of the ability of his business to sustain the burden, generously leaving him, of course, the privilege of abandoning his business as an alternative for going on at a loss. Within the limits of the minimum sum, he is precluded, under penalty of fine and imprisonment, from adjusting compensation to the differing merits of his employees. It compels him to pay at least the sum fixed in any event, because the employee needs it, but requires no service of equivalent value from the employee. * * * The law is not confined to the great and powerful employers but embraces those whose bargaining power may be as weak as that of the employee. It takes no account of periods of stress and business depression, of crippling losses, which may leave the employer himself without adequate means of livelihood. * * *

The feature of this statute, which perhaps more than any other, puts upon it the stamp of invalidity, is that it exacts from the employer an arbitrary payment for a purpose and upon a basis having no causal connection with his business, or the contract or the work the employee engages to do. The declared basis, as already pointed out, is not the value of the service rendered, but the extraneous circumstance that the employee needs to get a prescribed sum of money to insure her subsistence, health, and morals. * * * The necessities of the employee are alone considered, and these arise outside of the employment, are the same when there is no employment, and as great in one occupation as in another. Certainly the employer, by paying a fair equivalent for the service rendered, though not sufficient to support the employee, has neither caused nor contributed to her poverty. On the contrary, to the extent of what he pays, he has relieved it. In principle, there can be no difference between the case of selling labor and the case of selling goods. If one goes to the butcher, the baker, or grocer to buy food, he is morally entitled to obtain the worth of his money; but he is not entitled to more. If what he gets is worth what he pays, he is not justified in demanding more, simply because he needs more. * * *

Finally, it may be said that if, in the interest of the public welfare, the police power may be invoked to justify the fixing of a minimum wage, it may, when the public welfare is thought to require it, be invoked to justify a maximum wage. The power to fix high wages connotes, by like course of reasoning, the power to fix low wages. * * * If, for example, in the opinion of future lawmakers, wages in the building trades shall become so high as to preclude people of ordinary means from building and owning homes, an authority which sustains the minimum wage will be invoked to support a maximum wage for building laborers and artisans, and the same argument which has been here urged to strip the employer of his constitutional liberty of contract in one direction will be utilized to strip the employee of his constitutional liberty of contract in the opposite direction. A wrong decision does not end with itself; it is a precedent, and, with the swing of sentiment, its bad influence may run from one extremity of the arc to the other.

* * *

It follows, from what has been said, that the act in question passes the limit prescribed by the Constitution. * * *

■ MR. JUSTICE BRANDEIS took no part in the consideration or decision of these cases.

■ MR. CHIEF JUSTICE TAFT, dissenting.

I regret much to differ from the court in these cases. * * * Legislatures in limiting freedom of contract between employee and employer by a minimum wage proceed on the assumption that employees, in the class receiving least pay, are not upon a full level of equality of choice with their employer and in their necessitous circumstances are prone to accept pretty much anything that is offered. They are peculiarly subject to the overreaching of the harsh and greedy employer. The evils of the sweating system and of the long hours and low wages which are characteristic of it are well known. Now, I agree that it is a disputable question in the field of political economy how far a statutory requirement of maximum hours or minimum wages may be a useful remedy for these evils, and whether it may not make the case of the oppressed employee worse than it was before. But it is not the function of this court to hold congressional acts invalid simply because they are passed to carry out economic views which the court believes to be unwise or unsound.

* * *

■ MR. JUSTICE HOLMES, dissenting.

The question in this case is the broad one, whether Congress can establish minimum rates of wages for women in the District of Columbia with due provision for special circumstances, or whether we must say that Congress had no power to meddle with the matter at all. To me, * * * the power of Congress seems absolutely free from doubt. * * *

Contract is not specially mentioned in the text that we have to construe. It is merely an example of doing what you want to do, embodied in the word liberty. But pretty much all law consists in forbidding men to do some things that they want to do, and contract is no more exempt from law than other acts. * * * Usury laws prohibit contracts by which a man receives more than so much interest for the money that he lends. Statutes of frauds restrict many contracts to certain forms. Some Sunday laws prohibit practically all contracts during one-seventh of our whole life. Insurance rates may be regulated. * * * The size of a loaf of bread may be established. * * * The responsibility of employers to their employees may be profoundly modified. * * * [W]omen's hours of labor may be fixed; * * * and the principle was extended to men with the allowance of a limited overtime to be paid for 'at the rate of time and one-half of the regular wage.'

I confess that I do not understand the principle on which the power to fix a minimum for the wages of women can be denied by those who admit the power to fix a maximum for their hours of work. I fully assent to the proposition that here as elsewhere the distinctions of the law are distinctions of degree, but I perceive no difference in the kind or degree of interference with liberty, the only matter with which we have any concern, between the one case and the other. The bargain is equally affected whichever half you regulate. * * *

This statute does not compel anybody to pay anything. It simply forbids employment at rates below those fixed as the minimum requirement of health and right living. It is safe to assume that women will not be employed at even the lowest wages allowed unless they earn them, or unless the employer's business can sustain the burden. In short the law in its character and operation is like hundreds of so-called police laws that have been upheld. I see no greater objection to using a Board to apply the standard fixed by the Act than there is to the other commissions with which we have become familiar or than there is to the requirement of a license in other cases. * * *

I am of opinion that the statute is valid and that the decree should be reversed.

West Coast Hotel Co. v. Parrish

300 U.S. 379 (1937)

■ MR. CHIEF JUSTICE HUGHES delivered the opinion of the Court.

This case presents the question of the constitutional validity of the minimum wage law of the state of Washington. The act, entitled 'Minimum Wages for Women,' authorizes the fixing of minimum wages for women and minors. * * * It provides:

> 'Section 1. The welfare of the State of Washington demands that women and minors be protected from conditions of labor which have a pernicious effect on their health and morals. The State of Washington, therefore, exercising herein its police and sovereign power declares that inadequate wages and unsanitary conditions of labor exert such pernicious effect.
>
> 'Sec. 2. It shall be unlawful to employ women or minors in any industry or occupation within the State of Washington under conditions of labor detrimental to their health or morals; and it shall be unlawful to employ women workers in any industry within the State of Washington at wages which are not adequate for their maintenance.
>
> 'Sec. 3. There is hereby created a commission to be known as the 'Industrial Welfare Commission' for the State of Washington, to establish such standards of wages and conditions of labor for women and minors employed within the State of Washington, as shall be held hereunder to be reasonable and not detrimental to health and morals, and which shall be sufficient for the decent maintenance of women.'
>
> * * *

By a later act the Industrial Welfare Commission was abolished and its duties were assigned to the Industrial Welfare Committee consisting of the Director of Labor and Industries, the Supervisor of Industrial Insurance, the Supervisor of Industrial Relations, the Industrial Statistician, and the Supervisor of Women in Industry. * * *

Elsie Parrish was employed as a chambermaid and (with her husband) brought this suit to recover the difference between the wages paid her and the minimum wage fixed pursuant to the state law. The minimum wage was $14.50 per week of 48 hours. [West Coast Hotel] challenged the [constitutionality of the] act. * * *

[West Coast Hotel] relies upon the decision of this Court in *Adkins v. Children's Hospital*, 261 U.S. 525 (1923), which held invalid the District of Columbia Minimum Wage Act (40 Stat. 960). * * * The Supreme Court of Washington has upheld the minimum wage statute of that state. It has decided that the statute is a reasonable exercise of the police power of the state. In reaching that conclusion, the state court has invoked principles long established by this Court in the application of the Fourteenth Amendment. The state court has refused to regard the decision in the Adkins Case as determinative and has pointed to our decisions both before and since that case as justifying its position. We are of the opinion that this ruling of

the state court demands on our part a re-examination of the *Adkins* Case.
* * *

The principle which must control our decision is not in doubt. The constitutional provision invoked is the due process clause of the Fourteenth Amendment governing the states, as the due process clause invoked in the *Adkins* Case governed Congress. In each case the violation alleged by those attacking minimum wage regulation for women is deprivation of freedom of contract. What is this freedom? The Constitution does not speak of freedom of contract. It speaks of liberty and prohibits the deprivation of liberty without due process of law. In prohibiting that deprivation, the Constitution does not recognize an absolute and uncontrollable liberty. Liberty in each of its phases has its history and connotation. But the liberty safeguarded is liberty in a social organization which requires the protection of law against the evils which menace the health, safety, morals, and welfare of the people. Liberty under the Constitution is thus necessarily subject to the restraints of due process, and regulation which is reasonable in relation to its subject and is adopted in the interests of the community is due process.
* * *

This power under the Constitution to restrict freedom of contract has had many illustrations. That it may be exercised in the public interest with respect to contracts between employer and employee is undeniable. Thus statutes have been sustained limiting employment in underground mines and smelters to eight hours a day * * *; in requiring redemption in cash of store orders or other evidences of indebtedness issued in the payment of wages * * *; in forbidding the payment of seamen's wages in advance * * *; in making it unlawful to contract to pay miners employed at quantity rates upon the basis of screened coal instead of the weight of the coal as originally produced in the mine * * *; in prohibiting contracts limiting liability for injuries to employees * * *; in limiting hours of work of employees in manufacturing establishments * * *; and in maintaining workmen's compensation laws. * * * In dealing with the relation of employer and employed, the Legislature has necessarily a wide field of discretion in order that there may be suitable protection of health and safety, and that peace and good order may be promoted through regulations designed to insure wholesome conditions of work and freedom from oppression. * * *

The point that has been strongly stressed that adult employees should be deemed competent to make their own contracts was decisively met nearly forty years ago in *Holden v. Hardy*, 169 U.S. 366 (1898), where we pointed out the inequality in the footing of the parties. We said (*Id.* at 397):

> 'The legislature has also recognized the fact, which the experience of legislators in many states has corroborated, that the proprietors of these establishments and their operatives do not stand upon an equality, and that their interests are, to a certain extent, conflicting. The former naturally desire to obtain as much labor as possible from their employees, while the latter are often induced by the fear of discharge to conform to regulations which their judgment, fairly exercised, would pronounce to be detrimental to

> their health or strength. In other words, the proprietors lay down the rules, and the laborers are practically constrained to obey them. In such cases self-interest is often an unsafe guide, and the legislature may properly interpose its authority.'

And we added that the fact 'that both parties are of full age, and competent to contract, does not necessarily deprive the state of the power to interfere, where the parties do not stand upon an equality, or where the public health demands that one party to the contract shall be protected against himself.' 'The state still retains an interest in his welfare, however reckless he may be. The whole is no greater than the sum of all the parts, and when the individual health, safety, and welfare are sacrificed or neglected, the state must suffer.'

It is manifest that this established principle is peculiarly applicable in relation to the employment of women in whose protection the state has a special interest. That phase of the subject received elaborate consideration in *Muller v. Oregon*, 208 U.S. 412 (1908), where the constitutional authority of the state to limit the working hours of women was sustained. We emphasized the consideration that 'woman's physical structure and the performance of maternal functions place her at a disadvantage in the struggle for subsistence' and that her physical well being 'becomes an object of public interest and care in order to preserve the strength and vigor of the race.' We emphasized the need of protecting women against oppression despite her possession of contractual rights. We said that 'though limitations upon personal and contractual rights may be removed by legislation, there is that in her disposition and habits of life which will operate against a full assertion of those rights. * * *

This array of * * * principles * * * were thought by the dissenting Justices in the *Adkins* Case to demand that the minimum wage statute be sustained. The validity of the distinction made by the Court between a minimum wage and a maximum of hours in limiting liberty of contract was especially challenged. * * * That challenge persists and is without any satisfactory answer. * * * Mr. Justice Holmes, while recognizing that 'the distinctions of the law are distinctions of degree,' could 'perceive no difference in the kind or degree of interference with liberty, the only matter with which we have any concern, between the one case and the other. The bargain is equally affected whichever half you regulate.' * * *

One of the points which was pressed by the Court in supporting its ruling in the *Adkins* Case was that the standard set up by the District of Columbia Act did not take appropriate account of the value of the services rendered. * * *

The minimum wage to be paid under the Washington statute is fixed after full consideration by representatives of employers, employees, and the public. It may be assumed that the minimum wage is fixed in consideration of the services that are performed in the particular occupations under normal conditions. Provision is made for special licenses at less wages in the case of women who are incapable of full service. The statement of Mr. Justice Holmes in the *Adkins* Case is pertinent: 'This statute does not compel anybody to pay anything. It simply forbids employment at rates below those fixed as the minimum requirement of health and right living.

It is safe to assume that women will not be employed at even the lowest wages allowed unless they earn them, or unless the employer's business can sustain the burden. In short the law in its character and operation is like hundreds of so-called police laws that have been up-held.' * * * And Chief Justice Taft forcibly pointed out the consideration which is basic in a statute of this character: 'Legislatures which adopt a requirement of maximum hours or minimum wages may be presumed to believe that when sweating employers are prevented from paying unduly low wages by positive law they will continue their business, abating that part of their profits, which were wrung from the necessities of their employees, and will concede the better terms required by the law, and that while in individual cases, hardship may result, the restriction will enure to the benefit of the general class of employees in whose interest the law is passed, and so to that of the community at large.'

We think that the views thus expressed are sound and that the decision in the *Adkins* Case was a departure from the true application of the principles governing the regulation by the state of the relation of employer and employed. Those principles have been reenforced by our subsequent decisions. Thus, in *Radice v. New York*, 264 U.S. 292 (1924), we sustained the New York statute which restricted the employment of women in restaurants at night. In *O'Gorman & Young v. Hartford Fire Insurance Company*, 282 U.S. 251 (1931), [we] upheld an act regulating the commissions of insurance agents. * * * In *Nebbia v. New York*, 291 U.S. 502 (1934), [we upheld] the New York statute [that] provid[ed] for minimum prices for milk, * * * and we again declared that if such laws 'have a reasonable relation to a proper legislative purpose, and are neither arbitrary nor discriminatory, the requirements of due process are satisfied'; that 'with the wisdom of the policy adopted, with the adequacy or practicability of the law enacted to forward it, the courts are both incompetent and unauthorized to deal'; that 'times without number we have said that the Legislature is primarily the judge of the necessity of such an enactment, that every possible presumption is in favor of its validity, and that though the court may hold views inconsistent with the wisdom of the law, it may not be annulled unless palpably in excess of legislative power.' * * *

With full recognition of the earnestness and vigor which characterize the prevailing opinion in the *Adkins* Case, we find it impossible to reconcile that ruling with these well-considered declarations. What can be closer to the public interest than the health of women and their protection from unscrupulous and overreaching employers? And if the protection of women is a legitimate end of the exercise of state power, how can it be said that the requirement of the payment of a minimum wage fairly fixed in order to meet the very necessities of existence is not an admissible means to that end? The Legislature of the state was clearly entitled to consider the situation of women in employment, the fact that they are in the class receiving the least pay, that their bargaining power is relatively weak, and that they are the ready victims of those who would take advantage of their necessitous circumstances. * * *

There is an additional and compelling consideration which recent economic experience has brought into a strong light. The exploitation of a class of workers who are in an unequal position with respect to bargaining power and are thus relatively defenseless against the denial of a living wage is not only detrimental to their health and well being, but casts a direct burden for their support upon the community. What these workers lose in wages the taxpayers are called upon to pay. The bare cost of living must be met. We may take judicial notice of the unparalleled demands for relief which arose during the recent period of depression and still continue to an alarming extent despite the degree of economic recovery which has been achieved. It is unnecessary to cite official statistics to establish what is of common knowledge through the length and breadth of the land. * * * The community is not bound to provide what is in effect a subsidy for unconscionable employers. The community may direct its law-making power to correct the abuse which springs from their selfish disregard of the public interest. * * *

Our conclusion is that the case of *Adkins v. Children's Hospital* * * * should be, and it is, overruled. The judgment of the Supreme Court of the state of Washington is affirmed.

Affirmed.

■ MR. JUSTICE SUTHERLAND.

MR. JUSTICE VAN DEVANTER, MR. JUSTICE MCREYNOLDS, MR. JUSTICE BUTLER, and I think the judgment of the court below should be reversed.

* * *

In support of minimum-wage legislation, it has been urged, on the one hand, that great benefits will result in favor of underpaid labor, and, on the other hand, that the danger of such legislation is that the minimum will tend to become the maximum and thus bring down the earnings of the more efficient toward the level of the less-efficient employees. But with these speculations we have nothing to do. We are concerned only with the question of constitutionality.

That the clause of the Fourteenth Amendment which forbids a state to deprive any person of life, liberty, or property without due process of law includes freedom of contract is so well settled as to be no longer open to question. Nor reasonably can it be disputed that contracts of employment of labor are included in the rule. * * *

In the *Adkins* Case we * * * said that while there was no such thing as absolute freedom of contract, but that it was subject to a great variety of restraints, nevertheless, freedom of contract was the general rule and restraint the exception; and that the power to abridge that freedom could only be justified by the existence of exceptional circumstances. This statement of the rule has been many times affirmed; and we do not understand that it is questioned by the present decision.

We further pointed out four distinct classes of cases in which this court from time to time had upheld statutory interferences with the liberty of contract. They were, in brief, (1) statutes fixing rates and charges to be exacted by businesses impressed with a public interest; (2) statutes relating to contracts for the performance of public work; (3) statutes prescribing the character, methods, and time for payment of wages; and (4) statutes fixing hours of labor. * * * What is there said need not be repeated. It is enough for present purposes to say that statutes of the [fourth] class deal with an incident of the employment, having no necessary effect upon wages. The parties are left free to contract about wages, and thereby equalize such additional burdens as may be imposed upon the employer as a result of the restrictions as to hours by an adjustment in respect of the amount of wages. * * *

We then pointed out that minimum wage legislation such as that here involved does not deal with any business charged with a public interest, or with public work, or with a temporary emergency, or with the character, methods, or periods of wage payments, or with hours of labor, or with the protection of persons under legal disability, or with the prevention of fraud. It is, simply and exclusively, a law fixing wages for adult women who are legally as capable of contracting for themselves as men, and cannot be sustained unless upon principles apart from those involved in cases already decided by the court.

* * *

Whether this would be equally or at all true in respect of the statutes of some of the states we are not called upon to say. They are not now before us; and it is enough that it applies in every particular to the Washington statute now under consideration.

The Washington statute, like the one for the District of Columbia, fixes minimum wages for adult women. Adult men and their employers are left free to bargain as they please; and it is a significant and an important fact that all state statutes to which our attention has been called are of like character. The common-law rules restricting the power of women to make contracts have, under our system, long since practically disappeared. Women today stand upon a legal and political equality with men. There is no longer any reason why they should be put in different classes in respect of their legal right to make contracts; nor should they be denied, in effect, the right to compete with men for work paying lower wages which men may be willing to accept. And it is an arbitrary exercise of the legislative power to do so. * * *

Difference of sex affords no reasonable ground for making a restriction applicable to the wage contracts of all working women from which like contracts of all working men are left free. Certainly a suggestion that the bargaining ability of the average woman is not equal to that of the average man would lack substance. The ability to make a fair bargain, as every one knows, does not depend upon sex.

If, in the light of the facts, the state legislation, without reason or for reasons of mere expediency, excluded men from the provisions of the legislation, the power was exercised arbitrarily. On the other hand, if such legislation in respect of men was properly omitted on the ground that it would be unconstitutional, the same conclusion of unconstitutionality is inescapable in respect of similar legislative restraint in the case of women.

* * *

Finally, it may be said that a statute absolutely fixing wages in the various industries at definite sums and forbidding employers and employees from contracting for any other than those designated would probably not be thought to be constitutional. It is hard to see why the power to fix minimum wages does not connote a like power in respect of maximum wages. And yet, if both powers be exercised in such a way that the minimum and the maximum so nearly approach each other as to become substantially the same, the right to make any contract in respect of wages will have been completely abrogated.

Questions

1. The *Adkins* Court concluded that the minimum-wage law was "simply and exclusively a price-fixing law." How did the law fix prices? Are minimum-wage laws a form of price regulation?

2. In *Adkins*, Justice Sutherland wrote for the Court that "[t]he feature of this statute, which * * * puts upon it the stamp of invalidity, is that it exacts from the employer an arbitrary payment for a purpose and upon a basis having no causal connection with his business, or the contract or the work the employee engages to do." Dissenting, Justice Holmes responded to this argument writing: "This statute does not compel anybody to pay anything. It simply forbids employment at rates below those fixed as the minimum requirement of health and right living." Considering both arguments together, do minimum-wage salaries raise concerns regarding unemployment?

3. *Adkins* and *West Coast Hotel* were written in two different economic eras. The Court handed down *Adkins* in 1923, a few years before the Great Depression, and *West Coast Hotel* was written in 1937 when the United States was still recovering from the recession. Both decisions tied the analysis of "necessities" to the relative power of employers and employees. How did they factor potential economic recessions? Should economic recessions be a relevant consideration for state interference with employment agreements?

4. *Adkins* and *West Coast Hotel* raised the potential symmetry between minimum-wage and maximum-wage laws. In the wake of the Great Recession, there were many proposals to impose restrictions on executive compensation in the United States. Specifically, under the regulations of the Troubled Asset Relief Program (TARP), which structured a bailout for the financial sector and the car industry,[39] limits were imposed on compensation for executive and highly compensated employees at companies receiving TARP funds.[40] What views were expressed in *Adkins* and *West Coast Hotel* regarding the potential constitutionality of maximum-wage laws? Do these views apply to regulation of executive compensation?

§ 6.4 NATURAL MONOPOLY

§ 6.4.1 Market Concentration and Competitiveness

Our discussion of "unfair prices" stressed that, under some conditions, market participants may have the power to influence prices and other

39. The Emergency Economic Stabilization Act of 2008, Pub. L. No. 110–343, 122 Stat. 3765 (2008).

40. TARP Standards for Compensation and Corporate Governance, 31 C.F.R. 30 (Oct. 20, 2008).

contractual terms. In the past, economists believed that concentrated market structures explained anticompetitive conduct and poor performance.[41] Specifically, the premise was that when the number of firms in the market declines they are less likely to compete aggressively and more likely to collude.[42] Put simply, market competition was believed to be related to the number of market participants. As we saw, the Hawaii Legislature endorsed a similar premise and "concluded that concentrated land ownership was responsible for skewing the State's residential fee simple market, inflating land prices, and injuring the public tranquility and welfare."[43] During the last three decades of the twentieth century, economists have gradually abandoned this premise but it appears to defy death. Textbooks and policymakers link the number of market participants and market competitiveness.

The number of competitors, as well as the nature of the competition among them, is an outcome of the general sources of market inefficiencies. In the early twentieth century, pioneering carmakers, such as Henry Ford, faced entry from new entrepreneurs, such as the Dodge brothers. The manufacturing and pricing strategies of the first carmakers were influenced by the threat of competition from potential entry. By contrast, in Hawaii, landowners faced no threat of entry. The quantity of land in the islands could not have been increased. The landowners, therefore, were not concerned that their practices would draw competition.

Thus, it is not the number of market participants that determines market competitiveness. Rather, it is the threat of competition and market discipline that force competitiveness.[44] The problem is that the sources of market inefficiencies weaken the power of these disciplinary tools. They create barriers to entry and misguide the participants who are needed for market discipline.

§ 6.4.2 The Monopolist

In certain markets, it is efficient to have one seller (or one buyer). In such situations that market participant is a *natural monopolist*.[45] This happens when one firm can satisfy the entire demand, and its costs are

---

41. This approach was known as the Structure–Conduct–Performance ("S–C–P") paradigm. *See generally* JOE S. BAIN, BARRIERS TO NEW COMPETITION (1956); EDWARD S. MASON, ECONOMIC CONCENTRATION AND THE MONOPOLY PROBLEM (1964); Barak Orbach & Grace Campbell, *The Antitrust Curse of Bigness*, 85 SOUTHERN CALIFORNIA LAW REVIEW 605 (2012).

42. For the theoretical origins of the premise *see* ANTOINE AUGUSTINE COURNOT, RECHERCHES SUR LES PRINCIPES MATHÉMATIQUES DE LA THÉORIE DE RICHESSES (1838); Irving Fisher, *Cournot and Mathematical Economics*, 12 QUARTERLY JOURNAL OF ECONOMICS 119 (1898). For a general discussion of the relationship between the number of firms in the market and competition *see* Carl Shapiro, *Theories of Oligopoly Behavior, in* 1 HANDBOOK OF INDUSTRIAL ORGANIZATION 329 (Richard Schmalensee & Robert D. Willig eds., 1989).

43. Hawaii Housing Authority v. Midkiff, 467 U.S. 229, 232 (1984).

44. *See generally* WILLIAM J. BAUMOL ET AL., CONTESTABLE MARKETS AND THE THEORY OF INDUSTRY STRUCTURE (1982); Harold Demsetz, *Barriers to Entry*, 72 AMERICAN ECONOMIC REVIEW 47 (1982).

45. *See generally* Ronald R. Braeutigam, *Optimal Policies for Natural Monopolies*, in 2 HANDBOOK OF INDUSTRIAL ORGANIZATION 1289 (1989); Richard A. Posner, *Natural Monopoly and its Regulation*, 21 STANFORD LAW REVIEW 548 (1969).

lower than the combined costs of two or more firms that do that could perform the same tasks. To illustrate, consider a ferry route between two towns separated by a lake. Once the ferry is in the water, the marginal cost of adding a passenger is close to zero, up to the point of full capacity. If two ferries operate on the route and operate at a capacity below that of one ferry, they double the operation costs. The same analysis applies to all utility companies that provide cable services, gas, electricity, water, and other services. The utilization of more than one network of services would increase the operation costs, and require additional investments. Thus public utilities are natural monopolists. They may operate without any competition.

A complex set of laws regulate public utilities. These include common law doctrines of "common carriers," specific statutes, and many administrative rules. Because public utilities face no competition their rates are regulated and they are subject to many other constraints.[46]

Laboratories of Ice

New State Ice Co. v. Liebmann

285 U.S. 262 (1932)

■ MR. JUSTICE SUTHERLAND delivered the opinion of the Court.

The New State Ice Company, engaged in the business of manufacturing, selling, and distributing ice under a license or permit duly issued by the Corporation Commission of Oklahoma, brought this suit against Liebmann * * * to enjoin him from manufacturing, selling, and distributing ice within Oklahoma City without first having obtained a like license or permit from the commission. The license or permit is required by [a 1925] act of the Oklahoma Legislature. * * * That act declares that the manufacture, sale, and distribution of ice is a public business; that no one shall be permitted to manufacture, sell, or distribute ice within the state without first having secured a license for that purpose from the commission; that whoever shall engage in such business without obtaining the license shall be guilty of a misdemeanor, punishable by fine not to exceed $25, each day's violation constituting a separate offense, and that by general order of the commission, a fine not to exceed $500 may be imposed for each violation.

Section 3 of the act provides:

> 'That the Corporation Commission shall not issue license to any persons, firm or corporation for the manufacture, sale and distribution of ice, or either of them, within this State, except upon a hearing had by said Commission at which said hearing, competent testimony and proof shall be presented showing the necessity for

---

46. *See* Harold Demsetz, *Why Regulate Utilities?*, 11 JOURNAL OF LAW & ECONOMICS 55 (1968); George Priest, *The Origins of Utility Regulation and the "Theories of Regulation" Debate*, 36 JOURNAL OF LAW & ECONOMICS 289 (1993).

the manufacture, sale or distribution of ice, or either of them, at the point, community or place desired. If the facts proved at said hearing disclose that the facilities for the manufacture, sale and distribution of ice by some person, firm or corporation already licensed by said Commission at said point, community or place, are sufficient to meet the public needs therein, the said Corporation Commission may refuse and deny the applicant (application) for said license. In addition to said authority, the said Commission shall have the right to take into consideration the responsibility, reliability, qualifications and capacity of the person, firm or corporation applying for said license and of the person, firm or corporation already licensed in said place or community, as to afford all reasonable facilities, conveniences and services to the public and shall have the power and authority to require such facilities and services to be afforded the public; provided, that nothing herein shall operate to prevent the licensing of any person, firm or corporation now engaged in the manufacture, sale and distribution of ice, or either of them, in any town, city or community of this State, whose license shall be granted and issued by said Commission upon application of such person, firm or corporation and payment of license fee.'

The portion of the section immediately in question here is that which forbids the commission to issue a license to any applicant except upon proof of the necessity for a supply of ice at the place where it is sought to establish the business, and which authorizes a denial of the application where the existing licensed facilities 'are sufficient to meet the public needs therein.' * * *

It must be conceded that all businesses are subject to some measure of public regulation. And that the business of manufacturing, selling, or distributing ice, like that of the grocer, the dairyman, the butcher, or the baker, may be subjected to appropriate regulations in the interest of the public health cannot be doubted; but the question here is whether the business is so charged with a public use as to justify the particular restriction above stated.

In *Frost v. Corporation Commission*, 278 U. S. 515, 519–521 (1929), [we held that] engagement in the business is a privilege to be exercised only in virtue of a public grant, and not a common right to be exercised independently by any competent person conformably to reasonable regulations equally applicable to all who choose to engage therein.

The *Frost* Case is relied on here. That case dealt with the business of operating a cotton gin. It was conceded that this was a business clothed with a public interest, and that the statute requiring a showing of public necessity as a condition precedent to the issue of a permit was valid. But the conditions which warranted the concession there are wholly wanting here. It long has been recognized that mills for the grinding of grain or performing similar services for all comers are devoted to a public use and subject to public control, whether they be operated by direct authority of the state or entirely upon individual initiative. * * *

[*Frost* and other] cases, though not strictly analogous, furnish persuasive ground for upholding the declaration of the Oklahoma Legislature in respect of the public nature of cotton gins in that state. The production of cotton is the chief industry of the state of Oklahoma, and is of such paramount importance as to justify the assertion that the general welfare and prosperity of the state in a very large and real sense depend upon its maintenance. Cotton ginning is a process which must take place before the cotton is in a condition for the market. The cotton gin bears the same relation to the cotton grower that the old grist mill did to the grower of wheat. The individual grower of the raw product is generally financially unable to set up a plant for himself; but the service is a necessary one with which, ordinarily, he cannot afford to dispense. He is compelled, therefore, to resort for such service to the establishment which operates in his locality. So dependent, generally, is he upon the neighborhood cotton gin that he faces the practical danger of being placed at the mercy of the operator in respect of exorbitant charges and arbitrary control. The relation between the growers of cotton, who constitute a very large proportion of the population, and those engaged in furnishing the service, is thus seen to be a peculiarly close one in respect of an industry of vital concern to the general public. These considerations render it not unreasonable to conclude that the business 'has been devoted to a public use and its use thereby in effect granted to the public. * * *

We have thus, with some particularity, discussed the circumstances which, so far as the state of Oklahoma is concerned, afford ground for sustaining the legislative pronouncement that the business of operating cotton gins is charged with a public use, in order to put them in contrast with the completely unlike circumstances which attend the business of manufacturing, selling, and distributing ice. Here we are dealing with an ordinary business, not with a paramount industry, upon which the prosperity of the entire state in large measure depends. It is a business as essentially private in its nature as the business of the grocer, the dairyman, the butcher, the baker, the shoemaker, or the tailor, each of whom performs a service which, to a greater or less extent, the community is dependent upon and is interested in having maintained; but which bears no such relation to the public as to warrant its inclusion in the category of businesses charged with a public use. It may be quite true that in Oklahoma ice is, not only an article of prime necessity, but indispensable; but certainly not more so than food or clothing or the shelter of a home. And this court has definitely said that the production or sale of food or clothing cannot be subjected to legislative regulation on the basis of a public use; and that the same is true in respect of the business of renting houses and apartments, except as to temporary measures to tide over grave emergencies. * * *

It has been said that the manufacture of ice requires an expensive plant beyond the means of the average citizen, and that, since the use of ice is indispensable, patronage of the producer by the consumer is unavoidable. The same might, however, be said in respect of other articles clearly beyond the reach of a restriction like that here under review. * * * We know, since it is common knowledge, that today * * * electricity or gas is available (and one or the other is available in practically every part of the country), any one for a comparatively moderate outlay may have set up in his kitchen an appliance by means of which he may manufacture ice for himself. Under such circumstances it hardly will do to say that people generally are at the mercy of the manufacturer, seller, and distributer of ice for ordinary needs. Moreover, the practical tendency of the restriction * * * is to shut out new enterprises, and thus create and foster monopoly in the hands of existing establishments, against, rather than in aid of, the interest of the consuming public.

* * *

Stated succinctly, a private corporation here seeks to prevent a competitor from entering the business of making and selling ice. It claims to be endowed with state authority to achieve this exclusion. There is no question now before us of any regulation by the state to protect the consuming public either with respect to conditions of manufacture and distribution or to insure purity of product or to prevent extortion. The control here asserted does not protect against monopoly, but tends to foster it. The aim is not to encourage competition, but to prevent it; not to regulate the business, but to preclude persons from engaging in it. There is no difference in principle between this case and the attempt of the dairyman under state authority to prevent another from keeping cows and selling milk on the ground that there are enough dairymen in the business; or to prevent a shoemaker from making or selling shoes because shoemakers already in that occupation can make and sell all the shoes that are needed. We are not able to see anything peculiar in the business here in question which distinguishes it from ordinary manufacture and production. It is said to be recent; but it is the character of the business and not the date when it began that is determinative. It is not the case of a natural monopoly, or of an enterprise in its nature dependent upon the grant of public privileges. The particular requirement before us was evidently not imposed to prevent a practical monopoly of the business, since its tendency is quite to the contrary. Nor is it a case of the protection of natural resources. There is nothing in the product that we can perceive on which rest a distinction, in respect of this attempted control, from other products in common use which enter into free competition, subject, of course, to reasonable regulations prescribed for the protection of the public and applied with appropriate impartiality.

And it is plain that unreasonable or arbitrary interference or restrictions cannot be saved from the condemnation of that amendment merely by calling them experimental. It is not necessary to challenge the authority of the states to indulge in experimental legislation; but it would be strange and unwarranted doctrine to hold that they may do so by enactments which transcend the limitations imposed upon them by the Federal Constitution. The principle is imbedded in our constitutional system that there are certain essentials of liberty with which the state is not entitled to dispense in the interest of experiments. * * *

Decree affirmed.

■ MR. JUSTICE CARDOZO took no part in the consideration or decision of this case.

■ MR. JUSTICE BRANDEIS (dissenting).

* * * Under a license, so granted, the New State Ice Company is, and for some years has been, engaged in the manufacture, sale, and distribution of ice at Oklahoma City, and has invested in that business $500,000. While it was so engaged, Liebmann, without having obtained or applied for a license, purchased a parcel of land in that city and commenced the construction thereon of an ice plant for the purpose of entering the business in competition with the plaintiff. To enjoin him from doing so this suit was brought by the ice company. * * * Liebmann contends that the manufacture of ice for sale and distribution is not a public business; that it is a private business and, indeed, a common calling; that the right to engage in a common calling is one of the fundamental liberties guaranteed by the due process clause; and that to make his right to engage in that calling dependent upon a finding of public necessity deprives him of liberty and property in violation of the Fourteenth Amendment. Upon full hearing the District Court sustained that contention and dismissed the bill. * * * Its decree was affirmed by the Circuit Court of Appeals. * * * The case is here on appeal. In my opinion, the judgment should be reversed.

First. The Oklahoma statute makes entry into the business of manufacturing ice for sale and distribution dependent, in effect, upon a certificate of public convenience and necessity. Such a certificate was unknown to the common law. It is a creature of the machine age, in which plants have displaced tools and businesses are substituted for trades. The purpose of requiring it is to promote the public interest by preventing waste. Particularly in those businesses in which interest and depreciation charges in plant constitute a large element in the cost of production, experience has taught that the financial burdens incident to unnecessary duplication of facilities are likely to bring high rates and poor service.[1] There, cost is usually dependent, among other things, upon volume; and division of possible patronage among competing concerns may so raise the unit cost of operation as to make it impossible to provide adequate service at reasonable rates. The introduction in the United States of the certificate of public convenience and necessity marked the growing conviction that under certain circumstances free competition might be harmful to the community, and that, when it was so, absolute freedom to enter the business of one's choice should be denied.

Long before the enactment of the Oklahoma statute here challenged, a like requirement had become common in the United States in some lines of business. The certificate was required first for railroads; then for street railways; then for other public utilities whose operation is dependent upon the grant of some special privilege.[2] Latterly, the requirement has been

---

1. Compare SUMNER H. SLICHTER, MODERN ECONOMIC SOCIETY 56, 326–328 (1932); ELIOT JONES AND T. C. BIGHAM, PRINCIPLES OF PUBLIC UTILITIES 70 (1931); Eliot Jones, '*Is Competition in Industry Ruinous*,' 34 QUARTERLY JOURNAL OF ECONOMICS, 473, 488 (1920).

2. *See* Ford P. Hall, *Certificates of Convenience and Necessity*, 28 MICH. L. REV. 107, 276 (1929). * * * Professor Hall lists statutes of forty-three states, most of them enacted within the last 20 years, requiring a certificate for the operation of various classes of public utilities. Before the advent of the certificate of public convenience and necessity, similar but less

widely extended to common carriers by motor vehicle which use the highways, but which, unlike street railways and electric light companies, are not dependent upon the grant of any special privilege. In Oklahoma the certificate was required, as early as 1915, for cotton gins—a business then declared a public one, and, like the business of manufacturing ice, conducted wholly upon private property. * * * See *Frost v. Corporation Commission*, 278 U. S. 515 (1929). As applied to public utilities, the [constitutionality] of the requirement of the certificate has never been successfully questioned.

Second. Oklahoma declared the business of manufacturing ice for sale and distribution a 'public business'; that is, a public utility. So far as appears, it was the first state to do so. Of course, a Legislature cannot by mere legislative fiat convert a business into a public utility. * * * But the conception of a public utility is not static.[5] The welfare of the community may require that the business of supplying ice be made a public utility, as well as the business of supplying water or any other necessary commodity or service. If the business is, or can be made, a public utility, it must be possible to make the issue of a certificate a prerequisite to engaging in it.

Whether the local conditions are such as to justify converting a private business into a public one is a matter primarily for the determination of the state Legislature. Its determination is subject to judicial review; but the usual presumption of validity attends the enactment. The action of the state must be held valid unless clearly arbitrary, capricious or unreasonable. * * * Whether the grievances are real of fancied, whether the remedies are wise or foolish, are not matters about which the Court may concern itself.[7] * * *

Third. Liebmann challenges the statute—not an order of the Corporation Commission. If he had applied for a license and been denied one, we should have been obliged to inquire whether the evidence introduced before the commission justified it in refusing permission to establish an additional ice plant in Oklahoma City. As he did not apply, but challenges the statute itself, out inquiry is of an entirely different nature. Liebmann rests his defense upon the broad claim that the Federal Constitution gives him the right to enter the business of manufacturing ice for sale even if his doing so be found by the properly constituted authority to be inconsistent with the public welfare. He claims that, whatever the local conditions may demand,

---

flexible control over the entry of many public utilities into business was exercised through the grant of franchises, municipal or state. * * *

5. 'Neither is it a matter of any moment that no precedent can be found for a statute precisely like this. It is conceded that the business is one of recent origin, that its growth has been rapid, and that it is already of great importance.... It presents, therefore, a case for the application of a long-known and well-established principle in social science, and this statute simply extends the law so as to meet his new development of commercial progress.' *Munn v. Illinois*, 94 U. S. 113, 133 (1876). * * *

7. 'Whether the enactment is wise or unwise, whether it is based on sound economic theory, whether it is the best means to achieve the desired result, whether, in short, the legislative discretion within its prescribed limits should be exercised in a particular manner, are matters for the judgment of the legislature, and the earnest conflict of serious opinion does not suffice to bring them within the range of judicial cognizance.' *Chicago, Burlington & Quincy R. Co. v. McGuire*, 219 U. S. 549, 569 (1910).

to confer upon the commission power to deny that right is an unreasonable, arbitrary, and capricious restraint upon his liberty.

The function of the court is primarily to determine whether the conditions in Oklahoma are such that the Legislature could not reasonably conclude (1) that the public welfare required treating the manufacture of ice for sale and distribution as a 'public business'; and (2) that, in order to insure to the inhabitants of some communities an adequate supply of ice at reasonable rates, it was necessary to give the commission power to exclude the establishment of an additional ice plant in places where the community was already well served. Unless the Court can say that the Federal Constitution confers an absolute right to engage anywhere in the business of manufacturing ice for sale, it cannot properly decide that the legislators acted unreasonably without first ascertaining what was the experience of Oklahoma in respect to the ice business. * * * Our function is only to determine the reasonableness of the Legislature's belief in the existence of evils and in the effectiveness of the remedy provided. In performing this function we have no occasion to consider whether all the statements of fact which may be the basis of the prevailing belief are well-founded; and we have, of course, no right to weigh conflicting evidence.

(A) In Oklahoma a regular supply of ice may reasonably be considered a necessary of life, comparable to that of water, gas, and electricity. The climate, which heightens the need of ice for comfortable and wholesome living, precludes resort to the natural product. There, as elsewhere, the development of the manufactured ice industry in recent years has been attended by deep-seated alterations in the economic structure and by radical changes in habits of popular thought and living. Ice has come to be regarded as a household necessity, indispensable to the preservation of food and so to economical household management and the maintenance of health. Its commercial uses are extensive. In urban communities, they absorb a large proportion of the total amount of ice manufactured for sale. The transportation, storage, and distribution of a great part of the nation's food supply is dependent upon a continuous, and dependable supply of ice. It appears from the record that in certain parts of Oklahoma a large trade in dairy and other products * * * would be destroyed if the supply of ice were withdrawn. We cannot say that the Legislature of Oklahoma acted arbitrarily in declaring that ice is an article of primary necessity, in industry and agriculture as well as in the household, partaking of the fundamental character of electricity, gas, water, transportation, and communication.

Nor can the Court properly take judicial notice that, in Oklahoma, the means of manufacturing ice for private use are within the reach of all persons who are dependent upon it. Certainly it has not been so. In 1925 domestic mechanical refrigeration had scarcely emerged from the experimental stage.[15] Since that time, the production and consumption of ice manufactured for sale, far from diminishing, has steadily increased.[16] In

15. The total number of household refrigerators in the entire country manufactured and sold before 1920 was approximately 10,000. In 1924, the annual production reached 30,000; in 1925, 75,000. Electrical Refrigerating News, February 17, 1932.

16. The Secretary of the National Association of Ice Industries testified that the ice business for the last 11 years had increased upon an average of 5.35 per cent. each year; that

Oklahoma the mechanical household refrigerator is still an article of relative luxury.[17] Legislation essential to the protection of individuals of limited or no means is not invalidated by the circumstance that other individuals are financially able to protect themselves. The businesses of power companies and of common carriers by street railway, steam railroad, or motor vehicle fall within the field of public control, although it is possible, for a relatively modest outlay, to install individual power plants, or to purchase motor vehicles for private carriage of passengers or goods. The question whether in Oklahoma the means of securing refrigeration otherwise than by ice manufactured for sale and distribution has become so general as to destroy popular dependence upon ice plants is one peculiarly appropriate for the determination of its Legislature and peculiarly inappropriate for determination by this Court, which cannot have knowledge of all the relevant facts.

The business of supplying ice is not only a necessity, like that of supplying food or clothing or shelter, but the Legislature could also consider that it is one which lends itself peculiarly to monopoly. Characteristically the business is conducted in local plants with a market narrowly limited in area, and this for the reason that ice manufactured at a distance cannot effectively compete with a plant on the ground. In small towns and rural communities the duplication of plants, and in larger communities the duplication of delivery service, is wasteful and ultimately burdensome to consumers. At the same time the relative ease and cheapness with which an ice plant may be constructed exposes the industry to destructive and frequently ruinous competition. Competition in the industry tends to be destructive because ice plants have a determinate capacity, and inflexible fixed charges and operating costs, and because in a market of limited area the volume of sales is not readily expanded. Thus, the erection of a new plant in a locality already adequately served often causes managers to go to extremes in cutting prices in order to secure business. Trade journals and reports of association meetings of ice manufacturers bear ample witness to the hostility of the industry to such competition, and to its unremitting efforts, through trade associations, informal agreements, combination of delivery systems, and in particular through the consolidation of plants, to protect markets and prices against competition of any character.

* * *

---

in 1919 the per capita consumption of ice was 712 pounds; in 1929, 1,157 pounds. A great deal of the increase in consumption of ice in Oklahoma, another witness testified, was in rural communities and among urban dwellers of the poorer classes.

17. The number of domestic electric meters installed in Oklahoma as of August 31, 1930, was only 222,237. * * * The population of the state in 1930 was 2,396,000. * * * It is estimated that 965,000 household refrigerators were sold in 1931, of which only 10,146 were sold in Oklahoma. * * * Approximately 3,578,000 such refrigerators are now in use throughout the country. * * * From these figures it may be calculated that the number of refrigerators in use in Oklahoma is between 35,000 and 40,000. The average cost of a household electric refrigerator in 1925 was $425; in 1931, $245. * * * The price of ice for domestic use in Oklahoma varies from 40 to 70 cents the hundredweight. Few families use as much as three or four tons of ice in a year. In view of these facts, this Court can scarcely have judicial knowledge that in Oklahoma all families or businesses which are able to purchase ice are able to purchase a mechanical refrigerator. * * *

(B) The statute under review rests, not only upon the facts just detailed, but upon a long period of experience in more limited regulation dating back to the first year of Oklahoma's statehood. For 17 years prior to the passage of the act of 1925, the Corporation Commission * * * had exercised jurisdiction over the rates, practices, and service of ice plants, its action in each case, however, being predicated upon a finding that the company complained of enjoyed a 'virtual monopoly' of the ice business in the community which it served. The jurisdiction thus exercised was upheld by the Supreme Court of the state in *Oklahoma Light & Power Co. v. Corporation Commission*, 96 Okl. 19 (1923). The court said: 'The manufacture, sale and distribution of ice in many respects closely resembles the sale and distribution of gas as fuel, or electric current, and in many communities the same company that manufactures, sells, and distributes electric current is the only concern that manufactures, sells and distributes ice, and by reason of the nature and extent of the ice business it is impracticable in that community to interest any other concern in such business. In this situation, the distributor of such a necessity as ice should not be permitted by reason of the impracticability of any one else engaging in the same business to charge unreasonable prices, and if such an abuse is persisted in the regulatory power of the state should be invoked to protect the public.' * * *

By formal orders, the commission repeatedly fixed or approved prices to be charged in particular communities; required ice to be sold without discrimination and to be distributed as equitably as possible to the extent of the capacity of the plant; forbade short weights and ordered scales to be carried on delivery wagons and ice to be weighed upon the customer's request; and undertook to compel sanitary practices in the manufacture of ice and courteous service of patrons. Many of these regulations * * * are still in effect. Informally, the Commission adjusted a much greater volume of complaints of a similar nature. It appears from the record that for some years prior to the act of 1925 one day of each week was reserved by the commission to hear complaints relative to the ice business.

* * *

The enactment of the so-called Ice Act in 1925 enlarged the existing jurisdiction of the Corporation Commission by removing the requirement of a finding of virtual monopoly in each particular case, compare * * *; by conferring the same authority to compel adequate service as in the case of other public utilities; and by committing to the commission the function of issuing licenses equivalent to a certificate of public convenience and necessity. * * *

Fourth. Can it be said in the light of these facts that it was not an appropriate exercise of legislative discretion to authorize the commission to deny a license to enter the business in localities where necessity for another plant did not exist? The need of some remedy for the evil of destructive competition, where competition existed, had been and was widely felt. Where competition did not exist, the propriety of public regulation had been proven. Many communities were not supplied with ice at all. The particular remedy adopted was not enacted hastily. The statute was based upon a long-established state policy recognizing the public importance of the ice business, and upon 17 years' legislative and administrative experience in the regulation of it. The advisability of treating the ice business as a public utility and of applying to it the certificate of convenience and necessity had been under consideration for many years. Similar legislation had been enacted in Oklahoma under similar circumstances with respect to other public services. The measure bore a substantial relation to the evils found to exist. * * *

Fifth. The claim is that manufacturing ice for sale and distribution is a business inherently private, and, in effect, that no state of facts can justify denial of the right to engage in it. To supply one's self with water, electricity, gas, ice, or any other article is inherently a matter of private concern. So also may be the business of supplying the same articles to others for compensation. But the business of supplying to others, for compensation, any article or service whatsoever may become a matter of public concern. Whether it is, or is not, depends upon the conditions existing in the community affected. If it is a matter of public concern, it may be regulated, whatever the business. The public's concern may be limited to a single feature of the business, so that the needed protection can be secured by a relatively slight degree of regulation. * * * A regulation valid for one kind of business may, of course, be invalid for another; since the reasonableness of every regulation is dependent upon the relevant facts. * * *

Sixth. It is urged specifically that manufacturing ice for sale and distribution is a common calling; and that the right to engage in a common calling is one of the fundamental liberties guaranteed by the due process clause. To think of the ice-manufacturing business as a common calling is difficult; so recent is it in origin and so peculiar in character. Moreover, the Constitution does not require that every calling which has been common shall ever remain so. The liberty to engage in a common calling, like other liberties, may be limited in the exercise of the police power. The slaughtering of cattle had been a common calling in New Orleans before the monopoly sustained in *Slaughter-House Cases*, 83 U.S. 36 (1872), was created by the Legislature. Prior to the Eighteenth Amendment selling liquor was a common calling, but this Court held it to be consistent with the due process clause for a state to abolish the calling, *Bartemeyer v. Iowa*, 85 U.S. 129 (1873); * * * or to establish a system limiting the number of licenses, *Crowley v. Christensen*, 137 U. S. 86 (1890). * * *

It is settled that the police power commonly invoked in aid of health, safety, and morals extends equally to the promotion of the public welfare. The cases just cited show that, while ordinarily free competition in the common callings has been encouraged, the public welfare may at other times demand that monopolies be created. Upon this principle is based our whole modern practice of public utility regulation. * * * The certificate of public convenience and invention is a device—a recent social-economic invention—through which the monopoly is kept under effective control by vesting in a commission the power to terminate it whenever that course is required in the public interest. To grant any monopoly to any person as a favor is forbidden, even if terminable. But where, as here, there is reasonable ground for the legislative conclusion that, in order to secure a necessary service at reasonable rates, it may be necessary to curtail the right to enter the calling, it is, in my opinion, consistent with the due process clause to do so, whatever the nature of the business. The existence of such power in the Legislature seems indispensable in our ever-changing society.

Seventh. The economic emergencies of the past were incidents of scarcity. In those days it was pre-eminently the common callings that were the subjects of regulation. The danger then threatening was excessive prices. To prevent what was deemed extortion, the English Parliament fixed the prices of commodities and of services from time to time during the four centuries preceding the Declaration of Independence. Like legislation was enacted in the Colonies; and in the States, after the Revolution. * * *

Eighth. The people of the United States are now confronted with an emergency more serious than war. Misery is widespread, in a time, not of scarcity, but of overabundance. The long-continued depression has brought unprecedented unemployment, a catastrophic fall in commodity prices, and a volume of economic losses which threatens our financial institutions. Some people believe that the existing conditions threaten even the stability of the capitalistic system. Economists are searching for the causes of this disorder and are re-examining the basis of our industrial structure. Business men are seeking possible remedies. Most of them realize that failure to distribute widely the profits of industry has been a prime cause of our present plight. But rightly or wrongly, many persons think that one of the major contributing causes has been unbridled competition. Increasingly, doubt is expressed whether it is economically wise, or morally right, that men should be permitted to add to the producing facilities of an industry which is already suffering from overcapacity. In justification of that doubt, men point to the excess capacity of our productive facilities resulting from their vast expansion without corresponding increase in the consumptive capacity of the people. * * * Many insist there must be some form of economic control. There are plans for proration. There are many proposals for stabilization. And some thoughtful men of wide business experience insist that all projects for stabilization and proration must prove futile unless, in some way, the equivalent of the certificate of public convenience and necessity is made a prerequisite to embarking new capital in an industry in which the capacity already exceeds the production schedules.

Whether that view is sound nobody knows. The objections to the proposal are obvious and grave. The remedy might bring evils worse than the present disease. The obstacles to success seem insuperable. The economic and social sciences are largely uncharted seas. We have been none too successful in the modest essays in economic control already entered upon. The new proposal involves a vast extension of the area of control. Merely to acquire the knowledge essential as a basis for the exercise of this multitude of judgments would be a formidable task; and each of the thousands of these judgments would call for some measure of prophecy. Even more serious are the obstacles to success inherent in the demands which execution of the project would make upon human intelligence and upon the character of men. Man is weak and his judgment is at best fallible.

Yet the advances in the exact sciences and the achievements in invention remind us that the seemingly impossible sometimes happens. There are many men now living who were in the habit of using the age-old expression: 'It is as impossible as flying.' The discoveries in physical science, the triumphs in invention, attest the value of the process of trial and error. In large measure, these advances have been due to experimentation. In those fields experimentation has, for two centuries, been not only free but encouraged. Some people assert that our present plight is due, in part, to the limitations set by courts upon experimentation in the fields of social and economic science; and to the discouragement to which proposals for betterment there have been subjected otherwise. There must be power in the states and the nation to remold, through experimentation, our economic practices and institutions to meet changing social and economic needs. I cannot believe that the framers of the Fourteenth Amendment, or the states which ratified it, intended to deprive us of the power to correct the evils of technological unemployment and excess productive capacity which have attended progress in the useful arts.

To stay experimentation in things social and economic is a grave responsibility. Denial of the right to experiment may be fraught with serious consequences to the nation. It is one of the happy incidents of the federal system that a single courageous state may, if its citizens choose, serve as a laboratory; and try novel social and economic experiments without risk to the rest of the country. This Court has the power to prevent an experiment. We may strike down the statute which embodies it on the ground that, in our opinion, the measure is arbitrary, capricious, or unreasonable. We have power to do this, because the due process clause has been held by the Court applicable to matters of substantive law as well as to matters of procedure. But, in the exercise of this high power, we must be ever on our guard, lest we erect our prejudices into legal principles. If we would guide by the light of reason, we must let our minds be bold.

■ MR. JUSTICE STONE joins in this opinion.

Questions[47]

1. Writing for the *New State Ice* Court, Justice Sutherland could not "see anything peculiar in the business" of ice production in Oklahoma. Was ice production a natural monopoly in Oklahoma during the early twentieth century?
2. What is destructive and ruinous competition?

The Evolution of Monopolists

During the eighteenth and nineteenth centuries St. Louis, Missouri, served as strategic port city on the Mississippi River. In the late nineteenth century, it was the fourth largest city in the United States. The transporta-

47. A copy of the Oklahoma Act and materials related to the ice industry at the turn of the nineteenth century are available at *regti.me/liebmann* (case sensitive).

tion of commodities across the river to Illinois and other states was costly until the twentieth century.

In 1819, Samuel Wiggins secured from the Illinois Legislature *An Act to Authorize Samuel Wiggins to Establish a Ferry Upon the Waters of the Mississippi*. The statute granted Wiggins an exclusive right to operate ferries across the Mississippi River between Illinois and St. Louis. In 1820, the City of East St. Louis was established in Illinois across the Mississippi River from St. Louis. Wiggins and his associates established and operated a ferry business across the Mississippi River between the St. Louis and East St. Louis. In 1853, they convinced the legislature to enact another statute, *An act to incorporate the Wiggins Ferry Company*.[48] This Act, coupled with the prior one, allowed the Wiggins Ferry Company to enjoy the benefits of a secured monopoly that controlled all the traffic between St. Louis and Illinois.

In July 1866, Congress passed a statute authorizing the construction of several bridges across the Mississippi.[49] Specifically, the Act authorized *the Saint Louis & Illinois Bridge Company*, "or any other bridge company," "to erect, maintain, and operate a bridge across the Mississippi River, between the city of' Saint Louis, in the State of Missouri, and the city of East Saint Louis, in the State of Illinois."[50] On July 4, 1874, the world's longest bridge opened to traffic. The bridge was named *Eads Bridge*, after its chief engineer, James Buchanan Eads.[51] Eads Bridge introduced great technological efficiencies, and created competition for the Wiggins Ferry Company. In 1889, Jay Gould, a railroad tycoon, organized the Terminal Railroad Association of St. Louis ("TRRA") to acquire the Eads Bridge and consolidate control over railway transportation entering and leaving St. Louis. But the Eads Bridge was soon to face additional competition. In 1887, Congress authorized *the St. Louis Merchants Exchange* to build another bridge between St. Louis and East St. Louis, two miles away or more from the Eads Bridge.[52] Two of the key provisions of the statute provided:

Saint Louis Merchants' Bridge Company Authorized to bridge the Mississippi River.

SECTION 1. That the consent of Congress hereby given to the Saint Louis Merchants' Bridge Company of Saint Louis, Missouri, * * * or its assigns or successors, or any legally incorporated railroad company or companies which may be associated with it therein, to build a bridge * * * and maintain the same, across the Mississippi River at some suitable point between * * * the Ends Bridge * * * and the mouth of the Missouri River: *Provided*, That no bridge shall be constructed across the

48. Wiggins Ferry Co. v. City of E. St. Louis, 107 U.S. 365, 365 (1883).

49. An Act to Authorize the Construction of Certain Bridges, and to Establish them as Post Roads, 14 Stat. 244 (1866).

50. *Id.* § 11.

51. *See* John A. Kouwenhoven, *The Designing of the Eads Bridge*, 23 TECHNOLOGY & CULTURE 535 (1982). A short biography of James Buchanan Eads is available at *regti.me/J-B-Eads* (case sensitive).

52. An Act Authorizing the Construction of a Bridge Over the Mississippi River at Saint Louis, Missouri, 24 Stat. 375 (1887).

Mississippi River within two miles above or two miles below the * * * Eads Bridge.

* * *

Right of way to railroads.

SEC. 8. That all railroad companies desiring the use of said bridge shall have and be entitled to equal rights and privileges relative to the passage of railway trains over the same, and over the approaches thereto, upon payment of a reasonable compensation for such use. * * *

* * *

Pooling of earnings forbidden.

SEC. 11. [W]hereas a principal reason for giving authority to build the bridge herein contemplated is to secure reasonable rates and tolls for corporations and individuals for passing over the same, the Saint Louis Merchants' Bridge Company, or its successors or assigns, shall not agree or consent to the consolidation of this bridge with any other bridge across the Mississippi River, or to the pooling of the earnings of this bridge company with the earnings of any other bridge company on said river, nor shall any person who is or may be a stockholder or director or manager of any other bridge over said river be a stockholder or director or manager of the bridge herein provided for: *Provided*, That if this provision of this act shall at any time be violated in such violation shall, without legal proceeding, at once forfeit the privilege hereby granted, and-said bridge shall become the property of the United States, and the Secretary of War shall take possession of the same in the name and for the use of the United States.

Proviso. Violation for forfeit franchise.

* * * *Proviso*

SEC. 12. * * * *And it is further provided* that no bridge shall be constructed across the Mississippi River within two miles above or two miles below the bridge herein authorized.

The Merchants' Bridge opened in June 1890. In 1893, the restrictions on joint ownership of bridges were repealed. In that year, TRRA acquired the Merchants' Bridge.[53]

53. *See generally* ROBERT W. JACKSON, RAILS ACROSS THE MISSISSIPPI: A HISTORY OF THE ST. LOUIS BRIDGE (2001).

Figure 6.1
The Eads Bridge

BIRD'S-EYE VIEW OF THE BRIDGE.

Source: The Industries of St. Louis (1887).[54]

United States v. Terminal Railroad Association of St. Louis

224 U.S. 383 (1912)

■ MR. JUSTICE LURTON delivered the opinion of the court:

The United States filed this bill to enforce the provisions of the Sherman act of July 2, 1890, * * * against thirty-eight corporate and individual defendants named in the margin,[†] as a combination in restraint of interstate commerce and as a monopoly forbidden by that law. The cause

54. More images of the Eads Bridge are available at *regti.me/Eads–Bridge* (case sensitive).

† The Terminal Railroad Association of St. Louis; the St. Louis Merchants' Bridge Terminal Railway Company; the Wiggins Ferry Company; the St. Louis Bridge Company; the St. Louis Merchants' Bridge Company; the Missouri, Kansas, & Texas Railway Company; the St. Louis & San Francisco Railway Company; the Chicago & Alton Railway Company; the Baltimore & Ohio Southwestern Railroad Company; the Illinois Central Railroad Company; the St. Louis, Iron Mountain, & Southern Railway Company; the Chicago, Burlington, & Quincy Railway Company; the St. Louis, Vandalia, & Terre Haute Railroad Company; the Wabash Railroad Company; the Cleveland Cincinnati, Chicago, & St. Louis Railway Company; the Louisville & Nashville Railroad Company; the Southern Railway Company; the Chicago, Rock Island, & Pacific Railway Company; the Missouri Pacific Railway Company; the Central Trust Company of New York; A. A. Allen, S. M. Felton, A. J. Davidson, W. M. Green, J. T. Harahan, C. S. Clarke, H. Miller, Benjamin McKean, Joseph Ramsey, George E. Evans, C. E. Schaff, T. C. Powell, J. F. Stevens, A. G. Cochran, W. S. McChesney, Julius Walsh, V. W. Fisher and S. D. Webster.

was heard by the four circuit judges, who, being equally divided in judgment, dismissed the bill, without filing an opinion. From this decree the United States has appealed.

The principal defendant is the Terminal Railroad Association of St. Louis, hereinafter designated as the terminal company. It is a corporation of the state of Missouri, and was organized under an agreement made in 1889 between Mr. Jay Gould and a number of the defendant railroad companies for the express purpose of acquiring the properties of several independent terminal companies at St. Louis, with a view to combining and operating them as a unitary system.

The terminal properties first acquired and combined into one system by the terminal company comprised the following: The Union Railway & Transit Company of St. Louis and East St. Louis; the Terminal Railroad of St. Louis and East St. Louis; the Union Depot Company of St. Louis; the St. Louis Bridge Company; and the Tunnel Railroad of St. Louis. These properties included the great union station, the only existing railroad bridge—the Eads or St. Louis bridge—and every connecting or terminal company by means of which that bridge could be used by railroads terminating on either side of the [Mississippi River]. For a time this combination was operated in competition with the terminal system of the Wiggins Ferry Company, and upon the completion of the Merchants' bridge, in competition with it, and a system of terminals which were organized in connection with it. The Wiggins Ferry Company had for many years operated car transfer boats by means of which cars were transferred between St. Louis and East St. Louis.

Upon each side of the river it owned extensive railway terminal facilities, with which connection was maintained with the many railroads terminating on the west and east sides of the rivers, which gave such roads connection with each other, as well as access to many of the industrial and business districts on each side. In 1890 a third terminal system was opened up by the completion of a second railroad bridge over the Mississippi river at St. Louis, known as the Merchants' bridge. This was a railroad toll bridge, open to every railroad upon equal terms. That it might forever maintain the potentiality of competition as a railroad bridge, the act of Congress authorizing its construction provided that no stockholders in any other railway bridge company should become a stockholder therein. But as this was a mere bridge company, it was essential that railroad companies desiring to use it should have railway connections with it on each side of the river. For this purpose two or more railway companies were organized and lines of railway were constructed connecting each end of the Merchants' bridge with various railroad systems terminating on either side of the river. The Merchants' bridge and its allied terminals were thereby able to afford many, if not all, of the railroads coming into St. Louis, access to the business districts on both sides of the river, and connection with each other.

Thus, for a time, there existed three independent methods by which connection was maintained between railroads terminating on either side of the river at St. Louis: First, the original Wiggins Ferry Company, and its railway terminal connections; second, the Eads Railroad bridge and the several terminal companies by means of which railroads terminating at St.

Louis were able to use that bridge and connect with one another, constituting the system controlled by the terminal company; and, third, the Merchants' bridge and terminal facilities owned and operated by companies in connection therewith.

This resulted in some cases in an unnecessary duplication of facilities, but it at least gave to carriers and shippers some choice, a condition which, if it does not lead to competition in charges, does insure competition in service. Important as were the considerations mentioned, their independence of one another served to keep open the means for the entrance of new lines to the city, and was an obstacle to united opposition from existing lines. The importance of this will be more clearly seen when we come to consider the topographical conditions of the situation.

That the promoters of the terminal company designed to obtain the control of every feasible means of railroad access to St. Louis, or means of connecting the lines of railway entering on opposite sides of the river, is manifested by the declarations of the original agreement, as well as by the successive steps which followed. Thus, the proviso in the act of Congress authorizing the construction of the Merchants' bridge, which forbade the ownership of its stock by any other bridge company or stockholder in any such company, was eliminated by an act of Congress, and shortly thereafter the terminal company obtained stock control of the Merchants' Bridge Company, and of its related terminal companies, and likewise a lease.

The Wiggins Ferry Company owned the river front on the Illinois shore opposite St. Louis for a distance of several miles. It had on that side and on its own property, switching yards and other terminal facilities. From these yards extended lines of rails which connected with its car transfer boats and with the termini of railroads on the Illinois side. On the St. Louis side of the river it had like facilities by which it was in connection with railway lines terminating on that side. That company was consequently able to interchange traffic between the systems on opposite sides of the river, and to serve many industries. In 1892 the Rock Island Railroad Company endeavored to obtain an independent entrance to the city. For this purpose it sought to acquire the facilities owned by the Wiggins Ferry Company by securing a control of its capital stock. This was not deemed desirable by the railroad companies which jointly owned the terminal company's facilities, and to prevent this acquisition effort was made to secure control of the stock. The competition was fierce and the market price of the shares pushed to an abnormal price. The final result being in debt, an agreement was reached by which the Rock Island Company was admitted to joint ownership with the other proprietary companies in all of the terminal properties which were operated by the terminal company, or which should be acquired by it. The shares in the ferry company bought by the Rock Island were transferred to the terminal company at cost, and were paid for by that company. These shares, united with those which had been acquired by the terminal company, enabled the latter to absorb the properties of the ferry company, and thus the three independent terminal systems were combined into a single system.

We come, then, to the question upon which the case must turn: Has the unification of substantially every terminal facility by which the traffic of St. Louis is served resulted in a combination which is in restraint of trade within the meaning and purpose of the anti-trust act?

It is not contended that the unification of the terminal facilities of a great city where many railroad systems center is, under all circumstances and conditions, a combination in restraint of trade or commerce. Whether it is a facility in aid of interstate commerce or an unreasonable restraint, forbidden by the act of Congress, * * * will depend upon the intent to be inferred from the extent of the control thereby secured over instrumentalities which such commerce is under compulsion to use, the method by which such control has been brought about, and the manner in which that control has been exerted.

The consequences to interstate commerce of this combination cannot be appreciated without a consideration of natural conditions greatly affecting the railroad situation at St. Louis. * * * To the river the city owes its origin, and for a century and more its river commerce was predominant. It is now the great obstacle to connection between the termini of lines on opposite sides of the river and any entry into the city by eastern lines. The cost of construction and maintenance of railroad bridges over so great a river makes it impracticable for every road desiring to enter or pass through the city to have its own bridge. The obvious solution is the maintenance of toll bridges open to the use of any and all lines, upon identical terms. And so the commercial interests of St. Louis sought to solve the question, the system of carferry transfer being inadequate to the growing demands of an ever-increasing population. The first bridge, called the Eads bridge, was, and is, a toll bridge. Any carrier may use it on equal terms. But to use it there must be access over rails connecting the bridge and the railway. On the St. Louis side the bridge terminates at the foot of the great hills upon which the city is built; on the Illinois side ends in the low and wide valley of the Mississippi. This condition resulted in the organization of independent companies which undertook to connect the bridge on each side with the various railroad termini. On the Missouri side it was necessary to tunnel the hills, that the valley of Mill creek might be reached, where the roads from the west had their termini. Thus, though the bridge might be used by all upon equal terms, it was accessible only by means of the several terminal companies operating lines connecting it with the railroad termini.

This brought about a condition which led to the construction of the second bridge, the Merchants' bridge. This, too, was, and is, a toll bridge, and may be used by all upon equal terms. To prevent its control by the Eads Bridge Company, it was carefully provided that no stockholder in any other bridge company should own its shares. But this Merchants' bridge, like the Eads bridge, had not rail connections with any of the existing railroad systems, and these facilities, as in the case of the Eads bridge, were supplied by a number of independent railway companies who undertook to fill in the gaps between the bridge ends and the termini of railroads on both sides of the river. It must be also observed that these terminal companies were in many instances so supplied with switch connections as not only to connect with the bridge, but also served to connect such roads with each other and with the industries along their lines. Now, it is evident that these lines connecting railroad termini with the railroad bridges dominated the situation. They stood, as it were, just outside the gateway, and none could enter, though the gate stood open, who did not comply with their terms. The topographical situation making access to the city difficult does not end with the river. The city lies upon a group of great hills which hug the river closely and rapidly recede to the west. These hills are penetrated on the west by the narrow valley of Mill creek, which crosses the city about its center. Railways coming from the west use this valley, but its facilities are very restricted and now quite occupied. * * * Railroads coming from the east, northeast, and southeast have their termini in that valley. As a consequence, there have grown up numerous cities and towns of some consequence as manufacturing places, the chief of which is East St. Louis.

The result of the geographical and topographical situation is that it is, as a practical matter, impossible for any railroad company to pass through, or even enter St. Louis, * * * without using the facilities entirely controlled by the terminal company. * * * Not is this effect denied; for the learned counsel representing the proprietary companies, as well as the terminal company, say in their filed brief: 'There indeed is compulsion, but it is inherent in the situation. The other companies use the terminal properties because it is not possible to acquire adequate facilities for themselves. The cost to any one company is prohibitive.' Obviously, this was not true before the consolidation of the systems of the Wiggins Ferry Company and the Merchants' Bridge Company with the system theretofore controlled by the terminal company. * * * [B]before the three terminal systems were combined a considerable measure of competition for the business of the other companies [existed], and a larger power of competition, is undeniable. That the fourteen proprietary companies did not then have the power they now have to exclude either existing roads not in the combination, or new companies, from acquiring an independent entrance into the city, is also indisputable. The independent existence of these three terminal systems was therefore a menace to complete domination, as keeping open the way for greater competition. * * * To close the door to competition, large sums were expended to acquire stock control. For this purpose the obligations of the absorbed companies were assumed and new funds obtained by mortgages upon the unified system.

The physical conditions which compel the use of the combined system by every road which desires to cross the river, either to server the commerce of the city or to connect with lines separated by the river, is the factor which gives greatest color to the unlawfulness of the combination as now controlled and operated. If the terminal company was in law and fact the agent of all, the mere unification which has occurred would take on quite a different aspect. It becomes, therefore, of the utmost importance to know the character and purpose of the corporation which has combined all of the terminal instrumentalities upon which the commerce of a great city and gateway between the East and West must depend. The fact that the terminal company is not an independent corporation at all is of the utmost significance. There are twenty-four railroads converging at St. Louis. The relation of the terminal company is not one of impartiality to each of them. It was organized in 1889, at the instance of six of these railroad companies, for the purpose of acquiring all existing terminal instrumentalities for the benefit of the combination. * * * From time to time other companies came to an agreement with the original proprietors until, at the time this bill was filed, the properties unified were held for the joint use of the fourteen companies made defendants. * * *

Inasmuch as the directors of the terminal company consisted of one representative of each of the proprietary companies, selected by itself, it is plain that each of said companies had and still has a veto upon any joint use or control of terminals by any nonproprietary company.

* * *

By still another clause in the agreement the proprietary companies obligate themselves to forever use the facilities of the terminal company for all business destined to cross the river. This would seem to guarantee against any competitive system, since the companies to the agreement now control about one third of the railroad mileage of the United States.

* * *

The witness upon whom the defendants chiefly rely to uphold the advantages of the unified system * * * is an experienced railroad engineer and manager and is the railway expert of the municipal bridge and terminal board, a commission appointed under a city ordinance, headed by the mayor, to study and report legislation needed to relieve the terminal conditions of St. Louis. [H]e expresses the opinion that the terminals of railway lines in any large city should be unified as far as possible, and that such unification may be of the greatest public utility. * * * The witness, however, points out that such a terminal company should be the agent of every company, and, furthermore, that its service should not be for profit or gain. * * * The terminal properties in question are not so controlled and managed. * * * They are not under a common control and ownership.

* * *

There are certain practices of this terminal company which operate to the disadvantage of the commerce which must cross the river at St. Louis, and of nonproprietary railroad lines compelled to use its facilities. One of them grows out of the fact that the terminal company is a terminal company and something more. It does not confine itself to supplying and operating mere facilities for the interchange of traffic between railroads.

* * *

We come now to the remedy. * * * The government has urged a dissolution of the combination between the terminal company, the Merchants' Bridge Terminal Company, and the Wiggins Ferry Company. That remedy may be necessary unless one equally adequate can be applied. * * *

Plainly the combination * * * would not be an illegal restraint * * * if * * * a proper terminal association acting as the impartial agent of every line which is under compulsion to use its instrumentalities. [T]he violation of the statute * * * may be eliminated and the obvious advantages of unification preserved [through] a modification of the agreement between the terminal company and the proprietary companies [so that] the former [will serve as a] bona fide agent and servant of every railroad line which [will be able to] use its facilities. * * *

[T]he case is remanded to the district court, * * * directing the parties to submit to the court, within ninety days * * * a plan for the reorganization of the contract between the fourteen defendant railroad companies and the terminal company. * * *

First. By providing for the admission of any existing or future railroad to joint ownership and control of the combined terminal properties, upon such just and reasonable terms as shall place such applying company upon a plane of equality in respect of benefits and burdens with the present proprietary companies.

Second. Such plan of reorganization must also provide definitely for the use of the terminal facilities by any other railroad not electing to become a joint owner, upon such just and reasonable terms and regulations as will, in respect of use, character, and cost of service, place every such company upon as nearly an equal plane as may be with respect to expenses and charges as that occupied by the proprietary companies.

Third. By eliminating from the present agreement between the terminal company and the proprietary companies any provision which restricts any such company to the use of the facilities of the terminal company. * * *

Upon failure of the parties to come to an agreement * * * in substantial accord with this opinion and decree, the court will * * * make * * * order and decree for the complete disjoinder of the three systems, and their future operation as independent systems, as may be necessary, enjoining the defendants, singly and collectively, from any exercise of control or dominion over either of the said terminal systems, or their related constituent companies, through lease, purchase, or stock control, and enjoining the defendants from voting any share in any of said companies or receiving dividends, directly or indirectly, or from any future combination of the said systems, in evasion of such decree or any part thereof.

Questions

1. How did TRRA become a monopoly? Was TRRA a natural monopoly?

2. The *TRRA* Court was willing to consider the idea that "the terminals of railway lines in any large city should be unified as far as possible, and that such unification may be of the greatest public utility." What does this idea mean? Does executing this idea necessarily mean that one company in St. Louis should have controlled the bridges over the Mississippi River and the Wiggins Ferry Company?

3. What were conditions of the remedy stipulated by the *TRRA* Court? Did the Court establish a form of price regulation? Did the Court's solution protect the interests of the public and nonproprietary companies?

4. In May 1998, the U.S. Justice Department and twenty states filed a highly publicized antitrust lawsuit against Microsoft Corporation. At the time, the overwhelming majority of computer users worldwide used Microsoft's operating system, Windows. Most of the hardware and software they owned were compatible only with Windows.[55] The Justice Department and

---

55. *See* United States v. Microsoft, 253 F.3d 34 (D.C. Cir. 2001).

the states argued that Microsoft used its power in the market for operating system to influence other markets, such as the market for internet browsers and other important programs. In June 1998, Bill Gates, Microsoft's CEO, published an op-ed in *The Economist* defending his company.[56] Among other things Gates wrote:

> It is often argued that Microsoft should be deemed a regulated "essential facility." This too is weak. Essential-facility law primarily applies to a physical asset or facility (such as a bridge) that a company (or companies) denies to competitors, and which cannot be duplicated by those rivals. By contrast, Windows is a piece of intellectual property whose "facilities" are totally open to partners and competitors alike. Windows' programming interfaces are published free of charge, so millions of independent software developers can make use of its built-in facilities (*e.g.*, the user interface) in the applications they design. Those same interfaces are also provided freely to manufacturers of computer peripherals, who take similar advantage of them. And we license Windows cheaply to any PC maker that wants to use it, a strategy which has allowed computer makers such as Compaq and Dell to focus on improving their products.

(a) Bill Gates drew a distinction between a physical facility, such as a bridge, and an intangible facility, such as an operating system. To construct and operate a bridge over the Mississippi River or to operate ferries across the Mississippi, a business was required to obtained government licenses. TRRA controlled all rights granted by Congress, Missouri, and Illinois to maintain such businesses. Gates pointed out that "Windows is a piece of intellectual property." What are the similarities and differences between intellectual property and a franchise to operate a physical asset?

(b) TRRA organized 14 out of the 24 railroads that operated in the St. Louis area. Microsoft was the single owner of Windows. Should the ownership structure have any significance in the analysis of the monopolist?

(c) The *TRRA* Court observed that "[t]here are certain practices of this terminal company which operate to the disadvantage of the commerce which must cross the river at St. Louis, and of nonproprietary railroad lines compelled to use its facilities." It concluded that this could happen because "the terminal company is a terminal company and something more." Microsoft was also more than the owner of intellectual property rights in an operating system. It also owned intellectual property rights in an internet browser (Internet Explorer), office software (Office), and other software. The argument against Microsoft was that the company used Windows to channel consumers to use its products rather than the products of its competitors. In practice, many monopolies integrate "something more." For example, power companies have local monopolies over distribution of electricity and often also integrate production. Should natural monopolies be prohibited from integrating "something else"?

---

56. Bill Gates, *Compete, Don't Delete*, ECONOMIST, June 13, 1998, at 19.

(d) Was Microsoft a natural monopoly? Should the state regulate innovative technology companies as natural monopolies?

News Networks

In *International News Service v. Associated Press*, the Supreme Court established the misappropriation doctrine in unfair competition law. During the World War I, readers were particularly interested in international news. Many international news agencies located their central offices in London, but the British authorities did not allow all agencies to telegraph war reports to the United States. The Associated Press (AP) operated under fewer restrictions than other agencies. To compensate for the shortage of war materials, one of the censored agencies, International News Services (INS), bought early east coast editions of newspapers published by AP members and used the AP's war reports to serve its subscribers. Writing for the Court, Justice Mahlon Pitney declared that AP had "quasi property" in the news it gathered, and thus was entitled to prevent its competitors from distributing and reproducing that news. The Court limited this right and stated the right was limited in time and intended "only to * * * to prevent * * * competitor[s] from reaping the fruits of [AP's] efforts and expenditure." In essence, Justice Pitney accepted AP's argument that a person has the right to reap what he has sown, and rejected INS' argument that no person can have rights in public information that is not protected by copyrights.[57] The opinion illustrated that although Justice Pitney rejected the idea of property rights in the news, perceptions of unfair competition led him to create a judicial rule that protect "news gatherers" from free riders who are direct competitors.

International News Service v. Associated Press

248 U.S. 215 (1918)

■ MR. JUSTICE PITNEY delivered the opinion of the Court.

The parties are competitors in the gathering and distribution of news and its publication for profit in newspapers throughout the United States. The Associated Press, which was complainant in the District Court, is a cooperative organization, * * * its members being individuals who are either proprietors or representatives of about 950 daily newspapers published in all parts of the United States. * * * Complainant gathers in all parts of the world, by means of various instrumentalities of its own, by exchange with its members, and by other appropriate means, news and intelligence of current and recent events of interest to newspaper readers and distributes it daily to its members for publication in their newspapers. The cost of the

57. *See generally* Douglas G. Baird, Common Law Intellectual Property and the Legacy of International News Service v. Associated Press, 50 UNIVERSITY OF CHICAGO LAW REVIEW 411 (1983); Shyamkrishna Balganesh, "Hot News": The Enduring Myth of Property in News, 111 COLUMBIA LAW REVIEW 419 (2011); Richard A. Epstein, *International News Service v. Associated Press: Custom and Law as Sources of Property Rights in News*, 78 VIRGINIA LAW REVIEW 85 (1992).

service, amounting approximately to $3,500,000 per annum, is assessed upon the members and becomes a part of their costs of operation, to be recouped, presumably with profit, through the publication of their several newspapers. Under complainant's by-laws each member agrees upon assuming membership that news received through complainant's service is received exclusively for publication in a particular newspaper, language, and place specified in the certificate of membership, that no other use of it shall be permitted, and that no member shall furnish or permit any one in his employ or connected with his newspaper to furnish any of complainant's news in advance of publication to any person not a member. And each member is required to gather the local news of his district and supply it to the Associated Press and to no one else.

Defendant [International News Service] * * * is the gathering and selling of news to its customers and clients, consisting of newspapers published throughout the United States, under contracts by which they pay certain amounts at stated times for defendant's service. It has widespread news-gathering agencies; the cost of its operations amounts, it is said, to more than $2,000,000 per annum; and it serves about 400 newspapers located in the various cities of the United States and abroad, a few of which are represented, also, in the membership of the Associated Press.

The parties are in the keenest competition between themselves in the distribution of news throughout the United States; and so, as a rule, are the newspapers that they serve, in their several districts.

Complainant in its bill, defendant in its answer, have set forth in almost identical terms the rather obvious circumstances and conditions under which their business is conducted. The value of the service, and of the news furnished, depends upon the promptness of transmission, as well as upon the accuracy and impartiality of the news; it being essential that the news be transmitted to members or subscribers as early or earlier than similar information can be furnished to competing newspapers by other news services, and that the news furnished by each agency shall not be furnished to newspapers which do not contribute to the expense of gathering it. And further, to quote from the answer:

> 'Prompt knowledge and publication of worldwide news is essential to the conduct of a modern newspaper, and by reason of the enormous expense incident to the gathering and distribution of such news, the only practical way in which a proprietor of a newspaper can obtain the same is, either through co-operation with a considerable number of other newspaper proprietors in the work of collecting and distributing such news, and the equitable division with them of the expenses thereof, or by the purchase of such news from some existing agency engaged in that business.'

The bill was filed to restrain the pirating of complainant's news by defendant in three ways: First, by bribing employees of newspapers published by complainant's members to furnish Associated Press news to defendant before publication * * *; second, by inducing Associated Press members to violate its by-laws and permit defendant to obtain news before publication; and, third, by copying news from bulletin boards and from early editions of complainant's newspapers. * * *

The District Court * * * granted a preliminary injunction under the first and second heads, but refused at that stage to restrain the systematic practice admittedly pursued by defendant, of taking news bodily from the bulletin boards and early editions of complainant's newspapers and selling it as its own. * * *

The only matter that has been argued before us is whether defendant may lawfully be restrained from appropriating news taken from bulletins issued by complainant or any of its members, or from newspapers published by them, for the purpose of selling it to defendant's clients. Complainant asserts that defendant's admitted course of conduct in this regard both violates complainant's property right in the news and constitutes unfair competition in business. * * * As presented in argument, these questions are: (1) Whether there is any property in news; (2) Whether, if there be property in news collected for the purpose of being published, it survives the instant of its publication in the first newspaper to which it is communicated by the news-gatherer; and (3) whether defendant's admitted course of conduct in appropriating for commercial use matter taken from bulletins or early editions of Associated Press publications constitutes unfair competition in trade.

* * * Complainant's news matter is not copyrighted. * * * [A]ccording to complainant's contention, news is not within the operation of the copyright act. Defendant [maintains] that, assuming complainant has a right of property in its news, it can be maintained * * * only by being kept secret and confidential, and that upon the publication with complainant's consent of uncopyrighted news of any of complainant's members in a newspaper or upon a bulletin board, the right of property is lost, and the subsequent use of the news by the public or by defendant for any purpose whatever becomes lawful.

* * *

In considering the general question of property in news matter, it is necessary to recognize its dual character, distinguishing between the substance of the information and the particular form or collocation of words in which the writer has communicated it.

No doubt news articles often possess a literary quality, and are the subject of literary property at the common law; nor do we question that such an article, as a literary production, is the subject of copyright by the terms of the act as it now stands. * * *

But the news element-the information respecting current events contained in the literary production—is not the creation of the writer, but is a report of matters that ordinarily are *publici juris*; it is the history of the day. It is not to be supposed that the framers of the Constitution, when they empowered Congress 'to promote the progress of science and useful arts, by securing for limited times to authors and inventors the exclusive right to their respective writings and discoveries' (Const. art. 1, § 8, par. 8), intended to confer upon one who might happen to be the first to report a historic event the exclusive right for any period to spread the knowledge of it.

We need spend no time, however, upon the general question of property in news matter at common law, or the application of the copyright act, since it seems to us the case must turn upon the question of unfair competition in business. * * * The peculiar value of news is in the spreading of it while it is fresh; and it is evident that a valuable property interest in the news, as news, cannot be maintained by keeping it secret. * * * What we are concerned with is the business of making it known to the world, in which both parties to the present suit are engaged. That business consists in maintaining a prompt, sure, steady, and reliable service designed to place the daily events of the world at the breakfast table of the millions at a price that, while of trifling moment to each reader, is sufficient in the aggregate to afford compensation for the cost of gathering and distributing it, with the added profit so necessary as an incentive to effective action in the commercial world. The service thus performed for newspaper readers is not only innocent but extremely useful in itself, and indubitably constitutes a legitimate business. The parties are competitors in this field; and, on fundamental principles, applicable here as elsewhere, when the rights or privileges of the one are liable to conflict with those of the other, each party is under a duty so to conduct its own business as not unnecessarily or unfairly to injure that of the other.

Obviously, the question of what is unfair competition in business must be determined with particular reference to the character and circumstances of the business. * * * Regarding the news, * * * as but the material out of which both parties are seeking to make profits at the same time and in the same field, we hardly can fail to recognize that for this purpose, and as between them, it must be regarded as quasi property, irrespective of the rights of either as against the public.

* * * The question, whether one who has gathered general information or news at pains and expense for the purpose of subsequent publication through the press has such an interest in its publication as may be protected from interference, has been raised many times, although never, perhaps, in the precise form in which it is now presented.

* * * Not only do the acquisition and transmission of news require elaborate organization and a large expenditure of money, skill, and effort; not only has it an exchange value to the gatherer, dependent chiefly upon its novelty and freshness, the regularity of the service, its reputed reliability and thoroughness, and its adaptability to the public needs; but also, as is evident, the news has an exchange value to one who can misappropriate it.

The peculiar features of the case arise from the fact that, while novelty and freshness form so important an element in the success of the business, the very processes of distribution and publication necessarily occupy a good deal of time. Complainant's service, as well as defendant's, is a daily service to daily newspapers; most of the foreign news reaches this country at the Atlantic seaboard, principally at the city of New York, and because of this, and of time differentials due to the earth's rotation, the distribution of news matter throughout the country is principally from east to west; and, since in speed the telegraph and telephone easily outstrip the rotation of the earth, it is a simple matter for defendant to take complainant's news from bulletins or early editions of complainant's members in the eastern cities and at the mere cost of telegraphic transmission cause it to be published in western papers issued at least as early as those served by complainant. Besides this, and irrespective of time differentials, irregularities in telegraphic transmission on different lines, and the normal consumption of time in printing and distributing the newspaper, result in permitting pirated news to be placed in the hands of defendant's readers sometimes simultaneously with the service of competing Associated Press papers, occasionally even earlier.

Defendant insists that [once news is published,] complainant no longer has the right to control the use to be made of it; that when it thus reaches the light of day it becomes the common possession of all to whom it is accessible; and that any purchaser of a newspaper has the right to communicate the intelligence which it contains to anybody and for any purpose, even for the purpose of selling it for profit to newspapers published for profit in competition with complainant's members.

The fault in the reasoning lies in applying as a test the right of the complainant as against the public, instead of considering the rights of complainant and defendant. * * * [The] defendant * * * is taking material that has been acquired by complainant as the result of organization and the expenditure of labor, skill, and money, and which is salable by complainant for money, and * * * appropriating it and selling it as its own is endeavoring to reap where it has not sown. * * * Stripped of all disguises, the process amounts to an unauthorized interference with the normal operation of complainant's legitimate business precisely at the point where the profit is to be reaped, in order to divert a material portion of the profit from those who have earned it to those who have not; with special advantage to defendant in the competition because of the fact that it is not burdened with any part of the expense of gathering the news. The transaction speaks for itself and a court of equity ought not to hesitate long in characterizing it as unfair competition in business.

* * * The contention that the news is abandoned to the public for all purposes when published in the first newspaper is untenable. Abandonment is a question of intent, and the entire organization of the Associated Press negatives such a purpose. The cost of the service would be prohibited if the reward were to be so limited. No single newspaper, no small group of newspapers, could sustain the expenditure. Indeed, it is one of the most obvious results of defendant's theory that, by permitting indiscriminate publication by anybody and everybody for purposes of profit in competition with the news-gatherer, it would render publication profitless, or so little profitable as in effect to cut off the service by rendering the cost prohibitive in comparison with the return. * * *

[T]he view we adopt does not result in giving to complainant the right to monopolize either the gathering or the distribution of the news, or, without complying with the copyright act, to prevent the reproduction of its news articles, but only postpones participation by complainant's competitor in the processes of distribution and reproduction of news that it has not gathered, and only to the extent necessary to prevent that competitor from reaping the fruits of complainant's efforts and expenditure. * * *

Besides the misappropriation, there are elements of imitation, of false pretense, in defendant's practices. The device of rewriting complainant's news articles, frequently resorted to, carries its own comment. The habitual failure to give credit to complainant for that which is taken is significant. Indeed, the entire system of appropriating complainant's news and transmitting it as a commercial product to defendant's clients and patrons amounts to a false representation to them and to their newspaper readers that the news transmitted is the result of defendant's own investigation in the field. But these elements, although accentuating the wrong, are not the essence of it. It is something more than the advantage of celebrity of which complainant is being deprived.

The decree of the Circuit court of Appeals will be *affirmed.*

■ MR. JUSTICE CLARKE took no part in the consideration or decision of this case.

■ MR. JUSTICE HOLMES, dissenting.

When an uncopyrighted combination of words is published there is no general right to forbid other people repeating them—in other words there is no property in the combination or in the thoughts or facts that the words express. Property, a creation of law, does not arise from value, although exchangeable—a matter of fact. Many exchangeable values may be destroyed intentionally without compensation. Property depends upon exclusion by law from interference, and a person is not excluded from using any combination of words merely because some one has used it before, even if it took labor and genius to make it. If a given person is to be prohibited from making the use of words that his neighbors are free to make some other ground must be found. One such ground is vaguely expressed in the phrase unfair trade. This means that the words are repeated by a competitor in business in such a way as to convey a misrepresentation that materially injures the person who first used them, by appropriating credit of some kind which the first user has earned. * * *

Fresh news is got only by enterprise and expense. To produce such news as it is produced by the defendant represents by implication that it has been acquired by the defendant's enterprise and at its expense. When it comes from one of the great news collecting agencies like the Associated Press, the source generally is indicated, plainly importing that credit; and that such a representation is implied may be inferred with some confidence from the unwillingness of the defendant to give the credit and tell the truth. If the plaintiff produces the news at the same time that the defendant does, the defendant's presentation impliedly denies to the plaintiff the credit of collecting the facts and assumes that credit to the defendant. If the plaintiff is later in Western cities it naturally will be supposed to have obtained its information from the defendant. The falsehood is a little more subtle, the injury, a little more indirect, than in ordinary cases of unfair trade, but I think that the principle that condemns the one condemns the other. It is a question of how strong an infusion of fraud is necessary to turn a flavor into a poison. The dose seems to me strong enough here to need a remedy from the law. But as, in my view, the only ground of complaint that can be recognized without legislation is the implied misstatement, it can be corrected by stating the truth; and a suitable acknowledgment of the source is all that the plaintiff can require. I think that within the limits recognized by the decision of the Court the defendant should be enjoined from publishing news obtained from the Associated Press for ______ hours after publication by the plaintiff unless it gives express credit to the Associated Press; the number of hours and the form of acknowledgment to be settled by the District Court.

■ MR. JUSTICE MCKENNA concurs in this opinion.

■ MR. JUSTICE BRANDEIS, dissenting.

There are published in the United States about 2,500 daily papers. More than 800 of them are supplied with domestic and foreign news of general interest by the Associated Press—a corporation without capital stock which does not sell news or earn or seek to earn profits, but serves merely as an instrumentality by means of which these papers supply themselves at joint expense with such news. Papers not members of the Associated Press depend for their news of general interest largely upon agencies organized for profit. Among these agencies is the International News Service which supplies news to about 400 subscribing papers. It has, like the Associated Press, bureaus and correspondents in this and foreign countries; and its annual expenditures in gathering and distributing news is about $2,000,000. Ever since its organization in 1909, it has included among the sources from which it gathers news, copies (purchased in the open market of early editions of some papers published by members of the Associated Press and the bulletins publicly posted by them. These items, which constitute but a small part of the news transmitted to its subscribers, are generally verified by the International News Service before transmission; but frequently items are transmitted without verification; and occasionally even without being re-written. In no case is the fact disclosed that such item was suggested by or taken from a paper or bulletin published by an Associated Press member.

No question of statutory copyright is involved. The sole question for our consideration is this: Was the International News Service properly enjoined from using, or causing to be used gainfully, news of which it acquired knowledge by lawful means (namely, by reading publicly posted bulletins or papers purchased by it in the open market) merely because the news had been originally gathered by the Associated Press and continued to be of value to some of its members, or because it did not reveal the source from which it was acquired?

* * * News is a report of recent occurrences. The business of the news agency is to gather systematically knowledge of such occurrences of interest and to distribute reports thereof. The Associated Press contended that knowledge so acquired is property, because it costs money and labor to produce and because it has value for which those who have it not are ready to pay; that it remains property and is entitled to protection as long as it has commercial value as news; and that to protect it effectively, the defendant must be enjoined from making, or causing to be made, any gainful use of it while it retains such value. An essential element of individual property is the legal right to exclude others from enjoying it. If the property is private, the right of exclusion may be absolute; if the property is affected with a public interest, the right of exclusion is quali-

fied. But the fact that a product of the mind has cost its producer money and labor, and has a value for which others are willing to pay, is not sufficient to ensure to it this legal attribute of property. * * * The creations which are recognized as property by the common law are literary, dramatic, musical, and other artistic creations; and these have also protection under the copyright statutes. The inventions and discoveries upon which this attribute of property is conferred only by statute, are the few comprised within the patent law. * * * Protection * * * is [also] afforded where the suit is based upon breach of contract or of trust or upon unfair competition.

The knowledge for which protection is sought in the case at bar is not of a kind upon which the law has * * * conferred the attributes of property. * * *

The great development of agencies now furnishing country-wide distribution of news, the vastness of our territory, and improvements in the means of transmitting intelligence, have made it possible for a news agency or newspapers to obtain, without paying compensation, the fruit of another's efforts and to use news so obtained gainfully in competition with the original collector. The injustice of such action is obvious. But to give relief against it would involve more than the application of existing rules of law to new facts. It would require the making of a new rule in analogy to existing ones. * * * The[] the creation or recognition by courts of a new private right may work serious injury to the general public, unless the boundaries of the right are definitely established and wisely guarded. In order to reconcile the new private right with the public interest, it may be necessary to prescribe limitations and rules for its enjoyment; and also to provide administrative machinery for enforcing the rules. It is largely for this reason that, in the effort to meet the many new demands for justice incident to a rapidly changing civilization, resort to legislation has latterly been had with increasing frequency.

The rule for which the plaintiff contends would effect an important extension of property rights and a corresponding curtailment of the free use of knowledge and of ideas; and the facts of this case admonish us of the danger involved in recognizing such a property right in news, without imposing upon news-gatherers corresponding obligations. A large majority of the newspapers and perhaps half the newspaper readers of the United States are dependent for their news of general interest upon agencies other than the Associated Press. * * * [The new property rights that allows exclusion would force] subscribers of the International News Service [to] become members of the Associated Press, [or to vanish from the marketplace.]

A Legislature, urged to enact a law by which one news agency or newspaper may prevent appropriation of the fruits of its labors by another, would consider such facts and possibilities and others which appropriate inquiry might disclose. Legislators might conclude that it was impossible to put an end to the obvious injustice involved in such appropriation of news, without opening the door to other evils, greater than that sought to be remedied. Such appears to have been the opinion of our Senate which reported unfavorably a bill to give news a few hours' protection.[16] * * *

Or legislators dealing with the subject might conclude, that the right to news values should be protected to the extent of permitting recovery of damages for any unauthorized use, but that protection by injunction should be denied, just as courts of equity ordinarily refuse (perhaps in the interest of free speech) to restrain actionable libels, and for other reasons decline to protect by injunction mere political rights; and as Congress has prohibited courts from enjoining the illegal assessment or collection of federal taxes. If a Legislature concluded to recognize property in published news to the extent of permitting recovery at law, it might, with a view to making the remedy more certain and adequate, provide a fixed measure of damages, as in the case of copyright infringement.[22]

Or again, a Legislature might conclude that it was unwise to recognize even so limited a property right in published news as that above indicated; but that a news agency should, on some conditions, be given full protection of its business; and to that end a remedy by injunction as well as one for damages should be granted, where news collected by it is gainfully used without permission. If a Legislature concluded * * * that under certain circumstances news-gathering is a business affected with a public interest; it might declare that, in such cases, news should be protected against appropriation, only if the gatherer assumed the obligation of supplying it at reasonable rates and without discrimination, to all papers which applied therefor. If legislators reached that conclusion, they would probably go further, and prescribe the conditions under which and the extent to which the protection should be afforded; and they might also provide the administrative machinery necessary for insuring to the public, the press, and the news agencies, full enjoyment of the rights so conferred.

Courts are ill-equipped to make the investigations which should precede a determination of the limitations which should be set upon any

---

16. Senate Bill No. 1728, 48th Congress, First Session. The bill provides:

> SECTION 1. That any daily or weekly newspaper, or any association of daily or weekly newspapers, published in the United States or any of the territories thereof, shall have the sole right to print, issue, and sell, for the term of eight hours, dating from the hour of going to press, the contents of said daily or weekly newspaper, or the collected news of said newspaper association, exceeding one hundred words.
>
> 'SEC. 2. That for any infringement of the copyright granted by the first section of this act the party injured may sue in any court of competent jurisdiction and recover in any proper action the damages sustained by him from the person making such infringement, together with the costs of suit.

It was reported on April 18, 1884, by the Committee on the Library without amendment, and that it ought not to pass, Journal of the Senate. 48th Congress, First Session, p. 548. No further action was apparently taken on the bill. When the [the Copyright Act of 1909] was under consideration, there was apparently no attempt to include news among the subjects of copyright. * * *

22. * * * § 25 [of the Copyright Act of 1909] provides, as to the liability for the infringement of a copyright, that 'in the case of a newspaper reproduction of a copyrighted photograph such damages shall not exceed the sum of two hundred dollars nor be less than the sum of fifty dollars,' and that in the case of infringement of a copyrighted newspaper the damages recoverable shall be one dollar for every infringing copy, but shall not be less than $250 nor more than $5,000.

property right in news or of the circumstances under which news gathered by a private agency should be deemed affected with a public interest. Courts would be powerless to prescribe the detailed regulations essential to full enjoyment of the rights conferred or to introduce the machinery required for enforcement of such regulations. Considerations such as these should lead us to decline to establish a new rule of law in the effort to redress a newly disclosed wrong, although the propriety of some remedy appears to be clear.

Questions

1. Did the Justices in *Associated Press* believe the state should regulate the market for news? If so, why and how?

2. Associated Press (AP) and International News Service (INS) utilized network externalities in their operations.[58] But when AP pressed charges against INS, the term "externality" was not yet in use. What was the role of network externalities in the dispute between AP and INS? How did the Court (implicitly) address network externalities?

3. How should network externalities influence the analysis of natural monopolies? Could a news agency be a natural monopoly?

4. In *National Basketball Association v. Motorola, Inc.*, 105 F.3d 841 (2d Cir. 1997), the Second Circuit formulated the "hot news" doctrine, which builds on the framework of *International News Service*. Under the hot news doctrine, a news gatherer must meet five conditions to prevail with an "INS claim": (1) generating or collecting news at some cost or expense; (2) the news is highly time-sensitive; (3) the defendant's use of the news constitutes free-riding on the news gatherer's costly efforts to generate or collect it; (4) the defendant's use of the news is in direct competition with a product or service offered by the news gatherer; and (5) the ability of other parties to free-ride on the efforts of the news gatherer would so reduce the incentive to produce the product or service that its existence or quality would be substantially threatened.

What does the hot news doctrine add to the misappropriation doctrine? Does it establish monopolies in the market for news?

Telephone Networks

National Rural Telecom Association v. Federal Communications Commission

988 F.2d 174 (D.C. Cir. 1993)

■ STEPHEN F. WILLIAMS, CIRCUIT JUDGE:

At issue in this appeal are two Federal Communications Commission orders implementing "price cap" rate regulation for the interstate services

58. *See* § 3.2.4.

of local telephone exchange companies ("LECs"). Policy and Rules Concerning Rates for Dominant Carriers, Second Report and Order, 5 FCC Rcd 6786 (1990) ("LEC Price Cap Order"), on reconsideration, 6 FCC Rcd 2637 (1991) ("LEC Reconsideration Order"). Under the orders, all the Bell and GTE companies must shift to price cap regulation; all other LECs may but need not make the change. Although no party challenges the Commission's basic decision to move to price caps, petitioners here attack special aspects of the plan.

* * * Finding the Commission orders neither arbitrary nor capricious, we affirm.

Background

Rate-of-return regulation is based directly on cost. Firms so regulated can charge rates no higher than necessary to obtain "sufficient revenue to cover their costs and achieve a fair return on equity." * * * As one virtue of perfect competition is that it drives prices down to cost, rate-of-return regulation seems on its face a promising way to regulate natural monopolies, in principle roughly duplicating the benefits of competition.

By the late 1980s, however, the FCC began to take serious note of some of the inefficiencies inherent in rate-of-return regulation. First, the resulting cost incentives are perverse. Because a firm can pass any cost along to ratepayers (unless it is identified as imprudent), its incentive to innovate is less sharp than if it were unregulated. There is even a temptation toward "gold-plat[ing]"—using equipment or services that are not justifiable in purely economic terms, especially when their use improves the lot of management (elegant offices, company jets, etc.).

Second, rate-of-return regulation creates incentives for cost shifting that may defeat the regulatory purpose and have other ill effects. Firms can gain by shifting costs away from unregulated activities (where consumers would react to higher prices by reducing their purchases) into the regulated ones (where the price increase will cause little or no drop in sales because under regulation the prices are in a range where demand is relatively unresponsive to price changes). * * * Third, rate-of-return regulation is costly to administer, as it requires the agency endlessly to calculate and allocate the firm's costs. * * *

In 1987, then, the FCC began proceedings to explore price cap regulation as an alternative. * * * Under a price cap scheme, the regulator sets a maximum price, and the firm selects rates at or below the cap. Because cost savings do not trigger reductions in the cap, the firm has a powerful profit incentive to reduce costs. Nor is there any reward for shifting costs from unregulated activities into regulated ones, for the higher costs will not produce higher legal ceiling prices. Finally, the regulator has less need to collect detailed cost data from the regulated firms or to devise formulae for allocating the costs among the firm's services.

The above somewhat overstates the differences. Under rate-of-return regulation, the regulator sets ceilings on the basis of cost estimates, in turn based in large part on past costs. To the extent that a firm in any single period (i.e., between rate filings) can beat the estimates, it can keep the savings. Thus "regulatory lag" creates some incentive to economize under a rate-of-return scheme. But the incentive is muted, as a saving in one period will cause lower ceilings thereafter. On the other side, price cap regulation cannot quite live up to its promise as stated above. The Commission must select a formula for the cap—here it chose existing rates, *plus* an escalator based on general price inflation, *minus* an annual percentage reduction for expected savings from innovation and other economies. * * * Obviously no such formula can be perfect, so ultimately the Commission must check to see whether the cap has gotten out of line with reality. The prospect of that next overview may dampen firms' cost-cutting zeal.

In any event, the FCC in 1989 concluded that price cap regulation would on balance be an improvement over rate-of-return in terms of meeting its statutory goals. * * * Although the initial order applied price cap regulation only to AT & T, it made clear that the Commission also had the LECs in mind for future application. Then, in 1990 and 1991, the Commission extended price cap regulation to the LECs, though with a "more cautious and careful approach" in light of the variety of companies and the differences between the markets affected. *LEC Price Cap Order*, 5 FCC Rcd at 6787. * * *

The small telephone companies' claims

The National Rural Telecom Association and two other associations of small telephone companies challenge rules the Commission developed to govern the relation between price cap regulation and companies' mergers and acquisitions. These merger rules arise from two other features of the Commission's price cap plan for LECs—the "all or nothing rule" and the "permanent choice rule". Under all-or-nothing, an LEC choosing price cap regulation is required to shift all of its affiliates to price caps as well. The FCC feared that without this requirement, an LEC with affiliates under both regimes might attempt to shift costs from the price cap affiliate to the rate-of-return affiliate. * * *

The permanent-choice rule requires an LEC choosing price caps to remain under that regime. Without a bar against reversion to rate-of-return, the Commission was concerned that a firm might "game the system": build up its plant through capital investment under rate-of-return, then convert to price caps for the period during which the plant improvements pay off. Such behavior, in which an LEC would alternately "fatten up" and "slim down" * * * is a sequential version of the cost shifting that is conventionally an object of concern. Like the all-or-nothing rule, then, permanent-choice aimed at preserving the cost incentives that are central to price cap regulation.

The Commission found that these rules implied a special rule on mergers and acquisitions—the "forced conversion rule", 47 CFR § 61.41(c). Under this rule, when rate-of-return companies and price cap companies merge or acquire one another, the rate-of-return company must convert to price cap regulation within one year. For the purposes of the rule, the acquisition of even a *part* of an LEC's service area is treated as the acquisition of an entire LEC. * * * Of course an implication of the rule is that no company under price cap regulation can ever revert to rate-of-return through the device of acquiring, or merging with, a rate-of-return company.

It seems clear that in the absence of the forced conversion rule there would be at least some risk of evasion of the all-or-nothing and permanent-choice rules. Acquisition or merger without forced conversion would immediately create a dual-status firm—with the cost-shifting risk that all-or-nothing is designed to cure. And if successive mergers or acquisitions enabled a firm to shift back and forth between rate-of-return and price cap (as would be true if hybrid firms could satisfy the all-or-nothing rule by shifting to rate-of-return), there would be a risk of the sequential cost shifting that the permanent-choice rule seeks to prevent. Of course to say that there is a risk is not to say that the risk is so severe as to justify restrictions that materially impede otherwise desirable mergers and acquisitions; trade-offs must be made. Accordingly, the Commission said that it might waive the rule where the efficiencies of a transaction appeared to outweigh the "gaming the system" risks. *LEC Reconsideration Order*, 6 FCC Rcd at 2706 n. 207.

* * *

The small telephone companies * * * argue that even if cost shifting is a legitimate concern, the Commission could and should have relied on less drastic solutions. * * * [The court found their claims "far-fetched" and declined them all].

MCI's claims

To understand MCI's claims we must first examine some of the mechanics of the price cap scheme and their relation to the Commission's concerns. A price cap enables a firm to raise the price of a product or service, so long as the firm offsets any increase for one service with decreases for others within the comparison group selected by the regulator. Thus, if the firm in the benchmark period[2] provided 100 units of service *A* for $1 each and 100 units of service *B* for $2 each, for a total of $300, it could thereafter choose any *A–B* price combination that, *at the benchmark volume of sales,* would yield no more than $300. (For example, it could sell the *A* services at $.75 each and the *B* services at $2.25 each. 100*$.75=$75; 100*$2.25=$225; $75+$225=$300.) All the LECs provide multiple services. The broader the comparison group within which an LEC may use offsets, the greater its price-changing flexibility. At one extreme, the Commission could have imposed a single price cap reflecting the prices for all of an LEC's services, weighted for the volume of sales of each service in the initial benchmark period. At the other extreme, the FCC could have imposed a price cap on each individual service that an LEC provides, giving the LEC no flexibility whatever. In fact the Commission chose a middle course, dividing LEC services into four product "baskets".[3] A basket is a broad grouping of LEC services subject to its own price cap. *LEC Price Cap Order*, 5 FCC Rcd at 6811. The Commission set separate price caps for each

---

2. *I.e.*, the period to which the regulator looks for the market prices and quantities used to set the initial price caps.

3. The baskets are (1) common line services, (2) traffic sensitive services, (3) special access services, and (4) interexchange services. * * *

basket in order to limit an LEC's ability to cross subsidize among groups of services.

We here use the term cross-subsidization simply but consistently to refer to prices that are not based on each specific service's average costs, or, in the jargon of the trade, "fully distributed costs" or "FDCs". In a company producing multiple services, FDCs are computed by allocating to each service any costs exclusive to it, plus a share of joint costs (e.g., operating overhead) deemed proportionate by the regulator. Whereas above we consistently used the term cost shifting in contexts where the conduct was likely to be harmful (e.g., between differently regulated affiliates), something that any regulator would properly seek to reduce, we here use "cross-subsidization" as an entirely neutral term describing any deviation from fully distributed cost pricing.

As the Commission plainly and explicitly recognized, deviations from fully distributed costs are in certain respects highly desirable and may tend to maximize the consumer welfare created by a regulated natural monopoly. While in a competitive market consumer welfare is maximized by marginal cost prices, that option is not realistically available for regulators of a natural monopoly. Because a natural monopolist is operating in a range where average costs are declining, and therefore where marginal costs are below average costs, marginal cost pricing would not permit the firm to recover its total costs. * * * Thus the so-called "first best" efficient outcome is impossible, as its implementation would put the regulated firm out of business. As the Commission recognized, however, a regulator can realistically seek to achieve "second best" efficiency: the set of prices that allows the firm to recover its total costs while minimizing adverse effects on consumer surplus—the difference between the price of a good and what consumers would be willing to pay for that good. * * *

The orthodox concept of second best pricing is the inverse elasticity principle, or Ramsey pricing. The price increments over marginal cost are allocated in inverse proportion to the price elasticity of demand for the good or service, with the increments relatively high for services for which demand is inelastic, low for those for which demand is elastic. The upshot is to minimize the aggregate impact of the price increments on consumer demand and thereby maximize consumer surplus. As the Commission noted, a price cap regime is likely to induce companies to set Ramsey prices. Within the comparison group for which the price cap is defined (in the Commission's terms, within a "basket"), a firm can enhance its profits by increasing * * * the proportion of shared costs borne by the inelastic services; the effect of the decrease in sales there will (up to a point) be more than offset by the effect of the increase in sales due to corresponding price decreases for the price-elastic service. * * * The same price changes increase consumer surplus as well.

The Commission clearly adopted this basic understanding. It said, for example, that "the goal is to determine the 'second best' pricing methodology, one that permits the recovery of total company costs while minimizing the adverse impact on consumers' surplus." * * * It observed that price cap regulation "encourages efficient pricing by providing regulated carriers a measure of flexibility to adjust their rates to conform with prevailing market demand." * * * It also noted that "a carrier's ability to adjust prices constitutes one of the major benefits of incentive regulation." * * *

[MCI's claims focused on the validity of the pricing cap mechanism that adopted Ramsey pricing and the court rejected those claims].

The petitions for review are *dismissed.*

Questions

1. Define the terms "cross-subsidization," "fully distributed costs" (FDCs), and "cost shifting." What is the significance of these terms for the regulation of natural monopolies?

2. The *Averch–Johnson effect* refers to inefficiencies created by rate-of-return regulation: incentives for the regulated firm to make excessive investment in capital to inflate costs, in order to be able to raise its regulated rates.[59] *National Rural Telecom Association* involved two FCC's orders that implemented price-cap regulation, rather than rate-of-return regulation. Did the Averch–Johnson effect play a role in the FCC decision to adopt the orders or in the opinion of the court?

3. The *National Rural Telecom Association* court noted that the theoretical distinction between rate-of-return regulation and price-cap regulation "somewhat overstates the differences" between the schemes. Are the schemes related to each other? Why did regulated firms challenge a transition from one scheme to another if the differences among the schemes are not substantial?

4. What is the realistic pricing formula for natural monopolies? What is the difference between "first-best" and "second-best" solutions?

5. What is Ramsey pricing? Can a price cap regime induce Ramsey pricing? Can regulators induce Ramsey pricing? Is Ramsey pricing fair?

---

59. *See* Harvey Averch & Leland L. Johnson, *Behavior of the Firm Under Regulatory Constraint*, 52 AMERICAN ECONOMIC REVIEW 1052 (1962).

CHAPTER 7

LEGAL PATERNALISM

> *"But neither one person, nor any number of persons, is warranted in saying to another human creature of ripe years, that he shall not do with his life for his own benefit what he chooses to do with it."*
>
> —John Stuart Mill (1859)[1]
>
> *"Man is weak and his judgment is at best fallible."*
>
> —Justice Louis Brandeis (1932)[2]
>
> *"People, for reasons of their own, often fail to do things that would be good for them or good for society. Those failures—joined with the similar failures of others—can readily have a substantial effect on interstate commerce. Under the Government's logic, that authorizes Congress to use its commerce power to compel citizens to act as the Government would have them act.*
>
> *That is not the country the Framers of our Constitution envisioned."*
>
> —Chief Justice John Roberts (2012)[3]

§ 7.1 WHAT IS PATERNALISM?

Legal paternalism (*"paternalism"*) is regulation intended to protect the individual from self-inflicted harm or to coerce norms of morality.[4] Like all other regulations, paternalistic regulations intend to shape conduct and,

1. JOHN STUART MILL, ON LIBERTY 150 (1859).

2. New State Ice Co. v. Liebmann, 285 U.S. 262, 310 (1932).

3. National Federation of Independent Business v. Sebelius, 132 S.Ct. 2566, 2589 (2012).

4. *See generally* Paul Burrows, *Analyzing Legal Paternalism*, 15 INTERNATIONAL REVIEW OF LAW & ECONOMICS 489 (1995) ("An intervention will be labeled paternalistic if its intention (or one of its intentions) is to persuade, induce, or compel any individual to do something he would not otherwise have chosen to do, in order to bring benefits to that individual."); Gerald Dworkin, *Paternalism*, 56 MONIST 64 (1972) (defining paternalism as "the interference with the person's liberty of action justified by reasons referring exclusively to the welfare, good, happiness, needs, interests, or values of the person being coerced."); Ronald Dworkin, *Liberal Community*, 77 CALIFORNIA LAW REVIEW 479, 485 (1989) (distinguishing between volitional and critical paternalism. Volitional paternalism "supposes that coercion can sometimes help people achieve what they already want to achieve." "Critical paternalism supposes that coercion can sometimes provide people with lives that are better than the lives they now think good and coercion is therefore sometimes in their critical interests."); JOEL FEINBERG, HARM TO SELF 3–8 (1986); Joel Feinberg, *Legal Paternalism* 1 CANADIAN JOURNAL OF PHILOSOPHY 105, 105 (1971) (defining legal paternalism as a "principle [that] justifies state coercion to protect individuals from self-inflicted harm, or in its extreme version, to guide them, whether they like it or not, toward their own good."); Bernard Gert & Charles M. Culver, *Paternalistic Behavior*, 6 PHILOSOPHY & PUBLIC AFFAIRS 45 (1976).

as such, attempt to direct choices. Interference with choices in the form of coercion or influence, therefore, is not unique to paternalism. However, paternalism differs from other types of regulation in that it seeks to protect individuals from the consequences of their own actions, or at least pretends to do so.

Much of the discussion of paternalism builds on John Stuart Mill's 1859 work, *On Liberty*.[5] Mill considered "harm to others" as the only legitimate justification for regulation:

> That the only purpose for which [government] power can be rightfully exercised over any member of a civilized community, against his will, is to prevent *harm to others*. *His own good*, either physical or moral, is not a sufficient warrant. He cannot rightfully be compelled to do or forbear because it will be better for him to do so, because it will make him happier, because, in the opinions of others, to do so would be wise, or even right. These are good reasons for remonstrating with him, or reasoning with him, or persuading him, or entreating him, but not for compelling him, or visiting him with any evil in case he do otherwise.[6]

Some forms of self-inflicted harm may affect the well-being others. Mill therefore examined the question of whether gambling, drunkenness, incontinence, idleness, and uncleanliness, which could be "injurious to happiness," may justify an exception to the general objection to paternalism. He observed that "the mischief which a person does to himself, may seriously affect, both through their sympathies and their interests, those nearly connected with him, and in a minor degree, society at large." Mill maintained, however, that such forms of conduct, including "addiction to bad habits," "violate a distinct and assignable obligation to any other person or persons" and thus are similar to ordinary breach of contract and financial default.[7] This analogy, he maintained, meant that prevention of self-inflected harm cannot be a legitimate justification for regulation.

Further, Mill argued that morality does not offer a valid justification for regulation because there is no universal agreement as to what constitutes moral behavior:

> There are many who consider as an injury to themselves any conduct which they have a distaste for, and resent it as an outrage to their feelings. * * * But there is no parity between the feeling of a person for his own opinion, and the feeling of another who is offended at his holding it; no more than between the desire of a thief to take a purse, and the desire of the right owner to keep it. And a person's taste is as much his own peculiar concern as his opinion or his purse. * * * These teach that things are right because they are right; because we feel them to be so.[8]

---

5. *See, e.g.*, Richard J. Arneson, *Mill versus Paternalism*, 90 ETHICS 470 (1980); Gerald Dworkin, *Paternalism*, *id.*

6. JOHN STUART MILL, ON LIBERTY 22 (1859) (emphasis added).

7. *Id.* at 144–146.

8. *Id.* at 150–151.

In sum, John Stuart Mill articulated the classic argument against paternalism and interference in the judgment, choices, and preferences of individuals. State interference with human judgment, he posited, can do no good:

> [W]ith respect to his own feelings and circumstances, the most ordinary man or woman has means of knowledge immeasurably surpassing those that can be possessed by anyone else. * * * In this department, therefore, of human affairs, Individuality has its proper field of action. * * * Considerations to aid [a person's] judgment, exhortations to strengthen his will, may be offered to him, even obtruded on him, by others; but he himself is the final judge. All errors which he is likely to commit against advice and warning, are far outweighed by the evil of allowing others to constrain him to what they deem his good.[9]

As a practical matter, paternalism has always existed and will always be around. The broad objections to paternalism have fed an abstract critique of regulation, although these objections do not undermine the regulation of "harm to others," namely, externalities. Some conflate the terms "regulation" and "paternalism." The term "paternalism" itself is an unfortunate one, because it refers to two distinctive sources of motivations for regulation—self-inflicted harm and morality. Legal philosopher Joel Feinberg pointed out that "paternalism is something we often *accuse* people of. [The word] sounds so outrageous that we would expect hardly anyone to confess to even paternalistic tendencies, much less boldly affirm the paternalistic principle and wave the paternalistic banner."[10] Similarly, economist Paul Burrows observed that "[to] many economists 'paternalism' is a term of abuse. Paternalism is seen as illiberal, coercive, arrogant, and patronizing; it is thought to destroy autonomy and freedom, to display lack of respect to people, and to violate sacred consumer sovereignty."[11] H.L.A. Hart distinguished between "legal paternalism" that intends to prevent self-inflicted harm and "legal moralism" that targets inherently immoral conduct. He argued that paternalistic laws can be justifiable, while legal moralism is always unacceptable.[12] Ronald Dworkin, however, posited that "[e]very community has an ethical environment, and that environment makes a difference to the lives its members can lead."[13] Many other intellectual giants have also contributed their views to the debate over legal paternalism. Our goal here is to examine some implications of state interference with choices and preferences to prevent self-inflicted harm *or* perceived immoral conduct.

Paternalism is one of the most peculiar concepts in regulation. In many ways approaches toward paternalism explain the general controversy over regulation. Many people, who tend to be critical of regulation, find ways to rationalize coercion of morality. That is, they are generally uncomfortable

---

9. *Id.* at 137–138.

10. FEINBERG, HARM TO SELF, *supra* note 4, at 4.

11. Paul Burrows, *Patronising Paternalism*, 45 OXFORD ECONOMIC PAPERS 542 (1993).

12. H.L.A. HART, LAW, LIBERTY, AND MORALITY 30–34, 38 (1963).

13. Dworkin, *Liberal Community*, *supra* note 4, at 480.

with state interference with the freedom of choice, but they may feel rather strongly about regulating the conduct of those who do not comply with their views of morality.[14] By contrast, people who are comfortable with regulation as a means to protect the individual are not always attuned to the cost-effectiveness of the regulatory means and often deny the potential harms of their proposals.[15]

John Stuart Mill was very critical of the tendency of people to impose their views on others and to be dismissive of the views of others,[16] yet his own views on human rationality and the capacity to analyze information were uncompromising. Contrary to Mill's premises, bounded rationality, transaction costs, and inadequate information impair the judgment of all individuals. The starting point of our discussion is, therefore, that humans are not consistently rational.

§ 7.2 MORALITY

"I never supposed that government was permitted to sit in judgment on one's tastes or beliefs."

—Justice William Douglas[17]

The state's police powers intend to protect the safety, health, *morals*, and general welfare of the public. It is therefore expected that the state will protect the public morals. Should the majority's sentiments about morality define society's ethical environment even at the expense of certain groups? Anti-miscegenation laws imposed restrictions on personal relationships and were enforced in many states until 1967.[18] By implementing particular moral views, these laws aimed to regulate the sentiments of individuals and their ability to fulfill themselves. Laws that restrict same-sex relationships also justify intervention in personal relationships on moral grounds.[19] Are the moral rules that impose restrictions on personal relationships based on race and gender of the parties involved comparable? The answer may depend on point of view.

On July 4, 1910, Jack Johnson, the first black heavyweight champion of the world knocked out the "great white hope," Jim Jeffries. Within a few days many states and localities adopted censorship laws to bar the exhibi-

---

14. For the enforcement of social codes *see* Lawrence Lessig, *The Regulation of Social Meaning*, 62 UNIVERSITY OF CHICAGO LAW REVIEW 943 (1995); Barak Orbach, *On Hubris, Civility, and Incivility*, 54 ARIZONA LAW REVIEW 443 (2012).

15. *See* §§ 1.4, 1.5.

16. *See* § 2.1.

17. Paris Adult Theatre I v. Slaton, 413 U.S. 49, 72 (1973) (Douglas, J., dissenting).

18. *See* Pace v. Alabama, 106 U.S. 583 (1883); McLaughlin v. Florida 379 U.S. 184 (1964); Loving v. Virginia, 388 U.S. 1 (1967). *See generally* PEGGY PASCOE, WHAT COMES NATURALLY: MISCEGENATION LAW AND THE MAKING OF RACE IN AMERICA (2010).

19. *See, e.g.*, Varnum v. Brien, 763 N.W.2d 862 (Iowa 2009) (holding that statutory language limiting civil marriage to a man and a woman was unconstitutional); A.G. Sulberger, *Ouster of Iowa Judges Sends Signal to Bench*, N.Y. TIMES, Nov. 4, 2010, at A1; Perry v. Brown, 671 F.3d 1052 (9th Cir. 2012).

tion of the fight film that presented Johnson's black supremacy.[20] A few months later, because his relationships with white women, Johnson was the first person to be prosecuted and convicted for violating the White Slave Traffic Act.[21] Jack Johnson coped with laws that applied the moral sentiments of the majority of U.S. citizens at the time. Seventy years later, in *Bowers v. Hardwick*, Justice White stated that "[t]he law * * * is constantly based on notions of morality, and if all laws representing essentially moral choices are to be invalidated * * *, the courts will be very busy indeed."[22] The majority's moral choices, Justice White argued, should be honored.

Bowers involved the constitutionality of sodomy laws. Writing for the Court, Justice White stated that "homosexuals [have no fundamental right] to engage in acts of consensual sodomy [because] [p]roscriptions against [such] conduct have ancient roots." Seventeen years later, in *Lawrence v. Texas*, writing for the Court, Justice Kennedy stated that the framing of *Bowers* "discloses the Court's own failure to appreciate the extent of the liberty at stake."[23] Sodomy laws, he argued, "are * * * statutes that purport to do no more than prohibit a particular sexual act. Their penalties and purposes, though, have more far-reaching consequences, touching upon the most private human conduct, sexual behavior, and in the most private of places, the home. The statutes do seek to control a personal relationship that, whether or not entitled to formal recognition in the law, is within the liberty of persons to choose without being punished as criminals."

Dissenting, Justice Scalia argued that "[s]tate laws against bigamy, same-sex marriage, adult incest, prostitution, masturbation, adultery, fornication, bestiality, and obscenity are likewise sustainable only in light of *Bowers*' validation of laws based on moral choices. Every single one of these laws is called into question by today's decision."

Morality is a fixture of the legal system. However, it creates conflicts among social preferences and choices. Because social preferences and choices change over time, regulations that once were acceptable ways to coerce morality in one group in society sometimes retire in the hall of shame. By the same token, the absence of regulations that coerce morality may be judged in the similar manner. Conduct that was acceptable in the past may be regulated today and regarded as offensive and unacceptable. Examples include child labor, discrimination, bullying, and animal cruelty. Keepers of our normative virtues do not always appreciate the possibility that the values they fight for are not as universal as they may think.

---

20. *See* Barak Orbach, *The Johnson–Jeffries Fight and Censorship of Black Supremacy*, 5 NYU JOURNAL OF LAW & LIBERTY 270 (2010).

21. 36 Stat. 825 (1910).

22. Bowers v. Hardwick, 478 U.S. 186, 197 (1986).

23. Lawrence v. Texas, 539 U.S. 558 (2003). *See generally* WILLIAM M. ESKRIDGE, JR., DISHONORABLE PASSIONS: SODOMY LAWS IN AMERICA, 1861–2003 (2008).

The Kentucky Model

What is the relationship between alcohol and sodomy? In a 1993 landmark decision of the Kentucky Supreme Court, decided by a vote of four to three, the majority opinion stated that at the beginning of the twentieth century, "the use of alcohol was as much an incendiary moral issue as deviate sexual behavior in private between consenting adults is today." *Commonwealth v. Campbell*, 133 Ky. 50 (1909), and *Commonwealth v. Wasson*, 842 S.W.2d 487 (Ky. 1992), have historical significance in the development of standards of review for moral laws.

Commonwealth v. Campbell

Court of Appeals of Kentucky
133 Ky. 50 (1909)

The appellee, Peter Campbell, was arraigned before the police court of Nicholasville * * * under the following warrant: "Nicholasville Police Court. The Commonwealth of Kentucky, to the Chief of Police of Nicholasville, or to Any Sheriff, Coroner, Jailer, Marshal or Policeman in This State: You are commanded to arrest Peter Campbell and bring him before the Nicholasville police court to answer to the charge of said commonwealth * * * of a breach of the ordinances of said city, to wit: Bringing into the town of Nicholasville spirituous, vinous or malt liquors upon his person or as his personal baggage exceeding a quart in quantity * * *." He was tried and found guilty in the police court, and a fine of $100 assessed against him. Upon appeal to the Jessamine circuit court, the judgment of the police court was reversed, and the warrant dismissed. From this judgment the commonwealth has appealed.

The ordinance, by virtue of which the warrant was issued, is as follows:

> *An ordinance to regulate the carrying, moving, delivering, transferring or distributing intoxicating liquors in the town of Nicholasville.*
>
> Be it ordained by the board of councilmen of the town of Nicholasville:
>
> (1) It shall be unlawful for any person or persons, individuals or corporations, public or private carrier to bring into, transfer to any other person or persons, corporations, carrier or agent, or servant, deliver or distribute in the town of Nicholasville, Kentucky, any spirituous, vinous, malt or other intoxicating liquor, regardless of the name by which it may be called; either in broken or unbroken packages, provided individuals may bring into said town, upon their person or as their personal baggage, and for their own private use, such liquors in quantity not exceeding one quart.
>
> (2) Each package of such spirituous, vinous, malt or other intoxicating liquor, regardless of the name by which it may be called, whether broken or unbroken packages, brought into and transferred to other person or persons, corporations,

> carrier or agents, or servants, delivered or distributed in said town shall constitute a separate offense.
>
> (3) Any person or persons, individual or corporation, public or private carrier violating the provisions of this ordinance shall be fined not less than $50 nor more than $100 for each offense.
>
> (4) Provided the provisions of this ordinance do not apply to interstate commerce carriers when engaged in interstate commerce transportation.
>
> (5) This ordinance shall take effect and be in force from and after its passage and publication.
>
> Approved this 7th day of February, 1908.
>
> W. L. Steele, Mayor.

The following subsections of section 3490 [of Kentucky Statutes] are referred to in the briefs of counsel as having a bearing upon the question in hand:

> The board of council shall have power * * * within the city—
>
> (1) To pass ordinances not in conflict with the Constitution or laws of this state or of the United States, and to impose and collect license fees and taxes on stock used for breeding purposes, and on all franchises, trades, occupations and professions.
>
> (7) To prevent and remove nuisances at the cost of the owners or occupants, or of the parties upon whose ground they exist, and define and declare by ordinance what shall be a nuisance within the limits of the city, and to punish by fine any person for causing or permitting a nuisance.
>
> (27) The council shall have power, by ordinance, to license, permit, regulate or restrain the sale of all kinds of vinous, spirituous or malt liquors within the limits of the city, or to restrain or prohibit the sale thereof within one mile of the limits thereof, *provided* nothing herein shall be construed as granting the power or right to one town or city to license, permit, regulate, restrain or prohibit the sale of vinous, spirituous or malt liquors in any other town or city, and may fix the penalty or fine for violation of an ordinance under this section at any sum not exceeding one hundred dollars; *provided*, that no license to sell such liquors, to be drunk on the premises where sold, granted under this section, shall be for a less amount than two hundred and fifty dollars nor for a greater amount than one thousand dollars. * * *

Broadly stated, the question before us is whether or not it is competent for the Legislature to prohibit a citizen from having in his own possession spirituous liquor for his own use. * * * [I]f the citizen may be prohibited from having liquor in his possession, he can be prohibited from drinking it, because, of necessity, no one can drink that which he has not in his possession. So that if it is competent for [any] legislative body * * * to prohibit the citizen from having liquor in his own possession, then a new and more complete way has been discovered for the establishment of total prohibition. * * *

Before the present [State] Constitution, it was competent for the Legislature to prohibit the sale of liquor by retail in any county, town, or district without any vote being taken by the citizens, or without giving them any voice in the matter; but no one doubts that, under the present [State] Constitution, it is not competent for the Legislature, without a vote of the citizens, to declare the retailing of liquor in any part of the state unlawful. * * * It is self-evident that, if the Legislature may pass a general law prohibiting any citizen from possessing or using liquor in any quantity, this would in itself be the most perfect prohibition law possible, because no man could retail liquor without first having possession of it. We cannot believe that the framers of the Constitution intended to thus carefully take from the Legislature the power to regulate the sale of liquor, and at the same time leave with that department of the state government the greater power of prohibiting the possession or ownership of liquor. * * * The history of our state from its beginning shows that there was never even the claim of a right on the part of the Legislature to interfere with the citizen using liquor for his own comfort, provided that in so doing he committed no offense against public decency by being intoxicated; and we are of opinion that it never has been within the competency of the Legislature to so restrict the liberty of the citizen * * *. The Bill of Rights, which declares that among the inalienable rights possessed by the citizens is that of seeking and pursuing their safety and happiness, and that the absolute and arbitrary power over the lives, liberty, and property of freeman exists nowhere in a republic, not even in the largest majority, would be but an empty sound if the Legislature could prohibit the citizen the right of owning or drinking liquor, when in so doing he did not offend the laws of decency by being intoxicated in public. Man in his natural state has a right to do whatever he chooses and has the power to do. When he becomes a member of organized society, under governmental regulation, he surrenders, of necessity, all of his natural right the exercise of which is, or may be, injurious to his fellow citizens. This is the price that he pays for governmental protection, but it is not within the competency of a free government to invade the sanctity of the absolute rights of the citizen any further than the direct protection of society requires. Therefore the question of what a man will drink, or eat, or own, provided the rights of others are not invaded, is one which addresses itself alone to the will of the citizen. It is not within the competency of government to invade the privacy of a citizen's life and to regulate his conduct in matters in which he alone is concerned, or to prohibit him any liberty the exercise of which will not directly injure society.

* * *

Nothing that we have said herein is in derogation of the power of the state under the Constitution to regulate the sale of liquor, or any other use of it which in itself is inimical to the public health, morals, or safety; but as spirituous liquor is a legitimate subject of property, its ownership and possession cannot be denied when that ownership and possession is not in itself injurious to the public. The right to use liquor for one's own comfort, if the use is without direct injury to the public, is one of the citizen's natural and inalienable rights, guaranteed to him by the Constitution, and cannot be abridged as long as the absolute power of a majority is limited by our present Constitution. * * * Under our institutions there is no room for that inquisitorial and protective spirit which seeks to regulate the conduct of men in matters in themselves indifferent, and to make them conform to a standard, not of their own choosing, but the choosing of the lawgiver; that inquisitorial and protective spirit which seeks to prescribe what a man shall eat and wear, or drink or think, thus crushing out individuality and insuring Chinese inertia by the enforcement of the use of the Chinese shoe in the matter of the private conduct of mankind. We hold that the police power-vague and wide and undefined as it is-has limits, and in matters such as that we have in hand its utmost frontier is marked by the maxim: "*Sic utere tuo ut alienum non lædas.*"

The judgment of the circuit court, quashing the warrant in this case, is affirmed.

Commonwealth v. Wasson

Supreme Court of Kentucky
842 S.W.2d 487 (1992)

■ LEIBSON, JUSTICE.

* * * Lexington police were conducting a downtown undercover operation. Their modus operandi was to drive to a certain parking area, in plain clothes with microphones on their persons, and try to engage in conversation with persons passing by to see whether they would be solicited for sexual contact. The taped conversation between the undercover officer and [Jeffrey] Wasson covered approximately 20–25 minutes, toward the end of which Wasson invited the officer to "come home" to his residence. The officer then prodded Wasson for details, and Wasson suggested sexual activities which violated KRS 510.100 [that punishes "deviate sexual intercourse with another person of the same sex" as a criminal offense, and specifies "consent of the other person shall not be a defense"]. * * * The sexual activity was intended to have been between consenting adults. No money was offered or solicited.

[Wasson was charged with having solicited an undercover Lexington policeman to engage in deviate sexual intercourse. Wasson moved to dismiss charges on grounds that a statute criminalizing deviate sexual intercourse between consenting adults of the same sex, even if the act is committed in the privacy of a home, violates the Kentucky Constitution as: (1) an invasion of a constitutionally protected right of privacy; and (2) invidious discrimination in violation of constitutionally protected rights to equal treatment. The District Judge held that the statute violated Wasson's right of privacy, and dismissed the charges. The Circuit Court affirmed.]

Seven expert witnesses testified in support of Wasson's case: (1) a cultural anthropologist testified about the presence of homosexuals in every recorded human culture, including societies where they were rejected and those where they have been tolerated or even welcomed; (2) a Presbyterian minister discussed Biblical references, providing a modern interpretation that these references were not an indictment of homosexuals as such, but rather statements against aggression, inhospitality and uncaring relationships; (3) a social historian testified about the presence of homosexuals throughout the history of the United States, despite what was at times exceptionally strict punishment for homosexual acts; (4) a sociologist and sex researcher (a co-author of the Kinsey Report on homosexual behavior) testified that studies indicated " 'homosexuality' is just as deep-rooted as 'heterosexuality'," that it is not a choice and there is no "cure" for it, and that sexual acts prohibited to homosexuals by KRS 510.100, oral and anal sex, are practiced widely by heterosexuals; (5) a psychologist testified that homosexuality is no longer classified as a personality disorder by either the American Psychological Association or the American Psychiatric Association, and further, rather than being in and of themselves either harmful or pathological, the sexual acts outlawed by KRS 510.100 are a necessary adjunct to their sex life; (6) a therapist from a comprehensive care treatment center in Lexington, with fourteen years' experience counseling homosexual clients, testified that the statute criminalizing their sexual activities has an adverse impact on homosexuals and interferes with efforts to provide therapy to those who may need it; and (7) the Professor of Medicine at the University of Louisville, Chief of the Infectious Diseases section, testified at length about the origins and spread of AIDS, expressing the opinion that the statute in question offers no benefit in preventing the spread of the disease and can be a barrier to getting accurate medical histories, thus having an adverse effect on public health efforts.

The testimony from Wasson's expert witnesses is further substantiated by extensive citations to medical and social science literature and treatises supplied in Amicus Curiae Briefs filed by national and state associations of psychologists and clinical social workers, various national and state public health associations, and organizations covering a broad spectrum of religious denominations.[1]

The Commonwealth, on the other hand, presented no witnesses and offers no scientific evidence or social science data. Succinctly stated, its position is that the majority, speaking through the General Assembly, has the right to criminalize sexual activity it deems immoral, without regard to whether the activity is conducted in private between consenting adults and is not, in and of itself, harmful to the participants or to others; that, if not

1. Specifically, the associations and organizations represented on these Amici Curiae Briefs are: American Psychological Association, Kentucky Psychological Association, Kentucky Psychiatric Association, Kentucky Chapter of the National Association of Social Workers, and Kentucky Society for Clinical Social Workers; American Public Health Association, Community Health Trust, Inc., Heart To Heart, Inc., St. Jude Guild, Inc., and AIDS Education Coalition, Inc.; American Friends Service Committee, American Jewish Committee, Central Presbyterian Church, Louisville, First Unitarian Church of Louisville, Honesty, Louisville, Lexington Friends Meeting, Religious Society of Friends (Quakers), The United Church of Christ, Telos, Louisville, The Temple, Union of American Hebrew Congregations, Unitarian Universalist Association and Universalist Church of Lexington, Central Kentucky Council for Peace and Justice, Fellowship of Reconciliation, Central Kentucky and Louisville Chapters, Presbyterian Church [U.S.A.] and the United Methodist Church.

in all instances, at least where there is a Biblical and historical tradition supporting it, there are no limitations in the Kentucky Constitution on the power of the General Assembly to criminalize sexual activity these elected representatives deem immoral.

* * * The thrust of the argument advanced by the Commonwealth as a rational basis for criminalizing consensual intercourse between persons of the same sex, when the same acts between persons of the opposite sex are not punished, is that the level of moral indignation felt by the majority of society against the sexual preference of homosexuals justifies having their legislative representatives criminalize these sexual activities. The Commonwealth believes that homosexual intercourse is immoral, and that what is beyond the pale of majoritarian morality is beyond the limits of constitutional protection.

At the outset the subject is made difficult by a confusion of terms. KRS 510.100 is styled a "sodomy" statute, but its reach is not limited to the Biblical or traditional common law definition of the term. It punishes "deviate sexual intercourse with another of the same sex." * * * A significant part of the Commonwealth's argument rests on the proposition that homosexual sodomy was punished as an offense at common law, that it has been punished by statute in Kentucky since 1860, predating our Kentucky Constitution. * * * This, of course, would lend credence to the historical and traditional basis for punishing acts of sodomy, but for the fact that "sodomy" as defined at common law and in this 1860 statute is an offense significantly different from KRS 510.100, limited to *anal* intercourse between *men.* Unlike the present statute our common law tradition punished *neither oral copulation nor any form of deviate sexual activity between women.* The definitive Kentucky case on the subject is *Commonwealth v. Poindexter*, 133 Ky. 720 (1909), summarizing the common law and statutory background, and holding:

> "A penetration of the mouth is not sodomy."

In *Poindexter* two men were charged with sodomy "committed by the insertion of the private part of the one into the mouth of the other." The trial court dismissed the indictment as failing to state an offense, and our Court affirmed. * * * The Commentary to the Penal Code enacted in 1974 points out:

> "Under former Kentucky law penetration of the mouth was not sufficient.... Sodomy in the fourth degree ... broadens former Kentucky law by including oral copulation." Commentary, KRS 510.100.

Thus the statute in question here punishes conduct which has been historically and traditionally viewed as immoral, but much of which has never been punished as criminal.

The grounds stated by the District Court for striking down the statute as unconstitutional are:

> "KRS 510.100 clearly seeks to regulate the most profoundly private conduct and in so doing impermissibly invades the privacy of the citizens of this state.

Having so found, the Court need not address the other issues raised by the parties."

The Order expressing the judgment of the Fayette Circuit Court "agree[d] with that conclusion," and further held the statute "unjustifiably discriminates, and thus is unconstitutional under Sections 2 and 3 of our Kentucky Constitution." These Sections are:

> "§ 2. Absolute and arbitrary power over the lives, liberty and property of freemen exists nowhere in a republic, not even in the largest majority.
>
> § 3. All men, when they form a social compact, are equal. . . ."

* * * For reasons that follow, * * * we hold that the statute in question violates rights of equal protection as guaranteed by our Kentucky Constitution.

I. RIGHTS OF PRIVACY

No language specifying "rights of privacy," *as such,* appears in either the Federal or State Constitution. The Commonwealth recognizes such rights exist, but takes the position that, since they are implicit rather than explicit, our Court should march in lock step with the United States Supreme Court in declaring when such rights exist. Such is not the formulation of federalism. On the contrary, under our system of dual sovereignty, it is our responsibility to interpret and apply our state constitution independently. * * *

Kentucky cases recognized a legally protected right of privacy based on our own constitution and common law tradition long before the United States Supreme Court first took notice of whether there were any rights of privacy inherent in the Federal Bill of Rights. The first mention of a federal guarantee of the right of privacy is in the Dissenting Opinion of Justice Louis Brandeis in *Olmstead v. United States*, 277 U.S. 438, 478 (1928), in which he defined it as "the right to be let alone—the most comprehensive of rights and the right most valued by civilized men." Actual recognition by the majority as a working premise came much later in *Griswold v. Connecticut*, 381 U.S. 479 (1965).

* * *

Deviate sexual intercourse conducted in private by consenting adults is not beyond the protections of the guarantees of individual liberty in our Kentucky Constitution simply because "proscriptions against that conduct have ancient roots." *Bowers v. Hardwick*, 478 U.S. 186, 192 (1986). Kentucky constitutional guarantees against government intrusion address substantive rights. * * * Similarly, the Kentucky Constitution has a Preamble:

> We, the people of the Commonwealth of Kentucky, grateful to Almighty God for the civil, political and religious liberties we enjoy, and invoking the continuance of these blessings, do ordain and establish this Constitution.

But the Kentucky Constitution of 1891 does not limit the broadly stated guarantee of individual liberty to a statement in the Preamble. It amplifies the meaning of this statement of gratitude and purpose with a Bill of Rights in 26 sections, the first of which states:

> "§ 1. All men are, by nature, free and equal, and have certain inherent and inalienable rights, among which may be reckoned:
>
> First: The right of enjoying and defending their lives and liberties.
>
> . . .
>
> Third: The right of seeking and pursuing their safety and happiness.
>
> . . .
>
> § 2. Absolute and arbitrary power over the lives, liberty and property of freemen exists nowhere in a republic, not even in the largest majority."

* * *

The leading case on this subject is *Commonwealth v. Campbell*, 133 Ky. 50 (1909). At issue was an ordinance that criminalized possession of intoxicating liquor, even for "private use." Our Court held that the Bill of Rights in the 1891 Constitution prohibited state action thus intruding upon the "inalienable rights possessed by the citizens" of Kentucky. * * *

At the time *Campbell* was decided, the use of alcohol was as much an incendiary moral issue as deviate sexual behavior in private between consenting adults is today. Prohibition was the great moral issue of its time. It was addressed both in the 1891 Constitution and in the Nineteenth Amendment of the United States Constitution. In 1907, in *Board of Trustees of Town of New Castle v. Scott*, 125 Ky. 545 (1907), Chief Justice O'Rear passionately attacked the evil of alcohol in a pro-prohibition ruling interpreting Section 61 of the Kentucky Constitution, which provides for local option elections. He stated:

> "There is yet another view of the subject which we must assume was in the mind of the Convention. The liquor traffic had then [in 1891] come to be regarded as one of the most serious evils of the age, if not the most sinister menace to society that was known.
>
> . . .
>
> No other subject had been more clearly settled upon as being within the legitimate exercise of the police power of the state than the regulation of the sale and use of intoxicating liquors."

Notwithstanding their strong views that drinking was immoral, this same Court with these same judges, including Judge O'Rear, in the *Campbell* case recognized that private possession and consumption of intoxicating liquor was a liberty interest beyond the reach of the state.

Nor is the *Campbell* case an aberration. Subsequent cases cited and followed *Campbell*. In *Commonwealth v. Smith*, 163 Ky. 227 (1915), citing

Campbell, the Court declared a statute unconstitutional that had led to Smith being arrested for drinking beer in the backroom of an office:

> "The power of the state to regulate and control the conduct of a private individual is confined to those cases where his conduct injuriously affects others. With his faults or weaknesses, which he keeps to himself, and which do not operate to the detriment of others, the state as such has no concern."

The holding in *Smith* is that "the police power may be called into play [only] when it is reasonably necessary to protect the *public* health, or *public* morals, or *public* safety." [Emphasis added.]

The clear implication is that immorality in private which does "not operate to the detriment of others," is placed beyond the reach of state action by the guarantees of liberty in the Kentucky Constitution.

In *Hershberg v. City of Barbourville*, 142 Ky. 60 (1911), also citing *Campbell*, the Court declared an ordinance which purported to regulate cigarette smoking in such broad terms that it could be applied to persons who smoked in the privacy of their own home "unreasonably interfere[ed] with the right of the citizen to determine for himself such personal matters."

* * *

Modern legal philosophers [adopted] an enlightened paternalism, permitting the law to intervene to stop self-inflicted harm such as the result of drug taking, or failure to use seat belts or crash helmets, not to enforce majoritarian or conventional morality, but because the victim of such self-inflicted harm becomes a burden on society. * * *

We view the United States Supreme Court decision in *Bowers v. Hardwick*, 478 U.S. 186 (1986), [on which the Commonwealth is relying,] as a misdirected application of the theory of original intent. To illustrate: as a theory of majoritarian morality, miscegenation was an offense with ancient roots. It is highly unlikely that protecting the rights of persons of different races to copulate was one of the considerations behind the Fourteenth Amendment. Nevertheless, in *Loving v. Virginia*, 388 U.S. 1 (1967), the United States Supreme Court recognized that a contemporary, enlightened interpretation of the liberty interest involved in the sexual act made its punishment constitutionally impermissible.

According to *Bowers v. Hardwick*, "until 1961, all 50 States outlawed sodomy, and today, 25 States and District of Colombia continue to provide criminal penalties for sodomy performed in private and between consenting adults." 478 U.S. at 193–94. In the space of three decades half the states decriminalized this conduct, some no doubt in deference to the position taken by the American Law Institute in the Model Penal Code, Sec. 213.2:

> "Section 213.2 of the Model Code makes a fundamental departure from prior law in excepting from criminal sanctions deviate sexual intercourse between consenting adults." *American Law Institute, Model Penal Code and Commentaries*, Part II, 1980 Ed., pp. 362–63.

> "The usual justification for laws against such conduct is that, even though it does not injure any identifiable victim, it contributes to moral deterioration of society. One need not endorse wholesale repeal of all 'victimless' crimes in order to recognize that legislating penal sanctions solely to maintain widely held concepts of morality and aesthetics is a costly enterprise. It sacrifices personal liberty, not because the actor's conduct results in harm to another citizen but only because it is inconsistent with the majoritarian notion of acceptable behavior. * * * " *Id.* at 371–72.

* * *

II. EQUAL PROTECTION

[I]n *Bowers v. Hardwick*, the Equal Protection Clause was not implicated because the Georgia statute criminalized both heterosexual and homosexual sodomy. Unlike the Due Process Clause analysis provided in *Bowers v. Hardwick*, equal protection analysis does *not* turn on whether the law (KRS 510.100), transgresses "liberties that are 'deeply rooted in this Nation's history and tradition."

* * *

Certainly, the practice of deviate sexual intercourse violates traditional morality. But so does the same act between heterosexuals, which activity is decriminalized. Going one step further, *all* sexual activity between consenting adults outside of marriage violates our traditional morality. The issue here is not whether sexual activity traditionally viewed as immoral can be punished by society, but whether it can be punished solely on the basis of sexual preference.

The Commonwealth's argument against permitting sexual behavior preferred by homosexuals the protection of the Equal Protection Clause has centered solely on denying homosexuals status as a protected class, claiming society has a right to discriminate so long as such discrimination is not race related or gender related and this law punishes the act and not the preference of the actor. In *American Constitutional Law,* 2d ed. 1988, Laurence H. Tribe, p. 1616, the author answers the Commonwealth's claims:

> Not only is the characteristic of homosexuality or heterosexuality central to the personal identities of those singled out by laws based on sexual orientation, but homosexuals in particular seem to satisfy all of the Court's implicit criteria of suspectness. As subjects of age-old discrimination and disapproval, homosexuals form virtually a discrete and insular minority. Their sexual orientation is in all likelihood 'a characteristic determined by causes not within [their] control * * *,' and is, if not immutable, at least 'extremely difficult to alter * * *.' "

Professor Tribe's view is fully supported, not only by his own documentation, but by the testimony of record in this case and by the medical, scientific and social science data provided in the briefs filed herein by Amici

Curiae. The truth is, one's sexual partner is chosen usually, if not exclusively, based on sexual orientation. We cannot deny the evidence before us in analyzing how our state constitution should apply.

We do not speculate on how the United States Supreme Court as presently constituted will decide whether the sexual preference of homosexuals is entitled to protection under the Equal Protection Clause of the Federal constitution. We need not speculate as to whether male and/or female homosexuals will be allowed status as a protected class if and when the United States Supreme Court confronts this issue. They are a separate and identifiable class for Kentucky constitutional law analysis because no class of persons can be discriminated against under the Kentucky Constitution. * * *

The Commonwealth has tried hard to demonstrate a legitimate governmental interest justifying a distinction, but has failed. Many of the claimed justifications are simply outrageous: that "homosexuals are more promiscuous than heterosexuals, . . . that homosexuals enjoy the company of children, and that homosexuals are more prone to engage in sex acts in public." The only proffered justification with superficial validity is that "infectious diseases are more readily transmitted by anal sodomy than by other forms of sexual copulation." But this statute is not limited to anal copulation, and this reasoning would apply to male-female anal intercourse the same as it applies to male-male intercourse. The growing number of females to whom AIDS (Acquired Immune Deficiency Syndrome) has been transmitted is stark evidence that AIDS is not only a male homosexual disease. The only medical evidence in the record before us rules out any distinction between male-male and male-female anal intercourse as a method of preventing AIDS. The act of sexual contact is not implicated, per se, whether the contact is homosexual or heterosexual. In any event, this statute was enacted in 1974 before the AIDS nightmare was upon us. It was 1982 or 1983 before AIDS was a recognized diagnostic entity.

In the final analysis we can attribute no legislative purpose to this statute except to single out homosexuals for different treatment for indulging their sexual preference by engaging in the same activity heterosexuals are now at liberty to perform. By 1974 there had already been a sea change in societal values insofar as attaching criminal penalties to extramarital sex. The question is whether a society that no longer criminalizes adultery, fornication, or deviate sexual intercourse between heterosexuals, has a rational basis to single out homosexual acts for different treatment. Is there a rational basis for declaring this one type of sexual immorality so destructive of family values as to merit criminal punishment whereas other acts of sexual immorality which were likewise forbidden by the same religious and traditional heritage of Western civilization are now decriminalized? If there is a rational basis for different treatment it has yet to be demonstrated in this case. We need not sympathize, agree with, or even understand the sexual preference of homosexuals in order to recognize their right to equal treatment before the bar of criminal justice.

* * *

For the reasons stated, we affirm the decision of the Fayette Circuit Court, and the judgment on appeal from the Fayette District Court.

■ LAMBERT, JUSTICE, dissenting.

The issue here is not whether private homosexual conduct should be allowed or prohibited. The only question properly before this Court is whether the Constitution of Kentucky denies the legislative branch a right to prohibit such conduct. Nothing in the majority opinion demonstrates such a limitation on legislative prerogative.

To justify its view that private homosexual conduct is protected by the Constitution of Kentucky, the majority has found it necessary to disregard virtually all of recorded history, the teachings of the religions most influential on Western Civilization, the debates of the delegates to the Constitutional Convention, and the text of the Constitution itself. Rather than amounting to a decision based upon precedent as is suggested, this decision reflects the value judgment of the majority and its view that public law has no right to prohibit the conduct at issue here.

* * *

[T]his Court has strayed from its role of interpreting the Constitution and undertaken to make social policy. This decision is a vast extension of judicial power by which four Justices of this Court have overridden the will of the Legislative and Executive branches of Kentucky State Government and denied the people any say in this important social issue. No decision cited by the majority has ever gone so far and certainly none comes to mind. Where this slippery slope may lead is anybody's guess, but the ramifications of this decision will surely be profound.

For these reasons, I dissent.

■ WINTERSHEIMER, JUSTICE, dissenting.

I strongly dissent from the majority opinion because it totally misstates the case and proceeds to attack a statute that is not the direct subject of the criminal charge originally made in this case.

The majority opinion asserts that this is a case about privacy and yet it completely ignores that the criminal act for which the defendant was charged was a proposition made to a total stranger on a public street in downtown Lexington, Kentucky. Under such circumstances, there is no reasonable expectation of privacy.

Wasson solicited an undercover Lexington policeman in a parking lot in the Quality Street area to engage in deviate sexual intercourse. The charge against him was the solicitation to commit a criminal offense pursuant to K.R.S. 506.030. Solicitation to commit any crime on a public street in Lexington is simply not a private matter.

The majority opinion quickly departs from the solicitation aspect of the case, claiming it was not preserved, to something it prefers, the privacy issue, which it invented especially for this case.

The majority opinion lacks balance. It recognizes only one aspect of the equation of privacy. Every person is entitled to privacy to the degree that it does not invade the privacy of any other person. For every right there must be a corresponding responsibility. Here, we have a clear clash of rights. The public in general has a right to be free of solicitation from criminal acts and every individual has a right to conduct his or her own affairs.

* * *

There is a vast difference between liberty and license. License, in this context, means an excessive undisciplined freedom constituting an abuse of liberty. * * * The focus of the majority opinion is fuzzy. * * *

There must be an understanding that all persons are not alike but all have a right to live peacefully in our society. The judicial system falters if it does not observe such a right.

The judgment of the Fayette Circuit Court should be reversed with directions that the case be remanded to the Fayette District Court for trial on the merits.

Questions

1. The *Campbell* court stated: "We cannot believe that the framers of the [Kentucky] Constitution intended to * * * carefully take from the Legislature the power to regulate the sale of liquor, and at the same time leave with that department of the state government the greater power of prohibiting the possession or ownership of liquor." What is the logic behind this belief? Is it necessarily valid?

2. How did the *Campbell* court define "inalienable rights"? Do marijuana and other narcotics fall under this definition? Do saturated fat and cigarettes fall under this definition?

3. The *Wasson* court argued that *Campbell* is "the leading case on th[e] subject" of the state power to regulate "the conduct of a private individual." The *Campbell* court held that "the right to use liquor for one's own comfort, if the use is without direct injury to the public, is one of the citizen's natural and inalienable rights, guaranteed to him by the Constitution." Further, the court stressed that "[u]nder our institutions there is no room for [the] inquisitorial and protective spirit which seeks to regulate the conduct of men * * * and to make them conform to a standard, * * * which seeks to prescribe what a man shall eat and wear, or drink or think, thus crushing out individuality." By the time, the *Wasson* court was writing its decision relying on *Campbell*, the Food & Drug Administration had been regulating what people eating, drinking, and wearing for several decades. Was the *Campbell* court wrong in its analysis of regulation of the conduct a private individual? Could the *Wasson* court treat *Campbell* as a valid "leading case"?

4. The *Wasson* court refers to *Hershberg v. Barbourville*, 142 Ky. 60 (1911), in which a Kentucky court struck down an ordinance that banned smoking "a cigarette or cigarettes within the corporate limits of the city of Barbourville." The court held that

> The ordinance is so broad as to prohibit one from smoking a cigarette in his own home or on any private premises in the city. To prohibit the smoking of cigarettes in the citizen's own home or on other private premises is an invasion of his right to control his own personal indulgences. The city council is authorized by statute to enact and enforce all such local, police, sanitary, and other regulations as do not conflict with

> general laws. * * * But under this power it may not unreasonably interfere with the right of the citizen to determine for himself such personal matters. If the council may prohibit cigarette smoking in the city, it may prohibit pipe smoking or cigar smoking, or any other use of tobacco. The Legislature did not contemplate conferring such power upon the council. If the ordinance had provided a penalty for smoking cigarettes on the streets of the city, a different question would be presented; but whether such an ordinance would be valid is a question not now presented or decided.

Should all activities conducted at home be guarded and protected as "personal matters"?

5. The *Wasson* court refers to Justice Brandeis definition of "the right to be let alone" as "the most comprehensive of rights and the right most valued by civilized men." We have already seen that the "right to be let alone" means, among other things, "freedom to harm others," and sometimes also an expectation that the state will interfere with the liberty of others.[24] To illustrate, assume Gail likes the color black—for her outfit, home, bicycle, car, and everything else. Gail expresses her individualism and style with color. Everyone else in society finds the use of the color black immoral. Should society intervene in the freedom of Gail just to serve the majority's preferences? Should we protect Gail's freedom? The *Wasson* court rejected the argument that "what is beyond the pale of majoritarian morality is beyond the limits of constitutional protection." What types of preferences and values should courts protect? Should courts never respect the majority's values?

6. In *Ashcroft v. Free Speech Coalition*, 535 U.S. 234 (2002), the Supreme Court struck down the Child Pornography Prevention Act's ban on virtual (computer generated) child pornography. In response, in the PROTECT Act of 2003 Congress prohibited computer-generated child pornography when "such visual depiction is * * * indistinguishable from * * * that of a minor engaging in sexually explicit conduct." Five years later, in *United States v. Williams*, 553 U.S. 285 (2008), the Supreme Court held that the First Amendment does not protect offers or requests to trade in or transfer child pornography, including virtual child pornography. Are legal rules against virtual child pornography different from other moral rules?

Public Moral Code and Private Intimate Conduct

The traditional regulatory authorities of the state, as defined by the "police powers," include all reasonable actions needed to protect the safety, health, *morals*, and general welfare of the public. Does "the right to be let alone" protect the individual's choice of intimate conduct from coercive public moral codes?

24. *See* § 2.3.2.

Reliable Consultants, Inc. v. Earle

517 F.3d 738 (5th Cir. 2008)

■ REAVLEY, CIRCUIT JUDGE:

This case assesses the constitutionality of a Texas statute making it a crime to promote or sell sexual devices. The district court upheld the statute's constitutionality. * * * We reverse the judgment and hold that the statute has provisions that violate the Fourteenth Amendment of the U.S. Constitution.

I. The Statute

[The challenged statute criminalizes the selling, advertising, giving, or lending of a device designed or marketed for sexual stimulation unless the defendant can prove that the device was sold, advertised, given, or lent for a statutorily-approved purpose. The statute, however, does not prohibit the use or possession of sexual devices for any purpose. Violating the statute can result in punishment of up to two years in jail.]

* * * In 1985, the Texas Court of Criminal Appeals held that the statute did not violate an individual's right to privacy, concluding that there was no constitutional right to "stimulate ... another's genitals with an object designed or marketed as useful primarily for that purpose."[5] Later, in 1993, a narrow affirmative defense was added to protect those who promoted "obscene devices" for "a bona fide medical, psychiatric, judicial, legislative, or law enforcement purpose."

Besides Texas, only three states have a similar obscene-devices statute: Mississippi,[8] Alabama,[9] and Virginia.[10] The Mississippi supreme court has upheld its state's statute against First and Fourteenth Amendment challenges.[11] Neither the Alabama nor Virginia supreme court has entertained a challenge to its state's statute, but the Eleventh Circuit has rejected a Fourteenth Amendment challenge to Alabama's statute.[12] On the other hand, while the legislatures of Louisiana, Kansas, and Colorado had enacted obscene-devices statutes, each of their respective state supreme courts struck down its law on Fourteenth Amendment grounds.[13] Likewise, while

---

5. Yorko v. State, 690 S.W.2d 260, 263 (Tex.Crim.App.1985).

8. Miss.Code Ann. § 97–29–105.

9. Ala.Code § 13A–12–200.2.

10. Va.Code Ann. § 18.2–373.

11. PHE, Inc. v. State, 877 So.2d 1244, 1248–50 (Miss.2004).

12. *Williams v. Morgan*, 478 F.3d 1316 (11th Cir.2007), *cert. denied*, *Williams v. King*, 552 U.S. 814 (2007). The Williams case had previously been before the Eleventh Circuit, where the court held that the obscene-device ban did not burden a fundamental right. See *Williams v. Attorney General*, 378 F.3d 1232, 1233 (11th Cir.2004) (remanding the case to the district court).

13. *See State v. Brenan*, 772 So.2d 64, 72–76 (La.2000) (holding that the state's obscene-devices statute fails rational-basis review under the Fourteenth Amendment of the U.S. Constitution); *State v. Hughes*, 246 Kan. 607 (1990) (holding that the state's obscene-devices statute unconstitutionally burdens an individual's Fourteenth Amendment right to privacy); *People ex rel. Tooley v. Seven Thirty–Five East Colfax, Inc.*, 697 P.2d 348, 369–70 (Colo.1985) (same).

the Georgia legislature had passed an obscene-device statute, the Eleventh Circuit recently struck it down.[14]

II. This Proceeding

Reliable Consultants, Inc. * * * operates four retail stores in Texas that carry a stock of sexual devices. The sexual devices are for off-premise, private use. PHE, Inc. * * * is also engaged in the retail distribution of sexual devices. It operates no public facilities in Texas, but rather sells sexual devices by internet and mail, and it distributes sexual devices ordered in Texas by mail and common carrier. Reliable and PHE desire to increase their sale of, and advertising for, sexual devices in Texas, and they fear prosecution under the statute if they do so.

Reliable filed this declaratory action to challenge the constitutionality and enjoin the enforcement of the statutory provisions criminalizing the promotion of sexual devices. The complaint alleged that these provisions violate the substantive liberty rights protected by the Fourteenth Amendment and the commercial speech rights protected by the First Amendment. Later, PHE intervened as a plaintiff and sought similar relief.

Reliable and PHE contend that many people in Texas, both married and unmarried, use sexual devices as an aspect of their sexual experiences. For some couples in which one partner may be physically unable to engage in intercourse, or in which a contagious disease, such as HIV, precludes intercourse, these devices may be one of the only ways to engage in a safe, sexual relationship. Others use sexual devices to treat a variety of therapeutic needs, such as erectile dysfunction. Courts scrutinizing sexual-device bans in other states have explained that an "extensive review of the medical necessity for sexual devices" shows that "it is common for trained experts in the field of human sexual behavior to use sexual aids in the treatment of their male and female patients' sexual problems." Still other individuals use sexual devices for non-therapeutic personal reasons, such as a desire to refrain from premarital intercourse.[16]

The district court held, *inter alia,* that the statute does not violate the Fourteenth Amendment because there is no constitutionally protected right to publicly promote obscene devices. * * * [W]e hold that the statute violates the Fourteenth Amendment.

III. The Fourteenth Amendment

The Plaintiffs' claim is predicated upon the individual right under the Fourteenth Amendment to engage in private intimate conduct in the home without government intrusion. Because the asserted governmental interests for the law do not meet the applicable constitutional standard an-

---

14. *This That and the Other Gift and Tobacco, Inc. v. Cobb County*, 439 F.3d 1275, 1278 (11th Cir.2006).

16. A recent commentator points out that sexual devices, such as vibrators, were originally designed for medical purposes and they continue to be prescribed as such. Danielle J. Lindemann, *Pathology Full Circle: A History of Anti-Vibrator Legislation in the United States*, 15 Columbia Journal of Gender and Law 326, 327–30, 336–41 (2006). In the early to mid-twentieth century their use for sexual pleasure became well known, and in the 1960s advertising for such devices began to emphasize their sexual benefits.

nounced in *Lawrence v. Texas*, 539 U.S. 558 (2003), the statute cannot be constitutionally enforced.

The State argues that Plaintiffs, who distribute sexual devices for profit, cannot assert the individual rights of their customers. This argument fails under the Supreme Court precedent holding that (1) bans on commercial transactions involving a product can unconstitutionally burden individual substantive due process rights and (2) lawsuits making this claim may be brought by providers of the product. In the landmark 1965 case of *Griswold v. Connecticut*, 381 U.S. 479 (1965), which invalidated a ban on the *use* of contraceptives, the Court recognized that the plaintiff pharmacists "have standing to raise the constitutional rights of the married people with whom they had a professional relationship." Other Supreme Court cases hold that businesses can assert the rights of their customers and that restricting the ability to purchase an item is tantamount to restricting that item's use. In line with these cases, the statute must be scrutinized for impermissible burdens on the constitutional rights of those who wish to use sexual devices.

To determine the constitutional standard applicable to this claim, we must address what right is at stake. Plaintiffs claim that the right at stake is the individual's substantive due process right to engage in private intimate conduct free from government intrusion. The State proposes a different right for the Plaintiffs: "the right to stimulate one's genitals for non-medical purposes unrelated to procreation or outside of an interpersonal relationship."[23] The Court in *Lawrence*—where it overruled its decision in *Bowers v. Hardwick*, 478 U.S. 186 (1986), and struck down Texas's sodomy ban—guides our decision:

> To say that the issue in *Bowers* was simply the right to engage in certain sexual conduct demeans the claim the individual put forward, just as it would demean a married couple were it to be said marriage is simply about the right to have sexual intercourse. The laws involved in *Bowers* and here are, to be sure, statutes that purport to do no more than prohibit a particular sexual act. Their penalties and purposes, though, have more far-reaching consequences, touching upon the most private human conduct, sexual behavior, and in the most private of places, the home.[25]

The right the Court recognized was not simply a right to engage in the sexual act itself, but instead a right to be free from governmental intrusion regarding "the most private human contact, sexual behavior." That *Lawrence* recognized this as a constitutional right is the only way to make sense of the fact that the Court explicitly chose to answer the following question in the affirmative: "We granted certiorari . . . [to resolve whether] petitioners' criminal convictions for *adult consensual sexual intimacy* in the home

23. The State narrowly describes the right as the court did in Williams v. Attorney General of Alabama, 378 F.3d 1232 (11th Cir. 2004). Id. at 1235–38 (describing the right as the right to use sex toys).

25. *Lawrence*, 539 U.S. at 567.

violate their vital interests in liberty and privacy protected by the Due Process Clause of the Fourteenth Amendment."

The State also argues that Lawrence does not apply because the Court there was concerned with how the statute targeted a specific class of people. Justice O'Connor concurred in the majority's decision in *Lawrence* because she would have struck down the law on equal protection, not substantive due process, grounds. But the Court explicitly rested its holding on substantive due process, not equal protection. As discussed, the Court concluded that the sodomy law violated the substantive due process right to engage in consensual intimate conduct in the home free from government intrusion. Once *Lawrence* is properly understood to explain the contours of the substantive due process right to sexual intimacy, the case plainly applies.

Because of *Lawrence,* the issue before us is whether the Texas statute impermissibly burdens the individual's substantive due process right to engage in private intimate conduct of his or her choosing. Contrary to the district court's conclusion, we hold that the Texas law burdens this constitutional right. An individual who wants to legally use a safe sexual device during private intimate moments alone or with another is unable to legally purchase a device in Texas, which heavily burdens a constitutional right. This conclusion is consistent with the decision[] in * * * *Griswold*, where the Court held that restricting commercial transactions unconstitutionally burdened the exercise of individual rights. Indeed, under this statute it is even illegal to "lend" or "give" a sexual device to another person. This further restricts the exercise of the constitutional right to engage in private intimate conduct in the home free from government intrusion. It also undercuts any argument that the statute only affects public conduct.

[In *Lawrence*, the] Supreme Court * * * held that "individual decisions by married persons, concerning the intimacies of their physical relationship, even when not intended to produce offspring, are a form of 'liberty' protected by the Due Process Clause of the Fourteenth Amendment. Moreover, this protection extends to intimate choices by unmarried * * * persons." * * * We must apply *Lawrence* to the Texas statute.

The State's primary justifications for the statute are "morality based." The asserted interests include "discouraging prurient interests in autonomous sex and the pursuit of sexual gratification unrelated to procreation and prohibiting the commercial sale of sex."

These interests in "public morality" cannot constitutionally sustain the statute after *Lawrence*.[33] To uphold the statute would be to ignore the holding in *Lawrence* and allow the government to burden consensual private intimate conduct simply by deeming it morally offensive. In *Lawrence*, Texas's only argument was that the anti-sodomy law reflected the

---

33. The Eleventh Circuit disagreed in *Williams v. Morgan*, 478 F.3d 1316 (11th Cir.2007). * * * There, the court held that Alabama's interest in "public morality" was a constitutional justification for the state's obscene devices statute. * * * That fails to recognize the *Lawrence* holding that public morality cannot justify a law that regulates an individual's private sexual conduct and does not relate to prostitution, the potential for injury or coercion, or public conduct.

moral judgment of the legislature.[34] The Court expressly rejected the State's rationale by adopting Justice Stevens' view in *Bowers* as "controlling" and quoting Justice Stevens' statement that " 'the fact that the governing majority in a State has traditionally viewed a particular practice as immoral is not a sufficient reason for upholding a law prohibiting the practice.' "[35] Thus, if in *Lawrence* public morality was an insufficient justification for a law that restricted "adult consensual intimacy in the home," then public morality also cannot serve as a rational basis for Texas's statute, which also regulates private sexual intimacy.[36]

Perhaps recognizing that public morality is an insufficient justification for the statute after *Lawrence*, the State asserts that an interest the statute serves is the "protection of minors and unwilling adults from exposure to sexual devices and their advertisement." It is undeniable that the government has a compelling interest in protecting children from improper sexual expression.[37] However, the State's generalized concern for children does not justify such a heavy-handed restriction on the exercise of a constitutionally protected individual right. Ultimately, because we can divine no rational connection between the statute and the protection of children, and because the State offers none, we cannot sustain the law under this justification.

The alleged governmental interest in protecting "unwilling adults" from exposure to sexual devices is even less convincing. The [Supreme] Court has consistently refused to burden individual rights out of concern for the protection of "unwilling recipients." Furthermore, this asserted interest bears no rational relation to the restriction on sales of sexual devices because an adult cannot buy a sexual device without making the affirmative decision to visit a store and make the purchase.

The State argues that if this statute, which proscribes the distribution of sexual devices, is struck down, it is equivalent to extending substantive due process protection to the "commercial sale of sex." Not so. The sale of a device that an individual may choose to use during intimate conduct with a partner in the home is not the "sale of sex" (prostitution). Following the State's logic, the sale of contraceptives would be equivalent to the sale of sex because contraceptives are intended to be used for the pursuit of sexual gratification unrelated to procreation. This argument cannot be accepted as a justification to limit the sale of contraceptives. The comparison highlights

---

34. *See* Respondent's Brief, *Lawrence*, 539 U.S. 558 (No. 02–102), 2003 WL 470184, at *48 (internal footnote omitted) ("The prohibition of homosexual conduct in [the anti-sodomy statute] represents the reasoned judgment of the Texas Legislature that such conduct is immoral and should be deterred.... [L]ong-established principles of federalism dictate that the Court defer to the Texas Legislature's judgment and to the collective good sense of the people of the State of Texas, in their effort to enforce public morality and promote family values through the promulgation of penal statutes such as [the anti-sodomy statute].").

35. *Lawrence*, 539 U.S. at 577–78 (quoting *Bowers*, 478 U.S. at 216 (Stevens, J., dissenting)).

36. *See id.* at 564. The State offers cases for the general proposition that protecting morality is a legitimate governmental interest. *See, e.g., Paris Adult Theatre I v. Slaton*, 413 U.S. 49 (1973). Our holding in no way overtly expresses or implies that public morality can never be a constitutional justification for a law. We merely hold that after *Lawrence* it is not a constitutional justification for this statute.

37. *See, e.g., FCC v. Pacifica Found.*, 438 U.S. 726 (1978).

why the focus of our analysis is on the burden the statute puts on the individual's right to make private decisions about consensual intimate conduct. Furthermore, there are justifications for criminalizing prostitution other than public morality, including promoting public safety and preventing injury and coercion.

Just as in *Lawrence,* the State here wants to use its laws to enforce a public moral code by restricting private intimate conduct. The case is not about public sex. It is not about controlling commerce in sex. It is about controlling what people do in the privacy of their own homes because the State is morally opposed to a certain type of consensual private intimate conduct. This is an insufficient justification for the statute after *Lawrence.*

It follows that the Texas statute cannot define sexual devices themselves as obscene and prohibit their sale.[41] * * * Whatever one might think or believe about the use of these devices, government interference with their personal and private use violates the Constitution.

Appellants urge us to sustain their First Amendment claim to protect the advertisement of these devices. We decline to explore this claim because if it is necessary, it may be premature. Advertisements of the devices could be prohibited if they are obscene. * * * But the State may not prohibit the promotion or sale of a bed, even one specially designed or marketed for sexual purposes, by merely defining it as obscene. We have held here that the State may not burden the use of these devices by prohibiting their sale. If other issues need to be pursued, the parties are free to do so on remand in proceedings consistent with this decision.

Judgment REVERSED and the case REMANDED.

■ RHESA HAWKINS BARKSDALE, CIRCUIT JUDGE, concurring in part and dissenting in part:

* * * The [challenged] statute prohibits, *inter alia,* the sale or other promotion, such as advertising, of "obscene devices": those "designed or marketed as useful primarily for the stimulation of human genital organs". Tex. Penal Code Ann. § 43.21(a)(7); id. § 43.23; *see also id.* § 43.21(a)(1)(B)(ii). Such devices include, but are not limited to, "a dildo or artificial vagina". *Id.* at § 43.21 (a)(7). The statute provides an affirmative defense for persons who "possess[ ] or promote[ ] [obscene devices] ... for a bona fide medical, psychiatric, judicial, legislative, or law enforcement purpose". *Id.* at § 43.23(f).

Plaintiffs' complaints claim the statute unconstitutionally restricts commercial speech (advertising) under the First Amendment, as incorporated by the Fourteenth Amendment. The complaints also claim the "sale" portion of the statute violates substantive due process under the Fourteenth Amendment because it impinges upon the right to engage in private intimate conduct without governmental intrusion. * * *

---

41. *See State v. Brenan*, 772 So.2d 64, 74 (La.2000) (holding that "[t]he legislature cannot make a device automatically obscene merely through the use of labels"); *State v. Hughes*, 246 Kan. 607 (1990) ("The legislature may not declare a device obscene merely because it relates to human sexual activity.").

For starters, and contrary to the majority's position, * * * the proscribed conduct is *not* private sexual conduct. Instead, for obscene devices, the statute proscribes only the sale or other promotion (such as advertising) of those devices, including, but not limited to, a dildo or artificial vagina.

* * *

For the reasons stated by the Eleventh Circuit in its analysis of a statute materially identical to the one in issue, I conclude *Lawrence* declined to employ a fundamental-rights analysis, choosing instead to apply rational-basis review. *See Williams v. Attorney Gen. of Ala.*, 378 F.3d 1232, 1236 (11th Cir. 2004) (citation omitted); *see also Lawrence*, 539 U.S. at 578 ("The Texas statute furthers no *legitimate state interest* which can justify its intrusion into the personal and private life of the individual." (emphasis added)); *Lawrence*, 539 U.S. at 594 (Scalia, J. dissenting) ("Not once does [the Court] describe homosexual sodomy as a 'fundamental right' or a 'fundamental liberty interest,' nor does it subject the Texas statute to strict scrutiny. Instead, having failed to establish that the right to homosexual sodomy is 'deeply rooted in this Nation's history and tradition,' the Court concludes that the application of Texas's statute to petitioners' conduct fails the rational-basis test.").

Furthermore, as also held by the Eleventh Circuit, I agree that, "[t]o the extent *Lawrence* rejects public morality as a legitimate government interest, it invalidates only those laws that target conduct that is *both private and non-commercial*". *Williams v. Morgan*, 478 F.3d 1316, 1322 (11th Cir.) (emphasis added). * * * The Texas statute regulates, *inter alia,* the sale of what it defines as obscene devices. Obviously, such conduct is both public and commercial.

Therefore, I would hold: pursuant to the rational-basis standard of review, plaintiffs fail to state a substantive-due-process claim under the Fourteenth Amendment.

* * *

For the foregoing reasons, * * * the dismissal, however, of the Fourteenth Amendment substantive-due-process claim (sale) should be upheld. Therefore, I must respectfully dissent from my BROTHERS' invalidation of the statute on that basis.

Questions

1. State laws impose age restrictions on consensual sex.[25] For example, in Arizona, "[a] person commits sexual conduct with a minor by intentionally or knowingly engaging in sexual intercourse or oral sexual contact with any person who is under eighteen years of age."[26] In *Reliable Consultants*, the court was reluctant to uphold a statute that would "allow the government

---

25. *See generally* Catherine L. Carpenter, *On Statutory Rape, Strict Liability, and the Public Welfare Offense Model*, 53 AMERICAN UNIVERSITY LAW REVIEW 313 (2003); Russell L. Christopher & Kathryn H. Christopher, *The Paradox of Statutory Rape*, 87 INDIANA LAW JOURNAL 505 (2012).

26. Ariz. Rev. Stat. Ann. § 13–1405.

to burden consensual private intimate conduct simply by deeming it morally offensive" It reasoned that such holding "would be to ignore the holding in Lawrence." Are statutory rape laws inconsistent with this rationale?

2. Writing for the Court in *Bowers v. Hardwick*, 478 U.S. 186 (1986), Justice White argued that the moral choices of the majority should be honored. Justice White further warned that "if all laws representing essentially moral choices are to be invalidated * * *, the courts will be very busy indeed." Dissenting, Justice Stevens posited that "the fact that the governing majority in a State has traditionally viewed a particular practice as immoral is not a sufficient reason for upholding a law prohibiting the practice." In *Lawrence*, the Court endorsed Justice Stevens' view. The *Reliable Consultants* court stressed the differences between these positions and its commitment to follow *Lawrence*. Does a court need a sufficient reason to *uphold* a law representing moral choices? What is a sufficient reason to uphold or strike down laws representing moral choices?

3. Choices of the majority explain all financial bubbles. Every bubble is a consequence of some belief that "spreads by psychological contagion from person to person" and directs the majority to act in a particular way, which always results in great costs to society.[27]

(a) Should "beliefs" of the majority justify laws and regulation? Should laws resolve the majority from liability for acting on their beliefs in good faith?[28]

(b) Many argue that "scientific positions," which are arguably supported by facts, are biased and reflect beliefs.[29] Should the state regulate the distinction between facts and fiction; that is, should the reasonable person rely on facts? Assuming we should care about facts and reality, what is the adequate role of morality in law?

---

27. ROBERT J. SHILLER, IRRATIONAL EXUBERANCE 2 (2d ed. 2005) (defining "irrational exuberance"). *See generally* § 1.1.3 (the causes of the Great Recession).

28. Broadly speaking, under the business judgment rule, courts do not impose liability on corporate boards and managements for acting on their beliefs, as long as decisions were made in good faith by sufficiently informed, disinterested officers and directors. That is, to the extent officers and directors do not breach their fiduciary duties, they are unlikely to be liable for their decisions. *See generally* In re Walt Disney Co. Derivative Litigation, 907 A.2d 693 (Del. Ch. 2005).

29. *See, e.g.*, Brad Rodu, *Calculating the 'Big Kill,'* 30.4 REGULATION 16 (2007) (arguing that the customary methods used to estimate the number of deaths caused by smoking grossly inflate the figures); Stanley W. Trimble, *The Double Standard in Environmental Science*, 30.2 REGULATION 16 (2007) (criticizing the scientific community for being ideologically biased). *See also* Mohammadreza Hojat et al., *Impartial Judgment by the "Gatekeepers" of Science: Fallibility and Accountability in the Peer Review Process*, 8 ADVANCES IN HEALTH SCIENCES EDUCATION 75 (2003) (reviewing biases in the publication of academic works); Judith Warner, *Fact–Free Science*, N.Y. TIMES MAGAZINE, Feb. 27. 2011, at 11; Climate Change and the Integrity of Science, 328 SCIENCE 689 (2010) (a letter signed by 255 members of the U.S. National Academy of Sciences expressing concerns regarding the "escalation of political assaults on scientists" "driven by special interests or dogma, not by an honest effort to provide an alternative theory that credibly satisfies the evidence.")

Regulating What We Eat

In *Commonwealth v. Campbell*, a Kentucky court struck down a municipal ban on possession of alcohol, ruling that the ban in effect prohibited alcohol consumption. The court held that "[u]nder our institutions there is no room for [an] inquisitorial and protective spirit which seeks to regulate the conduct of men * * * and to make them conform to a standard, * * * which seeks to prescribe what a man shall eat and wear, or drink or think, thus crushing out individuality."

On April 26, 2006, by a vote of 48–to–1, the City Council of Chicago adopted an ordinance banning foie gras.[30] The ordinance's preamble provided:

> WHEREAS, The City of Chicago is a home rule unit of government pursuant to the 1970 Illinois Constitution * * *; and
>
> WHEREAS, Pursuant to its home rule power, the City of Chicago may exercise any power and perform any function relating to its government and affairs including protecting the health, safety and welfare of its citizens; and
>
> WHEREAS, The City of Chicago is home to many famous restaurants offering the finest cuisine and dining experiences to their customers; and
>
> WHEREAS, Millions of people visit Chicago every year, attending cultural events and dining in our legendary restaurants; and
>
> WHEREAS, Recently the media has shed light on the unethical practices of the care and preparation of the livers of birds; and
>
> WHEREAS, Birds, in particular geese and ducks, are inhumanely force fed, via a pipe inserted through their throats several times a day, in order to produce a rare delicacy, foie gas [*sic*], for restaurant patrons; and
>
> WHEREAS, Arguably our City's most renowned chef, Charlie Trotter, has stopped serving the delicacy, foie gas [*sic*], in his restaurants; and
>
> WHEREAS, Similar legislation requiring the ethical treatment of birds is being introduced throughout the United States; and
>
> * * *
>
> WHEREAS, According to a recent Zogby poll, nearly eighty percent (80%) of Americans, when educated about foie gras, support a ban on the force feeding of birds; and
>
> WHEREAS, The people of the City of Chicago and those who visit here have come to expect, and rightfully deserve, the highest quality in resources, service and fare; and

30. The ordinance is available at *regti.me/foie-gras* (case sensitive).

WHEREAS, By ensuring the ethical treatment of animals, who are the source of the food offered in our restaurants, the City of Chicago is able to continue to offer the best in dining experiences. * * *

Illinois Restaurant Association v. Chicago

United States District Court, N.D. Illinois
492 F.Supp.2d 891 (2007)

■ MANNING, DISTRICT JUDGE.

Foiegras, or "fatty liver," is produced using the French practice of gavage, which involves feeding ducks or geese with the goal of fattening their livers. The practice dates back to at least Roman times, when Pliny the Elder wrote of the practice of feeding geese dried figs to enlarge their livers. PLINY THE ELDER, NATURAL HISTORY, Book VIII, Ch. 77 (Teubner ed.1909). In the nineteenth century, the debate over the propriety of the practice continued, as Jean Anthelme Brillat–Savarin sided with the geese and ducks, writing that "[t]hey have not only been deprived of the means of reproduction, but they have been kept in solitude and darkness, and forced to eat until they were led to an unnatural state of fatness." PHYSIOLOGIE DU GOÛT (THE PHYSIOLOGY OF TASTE), SEC. III (1825). On the other hand, his contemporary, Charles Gerard, called the goose "an instrument for the output of a marvelous product, a kind of living hothouse in which there grows the supreme fruit of gastronomy." CHARLES GÉRARD, L'ANCIENNE ALSACE À TABLE (1862).

The debate rages on today, as the City of Chicago entered the fray in 2006 by enacting an ordinance banning the sale of foiegras at food dispensing establishments in the City. The Illinois Restaurant Association and Allen's New American Café sued the City in state court, claiming that the foiegras ordinance exceeded the City's police powers under the Illinois Constitution. * * * For the following reasons, the court finds that the foiegras ordinance is consistent with the Illinois and United States Constitutions. * * *

I. Background

* * * On April 26, 2006, the City Council enacted Ordinance PO–05–1895 ("the Ordinance"), which became effective on August 23, 2006. * * * The Ordinance amends the City's Municipal Code to add a section prohibiting the sale of foiegras at "food dispensing establishments" within the City and provides that any business that violates the Ordinance is subject to a fine of between $250 and $500 per offense.

* * * Foiegras is not produced in Chicago or Illinois. Instead, it is produced domestically at farms in California and New York and is produced and imported into the United States from farms in Canada and France. The production of foiegras in these out-of-state and foreign locations is lawful, and imported foiegras is subject to federal tariffs and other federal regulations allowing its importation for sale into the United States. Furthermore, the United States Department of Agriculture ("USDA") has found that foiegras is safe for human consumption.

The parties offer differing characterizations of the City Council's motives for passing the Ordinance. According to the plaintiffs, the City Council has never advanced any health, consumer protection, or fraud bases as justification for the Ordinance and no such justifications exist. Instead, the Ordinance is a "moral statement" which was passed "because of the purportedly inhumane manner in which foiegras is *produced*." * * *

On the other hand, the City points to the "WHEREAS" clauses of the Ordinance, which note the City Council's recognition that "the media has shed light on the unethical practices of the care and preparation of the livers of birds." * * * [T]he City Council identified a recent survey showing that nearly 80 percent of Americans oppose the treatment of geese and ducks whose livers become foiegras. * * *

The City Council [however] concluded that "[b]y ensuring the ethical treatment of animals, who are the source of the food offered in our restaurants, the City of Chicago is able to continue to offer the best in dining experiences." * * *

II. Discussion

* * *

B. The Illinois Constitution–Home Rule

* * * The plaintiffs contend that the Ordinance exceeds the City's home rule powers because it is not aimed at a legitimate local problem and has an impermissible extraterritorial effect since it is meant to affect the production process of foiegras, which only occurs outside Chicago. Under the Illinois Constitution of 1970, "a home rule unit may exercise any power and perform any function pertaining to its government and affairs including, but not limited to, the power to regulate for the protection of the public health, safety, morals and welfare...." * * * The City "is a home rule unit of local government under the 1970 Illinois Constitution." * * * Thus, the Ordinance does not violate the Illinois Constitution if it is within the scope of the City's broad home rule powers.

* * * The Illinois Supreme Court has emphasized that home rule units have expansive powers. * * * Because a home rule unit's powers are so broad, the constitutionality of its ordinances does not turn on a court's assessment of their wisdom or desirability. * * * Nevertheless, an ordinance enacted by a home rule unit must address a local problem, as opposed to a problem arising at the state or national level. * * * When determining whether an ordinance has a sufficient local angle for the purposes of home rule, the court must consider "[1] the nature and extent of the problem, [2] the units of government which have the most vital interest in its solution, and [3] the role traditionally played by local and statewide authorities in dealing with it." * * *

1. The Nature and Extent of the Problem

The Ordinance addresses sales of foiegras in Chicago and thus addresses a local aspect of the more general question as to whether foiegras should be available at the state or national level. * * * This is so even though foiegras sales are lawful elsewhere, as the fact that conduct is lawful outside the jurisdiction does not bar a home rule unit from enacting legislation which controls conduct inside its borders. * * * Similarly, the federal government's regulation of the safety of foiegras consumption does not preempt regulation of sales at the local level because Chicago is not enacting legislation directed at whether foiegras is fit for consumption. * * *

Moreover, the Ordinance states that because the vast majority of Americans oppose foiegras production, banning foiegras will enhance the reputation of restaurants in Chicago. Contrary to the plaintiffs' position, the City's expressed desire to use a foiegras ban to make a statement about the methods used to produce foiegras is a local interest since local political bodies traditionally enact legislation reflecting the perceived desires of their constituency, and the Ordinance reflects the City Council's belief that a majority of Chicagoans want to ban foiegras sales in Chicago. * * *

The Ordinance thus reflects the City Council's judgment that banning the sale of foiegras would benefit the City and advance the morals of the community. The court cannot sit as a superlegislature and determine if, in its judgment, the City Council was correct. * * * In other words, the Ordinance's constitutionality does not depend on whether the court or the parties agree as to its wisdom. The plaintiffs' numerous arguments regarding the desirability of a foiegras ban are, therefore, beside the point.

2. Who Has the Most Vital Interest in the Problem and Who Traditionally Deals With The Problem

The court next considers whether the Chicago City Council is the unit of government with the most vital interest in solving the problem at the heart of the Ordinance. Because the Ordinance regulates food which may be served in Chicago restaurants and sold in Chicago grocery stores, the Chicago City Council clearly meets this standard. * * * It is also the proper authority to address the problem because it is uniquely situated to govern the conduct of Chicago business establishments.

* * *

Accordingly, for the above reasons, the court finds that despite the Ordinance's extraterritorial effects, it is a valid exercise of Chicago's home rule powers under the Illinois Constitution because it is aimed at a sufficiently local problem. It thus reaches the argument to which the parties have devoted most of their energies: whether the Ordinance violates the United States Constitution.

C. The Federal Constitution—The Dormant Commerce Clause

The United States Constitution gives Congress the power to "regulate Commerce with foreign Nations, and among the several States." U.S. Const. Art. I, § 8. This portion of the Constitution is known as the Commerce Clause. Although the Commerce Clause does not limit the States' power to regulate commerce, it "has long been recognized as a self-executing limitation on the power of the States to enact laws imposing substantial burdens on [interstate] commerce." *S.-Cent. Timber Dev., Inc. v. Wunnicke*, 467 U.S. 82, 87 (1984). "This 'negative' aspect of the Commerce Clause is often referred to as the 'Dormant Commerce Clause' and is invoked to invalidate overreaching provisions of state regulation of commerce." * * *

The dormant Commerce Clause is generally analyzed using a two-tier approach. Under the first tier, the court must determine if the law at issue "directly regulates or discriminates against interstate commerce" or if "its effect is to favor in-state economic interests over out-of-state interests." *Brown-Forman Distillers Corp. v. New York State Liquor Auth.*, 476 U.S. 573, 579 (1986).

On the other hand, if a law indirectly affects interstate commerce and regulates evenhandedly, the line of cases which form the second tier potentially come into play. These cases require the court to examine whether the State's interest is legitimate and whether the burden on interstate commerce clearly exceeds the putative local benefits. * * *

The parties vigorously dispute what analysis is appropriate after the court determines that a law does not directly regulate or discriminate against extraterritorial commerce. * * * [T]he court finds that the Ordinance does not violate the dormant Commerce Clause because it does not regulate or discriminate against interstate commerce. * * *

III. Conclusion

The court's sole task is to evaluate the Ordinance's constitutionality. For the above reasons, it finds that Chicago's ban of foiegras sales in restaurants does not exceed the City's home rule powers or violate the dormant Commerce Clause. Thus, the Ordinance does not violate the Illinois or United States Constitutions. * * *

Notes

The Chicago's ban on foie gras was not as popular as the district court described it. Many people in the City opposed it. Many restaurants did not comply with the ban. The powerful mayor, Richard Daley, dismissed it as "the silliest law the City Council has ever passed." In May 2008, by a vote of 37–to–6, the City Council repealed the ordinance.

Questions

1. Chicago exercised its power to protect the public morals to ban foie gras. Was this ban substantially different from the bans discussed in *Campbell*, *Wasson*, and *Reliable Consultants*?

2. Senior city officials and many citizens were dismissive of the foie gras ban. It survived only two years. Nevertheless, the City used taxpayer money to defend the ban in court. Was the ban an effective way to promote its underlying goals?

§ 7.3 INALIENABILITY AND COMMODIFICATION

The Declaration of Independence declares that the rights to "life, liberty and the pursuit of happiness" are among the "unalienable rights" all people have (or more precisely, "all men" have).[31]

In a classic 1972 article about the classification of legal rights, Guido Calabresi and Douglas Melamed distinguished among property rules, liability rules, and inalienability rules.[32] A property rule protects the exclusive right of a person to decide how to use a particular entitlement, including trading this entitlement. Calabresi and Melamed observed that it "is the form of entitlement which gives rise to the least amount of state intervention: once the original entitlement is decided upon, the state does not try to decide its value."[33] A liability rule protects the right of a person to be compensated if another person destroys his entitlement. Calabresi and Melamed pointed out that "liability rules involve an additional stage of state intervention: not only are entitlements protected, but their transfer or destruction is allowed on the basis of a value determined by some organ of the state rather than by the parties themselves."[34] Inalienability rules refer to situations in which a transfer of an entitlement "is not permitted between a willing buyer and a willing seller"[35] and the entitlement cannot be waived, abandoned, relinquished, canceled, taken, or lost in any way. By definition, inalienability rules involve the greatest degree of state intervention, since the state is regulating or banning the transfer of entitlements. We have discussed a wide range of restrictions on transactions in entitlements from *Lochner* to *Adkins* and *West Coast Hotel*.[36] Inalienability rules are rather common. People cannot waive minimum standards of habitability, right to obtain a divorce, sue for relief under the bankruptcy laws, certain consumer rights, and many other entitlements.[37]

Calabresi and Melamed argued that externalities may explain inalienability rules: a trade in the entitlement would entail significant costs to third parties. To illustrate, using their example, "if Taney were allowed to sell his land to Chase, a polluter, he would injure his neighbor Marshall by lowering the value of Marshall's land. Conceivably, Marshall could pay Taney not to sell his land; but, because there are many injured Marshalls, [free riding] and information costs make such transactions practically impossible. * * * Barring the sale to polluters will be the most efficient [rule] because it is clear that avoiding pollution is cheaper than paying its costs—including its costs to the Marshalls."[38] Another category of cases refers to the "external harm of a moralism": "If Taney is allowed to sell himself into slavery, or to take undue risks of becoming penniless, or to sell a kidney, Marshall may be harmed, simply because Marshall is a sensitive

31. *See* § 2.2.1 (Sidebars 2–1, 2–2).

32. Guido Calabresi & A. Douglas Melamed, *Property Rules, Liability Rules, and Inalienability: One View of the Cathedral*, 85 HARVARD LAW REVIEW 1089 (1972).

33. *Id.* at 1092.

34. *Id.*

35. *Id.*

36. Lochner v. New York, 198 U.S. 45 (1905). Adkins v. Children's Hospital of the District of Columbia, 261 U.S. 525 (1923); West Coast Hotel Co. v. Parrish, 300 U.S. 379 (1937). *See supra* § 6.3.

37. *See generally* Anthony T. Kronman, *Paternalism and the Law of Contracts*, 92 YALE LAW JOURNAL 763 (1983).

38. Calabresi & Melamed, *supra* note 32, at 1111.

man who is made unhappy by seeing slaves, paupers, or persons who die because they have sold a kidney."[39]

Calabresi and Melamed distinguished the "external harm of a moralism" from paternalism, pointing out that the latter motivation for inalienability rules intends to prevent self-inflicted harm: "Here we are not talking about the offense to Marshall from Taney's choosing to read pornography, or selling himself into slavery, but rather the judgment that Taney was not in the position to choose best for himself when he made the choice for erotica or servitude."[40]

Fifteen years after Calabresi and Melamed published their famed article, Margaret Radin introduced the most influential explanation for inalienability rules to date: the concept of human flourishing, she argued, explains legal restrictions on transactions in entitlements.[41] Radin pointed out that inalienability rules negate a central characteristic of traditional property entitlements: commodification. In her words, "[w]hen something is noncommodifiable, market trading is a disallowed form of social organization and allocation. [It is placed] beyond supply and demand pricing, brokerage and arbitrage, advertising and marketing, stockpiling, speculation, and valuation in terms of the opportunity cost of production."[42] Radin observed that social choices about the characterization of entitlements are nuanced, and do not alternate between two options of completely commodified or completely noncommodified. Rather, "many things can be described as incompletely commodified—neither fully commodified nor fully removed from the market."[43] Examples for contested entitlements of commodification are infants and children, fetal gestational services, blood, human organs, human life, and sexual services.[44]

Legislatures, courts, and agencies frequently address questions related to inalienability and commodification. In many circumstances, these questions raise several rationales and themes. This Section illustrates two types of rules intended to promote inalienability and restrict commodification.

§ 7.3.1 "Some Things That Money Cannot Buy"

Is everything for sale? One of the arguments against cost-benefit analysis ("CBA") is that some things are priceless.[45] The essence of this

---

39. *Id.* at 1112.

40. *Id.* at 1113.

41. Margaret Jane Radin, *Market–Inalienability*, 100 HARVARD LAW REVIEW 1849 (1987).

42. *Id.* at 1855.

43. *Id.*

44. *See, e.g.*, Joel Feinberg, *Voluntary Euthanasia and the Inalienable Right to Life*, 7 PHILOSOPHY & PUBLIC AFFAIRS 93 (1978); Gary D. Glenn, *Abortion and Inalienable Rights in Classical Liberalism*, 20 AMERICAN JOURNAL OF JURISPRUDENCE 62 (1975); Elisabeth M. Landes & Richard A. Posner, *The Economics of the Baby Shortage*, 7 JOURNAL OF LEGAL STUDIES 323 (1978); Richard A. Posner, *The Regulation of the Market in Adoption*, 67 BOSTON UNIVERSITY LAW REVIEW 59 (1987); Carol Sanger, *Developing Markets in Baby–Making: In the Matter of Baby M*, 30 HARVARD JOURNAL OF LAW & GENDER 67 (2007); Lance K. Stell, *Dueling and the Right to Life*, 90 ETHICS 7 (1979).

45. *See* § 1.5.3.

critique is that the methodology is "producing prices for things that appear to be priceless."[46] In plain English, CBA is pricing "things" that have no markets and are noncommodifiable, because society bans the trade in such "things"—human lives, endangered species, certain environmental resources, and so forth. Alternatively, when CBA "tries to mimic a basic function of markets" it underprices valuable "things." This line of criticism relates to the absence of certain markets, but does not explain the regulations that restrict trade.

Inalienability means, among other things, that an entitlement cannot be traded. People object to trade in certain entitlements for many reasons that tend to be controversial, or at least to be challenged.[47] A long and bitter battle was needed until Congress passed the Thirteenth Amendment that bans slavery, or direct trading in humans.[48] To promote temperance, the Eighteenth Amendment prohibited "the manufacture, sale, or transportation of intoxicating liquors" in the United States and its territories, making illegal markets for alcohol a lucrative business until its repeal in 1933.[49] Congress has banned marijuana outright, recognizing no permissible medical exceptions.[50] Between 1996 and 2011, however, 16 states and the District of Columbia enacted laws that effectively allow patients to use and access medical marijuana despite federal law.[51] Markets for tradable permits, also known as cap-and-trade systems, use the pricing system to mitigate externality problems.[52] Tradable permits have been a target for criticism. Some perceive the commodification of permits to be immoral.[53] Others consider the commodification of permits as an illegitimate interference with the free market.[54] Congress, states and localities have introduced a diverse range of prohibitions against trade in plastic bags, pit bulls, trans

---

46. Frank Ackerman & Lisa Heinzerling, *Pricing the Priceless: Cost–Benefit Analysis of Environmental Protection*, 150 UNIVERSITY OF PENNSYLVANIA LAW REVIEW 1553, 1558 (2002). *See also* FRANK ACKERMAN & LISA HEINZERLING, PRICELESS: ON KNOWING THE PRICE OF EVERYTHING AND THE VALUE OF NOTHING (new ed., 2005).

47. *See, e.g.*, MICHAEL J. SANDEL, WHAT MONEY CAN'T BUY: THE MORAL LIMITS OF MARKETS (2012).

48. *See generally* MICHAEL VORENBERG, FINAL FREEDOM: THE CIVIL WAR, THE ABOLITION OF SLAVERY, AND THE THIRTEENTH AMENDMENT (2004).

49. *See generally* DANIEL OKRENT, LAST CALL: THE RISE AND FALL OF PROHIBITION (2011).

50. *See* Gonzales v. Raich, 545 U.S. 1 (2005); Ernest A. Young, *Just Blowing Smoke? Politics, Doctrine, and the Federalist Revival* after *Gonzales v. Raich*, 2005 SUPREME COURT REVIEW 1 (2005).

51. *See* THE MARIJUANA POLICY PROJECT, STATE-BY STATE MEDICAL MARIJUANA LAWS 2011 (2012); Robert Mikos, *On the Limits of Supremacy: Medical Marijuana and the States' Overlooked Power to Legalize Federal Crime*, 62 VANDERBILT LAW REVIEW 1421 (2009).

52. *See generally* William J. Baumol & and Wallace E. Oates, *The Use of Standards and Prices for Protection of the Environment*, 73 SWEDISH JOURNAL OF ECONOMICS 42 (1971); W. David Montgomery, *Markets in Licenses and Efficient Pollution Control Programs*, 5 JOURNAL OF ECONOMIC THEORY 395 (1972). Daniel D. Huppert, *An Overview of Fishing Rights*, 15 REVIEWS IN FISH BIOLOGY AND FISHERIES 201 (2005).

53. *See, e.g.*, Michael J. Sandel, *It's Immoral to Buy the Right to Pollute*, N.Y. TIMES, Dec. 15, 1997, at A23; SANDEL, WHAT MONEY CAN'T BUY, *supra* note 47. *See also* Robert E. Goodin, *Selling Environmental Indulgences*, 47 KYKLOS 573 (1994).

54. *See, e.g.*, *Sarah Palin, Copenhagen's Political Science*, WASHINGTON POST, Dec. 9, 2009, at A27.

fat, child pornography, sex toys, foie gras, tobacco products, high-capacity magazines for firearms, and many other things. Such inalienability rules have been frequently challenged. Like all other things in regulation, people feel very strongly about inalienability rules that are consistent or inconsistent with their views. As John Stuart Mill pointed out:

> But on every subject on which difference of opinion is possible, the truth depends on a balance to be struck between two sets of conflicting reasons. * * * [W]e do not [always] understand the grounds of our opinion. But when we turn to * * * to morals, religion, politics, social relations, and the business of life, three-fourths of the arguments for every disputed opinion consist in dispelling the appearances which favour some opinion different from it.[55]

Public views about inalienability rules and lack thereof change over time as they change about most things. Past inalienability rules may appear overly intrusive today, and the lack of some rules in the past is shocking and outrageous today.[56] Additionally, new technologies change the frontiers of externalities in many ways—old forms of externalities can be mitigated or eliminated, and new ones emerge.

Sidebar 7–1
Human Organs

What is the meaning of organ donation? "Peripheral blood stem cell apheresis" is a method of bone marrow transplant that avoids the need to invade the bone for marrow. In *Flynn v. Holder*, the plaintiffs argued that the method was needed to save lives and challenged the constitutionality of the ban on compensation for human organs in the National Organ Transplant Act ("NOTA"), as applied to bone marrow transplants.[57] The plaintiffs were parents of sick children who had diseases such as leukemia and a rare type of anemia, which can be fatal without bone marrow transplants, and an expert in bone marrow transplantation, who said that least one out of five of his patients died because no matching bone marrow donor can be found, and that many others have suffered from complications when the scarcity of matching donors compelled him to use imperfectly matched donors. The U.S. Attorney General responded that the statute plainly classifies "bone marrow" as an organ for which compensation is prohibited, and that the congressional determination is indeed rational. Specifically, the government argued that "Congress took the view that 'human body parts should not be viewed as commodities,' and had several policy reasons for disallowing compensation to donors,' which suffice to serve as a rational basis for the prohibition."

The challenged provision provides:

§ 274e. Prohibition of organ purchases
a) Prohibition

---

55. JOHN STUART MILL, ON LIBERTY 66–67 (1859).

56. *See, e.g.*, *The Decision of the Supreme Court in the School Cases—Declaration of Constitutional Principles*, 102 CONG. REC. 4459 (Mar. 12, 1956) (statement of Sen. Walter F. George introducing "The Southern Manifesto" into the Congressional Record, voicing a displeasure with the Supreme Court's decision to integrate public schools. The Southern Manifesto was endorsed by 19 Senators and 82 members of the House of Representatives, of whom 97 were Democrats and 2 were Republicans).

57. *See* Flynn v. Holder, 684 F.3d 852 (9th Cir. 2012); the National Organ Transplant Act, Pub. L. No. 98–507, 98 Stat. 2339 (1984).

It shall be unlawful for any person to knowingly acquire, receive, or otherwise transfer any human organ for valuable consideration for use in human transplantation if the transfer affects interstate commerce. The preceding sentence does not apply with respect to human organ paired donation.

(b) Penalties

Any person who violates subsection (a) of this section shall be fined not more than $50,000 or imprisoned not more than five years, or both.

(c) Definitions

For purposes of subsection (a) of this section:

(1) The term "human organ" means the human (including fetal) kidney, liver, heart, lung, pancreas, bone marrow, cornea, eye, bone, and skin or any subpart thereof and any other human organ (or any subpart thereof, including that derived from a fetus) specified by the Secretary of Health and Human Services by regulation.

(2) The term "valuable consideration" does not include the reasonable payments associated with the removal, transportation, implantation, processing, preservation, quality control, and storage of a human organ or the expenses of travel, housing, and lost wages incurred by the donor of a human organ in connection with the donation of the organ.

* * *[58]

Bone marrow transplants enable sick patients, whose own blood cells need to be killed, to produce new blood cells and save their lives. In the past, bone marrow donations entailed intrusive procedures that exposed the donors to risk and pain (the "aspiration method"). The peripheral blood stem cell apheresis requires injections of a medication into the donor's blood. This medication accelerates blood stem cell production in the marrow, so that more stem cells go into the bloodstream. Then, blood is withdrawn from the donor's vein and filtered through an apheresis machine to extract the blood stem cells. Complications for the donor are exceedingly rare. The compensation addressed in *Flynn* was the financial offer of MoreMarrowDonors.org, a California nonprofit corporation: $3,000 awards in the form of scholarships, housing allowances, or gifts to charities selected by donors of bone marrow cells. Holding that the ban on selling bone marrow does not encompass peripheral blood stem cells obtained through apheresis, the Ninth Circuit addressed the underlying rationale behind the ban:

> The policy concerns are obvious. * * * Congress may have been concerned that if donors could be paid, rich patients or the medical industry might induce poor people to sell their organs, even when the transplant would create excessive medical risk, pain, or disability for the donor. Or, looking from the other end, Congress might have been concerned that every last cent could be extracted from sick patients needful of transplants, by well-matched potential donors making "your money or your life" offers. The existing commerce in organs extracted by force or fraud by organ thieves might be stimulated by paying for donations. Compensation to donors might also degrade the quality of the organ supply, by inducing potential donors to lie about their medical histories in order to make their organs marketable. * * * Congress may have had philosophical as well as policy reasons for prohibiting compensation. People tend to have an instinctive revulsion at denial of bodily integrity, particularly removal of flesh from a human being for use by another, and most particularly "commodification" of such conduct, that is, the sale of one's bodily tissue. * * * These reasons are in some respects vague, in some speculative, and in some arguably misplaced. There are strong arguments for

58. 42 U.S.C.A. § 274e.

> contrary views. But these policy and philosophical choices are for Congress to make, not us. The distinctions made by Congress must have a rational basis, but do not need to fit perfectly with that rational basis, and the basis need merely be rational, not persuasive to all. Here, Congress made a distinction between body material that is compensable and body material that is not. The distinction has a rational basis, so the prohibition on compensation for bone marrow donations by the aspiration method does not violate the Equal Protection Clause.

The Ninth Circuit, however, pointed out that NOTA and the regulation omit blood from the list of examples of "human organs" banned for compensated donations. Thus, the court observed that "payment for blood donations has long been common, the silence * * * on compensating blood donors is loud." The court therefore concluded:

> It may be that "bone marrow transplant" is an anachronism that will soon fade away, as peripheral blood stem cell apheresis replaces aspiration as the transplant technique, much as "dial the phone" is fading away now that telephones do not have dials. Or it may live on, as "brief" does, even though "briefs" are now lengthy arguments rather than, as they used to be, brief summaries of authorities. Either way, when the "peripheral blood stem cell apheresis" method of "bone marrow transplantation" is used, it is not a transfer of a "human organ" or a "subpart thereof" as defined by the statute and regulation, so the statute does not criminalize compensating the donor.

In the Matter of Baby M

Supreme Court of New Jersey
109 N.J. 396 (1988)

In this matter the Court is asked to determine the validity of a contract that purports to provide a new way of bringing children into a family. For a fee of $10,000, a woman agrees to be artificially inseminated with the semen of another woman's husband; she is to conceive a child, carry it to term, and after its birth surrender it to the natural father and his wife. The intent of the contract is that the child's natural mother will thereafter be forever separated from her child. The wife is to adopt the child, and she and the natural father are to be regarded as its parents for all purposes. The contract providing for this is called a "surrogacy contract," the natural mother inappropriately called the "surrogate mother."

We invalidate the surrogacy contract because it conflicts with the law and public policy of this State. While we recognize the depth of the yearning of infertile couples to have their own children, we find the payment of money to a "surrogate" mother illegal, perhaps criminal, and potentially degrading to women. Although in this case we grant custody to the natural father, the evidence having clearly proved such custody to be in the best interests of the infant, we void both the termination of the surrogate mother's parental rights and the adoption of the child by the wife/stepparent. We thus restore the "surrogate" as the mother of the child. * * *

We find no offense to our present laws where a woman voluntarily and without payment agrees to act as a "surrogate" mother, provided that she is not subject to a binding agreement to surrender her child. Moreover, our holding today does not preclude the Legislature from altering the current statutory scheme, within constitutional limits, so as to permit surrogacy contracts. Under current law, however, the surrogacy agreement before us is illegal and invalid.

I.

FACTS

In February 1985, William Stern and Mary Beth Whitehead entered into a surrogacy contract. It recited that Stern's wife, Elizabeth, was infertile, that they wanted a child, and that Mrs. Whitehead was willing to provide that child as the mother with Mr. Stern as the father.

The contract provided that through artificial insemination using Mr. Stern's sperm, Mrs. Whitehead would become pregnant, carry the child to term, bear it, deliver it to the Sterns, and thereafter do whatever was necessary to terminate her maternal rights so that Mrs. Stern could thereafter adopt the child. Mrs. Whitehead's husband, Richard,[1] was also a party to the contract; Mrs. Stern was not. Mr. Whitehead promised to do all acts necessary to rebut the presumption of paternity under the Parentage Act. * * * Although Mrs. Stern was not a party to the surrogacy agreement, the contract gave her sole custody of the child in the event of Mr. Stern's death. Mrs. Stern's status as a nonparty to the surrogate parenting agreement presumably was to avoid the application of the baby-selling statute to this arrangement. * * *

Mr. Stern, on his part, agreed to attempt the artificial insemination and to pay Mrs. Whitehead $10,000 after the child's birth, on its delivery to him. In a separate contract, Mr. Stern agreed to pay $7,500 to the Infertility Center of New York ("ICNY"). The Center's advertising campaigns solicit surrogate mothers and encourage infertile couples to consider surrogacy. ICNY arranged for the surrogacy contract by bringing the parties together, explaining the process to them, furnishing the contractual form, and providing legal counsel.

The history of the parties' involvement in this arrangement suggests their good faith. William and Elizabeth Stern were * * * married in July 1974, having met at the University of Michigan, where both were Ph.D. candidates. Due to financial considerations and Mrs. Stern's pursuit of a medical degree and residency, they decided to defer starting a family until 1981. Before then, however, Mrs. Stern learned that she might have multiple sclerosis and that the disease in some cases renders pregnancy a serious health risk. Her anxiety appears to have exceeded the actual risk, which current medical authorities assess as minimal. Nonetheless that anxiety was evidently quite real, Mrs. Stern fearing that pregnancy might precipitate blindness, paraplegia, or other forms of debilitation. Based on the perceived risk, the Sterns decided to forego having their own children. The decision had special significance for Mr. Stern. Most of his family had

1. Subsequent to the trial court proceedings, Mr. and Mrs. Whitehead were divorced, and soon thereafter Mrs. Whitehead remarried. Nevertheless, in the course of this opinion we will make reference almost exclusively to the facts as they existed at the time of trial, the facts on which the decision we now review was reached. We note moreover that Mr. Whitehead remains a party to this dispute. For these reasons, we continue to refer to appellants as Mr. and Mrs. Whitehead.

been destroyed in the Holocaust. As the family's only survivor, he very much wanted to continue his bloodline.

Initially the Sterns considered adoption, but were discouraged by the substantial delay apparently involved and by the potential problem they saw arising from their age and their differing religious backgrounds. They were most eager for some other means to start a family.

The paths of Mrs. Whitehead and the Sterns to surrogacy were similar. Both responded to advertising by ICNY. The Sterns' response, following their inquiries into adoption, was the result of their long-standing decision to have a child. Mrs. Whitehead's response apparently resulted from her sympathy with family members and others who could have no children (she stated that she wanted to give another couple the "gift of life"); she also wanted the $10,000 to help her family.

Both parties, undoubtedly because of their own self-interest, were less sensitive to the implications of the transaction than they might otherwise have been. Mrs. Whitehead, for instance, appears not to have been concerned about whether the Sterns would make good parents for her child; the Sterns, on their part, while conscious of the obvious possibility that surrendering the child might cause grief to Mrs. Whitehead, overcame their qualms because of their desire for a child. At any rate, both the Sterns and Mrs. Whitehead were committed to the arrangement; both thought it right and constructive.

Mrs. Whitehead had reached her decision concerning surrogacy before the Sterns, and had actually been involved as a potential surrogate mother with another couple. After numerous unsuccessful artificial inseminations, that effort was abandoned. Thereafter, the Sterns learned of the Infertility Center, the possibilities of surrogacy, and of Mary Beth Whitehead. The two couples met to discuss the surrogacy arrangement and decided to go forward. On February 6, 1985, Mr. Stern and Mr. and Mrs. Whitehead executed the surrogate parenting agreement. After several artificial inseminations over a period of months, Mrs. Whitehead became pregnant. The pregnancy was uneventful and on March 27, 1986, Baby M was born.

Not wishing anyone at the hospital to be aware of the surrogacy arrangement, Mr. and Mrs. Whitehead appeared to all as the proud parents of a healthy female child. Her birth certificate indicated her name to be Sara Elizabeth Whitehead and her father to be Richard Whitehead. In accordance with Mrs. Whitehead's request, the Sterns visited the hospital unobtrusively to see the newborn child.

Mrs. Whitehead realized, almost from the moment of birth, that she could not part with this child. She had felt a bond with it even during pregnancy. Some indication of the attachment was conveyed to the Sterns at the hospital when they told Mrs. Whitehead what they were going to name the baby. She apparently broke into tears and indicated that she did not know if she could give up the child. She talked about how the baby looked like her other daughter, and made it clear that she was experiencing great difficulty with the decision.

Nonetheless, Mrs. Whitehead was, for the moment, true to her word. Despite powerful inclinations to the contrary, she turned her child over to the Sterns on March 30 at the Whiteheads' home.

The Sterns were thrilled with their new child. They had planned extensively for its arrival, far beyond the practical furnishing of a room for her. It was a time of joyful celebration—not just for them but for their friends as well. The Sterns looked forward to raising their daughter, whom they named Melissa. While aware by then that Mrs. Whitehead was undergoing an emotional crisis, they were as yet not cognizant of the depth of that crisis and its implications for their newly-enlarged family.

Later in the evening of March 30, Mrs. Whitehead became deeply disturbed, disconsolate, stricken with unbearable sadness. She had to have her child. She could not eat, sleep, or concentrate on anything other than her need for her baby. The next day she went to the Sterns' home and told them how much she was suffering.

The depth of Mrs. Whitehead's despair surprised and frightened the Sterns. She told them that she could not live without her baby, that she must have her, even if only for one week, that thereafter she would surrender her child. The Sterns, concerned that Mrs. Whitehead might indeed commit suicide, not wanting under any circumstances to risk that, and in any event believing that Mrs. Whitehead would keep her word, turned the child over to her. It was not until four months later, after a series of attempts to regain possession of the child, that Melissa was returned to the Sterns, having been forcibly removed from the home where she was then living with Mr. and Mrs. Whitehead, the home in Florida owned by Mary Beth Whitehead's parents.

The struggle over Baby M began when it became apparent that Mrs. Whitehead could not return the child to Mr. Stern. Due to Mrs. Whitehead's refusal to relinquish the baby, Mr. Stern filed a complaint seeking enforcement of the surrogacy contract. He alleged, accurately, that Mrs. Whitehead had not only refused to comply with the surrogacy contract but had threatened to flee from New Jersey with the child in order to avoid even the possibility of his obtaining custody. * * *

The Whiteheads immediately fled to Florida with Baby M. They stayed initially with Mrs. Whitehead's parents, where one of Mrs. Whitehead's children had been living. For the next three months, the Whiteheads and Melissa lived at roughly twenty different hotels, motels, and homes in order to avoid apprehension. From time to time Mrs. Whitehead would call Mr. Stern to discuss the matter; the conversations, recorded by Mr. Stern on advice of counsel, show an escalating dispute about rights, morality, and power, accompanied by threats of Mrs. Whitehead to kill herself, to kill the child, and falsely to accuse Mr. Stern of sexually molesting Mrs. Whitehead's other daughter.

Eventually the Sterns discovered where the Whiteheads were staying. * * * Police in Florida * * * forcibly remov[ed] the child from her grandparents' home. She was soon thereafter brought to New Jersey and turned over to the Sterns. * * * Mrs. Whitehead was awarded limited visitation with Baby M.

The Sterns' complaint, in addition to seeking possession and ultimately custody of the child, sought enforcement of the surrogacy contract. Pursuant to the contract, it asked that the child be permanently placed in their custody, that Mrs. Whitehead's parental rights be terminated, and that Mrs. Stern be allowed to adopt the child, *i.e.,* that, for all purposes, Melissa become the Sterns' child.

The trial took thirty-two days over a period of more than two months. * * * Soon after the conclusion of the trial, the trial court announced its opinion from the bench. * * * It held that the surrogacy contract was valid; ordered that Mrs. Whitehead's parental rights be terminated and that sole custody of the child be granted to Mr. Stern; and, after hearing brief testimony from Mrs. Stern, immediately entered an order allowing the adoption of Melissa by Mrs. Stern, all in accordance with the surrogacy contract. Pending the outcome of the appeal, we granted a continuation of visitation to Mrs. Whitehead, although slightly more limited than the visitation allowed during the trial. * * *

Mrs. Whitehead appealed. * * *

II.

INVALIDITY AND UNENFORCEABILITY OF SURROGACY CONTRACT

We have concluded that this surrogacy contract is invalid. Our conclusion has two bases: direct conflict with existing statutes and conflict with the public policies of this State, as expressed in its statutory and decisional law.

One of the surrogacy contract's basic purposes, to achieve the adoption of a child through private placement, though permitted in New Jersey "is very much disfavored." *Sees v. Baber*, 74 N.J. 201, 217 (1977). Its use of money for this purpose—and we have no doubt whatsoever that the money is being paid to obtain an adoption and not, as the Sterns argue, for the personal services of Mary Beth Whitehead—is illegal and perhaps criminal. * * * In addition to the inducement of money, there is the coercion of contract: the natural mother's irrevocable agreement, prior to birth, even prior to conception, to surrender the child to the adoptive couple. Such an agreement is totally unenforceable in private placement adoption. * * * Even where the adoption is through an approved agency, the formal agreement to surrender occurs only *after* birth * * *, and then, by regulation, only after the birth mother has been offered counseling. * * * Integral to these invalid provisions of the surrogacy contract is the related agreement, equally invalid, on the part of the natural mother to cooperate with, and not to contest, proceedings to terminate her parental rights, as well as her contractual concession, in aid of the adoption, that the child's best interests would be served by awarding custody to the natural father and his wife—all of this before she has even conceived, and, in some cases, before she has the slightest idea of what the natural father and adoptive mother are like.

The foregoing provisions not only directly conflict with New Jersey statutes, but also offend long-established State policies. These critical terms, which are at the heart of the contract, are invalid and unenforceable; the conclusion therefore follows, without more, that the entire contract is unenforceable.

A. Conflict with Statutory Provisions

The surrogacy contract conflicts with: (1) laws prohibiting the use of money in connection with adoptions; (2) laws requiring proof of parental unfitness or abandonment before termination of parental rights is ordered or an adoption is granted; and (3) laws that make surrender of custody and consent to adoption revocable in private placement adoptions.

(1) Our law prohibits paying or accepting money in connection with any placement of a child for adoption. *N.J.S.A.* 9:3–54a. Violation is a high misdemeanor. *N.J.S.A.* 9:3–54c. Excepted are fees of an approved agency (which must be a non-profit entity, *N.J.S.A.* 9:3–38a) and certain expenses in connection with childbirth. *N.J.S.A.* 9:3–54b.[4]

Considerable care was taken in this case to structure the surrogacy arrangement so as not to violate this prohibition. The arrangement was structured as follows: the adopting parent, Mrs. Stern, was not a party to the surrogacy contract; the money paid to Mrs. Whitehead was stated to be for her services—not for the adoption; the sole purpose of the contract was stated as being that "of giving a child to William Stern, its natural and biological father"; the money was purported to be "compensation for services and expenses and in no way . . . a fee for termination of parental rights or a payment in exchange for consent to surrender a child for adoption"; the fee to the Infertility Center ($7,500) was stated to be for legal representation, advice, administrative work, and other "services." Nevertheless, it seems clear that the money was paid and accepted in connection with an adoption.

The Infertility Center's major role was first as a "finder" of the surrogate mother whose child was to be adopted, and second as the arranger of all proceedings that led to the adoption. Its role as adoption finder is demonstrated by the provision requiring Mr. Stern to pay another $7,500 if he uses Mary Beth Whitehead again as a surrogate, and by ICNY's agreement to "coordinate arrangements for the adoption of the child by the

---

4. N.J.S.A. 9:3–54 reads as follows:

a. No person, firm, partnership, corporation, association or agency shall make, offer to make or assist or participate in any placement for adoption and in connection therewith

(1) Pay, give or agree to give any money or any valuable consideration, or assume or discharge any financial obligation; or

(2) Take, receive, accept or agree to accept any money or any valuable consideration.

b. The prohibition of subsection a. shall not apply to the fees or services of any approved agency in connection with a placement for adoption, nor shall such prohibition apply to the payment or reimbursement of medical, hospital or other similar expenses incurred in connection with the birth or any illness of the child, or to the acceptance of such reimbursement by a parent of the child.

c. Any person, firm, partnership, corporation, association or agency violating this section shall be guilty of a high misdemeanor.

wife." The surrogacy agreement requires Mrs. Whitehead to surrender Baby M for the purposes of adoption. The agreement notes that Mr. *and Mrs.* Stern wanted to have a child, and provides that the child be "placed" with Mrs. Stern in the event Mr. Stern dies before the child is born. The payment of the $10,000 occurs only on surrender of custody of the child and "completion of the duties and obligations" of Mrs. Whitehead, including termination of her parental rights to facilitate adoption by Mrs. Stern. * * *

Mr. Stern knew he was paying for the adoption of a child; Mrs. Whitehead knew she was accepting money so that a child might be adopted; the Infertility Center knew that it was being paid for assisting in the adoption of a child. The actions of all three worked to frustrate the goals of the statute. It strains credulity to claim that these arrangements, touted by those in the surrogacy business as an attractive alternative to the usual route leading to an adoption, really amount to something other than a private placement adoption for money.

The prohibition of our statute is strong. Violation constitutes a high misdemeanor, *N.J.S.A.* 9:3–54c, a third-degree crime, * * * carrying a penalty of three to five years imprisonment. * * * The evils inherent in baby-bartering are loathsome for a myriad of reasons. The child is sold without regard for whether the purchasers will be suitable parents. * * * The natural mother does not receive the benefit of counseling and guidance to assist her in making a decision that may affect her for a lifetime. In fact, the monetary incentive to sell her child may, depending on her financial circumstances, make her decision less voluntary. * * * Furthermore, the adoptive parents may not be fully informed of the natural parents' medical history.

Baby-selling potentially results in the exploitation of all parties involved. Conversely, adoption statutes seek to further humanitarian goals, foremost among them the best interests of the child. * * * The negative consequences of baby-buying are potentially present in the surrogacy context, especially the potential for placing and adopting a child without regard to the interest of the child or the natural mother.

(2) The termination of Mrs. Whitehead's parental rights, called for by the surrogacy contract and actually ordered by the court, * * * fails to comply with the stringent requirements of New Jersey law. Our law, recognizing the finality of any termination of parental rights, provides for such termination only where there has been a voluntary surrender of a child to an approved agency or to the Division of Youth and Family Services ("DYFS"), accompanied by a formal document acknowledging termination of parental rights, * * * or where there has been a showing of parental abandonment or unfitness. A termination may ordinarily take one of three forms: an action by an approved agency, an action by DYFS, or an action in connection with a private placement adoption. The three are governed by separate statutes, but the standards for termination are substantially the same, except that whereas a written surrender is effective when made to an approved agency or to DYFS, there is no provision for it in the private placement context. * * *

In this case a termination of parental rights was obtained not by proving the statutory prerequisites but by claiming the benefit of contractual provisions. [A] contractual agreement to abandon one's parental rights, or not to contest a termination action, will not be enforced in our courts. The Legislature would not have so carefully, so consistently, and so substantially restricted termination of parental rights if it had intended to allow termination to be achieved by one short sentence in a contract.

Since the termination was invalid, it follows, as noted above, that adoption of Melissa by Mrs. Stern could not properly be granted.

(3) The provision in the surrogacy contract stating that Mary Beth Whitehead agrees to "surrender custody ... and terminate all parental rights" contains no clause giving her a right to rescind. It is intended to be an irrevocable consent to surrender the child for adoption—in other words, an irrevocable commitment by Mrs. Whitehead to turn Baby M over to the Sterns and thereafter to allow termination of her parental rights. The trial court required a "best interests" showing as a condition to granting specific performance of the surrogacy contract. * * * Having decided the "best interests" issue in favor of the Sterns, that court's order included, among other things, specific performance of this agreement to surrender custody and terminate all parental rights.

Mrs. Whitehead, shortly after the child's birth, had attempted to revoke her consent and surrender by refusing, after the Sterns had allowed her to have the child "just for one week," to return Baby M to them. The trial court's award of specific performance therefore reflects its view that the consent to surrender the child was irrevocable. We accept the trial court's construction of the contract; indeed it appears quite clear that this was the parties' intent. Such a provision, however, making irrevocable the natural mother's consent to surrender custody of her child in a private placement adoption, clearly conflicts with New Jersey law.

* * *

It is clear that the Legislature so carefully circumscribed all aspects of a consent to surrender custody—its form and substance, its manner of execution, and the agency or agencies to which it may be made—in order to provide the basis for irrevocability. It seems most unlikely that the Legislature intended that a consent not complying with these requirements would also be irrevocable, especially where, as here, that consent falls radically short of compliance. * * *

These strict prerequisites to irrevocability constitute a recognition of the most serious consequences that flow from such consents: termination of parental rights, the permanent separation of parent from child, and the ultimate adoption of the child. * * * Because of those consequences, the Legislature severely limited the circumstances under which such consent would be irrevocable. * * *

Contractual surrender of parental rights is not provided for in our statutes as now written. * * * There is no doubt that a contractual provision purporting to constitute an irrevocable agreement to surrender custody of a child for adoption is invalid.

* * *

B. Public Policy Considerations

The surrogacy contract's invalidity * * * is further underlined when its goals and means are measured against New Jersey's public policy. The contract's basic premise, that the natural parents can decide in advance of birth which one is to have custody of the child, bears no relationship to the settled law that the child's best interests shall determine custody. * * * The fact that the trial court remedied that aspect of the contract through the "best interests" phase does not make the contractual provision any less offensive to the public policy of this State.

The surrogacy contract guarantees permanent separation of the child from one of its natural parents. Our policy, however, has long been that to the extent possible, children should remain with and be brought up by both of their natural parents. * * * This is not simply some theoretical ideal that in practice has no meaning. The impact of failure to follow that policy is nowhere better shown than in the results of this surrogacy contract. A child, instead of starting off its life with as much peace and security as possible, finds itself immediately in a tug-of-war between contending mother and father.[9]

The surrogacy contract violates the policy of this State that the rights of natural parents are equal concerning their child, the father's right no greater than the mother's. * * *

The policies expressed in our comprehensive laws governing consent to the surrender of a child * * * stand in stark contrast to the surrogacy contract and what it implies. Here there is no counseling, independent or otherwise, of the natural mother, no evaluation, no warning.

The only legal advice Mary Beth Whitehead received regarding the surrogacy contract was provided in connection with the contract that she previously entered into with another couple. Mrs. Whitehead's lawyer was referred to her by the Infertility Center, with which he had an agreement to act as counsel for surrogate candidates. His services consisted of spending one hour going through the contract with the Whiteheads, section by section, and answering their questions. Mrs. Whitehead received no further legal advice prior to signing the contract with the Sterns.

Mrs. Whitehead was examined and psychologically evaluated, but if it was for her benefit, the record does not disclose that fact. The Sterns regarded the evaluation as important, particularly in connection with the question of whether she would change her mind. Yet they never asked to see it, and were content with the assumption that the Infertility Center had made an evaluation and had concluded that there was no danger that the surrogate mother would change her mind. From Mrs. Whitehead's point of view, all that she learned from the evaluation was that "she had passed." It

---

9. And the impact on the natural parents, Mr. Stern and Mrs. Whitehead, is severe and dramatic. The depth of their conflict about Baby M, about custody, visitation, about the goodness or badness of each of them, comes through in their telephone conversations, in which each tried to persuade the other to give up the child. The potential adverse consequences of surrogacy are poignantly captured here—Mrs. Whitehead threatening to kill herself and the baby, Mr. Stern begging her not to, each blaming the other. The dashed hopes of the Sterns, the agony of Mrs. Whitehead, their suffering, their hatred—all were caused by the unraveling of this arrangement.

is apparent that the profit motive got the better of the Infertility Center. * * *

Under the contract, the natural mother is irrevocably committed before she knows the strength of her bond with her child. She never makes a totally voluntary, informed decision, for quite clearly any decision prior to the baby's birth is, in the most important sense, uninformed, and any decision after that, compelled by a pre-existing contractual commitment, the threat of a lawsuit, and the inducement of a $10,000 payment, is less than totally voluntary. Her interests are of little concern to those who controlled this transaction.

Although the interest of the natural father and adoptive mother is certainly the predominant interest, realistically the *only* interest served, even they are left with less than what public policy requires. They know little about the natural mother, her genetic makeup, and her psychological and medical history. Moreover, not even a superficial attempt is made to determine their awareness of their responsibilities as parents.

Worst of all, however, is the contract's total disregard of the best interests of the child. There is not the slightest suggestion that any inquiry will be made at any time to determine the fitness of the Sterns as custodial parents, of Mrs. Stern as an adoptive parent, their superiority to Mrs. Whitehead, or the effect on the child of not living with her natural mother.

This is the sale of a child, or, at the very least, the sale of a mother's right to her child, the only mitigating factor being that one of the purchasers is the father. Almost every evil that prompted the prohibition on the payment of money in connection with adoptions exists here.

The differences between an adoption and a surrogacy contract should be noted, since it is asserted that the use of money in connection with surrogacy does not pose the risks found where money buys an adoption. * * *

First, and perhaps most important, all parties concede that it is unlikely that surrogacy will survive without money. Despite the alleged selfless motivation of surrogate mothers, if there is no payment, there will be no surrogates, or very few. That conclusion contrasts with adoption; for obvious reasons, there remains a steady supply, albeit insufficient, despite the prohibitions against payment. The adoption itself, relieving the natural mother of the financial burden of supporting an infant, is in some sense the equivalent of payment.

Second, the use of money in adoptions does not *produce* the problem—conception occurs, and usually the birth itself, before illicit funds are offered. With surrogacy, the "problem," if one views it as such, consisting of the purchase of a woman's procreative capacity, at the risk of her life, is caused by and originates with the offer of money.

Third, with the law prohibiting the use of money in connection with adoptions, the built-in financial pressure of the unwanted pregnancy and the consequent support obligation do not lead the mother to the highest paying, ill-suited, adoptive parents. She is just as well-off surrendering the child to an approved agency. In surrogacy, the highest bidders will presumably become the adoptive parents regardless of suitability, so long as payment of money is permitted.

Fourth, the mother's consent to surrender her child in adoptions is revocable, even after surrender of the child, unless it be to an approved agency, where by regulation there are protections against an ill-advised surrender. In surrogacy, consent occurs so early that no amount of advice would satisfy the potential mother's need, yet the consent is irrevocable.

The main difference, that the unwanted pregnancy is unintended while the situation of the surrogate mother is voluntary and intended, is really not significant. * * *

Intimated, but disputed, is the assertion that surrogacy will be used for the benefit of the rich at the expense of the poor. *See, e.g.*, Radin, "*Market Inalienability*," 100 HARVARD LAW REVIEW 1849, 1930 (1987). In response it is noted that the Sterns are not rich and the Whiteheads not poor. Nevertheless, it is clear to us that it is unlikely that surrogate mothers will be as proportionately numerous among those women in the top twenty percent income bracket as among those in the bottom twenty percent. Put differently, we doubt that infertile couples in the low-income bracket will find upper income surrogates.

In any event, even in this case one should not pretend that disparate wealth does not play a part simply because the contrast is not the dramatic "rich versus poor." At the time of trial, the Whiteheads' net assets were probably negative—Mrs. Whitehead's own sister was foreclosing on a second mortgage. Their income derived from Mr. Whitehead's labors. Mrs. Whitehead is a homemaker, having previously held part-time jobs. The Sterns are both professionals, she a medical doctor, he a biochemist. Their combined income when both were working was about $89,500 a year and their assets sufficient to pay for the surrogacy contract arrangements.

The point is made that Mrs. Whitehead *agreed* to the surrogacy arrangement, supposedly fully understanding the consequences. Putting aside the issue of how compelling her need for money may have been, and how significant her understanding of the consequences, we suggest that her consent is irrelevant. There are, in a civilized society, some things that money cannot buy. In America, we decided long ago that merely because conduct purchased by money was "voluntary" did not mean that it was good or beyond regulation and prohibition. * * * Employers can no longer buy labor at the lowest price they can bargain for, even though that labor is "voluntary," * * * or buy women's labor for less money than paid to men for the same job, * * * or purchase the agreement of children to perform oppressive labor, * * * or purchase the agreement of workers to subject themselves to unsafe or unhealthful working conditions. * * * There are, in short, values that society deems more important than granting to wealth whatever it can buy, be it labor, love, or life. Whether this principle recommends prohibition of surrogacy, which presumably sometimes results in great satisfaction to all of the parties, is not for us to say. We note here only that, under existing law, the fact that Mrs. Whitehead "agreed" to the arrangement is not dispositive.

The long-term effects of surrogacy contracts are not known, but feared—the impact on the child who learns her life was bought, that she is the offspring of someone who gave birth to her only to obtain money; the impact on the natural mother as the full weight of her isolation is felt along with the full reality of the sale of her body and her child; the impact on the natural father and adoptive mother once they realize the consequences of their conduct. * * *

In sum, the harmful consequences of this surrogacy arrangement appear to us all too palpable. In New Jersey the surrogate mother's agreement to sell her child is void. Its irrevocability infects the entire contract, as does the money that purports to buy it.

III.

TERMINATION

* * * Nothing in this record justifies a finding that would allow a court to terminate Mary Beth Whitehead's parental rights under the statutory standard. * * * There is simply no basis * * * in the statute * * * to warrant termination of Mrs. Whitehead's parental rights. We therefore conclude that the natural mother is entitled to retain her rights as a mother.

* * *

V.

CUSTODY

* * * In this case, the trial court, believing that the surrogacy contract might be valid, and faced with the probable flight from the jurisdiction by Mrs. Whitehead and the baby if *any* notice were served, ordered, *ex parte,* * * * that custody be transferred immediately to Mr. Stern, rather than order[ed] Mrs. Whitehead not to leave the State. * * * Even her threats to flee should not suffice to warrant any other relief unless her unfitness is clearly shown. At most, it should result in an order enjoining such flight. The erroneous transfer of custody, as we view it, represents a greater risk to the child than removal to a foreign jurisdiction, unless parental unfitness is clearly proved. Furthermore, we deem it likely that, advised of the law and knowing that her custody cannot seriously be challenged at this stage of the litigation, surrogate mothers will obey any court order to remain in the jurisdiction.

VI.

VISITATION

* * * We * * * remand the visitation issue to the trial court for an abbreviated hearing and determination. * * *

CONCLUSION

This case affords some insight into a new reproductive arrangement: the artificial insemination of a surrogate mother. The unfortunate events that have unfolded illustrate that its unregulated use can bring suffering to all involved. Potential victims include the surrogate mother and her family, the natural father and his wife, and most importantly, the child. Although surrogacy has apparently provided positive results for some infertile couples, it can also, as this case demonstrates, cause suffering to participants, here essentially innocent and well-intended.

We have found that our present laws do not permit the surrogacy contract used in this case. Nowhere, however, do we find any legal prohibition against surrogacy when the surrogate mother volunteers, without any payment, to act as a surrogate and is given the right to change her mind and to assert her parental rights. Moreover, the Legislature remains free to deal with this most sensitive issue as it sees fit, subject only to constitutional constraints.

If the Legislature decides to address surrogacy, consideration of this case will highlight many of its potential harms. We do not underestimate the difficulties of legislating on this subject. In addition to the inevitable confrontation with the ethical and moral issues involved, there is the question of the wisdom and effectiveness of regulating a matter so private, yet of such public interest. Legislative consideration of surrogacy may also provide the opportunity to begin to focus on the overall implications of the new reproductive biotechnology—*in vitro* fertilization, preservation of sperm and eggs, embryo implantation and the like. The problem is how to enjoy the benefits of the technology—especially for infertile couples—while minimizing the risk of abuse. The problem can be addressed only when society decides what its values and objectives are in this troubling, yet promising, area.

Questions

1. What is the rationale for the prohibition against transactions in kids ("private placement adoption for money") according to the court in *Baby M*? Is there any cure for the reasons behind the prohibition?

2. In a provocative 1978 article Elisabeth Landes and Richard Posner criticized the regulation of child adoption, noting that the 1970s witnessed a "rapid development of the economic analysis of nonmarket behavior."[59] Prior to that article, Professor Posner had published several influential articles about the economics of regulation.[60] Landed and Posner's starting point was premise that the government could not do "a good job [in] regulating nonmarket behavior." They further explained that "if anything, the negative presumption created by numerous studies of economic regulation should carry over to the nonmarket sphere." To illuminate their view of burden of the regulatory system Landes and Posner opened their article writing:

> Sometimes natural parents do not want to raise their child; the typical case is where the birth is illegitimate. And in some cases

---

59. Elisabeth M. Landes & Richard A. Posner, *The Economics of the Baby Shortage*, 7 JOURNAL OF LEGAL STUDIES 323 (1978). *See also* Richard A. Posner, *The Regulation of the Market in Adoptions*, 67 BOSTON UNIVERSITY LAW REVIEW 59 (1987).

60. *See, e.g.*, Richard A. Posner, *Natural Monopoly and its Regulation*, 21 STANFORD LAW REVIEW 548 (1969); Richard A. Posner, *Theories of Economic Regulation*, 5 BELL JOURNAL OF ECONOMICS & MANAGEMENT SCIENCE 335 (1974).

> where the natural parents do raise the child initially, their custody is later terminated for one reason or another—death or other incapacity, abuse, or extreme indigence. In either case—the unwanted infant or the abused, neglected, or abandoned child—there are potential gains from trade from transferring the custody of the child to a new set of parents. Where the new parents assume full parental rights and obligations over the child, one speaks of adoption; where they obtain simply a temporary custody (usually being partially compensated for their custodial services by the state), one speaks of foster care. An alternative to foster care in a home is foster care in an institution. Ordinarily, potential gains from trade are realized by a process of voluntary transacting—by a sale, in other words. Adoptions could in principle be handled through the market and in practice, * * * there is a considerable amount of baby selling. But because public policy is opposed to the sale of babies, such sales as do occur constitute a "black market."

Do regulatory inefficiencies justify a repeal of *all* bans? Do black markets necessarily suggest that inalienability rules are unwarranted? Should we carry over premises regarding economic regulation to the nonmarket sphere?

3. In 1989, reviewing the *Baby M* decision, Judge Richard Posner concluded that "[s]o deficient is the court's reasoning that the explanation of its result must be sought elsewhere than in the analytical pros and cons of enforceable contracts of surrogate motherhood."[61] Judge Posner argued that "[t]he case for allowing people to make legally enforceable contracts of surrogate motherhood is straightforward. Such contracts would not be made unless the parties to them believed that surrogacy would be mutually beneficial." How did the *Baby M* court address this argument?

4. In May 2009, Judge Richard Posner[62] published his personal lessons from and reflections on the Great Recession in the book *A Failure of Capitalism*.[63] In his book Judge Posner concluded that "the depression [was] the result of normal business activity in a laissez-faire economic regime,"[64] since "rational maximization by businessmen and consumers, all pursuing their self-interest more or less intelligently within a framework of property and contract rights, can set the stage for an economic catastrophe."[65]

Considering this conclusion, is Judge Posner likely to maintain his 1989 critique of the *Baby M* decision? Is he likely to maintain his general critique of restrictions on surrogacy contracts?

---

61. Richard A. Posner, *The Ethics and Economics of Enforcing Contracts of Surrogate Motherhood*, 5 JOURNAL OF CONTEMPORARY HEALTH LAW AND POLICY 21, 31 (1989).

62. Professor Richard Posner was a judicial nominee to the Seventh Circuit of President Ronald Reagan. He assumed office in December 1981.

63. RICHARD A. POSNER, A FAILURE OF CAPITALISM: THE CRISIS OF '08 AND THE DESCENT INTO DEPRESSION (2009).

64. *Id.* at 235.

65. *Id.* at 111–112.

§ 7.3.2 *Suppression of Information*

Insufficient information impedes the functioning of markets. By extension, rather than banning transactions, the state can suppress information and supposedly accomplish a similar goal.

44 Liquormart, Inc. v. Rhode Island

517 U.S. 484 (1996)

■ JUSTICE STEVENS announced the judgment of the Court and delivered the opinion of the Court with respect to Parts I, II, VII, and VIII, an opinion with respect to Parts III and V, in which JUSTICE KENNEDY, JUSTICE SOUTER, and JUSTICE GINSBURG join, an opinion with respect to Part VI, in which JUSTICE KENNEDY, JUSTICE THOMAS, and JUSTICE GINSBURG join, and an opinion with respect to Part IV, in which JUSTICE KENNEDY and JUSTICE GINSBURG join.

We * * * hold that Rhode Island's statutory prohibition against advertisements that provide the public with accurate information about retail prices of alcoholic beverages is * * * invalid. Our holding rests on the conclusion that such an advertising ban is an abridgment of speech protected by the First Amendment and that it is not shielded from constitutional scrutiny by the Twenty-first Amendment.

I

In 1956, the Rhode Island Legislature enacted two separate prohibitions against advertising the retail price of alcoholic beverages. The first applies to vendors licensed in Rhode Island as well as to out-of-state manufacturers, wholesalers, and shippers. It prohibits them from "advertising in any manner whatsoever" the price of any alcoholic beverage offered for sale in the State; the only exception is for price tags or signs displayed with the merchandise within licensed premises and not visible from the street.[2] The second statute applies to the Rhode Island news media. It contains a categorical prohibition against the publication or broadcast of any advertisements-even those referring to sales in other States-that "make reference to the price of any alcoholic beverages."[3]

---

2. Rhode Island Gen. Laws § 3–8–7 (1987) provides:

"Advertising price of malt beverages, cordials, wine or distilled liquor.-No manufacturer, wholesaler, or shipper from without this state and no holder of a license issued under the provisions of this title and chapter shall cause or permit the advertising in any manner whatsoever of the price of any malt beverage, cordials, wine or distilled liquor offered for sale in this state; provided, however, that the provisions of this section shall not apply to price signs or tags attached to or placed on merchandise for sale within the licensed premises in accordance with rules and regulations of the department."

Regulation 32 of the Rules and Regulations of the Liquor Control Administrator provides that no placard or sign that is visible from the exterior of a package store may make any reference to the price of any alcoholic beverage. * * *

3. Rhode Island Gen. Laws § 3–8–8.1 (1987) provides:

"Price advertising by media or advertising companies unlawful.—No newspaper, periodical, radio or television broadcaster or broadcasting company or any other

* * *

II

Petitioners 44 Liquormart, Inc. (44 Liquormart), and Peoples Super Liquor Stores, Inc. (Peoples), are licensed retailers of alcoholic beverages. Petitioner 44 Liquormart operates a store in Rhode Island and petitioner Peoples operates several stores in Massachusetts that are patronized by Rhode Island residents. Peoples uses alcohol price advertising extensively in Massachusetts, where such advertising is permitted, but Rhode Island newspapers and other media outlets have refused to accept such ads.

Complaints from competitors about an advertisement placed by 44 Liquormart in a Rhode Island newspaper in 1991 generated enforcement proceedings that in turn led to the initiation of this litigation. The advertisement did not state the price of any alcoholic beverages. Indeed, it noted that "State law prohibits advertising liquor prices." The ad did, however, state the low prices at which peanuts, potato chips, and Schweppes mixers were being offered, identify various brands of packaged liquor, and include the word "WOW" in large letters next to pictures of vodka and rum bottles. Based on the conclusion that the implied reference to bargain prices for liquor violated the statutory ban on price advertising, the Rhode Island Liquor Control Administrator assessed a $400 fine.

After paying the fine, 44 Liquormart, joined by Peoples, filed this action against the administrator in the Federal District Court seeking a declaratory judgment that the two statutes and the administrator's implementing regulations violate the First Amendment and other provisions of federal law. * * *

[T]he District Judge * * * concluded that the price advertising ban was unconstitutional because it did not "directly advance" the State's interest in reducing alcohol consumption and was "more extensive than necessary to serve that interest." * * *

The Court of Appeals reversed. * * * We * * * granted certiorari.

III

Advertising has been a part of our culture throughout our history. * * * [It] was not until the 1970's, however, that this Court held that the First Amendment protected the dissemination of truthful and nonmisleading commercial messages about lawful products and services. * * *

Virginia State Board v. Virginia Citizens Consumer Council, Inc., 425 U.S. 748 (1976), reflected the conclusion that * * * the public's interest in receiving accurate commercial information, also supports an interpretation of the First Amendment that provides constitutional protection for the

---

person, firm or corporation with a principal place of business in the state of Rhode Island which is engaged in the business of advertising or selling advertising time or space shall accept, publish, or broadcast any advertisement in this state of the price or make reference to the price of any alcoholic beverages. Any person who shall violate any of the provisions of this section shall be guilty of a misdemeanor...." * * *

dissemination of accurate and nonmisleading commercial messages. We explained:

> "Advertising, however tasteless and excessive it sometimes may seem, is nonetheless dissemination of information as to who is producing and selling what product, for what reason, and at what price. So long as we preserve a predominantly free enterprise economy, the allocation of our resources in large measure will be made through numerous private economic decisions. It is a matter of public interest that those decisions, in the aggregate, be intelligent and well informed. To this end, the free flow of commercial information is indispensable."

The opinion further explained that a State's paternalistic assumption that the public will use truthful, nonmisleading commercial information unwisely cannot justify a decision to suppress it:

> "There is, of course, an alternative to this highly paternalistic approach. That alternative is to assume that this information is not in itself harmful, that people will perceive their own best interests if only they are well enough informed, and that the best means to that end is to open the channels of communication rather than to close them. If they are truly open, nothing prevents the 'professional' pharmacist from marketing his own assertedly superior product, and contrasting it with that of the low-cost, high-volume prescription drug retailer. But the choice among these alternative approaches is not ours to make or the Virginia General Assembly's. It is precisely this kind of choice, between the dangers of suppressing information, and the dangers of its misuse if it is freely available, that the First Amendment makes for us." *Id.*, at 770.

On the basis of these principles, our early cases uniformly struck down several broadly based bans on truthful, nonmisleading commercial speech, each of which served ends unrelated to consumer protection. * * *

Virginia Bd. of Pharmacy attributed the State's authority to impose [some types of commercial advertising] regulations in part to certain "common sense differences" that exist between commercial messages and other types of protected expression. * * * Our opinion noted that the greater "objectivity" of commercial speech justifies affording the State more freedom to distinguish false commercial advertisements from true ones, and that the greater "hardiness" of commercial speech, inspired as it is by the profit motive, likely diminishes the chilling effect that may attend its regulation, ibid.

* * *

In *Central Hudson Gas & Elec. Corp. v. Public Serv. Comm'n of N.Y.*, 447 U.S. 557 (1980), we * * * considered a regulation "completely" banning all promotional advertising by electric utilities. Our decision acknowledged the special features of commercial speech but identified the serious

First Amendment concerns that attend blanket advertising prohibitions that do not protect consumers from commercial harms.

Five Members of the Court recognized that the state interest in the conservation of energy was substantial, and that there was "an immediate connection between advertising and demand for electricity." * * * Nevertheless, they concluded that the regulation was invalid because respondent commission had failed to make a showing that a more limited speech regulation would not have adequately served the State's interest.[9]

In reaching its conclusion, the majority explained that although the special nature of commercial speech may require less than strict review of its regulation, special concerns arise from "regulations that entirely suppress commercial speech in order to pursue a nonspeech-related policy." In those circumstances, "a ban on speech could screen from public view the underlying governmental policy." * * *

IV

As our review of the case law reveals, Rhode Island errs in concluding that *all* commercial speech regulations are subject to a similar form of constitutional review simply because they target a similar category of expression. The mere fact that messages propose commercial transactions does not in and of itself dictate the constitutional analysis that should apply to decisions to suppress them. * * *

When a State regulates commercial messages to protect consumers from misleading, deceptive, or aggressive sales practices, or requires the disclosure of beneficial consumer information, the purpose of its regulation is consistent with the reasons for according constitutional protection to commercial speech and therefore justifies less than strict review. However, when a State entirely prohibits the dissemination of truthful, nonmisleading commercial messages for reasons unrelated to the preservation of a fair bargaining process, there is far less reason to depart from the rigorous review that the First Amendment generally demands.

Sound reasons justify reviewing the latter type of commercial speech regulation more carefully. * * * Our commercial speech cases have recognized the dangers that attend governmental attempts to single out certain messages for suppression. * * *

The special dangers that attend complete bans on truthful, nonmisleading commercial speech cannot be explained away by appeals to the "commonsense distinctions" that exist between commercial and noncommercial speech. * * * Regulations that suppress the truth are no less

---

9. In other words, the regulation failed the fourth step in the four-part inquiry that the majority announced in its opinion. It wrote:

> "In commercial speech cases, then, a four-part analysis has developed. At the outset, we must determine whether the expression is protected by the First Amendment. For commercial speech to come within that provision, it at least must concern lawful activity and not be misleading. Next, we ask whether the asserted governmental interest is substantial. If both inquiries yield positive answers, we must determine whether the regulation directly advances the governmental interest asserted, and whether it is not more extensive than is necessary to serve that interest." *Central Hudson*, 447 U.S., at 566.

troubling because they target objectively verifiable information, nor are they less effective because they aim at durable messages. As a result, neither the "greater objectivity" nor the "greater hardiness" of truthful, nonmisleading commercial speech justifies reviewing its complete suppression with added deference.

It is the State's interest in protecting consumers from "commercial harms" that provides "the typical reason why commercial speech can be subject to greater governmental regulation than noncommercial speech." *Cincinnati v. Discovery Network, Inc.*, 507 U.S. 410, 426 (1993). Yet bans that target truthful, nonmisleading commercial messages rarely protect consumers from such harms. Instead, such bans often serve only to obscure an "underlying governmental policy" that could be implemented without regulating speech. * * * In this way, these commercial speech bans not only hinder consumer choice, but also impede debate over central issues of public policy.* * *[13]

Precisely because bans against truthful, nonmisleading commercial speech rarely seek to protect consumers from either deception or overreaching, they usually rest solely on the offensive assumption that the public will respond "irrationally" to the truth. * * * The First Amendment directs us to be especially skeptical of regulations that seek to keep people in the dark for what the government perceives to be their own good. That teaching applies equally to state attempts to deprive consumers of accurate information about their chosen products:

> "The commercial marketplace, like other spheres of our social and cultural life, provides a forum where ideas and information flourish. Some of the ideas and information are vital, some of slight worth. But the general rule is that the speaker and the audience, not the government, assess the value of the information presented. Thus, even a communication that does no more than propose a commercial transaction is entitled to the coverage of the First Amendment. * * *" *Edenfield v. Fane*, 507 U.S. 761, 767 (1993).

V

In this case, there is no question that Rhode Island's price advertising ban constitutes a blanket prohibition against truthful, nonmisleading speech about a lawful product. There is also no question that the ban serves an end unrelated to consumer protection. Accordingly, we must review the price advertising ban with "special care," * * * mindful that speech prohibitions of this type rarely survive constitutional review.

The State argues that the price advertising prohibition should nevertheless be upheld because it directly advances the State's substantial interest in promoting temperance, and because it is no more extensive than necessary. Although there is some confusion as to what Rhode Island

---

13. This case bears out the point. Rhode Island seeks to reduce alcohol consumption by increasing alcohol price; yet its means of achieving that goal deprives the public of their chief source of information about the reigning price level of alcohol. As a result, the State's price advertising ban keeps the public ignorant of the key barometer of the ban's effectiveness: the alcohol beverages' prices.

means by temperance, we assume that the State asserts an interest in reducing alcohol consumption.[14]

In evaluating the ban's effectiveness in advancing the State's interest, we note that a commercial speech regulation "may not be sustained if it provides only ineffective or remote support for the government's purpose." * * * [W]e must determine whether the State has shown that the price advertising ban will *significantly* reduce alcohol consumption.

We can agree that common sense supports the conclusion that a prohibition against price advertising, like a collusive agreement among competitors to refrain from such advertising,[15] will tend to mitigate competition and maintain prices at a higher level than would prevail in a completely free market. Despite the absence of proof on the point, we can even agree with the State's contention that it is reasonable to assume that demand, and hence consumption throughout the market, is somewhat lower whenever a higher, noncompetitive price level prevails. However, without any findings of fact, or indeed any evidentiary support whatsoever, we cannot agree with the assertion that the price advertising ban will significantly advance the State's interest in promoting temperance.

Although the record suggests that the price advertising ban may have some impact on the purchasing patterns of temperate drinkers of modest means, * * * the State has presented no evidence to suggest that its speech prohibition will *significantly* reduce marketwide consumption.[16] * * * Moreover, the evidence suggests that the abusive drinker will probably not be deterred by a marginal price increase, and that the true alcoholic may simply reduce his purchases of other necessities.

---

14. Before the District Court, the State argued that it sought to reduce consumption among irresponsible drinkers. In its brief to this Court, it equates its interest in promoting temperance with an interest in reducing alcohol consumption among all drinkers. * * * The Rhode Island Supreme Court has characterized the State's interest in "promoting temperance" as both "the state's interest in reducing the consumption of liquor," * * * and the State's interest in discouraging "excessive consumption of alcoholic beverages." * * * A state statute declares the ban's purpose to be "the promotion of temperance and for the reasonable control of the traffic in alcoholic beverages." R.I. Gen. Laws § 3–1–5 (1987).

15. *See, e.g., Business Electronics Corp. v. Sharp Electronics Corp.*, 485 U.S. 717, 735 (1988) (considering restriction on price advertising as evidence of Sherman Act violation); *United States v. Sealy, Inc.*, 388 U.S. 350, 355 (1967) (same); *Blackburn v. Sweeney*, 53 F.3d 825, 828 (C.A.7 1995) (considering restrictions on the location of advertising as evidence of Sherman Act violation).

16. Petitioners' stipulation that they each expect to realize a $100,000 benefit per year if the ban is lifted is not to the contrary. The stipulation shows only that petitioners believe they will be able to compete more effectively for existing alcohol consumers if there is no ban on price advertising. It does not show that they believe either the number of alcohol consumers, or the number of purchases by those consumers, will increase in the ban's absence. Indeed, the State's own expert conceded that "plaintiffs' expectation of realizing additional profits through price advertising has no necessary relationship to increased overall consumption."

Moreover, we attach little significance to the fact that some studies suggest that people budget the amount of money that they will spend on alcohol. * * * These studies show only that, in a competitive market, people will tend to search for the cheapest product in order to meet their budgets. The studies do not suggest that the amount of money budgeted for alcohol consumption will remain fixed in the face of a marketwide price increase.

In addition, * * * the State has not identified what price level would lead to a significant reduction in alcohol consumption, nor has it identified the amount that it believes prices would decrease without the ban. Thus, the State's own showing reveals that any connection between the ban and a significant change in alcohol consumption would be purely fortuitous.

As is evident, any conclusion that elimination of the ban would significantly increase alcohol consumption would require us to engage in the sort of "speculation or conjecture" that is an unacceptable means of demonstrating that a restriction on commercial speech directly advances the State's asserted interest. * * * Such speculation certainly does not suffice when the State takes aim at accurate commercial information for paternalistic ends.

* * * It is perfectly obvious that alternative forms of regulation that would not involve any restriction on speech would be more likely to achieve the State's goal of promoting temperance. As the State's own expert conceded, higher prices can be maintained either by direct regulation or by increased taxation. Per capita purchases could be limited as is the case with prescription drugs. Even educational campaigns focused on the problems of excessive, or even moderate, drinking might prove to be more effective.

* * * [T]he State has failed to establish a "reasonable fit" between its abridgment of speech and its temperance goal. * * *

VI

The State responds by arguing that it merely exercised appropriate "legislative judgment" in determining that a price advertising ban would best promote temperance. * * * Rhode Island first argues that, because expert opinions as to the effectiveness of the price advertising ban "go both ways," * * * the ban constitute[s] a "reasonable choice" by the legislature. * * * The State next contends that precedent requires us to give particular deference to that legislative choice because the State could, if it chose, ban the sale of alcoholic beverages outright. * * * Finally, the State argues that deference is appropriate because alcoholic beverages are so-called "vice" products. * * * We consider each of these contentions in turn.

The State's first argument fails to justify the speech prohibition at issue. Our commercial speech cases recognize some room for the exercise of legislative judgment. However, Rhode Island errs in concluding that *United States v. Edge Broadcasting Co.*, 509 U.S. 418 (1993) and *Posadas de Puerto Rico Associates v. Tourism Co. of Puerto Rico*, 478 U.S. 328 (1986) establish the degree of deference that its decision to impose a price advertising ban warrants.

In *Edge*, we upheld a federal statute that permitted only those broadcasters located in States that had legalized lotteries to air lottery advertising. The statute was designed to regulate advertising about an activity that had been deemed illegal in the jurisdiction in which the broadcaster was located. * * * Here, by contrast, the commercial speech ban targets information about entirely lawful behavior.

Posadas is more directly relevant. There, a five-Member majority held that, under the *Central Hudson* test, it was "up to the legislature" to choose to reduce gambling by suppressing in-state casino advertising rather than engaging in educational speech. * * * Rhode Island argues that this logic demonstrates the constitutionality of its own decision to ban price advertising in lieu of raising taxes or employing some other less speech-restrictive means of promoting temperance.

The reasoning in *Posadas* does support the State's argument, but, on reflection, we are now persuaded that *Posadas* erroneously performed the First Amendment analysis. The casino advertising ban was designed to keep truthful, nonmisleading speech from members of the public for fear that they would be more likely to gamble if they received it. As a result, the advertising ban served to shield the State's antigambling policy from the public scrutiny that more direct, nonspeech regulation would draw. * * *

Given our longstanding hostility to commercial speech regulation of this type, *Posadas* clearly erred in concluding that it was "up to the legislature" to choose suppression over a less speech-restrictive policy. The *Posadas* majority's conclusion on that point cannot be reconciled with the unbroken line of prior cases striking down similarly broad regulations on truthful, nonmisleading advertising when non-speech-related alternatives were available. * * *

Because the 5–to–4 decision in Posadas marked such a sharp break from our prior precedent, and because it concerned a constitutional question about which this Court is the final arbiter, we decline to give force to its highly deferential approach.

Instead, in keeping with our prior holdings, we conclude that a state legislature does not have the broad discretion to suppress truthful, nonmisleading information for paternalistic purposes that the Posadas majority was willing to tolerate. As we explained in *Virginia Bd. of Pharmacy*, "[i]t is precisely this kind of choice, between the dangers of suppressing information, and the dangers of its misuse if it is freely available, that the First Amendment makes for us." * * *

We also cannot accept the State's second contention, which is premised entirely on the "greater-includes-the-lesser" reasoning endorsed toward the end of the majority's opinion in *Posadas*. There, the majority stated that "the greater power to completely ban casino gambling necessarily includes the lesser power to ban advertising of casino gambling." * * * It went on to state that "*because* the government could have enacted a wholesale prohibition of [casino gambling] it is permissible for the government to take the less intrusive step of allowing the conduct, but reducing the demand through restrictions on advertising." * * * The majority concluded that it would "surely be a strange constitutional doctrine which would concede to the legislature the authority to totally ban a product or activity, but deny to the legislature the authority to forbid the stimulation of demand for the product or activity through advertising on behalf of those who would profit from such increased demand." * * * On the basis of these statements, the State reasons that its undisputed authority to ban alcoholic beverages must include the power to restrict advertisements offering them for sale.

In *Rubin v. Coors Brewing Co.*, 514 U.S. 476 (1995), the United States advanced a similar argument as a basis for supporting a statutory prohibition against revealing the alcoholic content of malt beverages on product labels. We rejected the argument, noting that the statement in the *Posadas* opinion was made only after the majority had concluded that the Puerto Rican regulation "survived the *Central Hudson* test." * * * Further consideration persuades us that the "greater-includes-the-lesser" argument should be rejected for the additional and more important reason that it is inconsistent with both logic and well-settled doctrine.

Although we do not dispute the proposition that greater powers include lesser ones, we fail to see how that syllogism requires the conclusion that the State's power to regulate commercial *activity* is "greater" than its power to ban truthful, nonmisleading commercial *speech*. Contrary to the assumption made in *Posadas*, we think it quite clear that banning speech may sometimes prove far more intrusive than banning conduct. As a venerable proverb teaches, it may prove more injurious to prevent people from teaching others how to fish than to prevent fish from being sold. Similarly, a local ordinance banning bicycle lessons may curtail freedom far more than one that prohibits bicycle riding within city limits. In short, we reject the assumption that words are necessarily less vital to freedom than actions, or that logic somehow proves that the power to prohibit an activity is necessarily "greater" than the power to suppress speech about it.

As a matter of First Amendment doctrine, the *Posadas* syllogism is even less defensible. The text of the First Amendment makes clear that the Constitution presumes that attempts to regulate speech are more dangerous than attempts to regulate conduct. * * *

Thus, just as it is perfectly clear that Rhode Island could not ban all obscene liquor ads except those that advocated temperance, we think it equally clear that its power to ban the sale of liquor entirely does not include a power to censor all advertisements that contain accurate and nonmisleading information about the price of the product. As the entire Court apparently now agrees, the statements in the *Posadas* opinion on which Rhode Island relies are no longer persuasive.

Finally, we find unpersuasive the State's contention that, under *Posadas* and *Edge*, the price advertising ban should be upheld because it targets commercial speech that pertains to a "vice" activity. Respondents premise their request for a so-called "vice" exception to our commercial speech doctrine on language in Edge which characterized gambling as a "vice." * * * Respondents misread our precedent.

Moreover, the scope of any "vice" exception to the protection afforded by the First Amendment would be difficult, if not impossible, to define. Almost any product that poses some threat to public health or public morals might reasonably be characterized by a state legislature as relating to "vice activity." Such characterization, however, is anomalous when applied to products such as alcoholic beverages, lottery tickets, or playing cards that may be lawfully purchased on the open market. The recognition of such an exception would also have the unfortunate consequence of either allowing state legislatures to justify censorship by the simple expedient of placing the "vice" label on selected lawful activities, or requiring the federal courts to establish a federal common law of vice. * * *

VII

From 1919 until 1933, the Eighteenth Amendment to the Constitution totally prohibited "the manufacture, sale, or transportation of intoxicating liquors" in the United States and its territories. Section 1 of the Twenty-first Amendment repealed that prohibition, and § 2 delegated to the several States the power to prohibit commerce in, or the use of, alcoholic beverages.[21] The States' regulatory power over this segment of commerce is therefore largely "unfettered by the Commerce Clause." *Ziffrin, Inc. v. Reeves*, 308 U.S. 132, 138 (1939).

As is clear, the text of the Twenty-first Amendment supports the view that, while it grants the States authority over commerce that might otherwise be reserved to the Federal Government, it places no limit whatsoever on other constitutional provisions. Nevertheless, Rhode Island argues * * * that in this case the Twenty-first Amendment tilts the First Amendment analysis in the State's favor.

In * * * *California v. LaRue*, 409 U.S. 109 (1972), * * * five Members of the Court relied on the Twenty-first Amendment to buttress the conclusion that the First Amendment did not invalidate California's prohibition of certain grossly sexual exhibitions in premises licensed to serve alcoholic beverages. Specifically, the opinion stated that the Twenty-first Amendment required that the prohibition be given an added presumption in favor of its validity. * * * We are now persuaded that the Court's analysis in *LaRue* would have led to precisely the same result if it had placed no reliance on the Twenty-first Amendment.

Entirely apart from the Twenty-first Amendment, the State has ample power to prohibit the sale of alcoholic beverages in inappropriate locations.
* * *

[A]lthough the Twenty-first Amendment limits the effect of the dormant Commerce Clause on a State's regulatory power over the delivery or use of intoxicating beverages within its borders, "the Amendment does not license the States to ignore their obligations under other provisions of the Constitution." *Capital Cities Cable, Inc. v. Crisp*, 467 U.S. 691, 712 (1984). * * * Accordingly, we now hold that the Twenty-first Amendment does not qualify the constitutional prohibition against laws abridging the freedom of speech embodied in the First Amendment. The Twenty-first Amendment, therefore, cannot save Rhode Island's ban on liquor price advertising.

VIII

Because Rhode Island has failed to carry its heavy burden of justifying its complete ban on price advertising, we conclude that R.I. Gen. Laws §§ 3–8–7 and 3–8–8.1 (1989), as well as Regulation 32 of the Rhode Island Liquor Control Administration, abridge speech in violation of the First Amendment as made applicable to the States by the Due Process Clause of the Fourteenth Amendment. The judgment of the Court of Appeals is therefore reversed.

---

21. "Section 2. The transportation or importation into any State, Territory, or possession of the United States for delivery or use therein of intoxicating liquors, in violation of the laws thereof, is hereby prohibited." U.S. Const., Amdt. 21, § 2.

It is so ordered.

■ JUSTICE SCALIA, concurring in part and concurring in the judgment.

I share JUSTICE THOMAS's discomfort with the *Central Hudson* test, which seems to me to have nothing more than policy intuition to support it. I also share JUSTICE STEVENS's aversion towards paternalistic governmental policies that prevent men and women from hearing facts that might not be good for them. On the other hand, it would also be paternalism for us to prevent the people of the States from enacting laws that we consider paternalistic, unless we have good reason to believe that the Constitution itself forbids them. * * *

I believe, however, that JUSTICE STEVENS's treatment of the application of the Twenty-first Amendment to this case is correct, and accordingly join Parts I, II, VII, and VIII of JUSTICE STEVENS's opinion.

■ JUSTICE THOMAS, concurring in Parts I, II, VI, and VII, and concurring in the judgment.

In cases such as this, in which the government's asserted interest is to keep legal users of a product or service ignorant in order to manipulate their choices in the marketplace, the balancing test adopted in *Central Hudson Gas & Elec. Corp. v. Public Serv. Comm'n of N.Y.*, 447 U.S. 557 (1980), should not be applied, in my view. Rather, such an "interest" is *per se* illegitimate and can no more justify regulation of "commercial" speech than it can justify regulation of "noncommercial" speech.

I

In *Virginia Bd. of Pharmacy v. Virginia Citizens Consumer Council, Inc.*, 425 U.S. 748, 762 (1976), this Court held that speech that does " 'no more than propose a commercial transaction' " was protected by the First Amendment, and struck down a ban on price advertising regarding prescription drugs. The Court asserted that a "particular consumer's interest in the free flow of commercial information" may be as keen as, or keener than, his interest in "the day's most urgent political debate," * * * and that "the proper allocation of resources" in our free enterprise system requires that consumer decisions be "intelligent and well informed." * * * The Court also explained that, unless consumers are kept informed about the operations of the free market system, they cannot form "intelligent opinions as to how that system ought to be regulated or altered." * * * The Court sharply rebuffed the State's argument that consumers would make irresponsible choices if they were able to choose between higher priced but higher quality pharmaceuticals accompanied by high quality prescription monitoring services resulting from a "stable pharmacist-customer relationshi[p]," * * * on the one hand, and cheaper but lower quality pharmaceuticals unaccompanied by such services, on the other:

> "[T]he State's protectiveness of its citizens rests in large measure on the advantages of their being kept in ignorance. The advertising ban does not directly affect professional standards one way or the other. It affects them only through the reactions it is assumed people will have to the free flow of drug price information.

. . .

"There is, of course, an alternative to this highly paternalistic approach. That alternative is to assume that this information is not in itself harmful, that people will perceive their own best interests, if only they are well enough informed, and that the best means to that end is to open the channels of communication rather than to close them.... It is precisely this kind of choice, between the dangers of suppressing information, and the dangers of its misuse if it is freely available, that the First Amendment makes for us. Virginia is free to require whatever professional standards it wishes of its pharmacists; it may subsidize them or protect them from competition in other ways. But it may not do so by keeping the public in ignorance of the entirely lawful terms that competing pharmacists are offering. In this sense, the justifications Virginia has offered for suppressing the flow of prescription drug price information, far from persuading us that the flow is not protected by the First Amendment, have reinforced our view that it is." *Id.*, at 769–770 (citation omitted).

The Court opined that *false or misleading* advertising was not protected, on the grounds that the accuracy of advertising claims may be more readily verifiable than is the accuracy of political or other claims, and that "commercial" speech is made more durable by its profit motive. * * * The Court also made clear that it did not envision protection for advertising that proposes an illegal transaction. * * *

In case after case following *Virginia Bd. of Pharmacy*, the Court, and individual Members of the Court, have continued to stress the importance of free dissemination of information about commercial choices in a market economy; the antipaternalistic premises of the First Amendment; the impropriety of manipulating consumer choices or public opinion through the suppression of accurate "commercial" information; the near impossibility of severing "commercial" speech from speech necessary to democratic decisionmaking; and the dangers of permitting the government to do covertly what it might not have been able to muster the political support to do openly.

In other decisions, however, the Court has appeared to accept the legitimacy of laws that suppress information in order to manipulate the choices of consumers-so long as the government could show that the manipulation was in fact successful. *Central Hudson Gas & Elec. Corp. v. Public Serv. Comm'n of N.Y.*, 447 U.S. 557 (1980), was the first decision to clearly embrace this position, although the Court applied a very strict overbreadth analysis to strike down the advertising ban at issue.[3]

The Court has at times appeared to assume that "commercial" speech could be censored in a variety of ways for any of a variety of reasons. * * * I do not see a philosophical or historical basis for asserting that "commer-

3. The Court found that although the total effect of the advertising ban would be to decrease consumption, the advertising ban impermissibly extended to some advertising that itself might not increase consumption. * * *

cial" speech is of "lower value" than "noncommercial" speech. * * * Nor do I believe that the only explanations that the Court has ever advanced for treating "commercial" speech differently from other speech can justify restricting "commercial" speech in order to keep information from legal purchasers so as to thwart what would otherwise be their choices in the marketplace.

II

I do not join the principal opinion's application of the *Central Hudson* balancing test because I do not believe that such a test should be applied to a restriction of "commercial" speech, at least when, as here, the asserted interest is one that is to be achieved through keeping would-be recipients of the speech in the dark. * * *

III

Although the Court took a sudden turn away from *Virginia Bd. of Pharmacy* in *Central Hudson*, it has never explained why manipulating the choices of consumers by keeping them ignorant is more legitimate when the ignorance is maintained through suppression of "commercial" speech than when the same ignorance is maintained through suppression of "noncommercial" speech. The courts, including this Court, have found the *Central Hudson* "test" to be, as a general matter, very difficult to apply with any uniformity. * * * [T]he second prong of *Central Hudson* * * * apparently requires judges to delineate those situations in which citizens cannot be trusted with information, and invites judges to decide whether they themselves think that consumption of a product is harmful enough that it should be discouraged. In my view, the *Central Hudson* test asks the courts to weigh incommensurables—the value of knowledge versus the value of ignorance—and to apply contradictory premises—that informed adults are the best judges of their own interests, and that they are not. * * *

■ JUSTICE O'CONNOR, with whom THE CHIEF JUSTICE, JUSTICE SOUTER, and JUSTICE BREYER join, concurring in the judgment.

Rhode Island prohibits advertisement of the retail price of alcoholic beverages, except at the place of sale. The State's only asserted justification for this ban is that it promotes temperance by increasing the cost of alcoholic beverages. * * * I agree with the Court that Rhode Island's price-advertising ban is invalid. I would resolve this case more narrowly, however, by applying our established *Central Hudson* test to determine whether this commercial speech regulation survives First Amendment scrutiny.

Under that test, we first determine whether the speech at issue concerns lawful activity and is not misleading, and whether the asserted governmental interest is substantial. If both these conditions are met, we must decide whether the regulation "directly advances the governmental interest asserted, and whether it is not more extensive than is necessary to serve that interest." * * *

Given the means by which this regulation purportedly serves the State's interest, our conclusion is plain: Rhode Island's regulation fails First Amendment scrutiny. * * *

Coyote Publishing, Inc. v. Miller

598 F.3d 592 (9th Cir. 2010)

■ BERZON, CIRCUIT JUDGE:

[A]s long as poverty makes virtue hideous and the spare pocket-money of rich bachelordom makes vice dazzling, [the] daily hand-to-hand fight against prostitution with prayer and persuasion, shelters and scanty alms, will be a losing one.

—George Bernard Shaw, Preface to Mrs. Warren's Profession viii (1902)

The American experience with prostitution over the last hundred years is testament to the sagacity of Mr. Shaw. Even the coercive machinery of the criminal law, not yet arrayed against the sale of sexual services when Shaw penned *Mrs. Warren's Profession,* has not extinguished the world's oldest profession.

The State of Nevada, alone among the states, accommodates this reality by permitting the sale of sexual services in some of its counties.[1] Nevada combines partial legalization of prostitution with stringent licensing and regulation, including health screenings for sex workers, measures to protect sex workers from coercion, and—the aspect of Nevada law here challenged—restrictions on advertising by legal brothels. We must decide whether the advertising restrictions violate the First Amendment.

I.

A.

The sale of sexual services in Nevada is prohibited unless conducted in designated brothels licensed by a county. Nev.Rev.Stat. § 201.354(1). State law prohibits counties of more than 400,000 residents from issuing such licenses, * * * and counties with fewer than 400,000 residents are free to prohibit the sale of sexual services by local ordinance. The upshot is that licensed brothels do not operate in Clark County, which includes the city of Las Vegas, or in five of the sixteen remaining counties in Nevada.

State law establishes a strict regulatory regime governing brothels in the eleven counties that choose to license them. Sex workers are subject to mandatory health screening for sexually transmitted diseases, including HIV, * * * and brothel owners are liable for damages resulting from exposure to HIV. * * * Condom use is mandatory, * * * and all brothels must so notify customers. * * *

Several statutory provisions are directed to preventing coercion of sex workers by the operators of brothels and others. Section 201.300 makes criminal "pandering," defined to include, among other acts, inducing, persuading, encouraging, inveigling, or enticing a person to engage in the

1. From 1980 to 2009, so-called "indoor prostitution" was legal in Rhode Island. Due to a statutory amendment in 1980, prostitution itself was not expressly prohibited, although related activities such as "streetwalking" were. Whether this state of the law was an oversight is not altogether clear. Nevertheless, in 2009 the law was again amended and Rhode Island now outlaws prostitution as does every other state except Nevada. See R.I. Gen. Laws § 11-34.1-2 (2009). * * *

sale of sexual services. Nev.Rev.Stat. § 201.300; see also Nev.Rev.Stat. § 201.360 (prohibiting "placing" a person in a brothel). Detaining a person in a brothel because of debt is also forbidden. Nev.Rev.Stat. § 201.330. Section 201.320 makes it a crime to live from the earnings of a sex worker.[2]

The state's regulatory regime also restricts advertising by legal brothels. The principal restrictions are two: First, brothels are banned from advertising at all in counties where the sale of sexual services is prohibited by local ordinance or state statute. * * * Second, in counties where the sale of sexual services is permitted, brothels cannot advertise "[i]n any public theater, on the public streets of any city or town, or on any public highway." * * *

The statutes further provide that:

> Inclusion in any display, handbill or publication of the address, location or telephone number of a house of prostitution or of identification of a means of transportation to such a house, or of directions telling how to obtain any such information, constitutes prima facie evidence of advertising for the purposes of this section. Nev.Rev.Stat. § 201.430(3).

Persons in violation of the advertising restrictions are subject to criminal penalties, including fines and imprisonment.

B.

The publishers of two newspapers that circulate in areas of Nevada where prostitution is prohibited and the owner of a legal brothel in Nye County (all referred to, collectively, as Coyote Publishing) bring a facial challenge to * * * the advertising restrictions [arguing they] violate the First Amendment of the U.S. Constitution and Article I, Section 9, of the Nevada Constitution.[5]

On summary judgment, the district court declared the advertising restrictions unconstitutional. * * *

Nevada appeals. * * * [W]e conclude that Nevada's regulatory scheme is consistent with the First Amendment and so reverse the ruling of the district court.

II.

* * * For much of our history the First Amendment was thought not to apply to advertising. * * * More than thirty years ago, however, the Supreme Court determined that commercial speech is within the First Amendment's purview, albeit afforded only "a limited measure of protec-

2. Enforcement of these laws to protect sex workers appears to be lacking. Alexa Albert's study of one prominent brothel reports that pimps remained common and some assaults against sex workers still occurred, yet the authorities were rarely notified of these criminal violations. See ALEXA ALBERT, BROTHEL: MUSTANG RANCH AND ITS WOMEN 71–73, 153–54, 194 (2001).

5. Article I, Section 9 of the Nevada Constitution provides, in relevant part: "Every citizen may freely speak, write and publish his sentiments on all subjects being responsible for the abuse of that right; and no law shall be passed to restrain or abridge the liberty of speech or of the press." * * *

tion, commensurate with its subordinate position in the scale of First Amendment values." *Ohralik v. Ohio State Bar Ass'n*, 436 U.S. 447, 456 (1978). * * *

Speech is "commercial" if it does "no more than propose a commercial transaction." * * * Coyote Publishing contends that [the law] restricts more than pure commercial speech. * * *

The Nevada courts have not expressly adopted any limiting construction of section 201.430(3) that cabins its reach to only commercial speech. * * * Still, we are not persuaded that section 201.430 burdens any significant quantum of fully protected, non-commercial speech. * * *

In *44 Liquormart, Inc. v. Rhode Island*, 517 U.S. 484 (1996), a plurality of the Court considered and rejected the argument that the power to ban a vice activity necessarily includes the power to ban the accompanying commercial speech. * * * The plurality expressly * * * declar[ed] that "it is no answer [to First Amendment challenges] that commercial speech concerns products and services that the government may freely regulate...." * * *

Decisions since *44 Liquormart have* applied intermediate scrutiny to strike down restrictions on the advertising of "vice activities." * * * *See Greater New Orleans Broad. Ass'n, Inc. v. United States*, 527 U.S. 173, 195–96, (1999) (gambling); *Lorillard Tobacco Co. v. Reilly*, 533 U.S. 525, 566 (2001) (tobacco products). * * * Nevada also argues for an exception specific to prostitution. We agree that there are strong reasons why the sale of sexual services, in particular, ought to be treated differently than other advertising bans on "vice" activities.

The first derives from the degree of disfavor in which prostitution is held in our society, as reflected in law. In this respect, prostitution is sui generis. Forty-nine of the fifty states today prohibit all sales of sexual services. The federal government acknowledges the link between prostitution and trafficking in women and children, a form of modern day slavery. *See* U.S. Department of State, *The Link Between Prostitution and Sex Trafficking* (November 24, 2004). And federal law prohibits the transportation of persons in interstate or foreign commerce for the purpose of prostitution or other illegal sexual activity. White Slave Traffic Act, 36 Stat. 825, 18 U.S.C. § 2421–2124 (1910). Although Nevada has opted for partial legalization, Nevada too has taken significant steps to limit prostitution, including the total ban on the practice in by far the largest population center,[11] the permission to other counties to ban the practice, and the advertising restrictions here at issue.

The social condemnation of prostitution, therefore, is vastly more widespread—and vastly more consistent—than in the case of other categories of "vice" that courts have considered, such as alcohol, tobacco products, and gambling. This condemnation may be relevant to the degree of scrutiny applicable to these advertising restrictions. The protection of commercial speech is at least in part instrumental, in the sense that courts are concerned about the efficient allocation of the underlying good or

---

11. Clark County is home to 1,865,746 of the 2,600,167 people in Nevada, or approximately 72 percent of the state's population. * * *

service. As the Supreme Court recognized in *Virginia State Board v. Virginia Citizens Consumer Council, Inc.*, 425 U.S. 748, 765 (1976):

> Advertising, however tasteless and excessive it sometimes may seem, is nonetheless dissemination of information as to who is producing and selling what product, for what reason, and at what price. So long as we preserve a predominantly free enterprise economy, the allocation of our resources in large measure will be made through numerous private economic decisions.... To this end, the free flow of commercial information is indispensable.

* * * When the underlying service is of extremely little value, as demonstrated by near consensus within our society, the need for its efficient allocation and distribution is less compelling.

The nature of the market in sexual services, such as it is, provides an additional reason why the goal of efficiency applies with less force. In light of prevailing sexual mores, a highly transparent, and thus efficient, market for sex is a chimera. In this respect, sex is not a commodity. Commercial speech decisions routinely display concern over the risk of distortion of competitive markets. * * * In the context of the legal sale of sexual acts, in contrast, there is relatively little market competition to distort.[13]

Commercial speech doctrine also has been driven in part by objections to paternalistic regulatory policies, which assume that individual consumers need to be protected from their own choices. * * * Nevada's advertising restrictions, however, are not based on the premise that consumers of the advertising will act "irrationally" to their own detriment. Instead, as developed later, a central premise of the restrictions is that the advertising of prostitution is an integral aspect of, and exacerbates, the commodification of human sexuality on a society—wide basis. Regulations that are addressed to the third-party effects of private transactions, not to protecting people from themselves, are more likely to be consonant with First Amendment values.

Thus, two of the core justifications for protecting commercial speech—facilitating efficient market exchange and shunning paternalism—apply with less force in this context. * * * But they do not require that we discard the overall standard altogether rather than incorporating the points of distinction where they fit when applying that standard, as we shall do later in this opinion.

We * * * apply the familiar four-part test:

---

13. We make this observation in part because of the limited extent of the market, but also because of the lack of transparency inherent in commercial sexual transactions. Even in legal brothels in Nevada, for example, prices typically are not agreed upon until *after* a sex worker and client have removed to a private room. * * * We are, of course, aware of the existence of a vast illegal market in sexual acts, in Nevada and elsewhere. * * * Commercial speech doctrine, however, is not concerned with the efficient operation of illegal, "black" markets. *See United States v. Williams*, 553 U.S. 285 (2008) ("Offers to engage in illegal transactions are categorically excluded from First Amendment protection."). In any event, these markets, precisely because they are illegal, are less transparent and efficient than their size would otherwise predict.

> At the outset, we must determine whether the expression is protected by the First Amendment. For commercial speech to come within that provision, it at least must concern lawful activity and not be misleading. Next, we ask whether the asserted governmental interest is substantial. If both inquiries yield positive answers, we must determine whether the regulation directly advances the governmental interest asserted, and whether it is not more extensive than is necessary to serve that interest. *Central Hudson Gas & Elec. Corp. v. Public Service Commission of New York*, 447 U.S. 557, 566 (1980).

Because, as will appear, Nevada's interest in limiting the commodification of sex is important to the analysis at each step, we begin by assessing the substantiality of that interest. * * *

A.

We first consider whether Nevada has asserted substantial state interests in support of its advertising restrictions. Nevada relies largely on an asserted interest in limiting the commodification of sex.

We are aware of no case that considers the substantiality of a state's interest in preventing commodification—the turning of a good or service into a commodity to be bought and sold—for purposes of constitutional balancing. But the bedrock idea that "[t]here are, in a civilized society, some things that money cannot buy" is deeply rooted in our nation's law and public policy. *See In re Baby M,* 109 N.J. 396 (1988). The Thirteenth Amendment to the U.S. Constitution enshrines the principle that people may not be bought and sold as commodities. Payment for consent to adoption of a child is widely prohibited. * * * In many states, surrogacy contracts are unenforceable. * * * Federal law forbids the sale of human organs. * * *

These public policies may be motivated in part by concerns about the indirect consequences of permitting such sales, but they are also driven by an objection to their inherent commodifying tendencies—to the buying and selling of things and activities integral to a robust conception of personhood. *See Baby M*, 109 N.J. 396, (declaring paid surrogacy contracts "potentially degrading to women"); *see also* Margaret Jane Radin, Market–Inalienability, 100 HARVARD LAW REVIEW 1849, 1912 (1987) ("[W]e accept an inferior conception of personhood ... if we suppose people may freely choose to commodify themselves.").

Whether the law *ought* to treat sex as something, like babies and organs, that is "market-inalienable," or instead should treat it as equivalent to the sale of physical labor, is a question much contested among legal academics and philosophers. * * * But these questions are not for us to decide. In most cases that we can imagine—slavery, given the Thirteenth Amendment, being an obvious exception—including this one, it belongs to the political branches to fix the boundary between those human interactions governed by market exchange and those not so governed. In every state but Nevada, that boundary has been drawn so as to forbid such transactions entirely, including the proposing of such transactions through advertising. Nevada has, uniquely for this country, delineated a more nuanced boundary, but still seeks to closely confine the sale of sex acts, geographically, through restrictive licensing where legal, and through the advertising restrictions. We conclude that the interest in preventing the commodification of sex is substantial.

We emphasize that our holding is grounded in two distinctive characteristics of prostitution, each of which is critical to our conclusion:

First, prohibitions on prostitution reflect not a desire to discourage the underlying sexual activity itself but its *sale*. Prostitution without the exchange of money is simply sex, which in most manifestations is not a target of state regulators. * * * Second, public disapproval of prostitution's commodifying tendencies has an impressive historical pedigree. * * *

The sale of sex was not widely criminalized for much of our nation's history. Prostitution was instead covered only by prohibitions on vagrancy and "streetwalking"; the bans did not extend to brothels or other indoor locations in which sale of sex occurred. * * * The legal condemnation of prostitution as such did not arrive until after the Civil War, when a coalition of prominent abolitionists and feminists defeated attempts to license houses of prostitution in several states. * * *

The anti-commodification orientation of the early opponents of legalized prostitution was reflected in the nature of the criminal prohibitions adopted early in the twentieth century. Criminal laws were not directed at women themselves but at those profiting from "commercialized forms of vice." * * * In 1910, Congress passed the White Slave Traffic Act, underscoring the extent to which policymakers associated prostitution with involuntary servitude and the overriding concern with commercial manifestations of the practice, especially interstate and international trafficking in women. * * *

Though attitudes towards the sale of sexual services have continued to change and evolve since the early twentieth century, this history reinforces the conclusion that Nevada's objection is genuinely to the buying and selling of sex. Banning commodification of sex entirely is a substantial policy goal that all states but Nevada have chosen to adopt. Uniquely among the states, Nevada has not structured its laws to pursue this substantial state interest to the exclusion of all others. Rather, it has adopted a nuanced approach to the sale of sexual services, grounded in part in concern about the negative health and safety impacts of unregulated, illegal prostitution. By permitting *some* legal prostitution, Nevada has been able to subject a portion of the market for paid sex to extensive regulation, while continuing severely to limit the diffusion of sexual commodification through its banning of prostitution where by far most Nevadans live (and where most outsiders visit), Clark County.

Nevada has therefore struck its own idiosyncratic balance between various important but competing state interests. The state's dual approach does not make its asserted interest in limiting commodification of sex any less substantial than in the states that ban commercial sex transactions entirely. * * *

B.

* * * Nevada does not assert that the advertising of prostitution is false, deceptive, or misleading. * * *

C.

At step three * * * we ask whether Nevada's commercial speech restrictions "directly and materially advance[ ]" its asserted interest in limiting the commodification of sex. * * *

Increased advertising of commercial sex throughout the state of Nevada would increase the extent to which sex is presented to the public as a commodity for sale. * * * Nevada *might* be able to reduce the buying and selling of sex acts to a greater degree by instituting a complete ban on prostitution (although there has been no showing that the actual incidence of acts of prostitution, legal and illegal, in Nevada is greater than it would be under a total ban). But it has chosen to take an approach to reducing demand that will not short—circuit the health and safety gains that come with partial legalization.

Nevada's chosen approach directly and materially advances the state's policy of limiting commodification without undermining its competing health and safety goals. Common sense counsels that advertising tends to stimulate demand for products and services. Conversely, prohibitions on advertising tend to limit demand. * * * Reducing the demand for commercial sex acts in turn limits the commodification of sex.

At the same time, Nevada's decision to legalize prostitution obviously contributes to some extent to the commodification of sex. * * * [I]ncoherence in the operation of speech regulations can be fatal to the constitutionality of a scheme of regulation. In contrast, the fact that banning the underlying activity outright would also promote the interest advanced by restricting advertising does not by itself render a commercial speech regulation unconstitutional. * * * Here, the restrictions on prostitution advertising directly and materially advance Nevada's interest in limiting the commodification of sex.

Coyote Publishing suggests that Nevada's interest in limiting commodification is not materially advanced by the ban on brothel advertising in the counties where they are not legal because sexually suggestive material is already widely displayed in Nevada. The argument misses the point. Nevada seeks to limit the message that sex may be bought and sold. It does not object to sex per se, or to messages that utilize sexual innuendo to sell other products. The persistence of those other elements in Nevada society does not defeat Nevada's interest.

To be sure, there are goods and services for sale in the state of Nevada whose advertisement may contribute to the commodification of human sexuality but that escape the advertising ban at issue here—for example, shows featuring nude dancers. But Nevada asserts an interest in limiting the commodification of sexual acts; the buying and selling of nude images is a different concern. Nor is this distinction too fine for purposes of the First Amendment. It is the very distinction that drives the legislative choices of the many states that permit nude dancing but not prostitution.

In sum, we conclude that Nevada's substantial interest in limiting the commodification of sex is directly and materially advanced by the restrictions on brothel advertising.

D.

Finally, we must assess whether the restrictions on advertising are "more extensive than necessary" in light of Nevada's interests. * * * "The Government is not required to employ the least restrictive means conceivable," but "it must demonstrate narrow tailoring of the challenged regulation to the asserted interest—a fit that is not necessarily perfect, but reasonable. . . ." * * *

Nevada bans brothel advertising completely in counties where prostitution is illegal. In light of the fact that prostitution advertisements are themselves an aspect of the commodification harm that Nevada seeks to limit, we have no trouble concluding that the advertising restrictions are narrowly tailored. Every advertisement for prostitution that is not seen contributes to limiting the commodification of sex, both directly and by reducing demand.

Nevada's approach in counties where prostitution is legal is less straightforward. In those counties, legal brothels may advertise, but may not do so "[i]n any public theater, on the public streets of any city or town, or on any public highway." * * * This aspect of Nevada's scheme requires a more in-depth analysis of tailoring. * * *

Nevada's scheme does not suffer from these infirmities. Nevada's choice to pursue its state interests by regulating advertising rather than the alternative means of banning all prostitution directly is a unique one in this country, but not one without a well-developed policy basis: partial legalization and regulation serves Nevada's competing, substantial interests in preventing the spread of sexually transmitted disease and protecting sex workers from abuse. * * * The First Amendment does not require that a regulatory regime single-mindedly pursue one objective to the exclusion of all others to survive the intermediate scrutiny applied to commercial speech regulations.

In permitting some unobtrusive, non-public forms of advertising in counties where brothels are legal, Nevada has achieved "a fit that is not necessarily perfect, but reasonable." * * * By keeping brothel advertising out of public places, * * * but permitting other forms of advertising likely to reach those already interested in patronizing the brothels, Nevada strikes a balance between its interest in maintaining economically viable, legal, regulated brothels and its interest in severely limiting the commodification of sex.

* * *

III.

In sum, we hold that the restrictions on brothel advertising contained in Nevada Revised Statute * * * are consistent with the First Amendment.

REVERSED.

Questions

1. What is the "greater-includes-the-lesser" reasoning discussed in *44 Liquormat?* Did the *44 Liquormat* and *Coyote Publishing* Courts endorse this reasoning?

2. As an example of the reasoning behind its decision, the *44 Liquormat* Court noted that "a local ordinance banning bicycle lessons may curtail freedom far more than one that prohibits bicycle riding within city limits." Are bicycle lessons comparable to the advertising of retail price of alcoholic beverages? What are the similarities and differences between the two?

3. How did the *44 Liquormat* and *Coyote Publishing* Courts address the so-called "vice exception" to the commercial speech doctrine?

4. In *44 Liquormat*, Justice Thomas expressed the view that when "the government's asserted interest is to keep legal users of a product or service ignorant in order to manipulate their choices in the marketplace, * * * such an 'interest' is per se illegitimate and can no more justify regulation of 'commercial' speech." What were the positions of the plurality opinion in *44 Liquormat* and the *Coyote Publishing* court on this issue?

§ 7.4 BOUNDED RATIONALITY

> *"The Capacity of the human mind for formulating and solving complex problems is very small compared with the size of the problems whose solution is required for objectively rational behavior in the real world."*
>
> —Herbert Simon[66]

§ 7.4.1 Predictable Failures of the Pursuit of Self-Interest

Human cognitive abilities are finite. Our computational skills, analytical capacity, ability to absorb and digest information, and memories have boundaries.[67] Economist Herbert Simon named our limited capacity *bounded rationality*.[65] Contrary to the intuitive understanding of our human limitations, key approaches in regulation assume that individuals can make reasonably rational decisions. First and foremost, the strong beliefs in the pursuit of self-interest and the pursuit of happiness build on unrealistic assumptions regarding human intellect and conduct. Consequently, numerous controversies over regulation and specific regulatory policies are explicitly or implicitly about the legitimacy of this premise.[69] The perpetual nature of these controversies in itself underscores many of the ordinary boundaries of human rationality.[70] Indeed, the human tendency to seek and

66. Herbert Simon, Models of Men 198 (1957).

67. *See, e.g.*, René Marois & Jason Ivanoff, *Capacity Limits of Information Processing in the Brain*, 9 TRENDS IN COGNITIVE SCIENCES 296 (2005).

65. HERBERT A. SIMON, MODELS OF MAN 198 (1957). *See also* Herbert A. Simon, *A Behavioral Model of Rational Choice*, 69 QUARTERLY JOURNAL OF ECONOMICS 99, 99 (1955).

69. *See* Chapters 2 and 4.

70. *See generally* Barak Orbach & Frances R. Sjoberg, *Excessive Speech, Civility Norms, and the Clucking Theorem*, 44 CONNECTICUT LAW REVIEW 1 (2011).

interpret information in ways that are partial to existing beliefs, to which psychologists often refer as "confirmation bias," may be the most dominant aspect of approaches to regulation.[71] Regardless of their background and familiarity with relevant details, people have strong views about the desirable role of the state in society and particular regulatory policies. This is one form of bounded rationality.

To illustrate how bounded rationality may affect regulation consider the discussion of inalienability rules by Christine Jolls, Cass Sunstein, and Richard Thaler ("JS & T").[72] JS & T observed that a "pervasive feature of law is that mutually desired trades are blocked," and posited that "[p]erhaps most puzzling amidst this landscape—which includes bans on baby selling and vote trading, * * *—are bans on conventional 'economic' transactions, such as usurious lending, price gouging, and ticket scalping. * * * [E]conomists and economically oriented lawyers often view these laws as inefficient and anomalous." Their explanation for such restrictions on voluntary transactions was as follows:

> [L]laws banning usurious lending, price gouging, and ticket scalping [are outcomes of] perceived fairness. * * * In the case of each of these bans, the transaction in question is a significant departure from the usual terms of trade in the market for the good in question—that is, a significant departure from the "reference transaction." Behavioral analysis predicts that if trades are occurring frequently in a given jurisdiction at terms far from those of the reference transaction, there will be strong pressure for a law banning such trades. Note that the prediction is not that all high prices (ones that make it difficult or impossible for some people to afford things they might want) will be banned; what we predict will be banned are transactions at terms far from the terms on which those transactions generally occur in the marketplace.

JS & T's example presents regulations that reinforce bounded rationality and may preserve market inefficiencies. Economists regard such regulations as interference with the price system of the market that is likely to be counterproductive. Regulations, however, may also address bounded rationality, rather than being captured by human flaws. JS & T argued that "bounded rationality pushes toward a sort of anti-antipaternalism—a skepticism about antipaternalism, but not an affirmative defense of paternalism." Specifically, they stressed that many forms of bounded rationality call into question the idea of consumer sovereignty.

---

71. *See generally* Raymond S. Nickerson, *Confirmation Bias: A Ubiquitous Phenomenon in Many Guises*, 2 REVIEW OF GENERAL PSYCHOLOGY 175 (1998). *See also* Albert H. Hastorf & Hadley Cantril, *They Saw a Game: A Case Study*, 49 JOURNAL OF ABNORMAL & SOCIAL PSYCHOLOGY 129 (1954); Ziva Kunda, *The Case for Motivated Reasoning*, 108 PSYCHOLOGICAL REASONING 480 (1990); Peter Lamont, *The Making of Extraordinary Psychological Phenomena*, 48 JOURNAL OF THE HISTORY OF BEHAVIORAL SCIENCES 1 (2012); Hugo Mercier & Dan Sperber, *Why Do Humans Reasons? Arguments for an Argumentative Theory*, 34 BEHAVIOR & BRAIN SCIENCE 57 (2011).

72. Christine Jolls et al., *A Behavioral Approach to Law and Economics*, 50 STANFORD LAW REVIEW 1471 (1998).

Indeed, our ability to make rational decisions has many constraints. To begin with, rational decisionmaking requires well-defined preferences and goals that reflect true tradeoffs among available options; but we do not possess such clarity about our preferences and goals.[73] People generally exhibit a tendency to stick to existing circumstances and demonstrate a "status quo bias."[74] Framing and benchmarks influence simple and complex decisions.[75] We frequently fail to eliminate irrelevant alternatives from our decision process.[76] Because of scarcity of resources and time we develop and utilize rules of thumb (heuristics) on which we tend to rely too heavily.[77] We tend to be unrealistically optimistic about future events, to grossly underestimate ordinary risks, and to be overconfident about their relative abilities.[78] We all exhibit inconsistencies in our decisionmaking, experience challenges in making good intertemporal decisions, and struggle with exercising self-control.[79] We also often follow herd behavior.[80] And no person is exempt from human fallibility.[81] These are only some of our many cognitive limitations. The anti-antipaternalism argument states that the

---

73. *See generally* Daniel McFadden, *Rationality for Economists?*, 19 JOURNAL OF RISK & UNCERTAINTY 73 (1999); § 11.1.

74. *See* William Samuelson & Richard Zeckhauser, *Status Quo Bias in Decision Making*, 1 JOURNAL OF RISK & UNCERTAINTY 1 (1988).

75. *See generally* Daniel Kahneman & Daniel Tversky, *Choices, Values, and Frames*, 39 AMERICAN PSYCHOLOGIST 341 (1984); Richard Thaler, *Toward a Positive Theory of Consumer Choice*, 1 JOURNAL OF ECONOMIC BEHAVIOR AND ORGANIZATION 39 (1980); Amos Tversky & Daniel Kahneman, *The Framing of Decisions and the Psychology of Choice*, 211 SCIENCE 453 (1981).

76. *See* Amos Tversky, *Elimination by Aspects: A Theory of Choice*, 79 PSYCHOLOGICAL REVIEW 281 (1972); Amos Tversky & Itamar Simonson, *Context–Dependent Preferences*, 39 MANAGEMENT SCIENCE 1179 (1993).

77. *See generally* William J. Baumol & Richard E. Quandt, *Rules of Thumb and Optimally Imperfect Decisions*, 54 AMERICAN ECONOMIC REVIEW 23 (1964); Richard E. Nisbett et al., *The Use of Statistical Heuristics in Everyday Inductive Reasoning*, 90 PSYCHOLOGICAL REVIEW 339 (1983); Amos Tversky & Daniel Kahneman, *Judgment Under Uncertainty: Heuristics and Biases*, 185 SCIENCE 1124 (1974).

78. *See generally* Dan Lovallo & Daniel Kahneman, *Delusions of Success: How Optimism Undermines Executives Decisions*, 81(7) HARVARD BUSINESS REVIEW 56 (Jul. 2003); Frank P. McKenna, *It Won't Happen to Me: Unrealistic Optimism or Illusion of Control?* 84 BRITISH JOURNAL OF PSYCHOLOGY 39 (1993); Ola Svenson, *Are We All Less Risky and More Skillful Than Our Fellow Drivers?* 47 ACTA PSYCHOLOGICA 143 (1981); Neil D. Weinstein, *Unrealistic Optimism About Future Life Events*, 39 JOURNAL OF PERSONALITY & SOCIAL PSYCHOLOGY 806 (1980); Neil D. Weinstein, *Unrealistic Optimism About Susceptibility to Health Problems*, 5 JOURNAL OF BEHAVIORAL MEDICINE 441 (1982).

79. *See, e.g.*, Ted O'Donoghue & Matthew Rabin, *Doing It Now or Later*, 89 AMERICAN ECONOMIC REVIEW 103 (1999); Ted O'Donoghue & Matthew Rabin, *The Economics of Immediate Gratification*, 13 JOURNAL OF BEHAVIORAL DECISION MAKING 233 (2000).

80. *See, e.g.*, George A. Akerlof, *Procrastination and Obedience*, 81 AMERICAN ECONOMIC REVIEW 1 (1991); Abhijit V. Banerjee, A Simple Model of Herd Behavior, 107 QUARTERLY JOURNAL OF ECONOMICS 797 (1992); Sushil Bikhchandani et al., A *Theory of Fads, Fashion, Custom, and Cultural Change as Informational Cascades*, 100 JOURNAL OF POLITICAL ECONOMY 992 (1992); David S. Scharfstein & Jeremy C. Stein, *Herd Behavior and Investment*, 80 AMERICAN ECONOMIC REVIEW 465 (1990); SHILLER, IRRATIONAL EXUBERANCE, *supra* note 27.

81. *See generally* Raaj Kumar Sah and Joseph E. Stiglitz, *Human Fallibility and Economic Organization*, 74 AMERICAN ECONOMIC REVIEW 292 (1985); Raaj Kumar Sah, *Fallibility in Human Organizations and Political Systems*, 5 JOURNAL OF ECONOMIC PERSPECTIVES 67 (1991).

pursuit of self-interest may be unsuccessful in predictable patterns and may not necessarily serve the individual and society.

Building on the anti-antipaternalism argument, Sunstein and Thaler introduced a paternalistic approach that does not eliminate options; rather it utilizes regulatory mechanisms to manipulate choices in order to steer individuals toward those that are likely to enhance their well-being and away from those that are likely to adversely affect them. They named this framework "*libertarian paternalism*" because it imposes no restrictions on the freedom of choice.[82] Sunstein and Thaler justified this concept of paternalism with abundant empirical findings, which show that "in many domains, people lack clear, stable, or well-ordered preferences, and [w]hat they choose is strongly influenced by details of the context in which they make their choice, * * * and starting points." They argued that because "contextual influences render the very meaning of the term 'preferences' unclear," steering people's choices in welfare-promoting directions without eliminating choices is a desirable public policy. Sunstein and Thaler also introduced and popularized the concept of "*nudge*"—"any aspect of the choice architecture that alters people's behavior in a predictable way without forbidding any options or significantly changing their economic incentives."[83]

Mandatory disclosures are common nudges.[84] For example, the Nutrition Labeling and Education Act of 1990 (NLEA) requires most food products to include standardized nutrition labels.[85] The standardized labels include information about calories, total and saturated fats, cholesterol, sodium, and other nutrients. Another type of nudge is default rules that are designed to promote welfare, while maintaining simple opt-out options. For example, 401(k) participation is significantly higher when employees are automatically enrolled than when they need to take an action. Thus, because of the status quo bias and other reasons, the design of default rules influences outcomes.

Others proposed "asymmetric paternalism," referring to regulations that create "large benefits for those who make errors, while imposing little or no harm on those who are fully rational."[86] Proponents of this approach argue that certain regulatory areas, such as health and food regulations, "are heavily informed by scientific understanding (albeit an understanding sometimes captured by special interests) and by a widespread belief among professionals that average folks require information, prodding, and often

---

82. Cass R. Sunstein & Richard H. Thaler, *Libertarian Paternalism Is Not an Oxymoron*, 70 UNIVERSITY OF CHICAGO LAW REVIEW 1159 (2003).

83. RICHARD H. THALER & CASS R. SUNSTEIN, NUDGE: IMPROVING DECISIONS ABOUT HEALTH, WEALTH, AND HAPPINESS 6 (2008).

84. *See generally* David Weil et al., *The Effectiveness of Regulatory Disclosure Policies*, 25 JOURNAL OF POLICY ANALYSIS & MANAGEMENT 155 (2006); William M. Sage, *Regulating Through Information: Disclosure Laws and American Health Care*, 99 COLUMBIA LAW REVIEW 1701 (1999).

85. The Nutrition Labeling and Education Act of 1990, Pub. L. No. 101–535, 101 Stat. 2353 (1990).

86. Colin Camerer et al., *Regulation for Conservatives: Behavioral Economics and the Case for "Asymmetric Paternalism,"* 151 UNIVERSITY OF PENNSYLVANIA LAW REVIEW 1211, 1212 (2003).

regulation to improve their health and diet."[87] In some of these regulatory areas, paternalistic policies that mandate standardized disclosures and warnings have been successfully used for many years. These policies are asymmetrically paternalistic because they may benefit those who are likely to err and do not really burden others. Examples for strategies of asymmetric paternalism include: (1) default rules; (2) disclosures and reframing of information; (3) cooling-off periods; and (4) limiting consumer choices.[88] Both asymmetric and libertarian paternalism therefore rely on bounded rationality to justify regulation to eliminate self-inflicted harm caused by suboptimal choices. They differ from each other by the extent to which they preserve freedom of choice. Libertarian paternalism is supposedly less intrusive.

In sum, acknowledging our human limitations, psychologists, economists, and lawyers argue that traditional premises regarding rational decisionmaking are both counterintuitive and empirically unfounded.[89] Moreover, some of the cognitive limitations that prevent us from making rational decisions in our everyday life also explain common approaches to regulation, reasoning techniques, and unwillingness to reconsider firm positions.[90] There are many obvious promises in understanding our human limitations.

§ 7.4.2 Bounded Rationality in Action

Proposals to utilize bounded rationality in regulation have led to a broad range of critiques that question various aspects of state regulation, including the concentration of decisionmaking, slippery slopes, inefficiencies of the public sector, and general aversion of paternalism.[91] State agents—legislators, judges, and administrative agencies—are boundedly rational like all other humans. Can they regulate bounded rationality despite their own cognitive limitations? One way to think about this question is that boudedly rational regulators have always been regulating spheres of bounded rationality, even by choosing not to regulate such spheres. Thus, the institutional challenge is to recognize the limitations of boundedly rational regulators.

The following four cases illuminate a wide range of regulatory techniques that may be understood as attempts to exploit cognitive limitations or as being influenced by such limitations.

---

87. *Id.* at 1222.

88. *Id.* The term "cooling-off" periods refers to policies in which irrevocability of agreements cannot be waived, or agreements cannot be carried out. The boundaries on willpower and self-control provide the rationale for these policies. For elimination of choices *see* Joni Hersch, *Smoking Restrictions as a Self-Control Mechanism*, 31 JOURNAL OF RISK & UNCERTAINTY 5 (2005).

89. *See* DANIEL KAHNEMAN, THINKING, FAST AND SLOW (2011).

90. For reasoning biases *see* Kunda, *The Case for Motivated Reasoning*, *supra* note 66; Mercier & Sperber, *Why Do Humans Reasons?*, *supra* note 71.

91. *See generally* Edward L. Glaeser, *Paternalism and Psychology*, 73 UNIVERSITY OF CHICAGO LAW REVIEW 133 (2006).

Defunding Law

Palmer v. Thompson

403 U.S. 217 (1971)

■ MR. JUSTICE BLACK delivered the opinion of the Court.

In 1962 the city of Jackson, Mississippi, was maintaining five public parks along with swimming pools, golf links, and other facilities for use by the public on a racially segregated basis. Four of the swimming pools were used by whites only and one by Negroes only. Plaintiffs brought an action in the United States District Court seeking a declaratory judgment that this state-enforced segregation of the races was a violation of the Thirteenth and Fourteenth Amendments, and asking an injunction to forbid such practices. After hearings the District Court entered a judgment declaring that enforced segregation denied equal protection of the laws but it declined to issue an injunction.[1] The Court of Appeals affirmed, and we denied certiorari. The city proceeded to desegregate its public parks, auditoriums, golf courses, and the city zoo. However, the city council decided not to try to operate the public swimming pools on a desegregated basis. Acting in its legislative capacity, the council surrendered its lease on one pool and closed four which the city owned. A number of Negro citizens of Jackson then filed this suit to force the city to reopen the pools and operate them on a desegregated basis. The District Court found that the closing was justified to preserve peace and order and because the pools could not be operated economically on an integrated basis. It held the city's action did not deny black citizens equal protection of the laws. The Court of Appeals sitting en banc affirmed, six out of 13 judges dissenting. That court rejected the contention that since the pools had been closed either in whole or in part to avoid desegregation the city council's action was a denial of equal protection of the laws. We granted certiorari to decide that question. We affirm.

I

Petitioners rely chiefly on the first section of the Fourteenth Amendment which forbids any State to 'deny to any person within its jurisdiction the equal protection of the laws.' There can be no doubt that a major purpose of this amendment was to safeguard Negroes against discriminatory state laws-state laws that fail to give Negroes protection equal to that afforded white people. History shows that the achievement of equality for Negroes was the urgent purpose not only for passage of the Fourteenth Amendment but for the Thirteenth and Fifteenth Amendments as well. * * * Thus the Equal Protection Clause was principally designed to protect Negroes against discriminatory action by the States. * * * The question [here] is whether this closing of the pools is state action that denies 'the equal protection of the laws' to Negroes. It should be noted first that neither the Fourteenth Amendment nor any Act of Congress purports to impose an affirmative duty on a State to begin to operate or to continue to

1. Clark v. Thompson, 206 F.Supp. 539 (S.D.Miss.1962).

operate swimming pools. Furthermore, this is not a case where whites are permitted to use public facilities while blacks are denied access. It is not a case where a city is maintaining different sets of facilities for blacks and whites and forcing the races to remain separate in recreational or educational activities.[5] * * *

[W]e must agree with the courts below and affirm.

II

* * * Petitioners * * * claim that Jackson's closing of the public pools authorizes or encourages private pool owners to discriminate on account of race and that such 'encouragement' is prohibited. * * * In the first place there are no findings here about any state 'encouragement' of discrimination. * * * The implication of petitioners' argument appears to be that the fact the city turned over to the YMCA a pool it had previously leased is sufficient to show automatically that the city has conspired with the YMCA to deprive Negroes of the opportunity to swim in integrated pools. Possibly in a case where the city and the YMCA were both parties, a court could find that the city engaged in a subterfuge, and that liability could be fastened on it as an active participant in a conspiracy with the YMCA. We need not speculate upon such a possibility, for there is no such finding here. * * *

III

Petitioners have also argued that respondents' action violates the Equal Protection Clause because the decision to close the pools was motivated by a desire to avoid integration of the races. But no case in this Court has held that a legislative act may violate equal protection solely because of the motivations of the men who voted for it. The pitfalls of such analysis were set forth clearly in the landmark opinion of Mr. Chief Justice Marshall in *Fletcher v. Peck*, 10 U.S. 87 (1810), where the Court declined to set aside the Georgia Legislature's sale of lands on the theory that its members were corruptly motivated in passing the bill.

* * *

Petitioners have argued strenuously that a city's possible motivations to ensure safety and save money cannot validate an otherwise impermissible state action. This proposition is, of course, true. Citizens may not be compelled to forgo their constitutional rights because officials fear public hostility or desire to save money. * * * But the issue here is whether black citizens in Jackson are being denied their constitutional rights when the city has closed the public pools to black and white alike. Nothing in the history or the language of the Fourteenth Amendment nor in any of our prior cases persuades us that the closing of the Jackson swimming pools to all its citizens constitutes a denial of 'the equal protection of the laws.'

* * *

---

5. My Brother WHITE's dissent suggests that the pool closing operates unequally on white and blacks because, 'The action of the city in this case interposes a major deterrent to seeking judicial or executive help in eliminating racial restrictions on the use of public facilities.' * * * It is difficult to see the force of this argument since Jackson has desegregated its public parks, auditoriums, golf course, city zoo, and the record indicates it now maintains no segregated public facilities.

It has not been so many years since it was first deemed proper and lawful for cities to tax their citizens to build and operate swimming pools for the public. Probably few persons, prior to this case, would have imagined that cities could be forced by five lifetime judges to construct or refurbish swimming pools which they choose not to operate for any reason, sound or unsound. Should citizens of Jackson or any other city be able to establish in court that public, tax-supported swimming pools are being denied to one group because of color and supplied to another, they will be entitled to relief. But that is not the case here.

The judgment is affirmed.

■ MR. CHIEF JUSTICE BURGER, concurring.

I join the opinion of MR. JUSTICE BLACK, but add a brief comment.

The elimination of any needed or useful public accommodation or service is surely undesirable and this is particularly so of public recreational facilities. Unfortunately the growing burdens and shrinking revenues of municipal and state governments may lead to more and more curtailment of desirable services. Inevitably every such constriction will affect some groups or segments of the community more than others. To find an equal protection issue in every closing of public swimming pools, tennis courts, or golf courses would distort beyond reason the meaning of that important constitutional guarantee. To hold, as petitioners would have us do, that every public facility or service, once opened, constitutionally 'locks in' the public sponsor so that it may not be dropped * * * would plainly discourage the expansion and enlargement of needed services in the long run.

We are, of course, not dealing with the wisdom or desirability of public swimming pools; we are asked to hold on a very meager record that the Constitution requires that public swimming pools, once opened, may not be closed. But all that is good is not commanded by the Constitution and all that is bad is not forbidden by it. We would do a grave disservice, both to elected officials and to the public, were we to require that every decision of local governments to terminate a desirable service be subjected to a microscopic scrutiny for forbidden motives rendering the decision unconstitutional.

■ MR. JUSTICE BLACKMUN, concurring.

I, too, join MR. JUSTICE BLACK's opinion and the judgment of the Court.

Cases such as this are 'hard' cases for there is much to be said on each side. In isolation this litigation may not be of great importance; however, it may have significant implications.

The dissent of MR. JUSTICE WHITE rests on a conviction that the closing of the Jackson pools was racially motivated, at least in part, and that municipal action so motivated is not to be tolerated. That dissent builds to its conclusion with a detailed review of the city's and the State's official attitudes of past years.

MR. JUSTICE BLACK's opinion stresses, on the other hand, the facially equal effect upon all citizens of the decision to discontinue the pools. It also emphasizes the difficulty and undesirability of resting any constitutional decision upon what is claimed to be legislative motivation.

I remain impressed with the following factors: (1) No other municipal recreational facility in the city of Jackson has been discontinued. Indeed, every other service-parks, auditoriums, golf courses, zoo-that once was segregated, has been continued and operates on a nonsegregated basis. One must concede that this was effectuated initially under pressure of the 1962 declaratory judgment of the federal court. (2) The pools are not part of the city's educational system. They are a general municipal service of the nice-to-have but not essential variety, and they are a service, perhaps a luxury, not enjoyed by many communities. (3) The pools had operated at a deficit. It was the judgment of the city officials that these deficits would increase. (4) I cannot read into the closing of the pools an official expression of inferiority toward black citizens. * * * (5) The response of petitioners' counsel at oral argument to my inquiry* whether the city was to be 'locked in' with its pools for an indefinite time in the future, despite financial loss of whatever amount, just because at one time the pools of Jackson had been segregated, is disturbing.

There are, of course, opposing considerations enumerated in the two dissenting opinions. As my Brothers BLACK, DOUGLAS, and WHITE all point out, however, the Court's past cases do not precisely control this one. * * * I therefore vote to affirm.

■ MR. JUSTICE DOUGLAS, dissenting.

Jackson, Mississippi, closed all the swimming pools * * *, following a judgment of the Court of Appeals in Appeal *Clark v. Thompson*, 313 F.2d 637 (5th Cir. 1963), which affirmed the District Court's grant of a declaratory judgment that three Negroes were entitled to the desegregated use of the city's swimming pools. * * * No municipal swimming facilities have been opened to any citizen of either race since that time; and the city apparently does not intend to reopen the pools on an integrated basis.

That program is not, however, permissible if it denies rights created or protected by the Constitution. * * * I think that the plan has that constitutional defect; and that is the burden of this dissent.

* * *

May a State in order to avoid integration of the races abolish all of its public schools? That would dedicate the State to backwardness, ignorance,

* '**Q.** Mr. Rosen, if you were to prevail here, would the city of Jackson be locked in to operating the pools irrespective of the economic consequences of that operation?

'**A.** If the question is forever. If it was purely an economic problem, having nothing to do with race, or opposition to integration, they could handle that problem the way any community handles that problem, if it is purely an economic decision. But if it becomes a consideration of race, which creates the economic difficulties, then it seems to me that this Court in numerous decisions has answered that question. It answered it in Watson, it answered it in Brown, and it answered it in Green.

'**Q.** Well, this is in the premise of my question, for you to prevail here, this racial overtone, I will assume, you must concede must be present. Now suppose you prevail, and suppose they lose economically year after year by increasing amounts. Mr. question is, are they locked in forever?

'**A.** If the question is, are they locked in forever because of racial problems which cause a rise in economic difficulties in operating the pool, my answer is that they would be locked in.'
* * *

and existence in a new Dark Age. Yet is there anything in the Constitution that says that a State must have a public school system? Could a federal court enjoin the dismantling of a public school system? Could a federal court order a city to levy the taxes necessary to construct a public school system? Such supervision over municipal affairs by federal courts would be a vast undertaking, conceivably encompassing schools, parks, playgrounds, civic auditoriums, tennis courts, athletic fields, as well as swimming pools.

My conclusion is that the Ninth Amendment has a bearing on the present problem. It provides:

> 'The enumeration in the Constitution, of certain rights, shall not be construed to deny or disparage others retained by the people.'

Rights, not explicitly mentioned in the Constitution, have at times been deemed so elementary to our way of life that they have been labeled as basic rights. Such is the right to travel from State to State. * * * Such is also the right to marry. * * * The 'rights' retained by the people within the meaning of the Ninth Amendment may be related to those 'rights' which are enumerated in the Constitution. Thus the Fourth Amendment speaks of the 'right of the people to be secure in their persons, houses, papers, and effects' and protects it by well-known procedural devices. But we have held that that enumerated 'right' also has other facets commonly summarized in the concept of privacy. * * *

There is, of course, not a word in the Constitution, unlike many modern constitutions, concerning the right of the people to education or to work or to recreation by swimming or otherwise. Those rights, like the right to pure air and pure water, may well be rights 'retained by the people' under the Ninth Amendment. May the people vote them down as well as up?

* * *

In determining what municipal services may not be abolished the Court of Appeals drew the line between 'an essential public function' and other public functions. Whether state constitutions draw that line is not our concern. Certainly there are no federal constitutional provisions which make that distinction.

Closing of the pools probably works a greater hardship on the poor than on the rich; and it may work greater hardship on poor Negroes than on poor whites, a matter on which we have no light. Closing of the pools was at least in part racially motivated. And, as stated by the dissenters in the Court of Appeals:

> 'The closing of the City's pools has done more than deprive a few thousand Negroes of the pleasures of swimming. It has taught Jackson's Negroes a lesson: In Jackson the price of protest is high. Negroes there now know that they risk losing even segregated public facilities if they dare to protest segregation. Negroes will now think twice before protesting segregated public parks, segregated public libraries, or other segregated facilities. They must first decide whether they wish to risk living without the facility altogether, and at the same

> time engendering further animosity from a white community which has lost its public facilities also through the Negroes' attempts to desegregate these facilities.
>
> 'The long-range effects are manifold and far-reaching. If the City's pools may be eliminated from the public domain, parks, athletic activities, and libraries also may be closed. No one can say how many other cities may also close their pools or other public facilities. The City's action tends to separate the races, encourage private discrimination, and raise substantial obstacles for Negroes asserting the rights of national citizenship created by the Wartime Amendments.' * * *

That view has strong footing in our decisions. * * * When the effect is 'to chill the assertion of constitutional rights by penalizing those who choose to exercise them' * * * [the] state action is 'patently unconstitutional.'

While Chief Justice Marshall intimated in *Fletcher v. Peck*, 10 U.S. 87 (1810), that the motives which dominate or influence legislators in enacting laws are not fit for judicial inquiry, we do look closely at the thrust of a law to determine whether in purpose or effect there was an invasion of constitutional rights. * * * A candidate may be defeated because the voters are bigots. A racial issue may inflame a community causing it to vote a humane measure down. The federal judiciary cannot become involved in those kinds of controversies. The question for the federal judiciary is not what the motive was, put what the consequences are.

* * *

I conclude that though a State may discontinue any of its municipal services-such as schools, parks, pools, athletic fields, and the like—it may not do so for the purpose of perpetuating or installing apartheid or because it finds life in a multi—racial community difficult or unpleasant. If that is its reason, then abolition of a designated public service becomes a device for perpetuating a segregated way of life. That a State may not do.

* * *

■ MR. JUSTICE WHITE, with whom MR. JUSTICE BRENNAN and MR. JUSTICE MARSHALL join, dissenting.

I agree with the majority that the central purpose of the Fourteenth Amendment is to protect Negroes from invidious discrimination. Consistent with this view, I had thought official policies forbidding or discouraging joint use of public facilities by Negroes and whites were at war with the Equal Protection Clause. Our cases make it unquestionably clear, as all of us agree, that a city or State may not enforce such a policy by maintaining officially separate facilities for the two races. It is also my view, but apparently not that of the majority, that a State may not have an official stance against desegregating public facilities and implement it by closing those facilities in response to a desegregation order.

Let us assume a city has been maintaining segregated swimming pools and is ordered to desegregate them. Its express response is an official resolution declaring desegregation to be contrary to the city's policy and ordering the facilities closed rather than continued in service on a desegregated basis. To me it is beyond cavil that on such facts the city is adhering to an unconstitutional policy and is implementing it by abandoning the facilities. It will not do in such circumstances to say that whites and Negroes are being treated alike because both are denied use of public services. The fact is that closing the pools is an expression of official policy that Negroes are unfit to associate with whites. Closing pools to prevent interracial swimming is little different from laws or customs forbidding Negroes and whites from eating together or from co-habiting or intermarrying. * * * The Equal Protection Clause is a hollow promise if it does not forbid such official denigrations of the race the Fourteenth Amendment was designed to protect.

The case before us is little, if any, different from the case just described. Jackson, Mississippi, closed its swimming pools when a district judge struck down the city's tradition of segregation in municipal services and made clear his expectation that public facilities would be integrated. The circumstances surrounding this action and the absence of other credible reasons for the closings leave little doubt that shutting down the pools was nothing more or less than a most effective expression of official policy that Negroes and whites must not be permitted to mingle together when using the services provided by the city.

I am quite unpersuaded by the majority's assertion that it is impermissible to impeach the otherwise valid act of closing municipal swimming pools by resort to evidence of invidious purpose or motive. Congress has long provided civil and criminal remedies for a variety of official and private conduct. In various situations these statutes and our interpretations of them provide that such conduct falls within the federal proscription only upon proof of forbidden racial motive or animus. * * *

I

In May 1954, this Court held that '(s)eparate educational facilities are inherently unequal.' *Brown v. Board of Education*, 347 U.S. 483, 495 (1954). In a series of opinions following closely in time, the Court emphasized the universality and permanence of the principle that segregated public facilities of any kind were no longer permissible under the Fourteenth Amendment. * * *

The city of Jackson was one of many places where the consistent line of decisions following from Brown had little or no effect. Public recreational facilities were not desegregated although it had become clear that such action was required by the Constitution. As respondents state in their brief in this case:

> 'In 1963 the City of Jackson was operating equal but separate recreational facilities such as parks and golf links, including swimming pools. A suit was brought in the Southern District of Mississippi to enjoin the segregated operation of these facilities. The City of Jackson took the position in that litigation that the segregation of recreational facilities, if separate but equal recreational facilities were provided and if citizens

> voluntarily used segregated facilities, was constitutional.' * * *

This was nearly nine years after *Brown*. * * *

The suit respondents refer to was instituted in 1962 as a class action by three Negro plaintiffs who alleged that some city facilities—parks, libraries, zoo, golf courses, playgrounds, auditoriums, and other recreational complexes-were closed to them because of their race. The defendants were Jackson city officials. * * * The plaintiffs in that suit were successful. The District Court's opinion began by stating that Jackson was a city 'noted for its low crime rate and lack of racial friction except for the period in 1961 when the self-styled Freedom Riders made their visits.' * * * It was also stated that Jackson had racially exclusive neighborhoods, that as this residential pattern had developed the city had 'duplicated' its recreational facilities in white and Negro areas, and that members of each race 'have customarily used the recreational facilities located in close proximity to their homes.' The final finding of fact was that the 'defendants are not enforcing separation of the races in public recreational facilities in the City of Jackson. The defendants do encourage voluntary separation of the races.' * * *

It must be noted here that none of Jackson's public recreational facilities was desegregated until after the appellate proceedings in *Clark v. Thompson* were fully concluded. * * *

During May and June 1963, the Negro citizens of Jackson organized to present their grievances to city officials. On May 27, a committee representing the Negro community met with the mayor and two city commissioners. Among the grievances presented was a specific demand that the city desegregate public facilities, including the city-operated parks and swimming pools.

On the day following this meeting, the Jackson Daily News quoted the mayor as saying:

> "In spite of the current agitation, the Commissioners and I shall continue to plan and seek money for additional parks for our Negro citizens. Tomorrow we are discussing with local Negro citizens plans to immediately begin a new clubhouse and library in the Grove Park area, and other park and recreational facilities for Negroes throughout the City. We cannot proceed, however, on the proposed $100,000 expenditure for a Negro swimming pool in the Grove Park area as long as there is the threat of racial disturbances." * * *

On May 30, 1963, the same paper reported that the mayor had announced that '(p)ublic swimming pools would not be opened on schedule this year due to some minor water difficulty.' * * *

The city at this time operated five swimming facilities on a segregated basis. * * * In literature describing its Department of Parks and Recreation, the city stressed that '(*o*)ur $.10 and $.20 charge for swimming ... (is) the lowest to be found anywhere in the country. The fees are kept low in order to serve as many people as possible.' * * * Parks Director Kurts stated that for the years 1960, 1961, and 1962, the average annual expense to the city of operating [three] pools * * * was $10,000. The average annual revenue from [two of them] was $8,000 apiece; the average annual revenue from the Negro pool * * * was $2,300. Thus, for these three facilities, the city was absorbing an annual loss of approximately $11,700, and was doing so 'in order to serve as many people as possible.' * * *

In August 1965, petitioners brought the present class action in the Southern District of Mississippi. They challenged the closing of the pools and racial segregation in the city jail, seeking both declaratory and injunctive relief. The case was tried on affidavits and stipulations and submitted to the District Judge. * * * Mayor Thompson filed an affidavit which stated:

> 'Realizing that the personal safety of all of the citizens of the City and the maintenance of law and order would prohibit the operation of swimming pools on an integrated basis, and realizing that the said pools could not be operated economically on an integrated basis, the City made the decision subsequent to the *Clark* case to close all pools owned and operated by the City of members of both races.' * * *

Parks Director Kurts filed a similar affidavit, averring:

> 'That after the decision of the Court in the case of *Clark v. Thompson*, it became apparent that the swimming pools owned and operated by the City of Jackson could not be operated peacefully, safely, or economically on an integrated basis, and the City decided that the best interest of all citizens required the closing of all public swimming pools owned and operated by the City . . .'

Based on these affidavits, the District Judge found as a fact that the decision to close the pools was made after *Clark v. Thompson* and that the pools could not be operated safely or economically on an integrated basis. Accordingly, he held that petitioners were not entitled to any relief and dismissed the complaint. On appeal, a panel of the Court of Appeals for the Fifth Circuit affirmed. We granted certiorari to decide that issue, * * * and for the reasons that follow I would reverse.

II

* * * The officials' sworn affidavits, accepted by the courts below, stated that loss of revenue and danger to the citizens would obviously result from operating the pools on an integrated basis. Desegregation, and desegregation alone, was the catalyst that would produce these undesirable consequences. Implicit in this official judgment were assumptions that the citizens of Jackson were of such a mind that they would no longer pay the 10–or 20–cent fee imposed by the city if their swimming and wading had to be done with their neighbors of another race, that some citizens would direct violence against their neighbors for using pools previously closed to them, and that the anticipated violence would not be controllable by the authorities. Stated more simply, although the city officials knew what the Constitution required after *Clark v. Thompson* became final, their judg-

ment was that compliance with that mandate, at least with respect to swimming pools, would be intolerable to Jackson's citizens.

* * *

III

* * * Here, * * * the reality is that the impact of the city's act falls on the minority. Quite apart from the question whether the white citizens of Jackson have a better chance to swim than do their Negro neighbors absent city pools, there are deep and troubling effects on the racial minority that should give us all pause. [B]y closing the pools solely because of the order to desegregate, the city is expressing its official view that Negroes are so inferior that they are unfit to share with whites this particular type of public facility, though pools were long a feature of the city's segregated recreation program. But such an official position may not be enforced by designating certain pools for use by whites and others for the use of Negroes. * * *

IV

From what has been stated above, it is clear that the city's action in closing the pools because of opposition to the decision in *Clark v. Thompson* was 'an exercise of the state police power which trenches upon the constitutionally protected freedom from invidious official discrimination based on race.' * * * The city has only opposition to desegregation to offer as a justification for closing the pools, and this opposition operates both to demean the Negroes of Jackson and to deter them from exercising their constitutional and statutory rights. The record is clear that these public facilities had been maintained and would have been maintained but for one event: a court order to open them to all citizens without regard to race. I would reverse the judgment of the Court of Appeals and remand the cause for further proceedings.

Graphic Warnings

In June 2011, the Food and Drug Administration published a Final Rule requiring nine new visual warnings that would cover 50% of the front and back panels of every cigarette package manufactured and distributed in the United States on or after September 22, 2012.[92] The images are available at *regti.me/FDA-Warnings* (case sensitive). One of them is presented below.

---

92. Required Warnings for Cigarette Packages and Advertisements, 76 Fed.Reg. 36,628 (June 22, 2011), available at *regti.me/FDA-rule* (case sensitive).

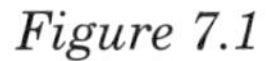

Figure 7.1

R.J. Reynolds Tobacco Co. v. United States Food and Drug Administration

845 F.Supp.2d 266 (D.D.C 2012)

■ RICHARD J. LEON, DISTRICT JUDGE.

Plaintiffs in this case ("plaintiffs") are five tobacco companies, which include the second-, third-, and fourth-largest tobacco manufacturers and the fifth-largest cigarette manufacturer in the United States. * * * In June 2011, defendant United States Food and Drug Administration ("FDA") published a Final Rule requiring (among other things) the display of nine new textual warnings—along with certain graphic images such as diseased lungs and a cadaver bearing chest staples on an autopsy table—on the top 50% of the front and back panels of every cigarette package manufactured and distributed in the United States on or after September 22, 2012. * * * Alleging that the Rule violates the First Amendment * * * plaintiffs moved for a preliminary injunction * * * enjoining the enforcement of the Rule until fifteen months after resolution of plaintiffs' claims on the merits. * * * As such, plaintiffs raised for the first time in our Circuit the question of whether the FDA's new and mandatory graphic images, when combined with certain textual warnings on cigarette packaging, are unconstitutional under the First Amendment. The Court granted plaintiffs' motion on November 7, 2011, * * * conclude[ing] that these mandatory graphic images violate the First Amendment by unconstitutionally compelling speech. For that and the other reasons stated herein, the Court GRANTS plaintiffs' Motion for Summary Judgment and DENIES the Cross–Motion for Summary Judgment.

BACKGROUND

I. Statutory and Regulatory History

A. The Act

The Family Smoking Prevention and Tobacco Control Act ("Act" or "the Act"), Pub.L. No. 111–31, 123 Stat. 1776 (2009), which President Obama signed into law on June 22, 2009, gives the FDA the authority to regulate the manufacture and sale of tobacco products, including cigarettes.

* * * Pursuant to that authority, Congress directed the Secretary of the U.S. Department of Health and Human Services ("the Secretary") to "issue regulations that require color graphics depicting the negative health consequences of smoking." * * * § 201(a) (amending 15 U.S.C. § 1333(d)); * * * In addition, Congress required all cigarette packages manufactured, packaged, sold, distributed, or imported for sale or distribution within the United States to bear one of the following nine textual warnings:

> **WARNING:** Cigarettes are addictive.
>
> **WARNING:** Tobacco smoke can harm your children.
>
> **WARNING:** Cigarettes cause fatal lung disease.
>
> **WARNING:** Cigarettes cause cancer.
>
> **WARNING:** Cigarettes cause strokes and heart disease.
>
> **WARNING:** Smoking during pregnancy can harm your baby.
>
> **WARNING:** Smoking can kill you.
>
> **WARNING:** Tobacco smoke causes fatal lung disease in non-smokers.
>
> **WARNING:** Quitting smoking now greatly reduces serious risks to your health.
>
> Act § 201(a) (amending 15 U.S.C. § 1333(a)(1)).

Congress required that these new textual warnings and graphic images occupy the top 50% of the front and back panels of all cigarette packages, Act § 201(a) (amending 15 U.S.C. § 1333(a)(2)), and the top 20% of all printed cigarette advertising, *id.* (amending 15 U.S.C. § 1333(b)(2)). It gave the FDA "24 months after the date of enactment" of the Act to issue regulations implementing the requirements of Section 201. Act § 201(a) (amending 15 U.S.C. § 1333(d)). * * * Finally, under the Act, the new textual warnings and graphic-image labels (and the related requirements) were scheduled to take effect 15 months after issuance of the Rule. * * *

B. The Rule

1. Proposed Rule

On November 12, 2010, the FDA submitted for public comment a Proposed Rule unveiling 36 graphic color images that could be displayed with the 9 new textual warnings created by Congress. * * * In addition, the Proposed Rule required cigarette packaging and advertising to include "a reference to a smoking cessation assistance resource" and set forth related requirements for what that resource must provide. * * * Finally, as part of its preliminary benefits analysis, the FDA estimated that "the U.S. smoking rate will decrease by ***0.212*** percentage points" as a result of the Proposed Rule, * * * (emphasis added), a statistic the FDA admits is "in general not statistically distinguishable from zero." * * *

2. Final Rule

After a period of notice and comment in which the FDA reviewed more than 1,700 comments, it published a Final Rule on June 22, 2011. * * * Of the 36 graphic images originally proposed, the FDA chose 9 for publication. * * *

In addition to being paired with one of the nine new textual warnings introduced by Congress, each of the graphic images prominently displays "1–800–QUIT–NOW": a telephone number the FDA selected to fulfill its own regulatory obligation to offer smoking cessation assistance on each package. * * * Based on the 15–month implementation period set out by Congress, *see* Act § 201(a) * * *, the new textual warnings and graphic images are scheduled to take effect for all cigarette packages manufactured on or after September 22, 2012, and for all cigarette packages introduced into commerce on or after October 22, 2012. * * * In response to the Final Rule, plaintiffs filed a Motion for Preliminary Injunction, which this Court granted on November 7, 2011. * * *

ANALYSIS

I. Standard of Review

Summary judgment is appropriate when the movant demonstrates that there is no genuine issue of material fact in dispute and that the moving party is entitled to judgment as a matter of law. * * *

II. First Amendment Claim

Plaintiffs oppose the placement of the Government-mandated warnings on the top 50% of the front and back portions of their cigarette packaging. * * * In particular, plaintiffs argue that the new Rule unconstitutionally compels speech, * * * and that such speech does not fit within the "commercial speech" exception under which certain types of Government-mandated, informational disclosures are evaluated under a less restrictive standard. * * * As a result, they argue, the Government's conduct must be analyzed under the strict scrutiny standard. * * * I agree.

A. Applicable Level of Scrutiny

A fundamental tenant of constitutional jurisprudence is that the First Amendment protects "both the right to speak freely and the right to refrain from speaking at all." * * * A speaker typically "has the autonomy to choose the content of his own message." * * * And, in fact, "[f]or corporations as for individuals, the choice to speak includes within it the choice of what not to say." *Pac. Gas & Elec. Co. v. Pub. Utils. Comm'n of Cal.*, 475 U.S. 1, 16 (1986) (plurality opinion). As plaintiffs so aptly stated, although "the Government may engage in [ ] advocacy using its own voice [,] . . . it may not force others, such as Plaintiffs, to serve as its unwilling mouthpiece." * * * *

In the arena of compelled commercial speech, however, narrow exceptions do exist and allow the Government to require certain disclosures to protect consumers from "confusion or deception." * * * Indeed, courts apply a lesser standard of scrutiny to this narrow category of compelled speech through which the Government may require disclosure only of "purely factual and uncontroversial information." * * * Even under this paradigm, however, compelled disclosures containing "purely factual and uncontroversial information" may still violate the First Amendment if they are "unjustified or unduly burdensome." * * * Unfortunately for the defendants, the images here neither meet the * * * standard, nor are narrowly tailored to avoid an undue burden to the plaintiffs' speech. How so?

First, after reviewing the evidence here it is clear that the Rule's graphic-image requirements are *not* the type of purely factual and uncontroversial disclosures that are reviewable under this less stringent standard. To the contrary, the graphic images here were neither designed to protect the consumer from confusion or deception, nor to increase consumer awareness of smoking risks; rather, they were crafted to evoke a strong emotional response calculated to provoke the viewer to quit or never start smoking. Indeed, a report by the Institute of Medicine—an authority chiefly relied upon by the Government—very frankly acknowledges this very purpose. * * * According to the IOM Report, "[i]t is time to state unequivocally that the primary objective of tobacco regulation is not to promote informed choice but rather to discourage consumption of tobacco products, especially by children and youths, as a means of reducing tobacco-related death and disease." * * * Further, "[e]ven though tobacco products are legally available to adults, the paramount health aim is to reduce the number of people who use and become addicted to these products, through a focus on children and youths," and, therefore, the "warnings must be designed to promote this objective." * * *

Not surprisingly the use of the graphic images accomplishes just that: an objective wholly apart from disseminating purely factual and uncontroversial information. That Dr. David Hammond—a researcher upon whom the Government relies—recommended that the graphic warnings should "elicit negative emotional reactions" to convince smokers to quit undercuts any argument that the images are purely factual. *See* David Hammond, *Health Warnings Messages on Tobacco Products: A Review,* 20 TOBACCO CONTROL 327, 331–32 (2011) ("Hammond Review"). * * * Indeed, the FDA measured the efficacy of the graphic images by their "salience," which the FDA defines in large part as a viewer's emotional reaction. * * *

Further, the graphic images are neither factual nor accurate. For example, the image of the body on an autopsy table suggests that smoking leads to autopsies; but the Government provides no support to show that autopsies are a common consequence of smoking. Indeed, it makes no attempt to do so. Instead, it contends that the image *symbolizes* that "smoking kills 443,000 Americans each year." * * * The image, however, does not provide that factual information. Similarly, the image of a man exhaling cigarette smoke through a tracheotomy hole in his throat is not being used to show a usual consequence of smoking. Instead, it is used to *symbolize* "the addictive nature of smoking"—a fact that is not accurately conveyed by the image. * * * Put simply, the Government fails to convey any factual information supported by evidence about the actual health consequences of smoking through its use of these graphic images.

The images, coupled with the placement of the toll free number, do not "promote informed choice" but instead advocate to consumers that they should "QUIT NOW." A telling example is the image depicting a man wearing a t-shirt that features a "no smoking" symbol and the words "I QUIT" next to the "1-800-QUIT-NOW" phone number. This image contains no factual information, and even the Government concedes this image "encourag[es] cessation." * * * Likewise, the Secretary and the Commissioner of the FDA ("the Commissioner") have acknowledged that the graphic images convey an anti-smoking message—specifically, the images were designed to: convey that "smoking is gross"; help "encourage smokers to quit"; "rebrand [ ] our cigarette packs"; and "dispel[ ] the notion that somehow [tobacco use] is cool." * * * Thus, while the line between the constitutionally permissible dissemination of factual information and the impermissible expropriation of a company's advertising space for Government advocacy can be frustratingly blurry, here the line seems quite clear. * * *

B. Analysis Under Strict Scrutiny

To withstand strict scrutiny, the Government carries the burden of demonstrating that the FDA's Rule is narrowly tailored to achieve a compelling government interest. * * * Unfortunately for the Government, it fails to satisfy this burden.

First, although the Government contends that it has a compelling interest—"conveying to consumers generally, and adolescents in particular, the devastating consequences of smoking and nicotine addiction." * * * To the contrary, it is clear that the Government's *actual* purpose is not to inform or educate, but rather to advocate a change in behavior—specifically to encourage smoking cessation and to discourage potential new smokers from starting. *See* IOM Report at 290–91 ("It is time to state unequivocally that the primary objective of tobacco regulation is not to promote informed choice but rather to discourage consumption of tobacco products, especially by children and youths, as a means of reducing tobacco-related death and disease."); Hammond Review at 331–32 (recommending that the graphic warnings should "elicit negative emotional reactions" to convince smokers to quit); 76 Fed.Reg. 36,633 (the purpose of the graphic warnings is to "discourage nonsmokers . . . from initiating cigarette use and to encourage current smokers to consider cessation"); Act § 3.9 (the purpose of the Act is "to promote cessation to reduce disease risk and the social costs associated with tobacco-related diseases"). The Government's reliance on the graphic images—which were chosen based on their ability to provoke emotion, a criterion that does not address whether the graphic images affect consumers' knowledge of smoking risks—coupled with the toll free number, further supports the conclusion that the Government's actual purpose is to convince consumers that they should "QUIT NOW." Indeed, at oral argument, the Government effectively conceded this purpose when it acknowledged: "Now, it's no secret that the Government wants people to stop smoking." * * * Although an interest in informing or educating the public about the dangers of smoking *might* be compelling, an interest in simply advocating that the public not purchase a legal product is not. However, even if the Government's interest is in fact "compelling," the Rule is clearly not narrowly tailored to achieve the Government's purpose. How so?

As I noted previously, "the sheer size and display requirements for the graphic images are anything but narrowly tailored." * * * Under the Rule, plaintiffs are forced to act as the Government's mouthpiece by dedicating the top 50% of the front and back of all cigarette packages manufactured and distributed in the United States to display the Government's anti-smoking message: *not* to purchase this product. These dimensions *alone* clearly demonstrate "that the Rule was designed to achieve the very objective articulated by the Secretary of Health and Human Services: to 'rebrand[ ] our cigarette packs,' treating (as the FDA Commissioner announced last year) 'every single pack of cigarettes in our country' as a 'mini-billboard.' A 'mini-billboard,' indeed, for its obvious anti-smoking agenda!" * * * The FDA's contention that neither it nor this Court has the authority to second-guess Congress, * * * even if the congressional mandate violates the First Amendment, is an oh-too-convenient dodge. * * * As the parties have conceded, there is no evidence that Congress even considered the First Amendment implications when drafting the Act. * * * To say the least, implementing a Final Rule consistent with a congressional mandate does not require a Court to hold that the Rule automatically passes constitutional muster. Congress must pass laws, and the FDA must implement final rules, that are consistent with the requirements of the Constitution. * * *

Finally, with respect to the content of the graphic images, it is curious to note that plaintiffs have offered several alternatives that are easily less restrictive and burdensome for plaintiffs, yet would still allow the Government to educate the public on the health risks of smoking without unconstitutionally compelling speech. First, the Government could disseminate its anti-smoking message itself, for example, by increasing its anti-smoking advertisements or issuing additional statements in the press urging consumers to quit smoking or both. * * * Although doing so might impose costs on the Government, * * * "[c]itizens may not be compelled to forgo their [First Amendment] rights because officials . . . desire to save money." *Palmer v. Thompson*, 403 U.S. 217, 226 (1971). Of course, by now it is clear that the Government's actual concern is not the potential for added cost as the FDA recently announced that it will be spending $600 million on a new—presumably believed to be effective—anti-smoking multimedia campaign. * * * Second, the Government could change the display requirements. Specifically, the Government could reduce the space appropriated for the proposed "warnings" to 20% of the packaging or require "warnings" only on the front or back of the packaging. * * * Third, the Government could change the content by selecting graphics that conveyed only purely factual and uncontroversial information rather than gruesome images designed to disgust the consumer. * * * Fourth, the Government could increase cigarette taxes. * * * And lastly, the Government could improve efforts to prevent the unlawful sale of cigarettes to minors. * * * Any one of these suggestions would be less restrictive than the Rule's current requirements. Unfortunately, because Congress did not consider the First Amendment implications of this legislation, it did not concern itself with how the regulations could be narrowly tailored to avoid unintentionally compelling commercial speech.

Therefore, because the Government has failed to carry both its burden of demonstrating a compelling interest and its burden of demonstrating that the Rule is narrowly tailored to achieve a constitutionally permissible form of compelled commercial speech, the Rule violates the First Amendment and plaintiffs' Motion for Summary Judgment must be, and is, GRANTED.

CONCLUSION

For all the foregoing reasons, plaintiffs' Motion for Summary Judgment * * * is GRANTED, and defendants' Cross–Motion for Summary Judgment * * * is DENIED. * * *

Informed Consent

The Texas' Woman's Right to Know Act supposedly intends to establish procedures of informed consent before abortion. Among other things, the statute requires physicians to provide women with a booklet with graphic images.[93]

Texas Medical Providers Performing Abortion Services v. Lakey

667 F.3d 570 (5th Cir. 2012)

■ EDITH H. JONES, CHIEF JUDGE:

Physicians and abortion providers—collectively representing all similarly situated Texas Medical Providers Performing Abortion Services ("TMPPAS")—sued the Commissioner of the Texas Department of State Health Services and the Executive Director of the Texas Medical Board (collectively "the State") under 42 U.S.C. § 1983 for declaratory and injunctive relief against alleged constitutional violations resulting from the newly-enacted Texas House Bill 15 ("the Act"), an Act "relating to informed consent to an abortion." H.B. 15, 82nd Leg. Reg. Sess. (Tex.2011). The district court granted a preliminary injunction against four provisions for violating the First Amendment. * * * We conclude * * * that Appellees failed to establish a substantial likelihood of success on any of the claims on which the injunction was granted, and therefore VACATE the preliminary injunction. For the sake of judicial efficiency, any further appeals in this matter will be heard by this panel.

Background

H.B. 15, passed in May 2011, substantially amended the 2003 Texas Woman's Right to Know Act ("WRKA"). The amendments challenged here are intended to strengthen the informed consent of women who choose to undergo abortions. The amendments require the physician "who is to perform an abortion" to perform and display a sonogram of the fetus, make audible the heart auscultation of the fetus for the woman to hear, and explain to her the results of each procedure and to wait 24 hours, in most cases, between these disclosures and performing the abortion. Tex. Health

---

93. A copy of the Act is available at *regti.me/TX–HB15* (case sensitive), and a copy of the booklet is available at *regti.me/TX–HB15–Materials* (case sensitive).

& Safety Code § 171.012(a)(4). A woman may decline to view the images or hear the heartbeat, § 171.0122(b), (c), but she may decline to receive an explanation of the sonogram images only on certification that her pregnancy falls into one of three statutory exceptions. * * *

Any woman seeking an abortion must also complete a form indicating that she has received the required materials, understands her right to view the requisite images and hear the heart auscultation, and chooses to receive an abortion. * * * The physician who is to perform the abortion must maintain a copy of this form, generally for seven years. * * *

If a woman ultimately chooses not to receive an abortion, the physician must provide her with a publication discussing how to establish paternity and secure child support. * * *

Finally, the Act amended the Texas Occupations Code to deny or revoke a physician's license for violating these provisions. Tex. Occ.Code § 164.055(a). The Act went into effect on September 1, 2011, and was scheduled to apply to abortions after October 1, 2011.

Appellees filed suit on June 13, requesting a preliminary injunction shortly thereafter. Following extensive briefing, the district court preliminarily enjoined the disclosure provisions of the Act described above on the ground that they "compel speech" in violation of the First Amendment. * * *

The State promptly appealed and sought a stay pending appeal, which the district court denied. A motions panel of this court carried with the case the motion to stay enforcement of the preliminary injunction, but also ordered expedited briefing and oral argument.

* * *

Standard of Review

"To be entitled to a preliminary injunction, the applicant [s] must show (1) a substantial likelihood that [they] will prevail on the merits, (2) a substantial threat that [they] will suffer irreparable injury if the injunction is not granted, (3) [their] substantial injury outweighs the threatened harm to the party whom [they] seek to enjoin, and (4) granting the preliminary injunction will not disserve the public interest." * * *

Discussion

I. First Amendment

Appellees contend that H.B. 15 abridges their First Amendment rights by compelling the physician to take and display to the woman sonogram images of her fetus, make audible its heartbeat, and explain to her the results of both exams. This information, they contend, is the state's "ideological message" concerning the fetal life that serves no medical purpose, and indeed no other purpose than to discourage the abortion. Requiring the woman to certify the physician's compliance with these procedures also allegedly violates her right "not to speak." In fashioning their First Amendment compelled speech arguments, which the district court largely accepted, Appellees must confront the Supreme Court's holding in *Planned Parenthood of Southeastern Pennsylvania v. Casey*, 505 U.S. 833 (1992), that reaffirmed a woman's substantive due process right to terminate a pregnancy but also upheld an informed-consent statute over precisely the same "compelled speech" challenges made here. Following *Casey*, an en banc decision of the Eighth Circuit has also upheld against a compelled speech attack another informed consent provision regulating abortion providers. *Planned Parenthood Minnesota, et al. v. Rounds*, 653 F.3d 662 (8th Cir.2011). We begin this analysis with *Casey*.

The law at issue in *Casey* required an abortion provider to inform the mother of the relevant health risks to her and the "probable gestational age of the unborn child." *Casey*, 505 U.S. at 881. The woman also had to certify in writing that she had received this information and had been informed by the doctor of the availability of various printed materials "describing the fetus and providing information about medical assistance for childbirth, information about child support from the father, and a list of agencies which provide adoption and other services as alternatives to abortion."[2] Planned Parenthood contended that all of these disclosures operate to discourage abortion and, by compelling the doctor to deliver them, violated the physician's First Amendment free-speech rights. Planned Parenthood urged application of the strict scrutiny test governing certain First Amendment speech rights. * * *

The *Casey* plurality's opinion concluded that such provisions, entailing "the giving of truthful, nonmisleading information" which is "relevant ... to the decision," did not impose an undue burden on the woman's right to an abortion and were thus permitted by the Fourteenth Amendment. * * * The requirement that the physician relay the probable age of the fetus furthered the legitimate end of "ensur[ing] that a woman apprehend the full consequences of her decision." * * * In other words, "informed choice need not be defined in such narrow terms that all considerations of the effect on the fetus are made irrelevant." * * * As the Court noted, such information "furthers the legitimate purpose of reducing the risk that a woman may elect an abortion, only to discover later, with devastating psychological consequences, that her decision was not fully informed." * * * States may further the "legitimate goal of protecting the life of the unborn" through "legislation aimed at ensuring a decision that is mature and informed, even when in doing so the State expresses a preference for childbirth over abortion." * * *

The plurality then turned to the petitioners'

> asserted First Amendment right of a physician not to provide information about the risks of abortion, and childbirth, in a manner mandated by the state. To be sure, the physician's First Amendment rights not to speak are implicated, * * * but only as part of the practice of medicine, subject to reasonable licensing and regulation by the State. * * * We see no constitutional infirmity in the requirement that the physician provide the information mandated by the state here. * * *

---

2. The description included a month by month explanation of prenatal fetal development.

The plurality response to the compelled speech claim is clearly not a strict scrutiny analysis. It inquires into neither compelling interests nor narrow tailoring. * * * The only reasonable reading of *Casey*'s passage is that physicians' rights not to speak are, when "part of the practice of medicine, subject to reasonable licensing and regulation by the State[.]" This applies to information that is "truthful," "nonmisleading," and "relevant . . . to the decision" to undergo an abortion. * * *

The Court's decision in *Gonzales v. Carhart*, 550 U.S. 124 (2007), reaffirmed *Casey*, as it upheld a state's "significant role . . . in regulating the medical profession" and added that "[t]he government may use its voice and regulatory authority to show its profound respect for the life within the woman." * * * The Court addressed in detail the justification for state regulations consistent with *Casey*'s reaffirming the right to abortion:

> Whether to have an abortion requires a difficult and painful moral decision. While we find no reliable data to measure the phenomenon, it seems unexceptionable to conclude that some women come to regret their choice to abort the infant life they once created and sustained. Severe depression and loss of esteem can follow.
>
> In a decision so fraught with emotional consequence some doctors may prefer not to disclose precise details of the means that will be used, confining themselves to the required statement of risks the procedure entails. From one standpoint this ought not to be surprising. Any number of patients facing imminent surgical procedures would prefer not to hear all details, lest the usual anxiety preceding invasive medical procedures become the more intense. This is likely the case with the abortion procedures here at issue [partial-birth abortions].
>
> . . . The State's interest in respect for life is advanced by the dialogue that better informs the political and legal systems, the medical profession, expectant mothers, and society as a whole of the consequences that follow from a decision to elect a late-term abortion.

Id. at 157–59, 1633–34 (citations omitted).

The import of these cases is clear. First, informed consent laws that do not impose an undue burden on the woman's right to have an abortion are permissible if they require truthful, nonmisleading, and relevant disclosures. Second, such laws are part of the state's reasonable regulation of medical practice and do not fall under the rubric of compelling "ideological" speech that triggers First Amendment strict scrutiny.[3] Third, "relevant" informed consent may entail not only the physical and psychological risks to the expectant mother facing this "difficult moral decision," but also the state's legitimate interests in "protecting the potential life within

3. *But see Casey*, 505 U.S. at 872 ("Even in the earliest stages of pregnancy, the State may enact rules and regulations designed to encourage her to know that there are philosophic and social arguments of great weight that can be brought to bear in favor of continuing the pregnancy to full term[.]").

her." * * * Finally, the possibility that such information "might cause the woman to choose childbirth over abortion" does not render the provisions unconstitutional. * * *

Fortifying this reading, the Eighth Circuit sitting en banc construed *Casey* and *Gonzales* in the same way:

> [W]hile the State cannot compel an individual simply to speak the State's ideological message, it can use its regulatory authority to require a physician to provide truthful, non-misleading information relevant to a patient's decision to have an abortion, *even if that information might also encourage the patient to choose childbirth over abortion.*

Planned Parenthood Minn. v. Rounds, 530 F.3d 724, 735 (8th Cir.2008) (en banc) (emphasis added). * * *

In contrast to the disclosures discussed in *Rounds*, H.B. 15 requires the taking and displaying of a sonogram, the heart auscultation of the pregnant woman's fetus, and a description by the doctor of the exams' results. That these medically accurate depictions are inherently truthful and non-misleading is not disputed.[4] * * * Unlike the plaintiffs in *Casey* and *Rounds*, the Appellees here do not contend that the H.B. 15 disclosures inflict an unconstitutional undue burden on a woman's substantive due process right to obtain an abortion. These omissions, together, are significant. If the disclosures are truthful and non-misleading, and if they would not violate the woman's privacy right under the *Casey* plurality opinion, then Appellees would, by means of their First Amendment claim, essentially trump the balance *Casey* struck between women's rights and the states' prerogatives. *Casey,* however, rejected any such clash of rights in the informed consent context.

Applying to H.B. 15 the principles of *Casey*'s plurality, the most reasonable conclusion is to uphold the provisions declared as unconstitutional compelled speech by the district court. To belabor the obvious and conceded point, the required disclosures of a sonogram, the fetal heartbeat, and their medical descriptions are the epitome of truthful, non-misleading information. They are not different in kind, although more graphic and scientifically up-to-date, than the disclosures discussed in *Casey*—probable gestational age of the fetus and printed material showing a baby's general prenatal development stages. Likewise, the relevance of these disclosures to securing informed consent is sustained by *Casey* and *Gonzales*, because both cases allow the state to regulate medical practice by deciding that

4. * * * Speech is ideological when it is "relating to or concerned with ideas" or "of, relating to, or based on ideology." * * * Of course, any fact may "relate" to ideas in some sense so loose as to be useless, but * * * "ideological" speech is speech which conveys a "point of view." * * * Though there may be questions at the margins, surely a photograph and description of its features constitute the purest conceivable expression of "factual information." If the sonogram changes a woman's mind about whether to have an abortion—a possibility which *Gonzales* says may be the effect of permissible conveyance of knowledge, * * * that is a function of the combination of her new knowledge and her own "ideology" ("values" is a better term), not of any "ideology" inherent in the information she has learned about the fetus.

information about fetal development is "relevant" to a woman's decision-making.

As for the woman's consent form, that, too, is governed by *Casey,* which approves the practice of obtaining written consent "as with any medical procedure." * * * H.B. 15 * * * requires that a pregnant woman certify in writing her understanding that (1) Texas law requires an ultrasound prior to obtaining an abortion, (2) she has the option to view the sonogram images, (3) she has the option to hear the fetal heartbeat, and (4) she is required to hear the medical explanation of the sonogram unless she falls under the narrow exceptions to this requirement.

To invalidate the written consent form as compelled speech would potentially subject to strict scrutiny a host of other medical informed-consent requirements. Appellees have offered no theory how the H.B. 15 informed-consent certification differs constitutionally from informed-consent certifications in general.

* * *

For all these reasons, we conclude that the enumerated provisions of H.B. 15 requiring disclosures and written consent are sustainable under *Casey,* are within the State's power to regulate the practice of medicine, and therefore do not violate the First Amendment. Appellees have not demonstrated a likelihood of success on the merits justifying the preliminary injunction.

* * *

Conclusion

Appellees failed to demonstrate constitutional flaws in H.B. 15. Accordingly, they cannot prove a substantial likelihood of success on each of their First Amendment and vagueness claims. This is fatal to their application for a preliminary injunction. Accordingly, we VACATE the district court's preliminary injunction, REMAND for further proceedings consistent with this opinion, and any further appeals in this matter will be heard by this panel.

■ PATRICK E. HIGGINBOTHAM, CIRCUIT JUDGE, concurring:

I join the panel opinion and with the freedom of writing without decisional force offer a different accent upon the appropriate role of the First Amendment in this case. To my eyes there are two settled principles in speech doctrine that inform our decision today. First, in protection of a valid interest the state need not remain neutral in its views and may engage in efforts to persuade citizens to exercise their constitutional right to choose a state-preferred course. Second, the state cannot compel a citizen to voice the state's views as his own. It is immediately apparent that both of these principles are implicated by state regulation of doctors' communications with their patients. It is equally apparent that, given the Supreme Court's decision in *Casey,* each is fully and appropriately abided today, without diminishing their vitality.

The doctor-patient relationship has long been conducted within the constraints of informed consent to the risks of medical procedures, as demanded by the common law, legislation, and professional norms. The doctrine itself rests on settled principles of personal autonomy, protected by a reticulated pattern of tort law, overlaid by both self—and state-imposed regulation. Speech incident to securing informed consent submits to the long history of this regulatory pattern.

The Court's decision in *Casey* accented the state's interest in potential life, holding that its earlier decisions * * * failed to give this interest force at all stages of a pregnancy and that in service of this interest the state may insist that a woman be made aware of the development of the fetus at her stage of pregnancy. Significantly, the Court held that the fact that such truthful, accurate information may cause a woman to choose not to abort her pregnancy only reinforces its relevance to an informed decision. Insisting that a doctor give this information in his traditional role of securing informed consent is permissible. * * *

Casey opens no unfettered pathway for states to suppress abortions through the medium of informed consent. * * * *Casey* recognized that frameworks for obtaining informed consent to abortion must leave the ultimate decision with the woman, whose fully informed decision cannot be frustrated by the state. Today we abide *Casey*, whose force much of the argument here fails to acknowledge. * * * We must and do apply today's rules as best we can without hubris and with less sureness than we would prefer, well aware that the whole jurisprudence of procreation, life and death cannot escape their large shrouds of mystery, yet, and perhaps not, to be lifted by advances of science.

Texas Medical Providers Performing Abortion Services v. Lakey

United States District Court, W.D. Texas
2012 WL 373132

■ SAM SPARKS, DISTRICT JUDGE.

BE IT REMEMBERED on January 20, 2012, the Court held a hearing. * * * [T]he Court now enters the following opinion and orders GRANTING the parties' motions to amend, and DISMISSING IN PART and GRANTING IN PART Defendants' motion for summary judgment.

Background

In this suit, Plaintiffs raise a variety of constitutional challenges to Texas House Bill Number 15, an Act "relating to informed consent to an abortion." Act of May 5, 2011, 82d Leg., R.S., ch. 73, 2011 Tex. Sess. Law Serv. ("H.B. 15" or "the Act"). Per their motion to amend, which the Court has granted, Plaintiffs abandon all claims except their First Amendment compelled speech claim. * * *

On June 30, 2011, Plaintiffs moved for a preliminary injunction based on these claims, and the Court, on August 30, 2011, granted Plaintiffs' motion in part, and denied it in part. * * * On January 10, 2012, a three-judge panel of the Fifth Circuit issued an opinion, vacating this Court's order, and remanding the case for further proceedings. * * * [T]he legal principles articulated by the panel left little room for meaningful discussion. * * *

Still pending are the parties' motions for summary judgment. * * * Resolution of the remainder calls for brief discussion of the Fifth Circuit panel's opinion.

I. First Amendment

In reversing this Court's temporary restraining order, Chief Judge Jones, writing for a majority of the panel, relied substantially on her interpretation of the Supreme Court's decision in *Planned Parenthood of Southeastern Pennsylvania v. Casey*, 505 U.S. 833 (1992)—an interpretation far more expansive than this Court's, but one which the Court must nevertheless apply.

Regarding Plaintiffs' First Amendment challenges, the panel distilled four "rules" from the Supreme Court's decisions in *Casey* and *Gonzales v. Carhart*, 550 U.S. 124 (2007):

> First, informed consent laws that do not impose an undue burden on the woman's right to have an abortion are permissible if they require truthful, nonmisleading, and relevant disclosures. Second, such laws are part of the state's reasonable regulation of medical practice and do not fall under the rubric of compelling "ideological" speech that triggers First Amendment strict scrutiny. Third, "relevant" informed consent may entail not only the physical and psychological risks to the expectant mother facing this difficult moral decision, but also the state's legitimate interests in protecting the potential life within her. Finally, the possibility that such information might cause the woman to choose childbirth over abortion does not render the provisions unconstitutional.

* * * These principles, taken together, describe a remarkable scope of state power in the context of regulating a woman's right to an abortion.[2] First, and most troubling, although the panel only specifically says strict scrutiny analysis does not apply to compelled speech by doctors where informed consent is concerned, it appears the panel has effectively eviscerated the protections of the First Amendment in the abortion context.[3]

---

2. The panel's conclusion is also remarkable because, unlike *Casey*, this Court's opinion had nothing to do with the Fourteenth Amendment abortion rights of women. However, because the Court is obligated to yield to the panel's judgment, it bears noting that regardless of one's feelings about abortion, or whether one believes it is moral or immoral, right or wrong, it remains a right protected by the United States Constitution, as recognized by the Supreme Court.

3. Two facts lead this Court to believe the panel did not reject strict scrutiny analysis in favor of some other First Amendment standard. First, and most obvious, the panel made no traditional First Amendment inquiry into the "fit" between the government's interests and the requirements of the Act. Second, as this Court noted in its opinion, Defendants in this case did not even attempt to justify the Act under such a framework, instead relying solely on *Casey*; and, of course, it would be very odd for the panel to base its decision on an argument not made by Defendants.

Apart from everything else, the Court questions whether the Supreme Court would have modified decades of First Amendment jurisprudence, through the incorporation of *Casey's* Fourteenth Amendment undue burden inquiry, without an explicit statement to that effect. That general point aside, however, specific language in *Casey* suggests the Supreme Court did not intend to analytically merge the First Amendment rights of doctors with the Fourteenth Amendment rights of women, even in the context of informed consent to an abortion: "a requirement that a doctor give a woman certain information as part of obtaining her consent to an abortion is, for constitutional purposes, no different from a requirement that a doctor give certain specific information about any medical procedure."[4] *Casey*, 505 U.S. at 884. * * * The above-quoted language from *Casey* suggests informed consent is informed consent, regardless of what medical procedure is involved; by contrast, the panel's opinion seems to create a special rule for informed consent for abortions. Consequently, this Court respectfully disagrees with the panel's conclusion on this point.[5]

Second, the Court observes that, by importing the panel's definition of "relevant" into its first rule, the result is that doctors may permissibly be compelled to parrot anything the state deems necessary to further its "legitimate interests in protecting the potential life within" the pregnant woman, provided the message does not impose an undue burden on the woman's right to have an abortion. That is, within the abortion context, the doctor's right to speak, or not to speak, is wholly dependent on the contours of a woman's right to an abortion.

Finally, the Court suggests the panel may have assumed away the Act's potential constitutional infirmities, both by equating doctors' First Amendment rights with women's Fourteenth Amendment rights, and by declining to give definite meaning to the phrase "reasonable regulation."

* * * [T]his Court is concerned with the panel's implicit conflation of "reasonable regulation of medical practice," with "truthful, nonmisleading, and relevant disclosures"—particularly given the panel's broad definition of "relevant" in this context. As this Court reads the panel's opinion, an extended presentation, consisting of graphic images of aborted fetuses, and heartfelt testimonials about the horrors of abortion, would be "truthful, nonmisleading, and relevant." Accordingly, the government could apparently require doctors personally to make such presentations prior to performing abortions, all under the rubric of "reasonable regulation of medical practice"—but only to the extent such presentations did not impose an

---

4. This statement not only calls into question the panel's decision to import Fourteenth Amendment undue burden analysis into the First Amendment inquiry, but also emphasizes the intrusive nature of H.B. 15: in no other medical context does the government go so far in telling doctors what they must, and must not, do. * * *

5. The Court also questions how a pregnant woman's informed consent, H.B. 15's nominal goal, is promoted by requiring "the physician who is to perform the abortion" to personally perform many of the mandated acts. If the Act is truly designed to inform women, and not simply to make abortions time-and cost-prohibitive for hospitals and clinics alike, it seems counter-productive to artificially limit the number of medically qualified people who can provide the relevant information. Informed consent requirements exist to protect the rights of patients, and to honor their autonomy, not to provide states with an excuse to impose heavy-handed, paternalistic, and impractical restrictions on the practice of medicine.

undue burden on the pregnant woman's right to an abortion. The concept that the government may make puppets out of doctors, provided it does not step on their patients' rights, is not one this Court believes is consistent with the Constitution, in the abortion context or otherwise.[8]

* * *

Conclusion

There can be little doubt that H.B. 15 is an attempt by the Texas Legislature to discourage women from exercising their constitutional rights by making it more difficult for caring and competent physicians to perform abortions. The added time and expense required by the Act; the random, unannounced searches of abortion facilities authorized thereby * * *; and its mandate to doctors, at the risk of license and criminal fine, to deliver a prescribed message to women seeking to exercise their constitutional rights, will naturally limit the number of competent physicians who are willing to perform abortions—which is, of course, the single purpose of the statute.[10] This Court continues to believe these requirements are impermissible; or, at the least, that *Casey* does not provide justification for them.

At bottom, it seems the panel conflated doctors' First Amendment rights with women's Fourteenth Amendment rights because it was concerned *Casey* could not stand otherwise:

> If the disclosures are truthful and non-misleading, and if they would not violate the woman's privacy right under the *Casey* plurality opinion, then Appellees would, by means of their First Amendment claim, essentially trump the balance *Casey* struck between women's rights and the states' prerogatives. *Casey,* however, rejected any such clash of rights in the informed consent context.

[This] Court disagrees with this assessment. There is no question *Casey* allows the government to limit a woman's constitutional right to an abortion, provided it does not impose an undue burden on that right. However, it does not follow (logically, if not legally) that the government can do anything it desires, within that boundary, to create such limits. Texas may be free to craft a law that imposes restrictions on women seeking abortions, but that does not mean it is equally free to craft a law that imposes affirmative duties on those who come into contact with them.

Even within the context of "informed consent," this Court believes doctors' First Amendment rights have a force independent of the rights of

---

8. Similarly, this Court wonders how "reasonable regulation of medical practice" can include statutory commands that preclude the use of reasoned medical judgment. * * * The Act's one-size-fits-all approach strikes this Court as being wholly inconsistent with reasonable regulation of medical practice. * * *

10. To clarify, the Court is not opposed to the Act's required disclosures as a categorical matter. Indeed, the mandated physician conduct and speech may well be appropriate in certain cases. However, they may equally well be injurious and destructive, mentally and physically, in others. This Court believes Texas overstepped its legitimate authority when it substituted its medical judgment for that of doctors, and imposed a uniform method of treatment for all patients, rather than allowing physicians to make medically appropriate, case-by-case determinations.

their patients. And while the *Casey* court saw "no constitutional infirmity in the requirement that the physician provide" "information about the risks of abortion, and childbirth, in a manner mandated by the State" in that case, * * * that holding does not strike this Court as blessing all "truthful, nonmisleading, and relevant" disclosures—as those terms are defined by the panel.

Finally, * * * H.B. 15, unlike the statute at issue in *Casey,* substantially impairs a doctor's exercise of his or her medical judgment. * * * The Act requires doctors to attempt to discourage their patients from obtaining abortions, in a variety of ways, even in cases where the doctors have determined that an abortion is, for any number of reasons, the best medical option. This one-size-fits-all approach seems to be the very antithesis of "reasonable regulation of medical practice."

Regardless of all the foregoing, however, this Court is required to defer to the panel's decision. And the Court believes the panel's opinion requires a grant of summary judgment in favor of Defendants.

Accordingly, * * * IT IS * * * ORDERED that Defendants' Motion for Summary Judgment is DISMISSED IN PART and GRANTED IN PART, as described above in this opinion.

Questions

1. How did the courts in *Palmer*, *R.J. Reynolds Tobacco*, and *Texas Medical Providers Performing Abortion Services* (Fifth Circuit and District Court) address the concepts of "choice," "market," and "state interference with choices"?

2. How did these courts perceive the meaning of paternalism? Did they implicitly or explicitly address or were influenced by bounded rationality?

3. What is the meaning of "compelled speech" discussed in *Palmer*, *R.J. Reynolds Tobacco*, and *Texas Medical Providers Performing Abortion Services*? Interest groups are routinely involved in the process of lawmaking,[94] and possibly were involved in the processes that led to the enactment of laws discussed in these cases. Should the state compel strong interest groups to deliver messages that serve the public?

---

94. *See generally* Barak Orbach, *Invisible Lawmakers*, 79 UNIVERSITY OF CHICAGO LAW REVIEW (2012).

PART III

Regulatory Methods

The Nirvana Fallacy

*"The view that * * * presents the relevant choice as between an ideal norm and an existing 'imperfect' institutional arrangement. This nirvana approach differs considerably from a comparative institution approach in which the relevant choice is between alternative real institutional arrangements. In practice, those who adopt the nirvana viewpoint seek to discover discrepancies between the ideal and the real and if discrepancies are found, they deduce that the real is inefficient."*

—Harold Demsetz[1]

On the Folly of Rewarding A, While Hoping for B

"Whether dealing with monkeys, rats, or human beings, it is hardly controversial to state that most organisms seek information concerning what activities are rewarded, and then seek to do (or at least pretend to do) those things, often to the virtual exclusion of activities not rewarded. The extent to which this occurs of course will depend on the perceived attractiveness of the rewards offered. * * *

Nevertheless, numerous examples exist of reward systems that are fouled up in that behaviors which are rewarded are those which the rewarder is trying to discourage, while the behavior he desires is not being rewarded at all."

—Steven Kerr[2]

---

1. Harold Demsetz, *Information and Efficiency: Another Viewpoint*, 12 Journal of Law & Economics 1, 1 (1969).

2. Steven Kerr, *On the Folly of Rewarding A, While Hoping for B*, 18 Academy for Management Journal 769 (1975).

CHAPTER 8

Bans, Mandates, and Permits

§ 8.1 Commands and Controls

Our discussion of the concept of "regulation" distinguished between command-and-control and incentive regulations.[1] We begin our review of regulatory methods with command and control regulations ("controls"). Controls are regulatory measures that dictate or proscribe conduct, or in other words, alter the set of practically feasible courses of action. In contrast, incentive regulations modify the consequences of actions to manipulate likely choices. Both controls and incentive regulations utilize legal sanctions and rewards to influence conduct.[2] Therefore, the distinction is sometimes a matter of degree of precision on a spectrum. Fundamentally, both types of measures use incentives.

Controls aim to eliminate or define possible choices. Therefore, most controls are crafted as rules. Standards require exercise of some discretion,[3] and do not work well for bright legal norms, such as "DO" and "DON'T DO." Consider the following example: If the goal is to outlaw driving above the speed limit, a rule that prohibits driving above a defined speed limit is likely to be superior than a standard that would prohibit driving at a speed "greater than is reasonable and proper under the conditions."[4]

In this Chapter, we will discuss the three basic forms of controls: *bans*, *mandates*, and *permits*. The term "bans" is self-explanatory. "Mandates" are requirements designed to compel a market participants to take a specific action. "Permits" refer to exemptions from regulatory constraints when certain conditions are met. The most common form of permits are permits to engage in activities that are generally banned, but permits may also mean exemptions from requirements to do something or other regulatory schemes.

Bans, permits, and mandates tend to be "bundled" or closely related. For example, most mandates and bans (if not all) have exceptions and loopholes that require "permits," or can be regarded as such—permits under particular circumstances.[5] Local laws that mandated smallpox vaccines had certain exceptions.[6] Similarly, the "individual mandates" under the Patient Protection and Affordable Care Act of 2010 have exceptions. In

---

1. *See* § 1.2.1.

2. *See generally* Brian Galle, *The Tragedy of the Carrots: Economics and Politics of the Choice of Price Instruments*, 64 Stanford Law Review 797 (2012).

3. *See* § 1.3.

4. *See* § 1.3 (Montana's Basic Rule).

5. *See generally* Leo Katz, *A Theory of Loopholes*, 39 Journal of Legal Studies 1 (2010).

6. *See, e.g.*, Jacobson v. Massachusetts, 197 U.S. 11 (1905).

the same spirit, during the Prohibition era, physicians had "permits" to prescribe alcohol. Their prescriptions were permits to circumvent a ban (*see Figure 8.1*).[7] We can also frame all bans as mandates and vice versa. As exemptions to bans and mandates, permits are always bundled with bans and mandates. Moreover, to receive a permit a person must meet certain conditions that may be additional bans and mandates. Thus, bans, mandates, and permits should be understood as elements in a regulatory scheme of control. Their framing may serve a purpose, but can be changed.

Figure 8.1
A Prohibition Era Prescription Form for "Medical Liquor"

ORIGINAL
PRESCRIPTION FORM FOR MEDICINAL LIQUOR

E231692

Rx

KIND OF LIQUOR QUANTITY DIRECTIONS

FULL NAME OF PATIENT DATE PRESCRIBED

PATIENTS ADDRESS
NUMBER STREET CITY STATE

ORIGINAL

PRESCRIBERS SIGNATURE PRESCRIBERS PERMIT NUMBER

PRESCRIBERS ADDRESS
NUMBER STREET CITY STATE

CANCELED

DRUG STORE NAME AS ON PERMIT PERMIT NUMBER

DISPENSERS SIGNATURE DATE FILLED AND CANCELED STRIP STAMP NUMBER

STORE ADDRESS
NUMBER STREET CITY STATE

SEE REVERSE SIDE FOR INSTRUCTIONS
DO NOT REFILL OR TRANSFER UNDER PENALTY

29

ISSUED UNDER AUTHORITY OF THE
NATIONAL PROHIBITION ACT

National Federation of Independent Business highlighted the unpopularity of controls. The case involved the controversy over the constitutionality of the "individual mandates" under the Patient Protection and Affordable Care Act of 2010—a requirement for minimum coverage of health insurance.[8] Chief Justice Roberts equated the individual mandates to a requirement to purchase "cars and broccoli." He therefore argued that "[u]nder the Government's theory, Congress could address the diet problem by ordering everyone to buy vegetables." At stake was the question whether uninsured people engage in commerce, when only in some proba-

7. *See* George Griffenhagen, *Medicinal Liquor in the United States*, 29 PHARMACY IN HISTORY 29 (1987); John P. Swann, *FDA and the Practice of Pharmacy: Prescription Drug Regulation Before the Durham–Humphrey Amendment of 1951*, 36 PHARMACY IN HISTORY 55 (1994).

8. National Federation of Independent Business v. Sebelius, 132 S.Ct. 2566 (2012).

bility they become ill and use medical facilities that are *required* to treat them. The dissent expressed one of the traditional critiques of controls:

> The Government presents the Individual Mandate as a unique feature of a complicated regulatory scheme governing many parties with countervailing incentives that must be carefully balanced. * * * This is not a dilemma unique to regulation of the health-insurance industry. Government regulation typically imposes costs on the regulated industry—especially regulation that *prohibits* economic behavior in which most market participants are already engaging. * * * And many industries so regulated face the reality that, without an artificial increase in demand, they cannot continue on. * * * Congress might protect the imperiled industry by prohibiting low-cost competition, or by according it preferential tax treatment, or even by granting it a direct subsidy.
>
> Here, however, Congress has impressed into service third parties, healthy individuals who could be but are not customers of the relevant industry, to offset the undesirable consequences of the regulation.

Our goal in this chapter is to understand the unpopularity and limitations of controls.

§ 8.2 BANS AND PROHIBITIONS

> *When the Eighteenth Amendment was passed, I earnestly hoped * * * that it would be generally supported by public opinion and thus the day be hastened when the value to society of men with minds and bodies free from undermining effects of alcohol would be generally realized. That this has not been the result, but rather that drinking generally has increased; that the speak-easy has replaced the saloon, not only unit for unit, but probably two-fold if not three-fold; that a vast army of lawbreakers has been recruited and financed on colossal scale; that many of our best citizens, piqued at what they regard as an infringement of their private rights, have openly and unabashed disregarded the Eighteenth Amendment; that as an inevitable result respect for all law has been greatly lessened; that crime has increased to an unprecedented degree—I have slowly and reluctantly come to believe.*
>
> —John D. Rockefeller, Jr.[9]

Bans, or prohibitions, diminish liberty. They eliminate certain choices. Although bans are common, in the United States, they connote an aggressive government intrusion upon privacy and liberty, and failing government policies. The term "Prohibition" frequently refers to the ban on the "manufacture, sale, or transportation of intoxicating liquors" by the Eighteenth Amendment between 1919 and 1933 (*see Figure 8.1*).[10]

---

9. A letter from John D. Rockefeller, Jr. to Nicholas Murray Butler, the President of Columbia University, dated June 6, 1932, available at *regti.me/JDR-ban* (case sensitive).

10. *See generally* DANIEL OKRENT, LAST CALL: THE RISE AND FALL OF PROHIBITION (2011).

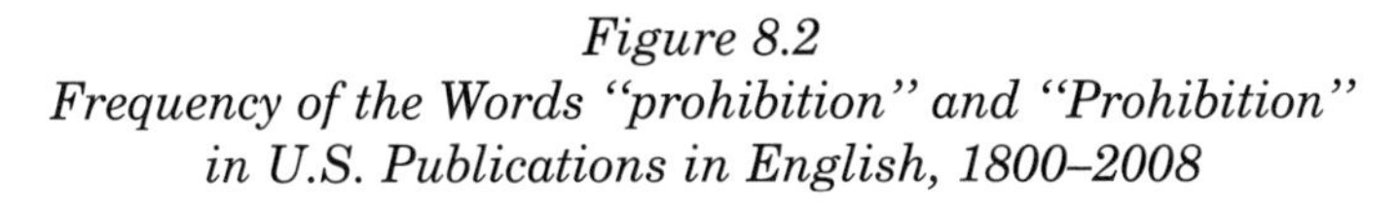

Figure 8.2
Frequency of the Words "prohibition" and "Prohibition" in U.S. Publications in English, 1800–2008

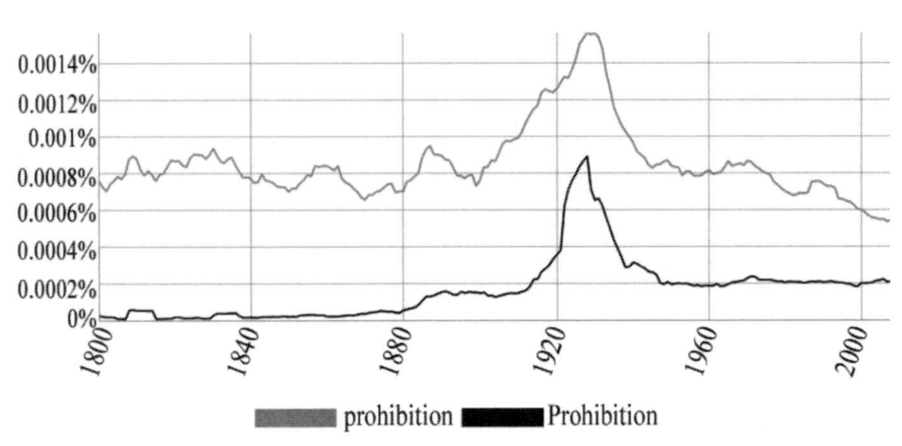

Source: Google Ngram.[11]

The traditional explanations for bans and prohibitions are: externalities,[12] rent seeking,[13] regulatory responses to public concerns,[14] morality,[15] bounded rationality,[16] and practical regulatory solutions to complex realities (second-best solutions).[17] Our discussion of externalities addressed a general category of bans under the common law maxim *sic utere tuo ut alienum non lædas*, "use your own in such a manner as not to injure another."[18] We have also discussed quite a few bans, such as anti-cartoon laws, the Atlanta's 1897 ban on ladies hats in theatres, the 2003 New York City prohibition against cellphones in places of public performance, the San Francisco 2007 ban on disposable shopping bags, anti-spitting laws, state sodomy laws, prohibitions against surrogacy contracts, the 2006 Chicago's ban on foie gras, and bans on the advertising of prostitution. Because bans can be unpopular, it is helpful to remember their wide spectrum. As Justice

11. For the methodology and its limitations *see* Jean–Baptiste Michel et al., *Quantitative Analysis of Culture Using Millions of Digitized Books*, 331 SCIENCE 176 (2011).

12. *See* William J. Boyes & Michael L. Marlow, *The Public Demand for Smoking Bans*, 88(1–2) PUBLIC CHOICE 57 (1996); JOEL FEINBERG, OFFENSE TO OTHERS (1985).

13. *See* George J. Stigler, *The Theory of Economic Regulation*, 2 BELL JOURNAL OF ECONOMICS & MANAGEMENT 1 (1971).

14. *See, e.g.*, Keith B. Leffler, *Physician Licensure: Competition and Monopoly in American Medicine*, 21 JOURNAL OF LAW & ECONOMICS 165 (1978).

15. *See* §§ 7.1–7.2.

16. *See* Douglas Gale, *Spoiled for Choice: Variety and Efficiency in Markets with Incomplete Information*, 51 RESEARCH IN ECONOMICS 41 (1997); Michael Spence, *Consumer Misperceptions, Product Failure, and Product Liability*, 77 REVIEW OF ECONOMIC STUDIES 561 (1977).

17. *See* Robin Hanson, *Warning Labels As Cheap–Talk: Why Regulators Ban Drugs*, 87 JOURNAL OF PUBLIC ECONOMICS 2013 (2003).

18. *See* § 3.2.1.

Holmes once observed: "But pretty much all law consists in forbidding men to do some things that they want to do."[19] Indeed, probably all people endorse *certain bans*, although they oppose others.

Pollution Regulation

Restrictions on the pollution levels that businesses emit can be controversial. Many argue such policies constitute excessive government intrusion upon liberty, that they unduly burden the economy, and that tend to result in job losses. The arguments for and against regulation of pollution have changed little during the past century. Over time, these debates seem to change with respect to the types of pollution subject to regulation. Bans are a common regulatory method used to address pollution. Among affected businesses, however, this response tends to be unpopular. To illustrate, consider *The Slaughter–House Cases*.[20] In the nineteenth century, when Louisiana banned slaughtering in New Orleans to improve the City's failing sanitary conditions, butchers filed almost 300 lawsuits to challenge the prohibition. Nuisance, liberty, and jobs were three key issues tied to the new regulatory framework.[21] Similarly, certain aspects of the controversy over regulation of greenhouse gas emission still implicate these issues with more elaborate arguments concerning the nature of the nuisance and its risk to jobs.

Pugh v. Des Moines

Supreme Court of Iowa
176 Iowa 593 (1916)

■ GAYNOR, JUSTICE.

The plaintiff filed the following petition, in which he made the city of Des Moines, the chief of police, the superintendent of public safety, and the police judge of the city defendants. * * * The plaintiff is a resident of the city, and brings this suit for the benefit of himself and other private automobile owners in the city. * * * Ordinance 1594 of [the] city * * * reads as follows:

> **SEC. 30.** No person shall between the hours of 7:00 o'clock a. m. and 6:30 o'clock p. m. leave standing upon any of the following streets any vehicle, whether in charge of a driver or not, to wit: [a list of streets in downtown Des Moines].
>
> (This section shall not be construed to prohibit vehicles in charge of a driver or other person from standing on said streets for not more than twenty minutes while such vehicle is being loaded or unloaded.)

---

19. Adkins v. Children's Hospital of the District of Columbia, 261 U.S. 525, 568 (1923) (Holmes, J., dissenting).

20. The Slaughter–House Cases, 83 U.S. 36 (1873).

21. *See* § 2.2.2a.

[**SEC. 31.**] No person shall between the hour of 7:00 o'clock a. m. and 6:30 o'clock p. m. leave standing any vehicle for a longer period than one hour on any of the following streets: [a list of streets that surround the streets in downtown Des Moines].

Provided, that the council may by ordinance designate portions of the streets named in this section as stands for vehicles used for the transportation of persons or property for hire.

[**SEC. 38.**] Any person violating any of the rules, regulations or provisions of this ordinance shall be punished by a fine of not less than one dollar nor more than fifty dollars, and shall stand committed until such fine and costs are paid.

* * *

[T]he plaintiff was an attorney at law residing in the city; maintained an office [in downtown Des Moines]; * * * he is the owner of a private passenger automobile carrying five persons; * * * [and] he used the * * * automobile in going to and from his office and elsewhere about the city and country in the practice of his profession. [W]hen [the] automobile was not in use during business hours, it frequently stands on West Fifth Street in the block where plaintiff's office is located [in streets in downtown Des Moines]; [and therefore] the use of [the] automobile is of value to the plaintiff.

[The plaintiff contends] that the * * * ordinance * * * prohibit or restrict the standing in the streets of a private automobile not used for hire, duly licensed, registered, and numbered under the state law, are in excess of the lawful power of the city and void. * * *

* * * Was there power in the city to pass and adopt the ordinance complained of? This presents two propositions: (1) The right of the city to exercise control over the streets and alleys within its corporate limits and to regulate their use; (2) the right of the citizen to the free and unobstructed use of the streets for unobstructed travel.

* * *

[T]he care and control of the highways, streets, and sidewalks within cities * * *, to the end that they may secure to the inhabitants and the general public the convenient and unobstructed use and enjoyment of those thoroughfares for their appropriate purposes. So the state, through its Legislature, has conferred upon cities the right to adopt ordinances to promote the order, comfort, and convenience of the inhabitants that are reasonable and not in conflict with the laws and policies of the state or in violation of private rights.

Separating in our minds for a moment the individual from the public as an aggregation, and looking now to the traveling public—those who use and have a right to use the streets and highways for the purposes for which they are set apart—the mind reaches the conclusion without any confusion of thought that the public have an untrammeled right to free and unobstructed transit over streets, sidewalks, and alleys. This is the primary and appropriate use to which they are generally put. Therefore whatever interferes, unreasonably or unnecessarily, with this use, is a nuisance which the council may prohibit by ordinance, and so it is made its duty to keep streets and sidewalks open and in repair and free from nuisance, to the end that this right may be secured.

* * * The ordinance in the instant case does not declare the obstruction of the streets by the parking of automobiles upon the streets a nuisance, but proceeds upon the theory that the general law so declares and provides. It simply forbids the obstruction, and declares that such obstruction shall be unlawful. This it does under the exercise of its police power. * * *

[Thus, the] public streets of a city are dedicated to public use, and are a public way from "side to side and end to end," and * * * any private use thereof which in any degree detracts from or hinders or prevents its free use as a public way to its full extent is, within the meaning of the law, an obstruction or incumbrance, and any obstruction or incumbrance for private purposes is in law a nuisance; * * * the city is given the exclusive care and control of the streets, and it is made its duty to keep them open and in repair and free from nuisance; [and] * * * the primary use or purpose for which streets are established is to afford the general traveling public a way of passage or travel, and the general traveling public are invested with the right to have them in repair and free from nuisance, that this right may be enjoyed.

This brings us to a consideration of the right of the individual in and to the use of the streets, separate and distinct from his right as a member of the general traveling public. * * *

In *Cohen v. Mayor of New York*, 113 N. Y. 532 (1889) the court said:

> "The storing of the wagon in a highway was a nuisance. The primary use of a highway is for the purpose of permitting the passing and repassing of the public, and it is entitled to the unobstructed and uninterrupted use of the entire width of the highway for that purpose."

The court further said:

> "It is no answer to the charge of nuisance that, even with the obstruction in the highway, there is still room for two or more wagons to pass, nor that the obstruction itself is not a fixture.... The highway may be a convenient place for the owner of carriages to keep them in, but the law, looking to the convenience of the greater number, prohibits any such use of the public streets."

The authorities seem uniform in holding that a person cannot carry on his business in a public street in such a way as to obstruct the street, either by placing actual physical obstructions upon it, or even in such a way as to collect crowds upon the walk, or in front of his business, or so as to interfere with the public travel. If he does, he is chargeable as for nuisance. The fact that the business is lawful does not justify him in interfering with or annoying the public in the obstruction of the free use of the streets. The right given the citizen is to use the public highway for travel, but not so as to impede the free passage of other citizens upon it generally.

* * * It is true that it provides that municipalities may not exclude the owner of an automobile from the free use of the public highway.

[It] is sufficient to say that this ordinance does not exact any fee, license, or permit from the owner of any automobile for the privilege of using the public streets. It does not exclude any automobile owner from the free use of the public streets. We interpret this to mean the free use for the purposes for which streets are primarily dedicated; the free use of the streets for public travel. Clearly it cannot mean that the city is prohibited from preventing the obstruction of its streets by the leaving of automobiles standing therein, to the hindrance and inconvenience of the general public in the use of the streets for travel.

* * *

The plaintiff's [last] contention * * * is that * * * all automobile owners and drivers are given full license to stop their cars upon the public streets when and where they please and for such a length of time as suits their pleasure and convenience, and to leave them standing there, though to the great prejudice and inconvenience of the general public desiring to use the streets for their primary purposes; and the city whose duty it is to keep the streets open and free from nuisance, is rendered as helpless as the shackled prisoner at the bar. The mere statement of the proposition is its own answer. [In plain English,] the argument [means] that the [state] has given to the automobile driver the free use of the public streets, and that the city has no power to exclude from the free use of the public streets. * * * The idea of the free use of a street does not involve the right to obstruct the free use of the street. If one man, in the exercise of his right to the free use of the street, can stable his automobile upon the public street and leave it standing there, any number of persons can exercise the same right, until a point is reached where the travel upon the street is absolutely obstructed. * * *

We * * * think the ordinance is reasonable in its provisions. * * *

Questions

1. Did the Des Moines Ordinance ban parking or imposed restriction on long-term parking in the down-town area?

2. Could or should have the *Pugh* court resorted to the common law maxim *sic utere tuo ut alienum non lædas* to explain the rationale underlying parking restrictions?

Banning Smoking in Public

In May 2005, a majority voters in Austin, Texas, won a divisive battle to ban smoking in public places. With 52% of the voters supporting the measure, the vote required the City to adopt an Ordinance that expanded the ban on smoking in public places. The new Ordinance took effect in

September 2005.[22] Among other terms, the 2005 Ordinance provided the following definitions:

> OPERATOR means the owner or person in charge of a public place or workplace, including an employer.
>
> * * *
>
> PUBLIC PLACE means an enclosed area to which the public is invited or in which the public is permitted, including but not limited to, banks, bars, educational facilities, health care facilities, laundromats, public transportation facilities, reception areas, restaurants, retail food production and marketing establishments, retail service establishments, retail stores, shopping malls, sports arenas, theaters, and waiting rooms. A private residence is not a "public place" unless it is used as a child care, adult day care, or health care facility.
>
> * * *
>
> SMOKING means inhaling, exhaling, burning, or carrying any lighted cigar, cigarette, pipe, weed, plant, or other combustible substance in any manner or form.

Section 10–6–2 of the Ordinance banned smoking in public:

> § 10–6–2 SMOKING PROHIBITED.
>
> (A) A person commits an offense if the person smokes in a public place.
>
> (B) A person commits an offense if the person smokes in an enclosed area in a building or facility owned, leased, or operated by the City.
>
> (C) A person commits an offense if the person smokes in an enclosed area of a workplace.
>
> (D) A person commits an offense if the person smokes within 15 feet from an entrance or openable window of an enclosed area in which smoking is prohibited.
>
> (E) The owner or operator of a public place commits an offense if the person fails to take necessary steps to prevent or stop another person from smoking in an enclosed area in a public place.

In response to inquiries from business owners, the City issued two sets of guidelines to clarify the meaning of the "necessary steps" provision (§ 10–6–2(E)). The guidelines required businesses to post no smoking signs and the City made such signs available.

---

22. A copy of the Ordinance is available at *regti.me/Austin–Smoking* (case sensitive).

Figure 8.3

City of Austin Smoking In Public Places Ordinance No. 050303-05
(Effective September 1, 2005)

NO SMOKING

This is a smoke-free establishment.

No Smoking within 15 feet of the entrance or openable window to this public place.

To report violations of the law, call 972-5600.

Roark & Hardee LP v. Austin

522 F.3d 533 (5th Cir. 2008)

■ CAROLYN DINEEN KING, CIRCUIT JUDGE:

Plaintiffs are owners of stand-alone bars in Austin, Texas. They filed this action against the City of Austin seeking a declaratory judgment and injunctive relief relating to the enforcement of Austin's ordinance prohibiting smoking in enclosed public places, including bars, restaurants, and workplaces. The district court declared the "necessary steps" provision of the ordinance unconstitutionally vague on its face and permanently enjoined the City of Austin from enforcing it. * * *

We REVERSE that portion of the district court's judgment declaring the "necessary steps" provision of the ordinance unconstitutionally vague, [and] VACATE the provision of the permanent injunction enjoining enforcement of said provision. * * *

I. FACTUAL AND PROCEDURAL BACKGROUND

On May 7, 2005, the citizens of Austin, Texas adopted the "Smoking in Public Places" ordinance (the "ordinance") by way of a ballot initiative.[1] The purpose of the ordinance is to protect persons in public places and employees in their occupational environments from second-hand smoke. The ordinance took effect on September 1, 2005, and its principal goal is to

---

1. As the district court pointed out, the fact that the ordinance was enacted via the voter initiative process placed the City in an unusual posture. The City Charter provides that an ordinance adopted via initiative cannot be amended or repealed until it has been in effect for two years. * * * Therefore, the City is in the position of defending the ordinance "as is" even though the City did not draft or enact it.

prohibit smoking in all "public place[s]" within the City of Austin (the "City").

The ordinance defines "public place" broadly to include any "enclosed area to which the public is invited or in which the public is permitted." * * * The ordinance expands the City's prior smoking ordinance, which gave those bars and restaurants with substantial revenue from the sale of alcoholic beverages the option of obtaining a permit to allow smoking. The new ordinance abolishes this permit option.

A violation of the ordinance is * * * punishable by a fine, not to exceed $2,000, or by revocation or suspension of the license or permit of a violating establishment by the city manager. * * * An individual violates the ordinance by smoking in a public place, * * * smoking in a building owned or operated by the City, * * * or smoking within fifteen feet of an entrance or openable window of a building in which smoking is prohibited. * * * In addition to the restrictions placed on individuals, the ordinance provides that an owner or operator of a public place violates the ordinance if he or she "fails to take *necessary steps* to prevent or stop another person from smoking in an enclosed area in a public place." * * * (emphasis added). Certain steps—including posting "no smoking" signs and removing ashtrays—are explicitly set out in the ordinance. * * *

Shortly after the ordinance took effect, [several bar owners and a couple of concerned citizens] filed suit in state court challenging the constitutionality of the ordinance and seeking a temporary restraining order and a declaratory judgment. * * * Plaintiffs alleged that the ordinance violated the First, Fourth, and Fourteenth Amendments, the Supremacy Clause, a number of federal statutes, as well as the Texas State Constitution, Texas statutes, and the Austin City Charter. The City subsequently removed the case to federal district court.

* * * The district court * * * enjoin[ed] two aspects of the penalty section of the ordinance. First, the district court concluded that the provision of the ordinance allowing the city manager to suspend or revoke the licenses or permits of "public places" violated the Due Process Clause of the Fourteenth Amendment and enjoined that provision to the extent that the City did not provide "expeditious judicial review." * * * Second, the district court enjoined the City from seeking fines of more than $500 * * *, so that the ordinance was in compliance with Texas Penal Code § 6.02(f).[6]

* * *

At trial, Plaintiffs focused their attack on the words "necessary steps" in § 10–6–2(E) of the ordinance. The City presented evidence that since the ordinance's passage, the City's Health and Human Services Department * * * had enacted two sets of guidelines to provide clarification of the "necessary steps" provision. The first set of guidelines provided: "Necessary steps include no smoking signs, absence of ash trays, asking the patron to stop smoking, asking the patron to leave the establishment if they refuse

6. Section 6.02(f) was enacted at the same time as the ordinance and provides that a municipal ordinance "may not dispense with the requirement of a culpable mental state if the offense is punishable by a fine exceeding [$500]." Tex. Pen.Code § 6.02(f).

to stop smoking and following your standard business practices for enforcing house rules." After receiving requests for more clarification, the second set of guidelines was released, which added the step of refusing service to a person who is smoking.[7]

The district court found that the issuance of these two additional sets of guidelines weighed in favor of finding the ordinance vague. * * * The district court held that the City could not provide "definitive guidance to business owners and operators about how they might avoid liability under the ordinance" or the precise actions required of business owners to satisfy the "necessary steps" standard and avoid prosecution. * * * Because the City had not provided business owners with clear guidance beyond the two actions specifically mentioned in the ordinance—posting no smoking signs and removing all ashtrays—the district court found the "necessary steps" provision of the ordinance facially vague and consequently unconstitutional. * * *

After the trial, the district court entered a judgment granting Plaintiffs a permanent injunction in three respects: (1) enjoining the City from enforcing the "necessary steps" provision against owners and operators of public places beyond the two steps of posting no smoking signs and removing ashtrays; (2) enjoining the City from suspending or revoking any city permits or licenses without providing "expeditious judicial review"; and (3) enjoining the City from imposing fines under the ordinance that violate Texas Penal Code § 6.02(f) by exceeding $500. * * *

II. DISCUSSION

* * *

Tasked with the difficult challenge of considering facial vagueness, the district court evaluated: (1) whether the ordinance's "necessary steps" provision provided fair notice that would enable ordinary people to understand the conduct prohibited; and (2) whether it authorized and encouraged arbitrary enforcement. * * * In holding that the City's "necessary steps" provision failed to satisfy this test, the court noted that neither the ordinance nor the guidelines contained an exclusive list or safe harbor provision, and that the guidelines were subject to amendment and differing interpretations. The district court's decision was greatly influenced by City officials who could not detail the steps that a business would have to

---

7. The second set of guidelines issued to Plaintiff bar owners on March 9, 2006, state:

Smoking in Public Places Ordinance No. 050303–05. Frequently Asked Questions.

After receiving requests for clarification, the City issued "further guidance" to business owner/operators which provided a "progressive enforcement process" for businesses to comply with the ordinance:

1. Post no-smoking signs and remove all ashtrays.

2. Verbally ask a patron who is smoking to extinguish the cigarette, cigar, smoking apparatus, etc. (Sign interpretation or in written form for the hearing impaired)

3. Refuse service to a person who is smoking.

4. Verbally ask anyone smoking to leave the premises. (Sign interpretation or in written form for the hearing impaired)

5. Apply standard business procedures in the same manner for violations of house rules or local ordinances or state laws.

implement to satisfy the "necessary steps" requirement under certain hypothetical fact scenarios.

The City asserts that the district court * * * failed to consider the complete legal test for facial vagueness. Specifically, the City * * * maintains that the ordinance is valid in many of its applications, and thus Plaintiffs cannot carry their burden. The City further contends that the "necessary steps" provision should be given its common, ordinary meaning and argues that owners and operators of bars are sufficiently capable of employing their experience and common sense to interpret their duties under the law to prohibit smoking in their establishments. *See Steffes v. City of Lawrence*, 284 Kan. 380 (2007) (holding that business owners must take enforcement efforts to prevent smoking in their establishments and that "common understanding and practice play a large role" in determining whether a business has complied with the ordinance).

Plaintiffs argue that the "necessary steps" provision establishes no standard at all. In fact, they contend, that it is a "tautology." According to Plaintiffs, the "ever-changing" guidelines are non-binding and thus fail to cure the vagueness of the "necessary steps" standard.

* * *

Plaintiffs assert that the ordinance violates their First Amendment right to be free from compelled speech. In particular, Plaintiffs allege that the guidelines compel them to speak against their will by mandating verbal confrontation with their patrons—verbally requesting them to stop smoking and to leave the premises. The district court rejected this argument in both the preliminary injunction order and its final judgment due to Plaintiffs' failure to provide useful evidence on the issue. We agree.

* * *

The ordinance's goal is to prohibit smoking in enclosed public places in order to protect the City's population from the harmful effects of secondhand smoke. To achieve that goal, the ordinance requires Plaintiffs to take the "necessary steps" to stop another person from smoking. Thus, as a general matter, the ordinance regulates Plaintiffs' conduct, not speech. Plaintiff bar owners and their employees remain free to express whatever views they have on the ordinance. And, although the amended guidelines call for Plaintiffs to "verbally" request smokers to extinguish cigarettes or leave the premises, this speech is plainly incidental to the ordinance's regulation of conduct. After all, the guidelines were amended to include these verbal requirements only after Plaintiffs "allegedly" experienced difficulty in implementing the ordinance. * * *

Plaintiffs further contend that the vagueness of the "necessary steps" provision permits unreasonable government interference in the operation of their businesses, a protected liberty interest. [In] *Stidham v. Texas Commission on Private Security*, 418 F.3d 486 (5th Cir.2005) * * * we "confirmed the principle that one has a constitutionally protected liberty interest in pursuing a chosen occupation." * * * Plaintiff bar owners may have a constitutionally protected interest in pursuing their chosen profession, that being the operation of a bar that provides alcohol and other entertainment, [but] the City's ordinance does not threaten to interfere with that interest. [T]he ordinance at issue here is not only authorized, but a valid exercise of the City's police power; it merely regulates smoking to minimize the adverse effects of second-hand smoke and does not threaten to infringe Plaintiffs' liberty interest in pursuing their chosen occupations. * * *

In evaluating vagueness, a reviewing court should consider: (1) whether the law "give[s] the person of ordinary intelligence a reasonable opportunity to know what is prohibited, so that he may act accordingly;" and (2) whether the law provides explicit standards for those applying them to avoid arbitrary and discriminatory applications. *Grayned v. City of Rockford*, 408 U.S. 104, 108–09 (1972). * * *

To begin, we note that the ordinance's goal, as a whole, is to prevent smoking in enclosed public places, so as to minimize the health hazards associated with second-hand smoke. * * * The title of the ordinance reveals that it is designed to prohibit "Smoking in Public Places," and the title of the section at issue, § 10–6–2, is even more explicit: "Smoking Prohibited." Furthermore, the language of the disputed subsection is sufficiently clear to put Plaintiffs on notice of what the statute governs and at whom it is directed. First, it is limited to "[t]he owner or operator of a public place," as defined in the ordinance, and second, it requires that said owner or operator "take necessary steps to prevent or stop another person from smoking in an enclosed area in a public place." § 10–6–2(E). * * *

Based on our conclusion that the district court erred in finding that the "necessary steps" provision in the ordinance is unconstitutionally vague, it was an abuse of discretion to grant a permanent injunction enjoining the City from enforcing that section of the ordinance.

Questions

1. Was Austin's ban on smoking in public places framed as a rule or standard? Can rules leave room for vagueness arguments?

2. What is the regulatory function of § 10–6–2(E)? Why does this provision impose liability on owners and operators of public places for the conduct of smokers?

3. In *R.J. Reynolds Tobacco Co. v. Food and Drug Administration*, 845 F.Supp.2d 266 (D.D.C. 2012), the court held that the FDA's mandated graphic warnings on every cigarette package manufactured and distributed in the United States unconstitutionally compelled speech.[23] The court condemned the warnings for "not 'promot[ing] informed choice' but instead advocate[ing] to consumers that they should 'QUIT NOW.' " Specifically, the court criticized the attempt to "force[ ] [tobacco manufacturers] to act as the Government's mouthpiece * * * to display the Government's anti-smoking message." Does this reasoning apply to Austin ordinance? How should we compare smoking bans and mandatory graphic warnings?

4. Read the following excerpt.

---

23. *See* § 7.4.2. The graphic warnings are available at *regti.me/FDA-Warnings* (case sensitive).

Thomas A. Lambert, *The Case Against Smoking Bans*, 29 REGULATION 34 (2006)

> [Many] localities and * * * states have enacted sweeping smoking bans. The bans generally forbid smoking in "public" places, which are defined to include not only publicly owned facilities but also privately owned properties to which members of the public are invited (e.g., bars, restaurants, hotel lobbies, etc.). Proponents of the bans insist that they are necessary to reduce risks to public health and welfare and to protect the rights of nonsmoking patrons and employees of the regulated establishments.
>
> Specifically, ban advocates have offered three justifications for government-imposed bans: First, they claim that such bans are warranted because indoor smoking involves a "negative externality." * * * In addition, advocates assert that smoking bans shape individual preferences against smoking, thereby reducing the number of smokers in society. Finally, proponents argue that smoking bans are justified, * * * simply because of the health risks associated with inhalation of environmental tobacco smoke (ETS), commonly referred to as "secondhand smoke."
>
> * * *
>
> Government-imposed smoking bans are unwise. Considered closely, the arguments used to justify them falter. The externality argument fails because indoor smoking creates, at worst, a pecuniary externality.† * * * Preference-shaping arguments are weak because heavy-handed government restrictions create a substantial risk of "norm backlash." Risk-based arguments are insufficient because the slight risks associated with ETS cannot justify the substantial privacy intrusion occasioned by sweeping smoking bans. In the end, a laissez-faire policy that would permit private business owners to tailor their own smoking policies according to the demands of their patrons is most likely to maximize social welfare by providing an optimal allocation of both smoking and smoke-free establishments.

(a) Can the market address problems arising from smoking in public places, assuming such problems exist?

(b) Many prohibitions have failed. Bans on alcohol, boxing, sodomy, adultery, and gambling are just a few examples. Is there any reason to believe that bans on smoking in public may succeed? Explain.

Regulating What We Eat

In 1901, Wilhelm Normann invented a "process for converting unsaturated fatty acids or their glycerides into saturated compounds." Normann

† ["Pecuniary externalities" refer to effects through the price system; that is, result in price increases or decreases. In perfectly competitive markets, people will be adequately compensated for risks created by smoking. This compensation is "pecuniary externalities." The argument is that, if smoking is not banned, employees at establishments that allow smoking will be compensated for the increased risk, and patrons will pay lower prices—BYO.]

was the head of the laboratory at Leprince & Siveke, a German food company. Normann's invention was quickly patented in Germany, Britain and other countries. *Unsaturated fatty acids*, also known as *trans fats*, were commercialized. Trans fats are the chemical compounds that make up fats. Fatty acids are chains of carbon atoms with hydrogen atoms attached to the carbon atoms. A "saturated" fatty acid has the maximum possible number of hydrogen atoms attached to every carbon atom. It is therefore said to be "saturated" with hydrogen atoms. Fatty acids are commonly used in margarines and commercial cooking. From the perspective of the food industry, trans fats are attractive because of their long shelf life, their stability during deep-frying, and their other properties valuable for large-scale food production. Studies unequivocally show that the consumption of trans fats "provides no apparent nutritional benefit and has considerable potential for harm."[24] The consumption of trans fats adversely affects several risk factors, and may substantially increase risk factors related to cardiovascular disease. Inevitably, the consumption of high levels of unsaturated fatty acids has statistically significant effects on health and life expectancy. Standardized, simple disclosures of tans-fats levels *may* help individuals compare among products (*see Figure 8.3*). An ordinary person can never fully estimate the risks associated with the consumption of trans fats, although she should know that any consumption has negative effects.

On July 11, 2003, the Food and Drug Administration (FDA) published a final rule requiring that the amount of trans fatty acids would be clearly stated on the nutritional labels of packaged food.[25]

---

24. *See generally* Dariush Mozaffrian et al., *Trans Fatty Acids and Cardiovascular Disease*, 354 NEW ENGLAND JOURNAL OF MEDICATION 1601 (2006) (surveying the literature).

25. Food & Drug Administration, Food Labeling: Trans Fatty Acids in Nutrition Labeling, Nutrient Content Claims, and Health Claims, 68 Fed.Reg. 41434 (July 11, 2003), available at *regti.me/trans-fatty* (case sensitive).

Figure 8.4
An FDA Mandated Nutrition Fact Label

Sample Label for
Macaroni and Cheese

Start Here

Nutrition Facts
Serving Size 1 cup (228g)
Servings Per Container 2

Amount Per Serving
Calories 250 Calories from Fat 110

% Daily Value*

Limit these Nutrients

Total Fat 12g	18%
Saturated Fat 3g	15%
Trans Fat 1.5g	
Cholesterol 30mg	10%
Sodium 470mg	20%
Total Carbohydrate 31g	10%
Dietary Fiber 0g	0%
Sugars 5g	
Protein 5g	
Vitamin A	4%
Vitamin C	2%
Calcium	20%
Iron	4%

Quick Guide to % DV

5% or less is low
20% or more is high

Get Enough of these Nutrients

Footnote

* Percent Daily Values are based on a 2,000 calorie diet. Your Daily Values may be higher or lower depending on your calorie needs:

	Calories:	2,000	2,500
Total Fat	Less than	65g	80g
Sat Fat	Less than	20g	25g
Cholesterol	Less than	300mg	300mg
Sodium	Less than	2,400mg	2,400mg
Total Carbohydrate		300g	375g
Dietary Fiber		25g	30g

Source: Food and Drug Administration.

New York City went further and banned trans fats in all food-service establishments located the City. Heart disease was New York City's leading cause of death. In 2004, for example, 23,000 New York City residents died from heart disease and nearly one-third of these individuals died before the age of 75. Studies showed that up to 23% of coronary heart disease events could be avoided by replacing trans fats with healthy alternatives. On December 5, 2006, the New York City Board of Health adopted a two-stage phase out of trans fat in all of the city's food-service establishments.[26] The City's Health Department issued guidelines for food establishments where it explained "how to comply" with the new regulation:

---

26. New York City Health Code § 81.08, available at *regti.me/NYC–TF1* (case sensitive).

Beginning July 1, 2007:

You may not use partially hydrogenated vegetable oils, shortenings, or margarines for frying, pan-frying (sautéing), grilling, or as a spread unless you have product labels or other documents from the manufacturer showing that these ingredients contain less than 0.5 grams of trans fat per serving.

You may continue to use trans fat-containing oils and shortenings for deep frying cake batter and yeast dough until the regulation takes full effect on July 1, 2008.

Beginning July 1, 2008:

No food containing partially hydrogenated vegetable oils, shortenings, or margarines with 0.5 grams or more trans fat per serving may be stored, used, or served by food service establishments. — The regulation does not apply to food served in the manufacturer's original, sealed packaging, such as a package of crackers or a bag of potato chips.[27]

The Ordinance provided:

Artificial trans fat restricted. No foods containing artificial trans fat * * * shall be stored, distributed, held for service, used in preparation of any menu item or served in any food service establishment or by any mobile food unit * * *, except food that is being served directly to patrons in a manufacturer's original sealed package.

New York City was the first American city to impose a partial ban on trans fats. Inspired by this model, states and other cities and states have adopted similar bans. Several national food chains have stopped using trans fats in all their locations.

By the nature of things, not all people have supported the trans-fats ban. Some have described it as representatives of a new regulatory trend that threatens society with "paternalistic slopes."[28] The argument is that modest and non-intrusive regulations may progress to intrusive, moral paternalism; therefore, hence society should avoid all forms of paternalistic regulations. In some states, the lobbying of restaurant owners has secured laws that prohibit municipalities from regulating the nutrients in food and beverages served locally.[29]

Questions

1. What are the motivations underlying the ban on trans fats in food establishments?

2. Alcohol, tobacco products, foie gras, and trans fats are routinely consumed by individuals. All are known to pose health risk, but at the moment of consumption they allow the individual to enjoy some moments of her "pursuit of happiness." This happiness may result from the joy of con-

---

27. The guidelines are available at *regti.me/NYC–TF2* (case sensitive).

28. *See* Douglas Glen Whitman & Mario J. Rizzo, *Paternalist Slopes*, 2 NYU JOURNAL OF LAW & LIBERTY 411, 443 (2007).

29. *See* Stephanie Storm, *Local Laws Fighting Fat Under Siege*, N.Y. TIMES, July 1, 2011, at B1.

sumption and its contribution to effectiveness in other things in life, such as social or professional success during the moment of consumption. How should we evaluate these benefits?

Restrictions on Relationships

It is often said that the dog is "a man's best friend." Nevertheless the state routinely interferes with such friendships, defining them as "ownership" and imposing restrictions on dog ownership.

Toledo v. Tellings

Supreme Court of Ohio
114 Ohio St.3d 278 (2007)

■ Justice Thomas J. Moyer.

[T]he city of Toledo, appeals from the judgment of the Court of Appeals of Lucas County that held [Ohio Revised Code] 955.11 and 955.22 and Toledo Municipal Code 505.14 unconstitutional. For the following reasons, we reverse the judgment of the court of appeals.

Appellee, Paul Tellings, a resident of the city of Toledo, owned three dogs identified as pit bulls. Tellings was charged by the city for violating Toledo Municipal Code 505.14(a) and R.C. 955.22. The Toledo Municipal Code limits ownership of vicious dogs, as defined in R.C. 955.11, or dogs commonly known as pit bulls or pit bull mixed breeds, to one in each household, and the Ohio Revised Code requires an owner of a pit bull to obtain liability insurance for damages, injuries, or death that might be caused by the dog.

Tellings challenged the constitutionality of Toledo Municipal Code 505.14(a) and R.C. 955.22 and 955.11(A)(4)(a)(iii), which includes pit bull in the definition of "vicious dog." * * *

R.C. 955.11 states:

> (A) As used in this section:
>
> * * *
>
> (4)(a) 'Vicious dog' means a dog that, without provocation and subject to division (A)(4)(b) of this section, meets any of the following:
>
> (i) Has killed or caused serious injury to any person;
>
> (ii) Has caused injury, other than killing or serious injury, to any person, or has killed another dog.
>
> (iii) Belongs to a breed that is commonly known as a pit bull dog. The ownership, keeping, or harboring of such a breed of dog shall be prima-facie evidence of the ownership, keeping, or harboring of a vicious dog.

R.C. 955.22(A) states:

> As used in this section, 'dangerous dog' and 'vicious dog' have the same meanings as in section 955.11 of the Revised Code.

Toledo Municipal Code 505.14(a) states:

> No person or organization or corporation shall own, keep, harbor or provide sustenance for more than one vicious dog, as defined by Ohio R.C. 955.11, or a dog commonly known as a Pit Bull or Pit Bull mixed breed dog, regardless of age, in the City of Toledo, with the exception of puppies commonly known as Pit Bull or Pit Bull mixed breed for which the owner has filed an ownership acknowledgement form in person with the Dog Warden of Lucas County, prior to reaching seven (7) days of age. The ownership of these puppies must be transferred according to Ohio R.C. 955.11 before they are three (3) months of age. Additionally, this section requires that all vicious dogs, as described in the Ohio Revised Code, or dogs commonly known as Pit Bull or Pit Bull mixed breed dogs are required, when off the owners' premises, to be securely confined as described in Ohio R.C. 955.22 and muzzled.

Our resolution of the issue presented turns on whether the statutes and the ordinance in question are valid exercises of police power by the state and the city. If R.C. 955.11 and 955.22 and Toledo Municipal Code 505.14 are rationally related to a legitimate interest of the state and the city in the public's health, safety, morals, or general welfare, they are constitutional. * * *

The Ohio Constitution provides for the exercise of state and local police power in derogation of the right to hold private property. Section 19, Article I of the Ohio Constitution states: "Private property shall ever be held inviolate, but subservient to the public welfare." "As a result of this subordination, police power regulations are upheld although they may interfere with the enjoyment of liberty or the acquisition, possession and production of private property." * * * Section 3, Article XVIII of the Ohio Constitution provides: "Municipalities shall have authority to exercise all powers of local self-government and to adopt and enforce within their limits such local police, sanitary and other similar regulations, as are not in conflict with general laws."

"Among the regulations which have been upheld as legitimate exercises of police power are those regulations addressing the ownership and control of dogs." * * * Despite the special relationships that exist between many people and their dogs, dogs are personal property, and the state or the city has the right to control those that are a threat to the safety of the community: "Although dogs are private property to a qualified extent, they are subject to the state police power, and 'might be destroyed or otherwise dealt with, as in the judgment of the legislature is necessary for the protection of its citizens.' ... [L]egislatures have broad police power to regulate all dogs so as to protect the public against the nuisance posed by a vicious dog." * * *

The state and the city have a legitimate interest in protecting citizens against unsafe conditions caused by pit bulls. We note that substantial reputable evidence was presented at the trial court by both parties: the parties produced 18 witnesses, dozens of exhibits were admitted into evidence, and more than 1,000 pages of testimony were taken. * * * The chief dog warden of Lucas County testified that (1) when pit bulls attack, they are more likely to inflict severe damage to their victim than other breeds of dogs, (2) pit bulls have killed more Ohioans than any other breed of dog, (3) Toledo police officers fire their weapons in the line of duty at pit bulls more often than they fire weapons at people and all other breeds of dogs combined, and (4) pit bulls are frequently shot during drug raids because pit bulls are encountered more frequently in drug raids than any other dog breed. * * *

The evidence presented in the trial court supports the conclusion that pit bulls pose a serious danger to the safety of citizens. The state and the city have a legitimate interest in protecting citizens from the danger posed by this breed of domestic dogs.

[T]he state and the city of Toledo possess the constitutional authority to exercise police powers that are rationally related to a legitimate interest in public health, safety, morals, or general welfare. Here, evidence proves that pit bulls cause more damage than other dogs when they attack, cause more fatalities in Ohio than other dogs, and cause Toledo police officers to fire their weapons more often than people or other breeds of dogs cause them to fire their weapons. We hold that the state of Ohio and the city of Toledo have a legitimate interest in protecting citizens from the dangers associated with pit bulls, and that R.C. 955.11(A)(4)(a)(iii) and 955.22 and Toledo Municipal Code 505.14 are rationally related to that interest and are constitutional.

* * *

■ JUSTICE MAUREEN O'CONNOR, concurring in judgment only.

I concur in judgment only to emphasize my disapproval of R.C. 955.11 (A)(4)(a)(iii), which identifies pit bulls as vicious animals per se.

Breed-specific prohibitions, limitations, and restrictions are justified by labeling dogs as "inherently dangerous" by virtue of the particular breed's alleged characteristics. Contrary to that assumption, dangerous animal behavior is the function of inherently dangerous dog owners, not inherently dangerous dogs.

The statistics offered at trial in this case may support a correlation between pit bulls and the frequency and severity of injuries they cause to people in urban settings, but they do not establish the conclusion that pit bulls must necessarily pose a danger. Indeed, experts in the canine field who rate the temperament of different breeds of dogs conclude that pit bulls have a better temperament than many other common breeds of dogs used as pets, including the miniature poodle and Shih–Tzu. * * *

A more thorough analysis of the dynamic would demonstrate that the danger posed is the result of some dog owners, including drug dealers, who deliberately increase the dog's aggression and lethality through abuse or other specific methods of training. Other owners simply fail to properly train and supervise the animal, thereby creating dangerous behavior by the dog.

Almost all domestic animals can cause significant injuries to humans, and it is proper to require that all domestic animals be maintained and controlled. Laws to that effect are eminently reasonable for the safety of citizens and of the animal. Because the danger posed by vicious dogs and pit bulls arises from the owner's failure to safely control the animal, rational legislation should focus on the owner of the dog rather than the specific breed that is owned.

Notes

In January 2009, Toledo amended its restrictions on the ownership of Pit Bulls, adding the following provisions:

> (b) Any Pit Bull which is outside the premises of the dog owner shall be kept on a leash and muzzled until the dog's return to the premises of ownership.
>
> (c) Whoever violates this section is guilty of a misdemeanor of the first degree. Each day that a violation of this section exists shall constitute a separate offense.
>
> (d) Any Pit Bull or Pit Bull mixed breed dog which has been seized in connection with a violation of this Section may be ordered destroyed or returned to its Owner only on the condition that the dog is first spayed or neutered at the owner's expense.
>
> * * *

In October 2010, the City passed Ordinance 389–10, which again amended its health code, repealed § 505.14, and created a comprehensive regulatory framework for dog ownership in Toledo. Ordinance 389–10 declares that "the City of Toledo finds that it is necessary to establish and implement regulations regarding dogs maintained within the City limits; that the property rights of owners or keepers and non-owners of dogs should be protected; and that the health, safety and welfare of the people residing in the City would be served by adoption of such an ordinance." The Ordinance defines the duties and responsibilities of dog owners, and specifically noted that "the owner is ultimately responsible for the behavior of the dog regardless of whether the owner or another member of the owner's household or a household visitor permitted the animal to engage in the behavior that is the subject of the violation."

Ordinance 389–10 further replaced the term "vicious dogs" with "dogs which pose a threat to public safety."[30] In doing so, this provision distinguished between "level-one" and "level-two" threat dogs and regulated the possession of such dogs.

> ***1706.03. Dogs which pose a threat to public safety.***
>
> *(a) Definitions.* * * *
>
> (1) A. "Level–One Threat." A dog * * * which, without provocation, and subject to subsection (b) of this section, has chased or approached a person, including a person on a bicycle, upon the

30. Toledo Municipal Health Code § 1706.03.

streets, sidewalks or any public or private property, other than the dog owner, keeper or harborer's property in either a menacing fashion or an apparent attitude of attack, or has attempted to bite or otherwise endanger any person. * * * A level-one threat dog may also be one who has repeatedly exhibited a propensity, tendency or disposition to attack, without provocation, or otherwise threatens the safety of humans or domestic animals.

B. "A Level–One Threat dog" does not include a police dog that has chased or approached * * * any person while the police dog is being used to assist law enforcement officers in the performance of their official duties.

(2) A. "Level–Two Threat." A dog * * * which, without provocation and subject to subsection (b) of this section, has killed or caused serious injury to any person; or has killed or caused serious injury to another dog;

B. "A Level–Two threat dog" does not include either of the following: (1) a police dog that has killed or caused serious injury to any person or that has caused injury, other than killing or serious injury, to any person or to another dog while the police dog is being used to assist law enforcement officers in the performance of their official duties; or (2) a dog that has killed or caused serious injury to any person while a person was committing or attempting to commit a criminal trespass or other criminal offense on the property of the owner, keeper or harborer of the dog.

* * *

(b) Determination of Dogs Which Pose a Threat to Public Safety.

* * * The Dog Warden, Commissioner of Health and/or Chief of Police, shall have the authority to determine whether any dog poses a threat to public safety. * * *

(c) Restrictions on Dogs Which Pose a Threat to Public Safety.

* * *

(1) Dogs classified as a threat to public safety shall be restrained, so as not to be at large by a physical device or structure, in a manner that prevents the dog from reaching within 10 feet of any public sidewalk or right of way, and must be located so as not to interfere with the public's legal access to the owner's or keeper's premises, whenever that dog is outside the owner, keeper or harborer's home and not on a leash. Level-one dogs shall be on a six (6) foot or shorter leash handled by an adult capable of controlling the dog, or shall be muzzled when off the property of the owner or keeper.

(2) * * * All dogs determined to be a Level–Two threat to public safety shall be spayed or neutered, unless exempted by a licensed veterinarian for health reasons.

In addition, the owner, keeper or harborer shall be required to obtain and maintain proof of public liability insurance in a minimum amount of $100,000.00. The owner, keeper or harborer shall not permit the dog to be off their premises unless the dog is humanely muzzled and restrained by an adequate leash and under the control of a capable person.

The Dog Warden, Commissioner of Health and/or Chief of Police may require the owner, keeper or harborer to satisfactorily complete a pet ownership program and other remedial measures which the Dog Warden, Commissioner of Health and/or Chief of Police finds are necessary and proper under the circumstances.

(3) To insure correct identification, all dogs that have been classified as threat to public safety shall be marked with a permanent identifying mark, micro-chipped, photographed, or may be fitted with a special tag or collar at the owner, keeper or harborer's expense.

* * *

(6) For 10 years from the date of release from incarceration or, if imprisonment was not ordered, then from the date of conviction, no person who has been convicted of a felony shall be allowed to own or have custody or possession of a dog that has not been spayed/neutered or that has been determined to be a threat to public safety.

(7) No owner, keeper or harborer shall have more than one dog on any premises which has been determined to be a Level–Two threat to public safety.

* * *

Questions

1. Does Toledo's regulation of dogs amount to some form of a "ban"? If so, what does the City ban?

2. In 1924, the Virginia legislature concluded that "human experience has demonstrated that heredity plays an important part in the transmission of insanity, idiocy, imbecility, epilepsy and crime" and that "the health of the individual patient and the welfare of society may be promoted in certain cases by * * * sterilization." Based on these findings, the legislature enacted the Virginia Sterilization Act of 1924. In *Buck v. Bell*, 274 U.S. 200 (1927), the Supreme Court upheld the constitutionality of the statute. Justice Holmes noted:

> We have seen more than once that the public welfare may call upon the best citizens for their lives. It would be strange if it could not call upon those who already sap the strength of the State for these lesser sacrifices, often not felt to be such by those concerned, to prevent our being swamped with incompetence. It is better for all the world, if instead of waiting to execute degenerate offspring for crime, or to let them starve for their imbecility, society can prevent those who are manifestly unfit from continuing their kind. The principle that sustains compulsory vaccination is broad enough to cover cutting the Fallopian tubes.

Does the regulation of breeds raise concerns regarding theories of the kind expressed in *Buck v. Bell*?[31]

The Incandescent Light Bulb

In 2007, global political and economic factors led to sudden sharp increases in energy prices. In the United States, gasoline prices reached unprecedented levels. In the background of a growing tension between the Democratic and Republican parties, Congress enacted the Energy Independence and Security Act of 2007, which included many measures designed to promote national energy efficiency and help the country to reduce its dependency on foreign oil. On December 18, 2007, President George W. Bush signed the Act into law.[32]

Sections 321 and 322 of the Energy Independence and Security Act introduced a multi-stage plan to phase out the incandescent light bulb. The Act did not outlaw or banned the manufacturing, distribution, or use incandescent light bulb. Rather, the Act revised the minimum efficiency standards applied to light bulbs sold in the United States.

Lighting technologies vary in several dimensions, including their lifetime, energy consumption, brightness, and efficiency. Lifetime is measured in hours of use. Energy consumption is measured in *watts*. Brightness is measured in *lumens*. And efficiency is measured by the energy used for lighting. The incandescent light bulb technology is quite inefficient: 10% of the energy consumed is used for light and 90% of the energy is lost as heat. Modern lighting technologies are superior to the wasteful incandescent light bulb by orders of magnitude, with respect to both lifetime and lumens per watt. Because incandescent light bulbs consume energy primarily for heat, their production of lumens per watt is very low.

The traditional incandescent light bulbs were highly standardized. Thus, people expect a 100–watt incandescent light bulb to produce more light than a 60–watt incandescent light bulb. The public references to brightness had therefore been in watts. Most people had no awareness of "lumens." As a result, consumers could not appreciate efficient light bulbs. To overcome this hurdle, manufacturers and retailers presented the capacity of efficient light bulbs in "hypothetical watts," the equivalent incandescent light bulb or a multiplier of a standard incandescent light bulb (*e.g.*, two 100–watt incandescent light bulbs). Moreover, high-wattage incandescent light bulbs are undesirable because of the heat they emit. Believing that wattage defines light bulbs, consumers had concerns about about the safety of powerful efficient light bulbs, since in they were presented as the equivalent of several incandescent light bulbs.

The Energy Independence and Security Act revised the federal definition of the term "general service lamp" to be:

---

31. North Carolina engaged in sterilization of human beings until the 1970s. *See* Kim Severson, *Thousands Sterilized, a State Weighs Restitution*, N.Y. TIMES, Dec. 10, 2011, at A1.

32. Pub. L. No. 110–140, 121 Stat. 1492 (2007).

(I) general service incandescent lamps;

(II) compact fluorescent lamps [(CFL)];

(III) general service light-emitting diode (LED or OLED) lamps; and

(IV) any other lamps that the Secretary [of Energy] determines are used to satisfy lighting applications traditionally served by general service incandescent lamps.[33]

The Act did not specify which bulbs should be manufactured and sold in the United States. Rather, it established a schedule of increased minimum efficiency requirements for general service lamps sold in the United States.

Effective Date	*Rated Lumens*	*Maximum Rated Wattage*	*Minimum Rated Lifetime (hours)*
January 1, 2012	1490-2600	72	1,000
January 1, 2013	1050-1489	53	1,000
January 1, 2014	750-1049	43	1,000
January 1, 2014	310-749	29	1,000

To improve the public understanding of lighting technologies, the Federal Trade Commission issued a rule that revised the labeling requirements for light bulbs and introduced a new set of standardized labels.[34]

Figure 8.5
The New Light Bulb Label

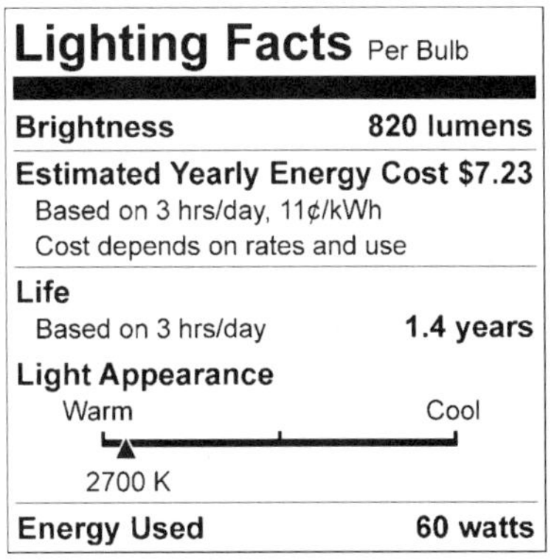

Lighting Facts Per Bulb

Brightness **820 lumens**

Estimated Yearly Energy Cost $7.23
Based on 3 hrs/day, 11¢/kWh
Cost depends on rates and use

Life
Based on 3 hrs/day **1.4 years**

Light Appearance
Warm Cool
2700 K

Energy Used **60 watts**

New Back

33. 42 U.S.C § 6291.

34. Federal Trade Commission, Appliance Labeling Rule, 16 C.F.R. 305 (July 19, 2010).

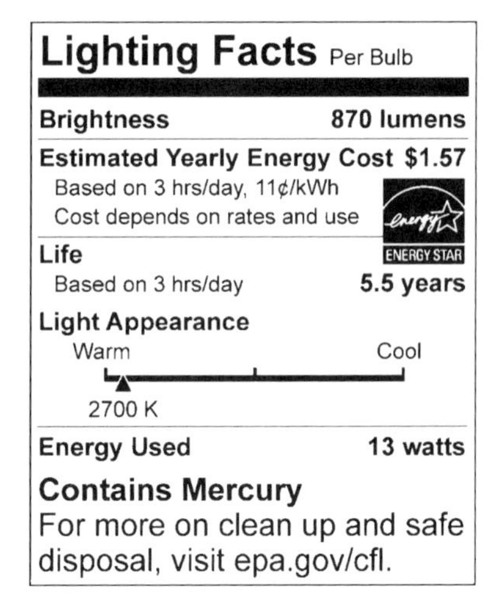

New Back Label for Bulbs Containing Mercury

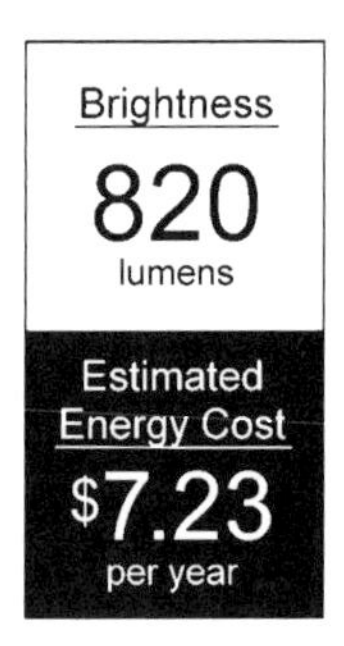

New Front

Source: The Federal Trade Commission

Sections 321 and 322 of the Energy Independence and Security Act, therefore, intended to facilitate a transition from a very inefficient technology to energy efficient ones. This regulatory scheme was not innovative in any meaningful way. Many regulatory frameworks establish new standards that intend to promote the public welfare through technological change.[35] For example, the Energy Policy and Conservation Act of 1975 established fuel economy standards that required American car manufacturers to reconfigure the design of their assembly lines.[36] This reform eliminated from the market several models of inefficient motor vehicles. Similarly, the Digital Television Transition and Public Safety Act of 2005 facilitated the digitization of television broadcasting.[37] This transition in turn interfered with the choices of those who had analogue televisions or wanted to have such televisions. Indeed, some opposed the Act for its interference in choices.[38]

The plan to retire the incandescent light bulb encountered fierce opposition. For many the plan symbolized aggressive intrusion upon personal liberty,[39] and some argued that the "federal government ha[d] no right to tell * * * any * * * citizen what type of light bulb to use at home,"[40] and that the "government ha[d] no business telling an individual what kind of light bulb to buy."[41] These views attracted many supporters in the 112th Congress. During 2011, Congress considered several initiatives to repeal, postpone, and defund the plan to increase the minimum efficiency standards of light bulbs.[42] In Arizona, the governor vetoed a bill would have exempted light bulbs manufactured in Arizona from federal regulation.[43]

35. *See* §§ 9.1, 9.3.

36. *See, e.g.*, Center for Biological Diversity v. National Highway Traffic Safety Administration, 538 F.3d 1172 (9th Cir. 2008), § 1.6.3 (discussing NHTSA's Average Fuel Economy Standards).

37. Pub. L. No. 109–171, 120 Stat. 21 (2006).

38. *See, e.g.*, TV Consumer Choice Act, H.R. 2354, 109th Cong., 1st Sess. (May 12, 2005) (proposing to repeal the Digital Television Transition and Public Safety Act).

39. Sean Collins Walsh, *House Votes to Hamper a Law on Light Bulbs*, N.Y. TIMES, July 16, 2011, at A2 (quoting Congressman Michael C. Burgess of Texas).

40. *See, e.g.*, Roger A. Pielke Jr., *Let There Be More Efficient Light*, N.Y. TIMES, March 11, 2011, at A27; Edward Wyatt, *Give Up Familiar Light Bulb?*, N.Y. TIMES, March 12, 2011, at A1; Andrew Rice, *Bulb In, Bulb Out*, N.Y. TIMES MAGAZINE, June 5, 2011, at 44.

41. Pielke Jr., *Let There Be More Efficient Light*, *id.* (quoting Congresswoman Michele Bachmann of Minnesota).

42. *See, e.g.*, the Light Bulb Freedom of Choice Act, S.395, 112 Cong. 1st Sess. (Feb. 17, 2011).

43. Governor Janice Brewer, Veto Letter on House Bill 2337 to Ken Bennett, Secretary of State (May 11, 2010). For discussion *see* Barak Orbach et al., *Arming States' Rights: Federalism, Private Lawmakers, and the Battering Ram Strategy*, 53 ARIZONA LAW REVIEW 1161, 1195–1996 (2010).

Notwithstanding this opposition, light bulbs sold in the United States are now required to be much more efficient than the incandescent light bulb.[44]

Questions

1. Prior to the implementation of the light bulb minimum efficiency standards, manufacturers chose not to commercialize efficient lighting technologies in large scale. Were they wrong? Was Congress "smarter than the market," or at least acted as if it were "smarter than the market"? What was the rationale behind the Congressional adoption of light bulb minimum efficiency standards?

2. Were the light bulb minimum efficiency standards designed to ban the traditional incandescent light bulb?

3. In the early twentieth century, the so-called "common drinking cup" was widespread in public places. The common drinking cups were durable cups available in public places for the use of any person. To protect the public health and improve hygiene, most states banned the common drinking cups and engaged in a massive campaign that explained the risks associated with the common drinking cup (See *Figure 8.5*).[45]

(a) Were the bans on the common drinking cup more legitimate than the light bulb minimum efficiency standards? (b) Was a campaign against the common drinking cup a legitimate use of public funds?

---

44. Materials concerning the incandescent light bulb controversy are available at *regti.me/l-bulb* (case sensitive).

45. *See, e.g.*, *The Drinking Cup Law*, N.Y. TIMES, Jan. 28, 1912, at 1.

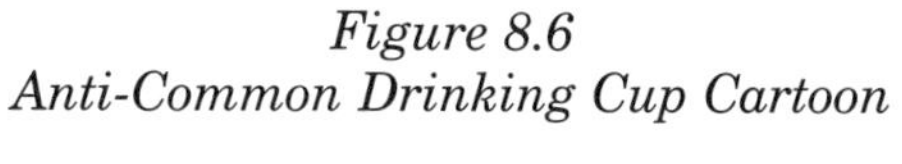

Figure 8.6
Anti-Common Drinking Cup Cartoon

Source: Cup-Campaigner, August 1910.

§ 8.3 MANDATES

Mandates are not uncommon. Mandatory insurance, compulsory education, and water fluoridation are three familiar examples. Mandates may be the most objectionable regulatory measures, although as we pointed out, they may be framed as bans. We have already discussed objections to mandates in two landmark Supreme Court decisions: *Jacobson v. Massachusetts*[46] and *National Federation of Independent Business* (NFIB).[47] In *NFIB*, the three opinions referred to *Wickard v. Filburn*.

46. *See* Jacobson v. Massachusetts, 197 U.S. 11 (1905).

47. *See* § 2.5.

Wickard v. Filburn

317 U.S. 111 (1942)

■ MR. JUSTICE JACKSON delivered the opinion of the Court.

The appellee filed his complaint against the Secretary of Agriculture of the United States [and others]. He sought to enjoin enforcement * * * of the marketing penalty imposed by the amendment of May 26, 1941, to the Agricultural Adjustment Act of 1938. * * * He also sought a declaratory judgment that the wheat marketing quota provisions of the Act * * * were unconstitutional. * * *

The appellee for many years past has owned and operated a small farm in Montgomery County, Ohio, maintaining a herd of dairy cattle, selling milk, raising poultry, and selling poultry and eggs. It has been his practice to raise a small acreage of winter wheat, sown in the Fall and harvested in the following July; to sell a portion of the crop; to feed part to poultry and livestock on the farm, some of which is sold; to use some in making flour for home consumption; and to keep the rest for the following seeding. The intended disposition of the crop here involved has not been expressly stated.

In July of 1940, pursuant to the Agricultural Adjustment Act of 1938, as then amended, there were established for the appellee's 1941 crop a wheat acreage allotment of 11.1 acres and a normal yield of 20.1 bushels of wheat an acre. He was given [a proper] notice. * * * He sowed, however, 23 acres, and harvested from his 11.9 acres of excess acreage 239 bushels, which under the terms of the Act as amended on May 26, 1941, constituted farm marketing excess, subject to a penalty of 49 cents a bushel, or $117.11 in all. * * *

The general scheme of the Agricultural Adjustment Act of 1938 as related to wheat is to control the volume moving in interstate and foreign commerce in order to avoid surpluses and shortages and the consequent abnormally low or high wheat prices and obstructions to commerce. * * *

It is urged that under the Commerce Clause of the Constitution Congress does not possess the power it has in this instance sought to exercise. The question would merit little consideration since our decision in *United States v. Darby*, 312 U.S. 100 (1941), sustaining the federal power to regulate production of goods for commerce except for the fact that this Act extends federal regulation to production not intended in any part for commerce but wholly for consumption on the farm. * * * [M]arketing quotas not only embrace all that may be sold without penalty but also what may be consumed on the premises. Wheat produced on excess acreage is designated as 'available for marketing' as so defined and the penalty is imposed thereon. * * *

At the beginning Chief Justice Marshall described the Federal commerce power with a breadth never yet exceeded. *Gibbons v. Ogden*, 22 U.S. 1 (1824). He made emphatic the embracing and penetrating nature of this power by warning that effective restraints on its exercise must proceed from political rather than from judicial processes. For nearly a century, however, decisions of this Court under the Commerce Clause dealt rarely with questions of what Congress might do in the exercise of its granted power under the Clause and almost entirely with the permissibility of state activity which it was claimed discriminated against or burdened interstate commerce. * * *

It was not until 1887 with the enactment of the Interstate Commerce Act that the interstate commerce power began to exert positive influence in American law and life. This first important federal resort to the commerce power was followed in 1890 by the Sherman Anti–Trust Act and, thereafter, mainly after 1903, by many others. These statutes ushered in new phases of adjudication, which required the Court to approach the interpretation of the Commerce Clause in the light of an actual exercise by Congress of its power thereunder. * * *

Whether the subject of the regulation in question was 'production,' 'consumption,' or 'marketing' is, therefore, not material for purposes of deciding the question of federal power before us. * * * [E]ven if appellee's activity be local and though it may not be regarded as commerce, it may still, whatever its nature, be reached by Congress if it exerts a substantial economic effect on interstate commerce and this irrespective of whether such effect is what might at some earlier time have been defined as 'direct' or 'indirect.' * * *

The wheat industry has been a problem industry for some years. * * * The decline in the export trade has left a large surplus in production which in connection with an abnormally large supply of wheat and other grains in recent years caused congestion in a number of markets; tied up railroad cars; and caused elevators in some instances to turn away grains, and railroads to institute embargoes to prevent further congestion.

Many countries, both importing and exporting, have sought to modify the impact of the world market conditions on their own economy. Importing countries have taken measures to stimulate production and self-sufficiency. The four large exporting countries of Argentina, Australia, Canada, and the United States have all undertaken various programs for the relief of growers. Such measures have been designed in part at least to protect the domestic price received by producers. Such plans have generally evolved towards control by the central government.[27]

In the absence of regulation the price of wheat in the United States would be much affected by world conditions. During 1941 producers who cooperated with the Agricultural Adjustment program received an average price on the farm of about $1.16 a bushel as compared with the world market price of 40 cents a bushel. * * *

The effect of consumption of homegrown wheat on interstate commerce is due to the fact that it constitutes the most variable factor in the

27. It is interesting to note that all of these have federated systems of government, not of course without important differences. In all of them wheat regulation is by the national government. In Argentina wheat may be purchased only from the national Grain Board. A condition of sale to the Board, which buys at pegged prices, is the producer's agreement to become subject to restrictions on planting. * * * The Australian system of regulation includes the licensing of growers, who may not sow more than the amount licensed, and who may be compelled to cut part of their crops for hay if a heavy crop is in prospect. * * *

disappearance of the wheat crop. Consumption on the farm where grown appears to vary in an amount greater than 20 per cent of average production. The total amount of wheat consumed as food varies but relatively little, and use as seed is relatively constant.

The maintenance by government regulation of a price for wheat undoubtedly can be accomplished as effectively by sustaining or increasing the demand as by limiting the supply. The effect of the statute before us is to restrict the amount which may be produced for market and the extent as well to which one may forestall resort to the market by producing to meet his own needs. That appellee's own contribution to the demand for wheat may be trivial by itself is not enough to remove him from the scope of federal regulation where, as here, his contribution, taken together with that of many others similarly situated, is far from trivial. * * *

It is well established by decisions of this Court that the power to regulate commerce includes the power to regulate the prices at which commodities in that commerce are dealt in and practices affecting such prices. One of the primary purposes of the Act in question was to increase the market price of wheat and to that end to limit the volume thereof that could affect the market. * * * Home-grown wheat in this sense competes with wheat in commerce. The stimulation of commerce is a use of the regulatory function quite as definitely as prohibitions or restrictions thereon. This record leaves us in no doubt that Congress may properly have considered that wheat consumed on the farm where grown if wholly outside the scheme of regulation would have a substantial effect in defeating and obstructing its purpose to stimulate trade therein at increased prices.

It is said, however, that this Act, forcing some farmers into the market to buy what they could provide for themselves, is an unfair promotion of the markets and prices of specializing wheat growers. It is of the essence of regulation that it lays a restraining hand on the self-interest of the regulated and that advantages from the regulation commonly fall to others. The conflicts of economic interest between the regulated and those who advantage by it are wisely left under our system to resolution by the Congress under its more flexible and responsible legislative process. Such conflicts rarely lend themselves to judicial determination. And with the wisdom, workability, or fairness, of the plan of regulation we have nothing to do. * * *

The statute is also challenged as a deprivation of property without due process of law contrary to the Fifth Amendment. * * * We do not agree. In its effort to control total supply, the Government gave the farmer a choice which was, of course, designed to encourage cooperation and discourage non-cooperation. * * * The farmer who produced in excess of his quota might escape penalty by delivering his wheat to the Secretary or by [complying with another statutory exemption]. * * * It is hardly lack of due process for the Government to regulate that which it subsidizes.

Questions

1. Was *Wickard* about bans or mandates?

2. The *Wickard* Court expresses the position that "the Government gave the farmer a choice." What was the significance of "choice" to the case?

§ 8.4 PERMITS AND ENTRY REGULATION

§ 8.4.1 Participation and Exclusion Through Permits

Permits are exemptions from regulatory constraints, specifically from bans and mandates. Thus, two meanings permits have are freedom to engage in a particular activity and freedom from a duty to engage in a particular activity. In this Section we will discuss permits to engage in business. The analysis can be expanded to other permits.

In any market, certain parties—ordinarily "sellers"—must make some investments in order to operate. They establish businesses (and their successors may acquire or lease these businesses). For example, a person who wishes to sell legal services acquires some knowledge and expertise. A person who wishes to serve diners with food opens a restaurant. And a person who wishes to manufacture cars builds a factory. In online markets, an intermediary like eBay.com may be the party that makes such an investment in infrastructure. Put simply, for a market to exist, some market participants must create infrastructure. Typically, the parties that make investments in infrastructure also have to obtain from permits, licenses, certificates, and other registration documents from the state. To illustrate, consider a restaurant in New York City. Before an aspiring restaurateur can open the establishment, she must not only secure 30 permits, registrations, licenses, and certificates from multiple city agencies, but also pass 23 inspections. This was the thicket she would have navigated in late 2010.[48]

The entry into many, if not most, markets is regulated. At least one permit, license, or certificate from the state is required to create and operate business. *Entry regulation* inevitably burdens businesses. When such barriers serves no viable purpose—or worse, serves the bureaucracy or some interest group—entry regulation can have significant negative effects on the economy.[49]

Entry regulation is one type of transaction costs the state generates and it raises concerns regarding bureaucratic inefficiencies and failures. For interest groups, entry regulation may be a boon. No corruption is needed: A sophisticated interest group has strategic opportunities for influence when a state organ must make hard choices about how to allocate resources.

---

48. *See* Diane Cardwell, *A New Team Helps Steer Restaurants Through a Thicket of Red Tape*, N.Y. TIMES, Dec. 28, 2010, at A18.

49. For the entry regulation and the bureaucracy *see* HERNANDO DE SOTO, THE OTHER PATH: THE INVISIBLE REVOLUTION IN THE THIRD WORLD (1989); Simeon Djankov, *The Regulation of Entry: A Survey*, 24 WORLD BANK RESEARCH OBSERVER 183 (2009); ANDREY SHLEIFER & ROBERT W. VISHNY, THE GRABBING HAND: GOVERNMENT PATHOLOGIES AND THEIR CURES (2002).

Entry regulation was featured in several cases we have already discussed. For example, *New State Ice v. Liebmann* involved the constitutionality of an Oklahoma law that required licensing from the State Corporation Commission of Oklahoma to manufacture, sell, or distribute ice in the Sooner State.[50] Writing for the Court, Justice Sutherland found the statute unconstitutional, expressing concerns regarding "the practical tendency of the restriction * * * to shut out new enterprises, and thus create and foster monopoly in the hands of existing establishments, against, rather than in aid of, the interest of the consuming public." In dissent, Justice Brandeis defended the concept of entry regulation by arguing that when substantial investment in infrastructure is needed, the "purpose of requiring [permits] is to promote the public interest by preventing waste." Writing during the Great Depression, Brandeis believed that excessive entry into a market might "expose[ ] the industry to destructive and frequently ruinous competition." In essence, he argued that the market for ice in Oklahoma City had the characteristics of a natural monopoly.

The *Terminal Railroad* case involved the consequences of entry regulation policies.[51] At the end of the nineteenth century, St. Louis, Missouri, was the fourth largest city in the country and an important center for trade on the Mississippi River. There were three ways to cross the Mississippi River from or to St. Louis: the Eads Bridge, the Merchants' Bridge, and the ferries of the Wiggins Ferry Company. To build another bridge or start a new ferry business, permits were required from Missouri, Illinois, and the federal government. Under existing laws, the Wiggins Ferry Company held an exclusive right to operate ferries across the Mississippi. Federal laws specifically provided that no bridge should "be constructed across the Mississippi River within two miles above or two miles below" the Eads Bridge or the Merchants' Bridge. The Terminal Railroad Association of St. Louis ("TRRA") dominated shipping commodities across the United States by taking control over the Eads Bridge, the Merchants' Bridge, and the Wiggins Ferry Company.

Several factors contributed to TRRA's formidable control over transportation across the Mississippi River. One of the most significant involved the failed management of rights by Missouri, Illinois, and the federal government. The 1887 federal law that authorized the construction of the Merchants' Bridge specifically banned "pooling of the earnings of this bridge * * * with the earnings of any other bridge * * * on said river." It also prohibited from the owners of the Merchants' Bridge to "be a stockholder or director or manager of any other bridge over said river." These restrictions were repealed in some mysterious fashion, allowing TRRA to acquire the Merchants' Bridge. Missouri and Illinois also accommodated TRRA's concentration of power.

Entry regulation is a favorite target for criticism, often for good reasons.[52] In some ways it is a mirror image of bans and prohibition: an activity is not allowed, unless it is specifically permitted.

---

50. New State Ice Co. v. Liebmann, 285 U.S. 262 (1932); *See* § 6.4.2.

51. *See* United States v. Terminal Railroad Association of St. Louis, 224 U.S. 383 (1912); § 6.4.2.

52. *See, e.g.*, MILTON FRIEDMAN, CAPITALISM AND FREEDOM 137–150 (1962); Morris M. Kleiner, *A License for Protection*, 29.3 REGULATION 17 (2006).

§ 8.4.2 Occupational Licensure

In *Butchers' Union Company v. Crescent City Co.*, Justice Field argued that "the right of men to pursue any lawful business or vocation in any manner not inconsistent with the equal rights of others" is among the constitutional "inalienable rights."[53] Of course, this right has never existed, or as some may argue, has never been respected. Entry regulation, including occupational licensure, has always created some impediments to pursue some lines of business. Consider the following list of occupations that New York State licensed, certified, and registered in 2012:

> acupuncturist, aquatic antifouling paint appplicator, architect, armored car guard, asbestos handler, athlete agent, audiologist, backflow prevention device tester, barber, blaster, boiler inspector, bus driver, certified athletic trainer, certified dental assistant, certified first responder, certified motor vehicle inspector, certified nurse aide, certified public accountant, certified shorthand reporter, chiropractor, clinical laboratory technologist, cytotechnologist, clinical laboratory technician, histological technician, commercial pesticide, cosmetologist, crane operator, credentialed alcoholism and substance abuse counselor, credentialed alcoholism and substance abuse prevention professional/specialist, dental hygienist, dentist, dietitian/nutritionist, driving school instructor, farrier, funeral director, groom, hazardous materials transporter, hearing aid dispenser, home inspector, horse driver, horse trainer, insurance adjuster, independent, insurance adjuster, insurance agent, insurance broker, insurance consultant, interior designer, jockey, jockey agent, land surveyor, landscape architect, lawyer, licensed clinical social worker, licensed creative arts therapist, licensed marriage and family therapist, licensed master social worker, licensed mental health counselor, licensed motor vehicle body damage estimator, licensed outdoor guide, licensed practical nurse, licensed psychoanalyst, radiographer, radiation therapist, nuclear medicine technologist, long term care ombudsman, massage therapist, medical physicist, midwife, milk gathering plant manager, milk laboratory technician, milk receiver, milk tester, nail specialists, nurse practitioner, nursing home administrator, occupational therapist, occupational therapy assistant, ophthalmic dispenser, optometrist, pharmacist, physical therapist, physical therapist assistant, physician, physician assistant, podiatrist, private investigator, professional engineer, psychologist, public librarian, public school administrator, public school teacher, race official, racetrack exercise rider, real estate appraiser, real estate broker, real estate salesperson, registered professional nurse, reinsurance intermediary, respiratory therapist, respiratory therapy technician, securi-

---

53. Butchers' Union Company v. Crescent City Co., 111 U.S. 746 (1884). Justice Field expressed this view already in his dissent in The Slaughter–House Cases, 83 U.S. 36 (1873). For the laissez-faire jurisprudence of Justice Stephen Field *see* Charles McCurdy, *Justice Field and the Jurisprudence of Government–Business Relations: Some Parameters of Laissez–Faire Constitutionalism*, 1863–1897, 61 JOURNAL OF AMERICAN HISTORY 970 (1975); Wallace Mandelson, *Mr. Justice Field and Laissez–Faire*, 36 VIRGINIA LAW REVIEW 45 (1950).

ty/fire alarm installer, security guard, security guard firearms instructor, security guard instructor, security peace officer, specialist assistant in acupuncture, specialist assistant in orthopedics, specialist assistant in radiology, specialist assistant in urology, speech language pathologist, truck driver, ultrasonic testing technician, vehicle escort driver, veterinarian, veterinary technician, wastewater treatment plant, operator, water treatment plant operator, water well contractor, waxer, weighmaster, welder, and workplace safety & loss prevention consultant.

Thus, the "right to pursue one of the ordinary trades or callings of life," is clearly *not* "a right appertaining solely to the individual pursuit of calling."[54] New York is regulating many occupations through licensing, certification, and registration. The terms "licensing," "certification," and "registration" have different meanings in the administration of entry regulation. *Licensing* is the most restrictive method of entry regulation. It requires any person wishing to engage in a particular occupation to obtain a *license* from a specific government agency. To receive a license, the applicant must usually meet a set of requirements, such as graduating from an approved educational institution, acquiring some work experience (*i.e.*, apprenticeship), passing various examinations, qualifying on certain personal prerequisites (*e.g.*, age, citizenship, and character), and paying fees. New York requires licensing from barbers, cosmetologists, dentists, nail specialists, lawyers and other professions. *Certification* is a regulatory method used for certain occupational titles (*e.g.*, a certified public accountant and a certified shorthand reporter). The entry into some occupations is not necessarily restricted by law, and certification adds credibility to those individuals in the trade. To receive the certificate, the applicant must meet the requirements of a state agency, trade association, or certification board. The requirements for certifications tend to be lower than those needed for licensing. *Registration* is the least restrictive method of entry regulation of occupations. Some occupations provide individuals with the opportunity to carry the title a "registered XYZ" (*e.g.*, a registered athlete agent in New York). The registration requirements are minimal and include fees and sometimes also references or other documentations. In practice, the actual classification of the permit is not especially important. Certificates or registrations may be required to do business.

Does society benefit from licensure? Is the licensure system cost-effective? By way of generalization, it may be fair to state that practitioners of licensed occupations tend to support occupational licensure on the grounds that it is in the public interest, whereas "outsiders" tend to feel that occupational licensure cripples competition and is a disservice to the public.[55]

---

54. The Slaughter–House Cases, 83 U.S. 36 (1873) (Field, J., dissenting) (arguing that the right to pursue one of the ordinary trade *is* "a right appertaining solely to the individual.")

55. *See, e.g.*, Alex Maurizi, *Occupational Licensing and the Public Interest*, 82 JOURNAL OF POLITICAL ECONOMY 399 (1974); Thomas G. Moore, *The Purpose of Licensing*, 4 JOURNAL OF LAW & ECONOMICS 93 (1961).

Dent v. West Virginia

129 U.S. 114 (1889)

This case comes from the supreme court of appeals of West Virginia. It involves the validity of the statute of that state which requires every practitioner of medicine in it to obtain a certificate from the state board of health that he is a graduate of a reputable medical college in the school of medicine to which he belongs; or that he has practiced medicine in the state continuously for the period of 10 years prior to the 8th day of March, 1881; or that he has been found, upon examination by the board, to be qualified to practice medicine in all its departments; and makes the practice of, or the attempt by any person to practice, medicine, surgery, or obstetrics in the state without such certificate, unless called from another state to treat a particular case, a misdemeanor punishable by fine or imprisonment, or both, in the discretion of the court. * * *

Under this statute, the plaintiff in error was indicted * * * for unlawfully engaging in the practice of medicine in that state in June, 1882. * * * [T]he defendant * * * engaged in the practice of medicine in the town of Newburg, Preston county, West Virginia, * * * and had been so engaged since the year 1876 continuously to the present time, and has during all said time enjoyed a lucrative practice, publicly professing to be a physician, prescribing for the sick, and appending to his name the letters, 'M. D.' * * * [He] has a diploma from the 'American Medical Eclectic College of Cincinnati, Ohio;' that he presented said diploma to the members of the board of health who reside in his congressional district, and asked for the certificate as required by law, but they, after retaining said diploma for some time, returned it to defendant with their refusal to grant him a certificate asked, because, as they claimed, said college did not come under the word 'reputable,' as defined by said board of health; that if the defendant had been or should be prevented from practicing medicine it would be a great injury to him, as it would deprive him of his only means of supporting himself and family; that at the time of the passage of the act of 1882 he had not been practicing medicine ten years, but had only been practicing six, as aforesaid, from the year 1876. * * * The [trial] court * * * sentenced the defendant to pay a fine of $50 and the costs of the proceedings. The case being taken on writ of error to the supreme court of appeals of the state, the judgment was affirmed, and to review this judgment the case is brought here.

■ MR. JUSTICE FIELD, after stating the facts as above, delivered the opinion of the court.

* * * The unconstitutionality asserted consists in its alleged conflict with the clause of the fourteenth amendment which declares that no state shall deprive any person of life, liberty, or property without due process of law; the denial to the defendant of the right to practice his profession without the certificate required constituting the deprivation of his vested right and estate in his profession, which he had previously acquired.

It is undoubtedly the right of every citizen of the United States to follow any lawful calling, business, or profession he may choose, subject only to such restrictions as are imposed upon all persons of like age, sex, and condition. This right may in many respects be considered as a distinguishing feature of our republican institutions. Here all vocations are open to every one on like conditions. All may be pursued as sources of livelihood, some requiring years of study and great learning for their successful prosecution. * * * The power of the state to provide for the general welfare of its people authorizes it to prescribe all such regulations as in its judgment will secure or tend to secure them against the consequences of ignorance and incapacity, as well as of deception and fraud. * * * The nature and extent of the qualifications required must depend primarily upon the judgment of the state as to their necessity. If they are appropriate to the calling or profession, and attainable by reasonable study or application, no objection to their validity can be raised because of their stringency or difficulty. It is only when they have no relation to such calling or profession, or are unattainable by such reasonable study and application, that they can operate to deprive one of his right to pursue a lawful vocation.

Few professions require more careful preparation by one who seeks to enter it than that of medicine. It has to deal with all those subtle and mysterious influences upon which health and life depend, and requires not only a knowledge of the properties of vegetable and mineral substances, but of the human body in all its complicated parts, and their relation to each other, as well as their influence upon the mind. The physician must be able to detect readily the presence of disease, and prescribe appropriate remedies for its removal. Every one may have occasion to consult him, but comparatively few can judge of the qualifications of learning and skill which he possesses. Reliance must be placed upon the assurance given by his license, issued by an authority competent to judge in that respect, that he possesses the requisite qualifications. Due consideration, therefore, for the protection of society may well induce the state to exclude from practice those who have not such a license, or who are found upon examination not to be fully qualified. * * * We perceive nothing in the statute which indicates an intention of the legislature to deprive one of any of his rights. No one has a right to practice medicine without having the necessary qualifications of learning and skill; and the statute only requires that whoever assumes, by offering to the community his services as a physician, that he possesses such learning and skill, shall present evidence of it by a certificate or license from a body designated by the state as competent to judge of his qualifications.

* * *

The law of West Virginia was intended to secure such skill and learning in the profession of medicine that the community might trust with confidence those receiving a license under authority of the state. Judgment affirmed.

Questions

1. Justice Field considered "the right of men to pursue any lawful business or vocation in any manner not inconsistent with the equal rights

of others" among the constitutional "inalienable rights."[56] Nevertheless, he endorsed occupational regulation. How did he justify this exception?

2. In his book *Capitalism and Freedom*, Milton Friedman wrote:

> I agree that the case for licensure is stronger in for medicine than for most other fields. Yet * * * even in medicine * * * licensure [is] undesirable.
>
> * * *
>
> The main argument [for licensure] is the existence of neighborhood effects. [Consider] the "incompetent" physician who produces an epidemic. Insofar as he harms only his patient, that is simply a question of voluntary contract and exchange between the patient and his physician. * * * However, it can be argued that if the physician treats his patient badly, he may unleash an epidemic that will cause harm to third parties who are not involved in the immediate transaction. * * * In practice, the major argument given for licensure * * * is not this one, * * * but rather a strictly paternalistic argument that has little or no appeal. Individuals, it is said, are incapable of choosing their own servants adequately, their own physician or plumber or barber. In order for a man to choose a physician intelligently he would have to be a physician himself. * * * [L]icensure is the key to the control that the medical profession can exercise over the number of physicians.[57]

Some possibly suffer from some shortage of hairstylists ("barbers"). Sometimes it may feel that certain hairstylists are busy or that there is no "good hairstylist" in town. But licensed hairstylists always seem to be available.

(a) Does this pattern suggest that individuals are indeed "incapable of choosing their own servants adequately"? (b) Do people choose their physicians, plumbers, and hairstylists in similar ways? (c) Does licensure necessarily imply that "people lack incapable of choosing their own servants adequately"?

S.S. Kresge Co. v. Couzens

290 Mich. 185 (1939)

■ SHARPE, JUSTICE.

The city of Detroit enacted Ordinance No. 170–C which became effective July 7, 1932. The ordinance, which is copied in the margin, provides for the licensing of those engaged in the florist business.

Ordinance No. 170–C

An Ordinance to provide for the regulation and licensing of florists and providing a penalty for the violation thereof.

---

56. Butchers' Union Company v. Crescent City Co., 111 U.S. 746 (1884).

57. MILTON FRIEDMAN, CAPITALISM AND FREEDOM 138–148 (1962),

It Is Hereby Ordained By the People of the City of Detroit:

SECTION 1. No person, firm or corporation shall engage in the florist business in the City of Detroit without first having obtained a license from the Mayor.

SECTION 2. A florist for the purpose of this ordinance shall mean all persons, firms or corporations, both principals and agents, who engage in the business of selling cut flowers and potted plants, and shall not be construed to mean or include market selling by persons selling such stock, * * * or producers, or their agents, * * * or producers or persons selling only dry bulbs, roots, tubers, corms, unpotted hardy perennials, bedding plants, deciduous plants, seedlings or evergreens, within the meaning of trees, shrubs, vines and vegetables or cereal plants.

SECTION 3. Every person of good moral character desiring to engage in the florist business in the City of Detroit shall make an application in writing to the Commissioner of Police for a license to engage in the florist business at least thirty (30) days before so engaging, stating the location and address at which he desires to engage in the business.

The Commissioner of Police may require, under oath if desired, information concerning the moral character and identification of the applicant. The Commissioner shall then transmit the results of such investigation to the Mayor together with his recommendation concerning the granting or refusing a license. The Mayor shall then issue a license to such applicant if he is found qualified for the same under the ordinance and has furnished the required bond as hereinafter set forth, or may refuse to issue a license if the applicant is not found qualified or has not fully complied with the ordinance. The moral character of the applicant shall be considered from the standpoint of protecting the public from dishonest or fraudulent conduct, or willful misrepresentations in the sale of cut flowers and potted plants.

SECTION 4. *Bond Required.* Before a license as herein provided, shall be issued, the applicant shall execute to the City of Detroit a good and sufficient bond for the period of one (1) year in the sum of Five Hundred ($500.00) Dollars, with good and sufficient surety, or sureties, to be approved by the Mayor as to the sufficiency of the surety or sureties, and to be approved by the Corporation Counsel or an Assistant Corporation Counsel, as to form; which bond shall be conditioned as to indemnify or reimburse any purchaser of goods, wares or merchandise in a sum equal to at least the amount of any payment or payments such purchaser may have been induced to make through misrepresentation as to the proper delivery or the kind, quality or value of such goods, wares or merchandise, made by the owners, or by their servants, agents or employees at the time of making the sale; and which bond shall be further conditioned for the faithful performance of all the terms and conditions and provisions of this ordinance.

SECTION 5. *License Fee.* A license fee of ten ($10.00) Dollars shall be charged for the issuance of this license which shall be granted for a period of one (1) year, but all licenses shall expire April first of each year.

SECTION 6. *License to Be Posted.* No person, firm or corporation shall engage in the florist business without first securing a license for each place to be operated and no license issued under this ordinance shall be transferable, nor shall be used by any persons, firm or corporation other than as named in the license and said licensee shall conspicuously display said license in his place of business so that the same is plainly visible to the public.

SECTION 7. *Complaint.* When any complaint is made that goods, wares or merchandise sold have not been delivered or have been misrepresented, or the ordinance violated in any way by the said license or any person acting in his behalf, it shall be the duty of the Commissioner of Police or any person authorized by him to make inquiries into the circumstances surrounding such loss, misrepresentation, or violation, and adjust the same and make such recommendation to the Mayor with respect to suspension or revocation of such license if such action is warranted by the facts: *Provided,* That no license shall be suspended or revoked without proper notice to the licensee and hearing provided before the Mayor or person authorized by him to conduct the same.

SECTION 8. *Penalty.* Any person, firm or corporation who shall violate any of the provisions of this ordinance or shall fail to comply with the same, shall upon conviction thereof, be punished by a fine of not more than One Hundred ($100.00) Dollars or by imprisonment in the Detroit House of Correction for a period of not to exceed ninety (90) days or by both such fine and imprisonment in the discretion of the Court.

S. S. Kresge Company, of Detroit, filed a * * * complaint in the circuit court of Wayne county to have the ordinance declared invalid and void and contends that the subject-matter contained in the ordinance is beyond the police power and amounts to an unreasonable interference with the rights of citizens to carry on a legitimate business; that the ordinance by including only persons 'selling cut flowers and potted plants' makes an arbitrary and unreasonable classification, constitutes class legislation, and conflicts with the Fourteenth amendment to the United States Constitution. * * * and that the ordinance is invalid because it exacts an excessive license fee.

Defendants contend that the ordinance was adopted to curb or eliminate fraudulent practices on the part of irresponsible, itinerant merchants engaged in the business of 'doping' flowers and selling them to an unsuspecting public and to prevent flower peddlers from engaging in the florist business without paying personal property tax.

An examination of the ordinance discloses that it prohibits the sale of cut flowers and potted plants except when the vendor is licensed by the mayor. It does not regulate the sale of cut flowers on the streets of the city of Detroit or the sale by temporary merchants who may rent store premises for short periods during the holiday seasons, except that they must comply with the act.

Citation of authority is unnecessary to establish the proposition that the sale of cut flowers and potted plants is a legitimate business and should remain unhampered by legislative action unless restrictions are required for the protection of the public. * * *

* * * The ordinance is * * * an 'unreasonable interference with the rights of citizens to carry on a legitimate business' and 'an attempt to stifle competition rather than to enforce reasonable and necessary regulations upon a business that is in need of regulation in order to afford protection to the public.' * * *

The purpose of the ordinance may be gleaned from the testimony of defendants' witness Brown:

> 'We were protecting our business by getting rid of these people who sold in the streets.... Mother's Day and Easter were the principal days that they hurt me, but during the week they hurt them all on those other corners. That is why the Florists Association lobbied this ordinance through.
>
> 'It is true that these second-hand flowers were sold at second-hand prices. They sold roses at twenty-five cents a dozen. I sold them for a dollar and a dollar and a half. They were selling second-hand roses and I was selling first-hand roses. It is true that that was just a depression condition. People would not buy dollar dozen roses during the depression as much as when times were good.'

And the witness Lutey who testified: 'There is nothing wrong with selling those imperfect roses as bull-heads at reduced prices. The object of this ordinance lobbied by my florist committee was to get rid of those merchants that sold that type of flower and old flowers. They were underselling our association of florists.'

The reasoning given in the case of *Chaddock v. Day*, 75 Mich. 527 (1889), again seems appropriate, we there said: 'It is quite common in these latter days for certain classes of citizens—those engaged in this or that business—to appeal to the government—national, state or municipal—to aid them by legislation against another class of citizens engaged in the same business, but in some other way. This class legislation, when indulged in, seldom benefits the general public, but nearly always aids the few for whose benefit it is enacted, not only at the expense of the few against whom it is ostensibly directed, but also at the expense and to the detriment of the many, for whose benefit all legislation should be. * * * '

The object of the present ordinance was not to protect the citizens of Detroit in their public health, safety, morals or general welfare, but was for the financial benefit of a few. * * * [W]e are constrained to hold that the ordinance involves the infringement of the right of property or business under the guise of police regulations and is therefore void.

Questions

1. Are there any good reasons to protect florists in stores from excessive competition?

2. Excessive use of licensure is rather common. Why did the florists in Detroit lose their privileges?

Dyrek v. Garvey

334 F.3d 590 (7th Cir. 2003)

■ HARLINGTON WOOD, JR., CIRCUIT JUDGE.

Appellant Gary Dyrek was employed by the Federal Aviation Administration ("FAA") as an Air Traffic Control Specialist ("ATCS"). FAA Air Traffic Control Specialists, also known as air traffic controllers, are responsible for directing air traffic, both on the ground and in the air. It is their duty to provide for the safe, orderly, and expeditious flow of air traffic across U.S. airspace. FAA rules and regulations require an air traffic controller to maintain a valid medical certificate to minimize the effects of health concerns on system safety.

Dyrek began working as an air traffic controller in 1981. During the time he worked at the FAA, Dyrek's work performance was never criticized. However, by letter dated March 14, 2000, Dyrek was informed he was being terminated from his position effective March 17, 2000, "because of [his] inability to meet medical standards required for Air Traffic Control Specialists." This termination letter was the culmination of nearly three years of discussions between Dyrek and the FAA regarding his health. In October 1993, Dyrek was diagnosed as having diabetes mellitus. In May 1997, Dyrek began taking daily injections of insulin for his diabetes. While the mere diagnosis of diabetes mellitus is a disqualifying condition for initial hire as an air traffic controller, an air traffic controller who becomes an insulin-using diabetic while employed by the FAA may maintain his or her medical certificate through "special consideration."[1]

By a letter dated June 30, 1997, the Regional Flight Surgeon's office temporarily withdrew Dyrek's medical clearance for safety-related duties, based on a review of a medical report from Dyrek's attending physician dated June 13, 1997 which stated Dyrek had been placed on insulin for his diabetes. According to the Regional Flight Surgeon's letter, laboratory results indicated unsatisfactory control of Dyrek's diabetes. * * *

When Dyrek's medical clearance was withdrawn, he was assigned to perform only limited "A-side duties." "A-side duties" do not include any responsibility for air traffic control, and a medical clearance is not required in order to perform "A-side duties." Prior to 1995, the FAA had "A-side positions" in which individuals performed only "A-side duties." This "A-side position" was a separate position from that of air traffic controller.

---

1. [A] medical clearance based on special consideration is granted based on a favorable review of an ATCS's medical history and a comprehensive medical evaluation. The ATCS must also demonstrate stable control of his diabetes through proper diabetes education and skills. If medical clearance is granted based on special consideration, the ATCS, his supervisors, and his coworkers must adhere to strict FAA guidelines throughout the workday to ensure the ATCS is maintaining stable control of his blood sugar to prevent dangerous diabetic complications that might interfere with air safety.

However, "A-side positions" were abolished by the FAA in 1995. Currently, air traffic controllers are required to perform "A-side duties" as a part of their job. The FAA and the National Air Traffic Controllers Association have an agreement that allows the FAA to assign air traffic controllers who are temporarily medically disqualified to perform only "A-side duties," which allows those air traffic controllers to continue working despite their lack of medical clearance.

According to the deposition testimony of Deputy Regional Flight Surgeon Dr. Robert Liska, prior to 1995, there were no insulin-using diabetic air traffic controllers who were medically certified to work in safety-related positions. However, the FAA periodically issued Medical Guideline Letters setting out medical protocols which would allow for certification of insulin-using air traffic controllers. These protocols were designed to collect and interpret information on a case-by-case basis and set forth standards to help the Regional Flight Surgeons in understanding whether an insulin-using individual was "safe" to perform safety-related air traffic control duties. For example, Medical Guideline Letter MGL–B–86, titled "Medical clearance; diabetic air traffic control specialists who use insulin" stated, "Clearance may be granted and shall be based on the medical history, on the results of a comprehensive medical evaluation, on documentation of proper education regarding diabetes, and on consideration of the diabetes control skills demonstrated by each subject ATCS." According to MGL–B–86, "Continued clearance requires control of diabetes with prevention of hypoglycemia through close monitoring and maintenance of appropriate blood glucose levels throughout every work day."

In 1997, Medical Guideline Letter MGL–B–5a–0026, titled "Guidance for Application of Medical Retention Standards for Air Traffic Control Specialists," was in effect. With respect to diabetes mellitus, MGL–B–5a–0026 states recurrent evidence of noncontrol, including blood sugar test results showing elevated Hemoglobin A1C ("A1C") levels and elevated fasting blood sugar ("FBS") levels, are grounds for disqualification. * * *

In response to the June 30, 1997 letter withdrawing his medical clearance, Dyrek submitted a medical report * * * from his endocrinologist Dr. Steven Bielski. By memo * * *, the office of the Regional Flight Surgeon notified Dyrek that, based on information contained in Dr. Bielski's * * * report, it had been determined that Dyrek's diabetes was "not well controlled." * * *

[During the following months, Dyrek and the FAA engaged in an extensive negotiation over his medical condition.] [O]n March 14, 2000, [Ralph] Davis, [Dyrek's supervisor and the Air Traffic Manager for the Chicago center,] issued his "Decision Letter" to Dyrek, stating he had considered Dyrek's * * * submissions, but nevertheless concluded Dyrek should be removed effective March 17, 2000. * * *

On October 12, 2000, Dyrek filed a two-count complaint in the United States District Court for the Northern District of Illinois against the FAA and FAA Administrator Jane Garvey ("the FAA"), alleg[ing] the FAA unlawfully discriminated against Dyrek because of his diabetes in violation of the Rehabilitation Act of 1973, the Americans with Disabilities Act ("ADA"), and Title VII of the Civil Rights Act of 1991. * * *

ANALYSIS

* * * The FAA contends Dyrek was terminated because he failed to submit documentation to establish his diabetes was under control, despite numerous requests for specific information. Dyrek does not dispute appellees' right to require that he controls his diabetes, nor does he challenge the FAA's heightened medical reporting requirements for insulin-using diabetics. Rather, he asserts appellees' proffered reason for his termination is pretextual, first, because there is no evidence in the record to show he was not controlling his diabetes and, secondly, because his diabetes was actually under control.

Absent direct evidence of pretext, Dyrek may show the FAA's proffered reason for his termination was pretextual by pointing to evidence which would tend to prove the proffered reason was factually baseless, not the actual motivation for the discharge, or insufficient to motivate the discharge. * * * This court does not sit as a super-personnel department; our only concern with respect to pretext is the honesty of an employer's explanation.

* * *

When asked at oral argument why Dyrek failed to provide the FAA with the requested documentation, counsel for Dyrek stated it was his belief that Dyrek's February 2000 submissions were sufficient to satisfy the FAA's request for a medical report. However, an examination of those submissions, which are included in the record, shows that they do not provide all of the information requested by the FAA. * * * Dyrek was given many opportunities to provide specific documentation, yet he failed to do so. * * *

Dyrek further contends his case of discrimination is bolstered by the fact he was not given another position within the FAA that did not require a medical clearance. We first address Dyrek's contention that "the position [he] held at the time he was fired" did not require a medical clearance. It is undisputed that the air traffic controller position requires a valid medical clearance. While "A-side duties" may be performed without a valid medical clearance, the record evidence clearly shows at the time Dyrek was terminated there was not a separate "A-side position" within the FAA. Furthermore, Dyrek concedes his assignment to another position was dependent upon the existence of a vacancy in a position that did not require a medical clearance, yet in his briefs on appeal he points to no evidence that could show such a vacancy existed at the time he made his request for an alternate assignment. * * * Viewed in the light most favorable to Dyrek, there is no evidence from which a reasonable trier of fact could conclude the FAA's proffered reason for Dyrek's termination was pretextual. * * *

Questions

1. Was Gary Dyrek's dispute with the FAA purely about termination of employment? Did the dispute involve occupational licensing?

2. Dyrek could not hold his position as an air traffic controller because of a change to his medical condition. The licensing requirements of many occupations refer to conditions at the point when an applicant obtains a license. These conditions include knowledge of certain standards within a given field and evaluation of the applicant's character. Do changes in these conditions disqualify licensed individuals? For example, how do states assure that lawyers maintain reasonable levels of knowledge after the law changes?

§ 8.4.3 Regulation through Permits

Permits are granted only when defined conditions are met. The state often regulates through such conditions. This Section illustrates the technique.

Dog Permits

On March 1, 1906, Kentucky Governor J.C.W. Beckham signed into law *An Act to Promote the Sheep Industry and to Provide a* Tax *On Dogs*.[58] Section 2 of the Act provided:

> The owner of every dog over four months of age shall pay a license tax thereon of one dollar. * * * Said license tax shall be due and collectible as other taxes, and collected by the sheriff and reported to the Auditor and paid to the Treasurer, but the sheriff shall keep such license tax on dogs separate from other funds, and so report to the Auditor and pay to the Treasurer, and the Treasurer and Auditor shall, keep separate accounts of such taxes by counties. The amount collected by license tax on dogs shall be used to indemnify losses by the killing or injuring of sheep by dogs. * * *

---

58. A copy of the Kentucky Dog Tax Law is available at *regti.me/KY-dog* (case sensitive).

Figure 8.6
Section 7 of the Kentucky "Dog Law"

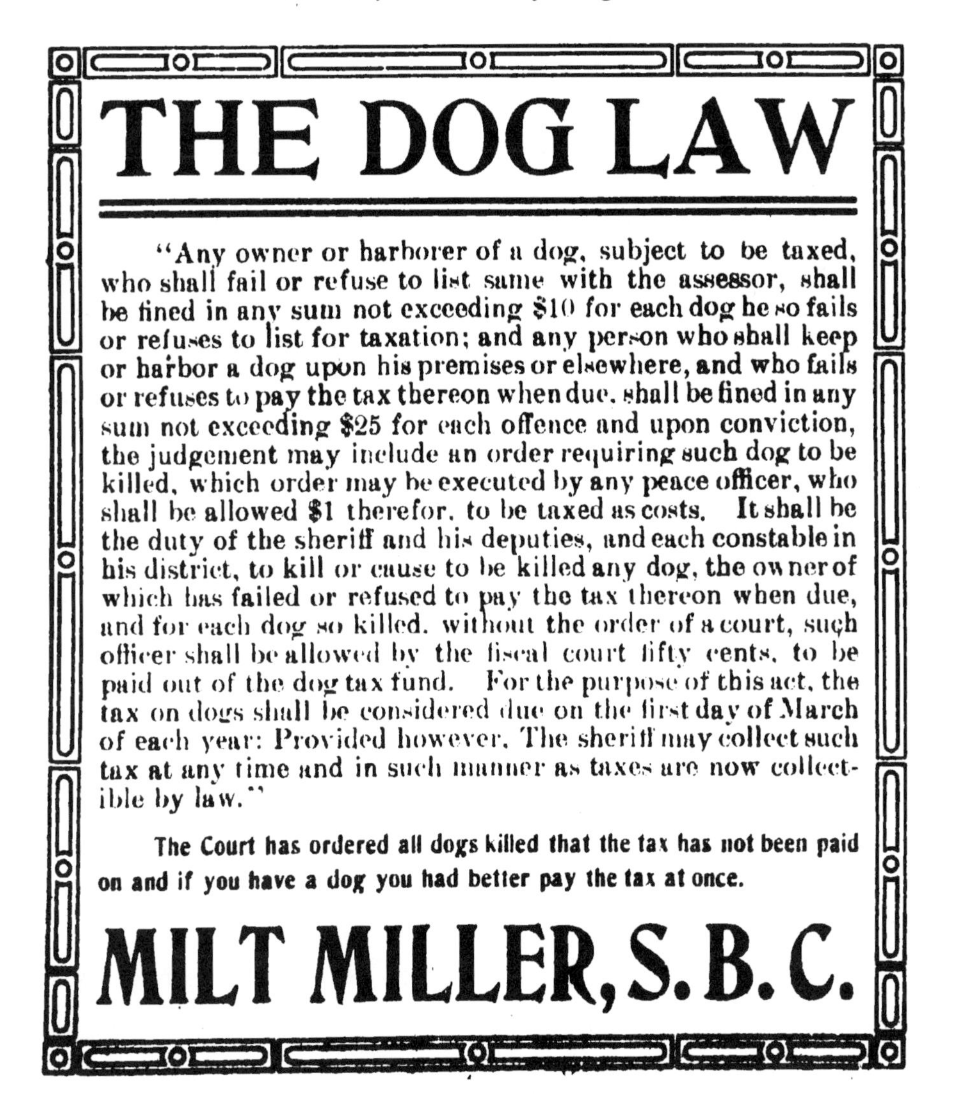

Source: A 1909 Advertisement.

McGlone v. Womack

Court of Appeals of Kentucky
129 Ky. 274 (1908)

■ BARKER, JUSTICE.

This action was instituted by * * * citizens of Carter County, Kentucky, and owners of dogs, to test the validity of an act of the General Assembly of the common-wealth of Kentucky approved March 1, 1906, entitled "*An act to promote the sheep industry and to provide a tax on dogs*." * * * By the first and second sections of the act a license tax of $1 per capita is required to be assessed upon every dog four months old within the common-wealth, which the owner of the animal is required to pay. This tax is required to be levied and collected as are other taxes, and paid over to the State Treasurer, but to be kept separate from the other public accounts and taxes by the Auditor and Treasurer. The funds thus raised are declared to be for the purpose of indemnifying losses by the killing or injuring of sheep by dogs. The third and fourth sections of the act provide how the losses by the killing of sheep by dogs shall be proved and paid; and, if there be any surplus after paying all losses occurring by the killing of sheep by dogs, it shall be paid over to the school fund of the county in which it was assessed. * * *

The first question to be determined is whether or not the statute before us is a revenue statute, or whether it was enacted for the purpose of police regulation. That it was not intended as a revenue statute is obvious from the most superficial reading. The title declares the purpose of the enactment to be the promotion of the sheep industry by the levy of a tax on dogs, and the body of the act shows clearly that its object is to remunerate the owners of sheep for any losses they may suffer by the killing of their sheep by dogs. The license tax imposed, then, was intended by the Legislature to be a regulation of dogs, and in this way to promote the sheep industry. This confronts us with the question as to whether or not it is within the competency of the Legislature to regulate dogs in the manner undertaken to be done in the statute before us. * * *

[W]e are of opinion that the regulation of dogs is within the police power of the state, and that it is competent for the Legislature to prohibit the keeping of dogs entirely, or, if it is necessary for the public welfare, any other regulation may be adopted which to the Legislature may seem most expedient for the promotion of that end. We are also of opinion that, the statute not being for revenue, but an exercise of the police power. * * * We do not think it can be doubted that, if it is competent for the Legislature to prohibit the ownership of dogs or to prohibit them running at large, it is also competent for it to impose any other regulation which in its wisdom is best adapted to promote the sheep industry. Therefore it seems to us competent for the Legislature to say to the owners of dogs in the state: "You may own dogs and you may permit them to run at large, but you must as a condition precedent to this privilege provide a fund by which their ravages on sheep may be paid for." That the state may do this legitimately seems quite clear, unless we are prepared to say that the less is not included in the greater, or a part in the whole. * * *

As we view it, the statute does not confer any special privilege on the owners of sheep. It merely protects these owners from the destruction of their property by dogs. It is the duty of the state to protect every citizen in his life, liberty, and property; and it certainly is within the competency of the Legislature to exercise the police power of the state to protect all property against the ravages of destructive animals. The question as to how this is to be done and what property is to be so protected is a matter of legislative discretion. Undoubtedly the sheep industry is a most important one to the whole state. All of our citizens are interested in an industry which supplies the market with wholesome meat, provides means of obtaining warm and comfortable clothing, and at the same time furnishes labor to the otherwise unemployed. * * * The fact that sheep are generally killed at night when it is impossible to ascertain the owner of the dog committing the ravage makes it necessary, if protection is to be had through this channel at all, that each owner of a dog should be required to contribute a small amount to a common fund dedicated to the remuneration of owners of sheep killed by unknown dogs. As said before, this is simply requiring the owners of dogs to make good the ravages of dangerous animals kept by them; and no citizen has just cause of complaint, if he keeps animals destructive to the property of others, that he is required to make good the damage done by them. The statute in truth, is but an enforcement of the maxim, "*sic utere tuo ut alienum non lædas,*" and, as such, its constitutionality is beyond successful question.

* * *

■ O'REAR, CHIEF JUSTICE (dissenting).

While admitting the scope of the police power in the state to regulate the ownership and control of property within its borders so as to minimize the injuries that may be inflicted on others because of the predatory nature of the property, still I am unable to go so far as the majority opinion does in this case. One man's property may need regulation for the public safety, but that is far from meaning that it may be taken from him and given to somebody else. * * * Dogs are personal property. * * * The state may regulate their ownership, as it may any other property; but I deny that it can regulate the ownership so as to confer the sole benefit directly and exclusively upon any other class of property. Nor can the fact that one class of property sometimes preys upon another class justify such legislation. Hogs are also a danger to other property. They may break into fields of corn and other grain and destroy them. Consequently the state may regulate the ownership of hogs by requiring them to be kept up by their owners, and may impose a liability on such owners for their depredations; but has the state the power to impose a license tax on hogs for the benefit of all who raise corn, or even of those engaged in raising corn who suffer damage by breachy hogs? * * * [Moreover, the] state has [no] power to tax one class of property and give the proceeds directly to owners of another class, upon the idea that the latter contribute more to the good of society. I submit that the state could not levy a tax or appropriate money out of the treasury (which is the same thing) for the benefit of unfortunate sheep owners who had lost their sheep by ravages of dogs or disease; nor for one any more than for the other. * * *

I do not believe such legislation is a valid exercise of the police power. We all recognize that sheep husbandry is a business of great value to the state. It may be admitted that the ownership of dogs is of doubtful value. The interests of the former as weighed against the latter may overwhelmingly preponderate from an economic standpoint. Notwithstanding all which, the principle of the law must be the same. It is unsafe to allow mere utilitarianism to bear down those safeguards of the citizens' rights-those checks imposed by the people in their Constitution against the power of the majority and in favor of the individual, that which gives, if anything gives, one man a right safe from the encroachment of all other men; that which recognizes the supreme right of individual taste and judgment in the matter of acquiring property and in the pursuit of happiness. * * *

Hence I feel constrained to dissent from the opinion delivered by the court in this case.

Questions

1. Observing that the legislature had the power to ban dogs, Justice Barker inferred that the legislature was "also competent * * * to impose any other regulation which in its wisdom [was] best adapted to promote the sheep industry." He argued that any other conclusion would mean that "the less is not included in the greater, or a part in the whole." Is this correct?

2. Was the Kentucky's dog law "an enforcement of the maxim, '*sic utere tuo ut alienum non lædas*,' and, as such, its constitutionality [should have been] beyond successful question," as the court concluded?[59]

3. Was regulation needed to protect the interest of the sheep industry? Could a Coasean bargaining have resolved the problems created by dogs?

4. In the late 1960s and early 1970s states introduced no-fault liability insurance requirements for drivers. Courts upheld the constitutionality of these insurance mandates.[60] Did Kentucky effectively establish a mandatory no-fault liability insurance requirement for dog owners? What were the likely effects of one rate for all dogs? Did the regulation reduce risks for the sheep industry?

Movie Censorship

On November 4, 1907, Chicago adopted a movie censorship ordinance. It was the first censorship regulation in the United States to require the review of motion pictures.

An Ordinance

*Prohibiting the exhibition of obscene and immoral [moving] pictures and regulating the exhibition of [moving] pictures of the classes and kinds commonly shown in * * * penny arcades.*

Be it ordained by the City Council of the City of Chicago:

SECTION 1. That it shall be unlawful for any person, firm or corporation to show or exhibit in a public place or in a place where the public is admitted anywhere in the City of Chicago any * * * moving picture * * *, whether an admission fee is charged or not,

---

59. For the maxim *sic utere tuo ut alienum non lædas* ("use your own in such a manner as not to injure another") *see* § 3.2.1.

60. *See* Bell v. Burson, 402 U.S. 535, 539 (1971) ("If the statute barred the issuance of licenses to all motorists who did not carry liability insurance or who did not post security, the statute would not, under our cases, violate the Fourteenth Amendment.") *See also* Gentile v. Altermatt, 169 Conn. 267 (1975); Montgomery v. Daniels, 38 N.Y.2d 41 (1975); Singer v. Sheppard, 464 Pa. 387 (1975); Lasky v. State Farm Ins. Co., 296 So.2d 9 (Fla., 1974); Manzanares v. Bell, 214 Kan. 589 (1974); Opinion of the Justices, May 14, 1973, 113 N.H. 205 (1973); Grace v. Howlett, 51 Ill.2d 478 (1972); Pinnick v. Cleary, 360 Mass. 1 (1971).

without first having secured a permit there-for from the Chief of Police of the City of Chicago.

SECTION 2. Before any such permit is granted, an application in writing shall be made therefor, and the * * * [moving] pictures * * * shall be shown to the Chief of Police who shall inspect, or cause to be inspected, such [moving] pictures and within three days after such inspection he shall either grant or deny the permit. In case a permit is granted it shall be in writing and in such form as the Chief of Police may prescribe.

SECTION 3. If [the moving] pictures for * * * which an application for a permit is made is immoral or obscene, it shall be the duty of the Chief of Police to refuse such permit, otherwise it shall be his duty to grant such permit.

SECTION 4. In case the Chief of Police shall refuse to grant a permit, the applicant may appeal to the Mayor. Such appeal shall be presented in the same manner as the original application to the Chief of Police. The action of the Mayor upon any application for a permit shall be final.

SECTION 5. * * * No fee or tax of any kind whatsoever shall be charged or exacted for [a] permit.

* * *

SECTION 7. The written permit herein provided for shall be posted at or near the entrance to the theatre, hall, room or place where any permitted [moving] pictures is being exhibited, at such a place and in such a position that it may easily and readily be read. * * *

SECTION 8. Anyone violating the terms of this ordinance shall be fined not less than fifty ($50.00) dollars nor more than one hundred ($100.00) dollars for each offense. Every day's exhibition of each picture or series of pictures without a permit shall be a distinct and separate offense.

* * *

Block v. Chicago

Supreme Court of Illinois
239 Ill. 251 (1909)

■ CARTWRIGHT, CHIEF JUSTICE.

The plaintiffs in error * * * filed their bill of complaint in the superior court of Cook county against the defendant in error, city of Chicago, alleging that they were engaged in the business of operating five and ten cent theaters in the city of Chicago, where moving pictures were displayed, and praying the court to enjoin the defendant in error from enforcing an ordinance entitled '*An ordinance prohibiting the exhibition of obscene and immoral [moving] pictures and regulating the exhibition of [moving] pictures of the classes and kinds commonly shown in * * * penny arcades*,' passed November 4, 1907. * * * The ground upon which the injunction was asked for was that the ordinance deprived the complainants of their rights under the Constitution, and was therefore void. * * *

The material facts * * * are as follows: The complainants are engaged in the business of operating five and ten cent theaters, where moving pictures are displayed by means of moving picture machines. * * * The pictures are displayed upon canvas and are taken from plays and dramas which the bill says are moral and in no way obscene. Among the pictures are pictures taken from the plays known as the 'James Boys' and the 'Night Riders,' displaying experiences connected with the history of this country. There had been, and at the time of the display of the pictures by complainants there were, certain plays and dramas being performed in certain playhouses in the city of Chicago of which the pictures were reproductions of parts. * * * The chief of police refused to grant a permit for the display of the pictures of the 'James Boys' and 'Night Riders,' and others used by the complainants, about 200 or 300 in all. * * * There are about 200 persons engaged in the same business in Chicago in addition to the complainants, all of whom are similarly situated, and the chief of police threatens to enforce the ordinance against all of them. At the same time permits to complainants were refused for the pictures named, some of the [moving] pictures prohibited were being shown in the city in stereoption views and stationary pictures. The bill alleges that the ordinance is void because it discriminates against the exhibiters of moving pictures, delegates discretionary and judicial powers to the chief of police, takes the property of complainants without due process of law, and is unreasonable and oppressive.

The purpose of the ordinance is to secure decency and morality in the moving picture business, and that purpose falls within the police power. It is designed as a precautionary measure to prevent exhibitions criminal in their nature and forbidden by the laws. Even the possession of an indecent picture is a crime * * *, and the offender may be confined in the county jail not more than six months or be fined not less than $100 nor more than $1,000 for each offense. The ordinance applies to five and ten cent theaters such as the complainants operate, and which, on account of the low price of admission, are frequented and patronized by a large number of children, as well as by those of limited means who do not attend the productions of plays and dramas given in the regular theaters. The audiences include those classes whose age, education, and situation in life specially entitle them to protection against the evil influence of obscene and immoral representations. The welfare of society demands that every effort of municipal authorities to afford such protection shall be sustained, unless it is clear that some constitutional right is interfered with. * * *

The ordinance, however, * * * contains no discrimination against persons of the same class or engaged in the same business. It applies alike to all persons engaged in the moving picture business. * * *

No wrong was done or threatened to the complainants, and the bill stated no ground for equitable interference.

Questions

1. The Illinois Supreme Court was convinced that movie theaters were "frequented and patronized by a large number of children, as well as by

those of limited means." How did this finding influence the court? Was the analysis of this finding consistent with the purposes of the ordinance?

2. Could Chicago censor films through bans? If so, how?

Tabooing Tattooing

Anderson v. Hermosa Beach

621 F.3d 1051 (9th Cir. 2010)

■ BYBEE, CIRCUIT JUDGE:

We address a question of first impression in our circuit: whether a municipal ban on tattoo parlors violates the First Amendment. Although courts in several jurisdictions have upheld such bans against First Amendment challenges, * * * we respectfully disagree. We hold that tattooing is purely expressive activity fully protected by the First Amendment, and that a total ban on such activity is not a reasonable "time, place, or manner" restriction.

I. BACKGROUND

Petitioner–Appellant Johnny Anderson seeks to establish a tattoo parlor in Defendant–Appellee City of Hermosa Beach (the "City"), but Hermosa Beach Municipal Code ("Code") § 17.06.070 effectively bans tattoo parlors. Anderson sued the City under 42 U.S.C. § 1983, alleging that § 17.06.070 is facially unconstitutional under the First and Fourteenth Amendments. * * *

A. *Tattooing*

A declaration provided by the City sums up well the process of tattooing:

> A tattoo is created by injecting ink into a person's skin. To do this, an electrically powered tattoo machine, often called a gun, moves a solid needle up and down to puncture the skin between 50 and 3,000 times per minute. The needle penetrates the skin by about a millimeter and deposits a drop of insoluble ink into the skin with each puncture. The ink is deposited in the dermis, which is the second layer of skin.... Because the skin has been punctured many times, the end result is essentially an open wound.

Tattooing carries the risk of infection and transmission of disease "if unsanitary conditions are present or unsterile equipment is used." * * * The City's declarations establish that tattooing can result in the transmission of such diseases as hepatitis, syphilis, tuberculosis, leprosy, and HIV. Reports from the Centers for Disease Control and Prevention and the Food and Drug Administration confirm the significant health risks of tattooing. * * *

In general, however, "tattooing is a safe procedure if performed under appropriate sterilized conditions." * * * "[T]attoo artists protect themselves and their clients when following safe and healthy practices," including "using sterile needles and razors, washing hands, wearing gloves, and keeping surfaces clean." * * *

B. *Tattooing Regulations*

Because of the potential health concerns implicated by tattooing, the State of California requires "[e]very person engaged in the business of tattooing ... [to] register ... with the county health department of the county in which that business is conducted," Cal. Health & Safety Code § 119303(a), and requires these county health departments to inspect the registered tattoo parlors, *id.* § 119304. A person engaged in a tattooing business "who fails to register as provided by Section 119303 ... [is] subject to a civil penalty of five hundred dollars ($500) per violation." *Id.* § 119306. Moreover, California makes it illegal to "tattoo[ ] or offer[ ] to tattoo a person under the age of 18 years." Cal. Penal Code § 653.

The City of Hermosa Beach lies within the County of Los Angeles ("the County"). According to a declaration by Claro Cartagena, an inspector of tattoo establishments for the County, there are nearly 300 tattoo establishments in the County and over 850 tattooists. However, Cartagena is the only inspector in the County monitoring the parlors. Many tattoo parlors have never been inspected and are subject to no regulations other than the requirement to register with the County. Thus, it is largely up to the owner of the tattoo establishment to sterilize his equipment and follow sterilization procedures. According to Cartagena, "While most tattoo establishments are clean and sanitary, others are not.... As in any field, there are those practitioners that are unscrupulous or incompetent and do not follow the proper sterilization processes strictly. This poses a risk for infection." Cartagena has also received complaints about illegal underage tattooing.

Although Los Angeles County generally permits tattooing businesses, the City of Hermosa Beach does not. Hermosa Beach Municipal Code § 17.06.070 provides: "Except as provided in this title, no building shall be erected, reconstructed or structurally altered, nor shall any building or land be used for any purpose except as hereinafter specifically provided and allowed in the same zone in which such building and land is located." The Code provides zoning for a wide variety of commercial uses, including movie theaters, restaurants, adult businesses, bars, fortune tellers, gun shops, and youth hostels. Hermosa Beach Mun. Code § 17.26.030. No provision of the zoning code, however, permits tattoo parlors, and as a result, these facilities are banned from Hermosa Beach under section 17.060.070. Indeed, on November 20, 2007, the City's Planning Commission adopted a resolution against amending the Code to permit tattoo parlors.

C. *Facts and Procedural History*

Plaintiff–Appellant Johnny Anderson presently co-owns a tattoo parlor in the City of Los Angeles, and seeks to establish a tattoo parlor in the City of Hermosa Beach. Anderson describes his own approach to tattooing in a declaration * * *:

> The tattoo designs that are applied by me are individual and unique creative works of visual art, designed by me in collaboration with the person who is to receive the tattoo. The precise design to be used is decided upon after discussion with the client and review of a draft of the design. The choices made by both me and by the recipient involve consideration of color, light, shape, size, placement on the body, literal meaning, symbolic meaning, historical allusion, religious import, and emotional content. I believe my designs are enormously varied and complex, and include realistic depictions of people, animals and objects, stylized depictions of the same things, religious images, fictional images, and geometric shapes and patterns.... Sometimes, several kinds of images are combined into a single tattoo or series of tattoos.... I have studied the history of tattooing, and I draw significantly on traditional Americana tattoo designs and on Japanese tattoo motifs in creating my images, while all the while trying to add my own creative input to make the designs my own.

* * *

II. FIRST AMENDMENT FRAMEWORK

The First Amendment, applied to the states through the Fourteenth Amendment, prohibits laws "abridging the freedom of speech." * * * The First Amendment clearly includes pure speech, but not everything that communicates an idea counts as "speech" for First Amendment purposes. * * *

III. ANALYSIS

We hold that Hermosa Beach Municipal Code § 17.06.070 is facially unconstitutional to the extent that it excludes tattoo parlors. First, we hold that tattooing is purely expressive activity rather than conduct expressive of an idea, and is thus entitled to full First Amendment protection. * * * Second, we hold that the City's total ban on tattooing is not a constitutional restriction on protected expression because it is not a reasonable "time, place, or manner" restriction.

A. *Tattooing as First Amendment Expression*

* * * The tattoo *itself,* the *process* of tattooing, and even the *business* of tattooing are not expressive conduct but purely expressive activity fully protected by the First Amendment.

1. The Tattoo

There appears to be little dispute that the tattoo itself is pure First Amendment "speech." The Supreme Court has consistently held that "the Constitution looks beyond written or spoken words as mediums of expression." * * *

Tattoos are generally composed of words, realistic or abstract images, symbols, or a combination of these, all of which are forms of pure expression that are entitled to full First Amendment protection. * * * We do not profess to understand the work of tattoo artists to the same degree as we know the finely wrought sketches of Leonardo da Vinci or Albrecht Dürer, but we can take judicial notice of the skill, artistry, and care that modern tattooists have demonstrated.

The principal difference between a tattoo and, for example, a pen-and-ink drawing, is that a tattoo is engrafted onto a person's skin rather than drawn on paper. This distinction has no significance in terms of the constitutional protection afforded the tattoo; a form of speech does not lose First Amendment protection based on the kind of surface it is applied to. It is true that the nature of the surface to which a tattoo is applied and the procedure by which the tattoo is created implicate important health and safety concerns that may not be present in other visual arts, but this consideration is relevant to the governmental interest *potentially justifying* a restriction on protected speech, not to whether the speech is constitutionally protected. We have little difficulty recognizing that a tattoo is a form of pure expression entitled to full constitutional protection.

2. The Tattooing Process

* * * Tattooing is a process like writing words down or drawing a picture except that it is performed on a person's skin. As with putting a pen to paper, the process of tattooing is not intended to "symbolize" anything. Rather, the entire purpose of tattooing is to produce the tattoo, and the tattoo cannot be created without the tattooing process any more than the Declaration of Independence could have been created without a goose quill, foolscap, and ink. Thus, as with writing or painting, the tattooing process is inextricably intertwined with the purely expressive product (the tattoo), and is itself entitled to full First Amendment protection.

* * *

3. The Business of Tattooing

Finally, the fact that the City's ban relates to tattooing *businesses* rather than the tattooing process itself[5] does not affect whether the activity regulated is protected by the First Amendment. * * * Thus, we conclude that the business of tattooing qualifies as purely expressive activity. * * * The business is subject to reasonable time, place, or manner restrictions * * *, but the fact that the tattoo is for sale does not deprive it of its First Amendment protection.

B. The City's Ban as a Time, Place, or Manner Restriction

Having determined that tattooing is protected by the First Amendment, our next inquiry is whether the City's total ban on tattooing is a constitutional restriction on free expression.

---

5. The City does not actually ban tattooing as such but simply does not permit tattoo parlors in its zoning regulations. In other words, so far as we can tell, the Code contains no provision that would prevent a person from performing a tattoo on a family member in his house for free. And the City's restrictions may not apply to cosmetic tattooing that may be performed in a doctor's office, clinic, or beauty parlor.

A regulation that restricts protected expression based on the content of the speech is constitutional only if it withstands strict scrutiny. * * * However, Anderson does not contend that Hermosa Beach Municipal Code § 17.06.070 is a content-based restriction on speech. *See supra* n. 4. Rather, he argues that the City's regulation is an unconstitutional restriction on a *means* of expression.

Accordingly, we must determine not whether the City's regulation survives strict scrutiny but whether the City's regulation is a reasonable "time, place, or manner" restriction on protected speech. * * *

The interplay between the Court's often rigid statements about total bans on modes of expression and its traditional "time, place, or manner" test is not entirely clear. However, we need not determine whether the City's regulation is *per se* unconstitutional as a total ban of a means of expression or whether it is subject to a particularly stringent test, because we hold that it fails under even the traditional "time, place, or manner" test. * * *

* * * The City's regulation bans all tattoo parlors, not just those conveying a particular kind of message or subject matter, and is purportedly justified based on health and safety concerns.

A reasonable "time, place, or manner" restriction must also be "narrowly tailored to serve a significant governmental interest." * * *

[T]he City argues, "there are insufficient resources to monitor the 8[5]0 tattooists operating in Los Angeles County, including the many who, like Plaintiff, are self-taught and operating in backrooms and basements." * * * [W]e cannot approve a total ban on protected First Amendment activity simply because of the government's failure to provide the resources it thinks are necessary to regulate it.

* * *

3. Alternative Channels

Even if the City's regulation were narrowly tailored to serve its health and safety interests, a reasonable "time, place, or manner" restriction on protected speech must also "leave open ample alternative channels for communication of the information." * * * The City argues that, although its regulation restricts tattooists' ability to apply images to human skin via the injection of ink, there are alternative means available for applying the exact same words, images, and symbols to skin, such as airbrushing or the use of natural henna paste to create temporary tattoos. * * * We disagree.

* * *

IV. CONCLUSION

In sum, we hold that the tattoo itself, the process of tattooing, and the business of tattooing are forms of pure expression fully protected by the First Amendment. We further hold that the City's total ban on tattoo parlors in Hermosa Beach is not a reasonable "time, place, or manner" restriction because it is substantially broader than necessary to achieve the City's significant health and safety interests and because it entirely forecloses a unique and important method of expression. * * * Thus, we hold that Hermosa Beach Municipal Code § 17.06.070 is facially unconstitutional to the extent that it excludes tattoo parlors. * * *

Questions

1. Did the dispute in Hermosa Beach involve a ban or a permit? What did the City try to accomplish with the regulation?

2. Until 2001, Massachusetts General Laws Annotated § 34 provided:

> Whoever, not being registered as a qualified physician * * *, marks the body of any person by means of tattooing, shall be punished by a fine of not more than three hundred dollars or by imprisonment for not more than one year, or both.

In *Lanphear v. Commonwealth*, the court declared the provision unconstitutional "as violative of the First Amendment of the United States Constitution and Article 16 of the Massachusetts Declaration of Rights."[61]

Unlike Hermosa Beach, Massachusetts specifically allowed tattooing in its jurisdiction and even addressed certain health risks associated with the business. Why did the court strike down § 34?

---

61. Lanphear v. Commonwealth, 2001 WL 36244749 (Mass. Super. 2001).

CHAPTER 9

STANDARD SETTING AND PRICE REGULATION

Should the state ever regulate the properties of products and services sold on the markets? When such properties interact with transaction costs, externalities, inadequate information, or bounded rationality, sound reasons may motivate regulation. When such properties interact with risk perceptions or morality, an excessive tendency to regulate often appears. State regulation is largely about properties of products and services. With the exception of paternalism, the purpose of regulation is to assure that the properties of products and services on the market meet the standards needed for the protection of "safety, health, morals, and general welfare of the public." This Chapter reviews some principles of regulation that govern properties of products and services, commonly known as "*standard setting*."

§ 9.1 STANDARD SETTING

> **stan·dard** (stan'därd). *n.* A flag, emblematic figure (as the Roman eagle), or other object raised on a pole to indicate the rallying point of an army, fleet, etc.; a distinctive flag or ensign, as of a king or a nation; * * * also, the authorized exemplar of a unit or measure; anything taken by general consent as a basis of comparison, or established as a criterion * * *; the legal rate of intrinsic value for coins; * * * a grade or level of excellence or advancement generally regarded as right or fitting (as, the *standard* of living in a community; *standard* of comfort; *standards* of education or of morals in the last century). * * *
>
> **stan·dard·ize** (stan'där-dīz). *v. t.*; *-ized, -izing.* To conform to or regulate by a standard; bring to or make of an established standard size, shape, weight, quality, strength, or the like (as, to *standardize* manufactured articles or parts). * * *
>
> —*The New Century Dictionary of the English Language* (1927)

Standard setting, the regulation of properties of products and services, means restrictions on the design and provision of particular products and services. Good standards may expand markets and enhance welfare by eliminating and mitigating sources of market inefficiencies. In his book, *Regulation and Its Reform*, Justice Stephen Breyer described the broad meaning of the term "standards:"

> Standards are aimed at objectives as diverse as increasing workplace and product safety, producing a cleaner environment, and providing consumers with better information. They may be enforced through criminal sanctions, withdrawal of a license, civil fines, or adverse publicity. They may be written broadly or narrowly, with widespread or limited application.[1]

"Standards" are properties of products and activities required or recommended for market participation.[2] In markets with binding standards, some authority outlaws, bars, or stigmatizes products and activities that one of their properties (or more) is not in compliance with the binding standard. For example, all cars sold in the United States must be equipped with seatbelts. Cars that do not meet this standard cannot be sold in the U.S. market. In markets with nonbinding standards, incompliance is possible but entry *may* be costly. For example, the United States Customary System of weights and measures consists of informal standards whose lack of adoption may be very costly for market participants. By contrast, since 1866, Congress has endorsed the metric system several times, but none of the regulatory endorsements has been binding. They have all remained somewhat irrelevant recommendations.[3] The USB ("Universal Serial Bus") is a nonbinding technological standard, whose specification was originally developed in the 1990s by Compaq, DEC, IBM, Intel, Microsoft, NEC, and Nortel. USB standardized the connections of computers and external devices. No manufacturer or user must adopt the USB standard, but it may be impossible to enter certain markets without its adoption. Today, the USB Implementers Forum, Inc. ("USB–IF"), a non-profit corporation founded by the group of companies that developed the original USB specification, continues to advance the USB standards in the market.

Standards dominate markets and society. There are standard time, standard weights and measures, standard holidays, standard currency, standard languages, standard equipment, community standards, and so forth. As these examples illustrate, standards have three types of sources: the government, private parties, and processes in society and the marketplace. When the state is not the source of a standard, it may still regulate some of its aspects to assure it is not used for exclusion or other improper purposes.[4] Standards of trade organizations illuminate this point. Trade organizations frequently adopt "professional standards" that benefit their members, exclude competition, and often disserve the public.[5]

---

1. STEPHEN BREYER, REGULATION AND ITS REFORM 96 (1982).

2. *See generally* DAVID HEMENWAY, INDUSTRY VOLUNTARY PRODUCT STANDARDS 4–7 (1975).

3. *See, e.g.*, Act to Authorize the Use of the Metric System of Weights and Measures, 14 Stat. 339 (1866); An Act to Declare a National Policy of Coordinating the Increasing Use of the Metric System in the United States, Pub L. No. 94–168, 89 Stat. 1007 (1975). *See also* JOHN QUINCY ADAMS, REPORT OF THE SECRETARY OF STATE UPON WEIGHTS AND MEASURES (Feb. 22, 1821), available at *regti.me/a-report* (case sensitive).

4. *See* LAWRENCE LESSIG, CODE: AND OTHER LAWS OF CYBERSPACE, VERSION 2.0 (2006).

5. *See, e.g.*, Bates v. State Bar of Arizona, 433 U.S. 350 (1977); Goldfarb v. Virginia State Bar, 421 U.S. 773 (1975); National Society of Professional Engineers v. United States, 435 U.S. 679 (1978). *See also* Hayne E. Leland, *Quacks, Lemons, and Licensing: A Theory of Minimum Quality Standards*, 87 JOURNAL OF POLITICAL ECONOMY 1328 (1979).

To illustrate government standard setting, consider five examples discussed in prior chapters: motor vehicle safety standards, fuel economy standards, light bulb efficiency standards, occupational licensing, and blue laws. First, the National Traffic and Motor Vehicle Safety Act of 1966 created the National Highway Traffic Safety Administration (NHTSA) and authorized it to establish "motor vehicle safety standards."[6] The Act defined these standards as "minimum standard[s] for motor vehicle performance, * * * which meet[] the need for motor vehicle safety." Second, pursuant to the Energy Policy and Conservation Act of 1975, NHTSA also issues fuel economy standards that define maximum thresholds for fuel consumption and greenhouse gas emissions for motor vehicles produced in the United States.[7] Third, sections 321 and 322 of the Energy Independence and Security Act of 2007 introduced a schedule for increasing minimum economy standards for light bulbs. Fourth, state laws require people who wish to engage in certain occupations to meet minimum standards, which do not always serve the public. And, finally, "Blue Laws" exclude Sundays from the service days of certain businesses.[8]

Despite the broad spectrum of standards, they can be divided into three general categories: quality standards, uniformity standards, and compatibility standards. *Quality standards* define normative thresholds of particular attributes. A failure to meet such thresholds means exclusion from the market or lack of accreditation. Examples for quality standards include the light bulb minimum efficiency standards, occupational licensing requirements, emissions standards, and community standards used to define obscenity.[9] *Uniformity standards* specify the attributes of certain properties that all product and services in the market must have. For example, in the 1883, the railroad industry standardized the time used in the United States to reduced transaction costs associated by lack of standardization (uniformity).[10] The railroad industry, however, also established uniform rates to increase its profits at the expense of the public. *Compatibility standards* assure that independent products or activities will fit each other and could operate together. The USB specification illuminates a compatibility standard. Compatibility standards facilitate network externalities: Under certain circumstances, when people use the same "standard" their independent choices have interrelated effects.[11]

In this Chapter, we will distinguish between two classes of properties of products and services: "prices" and "all other properties." The economic attributes of prices set them apart from all other properties.

---

6. The National Traffic and Motor Vehicle Safety Act of 1966, Pub L. No. 89–563, 80 Stat. 718 (1966). *See generally* JERRY L. MASHAW & DAVID L. HARFST, THE STRUGGLE FOR AUTO SAFETY (1990).

7. *See* Center for Biological Diversity v. National Highway Traffic Safety Administration, 538 F.3d 1172 (9th Cir. 2008).

8. *See* Hing v. Crowley, 113 U.S. 703 (1885); McGowan v. Maryland, 366 U.S. 420 (1961).

9. For community standards and obscenity *see* Miller v. California, 413 U.S. 15 (1973).

10. *See generally* IAN BARTKY, SELLING THE TRUE TIME: NINETEENTH-CENTURY TIMEKEEPING IN AMERICA (2000); MICHAEL O'MALLEY, KEEPING WATCH: A HISTORY OF AMERICAN TIME (1990). *See also* IAN BARTKY, ONE TIME FITS ALL: THE CAMPAIGNS FOR GLOBAL UNIFORMITY (2007).

11. *See* § 3.2.4.

Sidebar 9–1

Lord Kelvin and the Metric System

William Thomson was one of the most eminent physicists of the nineteenth century, enjoying a celebrity status during his time. In 1866, at age 42, for his many contributions to physics and science, Queen Victoria knighted him as Lord Kelvin. Thirty some years later, in 1900, addressing the British Association for Advancement of Science, Lord Kelvin famously declared: "There is nothing new to be discovered in physics now. All that remains is more and more precise measurement." Five years later, Albert Einstein published his special theory of relativity and introduced the equation $E=mc^2$.

In April 1896, *The London Times* published a four-part article criticizing popular proposals to require the metric system by law. Two days after the publication of the fourth part, *The Times* published an editorial, acknowledging that "[m]en of science all over the world have gradually adopted [the metric system] for their own purposes, and have found their convenience in so doing." It warned, however, that "[m]en of science use the metric system for processes of measurement, not for processes of exchange. * * * There can be no good reason * * * for accepting their judgment as conclusive." *The Times* expressed strong concerns regarding the "poor fellow [who] has his own convenience in view, [but] under compulsion * * * will be induced to change his ways." Responding to those publications, Lord Kelvin sent a letter to the editor of *The Times*:

> **TO THE EDITOR OF THE TIMES**
> Sir, In your very interesting leading article on the metric system * * * you treat, in what seems to me a thoroughly clear and fair manner, the question at issue in respect to the demand for legislation on the subject.
>
> [Y]ou rightly give prominence to consideration for the consideration of the poorer classes. * * * If it were true that the adoption of the metric system would be hurtful, or even seriously inconvenient to them, that would be a strong reason against its being adopted in England. But in this respect, we have, happily, a very large experience, and I believe it is quite certain that among the Germans, Italians, Portuguese, and other European peoples who have had the practical wisdom to follow the French in the metric system, all classes are thoroughly contented with it, and find it much more convenient for every-day use than the systems which they abandoned in adopting it. * * *
>
> The great advantage of the metric system is its uniform simplicity. * * * But now, considering the wants and the convenience of the whole population, think of the vast contrast between practically valuable simplicity of the metric system and truly monstrous complexity of the British measurements in miles, furlongs, chains, poles, yards, feet, inches, * * * etc. Looking at the question from all sides, and considering all circum-

stances, I believe it will be found that the thorough introduction of the metric system, for general use in Great Britain, will be beneficial for all classes; and that the benefit will, in the course of a few weeks, be found to more than compensate any trouble involved in making the change.

I am your obedient servant,

KELVIN.[12]

§ 9.2 PRICE REGULATION

The concept of "price regulation" is often misunderstood for two primary reasons. First, people tend to have strong feelings about the prices they pay and the nature of market prices, while these "feelings" are subjective and may be divorced from reality. Second and relatedly, many people possess strong views about price regulations, their potential benefits and their likely costs, although these views are mostly abstract and not necessarily supported by economic theory and factual analyses.

Prices—payments that are paid or received for goods and services—are rarely a source of any problem. When prices *appear* unfair, too high, too low, unstable, or inadequate in some other way, they are ordinarily symptoms of problems in the market system.[13] When they *appear* fair and competitive, the market may still suffer from serious problems.

The starting point of any price analysis is the recognition that "adequacy" of prices tends to be a matter of perspective—buyers and sellers may disagree about the adequacy of the same price.[14] Additionally, perceptions of prices may be divorced from values for many reasons. To illustrate, we mention four reasons. First, the framing of information, including advertising and payment schedules, confuses people when they rank alternatives.[15] Second, people tend to think in terms of nominal prices rather than values, discounting the value of time and ignoring the significance of means of payment and other factors.[16] Third, people sometimes follow trends in fashion, status expenditures, investments, and other cultural

12. The 1896 publications in *The London Times are available at regti.me/k-metric* (case sensitive).

13. *See* § 6.2.

14. *See, e.g.*, Daniel Kahneman et al., *Fairness as a Constraint on Profit Seeking*, *supra* note 11; Daniel Kahneman et al., *The Endowment Effect, Loss Aversion, and the Status Quo Bias*, 5 JOURNAL OF ECONOMIC PERSPECTIVES 193 (1991); SARAH MAXWELL, THE PRICE IS WRONG: UNDERSTANDING WHAT MAKES A PRICE SEEM FAIR AND THE TRUE COST OF UNFAIR PRICING (2008).

15. *See* DANIEL KAHNEMAN & AMOS TVERSKY, CHOICES, VALUES, AND FRAMES (2000).

16. *See, e.g.*, Ernest Fehr & Jean-Robert Tyran, *Does Money Illusion Matter?*, 91 AMERICAN ECONOMIC REVIEW 1239 (2001); Eldar Shafir et al. *Money Illusion*, 103 QUARTERLY JOURNAL OF ECONOMICS 341 (1997).

signals.[17] And, fourth, people tend to struggle with price adjustments that adversely affect them (*e.g.*, a salary cut vs. a raise).[18] Put simply, personal views regarding prices are not necessarily reliable.

Government price regulation is conducted in two patterns: *regulation of prices* and *regulation through prices*. *Regulation of prices* is used to address concerns over inadequate prices, and is a form of command-and-control regulation that utilizes prices to manipulate incentives. *Regulation through prices* is a form of incentive regulation that utilizes prices to manipulate incentives. We have already discussed several examples of price regulation. *Adkins* and *West Coast Hotel* involved the constitutionality of minimum wages.[19] *National Rural Telecom Association* addressed the FCC's price-cap policy.[20] The proposed Green Fee on disposable shopping bags in Seattle intended to use prices to influence choices.[21] The Kentucky Dog Law taxed dog owners and inevitably influenced their incentives.[22] As the examples illuminate, some forms of price regulations may be presented as both regulation of prices and regulation through prices.

When the state regulates prices it may set fixed prices, set minimum or maximum prices, or change the level of prices through taxes and subsidies. We follow this classification.

Munn v. Illinois (1876)

Munn v. Illinois (1876) is a cornerstone of the Supreme Court regulatory jurisprudence.[23] The Court upheld the constitutionality of an 1871 Illinois statute that set maximum prices for grain elevators in Chicago, and held that when private property is "affected by with a public interest" it is subject to state police powers.

When Illinois adopted the statute, grain was a valuable source of capital and a key basis for trade in the United States. Chicago was the world's largest market for grain trade. Chicago gained preeminence because of its location and maintained it with superior storage and delivery facilities. One of the most important delivery facilities was the grain elevator.[24] The *Munn* Court recognized the significance of grain elevators:

---

17. *See* ROBERT J. SHILLER, IRRATIONAL EXUBERANCE 2 (2d ed. 2005) Sushil Bikhchandani et al., A *Theory of Fads, Fashion, Custom, and Cultural Change as Informational Cascades*, 100 JOURNAL OF POLITICAL ECONOMY 992 (1992); § 1.1.3a.

18. *See, e.g.*, Daniel W. Carlton, *The Rigidity of Prices*, 76 AMERICAN ECONOMIC REVIEW 637 (1986).

19. Adkins v. Children's Hospital of the District of Columbia, 261 U.S. 525 (1923); West Coast Hotel Co. v. Parrish, 300 U.S. 379 (1937). *See* § 6.3.

20. National Rural Telecom Association v. Federal Communications Commission, 988 F.2d 174 (D.C. Cir. 1993). *See* § 6.4.

21. *See* § 2.2.2c.

22. McGlone v. Womack, 129 Ky. 274 (1908). *See* § 8.2.2.

23. Munn v. Illinois, 94 U.S. 113 (1876). For a detailed description of the facts and the issues behind the case *see* Edmund W. Kitch & Clara Ann Bowler, *The Facts of Munn v. Illinois*, 1978 SUPREME COURT REVIEW 313 (1978).

24. *See generally* WILLIAM J. BROWN, AMERICAN COLOSSUS: THE GRAIN ELEVATOR, 1843 TO 1943 (rev. ed. 2010); Guy A. Lee, *The Historical Significance of the Chicago Grain Elevator System*, 11 AGRICULTURAL HISTORY 16 (1937).

> The quantity [of grain] received in Chicago has made it the greatest grain market in the world. This business has created a demand for means by which the immense quantity of grain can be handled or stored, and these have been found in grain warehouses, which are commonly called elevators, because the grain is elevated from the boat or car, by machinery operated by steam, into the bins prepared for its reception, and elevated from the bins, by a like process, into the vessel or car which is to carry it on.

The Illinois Legislature declared that "[a]ll elevators or storehouses where grain or other property is stored for a compensation * * * are * * * public warehouses." It created a simple regulatory framework that addressed several issues related to transportation, trade, storage, and set maximum rates for grain elevators. Writing for the Court Chief Justice Morrison Waite accepted the proposition that, although grain elevators were private property, their regulation was justified because they were clothed with a public interest. In doing so, Chief Justice Waite created the "affected by with a public interest" doctrine.[25] He found support for the doctrine in the common law maxim *sic utere tuo ut alienum non laedas*, use your own property in such manner as not to injure that of another.[26] Put simply, whenever one's property is utilized in a manner that affects the public, that property may be subject to state regulation, including price regulation.

Dissenting, Justice Field argued that the majority's ruling amounted to a taking:

> The doctrine * * * of this court, that, whenever one's property is used in such a manner as to affect the community at large, it becomes by that fact clothed with a public interest * * * appear to me to destroy, for all useful purposes, the efficacy of the constitutional guaranty. All that is beneficial in property arises from its use, and the fruits of that use; and whatever deprives a person of them deprives him of all that is desirable or valuable in the title and possession.

---

25. *See* pp. 267–270.

26. *See* § 3.2.1.

Figure 9.1
The First Shipment of Grain from Chicago (1839)

Source: A.T. Andreas History of Chicago from the Earliest Period to the Present Time (1884).

Munn established the power of the state to regulate prices, without addressing meaning of reasonable price regulation. In subsequent decisions the Court held that when the rates the state set must be "just and reasonable."[27]

§ 9.2.1 *Regulation of Prices*

In 1962, George Stigler and Claire Friedland published article titled *What Can Regulators Regulate?*, finding that regulation of power companies had not led to any significant effects on industry performance, and specifically that the price regulation had no significant effect.[28] The finding that regulation has modest to negligible effects on prices has been cited ever since to support the proposition that regulation is ineffective. Can we conclude from this study that all forms of regulations of prices are ineffective? Probably not.

For example, empirical findings regarding the efficacy of ratemaking of power companies have little to do with the economic effects of state minimum wage laws passed during the first half of the twentieth century. Moreover, methodologies used for ratemaking until the 1960s were profoundly different from today's methodologies. Computers were not really

---

27. *See* Smyth v. Ames, 169 U.S. 466 (1898) ("fair value"); McCardle v. Indianapolis Water Co., 272 U.S. 400 (1926); Federal Power Commission v. Hope Natural Gas Co., 320 U.S. 591 (1944).

28. George J. Stigler & Claire Friedland, *What Can Regulators Regulate? The Case of Electricity*, 5 JOURNAL OF LAW & ECONOMICS 1 (1962).

available or useful. Economics and applied statistics were not nearly as advanced as today. Moreoever, a century of experience was not available yet for regulators. No doubt, past schemes of price regulation had little to do with economics. But past methodologies are not the ones that should be evaluated today.

Until the 1980s, the traditional methods of regulation of prices were rather prevailing in the United States. The regulatory system relied mostly on command-and-control regulations, and price controls were only natural in this system. The federal government, states, and localities regulated prices of particular industries and sectors, or in response to changes in economic conditions (*e.g.*, recessions).[29] One of the many changes the deregulation wave of the 1980s brought was new approaches to price regulation. Our discussion of the FCC's maximum price cap policy illuminates one aspect of this change.

Regulation of prices fails when it ignores differences among products or does not respond to changes over time. This was a key reason for past failures. Most markets offer differentiated products and introduce innovation at some rate. If we have one price for all oranges and another price for all apples, we should expect to have fewer varieties of lower quality. In such markets, the state cannot devise a menu of rates that would be sufficiently sensitive to all differences among products. Put simply, product characteristics dictate the potential effectiveness of regulation of prices.

§ 9.2.1a Ratemaking

Ratemaking is the most extreme form of price regulation: The state set prices for goods and services. Because ratemaking requires standardization of "units"—products or services, it has been used mostly for utilities and transportation. Two primary challenges in ratemaking are: (1) minimizing the capture of the regulator by the regulated industry and firms, and (2) encouraging innovation and efficiency although the ratemaking takes into account the costs of the regulated firm.[30]

Fire Insurance

Urban fires destroyed, demolished, and ravaged substantial portions of many cities in the United States until the 1920s. Among the disasters on this list are the Great Fire of New York City (1776), the Second Great Fire of New York City (1835), the Great Chicago Fire of 1871, the Great Boston Fire of 1872, the Great Seattle Fire of 1889, the Great Baltimore Fire of 1904, and the Great Atlanta Fire of 1917. The 1906 San Francisco Earth-

29. *See, e.g.*, Nathan Isaacs, *Price Control By Law*, 18 HARVARD BUSINESS REVIEW 504 (1940); William K. Jones, *Government Price Controls and Inflation: A Prognosis Based on the Impact of Controls in the Regulated Industries*, 65 CORNELL LAW REVIEW 303 (1980).

30. The Averch–Johnson effect refers to incentives of regulated firms to inflate costs when ratemaking is using cost-plus formulas. *See generally* Harvey Averch & Leland L. Johnson, *Behavior of the Firm Under Regulatory Constraint*, 52 AMERICAN ECONOMIC REVIEW 1052 (1962).

quake was followed by fire that destroyed most buildings. Urbanization and the new technologies of the nineteenth century gradually increased risks of fire. Society, however, had not developed corresponding measures—appropriate regulatory frameworks—to reduce the risk of fire.[31]

The risk of fire made fire insurance an important financial instrument to individuals and the economy.[32] As such, the provision and accessibility of fire insurance was also perceived as an important public interest. All states regulated various aspects of the activities of fire insurance companies, including their rates.[33]

The ratemaking process of fire insurance introduced inefficiencies. The standardization of rates left many individuals and businesses overinsured or underinsured, and created peculiar incentives for property owners.[34] Moreover, the process itself frequently facilitated collusion among insurance companies.[35] At least until the second half of the twentieth century, the regulation of fire insurance had many apparent problems. However, it is unclear that a market with no regulation would have been a better alternative. The regulation of the fire insurance industry was a mixed bag: it assured the capitalization of insurance companies and consumer rights, but it also presented inefficiencies. Materials about urban fires and fire insurance are available at *regti.me/fire-insurance* (case sensitive).

German Alliance Insurance Co. v. Lewis

233 U.S. 389 (1914)

■ Statement by MR. JUSTICE MCKENNA:

Bill in equity to restrain the enforcement of the provisions of [a 1909] act of the state of Kansas entitled, '*An Act Relating to Fire Insurance, and to Provide for the Regulation and Control of Rates of Premium Thereon, and to Prevent Discriminations Therein.*' * * *

The grounds of the bill are that the act offends the Constitution of the state and of the United States.

A summary of the requirements of the act is as follows:

> **SEC. 1**. Every fire insurance company shall file with the superintendent of insurance general basis schedules showing the rates on all risks insurable by such company in the state, and all the

31. *See, e.g.*, Everett, U. Crosby, *Fire Prevention*, 26 ANNALS OF THE AMERICAN ACADEMY OF POLITICAL & SOCIAL SCIENCE 224 (1905).

32. *See, e.g.*, Ralph H. Blanchard, *Insurance of the Catastrophe Hazard*, 70 ANNALS OF THE AMERICAN ACADEMY OF POLITICAL & SOCIAL SCIENCE 220 (1917); A. F. DEAN, PHILOSOPHY OF FIRE INSURANCE (1925); F. C. Oviatt, *Historical Study of Fire Insurance in the United States*, 26 ANNALS OF THE AMERICAN ACADEMY OF POLITICAL & SOCIAL SCIENCE 155 (1905).

33. *See, e.g.*, George Uriel Crocker, *Does Fire Insurance Cost Too Much?*, 160 NORTH AMERICAN REVIEW 470 (1895); Robert Riegel, *The Regulation of Fire Insurance Rates*, 130 ANNALS OF THE AMERICAN ACADEMY OF POLITICAL & SOCIAL SCIENCE114 (1927).

34. *See, e.g.*, W.F. Gephart, *Fire Insurance Rates and State Regulation*, 28 QUARTERLY JOURNAL OF ECONOMICS 447 (1914).

35. *See, e.g.*, Werner Sichel, *Fire Insurance: Imperfectly Regulated Collusion*, 33 JOURNAL OF RISK & INSURANCE 95 (1966).

conditions which affect the rates or the value of the insurance to the assured.

SEC. 2. No change shall be made in the schedules except after ten days' notice to the superintendent, which notice shall state the changes proposed and the time when they shall go into effect. The superintendent may allow changes upon less notice.

SEC. 3. When the superintendent shall determine any rate is excessive or unreasonably high, or not adequate to the safety or soundness of the company, he is authorized to direct the company to publish and file a higher or lower rate, which shall be commensurate with the character of the risk; but in every case the rate shall be reasonable.

SEC. 4. No company shall engage or participate in insurance on property located in the state until the schedules of rates be filed, nor write insurance at a different rate than the rate named in the schedules, or refund or remit in any manner or by any device any portion of the rates; or extend to any insured or other person any privileges, inducements, or concessions except as specified in the schedules.

SEC. 5. Any company making insurance where no rate has been filed shall, within thirty days after entering into such contract, file with the superintendent a schedule of such property, showing the rate and such information as he may require. The schedule shall conform to the general basis of schedules, and shall constitute the permanent rate of the company.

SEC. 6. The schedules shall be open to the inspection of the public, and each local agent shall have and exhibit to the public copies thereof relative to all risks upon which he is authorized to write insurance.

SEC. 7. No company shall, directly or indirectly, by any special rate or by any device, charge or receive from any person a different rate of compensation for insurance than it charges or receives from any other person for like insurance or risks of a like kind and hazard under similar circumstances and conditions in the state. Any company violating this provision shall be deemed guilty of unjust discrimination, which is declared unlawful.

SEC. 8. The superintendent may, if he finds that any company, or any officer, agent, or representative thereof, has violated any of the provisions of the act, revoke the license of such offending company, officer, or agent, but such revocation shall not affect liability for the violation of any other section of the act; and provided that any action, decision, or determination of the superintendent under the provisions of the act shall be subject to review by the courts of the state as provided in the act.

* * *

SEC. 10. Infractions of the act are declared to be misdemeanors and punishable by a fine not exceeding $100 for each offense, provided that if the conviction be for an unlawful discrimination, the punishment may be by a fine or by imprisonment in the county jail not exceeding ninety days, or by both fine and imprisonment.

SEC. **11**. No person shall be excused from testifying at the trial of any other person on the ground that the testimony may incriminate him, but he shall not be prosecuted on account of any transaction about which he may testify, except for perjury committed in so testifying; 'provided, that nothing in this act shall affect farmers' mutual insurance companies, organized and doing business under the laws of this state, and insuring only farm property.'

The bill alleged that it was brought by the German Alliance Insurance Company in behalf of itself and all other companies and corporations conducting a similar business and similarly situated. * * *

Complainant argues that the respondent is not possessed of the requisite information or special training necessary to qualify for [risk analysis], and any conclusion to which he might come would be a mere guess or arbitrary determination; and the provisions of the act can only be properly administered in any event by the employment by the state of a corps of inspectors and experts specially trained in the business of fixing rates of fire insurance.

* * *

The business of fire insurance is private, with which the state has no right to interfere, and the right to fix by private contract the rate of premium is a property right of value; the business is not a monopoly, either legally or actually; it may not be legally conducted by the national government or by the state of Kansas or other states under their respective constitutions, and is not a business included within the functions of government. Neither Complainant nor others engaged in fire insurance receive or enjoy from the state of Kansas or any government, state or national, any privilege or immunity not in like manner and to like extent received and enjoyed by all other persons, partnerships, and companies, incorporated or unincorporated, respectively, engaged in the conduct of other lines of private business and enterprises. Complainant, therefore, is deprived of one of the incidents of liberty and of its property without due process of law, in violation of the 14th Amendment to the Constitution of the United States.

* * *

■ After stating the case as above, MR. JUSTICE MCKENNA delivered the opinion of the court:

* * * The basic contention is that the business of insurance is a natural right, receiving no privilege from the state, is voluntarily entered into, cannot be compelled, nor can any of its exercises be compelled; that it concerns personal contracts of indemnity against certain contingencies merely. Whether such contracts shall be made at all, it is contended, is a matter of private negotiation and agreement, and necessarily there must be freedom in fixing their terms. And 'where the right to demand and receive service does not exist in the public, the correlative right of regulation as to

rates and charges does not exist.' Many elements, it is urged, determine the extending or rejection of insurance; the hazards are relative and depend upon many circumstances upon which there may be different judgments, and there are personal considerations as well—'*moral hazards*,' as they are called.

It is not clear to what extent some of these circumstances are urged as affecting the power of regulation in the state. It would seem to be urged that each risk is individual, and no rule of rates can be formed or applied. The bill asserts the contrary. It in effect admits that there can be standards and classification of risks, determined by the law of averages. Indeed, it is a matter of common knowledge that rates are fixed and accommodated to those standards and classifications in pre-arranged schedules, and, granted the rates may be varied in particular instances, they are sufficiently definite and applicable as a general and practically constant rule. They are the product, it is true, of skill and experience, but such skill and experience a regulating body may have as well as the creating body. * * * It would * * * be a strained contention that the government could not avail itself, in the exercise of power it might deem wise to exert, of the skill and knowledge possessed by the world. We may put aside, therefore, all merely adventitious considerations and come to the bare and essential one, whether a contract of fire insurance is private, and as such has constitutional immunity from regulation. Or, to state it differently and to express an antithetical proposition, is the business of insurance so far affected with a public interest as to justify legislative regulation of its rates? And we mean a broad and definite public interest. In some degree the public interest is concerned in every transaction between men, the sum of the transactions constituting the activities of life. But there is something more special than this, something of more definite consequence, which makes the public interest that justifies regulatory legislation. We can best explain by examples. The transportation of property—business of common carriers—is obviously of public concern, and its regulation is an accepted governmental power. The transmission of intelligence is of cognate character. There are other utilities which are denominated public, such as the furnishing of water and light, including in the latter gas and electricity. We do not hesitate at their regulation nor of the fixing of the prices which may be charged for their service. The basis of the ready concession of the power of regulation is the public interest. This is not denied, but its application to insurance is so far denied as not to extend to the fixing of rates. * * *

Munn v. Illinois, 94 U. S. 113 (1877), is an instructive example of legislative power exerted in the public interest. The Constitution of Illinois declared all elevators or storehouses, where grain or other property was stored for a compensation, to be public warehouses, and a law was subsequently enacted fixing rates of storage. In other words, that which had been private property had from its uses become, it was declared, of public concern, and the compensation to be charged for its use prescribed. The law was sustained against the contention that it deprived the owners of the warehouses of their property without due process of law. We can only cite the case and state its principle, not review it at any length. The principle was expressed to be, quoting Lord Chief Justice Hale, 'that when private property is 'affected with a public interest, it ceases to be *juris privati*' only' and it becomes 'clothed with a public interest when used in a manner to make it of public consequence, and affect the community at large;' and, so using it, the owner 'grants to the public an interest in that use, and must submit to be controlled by the public for the common good.'† * * *

Against [the] conservatism of the mind which puts to question every new act of regulating legislation, and regards the legislation invalid or dangerous until it has become familiar, government—state and national—has pressed on in the general welfare; and our reports are full of cases where in instance after instance the exercise of regulation was resisted and yet sustained against attacks asserted to be justified by the Constitution of the United States. The dread of the moment having passed, no one is now heard to say that rights were restrained or their constitutional guaranties impaired.

* * * It would be a bold thing to say that the principle is fixed, inelastic, in the precedents of the past, and cannot be applied though modern economic conditions may make necessary or beneficial its application. In other words, to say that government possessed at one time a greater power to recognize the public interest in a business and its regulation to promote the general welfare than government possesses today. We proceed, then, to consider whether the business of insurance is within the principle.

A contract for fire insurance is one for indemnity against loss, and is personal. * * * Its personal character certainly does not of itself preclude regulation, for there are many examples of government regulation of personal contracts. * * * We need only say that there was quite early (in Massachusetts, 1837, New York, 1853) state provision for what is known as the unearned premium fund or reserve; then came the limitation of dividends, the publishing of accounts, valued policies, standards of policies, prescribing investment, requiring deposits in money or bonds, confining the business to corporations, preventing discrimination in rates, limitation of risks, and other regulations equally restrictive. In other words, the state has stepped in and imposed conditions upon the companies, restraining the absolute liberty which businesses strictly private are permitted to exercise.

Those regulations exhibit it to be the conception of the lawmaking bodies of the country without exception that the business of insurance so far affects the public welfare as to invoke and require governmental regulation. * * * The universal sense of a people cannot be accidental; its persistence saves it from the charge of unconsidered impulse, and its estimate of insurance certainly has substantial basis. Accidental fires are inevitable and the extent of loss very great. The effect of insurance—indeed, it has been said to be its fundamental object—is to distribute the loss over as wide an area as possible. In other words, the loss is spread over the country, the disaster to an individual is shared by many, the disaster to a community shared by other communities; great catastrophes are thereby lessened, and, it may be, repaired. In assimilation of insurance to a tax, the companies have been said to be the mere machinery by which the inevitable losses by fire are distributed so as to fall as lightly as possible on the public

† [For the "affected with a public interest" doctrine *see* pp. 267–270.—BYO.]

at large, the body of the insured, not the companies, paying the tax. Their efficiency, therefore, and solvency, are of great concern. The other objects, direct and indirect, of insurance, we need not mention. Indeed, it may be enough to say, without stating other effects of insurance, that a large part of the country's wealth, subject to uncertainty of loss through fire, is protected by insurance. * * * We can see, therefore, how it has come to be considered a matter of public concern to regulate it, and, governmental insurance has its advocates and even examples. Contracts of insurance, therefore, have greater public consequence than contracts between individuals to do or not to do a particular thing whose effect stops with the individuals. We may say in passing that when the effect goes beyond that, there are many examples of regulation. * * *

The principle we apply is definite and old, and has [many] illustrating examples. * * * [W]e have tried to confine our decision to the regulation of the business of insurance, [which is] 'clothed with a public interest,' and therefore subject 'to be controlled by the public for the common good.' * * *

We may venture to observe that the price of insurance is not fixed over the counters of the companies by what Adam Smith calls the higgling of the market, but formed in the councils of the underwriters, promulgated in schedules of practically controlling constancy which the applicant for insurance is powerless to oppose, and which, therefore, has led to the assertion that the business of insurance is of monopolistic character and that 'it is illusory to speak of a liberty of contract.' It is in the alternative presented of accepting the rates of the companies or refraining from insurance. * * *

The [Kansas] statute seeks to secure rates which shall be reasonable both to the insurer and the insured, and as a means to this end it prescribes equality of charges, forbids initial discrimination or subsequently by the refund of a portion of the rates, or the extension to the insured of any privilege; to this end it requires publicity in the basic schedules and of all of the conditions which affect the rates or the value of the insurance to the insured, and also adherence to the rates as published. Whether the requirements are necessary to the purpose, or—to confine ourselves to that which in under review—whether rate regulation is necessary to the purpose, is a matter for legislative judgment, not judicial. Our function is only to determine the existence of power.

* * *

■ MR. JUSTICE LAMAR, dissenting:

I dissent from the decision and the reasoning upon which it is based. The case does not deal with a statute affecting the safety or morals of the public. It presents no question of monopoly in a prime necessity of life, but relates solely to the power of the state to fix the price of a strictly personal contract. The court holds that fire insurance, though personal, is affected with a public interest, and therefore that the business may not only be regulated, but that the premium or price to be paid to the insurer for entering into that personal contract can be fixed by law.

The fixing of the price for the use of private property is * * * a taking [and] has always heretofore been thought to be permissible only when it was for a public use. But the court in this case holds that there is no distinction between the power to take for public use and the power to regulate the exercise of private rights for the public good. That is the fundamental proposition on which the case must stand, and the decision must therefore be considered in the light of that ruling and of the results which must necessarily flow from the future application of that principle. For if the power to regulate, in the interest of the public, comprehends what is intended in the power to take property for public use, it must inevitably follow that the price to be paid for any service or the use of any property can be regulated by the general assembly. This is so because the power of regulation is all-pervading, as witness the statute of frauds, the recording acts, weight and measure laws, pure food laws, hours of service laws, and innumerable other enactments of that class. * * *

[Indeed,] insurance is a contract of indemnity, and personal, [and] its personal character has not been thought to preclude the many regulatory measures adopted and sustained during the past hundred years.

* * * But it is equally true that * * * rate-making is no new thing, and neither is insurance. [The use of insurance] in protecting the owner of property against loss; its value as collateral in securing loans; its method of averages and distributing the risk between many persons widely separated, and all contributing small premiums in return for the promise of a large indemnity, has been known for centuries. * * *

The character of insurance, therefore, as a private and personal contract of indemnity, has, not been changed by its magnitude or by the fact that more policies and for greater amounts are now written than in the centuries during which no effort has ever before been made to fix their rates. It is, however, undoubtedly true that during all of that period *regulatory statutes* were, from time to time, adopted to protect the public against conditions and practices which were subject to regulation. The public had no means of knowing whether these corporations were solvent or not, and statutes were passed to require a publication of the financial condition. The policies were long and complicated, with exceptions and qualifications and provisos. They were often unread by the policy holder and sometimes not understood when read. Statutes were accordingly passed providing for a standard form of policy in order to protect the assured against his inexperience, to prevent hard bargains, and to avoid vexatious litigation; and as similar evils appear they may be dealt with by regulatory or prohibitory legislation just as statutes were passed, and can still be passed to punish combinations, pooling arrangements, and all those practices which amount to unfair competition.

* * * And if, as seems to be implied, the fact that a business may be regulated is to be the test of the power to fix rates, it would follow, since all can be regulated, the price charged by all can be regulated. Or if great size is the test, if the number of customers is the test, if the scope of the business throughout the nation is the test, if the contributions of the many to the value of the business is the test—or if it takes a combination of all to meet the condition—then every business with great capital and many customers distributed throughout the country, and making a large business possible, must be treated as affected with a public interest, and the price of

the goods on its shelves can be fixed by law. Then could the price of newspapers, magazines, and the like be fixed, because certainly nothing is more affected with a public interest, nothing is so dependent on the public, nothing reaches so many persons, and so profoundly affects public thought and public business. Such a business is, indeed, affected with a public interest—justifying regulation * * *, but not the fixing of the price of the paper or periodical or the rates of advertising. For great and pervasive as is the power to regulate, it cannot override the constitutional principle that private property cannot be taken for private purposes. * * *

[But] the size of the business in unimportant, for the fares of a cabman, employing a broken-down horse and a dilapidated vehicle, can be fixed by law as well as the rates of a railroad with millions of capital and thousands of cars transporting persons and property across the continent.

The fact that rate statutes, enacted and sustained since the adoption of constitutional government in this country, all had some reference to transportation or distribution, is a practical illustration of the accepted meaning of 'public use.' * * *

[T]he contract of insurance is private and personal, [and] it is almost a contradiction in terms to say that the private contract is public, or that a business which consists in making such private contracts is public in the constitutional sense. * * * If the company has the discretion to insure or the right to refuse to insure, then, by the very definition of the terms, it is not a public business. If, on the other hand, the company is obliged to insure bad risks or the property of men of bad character, of doubtful veracity, or known to be careless in their handling of property, the law would be an arbitrary exertion of power in compelling men to enter into contract with persons with whom they did not choose to deal where confidence is the very foundation of a contract of indemnity. Indeed, it seems to be conceded that a person owning property is not entitled to demand insurance as a matter of right. If not, the business is not public, and not within the provision of the Constitution which only authorizes the taking of property for public purposes—whether the taking be of the fee, for a lump sum assessed in condemnation proceedings, or whether the use be taken by rate regulation, which is but another method of exercising the same power. * * *

Questions

1. We defined systemic risk as a form of network externality. Under certain circumstances, the use of a system by one person affects the marginal risk of all other users.[36] Did American cities until the 1920s presented a systemic risk of urban fires? Could the state regulate such a systemic risk?

2. Taxicab rates have been regulated throughout the history of the service. The overwhelming majority of cities with taxicabs supersede market price system with administrative ratemaking. Are they all wrong or do they promote market efficiency?

---

36. *See* § 4.6.

§ 9.2.1b Price Floors and Ceilings

Do price floors and ceilings (minimum and maximum prices) substantially differ from ratemaking? If we set a price floor sufficiently high or price ceiling sufficiently low, it will be equivalent to ratemaking. It is unclear why that would ever happen. Price floors and ceilings may be crude regulatory instruments that increase costs or reduce profitability. However, their use may also be more nuanced. Anti-discrimination laws are in effect price-floor laws. For example, the Age Discrimination in Employment Act provides that "[i]t shall be unlawful for an employer * * * to reduce the wage rate of any employee in order to comply with this [Act]."[37] Usury laws regulate the maximum lending rate and the penalties imposed for default.[38] Under the regulations of the Troubled Asset Relief Program (TARP), which structured a bailout for the financial sector and the car industry,[39] limits were imposed on compensation for executives and highly compensated employees at companies receiving TARP funds.[40]

Price floors and ceilings, therefore, *may* function very differently from ratemaking.[41] The FCC's price cap policy, discussed in *National Rural Telecom Association*, intended, among other things, to incentivize regulated firms to cut their operation costs.[42] Anti-discrimination laws and minimum wage laws are motivated by a wide range of rationales other than addressing inadequate prices. The label of a regulatory instrument does not necessarily reveal much about it.

In re Kazas

District Court of Appeal, Fourth District, California
22 Cal.App.2d 161 (1937)

■ MARKS, JUSTICE.

This is an original proceeding wherein petitioner seeks release from confinement under the charge of violating the provisions of Ordinance No. 495, New Series, of the City of Bakersfield.

We quote the pertinent provisions of this ordinance as follows:

---

37. 29 U.S.C. § 623.

38. *See* Efraim Benmelech & Tobias J. Moskowitz, *The Political Economy of Financial Regulation: Evidence from U.S. State Usury Laws in the 19th Century*, 65 JOURNAL OF FINANCE 1029 (2010); Richard Hynes & Eric A. Posner, *The Law and Economics of Consumer Finance*, 4 AMERICAN LAW & ECONOMICS REVIEW 168 (2002).

39. The Emergency Economic Stabilization Act of 2008, Pub. L. No. 110–343, 122 Stat. 3765 (2008).

40. TARP Standards for Compensation and Corporate Governance, 31 C.F.R. 30 (Oct. 20, 2008).

41. *See, e.g.*, Timothy J. Brennan, *Regulating By Capping Prices*, 1 JOURNAL OF REGULATORY ECONOMICS 133 (1989); Lorenzo Brown, *Improved and Practical Incentive Regulation*, 3 JOURNAL OF REGULATORY ECONOMICS 323 (1991).

42. National Rural Telecom Association v. Federal Communications Commission, 988 F.2d 174 (D.C. Cir. 1993). *See* § 6.4.

SECTION 1. The existence of a national, state and local emergency productive of widespread unemployment and disorganization of trade and industry which affects the peace and welfare of all the people of this city, is hereby recognized, and among the trades and industries particularly affected are those in which service is rendered to the public without necessarily involving the sale, manufacture or transportation of merchandise or commodities. The practice of barbering is a trade so affected and in which there is widespread unemployment and economic distress, and the owners, operators and managers of more than eighty per cent of the barber shops in the City of Bakersfield have applied to the City Council for the establishment of a code of fair competition for barber shops and the practice of barbering in the City of Bakersfield. For the purpose of ameliorating such conditions it is necessary and desirable to establish a code of fair competition applicable to such barber shops and the practice of barbering in the City of Bakersfield.

SECTION 2. As used herein, the practice of barbering is hereby defined to be any of or any combination of the following practices for the hire or reward:

Shaving or trimming the beard or cutting the hair;

Giving facial and scalp massages or treatments with oils, creams, lotions or other preparations either by hand or mechanical appliances;

Singeing, shampooing, arranging, dressing, curling, waving or dyeing the hair or applying hair tonics; provided that the word 'waving' as herein used does not include permanent waving;

Applying cosmetic preparations, antiseptics, powders, oils, clays or lotions to scalp, face or neck.

As used herein the term 'barber–shop' is hereby defined to embrace and include any establishment or place of business wherein the practice of barbering as hereinabove defined is engaged in or carried on.

SECTION 3. (a) All barber shops in the City of Bakersfield shall charge and receive compensation for barbering services therein rendered, not less than the prices set forth in the following schedule:

Haircut .... 50¢
Shave .... 35¢
No service rendered for less than .... 25¢

(b) No combination of services mentioned in the foregoing schedule shall be rendered for a price less than the total of the minimum price which may be charged for each such service separately.

(c) The allowance of rebates, refunds or unearned discounts or the use of any method of subterfuge to defeat the prices specified in the foregoing schedule shall constitute a violation of this act.

(d) This ordinance shall have no application to services rendered by student barbers or operators in any regularly established barber school or school of cosmetology in this city. . . .

SECTION 5. Any person, firm or corporation violating any of the provisions of this ordinance shall be guilty of a misdemeanor and upon conviction thereof shall be punishable by a fine of not more than One Hundred Dollars ($100.00) or by imprisonment in the County Jail for not more than thirty (30) days, or by both such fine and imprisonment. Each and every day's continuance of such violation shall constitute a separate offense.

Petitioner is a barber with an established place of business in the city of Bakersfield. He is charged with having cut the hair of N. J. Nichols for 35 cents, and with having shaved him for 25 cents.

* * * If the ordinance can be sustained as constitutional, it must be because it is a reasonable exercise of the police power of the city of Bakersfield. * * *

The police powers extend to legislation promoting the public health, safety, morals, and general welfare of a people. If the ordinance in question is a legal exercise of the police power, it must be because it tends to promote the general welfare of the people of Bakersfield. It does not pretend to concern itself with the health, safety, or morals of the people. The health and sanitary legislation applying to barber shops is found elsewhere. * * *

The record before us shows that at the time of the adoption of the ordinance there were forty-six barber shops in the city of Bakersfield; that forty-three of them petitioned the city council for the enactment of an ordinance establishing a code of fair competition for the barber trade; that the ordinance was thereafter enacted. It is not in evidence that the city council made, or caused to be made, any investigation of any condition of unemployment in the barber trade in Bakersfield, its need of the ordinance or the effect of the enactment on barbers, their patrons, or the general public. We may take judicial notice that the population of Bakersfield is about twenty-five thousand.

It is clear that the ordinance had as its sole object the attempt to regulate prices charged by barbers. It fixed a minimum below which no barber could go without subjecting himself to the penalties provided in section five. It took no cognizance of differences in skill possessed by different members of the trade, differences in equipment in separate shops, or differences in costs in conducting any of them. Figuratively speaking, it attempted to pour all barbers and barber shops into a common mold, turning them out exactly alike regardless of skill or efficiency of operation, excellence and completeness of equipment, desirability of location, or expense of conducting business.

* * *

The reasons for the passage of the ordinance in question here are set forth in its section one. The existence of a state, national, and local emergency that has produced widespread unemployment and disorganization of trade and industry which affects the peace and welfare of all the people of Bakersfield is there declared; that barbering is a trade thus affected; that for ameliorating such condition in that trade it is necessary that a code of fair competition be adopted for barbers is also declared.

Since early in 1933 it has almost become a legislative habit to adopt laws and ordinances containing declarations of such an emergency in almost the exact language used by the Bakersfield city council. In some instances that legislation was enacted after much study, investigation, taking of evidence, and the making of findings by a fact finding body, which findings fully justified the legislative conclusion. * * * In other cases the laws were just enacted.

In considering this subject we should weigh the words of the Supreme Court of the United States in Action Home *Building & Loan Ass'n v. Blaisdell*, 290 U.S. 398 (1934):

> "Emergency does not create power. Emergency does not increase granted power or remove or diminish the restrictions imposed upon power granted or reserved. The Constitution was adopted in a period of grave emergency. Its grants of power to the federal government and its limitations of the power of the States were determined in the light of emergency, and they are not altered by emergency. What power was thus granted and what limitations were thus imposed are questions which have always been, and always will be, the subject of close examination under our constitutional system.

* * * The question of the existence of the emergency resulting from the recent widespread and disastrous financial depression has been in sharp dispute for at least the past nine months. It has been asserted that we have now emerged from the depression and only need to guard against following a path that will lead into another. Departments of our national government have reported prices of many commodities climbing towards the peak that preceded the disastrous break of 1929. It is confidently asserted that the financial condition of the great farm population and of those engaged in many industries has reached a point that must be regarded as normal. While there is unemployment, its extent is not definitely known. Some economists point to the fact that we have always had and always will have unemployment because of the refusal of some and the incapacity of others to work. They maintain that under our present social, industrial, and economic structure the present condition of unemployment is near normal. On the other hand, these assertions are all denied by many whose opinions are entitled to great weight.

Under such confusion of thought and statement we would hesitate to hold that a court could take judicial notice of and declare the existence of an emergency arising from the recent depression. It should follow that little importance should be attached to the declaration of an emergency by the city council of the city of Bakersfield as the ordinance in question was passed on March 17, 1937, several months after the debate to which we have alluded became vocal. * * *

However, we do not regard the declaration of an emergency by the city council of Bakersfield necessarily of controlling importance here. [An] emergency might serve as the occasion for bringing into activity the latent power to legislate for the public welfare. * * * The term "public welfare" has never been given a fixed or static definition. * * *

We may [however] fairly conclude that the term "general welfare" means just what it literally implies, namely, that legislation to be justified and supported by that term must at least promote the welfare of the general public as contrasted with that of a small percentage or insignificant numerical proportion of the citizenry. * * *

When we apply these descriptions of "general welfare" to the facts of the instant case, we conclude that the legislation in question here does not fall within their terms. The ordinance does not purport to promote the prosperity of the citizens of Bakersfield nor of any considerable class of them. It concerns itself with the welfare of a small group within a class. If we assume that there exists in Bakersfield the deplorable and chaotic condition of trade and industry which the ordinance portrays, we are confronted by the question: What specific remedy is proposed by the ordinance? We are advised that there are forty-six barber shops in Bakersfield. The barbers and their families could not compose more than 2% of the population of the city. The ordinance is a price fixing ordinance for barbers alone. The ordinance legislates for the benefit of barbers alone. It recites that there is wide unemployment in the barbering trade. To ameliorate that condition it fixes a minimum price to be charged for haircuts and shaves. The ordinance does not purport to consider the welfare of the other 98% of the population of the city nor the effect on them of fixing the minimum prices to be charged for cutting their hair or shaving their masculine faces. We conclude that on the face of the ordinance it affirmatively appears that the legislation was not intended to promote the general welfare of the people of Bakersfield, but only a small group composing a very small proportion of the population of that city.

We find nothing unreasonable, unjust, or oppressive in the minimum prices fixed, and that feature of the case does not enter into our reasoning and has not influenced our conclusions. * * *

State Board of Dry Cleaners v. Thrift–D–Lux Cleaners

Supreme Court of California
40 Cal.2d 436 (1953)

■ SHENK, JUSTICE.

[T]he Dry Cleaners' Act of 1945 [includes minimum price provisions] under which the plaintiff sought injunctive relief against the defendant's alleged violations of that Act. * * *

The Act provides for the creation of a State Board of Dry Cleaners consisting of seven members: one from the general public; two owners of retail plants; two owners of wholesale plants; and two owners of shops. Article 5, in Sections 9560 through 9567, provides for "*Minimum Price Schedules.*" * * * [Section 9563 provides:

> "The board may establish minimum price schedules for the various items of cleaning, dyeing and pressing services for any * * * area as may be determined by the board upon the filing of a petition with it, requesting a minimum price schedule for that * * * area signed by seventy-five per cent (75%) or more of the persons engaged in the industry in that * * * area."]

* * *

In July, 1947, 75 per cent of those licensed by the board in numerous cities in Los Angeles County petitioned the board to establish minimum prices in both wholesale and retail fields. Basing its action upon its own cost surveys, the board established and published its minimum Price Schedules. In September, 1949, the board filed a complaint charging the defendants with violations of the price schedule and with threats to continue to do so. The board had established a minimum price to be paid for cleaning and pressing a man's suit at $1.00. The defendant Thrift–D–Lux Cleaner was charging 69 cents for the same service.

If the statute can be sustained as constitutional it is because it is a reasonable exercise of the police power of the state. * * * Under the law generally that power extends to legislation enacted to promote the public health, safety, morals and general welfare.

It is first contended by the plaintiff that the price fixing features of the statute were designed to protect the public health and safety. The statutory law in California meets this contention head on for it has made detailed and adequate provisions elsewhere for the protection of the public's health and safety through the regulation of the dry cleaning industry. * * * [The price fixing feature of the statute] constitute an unnecessary and unreasonable restriction on the pursuit of private and useful business activities. The asserted objectives of those portions of the statute are not in fact their real objective. There is * * * nothing relating to the price charged for such services that has any real or substantial relationship to the public health or safety.

The proponents of the validity of the statute would justify it in the light of troubled conditions which they claim existed prior to World War II, although they are adverse to applying legal concepts generally accepted during that same period. The statute does not purport to be nor can it be justified as a war or emergency measure. During periods of emergency such as a state of war or of general economic distress the courts have recognized a broad legislative discretion dealing with such situations in the interest of the public welfare. It does not appear that at the time this legislation was enacted there was any such general emergency affecting all private businesses alike. There is nothing in the dry cleaning business which distinguishes it from the multitude of other businesses offering services to the general public. The disturbances and violence which are said to have existed in the dry cleaning business during the period of economic stress prior to the last World War were common to other businesses. It is important to note that the statute itself in no way purports to prevent destructive and unfair competition or to suppress violence.

It is claimed that the price-fixing portions of the statute were enacted to provide for the general welfare. But a legislative body may not, under the guise of providing for this component of the police power, impose unnecessary and unreasonable restrictions upon the pursuit of these useful activities. If a statute has no real or substantial relation to any legitimate police power objective, it is the duty of the court to so declare. * * *

It is argued that the "affected with a public interest" doctrine was abandoned in the *Nebbia* case. On the contrary that case may be cited merely for an interpretation of that doctrine.† * * * [This] does not imply that some particular industries are and others are not subject to control. It means that where the control is for the public good any industry may be regulated, provided there is "adequate reason" for it. That "adequate reason" can only be to achieve a purpose within the police power of the state. The test emphasizes that the control must be for the "public good." When the "affected with a public interest" doctrine is applied in this sense it is an adequate and proper test. As it was traditionally applied to confine regulation to only those industries in the nature of public utilities it is admittedly no longer so limited.

Regardless of the legal terminology used in defining the test employed, any legislation to be justified and supported by the concept of "general welfare" must aim to promote the welfare of a properly classified segment of the general public as contrasted with that of a small percentage or a special class of the body politic where no such classification can be justified. * * *

The statute before us * * * seeks to establish * * * a single grade of work in the dry cleaning industry and to eliminate the economical cleaning job. It does not take into consideration the "skill or efficiency of operation, excellence and completeness of equipment, desirability of location or expense of conducting business." It does not consider that a substantial group of the public may choose to purchase a cheaper grade of cleaning for particular garments, knowing that they are not obtaining the quality of service offered by more expensive establishments. * * *

It must be concluded that the price fixing provision of the statute here involved is invalid because it is not, by any recognized or recognizable standard, an enactment providing for the public health, safety, morals, or general welfare.

The defendant points to another ground upon which the invalidity of the statute may well be based. Section 9564 of the code requires that the "board shall investigate and ascertain those minimum prices which will enable cleaners, dyers, or pressers in that ... area to furnish modern, proper, healthful and sanitary services, using such appliances and equipment as will minimize the danger to public health and safety incident to such services." However, "one person may not be entrusted with the power to regulate the business of another, and especially of a competitor. * * *" *Carter v. Carter Coal Co.*, 298 U.S. 238, 311 (1936). * * * Where the Legislature attempts to delegate its powers to an administrative board

† [In Nebbia v. New York, 291 U.S. 502 (1934), the Supreme Court repudiated the logic of the "affected with a public interest" doctrine and held it had no particular meaning.]

made up of interested members of the industry, the majority of which can initiate regulatory action by the board in that industry, that delegation may well be brought into question.

From the foregoing it follows that the price fixing provisions of the statute under attack must fall on the constitutional grounds stated. * * *

■ TRAYNOR, JUSTICE, dissenting.

In my opinion the minimum price provisions of the Dry Cleaners' Act of 1945 do not violate the due process clause of either the United States Constitution or the California Constitution.

The Legislature has power to determine the rights of persons, subject only to the limitations of the United States Constitution and the California Constitution. * * * A statute regulating commercial transactions does not violate the due process clause of either Constitution unless it is proved so unreasonable as to dispel the presumption that it rests upon some rational basis within the knowledge and experience of the legislators. * * * Judicial inquiry "where the legislative judgment is drawn into question, must be restricted to the issue whether any state of facts either known or which could reasonably be assumed affords support for it." * * * The statute in the present case, like any other regulation of private enterprise, must be considered in this light.

Although early decisions held that prices could not be regulated unless the industry was clothed with a public interest * * *, the United States Supreme Court discarded that test in *Nebbia v. New York*, 291 U.S. 502 (1934). * * * The Legislature, therefore, is clearly empowered to prevent destructive price cutting, which has demoralizing effects on business itself and on its service to the public.

The dry cleaning industry has an unhappy history of ruthless competition marked by destructive price cutting and retaliatory sabotage. Early attempts at voluntary price regulation by internal agreements were struck down by the courts. (*Endicott v. Rosenthal*, 216 Cal. 721 (1932)) * * * Thereafter, price cutting was fought by sabotage. The chaotic state of the industry was brought to light in *People v. Cowan*, 38 Cal. App. 2d 231 (1940), a murder prosecution arising out of an attempt to sabotage a dry cleaner who cut his prices. * * * It was * * * revealed that a substantial number of industry members were guilty of unlawful attacks on retailers who cut prices. The industry thereafter, from 1941–1945, achieved stabilization under price regulation by the Office of Price Administration. After the cessation of O.P.A. regulation, the statute now held unconstitutional constitutional was passed by unanimous vote of both houses of the Legislature and signed by the Governor.

The dry cleaning business is highly vulnerable to price wars and their attendant evils. The industry represents millions of dollars in plants and equipment and requires the labor of thousands of skilled workers. It is subject to intense short-period fluctuations. The dry cleaner cannot hedge against these fluctuations by stock-piling inventory or by large-scale buying of raw materials. He cannot supply his market in advance, lay off help, and wait for demand to catch up with supply as a manufacturer ordinarily can. A dry cleaner is under constant pressure to cut his prices, increase his volume, and reduce his costs. Other cleaners follow suit and the price cuts inevitably result in downgrading of service. The cleaning industry is particularly susceptible to down-grading: its processes are highly specialized and it is difficult to police against slipshod performance or to detect it. Destructive price cutting quickly starts a vicious train of sabotage, violence, eventual bankruptcy for many cleaners, and disruption of a service industry essential to the public health.

The statute sets the minimum price schedule as low as is consistent with efficient and sanitary service. * * * Prices can be fixed only after a cost survey and due investigation by the board. * * * If the board should abuse the discretion vested in it, its action is subject to judicial correction. The statute thus limits the competitive struggle in the industry to the quality of service offered to the public.

The Legislature could reasonably conclude that the economic waste, the loss of property, the violation of law, the threat to health and public convenience, could be prevented by elimination of price warfare through establishment of minimum price schedules. It could reasonably conclude that a measure of economic security would encourage compliance with health and safety regulations and the maintenance of the industry's capacity to meet the fluctuating demand of the public at reasonable prices. * * *

Most of the cases holding statutes regulating dry cleaning and barber prices unconstitutional were decided in 1937 or earlier, before the decision in *West Coast Hotel Co. v. Parrish*, 300 U.S. 379 (1937), [and were overruled in that decision].

The United State Supreme Court, however, no longer adheres to the constitutional doctrine expressed in the *Lochner* and similar cases. * * * [The Court endorsed the] constitutional principle that states have power to legislate against what are found to be injurious practices in their internal commercial and business affairs, so long as their laws do not run afoul of some specific federal constitutional prohibition, or of some valid federal law. * * *

As an alternative ground of decision, the majority opinion states that the Dry Cleaners' Act "may well be" unconstitutional because it "assumes to confer legislative authority upon those who are directly interested in the operation of the regulatory rule and its penal provisions with no guide for the exercise of the delegated authority."

The members of the State Board of Dry Cleaners are appointed by the Governor and approved by the Senate. They are officials of the state, paid by the state for administering the law, and their acts are reviewed by the judiciary. The fact that six members of the board must be members of the cleaning industry has no constitutional significance. * * *

The fact that price regulation is initiated at the insistence of 75 per cent of the cleaners in the area does not present constitutional difficulties. Whatever their special interest in articulating the problem, it remains a general one, of the greatest concern to the public. Governmental processes are commonly set in motion by the petition, complaint, or other action by some individual or group.

The provision in the present statute does no more than relieve the board from making an expensive survey at the instance of a few cleaners, and allows it to act only when the need for regulation is apparent to a substantial number of those who would be affected. Far from unlawfully delegating authority, the Legislature has merely restricted its regulations by withholding their operation from a given area until 75 per cent of the cleaners favor it. * * *

The real basis for the result reached by the majority opinion is an adherence to an economic view that minimum price legislation is not in the best interests of the general public. But as Mr. Justice Holmes long admonished, the economic and moral beliefs of the judiciary are not embedded in the Constitution. There is no reason to suppose that judges are better qualified than legislators to determine what social and economic programs should be adopted by the State of California.

* * *

Questions

1. What were the reasons for and against minimum prices *Kazas* and *Thrift–D–Lux*?

2. Dissenting in *New State Ice v. Liebmann*, Justice Brandeis wrote: "The people of the United States are now confronted with an emergency more serious than war. Misery is widespread, in a time, not of scarcity, but of overabundance. * * * Many insist there must be some form of economic control. * * * Denial of the right to experiment may be fraught with serious consequences to the nation."[43] In *Kazas* and *Thrift–D–Lux*, the courts rejected the argument that emergency situations warrant price controls. Should the state regulate prices during emergencies?

Price Gouging

> **Prof-it-eer'**, *n.* One who seeks or extracts exorbitant profits, by taking advantage of public necessity.
>
> —The New Century Dictionary (1927)

Price gouging, or *profiteering*, occurs when sellers sharply increase prices of goods and services in response to conditions of shortage or anticipated shortage. For example, complaints about gouging frequently follow tropical storms when products and services are in shortage. People tend to feel that the price increases that respond to the shortage are unfair.[44] Price gouging has always existed and, as long as people pursue their self-interest, it will always exist. Anti-price gouging sentiments have always been powerful, as well.

---

43. New State Ice Co. v. Liebmann, 285 U.S. 262 (1932), § 6.4.2.

44. *See* Jeremy Snyder, *What's the Matter with Price Gouging?*, 19 BUSINESS ETHICS QUARTERLY 275 (2009); Matt Zwolinski, *The Ethics of Price Gouging*, 18 BUSINESS ETHICS QUARTERLY 347 (2008). *See also* Daniel Kahneman et al., *Fairness as a Constraint on Profit Seeking: Entitlements in the Market*, 76 AMERICAN ECONOMIC REVIEW 728 (1986).

Today, most states have anti-price gouging statutes. The overwhelming majority of these statutes were adopted during the first decade of the twenty-first century in response to perceived profiteering during times of shortage created by natural disasters and sharp increases in gasoline prices. There are three categories of contemporary U.S. anti-gouging laws: (1) price percentage caps, (2) bans on unconscionable price increases, and (3) bans on price increases.[45]

(1) Price Percentage Caps. Several states restrict price increases during defined periods. The defined periods typically refer to the duration of a declared state of emergency, and in some states defined periods before and after that timeframe. The percentage caps range from 10% to 25%. For example, the California anti-price gouging law provides:

(a) The Legislature hereby finds that during emergencies and major disasters, including, but not limited to, earthquakes, fires, floods, or civil disturbances, some merchants have taken unfair advantage of consumers by greatly increasing prices for essential consumer goods and services. While the pricing of consumer goods and services is generally best left to the marketplace under ordinary conditions, when a declared state of emergency results in abnormal disruptions of the market, the public interest requires that excessive and unjustified increases in the prices of essential consumer goods and services be prohibited. *It is the intent of the Legislature in enacting this act to protect citizens from excessive and unjustified increases in the prices charged during or shortly after a declared state of emergency for goods and services that are vital and necessary for the health, safety, and welfare of consumers.* Further it is the intent of the Legislature that this section be liberally construed so that its beneficial purposes may be served.

(b) Upon the proclamation of a state of emergency * * * and for a period of 30 days following that declaration, it is unlawful for a person, contractor, business, or other entity to sell or offer to sell any consumer food items or goods, goods or services used for emergency cleanup, emergency supplies, medical supplies, home heating oil, building materials, housing, transportation, freight, and storage services, or gasoline or other motor fuels for a price of more than 10 percent above the price charged by that person for those goods or services immediately prior to the proclamation of emergency. However, a greater price increase is not unlawful if that person can prove that the increase in price was directly attributable to additional costs.

* * *

(f) A violation of this section is a misdemeanor punishable by imprisonment in a county jail for a period not exceeding one year, or by a fine of not more than ten thousand dollars ($10,000), or by both that fine and imprisonment.

---

45. *See generally* Emily Bae, *Are Anti–Price Gouging Legislations Effective Against Sellers During Disasters?*, 4 ENTREPRENEURIAL BUSINESS LAW JOURNAL 79 (2009).

* * *

(h) For the purposes of this section, the following terms have the following meanings:

(1) "***State of emergency***" means a natural or manmade disaster or emergency resulting from an earthquake, flood, fire, riot, or storm for which a state of emergency has been declared by the President of the United States or the Governor of California.

* * *

(3) "***Consumer food item***" means any article that is used or intended for use for food, drink, confection, or condiment by a person or animal.

* * *

(5) "***Emergency supplies***" includes, but is not limited to, water, flashlights, radios, batteries, candles, blankets, soaps, diapers, temporary shelters, tape, toiletries, plywood, nails, and hammers.

(6) "***Medical supplies***" includes, but is not limited to, prescription and nonprescription medications, bandages, gauze, isopropyl alcohol, and antibacterial products.

(7) "***Building materials***" means lumber, construction tools, windows, and anything else used in the building or rebuilding of property.

(8) "***Gasoline***" means any fuel used to power any motor vehicle or power tool.

(9) "***Transportation, freight, and storage services***" means any service that is performed by any company that contracts to move, store, or transport personal or business property or rents equipment for those purposes.(10) "Housing" means any rental housing leased on a month-to-month term. * * *[46]

(2) Bans on Unconscionable Price Increases. Many states have incorporated fairness perceptions into their anti-price gouging statutes. These statutes explicitly use subjective perspective to define price gouging. For example, the New York anti-gouging statute provides:

1. Legislative findings and declaration. The legislature hereby finds that during periods of abnormal disruption of the market caused by strikes, power failures, severe shortages or other extraordinary adverse circumstances, some parties within the chain of distribution of consumer goods have taken unfair advantage of consumers by charging grossly excessive prices for essential consumer goods and services. * * *

2. During any abnormal disruption of the market for consumer goods and services vital and necessary for the health, safety

46. Cal. Penal Code § 396 (emphasis added).

> and welfare of consumers, no party within the chain of distribution of such consumer goods or services or both shall sell or offer to sell any such goods or services or both for an amount which represents an *unconscionably excessive price*.
>
> For purposes of this section, the phrase "*abnormal disruption of the market*" shall mean any change in the market, whether actual or imminently threatened, resulting from stress of weather, convulsion of nature, failure or shortage of electric power or other source of energy, strike, civil disorder, war, military action, national or local emergency, or other cause of an abnormal disruption of the market which results in the declaration of a state of emergency by the governor.
>
> [T]he term *consumer goods and services* shall mean those used, bought or rendered primarily for personal, family or household purposes. * * *
>
> 3. Whether a price is unconscionably excessive is a question of law for the court. * * * The court's determination that a violation of this section has occurred shall be based on any of the following factors:
>
> (i) that the amount of the excess in price is unconscionably extreme; or
>
> (ii) that there was an exercise of unfair leverage or unconscionable means; or
>
> (iii) a combination of both factors in subparagraphs (i) and (ii) of this paragraph. * * *[47]

To illustrate the logic of the statute consider the events that followed Hurricane Gloria that struck the East Coast in September 1985, and left much of Long Island without electrical power between September 27 and October 8. Beginning on September 26, in anticipation of the storm, and continuing through October 5, an electric generator dealer sold approximately 100 generators at inflated prices ranging from 4% to 67% over the "base prices" for those models. The dealer was prosecuted for price gouging and was found guilty for charging unconscionably excessive prices during power outages. Explaining the judgment, the New York court wrote: "The situation [was] ripe for overreaching by the merchant, who enjoy[ed] a temporary imbalance in bargaining power by virtue of an abnormal level of demand, in terms of both the number of consumers who desire the item and the sense of urgency that increases that desire."[48]

Massachusetts' anti-price gouging law is particularly unique. It is in the form of a regulation the Attorney General promulgated in response to the oil price increases that followed Hurricane Katrina.[49] This regulation provides:

47. N.Y. Gen. Bus. Law § 396–r (emphasis added).

48. People v. Two Wheel Corp., 71 N.Y.2d 693 (1988).

49. *See* Peter J. Howe, *Romney Warns Suppliers Against Price Gouging*, BOSTON GLOBE, Sept. 3, 2005, at A10. The Massachusetts consumer protection statute authorizes the Attorney General to create rules in furtherance of statute. Mass. Gen. Laws ch. 93A, § 2(a).

(1) It shall be an unfair or deceptive act or practice, during any market emergency, for any petroleum-related business to sell or offer to sell any petroleum product for an amount that represents an *unconscionably high price*.

(2) A price is unconscionably high if:

(a) the amount charged represents a *gross disparity* between the price of the petroleum product and

1. the price at which the same product was sold or offered for sale by the petroleum-related business in the usual course of business immediately prior to the onset of the market emergency, or

2. the price at which the same or similar petroleum product is readily obtainable by other buyers in the trade area; and

(b) the disparity is not substantially attributable to increased prices charged by the petroleum-related business suppliers or increased costs due to an abnormal market disruption.[50]

In *White v. R.M. Packer Co.*, the First Circuit interpreted the meaning of the term "gross disparity" in the regulation and ruled that "nothing in the regulation suggests that increases in gross margin alone, in the absence of any price increase and simultaneous with declining retail prices, can support a price-gouging claim."[51]

(3) Bans on Price Increases. Several states prohibit any price increases during times of emergency. For example, Connecticut law addresses price gouging in its old name "profiteering" and sets a strict prohibition on price increases:

> No person, firm or corporation shall increase the price of any item * * * in an area which is the subject of any disaster emergency declaration issued by the Governor. * * * Nothing in this section shall prohibit the fluctuation in the price of items sold at retail which occurs during the normal course of business. * * *[52]

Questions

1. What are the differences among the three types of anti-price gouging laws? Is any one of them better or worse than the others?

2. The U.S. entry into World War I increased the perceived rate of price gouging ("profiteering") in all American industries. Delivering the State of the Union Address, in December 1917, President Woodrow Wilson noted:

> Recent experience has convinced me that the Congress must * * * authorize[e] the Government to set limits to prices. The law of supply and demand, I am sorry to say, has been replaced by the law of unrestrained selfishness. While we have eliminated profit-

---

50. 940 Mass. Code Regs. § 3.18 (emphasis added).

51. White v. R.M. Packer Co., Inc., 635 F.3d 571 (1st Cir. 2011).

52. Conn. Gen. Stat. § 42–230.

eering in several branches of industry it still runs impudently rampant in others.

In June 1918, the Federal Trade Commission submitted to the Senate a highly publicized study of profiteering.[53] The Commission declared that it "has reason to know that profiteering exists," and that "[m]uch of it is due to advantages taken of the necessities of the times as evidenced in the war pressure for heavy production." The Commission further found that some of the profiteering "is attributable to inordinate greed and barefaced fraud." A 1920 *New York Times* article warned readers about a relatively unnoticed type of profitmaking:

Profiteering in Cents

> [The] profiteering in the small necessities of life probably costs you more each year in dollars and cents than profiteering in coal, food, and clothing.
>
> Consider for a moment the one item of soap. One brand before the war sold for 5 cents a cake. * * * Now it sells for 10 cents a cake, an increase in price of 100 per cent. Other soaps have risen at the same rate.
>
> * * * The profiteer in small things * * * calculates upon the carelessness of the average American about details of economy and upon fact that the purchase price is in cents. He knows that if the American has the money in his pocket he will hand it out with simply a mental shrug in protest. * * *
>
> The remedy may lie in arousing the public, in getting newspaper notice and in having Government inspection. * * *
>
> Profiteering in small things is so widespread that to tolerate it is becoming a habit with the buying public. * * * What is to be done about it? Government regulation of some kind.[54]

(a) Does profiteering in cents warrant government regulation of some kind? (b) Does price gouging result in any effects other than redistribution of wealth? (c) Why does price gouging tend to have support for government intervention in the market price system?

The Durbin Amendment

In the 1970s, automated teller machines (ATMs) proliferated the country and reduced the use of paper checks. ATMs were "state of art in electronic banking services."[55] They were "are electronic terminals through which consumers [could] withdraw cash from, make deposits to, transfer funds between, and often make payments from, their various accounts at a bank or other financial institution. Customer access at an ATM [was]

---

53. Federal Trade Commission, *Profiteering* (June 1918).

54. M. Theresa Dallam, *Profiteering in Cents*, N.Y. TIMES, Sept. 12, 1920, at 10.

55. Roland E. Brandel & Eustace A. Olliff III, *The Electronic Fund Transfer Act: A Primer*, 40 OHIO STATE LAW JOURNAL 531, 533 (1979).

achieved by inserting a special [electronic fund transfer (EFT)] card and pushing buttons to enter a secret personal identification number (PIN). ATMs frequently operate[ed] around-the-clock."[56] To enhance consumer confidence in electronic banking services, Congress passed the Electronic Fund Transfer Act of 1978 (EFTA). The stated congressional purpose of the EFTA was "to provide a basic framework establishing the rights, liabilities, and responsibilities of participants in electronic fund transfer systems."[57] Electronic fund transfers have dramatically evolved since the late 1970s, predominately due to the rise of credit cards and electronic commerce.

When a consumer makes a transaction with a credit or debit card, the merchant does not receive the full purchase amount. A portion of the transaction (a "*discount fee*") is deducted and distributed among the merchant's financial institution, the financial institution that issued the card (the "*issuer*"), and the card network that processes the transaction (the "*payment card network*")—Visa, MasterCard, American Express, or another network. The majority of this amount generally is called the *interchange fee* and goes to the issuer.

The discount and interchange fees are essentially negotiated transaction costs. The merchants pay financial institutions a portion of each transaction for processing payments (*see Figure 9.2*). However, the services extended by financial institutions are substantial and go beyond saving of transaction costs to merchants and consumers. The use of cards enhances security and expands the scope of the markets.

Figure 9.2
Transfer of Fees in a Credit Card Transaction

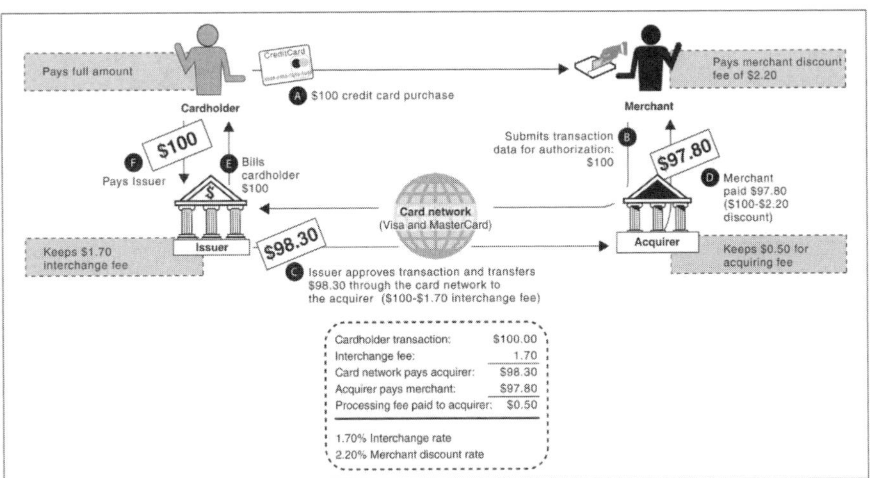

Source: U.S. Government Accountability Office.

56. *Id.*

57. EFTA § 902.

Credit card companies utilize network externalities to economize transaction costs in commerce, and spread risks associated with credit.[58] They typically argue that their revenues merely constitute reasonable commissions on these services. This argument has been framed in many elaborate ways, but has not changed in nature.[59] The argument, however, is somewhat simplistic. The nexus of contracts and infrastructure that builds a credit card network is all about transaction costs, and as such imperfect competition defines it. In imperfect markets, a market participant that is in a position to exploit a source of market inefficiency, such as transaction costs, can also extract value from other participants. The reason is that such party effectively controls entry to the market.[60] From the economic perspective, the financial institutions in the credit card markets are in a strategic position to squeeze value from consumers, including indirectly through interchange fees. Indeed, with the expanded use of credit cards, interchange fees have increased.

In May 2009, Congress passed and the President signed the Credit Card Accountability Responsibility and Disclosure Act of 2009 ("Credit CARD" Act), which banned and curbed many of the practices of the credit card companies.[61] Section 501 of the CARD Act directed the Comptroller General to "conduct a study on the use of credit by consumers, interchange fees, and their effects on consumers and merchants."

In November 2009, the Government Accountability Office (GAO) issued a report, concluding that the significant network effects in the market empowered the payment card networks and allowed them to continuously increase the amount of interchange fees charged from merchants.[62] Further, the report concluded that interchange fees were among the most profitable activities for banks, and a significant source of revenue for small banks and credit unions.

In July 2010, Congress passed the Dodd–Frank Wall Street Reform and Consumer Protection Act.[63] The Dodd–Frank Act introduced massive financial reforms, and for that it has been a subject for objections and critique.[64] Section 1075 of the Dodd–Frank Act, named the *Durbin Amendment* after its sponsor Senator Richard Durbin of Illinois, amended EFTA.[65] The Durbin Amendment requires the Board of Governors of the Federal Reserve System to regulate interchange fees, and specifically to "prescribe regulations * * * regarding any interchange transaction fee that an issuer

---

58. *See* § 3.2.4.

59. *See, e.g.*, DAVID S. EVANS & RICHARD S. SCHMALENSEE, PAYING WITH PLASTIC: THE REVOLUTION IN BUYING AND BORROWING (2d ed., 2004).

60. *See* § 6.2.

61. Pub. L. No. 111–24, 123 Stat. 1734 (2009).

62. Government Accountability Office, Credit Cards: Rising Interchange Fees Have Increased Costs for Merchants, but Options for Reducing Fees Pose Challenges (November 2009), available at *regti.me/GAO-IF* (case sensitive). *See also* Kendall v. Visa U.S.A., Inc., 518 F.3d 1042 (9th Cir. 2008). For network effects *see* § 3.2.4.

63. The Dodd–Frank Wall Street Reform and Consumer Protection Act, Pub. L. No. 111–203, 124 Stat. 1376 1075 (2010).

64. *See, e.g.*, A Bill to Repeal the Dodd–Frank Wall Street Reform and Consumer Protection Act, H.R. 87, 112th Cong. 1st Sess. (Jan. 5, 2011).

65. A copy of the Durbin amendment is available at *regti.me/durbin1075* (case sensitive).

may receive or charge with respect to an electronic debit transaction."[66] These regulations should "establish standards for assessing whether the amount of any interchange transaction fee * * * is reasonable and proportional to the cost incurred by the issuer with respect to the transaction."[67]

In July 2011, the Federal Reserve Board issued its final rule on interchange fees.[68] Under this rule, the maximum permissible interchange fee that an issuer may receive for an electronic debit transaction is the sum of 21 cents per transaction and 5 basis points (0.05%) multiplied by the value of the transaction. For credit card companies, the rule meant a cap of cap of 21 to 24 cents fee per debit transaction, down from an average of 44 cents per transaction.[69]

In late September 2011, Bank of America, the nation's largest commercial bank at the time, announced that it would charge a $5 monthly fee on debit cards, stating that the bank is "adjusting [its] pricing to reflect today's economics."[70] Other big banks followed.[71] Within a few weeks, public outrage persuaded all banks to withdraw from the idea of charging monthly debit card fees.[72]

Questions

1. Professor Richard Epstein argued that "[t]he Durbin Amendment's regulation of debit interchange [fees] represents a radical effort to extend price regulation to areas in which it has never been attempted before."[73] Price regulation may not be popular, and may even be undesirable. However, it has been around for centuries. What is so radical in the Durbin Amendment?

2. What is the regulatory significance of the failed plan of commercial banks to charge a $5 monthly fee on debit cards?

---

66. 15 U.S.C. § 1603o–2.

67. *Id.* In June 2011, the Eight Circuit upheld the constitutionality of the Durbin Amendment. *See* TCF National Bank v. Bernanke, 643 F.3d 1158 (8th Cir. 2011).

68. Board of Governors of the Federal Reserve System, Debit Card Interchange Fees and Routing, 12 C.F.R. 235 (July 20, 2011).

69. *See* Edward Wyatt, *Fed Halves Debit Card Bank Fees*, NEW YORK TIMES, Jun. 30, 2011, at B1.

70. Ylan Q. Mui, *Bank of America Plans $5 Monthly Fee on Debit Cards*, WASHINGTON POST, Sept. 30, 2011, at A1.

71. *See* Tara Siegel Bernard & Ben Protess, *Banks to Make Customers Pay Debit Card Fee*, NEW YORK TIMES, Sept. 30, 2011, at A1; Andrew R. Johnson, *Banks Plan New Fees For Using Debit Cards*, WALL STREET JOURNAL, Sept. 2011, 2011, at A1.

72. *See* Tara Siegel Bernard, Bank of America Drops Plan for Debit Card Fee, NEW YORK TIMES, Nov. 2, 2011, at A1; Robin Sidel, *Big Banks Blink on New Card Fees*, WALL STREET JOURNAL, Oct. 28, 2011, at C1.

73. Richard A. Epstein, *The Dangerous Experiment of the Durbin Amendment*, 34.1 REGULATION 24, 29 (2011).

§ 9.2.2 *Regulation Through Prices and Taxes*

Ronald Coase's critique of Arthur Cecil Pigou is largely about the concept of regulation through prices.[74] Pigou proposed to impose taxes on sources of externalities to encourage them to internalize the costs of their actions. In contrast, Coase argued that private parties could resolve externalities through private bargaining. The Pigonvian taxes are regulation through prices, since they increase the cost of operation for firms and individuals. Coase resented the idea of state intervention in the market price system.[75]

The real world frequently does not accommodate efficient private bargaining. Transaction costs, inadequate information, bounded rationality, and specific preferences frequently impede and reduce the value of exchanges. The state routinely utilizes the price system to compensate for inherent market inefficiencies. For example, eleven states have adopted container-deposit laws that alter beverage prices and create financial incentives to ensure large-scale recycling of beverage containers.[76] All states impose excise taxes on cigarettes to discourage smoking and to collect revenues from addicted smokers. As of January 1, 2012, the median tax rate was $1.25 per pack of cigarettes, with Missouri charging the lowest tax at 17¢ per pack and New York charging the highest tax rate at $4.35 per pack.

Some believe that regulation through prices (or taxes) can only serve interest groups, because "as a rule, regulation is acquired by the industry and is designed and operated primarily for its benefit."[77] When price regulation is available, rent seeking becomes a viable strategy for interest groups.[78] As we saw, during the 1930s, the barbers of Bakersfield, California, secured from the City Council a minimum-rates ordinance to protect their financial interests. Similarly, since 1916, oil companies have been receiving federal subsidies and tax breaks.[79] In May 2011, while Congress engaged in massive budget cuts, the big oil companies persuaded members of Congress not to eliminate any tax breaks.[80]

Our discussion in this Section illustrates some of the key issues that regulation through prices raises.

---

74. *See* § 3.1.2.

75. For a modern theoretical analysis *see* Steven Shavell, *Corrective Taxation versus Liability*, 101 AMERICAN ECONOMIC REVIEW 273 (2011).

76. *See generally* W. Kip Viscusi, *Promoting Recycling: Private Values, Social Norms, and Economic Incentives*, 101 AMERICAN ECONOMIC REVIEW 65 (2011).

77. Stigler, *The Theory of Economic Regulation*, 2 BELL JOURNAL OF ECONOMIC & MANAGEMENT SCIENCE 3, 5 (1971).

78. *See generally* Jeremy Bulow & Paul Klemperer, *Regulated Prices, Rent Seeking, and Consumer Surplus*, 120 JOURNAL OF POLITICAL ECONOMY 160 (2012).

79. *See* Molly F. Sherlock, Energy Tax Policy: Historical Perspectives on Current Status of Energy Tax Expenditure, Congressional Research Service (May 2, 2011).

80. *See* John M. Broder, *Oil Executives, Defending Tax Breaks, Say They'd Cede Them If Everyone Did*, N.Y. TIMES, May, 13, 2011, at B4; *A Big Whine from Big Oil*, N.Y. TIMES, May 15, 2011, at WK7; Curl Hulse, *Senate Refuses to End Tax Breaks for Big Oil*, N.Y. TIMES, May 18, 2011, at A13. *See also* End Big Oil Tax Subsidies Act of 2011, H.R. 601, 112th Cong. (2011); Oil and Gas Tax Incentives and Rising Energy Prices, Hearing Before S. Comm. on Finance (May. 12, 2011) (statement of Rex W. Tillerson, the Chairman and CEO of Exxon Mobil. Tillerson argued that the elimination of the tax breaks to the five big energy companies would be "misinformed and discriminatory.")

§ 9.2.2a Sin Taxes

Under the 1906 Kentucky Dog Tax Law, dog owners paid an annual "license tax" of $1 per dog to indemnify for injury and killing losses of sheep caused by dogs. Because of the frequent "sins" of dogs in Kentucky and the significance of sheep to the state economy, the legislature decided to tax dog owners and use the tax funds exclusively to the benefit of sheep owners.[81] "Sin taxes" are, indeed, a traditional regulatory method. Federal and state governments use explicit forms of sin taxes when they impose excise taxes on goods and services, such as tobacco products, alcohol, soda, candies, hotels, air transportation, and shopping bags.[82]

Sin taxes have three general purposes: (1) reduce the consumption of certain products; (2) compensate for the costs of the "sin" by collecting revenues; and (3) exploit sins to collect revenues. As the example of the Kentucky Dog Tax Law illustrates, when the government designs a sin tax, it often utilizes it for multiple purposes. Similarly, the District of Columbia's Anacostia River Clean Up and Protection Act of 2009 was enacted to reduce the use of "disposable carryout bags" and to create a fund for the purpose of cleaning and maintaining the Anacostia River. It does so by imposing a 5¢ fee per disposable bag from.[83]

In the United States, the use of sin taxes has substantially expanded since the beginning of the twenty-first century.[84] This expansion is consistent with the general trend toward incentive regulation, and can also be attributed to state needs to increase tax revenues.

The contemporary sin taxes are diverse and often controversial. For example, recognizing obesity as a national epidemic, many states have adopted various schemes of sin taxes that intend to steer people away from unhealthy food and toward healthier food.[85] By contrast, food manufacturers have been feeding individual fears of regulation and have mobilized effective campaigns against taxes and interference with the freedom of choice.[86]

---

81. *See* McGlone v. Womack, 129 Ky. 274 (1908). A copy of the Kentucky Dog Tax Low is available at *regti.me/KY-dog* (case sensitive). *See also* § 8.2.2.

82. *See generally* James R. Hines Jr. *Taxing Consumption and Other Sins*, 21 JOURNAL OF ECONOMIC PERSPECTIVES 49 (2007).

83. A copy of the Anacostia River Clean Up and Protection Act of 2009 is available at *regti.me/Anacostia* (case sensitive).

84. *See, e.g.*, Mark Bitman, *Bad Food? Tax It*, N.Y. TIMES, July 24, 2011, at S1.

85. *See, e.g.*, Kelly D. Brownell et al., *Ounces of Prevention—The Public Policy Case for Taxes on Sugared Beverages*, 360 NEW ENGLAND JOURNAL OF MEDICINE 1805 (2009); Kelly D. Brownell et al., *The Public Health and Economic Benefits of Taxing Sugar-Sweetened Beverages*, 361 NEW ENGLAND JOURNAL OF MEDICINE 1599 (2009).

86. *See, e.g.*, Muhtar Kent, *Coke Didn't Make America Fat*, WALL STREET JOURNAL, Oct. 7, 2010, at A17 (Mr. Kent is the Chairman and CEO of the Coca-Cola Company); Amemona Hartocollis, *Failure of State Soda Tax Plan Reflects Power of an Antitax Message*, N.Y. TIMES, July 3, 2010, at A14; Robert Pear, *Soda Drink Industry Fights Proposed Food Stamp Ban*, N.Y. TIMES, Apr. 30, 2011, at A11. *See also* Jonathan Klick & Eric A. Helland, *Slim Odds*, 34(1) REGULATION 20 (2011); Michael L. Marow & Alden F. Shiers, *Would Soda Taxes Really Yield Health Benefits?*, 33(1) REGULATION 34 (2010).

The concept of "sin" is of course relative. Since 2004, Utah has been collecting a 10% tax on any amount paid to or charged by a "sexually explicit businesses" for admission fee, user fee, any sale or service.[87] The state tax code defines "sexually explicit business" as a "business at which any nude or partially denuded individual * * * performs any service."[88] Tax revenues collected from sexually explicit businesses are invested in the "Sexually Explicit Business and Escort Service Fund" that Utah is using for "treatment services" for convicted sex offenders and for any task force administered through the Attorney General Office.[89] Texas joined Utah in 2007, starting collecting an excise tax of $5 for each entry by each customer admitted to a "sexually oriented business," which is a "a nightclub, bar, restaurant, or similar commercial enterprise that * * * provides * * * live nude entertainment * * * [and] authorizes on-premises consumption of alcoholic beverages."[90] The first $25 million received from this so-called "pole tax" are deposited in the state sexual assault program fund, and any excess amounts will diverted into the state fund for "assistance to low-income persons."[91] The Utah and Texas statutes survived challenges in state courts.[92]

Child Labor

In many ways, the American history of illegalization of child labor is typical to industrialized nations. Child labor was not banned until such labor was not economically valuable.[93] Congress first attempted to reduce the value of child labor with the Keating–Owen Child Labor Act of 1916, which banned from interstate commerce goods produced by child labor.[94] Following a line of precedents that allowed only a narrow interpretation of the Commerce Clause, in *Hammer v. Dagenhart*, the Supreme Court held the act unconstitutional.[95] Responding to *Hammer*, in February 1919, Congress passed the Child Labor Tax Law, which imposed an excise tax of 10% on the net profits of firms that employed children of certain age or in certain hours.

---

87. Utah Code Ann. § 59–27–103.

88. Utah Code Ann. § 59–27–102.

89. Utah Code Ann. § 59–27–105. Under the statute, Utah can allocate to the Attorney General Office no more than 15% of the money in the fund.

90. Tex. Bus. & Com. Code Ann. §§ 102.051–052.

91. Tex. Bus. & Com. Code Ann. §§ 102.054, 055.

92. *See* TDM, Inc. v. Tax Commission, 2004 UT App. 433 (2004); Combs v. Texas Entertainment Association, Inc., 347 S.W.3d 277 (Tex. 2011).

93. *See generally* HUGH D. HINDMAN, CHILD LABOR: AN AMERICAN HISTORY (2002); KRISTE LINDENMEYER, A RIGHT TO CHILDHOOD: THE U.S. CHILDREN'S BUREAU AND CHILD WELFARE, 1912–1946 (1997).

94. An Act to Prevent Interstate Commerce in the Product of Child Labor, and for Other Purposes, Pub L. No. 64–249, 39 Stat. 675 (1916).

95. Hammer v. Dagenhart, 247 U.S. 251 (1918).

Bailey v. Drexel Furniture Co.
Child Labor Tax Case

259 U.S. 20 (1922)

■ MR. CHIEF JUSTICE TAFT delivered the opinion of the Court.

* * * The Child Labor Tax Law is title No. XII of an act entitled '*An act to provide revenue and for other purposes*,' approved February 24, 1919. * * * The heading of the title is '*Tax on Employment of Child Labor*.' It begins with section 1200 and includes eight sections. Section 1200 is as follows:

> SEC. **1200**. That every person * * * operating (a) any mine or quarry situated in the United States in which children under the age of sixteen years have been employed or permitted to work during any portion of the taxable year; or (b) any mill, cannery, workshop, factory, or manufacturing establishment situated in the United States in which children under the age of fourteen years have been employed or permitted to work, or children between the ages of fourteen and sixteen have been employed or permitted to work more than eight hours in any day or more than six days in any week, or after the hour of seven o'clock post meridian, or before the hour of six o'clock ante meridian, during any portion of the taxable year, shall pay for each taxable year, in addition to all other taxes imposed by law, an excise tax equivalent to 10 per centum of the entire net profits received or accrued for such year from the sale or disposition of the product of such mine, quarry, mill, cannery, workshop, factory, or manufacturing establishment.

Section 1203 relieves from liability to the tax any one who employs a child, believing him to be of proper age relying on a certificate to this effect issued by persons prescribed by a board consisting of the Secretary of the Treasury, the Commissioner of Internal Revenue, and the Secretary of Labor, or issued by state authorities. The section also provides in paragraph (b) that—

> The tax imposed by this title shall not be imposed in the case of any person who proves to the satisfaction of the Secretary that the only employment or permission to work which but for this section would subject him to the tax, has been of a child employed or permitted to work under a mistake of fact as to the age of such child and without intention to evade the tax.

Section 1206 gives authority to the Commissioner of Internal Revenue, or any other person authorized by him 'to enter and inspect at any time any mine, quarry, mill, cannery, workshop, factory or manufacturing establishment.' The Secretary of Labor, or any person whom he authorizes, is given like authority in order to comply with a request of the Commissioner to make such inspection and report the same. Any person who refuses entry or obstructs inspection is made subject to fine or imprisonment or both.

The law is attacked on the ground that it is a regulation of the employment of child labor in the states—an exclusively state function under the federal Constitution and within the reservations of the Tenth Amendment. * * * We must construe the law and interpret the intent and meaning of Congress from the language of the act. * * * Does this law impose a tax with only that incidental restraint and regulation which a tax must inevitably involve? Or does it regulate by the use of the so-called tax as a penalty? If a tax, it is clearly an excise. If it were an excise on a commodity or other thing of value, we might not be permitted under previous decisions of this court to infer solely from its heavy burden that the act intends a prohibition instead of a tax. But this act is more. It provides a heavy exaction for a departure from a detailed and specified course of conduct in business. That course of business is that employers shall employ in mines and quarries, children of an age greater than 16 years; in mills and factories, children of an age greater than 14 years, and shall prevent children of less than 16 years in mills and factories from working more than 8 hours a day or 6 days in the week. If an employer departs from this prescribed course of business, he is to pay to the government one-tenth of his entire net income in the business for a full year. The amount is not to be proportioned in any degree to the extent or frequency of the departures, but is to be paid by the employer in full measure whether he employs 500 children for a year, or employs only one for a day. Moreover, if he does not know the child is within the named age limit, he is not to pay; that is to say, it is only where he knowingly departs from the prescribed course that payment is to be exacted. Scienters are associated with penalties, not with taxes. The employer's factory is to be subject to inspection at any time not only by the taxing officers of the Treasury, the Department normally charged with the collection of taxes, but also by the Secretary of Labor and his subordinates, whose normal function is the advancement and protection of the welfare of the workers. In the light of these features of the act, a court must be blind not to see that the so-called tax is imposed to stop the employment of children within the age limits prescribed. Its prohibitory and regulatory effect and purpose are palpable. All others can see and understand this. How can we properly shut our minds to it?

* * * Grant the validity of this law, and all that Congress would need to do, hereafter, in seeking to take over to its control any one of the great number of subjects of public interest, jurisdiction of which the states have never parted with, and which are reserved to them by the Tenth Amendment, would be to enact a detailed measure of complete regulation of the subject and enforce it by a so-called tax upon departures from it. To give such magic to the word 'tax' would be to break down all constitutional limitation of the powers of Congress and completely wipe out the sovereignty of the states.

The difference between a tax and a penalty is sometimes difficult to define, and yet the consequences of the distinction in the required method of their collection often are important. * * * Taxes are occasionally imposed in the discretion of the Legislature on proper subjects with the primary motive of obtaining revenue from them and with the incidental motive of discouraging them by making their continuance onerous. They do not lose their character as taxes because of the incidental motive. But there comes a time in the extension of the penalizing features of the so-called tax when it loses its character as such and becomes a mere penalty, with the characteristics of regulation and punishment. Such is the case in the law before us. Although Congress does not invalidate the contract of employment or expressly declare that the employment within the mentioned ages is illegal, it does exhibit its intent practically to achieve the latter result by adopting the criteria of wrongdoing and imposing its principal consequence on those who transgress its standard.

* * * For the reasons given, we must hold the Child Labor Tax Law invalid. * * *

§ 9.2.2b Rent Seeking

Price regulation is fertile domain for rent seeking because it potentially offers direct wealth transfers. In the case of the Bakersfield barbers, the minimum rates the City Council established allegedly contributed to the well being of the members of the trade.[96] And the 1906 Kentucky Dog Tax Law benefitted sheep owners through the indemnification fund. Rent seeking, however, may be used not only to extract direct benefits through regulation, but also punish a rival industry through taxes.

Butter and Margarine

Invented in the late 1860s in France, margarine was made from oleo (refined caul fat of beef). The product was colored in yellow and commercialized as a butter substitute.[97] Margarine's journey to American table was long and dreadful. The American dairy industry considered margarine a threat to one of its flagship products and campaigned federal and state lawmakers to pass and maintain anti-margarine laws.[98] Anti-margarine laws primarily used taxes to inflate the price of butter substitutes and increase the costs of businesses participating in the production and trade of those products. They used some additional creative features. For example, Minnesota, New Hampshire, South Dakota, Vermont, and West Virginia required margarine to be colored in pink. But, primarily the laws used taxes to make margarine less attractive for consumers.

At the federal level, in 1886, Congress enacted the Oleomargarine Act, which imposed a tax of 2¢ per pound on all margarine produced in the United States and 15¢ per pound on imported margarine.[99] Additionally,

96. In re Kazas, 22 Cal.App.2d 161 (1937); *See* § 9.1.2.

97. *See generally* KATHARINE SNODGRASS, MARGARINE AS A BUTTER SUBSTITUTE (1930).

98. *See* Geoffrey Miller, *Public Choice at the Dawn of the Special Interest State: The Story of Butter and Margarine*, 77 CALIFORNIA LAW REVIEW 83 (1989); Frederic P. Storke, Oleomargarine and the Law, 18 ROCKY MOUNTAIN LAW REVIEW 79 (1946).

99. 24 Stat. 209 (1886), available at *regti.me/ol1886* (case sensitive).

the 1886 Act imposed "special taxes" on manufacturers and distributors of margarine, and retailers who sold the product. Manufacturers were required to post bonds and maintain detailed records. The Oleomargarine Act of 1902 amended the 1886 Act and introduced a differential tax—10¢ per pound on yellow margarine and a ¼¢ per pound on uncolored product.[100] For some time, coconut margarine benefitted from some loopholes and the industry quickly developed. However, the dairy industry diligently persuaded Congress to close these loopholes and tax imported coconuts.

The states were as creative as Congress and further increased local prices of butter substitutes. All states except Arizona enacted statutes taxing and regulating butter substitutes.[101] In 1923, Washington voters rejected a referendum to impose excise tax on butter substitutes. Eight years later, in 1931, the Washington Legislature passed an act imposing an excise tax of 15 cents per pound on butter substitutes.[102] At the time, *Nucoa* was the most dominant brand of margarine sold in Washington State.

---

100. 32 Stat. 193 (1902), available at *regti.me/ol1902* (case sensitive).

101. *See generally* CARTER LITCHFIELD, HISTORY OF OLEOMARGARINE TAX STAMPS AND LICENSES IN THE UNITED STATES (1987).

102. A copy of the statute is available at *regti.me/WA-butter* (case sensitive).

Figure 9.3
A Nucoa Advertisement (1920)

FOR YOUR PROTECTION

WHY do you have to pay 10c a pound more for colored NUT BUTTER, than you do for the WHITE? BECAUSE the Federal Government compels the manufacturer to pay a tax of 10c a pound on every pound he colors. The NATURAL color of NUT BUTTER is WHITE, the same as the meat of the cocoanut. Save this 10c and COLOR YOUR OWN NUT BUTTER—you will be doing a real service in helping reduce the high cost of living.

YOUR dealer will furnish you color capsules containing exactly the same color as used in every pound of creamery butter, free. Coloring process simple. Details surround each print, COLORING ADDS NOTHING TO THE TASTE, it simply makes it pleasing to the eye.

NUCOA stands for the highest grade of NUT BUTTER ever churned. It is Butter's successor. Just think, every day over 300,000 pounds of NUCOA is consumed in the United States.

IT JUST MUST BE GOOD

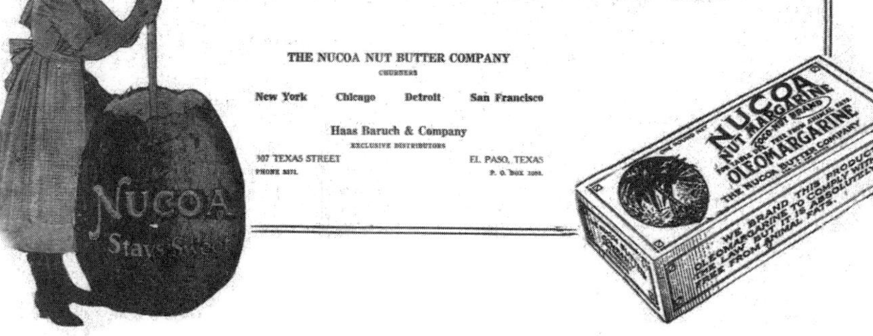

A. Magnano Co. v. Hamilton

292 U.S. 40 (1934)

■ MR. JUSTICE SUTHERLAND delivered the opinion of the Court.

Appellant assails as invalid a statute of the state of Washington which levies an excise tax of 15 cents per pound on all butter substitutes sold within the state. * * * Section 10 of the act provides that the tax shall not be imposed on butter substitutes when sold for exportation to any other state, territory, or nation; and any payment or the doing of any act which would constitute an unlawful burden upon the sale or distribution of butter substitutes in violation of the Constitution or laws of the United States is by section 13 excluded from the operation of the act. Violation of any provision of the act is denounced as a gross misdemeanor.

Appellant is a Washington corporation, and has for many years been engaged in importing and selling 'Nucoa,' a form of oleomargarine. Prior to the passage of the act, it had derived a large annual net profit from sales made within the state. Since then, claiming the tax to be prohibitive, it has made no intrastate sales and no effort to do so. 'Nucoa' is a nutritious and pure article of food, with a well-established place in the dietary.

Suit was brought to enjoin the enforcement of the act, on the ground that it violates the Federal Constitution in the following particulars: (1) That the imposition of the tax has the effect of depriving complainant of its property without due process of law and of denying to it the equal protection of the laws, in violation of the Fourteenth Amendment; (2) that the tax is not levied for a public purpose, but for the sole purpose of burdening or prohibiting the manufacture, importation, and sale of oleomargarine, in aid of the dairy industry; [and] (3) that the act imposes an unjust and discriminatory burden upon interstate commerce. * * *

First. We put aside at once all of the foregoing contentions, except the one relating to due process of law, as being plainly without merit. (1) In respect of the equal protection clause it is obvious that the differences between butter and oleomargarine are sufficient to justify their separate classification for purposes of taxation. (2) That the tax is for a public purpose is equally clear, since that requirement has regard to the use which is to be made of the revenue derived from the tax, and not to any ulterior motive or purpose which may have influenced the Legislature in passing the act. And a tax designed to be expended for a public purpose does not cease to be one levied for that purpose because it has the effect of imposing a burden upon one class of business enterprises in such a way as to benefit another class. (3) The act, considered as a whole, clearly negatives the idea that a burden is imposed upon interstate commerce. * * * The tax is confined to sales within the state, * * * has no application to sales of oleomargarine to be either imported or exported in interstate commerce. * * *

Collateral purposes or motives of a Legislature in levying a tax of a kind within the reach of its lawful power are matters beyond the scope of judicial inquiry. * * * Nor may a tax within the lawful power of a state be judicially stricken down under the due process clause simply because its enforcement may or will result in restricting or even destroying particular occupations or businesses. * * * *Child Labor Tax Case*, 259 U.S. 20, 38, 40–43 (1922), unless, indeed, as already indicated, its necessary interpretation and effect be such as plainly to demonstrate that the form of taxation was adopted as a mere disguise, under which there was exercised, in reality, another and different power denied by the Federal Constitution to the state. The present case does not furnish such a demonstration.

* * *

The statute here * * * is in form plainly a taxing act, with nothing in its terms to suggest that it was intended to be anything else. It must be construed, and the intent and meaning of the Legislature ascertained, from the language of the act, and the words used therein are to be given their ordinary meaning unless the context shows that they are differently used. * * * If the tax imposed had been 5 cents instead of 15 cents per pound, no one, probably, would have thought of challenging its constitutionality or of suggesting that under the guise of imposing a tax another and different power had in fact been exercised. If a contrary conclusion were reached in the present case, it could rest upon nothing more than the single premise that the amount of the tax is so excessive that it will bring about the destruction of appellant's business, a premise which, standing alone, this court heretofore has uniformly rejected as furnishing no juridical ground for striking down a taxing act. * * *

From the beginning of our government, the courts have sustained taxes although imposed with the collateral intent of effecting ulterior ends which, considered apart, were beyond the constitutional power of the lawmakers to realize by legislation directly addressed to their accomplishment. Those decisions * * * rule the present case.

§ 9.2.2c Internalization

In imperfect markets, individuals and firms do not fully internalize the costs and benefits of their choices. As a result, when they promote their private interests, they frequently do *not* promote the interests of society as a whole.[103] No "invisible hand" corrects actions or compensates for their consequences.[104] For example, urban butchers of the nineteenth century did not internalize the nuisance costs they produced and gradually created large-scale health hazards.[105] By using price regulation, the state frequently attempts to encourage internalization by calibrating perceived costs. Common measures include "Pigonvian taxes"—taxes designed to compensate for the costs of externalities—and improved allocation of payments for services.

Again, the contemporary taxes on plastic bags offer examples of internalization. Another example is the 2009 San Francisco Cigarette Butt Tax. San Francisco estimated that cigarette butts and related packaging constituted 25% of the litter collected from the sidewalks, gutters, and public places of San Francisco. The City therefore attributed 25% of its total expenditures related to removing litter to cigarette litter. Using these figures, San Francisco calculated that a fee of 22¢ per pack of cigarettes sold in the City would offset the City's cigarette litter abatement costs. After an extensive debate, in July 2009 the City's Board of Supervisors unanimously passed an ordinance that imposes a 20¢ fee on every pack of cigarettes sold in the City.[106]

Similarly, regulations addressing traffic congestion also tend to use prices. Roads have limited capacity and, thus, "free roads," frequently result in excess demand during certain hours. This problem of congestion network effects (negative network externalities) entails substantial monetary and many other costs, such as time, reduced productivity, increased risks, and pollution.[107] Possible solutions for congestion include expansion

103. *See* Chapter 3.

104. *See* § 2.2.1.

105. *See* § 2.2.2a.

106. Cigarette Litter Abatement Fee Ordinance, San Francisco Ord. No. 173–09 (June 6, 2009), available at *regti.me/SF-CBTax* (case sensitive).

107. For network effects *see* § 3.2.4. Another way to say the same thing is that free roads often lead to the tragedy of commons. *See* § 3.2.3.

of roads and public transportation, and an excise tax on use of public roads. *Congestion pricing* is a regulatory method that supersedes the free road system to account for congestion externalities. The general principle of congestion pricing is simple: drivers pay a "user fee" to enter busy roads or nonresidential urban areas. The user fee according to the congestion level and may be zero during the night and other slow times.[108] Pigou already proposed congestion pricing. It has been successfully implemented in London, Milan, and other cities. In New York City, a 2008 proposal to implement congestion pricing failed.[109] Many people find congestion pricing objectionable because it is a price regulation method that intends to alter individual behavior based on the ability and willingness to pay.[110]

Internalization through price regulation, therefore, is a standard economic instrument, which remains controversial.

Pay as You Throw

Pay-as-you-throw (PAYT) is a waste management concept that many communities across the United States have been using since 1916.[111] PAYT's principle is that a person must pay for each container of waste she generates, rather than paying a flat fee to the waste management company—directly or indirectly through property taxes.

The simple rationale behind PAYT is that it provides individuals and firms with incentives to reduce waste and it efficiently allocates the costs of waste collection based on the supply of waste. PAYT influences choices of individuals and firms as they internalize the costs of waste production. Under the traditional system of waste management, individuals and firms are oblivious to the costs of waste production because they pay uniformly for all levels of waste. PAYT is indeed a regulatory system, yet it provides decisionmakers with "prices" for a particular set of decisions.

To illustrate the design of a PAYT program consider the "Recycle Plus Program" of San Jose, California. In 1993, the City adopted an ordinance that, among other things provides:

---

108. *See generally* Anthony Downs, *The Law of Peak–Hour Express–Way Congestion*, 14 TRAFFIC QUARTERLY 392 (1962); Jonathan Leape, *The London Congestion Charge*, 20 JOURNAL OF ECONOMIC PERSPECTIVES 157 (2006).

109. *See* Nicholas Confessore, $8 Traffic Fee for Manhattan Fails in Albany, N.Y. TIMES, Apr. 8, 2008, at A1; Ted Mann, *Advocate Finds Tolls a Tough Sell*, WALL STREET JOURNAL, March 22, 2012, at A17. *See also* William Neuman, Many Hurdles, Legal and Political, to Bridge Tolls, N.Y. TIMES, Dec. 7, 2008, at A47.

110. *See, e.g.*, Richard L. Brodsky, An Inquiry Into Congestion Pricing As Proposed in PlaNYC 2030 and S.6068 (July 9, 2007), available *regti.me/b-report* (case sensitive); MICHAEL J. SANDEL, WHAT MONEY CAN'T BUY: THE MORAL LIMITS OF MARKETS (2012).

111. A 2006 EPA report found that 7,095 communities had implemented PAYT programs, covering over 25% of the U.S. population. A copy of the report is available at *regti.me/payt2006* (case sensitive). *See also* John E. Schneider et al., *Tobacco Litter Costs and Public Policy: A Framework and Methodology for Considering the Use of Fees to Offset Abatement Costs*, 20 TOBACCO CONTROL i36 (2011).

Solid Waste Management

9.10.1000 Collection agreement required.

A. No person shall engage in the business of collection of residential solid waste unless such person is authorized to do so pursuant to a collection agreement then existing between such person and the city.

* * *

C. The city council may, by resolution, establish fees to be paid by persons engaged in the business of collection of residential solid waste. Such fees shall be for the privilege of engaging in such business within the city and shall be due and payable at such times and in such manner as determined by the council.

* * *

9.10.1040 Solid waste collection setouts.

No owner of any residential premises and no generator of solid wastes generated at residential premises shall set out solid wastes for collection, nor shall any such owner or generator permit the set-out of solid wastes at any residential premises in such owner's or generator's possession or control, except in accordance with the provisions of this part.

9.10.1050 Garbage containers permitted.

A. No owner of a single-family dwelling and no generator of any solid waste generated at such premises shall set out garbage for collection except in a container meeting one of the following descriptions:

1. A wheeled garbage disposal cart provided by the city or by the city's authorized residential solid waste collector, which together with its contents does not exceed the following weight limits:

    a. Eighty pounds for a cart with a capacity of twenty gallons;

    b. One hundred pounds for a cart with a capacity of thirty-two gallons;

    c. One hundred seventy-five pounds for a cart with a capacity of sixty-four gallons; or

    d. Two hundred fifty pounds for a cart with a capacity of ninety-six gallons.

2. A plastic garbage disposal bag approved by the city or by the city's authorized residential solid waste collector, which together with its contents does not exceed a weight of sixty pounds.

B. No owner of a multifamily dwelling and no generator of any solid waste generated at such premises shall set out garbage for collection except in a container meeting one of the following descriptions:

* * *

1. A wheeled garbage disposal cart provided by the city or by the city's authorized residential solid waste collector, whose contents do not exceed a weight of one hundred pounds for each thirty-two gallons of capacity.

2. A garbage disposal bin provided by the city or by the city's authorized residential solid waste collector.

3. A garbage disposal bin provided by the multifamily dwelling owner or management which meets specifications approved by the director [of environmental services].

* * *

9.10.1100 Placement of solid waste.

* * * No person shall keep any garbage container, nor permit any garbage container to remain, in the street or upon the public parkway except during the period from noon on the day preceding the scheduled collection day to noon on the day immediately following collection.

9.10.1120 Residential source reduction and recycling fee.

* * * Each residential solid waste generator in the city shall pay a source reduction and recycling fee as set forth in the schedule of fees adopted by resolution of the city council. * * *

San Jose has several schedules of "garbage rates" that the City Council updates periodically.[112] For example, as of early 2012, the rates for single-family homes were:

---

112. A guide for the 2012 rates is available at *regti.me/SJ–RP2011* (case sensitive).

Collection Service	Monthly Rate Effective August 1, 2011
Garbage	
* Monthly fees are represented here. Your bill statement reflects a 2-month billing period.	
20-gallon cart	$28.23
32-gallon cart	$29.95
64-gallon cart	$59.90
96-gallon cart	$89.85
Extra Garbage Sticker	$6.25 each
Recycling	
Any size cart (32-, 64-, 96-gallon)	Included with garbage fee
Yard Trimmings	
Subscription cart (optional) Any size cart (32-, 64-, 96-gallon)	$4.35/month
Loose in the street	Included with garbage fee
Large Items (e.g., tires, furniture)	
Up to 3 large items Call 535-3500 for more information and to set up a collection appointment	$25.00
On-Premise Collection	
20-gallon cart	$89.23
32-gallon cart	$90.95
64-gallon cart	$120.90
96-gallon cart	$150.85
Household Hazardous Waste	
Call the County at 299-7300 to schedule a free drop-off appointment	Free

Questions

1. In the process of creating a PAYT program, San Jose established strict standards for how waste can be set out. Individuals lost their freedom of choice and no longer can use their garbage container of their liking. Was this particular interference with preferences (or intrusion upon liberty) necessary? Why?

2. The business of waste collection has not always been regulated. Can we expect municipal-waste-collection markets to be efficient? How would waste collection services be priced in a free market?

§ 9.3 QUALITY AND OTHER STANDARDS

The discussion of price regulation can also serve as the basis for the analysis of standard setting of all other properties of products and services. The problems and characteristics of price regulation tend to appear in properties.

Bread Standardization

Should the government tell us what sizes of bread we can buy? Should bakeries and consumers have the liberty to choose the sizes and weights of loaves of bread? Some may argue that government standardization of weights of loaves of bread "abridges the right * * * to manufacture loaves of bread of such size or weight as [bakers] may deem most salable; * * * places a limitation upon the capacity * * * to carry on a lawful business; [and] is not within the police powers of the state."[113] Others argue that "[t]he police power of a state is not confined to regulations looking to the preservation of life, health, good order, and decency," and can be used for "any reasonable preventive remedy when the frequency of * * * frauds, or the difficulty experienced by individuals in circumventing them, is so great that no other means will prove efficacious."[114] In other words, when uniform standards reduce transaction costs and compensate for inadequate information, they may also be used as means to reduce fraud, deception, and confusion.

In Chicago, an "immemorial custom" obligated bakers to sell a 16–ounce loaf of bread for 5¢. In late 1907, the City Council considered standardizing the weights of loaves of bread. The weight of a 5¢ loaf of bread sold in the City ranged from 12 to 16 ounces, although consumers expected to receive 16–ounce loaves. Consumers felt deceived about the "short weight" bread. The City Council indeed had received hundreds of complaints about short-weight loaves.

In defense of the so-called short-weight loaves, the City bakers argued that they "should be allowed to meet the fluctuations in the price of flour and labor by varying the size of the loaves," but that "it was impossible to raise the price."[115] Mathias Schmidinger, the President of the Master Baker's Association, fought aggressively and vigorously against the ordinance for the members of his trade. In addressing the City Council, he warned them about the potential consequences of regulating bread:

> We don't want to deceive the people, and we don't. We don't sell a pound of bread. We sell a 5 cents worth of bread, and we give as good quality as we can and as much of it as we can for 5 cents.

---

113. People v. Wagner, 86 Mich. 594 (1891) (summarizing arguments against an ordinance that regulated weights of loaves of bread).

114. *Id.* (upholding the constitutionality of an ordinance that regulates loaves of bread).

115. *Court Will Test Bread Ordinance*, CHICAGO DAILY TRIBUNE, Dec. 18, 1907, at 5.

> People don't buy bread by weight. They buy it by 5 cents worth. * * * [I]f a sixteen ounce standard is fixed by law, up goes the price to 6 cents, and the people won't stand for it.[116]

The Aldermen were unsure about the constitutionality of the proposed ordinance. Some of them believed that it would be "futile" and that the best the City could accomplish "by regulation [was] the labeling of the loaves to indicate to the purchaser how much bread he is getting for 5 cents."[117] The Council and the bakers, therefore, reached a compromise: The Council passed the ordinance agreeing that the bakers would test it in court. Mathias Schmidinger, on behalf of the bakers, won in the Illinois Circuit Court. For the court, Judge Windes wrote: "There can be no question that [this ordinance] deprives manufacturers of bread of their right under the constitutional provisions to contract for the sale of bread of different sizes."[118] The Illinois Supreme Court reversed,[119] and Schmidinger continued to the U.S. Supreme Court.

Schmidinger v. Chicago

226 U.S. 578 (1913)

■ MR. JUSTICE DAY delivered the opinion of the court:

The City of Chicago instituted suit against the plaintiff in error * * * to recover penalties for certain violations of an ordinance of that city. The [alleged] violations * * * [refer to] the making and selling of loaves of bread differing in weight from the weights prescribed by the ordinance. * * *

The ordinance in question, passed January 6, 1908, undertakes to regulate the sale of bread in the loaf within the City of Chicago, and the parts pertinent to the present case provide:

> **SECTION 2.** Every loaf of bread made or procured for the purpose of sale, sold, offered or exposed for sale, in the City of Chicago, shall weigh a pound avoirdupois (except as hereinafter provided), and such loaf shall be considered to be the standard loaf of the City of Chicago. Bread may also be made or procured for the purpose of sale, sold, offered or exposed for sale, in half, three-quarter, double, triple, quadruple, quintuple, or sextuple loaves, and in no other way. Every loaf of bread made or procured for the purpose of sale, sold, offered or exposed for sale, in the city, shall have affixed thereon in a conspicuous place a label at least 1 inch square, or, if round, at least 1 inch in diameter, upon which label there shall be printed in plain type . . . the weight of the loaf in pound, pounds, or fraction of a pound avoirdupois, whether the loaf be a standard

116. *16 Ounces, 6 Cents; Say City Bakers*, CHICAGO DAILY TRIBUNE, Dec. 11, 1907, at 9.

117. *Court Will Test Bread Ordinance*, *supra* note 115.

118. *Bread Ordinance Invalid; Limits Right of Contract*, CHICAGO DAILY TRIBUNE, May 28, 1908, at 11.

119. City of Chicago v. Schmidinger, 243 Ill. 167 (1909).

> loaf or not. The business name and address of the maker, baker, or manufacturer of the loaf shall also be printed plainly on each label.
>
> **SECTION 3**. Every maker, baker, or manufacturer of bread, every proprietor of a bakery or bakeshop, and every seller of bread in the City of Chicago, shall keep scales and weights, suitable for the weighing of bread, in a conspicuous place in his bakery, bakeshop, or store, and shall, whenever requested by the buyer, and in the buyer's presence, weigh the loaf or loaves of bread sold or offered for sale.
>
> **SECTION 4**. If any person, firm, or corporation shall make or procure for the purpose of sale, sell, offer or expose for sale, within the City of Chicago . . . any bread the loaf or loaves of which are not standard * * * as defined in § 2 of this ordinance, * * * or any bread the loaf or loaves of which do not have affixed thereon the label marked as hereinbefore provided, contrary to the provisions of this ordinance, such person, firm, or corporation shall be fined not less than $10 nor more than $100 for each offense.
>
> **SECTION 5**. The provisions of this ordinance . . . shall not apply to . . . what is commonly known as 'stale bread,' sold as such, provided the seller shall, at the time of sale, expressly state to the buyer that the bread so sold is stale bread.

The objections of a Federal character arise from alleged violations of the Fourteenth Amendment to the Constitution of the United States. The plaintiff in error avers that * * * the ordinance is an unreasonable and arbitrary exercise of the police power, and constitutes an unlawful interference with the freedom of contract included in the protection secured to the individual under that Amendment. * * *

At the hearing the plaintiff in error introduced testimony which tended to establish the following facts: There are between 800 and 1,000 bakers in the City of Chicago, together making about 50 per cent of the bread consumed in that city. Bread is sold in Chicago in large quantities at certain prices per loaf, 95 per cent of the bread made by the bakers, outside of the restaurant business, consisting of loaves sold for 5 cents or multiples thereof, and 85 per cent of such bread being sold for 5 cents a loaf. The 5–cent loaf weighs about 14 ounces when baked, and the weight of the bread in the loaf varies and is adjusted in accordance with the fluctuations in the price of raw material, labor, and other elements of expense of production, and the different qualities of bread, and as a result of competition. There is a considerable demand in Chicago, especially in the restaurant trade, for bread in weights differing from those fixed by the ordinance. In some parts of the city bread weighing 7 pounds is commonly sold. The moisture in the bread after it leaves the oven causes very appreciable shrinkage in weight, the extent of which depends upon the quality and size of the loaf, the atmospheric condition, and the dryness and temperature of the place where kept. It appears that, in order to insure bread of the standard weight of 16 ounces, it is necessary to scale the dough before baking at about 20 ounces.

The record also shows that although the price of bread sold by the loaf in Chicago has generally been 5 cents or some multiple thereof, loaves of bread weighing approximately 1 pound have been sold for 5, 6, and 7 cents at different times.

The right of state legislature or municipalities acting under state authority to regulate trades and callings in the exercise of the police power is too well settled to require any extended discussion. * * *

The making and selling of bread, particularly in a large city, where thousands of people depend upon their supply of this necessary of life by purchase from bakers, is obviously one of the trades and callings which may be the subject of police regulation. This general proposition is conceded by counsel for plaintiff in error, but it is contended that the limitation of the right to sell bread which this ordinance undertakes to make in fixing a standard loaf of 16 ounces and other half, three-quarter, double, triple, quadruple, quintuple, or sextuple loaves, is such an unreasonable and arbitrary exercise of legislative power as to render it unconstitutional and void. This court has frequently affirmed that the local authorities intrusted with the regulation of such matters, and not the courts, are primarily the judges of the necessities of local situations calling for such legislation, and the courts may only interfere with laws or ordinances passed in pursuance of the police power where they are so arbitrary as to be palpably and unmistakably in excess of any reasonable exercise of the authority conferred. * * *

Furthermore, laws and ordinances of the character of the one here under consideration, and tending to prevent frauds, and requiring honest weights and measures in the sale of articles of general consumption, have long been considered lawful exertions of the police power. *McLean v. Arkansas*, 211 U.S. 539 (1909). * * * Laws prescribing standard sizes of loaves of bread, and prohibiting, with minor exceptions, the sale of other sizes, have been sustained in the courts of Massachusetts and Michigan. *Commonwealth v. McArthur*, 152 Mass. 522 (1890); *People v. Wagner*, 86 Mich. 594 (1891).

It is contended, however, that there are special circumstances in this case that take it out of this rule. The record shows, as we have already said, that the loaf of bread most largely sold in Chicago costs 5 cents, and when it reaches the consumer is generally 14 ounces in weight; and it is urged that to make a loaf of the standard size of 1 pound, as required by the ordinance, would be extremely inconvenient at least, owing to changes and evaporation after the loaf is baked, and that to insure a loaf of full standard size it would be necessary to use 20 ounces of dough. But inconveniences of this kind do not vitiate the exercise of legislative power. The local legislature is presumed to know what will be of the most benefit to the whole body of citizens. Evidently, the council of the City of Chicago has acted with the belief that a full pound loaf, with the variations provided, would furnish the best standard. It has not fixed the price at which bread may be sold. It has only prescribed that the standard weight must be found in the loaves of the sizes authorized. To the argument that to make exactly 1 pound loaves is extremely difficult, if not impracticable, the supreme court of Illinois has answered, and this construction is binding upon us, that the ordinance is not intended to limit the weight of a loaf to a pound or the fractional part or multiple of a pound, but that the ordinance was passed with a view only to prevent the sale of loaves of bread which are short in weight. Thousands of transactions in bread in the City of Chicago are with people who buy in small quantities, perhaps a loaf at a time, and, exercising the judgment which the law imposed in it, the council has passed an ordinance to require such people to be sold loaves of bread of full weight. We cannot say that the fixing of these standards in the exercise of the legislative discretion of the council is such an unreasonable and arbitrary exercise of the police power. * * *

It is further urged that this ordinance interferes with the freedom of contract guaranteed by the Fourteenth Amendment, for it is said that there is a demand for loaves of bread of sizes other than those fixed in the ordinance, which demand exists among many people and also among contractors whose business requires special sizes to be made for them. This court has had frequent occasion to declare that there is no absolute freedom of contract. The exercise of the police power fixing weights and measures and standard sizes must necessarily limit the freedom of contract which would otherwise exist. Such limitations are constantly imposed upon the right to contract freely, because of restrictions upon that right deemed necessary in the interest of the general welfare. So long as such action has a reasonable relation to the exercise of the power belonging to the local legislative body, and is not so arbitrary or capricious as to be a deprivation of due process of law, freedom of contract is not interfered with in a constitutional sense. * * *

Questions

1. Sections 2 and 3 of the Chicago Ordinance required labeling of all loaves and keeping "scales and weights, suitable for the weighing of bread, in a conspicuous place" available for all consumers. What was the purpose of these requirements?

2. If short-weight loaves presented a problem in Chicago, why did consumers not demand bakers to disclose the weight of loaves? If the short-weight loaves presented an economic problem, one may argue that they also created economic opportunities for entrepreneurial bakers. Why such bakers did not emerge?

3. Nobel laureate Thomas Schelling observed that "[t]here is of course a strong sentiment against antibusiness regulation. There is apprehension, not always unjustified, that when government intrudes into a field of production it bodes ill for the companies intruded on. This attitude may not have much to do with profits: people don't like, or pretend not to like, being told what to do. One is provoked to wonder * * * whether government regulation is quiet menacing as it is seen to be." Schelling pointed out that "[a] 'responsible' firm can wish to comply with some social standards but refuse to adopt them unilaterally while its competitors ignore them." Thus, he argued, that "standards, once adopted by all, may not always turn out to be onerous. Often measures that perforce increase business costs * * * turn out to be neutral or even beneficial in relation to business profits."[120]

---

120. THOMAS C. SCHELLING, *Command and Control* 27, 51 in CHOICES AND CONSEQUENCES (1984).

(a) Does the standardization of loaves of bread fit the dynamics described by Schelling? (b) What is a "responsible firm"? To which social standards should firms adhere? (c) Why may firms ever be reluctant to unilaterally adopt standards, if universally adopted would be neutral or beneficial? (d) How could a Chicago baker in the early twentieth century benefit from disclosing the weights of the loaves she sold?

Water Fluoridation

Can the government mandate that individuals purchase and use particular products? Standard setting may entail such a requirement. Mandatory vaccines, for example, fit this description. Waste collection programs also tend to be mandatory: A person cannot always opt out from the local program because she is not interested in purchasing the offered waste collection services. Fluoride is a supplement that states and localities choose to add to water, effectively mandating that local residents pay for the fluoride through their taxes and receive fluoridated water. Fluoridation, a government-mandated medical supplement, directly conflicts with some interpretations of the "right to be let alone" and the inalienable right to the pursuit of happiness.[121] This is one practical meaning of government standard setting.

At the end of 1999, the Centers for Diseases Control and Prevention (CDC) announced the "Ten Great Public Health Achievements" in the United States during the twentieth century. The ninth great achievement was fluoridation of drinking water to prevent dental caries. Empirical evidence unequivocally showed that fluoridation of community drinking water was "a major factor responsible for the decline in dental caries (tooth decay) during the second half of the 20th century."[122] In January 2011, the Department of Health and Human Services (HHS) and the Environmental Protection Agency (EPA) announced "new scientific assessments and ac-

---

121. For the "right to be let alone" *see* Olmstead v. United States, 277 U.S. 438, 478 (1928) (Brandeis, J., dissenting), § 2.3.2. For the right to the pursuit of happiness *see* § 2.2.1 (Sidebars 2–1, 2–2).

122. *See Fluoridation of Drinking Water to Prevent Dental Caries*, 48 MORBIDITY & MORTALITY WEEKLY REPORT 933 (Oct. 22, 1999).

tions on fluoride,"[123] and lowered their recommendation for fluoride concentration in drinking water.[124]

Since 1945, local governments in the United States have added fluoride to drinking water to prevent cavities.[125] The CDC estimated that at the end of 2010, 66.2% of the entire American population received fluoridated water. 73.9% of the population receiving water from public water systems received fluoridated water. However, in the wake of the Great Recession, financial problems of localities and hostility toward regulation led quite a few localities to eliminate fluoridation programs.[126]

Excessive amount of fluoride intake causes enamel fluorosis. Yet, the benefits of supplementing water with fluoride have dwarfed all such potential costs any accidents if such happen.[127] Since the 1940s, however, water fluoridation has been a source of bitter controversy. The fluoridation opponents argue that fluoridation violates the individual's right to informed consent to medication and make numerous medical claims about fluoridation.[128]

Paduano v. City of New York

Supreme Court, New York County, New York
257 N.Y.S.2d 531 (1965)

■ JOSEPH A. BRUST, JUSTICE.

In this action wherein plaintiffs, as taxpayers, seek to enjoin * * * the proposed program for the fluoridation of the municipal water supply of New York City. * * *

The fluoridation program proposed for this City was formally authorized by a new section 141.08, of the New York City Health Code enacted by the New York City Board of Health on April 7, 1964, which provides as follows:

---

123. U.S. Department of Health and Human Services & Environmental Protection Agency, HHS and EPA Announce New Scientific Assessments and Actions on Fluoride, Press Release, Jan. 7, 2011. *See also* Timothy W. Martin, *Government Advises Less Fluoride in Water*, WALL STREET JOURNAL, Jan. 8–9, 2011, at A3.

124. U.S. Department of Health and Human Services, Proposed HHS Recommendation for Fluoride Concentration in Drinking Water for Prevention of Dental Caries, 76 Fed.Reg. 2383 (Jan. 13, 2011).

125. *See* H. ALLAN FREEZE & JAY H. LEHR, THE FLUORIDE WARS (2009).

126. *See, e.g.*, Lizette Alvarez *Looking to Save Money, More Places Decide to Stop Fluoridating the Water*, N.Y. TIMES, Oct. 14, 2011, at A20.

127. *See, e.g.*, NATIONAL RESEARCH COUNCIL, FLUORIDE IN DRINKING WATER: A SCIENTIFIC REVIEW OF EPA'S STANDARDS (2006); Herschel S. Horowitz, *The Effectiveness of Community Water Fluoridation in the United States*, 56 JOURNAL OF HEALTH DENTISTRY 253 (1996); Ernest Newburn, *What We Know and Do Not Know About Fluoride*, 70 JOURNAL OF HEALTH DENTISTRY 227 (2010).

128. *See generally* FREEZE & JAY H. LEHR, THE FLUORIDE WARS, *supra* note 125.

Section 141.08 Fluoridation of public water supply

> The public water supply of the city of New York shall be fluoridated in the following manner:
>
> A fluoride compound shall be added which will provide in such water supply a concentration of approximately 1.0 part per million of the fluoride ion, provided, however, that the concentration of such ion shall not exceed 1.5 parts per million.

This amendment was filed with the City Clerk of the City of New York on April 7, 1964 and took effect on that date in accordance with the provisions of Section 558 of the New York City Charter.

The authority of the Board of Health to act in this general area is derived from Sections 555–558 of the New York City Charter. Section 558, subdivision a, provides that the New York City Health Code 'shall have the force and effect of law.'

While the New York City Sanitary Code (the predecessor of the present City Health Code, which superseded the Sanitary Code as of October 1, 1959) was in effect, it was repeatedly declared that the Sanitary Code and amendments thereto, had the force of state law. * * *

The power of the Board to enact provisions for the furtherance and protection of health has long been established as a constitutional exercise of power (*Metropolitan Board of Health v. Heister*, 37 N.Y. 661 (1868) * * *).

Article 17, Section 3, of the State Constitution, effective January 1, 1939, provides:

> The protection and promotion of the health of the inhabitants of the state are matters of public concern and provision therefor shall be made by the state and by such of its subdivisions and in such manner, and by such means as the legislature shall from time to time determine.

Concerning this provision, it is stated in the revised record of the 1938 Constitutional Convention, * * * that it was to validate the police power as then 'practiced in the State of New York' and, when applied to public health, such police power is not merely the power to restrain and regulate the use of property, but is rather 'a constructive program for the promotion of positive health.'

* * *

Regardless of its validity, the fluoridation program is obviously directed towards the 'security of the life and health' of the citizens of New York City, and is an attempt to cope with the serious and growing public health problem of tooth decay and dental neglect, particularly among children. To hold otherwise would require a finding that fluoridation, regardless of its merits, is a measure which has no direct bearing on a public health problem. Adopting plaintiffs' substantive arguments at face value arguendo, the most that could be said is that there is a strong difference of opinion as to the value of fluoridation and that it may not be the best means of attacking the problem of tooth decay and dental neglect. However the problem still remains fundamentally one of health and is therefore within the jurisdiction of the New York City Department of Health.

This Court finds that the aforementioned new Section 141.08 of the New York City Health Code offends no public policy of this State, contravenes no prevailing State statute or municipal ordinance and is not in excess of the Health Department's power. * * *

[Another] cause of action is based on plaintiffs' allegations and contentions (a) that other methods of reducing tooth decay are available; (b) that fluoridation is discriminatory in that it allegedly benefits children only; (c) that fluoridation unlawfully imposes medication on plaintiffs against their will; and finally, (d) that fluoridation 'is or may be' dangerous to health. Plaintiffs also contend, in an affidavit submitted herein by a non-party, that the religious freedom of certain groups in the community will be unconstitutionally impaired by fluoridation. However, no such allegation is set forth in the complaint and, accordingly, this issue is not properly before this court at this time. This court may only concern itself with the issues raised by the pleadings.*

Plaintiffs allege, in effect, on the basis of these contentions, that the city's fluoridation program violates the privileges and immunities clause of the Fourteenth Amendment to the Federal Constitution and also the New York State Constitution, Article I, Section 1, the equal protection clauses of both constitutions, and the due process clause of the Fourteenth Amendment to the United States Constitution. Finally, plaintiffs also claim that the city's fluoridation program violates the New York City Public Health Law in that the city allegedly lacks the power to add any substance to its water supplies which is not related to prevention of waterborne disease or maintenance of the purity and potability of such water supplies.

Both parties hereto have submitted a mass of documentary evidence attesting to the point of view advanced by each as to the beneficial or possibly detrimental nature of fluoridation. * * * It has already been noted that the Board of Health has the power to, and did, act in legislative capacity under State legislative authority. It is not disputed that the matter of tooth decay and dental neglect among 500,000 of the City's children presents a growing public health problem. * * * The record discloses that 48,000,000 people in the United States and Canada have been consuming municipally fluoridated water for years without any substantial evidence of harm to health and that 7,000,000 additional people in this country have, for generations, consumed naturally fluoridated waters with a content similar to, or greater than, the one-part-per-million level contemplated for New York City also without any verified harm to health.

Fluoridation as a public health practice has been exercised in the United States for almost twenty years. It is not disputed that dental caries affect a substantial percentage of our population, particularly the more disadvantaged who are not disposed or able to undertake programs of proper dental care. It is also clear that fluoridation is effective in combatting dental caries among the young, and its effects last through adulthood. Fluoridation of the water supply is also the most efficacious, probably the

---

* It appears that the allegation of infringement of religious liberty has been determined adversely in other courts and that those determinations, in effect, were affirmed by the United States Supreme Court in its dismissal of the appeal on *Kraus v. Cleveland*, 163 Ohio St. 559 (1955). * * *

cheapest, and may be the only practical method of insuring the administration of this drug to the very young.

Plaintiffs assert that other means are available whereby fluorides may be provided for those desirous of using them. But the question before this Court is solely whether the means proposed herein are lawful. The existence of other possible remedies is not relevant. * * * In *Jacobson v. Massachusetts*, 197 U.S. 11 (1905), it was stated:

> Since ... vaccination, as a means of protecting a community against smallpox, finds strong support in the experience of this and other countries, no court, much less a jury, is justified in disregarding the action of the legislature simply because in its or their opinion that particular method was—perhaps, or, possibly—not the best either for children or adults.

As to plaintiffs' claim that fluoridation is discriminatory for it benefits children only, all that need be said is, that in the usual course, children become adults and that fluoridation will, commencing with the date of its adoption, ultimately affect all.

Plaintiffs lay special emphasis upon 'individual liberty' and the compulsive aspect of municipal fluoridation in shrinking this area. In support of this, plaintiffs quote from *Jacobson v. Massachusetts*, wherein the Supreme Court held constitutional a regulation requiring vaccination, as follows:

> There is, of course, a sphere within which the individual may assert the supremacy of his own will, and rightfully dispute the authority of any human government—especially of any free government existing under a written constitution, to interfere with the exercise of that will.
>
> However, this Court also stated:
>
> But it is equally true that in every well-ordered society charged with the duty of conserving the safety of its members the rights of the individual in respect to his liberty may at times, under the pressure of great dangers, be subjected to such restraint, to be enforced by reasonable regulations, as the safety of the general public may demand.

The Court of Appeals of this State similarly upheld the propriety and constitutionality of a vaccination statute (*Viemeister v. White*, 179 N.Y. 235 (1904)), stating:

> When the sole object and general tendency of legislation is to promote the public health, there is no invasion of the Constitution, even if the enforcement of the law interferes to some extent with liberty or property.

It is true that the issues presented in the aforementioned *Jacobson* and *Viemeister* cases involved communicable infectious diseases and did not involve a disease such as dental caries, which admittedly is not a communicable infectious disease. At the worst, if unchecked, dental caries can cause a degeneration of the physical condition of the individual, but its effect upon society generally is, at its best, quite indirect. * * *

As far as this court can determine, the highest courts of our State and of the United States have not yet decided whether a State, in the proper exercise of the police power, can force individuals to take medication in these non-contagious diseases which are not extremely debilitating to the individual concerned and which can be prevented by other readily available and inexpensive means. Some have argued that in so doing, the government is confusing expediency with obligation, and stepping out of a role of protector of the individual's rights, to one as arbiter of them. They assert that if this right of the State is upheld, it may equally interdict the use of tobacco, alcohol or rich foods, and introduce into the water supply aspirin to prevent headaches, or any other drug that may be developed in the future to prevent any type of disease, such as allergies, etc. It should be here noted that if the condition attacked were in the nature of an 'adult' disease, rather than, as in the instant case, one where the treatment, to be efficacious, must be given to the very young, different considerations would be present. However, the health of our children is a legitimate area of public and governmental concern, whether under the police power of the State, or in the exercise of the State's power to protect the general welfare. It is not shocking to realize that the State, acting in the interest of children, too young to be *sui juris*, may intervene in the parental area.

This question has been presented to the highest courts of several other states and it has been universally held that fluoridation does not unconstitutionally invade the rights of the citizens. * * * [T]he approach of the courts has been to uphold fluoridation if it could be found that fluoridation was a reasonable method of preventing a widespread detrimental health condition which the executive or legislative branches of the government believed desirable to treat. In effect, the courts have therefore generally held that their review of fluoridation measures are subject to the same limitations as to scope that exist in the customary review of administrative actions. It should also be noted at this point that the United States Supreme Court has either dismissed appeals or denied certiorari in cases which squarely presented as the primary or sole question for review the constitutionality of fluoridation of a water supply. * * * While denials of certiorari do not constitute decisions on the merits, it is clear that the Supreme Court has repeatedly held that no substantial Federal questions are presented by objections to fluoridation.

The question of the desirability of fluoridation is immaterial. In the face of the overwhelming precedents * * *, and in accordance with general principles of *stare decisis*, this court sitting at Special Term, feels constrained to deny plaintiffs' application for a temporary injunction and to grant defendants' motion for a dismissal of the complaint. Until the scientific evidence as to the deleterious effects of fluoridation reaches beyond the purely speculative state now existing, decisional law mandates the holding that the controversy should remain within the realm of the legislative and executive branches of government. While the courts do not have a right to impose fluoridation upon anyone, judicial restraint requires us to adhere to the uniform decision holding that the executive and legislative branches of government do—at least until some proof is adduced that fluoridation has harmful side effects and therefore is not in the interests of the community. In so holding, the Court is aware that no truly applicable analogy exists in other areas of judicially approved government-mandated action. In other cases, where the citizenry is mandated to do something primarily for the benefit of the individual citizen and with at most an indirect effect on society generally, alternatives are usually provided for those members of the public who do not wish to submit themselves to such requirements. For example, the case of compulsory education with the alternative of sending a child to private school comes to mind. This Court is also aware that if such harmful effects become evident in the future, almost by definition, damage will have already befallen those forced to partake of fluoridated water by the action herein upheld. However, courts are traditionally, and with good cause, reluctant to act until the harm threatened becomes real, evident, and imminent.

For the reasons above noted, the plaintiffs' motion for temporary injunction is denied, and defendants' cross motion to dismiss the complaint is granted.

Coshow v. Escondido

Court of Appeal, Fourth District, Division 1, California
132 Cal.App.4th 687 (2005)

■ HALLER, JUDGE.

Paul Coshow and several other residents of Escondido, California (collectively Coshow) sued the City of Escondido (City) and the California Department of Health Services (Department) for declaratory and injunctive relief, challenging the City's plan to fluoridate its drinking water with hydrofluorosilicic acid (HFSA) and claiming the use of HFSA violates their constitutional rights and exposes the general public to unnecessary health risks. * * *

[W]e conclude Coshow cannot state a cause of action for violations of fundamental constitutional rights or a violation of Penal Code section 374.8. * * *

FACTUAL AND PROCEDURAL BACKGROUND

City operates a community water system serving about 130,000 people through nearly 25,000 service connections. In June 2001, City directed its staff to implement a fluoridation plan in compliance with the California Safe Drinking Water Act (SDWA) * * *, which requires fluoridation of each public water system having at least 10,000 service connections. * * *

In September 2001, Coshow filed a complaint for declaratory relief, alleging City's plan to fluoridate its water was unconstitutional and illegal because mass fluoridation of the water supply presents a reasonable certainty of harm to City's residents, including permanent dental scarring, genetic damage, cancer and other ailments. [After a lengthy battle, the court] concluded as a matter of law that Coshow failed to state causes of action for declaratory or injunctive relief.

DISCUSSION

* * *

III

Coshow Cannot State a Cause of Action for Declaratory or Injunctive Relief Based on a Violation of a Fundamental Constitutional Right

Coshow contends he stated a cause of action for violation of a fundamental constitutional right by alleging City's conduct of dumping dangerous levels of arsenic into the public water supply severely and negatively impacts his bodily integrity and that of every other citizen served by City's water supply. He asserts he is being forced, without his consent, to drink the municipal water containing a drug—HFSA—that has never been tested or approved by the FDA to treat dental caries and which is dangerous to his health and the health of other residents.

A

The Safe Drinking Water Act and Its Implementing Regulations

Congress enacted the Safe Drinking Water Act (federal SDWA) (42 U.S.C., § 300f *et seq.*) in 1974 to establish uniform quality standards for the public water systems in the United States and to reduce contamination in drinking water. The federal SDWA prohibits states from enacting drinking water laws less stringent than those established by the Environmental Protection Agency (EPA). * * *

In 1976, the Legislature enacted California's SDWA, declaring water delivered by public water systems in this state should be at all times pure, wholesome and potable, and adopting procedures to be followed in an effort to accomplish this objective. * * * The SDWA was meant to reduce to the lowest level feasible all concentrations of toxic chemicals in drinking water that may cause cancer, birth defects and other chronic diseases. * * * In this regard, the SDWA "establishes standards at least as stringent as the federal SDWA and is intended to be 'more protective of public health' than the minimum federal standards." (*Hartwell Corp. v. Superior Court*, 27 Cal. 4th 256 (2002). Because the SDWA is a remedial act intended to protect the public from contamination of its drinking water, we are required to construe it broadly to accomplish its protective purpose. * * *

In the SDWA, the Legislature delegated to Department "the initial and primary authority, and the corresponding responsibility, for establishing drinking water standards. * * * Courts must respect this primary delegation of authority." * * * One of Department's responsibilities under the SDWA is to establish "primary drinking water standards that include the maximum levels of contaminants which, in [its] judgment, may have an adverse effect on the health of persons." * * * Department is also responsible for reviewing and revising public health goals for contaminants in drinking water, including preparing health risk assessments for any contaminants deemed carcinogenic or acutely toxic. * * * With respect to acutely toxic substances, the maximum contaminant level (MCL) is set at a level that will avoid any known or anticipated adverse effects on public health with an adequate margin of safety. (Cal. Health & Safety Code § 116365(a)(1)). With respect to carcinogens, the MCL is set at a level that will avoid any risk to public health. (Cal. Health & Safety Code § 116365(a)(2)). * * *

Effective September 29, 1996, Section 116410 was added to the SDWA, requiring public water systems with at least 10,000 service connections to be fluoridated "to promote the public health of Californians of all ages through the protection and maintenance of dental health, a paramount issue of statewide concern." (§ 116410 (a)). This provision requires Department to adopt regulations mandating the fluoridation of public water systems. * * *

Although fluoridation has been and continues to be a controversial issue, "[c]ourts through[out] the United States have uniformly held that fluoridation of water is a reasonable and proper exercise of the police power in the interest of public health. * * * The matter is no longer an open question." (*Beck v. City Council of Beverly Hills*, 30 Cal. App. 3d 112 (Ct. App. 1973); see also *De Aryan v. Butler*, 119 Cal. App. 2d 674 (1953) (addition of fluoride to water supply, as directed by resolution of city council, was valid exercise of police power of City of San Diego)).

The *manner* of fluoridation, challenged by Coshow in this case, is also prescribed by the SDWA and its implementing regulations, which mandate the concentration of fluoride in drinking water supplied to the public. * * * For example, the regulations adopted by Department set forth the optimal fluoride levels based on daily air temperatures. * * * Additionally, the regulations contain extensive monitoring and compliance requirements * * * and impose stringent record-keeping, reporting and notification requirements for fluoridating water systems. * * * Although the SDWA and its implementing regulations provide specific mechanisms to ensure the drinking water is safe for all consumers, including City's residents, the water need not be completely free of contaminants for which there are MCL's and detection limits. "While pure water is an objective of the state, statutory and regulatory standards do not require that water be entirely pure; and few, if any, water supplies are entirely clear of a broad range of contaminants. * * * " (*Western States Petroleum Association v. Department of Health Services*, 99 Cal. App. 4th 999 (2002). Before a particular chemical is added to drinking water as part of the treatment process, it must first be tested and certified as meeting the specifications of the American National Standard Institute/National Sanitation Foundation Standard 60 (ANSI/NSF 60). * * * HFSA meets this standard as an approved chemical additive under the regulations, and Coshow does not claim otherwise. * * * Thus, the statutory and regulatory schemes allow fluoridating agents, including HFSA, to contain contaminants (such as arsenic and lead) as long as those agents comply with MCL's and detection limits.

B

City's Choice of HFSA as a Fluoridation Agent is a Legislative Function

* * * Coshow contends he [is] entitled to a declaratory judgment that City's admitted conduct of "discharging arsenic into the water," through

the use of HFSA as required and approved by Department, violates his fundamental constitutional rights. Regardless of how Coshow frames his argument, his objection is, in essence, to the particular chemical chosen to comply with the legislatively mandated fluoridation plan. However, that choice necessarily involved a determination and weighing of facts and policies pertaining to fluoridation of water supplies. "This is a distinctively legislative process, and a court does not have the authority to exercise its independent judgment with respect to the performance of legislative functions." * * *

The record shows Coshow sued City in September 2001 after it directed its staff to implement a fluoridation plan. * * * Coshow initially challenged the constitutionality of fluoridation in general, but when unsuccessful on that ground, Coshow's lawsuit evolved into a challenge to the particular fluoridation chemical used (HFSA). * * *

Coshow Cannot State a Claim for Violation of the Right to Privacy or Bodily Integrity

In an attempt to state a cause of action for declaratory and injunctive relief based on a constitutional violation, Coshow characterizes City's fluoridation plan as "forced medication" with potential adverse consequences to human health, or with a chemical that has not been approved by the FDA for such medicinal purposes, thereby implicating his fundamental rights to bodily integrity and privacy under the Ninth and Fourteenth Amendments to the United States Constitution and * * * the California Constitution. He claims the right to be free from forced medication contaminated with arsenic is a fundamental one, requiring strict scrutiny review.

1. No fundamental constitutional right is involved here

The guarantee of due process of law includes a substantive component which prohibits the government from infringing on certain "fundamental" liberty interests unless the infringement is narrowly tailored to serve a compelling state interest. * * * Only rights " 'deeply rooted in this Nation's history and tradition' " and " 'implicit in the concept of ordered liberty' " are recognized as fundamental. * * *

Coshow alleges City's use of HFSA to fluoridate the public drinking water violates his fundamental right "to preserve [his] health from such government-imposed practices as may prejudice or annoy it." However, given this vague and general assertion of a fundamental liberty interest, we must heed the Supreme Court's advice against expanding "the concept of substantive due process because guideposts for responsible decisionmaking in this unchartered area are scarce and open-ended." (*Collins v. Harker Heights*, 503 U.S. 115 (1992)). When we view the asserted right in the factual context of this case, it is evident Coshow is seeking to establish a right to public drinking water of a certain quality or, more specifically, a right to drinking water uncontaminated with HFSA.

In determining whether this right is fundamental, we do not compare its "relative societal significance" to other public entitlements, nor do we consider whether public drinking water free of HFSA is as important a right as any other constitutionally protected right. * * * Rather, we assess whether there is such a right "explicitly or implicitly guaranteed by the Constitution." * * * We conclude no such fundamental right exists.

* * *

2. *Fluoridation using HFSA is not forced medication*

Coshow contends he is being forced, without his consent, to drink the municipal water containing a drug which has never been tested or approved by the FDA to treat dental caries and which is dangerous to his health and the health of other residents because of the high levels of arsenic in HFSA. He asserts the use of municipal water as the drug delivery system is forced medication in violation of his constitutional rights.

"[A] competent adult has the right to refuse medical treatment, even treatment necessary to sustain life." * * * However, the right to be free from forced medication is not a fundamental constitutional right in the context of adding fluoride or other chemicals to public drinking water. City's use of HFSA to fluoridate its drinking water does not *force* Coshow to do anything. Fluoridation occurs before it enters each household and stops with the water faucet. The HFSA in the water is not directly introduced into Coshow's or other residents' bloodstreams. Because Coshow is not compelled to drink the fluoridated water, his freedom to choose not to ingest HFSA remains intact. * * *

The statutes and regulations requiring fluoridation of public water supplies as a means of combating dental caries is a valid exercise of the state's police power with respect to public health. In this regard, chemicals, which in their concentrated or basic state may be poisonous, are often introduced into water for the purpose of purification or to protect and preserve health. * * * When used in an extensively regulated fluoridation program which complies with the SDWA, Department ensures the type and amount of any chemicals introduced into the public water supply are not impure or dangerous to the public. We presume Department will act properly and perform its duty to ensure "the condition of the water, as ultimately distributed, is one of purity and potability." * * * Thus, introducing chemicals such as HFSA into the public drinking water does not constitute an infringement of the constitutional right of privacy to be free from forced medication.

* * *

V

City's Use of HFSA, as Approved by Department, Was Not an Illegal Expenditure of Public Funds

In his fourth amended complaint, Coshow unsuccessfully sought injunctive relief against City on the ground its use of HFSA to fluoridate the drinking water is an illegal expenditure of public funds because it violates Penal Code section 374.8. That statute creates criminal penalties for any person who knowingly causes any hazardous substance to be deposited into the waters of the state. (Pen.Code, § 374.8(b)). * * *

Here, City's exercise of its police power to fluoridate the water using HFSA cannot constitute illegal conduct. * * *

The judgment is affirmed.

Questions

1. What types of standards do fluoridation plans involve?

2. How did the *Paduano* and *Coshow* courts address concerns regarding paternalism, slippery slopes, cost-benefit analysis, and the "right to be let alone"?

3. 40 years separated *Paduano* and *Coshow*. Long before *Padunano*, many courts strongly rejected arguments against the constitutionality of fluoridation. The arguments have not changed much during the 40 years that followed *Pandunano*, and numerous courts rejected them. Does a failure of standards facilitate or accommodate the repeat lawsuits against fluoridation?

CHAPTER 10

INFORMATION REGULATION

"[T]here is little quarrel with governmental efforts to help consumers obtain necessary information when the information is in fact needed and the intervention lowers the cost of providing it."

—Stephen Breyer[1]

§ 10.1 INFORMATION AND BELIEFS

The performance of markets and society depends on the adequacy of information people have, and their ability to make good decisions. Information regulation is a particular type of government standard setting.[2] Through bans, quality, uniform, and compatibility standards, the state acts to improve and suppress information in markets and society. Information regulation, however, is not a cure for every information inadequacy. First, inadequate information may motivate regulation, but in itself cannot justify any regulation;[3] rather, it is the availability of cost-effective regulatory measures that may justify regulation.[4] Second, information regulation does not always provide effective means to address inadequate information; rather, other regulatory methods provide simple solutions to informational problems.

To illustrate some of the issues, consider the problem of short-weight bread in the early twentieth century.[5] In most major cities, bakers were selling 5¢ loaves, adjusting the size in response to "the fluctuations in the price of flour and labor," and other things. Consumers felt deceived since the 5¢ bread was regarded as a 16–ounce loaf, although loaves often weighed as little as 12 ounces. In a world of perfect information, the short-weight problem would not have existed. At the turn of the twentieth century, localities addressed the informational problem in the bread market by standardizing the sizes of bread, mandating labeling, and requiring scales in "a conspicuous place" at every point of sale. The key feature of the solution—standardization of loaf weight—was *not* a form of information regulation. It regulated properties of bread, not properties of information.

---

1. STEPHEN BREYER, REGULATION AND ITS REFORM 28 (1982).

2. For standard setting *see* § 9.1.

3. *See generally* Alan Schwartz & Louis L. Wilde, *Intervening in Markets on the Basis of Imperfect Information: A Legal and Economic Analysis*, 127 UNIVERSITY OF PENNSYLVANIA LAW REVIEW 630 (1979).

4. *See* §§ 1.6 (cost-benefit analysis), II.0 (motivations vs. justifications).

5. *See* Bread Standardization, § 9.3. *See also* Timothy Messer–Kruse, *The Crusade for Honest Weight: The Origins of an Overlooked Progressive Movement*, 5 JOURNAL OF THE GILDED AGE AND PROGRESSIVE ERA 241 (2006). Materials about the short-weight bread problem are available at *regti.me/sw-bread* (case sensitive).

Other features of the solution—the requirements for standardized labeling and scales—were forms of information regulation. They intended to reduce costs associated with communicating information about the size of bread, including the costs of fraud.

Information regulation, therefore, is not always the instrument used to address inadequate information. When the state utilizes information regulation, it deploys measures of *centralized information regulation* and *decentralized information regulation*. Centralized measures refer to (1) control of the state over the production of information, and (2) suppression of information. For example, the Center for Disease Control and Prevention (CDC) produces information regarding health risks and relies on market institutions, such as media and physicians, to disseminate this information to the public. Similarly, the U.S. Food and Drug Administration (FDA) regulates tobacco warnings. It defines the specifications of the warnings tobacco companies must print on products and include in advertisements.[6] By contrast, the state also promulgates laws that suppress information or allow private parties to suppress information. Examples of such regulations we have already discussed include liability for fraud,[7] anti-cartoon laws,[8] prohibitions against advertising of retail alcohol prices,[9] restrictions on advertising of legal brothels,[10] the FCC's indecency policy,[11] and movie censorship.[12]

Decentralized measures, in turn, refer to standardization of information produced by private entities. Here, the state does not produce or dictate the information; rather, it sets standards that define the form in which the information should be provided and sometimes impose disclosure duties. For example, the 1908 Chicago bread ordinance required bakers to "affix[ ] * * * in a conspicuous place [on the bread] a label at least 1 inch square, or, if round, at least 1 inch in diameter, upon which label there shall be printed in plain type * * * the weight of the loaf * * * [and] whether the loaf be a standard loaf or not." Similarly, the 2007 federal minimum efficiency standards for light bulbs were supplemented with new labeling requirements for light bulbs.[13]

But even when information is available, bounded rationality may impede the ability to process it, as demonstrated by our discussion of the minimum efficiency standards for light bulbs. The entrenched habit of using energy units (watts) to evaluate light emitted from light bulbs, led consumers to continue using incandescent light bulb and kept them away

---

6. 10. U.S.C. § 654 (repealed).

7. *See* § 5.2.

8. *See* § 2.4.2a.

9. *See* 44 Liquormart, Inc. v. Rhode Island, 517 U.S. 484 (1996); § 7.3.2.

10. *See* Coyote Publishing, Inc. v. Miller, 598 F.3d 592 (9th Cir. 2010); § 7.3.2.

11. *See* Fox Television Stations, Inc. v. Federal Communications Commission, 613 F.3d 317 (2d Cir. 2010); § 1.4.

12. *See* Tennessee Movie Rating Law, Tenn. Code Ann. § 39–17–907; § 1.4; Block v. Chicago, 239 Ill. 251 (1909); § 8.2.2.

13. *See* Federal Trade Commission, Appliance Labeling Rule, 16 C.F.R. 305 (July 19, 2010); the Incandescent Light Bulb, § 8.1.

from efficient light bulbs—their use of energy is relatively low (measured in watts) and consumers did not appreciate units of brightness (lumens). The federal minimum efficiency standards intended to overcome this impediment, while using the opportunity of transition to change the public informational references. To a large extent, the vocal battle against these efficiency standards reflected a combination of disregard and misunderstanding of information. Materials about the light bulb controversy are available at *regti.me/l-bulb* (case sensitive).

Thus, when we consider the use of information and knowledge in society, we should keep in mind realistic human constraints.[14] Specifically, the ability to process complex information—including complex disclosures—is limited and varies substantially in the population. Information tends to be effective when it is embedded in everyday decisionmaking routines, such as bread shopping, and less effective when it is embedded in infrequent procedures, such as light bulb purchases. Moreover, people tend to see in information what they want and expect to see,[15] and often argue strongly for positions they are unwilling to or cannot evaluate.[16] Francis Bacon, John Stuart Mill, and many other thinkers addressed this point in their writing.[17] Friedrich Hayek famously framed it as follows:

> *If* we possess all the relevant information, *if* we can start out from a given system of preferences and *if* we command complete knowledge of available means, the problem which remains is purely one of logic.[18]

Put simply, regulation of information cannot always accomplish its goals, because of the constraints on rational decisionmaking.

The general principles of information regulation are as follows. First, decentralization of knowledge and information is necessary for informed decisions and for timely "adaptation to changes in the particular circumstances of time and place."[19] Second, information regulation should be deployed to help individuals to obtain adequate information through stan-

---

14. *See* Michael J. Fishman & Kathleen M. Hagerty, *Mandatory Versus Voluntary Disclosure in Markets with Informed and Uninformed Customers*, 19 JOURNAL OF LAW, ECONOMICS & ORGANIZATION 45 (2003); Douglas Gale, *Spoiled for Choice: Variety and Efficiency in Markets with Incomplete Information*, 51 RESEARCH IN ECONOMICS 41 (1997); Howard Latin, *"Good" Warnings, Bad Products, and Cognitive Limitations*, 41 UCLA LAW REVIEW 1193 (1994); David Weil et al., *Effectiveness of Regulatory Disclosure Policies*, 25 JOURNAL OF POLICY ANALYSIS & MANAGEMENT 155 (2006).

15. *See, e.g.*, Albert H. Hastorf & Hadley Cantril, *They Saw a Game: A Case Study*, 49 JOURNAL OF ABNORMAL & SOCIAL PSYCHOLOGY 129 (1954); John Heil, *Seeing Is Believing*, 19 AMERICAN PHILOSOPHICAL QUARTERLY 229 (1982); Dan Lovallo & Daniel Kahneman, *Delusions of Success: How Optimism Undermines Executives' Decisions*, 81(7) HARVARD BUSINESS REVIEW 56 (July 2003); Raymond S. Nickerson, *Confirmation Bias: A Ubiquitous Phenomenon in Many Guises*, 2 REVIEW OF GENERAL PSYCHOLOGY 175 (1998); Neil D. Weinstein, *Unrealistic Optimism About Future Life Events*, 39 JOURNAL OF PERSONALITY & SOCIAL PSYCHOLOGY 806 (1980).

16. *See, e.g.*, Hugo Mercier & Dan Sperber, *Why Do Humans Reasons? Arguments for an Argumentative Theory*, 34 BEHAVIOR & BRAIN SCIENCE 57 (2011).

17. *See* § 2.1.

18. F.A. Hayek, *The Use of Knowledge in Society*, 35 AMERICAN ECONOMIC REVIEW 519, 519 (1945).

19. Hayek, *The Use of Knowledge in Society*, *supra* note 18.

dard setting, rather than used as a "central planning" or "thought control" instrument.[20] Third, state provision of information may be efficient in very limited circumstances, when the markets fail to produce valuable information and the state can cost-effectively produce such information.[21] Fourth, state investments in production of valuable information are necessary. Absent state support in R & D, arts, and education, the level of information produced in society would be suboptimal.[22] Fifth, certain categories of information warrant suppression. Examples include fraud, misrepresentations, invasion of privacy, libel, child pornography incitement, fighting words, national secrets, and trade secrets.

Our goal in this Chapter is to understand the distinction between centralized and decentralized information regulation.

Personal Hygiene

Lewis M. Terman, *Social Hygiene: The Real Conservation Problem*, 198 NORTH AMERICAN REVIEW 404 (1913).

The prevention of waste promises to become the dominant issue of our entire political and industrial situation. * * * The popular notions of personal hygiene [however] are little better than a seething welter of ignorance and superstition, not all of which is confined to the confessedly uneducated. To the average person, certainly, the phenomena of life, growth, decay, and death are still strange mysteries. In popular superstition various disease entities have replaced the numerous spirit entities of old as irrational forces with which man is doomed to wage blind and uncertain combat.

The cost of this ignorance in money, sickness, death, and grief is stupendous. Basing his estimate upon statistics of mortality for ninety different diseases and accepting the expert opinion of numerous medical specialists as to the ratio of preventability for these diseases, Professor Irving Fisher has reckoned that the general adoption of a few well-established hygienic principles would add fifteen years to the average span of human life.† For the most part these fifteen lost years would be years of economic productivity. It is evident that every premature death entails an economic loss upon society, varying according to the age of the person

---

20. *See, e.g.*, Howard Beales et al., *The Efficient Regulation of Consumer Information*, 24 JOURNAL OF LAW & ECONOMICS 491 (1981); Colin Camerer et al., *Regulation for Conservatives: Behavioral Economics and the Case for "Asymmetric Paternalism,"* 151 UNIVERSITY OF PENNSYLVANIA LAW REVIEW 1211, 1212 (2003); Hayek, *The Use of Knowledge in Society*, *supra* note 18; Cass R. Sunstein & Richard H. Thaler, *Libertarian Paternalism Is Not an Oxymoron*, 70 UNIVERSITY OF CHICAGO LAW REVIEW 1159 (2003). *See also* American Booksellers Association, Inc. v. Hudnut, 771 F.2d 323, 328 (7th Cir. 1985) (Easterbrook, J.) (striking down a pornography ordinance, describing its purpose as "thought control.").

21. *See* § 3.1.2c (public goods).

22. *See generally* Kenneth Arrow, *Economic Welfare and the Allocation of Resources for Invention*, in THE RATE AND DIRECTION OF INVENTIVE ACTIVITY: ECONOMIC AND SOCIAL FACTORS 609 (Richard R. Nelson ed. 1962).

† [Referring to IRVING FISHER, ECONOMIC ASPECT OF LENGTHENING HUMAN LIFE (1909)—BYO.]

dying. * * * But this is not half the story of waste. For each unnecessary death there are several cases of unnecessary illness, the total cost of which, counting medical attention and wages lost, amounts to about one billion dollars more. * * * America's leading prophet of personal hygiene believes that it is within the power of the average individual to double his economic efficiency by better methods of living and working.[††] Apart from this we suffer an aggregate calculable loss from preventable illness and death of at least two billion dollars per year, or nearly four times the sum spent for public education. * * *

Waste of life or health, far more than waste of the earth's natural resources, involves grief and moral suffering of a kind not commensurable with gold. * * * Whatever advances bacteriology may make, this needless slaughter will continue little abated unless the new generation is educated to a different hygienic viewpoint. There is no other agency that can perform the function of the public school in this respect. The time is at hand for the school to make a nation-wide campaign for the hygienic enlightenment of the young.

In December 1913, a few months after the publication of Terman's article, together with a notable physician, Eugene Fisk, Professor Irving Fisher founded *the Life Extension Institute* "on the basis of a self-sustaining philanthropy" to "maintain a central clearinghouse of information regarding hygiene and how to live." Philanthropists, business leaders, and eminent scientists backed the Institute with capital and ideological support. Former President William Taft, who eight years later would become the Chief Justice of the United States Supreme Court, served as a Chairman of the Board of Directors of the Institute.[23] The Institute engaged in aggressive advocacy activities, including advertisements in major newspapers.[24]

Fisher and Fisk also co-authored, a book entitled, *How to Live*, whose purpose, they wrote, was "to spread knowledge of *Individual Hygiene* and thus to promote the aims of the Life Extension Institute * * *: (1) to provide the individual and the physician with the latest and best conclusions on individual hygiene; (2) to ascertain the exact and special needs of

†† [Today, Professor Fisher's work is credited for contributing to the increased productivity and longevity in the United States during the twentieth century. *See* William D. Nordhaus, *Irving Fisher and the Contribution of Improved Longevity to Living Standards*, 64 AMERICAN JOURNAL OF SOCIOLOGY & ECONOMICS 367 (2005). On October 23, 1929, a few days before the stock market crash of 1929 Irving Fisher made a famous statement: "Stock prices have reached what looks like a permanently high plateau." Nevertheless, contemporary economists argue that he "experienced the fate of a prophet." *See* William J. Barber, *Irving J. Barber of Yale*, 64 AMERICAN JOURNAL OF SOCIOLOGY & ECONOMICS 43 (2005).—BYO.]

23. *See Has Sweeping Plan to Lengthen Lives*, THE SUN, Dec. 30, 1913, at 6; *National Society to Conserve Life*, N.Y. TIMES, Dec. 30, 1913, at 2; *The Life Extension Institute*, N.Y. TIMES, Dec. 31, 1913, at 8. Resources related to the Board of Directors and Hygiene Reference Board of the Institute are available at *regti.me/Life-EI* (case sensitive).

24. Examples of advertisements of the Institute are available at *regti.me/LEI-ads* (case sensitive). For the Institute and its mission *see* Helen Zoe Veit, *"Why Do People Die?" Rising Life Expectancy, Aging and Personal Responsibility*, 45 JOURNAL OF SOCIAL HISTORY 1026 (2012).

the individual through periodic health examinations; (3) to induce all persons who are found to be in need of medical attention to visit their physicians."[25] The book was an instant best seller and kept selling new prints for over a decade. Some of the ideas in the book extend well beyond personal hygiene. For example, in the last chapter dedicated to eugenics, Fisher and Fisk expressed their support in sterilization, a view that was within the mainstream norm at the time.[26] True to their dedication to information, Fisher and Fisk advocated the advantages of eugenics and proper education:

> Certain races of men, without consciousness of their action, have varied in the character of their choices (sex selection) in such a way as to bring about varied conditions in their races, with respect to resistance to disease, of mental capacity and to moral quality. The Mongolian differs from the Hebrew, the Anglo–Saxon differs from the African. It depends largely upon the action of those now upon the earth, who are now making their choices of marriage, as to whether the races of the future shall be physical, mental or moral weaklings, or whether they shall be physically brave and hardy, mentally broad and profound, and morally sterling.
>
> To summarize: There are three main lines along which eugenic improvement of the race may be attained: (1) Education of all people on the inheritability of traits; (2) segregation of defectives so that they may not mingle their family traits with those on sound lines; (3) sterilization of certain gross and hopeless defectives, to preclude the propagation of their type.

The significance Fisher and Fisk attributed to this issue is reflected in the book's closing conclusion: "There would seem to be great need of State Eugenic Boards, to correlate and to promote these activities, in the interests of the future population, and to give expert advice as to how to legislate wisely, and individual advice as to how to mate wisely."[27] Eugene Fisk died unexpectedly in his early sixties. In the summer of 1931, on his way to the Museum of Hygiene in Dresden, he collapsed and passed away a few days later. Cause of death: cerebral hemorrhage.[28]

Questions

1. Is personal hygiene a consequence of rational choices? Would adequate information induce people to make ideal decisions with respect to their personal hygiene? What is the ideal level of personal hygiene?

---

25. IRVING FISHER & EUGENE LYMAN FISK, HOW TO LIVE: RULES FOR HEALTHFUL LIVING BASED ON MODERN SCIENCE ix (1915).

26. *See, e.g.*, Buck v. Bell, 274 U.S. 200 (1927) (upholding the constitutionality of the Virginia Sterilization Act). Relying on *Jacobson v. Massachusetts*, 197 U.S. 11 (1905), in *Buck*, Justice Holmes concluded: "The principle that sustains compulsory vaccination is broad enough to cover cutting the Fallopian tubes. * * * Three generations of imbeciles are enough." *See* PAUL A. LOMBARDO, THREE GENERATIONS, NO IMBECILES: EUGENICS, THE SUPREME COURT, AND BUCK V. BELL (2008).

27. FISHER & FISK, HOW TO LIVE, *supra* note 25, at 323–324.

28. *See* Veit, *Why Do People Die?*, *supra* note 24.

2. Personal hygiene is a risk factor that influences longevity and quality of life. Empirical evidence shows that people who maintain low levels of personal hygiene tend to take risks that other people are less likely to take, such as smoking and no-use of seatbelts.[29] During the 1910s, when Professor Terman published his article and the Life Extension Institute was founded, regulation of personal hygiene became prevalent. Many states outlawed the public drinking cup and banned spitting in public.[30] (a) Was the purpose of personal hygiene education to warn individuals about risky choices? (b) Should the state engage in paternalistic regulation to enhance personal hygiene? (c) The principles Fisher and Fisk promoted led them to believe that State Eugenic Boards should give "individual advice as to how to mate wisely." Risks associated with many genetic diseases can be reduced thorough genetic counseling.[31] Is the proposal of Fisher and Fisk regarding State Eugenic Boards profoundly different from informing people about the significance of personal hygiene?

3. Professor Terman was a pioneer in educational psychology. In his article, Terman called for a "nation-wide campaign for the hygienic enlightenment of the young." Fisher and Fisk founded central private clearinghouse of information that intended to enlighten the entire nation. Why would state regulation be ever needed if private institutions can provide the public with information?

§ 10.2 CENTRALIZED INFORMATION REGULATION

Centralized information regulation may be efficient under certain circumstances. For example, when information has the characteristics of public good, markets may not produce it, and centralized information regulation may be needed. Information about foodborne outbreaks, epidemics, and general health risks falls into this category. Market institutions may have incentives to collect and disseminate such information, but such institutions do not exist. To illustrate the problem, consider the 2010 salmonella outbreak. CDC coordinates a national network of public health and food regulatory agency laboratories (PulseNet). During May and June 2010, CDC received several alerts about Salmonella Enteridis infections and identified several clusters of infections. In July 2010, using data from PulseNet, CDC identified a nationwide sustained increase in the number of Salmonella Enteridis outbreaks of a particular strain. CDC issued alerts and launched an investigation that identified three egg farms in Iowa as the source of the outbreak strain. Under pressure from the FDA, CDC, and the press, Wright County Egg, the company that owned the three egg farms, recalled more than half a billion eggs. From May 1 to November 30,

29. *See, e.g.*, Lisa R. Anderson & Jennifer M. Mellor, *Predicting health behaviors with an experimental measure of risk preference*, 27 JOURNAL OF HEALTH ECONOMICS 1260 (2008); Joni Hersch & W. Kip Viscusi, *Smoking and Other Risky Behaviors*, 28 JOURNAL OF DRUG ISSUES 645 (1998).

30. For the public drinking cup *see* § 3.2.1b (regulation of social diseases), § 8.1 (Figure 8.5). For the rise of anti-spitting laws *see* § 4.2.

31. *See, e.g.*, Muin J. Koury et al., *Population Screening in the Age of Genomic Medicine*, 348 NEW ENGLAND JOURNAL OF MEDICINE 50 (2003).

2010, a total of 3,578 illnesses were reported across the country. Market institutions cannot efficiently respond to outbreaks for the purpose of producing the relevant information.[32]

Centralized information regulation, however, may be overly used and misused. In the first place, the production of information should not be centralized. When it is centralized because of the characteristics of the market, then a natural monopoly may still be the superior option for the production of information. For example, *International News Service v. Associated Press*, 248 U.S. 215 (1918), involved the control over the production of international news during World War I. Obviously, the government should not control the production of news. Moreover, the state has the power to suppress information, through direct censorship, defunding programs and institutions, and other means. Centralized suppression of information may have negative consequences.

Advertising

In July 1919, Pennsylvania passed the following statute:

AN ACT

Prohibiting advertisements relating to the treatment of diseases of the generative organs, and prescribing penalties

SECTION 1. Be it enacted, etc., That it shall be unlawful for any person * * * to advertise, in any manner whatsoever, representing such person * * * as being engaged in the business or profession of treating diseases of the generative organs of either sex; and it shall be unlawful for any person * * * operating a printing establishment to insert such advertisement in any publication issued by such printing establishment.

SECTION 2. Any individual, or the members or agents of any [organization or corporation] or the officers or directors or agents of any corporation, violating the provisions of this act, shall be guilty of a misdemeanor, and, upon conviction, shall be sentenced to pay a fine not exceeding one thousand dollars, and to imprisonment for a period not exceeding one year.

Until 1977, professional advertising was frequently banned. Dentists, lawyers, ophthalmologist, and other professionals could not advertise their services.[33] In *Bates v. State Bar of Arizona*, 433 U.S. 350 (1977), the Supreme Court held that professional advertising that is not misleading falls within the scope of the First Amendment. Nevertheless, in *Coyote Publishing, Inc. v. Miller*, 598 F.3d 592 (9th Cir. 2010), the Ninth Circuit

---

32. A timeline of the CDC's work during the 2010 outbreak is available at *reg-ti.me/2010SE* (case sensitive).

33. *See, e.g.*, Semler v. Oregon State Board of Dental Examiners, 294 U.S. 608 (1935); Williamson v. Lee Optical of Oklahoma, 348 U.S. 483 (1955).

upheld the constitutionality of restrictions on advertising of legal brothels.[34]

Questions

1. Should the state regulate the advertising of any lawful businesses or occupations? Should the state ban the advertising of any lawful businesses or occupation?

2. Should the state ban the advertising of any lawful products?

3. Radar detectors are electronic devices used to detect whether law enforcement officials are monitoring a driver's speed. Their primary purpose is to undermine law enforcement. Should their advertising benefit from the protection of the First Amendment?

Education and the State

> *"There is no doubt as to the power of a State, having a high responsibility for education of its citizens, to impose reasonable regulations for the control * * * of basic education."*
>
> —Chief Justice Warren Burger[35]

Does academic freedom encompass the right of the state to impose constraints on knowledge in public schools to advance particular views and beliefs? Consider a 2010 Arizona statute relating to school curriculum.[36] The Arizona Legislature declared its purpose: "[P]ublic school pupils should be taught to treat and value each other as individuals and not be taught to resent or hate other races or classes of people."[37] To promote this goal, the statute provides that "[a] school district or charter school in this state shall not include in its program of instruction any courses or classes that include any of the following:"

1. Promote the overthrow of the United States government.
2. Promote resentment toward a race or class of people.
3. Are designed primarily for pupils of a particular ethnic group.
4. Advocate ethnic solidarity instead of the treatment of pupils as individuals.[38]

When the Arizona Governor signed the bill into law, her spokesman released a statement to the press saying: "Governor Brewer signed the bill because she believes, and the legislation states, that public school students

---

34. *See* § 7.3.2.

35. Wisconsin v. Yoder, 406 U.S. 205, 213 (1972).

36. School Curriculum, 2010 Ariz. Legis. Serv. Ch. 311 (H.B. 2281), available at *regti.me/AZ-HB2281* (case sensitive).

37. Ariz. Rev. Stat. Ann. § 15-111.

38. Ariz. Rev. Stat. Ann. § 15-112.

should be taught to treat and value each other as individuals and not be taught to resent or hate other races or classes of people."[39]

State regulation of public school curriculum is a centralized form of information regulation. In the famous *Scope* trial, Tennessee made it "unlawful for any teacher in any of the Universities, Normals and all other public schools of the state which are supported in whole or in part by the public school funds of the state, to teach any theory that denies the story of the divine creation of man as taught in the Bible and to teach instead that man has descended from a lower order of animals."[40] State laws that censor knowledge to preserve and promote ideologies and beliefs are common.

Edwards v. Aguillard

482 U.S. 578 (1987)

■ JUSTICE BRENNAN delivered the opinion of the Court.[†]

The question for decision is whether Louisiana's "Balanced Treatment for Creation–Science and Evolution–Science in Public School Instruction" Act (Creationism Act), La.Rev.Stat.Ann. §§ 17:286.1–17:286.7,[*] is facially invalid as violative of the Establishment Clause of the First Amendment.

I

The Creationism Act forbids the teaching of the theory of evolution in public schools unless accompanied by instruction in "creation science." § 17:286.4A. No school is required to teach evolution or creation science. If either is taught, however, the other must also be taught. * * * The theories of evolution and creation science are statutorily defined as "the scientific evidences for [creation or evolution] and inferences from those scientific evidences." §§ 17.286.3(2) and (3).

Appellees, who include parents of children attending Louisiana public schools, Louisiana teachers, and religious leaders, challenged the constitutionality of the Act in District Court, seeking an injunction and declaratory relief.[1] Appellants, Louisiana officials charged with implementing the Act, defended on the ground that the purpose of the Act is to protect a legitimate secular interest, namely, academic freedom. Appellees attacked the Act as facially invalid because it violated the Establishment Clause and made a motion for summary judgment. The District Court granted the motion. The court held that there can be no valid secular reason for

---

39. Tamar Lewin, *Citing Individualism, Arizona Tries to Rein in Ethnic Studies in School*, N.Y. TIMES, May 14, 2010, at A13.

40. *See* Scopes v. State, 154 Tenn. 105 (1927). *See also* EDWARD J. LARSON, SUMMER FOR GODS (1997).

† JUSTICE O'CONNOR joins all but Part II of this opinion.

* [A copy of the statute is available at *regti.me/LA-BTA* (case sensitive).—BYO.]

1. Appellants, the Louisiana Governor, the Attorney General, the State Superintendent, the State Department of Education and the St. Tammany Parish School Board, agreed not to implement the Creationism Act pending the final outcome of this litigation. The Louisiana Board of Elementary and Secondary Education, and the Orleans Parish School Board were among the original defendants in the suit but both later realigned as plaintiffs.

prohibiting the teaching of evolution, a theory historically opposed by some religious denominations. * * * We * * * affirm.

II

The Establishment Clause forbids the enactment of any law "respecting an establishment of religion." The Court has applied a three-pronged test to determine whether legislation comports with the Establishment Clause. First, the legislature must have adopted the law with a secular purpose. Second, the statute's principal or primary effect must be one that neither advances nor inhibits religion. Third, the statute must not result in an excessive entanglement of government with religion. * * * State action violates the Establishment Clause if it fails to satisfy any of these prongs.

In this case, the Court must determine whether the Establishment Clause was violated in the special context of the public elementary and secondary school system. States and local school boards are generally afforded considerable discretion in operating public schools. * * * The Court has been particularly vigilant in monitoring compliance with the Establishment Clause in elementary and secondary schools. Families entrust public schools with the education of their children, but condition their trust on the understanding that the classroom will not purposely be used to advance religious views that may conflict with the private beliefs of the student and his or her family. Students in such institutions are impressionable and their attendance is involuntary. * * *

Therefore, in employing the three-pronged * * * test, we must do so mindful of the particular concerns that arise in the context of public elementary and secondary schools. * * *

III

* * * True, the Act's stated purpose is to protect academic freedom. * * * This phrase might, in common parlance, be understood as referring to enhancing the freedom of teachers to teach what they will. The Court of Appeals, however, correctly concluded that the Act was not designed to further that goal. We find no merit in the State's argument that the "legislature may not [have] use[d] the terms 'academic freedom' in the correct legal sense. They might have [had] in mind, instead, a basic concept of fairness; teaching all of the evidence." * * * Even if "academic freedom" is read to mean "teaching all of the evidence" with respect to the origin of human beings, the Act does not further this purpose. The goal of providing a more comprehensive science curriculum is not furthered either by outlawing the teaching of evolution or by requiring the teaching of creation science.

A

It is clear from the legislative history that the purpose of the legislative sponsor, Senator Bill Keith, was to narrow the science curriculum. During the legislative hearings, Senator Keith stated: "My preference would be that neither [creationism nor evolution] be taught." * * * Such a ban on teaching does not promote—indeed, it undermines—the provision of a comprehensive scientific education.

It is equally clear that requiring schools to teach creation science with evolution does not advance academic freedom. The Act does not grant teachers a flexibility that they did not already possess to supplant the present science curriculum with the presentation of theories, besides evolution, about the origin of life. Indeed, the Court of Appeals found that no law prohibited Louisiana public school teachers from teaching any scientific theory. As the president of the Louisiana Science Teachers Association testified, "[a]ny scientific concept that's based on established fact can be included in our curriculum already, and no legislation allowing this is necessary." The Act provides Louisiana school teachers with no new authority. Thus the stated purpose is not furthered by it.

Furthermore, the goal of basic "fairness" is hardly furthered by the Act's discriminatory preference for the teaching of creation science and against the teaching of evolution.[7] While requiring that curriculum guides be developed for creation science, the Act says nothing of comparable guides for evolution. * * * Similarly, resource services are supplied for creation science but not for evolution. Only "creation scientists" can serve on the panel that supplies the resource services. The Act forbids school boards to discriminate against anyone who "chooses to be a creation-scientist" or to teach "creationism," but fails to protect those who choose to teach evolution or any other non-creation science theory, or who refuse to teach creation science.

If the Louisiana Legislature's purpose was solely to maximize the comprehensiveness and effectiveness of science instruction, it would have encouraged the teaching of all scientific theories about the origins of humankind. But under the Act's requirements, teachers who were once free to teach any and all facets of this subject are now unable to do so. Moreover, the Act fails even to ensure that creation science will be taught, but instead requires the teaching of this theory only when the theory of evolution is taught. Thus * * * the Act does not serve to protect academic freedom, but has the distinctly different purpose of discrediting "evolution by counterbalancing its teaching at every turn with the teaching of creationism."

B

* * * There is a historic and contemporaneous link between the teachings of certain religious denominations and the teaching of evolution.[9] It was this link that concerned the Court in *Epperson v. Arkansas*, 393 U.S. 97 (1968), which also involved a facial challenge to a statute regulating the teaching of evolution. In that case, the Court reviewed an Arkansas statute that made it unlawful for an instructor to teach evolution or to use a

7. The Creationism Act's provisions appear among other provisions prescribing the courses of study in Louisiana's public schools. These other provisions, similar to those in other States, prescribe courses of study in such topics as driver training, civics, the Constitution, and free enterprise. None of these other provisions, apart from those associated with the Creationism Act, nominally mandates "equal time" for opposing opinions within a specific area of learning. * * *

9. See McLean v. Arkansas Bd. of Ed., 529 F. Supp. 1255 (E.D. Ark. 1982) (reviewing historical and contemporary antagonisms between the theory of evolution and religious movements).

textbook that referred to this scientific theory. Although the Arkansas antievolution law did not explicitly state its predominant religious purpose, the Court could not ignore that "[t]he statute was a product of the upsurge of 'fundamentalist' religious fervor" that has long viewed this particular scientific theory as contradicting the literal interpretation of the Bible.[10] After reviewing the history of antievolution statutes, the Court determined that "there can be no doubt that the motivation for the [Arkansas] law was the same [as other anti-evolution statutes]: to suppress the teaching of a theory which, it was thought, 'denied' the divine creation of man." The Court found that there can be no legitimate state interest in protecting particular religions from scientific views "distasteful to them," * * * and concluded "that the First Amendment does not permit the State to require that teaching and learning must be tailored to the principles or prohibitions of any religious sect or dogma." * * *

These same historic and contemporaneous antagonisms between the teachings of certain religious denominations and the teaching of evolution are present in this case. The preeminent purpose of the Louisiana Legislature was clearly to advance the religious viewpoint that a supernatural being created humankind. The term "creation science" was defined as embracing this particular religious doctrine by those responsible for the passage of the Creationism Act. Senator Keith's leading expert on creation science, Edward Boudreaux, testified at the legislative hearings that the theory of creation science included belief in the existence of a supernatural creator. * * * Senator Keith also cited testimony from other experts to support the creation-science view that "a creator [was] responsible for the universe and everything in it." * * * The legislative history therefore reveals that the term "creation science," as contemplated by the legislature that adopted this Act, embodies the religious belief that a supernatural creator was responsible for the creation of humankind.

Furthermore, it is not happenstance that the legislature required the teaching of a theory that coincided with this religious view. The legislative history documents that the Act's primary purpose was to change the science curriculum of public schools in order to provide persuasive advantage to a particular religious doctrine that rejects the factual basis of evolution in its entirety. The sponsor of the Creationism Act, Senator Keith, explained during the legislative hearings that his disdain for the theory of evolution resulted from the support that evolution supplied to views contrary to his own religious beliefs. According to Senator Keith, the theory of evolution was consonant with the "cardinal principle[s] of religious humanism, secular humanism, theological liberalism, aetheistism [*sic*]." * * * The state senator repeatedly stated that scientific evidence supporting his religious views should be included in the public school curriculum to redress the fact that the theory of evolution incidentally coincided with what he characterized as religious beliefs antithetical to his own. The legislation therefore sought to alter the science curriculum to

10. The Court evaluated the statute in light of a series of antievolution statutes adopted by state legislatures dating back to the Tennessee statute that was the focus of the celebrated *Scopes* trial in 1925. * * * The Court found the Arkansas statute comparable to this Tennessee "monkey law." * * *

reflect endorsement of a religious view that is antagonistic to the theory of evolution.

In this case, the purpose of the Creationism Act was to restructure the science curriculum to conform with a particular religious viewpoint. Out of many possible science subjects taught in the public schools, the legislature chose to affect the teaching of the one scientific theory that historically has been opposed by certain religious sects. * * * [T]he Creationism Act is designed *either* to promote the theory of creation science which embodies a particular religious tenet by requiring that creation science be taught whenever evolution is taught *or* to prohibit the teaching of a scientific theory disfavored by certain religious sects by forbidding the teaching of evolution when creation science is not also taught. The Establishment Clause, however, "forbids *alike* the preference of a religious doctrine *or* the prohibition of theory which is deemed antagonistic to a particular dogma." * * * Because the primary purpose of the Creationism Act is to advance a particular religious belief, the Act endorses religion in violation of the First Amendment.

We do not imply that a legislature could never require that scientific critiques of prevailing scientific theories be taught. * * * But because the primary purpose of the Creationism Act is to endorse a particular religious doctrine, the Act furthers religion in violation of the Establishment Clause. * * *

V

The Louisiana Creationism Act advances a religious doctrine by requiring either the banishment of the theory of evolution from public school classrooms or the presentation of a religious viewpoint that rejects evolution in its entirety. The Act violates the Establishment Clause of the First Amendment because it seeks to employ the symbolic and financial support of government to achieve a religious purpose. The judgment of the Court of Appeals therefore is *Affirmed.*

■ JUSTICE POWELL, with whom JUSTICE O'CONNOR joins, concurring.

I write separately to note certain aspects of the legislative history, and to emphasize that nothing in the Court's opinion diminishes the traditionally broad discretion accorded state and local school officials in the selection of the public school curriculum.

I

* * *

A

* * * The Balanced Treatment for Creation–Science and Evolution–Science Act (Act or Balanced Treatment Act), * * * provides in part:

> [P]ublic schools within [the] state shall give balanced treatment to creation-science and to evolution-science. Balanced treatment of these two models shall be given in classroom lectures taken as a whole for each course, in textbook materials taken as a whole for each course, in library materials taken as a whole for the sciences

> and taken as a whole for the humanities, and in other educational programs in public schools, to the extent that such lectures, textbooks, library materials, or educational programs deal in any way with the subject of the origin of man, life, the earth, or the universe. When creation or evolution is taught, each shall be taught as a theory, rather than as proven scientific fact.

"Balanced treatment" means "providing whatever information and instruction in both creation and evolution models the classroom teacher determines is necessary and appropriate to provide insight into both theories in view of the textbooks and other instructional materials available for use in his classroom." § 17:286.3(1). "Creation-science" is defined as "the scientific evidences for creation and inferences from those scientific evidences." § 17:286.3(2). "Evolution-science" means "the scientific evidences for evolution and inferences from those scientific evidences." § 17:286.3(3).

Although the Act requires the teaching of the scientific evidences of both creation and evolution whenever either is taught, it does not define either term. * * * The "doctrine or theory of creation" is commonly defined as "holding that matter, the various forms of life, and the world were created by a transcendent God out of nothing." Webster's Third New International Dictionary 532 (unabridged 1981). "Evolution" is defined as "the theory that the various types of animals and plants have their origin in other preexisting types, the distinguishable differences being due to modifications in successive generations." * * * Thus, the Balanced Treatment Act mandates that public schools present the scientific evidence to support a theory of divine creation whenever they present the scientific evidence to support the theory of evolution. * * * From the face of the statute, a purpose to advance a religious belief is apparent.

A religious purpose alone is not enough to invalidate an act of a state legislature. The religious purpose must predominate. * * * The Act contains a statement of purpose: to "protec[t] academic freedom." § 17:286.2. This statement is puzzling. Of course, the "academic freedom" of teachers to present information in public schools, and students to receive it, is broad. But it necessarily is circumscribed by the Establishment Clause. "Academic freedom" does not encompass the right of a legislature to structure the public school curriculum in order to advance a particular religious belief. * * * Nevertheless, I read this statement in the Act as rendering the purpose of the statute at least ambiguous. Accordingly, I proceed to review the legislative history of the Act.

B

In June 1980, Senator Bill Keith introduced Senate Bill 956 in the Louisiana Legislature. The stated purpose of the bill was to "assure academic freedom by requiring the teaching of the theory of creation ex nihilo in all public schools where the theory of evolution is taught."[2] The

---

2. Creation "*ex nihilo*" means creation "from nothing" and has been found to be an "inherently religious concept." *McLean v. Arkansas Board of Education*, 529 F.Supp. 1255, 1266 (ED Ark. 1982). The District Court in McLean found:

bill defined the "theory of creation ex nihilo" as "the belief that the origin of the elements, the galaxy, the solar system, of life, of all the species of plants and animals, the origin of man, and the origin of all things and their processes and relationships were created ex nihilo and fixed by God." * * * This theory was referred to by Senator Keith as "scientific creationism." * * *

While a Senate committee was studying scientific creationism, Senator Keith introduced a second draft of the bill, requiring balanced treatment of "evolution-science" and "creation-science." * * * Although the Keith bill prohibited "instruction in any religious doctrine or materials," * * * defined "creation-science" to include

> "the scientific evidences and related inferences that indicate (a) sudden creation of the universe, energy, and life from nothing; (b) the insufficiency of mutation and natural selection in bringing about development of all living kinds from a single organism; (c) changes only within fixed limits or originally created kinds of plants and animals; (d) separate ancestry for man and apes; (e) explanation of the earth's geology by catastrophism, including the occurrence of a worldwide flood; and (f) a relatively recent inception of the earth and living kinds."

Significantly, the model Act on which the Keith bill relied was also the basis for a similar statute in Arkansas. See *McLean v. Arkansas Board of Education*, 529 F.Supp. 1255 (ED Ark. 1982). The District Court in *McLean* carefully examined this model Act, particularly the section defining creation science, and concluded that "[b]oth [its] concepts and wording ... convey an inescapable religiosity." *Id.*, at 1265. The court found that "[t]he ideas of [this section] are not merely similar to the literal interpretation of Genesis; they are identical and parallel to no other story of creation." *Ibid.*

The complaint in *McLean* was filed on May 27, 1981. On May 28, the Louisiana Senate committee amended the Keith bill to delete the illustrative list of scientific evidences. According to the legislator who proposed the amendment, it was "not intended to try to gut [the bill] in any way, or defeat the purpose [for] which Senator Keith introduced [it]," * * * and was not viewed as working "any violence to the bill." * * * Instead, the concern was "whether this should be an all inclusive list." *Ibid.*

The legislature then held hearings on the amended bill that became the Balanced Treatment Act under review. The principal creation scientist to testify in support of the Act was Dr. Edward Boudreaux. He did not elaborate on the nature of creation science except to indicate that the "scientific evidences" of the theory are "the objective information of science [that] point[s] to conditions of a creator." * * * He further testified that the recognized creation scientists in the United States, who "numbe[r]

"The argument that creation from nothing in [§] 4(a)(1) [of the substantially similar Arkansas Balanced Treatment Act] does not involve a supernatural deity has no evidentiary or rational support. To the contrary, 'creation out of nothing' is a concept unique to Western religions. In traditional Western religious thought, the conception of a creator of the world is a conception of God. Indeed, creation of the world 'out of nothing' is the ultimate religious statement because God is the only actor." *Id.*, at 1265.

something like a thousand [and] who hold doctorate and masters degrees in all areas of science," are affiliated with either or both the Institute for Creation Research and the Creation Research Society. * * * Information on both of these organizations is part of the legislative history, and a review of their goals and activities sheds light on the nature of creation science as it was presented to, and understood by, the Louisiana Legislature.

The Institute for Creation Research is an affiliate of the Christian Heritage College in San Diego, California. The Institute was established to address the "urgent need for our nation to return to belief in a personal, omnipotent Creator, who has a purpose for His creation and to whom all people must eventually give account." * * * A goal of the Institute is "a revival of belief in special creation as the true explanation of the origin of the world." Therefore, the Institute currently is working on the "development of new methods for teaching scientific creationism in public schools." * * * The Creation Research Society (CRS) is located in Ann Arbor, Michigan. A member must subscribe to the following statement of belief: "The Bible is the written word of God, and because it is inspired throughout, all of its assertions are historically and scientifically true." * * * To study creation science at the CRS, a member must accept "that the account of origins in Genesis is a factual presentation of simple historical truth."[3]

C

* * * My examination of the language and the legislative history of the Balanced Treatment Act confirms that the intent of the Louisiana Legislature was to promote a particular religious belief. * * * Whatever the academic merit of particular subjects or theories, the Establishment Clause limits the discretion of state officials to pick and choose among them for the purpose of promoting a particular religious belief. The language of the statute and its legislative history convince me that the Louisiana Legislature exercised its discretion for this purpose in this case.

II

Even though I find Louisiana's Balanced Treatment Act unconstitutional, I adhere to the view "that the States and locally elected school boards should have the responsibility for determining the educational policy of the public schools."

---

3. The District Court in McLean noted three other elements of the CRS statement of belief to which members must subscribe:

> " '[i] All basic types of living things, including man, were made by direct creative acts of God during Creation Week as described in Genesis. Whatever biological changes have occurred since Creation have accomplished only changes within the original created kinds. [ii] The great Flood described in Genesis, commonly referred to as the Noachian Deluge, was an historical event, world-wide in its extent and effect. [iii] Finally, we are an organization of Christian men of science, who accept Jesus Christ as our Lord and Savior. The account of the special creation of Adam and Eve as one man and one woman, and their subsequent Fall into sin, is the basis for our belief in the necessity of a Savior for all mankind. Therefore, salvation can come only thru (sic) accepting Jesus Christ as our Savior.' " * * *

[S]choolchildren can and should properly be informed of all aspects of this Nation's religious heritage. I would see no constitutional problem if schoolchildren were taught the nature of the Founding Fathers' religious beliefs and how these beliefs affected the attitudes of the times and the structure of our government. Courses in comparative religion of course are customary and constitutionally appropriate. In fact, since religion permeates our history, a familiarity with the nature of religious beliefs is necessary to understand many historical as well as contemporary events. In addition, it is worth noting that the Establishment Clause does not prohibit *per se* the educational use of religious documents in public school education. * * *

III

In sum, I find that the language and the legislative history of the Balanced Treatment Act unquestionably demonstrate that its purpose is to advance a particular religious belief. * * * Accordingly, I concur in the opinion of the Court and its judgment that the Balanced Treatment Act violates the Establishment Clause of the Constitution.

■ JUSTICE WHITE, concurring in the judgment.

As it comes to us, this is not a difficult case. Based on the historical setting and plain language of the Act both courts construed the statutory words "creation science" to refer to a religious belief, which the Act required to be taught if evolution was taught. In other words, the teaching of evolution was conditioned on the teaching of a religious belief. Both courts concluded that the state legislature's primary purpose was to advance religion and that the statute was therefore unconstitutional under the Establishment Clause. * * * I agree that the judgment of the Court of Appeals must be affirmed.

■ JUSTICE SCALIA, with whom THE CHIEF JUSTICE joins, dissenting.

Even if I agreed with the questionable premise that legislation can be invalidated under the Establishment Clause on the basis of its motivation alone, without regard to its effects, I would still find no justification for today's decision. The Louisiana legislators who passed the "Balanced Treatment for Creation–Science and Evolution–Science Act" (Balanced Treatment Act), * * * each of whom had sworn to support the Constitution, were well aware of the potential Establishment Clause problems and considered that aspect of the legislation with great care. After seven hearings and several months of study, resulting in substantial revision of the original proposal, they approved the Act overwhelmingly and specifically articulated the secular purpose they meant it to serve. Although the record contains abundant evidence of the sincerity of that purpose * * * the Court today holds, essentially on the basis of "its visceral knowledge regarding what *must* have motivated the legislators," * * * that the members of the Louisiana Legislature knowingly violated their oaths and then lied about it. I dissent. Had requirements of the Balanced Treatment Act that are not apparent on its face been clarified by an interpretation of the Louisiana Supreme Court, or by the manner of its implementation, the Act might well be found unconstitutional; but the question of its constitutionality cannot rightly be disposed of on the gallop, by impugning the motives of its supporters.

* * *

If one adopts the obviously intended meaning of the statutory term "academic freedom," there is no basis whatever for concluding that the purpose they express is a "sham." * * * To the contrary, the Act pursues that purpose plainly and consistently. It requires that, whenever the subject of origins is covered, evolution be "taught as a theory, rather than as proven scientific fact" and that scientific evidence inconsistent with the theory of evolution (viz., "creation science") be taught as well. * * * Living up to its title of "*Balanced Treatment* for Creation–Science and Evolution–Science Act," * * * it treats the teaching of creation the same way. * * *

We have * * * no adequate basis for disbelieving the secular purpose set forth in the Act itself, or for concluding that it is a sham enacted to conceal the legislators' violation of their oaths of office. I am astonished by the Court's unprecedented readiness to reach such a conclusion, which I can only attribute to an intellectual predisposition created by the facts and the legend of *Scopes v. State*, 154 Tenn. 105, 289 S.W. 363 (1927)—an instinctive reaction that any governmentally imposed requirements bearing upon the teaching of evolution must be a manifestation of Christian fundamentalist repression. In this case, however, it seems to me the Court's position is the repressive one. The people of Louisiana, including those who are Christian fundamentalists, are quite entitled, as a secular matter, to have whatever scientific evidence there may be against evolution presented in their schools, just as Mr. Scopes was entitled to present whatever scientific evidence there was for it. Perhaps what the Louisiana Legislature has done is unconstitutional because there is no such evidence, and the scheme they have established will amount to no more than a presentation of the Book of Genesis. But we cannot say that on the evidence before us. * * * Infinitely less can we say (or should we say) that the scientific evidence for evolution is so conclusive that no one could be gullible enough to believe that there is any real scientific evidence to the contrary, so that the legislation's stated purpose must be a lie. Yet that illiberal judgment, that *Scopes*-in-reverse, is ultimately the basis on which the Court's facile rejection of the Louisiana Legislature's purpose must rest.

* * *

Because I believe that the Balanced Treatment Act had a secular purpose, * * * I would reverse the judgment of the Court of Appeals and remand for further consideration. * * *

On June 25, 2008 Louisiana Governor Bobby Jindal signed into law the *Louisiana Science Education Act*.[41]

---

41. La. Rev. Stat. Ann. § 17:285.1.

Louisiana Science Education Act

AN ACT

To enact R.S. 17:285.1, relative to curriculum and instruction; to provide relative to the teaching of scientific subjects in public elementary and secondary schools; to promote students' critical thinking skills and open discussion of scientific theories; to provide relative to support and guidance for teachers; to provide relative to textbooks and instructional materials; to provide for rules and regulations; to provide for effectiveness; and to provide for related matters.

Be it enacted by the Legislature of Louisiana:

* * *

285.1. Science education; development of critical thinking skills

A. This Section shall be known and may be cited as the "Louisiana Science Education Act."

B. (1) The State Board of Elementary and Secondary Education, upon request of a city, parish, or other local public school board, shall allow and assist teachers, principals, and other school administrators to create and foster an environment within public elementary and secondary schools that promotes critical thinking skills, logical analysis, and open and objective discussion of scientific theories being studied including, but not limited to, evolution, the origins of life, global warming, and human cloning.

(2) Such assistance shall include support and guidance for teachers regarding effective ways to help students understand, analyze, critique, and objectively review scientific theories being studied, including those enumerated in Paragraph (1) of this Subsection.

C. A teacher shall teach the material presented in the standard textbook supplied by the school system and thereafter may use supplemental textbooks and other instructional materials to help students understand, analyze, critique, and review scientific theories in an objective manner, as permitted by the city, parish, or other local public school board unless otherwise prohibited by the State Board of Elementary and Secondary Education.

D. This Section shall not be construed to promote any religious doctrine, promote discrimination for or against a particular set of religious beliefs, or promote discrimination for or against religion or nonreligion.

* * *

Questions

1. Vaccines have made many diseases preventable. In 1954, two prominent members from the Department of Epidemiology at Harvard School of Public Health noted that "measles is as inevitable as death and taxes."[42]

---

42. Frank L. Babbot, Jr. & John E. Gordon, *Modern Measles*, 268 AMERICAN JOURNAL OF THE MEDICAL SCIENCES 361 (1954).

Developed in the late 1960s, the measles, mumps, and rubella (MMR) vaccination changed that and quickly became a standard childhood vaccine. In February 1998, a group of researchers, led by Dr. Andrew J. Wakefield, published in the prestigious medical journal *The Lancet* an article that linked the MMR vaccination to autism.[43] Although the article's methodology was questionable, it spurred a public scare. In the years that followed, epidemiological studies consistently found no evidence of a link between the MMR vaccine and autism. In January 2010, a Fitness to Practise Panel of the UK General Medical Council issued a judgment determining that the researchers had no evidence to support their claims. A few days later *The Lancet* retracted the 1998 article, stating: "Following the judgment of the UK General Medical Council's Fitness to Practise Panel, * * * it has become clear that several elements of the 1998 paper by Wakefield et al. are incorrect. * * * In particular, the claims in the original paper * * * have been proven to be false. Therefore we fully retract this paper from the published record."[44] Subsequently, the General Medical Council revoked Wakefield's medical license after a lengthy hearing, citing numerous ethical violations that tainted his work, such as failing to disclose financial interests.[45] The MMR vaccine scare created uncertainty regarding the safety of the MMR vaccine and vaccines in general, resulting in increased litigation, public campaigns, and some reduced use of vaccination.[46]

(a) Should the state suppress false scientific claims that create risks to people who believe them and others? (b) Can the state suppress any false claims?

2. In 2012, when this book was printed, the most common sexually transmitted infection in the United States and the major cause of cervical cancer was the human papillomavirus (HPV).[47] In June 2006, the FDA approved the use of a commercial HPV vaccine for females aged 9 to 26 years to prevent four common threads of HPV. Later that month, the Advisory Committee on Immunization Practices (ACIP) recommended routine vaccination of females aged 11 to 12 years.[48] In October 2011, ACIP

---

43. A. J. Wakefield et al., *Ileal-Lymphoid-Nodular Hyperplasia, Non-Specific Colitis, and Pervasive Developmental Disorder in Children*, 351 LANCET 637 (1998).

44. *Retraction*, 375 LANCET 445 (Feb. 6, 2010).

45. *See* Brian Deer, *How the Case Against the MMR Vaccine Was Fixed*, 342 BRITISH MEDICAL JOURNAL 77 (Jan. 8, 2011); *generally* Susan Dominus, *The Denunciation of Dr. Wakefield*, NEW YORK TIMES MAGAZINE, April 24, 2011, at 36.

46. *See generally* INSTITUTE OF MEDICINE, IMMUNIZATION, SAFETY REVIEW: VACCINES AND AUTISM (2004); KATHLEEN STRATTON, ADVERSE EFFECTS OF VACCINES: EVIDENCE AND CAUSALITY (2011). *See also* Cedillo v. Secretary of Health and Human Services, 617 F.3d 1328 (Fed. Cir. 2010); Bruesewitz v. Wyeth LLC, 131 S.Ct. 1068 (2011); Graves v. Secretary of Dept. of Health and Human Services, 2011 WL 3010753 (2011). *See also* Illana Ritov & Jonathan Baron, *Reluctance to Vaccinate: Omission Bias and Ambiguity*, 3 JOURNAL OF BEHAVIORAL DECISION MAKING 263 (1990).

47. *See generally* Anil K. Chaturvedi et al., *Human Papillomavirus and Rising Oropharyngeal Cancer Incidence in the United States*, 29 JOURNAL OF CLINICAL ONCOLOGY 4294 (2011).

48. *See generally* James Colgrove et al., *HPV Vaccination Mandates—Lawmaking Amid Political and Scientific Controversy*, 638 NEW ENGLAND JOURNAL OF MEDICINE 785 (2010); Barbara A. Slade et al., Postlicensure Safety Surveillance for Quadrivalent Human Papillomavirus Recombinant Vaccine, 302 JAMA 750 (2009); Win Techakehakij & Roger D. Feldman, *Cost-Effectiveness of HPV Vaccination Compared With Pap Smear Screening on a National Scale: A Literature Review*, 26 VACCINE 6258 (2008).

recommended routine vaccination of males aged 11 to 12.[49] Shortly after the approval of the HPV vaccine, many states considered and some adopted laws that added the HPV vaccine to the list of school vaccination requirements.[50] The HPV vaccine—and much more so initiatives to mandate it—sparked a bitter public debate that included skepticism about the efficacy of the vaccine, concerns regarding side effects, and resentment toward mandatory vaccinations. The American Academy of Pediatrics, the Centers for Disease Control and Prevention (CDC), and the American Academy of Family Physicians "recommend that girls receive HPV vaccine around age 11 or 12 because this is the age at which the vaccine produces the best immune response in the body, and because it's important to protect girls well before the onset of sexual activity."[51]

(a) Should the state suppress denials of scientific knowledge that can save lives? (b) Can the state define scientific knowledge for school districts? (c) Should the state protect children from risky denials of scientific knowledge?

§ 10.3 Decentralized Information Regulation

Decentralized information regulation is a common regulatory method. Market discipline does not force participants to disclose relevant negative information.[52] For example, tobacco companies have never voluntarily disclosed information about the negative effects of smoking and effectively denied them for decades. People convicted of sex crimes against minors are unlikely to voluntarily share their criminal records with the public. Many parents, however, believe such records should be made public. Publicly traded companies are likely to share with the public good news, but are much less likely to share bad news. Sexually transmitted diseases (STDs) are spread, among other reasons, because carriers fail to disclose their condition to their sexual partners. In any context of social exchange or commercial transaction, under some circumstances, a party may refrain from disclosing relevant information, or may not disclose it clearly. Decentralized information regulation intends to resolve such problems.

To be sure, decentralized information regulation may also be misused and abused.[53] Specifically, many criticize the use of mandatory disclo-

---

49. *See Recommendations on the Use of Quadrivalent Human Papillomavirus Vaccine in Males—Advisory Committee on Immunization Practices (ACIP), 2011*, 60 MORBIDITY AND MORTALITY WEEKLY REPORT 1705 (Dec. 23, 2011).

50. *See generally* James G. Hodge, Jr. et al., *School Vaccination Requirements: Historical, Social, and Legal Perspectives*, 90 KENTUCKY LAW JOURNAL 831 (2001–2002).

51. *See American Academy of Pediatrics Statement on HPV Vaccine* (Sept. 13, 2011). *See also* Colgrove et al., *HPV Vaccination Mandates*, *supra* note 106.

52. *See* Boyan Jovanovic, *Truthful Disclosure of Information*, 13 BELL JOURNAL OF ECONOMICS 36 (1982); Paul R. Milgrom, *Good News and Bad News: Representation Theorems and Applications*, 12 BELL JOURNAL OF ECONOMICS 380 (1981).

53. *See, e.g.*, Paul G. Mahoney, *The Political Economy of the Securities Act of 1933*, 30 JOURNAL OF LEGAL STUDIES 1 (2001).

sures.[54] The critique of mandatory disclosure tends to focus on the costs of producing the disclosures, their limited effectiveness with the target audience, and their strategic use against the parties they intend to protect.[55] A legally informed person ordinarily has no remedies for risks he took. Indeed, numerous examples support the critique of mandatory disclosures. For example, item-pricing laws (IPLs) require a price tag on every item sold by a retailer. A comprehensive empirical study of IPLs found that they tend to lead to higher prices.[56] Congress passed the Credit Card Accountability Responsibility and Disclosure ("Credit CARD") Act of 2009 primarily because consumers could not process the disclosures of credit card companies.[57] In a very different domain, many argue that state informed consent statutes, which expose women who choose to undergo abortions to emotionally loaded information, do not add relevant information. Rather, they intend to manipulate choices through emotions.[58] As our starting point states, information regulation is not a cure for every illness and should be used cautiously due to the constraints on human rationality. However, mandatory disclosures can be efficient and can be instrumental to overcome market distortions caused by bounded rationality.[59] Moreover, in a world of second-best solutions, mandatory disclosures may be very imperfect but may be the only regulatory instrument the state can adopt, because others are perceived more intrusive.

---

§ 10.3.1 Warnings

Skyhook Corp. v. Jasper

Supreme Court of New Mexico
90 N.M. 143 (1977)

■ OMAN, CHIEF JUSTICE.

This is an action for claimed wrongful death brought by plaintiff (Jasper), as administrator of the estate and personal representative of Malvin Mack Brown, deceased. * * * Decedent was employed by Electrical Products Signs, Inc. (Signs, Inc.) as an apprentice sign installer. On January 11, 1973, he was assisting a journeyman installer of signs (Pulis),

---

54. *See, e.g.*, Omri Ben–Sahar & Carl E. Schneider, *The Failure of Mandated Disclosure*, 159 UNIVERSITY OF PENNSYLVANIA LAW REVIEW 647 (2011); Samuel Issacharoff & George Loewenstein, *Unintended Consequences of Mandatory Disclosure*, 73 TEXAS LAW REVIEW 753 (1995).

55. *See generally* Vincent P. Crawford & Joel P. Sobel, *Strategic Information Transmission*, 50 ECONOMETRICA 1431 (1982).

56. *See* Mark Bergen et al., *When Little Things Mean a Lot: On the Efficiency of Item–Pricing Laws*, 51 JOURNAL OF LAW & ECONOMICS 209 (2008).

57. For problems in the market for consumer credit *see* Oren Bar–Gill & Elizabeth Warren, *Making Credit Safer*, 157 UNIVERSITY OF PENNSYLVANIA LAW REVIEW 1 (2008).

58. *See* Texas Medical Providers Performing Abortion Services v. Lakey, 667 F.3d 570 (5th Cir. 2012); Texas Medical Providers Performing Abortion Services v. Lakey, 2012 WL 373132 (W.D. Texas, Feb. 6, 2012); § 7.4.2.

59. *See, e.g.*, Michael Greenstone et al., *Mandated Disclosure, Stock Returns, and the 1964 Securities Acts Amendments*, 121 QUARTERLY JOURNAL OF ECONOMICS 399 (2006); Alan Mathios, *The Impact of Mandatory Disclosure Laws on product Choices: An Analysis of the Salad Dressing Market*, 43 JOURNAL OF LAW & ECONOMICS 651 (2000); Emir Kamenica et al., *Helping Consumers Know Themselves*, 101 AMERICAN ECONOMIC REVIEW 417 (2011).

also employed by Signs, Inc., to install a Phillips 66 Sign at a service station near Springer, New Mexico.

A hole had been dug in the ground in which to place the heavy signpost, a metal pipe, in an upright position. Pulis and decedent were using a 100 foot telescoping crane rig to lift and place the signpost in the hole. This crane was manufactured by Skyhook and sold by it to Signs, Inc., in January 1968. A clearly visible written warning appeared on the boom. In this warning it was stated:

> 'All equipment shall be so positioned, equipped or protected so no part shall be capable of coming within ten feet of high voltage lines.'

Pulis was aware of and had read the warning, and the evidence is to the effect that decedent also had seen and was aware of the warning, since it was clearly visible and decedent had previously worked on and had operated the rig. Both Pulis and decedent knew of the presence of overhead high voltage lines, since they had been warned of the presence of these lines by the operator of the Phillips 66 station at which the sign was being installed. The station operator had warned then that they should operate the equipment ten feet from these high voltage lines.

Pulis and decedent positioned the crane so that, in the judgment of Pulis, the crane was ten or twelve feet from the power lines. However, no measurements were made to assure that the positioned distance of the crane from the power lines was sufficient to prevent any portion of the equipment from coming within ten feet of these lines, even though a tape measure was kept in the cab of the rig for the purpose of making these measurements. Pulis then hoisted the signpost with the crane and began swinging it toward the hole in which it was to be positioned. As he was swinging the signpost toward the hole, he heard decedent scream. Decedent, who was guiding the signpost by hand toward the hole, was electrocuted when the lift cable came in contact with the overhead power line. A 'tag line' or 'guide rope,' which was not an effective conductor of electricity and which decedent could have used to guide the signpost to the hole, was available, but was not ordinarily used by the helper in setting a post. There were also other measures commonly known, and known at least to Pulis, which could have been taken to avert the electrocution of decedent.

Decedent had been warned by his father of the dangers in operating crane too near high voltage lines. The rig had been used by Signs, Inc. for the purpose of erecting signs for a period of five years, and no such accident or incident had ever previously occurred.

Plaintiff sought recovery from Skyhook on the theory of strict tort liability for failing to equip its crane, at the time of its sale to Signs, Inc. in January 1968, with either an 'insulated link' or a 'proximity warning device.' An insulated link is a device installed on a crane to isolate the lifting hook from the lifting line or cable, so that there is no electrical continuity between the crane boom or lifting cable and the load being lifted. In January 1968, no crane manufacturer installed insulated links as standard equipment, but they were available to a purchaser of a crane at an additional cost of $300 to $400, depending on the size of the link.

A proximity warning device is an alarm warning system activated by the electrostatic field of overhead power lines. The use of this device requires that the crane be positioned at the minimum distance desired from the power line and the device then set for operation. If properly set, it will warn the operator by sound and lights when the equipment encroaches on the minimum preset distance from the power line. At the time of the sale of the crane to Signs, Inc., no crane manufacturer offered this device as either standard or optional equipment, but it could be purchased for approximately $700.

* * *

[T]he question to be resolved is whether the evidence created an issue of fact as the liability of Skyhook under [Restatement (Second) of Torts] § 402A. * * * The pertinent portions of this section of the Restatement provide:

> **Special Liability of Seller of Product for Physical Harm to User or Consumer.**
>
> (1) One who sells any product in a defective condition unreasonably dangerous to the user or consumer or to his property is subject to liability for physical harm thereby caused to the ultimate user or consumer, or to his property, if
>
> (a) the seller is engaged in the business of selling such a product, and
>
> (b) it is expected to and does reach the user or consumer without substantial change in the condition in which it is sold.

There is no question about the sale of the rig by Skyhook to Sings, Inc; no question that Skyhook was engaged in the business of selling these rigs; no question that decedent was using the crane rig at the time of his death; and no question about any substantial change having been effected in the rig from the day of its sale to Signs, Inc. in January 1968 to January 11, 1973, the date of the unfortunate accident. Therefore the only issue under § 402A, which must be determined, is whether the crane was in a defective condition which made it unreasonably dangerous to the user.

First, we must decide whether the failure of a seller to include an optional safety device as a part of the product may be considered as a sale of the product in a 'defective condition.' * * * However, we are of the opinion that a failure to incorporate into a product a safety feature or device may constitute a defective condition of the product. Obviously, the test of whether or not such a failure constitutes a defect is whether the product, absent such feature or device, is unreasonably dangerous to the user or consumer or to his property.

* * * The fact that the accident did occur is not in itself sufficient, in the light of hindsight, to support a finding that the crane rig was unreasonably dangerous. Almost everything, if not everything, we use or consume can cause injury, or even death, if used excessively or improperly.

The crane rig had been used by Signs, Inc. for five years, had performed well, and no injury had resulted. Obviously, it was not unreasonably dangerous within the contemplation of the ordinary consumer or user of such a rig when used in the ordinary ways and for the ordinary purposes for which such a rig is used. * * * Furthermore, even though Skyhook had knowledge that the rig might be used in areas where overhead high voltage lines were present, it placed on the boom a clearly visible written warning that 'all equipment shall be so positioned, equipped or protested so that no part shall be capable of coming within ten feet of high voltage lines.' There is no contention that this warning was inadequate, had it been heeded. Skyhook, as the seller, could reasonably assume that the warning would be read and heeded. And had it been heeded, the crane rig was not in a defective condition nor unreasonably dangerous. * * *

The above reasons are sufficient in themselves to dispose of this case, but we have more here. Both Pulis and decedent had the presence of the high voltage lines called to their attention, both knew the dangers of high voltage electricity—as does every ordinary adult in this present day society in New Mexico in which electricity is used so commonly for so many purposes—and together they positioned the crane rig away—but not far enough away—from these high voltage lines. There is no duty to warn of dangers actually known to the user of a product, regardless of whether the duty rests in negligence or on strict liability under § 402A. * * *

Since there was no defect in the crane rig unreasonably dangerous to the decedent within the contemplation of the strict liability concept enunciated in § 402A, there was no culpable conduct on the part of Skyhook which could have proximately caused the accident and the resulting death. * * *

In a case with a factual situation surprisingly similar to that in the present case and in which the § 402A claim of strict liability was predicated upon the absence of the same type of safety devices as those involved in the present claim, the Supreme Court of Minnesota, in its opinion holding as a matter of law that the defendant there involved was not liable under either strict liability or negligence, stated:

> 'Here the manufacturer warned against using the product within 6 feet of any power lines. (This warning was contained in the Operator's Instruction Manual, whereas in the present case it was placed in a clearly visible position on the crane boom.) Additionally, Barton, the employer, and plaintiff, its employee, knew of the danger involved.
>
> 'We hold that American Hoist did not owe the injured plaintiff any duty to install safety devices on its crane to guard against the risk of electrocution when the record demonstrated that risk was: (1) Obvious; (2) known by all of the employees involved; and (3) specifically warned against in American Hoist's operations manual....'
>
> *Halvorson v. American Hoist & Derrick Co., Minn.*, 240 N.W.2d 303, 308 (1976).

[W]e take the same position in the present case as that taken by the Minnesota court in the *Halvorsen* case. Since we hold that there was no defective condition in the crane rig which was unreasonably dangerous to the decedent as a user thereof, we need not and do not consider the other issues raised in the appeal or in the petition for writ of certiorari. * * *

IT IS SO ORDERED.

Klopp v. Wackenhut Corp.

Supreme Court of New Mexico
113 N.M. 153 (1992)

■ RANSOM, CHIEF JUSTICE.

Nancy Klopp [sued] Trans World Airlines, Inc. [(TWA)] and Wackenhut Corporation. * * * for personal injuries sustained when she tripped over the stanchion base of a metal detector at an airport security station. Wackenhut operated the security station for TWA. * * *

TWA and Wackenhut argued that the stanchion base of the metal detector was open and obvious and, because there was no reason to believe it constituted a danger, no duty of care was owed to Klopp. * * *

Klopp contends that, under the evidence * * *, fact questions existed whether the protruding stanchion base involved an unreasonable risk of danger, and whether TWA reasonably could have anticipated that a passenger's attention may be distracted from that danger, or that such person would forget the danger she had discovered. * * * We agree with Klopp that * * * the issue of the open and obvious danger rule under comparative negligence is properly before this Court.

* * * The Defense Lawyers Association argues that, in both premises liability and products liability cases, New Mexico courts long have considered that the open and obvious danger rule applies to that portion of the negligence formula concerning the duty of the landowner or supplier *to warn* of known, or open and obvious dangers. *Skyhook Corp. v. Jasper*, 90 N.M. 143 (1977); [and many other cases]. In this case, however, we address the duty issue irrespective of a specific duty to warn. If the nature of the risk would not be made more obvious through the giving of additional warning, then the giving of a warning would be a false issue. But this is not dispositive of whether ordinary care has been exercised to keep the premises safe.

* * * Simply by making hazards obvious to reasonably prudent persons, the occupier of premises cannot avoid liability to a business visitor for injuries caused by dangers that otherwise may be made safe through reasonable means. A risk is not made reasonable simply because it is made open and obvious to persons exercising ordinary care. *See Fabian v. E.W. Bliss Co.*, 582 F.2d 1257, 1263 (10th Cir.1978) (manufacturer has duty to use reasonable care in design of its products, and that duty is not changed because any risk from use of products might be obvious). Cases that appear to have held the duty to avoid unreasonable risk of injury to others is satisfied by an adequate warning are overruled by us today. *E.g., Skyhook Corp. v. Jasper*, 90 N.M. 143 (1977) (no duty to make product safe when risk is obvious, known, and specifically warned against); *Garrett v. Nissen*

Corp., 84 N.M. 16 (1972) (if duty to warn is satisfied, then there is no defect in product). Moreover, we think that some degree of negligence on the part of all persons is foreseeable, just like the inquisitive propensities of children, and thus, should be taken into account by the occupant in the exercise of ordinary care.

* * *

Question

Credit products may be very unsafe and dangerous. No recession has ever been the outcome of risks inherent to cranes, metal detectors, infant car seats, aspirin.[60] In contrast, excessive use of credit is a periodical phenomenon that creates bubbles and brings about recessions.[61] Even without changes in the economy, the personal costs of risks associated with credit may be substantial. Credit disclosures are mandatory and heavy regulated.[62] Can regulators (including courts) apply the rule of *Klopp v. Wackenhut Corp.* to financial institutions?

§ 10.3.2 Disclosures

Grade Cards and Restaurant Hygiene

Hygiene inspections have become an ordinary ordeal for restaurants in modern times. In December 1997, the Los Angeles County Board of Supervisors passed an ordinance requiring restaurants to display "grade cards" issued following hygiene inspections. The grade cards disclose the outcome of the most recent inspection, and restaurants must. The Ordinance provides:

> **8.04.225 Grading, scoring method and letter grade card.**
>
> A. "*Grading*" means the letter grade issued by the county health officer at the conclusion of the routine inspection of a food facility. The grade shall be based upon the scoring method * * * resulting from the food official inspection report and shall reflect the food facility's degree of compliance with all applicable federal, state and local statutes, orders, ordinances, quarantines, rules, regulations, or directives relating to the public health.
>
> C. "*Letter grade card*" means a card that may be posted by the county health officer at a food facility upon completion of a routine inspection that indicates the letter grade of the facility as determined by the county health officer using the scoring method set forth in this section. * * *
>
> D. The county health officer, in his discretion, may immediately close any food facility which, upon completion of the routine

---

60. In the past, some recessions had no identified causes. *See* § 1.1.1.

61. *See generally* CARMEN M. REINHART & KENNETH S. ROGOFF, THIS TIME IS DIFFERENT (2009); § 1.1.

62. A sample of credit card agreements is available at *regti.me/CC-agreements* (case sensitive).

inspection, does not achieve at least a "*C*" grade as defined herein. Nothing in this provision shall prohibit the county health officer from immediately closing any food facility if, in his discretion, immediate closure is necessary to protect the public health.

E. The letter grade for a food facility shall be based upon the final numerical percentage score set forth in the food official inspection report, as follows:

1. A grade of "*A*" shall indicate a final score of 90 percent or higher as determined by the county health officer;

2. A grade of "*B*" shall indicate a final score less than 90 percent but not less than 80 percent as determined by the county health officer;

3. A grade of "*C*" shall indicate a final score less than 80 percent but not less than 70 percent as determined by the county health officer.

Studies of the Los Angeles County grade card system found that its introduction followed by an increase in inspection scores and a decrease in the number of foodborne illnesses hospitalization.[63] Inspired by Los Angeles County, localities across the country began adopting similar systems.

In 2010, New York City adopted the letter grading system. The City's Department of Health and Mental Hygiene began issuing and requiring restaurants to post grade cards. The City also released apps for iPhones and iPads: *ABCEats*. Available on iTunes, the app attempts to allure users with the promise:

> Find restaurant grades and detailed inspection reports for each of the City's 24,000 restaurants using the NYC Health Department's free mobile restaurant inspection app. Check inspection letter grades at restaurants near your current location or search by restaurant name or neighborhood. Information is updated daily, so you'll have the latest results.

Calorie Labeling in Food Establishments

How much weight would you gain by eating an extra chocolate chip cookie every day for life? How much weight would you lose if you cut an unhealthy item from your daily menu? You just don't know.[64] Chocolate chip cookies come in many forms and sizes. Your favorite chocolate chip cookie, however, is likely to account for a noticeable percentage of your recommended daily caloric intake, probably 10% or more. In the long run, a decision about the daily consumption of a chocolate chip cookie will be

---

63. *See* Ginger Zhe Jin & Phillip Leslie, *The Effect of Information on Product Quality: Evidence from Restaurant Hygiene Grade Cards*, 118 QUARTERLY JOURNAL OF ECONOMICS 409 (2003); Paul A. Simon et al., *Impact of Restaurant Hygiene Grade Cards on Foodborne-Disease Hospitalization in Los Angeles County*, 67 JOURNAL OF ENVIRONMENTAL HEALTH 32 (2005).

64. *See generally* Martijn B. Katan & David S. Ludwig, *Extra Calories Cause Weight Gain—But How Much?*, 303 JAMA 65 (2010).

noticeable in your waistline. By extension, the decision to consume "less" calories every day will result in loss of weight.

Since the early 1970s, obesity rates in the United States have more than doubled.[65] Obesity is identified as a national epidemic. Overweight people are at increased risk for diabetes, heart disease, stroke, high blood pressure, arthritis, and cancer. In 2006, 21% of kindergarten children in New York City were obese. Experts and health authorities around the country were expressing concerns about the vulnerability of the population born after 2000 to develop certain health conditions over time, particularly diabetes. Much of the increased in obesity in the United States is attributed to a dramatic expansion in consumption of calories driven by a change from homemade food to commercial food.[66]

On December 5, 2006, the Department of Health and Mental Hygiene at the New York City Board of Health ("the Department") adopted Regulation 81.50, which standardized voluntary disclosures of calorie information at food service establishments. The Regulation applied only to standardized menu items "for which calorie content information is made publicly available on or after March 1, 2007,"[67] since disclosures can be made only for standardized items. It affected an estimated 2,375 food service establishments out of over 23,000 permitted establishments in the City. The New York State Restaurant Association ("NYSRA"), a trade association of over 7,000 restaurants, challenged the City's choice of methods for combating obesity. NYRSA argued that caloric intake is just one component of a healthy lifestyle, that it is far from clear that consumers can effectively utilize caloric information, and that the Regulation would have adverse effects and confuse consumers. NYRSA also argued that Regulation 81.50 was invalid, because the Nutrition Labeling and Education Act of 1990 ("NLEA") preempted regulation of voluntary disclosures of calorie disclosures by states and localities. The New York District Court ruled in favored of NYRSA, finding that the Regulation was expressly preempted by NLEA.[68]

On January 22, 2008, the Department adopted a new regulation mandating disclosure of calorie information. The revised Regulation 81.50 applied to food service establishments belong to a chain with fifteen branches or more nationwide that offer for substantially the same menu items.[69]

---

65. *See generally* David M. Cutler et al., *Why Have Americans Become More Obese?*, 17 JOURNAL OF ECONOMIC PERSPECTIVES 93 (2003). Data about trends in obesity in the United States between 1985 and 2010 is available at *regti.me/obesity2010* (case sensitive).

66. David M. Cutler et al., *Why Have Americans Become More Obese*, *id.*

67. The regulation and notice of adoption are available at *regti.me/81–50–2006* (case sensitive).

68. New York State Restaurant Association v. New York City Board of Health, 509 F. Supp. 2d 351 (S.D.N.Y. 2007).

69. The notice of adoption is available at *regti.me/81–50–2008* (case sensitive). The City also issued a "calorie compliance guide" for food establishments that is available at *regti.me/NYC-ccg* (case sensitive). *See also* Michelle M. Mello, *New York City's War on Fat*, 360 NEW ENGLAND JOURNAL OF MEDICINE 2016 (2009).

Health Code of the City of New York

81.50 Posting of calorie information.

(a) **Definitions and construction of words and terms used in this section.**

(1) **Covered food service establishment** shall mean a food service establishment within the City of New York that is one of a group of 15 or more food service establishments doing business nationally, offering for sale substantially the same menu items, in servings that are standardized for portion size and content, that operate under common ownership or control, or as franchised outlets of a parent business, or do business under the same name.

(2) **Menu** shall mean a printed list or pictorial display of a food item or items, and their price(s), that are available for sale from a covered food service establishment and shall include menus distributed or provided outside of the establishment.

(3) **Menu board** shall mean any list or pictorial display of a food item or items and their price(s) posted in and visible within a covered food service establishment or outside of a covered food service establishment for the purpose of ordering from a drive-through window.

(4) **Menu item** shall mean any individual food item, or combination of food items, listed or displayed on a menu board or menu that is/are sold by a covered food service establishment.

(5) **Food item tag** shall mean a label or tag that identifies any food item displayed for sale at a covered food service establishment.

(b) **Scope and applicability**. This section shall apply to menu items that are served in portions the size and content of which are standardized at a covered food service establishment. This section shall not apply to menu items that are listed on a menu or menu board for less than 30 days in a calendar year.

(c) **Posting calorie information for menu items**. All menu boards and menus in any covered food service establishment shall bear the total number of calories derived from any source for each menu item they list. Such information shall be listed clearly and conspicuously, adjacent or in close proximity such as to be clearly associated with the menu item, using a font and format that is at least as prominent, in size and appearance, as that used to post either the name or price of the menu item.

(1) **Calculating calories**. Calorie content values (in kcal) required by this section shall be based upon a verifiable analysis of the menu item, which may include the use of nutrient databases, laboratory testing, or other reliable methods of analysis, and shall be rounded to the nearest ten (10) calories for calorie content values above 50 calories and to the

nearest five (5) calories for calorie content values 50 calories and below.

(2) **Food item tags**. When a food item is displayed for sale with a food item tag, such food item tag shall include the calorie content value for that food item in a font size and format at least as prominent as the font size of the name of the food item.

(3) **Drive-through windows**. Calorie content values at drive-through windows shall be displayed on either the drive through menu board, or on an adjacent stanchion visible at or prior to the point of ordering, so long as the calorie content values are as clearly and conspicuously posted on the stanchion adjacent to their respective menu item names, as the price or menu item is on the drive through menu board.

(4) **Range of calorie content values for different flavors, varieties and combinations**.

(i) **Different flavors and varieties**. For menu items offered in different flavors and varieties, including, but not limited to, beverages, ice cream, pizza, and doughnuts, the range of calorie content values showing the minimum to maximum numbers of calories for all flavors and varieties of that item shall be listed on menu boards and menus for each size offered for sale, provided however that the range need not be displayed if calorie content information is included on the food item tag identifying each flavor or variety of the food item displayed for sale, in accordance with paragraph (2) of this subdivision.

(ii) **Combinations**. For combinations of different food items listed or pictured as a single menu item, the range of calorie content values showing the minimum to maximum numbers of calories for all combinations of that menu item shall be listed on menu boards and menus. If there is only one possible calorie total for the combination, then that total shall be listed on menu boards and menus.

(d) **Effective date**. This section shall take effect on March 31, 2008.

(e) **Severability**. If any provision of this section, or its application to any person or circumstance, is held invalid by any court of competent jurisdiction, the remaining provisions or the application of the section to other persons or circumstances shall not be affected.

New York State Restaurant Association v. New York City Board of Health

556 F.3d 114 (2d Cir. 2009)

■ POOLER, CIRCUIT JUDGE:

In this case, the New York State Restaurant Association ("NYSRA"), a not-for-profit business association of over 7,000 restaurants, challenges the constitutionality of New York City Health Code § 81.50, which requires roughly ten percent of restaurants in New York City, including chains such as McDonald's, Burger King and Kentucky Fried Chicken, to post calorie content information on their menus and menu boards. *See* New York City, N.Y., Health Code tit. 24, § 81.50 (2008) ("Regulation 81.50"). NYSRA contends that Regulation 81.50 is unconstitutional because it is: (1) preempted by federal laws, specifically the Nutrition Labeling and Education Act of 1990 ("NLEA"), and (2) infringes on its member restaurants' First Amendment rights. * * * [W]e conclude that Regulation 81.50 survives both challenges. As we will explain, the federal statutory scheme regulating labeling and branding of food is a labyrinth and interpreting the statute are a series of agency regulations that sometimes appear to conflict and are difficult to harmonize. It is our view, however, that Congress intended to exempt restaurant food from the preemption sections that are necessary to allow food to be sold interstate. In requiring chain restaurants to post calorie information on their menus, New York City merely stepped into a sphere that Congress intentionally left open to state and local governments. Furthermore, although the restaurants are protected by the Constitution when they engage in commercial speech, the First Amendment is not violated, where as here, the law in question mandates a simple factual disclosure of caloric information and is reasonably related to New York City's goals of combating obesity.

I. Background

A. Federal Statutory Scheme: the Nutrition Labeling and Education Act of 1990

The Federal Food, Drug, and Cosmetic Act (the "FDCA"), enacted in 1938, generally prohibits misbranding of food. Our discussion focuses on two sections of that act—(q) and (r)—which were added in 1990 through the passage of the Nutrition Labeling and Education Act (the "NLEA"), Pub.L. No. 101–535, 104 Stat. 2353 (1990). The NLEA sought "to clarify and to strengthen the Food and Drug Administration's legal authority to require nutrition labeling on foods, and to establish the circumstances under which claims may be made about nutrients in foods." H.R.Rep. No. 101–538, at 7 (1990). * * *

Sections 343(q) and (r) and their related preemption provisions, Sections 343–1(a)(4) and (a)(5),† are the statutory bases from which the

† [Sections 343–1(a)(4) and (a)(5) are the respective preemption provisions of Sections 343(q) and (r) and at the time of the trial provided:

preemption questions in this case stem. Section 343(q), entitled "[n]utrition information," addresses mandatory information on nutrients, and requires that basic nutrition facts be disclosed for most foods. The general public is well-acquainted with this provision through the "Nutrition Facts" panel on packaged foods that informs buyers of the "the total number of calories" per serving, along with the quantities of various nutrients contained in the foods. 21 U.S.C. § 343(q). Restaurants, NYSRA's membership, are exempt from Section 343(q)'s mandatory nutrition information labeling requirements; they do not have to attach a Nutrition Facts panel to food they serve. * * *

Nutrition Facts

Serving Size 1 cup (228g)
Servings Per Container about 2

Amount Per Serving	
Calories 250	Calories from Fat 110
	% Daily Value*
Total Fat 12g	**18%**
Saturated Fat 3g	**15%**
Trans Fat 3g	
Cholesterol 30mg	**10%**
Sodium 470mg	**20%**
Total Carbohydrate 31g	**10%**
Dietary Fiber 0g	**0%**
Sugars 5g	
Proteins 5g	
Vitamin A	4%
Vitamin C	2%
Calcium	20%
Iron	4%

* Percent Daily Values are based on a 2,000 calorie diet. Your Daily Values may be higher or lower depending on your calorie needs:

	Calories:	2,000	2,500
Total Fat	Less than	65g	80g
Saturated Fat	Less than	20g	25g
Cholesterol	Less than	300mg	300mg
Sodium	Less than	2,400mg	2,400mg
Total Carbohydrate		300g	375g
Dietary Fiber		25g	30g

Section 343(r), entitled "[n]utrition levels and health-related claims," addresses voluntary information, that is, those claims that a food purveyor

---

(a) [N]o State or political subdivision of a State may directly or indirectly establish under any authority or continue in effect as to any food in interstate commerce—

* * *

(4) any requirement for nutrition labeling of food that is not identical to the requirement of section 343(q) of this title, * * *, or

(5) any requirement respecting any claim of the type described in section 343(r)(1) of this title, made in the label or labeling of food that is not identical to the requirement of section 343(r) of this title. * * *—BYO.]

may choose to add to its product label about the nutrient content (for example, "low sodium") or health benefits (for example, "fiber reduces cholesterol") of its product. * * *

Though appearing complex, th[e] scheme is simple when it comes to restaurant food—the NLEA *does not* regulate nutrition information labeling on restaurant food, and states and localities are free to adopt their own rules. The NLEA, however, *does* generally regulate nutrition content claims on restaurant foods, and states and localities may only adopt rules that are identical to those provided in the NLEA.

B. New York City Adopts Regulations Governing Calorie Labeling in Restaurants; NYSRA Challenges those Regulations.

Seeking to combat rising rates of obesity and associated health care problems, in December 2006, the New York City Board of Health adopted the precursor to the current Regulation 81.50, by amending Article 81 of the Health Code and adding a new Section 81.50.The 2006 regulation, which was to be—

> come effective on July 1, 2007, mandated that *any* food service establishment *voluntarily* publishing calorie information post such information on its menus and menu boards. This regulation was met with vigorous objection from the restaurants and prompted many to stop voluntarily making such information available. On behalf of the restaurants, NYSRA subsequently sued the New York City Board of Health, the New York City Department of Health and Mental Hygiene, and Thomas R. Frieden (also appellees here, together "New York City" or the "City") in the Southern District of New York. In a decision issued on September 11, 2007, the district court concluded that Regulation 81.50 as adopted was preempted by 21 U.S.C. § 343–1(a)(5)—the claims preemption provision—because, to the extent it applied only to restaurants that had voluntarily provided calorie information, it regulated nutrient content claims. *N.Y. State Rest. Ass'n v. N.Y. City Bd. of Health (NYSRA I)*, 509 F.Supp.2d 351, 361–63 (S.D.N.Y.2007). However, in so holding, the district court stated that
>
> By making its requirements contingent on a voluntary claim, Regulation 81.50 directly implicates [Section] 343(r) and its corresponding preemption provision. New York City, although free to enact mandatory disclosure requirements of the nature sanctioned by [Section] 343(q) (and proposed or enacted in other jurisdictions), has adopted a regulatory approach that puts it in the heartland of [Section] 343(r) and has subjected its regulation to preemption. * * *

Having decided for NYSRA on preemption, the district court did not reach NYSRA's First Amendment claim.

Taking its cue from the district court's opinion, on January 22, 2008, the New York City Board of Health repealed and modified the 2006 regulation, producing the current version of Regulation 81.50. * * * The revised Regulation 81.50 requires all chain restaurants with fifteen or more establishments nationally to make statements showing calorie content in the precise manner prescribed by the regulation. For those restaurants covered by the regulation, the calorie information must be presented clearly and conspicuously, adjacent or in close proximity to the menu item, and the font and format of calorie information must be as prominent in size and appearance as the name or price of the menu item. * * * Now, every time New Yorkers walk into or use the drive-through of certain chain restaurants, they are informed, for instance, that the taco salad contains 840 calories, the sausage and egg breakfast sandwich contains 450 calories, and the premium hamburger sandwich with mayonnaise contains 670 calories but without mayonnaise contains 510 calories. Regulation 81.50 expressly permits the restaurants to provide "additional nutritional information" and to "provid[e] ... disclaimer[s] stating that there may be variations in calorie content values across servings based on slight variations in serving size, quantity of ingredients, or special ordering."

NYSRA's member restaurants, some of which already provided nutrition information to their customers, just not on their menus and menu boards, were not much happier with the City's latest effort at calorie disclosure on menus and menu boards specifically. * * **

II. Discussion

* * * As will be discussed, Regulation 81.50 is not preempted nor does it violate the restaurants' First Amendment rights.

A. Preemption

Under the Supremacy Clause of the United States Constitution, "state laws that conflict with federal law are without effect," *Altria Group, Inc. v. Good*, 555 U.S. 70 (2008) * * * Helpfully, the NLEA is clear on preemption, stating that it "shall not be construed to preempt any provision of State law, unless such provision is *expressly preempted* under [21 U.S.C. § 343–1(a)] of the [FDCA]." * * * As already noted, as it pertains to restaurants, the NLEA does not preempt New York City from adopting its own requirements for nutrition information labeling, * * * *but* it does generally preempt it from adopting different rules for nutrient content claims. * * * In light of the NLEA's express preemption provisions, therefore, the issue in this case is less whether the NLEA is clear on preemption, but more whether the quantitative calorie disclosures Regulation 81.50 mandates that chain restaurants place on their menus and menu boards are "claims" falling under Section 343(r) and are thus preempted, or are "nutrition information" falling under Section 343(q) and thus are not preempted. Since NYSRA's argument that Regulation 81.50 pertains to claims turns primarily on the meaning of "claim" as used in the NLEA, some exposition of that term, especially as compared to the meaning of "nutrition information," is required.

As explained, the NLEA defines nutrition "information," to include "the total number of calories" in a food product. * * * Nutrition "claims" are statements "made in the label or labeling of the food which expressly or by implication ... *characterize[]* the level of any nutrient which is of the type required by [Section 343(q)]." 21 U.S.C. § 343(r)(1)(A) (emphasis added). However, "[a] statement of the type required by [Section 343(q)] that appears as part of the nutrition information required or permitted by such paragraph is *not a claim.*" *Id.* § 343(r)(1) (emphasis added).

An initial reading of these sections of the statute suggests a quantitative-qualitative distinction according to which nutrition "information" refers to quantitative statements such as "100 calories" and nutrition "claims" refers to descriptive or qualitative statements, such as "heart healthy." * * * By that view, Regulation 81.50, a regulation which merely requires the disclosure of quantitative information listed in Section 343(q), would not be preempted by the NLEA.

Such a simple path is not to be ours, however, because the FDA, as the agency charged with implementing the FDCA and NLEA, has defined "claims" with more nuance. * * * In several regulations, the FDA embraces the quantitative-qualitative distinction using terms such as "characterizes," "describes," and "suggests," to define claims. In listing terms that characterize nutrient levels, the regulations point to terms and phrases such as "rich in," "excellent source of," "enriched," "fortified." * * * As is particularly pertinent here, the regulations describe "calorie content claims" to include " 'calorie free,' 'free of calories,' ... 'without calories,' 'trivial source of calories,' 'negligible source of calories,' [and] 'dietarily insignificant source of calories.' " Further, the regulations that discuss the labeling requirements for restaurants making nutrient content claims differentiate between "nutrient amounts" (a phrase indicative of a quantitative statement), and "claims," by permitting restaurants to provide "the nutrient amounts that are the basis for the claim." * * *

But, other FDA regulations provide for a definition of claims that includes quantitative statements of the sort listed in Section 343(q). * * *

Though we might have interpreted the NLEA differently, we owe deference to the FDA's reading, as it has some support in the statute. * * * Thus, like the district court, we conclude that "under the FDA regulations, statements as to nutrient amount, including calorie content, may be a 'claim' subject to the requirements of [Section] 343(r) and its implementing regulations." *NYSRA I*, 509 F.Supp.2d at 360.

* * *

That our decision might result in NYSRA's members being subject to multiple, inconsistent local regulations is the result of the choice that Congress made to permit localities to mandate restaurants to disclose nutrition information about the food they serve. It is not a permissible basis to conclude that the NLEA preempts Regulation 81.50.

* * *

B. First Amendment

NYSRA's other objection to Regulation 81.50 is that it impermissibly infringes on NYSRA's member restaurants' First Amendment rights. It is undisputed that commercial speech is entitled to the protection of the First Amendment. * * * As commercial speech is speech that proposes a commercial transaction, and Regulation 81.50 "requires disclosure of calorie information in connection with a proposed commercial transaction—the sale of a restaurant meal," * * * the form of speech affected by Regulation 81.50 is clearly commercial speech. However, the protection afforded commercial speech is "somewhat less extensive than that afforded noncommercial speech. And, within the class of regulations affecting commercial speech, we accord varying levels of protection depending on the type of commercial speech at issue.

[NYSRA] argues that Regulation 81.50 should be subjected to heightened scrutiny, and not, as the district court concluded, "rationality." * * * [T]his Circuit [however] held that rules "mandating that commercial actors disclose commercial information" are subject to the rational basis test. *Nat'l Elec. Mfrs. Ass'n v. Sorrell*, 272 F.3d 104, 114–15 (2d Cir. 2001). We explained that:

> Commercial disclosure requirements are treated differently from restrictions on commercial speech because mandated disclosure of accurate, factual, commercial information does not offend the core First Amendment values of promoting efficient exchange of information or protecting individual liberty interests. Such disclosure furthers, rather than hinders, the First Amendment goal of the discovery of truth and contributes to the efficiency of the "marketplace of ideas." Protection of the robust and free flow of accurate information is the principal First Amendment justification for protecting commercial speech, and requiring disclosure of truthful information promotes that goal. In such a case, then, less exacting scrutiny is required than where truthful, nonmisleading commercial speech is restricted.

* * * NYSRA [contends that its] member restaurants, which do not believe that disclosing calorie information would reduce obesity, and would prefer to provide complete nutrition information, [but] are instead forced, as counsel informed us during oral argument, to "cram" calorie information "down the throats" of their customers.

* * * NYSRA does not contend that disclosure of calorie information is not "factual"; it only claims that its member restaurants do not want to communicate to their customers that calorie amounts should be prioritized among other nutrient amounts, such as those listed in Section 343(q)'s Nutrition Fact panel. However, the First Amendment does not bar the City from compelling such "under-inclusive" factual disclosures, * * * where as discussed below, the City's decision to focus its attention on calorie amounts is rational.

C. Rational Basis Review

Accordingly, rational basis applies and NYSRA concedes that it will not prevail if we apply that test. Our review reveals the concession to be warranted; New York City has plainly demonstrated a reasonable relationship between the purpose of Regulation 81.50's disclosure requirements and the means employed to achieve that purpose. Citing what it termed an "obesity epidemic," New York City enacted Regulation 81.50 to: (1) reduce consumer confusion and deception; and (2) to promote informed consumer decision-making so as to reduce obesity and the diseases associated with it. * * * First, that obesity is epidemic and is a serious and increasing cause of disease; in New York City, 54% of adults, and 43% of elementary school children are overweight or obese and obesity is a contributing factor for heart disease, diabetes, stroke, and cancer, which caused 70% of deaths in New York City in 2005. Second, that the obesity epidemic is mainly due to excess calorie consumption, often resulting from meals eaten away from the home. Americans, including New Yorkers, are eating out more than in the past and when doing so, typically eat more than they do at home, and in just one meal ordered in a fast food restaurant, might consume more than the advised daily caloric intake. Third, that chain restaurants serve food that is associated with excess calorie consumption and weight gain. Fourth, that consumers' distorted perceptions about how many calories food contained led to unhealthy food choices. Fifth, that providing calorie information, similar to that provided in the NLEA's Nutrition Fact panel, at the point-of-decision would help consumers make informed, healthier food choices. Finally, it noted that voluntary activities by restaurants were "woefully inadequate" and failed to inform the vast majority of customers, only 3.1% of whom in a study, reported noticing calorie information, and that leading health authorities recommend posting calorie information at the point of purchase.

New York City was not alone in making these observations. A 2006 FDA-commissioned report concluded that "obesity has become a public health crisis of epidemic proportions." * * * In addition, a 2005 study by the Centers for Disease Control and Prevention (the "CDC") estimated that approximately 112,000 deaths in 2000 were associated with obesity in the United States. * * * Another study concluded that rising obesity rates led to increasing diabetes rates, finding that as of 2005, 15.8 million Americans had diabetes, almost triple the number from 1980. * * * Yet another study concluded that with these increased rates of obesity and associated health problems, have come increased health-care costs. * * *

Further, studies have linked obesity to eating out. * * * Indeed, NYSRA's expert does not assert that provision of information about the calorie content of food at the point of purchase in restaurants will not be beneficial in reducing obesity levels, and only states that it might not.

In view of all the above findings, Regulation 81.50's calorie disclosure rules are clearly reasonably related to its goal of reducing obesity. We thus conclude that NYSRA has not demonstrated a likelihood of success on its First Amendment claims and affirm the district court's denial of an injunction.

III. Conclusion

For the reasons stated above, we reject NYSRA's challenge to Regulation 81.50 because we conclude that it is not preempted by the NLEA and does not violate NYSRA's member restaurants' First Amendment rights. * * *

* * *

In July 2009, a few months after the Second Circuit handed down its decision, *Science* magazine published a pioneering study that examined the effects of caloric restrictions on aging in a primate species. The study was conducted in a population of rhesus monkeys over a period of 20 years. It found that a moderate caloric restriction lowered the incidence of aging-related deaths and delayed the onset of age-associated pathologies. Specifically, a moderate calorie restriction reduced the incidence of diabetes, cancer, cardiovascular disease, and brain atrophy. The study demonstrated that caloric restrictions slow aging in a primate species.[70] Concluding their article, the authors wrote: "Our data indicate that adult-onset [a] moderate [caloric restriction] delays the onset of age-associated pathologies and promotes survival in a primate species. * * * Given the obvious parallels between rhesus monkeys and humans, the beneficial effects of [caloric restriction] may also occur in humans. This prediction is supported by studies of people on [a] long-term [caloric restriction], who show fewer signs of cardiovascular aging. The effect of controlled [a] long-term [caloric restriction] on maximal life span in humans may never be known, but our extended study will eventually provide such data on rhesus monkeys."

When New York City adopted its restaurant calorie labeling regulation, it acted under scientific uncertainty. The City could not prove that the regulatory measure would prolong lives or enhance health.[71] Critics argued that restaurants should not be blamed for obesity, that most people cannot calculate the number of calories they consume a day, and that people tend to compensate for the conscious reduction of calories. Overall, however, the medical community embraced and praised the regulation.[72] The Patient Protection and Affordable Care Act amended the Federal Food, Drug, and Cosmetic Act to require disclosure of calorie and other nutrition information in food chain establishments with more than 20 locations and in vending machines.[73]

Questions

1. What are the similarities and differences between restaurant hygiene grade cards and calorie labeling menus?

2. In 2011, New York City announced that teachers' performance assessments would be made public. The state courts upheld the decision, holding that "[p]ublic agency records, like the ones at issue here, are presumptively open for public inspection and copying, and the party seeking an exemption from disclosure has the burden of proving entitlement to the exemption."[74] Responding to this decision, Bill Gates, Microsoft founder and a philanthropist, published an op-ed in *The New York Times* entitled, *Shame Is Not the Solution*.[75] In his op-ed Mr. Gates wrote:

---

70. *See* Ricki J. Colman et al., *Caloric Restrictions Delays Disease Onset and Mortality in Rhesus Monkeys*, 325 SCIENCE 201 (2009).

71. *See, e.g.*, David S. Ludwig & Kelly D. Bronwell, *Public Health Action Amid Scientific Uncertainty*, 302 JAMA 434 (2009).

72. *See, e.g.*, Linda Van Horn, *Calories Count*, 306 JAMA 315 (2011).

73. *See generally* Marion Nestle, *Health Care Reform in Action—Calorie Labeling Goes National*, 362 NEW ENGLAND JOURNAL OF MEDICINE 2343 (2010).

74. Mulgrew v. Board of Education of City School District of City of New York, 928 N.Y.S.2d 701, 702 (2011), *leave to appeal denied*, 18 N.Y.3d 806 (2012).

75. Bill Gates, *Shame Is Not the Solution*, N.Y. TIMES, Feb. 23, 2012, at A27, available at *regti.me/Gates–Q* (case sensitive).

I am a strong proponent of measuring teachers' effectiveness, and my foundation works with many schools to help make sure that such evaluations improve the overall quality of teaching. But publicly ranking teachers by name will not help them get better at their jobs or improve student learning. On the contrary, it will make it a lot harder to implement teacher evaluation systems that work.

In most public schools today, teachers are simply rated "satisfactory" or "unsatisfactory," and evaluations consist of having the principal observe a class for a few minutes a couple of times each year. Because we are just beginning to understand what makes a teacher effective, the vast majority of teachers are rated "satisfactory." * * *

Putting sophisticated personnel systems in place is going to take a serious commitment. Those who believe we can do it on the cheap—by doing things like making individual teachers' performance reports public—are underestimating the level of resources needed to spur real improvement.

(a) Does Mr. Gates' critique of the disclosure of teachers' performance assessments also apply to restaurant hygiene grade cards and calorie labeling menus? (b) What are the characteristics of effective disclosures?

3. In 2001–2002, a series of corporate and accounting scandals involving famous corporations like Enron, Tyco International, Adelphia, and WorldCom shook the stock market and the nation. These scandals involved publically traded companies that deceived the public and regulatory agencies by "cooking the books." Simply put, the companies released financial statements that did not reflect their actual situation. These companies' top executives led the corruption that ultimately cost investors billions of dollars and undermined the public's confidence in financial markets. In response to the series of scandals, In July 2002, Congress passed the Company Accounting Reform and Investor Protection Act of 2002, commonly known as the Sarbanes–Oxley Act, or SOX. Section 302 of the Sarbanes–Oxley Act (15 U.S.C. § 7241) provides:

§ 7241. Corporate responsibility for financial reports

The [Securities and Exchange] Commission shall, by rule, require, for each company filing periodic reports under * * * the Securities Exchange Act of 1934 * * *, that the principal executive officer or officers and the principal financial officer or officers, or persons performing similar functions, certify in each annual or quarterly report filed or submitted under either such section of such Act that—

(1) the signing officer has reviewed the report;

(2) based on the officer's knowledge, the report does not contain any untrue statement of a material fact or omit to state a material fact necessary in order to make the statements made, in light of the circumstances under which such statements were made, not misleading;

(3) based on such officer's knowledge, the financial statements, and other financial information included in the report, fairly present in all material respects the financial condition and results of operations of the [corporation] as of, and for, the periods presented in the report;

(4) the signing officers—

(A) are responsible for establishing and maintaining internal controls;

(B) have designed such internal controls to ensure that material information relating to the [corporation] is made known to [the signing officers];

(C) have evaluated the effectiveness of the [corporation]'s internal controls as of a date within 90 days prior to the report; and

(D) have presented in the report their conclusions about the effectiveness of their internal controls based on their evaluation as of that date.

(a) What are the potential cons and pros of imposing personal responsibility on the senior management for the accuracy of the company's disclosure? (b) Studies show that calorie labeling of food establishments are not always accurate, and for certain types of food are frequently understated.[76] Should New York City impose liability on senior officers of restaurant chains for inaccuracies in their calorie disclosures?

---

76. *See, e.g.*, Lorien E. Urban et al., *Accuracy of Stated Energy Contents of Restaurant Foods*, 306 JAMA 287 (2011).

CHAPTER 11

PREFERENCE SHAPING

A famous Latin maxim provides: *De gustibus non est disputandum*—there's no arguing about taste. The maxim serves as practical advice for parties with incompatible tastes: quarrels over preferences are pointless. Economists George Stigler and Gary Becker explained the maxim: "[O]ne does not argue over tastes for the same reason that one does not argue over the Rocky Mountains—both are there, will be there next year, too, and are the same to all men."[1] Preferences, however, *do* change and evolve and, as we shall see, the state utilizes a wide range of regulatory measures in an effort to alter preferences.[2]

Our discussion thus far has focused on interference with choices through incentive regulations and command-and-control measures. We conclude this book with a discussion about preference-shaping regulations.

§ 11.1 DO WE HAVE DEFINED PREFERENCES?

Preferences are reasons for conduct; attributes of individuals that account for the actions they take. Beliefs, taste, passion, desire, and other forces may cause a person to prefer *X* to *Y*. Some preferences are stable and may drive a person to choose *X* over *Y* in every situation throughout her life. Other preferences are situational and may be unstable. For example, food preferences are generally unstable and can be influenced by experiences, beliefs, and information.[3] A person may always prefer chocolate to vanilla ice cream, but her preference for alcohol over water may depend on the time of day and social circumstances. Moreover, her taste for alcohol may evolve—she may acquire alcohol addiction, or lose her interest in alcohol altogether. In contrast, sexual orientation shapes preferences that are rather stable; information cannot change such preferences.[4] Experi-

1. George J. Stigler & Gary S. Becker, *De Gustibus Non Est Disputandum*, 67 AMERICAN ECONOMIC REVIEW 76 (1977).

2. *See* Samuel Bolwes, *Endogenous Preferences: The Cultural Consequences of Markets and other Economic Institutions*, 36 JOURNAL OF ECONOMIC LITERATURE 75 (1998); Ernest Fehr & Karla Hoff, *Tastes, Castes and Culture: The Influence of Society on Preferences*, 121 ECONOMIC JOURNAL 396 (2011).

3. *See* P. Rozin & T. A. Vollmecke, *Food Likes and Dislikes*, 6 ANNUAL REVIEW OF NUTRITION 433 (1986).

4. *See generally* American Psychological Association, *Resolution on Appropriate Affirmative Responses to Sexual Orientation Distress and Change Efforts* (August 5, 2009), available at *regti.me/APA2009* (case sensitive).

ences, information, and knowledge, however, tend to shape attitudes toward members of the LGBT community.[5]

Preferences, as reasons for conduct, are intricate, yet people's choices do not necessarily reflect their preferences. Many factors may bring a person to make a choice that does not reflect his preferences. Here, we provide four examples. First, choices are vulnerable to the framing of situations and alternatives. A person may *express* opposite preferences among different frames of the same alternative,[6] or choose a specific alternative because of its salient presentation.[7] Second, compulsion, addiction, habit, and other psychological dispositions cause people to act in ways that may be inconsistent with their preferences. Third, one's social identity influences her internal expectations and affects her choices. Studies show that people tend to conform to their social identity in a manner that drives their conduct, often in the face of adverse preferences.[8] Fourth, so-called "moral choices"—religious or social norms—are sufficiently powerful to direct conduct, but they do not necessarily reflect or change preferences.[9] Pressures for social conformity can be powerful.[10]

Moreover, people are frequently in denial about their preferences and cannot explain their choices. For example, eating, physical exercise, and work habits are significant dimensions of life in which people's perceptions of their own preferences tend to be inconsistent with their actual choices. Most people also do not like to admit to themselves and others that they have prejudice, even though prejudice is rather common.[11] That is, people tend to be "dishonest" about their preferences with themselves and others, including about their tolerance toward others' preferences.[12] Yet, people also tend to dislike dishonesty.[13]

---

5. *See, e.g.*, American Psychiatric Association, *Position Statement on Support of Legal Recognition of Same–Sex Civil Marriage* (July 2005); Sheryl Gay Stolberg, *For President, Gay Marriage Views Evolve*, N.Y. TIMES, June 19, 2011, at A1; Carol E. Lee, *Obama Backs Gay Marriage*, WALL STREET JOURNAL, May 10, 2012, at A1; Erik Eckholm, *Rift Forms in Movement as Belief in Gay 'Cure' Is Renounced*, N.Y. TIMES, July 7, 2012, at A9.

6. *See* Amos Tversky & Daniel Kahnemn, *The Framing of Decisions and the Psychology of Choice*, 211 SCIENCE 453 (1981); Amos Tversky & Daniel Kahnemn, Rational Choice and the Framing of Decisions, 59 JOURNAL OF BUSINESS S251 (1986).

7. *See* Dan Ariely et al., *"Coherent Arbitrariness": Stable Demand Curves Without Stable Preferences*, 118 QUARTERLY JOURNAL OF ECONOMICS 73 (2003).

8. *See* Karla Hoff & Priyanka Pandey, *Discrimination, social identity, and durable inequalities,* 96 AMERICAN ECONOMIC REVIEW 206 (1996). *See also* GLENN LOURY, THE ANATOMY OF RACIAL INEQUALITY (2002).

9. *See, e.g.*, Bowers v. Hardwick, 478 U.S. 186 (2003); Lawrence v. Texas, 539 U.S. 558 (2003).

10. *See* Solomon E. Asch, *Opinions and Social Pressure*, 193 SCIENTIFIC AMERICAN 31 (1955).

11. *See, e.g.*, GORDON W. ALLPORT, THE NATURE OF PREJUDICE (1954); Gordon W. Allport & J. Michael Ross, *Personal Religious Orientation and Prejudice*, 5 JOURNAL OF PERSONALITY & SOCIAL PSYCHOLOGY 432 (1967); Marillynn B. Brewer, *The Psychology of Prejudice: Ingroup Love or Outgroup Hate?*, 55 JOURNAL OF SOCIAL ISSUES 429 (1999); Christian S. Crandall, *Prejudice Against Fat People: Ideology and Self–Interest*, 66 JOURNAL OF PERSONALITY & SOCIAL PSYCHOLOGY 882 (1994); Henri Tajfel, *Cognitive Aspects of Prejudice*, 25 JOURNAL OF SOCIAL ISSUES 79 (1969).

12. *See generally* DAN ARIELY, THE HONEST TRUTH ABOUT DISHONESTY: HOW WE LIE TO EVERYONE—ESPECIALLY OURSELVES (2012); SISSELA BOK, LYING: MORAL CHOICE IN PUBLIC AND PRIVATE LIFE (1999); TIMUR KURAN, PRIVATE TRUTHS, PUBLIC LIES: THE SOCIAL CONSEQUENCES OF PREFERENCE FALSIFICATION (1997).

13. *See, e.g.*, United States v. Alvarez, 132 S.Ct. 2537 (2012).

In sum, our views and beliefs are often more self-defined than some of our so-called preferences. We may not fully understand the reasons underlying our choices, but we know that that these reasons are not necessarily "wired" in us. At the very least, information and knowledge may influence certain preferences and choices.

Sidebar 11–1
What Are the Preferences of Motorcyclists?

The likelihood of surviving a motorcycle accident is relatively low. In 2009, Motorcycles accounted for about 0.7% miles traveled by motor vehicles in the United States, but motorcycle accidents accounted for 13% of all motor vehicle accident fatalities and 4% of all motor vehicle accident injuries (*see Figure 11–1*).

From 1998 to 2008, the motorcycle fatality rate—the percentage of motorcyclist fatalities in motor vehicle accidents—increased by 158%. During this period, the motorcycle injury rate went up by 167%, and the motorcycle miles traveled rate went up by 79%. In 2009, the fatality rate dropped by 14%. Motorcycle riding is substantially riskier than driving in other motor vehicles. Per motor vehicle mile traveled, motorcyclists are about 25 more likely than car drivers and passengers to be involved in a fatal traffic accident.

The National Highway Traffic Safety Administration estimated that, in 2009, helmets saved the lives of 1483 motorcyclists and, "[i]f all motorcyclists had worn helmets, an additional 732 lives [16% of motorcycle fatalities, or 2.2% of total motor vehicle fatalities] could have been saved."[14] 20 states, the District of Columbia and Puerto Rico have universal helmet laws that require all motorcycle riders to wear helmets. In states with no universal helmet laws, many motorcycle riders do not wear helmets. Every year, motorcycle accidents cost taxpayers substantial sums of resources. On average, the costs are considerably lower in states that adopted universal helmet laws.[15]

Do the fatality rates of motorcyclists reveal something about their preferences? Does the increase in motorcycle ownership during the first decade of the twenty-first century provide any information about changes in the preferences of the population? Does helmet wearing necessarily provide information about the preferences of motorcyclists? Do universal helmet laws provide information about the preferences of lawmakers? Should all states have universal helmet laws?

---

14. National Highway Traffic Safety Administration, *Traffic Safety Facts: 2009 Data, Motorcycles* (October, 2011).

15. *See, e.g.*, Rebecca B. Neumann & Ruth A. Shultz, *Helmet Use Among Motorcyclists Who Died in Crashes and Economic Cost Savings Associated With State Motorcycle Helmet Laws—United States, 2008–2010*, 61 MORBIDITY & MORTALITY WEEKLY REPORT 425 (June 15, 2012).

Figure 11.1

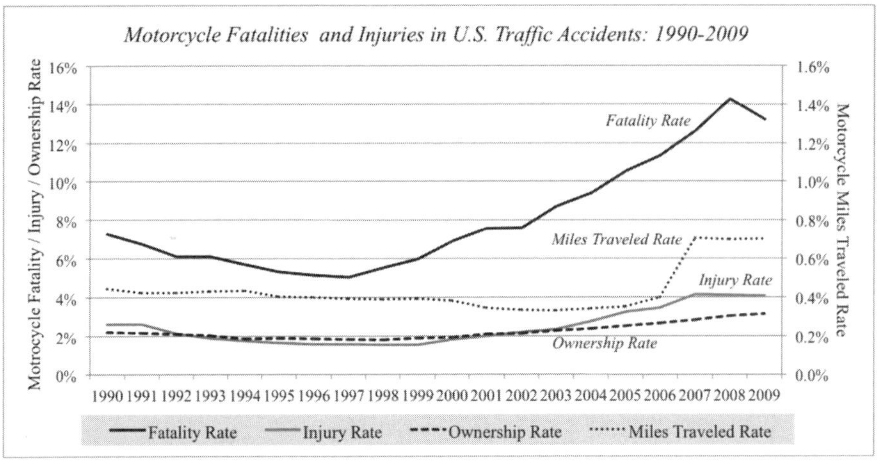

Motorcycle Fatalities and Injuries in U.S. Traffic Accidents: 1990-2009

Source: The Bureau of Transportation Statistics.

§ 11.2 WHY REGULATE PREFERENCES?

§ 11.2.1 Addressing Conflicting Preferences

We have already seen that preference diversity may lead to conflicts.[16] We used a simple hypothetical to illustrate Amartya Sen's Liberal Paradox:[17]

> Consider Alexis, who likes the color black—for her outfit, home, bicycle, car, and everything else. Alexis expresses her individualism and style with color. Alas, everyone else in society finds the color black terribly depressing. Should society intervene in the freedom of Alexis (and individuals with similar preferences) to serve the majority's preferences?

For the majority, altering Alexis' preferences may be a convenient solution to the problem, if such solution is attainable. Alternatively, the majority may compel Alexis to use unwanted colors. Some may consider modification of Alexis' preferences more intrusive than forcing her to use unwanted colors. Of course, the majority can also "subsidize" Alexis and tolerate her color preferences. What option should society choose?

To make the hypothetical more realistic, replace "Alexis" with "an avid motorcyclist" and "likes the color black" with "likes riding her motorcycle with no helmet."[18] Professor Laurence Tribe pointed out that "[in] a society unwilling to abandon bleeding bodies on the highway, the motorcyclist or driver who endangers himself plainly imposes costs on

---

16. *See* §§ 2.3.2, 3.1. *See also* DAVID HUME, OF THE STANDARD OF TASTE (1757).

17. *See* Amartya Sen, *The Impossibility of a Paretian Liberal*, 78 JOURNAL OF POLITICAL ECONOMY 152 (1970). *See also* Amartya Sen, *Freedom of Choice: Concept and Content*, 32 EUROPEAN ECONOMIC REVIEW 269 (1988).

18. For these preferences in practice *see* § 4.5.

others."[19] Should society mandate helmets? Wouldn't it be better if society could cause motorcyclists to want to wear helmets? Another alternative is to persuade society to abandon bleeding motorcyclists who cannot pay medical bills, or perhaps only bleeding "helmetless motorcyclists" who cannot pay medical bills.

Consider now the preference for health insurance. The 2012 health-care decision was supposedly all about preferences.[20] The analysis of the individual mandate provision relied on the premise that some individuals prefer to be uninsured. The plaintiffs argued that, by requiring minimum essential health insurance coverage, Congress compelled individuals to purchase a product they do not want. Similarly, the analysis of the Medicaid expansion provision rested on the premise that at least some states had a preference not to expand their Medicaid programs.

The Supreme Court decision consisted of three opinions. Chief Justice Roberts charged that by requiring health insurance, Congress compelled individuals to purchase "an unwanted product." Responding to this description, Justice Ginsburg maintained that preferences to be uninsured, if such exist, are unstable over time; and time-inconsistent preferences of this kind impose costs on society:

> If unwanted today, medical service secured by insurance may be desperately needed tomorrow. Virtually everyone * * * consumes health care at some point in his or her life. Health insurance is a means of paying for this care, nothing more. In requiring individuals to obtain insurance, Congress is * * * not mandating the purchase of a discrete, unwanted product. Rather, Congress is merely defining the terms on which individuals pay for an interstate good they consume: Persons subject to the mandate must now pay for medical care in advance (instead of at the point of service) and through insurance (instead of out of pocket).

The dissenters—Justices Scalia, Kennedy, Thomas, and Alito—supposedly attributed at least some of this time-inconsistency to the statutory protection of individuals with preexisting conditions established by the Patient Protection and Affordable Care Act of 2010:

> Under ordinary circumstances, * * * insurers would * * * charg[e] high premiums to individuals with pre-existing conditions. The Act seeks to prevent this. * * * Aside from the rough proxies of age and tobacco use * * *, the Act does not allow an insurer to factor the individual's health characteristics into the price of his insurance premium. This creates a new incentive for young and healthy individuals without pre-existing conditions. The insurance premiums for those in this group will not reflect their own low actuarial risks but will subsidize insurance for others in the pool. Many of them may decide that purchasing health insurance is not an economically sound decision. * * * But without the contribution of above-risk premiums from the young and healthy,

---

19. LAURENCE H. TRIBE, AMERICAN CONSTITUTIONAL LAW 1372 (2d ed. 1988).

20. National Federation of Independent Business v. Sebelius, 132 S.Ct. 2566 (2012), § 2.6.

> the * * * insurers [will not be able] to take on high-risk individuals without a massive increase in premiums.

That is, the dissenters essentially endorsed the view that health insurance may be an "unwanted product." More precisely, the dissenters argued that health insurance may be an unwanted product for young and healthy individuals.

We need not evaluate these judicial views of human preferences. Under any set of assumptions, uninsured individuals make choices that impose costs on others. One of the reasons for "cost-shifting" is that state and federal laws require hospitals to provide emergency services to individuals without regard to their ability to pay. These laws reflect a societal preference not to abandon dying people, especially bleeding ones. The dissenters implicitly criticized these laws, pointing out that "Government regulation typically imposes costs on the regulated industry—especially regulation that prohibits economic behavior in which most market participants are already engaging."

The examples of color, helmet, and health insurance preferences illustrate the choices society must make when preference diversity creates conflicts; that is, when unrestricted freedom of some individuals is likely to result in harm to others. Our point here is that, regardless of one's views of particular preferences, in each case of preference diversity society makes a choice among four primary options: (a) preserving liberty and accommodating harm, (b) imposing restriction on individual liberty to reduce the scope of potential externalities, (c) altering some preferences, and (d) adopting a nuanced regulatory scheme that includes a combination of (a), (b), and (c).

§ 11.2.2 Debiasing Bounded Rationality

In August 1992, the Council of Representatives of the American Psychological Association adopted the following resolution:

> **Resolution on the Use of Psychology to Market Tobacco Products**
>
> WHEREAS three successive Surgeons General of the United States have determined that tobacco products pose a threat to the public health of Americans; and WHEREAS some members of this Association have assisted in applying psychology to the marketing of tobacco products with special targeting of youth, women, and members of ethnic minority groups, now therefore,
>
> The American Psychological Association urges our colleagues who are using psychological techniques to assist in the marketing of tobacco products to take cognizance of the public welfare and consider voluntarily suspending all efforts at using psychological techniques as a matter of conscience.

Logic dictates that methods used to steer people to make decisions that undermine their own well being can be utilized to protect the public welfare as well.

In many dimensions of life, bounded rationality impairs our decision-making. We often have access to the relevant information and even possess such information, yet we fail to make rational decisions.[21] We all know that smoking is the leading cause of preventable morbidity and mortality in the United States, yet about one out of five adults is a smoker.[22] We know, or should know, that an increase in calorie consumption, which is not accompanying with other lifestyle changes, results in weight gain.[23] Nevertheless, most of us are not mindful of our daily calorie intake. We all know that certain *consistent* patterns of conduct, such as saving, health maintenance, studying, and working—will serve us in the long term. But we pursue immediate gratification and sacrifice our long-term well-being.[24]

Debiasing through regulation—steering people toward rational decisions—is one instrument the state can utilize to promote the public welfare.[25] There are many debiasing techniques and strategies,[26] but essentially they all seek to identify and compensate for behavioral patterns that fail people.[27] For example, the use of graphic warnings and the regulation of disclosures and representations have substantial influence on choices.[28] The FDA utilized these techniques in its 2011 graphic warnings campaign concerning smoking risks.[29] Distinctly, state abortion informed-consent statutes use such strategies to influence decisions. Regardless of how one may feel about abortions, abortion informed consent statutes do not address bounded rationality. They are designed to impact women's views concerning the morality of abortion.[30]

---

21. *See generally* § 7.4.

22. Brian King et al., *Current Cigarette Smoking Among Adults Aged≥18 Years: United States, 2005–2010*, 60 MORBIDITY & MORTALITY WEEKLY REPORT 1207 (Sept. 9 2011).

23. *See generally* Martijn B. Katan & David S. Ludwig, *Extra Calories Cause Weight Gain—But How Much?*, 303 JAMA 65 (2010); MARION NESTLE & MADLEN NESHEIM, WHY CALORIES COUNT: FROM SCIENCE TO POLITICS (2012); § 10.3.2.

24. *See, e.g.*, Ted O'Donoghue & Matthew Rabin, *The Economics of Immediate Gratification*, 13 JOURNAL OF BEHAVIORAL DECISION MAKING 233 (2000); Thomas C. Schelling, *Self-Command in Practice, in Policy, and in a Theory of Rational Choice*, 74 AMERICAN ECONOMIC REVIEW 1 (1984).

25. *See* Christine Jolls & Cass R. Sunstein, *Debiasing Through Law*, 35 JOURNAL OF LEGAL STUDIES 199 (2006).

26. *See, e.g.*, Colin Camerer et al., *Regulation for Conservatives: Behavioral Economics and the Case for "Asymmetric Paternalism,"* 151 UNIVERSITY OF PENNSYLVANIA LAW REVIEW 1211, 1212 (2003); RICHARD H. THALER & CASS R. SUNSTEIN, NUDGE: IMPROVING DECISIONS ABOUT HEALTH, WEALTH, AND HAPPINESS 6 (2008).

27. *See generally* Baruch Fischhoff, *Debiasing*, in JUDGMENT UNDER UNCERTAINTY: HEURISTICS AND BIASES 422 (Daniel Kahneman et al. eds., 1982).

28. *See, e.g.*, Marion Nestle & David S. Ludwig, *Front-of-Package Food Labels*, 303 JAMA 771 (2010).

29. *See* R.J. Reynolds Tobacco Co. v. U.S. Food & Drug Administration, 845 F. Supp. 2d 266 (D.D.C. 2012). Copies of the FDA's 2011 graphic warnings are available at *regti.me/FDA-Warnings* (case sensitive).

30. *See, e.g.*, Texas Medical Providers Performing Abortion Services v. Lakey, 667 F.3d 570 (5th Cir. 2012). A copy of the Texas Woman's Right to Know Act is available at *regti.me/TX-HB15* (case sensitive).

§ 11.3 TRADITIONAL PREFERENCE SHAPING

The concept of preference shaping through law is rather old.[31] For example, in the late eighteenth century, Jeremy Bentham wrote on the "proportion between punishments and offences." Bentham argued that sometimes a punishment should be "stretched a little," where it is "calculated to answer the purpose of a moral lesson."[32] Bentham further clarified the meaning of a punishment for a moral lesson:

> A punishment may be said to be calculated to answer the purpose of a moral lesson, when, by reason of the ignominy it stamps upon the offence, it is calculated to inspire the public with sentiments of aversion towards those pernicious habits and dispositions with which the offence appears to be connected and thereby to inculcate the opposite beneficial habits and dispositions.[33]

The principle underlying preference shaping through law is that the legal system does more than allocating payoffs—penalties and rewards—to direct the cost-benefit analysis of individuals.[34] Utilizing intuitive psychological mechanisms that shape human preferences, the legal system influences the tastes for choices. The most popular techniques are repetition and strong emotions. While these techniques are old and intuitive, modern psychology has proved their efficiency and provided tools to improve traditional methods.[35]

Finally, like all regulatory methods, preference shaping is controversial, and may be misused or abused.[36] Consider, for example, *American Booksellers Association v. Hudnut*.[37] In *Hudnut*, Judge Frank Easterbrook struck down an anti-pornography ordinance that did "not refer to the prurient interest, to offensiveness, or to the standards of the community." Rather, the ordinance banned "the graphic sexually explicit subordination of women." Judge Eaterbrook held that "[u]nder the ordinance graphic sexually explicit speech is 'pornography' or not depending on the perspec-

---

31. *See, e.g.*, Jean Hampton, *The Moral Education Theory of Punishment*, 13 PHILOSOPHY & PUBLIC AFFAIRS 208 (1984). *See generally* John C. Harsanyi, *Welfare Economics of Variable Tastes*, 21 REVIEW OF ECONOMIC STUDIES 204 (1953–1954).

32. JEREMY BENTHAM, AN INTRODUCTION TO THE PRINCIPLES OF MORALS AND LEGISLATION 88 (rev. ed. 1789).

33. *Id.*

34. *See generally* Oren Bar–Gill & Chaim Fershtman, *Law and Preferences*, 20 JOURNAL OF LAW, ECONOMICS & ORGANIZATION 331 (2004); Robert Cooter, *Expressive Law and Economics*, 27 JOURNAL OF LEGAL STUDIES 585 (1998); Dan M. Kahan, *What Do Alternative Sanctions Mean?*, 63 UNIVERSITY OF CHICAGO LAW REVIEW 591 (1996); Cass R. Sunstein, *The Expressive Function of Law*, 144 UNIVERSITY OF PENNSYLVANIA LAW REVIEW 2021 (1996).

35. *See, e.g.*, George Loewenstein, *Out of Control: Visceral Influences on Behavior*, 65 ORGANIZATIONAL & HUMAN DECISION PROCESSES 272 (1996); Robert B. Zajonc, *Attitudinal Effects of Mere Exposure*, 9 JOURNAL OF PERSONALITY & SOCIAL PSYCHOLOGY S1 (1968).

36. *See, e.g., Lawrence Lessig, The Regulation of Social Meaning*, 62 UNIVERSITY OF CHICAGO LAW REVIEW 943 (1995).

37. American Booksellers Association, Inc. v. Hudnut, 771 F.2d 323 (7th Cir. 1985).

tive the author adopts." "This," he argued, "is thought control." Anti-pornography laws generally intend to shape preferences and attitudes. With preference shaping, it is often difficult to distinguish between desirable regulation that protects the public welfare and "thought control."

Influencing people's preferences and tastes is a delicate task. Advertisers and marketing professionals supposedly have an expertise in the area. Lawmakers, judges, and bureaucrats may have ambitions but do not always have the practical knowledge and experience in the area. We will examine a few common instruments the state utilizes for preference shaping.

§ 11.4 Censorship

Censorship has always been a popular instrument to influence tastes, views, and attitudes. It is still in use.[38]

Maryland v. West

9 Md.App. 270 (1970)

■ MORTON, JUDGE.

The single issue presented in this case involves the constitutionality [of Maryland] blasphemy statute. * * * The record indicates that the petitioner below was convicted by a local trial magistrate of disorderly conduct, resisting arrest and blasphemy. The fine of $25.00 for disorderly conduct was paid and the sentence of thirty days imprisonment for resisting arrest was served and the $25.00 fine for that conviction paid. After the time for taking an appeal had expired, he filed a Post Conviction petition contesting the legality of his conviction for blasphemy and the imposition of the $25.00 fine and thirty day consecutive jail sentence. * * *

The statute under which the petitioner below was convicted (Md.Code, Art. 27, § 20) provides:

> If any person, by writing or speaking, shall blaspheme or curse God, or shall write or utter any profane words of and concerning our Saviour Jesus Christ, or of and concerning the Trinity, or any of the persons thereof, he shall on conviction be fined not more than one hundred dollars, or imprisoned not more than six months, or both fined and imprisoned as aforesaid, at the discretion of the court.

The concept underlying the blasphemy statute goes back into Maryland history some 300 years and would appear to have had its origin in a 1649 enactment of the Colonial legislature entitled 'An Act Concerning Religion' which provided for punishment 'with Death, and Conviscation of Lands and Goods to the Lord Proprietary' of anyone found guilty of committing 'Blasphemy against GOD, or denying the Holy TRINITY, or the Godhead of any of the Three Persons * * *.'

---

38. *See, e.g.*, the FCC's indecency policy, § 1.4.

Over a half century later, the concept of scienter was inserted into the law and the penalty provisions changed by Chapter 16 of the Acts of 1723 which provided, inter alia, that 'if any person shall hereafter, within this province, wittingly maliciously and advisedly, by writing or speaking, blaspheme or curse God, or deny our Saviour Jesus Christ to be the Son of God, or shall deny the Holy Trinity, the Father, Son and Holy Ghost,' he shall upon conviction 'for the first offense, be bored through the tongue * * * (and) for the second offense * * * shall be stigmatized by burning in the forehead with the letter B * * * and that for the third offense * * * shall suffer death without the benefit of the clergy.'

Except for the penalty provisions, it is apparent that the present statute remains in substantially the same form as its predecessor statutes. It is equally apparent that the statute's historical roots, as evidenced by the title of the original Act, were imbedded in the firm conviction of its original and subsequent framers that legislative fiat was necessary and desirable to preserve the sanctity of the Christian religion; and the sanctions invoked by the statute demonstrate the depth and earnestness of their feelings towards the Christian religion.

The First Amendment to the Federal Constitution provides, in part: 'Congress shall make no law respecting an establishment of religion, or prohibiting the free exercise thereof; * * *.' * * * When the power, prestige and support of government is placed behind a particular religious belief, there inevitably occurs a breach of the 'wall of separation' which, according to Thomas Jefferson, the framers of the First Amendment intended to erect and forever maintain between Church and State. * * * In short, the provisions of the First Amendment require the States and the Federal Government to assume a 'neutral position' with respect to an individual and his religion. * * *

The Free Exercise Clause, likewise considered many times here, withdraws from legislative power, state and federal, the exertion of any restraint on the free exercise of religion. Its purpose is to secure religious liberty in the individual by prohibiting any invasions thereof by civil authority. Hence it is necessary in a free exercise case for one to show the coercive effect of the enactment as it operates against him in the practice of his religion. The distinction between the two clauses is apparent—a violation of the Free Exercise Clause is predicated on coercion while the Establishment Clause violation need not be so attended.'

[It is apparent] both from a literal reading of the statute and when considered in its historical setting, that there has not been and could not be, short of legislative action, any infusion of a secular purpose into the statute in its present form. The statute does not purport to relate the blasphemous utterances therein proscribed to the prevention of violence or breaches of the public peace or to enabling persons of the Christian or other faiths to worship unmolested, or to preserve the orderliness of our society. It plainly and unequivocally makes it a crime for any person to blaspheme or curse God, whether orally or in writing, or to 'write or utter profane words of and concerning our Saviour Jesus Christ, or of and concerning the Trinity, or any person thereof * * *.' The setting or circumstances in which the writing or utterance occurs is unrestricted. It simply and categorically proscribes such utterances under any and all circumstances.

Patently, the statute was intended to protect and preserve and perpetuate the Christian religion in this State. It obviously was intended to serve and, if allowed to stand, would continue to serve as a mantle of protection by the State to believers in Christian orthodoxy and extend to those individuals the aid, comfort and support of the State. This effort by the State of Maryland to extend its protective cloak to the Christian religion or to any other religion is forbidden by the Establishment and Free Exercise Clauses of the First Amendment. * * *

Questions

1. In 1971, Chief Justice Warren Burger defined "civility" as "the very glue that keeps an organized society from flying apart."[39] People often express concerns regarding the decline of civility norms in our society. Should the state censor uncivil forms of expressions?

2. In September 2002, New Jersey Governor signed into law an anti-bullying statute.[40] The statute defines "*harassment, intimidation or bullying*" as

> any gesture or written, verbal or physical act that is reasonably perceived as being motivated either by any actual or perceived characteristic, such as race, color, religion, ancestry, national origin, gender, sexual orientation, gender identity and expression, or a mental, physical or sensory handicap, or by any other distinguishing characteristic, that takes place on school property, at any school-sponsored function or on a school bus and that:
>
> a. a reasonable person should know, under the circumstances, will have the effect of harming a student or damaging the student's property, or placing a student in reasonable fear of harm to his person or damage to his property; or
>
> b. has the effect of insulting or demeaning any student or group of students in such a way as to cause substantial disruption in, or substantial interference with, the orderly operation of the school.

The statute further requires each school district to adopt a "policy prohibiting harassment, intimidation or bullying on school property, at a school-sponsored function or on a school bus." The policy must include the following components:

> (1) a statement prohibiting harassment, intimidation or bullying of a student;
>
> (2) a definition of harassment, intimidation or bullying no less inclusive than that set forth in * * * this act;
>
> (3) a description of the type of behavior expected from each student;

---

39. Warren E. Burger, *The Necessity for Civility*, 52 F.R.D. 211, 215 (1971).

40. A copy of the statute is available at *regti.me/NJ2002* (case sensitive).

(4) consequences and appropriate remedial action for a person who commits an act of harassment, intimidation or bullying;

(5) a procedure for reporting an act of harassment, intimidation or bullying, including a provision that permits a person to report an act of harassment, intimidation or bullying anonymously; * * *

(6) a procedure for prompt investigation of reports of violations and complaints * * *

(7) the range of ways in which a school will respond once an incident of harassment, intimidation or bullying is identified;

(8) a statement that prohibits reprisal or retaliation against any person who reports an act of harassment, intimidation or bullying and the consequence and appropriate remedial action for a person who engages in reprisal or retaliation;

(9) consequences and appropriate remedial action for a person found to have falsely accused * * *

In 2010, the New Jersey legislature amended the law, requiring training for most public school employees on how to spot bullying and mandating that all school districts form "school safety teams" to review complaints.[41] The 2010 statute, the Anti–Bullying Bill of Rights Act, also imposes liability on administrators who fail to investigate complaints. (a) Is the New Jersey anti-bullying law designed to shape preferences or to control conduct? (b) Does the anti-bullying law impose censorship or try to enforce civility norms? (c) In August 2011, Standard & Poor's removed the United States from its list of risk-free borrowers because its analysis showed that "political brinkmanship" made governance and policymaking in the United States "less stable, less effective, and less predictable, than what [was] previously believed."[42] Should Congress regulate the political bullying and childish conduct among its members?

§ 11.5 COMPULSORY EXPRESSIONS

We have already referred to two forms of compulsory expressions: mandatory disclosures and warnings. These forms of expressions may intend to influence the choices, and possibly the preferences, of their recipients. In some instances, however, the purpose of the expression is to influence the person who is required to make it.

The Pledge of Allegiance

In September 1892, as part of the commemoration of the 400th anniversary of Christopher Columbus's discovery of America, Francis Bella-

41. A copy of the New Jersey's Anti–Bullying Bill of Rights Act is available at *regti.me/NJ–ABBRA* (case sensitive).

42. Nikola G. Swann & John Chambers, *United States of America Long–Term Rating Lowered to 'AA+' on Political Risks and Rising Debt Burden*, STANDARD & POOR'S (Aug. 5, 2011), available at *regti.me/US-rating1* (case sensitive).

my, a Christian socialist and a popular author, published *The Pledge of Allegiance* in *The Youth Companion*. The Pledge of Allegiance quickly became a patriotic expression of loyalty. In April 1898, as the United States was preparing for the Spanish–American War, New York passed *An Act to Provide for the Display of the United States Flag on the Schoolhouses of the States*.[43] The stated purpose of the statute was to "encourage patriotic exercises in [public] schools." Section 3 of the Act provided:

> **Patriotic Exercises.**
>
> It shall be the duty of the state superintendent of public instruction to prepare, for the use of public schools of the state, a program providing for a salute to the flag at the opening of each day of school and such other patriotic exercises as may be deemed by him to be expedient. * * *

New York became the first state to require the Pledge of Allegiance in public schools. Other states followed.

Minersville School District v. Gobitis

310 U.S. 586 (1940)

■ MR. JUSTICE FRANKFURTER delivered the opinion of the Court.

A grave responsibility confronts this Court whenever in course of litigation it must reconcile the conflicting claims of liberty and authority. But when the liberty invoked is liberty of conscience, and the authority is authority to safeguard the nation's fellowship, judicial conscience is put to its severest test. Of such a nature is the present controversy.

Lillian Gobitis, aged twelve, and her brother William, aged ten, were expelled from the public schools of Minersville, Pennsylvania, for refusing to salute the national flag as part of a daily school exercise. The local Board of Education required both teachers and pupils to participate in this ceremony. The ceremony is a familiar one. The right hand is placed on the breast and the following pledge recited in unison: 'I pledge allegiance to my flag, and to the Republic for which it stands; one nation indivisible, with liberty and justice for all.' While the words are spoken, teachers and pupils extend their right hands in salute to the flag. The Gobitis family are affiliated with 'Jehovah's Witnesses', for whom the Bible as the Word of God is the supreme authority. The children had been brought up conscientiously to believe that such a gesture of respect for the flag was forbidden by command of scripture.[1]

The Gobitis children were of an age for which Pennsylvania makes school attendance compulsory. Thus they were denied a free education and

---

43. A copy of the New York statute is available at *regti.me/NYpledge* (case sensitive).

1. Reliance is especially placed on the following verses from Chapter 20 of Exodus:

3. Thou shalt have no other gods before me.

4. Thou shalt not make unto thee any graven image, or any likeness of any thing that is in heaven above, or that is in the earth beneath, or that is in the water under the earth:

5. Thou shalt not bow down thyself to them, nor serve them: . . .

their parents had to put them into private schools. To be relieved of the financial burden thereby entailed, their father, on behalf of the children and in his own behalf, brought this suit. * * *

We must decide whether the requirement of participation in such a ceremony, exacted from a child who refuses upon sincere religious grounds, infringes without due process of law the liberty guaranteed by the Fourteenth Amendment.

Centuries of strife over the erection of particular dogmas as exclusive or all-comprehending faiths led to the inclusion of a guarantee for religious freedom in the Bill of Rights. The First Amendment, and the Fourteenth through its absorption of the First, sought to guard against repetition of those bitter religious struggles by prohibiting the establishment of a state religion and by securing to every sect the free exercise of its faith. So pervasive is the acceptance of this precious right that its scope is brought into question, as here, only when the conscience of individuals collides with the felt necessities of society.

Certainly the affirmative pursuit of one's convictions about the ultimate mystery of the universe and man's relation to it is placed beyond the reach of law. Government may not interfere with organized or individual expression of belief or disbelief. * * *

But the manifold character of man's relations may bring his conception of religious duty into conflict with the secular interests of his fellow-men. When does the constitutional guarantee compel exemption from doing what society thinks necessary for the promotion of some great common end, or from a penalty for conduct which appears dangerous to the general good? To state the problem is to recall the truth that no single principle can answer all of life's complexities. The right to freedom of religious belief, however dissident and however obnoxious to the cherished beliefs of others—even of a majority—is itself the denial of an absolute. But to affirm that the freedom to follow conscience has itself no limits in the life of a society would deny that very plurality of principles which, as a matter of history, underlies protection of religious toleration. * * * Our present task then, as so often the case with courts, is to reconcile two rights in order to prevent either from destroying the other. But, because in safeguarding conscience we are dealing with interests so subtle and so dear, every possible leeway should be given to the claims of religious faith.

In the judicial enforcement of religious freedom we are concerned with a historic concept. * * * The religious liberty which the Constitution protects has never excluded legislation of general scope not directed against doctrinal loyalties of particular sects. Judicial nullification of legislation cannot be justified by attributing to the framers of the Bill of Rights views for which there is no historic warrant. Conscientious scruples have not, in the course of the long struggle for religious toleration, relieved the individual from obedience to a general law not aimed at the promotion or restriction of religious beliefs. * * * Even if it were assumed that freedom of speech goes beyond the historic concept of full opportunity to utter and to disseminate views, however heretical or offensive to dominant opinion, and includes freedom from conveying what may be deemed an implied but rejected affirmation, the question remains whether school children, like the

Gobitis children, must be excused from conduct required of all the other children in the promotion of national cohesion. We are dealing with an interest inferior to none in the hierarchy of legal values. National unity is the basis of national security. To deny the legislature the right to select appropriate means for its attainment presents a totally different order of problem from that of the propriety of subordinating the possible ugliness of littered streets to the free expression of opinion through distribution of handbills. * * *

Situations like the present are phases of the profoundest problem confronting a democracy—the problem which Lincoln cast in memorable dilemma: 'Must a government of necessity be too strong for the liberties of its people, or too weak to maintain its own existence?' No mere textual reading or logical talisman can solve the dilemma. And when the issue demands judicial determination, it is not the personal notion of judges of what wise adjustment requires which must prevail.

* * * The ultimate foundation of a free society is the binding tie of cohesive sentiment. Such a sentiment is fostered by all those agencies of the mind and spirit which may serve to gather up the traditions of a people, transmit them from generation to generation, and thereby create that continuity of a treasured common life which constitutes a civilization. 'We live by symbols.' The flag is the symbol of our national unity, transcending all internal differences, however large, within the framework of the Constitution. * * *

The case before us must be viewed as though the legislature of Pennsylvania had itself formally directed the flag-salute for the children of Minersville; had made no exemption for children whose parents were possessed of conscientious scruples like those of the Gobitis family; and had indicated its belief in the desirable ends to be secured by having its public school children share a common experience at those periods of development when their minds are supposedly receptive to its assimilation, by an exercise appropriate in time and place and setting, and one designed to evoke in them appreciation of the nation's hopes and dreams, its sufferings and sacrifices. The precise issue, then, for us to decide is whether the legislatures of the various states and the authorities in a thousand counties and school districts of this country are barred from determining the appropriateness of various means to evoke that unifying sentiment without which there can ultimately be no liberties, civil or religious. To stigmatize legislative judgment in providing for this universal gesture of respect for the symbol of our national life in the setting of the common school as a lawless inroad on that freedom of conscience which the Constitution protects, would amount to no less than the pronouncement of pedagogical and psychological dogma in a field where courts possess no marked and certainly no controlling competence. The influences which help toward a common feeling for the common country are manifold. Some may seem harsh and others no doubt are foolish. Surely, however, the end is legitimate. And the effective means for its attainment are still so uncertain and so unauthenticated by science as to preclude us from putting the widely prevalent belief in flag-saluting beyond the pale of legislative power. It mocks reason and denies our whole history to find in the allowance of a requirement to salute our flag on fitting occasions the seeds of sanction for obeisance to a leader.

The wisdom of training children in patriotic impulses by those compulsions which necessarily pervade so much of the educational process is not for our independent judgment. Even were we convinced of the folly of such a measure, such belief would be no proof of its unconstitutionality. For ourselves, we might be tempted to say that the deepest patriotism is best engendered by giving unfettered scope to the most crochety beliefs. Perhaps it is best, even from the standpoint of those interests which ordinances like the one under review seek to promote, to give to the least popular sect leave from conformities like those here in issue. But the court-room is not the arena for debating issues of educational policy. It is not our province to choose among competing considerations in the subtle process of securing effective loyalty to the traditional ideals of democracy, while respecting at the same time individual idiosyncracies among a people so diversified in racial origins and religious allegiances. So to hold would in effect make us the school board for the country. That authority has not been given to this Court, nor should we assume it.

We are dealing here with the formative period in the development of citizenship. Great diversity of psychological and ethical opinion exists among us concerning the best way to train children for their place in society. Because of these differences and because of reluctance to permit a single, iron-cast system of education to be imposed upon a nation compounded of so many strains, we have held that, even though public education is one of our most cherished democratic institutions, the Bill of Rights bars a state from compelling all children to attend the public schools. * * * But it is a very different thing for this Court to exercise censorship over the conviction of legislatures that a particular program or exercise will best promote in the minds of children who attend the common schools an attachment to the institutions of their country. * * *

■ MR. JUSTICE STONE (dissenting).

* * * Two youths, now fifteen and sixteen years of age, are by the judgment of this Court held liable to expulsion from the public schools and to denial of all publicly supported educational privileges because of their refusal to yield to the compulsion of a law which commands their participation in a school ceremony contrary to their religious convictions. They and their father are citizens and have not exhibited by any action or statement of opinion, any disloyalty to the Government of the United States. They are ready and willing to obey all its laws which do not conflict with what they sincerely believe to be the higher commandments of God. It is not doubted that these convictions are religious, that they are genuine, or that the refusal to yield to the compulsion of the law is in good faith and with all sincerity. It would be a denial of their faith as well as the teachings of most religions to say that children of their age could not have religious convictions.

The law which is thus sustained is unique in the history of Anglo–American legislation. It does more than suppress freedom of speech and more than prohibit the free exercise of religion. * * * For by this law the state seeks to coerce these children to express a sentiment which, as they interpret it, they do not entertain, and which violates their deepest religious convictions. * * * Since the state, in competition with parents, may through teaching in the public schools indoctrinate the minds of the young, it is said that in aid of its undertaking to inspire loyalty and devotion to constituted authority and the flag which symbolizes it, it may coerce the pupil to make affirmation contrary to his belief and in violation of his religious faith. And, finally, it is said that since the Minersville School Board and others are of the opinion that the country will be better served by conformity than by the observance of religious liberty which the Constitution prescribes, the courts are not free to pass judgment on the Board's choice.

* * * The guaranties of civil liberty are but guaranties of freedom of the human mind and spirit and of reasonable freedom and opportunity to express them. * * * If these guaranties are to have any meaning they must, I think, be deemed to withhold from the state any authority to compel belief or the expression of it where that expression violates religious convictions, whatever may be the legislative view of the desirability of such compulsion.

History teaches us that there have been but few infringements of personal liberty by the state which have not been justified, as they are here, in the name of righteousness and the public good, and few which have not been directed, as they are now, at politically helpless minorities. * * * The Constitution may well elicit expressions of loyalty to it and to the government which it created, but it does not command such expressions or otherwise give any indication that compulsory expressions of loyalty play any such part in our scheme of government as to override the constitutional protection of freedom of speech and religion. * * *

But even if this view be rejected and it is considered that there is some scope for the determination by legislatures whether the citizen shall be compelled to give public expression of such sentiments contrary to his religion, I am not persuaded that we should refrain from passing upon the legislative judgment 'as long as the remedial channels of the democratic process remain open and unobstructed.' This seems to me no more than the surrender of the constitutional protection of the liberty of small minorities to the popular will. We have previously pointed to the importance of a searching judicial inquiry into the legislative judgment in situations where prejudice against discrete and insular minorities may tend to curtail the operation of those political processes ordinarily to be relied on to protect minorities. * * * Here we have such a small minority entertaining in good faith a religious belief, which is such a departure from the usual course of human conduct, that most persons are disposed to regard it with little toleration or concern. In such circumstances careful scrutiny of legislative efforts to secure conformity of belief and opinion by a compulsory affirmation of the desired belief, is especially needful if civil rights are to receive any protection. * * *

West Virginia State Board of Education v. Barnette

319 U.S. 624 (1943)

■ MR. JUSTICE JACKSON delivered the opinion of the Court.

Following the decision by this Court on June 3, 1940, in *Minersville School District v. Gobitis*, * * * the West Virginia legislature amended its statutes to require all schools therein to conduct courses of instruction in history, civics, and in the Constitutions of the United States and of the State 'for the purpose of teaching, fostering and perpetuating the ideals, principles and spirit of Americanism, and increasing the knowledge of the organization and machinery of the government.' Appellant Board of Education was directed, with advice of the State Superintendent of Schools, to 'prescribe the courses of study covering these subjects' for public schools. The Act made it the duty of private, parochial and denominational schools to prescribe courses of study 'similar to those required for the public schools.'[1]

The Board of Education on January 9, 1942, adopted a resolution containing recitals taken largely from the Court's *Gobitis* opinion ordering that the salute to the flag become 'a regular part of the program of activities in the public schools,' that all teachers and pupils 'shall be required to participate in the salute honoring the Nation represented by the Flag; provided, however, that refusal to salute the Flag be regarded as an Act of insubordination, and shall be dealt with accordingly.'[2]

---

1. § 1734, West Virginia Code (1941 Supp.):

In all public, private, parochial and denominational schools located within this state there shall be given regular courses of instruction in history of the United States, in civics, and in the constitutions of the United States and of the state of West Virginia, for the purpose of teaching, fostering and perpetuating the ideals, principles and spirit of Americanism, and increasing the knowledge of the organization and machinery of the government of the United States and of the state of West Virginia. * * *

2. The text is as follows:

WHEREAS, The West Virginia State Board of Education holds in highest regard those rights and privileges guaranteed by the Bill of Rights in the Constitution of the United States of America and in the Constitution of West Virginia, specifically, the first amendment to the Constitution of the United States as restated in the fourteenth amendment to the same document and in the guarantee of religious freedom in Article III of the Constitution of this States, and

WHEREAS, The West Virginia State Board of Education honors the broad principle that one's convictions about the ultimate mystery of the universe and man's relation to it is placed beyond the reach of law; that the propagation of belief is protected whether in church or chapel, mosque or synagogue, tabernacle or meeting house; that the Constitutions of the United States and of the State of West Virginia assure generous immunity to the individual from imposition of penalty for offending, in the course of his own religious activities, the religious views of others, be they a minority or those who are dominant in the government, but

WHEREAS, The West Virginia State Board of Education recognizes that the manifold character of man's relations may bring his conception of religious duty into conflict with the secular interests of his fellowman; that conscientious scruples have not in the course of the long struggle for religious toleration relieved the individual from obedience to the general law not aimed at the promotion or restriction of the religious beliefs; that the mere possession of convictions which contradict the relevant concerns

The resolution originally required the 'commonly accepted salute to the Flag' which it defined. Objections to the salute as 'being too much like Hitler's were raised by the Parent and Teachers Association, the Boy and Girl Scouts, the Red Cross, and the Federation of Women's Clubs.[3] Some modification appears to have been made in deference to these objections, but no concession was made to Jehovah's Witnesses. What is now required is the 'stiff-arm' salute, the saluter to keep the right hand raised with palm turned up while the following is repeated: 'I pledge allegiance to the Flag of the United States of America and to the Republic for which it stands; one Nation, indivisible, with liberty and justice for all.'

Failure to conform is 'insubordination' dealt with by expulsion. Readmission is denied by statute until compliance. Meanwhile the expelled child is 'unlawfully absent'[5] and may be proceeded against as a delinquent. His

---

of political society does not relieve the citizen from the discharge of political responsibility, and

WHEREAS, The West Virginia State Board of Education holds that national unity is the basis of national security; that the flag of our Nation is the symbol of our National Unity transcending all internal differences, however large within the framework of the Constitution; that the Flag is the symbol of the Nation's power; that emblem of freedom in its truest, best sense; that it signifies government resting on the consent of the governed, liberty regulated by law, protection of the weak against the strong, security against the exercise of arbitrary power, and absolute safety for free institutions against foreign aggression, and

WHEREAS, The West Virginia State Board of Education maintains that the public schools, established by the legislature of the State of West Virginia under the authority of the Constitution of the State of West Virginia and supported by taxes imposed by legally constituted measures, are dealing with the formative period in the development in citizenship that the Flag is an allowable portion of the program of schools thus publicly supported.

Therefore, be it RESOLVED, That the West Virginia Board of Education does hereby recognize and order that the commonly accepted salute to the Flag of the United States-the right hand is placed upon the breast and the following pledge repeated in unison: 'I pledge allegiance to the Flag of the United States of America and to the Republic for which it stands; one Nation, indivisible, with liberty and justice for all'—now becomes a regular part of the program of activities in the public schools, supported in whole or in part by public funds, and that all teachers as defined by law in West Virginia and pupils in such schools shall be required to participate in the salute honoring the Nation represented by the Flag; provided, however, that refusal to salute the Flag be regarded as an act of insubordination, and shall be dealt with accordingly.

3. The National Headquarters of the United States Flag Association takes the position that the extension of the right arm in this salute to the flag is not the Nazi–Fascist salute, 'although quite similar to it. In the Pledge to the Flag the right arm is extended and raised, palm Upward, whereas the Nazis extend the arm practically straight to the front (the finger tips being about even with the eyes), palm Downward, and the Fascists do the same except they raise the arm slightly higher.' James A. Moss, The Flag of the United States: Its History and Symbolism 108 (1914).

5. § 1851(1), West Virginia Code (1941 Supp.):

If a child be dismissed, suspended, or expelled from school because of refusal of such child to meet the legal and lawful requirements of the school and the established regulations of the county and/or state board of education, further admission of the child to school shall be refused until such requirements and regulations be complied with. Any such child shall be treated as being unlawfully absent from the school during the time he refuses to comply with such requirements and regulations, and parents or guardians are liable to prosecution, and if convicted are subject to fine not exceeding $50 and jail term not exceeding thirty days.

Appellees, citizens of the United States and of West Virginia, brought suit * * * for themselves and others similarly situated asking its injunction to restrain enforcement of these laws and regulations against Jehovah's Witnesses. The Witnesses are an unincorporated body teaching that the obligation imposed by law of God is superior to that of laws enacted by temporal government. Their religious beliefs include a literal version of Exodus, Chapter 20, verses 4 and 5, which says: 'Thou shalt not make unto thee any graven image, or any likeness of anything that is in heaven above, or that is in the earth beneath, or that is in the water under the earth; thou shalt not bow down thyself to them nor serve them.' They consider that the flag is an 'image' within this command. For this reason they refuse to salute it.

Children of this faith have been expelled from school and are threatened with exclusion for no other cause. Officials threaten to send them to reformatories maintained for criminally inclined juveniles. Parents of such children have been prosecuted and are threatened with prosecutions for causing delinquency.

* * *

The freedom asserted by these appellees does not bring them into collision with rights asserted by any other individual. It is such conflicts which most frequently require intervention of the State to determine where the rights of one end and those of another begin. But the refusal of these persons to participate in the ceremony does not interfere with or deny rights of others to do so. Nor is there any question in this case that their behavior is peaceable and orderly. The sole conflict is between authority and rights of the individual. The State asserts power to condition access to public education on making a prescribed sign and profession and at the same time to coerce attendance by punishing both parent and child. The latter stand on a right of self-determination in matters that touch individual opinion and personal attitude.

As the present Chief Justice said in dissent in the *Gobitis* case, the State may 'require teaching by instruction and study of all in our history and in the structure and organization of our government, including the guaranties of civil liberty which tend to inspire patriotism and love of country.' Here, however, we are dealing with a compulsion of students to declare a belief. They are not merely made acquainted with the flag salute so that they may be informed as to what it is or even what it means. The issue here is whether this slow and easily neglected route to aroused loyalties constitutionally may be short-cut by substituting a compulsory salute and slogan.[12] * * *

---

any person having legal or actual control of such child shall be liable to prosecution under the provisions of this article for the absence of such child from school.

12. The Resolution of the Board of Education did not adopt the flag salute because it was claimed to have educational value. It seems to have been concerned with promotion of national unity (see footnote 2), which justification is considered later in this opinion. No information as to its educational aspect is called to our attention except Olander, *Children's*

There is no doubt that, in connection with the pledges, the flag salute is a form of utterance. Symbolism is a primitive but effective way of communicating ideas. The use of an emblem or flag to symbolize some system, idea, institution, or personality, is a short cut from mind to mind. Causes and nations, political parties, lodges and ecclesiastical groups seek to knit the loyalty of their followings to a flag or banner, a color or design. The State announces rank, function, and authority through crowns and maces, uniforms and black robes; the church speaks through the Cross, the Crucifix, the altar and shrine, and clerical reiment. Symbols of State often convey political ideas just as religious symbols come to convey theological ones. Associated with many of these symbols are appropriate gestures of acceptance or respect: a salute, a bowed or bared head, a bended knee. A person gets from a symbol the meaning he puts into it, and what is one man's comfort and inspiration is another's jest and scorn.

* * * Here * * * the State * * * employs a flag as a symbol of adherence to government as presently organized. It requires the individual to communicate by word and sign his acceptance of the political ideas it thus bespeaks. Objection to this form of communication when coerced is an old one, well known to the framers of the Bill of Rights.

It is also to be noted that the compulsory flag salute and pledge requires affirmation of a belief and an attitude of mind. It is not clear whether the regulation contemplates that pupils forego any contrary convictions of their own and become unwilling converts to the prescribed ceremony or whether it will be acceptable if they simulate assent by words without belief and by a gesture barren of meaning. It is now a commonplace that censorship or suppression of expression of opinion is tolerated by our Constitution only when the expression presents a clear and present danger of action of a kind the State is empowered to prevent and punish. It would seem that involuntary affirmation could be commanded only on even more immediate and urgent grounds than silence. But here the power of compulsion is invoked without any allegation that remaining passive during a flag salute ritual creates a clear and present danger that would justify an effort even to muffle expression. To sustain the compulsory flag salute we are required to say that a Bill of Rights which guards the individual's right to speak his own mind, left it open to public authorities to compel him to utter what is not in his mind.

* * *

Struggles to coerce uniformity of sentiment in support of some end thought essential to their time and country have been waged by many good as well as by evil men. Nationalism is a relatively recent phenomenon but at other times and places the ends have been racial or territorial security, support of a dynasty or regime, and particular plans for saving souls. * * * Those who begin coercive elimination of dissent soon find themselves

---

Knowledge of the Flag Salute, 35 Journal of Educational Research, 300, 305, which sets forth a study of the ability of a large and representative number of children to remember and state the meaning of the flag salute which they recited each day in school. His conclusion was that it revealed 'a rather pathetic picture of our attempts to teach children not only the words but the meaning of our Flag Salute.'

exterminating dissenters. Compulsory unification of opinion achieves only the unanimity of the graveyard.

* * *

The case is made difficult * * * because the flag involved is our own. Nevertheless, we apply the limitations of the Constitution with no fear that freedom to be intellectually and spiritually diverse or even contrary will disintegrate the social organization. To believe that patriotism will not flourish if patriotic ceremonies are voluntary and spontaneous instead of a compulsory routine is to make an unflattering estimate of the appeal of our institutions to free minds. We can have intellectual individualism and the rich cultural diversities that we owe to exceptional minds only at the price of occasional eccentricity and abnormal attitudes. When they are so harmless to others or to the State as those we deal with here, the price is not too great. But freedom to differ is not limited to things that do not matter much. That would be a mere shadow of freedom. The test of its substance is the right to differ as to things that touch the heart of the existing order.

If there is any fixed star in our constitutional constellation, it is that no official, high or petty, can prescribe what shall be orthodox in politics, nationalism, religion, or other matters of opinion or force citizens to confess by word or act their faith therein. * * *

We think the action of the local authorities in compelling the flag salute and pledge transcends constitutional limitations on their power and invades the sphere of intellect and spirit which it is the purpose of the First Amendment to our Constitution to reserve from all official control.

* * *

■ MR. JUSTICE BLACK and MR. JUSTICE DOUGLAS, concurring.

We are substantially in agreement with the opinion just read, but since we originally joined with the Court in the *Gobitis* case, it is appropriate that we make a brief statement of reasons for our change of view.

Reluctance to make the Federal Constitution a rigid bar against state regulation of conduct thought inimical to the public welfare was the controlling influence which moved us to consent to the *Gobitis* decision. Long reflection convinced us that although the principle is sound, its application in the particular case was wrong. We believe that the statute before us fails to accord full scope to the freedom of religion secured to the appellees by the First and Fourteenth Amendments.

The statute requires the appellees to participate in a ceremony aimed at inculcating respect for the flag and for this country. The Jehovah's Witnesses, without any desire to show disrespect for either the flag or the country, interpret the Bible as commanding, at the risk of God's displeasure, that they not go through the form of a pledge of allegiance to any flag. The devoutness of their belief is evidenced by their willingness to suffer persecution and punishment, rather than make the pledge.

No well-ordered society can leave to the individuals an absolute right to make final decisions, unassailable by the State, as to everything they will or will not do. The First Amendment does not go so far. Religious faiths, honestly held, do not free individuals from responsibility to conduct themselves obediently to laws which are either imperatively necessary to protect society as a whole from grave and pressingly imminent dangers or which, without any general prohibition, merely regulate time, place or manner of religious activity. Decision as to the constitutionality of particular laws which strike at the substance of religious tenets and practices must be made be this Court. The duty is a solemn one, and in meeting it we cannot say that a failure, because of religious scruples, to assume a particular physical position and to repeat the words of a patriotic formula creates a grave danger to the nation. Such a statutory exaction is a form of test oath, and the test oath has always been abhorrent in the United States.

Words uttered under coercion are proof of loyalty to nothing but self-interest. Love of country must spring from willing hearts and free minds, inspired by a fair administration of wise laws enacted by the people's elected representatives within the bounds of express constitutional prohibitions. These laws must, to be consistent with the First Amendment, permit the widest toleration of conflicting viewpoints consistent with a society of free men.

Neither our domestic tranquillity in peace nor our martial effort in war depend on compelling little children to participate in a ceremony which ends in nothing for them but a fear of spiritual condemnation. If, as we think, their fears are groundless, time and reason are the proper antidotes for their errors. The ceremonial, when enforced against conscientious objectors, more likely to defeat than to serve its high purpose, is a handy implement for disguised religious persecution. As such, it is inconsistent with our Constitution's plan and purpose.

■ MR. JUSTICE FRANKFURTER, dissenting.

One who belongs to the most vilified and persecuted minority in history is not likely to be insensible to the freedoms guaranteed by our Constitution. Were my purely personal attitude relevant I should wholeheartedly associate myself with the general libertarian views in the Court's opinion, representing as they do the thought and action of a lifetime. But as judges we are neither Jew nor Gentile, neither Catholic nor agnostic. We owe equal attachment to the Constitution and are equally bound by our judicial obligations whether we derive our citizenship from the earliest or the latest immigrants to these shores. As a member of this Court I am not justified in writing my private notions of policy into the Constitution, no matter how deeply I may cherish them or how mischievous I may deem their disregard. They duty of a judge who must decide which of two claims before the Court shall prevail, that of a State to enact and enforce laws within its general competence or that of an individual to refuse obedience because of the demands of his conscience, is not that of the ordinary person. It can never be emphasized too much that one's own opinion about the wisdom or evil of a law should be excluded altogether when one is doing one's duty on the bench. The only opinion of our own even looking in that direction that is material is our opinion whether legislators could in reason have enacted such a law. In the light of all the circumstances, including the history of this question in this Court, it would require more daring than I possess to deny that reasonable legislators could have taken the action which is before us for review. Most unwillingly, therefore, I must differ from my brethren with regard to legislation like this. I cannot bring my mind to believe that the 'liberty' secured by the Due Process Clause gives this Court authority to deny to the State of West Virginia the attainment of that which we all recognize as a legitimate legislative end, namely, the promotion of good citizenship, by employment of the means here chosen. * * *

An act compelling profession of allegiance to a religion, no matter how subtly or tenuously promoted, is bad. But an act promoting good citizenship and national allegiance is within the domain of governmental authority and is therefore to be judged by the same considerations of power and of constitutionality as those involved in the many claims of immunity from civil obedience because of religious scruples.

That claims are pressed on behalf of sincere religious convictions does not of itself establish their constitutional validity. Nor does waving the banner of religious freedom relieve us from examining into the power we are asked to deny the states. Otherwise the doctrine of separation of church and state, so cardinal in the history of this nation and for the liberty of our people, would mean not the disestablishment of a state church but the establishment of all churches and of all religious groups.

The subjection of dissidents to the general requirement of saluting the flag, as a measure conducive to the training of children in good citizenship, is very far from being the first instance of exacting obedience to general laws that have offended deep religious scruples. Compulsory vaccination, see *Jacobson v. Massachusetts*, 197 U.S. 11 (1905), food inspection regulations, * * * the obligation to bear arms, * * * compulsory medical treatment—these are but illustrations of conduct that has often been compelled in the enforcement of legislation of general applicability even though the religious consciences of particular individuals rebelled at the exaction.

Law is concerned with external behavior and not with the inner life of man. It rests in large measure upon compulsion. * * * The state is not shut out from a domain because the individual conscience may deny the state's claim. * * *

We are told that a flag salute is a doubtful substitute for adequate understanding of our institutions. * * * We may deem it a foolish measure, but the point is that this Court is not the organ of government to resolve doubts as to whether it will fulfill its purpose. Only if there be no doubt that any reasonable mind could entertain can we deny to the states the right to resolve doubts their way and not ours.

* * *

We are told that symbolism is a dramatic but primitive way of communicating ideas. Symbolism is inescapable. Even the most sophisticated live by symbols. But it is not for this Court to make psychological judgments as to the effectiveness of a particular symbol in inculcating concededly indispensable feelings, particularly if the state happens to see fit to utilize the symbol that represents our heritage and our hopes. And surely only flippancy could be responsible for the suggestion that constitutional validity of a requirement to salute our flag implies equal validity of a requirement to salute a dictator. The significance of a symbol lies in what it represents. To reject the swastika does not imply rejection of the Cross. * * * To deny the power to employ educational symbols is to say that the state's educational system may not stimulate the imagination because this may lead to unwise stimulation.

* * *

Of course patriotism cannot be enforced by the flag salute. But neither can the liberal spirit be enforced by judicial invalidation of illiberal legislation. Our constant preoccupation with the constitutionality of legislation rather than with its wisdom tends to preoccupation of the American mind with a false value. The tendency of focusing attention on constitutionality is to make constitutionality synonymous with wisdom, to regard a law as all right if it is constitutional. Such an attitude is a great enemy of liberalism. Particularly in legislation affecting freedom of thought and freedom of speech much which should offend a free-spirited society is constitutional. Reliance for the most precious interests of civilization, therefore, must be found outside of their vindication in courts of law. Only a persistent positive translation of the faith of a free society into the convictions and habits and actions of a community is the ultimate reliance against unabated temptations to fetter the human spirit.

Questions

1. Laws requiring students to participate in the recitation of the Pledge of Allegiance intend to foster patriotism in a particular way. Under *Barnette*, can states adopt alternative mandatory measures that foster patriotism and develop enmity toward national enemies? For example, can states design curricula with movies that evoke patriotic sentiments and present the enemy in a negative way?

2. Many states established and some still maintain abstinence-until-marriage education programs. For example, the Texas law provides:

> * * *
>
> (e) Any course materials and instruction relating to human sexuality, sexually transmitted diseases, or human immunodeficiency virus or acquired immune deficiency syndrome shall be selected by the board of trustees with the advice of the local school health advisory council and must:
>
> (1) present abstinence from sexual activity as the preferred choice of behavior in relationship to all sexual activity for unmarried persons of school age;
>
> (2) devote more attention to abstinence from sexual activity than to any other behavior;
>
> (3) emphasize that abstinence from sexual activity, if used consistently and correctly, is the only method that is 100 percent effective in preventing pregnancy, sexually transmitted diseases, infection with human immunodeficiency virus or acquired immune deficiency syndrome, and the emotional trauma associated with adolescent sexual activity;

(4) direct adolescents to a standard of behavior in which abstinence from sexual activity before marriage is the most effective way to prevent pregnancy, sexually transmitted diseases, and infection with human immunodeficiency virus or acquired immune deficiency syndrome; and

(5) teach contraception and condom use in terms of human use reality rates instead of theoretical laboratory rates, if instruction on contraception and condoms is included in curriculum content.

(f) A school district may not distribute condoms in connection with instruction relating to human sexuality.

(g) A school district that provides human sexuality instruction may separate students according to sex for instructional purposes.[43]

In *Barnette*, Justice Jackson wrote: "If there is any fixed star in our constitutional constellation, it is that no official, high or petty, can prescribe what shall be orthodox in politics, nationalism, religion, or other matters of opinion. * * * " Are abstinence-until-marriage education programs consistent with the Court's ruling in *Barnette*?

Live Free or Die

Figure 11.2
New Hampshire Emblem

In May 1945, the New Hampshire legislature passed *An Act Establishing the State Emblem*. The Act provided that:

---

43. Tex. Educ. Code Ann. § 28.004.

> The state emblem shall be of the following design: Within an elliptical panel, the longest dimension of which shall be vertical, there shall appear an appropriate replica of the Old Man of the Mountain; surrounding the inner panel, and enclosed within another ellipse, there shall be at the bottom of the design the words of any state motto which may be adopted by the general court; and at the top of the design, between the inner and outer elliptical panels, the words, New Hampshire, appropriately separated from the motto, if adopted, by one star on each side. Said emblem may be placed on all printed or related material issued by the state and its subdivisions relative to the development of recreational, industrial, and agricultural resources of the state.[44]

A week later, the legislature adopted *An Act Establishing the State Motto*. This Act provided that "[t]he words 'Live Free or Die,' written by General John Stark, July 31, 1809, shall be the official motto of the state."[45]

Twenty-four years later, in 1969, the New Hampshire Legislature amended the statutory requirements relating to motor vehicle license plates to provide:

> Every vehicle driven in or on any way in this state, if required to be registered hereunder, shall have displayed conspicuously thereon a number plate or plates. * * * [N]umber plates for passenger vehicles shall have the state motto "Live Free or Die" written thereon. The plate shall be kept clean.[46]

Wooley v. Maynard

430 U.S. 705 (1977)

■ MR. CHIEF JUSTICE BURGER delivered the opinion of the Court.

The issue on appeal is whether the State of New Hampshire may constitutionally enforce criminal sanctions against persons who cover the motto "Live Free or Die" on passenger vehicle license plates because that motto is repugnant to their moral and religious beliefs.

(1)

Since 1969 New Hampshire has required that noncommercial vehicles bear license plates embossed with the state motto, "Live Free or Die."[1] N.H. Rev. Stat. Ann. § 263:1 (Supp. 1975). Another New Hampshire statute makes it a misdemeanor "knowingly (to obscure) . . . the figures or letters on any number plate." N.H. Rev. Stat. Ann. § 262:27–c (Supp.

---

44. N.H. Rev. Stat. Ann. § 3:1.

45. N.H. Rev. Stat. Ann. § 3:8.

46. N.H. Rev. Stat. Ann. § 261:75. An image of a "Live Free or Die" plate is available at *regti.me/NHPlate* (case sensitive).

1. License plates are issued without the state motto for trailers, agricultural vehicles, car dealers, antique automobiles, the Governor of New Hampshire, its Congressional Representatives, its Attorney General, Justices of the State Supreme Court, veterans, chaplains of the state legislature, sheriffs, and others.

1975). The term "letters" in this section has been interpreted by the State's highest court to include the state motto. *State v. Hoskin*, 112 N.H. 332 (1972).

Appellees George Maynard and his wife Maxine are followers of the Jehovah's Witnesses faith. The Maynards consider the New Hampshire State motto to be repugnant to their moral, religious, and political beliefs,[2] and therefore assert it objectionable to disseminate this message by displaying it on their automobiles.[3] Pursuant to these beliefs, the Maynards began early in 1974 to cover up the motto on their license plates.

On November 27, 1974, Mr. Maynard was issued a citation for violating § 262:27–c. On December 6, 1974, he appeared pro se in Lebanon, N.H., District Court to answer the charge. After waiving his right to counsel, he entered a plea of not guilty and proceeded to explain his religious objections to the motto. The state trial judge expressed sympathy for Mr. Maynard's situation, but considered himself bound by the authority of *State v. Hoskin*, *supra*, to hold Maynard guilty. A $25 fine was imposed, but execution was suspended during "good behavior."

On December 28, 1974, Mr. Maynard was again charged with violating § 262:27–c. He appeared in court on January 31, 1975, and again chose to represent himself; he was found guilty, fined $50, and sentenced to six months in the Grafton County House of Corrections. The court suspended this jail sentence but ordered Mr. Maynard to also pay the $25 fine for the first offense. Maynard informed the court that, as a matter of conscience, he refused to pay the two fines. The court thereupon sentenced him to jail for a period of 15 days. He has served the full sentence.

Prior to trial on the second offense Mr. Maynard was charged with yet a third violation of § 262:27–c on January 3, 1975. He appeared on this complaint on the same day as for the second offense, and was, again, found guilty. This conviction was "continued for sentence" so that Maynard received no punishment in addition to the 15 days.

* * *

(4)

The District Court held that by covering up the state motto "Live Free or Die" on his automobile license plate, Mr. Maynard was engaging in symbolic speech and that "New Hampshire's interest in the enforcement of its defacement statute is not sufficient to justify the restriction on (appellee's) constitutionally protected expression." *Maynard v. Wooley*, 406 F.

---

2. Mr. Maynard described his objection to the state motto:

"(B)y religious training and belief, I believe my 'government' Jehovah's Kingdom offers everlasting life. It would be contrary to that belief to give up my life for the state, even if it meant living in bondage. Although I obey all laws of the State not in conflict with my conscience, this slogan is directly at odds with my deeply held religious convictions.

". . . I also disagree with the motto on political grounds. I believe that life is more precious than freedom." Affidavit of George Maynard, App. 3.

3. At the time this suit was commenced appellees owned two automobiles, a Toyota Corolla and a Plymouth station wagon. Both automobiles were registered in New Hampshire where the Maynards are domiciled.

Supp. 1381, at 1389 (D.N.H. 1976). We find it unnecessary to pass on the "symbolic speech" issue, since we find more appropriate First Amendment grounds to affirm the judgment of the District Court. We turn instead to what in our view is the essence of appellees' objection to the requirement that they display the motto "Live Free or Die" on their automobile license plates. This is succinctly summarized in the statement made by Mr. Maynard in his affidavit filed with the District Court:

> "I refuse to be coerced by the State into advertising a slogan which I find morally, ethically, religiously and politically abhorrent." App. 5.

We are thus faced with the question of whether the State may constitutionally require an individual to participate in the dissemination of an ideological message by displaying it on his private property in a manner and for the express purpose that it be observed and read by the public. We hold that the State may not do so.

A

We begin with the proposition that the right of freedom of thought protected by the First Amendment against state action includes both the right to speak freely and the right to refrain from speaking at all. * * *

The Court in *West Virginia State Board of Education v. Barnette*, 319 U.S. 624 (1943), was faced with a state statute which required public school students to participate in daily public ceremonies by honoring the flag both with words and traditional salute gestures. [T]the Court held that "a ceremony so touching matters of opinion and political attitude may (not) be imposed upon the individual by official authority under powers committed to any political organization under our Constitution." Compelling the affirmative act of a flag salute involved a more serious infringement upon personal liberties than the passive act of carrying the state motto on a license plate, but the difference is essentially one of degree. Here, as in *Barnette*, we are faced with a state measure which forces an individual, as part of his daily life indeed constantly while his automobile is in public view to be an instrument for fostering public adherence to an ideological point of view he finds unacceptable. In doing so, the State "invades the sphere of intellect and spirit which it is the purpose of the First Amendment to our Constitution to reserve from all official control." *Barnette*, at 642.

New Hampshire's statute in effect requires that appellees use their private property as a "mobile billboard" for the State's ideological message or suffer a penalty, as Maynard already has. As a condition to driving an automobile a virtual necessity for most Americans the Maynards must display "Live Free or Die" to hundreds of people each day.[11] The fact that most individuals agree with the thrust of New Hampshire's motto is not the test; most Americans also find the flag salute acceptable. The First Amendment protects the right of individuals to hold a point of view

---

11. Some States require that certain documents bear the seal of the State or some other official stamp for purposes of recordation. Such seal might contain, albeit obscurely, a symbol or motto having political or philosophical implications. The purpose of such seal, however, is not to advertise the message it bears but simply to authenticate the document by showing the authority of its origin.

different from the majority and to refuse to foster, in the way New Hampshire commands, an idea they find morally objectionable.

B

Identifying the Maynards' interests as implicating First Amendment protections does not end our inquiry however. We must also determine whether the State's countervailing interest is sufficiently compelling to justify requiring appellees to display the state motto on their license plates. * * * The two interests advanced by the State are that display of the motto (1) facilitates the identification of passenger vehicles,[12] and (2) promotes appreciation of history, individualism, and state pride.

The State first points out that passenger vehicles, but not commercial, trailer, or other vehicles are required to display the state motto. Thus, the argument proceeds, officers of the law are more easily able to determine whether passenger vehicles are carrying the proper plates. However, the record here reveals that New Hampshire passenger license plates normally consist of a specific configuration of letters and numbers, which makes them readily distinguishable from other types of plates, even without reference to the state motto.[13] Even were we to credit the State's reasons and "even though the governmental purpose be legitimate and substantial, that purpose cannot be pursued by means that broadly stifle fundamental personal liberties when the end can be more narrowly achieved. The breadth of legislative abridgment must be viewed in the light of less drastic means for achieving the same basic purpose." *Shelton v. Tucker*, 364 U.S. 479, 488 (1960) (footnotes omitted).

The State's second claimed interest is not ideologically neutral. The State is seeking to communicate to others an official view as to proper appreciation of history, state pride, and individualism. Of course, the State may legitimately pursue such interests in any number of ways. However, where the State's interest is to disseminate an ideology, no matter how acceptable to some, such interest cannot outweigh an individual's First Amendment right to avoid becoming the courier for such message.[14]

We conclude that the State of New Hampshire may not require appellees to display the state motto[15] upon their vehicle license plates. * * *

---

12. The Chief of Police of Lebanon, N. H., testified that "enforcement of the motor vehicle laws is facilitated by the State Motto appearing on noncommercial license plates, the benefits being the ease of distinguishing New Hampshire license plates from those of similar colors of other states and the ease of discovering misuse of license plates, for instance, the use of a 'trailer' license plate on a non-commercial vehicle." * * *

13. New Hampshire passenger vehicle license plates generally consist of two letters followed by four numbers. No other license plate category displays this combination, and no other category bears the state motto. * * * However, of the approximately 325,000 passenger plates in New Hampshire, 9,999 do not follow the regular pattern, displaying numbers only, preceded by no letters. * * *

14. Appellants do not explain why advocacy of these values is enhanced by display on private citizens' cars but not on the cars of officials such as the Governor, Supreme Court Justices, Members of Congress and sheriffs. *See* n. 1, *supra*.

15. It has been suggested that today's holding will be read as sanctioning the obliteration of the national motto, "In God We Trust" from United States coins and currency. That

■ MR. JUSTICE REHNQUIST, with whom MR. JUSTICE BLACKMUN joins, dissenting.

The Court holds that a State is barred by the Federal Constitution from requiring that the state motto be displayed on a state license plate. The path that the Court travels to reach this result demonstrates the difficulty in supporting it. The Court holds that the required display of the motto is an unconstitutional "required affirmation of belief." * * *

The logic of the Court's opinion leads to startling, and I believe totally unacceptable, results. For example, the mottoes "In God We Trust" and "E Pluribus Unum" appear on the coin and currency of the United States. I cannot imagine that the statutes, see 18 U.S.C. §§ 331 and 333, proscribing defacement of United States currency impinge upon the First Amendment rights of an atheist. The fact that an atheist carries and uses United States currency does not, in any meaningful sense, convey any affirmation of belief on his part in the motto "In God We Trust." Similarly, there is no affirmation of belief involved in the display of state license tags upon the private automobiles involved here. * * *

Questions

1. What motor vehicles were required to have the New Hampshire state motto on the license plate? How did New Hampshire justify the distinction among categories of motor vehicles?

2. Did the requirement to have the motto "Live Free Or Die" on license plates promote freedom? What was the purpose of the requirement?

3. The motto "In God We Trust" first appeared on coins in April 1864, when the federal Mint Director released the 2–cent coin. In early 1907, the Department of Treasury announced it would introduce a new design of a double-eagle gold dollar. President Roosevelt instructed the Treasury to design the coin without the motto. In November 1907, the President released to the press a letter he wrote in reply to one of the many inquiries he had received from citizens regarding the issue.

> Dear Sir:
>
> When the question of the new coinage came up we looked into the law and found there was no warrant therein for putting 'In God We Trust' on the Coins. As the custom, although without legal warrant, had grown up, however, I might have felt at liberty to keep the inscription had I approved of its being on the coinage. But as I did not approve of it, I did not direct that it should again be put on.
>
> My own feeling in the matter is due to my very firm conviction that to put such a motto on coins, or to use it in any kindred manner, not only does no good, but does positive harm, and is in effect irreverence which comes dangerously near to sacrilege. A

---

question is not before us today but we note that currency, which is passed from hand to hand, differs in significant respects from an automobile, which is readily associated with its operator. Currency is generally carried in a purse or pocket and need not be displayed to the public. The bearer of currency is thus not required to publicly advertise the national motto.

beautiful and solemn sentence, such as the one in question, should be treated and uttered only with that the fine reverence, which necessarily implies certain exaltation of spirit. Any use which tends to cheapen it, and above all, any use which tends to secure its being treated in a spirit of levity is, from every standpoint, profoundly to be regretted.

It is a motto which it is indeed well to have inscribed on our great national monuments, in our temples of justices, in our legislative halls, and in buildings such as those at West Point and Annapolis—in short, wherever it will tend to arouse and inspire a lofty emotion in those who look thereon. But it seems to me eminently unwise to cheapen such a motto by use on coins, just as it would be cheapen it by use on postage stamps or advertisements.

In all my life I have never heard any human speak reverently of this motto on the coins, or show any sign of its having appealed to any high emotion to him. But I have literally hundreds of times heard of it used as an occasion of, and incitement to, the sneering ridicule which it is above all things undesirable. * * *

Sincerely yours,

THEODORE ROOSEVELT

President Roosevelt's decision was unpopular. In May 1908, Congress enacted a law requiring that the motto "In God We Trust" would appear on all coins of dominations, upon which the motto had previously appeared.[47] On November 2, 2011, Congress adopted a resolution "[r]eaffirming 'In God We Trust' as the official motto of the United States and supporting and encouraging the public display of the national motto in all public buildings, public schools, and other government institutions."[48] The resolution briefly described the significance of the national motto and, among other things, stated that "if religion and morality are taken out of the marketplace of ideas, the very freedom on which the United States was founded cannot be secured."

In *Wooley v. Maynard*, Justice Rehnquist wrote: "The fact that an atheist carries and uses United States currency does not, in any meaningful sense, convey any affirmation of belief on his part in the motto 'In God We Trust.' " What is the purpose of having the national motto on coins and currency? Does the fact that an atheist carries and uses U.S. currency convey any message?

Cigarettes in Pharmacies

In July 2008, the San Francisco Board of Supervisors lawmakers voted to make the City the first in the nation to ban the sale of tobacco products

---

47. Pub. L. No. 60–120, 35 Stat. 164 (May 18, 1908).

48. H. Con. Res. 13, 112 Cong. (Nov. 2, 2011), available at *regti.me/IGT2011* (case sensitive).

at pharmacies.[49] Mayor Gavin Newsom, who proposed the ban, stated its rationale: "A pharmacy is a place you should go to get better, not to get cancer." Philip Morris and Walgreen separately challenged the constitutionality of the ban.

Walgreen Co. v. San Francisco

Court of Appeal, First District, Division 3, California
185 Cal.App.4th 424 (2010)

■ McGUINESS, PRESIDING JUSTICE

In this appeal we consider a challenge to an ordinance enacted by the City and County of San Francisco (the City) banning the sale of tobacco products in certain retail establishments that contain a pharmacy. The ordinance is premised on the notion that a retail store conveys tacit approval of tobacco use when it sells prescription drugs as well as tobacco products. Appellant Walgreen Co. (Walgreens) contends the ordinance violates the equal protection clauses of the federal and state constitutions, arguing there is no rational basis for prohibiting its stores with pharmacies from selling tobacco products while allowing such sales at "general grocery" stores and "big box" stores that contain pharmacies. * * *

[W]e agree with Walgreens that its complaint adequately states a cause of action alleging an equal protection violation. * * * There is no rational basis to believe the supposed implied message conveyed by selling tobacco products at a Walgreens that has a licensed pharmacy in the back of the store is different in any meaningful way from the implied message conveyed by selling such products at a supermarket or big box store that contains a licensed pharmacy. * * *

FACTUAL AND PROCEDURAL BACKGROUND

The legislation challenged in this appeal, City Ordinance No. 194–08 (hereafter the ordinance), amended the San Francisco Health Code to provide that "No person shall sell tobacco products[1] in a pharmacy, except as provided in [San Francisco Health Code] Sec. 1009.93." * * * The term "pharmacy" is defined in the ordinance to refer to the entire retail establishment that includes the portion normally referred to as a pharmacy, giving rise to some confusion in terminology.[2] TO AVOID CONFUSION and be consistent with the language of the ordinance, we shall refer to the section of a retail establishment in which a licensed pharmacist prepares and sells prescription pharmaceuticals as a "licensed pharmacy," in contrast to the entire store containing a licensed pharmacy, which the ordi-

49. A copy of the ordinance is available at *regti.me/sf-194-08* (case sensitive).

1. "Tobacco Product" is defined as "any substance containing tobacco leaf, including but not limited to cigarettes, cigars, pipe, tobacco, snuff, chewing tobacco, and dipping tobacco." (S.F. Health Code, § 1009.91(f).)

2. "Pharmacy" is defined as "a retail establishment in which the profession of pharmacy by a pharmacist licensed by the State of California in accordance with the Business and Professions Code is practiced and where prescriptions are offered for sale. A pharmacy may also offer other retail goods in addition to prescription pharmaceuticals. For purposes of this Article, 'pharmacy' includes retail stores commonly known as drugstores." (S.F. Health Code, § 1009.91(e).)

nance labels a "pharmacy." The prohibition on sales of tobacco products is not limited to the licensed pharmacy portion of a store but instead applies to the establishment as a whole.

In addition to traditional independent pharmacies, which sell little more than prescription drugs, over-the-counter medications, and personal care items, the term "pharmacy" encompasses chain stores, supermarkets, and big box stores that sell a variety of products such as food, beverages, paper goods, and miscellaneous items in addition to prescription drugs. However, although a "general grocery store"[3] or a "big box store"[4] that contains a licensed pharmacy qualifies as a "pharmacy" under the ordinance, the ordinance specifically excludes these establishments from the prohibition on sales of tobacco products. (S.F. Health Code, § 1009.93.) As a result, the ordinance prohibits a Walgreens that contains a licensed pharmacy from selling tobacco products but imposes no such limitation on a Safeway supermarket or a Costco big box store that contains a licensed pharmacy.

The legislative findings associated with the ordinance cite the adverse health effects associated with tobacco use. The principal finding upon which the ordinance is premised states: "Through the sale of tobacco products, pharmacies convey tacit approval of the purchase and use of tobacco products. This approval sends a mixed message to consumers who generally patronize pharmacies for health care services." As further support for the ordinance, the City's Board of Supervisors (Board of Supervisors or Board) also found that "[p]harmacies and drugstores are among the most accessible and trusted sources of health information among the public," and that "[c]linicians can have a significant effect on smokers' probability of quitting smoking."

As reflected in the legislative findings, various medical and pharmaceutical organizations advocate prohibiting sales of tobacco products in pharmacies. Among the organizations supporting such a prohibition are the Tobacco Education and Research Oversight Committee for California, the American Pharmacists Association, the California Pharmacists Association, and the California Medical Association. As far back as 1970 the American Pharmaceutical Association declared that "mass display of cigarettes in pharmacies is in direct contradiction to the role of a pharmacy as a public health facility."

As support for distinguishing between chain drugstores,[5] on the one hand, and general grocery stores and big box stores on the other hand, the

---

3. "General Grocery Store" is defined to have "the same meaning as set forth in [San Francisco] Planning Code Section 790.102(a) or any successor provisions." (S.F. Health Code, § 1009.91(c).) Section 790.102(a)(1) of the San Francisco Planning Code, in turn, defines "General Grocery Store" as "[a]n individual retail food establishment that: [¶] (A) Offers a diverse variety of unrelated, non-complementary food and non-food commodities, such as beverages, dairy, dry goods, fresh produce and other perishable items, frozen foods, household products, and paper goods; [¶] (B) May provide beer, wine, and/or liquor sales for consumption off the premises . . .; (C) Prepares minor amounts or no food on-site for immediate consumption; and [¶] (D) Markets the majority of its merchandise at retail prices."

4. "Big Box Store" is defined as "a single retail establishment occupying an area in excess of 100,000 gross square feet." (S.F. Health Code, § 1009.91(a).)

5. Neither the ordinance nor the legislative findings define the terms "drugstore" or "chain drugstore." Nevertheless, based on the text of the legislative findings, the City ordinance contains a finding that prescription drug sales comprise a much larger part of the business of chain drugstores, as follows: "Prescription drug sales for chain drugstores represent a significantly higher percentage of total sales than for grocery stores and big box stores that contain pharmacies. According to the 2007 Rite Aid Annual Report, prescription drug sales represented 63.7% of total sales in fiscal 2007. Walgreen's 2007 Annual Report documented prescription sales as approximately 65% of net sales that year. Pharmacy sales at Safeway have been estimated at 7.5% of annual volume. Costco's prescription sales generated 1.5% of total revenue in 2002."

During public hearings on the ordinance, one of it main proponents, Dr. Mitchell Katz, the City's Director of Public Health * * * [was] asked * * * why the legislation did not cover all stores containing a pharmacy[.] Dr. Katz responded as follows: "What I was trying to do in our work in fashioning the legislation was focusing on the group where I thought the case was strongest. We all go to supermarkets. We all go to warehouse stores. They get a cross section of people. We teach our children that supermarkets, wholesale stores, they're places you to go to buy everything. When it comes [to] pharmacies, I feel that our children, our teenagers get a different message.... What we're trying to say is these places market themselves as health-promoting businesses. They're not Walgreens General Store. They're not Rite Aid. They're Walgreens pharmacy. They're Rite Aid pharmacy. The ['P]harmacy America [T]rusts' and so it sends a very different message. Certainly in the future if we have success and I believe we would, just like San Francisco was the leader and then broaden[ed] the legislation ... around second hand smoke.... [W]e focus on that group we thought was most compelling."

On September 8, 2008, Walgreens filed a complaint seeking to invalidate the ordinance. Walgreens also moved for a preliminary injunction to prevent the ordinance from taking effect. The trial court denied the application for a preliminary injunction on September 30, 2008. The ordinance took effect the following day. Walgreens thereafter filed a first amended complaint (hereafter the complaint).

Walgreens alleges in the complaint that it operates licensed pharmacies in 52 of its 54 full-service stores in the City. The two Walgreens stores that do not operate pharmacies are exempt from the prohibition on selling tobacco. Walgreens contends that licensed pharmacies could also be found in the City at one Costco big box store, one pharmacy operated by Longs Drugs, two Lucky supermarket stores, ten Safeway stores, and six Rite–Aid stores.[6] Walgreens asserts that its stores containing licensed pharmacies

---

classifies chain stores such as Walgreens and Rite Aid as "chain drugstores," whereas Safeway and Costco are not considered "chain drugstores," even though they are chains and may contain a licensed pharmacy.

6. The complaint neglects to mention independent pharmacies covered by the ordinance. Dr. Katz testified that there were 16 independent pharmacies in the City at the time the ordinance was enacted. Only four of those independent pharmacies were still selling tobacco products at the time the ordinance was enacted. * * * Walgreens's tally omits the 12 independent pharmacies that had voluntarily chosen not to sell tobacco products even before the ordinance was enacted. Regardless of how one calculates the number of pharmacies subject to the ban on sales of tobacco products, the fact remains that * * * Walgreens operates over

are similar in all relevant respects to the 12 grocery stores and one big box store that are specifically exempt from the ordinance. Among other things, at both Walgreens and the exempt grocery stores, the licensed pharmacy is located in the back of the store, whereas tobacco products were sold in the front of a Walgreens store prior to the effective date of the ordinance. Tobacco products were not sold by pharmacists at Walgreens but instead were "clerk served," meaning that a customer would have to request to purchase a tobacco product from a clerk or checkout attendant. * * *

The trial court [dismissed the complaint and entered] judgment in the City's favor.

DISCUSSION

* * *

II. EQUAL PROTECTION

Walgreens contends the challenged ordinance violates the equal protection clauses of the federal and state constitutions, asserting that the disparate treatment of different types of stores containing pharmacies is not rationally related to a legitimate legislative end. For the reasons that follow, we agree that Walgreens's complaint adequately states an equal protection violation.

A. Applicable Legal Principles

The Fourteenth Amendment to the United States Constitution provides that "No State shall . . . deny to any person within its jurisdiction the equal protection of the laws." The California Constitution likewise prohibits the denial of equal protection. * * *

" 'The first prerequisite to a meritorious claim under the equal protection clause is a showing that the state has adopted a classification that affects two or more *similarly situated* groups in an unequal manner.' * * *

The City concedes that, for purposes of the challenged ordinance, all retail establishments containing licensed pharmacies are similarly situated. * * *

B. Asserted Rational Grounds for Exempting General Grocery Stores and Big Box Stores from Ban on Sales of Tobacco Products

We now turn to the question of whether there is a rational basis for exempting general grocery stores and big box stores that contain licensed pharmacies from the ban on sales of tobacco products applicable to all other retail establishments containing licensed pharmacies. * * * What must be decided here is whether the legitimate objectives of discouraging smoking and avoiding the suggestion that a health care purveyor approves of cigarette smoking provides a rational justification for prohibiting retail establishments such as Walgreens—which contains a licensed pharmacy in the rear of the store—from selling tobacco products, while permitting a

---

three-quarters of the pharmacies covered by the ordinance (58 out of approximately 75), including all but one of the chain drugstores prohibited from selling tobacco products.

competing retail establishment such as Safeway or Costco—which sells many of the same products and also has a licensed pharmacy on premises—to sell the very same tobacco products.

The City defends the distinction drawn in the ordinance by asserting that the Board of Supervisors "rationally could have concluded that the sale of cigarettes by drug stores like Walgreens sends the wrong message about cigarettes *more strongly* than does the sale of cigarettes by big box stores or grocery stores, even if those stores too have pharmacies in them." (Italics added.) What the City seems to mean is that customers, particularly "impressionable young people," are more likely to perceive a tacit message that smoking is not harmful when tobacco products are sold in a store the public associates with the sale of health-related products, and a "drugstore" such as Walgreens carries such an association more so than does a supermarket such as Safeway.

The City's premise contradicts the allegation in Walgreens's complaint that "the implied message, if any, conveyed by the sale of tobacco products at a Walgreens [is not] different from the implied message, if any, conveyed by the sale of tobacco products at the exempted stores with [licensed] pharmacies." We must accept Walgreens's allegation as true. * * * More importantly, allegations in the complaint concerning the similarities between Walgreens and general grocery stores support the contention there is no difference in any implied message that might be conveyed by selling tobacco products in the two types of stores. These allegations appear to be beyond dispute, with the City conceding that similarities exist. Thus, for example, at both Walgreens and the exempt general grocery stores, the licensed pharmacy is located in the back of the store, whereas tobacco products were sold in the front of Walgreens stores prior to the effective date of the ordinance and had to be requested from a clerk. Stores subject to the ordinance and grocery stores exempt from it typically advertise themselves as health-promoting and have signage on the outside of the store advertising the licensed pharmacy within. Indeed, Safeway advertised itself as promoting "Healthy Living." Like stores exempt from the ordinance that do not devote a significant percentage of their floor space to their licensed pharmacies, Walgreens devotes less than 10 percent of the total "front area" of its stores to the licensed pharmacy. In addition, 90 percent of the transactions at Walgreens's stores in the City do not involve a purchase from the licensed pharmacy.

Furthermore, * * * the majority of [Walgreens's] stores in San Francisco meet the primary criteria for the ordinance's definition of "general grocery store," which the ordinance exempts from the ban on sales of tobacco products. Walgreens alleges that the majority of its stores meet the four criteria defining a general grocery store because they "(A) exceed 5,000 gross square feet; (B) offer a diverse variety of unrelated, non-complementary food and non-food commodities, such as beverages, dairy, dry goods, fresh produce and other perishable items, frozen foods, household products, and paper goods; (C) prepare no food on-site for immediate consumption; and (D) market all of their merchandise at retail prices." Walgreens purportedly does not come within the definition of "general grocery store" only because of the peculiar distinction that it is not a "retail food establishment" but instead is a retail store that sells food. The distinction apparently turns upon whether the establishment primarily sells foodstuffs.[9]

The increasingly blurred distinction between Walgreens and general grocery stores is much like the growing similarities over time between hotels and motels, which the appellate court addressed in *Gawzner Corp. v. Minier*, 45 Cal. App. 3d 903 (Ct. App. 1975). There, the court held that a statute regulating the content of outdoor rate advertising by motels but not hotels violated equal protection and could not be enforced. The proffered justification for the distinction was that hotels do not seek the business of the motoring public and therefore have no need to display rate signs to appeal to passing motorists. The court rejected this reasoning as "patently untrue in California in the year 1975." According to the court, "Just as motels have expanded their services to compete with hotels, hotels have added parking facilities to compete with motels." The court concluded that although a hotel is obviously different from a motel in terms of size, diversity of services, and facilities, they both "rely to a large degree upon the motoring public for business." Thus, "[w]ith respect to the avowed purpose of [the statute], hotels and motels are similarly situated."

Likewise, based on an objective comparison of the stores, a Walgreens store and a general grocery store are similarly situated with respect to the purpose of the ordinance. There is no reason to believe the implied message conveyed by a Walgreens that sells tobacco products is any different from the implied message conveyed by a supermarket or big box store that sells such items. * * * Here, there is no reasonably conceivable factual basis for finding that the purported implied message approving tobacco use is "stronger" at a Walgreens than it is at a supermarket containing a licensed pharmacy.

Walgreens attacks not only the exemption for general grocery stores and big box stores but also claims the very premise of the legislation is questionable. According to Walgreens, "It is simply not credible that 'pharmacies convey tacit approval of the purchase and use of tobacco products' ... given the decades of anti-smoking media campaigns and warnings that would counteract any such implied message." The premise underlying the prohibition on sales of tobacco products in pharmacies may not be universally accepted. Nonetheless, the government unquestionably has a legitimate interest in discouraging tobacco use. Here, the City made a determination that prohibiting sales of tobacco products in pharmacies furthers that legitimate interest, a determination supported by numerous professional medical and pharmaceutical organizations. While that assessment may be subject to debate—and indeed was debated by members of the City's Board of Supervisors—it does not violate any constitutional principle.

* * * In this case, the City has relied upon a premise that is itself subject to debate to support narrow distinctions the generic premise simply

9. The City offers no explanation of the product mix that would be necessary for a store to be considered a "retail food establishment," a troubling ambiguity as hybrid forms of retail stores offering food items continue to appear in the marketplace. * * *

does not support. With the image of a small, traditional independent pharmacy in mind—one that primarily sells pharmaceutical prescriptions, over-the-counter medications, personal care items, and little more—the justification for precluding customers from obtaining the impression that the licensed pharmacist endorses the use of tobacco products can be readily understood. There is an unmistakable difference, however, between the traditional independent pharmacy selling predominantly pharmaceuticals and contemporary chain stores that sell a far greater variety of merchandise, including foodstuffs as well as prescription drugs. The premise underlying the ordinance—that pharmacies selling tobacco products convey tacit approval of tobacco use—has a questionable application to stores such as Walgreens, and it certainly does not support the narrow distinction in the ordinance between stores such as Walgreens and general grocery stores.
* * *

The only explanation the City advances as to why it is plausible to assume that, despite their similarities, stores such as Walgreens are more likely than a supermarket such as Safeway or a big box store such as Costco to convey the tacit message that smoking is not harmful is that a greater percentage of Walgreens's sales revenue is derived from prescription drugs than is true of Safeway or Costco.[11]

But why do these revenue percentages indicate that customers receive a different message concerning the safety of tobacco products sold at a store such as Walgreens than the message received by customers of Safeway or Costco? A customer normally would not be aware of the percentage of pharmacy sales at the different types of stores. The City agrees that the percentage of a store's revenue attributable to pharmacy sales does not *cause* a customer to perceive the various types of stores differently. It claims, however, that the comparison of revenues attributable to pharmacy sales reflects the fact that stores such as Walgreens are *in fact* different from grocery and big box stores. That undoubtedly is true, but it begs the question: why do the different sales percentages indicate that purchasers at the different establishments receive different messages concerning the safety of tobacco products they sell? The public may more closely identify a Walgreens with a licensed pharmacy than a Safeway with a licensed pharmacy, since most Walgreens contain a pharmacy and that is not true of most grocery stores and likely is not true of what have come to be known as supermarkets or big box stores. But the fact that the public considers it more likely to find a licensed pharmacy in a Walgreens than in a supermarket, or is more likely to purchase prescription drugs at a Walgreens than a supermarket, does not rationally explain why in those stores that contain a licensed pharmacy, the implied approval of smoking is greater in one than the other.
* * *

Other reasons offered by the City to justify the classification among pharmacies are no more persuasive. According to the City, one could

---

11. By Walgreens's estimates, pharmacy sales comprise slightly over half of the sales revenue at its San Francisco stores. According to the recitals in the City's ordinance, pharmacy sales at Safeway are estimated to be "7.5% of annual volume" and prescription sales generated "1.5% of total revenue in 2002" at Costco.

rationally conclude that a ban on sales of tobacco products in stores such as Walgreens and Rite–Aid would serve the purpose of limiting the exposure of sick people to cigarettes. The City reasons that customers of Walgreens and Rite–Aid are more likely to be sick than customers of general grocery stores and big box stores. The contention lacks merit. Sick people who go to a licensed pharmacy at a Safeway or Costco are just as likely to be exposed to tobacco products as those who went to a Walgreens. Moreover, there is no reason to believe supermarkets and big box stores have fewer sick customers than Walgreens. People who are sick still need to buy food and will be exposed to tobacco products at the supermarket when they do their grocery shopping, regardless of whether they also patronize the store for pharmacy services. * * *

For the reasons set forth above, Walgreens's complaint adequately states causes of action for a violation of the equal protections provisions of the United States and California constitutions. * * *

In August 2010, responding to the decision of the Court of Appeal, the Board of Supervisors revised its 2008 ordinance and removed the exceptions for big box stores and grocery stores.[50] Walgreen, Safeway, and Costco removed all tobacco products from the shelves in their stores that have a pharmacy.

Questions

1. In *Wooley v. Maynard*, the Supreme Court held that the state could not require a person to display an ideological message on his private property "in a manner and for the express purpose that it be observed and read by the public." San Francisco imposed restrictions on property supposedly to prevent communication of a particular message. Is censorship of messages more legitimate than requirements for messages? Could Walgreen argue that the San Francisco ban on tobacco in pharmacies was equivalent to New Hampshire requirement for the state motto on license plates?

2. All know that smoking and exposure to tobacco smoke are associated with substantially increased risk of premature death from chronic diseases. Nevertheless, about 19% of the adults in United States are smokers. Is the San Francisco restriction on sales of tobacco products likely to change the conduct of any smoker? What is the purpose of the ban?

§ 11.6 VOLUNTARY EXPRESSIONS

Mandatory expressions intend to influence the preferences of the individuals who are required to utter them *or* the preferences of others. In the case of voluntary expressions, the state creates a framework for expressions that have the power to influence tastes. By definition, unlike

---

50. A copy of the 2010 ordinance is available at *regti.me/sf-245-10* (case sensitive).

mandatory expressions, regulatory frameworks governing voluntary expressions are designed to apply only to interested individuals. A potential problem with such designs is that nonparticipants may feel excluded from group activities. Again, the Pledge of Allegiance has been used for the technique.

The Pledge of Allegiance

In the aftermath of September 11, 2001, many states adopted new laws that established non-compulsory frameworks for the recitation of the Pledge of Allegiance in public law schools. New Hampshire was among these states.

Freedom From Religion Foundation v. Hanover School District

626 F.3d 1 (1st Cir. 2010)

■ LYNCH, CHIEF JUDGE.

The question presented is whether the New Hampshire School Patriot Act, N.H.Rev.Stat. Ann. § 194:15–c ("the New Hampshire Act"), which requires that the state's public schools authorize a period during the school day for students to voluntarily participate in the recitation of the Pledge of Allegiance, violates the First * * * to the Constitution of the United States. We hold that the statute is constitutional and affirm entry of judgment for defendants.

I.

Plaintiffs are The Freedom From Religion Foundation, its members Jan and Pat Doe, and their three children who attend New Hampshire public schools (collectively "FFRF"). Jan and Pat Doe identify themselves as atheist and agnostic, respectively, and their children as either atheist or agnostic. * * * Pursuant to the New Hampshire Act, the Pledge of Allegiance ("the Pledge") is routinely recited in the Doe children's classrooms under the leadership of their teachers.

The full text of the New Hampshire Act, enacted in 2002, is as follows:

> I. As a continuation of the policy of teaching our country's history to the elementary and secondary pupils of this state, this section shall be known as the New Hampshire School Patriot Act.
>
> II. A school district shall authorize a period of time during the school day for the recitation of the pledge of allegiance. Pupil participation in the recitation of the pledge of allegiance shall be voluntary.
>
> III. Pupils not participating in the recitation of the pledge of allegiance may silently stand or remain seated but shall be required to respect the rights of those pupils electing to participate. If this paragraph shall be declared to be unconstitutional or

otherwise invalid, the remaining paragraphs in this section shall not be affected, and shall continue in full force and effect.

N.H.Rev.Stat. Ann. § 194:15–c.

Several aspects of the statute are worth note. By expressly requiring that student participation in the recitation of the Pledge be voluntary, New Hampshire has created a framework in which a school or educator would violate state law by any actions that rendered student participation involuntary. In addition, the statute allows any student not to participate in the recitation of the Pledge regardless of the student's reasons for non-participation. Those who do not participate may either stand silently or remain seated. The only obligation imposed on non-participants is that they respect the rights of those students electing to participate.

The New Hampshire Act itself does not identify the words of the Pledge or otherwise specify which words should be used. The parties accept that the words of the Pledge that are used in New Hampshire schools are those codified in federal law: "I pledge allegiance to the Flag of the United States of America, and to the Republic for which it stands, one Nation under God, indivisible, with liberty and justice for all." 4 U.S.C. § 4 ("the federal Pledge statute"). The Pledge, which dates to 1892, was first codified in 1942 to clarify the "rules and customs pertaining to the display and use of the flag of the United States of America." See Act of June 22, 1942, Pub.L. No. 77–623, 56 Stat. 377. The words "under God" were added in 1954. See Act of June 14, 1954, Pub.L. No. 83–396, 68 Stat. 249.

* * *

II.

A. *The Pledge Does not Violate the Establishment Clause*

Under the Establishment Clause, "Congress shall make no law respecting an establishment of religion." U.S. Const. amend. I. Although applicable originally only against the federal government, the Establishment Clause was incorporated to apply to the states by the Fourteenth Amendment.

In determining whether a law runs afoul of this prohibition, the Supreme Court has articulated three interrelated analytical approaches: the three-prong analysis set forth in *Lemon v. Kurtzman*, 403 U.S. 602, 612–13 (1971); the "endorsement" analysis, first articulated by Justice O'Connor in her concurrence in *Lynch v. Donnelly*, 465 U.S. 668, 688 (1984) * * *; and the "coercion" analysis of *Lee v. Weisman*, 505 U.S. 577, 587 (1992). Before applying the three approaches to the case before us, we first address a few general matters.

FFRF's argument is that the School Districts' Pledge practices pursuant to the New Hampshire Act are religious for purposes of the First Amendment because the Pledge itself is a religious exercise in that it uses the phrase "under God." FFRF argues that despite the voluntary nature of any student participation in the Pledge, the result is nonetheless the establishment by the state of religion.

As to the first part of the argument, we begin with the unremarkable proposition that the phrase "under God" has some religious content. In our view, mere repetition of the phrase in secular ceremonies does not by itself deplete the phrase of all religious content. A belief in God is a religious belief. * * *

The Pledge and the phrase "under God" are not themselves prayers, nor are they readings from or recitations of a sacred text of a religion. That fact does not itself dispose of the constitutional question either. * * * The question is where along this spectrum of cases falls the voluntary, teacher-led recitation of the Pledge, including the phrase "under God," by pupils in New Hampshire's public schools. We turn to the Court's different analytical measures for Establishment Clause claims.

1. The Three–Factored Lemon Analysis

Under the *Lemon* analysis, a court must consider three factors: "First, the statute must have a secular legislative purpose; second, its principal or primary effect must be one that neither advances nor inhibits religion; finally, the statute must not foster 'an excessive government entanglement with religion.' " * * *

FFRF concedes that the New Hampshire Act has a secular purpose—the promotion of patriotism—but insists that this does not end the inquiry. FFRF argues that Congress had an impermissible religious purpose when it added the words "under God" to the text of the Pledge in 1954, and that this fact must be considered in our analysis. Even if so, the argument does not go to the first factor. We look at the purpose of New Hampshire when it enacted the statute in 2002, in the aftermath of the tragedy of September 11, 2001. Because FFRF has stipulated that New Hampshire had a secular purpose, its claim of impermissible governmental purpose clearly fails on the first prong of *Lemon*.

FFRF argues, under the second factor, that the principal or primary effect of the New Hampshire Act is the advancement of religion. The Pledge's affirmation that ours is a "nation, under God" is not a mere reference to the fact that many Americans believe in a deity, nor to the undeniable historical significance of religion in the founding of our nation. * * *

In looking at the effect of the state's creation of a daily period for the voluntary recitation of the Pledge, we must consider the text as a whole and must take account of context and circumstances. * * * It takes more than the presence of words with religious content to have the effect of advancing religion, let alone to do so as a primary effect.

As to context, there is no claim that a student is required to advance a belief in theism (or monotheism), nor is there any claim that a student is even encouraged by the faculty to say the Pledge if the student chooses not to do so.

By design, the recitation of the Pledge in New Hampshire public schools is meant to further "the policy of teaching our country's history to the elementary and secondary pupils of this state." N.H.Rev.Stat. Ann. § 194:15–c. "The very purpose of a national flag is to serve as a symbol of our country." *Elk Grove Unified Sch. Dist. v. Newdow*, 542 U.S. 1, 6 (2004). * * * As the Court has observed, "the Pledge of Allegiance evolved as a common public acknowledgment of the ideals that our flag symbolizes. Its recitation is a patriotic exercise designed to foster national unity and pride in those principles." *Id.* In reciting the Pledge, students promise fidelity to our flag and our nation, not to any particular God, faith, or church.

The New Hampshire School Patriot Act's primary effect is not the advancement of religion, but the advancement of patriotism through a pledge to the flag as a symbol of the nation.

2. *The Endorsement Analysis*

Under the related endorsement analysis, courts must consider whether the challenged governmental action has the purpose or effect of endorsing, favoring, or promoting religion. * * *

At the heart of FFRF's claim is its argument that those students who choose not to recite the Pledge for reasons of non-belief in God are quite visibly differentiated from other students who stand and participate. The result, FFRF argues, is that the recitation of the Pledge makes the Doe children outsiders to their peer group on the grounds of their religion.

FFRF's premise is that children who choose not to recite the Pledge become outsiders based on their beliefs about religion. That premise is flawed. Under the New Hampshire Act, both the choice to engage in the recitation of the Pledge and the choice not to do so are entirely voluntary. The reasons pupils choose not to participate are not themselves obvious. There are a wide variety of reasons why students may choose not to recite the Pledge, including many reasons that do not rest on either religious or anti-religious belief. These include political disagreement with reciting the Pledge, a desire to be different, a view of our country's history or the significance of the flag that differs from that contained in the Pledge, and no reason at all. Even students who agree with the Pledge may choose not to *recite* the Pledge. Thus, the Doe children are not *religiously* differentiated from their peers merely by virtue of their non-participation in the Pledge.

Furthermore, the constitutionality of a state statute does not turn on the *subjective* feelings of plaintiffs as to whether a religious endorsement has occurred. Rather, in the endorsement analysis, the court assumes the viewpoint of an "objective observer acquainted with the text, legislative history, and implementation of the statute." * * *

Adopting the view of the objective observer fully aware of the relevant circumstances, we conclude there has been no endorsement of religion. The state legislature passed the New Hampshire Act in the aftermath of September 11, 2001 with the intent of fostering patriotism, * * * and that is the statute's effect. Taken in the context of the words of the whole Pledge, the phrase "under God" does not convey a message of endorsement.

* * * Here, the words "under God" appear in a pledge to a flag—itself a secular exercise, accompanied by no other religious language or symbolism.

We reject FFRF's claim of unconstitutional endorsement.

3. *The Coercion Analysis*

Relying heavily on *Lee*, FFRF finally argues that the recitation of the Pledge in public school classrooms unconstitutionally coerces the Doe children to "recite a purely religious ideology."

Coercion need not be direct to violate the Establishment Clause, but rather can take the form of "subtle coercive pressure" that interferes with an individual's "real choice" about whether to participate in the activity at issue. In public schools, this danger of impermissible, indirect coercion is most pronounced because of the "young impressionable children whose school attendance is statutorily compelled." As *Lee* stated, "prayer exercises in public schools carry a particular risk of indirect coercion. The concern may not be limited to the context of schools, but it is most pronounced there."

* * *

The *Lee* * * * Court found that students were being coerced into silence during the saying of the prayer; that silence was, in the eyes of the community, functionally identical to participation in the prayer; and that therefore, students were being functionally coerced into participation in the prayer in violation of the Constitution.

A key premise is different here. While in *Lee*, "the act of standing or remaining silent was an expression of participation in the rabbi's prayer," silence by students is not an expression of participation in the Pledge. Rather, a student who remains silent during the saying of the Pledge engages in overt non-participation by doing so, and this non-participation is not itself an expression of either religious or non-religious belief.

FFRF's claim of unconstitutional coercion under Lee fails.

B. *The Pledge Does Not Violate the Free Exercise Clause*

Under the Free Exercise Clause, the government may not "(1) compel affirmation of religious beliefs; (2) punish the expression of religious doctrines it believes to be false; (3) impose special disabilities on the basis of religious views or religious status; or (4) lend its power to one side or the other in controversies over religious authorities or dogma." *Parker v. Hurley*, 514 F.3d 87, 103 (1st Cir. 2008). * * *

In *Parker*, we explained that "[p]ublic schools are not obliged to shield individual students from ideas which potentially are religiously offensive, particularly when the school imposes no requirement that the student agree with or affirm those ideas, or even participate in discussions about them." Because the Doe children allege mere exposure to the religious content of the Pledge, they cannot state a claim under the Free Exercise Clause, nor can their parents, as "the mere fact that a child is exposed on occasion in public school to a concept offensive to a parent's religious belief does not inhibit the parent from instructing the child differently."

* * *

III.

We hold that the New Hampshire School Patriot Act and the voluntary, teacher-led recitation of the Pledge by the state's public school students do not violate the Constitution. * * *

Questions

1. "As a continuation of the policy of teaching our country's history," the New Hampshire School Patriot Act was enacted in response to the tragedy of September 11, 2011. Indeed, the First Circuit stressed that "[b]y design, the recitation of the Pledge in New Hampshire public schools is meant to further 'the policy of teaching our country's history. * * * " Was the New Hampshire School Patriot Act designed to further the teaching of our country's history? What in the statute's design persuaded the court that it had the power to promote the teaching of national history? What were the Act's goals?

2. The First Circuit supposedly ruled that the statutory framework of New Hampshire protects children who chose not to participate in the recitation of the Pledge of Allegiance. Does the Act adequately protect children?

§ 11.7 Curbing Immediate Gratification Options

Most people encounter self-control problems in several dimensions of life and a tendency to pursue immediate gratification at the expense of long-term benefits.[51] We cannot or do not want to suppress the taste for immediate gratification. Rules that encourage people to develop self-control are nothing new. Indeed, the Old Testament is replete with examples. Experience shows that it is difficult to eradicate "bad habits."

Small Stake Gambling

In 1991, Colorado amended its constitution to permit gambling in the state under the following restrictions:

> (1) [L]imited gaming in the City of Central, the City of Black Hawk, and the City of Cripple Creek shall be lawful as of October 1, 1991.
>
> * * *
>
> (3) Limited gaming shall be subject to the following:
>
> (a) Limited gaming shall take place only in the existing Colorado cities of: the City of Central, county of Gilpin, the City of Black

51. *See* O'Donoghue & Rabin, *The Economics of Immediate Gratification*, *supra* note 24; Schelling, *Self-Command in Practice, in Policy, and in a Theory of Rational Choice*, *supra* note 24.

Hawk, county of Gilpin, and the City of Cripple Creek, county of Teller. * * *

(c) No more than thirty-five percent of the square footage of any building and no more than fifty percent of any one floor of such building, may be used for limited gaming.

(d) Limited gaming operations shall be prohibited between the hours of 2:00 o'clock a.m. and 8:00 o'clock a.m.

(e) Limited gaming may occur in establishments licensed to sell alcoholic beverages.

(4) As certain terms are used in regards to limited gaming:

* * *

(b) "Limited gaming" means the use of slot machines and the card games of blackjack and poker, each game having a maximum single bet of five dollars.

(c) "Slot machine" means any mechanical, electrical, video, electronic, or other device, contrivance, or machine which, after insertion of a coin, token, or similar object, or upon payment of any required consideration whatsoever by a player, is available to be played or operated, and which, whether by reason of the skill of the player or application of the element of chance, or both, may deliver or entitle the player operating the machine to receive cash premiums, merchandise, tokens, redeemable game credits, or any other thing of value other than unredeemable free games, whether the payoff is made automatically from the machines or in any other manner.

* * *

In 2008, a coalition of casinos financed a campaign to promote a ballot measure that raised betting limits from $5 to $100 and removed the restrictions from the hours of operation. The measure, *Colorado Gaming, Amendment 50*, appeared on the November 2008 ballot and received almost 59% of the votes.[52]

Questions

1. What was the purpose of the original limited gaming law?

2. What is the purpose of the 2008 limited gaming law?

3. In the summer of 2012, New York Mayor Michael Bloomberg introduced a new regulatory proposal: a ban on big sizes of sugary drinks. Under the Mayor's plan, the City would enact a ban on the sale of large sodas and other sugary drinks at restaurants, movie theaters, and street carts to combat rising obesity. The measure would not apply to diet sodas, fruit juices, dairy based drinks like milkshakes, or alcoholic beverages; it would also not extend to beverages sold in grocery or convenience stores. What are the similarities and differences between the proposal and limited gaming law?

---

52. A copy of the ballot measure is available at *regti.me/CO-Am50* (case sensitive).

INDEX

References are to pages

ABORTION
Informed consent, information disclosure mandate, 415, 620

ACCIDENT LAW
Calabresi, Guido
Generally, 356
Axiomatic principal function, 402

ADD-ON STRATEGY
Pricing, 446

ADHESIVE CONTRACTS
Unconscionability doctrine, 472

ADMINISTRATIVE AGENCIES
Chevron deference to statutory interpretations of, 43
Delegation doctrine, 42
Standard of review of agency actions, 131

ADMIRALTY LAW
Seaworthiness, information insufficiency, 413, 415

ADOPTION REGULATIONS
Posner, Richard, 576

ADULT FILMS
See Sexually Oriented Businesses, this index

ADVERTISING
Cigarette packaging and advertising, graphic warnings on, 614
First Amendment protections, 579, 764
Information regulation, 764
Professional advertising regulation, 764
Prostitution advertising, 591
Suppression of information, regulation through, 578

AFFORDABLE CARE ACT
See also Health Insurance Regulation, this index
Mandates, 19, 231, 258
Regulatory authority challenge, 231
Scalia dissent, 257
Subsidies, 243, 248, 259

AGRICULTURAL ADJUSTMENT ACT
Commerce Clause authority, 662

AIR POLLUTION
See Clean Air Act, this index

AIR TRAFFIC CONTROLLERS
Permits and entry regulation, 675

ALCOHOL
Brewer regulations, 154
Eighteenth Amendment Prohibition, 561, 634
Possession regulation, 532
Suppression of information, regulation through, 578

ANIMAL RIGHTS REGULATION
Interest groups, 202

ANTI-CARTOON LAWS
Speech, freedom of, 175

ANTI-SPITTING LAWS
Generally, 363

ANTITRUST LAW
Gates, Bill, Microsoft litigation, 511
Market power, 452, 456
Microsoft litigation, 510
Misappropriation doctrine, 512, 521
Parker immunity, 217
Per se violations, 452
Scalia, per se violations, 452
State action immunity, 217
Tying arrangements, 447

ARBITRAGE
Price regulation, 466
Regulatory, 108

ASYMMETRIC INFORMATION
See Information, this index

AUTHORITY TO REGULATE
Generally, 40
Affordable Care Act challenge, 231
Chevron deference to administrative agencies, 43
Commerce Clause, this index
Delegation doctrine, 42
Federal preemption, 41
Federal Regulatory Authority, this index
Police Power, this index
Public interest, 267
Public interest doctrine, 268
State Regulatory Authority, this index
Statutory interpretation authority of administrative agencies, 43
Tobacco
Generally, 43 et seq.

AUTHORITY TO REGULATE—Cont'd
Tobacco—Cont'd
Federal regulatory authority, 61

AUTOMATED TELLER MACHINES
Price regulation, 722

AUTOMOBILE AND TRAFFIC REGULATIONS
Motorcycle Helmets, this index
No-fault liability insurance requirements, 682
Risk perceptions, 382
Rules vs standards
Generally, 77
Due Process Clause limitations, 80
Seatbelt laws, 390, 692

BAILOUTS
See also Government Relief, this index; Subsidies, this index
European financial crisis, 403
Government bailouts of financial institutions, moral hazard problems, 402

BAKERS
Bakeshop Act, police power limitations on state regulatory authority, 25
Labor regulation, 25, 155
Sanitary regulations, 155
Short-weight laws, 740

BANKING SYSTEM
See Financial Institutions, this index

BANS
Generally, 632 et seq.
Common drinking cups, 324, 660
Definition, 632
Eighteenth Amendment, 634
Fatty acids, 648
Holmes on prohibitory laws, 22
Incandescent light bulbs, 656
Phase-outs, 656
Pit bull bans, 650
Pollution regulation, 636
Prohibitions
Generally, 634
Holmes on prohibitory laws, 22
Smoking in public, 639, 646
Spitting, 363
Sterilization laws, 655
Sugary drinks, supersize bans, 845
Supersize sugary drinks, 845
Tattooing, 685
Unconscionable price increases, 719

BARBERSHOPS
Price regulation, 708

BARGINING
Coasean, 281
Rhetoric of price bargaining, 471 et seq.
Standardized transactions circumventing, 473
Unequal bargaining power distortions, 471

BEDBUGS
Disclosure regulations, 421

BEGGING
Social preferences motivating regulations, 275

BEST AVAILABLE TECHNOLOGY
Cost-benefit analysis, 123, 128
Scalia on, 123

BEZZLE
Interest groups, effects of bezzle inventory fluctuations, 200

BIAS
Bounded rationality, debiasing, 804
Debiasing through regulation, 805
Informational externalities associated with, 406
Informational externalities associated with cognitive biases, 406
Judicial bias claim, 220, 225
Optimism bias, 359
Reasoning to serve rather than reexamine
Irrational exuberance, 15
Risk perception, 382
Risk, cognitive biases affecting perception, 359

BLASPHEMY LAWS
First Amendment, 808
Historical background, 807

BLOOD
Commodification restraints, 560

BLUE LAWS
See Sunday Laws, this index

BONO RULE
Direct and indirect regulation, 93

BOUNDED RATIONALITY
Generally, 599 et seq.
Ability to process information, bounded rationality constraining, 445
Anti-antipaternalism, 600
Barak on boundaries of human rationality, 599
Cognitive limitations, 601
Debiasing, 804
Definition, 599
Defunding law, 604
Failures of self-interest pursuit, 599
Graphic warnings on cigarette packaging and advertising, 614
Market inefficiency sources, 464
Nudging choices, 602
Price distortions, 464
Price perceptions, 695
Regulations reinforcing, 600
Regulatory utilization, 603
Risk, bounded rationality impacting perception, 359
Tobacco regulation, graphic warnings, 614
Utilization in regulations, 603

BRANDEIS, LOUIS, JUSTICE
Dangers of regulation, 2
Experimental state regulations, 60

BRANDEIS, LOUIS, JUSTICE—Cont'd
News networks, natural monopoly determinations, 518
Paternalism, 527
Permits and entry regulation, 666
Privacy law, 186
Public utilities regulations, 494
Right to be let alone, 161, 411, 545
State regulations, experimental, 60
Working hour regulations, Brandeis brief, 34, 473

BREAD, SHORT-WEIGHT
See Bakers, this index

BREWERS
See also Alcohol, this index
Regulation, 154

BREYER, STEPHEN, JUSTICE
Cost-benefit analysis, 126
First Amendment, commercial speech cases, 590
Justification for regulation, 272
Standards, 692
Tobacco, federal regulatory authority, 67

BRIBERY
Institutional weaknesses, 191

BUBBLES
Generally, 15, 21
Herd behavior, 406

BUREAUCRACY
See also Government Failure, this index; Public Decisionmakers, this index
Entry regulations, purposeless, 665
Inefficiency, 165
Transaction costs, 281

BUTCHERS
See also Slaughterhouses, this index
Self-interest, 150
Slaughter-House Cases, 152

BUTTER LAWS
Interest groups, regulation aiding, 163
Kaldor-Hicks principles, 163
Rent seeking, 731

CALABRESI, GUIDO
Accident law
Generally, 356
Axiomatic principal function, 402
Classification of legal rights, 559
Inalienable rights, 559

CALORIE LABELING
Generally, 785
Federal and state regulation, 789
First Amendment challenge, 793

CANCER RISK
Cost-benefit analysis conflicts
Generally, 118
Delaney Clause, 119
Smoking, 44

CAP-AND-TRADE POLLUTION PERMITS
Commodification criticisms, 561

CAPTURE THEORY
Generally, 199
See also Conflicts of Interest, this index; Self-Interest, this index
Delegation doctrine, delegations to conflicted agencies, 715
Interstate Commerce Commission, 199
Judicial perceptions, 384
Scientific understanding, captured, 602
Stigler, George, 199

CARTOONS
See Anti-Cartoon Laws, this index

CATASTROPHES
Risks, 285
Systemic risks, 403

CAVEAT EMPTOR
Historical background, 417
Implied warranties, 419

CEILINGS
See Price, this index

CELLPHONES IN THEATERS
Generally, 301

CENSORSHIP
See also Information Regulation, this index
Blasphemy statutes, 807
Pornography laws, preference shaping effects, 806
Preference shaping, 807

CENTERS FOR DISEASE CONTROL AND PREVENTION (CDC)
Information production, 410
Information regulation, 758

CERTIFICATES
See also Permits and Entry Regulation, this index
Definition of certification, 668

CHEVRON DEFERENCE
Statutory interpretation authority of administrative agencies, 43

CHILD LABOR REGULATION
Generally, 728

CHILD PORNOGRAPHY LAWS
Generally, 545

CHILDREN
See Infants and Children, this index

CIGARETTES
Smoking in Public, this index
Tobacco Regulations, this index

CINCH BILLS
Institutional weaknesses, 193

CIRCUMVENTION
Network effects, 350

CLEAN AIR ACT (CAA)
Cap-and-trade pollution permits, commodification criticisms, 561
Fuel economy standards, 693
Greenhouse gas regulation, 136, 139
Nuisance law vs regulatory remedies, 294
Regulation loopholes, 129, 134

CLEAN WATER ACT (CWA)
See Best Available Technology, this index

COASE, RONALD
Bargaining, Coasean, 281
Cost-benefit analyses, 280
Pigou views contrasted, 280, 725
Positive externalities, 282
Price, supply-demand relationships, 461
Social costs, 279

COASE THEOREM
Generally, 279
Information-improving regulation, 404
Market efficiency, 218
Regulation, information-improving, 404
Stigler on, 281
Transaction costs, 281

COGNITIVE BIAS
See Bias, this index

COGNITIVE LIMITATIONS
Bounded rationality, 601

COLLECTIVE ACTION
Generally, 202
Social norms directing, 272
State vs private exercises, 271
Tragedy of the Commons, this index

COMMAND AND CONTROL
Generally, 632
Bans, this index
Common drinking cup bans, 324, 660
Fatty acids ban, 648
Incandescent light bulbs ban, 656
Incentive regulations compared, 24
Incentive regulations distinguished, 632
Information improving regulation compared, 404
Mandates, this index
Permits and Entry Regulation, this index
Pit bull bans, 650
Pollution regulation, 636
Price regulation through, 699
Rules vs standards, 632
Smoking in public, 639, 646
Sterilization laws, 655
Vaccinations, 412

COMMERCE CLAUSE
Agricultural Adjustment Act, 662
Dormant Commerce Clause restraints on state regulatory powers, 557
Economic regulation, 248
Orbach, Barak, Commerce Clause regulatory authority of federal government, 41

COMMERCIAL SPEECH
See First Amendment, this index

COMMODIFICATION
Generally, 558
See also Inalienable Rights, this index
Blood, market restraints, 560
Cap-and-trade pollution permits, 561
Cost-benefit analysis, priceless things problem, 560
Eighteenth Amendment alcohol restrictions, 561
Endangered species, market restraints, 561
Fetal gestational services, market restraints, 560, 564
Human flourishing concept, 560
Human life, market restraints, 560, 561
Human organs, market restraints, 560, 562
Incomplete commodification, 560
Infants and children, market restraints, 560, 576
Marijuana laws, 561
Prostitution
Market restraints, 560, 595
Regulation, 595
Suppression of information, 578 et seq.
Thirteenth Amendment ban of slavery, 561

COMMON DRINKING CUPS
Bans, 324, 660

CONFLICTS OF INTEREST
See also Capture Theory, this index; Self-Interest, this index
Delegation of regulatory authority to conflicted agencies, 715
Judges, 220
Private interests, conflicting, 160
Public decisionmaker, self-interested, 169

CONFUSING INFORMATION
See Information, this index

CONGESTION PRICING
Generally, 736

CONSEQUENCES OF REGULATION
See Unintended Consequences, this index

CONSTITUTIONAL LAW
Commerce Clause, this index
Delegation Doctrine, this index
Dormant Commerce Clause restraints on state regulatory powers, 557
Due Process, this index
Equal Protection, this index
Freedom of Contract, this index
Indian Land Consolidation Act, 334, 465
Overbreadth doctrine, 209
Police Power, this index
Preemption, this index
Privacy, this index
Supremacy Clause, 45
Vagueness doctrine, 80, 95

CONSUMER PROTECTION
Bargaining, standardized transactions circumventing, 473
Commercial speech regulation, 582
Information Regulation, this index
Information suppression, consumer protection rationale, 582

CONSUMER PROTECTION—Cont'd
Price unfairness, 472
Quality Standards, this index
Sales, unequal bargaining power distortions, 471
Standardized transactions circumventing bargaining, 473
Suppression of information, consumer protection rationale, 582
Unconscionability doctrine, 472

CONTRACT FREEDOM
See Freedom of Contract, this index

COORDINATION BREAKDOWNS
Generally, 328
Indian Land Consolidation Act, 334, 465

COPYRIGHT LAW
Contributory infringement liability as indirect regulation, 86

COST-BENEFIT ANALYSIS (CBA)
Generally, 113
Best available technology regulations, 123, 128
Breyer on scope of legislative requirement, 126
Cancer risk conflicts
Generally, 118
Delaney Clause, 119
Coase Theorem, 280
Corporate average fuel economy standards, 128
Counterintuitive aspects, 116
Delaney Clause, 118
Environmental Protection Agency applications, 119, 123
Executive Order 12866, 115
Government failures, cost-benefit analysis test, 226, 265
Greenhouse gas emission regulations, 136
Human papillomavirus vaccine regulations applicability, 122
Interest group conflicts, 117
Intuition-based regulation, 114
Irreversible harms problems, 118
Kaldor-Hicks efficiency compared, 162
Learned Hand formula, 113
Methodologies, 116, 117
Policy debates, 116
Precautionary Principle conflicts, 118
Priceless things problem, 560
Pricing uncertainties and ethical concerns, 117
Risk, 375
Social cost measurements, 117

COSTS
Ignorance, 760
Information gathering, 410
Opportunity, 560
Research, 410
Risk management, 375
Social costs, 279
Switching, 350, 450
Transaction Costs, this index

CREDIT CARD ACCOUNTABILITY RESPONSIBILITY AND DISCLOSURE ACT OF 2009
Confusing information, 446

DAIRY REGULATIONS
See Butter Laws

DANGERS OF REGULATION
Brandeis, Louis, Justice, 2

DECISIONMAKING
Information and, 409
Informed decisionmaking, necessity of decentralized information for, 759
Insufficient information, 411
Public Decisionmakers, this index

DECODING
Network effects, 350

DEFAMATION
Public official criticisms, freedom of speech, 173

DEFAULT RULES
Outcome influencing, 602

DEFINITIONS
Add-on strategy, 446
Ban, 632
Bounded rationality, 599
CAA, 139
Catastrophic risk, 285
CDC, 320
Centralized information regulation, 758
Certification, 668
Cinch bills, 193
Collective action problems, 202
Command-and-control regulation, 24
Coordination breakdown, 328
CRC, 356
Critical paternalism, 527
Cross-subsidization, 525
CWA, 127
Decentralized information regulation, 758
DMCA, 352
Earmark, 200
EPA, 119
Externality, 276, 278
FCC, 42
General risk, 400
Gini Index, 6
Government failure, 226
Hazard, 357
Herd behavior, 406
Heuristics, 601
HPV, 777
ICC, 197
Inadequate information, 404
Inalienability, 561
Incentive regulation, 24
Indirect regulation, 81
Infrastructure, 665
Kaldor-Hicks efficiency, 162
LHPA, 364
Licensing, 668
Macroeconomics, 5
Mandate, 632

DEFINITIONS—Cont'd
Market power, 464
MMR, 321
Natural monopolist, 489
Negative externality, 282
Network effect, 348
NHTSA, 128
NLEA, 602
Non-exclusivity and non-rivalry, 283
Nudge, 602
Pareto efficiency, 161
Parker immunity, 217
Patent troll, 306
Paternalism, 527
Path dependence, 349
Permit, 632, 665
Police power, 40
Positive externality, 282
PP, 118
Preferences, definitional problems, 602
Price gouging, 717
Private net product, 277
Profiteering, 717
Public business, 495
Registration, 668
Regulatees, 70
Regulation
Generally, 2 et seq.
Holmes view, 22
Scalia view, 258
Regulation, this index
Regulatory arbitrage, 108
Rent, 463
Rent seeking, 198, 463
Risk, 357, 358, 409
Rule, 74
SIFI, 401
Social net product, 277
Social welfare, 282
Standard, 74, 691
Systemic risk, 400
TARP, 488
TBTF, 401
TRRA, 504
Uncertainty, 358, 409
Volitional paternalism, 527

DEFUNDING LAW
Segregated public facilities, 604

DELANEY CLAUSE
Cost-benefit analysis, cancer risk conflicts, 119

DELEGATION DOCTRINE
Authority to regulate, 42
Conflicted agencies, delegation to, 715
Sunstein on, 42

DIFFERENTIATION
Price, preferences for differentiation distorting, 464

DIGITAL MILLENNIUM COPYRIGHT ACT (DMCA)
Generally, 352

DIRECT AND INDIRECT REGULATION
Generally, 81 et seq.
See also Litigation, Regulation Through, this index
Bono rule, 93
Censorship through indirect regulation, 84
Copyright law, contributory infringement, 86
Federal Communication Commission censorship by indirect regulation, 93
Posner, Richard, 86
Vicarious liability as indirect regulation, 82

DISCLOSURE
Generally, 784 et seq.
See also Information Regulation, this index
Calorie Labeling, this index
Compulsory expressions shaping preferences, 810
First Amendment challenge to disclosure mandates, 793
Mandates, First Amendment challenge, 793
Nutrition Labeling and Education Act, 789
Preferences, compulsory expressions shaping, 810
Premises liability warnings duties, 783
Products liability warnings duties, 779
Public corporation financial disclosures, 797
Restaurant hygiene inspections, 784
Unintended consequences of mandatory disclosure, 778
Warnings duties and tort liability
Premises liability, 783
Products liability, 779

DISCOUNTS
Surcharges and, confusing information, 445

DOGS
Kentucky Dog Tax, 678, 696, 727
Pit bull bans, 650

DRY CLEANERS
Price regulation, 712

DUE PROCESS
Automobile traffic regulations, 80
Clarity in regulation, 105
Equal protection compared, 541
Fair notice of regulations, 106
Flag salute mandate challenge, 811
Freedom of contract, 486
Judicial bias claim, 220, 225
Margarine tax, 733
Permits and entry regulation challenges, 669
Privacy law, 397
Public utilities regulation challenges, 494
Substantive due process, 501, 548

DURBIN AMENDMENT
Automated teller machines, price regulation, 722
Interchange transaction fees, price regulation, 722

EARMARKS
Generally, 200

ECONOMIC REGULATION
Commerce Clause authority to regulate, 248
Historical background, 33, 251
Justifications, 271
Social regulation distinguished, 275

EDUCATION
See also Preferences, this index
Mandates, 661

EFFECTS
Entitlements, effects on others, 297
Entry regulation, negative effects, 665
Irrational exuberance, bubble effect, 15
Litigation, regulatory effects, 219
Markets forces, regulatory effects, 144
Markets inefficiencies, disruptive effect, 465
Network Effects, this index
Preference shaping. See Preferences, this index
Vicarious liability, indirect regulation effect, 82

EFFICIENCY
Bureaucratic inefficiencies, 165

EFFICIENCY STANDARDS
Fuel, 128, 693
Informational, 404
Light bulbs, 350, 656, 693, 758
Lock-ins of inefficient standards, 350

EIGHTEENTH AMENDMENT
Alcohol prohibition, 634

ELECTRONIC FUND TRANSFER ACT
Price regulation, 723

EMERGENCIES
Price regulation, emergencies justifying, 717

EMERGENCY ECONOMIC STABILIZATION ACT
Financial institutions too big to fail, 401
Great Recession, 201
Systemic risk, 401

EMINENT DOMAIN
Hawaii, 457
Indian Land Consolidation Act, 334, 465
Kaldor-Hicks improvements, 162

ENDANGERED SPECIES
Commodification restraints, 561

ENERGY INDEPENDENCE AND SECURITY ACT
Incandescent light bulb bans, 656

ENTITLEMENTS
Effects on others, 297

ENTRY REGULATIONS
See Permits and Entry Regulation, this index

ENVIRONMENTAL PROTECTION AGENCY (EPA)
Cost-benefit analysis applications, 119, 123
Endangerment findings, 139
Greenhouse Gas Regulations, this index

ENVIRONMENTAL REGULATION
Best Available Technology, this index
Clean Air Act, this index
Pay-as-you-throw laws, 24, 736
Pollution, 636
Self-interest conflicts with public interests, 157

EQUAL PROTECTION
Due Process Clause protections compared, 541
Homosexuality laws challenge, 541
Pharmacy cigarette sales ban challenge, 830
Segregation challenges, 604

EUGENICS REGULATIONS
Social preferences motivations, 274

EUROPEAN FINANCIAL CRISIS
Bailouts, 403

EVOLUTION
Creationism laws, 766, 772
False claims, 445

EXCESSIVE CONFIDENCE
Risk analysis, 356

EXCLUDABILITY
Tragedies of commons and anticommons, 330

EXECUTIVE ORDER 12291
Limitations on regulation, 23

EXECUTIVE ORDER 12866
Cost-benefit analysis, 115

EXTERNALITIES
Generally, 274 et seq.
Biases, informational externalities associated with, 406
Cellphones in theaters, 301
Coordination breakdowns, 328
Definition, 276, 278
Entitlements and effects on others, 297
Fish and game regulation, 330
Heuristics, informational externalities associated with, 406
Inalienable rights, externalities explaining, 559
Informational
  Biases, informational externalities associated with, 406
  Negative informational externalities motivating regulation, 405
Internalization and, 279
John Stuart Mill, 276
Justification for regulation, 286
Ladies' hats regulation, 298
Moralism, external harms of, 559
Negative externalities
  Generally, 282, 405
  Sic utere tuo ut alienum non laedas, 288
Network Effects, this index
Non-exclusive and non-rivalrous positive externalities, 283
Pecuniary, 646
Pigou on, 277

EXTERNALITIES—Cont'd
Positive externalities, non-exclusivity and non-rivalry, 283
Positive informational externalities motivating regulation, 405
Railroad transportation risks, 292
Self-interest, societal consequences, 277
Sic utere tuo ut alienum non laedas, 288
Social disease regulation, 322
Social Regulation, this index
Societal consequences of self-interest, 277
Tragedy of the Anticommons, this index
Tragedy of the Commons, this index
Urban nuisances, 303

FABLE OF THE BEES
Generally, 286

FABLE OF THE KEYS
Generally, 349

FALLIBILITY
See also Government Failure, this index
Coordination breakdowns, 328
Great Recession, regulatory failures, 19
Market inefficiency sources, 464

FAMILY SMOKING PREVENTION AND TOBACCO CONTROL ACT
Graphic warnings on cigarette packaging and advertising, 614

FEDERAL COMMUNICATIONS COMMISSION (FCC)
Censorship by indirect regulation, 93
Free speech challenges to regulations, 103
Indecency policy
Generally, 42, 161
First Amendment challenge, 95, 101
Price cap orders, 521
Price ceilings, 521, 696

FEDERAL DEPOSIT INSURANCE CORPORATION (FDIC)
Creation, 4

FEDERAL FOOD, DRUG, AND COSMETIC ACT
See Food and Drug Administration, this index

FEDERAL PREEMPTION
See Preemption, this index

FEDERAL REGULATORY AUTHORITY
Affordable Care Act challenge, 231
Breyer on tobacco regulation, 67
Calorie labeling, state regulatory authority distinguished, 789
Commerce Clause, this index
Marijuana, state regulatory authority distinguished, 561
Preemption, this index
Prostitution, state regulatory authority distinguished, 591
Public interest era of regulation, 277
Safe Drinking Water Act, 752
State regulatory authority distinguished
Generally, 40

FEDERAL REGULATORY AUTHORITY—Cont'd
State regulatory authority distinguished—Cont'd
See also Preemption, this index
Calorie labeling, 789
Marijuana, 561
Prostitution, 591
Taxing power, 261
Tobacco regulation, 50 et seq.
Vaccine regulations, 227, 265

FERRIES
Natural monopolies, 501

FETAL GESTATIONAL SERVICES
Commodification restraints, 560, 564

FIELD, STEPHEN JOHNSON, JUSTICE
Inalienable right of the pursuit of happiness, 418
Inalienable rights, 667
Liberty of contract, 37
Permits and entry regulation, 669
Price regulation, 697
Public interests justifying regulation, 268

FINANCIAL CRISIS INQUIRY COMMISSION
Generally, 16

FINANCIAL INSTITUTIONS
See also Great Recession, this index
Automated teller machines, price regulation, 722
Credit Card Accountability Responsibility and Disclosure Act of 2009, 446
Electronic Fund Transfer Act, price regulation, 723
Emergency Economic Stabilization Act, 401
Gini Index, 6
Government bailouts, moral hazard problems, 402
Macroeconomics, 5
Moral hazard problems, government bailouts, 402
Price regulation, automated teller machines, 722
Regulation, historical background, 4
Risk, management practices, 5
Systemically important, too big to fail syndrome, 401

FIRE INSURANCE
Generally, 264
Ratemaking, 699

FIREARMS REGULATION
Litigation, regulatory effects, 219

FIRST AMENDMENT
Advertising protection, 764
Advertising protections, 579
Anti-cartoon laws, 175
Blasphemy laws, 808
Commercial speech
Generally, 547, 582
Breyer on, 590
Compelled, 616

FIRST AMENDMENT—Cont'd
Commercial speech—Cont'd
  Disclosure mandates, 793
  Four-part analysis, 581
  Graphic warnings on cigarette packaging and advertising, 616
  Mandated disclosure, 793
  Prostitution advertising, 591
  Scalia on, 588
Crush videos regulation, 203, 205
Disclosure mandates, 793
FCC indecency policy challenge, 95, 101
Federal Communication Commission regulations, free speech challenges, 103
Flag salute mandate challenges, 816
Interest group legal restrictions, free speech challenges, 198
License plate motto challenge, 824
Mandated disclosures, 793
Movie censorship challenge, 683
Obscenity exception, 209
Overbreadth doctrine, 209
Prostitution advertising, 591
Public officials' defamation claims, 173
Scalia, commercial speech cases, 588
Sexual stimulation device laws challenge, 546
Sherman Act conflicts, 216
Standard of review of challenged restrictions, 616
Stolen Valor Act, 437

FISH AND GAME REGULATION
  Generally, 330
Institutional weaknesses, 166

FLAG SALUTE MANDATES
Due process challenge, 811
First Amendment challenge, 816

FLORISTS
Permits and entry regulation, 671

FLU
See Influenza, this index

FLUORIDE
  Generally, 745
Police power authority, 753

FOIE GRAS
Morality, 554

FOOD AND DRUG ADMINISTRATION (FDA)
Bounded rationality, nudging choices, 602
Effectiveness of regulations, 372
Fatty acid regulations, 646
Fatty acids ban, 648
Foie gras bans, 554
Graphic warnings on cigarette packaging and advertising, 614
Historical background, 370
Premarketing approval regulations, 372
Regulations, effectiveness determinations, 372
Safety determinations, 372

FORD CORPORATION
Shareholders' rights, 466

FRAUD LIABILITY
Misleading information, 425

FREEDOM OF CONTRACT
Due Process clause, 486
Field on, 37
Holmes on, 31
Liberty of contract, 473
Market inefficiencies, theories rejecting, 473
Minimum wage laws challenges, 474, 482
Regulatory authority limitation, 28
Sunday laws, 32, 37

GATES, BILL
Microsoft, antitrust litigation, 511

GINI INDEX
Generally, 6

GLASS-STEAGALL ACT
Enactment, 4

GOUGING
See Price, this index

GOVERNMENT
Bureaucracy, this index
Federal Regulatory Authority, this index
Public Decisionmakers, this index
State Regulatory Authority, this index

GOVERNMENT FAILURE
  Generally, 225
Cost-benefit analysis test, 226, 265
Definition, 226
Hurricane Katrina, 286, 403
Limits of government, John Stuart Mill, 137
Market failure parallels, 226
Mill on limits of government, 137
Overenforcement and underenforcement, 226
Price regulation, failure to account for innovation, 699
Underenforcement and overenforcement, 226
Vaccine regulations, 227, 265

GOVERNMENT RELIEF
  Generally, 400 et seq.
  See also Bailouts, this index; Subsidies, this index
Emergency Economic Stabilization Act, 401
Great Depression, 486
Recession responses, 21
Too big to fail syndrome, 401
Troubled Asset Relief Program, 488, 708

GRAPHIC WARNINGS
See Warnings, this index

GREAT DEPRESSION
Historical background, 3

GREAT RECESSION
  Generally, 3 et seq.
Causes, 12
Costs, 10
Emergency Economic Stabilization Act, 201, 401
Financial Crisis Inquiry Commission, 16
Financial firms, risk taking, 363
Irrational exuberance, 15

GREAT RECESSION—Cont'd
Posner, Richard, 577
Regulatory failures, 19
Regulatory responses to recessions, 21
Risk perception, 15
Risk taking by financial firms, 363

GREENHOUSE GAS REGULATIONS
Cost-benefit analysis, 136
Endangerment finding, 139

HAPPINESS
See Pursuit of Happiness, this index

HAZARD
See also Risk, this index
Definition, 357

HEALTH INSURANCE REGULATION
See also Affordable Care Act, this index
Mandated self-protection, 399
National controversy on health care reform, 231
Preferences for health insurance, 803

HEALTH REGULATION
Centers for Disease Control and Prevention, this index
Sanitary Regulations, this index
Vaccination Regulations, this index
Water fluoridation, 745

HERD BEHAVIOR
Generally, 406

HEURISTICS
Definition, 601
Informational externalities associated with, 406
Risk, heuristics impacting perception, 359

HISTORICAL BACKGROUND
Banking system, 3
Blasphemy statutes, 807
Caveat emptor
Generally, 417
Implied warranties, 419
Child labor, 728
Economic regulation, 33, 251
Financial regulation, 4
Food and drug regulation, 370
Great Depression, 3
Great Recession, 3
Lochner era, 25, 33
Monopolists, 501
Movie censorship, 682
Party politics, 175
Price regulation, 466
Privacy law, 186
Public interest era of regulation, 277
Railroad transportation, 292
Sanitary regulation, 153
Sexually transmitted disease regulation, 322
Slaughterhouse regulation, 151, 292
Sodomy law challenges, 531, 548
Vaccine regulations, 227

HOLMES, OLIVER WENDELL, JUSTICE
Liberty of contract as regulatory authority limitation, 31
Minimum wage laws, 481
Prohibitory laws, 22
Sterilization laws, 655
Ticket resale regulation, 273

HOMOSEXUALITY LAWS
Equal Protection Clause challenges, 541
Privacy right challenges, 535
Sodomy Laws, this index

HOT NEWS DOCTRINE
Generally, 521

HUMAN LIFE
Commodification restraints, 560, 561

HUMAN ORGANS
Commodification restraints, 560, 562

HUMAN PAPILLOMAVIRUS (HPV) VACCINATION
Generally, 322, 777
Cost-benefit analysis applicability to vaccine regulations, 122

HURRICANE KATRINA
Government failures, 286, 403

HYGIENE
See also Sanitary Regulations, this index
Personal
Generally, 760
Anti-spitting laws, 363
Restaurant hygiene inspections, 784
Social, common drinking cup bans, 324, 660

ILLUSION OF CONTROL
Risk perception overconfidence, 359

INADEQUATE INFORMATION
See Information, this index

INALIENABLE RIGHTS
Generally, 148, 558
See also Commodification, this index
Calabresi on, 559
Cost-benefit analysis, priceless things problem, 560
Eighteenth Amendment alcohol restrictions, 561
Externalities explaining, 559
Field on
Generally, 667
Pursuit of happiness, 418
Human flourishing concept, 560
Marijuana laws, 561
Mill on, 562
Paternalism as motivation, 560
Pursuit of happiness as, 418
Regulatory protections, 148
Sunstein on, 600
Suppression of information, 578 et seq.
Thirteenth Amendment ban of slavery, 561
Transfer regulations, 559
Waiver restrictions, 559

INCANDESCENT LIGHT BULBS
See Efficiency Standards, this index

INCENTIVE REGULATION
Command-and-control regulation compared, 24
Command-and-control regulation distinguished, 632
Subsidies, this index
Taxes, this index

INDECENCY
See Federal Communications Commission, this index

INDIAN LAND CONSOLIDATION ACT
Constitutionality, 334, 465

INDIRECT REGULATION
Generally, 81
See also Direct and Indirect Regulation, this index

INFANTS AND CHILDREN
Commodification restraints, 560, 576
Labor regulation, 728
Pornography laws, 545
Statutory rape, 552

INFLUENCE GROUPS
See Interest Groups, this index

INFLUENZA
Generally, 320
Anti-spitting laws, 363
Centers for Disease Control and Prevention, this index
Vaccination Regulations, this index

INFORMATION
Generally, 404 et seq.
See also Information Regulation, this index
Ability to process information, bounded rationality constraining, 445
Abortion information mandate, 415, 620
Abortion regulation, information-based, 415
Admiralty law test of seaworthiness, insufficient information, 413, 415
Advertising, suppression of information, regulation through, 578
Asymmetry
Generally, 416
Bedbugs, disclosure regulations, 421
Caveat emptor
Generally, 417
Implied warranties, 419
Justifications for regulation, 417
Market impacts, 418
Voluntary and involuntary relationships, 416
Bedbugs, disclosure regulations, 421
Biases, informational externalities associated with, 406
Bounded rationality constraining ability to process information, 445
Caveat emptor
Generally, 417
Implied warranties, 419

INFORMATION—Cont'd
Centers for Disease Control and Prevention information production, 410
Choices of others, insufficient information, 411
Command-and-control regulation, information improving regulation compared, 404
Commercial speech. See First Amendment, this index
Confusing
Generally, 445 et seq.
Credit Card Accountability Responsibility and Disclosure Act of 2009, 446
Pricing, 445
Regulation motivation and justification, 447
Surcharges and discounts, 445
Tying arrangements, antitrust law, 447
Consumer protection as grounds for suppression of information, 582
Costs of ignorance, 760
Costs of information gathering, 410
Credit Card Accountability Responsibility and Disclosure Act of 2009, 446
Decisionmaking of others, insufficient information, 411
Decisionmaking under ignorance, 409
Discounts and surcharges, confusing information, 445
Effectiveness variables, 759
Efficiency, informational, 404
Failures, market inefficiency sources, 464
Fraud liability, misleading information, 425
Free speech. See First Amendment, this index
Heuristics, informational externalities associated with, 406
Ignorance, uncertainty as, 409
Inadequate
Generally, 404 et seq.
Biases, informational externalities associated with, 406
Definition, 404
Externalities, informational, associated with heuristics and cognitive biases, 406
Heuristics, informational externalities associated with, 406
Measles, mumps, and rubella vaccinations, 408
Negative informational externalities motivating regulation, 405
Positive informational externalities motivating regulation, 405
Price, inadequate information distorting, 464
Regulation motivating, 404
Insufficient
Generally, 409 et seq.
Admiralty law test of seaworthiness, 413, 415
Centers for Disease Control and Prevention information production, 410
Choices of others, 411
Costs of information gathering, 410

INFORMATION—Cont'd
Insufficient—Cont'd
Decisionmaking of others, 411
Decisionmaking under ignorance, 409
Market as information source, reliability, 410
Motivation vs justification for regulations, 409
Others' choices, 411
Research costs, 410
Risk perception uncertainty and ignorance affecting, 409
Smoking, second-hand smoke risks, 411
Tort law standard of care issues, 413, 415
Vaccine skepticism, 411
Involuntary relationships, asymmetric information, 416
Justification vs motivation for regulations, 409
Justifications for regulation, asymmetric information, 417
Lying. Misleading, below
Market as information source, reliability, 410
Market impacts of asymmetric information, 418
Measles, mumps, and rubella vaccinations, inadequate information, 408
Misleading
Generally, 424
Fraud liability, 425
Stolen Valor Act, 437
Tobacco risk information, 425 et seq.
Motivation for regulation, 406
Motivation vs justification for regulations, 409
Negative informational externalities motivating regulation, 405
Network externalities, information control concerns, 406
Others' choices, insufficient information, 411
Positive informational externalities motivating regulation, 405
Preferences, information effects, 799
Pricing
Add-on strategy, 446
Confusing information, 445
Inadequate information distorting, 464
Prostitution advertising, 591
Regulation
Information-improving, 404
Motivation for, 406
Research costs, 410
Risk perception, uncertainty and ignorance affecting, 409
Self-interest, information withholding and, 405
Smoking, second-hand smoke risks, 411
Stolen Valor Act, 437
Suppression of information
Generally, 578 et seq.
See also Censorship, this index
Advertising, 578
Consumer protection rationale, 582
Prostitution advertising, 591
Surcharges and discounts, confusing information, 445

INFORMATION—Cont'd
Tobacco risk information, 425 et seq.
Tort law standard of care issues, insufficient information, 413, 415
Uncertainty and ignorance, 409
Uncertainty and ignorance affecting risk perception, 409
Vaccine skepticism, insufficient information, 411
Voluntary relationships, asymmetric information, 416

INFORMATION REGULATION
Generally, 757 et seq.
See also Disclosure, this index
Advertising, 764
Calorie Labeling, this index
Censorship. Suppression, below
Center for Disease Control and Prevention, 758
Centralized
Generally, 763 et seq.
Advertising regulation, 764
Decentralized information regulation distinguished, 758
Definition, 758
Education and the state, 765
Overuse and misuse, 764
School curriculum, 765
Suppression, 764
Use and misuse, 764
Costs of ignorance, 760
Decentralized
Generally, 778
Abuse and misuse, 778
Calorie labeling in food establishments, 785
Centralized information regulation distinguished, 758
Definition, 758
Disclosure failures, 778
Necessity for informed decisionmaking, 759
Public corporation financial disclosures, 797
Standard setting for, 758
Unintended consequences of mandatory disclosure, 778
Education and the state, 765
Effectiveness variables, 759
False medical information suppression, 777
Fraudulent information suppression, 760
Inadequate information motivating regulation, 757
Informed decisionmaking, necessity of decentralized information for, 759
Misuse
Centralized regulation, 764
Decentralized regulation, 778
Motivation for regulation, inadequate information, 757
Premises liability warnings duties, 783
Private information dissemination. Decentralization, above
Products liability warnings duties, 779
Public corporation financial disclosures, 797

INFORMATION REGULATION—Cont'd
Public information dissemination. Centralization, above
Quality regulation compared, 757
School curriculum, 765
Standard setting
Generally, 757
Decentralized information, 758
Suppression
See also Censorship, this index
Centralized, 764
False medical information, 777
Fraudulent information, 760
Regulations, 758
Unintended consequences of mandatory disclosure, 778
Warnings duties
Premises liability, 783
Products liability, 779

INFORMED CONSENT
Generally, 416
Abortion information mandate, 415, 620
Fluoridation opponents, 746

INFRASTRUCTURE, MARKETS
Control, 724
Creation, 665

INJUNCTIONS
Societal interests, injunctions affecting, 307

INSTITUTIONAL WEAKNESSES
Generally, 165 et seq.
Agreements with interest groups, 211
Anti-cartoon laws, 175
Benevolent public decisionmaker principle, 166
Bribery, 191
Cinch bills, 193
Conflicts of interest, self-interested public decisionmakers, 169
Earmarks, 200
Fishery management regulations, 166
Government Failure, this index
Interest groups
Agreements with, 211
Pressures, 197
Regulatory capture, 199
Rent seeking activities, 198
Judiciary and interest groups, 218
Lobbyists, cinch bills, 193
Public officials, defamation claims, 173, 188
Regulatory capture by interest groups, 199
Rent seeking activities of interest groups, 198
Self-interested public decisionmaker, 169
Self-serving regulations, 171
Tobacco regulation agreements with interest groups, 211

INSUFFICIENT INFORMATION
See Information, this index

INSURANCE
Adhesive contracts, 472
Affordable Care Act, this index
Fire Insurance, this index
Health Insurance Regulation, this index

INSURANCE—Cont'd
Mandates, 661
Moral hazard, 703
No-fault liability insurance requirements, 682
Ratemaking, fire insurance, 699
Risk management, 358

INTEREST GROUPS
Agreements with, 211
Animal rights regulation, 202
Bezzle inventory fluctuations, 200
Butter laws, 163, 731
Collective action problems, 202
Cost-benefit analysis conflicts, 117
Earmarks, 200
Entry regulation advantages, 665
Free speech challenges to legal restrictions, 198
Institutional weakness pressures, 197
Judicial election activities, 219
Legal disputes, rule-setting uses, 218
Margarine regulations, 163
Orbach on, 198
Regulatory capture, 199
Rent seeking activities, 198, 463

INTERNALITIES
See also Externalities, this index
Externalization and, 279
Price regulation, internalization, 735

INTERSTATE COMMERCE COMMISSION (ICC)
Generally, 197, 466
Capture theory, 199

INTUITION-BASED REGULATION
Cost-benefit analysis, 114

INVISIBLE HAND METAPHOR
Smith, Adam, 144

IRRATIONAL EXUBERANCE
Generally, 21
See also Great Recession, this index
Bubble effect, 15
Herd behavior, 406

JUDICIARY
Decisions, regulatory effects, 25
Interest groups and
Generally, 218
Conflicts of interests of judges, 220
Elected judges, campaign contributions, 219
Litigation, Regulation Through, this index

JUSTIFICATION FOR REGULATION
Asymmetric information, 417
Breyer, 272
Confusing information, regulation motivation and justification, 447
Economic regulation, 271
Emergencies justifying price regulation, 717
Externalities, 286
Hollow justifications, 270
Information asymmetries, 417
Motivation for regulation compared, 273

JUSTIFICATION FOR REGULATION —Cont'd
Motivation for regulation distinguished
Generally, 267
Insufficient information problems, 409
Permits and entry regulation, 668
Price regulation, emergencies justifying, 717
Public goods, 284

KALDOR-HICKS
Efficiency
Generally, 162
Cost-benefit analysis compared, 162
Principle
Butter laws, 163
Precautionary Principle compared, 164

KENTUCKY DOG TAX LAW
Generally, 678, 696, 727

LABOR REGULATIONS
Bakers, 25, 155
Brandeis brief, 34, 473
Child labor, 728
Freedom of contract challenges, 474, 482
Minimum Wage Laws, this index
Sunday laws, 164

LADIES' HATS REGULATION
Externalities, 298

LADIES' HEALTH PROTECTIVE ASSOCIATION (LHPA)
Anti-spitting campaign, 364

LAISSEZ FAIRE
Field on, 667
Lochner era, 33
New Deal era, 34, 577

LAND OWNERSHIP CONCENTRATION
Rent effects, 334, 465

LEARNED HAND FORMULA
Cost-benefit analysis, 113

LEGAL PATERNALISM
See Paternalism, this index

LIABILITY
Direct and Indirect Regulation, this index
Litigation, Regulation Through, this index

LIABILITY RULES
Calabresi on, 559

LIBERAL PARADOX
Pareto efficiency, 274

LIBERTY OF CONTRACT
See Freedom of Contract, this index

LICENSURE
Generally, 667
See also Permits and Entry Regulation, this index

LIFE EXTENSION INSTITUTE
Personal hygiene, 761

LIGHT BULBS
See Efficiency Standards, this index

LITIGATION, REGULATION THROUGH
See also Direct and Indirect Regulation, this index
Admiralty law seaworthiness, information insufficiency, 413, 415
Firearms litigation, regulatory effects, 219
Injunctions affecting societal interests, 307
Judicial decisions, regulatory effects, 25
Premises liability warnings duties, 783
Products liability warnings duties, 779
Societal interests, injunctions affecting, 307
Tort liability and warnings duties
Premises liability, 783
Products liability, 779
Vicarious liability as indirect regulation, 82

LOBBYISTS
Cinch bills, 193
Interest Groups, this index

LOCHNER ERA
Historical background, 25, 33

LOCK-INS
Inefficient standards, 350
Metric system proposals, 694

LONDON MILLENNIUM BRIDGE (LMB)
Systemic risk, 400

LOOPHOLES
Clean Air Act regulation, 129, 134
Margarine regulation, 732
Price regulation, 466

MACROECONOMICS
Generally, 5

MANDATES
Generally, 632 et seq., 661
Affordable Care Act, 19, 231, 258
Agricultural Adjustment Act, 662
Calorie Labeling, this index
Definition, 632
Disclosure mandates, First Amendment challenge, 793
Due process, flag salute challenge, 811
Education, 661
Flag salute
Due process challenge, 811
First Amendment challenge, 816
Individual mandate, Affordable Care Act, 258
Insurance, 661
License plate mottos, First Amendment challenge, 824
Vaccination regulations, 227, 315
Water fluoridation, 745

MARGARINE
See Butter Laws, this index

MARIJUANA LAWS
Federal vs state regulation, 561

MARKETS
Asymmetric information impacts, 418
Competitive level and price, 464
Competitiveness relationships of participants, 489

MARKETS—Cont'd
Costs, this index
Efficiency, Coase Theorem, 218
Entry regulations. See Permits and Entry Regulation, this index
Failures
Government failure parallels, 226
Motivations for regulation, 270
Regulatory responses, 23
Forces, regulatory effects, 144
Impacts of asymmetric information, 418
Inefficiencies
Disruptive effect, 465
Theories rejecting, 473
Information source reliability, 410
Infrastructure
Control, 724
Creation, 665
Participants, competitiveness relationship, 489
Permits and Entry Regulation, this index
Power, market
See also Antitrust Law, this index
Definition, 464
Natural Monopoly, this index
Price influencing, 464
Unequal bargaining power distortions, 471
Regulatory effects of market forces, 144
Reliability as information source, 410
Transaction Costs, this index

MEASLES, MUMPS, AND RUBELLA (MMR)
False medical information, 777
Vaccination
Generally, 321
Information inadequacies, 408

MEDICINE, PRACTICE OF
Permits and entry regulation, 669

METHODS OF REGULATION
Generally, 631 et seq.
Bans, this index
Command and Control, this index
Incentive Regulation, this index
Mandates, this index
Permits and Entry Regulation, this index
Rewards, 631
Standard Setting, this index
Subsidies, this index

METRIC SYSTEM
Standard setting, 694

MICROSOFT
Antitrust litigation, 510

MILL, JOHN STUART
Externalities, 276
Government, limits of, 137
Inalienable rights, 562
Paternalism, 527
Self-protection regulations, 398

MINE SAFETY REGULATION
Generally, 379
Police power enforcement, 381
Risk perception and management, 375

MINIMUM WAGE LAWS
Freedom of contract challenges, 474, 482
Holmes on, 481

MISAPPROPRIATION DOCTRINE
Antitrust law, 512, 521

MISLEADING INFORMATION
See Information, this index

MONOPOLIES
See Antitrust Law, this index
Historical background, 501
Hot news doctrine, 521
Microsoft operating system as natural monopoly, 510
Natural Monopoly, this index
Network externalities, natural monopoly analyses, 521
News networks, natural monopoly determinations, 512

MORAL HAZARD
Financial institutions, government bailouts, 402
Insurance underwriting, 703

MORALITY
Generally, 530 et seq.
Alcohol possession regulation, 532
Anti-miscegenation laws, 530
Child pornography laws, 545
Conflicting social preferences, 531
External harms of moralism, 559
Foie gras bans, 554
Homosexuality laws, 535
Paternalism issues distinguished, 529
Police power exercises to protect public morals, 530
Preferences, moral choice conflicts, 800
Public moral code and private intimate conduct, 545
Sexual stimulation device laws, 546
Social preferences conflicts, 531
Sodomy laws, 531
Statutory rape laws, morality aspects, 552

MOTION PICTURE CENSORSHIP
Indirect regulation, 84

MOTIVATION FOR REGULATION
Generally, 267 et seq.
Confusing information, regulation motivation and justification, 447
Eugenics regulations, social preferences motivations, 274
Externalities, this index
Hollow justifications, 270
Inadequate information, 757
Information regulations, 406
Justifications compared, 273
Justifications distinguished
Generally, 267
Insufficient information problems, 409
Market failures, 270
Negative informational externalities, 405

MOTIVATION FOR REGULATION —Cont'd
Network externalities, 350
Positive informational externalities, 405
Preferences, 802
Public goods, 284
Public interest authority for regulation, 267
Public interest doctrine, 268, 269
Rent, price, and motivations for regulation, 463
Self-inflicted harms reductions, 270
Sin taxes, 727
Social preferences motivations, eugenics regulations, 274
Standard setting, 691
Ticket resale regulation, 273
Uncompensated effects on others' well being, 270
Unfair price as, 464

MOTORCYCLE HELMETS
Preferences of motorcyclists, 801
Regulations, 385, 393, 396
Risk perception, 385

MOVIE CENSORSHIP
First Amendment challenge, 683
Historical background, 682

NATIONAL BANKING ACT
Enactment, 4

NATIONAL CONTROVERSY
Generally, 231 et seq.
Health care reform, 231

NATIONAL HIGHWAY TRAFFIC SAFETY ADMINISTRATION (NHTSA)
Creation, 382
Safety standards, 693

NATIONAL RESEARCH COUNCIL'S COMMITTEE ON RISK CHARACTERIZATION (CRC)
Generally, 356

NATURAL MONOPOLY
Generally, 488
Definitions, 489
Demand requirements for licensed activities, 490
Evolution of monopolists, 501
Ferries, 501
Hot news doctrine, 521
Licensed activities, demand requirements for, 490
Microsoft operating system as, 510
Network externalities, natural monopoly analyses, 521
New networks, 512
Public convenience and necessity determinations, 490
Public utilities, 490

NETWORK EFFECTS
Generally, 348
Circumvention, 350
Congestion network effects, 350
Consumption network effects, 349, 350

NETWORK EFFECTS—Cont'd
Decoding, 350
Definition, 348
Digital Millennium Copyright Act, 352
Information control concerns, 406
Lock-ins of standards, 350
Motivations for regulation, 350
Natural monopoly analyses, 521
News networks, natural monopoly determinations, 521
Path dependence, 349, 350
Positive network externalities, 349
Switching costs, 350
Systemic risk as, 400

NEWS NETWORKS
Natural monopoly determinations, 512

NIRVANA FALLACY
Generally, 631

NOERR-PENNINGTON IMMUNITY
Generally, 216
State action immunity compared, 218

NUDGE
Bounded rationality, nudging choices, 602

NUISANCE LAW
Permanent damages vs injunctive remedies, 296
Sic utere tuo ut alienum non laedas, 293
Urban nuisances, 303

NUTRITION
Labeling disclosures
Generally, 602
State law requirements, 789
Trans fatty acids, 647
Supersize sugary drinks bans, 845

NUTRITION LABELING AND EDUCATION ACT (NLEA)
Generally, 602, 789

OBSCENITY
Federal Communications Commission, this index
Freedom of speech, obscenity exception, 209, 210

OCCUPATIONAL LICENSURE
Generally, 667
See also Permits and Entry Regulation, this index

OPPORTUNITY COST
Generally, 560

ORBACH, BARAK
Animal rights regulation, interest group pressures, 202
Boundaries of human rationality, 599
Commerce Clause regulatory authority of federal government, 41
Interest groups, 198

OVERBREADTH DOCTRINE
Speech, freedom of, 209

OVERENFORCEMENT
Government failures, 226

PARETO
Efficiency
Generally, 161
Liberal paradox, 274
Police power breadth and scope, 274
Principle
Precautionary Principle compared, 164
Right to be let alone, 162

PARKER IMMUNITY
Antitrust law, 217

PARTY POLITICS
See also Interest Groups, this index
Historical background, 175

PATENT TROLLS
Generally, 306

PATERNALISM
Generally, 527 et seq.
See also Self-Protection Regulations, this index
Asymmetric paternalism, 602, 603
Bounded rationality and anti-antipaternalism, 600
Brandeis on, 527
Critical paternalism, 527
Default rules, outcome influences, 602
Definition, 527
Inalienable rights, paternalism as motivation, 560
Indirect public impacts of self-inflicted harm, 528
Libertarian paternalism
Generally, 603
Sunstein on, 602
Mill, John Stuart, 527
Morality
See also Morality, this index
Paternity issues distinguished, 529
Negative connotations of term, 529
Regulation and, conflation of terms, 529
Sunstein on libertarian paternalism, 602
Volitional paternalism, 527

PATH DEPENDENCE
Generally, 349

PATIENT PROTECTION AND AFFORDABLE CARE ACT
See Affordable Care Act, this index

PAY-AS-YOU-THROW LAWS (PAYT)
Environmental regulation, 24, 736

PERMITS AND ENTRY REGULATION
Generally, 632, 665
Affirmative and negative permits, 665
Air traffic controllers, 675
Brandeis, Louis, Justice, 666
Certification defined, 668
Definitions, 632, 665
Dog permits, 678
Due process challenges, 669
Field on, 669

PERMITS AND ENTRY REGULATION —Cont'd
Florists, 671
Interest groups advantages of entry regulation, 665
Justification for regulation, 668
Licensing defined, 668
Medicine, 669
Movie censorship, 682
Negative and affirmative permits, 665
Negative effects of entry regulation, 665
No-fault liability insurance requirements, 682
Occupational licensure, 667
Police power authority, 671
Public interest justifications, 668
Public necessity determinations, 494
Public utilities, 490, 666
Purposeless, 665
Registration defined, 668
Regulation through permits, 678
Tattooing, 685
Terminal Railroad Association of St. Louis prosecution, 504, 666
Transaction costs, entry regulation as, 665

PERSONS SUBJECT TO REGULATION
Generally, 70
Rules vs standards governing, 75

PHYSICIANS
Permits and entry regulation, 669

PIGOU, ARTHUR CECIL
Coase views contrasted, 280, 725
Congestion pricing, 736
Externalities, 277
Self-interest conflicts with public interests, 147

PIGOVIAN TAX
Generally, 726

PIT BULL BANS
Generally, 650

PLASTIC BAG
Regulation, unintended consequences, 108

PLEDGE OF ALLEGIANCE LAWS
Compulsory expression shaping preferences, 810
Voluntary expression shaping preferences, 839

POLICE POWER
Generally, 40
Breadth and scope, 274
Dog permits, 678
Dormant Commerce Clause restraints, 557
Federal and state regulatory authority distinguished, 40
Limitations on state regulatory authority, 25
Mine safety regulation, 381
Morality, exercises to protect, 530
Permits and entry regulation, 671
Price ceilings, 696
Public interest, 269

POLICE POWER—Cont'd
Self-protection regulations, police power authority to enforce, 386
Sic utere tuo ut alienum non laedas justification for exercises, 310
Slaughterhouses regulation, 290
Water fluoridation, 753

POLITICS
Historical background of party politics, 175
Interest Groups, this index

POLLUTION REGULATION
Generally, 636

POSNER, RICHARD
Adoption regulations, 576
Direct and indirect regulation, 86
Great Recession, 577
Market power, 464

PRECAUTIONARY PRINCIPLE (PP)
Cost-benefit analysis conflicts, 118
Pareto and Kaldor-Hicks principles compared, 164
Sic utere tuo ut alienum non laedas compared, 291

PREEMPTION
Generally, 41
Scalia on, 49
Supremacy Clause, 45
Tort claims based on state common law, 43, 60
Tort claims based on state regulations, 50, 60

PREFERENCES
Generally, 799 et seq.
Abstinence education, 823
Abuse or misuse of preference shaping, 806
Addressing conflicting preferences, 802
Altering through regulatory measures, 799
Bounded rationality, debiasing, 804
Censorship shaping, 807
Compulsory expressions shaping preferences, 810 et seq.
Conflicting preferences, addressing, 802
Curbing immediate gratification options, 844
Debiasing bounded rationality, 804
Debiasing through regulation, 805
Defined preferences, 799
Definitional problems, 602
Denial of, 800
Eugenics regulations, social preferences motivations, 274
Flag salute mandates shaping
Due process challenge, 811
First Amendment challenge, 816
Gambling preferences, shaping, 844
Health insurance preferences, 803
Immediate gratification options, curbing, 844
Information effects, 799
License plate mottos, First Amendment challenge, 824
Moral choice conflicts, 800
Morality, social preferences conflicts, 531
Motivations for regulating, 802
Pledge of Allegiance laws

PREFERENCES—Cont'd
Pledge of Allegiance laws—Cont'd
Compulsory expression shaping, 810
Voluntary expression shaping, 839
Pornography laws, shaping effects, 806
Prejudice, 800
Regulatory measures to alter, 799
Shaping
Generally, 799 et seq.
Abstinence education, 823
Abuse or misuse of preference shaping, 806
Censorship, 807
Compulsory expressions, 810 et seq.
Curbing immediate gratification options, 844
Eugenics regulations, social preferences motivations, 274
Flag salute mandates
Due process challenge, 811
First Amendment challenge, 816
Gambling preferences, 844
Immediate gratification options, curbing, 844
License plate mottos, First Amendment challenge, 824
Pledge of Allegiance laws
Compulsory expression, 810
Voluntary expression shaping, 839
Pornography laws, shaping effects, 806
Social preferences motivations, eugenics regulations, 274
Traditional preference shaping, 806
Voluntary expressions, 838
Social preferences motivations
Begging, 275
Eugenics, 274
Morality, social preferences conflicts, 531
Ugly laws, 275
Stable and unstable, 799
Steering, 805
Stigler, George, 799
Traditional preference shaping, 806
Voluntary expressions shaping preferences, 838
Why regulate, 802

PRESS AND SPEECH FREEDOMS
See First Amendment, this index

PRESSURE GROUPS
See Interest Groups, this index

PRICE
Generally, 457 et seq.
Adhesive contracts, price unfairness, 472
Arbitrage, regulatory, 466
Bargaining
Rhetoric of, 471 et seq.
Standardized transactions circumventing, 473
Bounded rationality
Price distortions, 464
Price perceptions, 695
Caps and ceilings
Generally, 708 et seq.

PRICE—Cont'd
Caps and ceilings—Cont'd
Federal Communications Commission price cap orders, 521
Federal Communications Commissions, 521, 696
Gouging, 717, 722
Increase caps, 718
Police power authority, 696
Profiteers, 717, 722
Public interest justifying, 696
Rate-of-return regulation and price-cap regulation distinguished, 522, 526
Unconscionable price increases, 719
Coase on supply-demand relationships, 461
Competitive level, 464
Congestion pricing, 736
Differentiation preferences distorting, 464
Distortions, 464
Efficacy of price regulation, 465
Fallibility distorting, 464
Federal Communications Commission price cap orders, 521
Floors, 708 et seq.
Gouging, 717, 722
Inadequate information distorting, 464
Interstate Commerce Act regulation of perceived unfairness, 466
Land ownership concentration, rent effects, 334, 465
Loopholes, 466
Market inefficiencies
Disrupting, 465
Distorting, 464
Freedom of contract theories rejecting, 473
Maximums. Caps and ceilings, above
Minimum wage laws, 474, 482
Motivation for regulation, unfair price as, 464
Natural Monopoly, this index
Of prices, regulation, 696
Perceptions
Bounded rationality, 695
Unfair prices, 464
Power influencing, 464
Preferences for differentiation distorting, 464
Problems, regulations, 466
Profiteers, 717, 722
Ramsey pricing, 525
Ratemaking, 699
Rate-of-return regulation and price-cap regulation distinguished, 522, 526
Regulation
Generally, 695 et seq.
Arbitrage, regulatory, 466
Automated teller machines, 722
Barbershops, 708
Child labor regulation, 728
Command and control approach, 699
Congestion pricing, 736
Dry cleaners, 712
Durbin Amendment, this index
Efficacy, 465
Electronic Fund Transfer Act, 723
Emergencies justifying, 717
Field on, 697

PRICE—Cont'd
Regulation—Cont'd
Fire insurance, ratemaking, 699
Gouging, 717, 722
Historical background, 466
Innovation, failure to account for, 699
Internalization, 735
Loopholes, 466
Problems created by, 466
Profiteers, 717, 722
Quality standards, price regulation relationships, 740
Ratemaking, 699
Rent seeking opportunities, 731
Sin taxes, 727
Stigler on effects of price regulation, 698
Taxes, regulation through, 725
Taxicab services, 707
Through prices, regulation, 696
Two patterns of price regulation, 696
Unconscionable price increases, 719
Unintended consequences, 466
Rent, price, and motivations for regulation, 463
Rent relationships, 463
Rents, land ownership concentration affecting, 334, 465
Rhetoric of bargaining, 471 et seq.
Sherman Act regulation of perceived unfairness, 466
Standardization of transactions, price unfairness, 473
Standardized transactions circumventing bargaining, 473
Subjectivity of price perceptions, 695
Supply-demand relationships, Coase, 461
Through prices, regulation, 696
Transaction costs distorting, 464
Unconscionability doctrine
Price increases, 719
Price unfairness, 472
Unequal bargaining power distortions, 471
Unfair
Generally, 457 et seq.
Adhesive contracts, 472
Bounded rationality and price perceptions, 695
Gouging, 717, 722
Interstate Commerce Act regulation, 466
Minimum wage laws, 474, 482
Motivation for regulation, 464
Natural Monopoly, this index
Perceptions
Generally, 464
Bounded rationality, 695
Profiteers, 717, 722
Regulatory solutions, problems created by, 466
Sherman Act regulation, 466
Standardization of transactions, 473
Subjectivity of price perceptions, 695
Unconscionability doctrine, 472
Unintended consequences of regulation, 466

PRICING
Add-on strategy, 446
Confusing information, 445

PRIVACY
See also Right to be Let Alone, this index
Brandeis, Louis, Justice, 186
Due process protection, 397
Homosexuality laws, privacy right challenges to enforcement, 535
Sexual stimulation device laws challenge, 546

PRIVATE INTERESTS
Conflicting, 160

PROHIBITIONS
See Bans, this index

PROPERTY RULES
Calabresi on, 559

PROSTITUTION
Advertising restrictions, 591
Commodification restraints, 560, 595

PUBLIC BUSINESSES
Definition, 495

PUBLIC CORPORATIONS
Financial disclosure regulations, 797

PUBLIC DECISIONMAKERS
Generally, 160
Benevolent public decisionmakers, 166
Judges as, 219
Private vs public interest promotion, 163, 197
Self-interested, 169

PUBLIC GOOD
Justifications for regulation, 284
Motivations for regulation, 284
Non-exclusivity and non-rivalry, 283
Risk management functions, 285

PUBLIC HARMS
Indirect impacts of self-inflicted harm, 528

PUBLIC INTEREST
See also Societal Interests, this index
Authority for regulation, 267
Field, Stephen Johnson on public interests justifying regulation, 268
Historical background, public interest era of regulation, 277
Motivations for regulation, public interest doctrine as, 268
Pigou, self-interest conflicts with public interests, 147
Police power authority, 269
Price ceilings, public interest justifying, 696
Self-interests conflicts, 147, 157

PUBLIC OFFICIALS' DEFAMATION CLAIMS
Generally, 188
Speech, freedom of, 173

PUBLIC UTILITIES
Brandeis on regulations, 494
Convenience and necessity determinations, 490
Natural monopolies, 490
Permits and entry regulation, 490, 666

PUBLIC UTILITIES—Cont'd
Public convenience and necessity determinations, 490
Ratemaking price regulation, 699
Regulations
Brandeis on, 494
Due Process Clause challenges, 494

PURSUIT OF HAPPINESS
Bounded rationality
Failures of self-interest pursuit, 599
Failures of self-interest pursuit
Bounded rationality, 599
Field, Stephen Johnson, Justice
Inalienable right of the pursuit of happiness, 418
Inalienable right
Generally, 148
Field, Stephen Johnson, Justice, 418

QUALITY STANDARDS
Generally, 740 et seq.
Bread, 740
Price regulation relationships, 740
Regulation of quality, information regulation compared, 757
Water fluoridation, 745

RAILROADS
See also Interstate Commerce Commission, this index
Gauge standards, 350
Historical background, 292
Price unfairness perceptions, 466
Terminal Railroad Association of St. Louis, Sherman Act prosecution, 504

RAMSEY PRICING
Generally, 525

RATEMAKING
Fire insurance, 699
Price regulation, 699
Taxicab services, 707

RATIONALITY
See Bounded Rationality, this index
Bounded rationality constraining ability to process information, 445

RECESSIONS
Great Depression, 3
Great Recession, this index
Regulatory responses, 21

REGISTRATION
Definition, 668

REGULATEES
See Persons Subject to Regulation, this index

REGULATION
Authority to Regulate, this index
Definitions
Generally, 2 et seq.
Holmes view, 22
Scalia view, 258
Economic Regulation, this index
Federal Regulatory Authority, this index
Incentive Regulation, this index

REGULATION—Cont'd
Information Regulation, this index
Justification for Regulation, this index
Litigation, Regulation Through, this index
Methods of Regulation, this index
Motivation for Regulation, this index
Price regulation. See Price, this index
Social Regulation, this index
State Regulatory Authority, this index

REGULATORY CAPTURE
See Capture Theory, this index

RELIGIOUS FREEDOMS
See First Amendment, this index

RENT
Definition, 463
Implied warranties, rented property, 419
Land ownership concentration affecting, 334, 465
Price and motivations for regulation, 463
Price relationships, 463

RENT SEEKING
Generally, 198
Definition, 463
Interest group activities, 463
Margarine regulation, 731
Price regulation opportunities, 731

RESTRAINTS OF TRADE
See Antitrust Law, this index
Noerr-Pennington immunity, 216
Tobacco regulation, price-fixing challenge to Master Settlement Agreement, 211

REWARDS
Regulation through, 631

RIGHT TO BE LET ALONE
Brandeis on, 161, 411, 545
Pareto principle, 162
Self-protective regulations, 390

RISK
See also Safety Regulations, this index
Ability to pay costs of management, 375
Analyzing risks, techniques available for, 356
Assessment. Perception, below
Assumption of reasonable risk, safety as, 356
Automobile safety regulation, 382
Aversion to risk, 362
Bounded rationality impacting perception, 359
Cancer risk, cost-benefit analysis conflicts
Generally, 118
Delaney Clause, 119
Catastrophic failures
Generally, 285
Systemic risk, 403
Chance and hope, 370
Characterization, 357
Cognitive biases affecting perception, 359
Cognitive biases influencing analysis, 406
Conflicting values and disbelief, 382
Cost-benefit analysis, 375
Definitions
Generally, 357

RISK—Cont'd
Definitions—Cont'd
General risk, 400
Systemic risk, 400
Denial of risk, 362
Disbelief and conflicting values, 382
Epidemics risk of, 363
Excessive confidence in analyzing risks, 356
Financial institutions
Management practices, 5
Risk taking, 363
General risk, 400
Great Recession, financial firm risk taking, 363
Hazard defined, 357
Health care risk perception, 356
Health risks and regulation, 360
Heuristics impacting perception, 359
Heuristics influencing analysis, 406
Hope and chance, 370
Ignorance and risk perception, 409
Improved understanding of risk analysis, 361
Individual management, 356
Insurance management, 358
Labor, risk-compensation theory, 35
London Millennium Bridge, systemic risk, 400
Management
Ability to pay costs of, 375
Analyzing risks, techniques available for, 356
Anti-spitting laws, 363
Financial institutions, management practices, 5
Individual, 356
Insurance, 358
Market solutions to systemic risk, 400
Mine safety regulation, 375
Misuse of risk, 363
Pooling of risks, 358
Public goods, risk management functions, 285
Systemic risk, market solutions, 400
Taxation vs regulation of risky behavior, 399
Techniques available for analyzing risks, 356
Willingness to pay costs of, 375
Market solutions to systemic risk, 400
Mine safety regulation, 375
Misperceptions and regulation, 360
Misuse of risk, 363
National Research Council's Committee on Risk Characterization, 356
Perception
Automobile safety regulation, 382
Bounded rationality impacting, 359
Cognitive biases affecting, 359
Cognitive biases influencing, 406
Conflicting values and disbelief, 382
Disbelief and conflicting values, 382
Excessive confidence in analyzing risks, 356
Great Recession, 15
Health care, 356
Heuristics impacting, 359

RISK—Cont'd
Perception—Cont'd
Heuristics influencing, 406
Ignorance and, 409
Improved understanding of risk analysis, 361
Mine safety regulation, 375
Misperceptions and regulation, 360
Uncertainty and, 358, 409
Pooling of risks, 358
Public goods, risk management functions, 285
Railroad transportation, 292
Self-protection regulations, taxation vs regulation of risky behavior, 399
Systemic risk
Generally, 400
Catastrophic failures, 403
Definition, 400
Emergency Economic Stabilization Act, 401
Financial institutions, systemically important, 401
London Millennium Bridge, 400
Market solutions, 400
Network externality characterization, 400
Too big to fail syndrome, 401
Techniques available for analyzing risks, 356
Tobacco regulation, risk information, 425 et seq.
Trade in risks, 357
Uncertainty distinguished, 358, 409
Values, conflicting values and disbelief, 382
Willingness to pay costs of management, 375

RIVALRY
Tragedies of commons and anticommons, 330

ROUTINE CHANGE
Metric system proposals, 694

RULES VS STANDARDS
Generally, 74
Automobile traffic regulation, 77, 80
Command-and-control regulation, 632
Due Process Clause limitations, 80

SAFE DRINKING WATER ACT
Federal regulatory authority, 752

SAFETY REGULATIONS
Generally, 355 et seq.
Assumption of reasonable risk, safety as, 356
Automobile safety, risk perceptions, 382
Foods and drugs, 372
Mining activities, 375
Motorcycle Helmets, this index
National Highway Traffic Safety Administration, 693
Risk perceptions, 382
Seatbelt laws, 390
Self-protection regulations
See also Self-Protection Regulations, this indcx
Police power authority to enforce, 386

SALES
Consumer Sales, this index
Markets, this index
Price, this index

SANITARY REGULATIONS
Bakers, 155
Historical background, 153
Restaurant hygiene inspections, 784
Social diseases, 322

SCALIA, ANTONIN, JUSTICE
Affordable Care Act, 257
Antitrust law, per se violations, 452
Best available technology regulations, 123
Commercial speech cases, 588
Federal preemption, 49
Sodomy laws, 531

SECOND-BEST SOLUTIONS
Generally, 271, 272
Flawed regulation vs no regulation, 199

SEGREGATION
Equal Protection Clause challenges, 604

SELF-INFLICTED HARMS REDUCTIONS
Motivations for regulation, 270

SELF-INTEREST
Bounded rationality, failures of self-interest pursuit, 599
Butchers, 150
Coordination breakdowns in pursuit of, 328
Earmarks, 200
Failures of self-interest pursuit, bounded rationality, 599
Information withholding and, 405
Pigou, self-interest conflicts with public interests, 147
Private and social net products, 277
Public interest conflicts, 147, 157
Societal consequences, 277

SELF-PROTECTION REGULATIONS
See also Paternalism, this index
Health insurance mandates, 399
Mill, John Stuart, 398
Minimum Wage Laws, this index
Motorcycle Helmets, this index
Police power, 386
Right to be let alone, 390
Seatbelt laws, 390
Taxation vs regulation of risky behavior, 399
Tobacco Regulations, this index

SELF-SERVING REGULATIONS
Institutional weaknesses, 171

SEXUAL STIMULATION DEVICE LAWS
Constitutionality, 546

SEXUALLY ORIENTED BUSINESSES
Prostitution, this index
Sexually transmitted disease regulation
Generally, 38
Historical background, 322
Sin taxes, 728

SHAPING PREFERENCES
See Preferences, this index

SHAREHOLDERS' RIGHTS
Ford corporation, 466

SHERMAN ACT
See also Antitrust Law, this index
Freedom of speech conflicts, 216
Per se violations, 218
Perceived price unfairness regulation, 466
Terminal Railroad Association of St. Louis prosecution, 504

SIC UTERE TUO UT ALIENUM NON LAEDAS
Generally, 288
Nuisance law, 293
Police power enforcement, 310
Precautionary Principle compared, 291

SIN TAXES
Generally, 727
Child labor regulation, 728
Sexually explicit businesses, 728

SLAUGHTER-HOUSE CASES
Butchers, 152

SLAUGHTERHOUSES
Police power regulation, 290
Regulation, historical background, 151, 292
Self-interested public decisionmakers, 170

SMALLPOX VACCINATIONS
Federal regulations, 265
State regulations, 313

SMITH, ADAM
Invisible hand metaphor, 144

SMOKING IN PUBLIC
See also Tobacco Regulations, this index
Bans, 639, 646

SOCIAL NORMS
Collective action directing, 272

SOCIAL PREFERENCES
See Preferences, this index

SOCIAL REGULATION
Generally, 275
Bargaining, Coasean, 281
Begging regulations, 275
Coasean bargaining, 281
Economic regulation distinguished, 275
Private and social interests, 277
Private and social net products, 277
Public goods, 282
Self-interest, societal consequences, 277
Ugly laws, 275
Uncompensated effects on others' well-being, 277

SOCIAL WELFARE
Definition, 282

SOCIETAL INTERESTS
Generally, 270
See also Public Interest, this index

SOCIETAL INTERESTS—Cont'd
Injunctions affecting, 307
Self-interest, societal consequences, 277

SODOMY LAWS
Challenges, historical background, 531, 548

SPECIAL INTERESTS
Capture Theory, this index
Interest Groups, this index

SPEECH AND PRESS FREEDOMS
See First Amendment, this index

SPITTING
Anti-spitting laws, 363

STANDARD OF REVIEW
Administrative agency actions, 131
First Amendment challenges, 616

STANDARD SETTING
Generally, 691
Breyer on standards, 692
Definitions, 691
Efficiency Standards, this index
Fuel economy standards, 693
Information regulation
Generally, 757
Decentralized information, 758
Light bulbs, 693
Metric system, 694
Motivation for regulation, 691
Quality Standards, this index
Seatbelts, 692

STANDARDS
Efficiency Standards, this index
Lock-ins of inefficient standards, 350
Quality Standards, this index
Railway gauge standards, 350
Ratemaking price regulation, 699
Rules vs standards, 74

STATE ACTION IMMUNITY
Noerr-Pennington immunity compared, 218

STATE REGULATORY AUTHORITY
Brandeis on experimental state regulations, 60
Calorie labeling, 789
Dormant Commerce Clause restraints, 557
Experimental, 60
Federal regulatory authority distinguished
Generally, 40
See also Preemption, this index
Calorie labeling, 789
Marijuana, 561
Prostitution, 591
Marijuana, 561
Preemption, this index
Prostitution, 591
Vaccinations, 313

STATUTORY RAPE LAWS
Morality aspects, 552

STERILIZATION LAWS
Generally, 655
Holmes on, 655

STIGLER, GEORGE
Coase Theorem, 281
Preferences, 799
Price regulation effects, 698
Regulatory capture, 199

STOLEN VALOR ACT
Freedom of speech challenge, 437

SUBSIDIES
Generally, 696
See also Bailouts, this index
Affordable Care Act, 243, 248, 259
Cross-subsidization, 525
Incentive regulations, 24

SUNDAY LAWS
Labor regulations, 164
Liberty of contract, 32, 37

SUNSTEIN, CASS
Cost-benefit analysis, 116
Delegation doctrine, 42
Inalienability rules, 600
Libertarian paternalism, 602
Rules vs standards, 74

SUPPRESSION OF INFORMATION
See Information, this index

SURCHARGES
Discounts and confusing information, 445

SWITCHING COSTS
Generally, 350, 450

SYSTEMICALLY IMPORTANT FINANCIAL INSTITUTIONS (SIFI)
Too big to fail syndrome, 401

TASTE
See Preferences, this index

TATTOOING
Permits and entry regulation, 685

TAXATION
Child labor regulation, 728
Congestion pricing, 736
Due process challenge to margarine tax, 733
Kentucky Dog Tax, 678, 696, 727
Litter taxes, 735
Margarine regulation
Generally, 731
Due process challenge, 733
Pay-as-you-throw laws, 24, 736
Regulation through, 725
Sin Taxes, this index

TAXICAB SERVICES
Ratemaking, 707

TELECOMMUNICATION REGULATIONS
FCC price cap orders, 521

TERMINAL RAILROAD ASSOCIATION OF ST. LOUIS (TRRA)
Permits and entry regulation, 504, 666
Sherman Act prosecution, 504

TICKET RESALE REGULATION
Motivation for regulation, 273

TOBACCO REGULATIONS
Agreements with interest groups, 211
Authority to regulate, 43 et seq.
Bans on smoking in public, 639, 646
Breyer on federal regulatory authority, 67
Federal regulation, preemptive effects, 50 et seq.
Federal regulatory authority, 61
Fraud liability for misleading information, 425 et seq.
Graphic warnings, 614
Informational problems, second-hand smoke risks, 411
Legal disputes, rule-setting uses, 219
Litter taxes, 735
Manufacturing restrictions, 307
Pharmacy sales ban, equal protection challenge, 830
Price-fixing challenge to Master Settlement Agreement, 211
Risk information, 425 et seq.
Second-hand smoke risks, informational problems, 411
Smoking in public bans, 639, 646

TOO BIG TO FAIL SYNDROME (TBTF)
Financial institutions, systemic risk, 401

TORT LAW
See Litigation, Regulation Through, this index

TRAFFIC
Congestion pricing, 736

TRAGEDY OF THE ANTICOMMONS
Generally, 329
Excludability and rivalry, 330

TRAGEDY OF THE COMMONS
Generally, 328
Excludability and rivalry, 330

TRANS FATS
Nutrition labeling requirements, 647

TRANSACTION COSTS
Bureaucracy, 281
Coase Theorem, 281
Entry regulation as transaction cost, 665
Market impeding, 271
Market inefficiency sources, 464
Permit regulations as transaction cost, 665
Price, transaction costs distorting, 464

TROUBLED ASSET RELIEF PROGRAM (TARP)
Generally, 488, 708

UGLY LAWS
Social preferences motivations, 275

UNCERTAINTY
Risk distinguished, 358, 409

UNCONSCIONABILITY DOCTRINE
Bans on unconscionable price increases, 719
Price unfairness, 472

UNDERENFORCEMENT
Government failures, 226

UNFAIR PRICE TERMS
See Price, this index

UNINTENDED CONSEQUENCES
Generally, 107
Mandatory disclosure, 778
Plastic bag regulation, 108
Price regulation, 466
Regulatory arbitrage, 108

VACCINATION REGULATIONS
Command-and-control approach, 412
Federal regulatory authority, 227, 265
Government failures, 227, 265
Historical background, 227
Human papillomavirus vaccination, 322, 777
Information insufficiencies and vaccine skepticism, 411
Mandates, 227, 315
Measles, mumps, and rubella vaccination
Generally, 321

VACCINATION REGULATIONS—Cont'd
Measles—Cont'd
Information inadequacies, 408
Smallpox, 265, 313
State regulatory authority, 313

VICARIOUS LIABILITY
Indirect regulation effect, 82

WAIVERS
Inalienable rights, waiver restrictions, 559

WARNINGS
Compulsory expressions shaping preferences, 810
Graphic
Abortion information mandates, 415, 620
Cigarette packaging and advertising, 614
Preferences, compulsory expressions shaping, 810
Tort liability
Premises liability, 783
Products liability, 779

WARRANTY
Implied warranties, 419

WATER FLUORIDATION
Generally, 745
Police power authority, 753

†